W9-BZN-178

Handbook for Auditors

HF5667
H26

Handbook for Auditors

JAMES A. CASHIN *editor-in-chief*
Professor and Past Chairman
Department of Accounting, Hofstra University

McGRAW-HILL BOOK COMPANY
New York St. Louis San Francisco Düsseldorf Johannesburg
Kuala Lumpur London Mexico Montreal New Delhi
Panama Rio de Janeiro Singapore Sydney Toronto

170194

AUG 7 1972

HANDBOOK FOR AUDITORS

Copyright © 1971 by McGraw-Hill, Inc. All Rights Reserved. Printed in the United States of America. No part of this publication may be reproduced, stored in a retrieval system, or transmitted, in any form or by any means, electronic, mechanical, photocopying, recording, or otherwise, without the prior written permission of the publisher. *Library of Congress Catalog Card Number* 73-116660

07-010200-7

1234567890 MAMB 754321

This book was set in Linofilm Caledonia by Quinn & Boden Company, Inc., and printed and bound by The Maple Press Company. The editors were M. Joseph Dooher and Frank Purcell. The designer was Naomi Auerbach. Stephen J. Boldish supervised production.

Contents

Board of Advisors

Independent Auditing

FREDERICK E. HORN	*Director of Personnel Education Arthur Young & Company*
JOSEPH L. ROTH	*Partner, Price Waterhouse & Co.*

Internal Auditing

DONALD E. DOOLEY	*Headquarters Administrative Service Manager Weyerhaeuser Company*
JOHN J. KEARNEY, JR.	*Secretary and General Auditor Long Island Lighting Company*

Governmental Auditing

ROBERT G. ALLYN	*Executive Secretary, New York State Board of Certified Public Accountant Examiners*
ELLSWORTH H. MORSE, JR.	*Director, Office of Policy and Special Studies, U.S. General Accounting Office*

Education

VICTOR Z. BRINK	*Professor of Business, Graduate School of Business, Columbia University*
LAWRENCE L. VANCE	*Professor of Accounting, Graduate School of Business Administration University of California, Berkeley*

Contributors

ROBERT G. ALLYN
Executive Secretary, New York State Board of CPA Examiners (CHAPTER 44)

R. J. ANDERSON
Partner, Clarkson, Gordon & Co. (CHAPTER 49)

SIDNEY S. BAURMASH
Deputy Director of Audits, U.S. Department of Commerce (CHAPTER 8)

LEOPOLD A. BERNSTEIN
Professor of Accounting, Baruch College, The City University of New York, and Research Consultant, Lybrand Ross Bros. & Montgomery (CHAPTER 48)

MAX BLOCK
Editor, The New York Certified Public Accountant (CHAPTER 40)

HOWARD J. BROWN
Assistant Professor of Accounting, Hofstra University (CHAPTER 4)

THOMAS BURGESS, JR.
Auditor, Mutual of New York (CHAPTER 7)

KENNETH S. CALDWELL
Principal, Ernst & Ernst (CHAPTER 52)

N. T. CAMPBELL
Audit Zone Manager, IBM Corporation (CHAPTER 33)

EDWARD DARCEY
Partner, Haskins & Sells (CHAPTER 20)

GORDON B. DAVIS
Professor and Director of the Management Information Systems Research Center, University of Minnesota (CHAPTER 16)

E. J. DeMARIS
Professor and Head, Department of Accountancy, University of Illinois (CHAPTER 25)

CHARLES FABRIZIO
Manager, Internal Audits, Warner-Lambert Pharmaceutical Company (CHAPTER 34)

IRVING L. FANTL
Associate Professor of Accounting, Seton Hall University (CHAPTER 19)

SAUL FELDMAN
Assistant Professor of Accounting, Hofstra University (CHAPTER 27)

W. C. FLEWELLEN, JR.
Dean, College of Business Administration, University of Georgia (CHAPTER 18)

B. BERNARD GREIDINGER
Professor of Accounting, New York University Graduate School of Business Administration (CHAPTER 45)

E. GEORGE HAKULA
General Auditor, General Foods Corporation (CHAPTER 35)

CARL D. HARNICK
Partner, Arthur Young & Company (CHAPTER 39)

FREDERICK E. HORN
Director of Personnel Education, Arthur Young & Company (CHAPTER 9)

MARTIN IVES
Deputy Comptroller, State of New York (CHAPTER 8)

LOUIS H. JORDAN
Professor of Accounting, Graduate School of Business, Columbia University (CHAPTER 2)

JOEL KAUFFMAN
Associate Professor of Economics, Hunter College, The City University of New York (CHAPTER 5)

JOHN J. KEARNEY, JR.
Secretary and General Auditor, Long Island Lighting Company (CHAPTER 32)

FRANK W. KOLMIN
Professor of Accounting and Finance and Director of Accounting Programs, School of Business, State University of New York at Albany (CHAPTER 29)

NEALE KURLANDER
Associate Professor of Business Administration and Director, Accounting Program, Adelphi University (CHAPTER 17)

IRA M. LANDIS
Partner, Alexander Grant & Company (CHAPTER 11)

BERNHARD C. LEMKE
Professor of Accounting, Graduate School of Business Administration, Michigan State University (CHAPTER 37)

WILLIAM C. LINS
Professor of Accounting, Graduate School of Business Administration, Rutgers University (CHAPTER 36)

EDWARD S. LYNN
Professor of Accounting, The University of Arizona (CHAPTER 6)

ROBERT L. MAY
Partner, Arthur Andersen & Co. (CHAPTER 23)

ELLSWORTH H. MORSE, JR.
Director, Office of Policy and Special Studies, U.S. General Accounting Office (CHAPTER 50)

MARY E. MURPHY
Professor of Accounting, California State College, Los Angeles (CHAPTER 38)

EDWARDS B. MURRAY
Manager, Corporate Audit Staff, General Electric Company (CHAPTER 30)

FREDERICK L. NEUMANN
Associate Professor of Accountancy, University of Illinois (CHAPTER 25)

OSWALD NIELSEN
Professor of Accounting, Graduate School of Business, Stanford University (CHAPTER 10)

ALPHONSE L. NIGRA
Audit Manager, Allied Chemical Corporation (CHAPTER 15)

R. FRANK PAGE
Associate Professor of Accounting, University of Missouri, St. Louis (CHAPTER 3)

JENNIE M. PALEN
Certified Public Accountant (CHAPTER 41)

WYMAN G. PATTEN
Partner, Price Waterhouse & Co. (CHAPTER 22)

JAMES W. PATTILLO
Professor of Accounting, Louisiana State University at Baton Rouge (CHAPTER 14)

SAMUEL PERSON
Associate Professor of Accounting and Director of Business Administration, Dowling College (CHAPTER 43)

JEROME K. PESCOW
Assistant Professor, Hofstra University (CHAPTER 46)

GERALD P. ROONEY
Partner, Peat, Marwick, Mitchell & Co. (CHAPTER 28)

LAWRENCE B. SAWYER
Supervising Auditor, Lockheed-California Company (CHAPTER 51)

DANIEL A. SCHAEFFER
Partner, Richard A. Eisner & Company (CHAPTER 24)

ROBERT E. SCHLOSSER
Director, Professional Development Division, American Institute of Certified Public Accountants (CHAPTER 1)

DAVID M. SCHOEN
Senior Accountant, Ernst & Ernst (CHAPTER 21)

HOWARD F. STETTLER
Professor of Business Administration, The University of Kansas (CHAPTER 12)

M. TABIBIAN
Partner, Touche Ross & Co. (CHAPTER 26)

L. H. TOLER
Department Head, Accounting Department, Mississippi State University (CHAPTER 18)

JOHN E. ULLMANN
Chairman, Department of Management, Marketing and Business Statistics, Hofstra University (CHAPTER 47)

ROBERT W. VANASSE
Professor of Accounting, California State College, Fullerton (CHAPTER 13)

DOYLE Z. WILLIAMS
Associate Professor of Accounting, Texas Tech University (CHAPTER 43)

DUANE E. WILSON
Chief Auditor–Chicago, Standard Oil Company (Indiana) (CHAPTER 31)

MARILYNN G. WINBORNE
Professor of Accounting, The University of Arizona (CHAPTER 6)

CORNELL G. WRIGHT
Partner, Ernst & Ernst (CHAPTER 21)

PERCY B. YEARGAN
Professor and Head, Department of Accounting, University of Georgia (CHAPTER 3)

CHARLES H. ZWICKER
Professor of Accounting and Chairman, Accounting Department, C. W. Post College of Long Island University (CHAPTER 42)

Consultants

ROBERT N. ANTHONY
Professor of Business Administration, Harvard Business School

RAYMOND S. BABAYAN
Director of Management Controls, American Machine & Foundry Company

JOHN H. BARRY
General Auditor and Assistant Controller, Mobil Oil Corporation

ROBERT I. BEGGS
Consultant, Education and Training, General Electric Company

ARTHUR BETTAUER
Partner, Price Waterhouse & Co.

FRANCIS M. BRADY, JR.
Assistant Professor of Accounting, Lehigh University

FRANK A. BRUNI
Principal, Haskins & Sells

JOHN W. BUCKLEY
Chairman, Department of Accounting, Graduate School of Business Administration, University of California, Los Angeles

VICTOR N. CANNIZZARRO
Assistant Treasurer, North American Philips Company, Inc.

STUART A. CASHIN, JR.
Partner, Windham, Brannon, Cashin & Duval

JAMES J. CONNOLLY
Manager, Price Waterhouse & Co.

SIDNEY DAVIDSON
Dean, Graduate School of Business, University of Chicago

JOHN P. DEEHAN
Past Chairman, Department of Accounting, Seton Hall University

JOSEPH H. DWORETSKY
Director, Division of Business Administration, Long Island University

GUNNAR A. EKBERG
Professor of Accounting, Pace College

WILLIAM L. FURLONG
Professor of Accounting, Georgia State University

ALLEN R. GALLOWAY
Partner, Kelley & Galloway

WILLIAM D. GASSER
Associate Professor of Accounting, Rochester Institute of Technology

JEFFREY L. GOLDBERG
Vice President–Finance and Director, Granite Management Services

GUSTAV A. GOMPRECHT
Managing Partner, Main LaFrentz & Co.

SEYMOUR GROSS
Partner, Sommer, Gross & Kleinman

GEORGE A. GUSTAFSON
Assistant Professor of Accounting, California State College, Fullerton

WILLIAM D. HALL
Partner, Arthur Andersen & Co.

HERBERT H. HALPERN
Internal Auditor, General Adjustment Bureau

ROBERT HAMPTON III
Partner, S. D. Leidesdorf & Co.

THOMAS W. HILL, JR.
Partner, Spear and Hill

LEONARD H. JACOBY
Auditing Supervisor, Shell Oil Company

DAN JOSEPH, JR.
Director, Ohio State Board of Accountancy

JAMES W. KELLEY
Assistant Professor of Accounting, University of Georgia

MAC KIRSCHBAUM
Manager, J. K. Lasser & Company

ROBERT KRANZLER
Partner, Laventhol Krekstein Horwath & Horwath

WILLIAM C. LINS
Professor of Accounting, Graduate School of Business Administration, Rutgers University

LESLIE R. LOSCHEN
Associate Professor of Accounting, University of Southern California

HOWARD D. LOWE
Chairman, Department of Accounting, University of Hawaii

JOSEPH P. MARUSAK
Manager of Auditing, NACPG, The Singer Company

STANLEY H. MEYER
Certified Public Accountant, and Lecturer, Hofstra University

ELLSWORTH H. MORSE, JR.
Director, Office of Policy and Special Studies, U.S. General Accounting Office

CORINE NORGAARD
Assistant Professor of Accounting, University of Connecticut

RICHARD V. NORTHRUP
Associate Professor, The Ohio State University

PAUL R. OKEN
Partner, A. M. Pullen & Company

JOHN W. PAIGE
Director of Division of Professional Licensing Service, New York State Department of Education

JAMES M. PETTIT
Manager, Audit Section, Grumman Aircraft Engineering Corporation

CARL A. POLSKY
Assistant Professor of Accounting, Wharton School, University of Pennsylvania

RAY M. POWELL
Head, Department of Accountancy, University of Notre Dame

JOSEPH L. ROTH
Partner, Price Waterhouse & Co.

ALFRED O. SAVAGE
Comptroller, Standard Oil Company (N.J.)

ZACHARY S. SCHEER
Partner, J. K. Lasser & Company

FRANCIS E. SCHNEIDER
Manager of Internal Auditing Department, Union Carbide Corporation

RICHARD SCHWARTZ
Partner, S. D. Leidesdorf & Co.

ELLIOTT C. SEROTTA
Partner, Serotta, Maddocks and Serotta

MARION W. SPRAGUE
President, Funding Systems Corporation

RICHARD T. STELTER
Partner, Byrnes & Baker

STANLEY B. TUNICK
Chairman, New York State Board of Certified Public Accountant Examiners

JOSEPH J. WASSERMAN
President, Computer Audit Systems, Inc.

DOYLE Z. WILLIAMS
Associate Professor of Accounting, Texas Tech University

ROGER H. WILLIS
Director of Internal Auditing, National Dairy Products Corporation

HERBERT WITT
Regional Auditor, U.S. Department of Health, Education and Welfare

IVOR B. WRIGHT
Partner, Smith and Harder

Preface

This handbook is designed to fill a substantial void that has existed to date in the field of auditing. For many years there have been accounting handbooks, cost handbooks, finance handbooks, etc., but to date there has been no handbook covering all branches of auditing. Auditing differs from accounting in that the branches or segments are more distinct. There are independent auditors, internal auditors, and governmental auditors, each with his own professional organization and literature. However, there is much overlapping as the independent auditor often uses the operational approach of the internal auditor, especially in performing management services or special audits. The internal auditor may use the financial approach in the verification of the cash balance, or the operational approach in evaluating and recommending ways of accelerating cash flow. The governmental auditor may use the financial approach similar to that of the CPA, or he may use the operational approach within his own agency, or at some other unit. Up to this time no handbook has included all these phases of auditing.

With the greatly increased liability exposure of the auditor it is more important than ever before that there be no gaps in the total audit program. Therefore it is well for the independent auditor to know what the internal auditor is doing and for the internal auditor to be familiar with the independent auditor's range of work. Thus serious problems may be averted and closer cooperation fostered. To provide better balance and more comprehensive coverage in each chapter the talents of the practitioner and teacher have been carefully integrated. For example, if the chapter was written by a practitioner, such as a CPA, an internal auditor, or a governmental auditor, the consultant was a teacher. If the chapter was written by a teacher, the consultant was a practitioner.

As indicated, the handbook will be useful to all auditors, including the large number of auditors in specialized fields. Any auditor on the job will find that he will have a comprehensive source of authoritative reference at his fingertips throughout the audit. Accountants, corporate officers, lawyers, and others interested in particular source material will find the handbook references and text a mine of information. Teachers and students alike are provided with important supplemental material and references for the auditing course.

The development and application of new technology and techniques have had an important effect on the whole field of auditing. The impact of computerized systems, statistical sampling, and other developments is described in detail in individual chapters. The procedures for evaluating the internal controls relating to the computer are described broadly in the internal control chapter and in detail in the computer systems chapter. The procedures concerned with computer output are described, where appropriate, in the respective technical chapters. The ways of utilizing the computer in the audit, such as with the generalized computer program, are described in the computer systems chapter.

The field of auditing has always encompassed a very wide range of sophistication. Many practitioners and firms use the latest techniques, such as quantitative analysis, management auditing, and operational auditing, in their audits. Other practitioners are content with the traditional approach. I strongly believe that a handbook should not only present the best present practice but encourage and make readily available the new trends which are now discernible and are being used by leaders in the field and which will be common practice five or ten years from now.

An entire section, Part Six, "Horizons for Auditing," consisting of seven chapters, is devoted to the future developments in auditing. In this part, "Horizons for a Profession," the research study by Roy and MacNeill, is used as a frame of reference. The first chapter, "The Common Body of Auditing Knowledge," summarizes the conclusions and recommendations of the study, particularly with reference to auditing. Topics which will be of major importance to auditors of the future are well covered in the following six chapters: "Quantitative Analysis"; "Ratio, Change, and Trend Analysis"; "Analytical Auditing—The Flow-chart Approach"; "Management Performance Auditing"; "Operational Auditing"; and "Planning, Programming, and Budgeting Systems."

A large number of references are included. First, there are the specific references in the text and footnotes; second, there are the general references in a broad bibliography at the end of each chapter. The reader may wish to become familiar with the background, history, and development of a topic which, for practical purposes, cannot be covered in a handbook. The bibliographies have been arranged in a manner that will be most useful to the auditor. Each bibliography is divided into three distinct groups: (1) official opinions, statements, pronouncements, etc.; (2) authoritative texts, brochures, etc.; and (3) magazine articles relating to current developments. The first two groups are arranged alphabetically, and the last group is arranged chronologically, so that an auditor interested in current material will not have to look through a number of items with which he is not presently concerned.

A special debt is owed to the following members of the Board of Advisors for their valuable help in structuring the handbook and in suggesting contributors and consultants: Mr. Joseph L. Roth of Price Waterhouse & Co.; Professor Lawrence L. Vance of the Graduate School of Business Administration, University of California, Berkeley; and Mr. Frederick E. Horn of Arthur Young & Company.

Appreciation is expressed to the American Institute of Certified Public Accountants for permission to use various Institute publications. Thanks also go to the Financial Executives Institute, The Institute of Internal Auditors, the Federal Government Accountants Association, the U.S. General Accounting Office, and others for permission to use their published material.

Special thanks must go to my wife, Dorothy, for her patience and forbearance during the long period of preparation, and also for her help in typing parts of the manuscript.

I wish to thank my secretary, Mrs. Frieda Payne, for her helpfulness and Mrs. Sophie Wetter for typing various parts of the manuscript. Thanks are also due the following outstanding Hofstra students who helped with the voluminous task of proofreading: Messrs. John Connolly, Jr., Kenneth Shavelson, Joseph Wenk, and Miss Nannette Stvartak.

Last and most important, I wish to thank the contributors and consultants for the high quality of their material and for their understanding and patience during the manuscript editing. It is mostly because of their efforts that I believe the result will be an important contribution to our profession and hopefully will help compensate for the tremendous amount of work put forth by so many, for so long.

James A. Cashin

Part One

Principles, Standards, and Responsibilities

Chapter 1

The Field of Auditing

ROBERT E. SCHLOSSER

Director, Professional Development Division, American Institute of Certified Public Accountants

GENERAL

The Nature of Auditing. Auditing has been defined as being "concerned with the verification of accounting data, with determining the accuracy and reliability of accounting statements and reports."[1] A more comprehensive

[1] R. K. Mautz, *Fundamentals of Auditing*, 2d ed., New York, John Wiley & Sons, Inc., 1964, p. 1.

concept would consider auditing to be a systematic examination of financial statements, records, and related operations to determine adherence to generally accepted accounting principles, management policies, or stated requirements.

At the outset it should be clear that auditing is not a subdivision or a continuation of the field of accounting.

> The relationship of auditing to accounting is close, yet their natures are very different; they are business associates, not parent and child. Accounting includes the collection, classification, summarization, and communication of financial data; it involves the measurement and communication of business events and conditions as they affect and represent a given enterprise or other entity. The task of accounting is to reduce a tremendous mass of detailed information to manageable and understandable proportions. Auditing does none of these things. Auditing must consider business events and conditions, too, but it does not have the task of measuring or communicating them. Its task is to review the measurements and communications of accounting for propriety. Auditing is analytical; it is critical, investigative, concerned with the basis for accounting measurements and assertions. Auditing emphasizes proof, the support for financial statements and data. Thus, auditing has its principal roots, not in accounting which it reviews, but in logic on which it leans heavily for ideas and methods.[2]

An auditor engaged to review financial statements, management policies, or specific procedures must concern himself with gathering sufficient evidence about the object of his review so that he can render a professional opinion about it.

The *purpose* of any kind of audit is to add some degree of validity to the object of the review. Financial statements are free from management bias if reviewed by an independent auditor; management policies are carried out more effectively if procedures governed by the policies are subject to review; financial reports of government agencies have a higher degree of validity if they have been reviewed by a third party. Published financial statements, for example, are a series of claims or representations asserted to be a fair presentation of financial position for specific dates and results of operations for specific time segments. An audit of these representations is an effort to determine whether the financial statements are fair presentations for the dates and periods claimed. In any presentation of financial information—internal or external—or in the operation of internal control activities, individuals could be guilty of (1) personal bias, (2) self-interest, (3) carelessness, and (4) dishonesty.[3] The principal *objective* of an audit is to eliminate these four causes of distortion of the facts.

The Philosophy of Auditing.[4] In developing their "philosophy of auditing," Mautz and Sharaf hold that there are five "primary concepts in auditing":

1. Evidence
2. Due audit care
3. Fair presentation
4. Independence
5. Ethical conduct

Evidence. This "includes all influences on the mind of an auditor which affect his judgment about the truthfulness of . . . propositions, submitted to

[2] R. K. Mautz and Hussein A. Sharaf, *The Philosophy of Auditing*, Chicago, American Accounting Association, 1961, p. 14.

[3] Howard F. Stettler, *Systems Based Independent Audits*, Englewood Cliffs, N.J., Prentice-Hall, Inc., 1967, p. 1.

[4] Mautz and Sharaf, *op. cit.*

him for review." The auditor is not searching for concrete, absolute proof. He is looking for that which is required to assure a reasonable and competent man of the fairness of management's financial representations and/or adequacy of internal control activities.

Due audit care. This is concerned with the extent of the examination required in conducting an audit. More simply stated, this concept deals with the problem of determining when enough evidence has been collected to constitute sufficient proof. While there can be guidelines to aid the auditor in making this decision, the only rule that really can exist is that the auditor himself must be adequately convinced that the financial statements represent a fair presentation or that the procedures examined are being followed in accordance with management policy.

A part of the concept of due care is the idea that "due audit care" is expected to be carried out by a *reasonable man* who has "adequate technical training and proficiency as an auditor."[5] In undertaking a review of a financial or operational area, there is no such thing as absolute proof. There can only be a qualitative or a quantitative probability that a representation is true. The minimum degree of probability acceptable to the auditor is that degree any *reasonable man* would accept as being the minimum. The concept of due audit care, therefore, is concerned with the extent of examination required to establish that financial and operational representations are true within review limits acceptable to a reasonable man.

Fair presentation. This concerns the following three concepts of auditing:

1. Accounting propriety
2. Adequate disclosure
3. Audit obligation

ACCOUNTING PROPRIETY: In an effort to summarize the concept of accounting propriety, that is, conformance with generally accepted accounting principles, it is helpful to abstract from accepted accounting practices the essence of the principles now before us. The principles we now have are primarily concerned with two broad areas of accounting: the first may be called accounting methods, the second financial-statement presentation. *Accounting methods* include such practices as account classification, transaction analysis, the practice of capitalizing the cost of long-lived assets and subsequently amortizing these costs through depreciation charges, the use of accruals and deferrals, the consideration of inventory in income determination, methods of pricing inventories, and the like. Unless acceptable accounting methods are followed, reliable data will not result. *Financial-statement presentation* is concerned with balance sheet classifications, the treatment of unusual gains and losses for income-statement purposes, the disclosure of contingent liabilities, indication of valuation bases in the balance sheet, and similar matters. Even with reliable data, unsatisfactory financial-statement presentation may conceal useful information or even be misleading and deceitful.

In each area, the goal of generally accepted accounting principles is to provide financial statement data which faithfully portray the realities of enterprise operations and financial condition. The essence of these principles can therefore be presented in the following statements of Mautz and Sharaf, pages 168–169:

[5] Statements on Auditing Procedure No. 33, *Auditing Standards and Procedures*, AICPA (Committee on Auditing Procedure), New York, 1963, p. 18.

1. Acceptable accounting methods are those which realistically recognize enterprise transactions and their effects as they occur, and which, through the use of the accrual system, relate efforts (costs) and accomplishments (revenues) on the basis of their pertinence to one another within time periods.

2. Acceptable financial statement presentations are those which, without favoritism or bias, report as fairly as possible data obtained through acceptable accounting methods to those having a legitimate interest in the results of enterprise operations and enterprise financial position.

In these statements we find the basic ideas of the concept of accounting propriety. To the extent that the presentations submitted to an auditor meet these requirements, they can be said to "present fairly," to meet the requirements of accounting propriety. But if he finds that they fail to meet those requirements he must reject them and call for their improvement. The auditor's concern must be with the goals of generally accepted principles, not with their letter. An approach sometimes followed is one that finds acceptable any method or presentation that is "not misleading." Such a negative attitude should not be condoned and certainly does not satisfy the concept of accounting propriety. Surely the auditor should insist upon something more constructive than the mere absence of injury; unless a practice actually aids and furthers understanding, it should be held deficient.

ADEQUATE DISCLOSURE: The concept of adequate disclosure embraces the idea that the auditor has not performed his function regarding the disclosure of financial information to third parties unless he has:

(1) assured himself that sufficient information for investment decisions under current market conditions has been made available,

(2) indicated his ability and willingness as an expert to subject that information to review and thereafter to express his professional opinion as to its reliability, and

(3) adopted throughout an attitude of protecting the interests of investors to the best of his professional abilities.

Mautz and Sharaf couched the concept of adequate disclosure in terms of the relationship of the certified public accountant to readers of published financial reports. It should be evident, however, that the above three standards, with slight modifications, apply equally to nonpublic auditors. The nonpublic auditor has not performed his function regarding adequate disclosure unless he has (1) assured himself that sufficient information for management decisions under current market and operating conditions has been made available, (2) (unchanged from above), and (3) adopted throughout an attitude of protecting the interests of stockholders or taxpayers to the best of his professional abilities.

AUDIT OBLIGATION: In order to carry out the concept of audit obligation, the auditor must take steps to protect those who read his report from being misled either on the extent of his examination or the nature of his opinion.

Independence. The concept of *independence* is extremely important to auditors, independent of management, who have extensive responsibilities to third parties. Nevertheless, a degree of independence is necessary for those auditors working as employees in business or those performing audit functions for government. In order to perform a proper review, the auditor must not be influenced by anyone in the unit under review. This means that the auditor should have an "independence of approach" and be free from "bias and prejudice." Because of its vital importance to the independent auditor, a more complete discussion of independence is contained in Chapter 6.

Ethical conduct. This basic auditing concept embraces the idea that the auditor must carry out his work within the framework of a professional code of ethics. As Mautz and Sharaf point out, page 237,

Professional ethics are but a special application of general ethics. General ethics emphasize that there are certain guides by means of which an individual can govern his conduct. Knowledge of the ultimate outcome of his actions on himself and others, awareness of the requirements of the society in which he lives, respect for divine law, acceptance of duty, obligation to act toward others as one would want all men to act at all times, and recognition of the norms of ethical conduct in the society in which one operates all aid the individual to attain a high degree of ethical conduct.

General Objectives of Auditing. As Holmes points out, "The immediate objectives of an audit are to ascertain the reliability of the financial statements, and to render an opinion of the fairness of presentation of those statements."[6] While these objectives seem more appropriate as objectives of "external auditing" (see "Branches of Auditing" below), they are valid objectives for all branches of auditing. More importantly, Holmes points out that "the long-range objectives of an audit should be to serve as a guide to management's future decisions in all financial matters, such as controlling, forecasting, analyzing, and reporting. These objectives have as their purposes the improvement of performances."[7]

History and Development of Auditing. There is evidence that auditing of a sort was done in ancient times. The fact that early rulers required that their household accounts be kept by two scribes independently is evidence that some measures were taken to prevent defalcations in these accounts. As commerce developed so did the need for independent reviews to ascertain the accuracy and reliability of the records kept of the various commercial ventures. Professional auditing was enhanced through the British Companies Act of 1862 and the general recognition, during the period leading up to the act, that "an orderly and standardized system of accounting was desirable for both accurate reporting and fraud prevention."[8] Also, there was "a general acceptance of the need for an independent review of the accounts for both large and small enterprises."[9] From 1862 to 1905, professional auditing grew and flourished in England, and it was introduced in the United States around 1900. In England considerable emphasis was still placed on the detection of fraud, but auditing in the United States took an independent turn away from fraud detection as a primary objective of auditing. In 1912, Montgomery said,

> In what might be called the formative days of auditing, students were taught that the chief objects of an audit were:
> 1. Detection and prevention of fraud
> 2. Detection and prevention of errors, but in recent years there has been a decided change in demand and service. Present-day purposes are:
> 1. To ascertain actual financial condition and earnings of an enterprise.
> 2. Detection of fraud and errors, but this is a minor objective.[10]

This change in audit objective continued to develop, not without opposition, to about 1940. At this time, "there was a fair degree of agreement that the auditor could not and should not be primarily concerned with the detection

[6] Arthur W. Holmes, *Basic Auditing Principles,* 3d ed., Homewood, Ill., Richard D. Irwin, Inc., 1966, p. 2.

[7] *Ibid.*

[8] R. Gene Brown, "Changing Audit Objectives and Techniques," *The Accounting Review,* October, 1962, p. 697. The contributing author has relied heavily on R. Gene Brown's article, which is well researched and documented for the entire history section.

[9] *Ibid.*

[10] Robert H. Montgomery, *Auditing Theory and Practice,* 8th ed., New York, The Ronald Press Company, 1912, p. 13.

of fraud."[11] More importantly, the primary objective of an independent audit should be to review the financial position and results of operation as indicated by the financial statements of the client so that an opinion on the fairness of such presentations can be rendered to the many publics of the client. Table 1 is a tabulation of the evolution of auditing objectives and techniques.

TABLE 1 Evolution of Auditing Objectives and Techniques

Period	Stated audit objectives	Extent of verification	Importance of internal control
Ancient–1500	Detection of fraud	Detailed	Not recognized
1500–1850	Detection of fraud	Detailed	Not recognized
1850–1905	Detection of fraud Detection of clerical errors	Some tests, primarily detailed	Not recognized
1905–1933	Determination of fairness of reported financial position Detection of fraud and errors	Detailed and testing	Slight recognition
1933–1940	Determination of fairness of reported financial position Detection of fraud and errors	Testing	Awakening of interest
1940–1960	Determination of fairness of reported financial position	Testing	Substantial emphasis

SOURCE: *The Accounting Review*, October, 1962, pp. 696–703.

In summarizing his article, Brown remarked,

In most professions it is rather difficult to predict the future, but there are some significant trends revealed by the history of auditing which should carry forward into succeeding years. Interpreted in line with changing audit objectives and techniques these trends seem to indicate:

1. The first and foremost audit objective will remain the determination of the fairness of financial statement representations.

2. Reliance on the system of internal controls will increase. The audit will be primarily a system of audit procedures. Detailed testing will take place only insofar as it is required to detect irregularities, errors, or to evaluate the effectiveness of the internal controls.

3. Since the fairness of the financial statement representations is affected by all material misstatements, there will be acceptance of the general responsibility of the auditor to perform tests to detect material defalcations and errors if they exist. This will be incorporated as a supplementary audit objective.[12]

Parallel to the growth of independent auditing in the United States, internal and governmental auditing developed and became part of the field of auditing. As independent auditors recognized the importance of good internal control and its bearing on the extent of testing necessary in the independent audit, they supported the growth of auditing departments within client organizations who would be charged with the development and maintenance of good internal control procedures apart from the general accounting department. Progressive companies fostered the expansion of

[11] Brown, *op. cit.*, p. 700.
[12] *Ibid.*, p. 708.

the activities of internal audit departments into areas which are beyond the scope of the accounting system. Today many internal audit departments are reviewers of all phases of corporate operations, of which financial operations are a part.

Governmental auditing was officially recognized in 1921 when the Congress of the United States established the General Accounting Office.

> This law . . . directed the Comptroller General, among other things, to investigate all matters relating to the receipt, disbursement and application of public funds. Later legislation extended and clarified his audit authority, particularly with respect to Government corporations, but the 1921 law laid the primary foundation for a broad scope of auditing that went beyond accounting, financial matters and legal compliance.[13]

A recent survey showed that there were more than 75 separate audit organizations in the federal government.

Relationship to Internal Control. In Table 1 it can be observed that the objectives of external auditing changed from emphasis on fraud detection to a professional review of financial statements by an expert, so that a professional opinion indicating that financial condition and results of operation have been fairly presented can be given. The change in objective was effected because auditors recognized the importance of good internal control.

Internal control is "the plan of organization and all of the co-ordinate methods and measures adopted within a business to safeguard its assets, check the accuracy and reliability of its accounting data, promote operational efficiency, and encourage adherence to prescribed managerial policies."[14] If the system of internal control is adequate, the probability that fraud or other errors exist in any magnitude is remote. Relying on the absence of fraud and data processing error, the independent auditor can spend more of his time gathering evidence concerning the fairness of the presentation of financial position and results of operations.

Independent auditors (private or governmental) must review the system of internal control in each engagement and based on its adequacy develop the scope of their examination. Internal auditors are usually given the responsibility (among others) to design, implement, review, and revise the system of internal control in their company or agency.

The Opinion of the Independent Auditor. Although it is true that everyone engaged in auditing activities uses many common techniques and issues reports of his findings, the function of the report issued by an independent auditor sets it apart from all others. "It is the sole outward evidence of the major activity of the public accounting profession, and it is heavily relied upon whenever financial decisions are based upon financial statements."[15] The independent auditor's report, or "certificate," is issued only after an investigation of the representations made by his client on its financial position and results of operations as evidenced by published financial statements. The independent auditor must state that "our examination was made in accordance with generally accepted auditing standards, and accordingly included such tests of the accounting records and such other auditing procedures as we considered necessary in the circumstances." If, after his review of his client's financial position and results of operations, he is in

[13] Ellsworth H. Morse, Jr., "GAO Audits of Management Performance," *The Journal of Accountancy*, October, 1961, pp. 42–43.

[14] Statements on Auditing Procedure No. 33, p. 27.

[15] Stettler, *op. cit.*, p. 6.

agreement with the representations, he must state this in his report. It should read substantially as follows:

In our opinion, the accompanying balance sheet and statements of income and retained earnings present fairly the financial position of ABC Company at December 31, 19__, and the results of its operations for the year then ended, in conformity with generally accepted accounting principles applied on a basis consistent with that of the preceding year.

More on the opinion of the independent auditor will be covered in Chapter 6.

AUDITING CLASSIFICATIONS

Branches of Auditing. Auditing as a field of endeavor is concerned with reviewing the way in which business events have been measured and communicated. It is also concerned with reviewing the adequacy and reliability of management information systems and operating procedures. In short, the field of auditing encompasses all review functions. Obviously, more than one group of professionals are concerned with auditing and the conduct of audits. Professional auditing can be classified generally into three branches according to those performing the audit. These are:

1. Independent auditing
2. Internal auditing
3. Governmental auditing

Essentially, the services performed by auditors in each of the above three branches are similar, and yet each branch has separate and distinct responsibilities and differing degrees of independence.

Independent auditing. This is auditing as carried out by certified public accountants who "are independent contractors who, after adequate examination and investigation, offer a professional opinion as to whether the concern's financial statements . . . present fairly the results of operations and the financial condition of the enterprise."[16] Although the independent auditor is hired by an enterprise to perform his services, he is primarily responsible to the public who rely on his opinion concerning the financial statements. In other review matters he is primarily responsible to his client. It is because of this primary responsibility to third parties that the independent auditor must be, in fact and in appearance, independent of the client who has hired him.

Internal auditing. The Institute of Internal Auditors delineates the *internal audit branch* of the field of auditing as "an independent appraisal activity within an organization for the review of accounting and other operations as a basis for service to management. It is a managerial control, which functions by measuring and evaluating the effectiveness of other controls." Francis J. Walsh, Jr., lists five primary objectives of an internal auditing program:

1. Determine the adequacy of the system of internal control.
2. Investigate compliance with company policies and procedures.
3. Verify the existence of assets, see that proper safeguards for assets are maintained and prevent or discover fraud.
4. Check on the reliability of the accounting and reporting system.
5. Report findings to management and recommend corrective action where necessary.[17]

[16] Mautz, *op. cit.*, p. 5.

[17] Francis J. Walsh, Jr., *Internal Auditing,* Business Policy Study No. 111, New York, National Industrial Conference Board, Inc., 1963, p. 5.

Governmental auditing. This is the most comprehensive of the three branches of auditing. Many government agencies have internal auditing departments which are expected to confine their investigations to the specific agency. Other governmental units such as the GAO (General Accounting Office) are set up for the express purpose of performing audits of other governmental units and of the private enterprises who do business with the government where the right of the governmental unit to perform such audits is a prerequisite for contract awards.

More will be discussed about each of the branches of auditing in following chapters, but it should be apparent from the brief discussion above that

> the similarities in the work of auditors in these several fields are far more important than the differences. All those engaged in actual auditing activities are concerned with audit evidence, collect it through application of the same basic techniques, and have similar problems of report writing and program planning. Certain essentials must receive first attention, therefore, regardless of which field of auditing constitutes the auditor's major interest.[18]

Kinds of Audits. An audit, as described above, is a review designed to add some degree of validity to the object of the review. Audits can be classified according to the audit emphasis into the following groups:

1. Financial
2. Operational
3. Compliance
4. Performance
5. Special reviews

A *financial audit* is a review of the representations made on published financial statements. As was described above, this particular kind of audit must be made in accordance with generally accepted auditing standards. Although such an audit could be performed by internal or governmental auditors, a lesser degree of independence implicit in their relationship to the unit being audited may mitigate the reliability of their report. A financial audit is not a detailed review in any way. It is a test of accounting and other related records. The scope of these tests is determined by the auditor based on his own judgment and experience.

An *operational audit* is a review of an area or operation which is not usually under the jurisdiction of a controller or treasurer in a business enterprise or governmental unit. Frederic E. Mints, Resident Internal Auditor of Lockheed Aircraft Corporation, has stated:

> So when I use the term "operational audit" or perhaps "audit of other operations," you will understand that I am thinking primarily of the areas or types of activities to be audited and that I intend to refer to reviews of activities other than those usually under the jurisdiction of the company's controller or treasurer.[19]

As a point of clarification, Mints adds a statement:

> In talking about an operational audit I am not suggesting that the auditor attempt to make an appraisal of the technical skills of engineers, machinists, geologists, or other specialists. Rather I mean that he should make an appraisal of the way in which a particular operation or activity is administered—whether its objectives have been clearly defined in conformance with sound business principles and communicated to all concerned; whether the policies under which it operates conform to the established

[18] Mautz, *op. cit.*

[19] Frederic E. Mints, "New Developments in Operational Auditing," *The Internal Auditor*, June, 1960, p. 9.

objectives; whether those policies are implemented by specific procedures and whether those procedures are followed as intended; whether necessary administrative information is accumulated by orderly methods; and whether management is provided with adequate, timely and accurate reports containing information on matters of primary concern.[20]

A *compliance audit* is one designed to determine if certain contractual agreements have been kept. For example, many contracts let by the federal government contain certain statements which tie the amount to be paid out under the contract to specific performance of the contractor. Quality of product and cost to produce are but two examples of many determinants governing the amounts to be paid out in such contracts. A compliance audit seeks to determine if the terms of the contract have been kept. One agency of the federal government is set up for the express purpose of performing compliance audits—The Defense Contract Audit Agency.

A *performance audit* is one which is not tied to written contracts. Much of the work of the internal auditor is concerned with performance auditing. In order to bring about effective internal control in an organization, many people must perform specified control activities. Performance auditing is concerned with determining how well these control activities are carried out. For example, the comparison of purchase order, invoice, and receiving report is essential to proper control over cash disbursements. A review of the performance of this activity is an appropriate performance audit.

A *special review* is a miscellaneous category that includes audits which are not considered as financial, operational, compliance, or performance audits. An auditor's competence to do a particular review and whether his independence is essential to the review would be the only limiting features pertaining to the review. For example, many auditors would not be competent to recommend a new plant location. Some, however, through the application of appropriate techniques, could make a valid recommendation.

AUDITING FUNDAMENTALS

Guides and Methodology of Auditing. There are four general types of guides used by auditors. They are:

1. Principles
2. Standards
3. Techniques
4. Procedures

Each type of guide is different and distinct, yet they are all connected so as to form the overall guide for auditors.

C. A. Moyer distinguished among the four types of guides as follows:

Auditing *Principles* are the basic premises of Auditing which indicate the purpose and objectives of auditing. Auditing *Standards* are criteria or measures of performance. Principles define objectives; standards set up criteria to be observed in accomplishing these objectives. Auditing *Techniques* are the devices or methods available to the auditor for obtaining competent evidential matter. They are the working tools of the auditor. Auditing *Procedures* are ways of applying techniques to particular phases of a particular audit. The procedures adopted in different engagements result from the judicious application of the available techniques.[21]

[20] *Ibid.*

[21] C. A. Moyer, "Relationship of Audit Programs to Audit Standards, Principles, Techniques, and Procedures," *The Journal of Accountancy* (AICPA, New York), December, 1952, p. 687.

In using these types of guides, an audit program will not merely be a listing of procedures. Instead, it will be a plan of action in which recognized *principles* imply certain levels of achievement—*standards*—and which utilizes various *techniques* so that *procedures* selected will secure adequate audit evidence.

No one has formulated a formal set of auditing principles. However, Mautz and Sharaf have come very close to a set of principles in developing their five "primary concepts in auditing" (see pages 1-4 to 1-7). That these concepts are principles is evidenced by the fact that the generally accepted auditing standards which have been developed by the American Institute of Certified Public Accountants (AICPA) are minimum levels of achievement covering the five conceptual areas of evidence, due care, fair presentation, independence, and ethical conduct. The full text of the audit standards follows:

I. *General Standards*

1. The examination is to be performed by a person or persons having adequate technical training and proficiency as an auditor.
2. In all matters relating to the assignment an independence in mental attitude is to be maintained by the auditor or auditors.
3. Due professional care is to be exercised in the performance of the examination and the preparation of the report.

II. *Standards of Field Work*

1. The work is to be adequately planned and assistants, if any, are to be properly supervised.
2. There is to be a proper study and evaluation of the existing internal control as a basis for reliance thereon and for the determination of the resultant extent of the tests to which auditing procedures are to be restricted.
3. Sufficient competent evidential matter is to be obtained through inspection, observation, inquiries and confirmations to afford a reasonable basis for an opinion regarding the financial statements under examination.

III. *Standards of Reporting*

1. The report shall state whether the financial statements are presented in accordance with generally accepted principles of accounting.
2. The report shall state whether such principles have been consistently observed in the current period in relation to the preceding period.
3. Informative disclosures in the financial statements are to be regarded as reasonably adequate unless otherwise stated in the report.
4. The report shall either contain an expression of opinion regarding the financial statements, taken as a whole, or an assertion to the effect that an opinion cannot be expressed. When an overall opinion cannot be expressed, the reasons therefor should be stated. In all cases where an auditor's name is associated with financial statements the report should contain a clear-cut indication of the character of the auditor's examination, if any, and the degree of responsibility he is taking.

It should be apparent from a review of the above standards that the general standards and the standards of fieldwork apply to all types of auditing. The reporting standards apply primarily to independent auditing. Using the concept of "fair presentation" as developed by Mautz and Sharaf, the following reporting standards seem appropriate for those audits which are not independent reviews of financial position and results of operations:

1. The report shall state whether the segment of the data processing system or other operation under review is being carried out in accordance with company, regulatory, or contractual policy.
2. The report shall state whether such policies have been consistently observed.

3. The report shall contain clear and concise recommendations, if any are necessary, for improving the segment of the data processing system or other operation under review.

Audit *techniques* and audit *procedures* are as closely related as principles and standards. Audit techniques are tools which can be used on specific audit engagements. Mautz lists the following audit techniques:[22]

1. Physical examination and count
2. Confirmation
3. Examination of authoritative documents and comparison with the record
4. Recomputation
5. Retracing bookkeeping procedures
6. Scanning
7. Inquiry
8. Examination of subsidiary records
9. Correlation with related information
10. Observation of pertinent activities and conditions

Audit procedures are the specific means used to carry out a specific audit technique. For example, on a specific engagement, *positive*-type confirmation requests instead of *negative*-type requests could be used to implement the technique of confirmation. A physical examination could be carried out in one situation if the auditor merely viewed certain items, but in another situation, the auditor might deem it necessary to view *and* handle certain items.

AUDITING PATTERN

In general, the pattern of any audit consists of three phases:

1. Planning the fieldwork
2. Carrying out the fieldwork
3. Rendering the auditor's report

Planning the Fieldwork. This has as its objective the preparation of an audit program so that the most effective and efficient audit possible is carried out. Ideally, an audit program should be a comprehensive outline of the work to be done in a specific engagement which when completed will permit the proper report to be issued. In the case of an audit program for an independent opinion audit, sufficient investigative measures must be taken to permit an opinion to be rendered on the client's financial statements. In the case of an audit program for an internal auditor undertaking a performance audit, the audit program should contain measures which, upon completion, will permit an informative report to be written concerning the specific procedure(s) reviewed. It is the audit program which is the basis for planning audit work and against which supervision and control can be measured.

Because of the unique nature of every audit engagement, an audit program should be tailor-made to fit each situation. "Among the factors which must be considered in preparing an audit program are internal control, the client's accounting procedures, the timing of the work in relation to the balance sheet date, any special instructions, and the size, nature, and extent of the client's operations."[23] Once an audit program is approved by the auditor in charge of the engagement, various tasks can be assigned to assistants.

[22] Mautz, *op. cit.*, pp. 76–77.
[23] Stettler, *op. cit.*, p. 126.

Carrying Out the Fieldwork. In an independent audit this is usually under the supervision of a senior or supervising auditor. It is his responsibility to direct the staff assigned to the particular engagement and to select the specific procedures which must be undertaken to assemble the appropriate audit evidence. It is also the responsibility of the senior auditor to do a field review of all audit working papers to see that all the steps called for in the audit program have been completed properly and that the conclusions drawn and included in the working papers are supported by evidence contained in the working papers. When the fieldwork is completed, a draft opinion is prepared and submitted to the auditor in charge of the engagement along with the working papers for his review.

Rendering the Auditor's Report. This is the responsibility of the auditor in charge of the engagement. When the draft opinion and working papers are submitted to him for review, he must determine that all the steps in the audit program have been completed and properly initialed by the staff member carrying out each step. He then will make a thorough review of the working papers to determine if his interpretations of the evidence presented agree with the conclusions reached by the senior auditor during the field review of the working papers. Any questions, of course, must be resolved through consultation with the senior auditor. At times it is necessary to do additional fieldwork in order to answer some of the questions arising in this review. Once the auditor in charge is satisfied, the appropriate report is rendered to the client. Usually this report is a short-form unqualified opinion on the financial statements. Chapter 40 contains a sample wording of this type of opinion as well as other types of short-form opinions and a discussion of long-form reports.

AUDITING RELATIONSHIPS

Responsibilities to Various Groups. As previously noted, the objective of the independent auditor is to add validity to the fairness of his client's financial statements by giving an opinion on these statements. Shareholders, to whom the financial statements are primarily directed, can rely on the accuracy of the audited financial representations to the degree which would be demanded by any reasonable man. In effect, the auditor is substituting his personal examination and opinion for that of each shareholder or for anyone having an interest in the financial statements. Shareholders and other interested publics might use the statements for the following purposes: [24]

1. A report of stewardship
2. A basis for fiscal policy
3. A device to determine the legality of dividends
4. A guide to wise dividend action
5. A basis for the granting of credit
6. Information for prospective investors in an enterprise
7. A guide to the value of investments already made
8. An aid to government supervision
9. A basis for price or rate regulation
10. A basis for taxation

It is possible to classify the user of published financial information according to the 10 uses and delineate at least 10 reporting publics.

[24] Norton M. Bedford, *Income Determination Theory,* Reading, Mass., Addison-Wesley Publishing Company, Inc., 1965, p. 13.

If each of these publics had the ability and/or time to examine the financial statements personally in the manner in which the independent auditor does, it would be unnecessary for the auditor to perform his audit; but this would be impossible. Thus, the value of the independent audit lies in the confidence the various publics have in the independent auditor and his opinion. The fairness of the auditor's opinion has value only if the auditor has not subordinated his independent attitude to the will of the client or created the situation where he is performing management duties for the client and thus auditing his own work. If ever the various publics lost confidence in the reliability and validity of the auditor's opinion, the auditor could not perform his function.

Carey and Doherty claim that "the auditor must assess his relationships with his client to determine whether his opinion would be *considered* objective and unbiased by one who had knowledge of all the facts. In other words, he must not only be independent, but must not *appear* to be otherwise."[25] Carey and Doherty have interpreted the professional responsibility auditors must accept as prescribed by the Code of Professional Ethics of the AICPA.

By fufilling these professional responsibilities, the auditor fulfills certain responsibilities to his client, to his profession, and to himself. To his *client*, the auditor's opinion adds assurance to the fairness of its own financial representations.

To his profession, the independent auditor has the responsibility of fulfilling his obligations to the public so that the profession may continue to have the stature of a profession.

The most important responsibility of an independent auditor is to himself. It is his opinion that is being substituted for the opinion of various publics and his client. Thus, he has the responsibility to himself to uphold the value of his opinion. The fundamental value of an audit is in the value of the auditor's responsibility to himself. Once the auditor fails to remain responsible to himself, his entire value to his various publics is lost.

A. C. Littleton summarized more specific audit responsibilities in his article, "Vocabulary of Auditing Techniques."[26] He said that the auditor has the duty to *ascertain facts, examine evidence,* and *report opinions* to the public. To the client, he must *confer, consult,* and *advise,* while to his profession, he has the duty to *detect, understand,* and *judge.*

Besides professional responsibility to the public, to his client, to his profession, and to himself, the independent auditor has certain legal responsibilities. The English court case of *Kingston Cotton Mill Co.* summarizes nicely the auditor's liability to his client. "An auditor is not bound to do more than exercise reasonable care and skill in making inquiries and investigations. He is not an insurer; he does not guarantee that the books do correctly show the true position of the company's affairs; he does not guarantee that his balance sheet is accurate according to the books of the company. The accountant is a watch-dog, but not a bloodhound."[27] The *Craig-Anyon* case[28] pointed out that the plaintiffs should not be allowed to recover for losses

[25] John L. Carey and William O. Doherty, *Ethical Standards of the Accounting Profession*, New York, AICPA, 1966, p. 20.

[26] A. C. Littleton, "Vocabulary of Auditing Techniques," *The New York Certified Public Accountant* (New York Society of Certified Public Accountants), November, 1947, p. 639.

[27] *Kingston Cotton Mill Co.*, 2 Ch. 279 (CA), 22 Acct. L.R. 77 (1896).

[28] 212 App. Div. 55, 208 N.Y.S. 259 (1st Dep't 1925), *aff'd without opinion* 242 N.Y. 569, 152 N.C. 431 (1926).

which they could have avoided by the exercise of (their own) reasonable care. The *National Surety Corporation* case[29] noted, however, that "negligence of the employer is a defense (for the CPA) only when it has contributed to the accountant's failure to perform his contract and to report the truth."

The accountant's liability to third parties, by common law, was summarized by Saul Levy as follows:

> . . . we still have the possibility of liability for mere negligence if the particular third party, or a limited group of which he was a member, was known to the accountant with sufficient definiteness as a party for whose primary benefit the certified statement of the accountant was intended.
>
> The *Ultramares* case held that a false representation of fact as of knowledge creates liability even if believed to be true. This rule emphasizes the vital distinction between representations of fact and expression of opinions.
>
> . . . The principle that there is liability for fraud to persons outside the privity of contract, that gross negligence may be evidence of fraud, that even the expression of opinions may be a fraudulent representation if there is not a sincere and honest belief in that opinion—are all long established in the law.[30]

The accountant, though, has been assigned legal liability by the enactment of the 1933 Securities Act (which deals with the issuance of new securities) and by the Securities Exchange Act of 1934 (which deals with the exchange of existing securities). These acts have the general effect that "insofar as the work of the accountant falls within the jurisdiction of (these acts) there can be liability for mere negligence as well as for fraud, to certain large classes of third parties, namely the purchasers and owners of securities."[31]

Two other areas of legal liability might arise. They are (1) the ownership of the accountant's working papers and (2) the extent of the confidential relationship rights between the accountant and his client. The first was answered in the *Ipswich Mills* case,[32] stating that "in view of the potential importance of the accountant's working papers, many states have confirmed their ownership by the accountant through specific statutory enactment. Even in the absence of such statutory provisions, however, the courts have recognized and upheld such ownership by the accountant."[33] The second was answered in the *Frye* case,[34] which "emphasized that neither the confidential nature of the accountant's working papers, nor the personal ownership of them by the accountant was sufficient legal reasons for refusal by the accountant to divulge their contents in a judicial proceeding to which they were relevant."[35]

In summary, it is the accountant's assumption of responsibility that has created (1) the value of his opinion and (2) the degree of reliance upon it that the public has assumed.

Relationship to Other Fields. Auditing, although distinct in itself, is related to other disciplines and relies on many of the techniques of those other fields. For instance, statistical sampling is a prime example. Basically, the application of statistical sampling adds quantitative analysis to areas of auditing that formerly were based solely on qualitative methods. "It provides a

[29] *National Surety Corp. v. Lybrand,* 256 App. Div. 226, 9 N.Y.S. 2d 554 (1st Dep't 1939).

[30] Saul Levy, *Accountants' Legal Responsibility,* New York, American Institute of Accountants, 1954, p. 43.

[31] *Ibid.,* p. 45.

[32] 260 Mass. 453, 157 N.E. 604 (1927).

[33] Levy, *op. cit.,* p. 54.

[34] *Ibid.,* p. 61.

[35] *Ibid.*

means of measuring mathematically the extent of the uncertainty that results from examining only a part of the data, instead of all of it."[36] It must be noted, though, that statistical sampling is not a mechanical means of replacing the auditor's judgment but instead will supplement this judgment and aid in its application.

Until recently, there has been a tendency for auditors to accept these new techniques reluctantly. However, as Trueblood and Cyert noted,

> Would it not be difficult for the profession to justify its failure to use a technique found to be of such material help in other professional fields? . . . What would happen if, in a court proceeding involving accountants' liability, a competent statistician were to demonstrate mathematically that the auditor's sampling procedures or conclusions (which had been based on his qualitative judgment) were not statistically justifiable?[37]

But the basis for acceptance by the auditor should go far beyond any legal liability. The auditor has a professional responsibility to satisfy himself as to the authenticity of available evidence. Because of the time and cost limitation of an audit, it is impossible for the auditor to conduct a complete detailed audit, but instead he must rely on tests. Therefore, since the auditor does rely on tests as a basis for making his judgment, it is inconceivable that he should not use all available and statistically sound procedures to aid him in (1) calculating the sample size, (2) selecting the sample (i.e., which items should be sampled), and (3) evaluating the results. And these three aids form the basis for statistical sampling. A more complete explanation of the use of statistics in auditing is given in Chapter 15.

Auditing is also related to the field of management advisory services. It is here that the auditor extends his services to the field of advising management in those areas where a client needs an independent review. The independent auditor has always offered his services in certain limited areas such as advising the client how to improve its system of internal control. But within the past 10 years, he has been extending these services to areas farther and farther away from what traditionally has been considered the domain of the auditor. Some accounting firms have been advising the client how to organize its firm, how to spend its money, and even how to design its buildings.

An extension of service by the independent auditor poses two questions: (1) What effect does the offering of management advisory services have on the independence of the auditor? (2) Does the auditor possess the competence to offer such services?

Charles Crumley posed a line of reasoning in *The CPA*, a newsletter of the AICPA, in answer to the first question. In essence, he pointed out that if the public expects the CPA to stay, in fact, independent of all connections whatsoever with management, the CPA must curtail many of those services which have traditionally been considered a main part of his auditing service. If this independence is truly enforced, the CPA could never advise the client how to improve his system of internal control or advise him how to set up a system of accounts. But this degree of independence is not needed, the reason being that the public accountant has the professional responsibility to stay independent in attitude so as to prevent him from subordinating his opinion to the will of the client and creating the situation where he is per-

[36] K. Stringer, "Some Basic Concepts of Statistical Sampling in Auditing," *The Journal of Accountancy*, November, 1961, p. 63.

[37] R. Trueblood and R. Cyert, *Sampling Techniques in Accounting*, Englewood Cliffs, N.J., Prentice-Hall, Inc., 1957, p. 61.

forming management duties for the client and thus auditing his own work. To ensure this independence, the CPA must assure himself that his services remain in the "fact-finding" and advisory role. If, at any time, the CPA becomes a de facto manager, in that his advice is being taken and accepted blindly, he must relinquish either his advisory or his audit service. If he does not relinquish one of the two, he will, in fact, be auditing his own work. Often smaller companies will contract these services from a CPA firm because it does not have enough management depth to perform certain functions. And it is exactly these firms, because of their lack of depth, that tend to accept the CPA's advice blindly and force him into the position of becoming a de facto manager. The CPA must tread carefully in these situations.

The second question posed concerning the auditor's competence to perform management advisory services cannot be answered with a simple "yes" or "no." Different auditors will have different competence levels in the broad field of management advisory services. It seems, however, that the two general auditing standards covering competence and due care apply equally to management advisory services and tax services as well as to auditing. An auditor offering service in an area in which he is not competent to perform is performing substandard work and, in effect, is guilty of violating the standards of his profession.

The internal or governmental auditor need not be as concerned as the independent auditor regarding the question of independence. However, audits performed by the General Accounting Office, for example, do possess a degree of independence comparable with that of the CPA. Regarding the question of competence, it is incumbent on both independent and non-independent auditors equally to be competent in a specific area of management advisory services before undertaking the assignment.

Relationships among Auditors. Earlier in this chapter, three principal branches of auditing were discussed—external, internal, and governmental auditing. In any independent opinion audit it is quite possible that all branches of auditing could contribute to the final report of the independent (external) auditor. For example, the second standard of fieldwork states: "There is to be a proper study and evaluation of the existing internal control as a basis for reliance thereon and for the determination of the resultant extent of tests to which auditing procedures are to be restricted."[38] The existence of a sound, well-functioning internal audit department gives added assurance to the external auditor that internal control activities are being reviewed by the internal auditors periodically and are being improved as necessary. Stettler points out, "Of course, reliance can be placed on the internal auditor's work only after the scope and thoroughness of the work have been carefully reviewed by the independent auditor."[39] Nevertheless, internal auditors contribute greatly to the independent audit engagement. A similar relationship with the same reliance precautions exists between governmental auditors and independent auditors. Proper coordination of work done by internal or governmental auditors can contribute to a more efficient and effective external audit.

In many independent audits it is necessary for the external auditor to coordinate work done on his behalf by other firms of certified public accountants. This is permitted under the AICPA Code of Professional Ethics according to Article 2, Section 01, which reads:

[38] Statements on Auditing Procedures No. 33, p. 16.
[39] Stettler, *op. cit.*, p. 78.

In obtaining sufficient information to warrant expression of an opinion, he (the independent auditor) may utilize, in part, to the extent appropriate in the circumstances, the reports or other evidence of auditing work performed by another certified public accountant, or firm of public accountants, at least one of whom is a certified public accountant, who is authorized to practice in a state or territory of the United States or the District of Columbia, and whose independence and professional reputation he has ascertained to his satisfaction.[40]

It is essential, therefore, that the work of other CPAs be coordinated closely with the work of the independent auditor who is primarily responsible for the engagement.

BIBLIOGRAPHY

Code of Professional Ethics, AICPA (Committee on Professional Ethics), New York, 1967.

Statements on Auditing Procedure No. 33, *Auditing Standards and Procedures,* AICPA (Committee on Auditing Procedure), New York, 1963.

Walsh, Francis J., Jr.: *Internal Auditing,* Business Policy Study No. 111, New York, National Industrial Conference Board, Inc., 1963.

Bedford, Norton M.: *Income Determination Theory,* Reading, Mass., Addison-Wesley Publishing Company, Inc., 1965.

Cashin, James A., and Garland C. Owens: *Auditing,* 2d ed., New York, The Ronald Press Company, 1963.

Holmes, Arthur W.: *Basic Auditing Principles,* 3d ed., Homewood, Ill., Richard D. Irwin, Inc., 1966.

Mautz, R. K.: *Fundamentals of Auditing,* 2d ed., New York, John Wiley & Sons, Inc., 1964.

Mautz, R. K., and Hussein A. Sharaf: *The Philosophy of Auditing,* Chicago, American Accounting Association, 1961.

Montgomery, Robert H.: *Auditing Theory and Practice,* 8th ed., New York, The Ronald Press Company, 1912.

Stettler, Howard F.: *Systems Based Independent Audits,* Englewood Cliffs, N.J., Prentice-Hall, Inc., 1967.

Mints, Frederic E.: "New Developments in Operational Auditing," *The Internal Auditor* (The Institute of Internal Auditors, New York), June, 1960.

Morse, Ellsworth H., Jr.: "GAO Audits of Management Performance," *The Journal of Accountancy* (AICPA), October, 1961.

Brown, R. Gene: "Changing Audit Objectives and Techniques," *The Accounting Review,* October, 1962.

Schlosser, Robert E., and Associates: "An Historical Approach to the Concept of Independence," *The New York Certified Public Accountant,* July, 1969.

Littleton, A. C.: "Factors Limiting Accounting," *The Accounting Review,* July, 1970.

[40] Code of Professional Ethics, AICPA (Committee on Professional Ethics), New York, 1967, p. 7.

Chapter **2**

Principles and Consistency

LOUIS H. JORDAN

Professor of Accounting, Graduate School of Business,
Columbia University

ACCOUNTING PRINCIPLES

The Auditor's Opinion. The independent auditor in expressing an opinion on financial statements typically indicates whether they present financial information "fairly in conformity with generally accepted accounting principles." Consequently, generally accepted accounting principles play a key role in the auditor's attest function. As an expert accountant, the independent auditor must be expert in the area of accounting principles, knowing which of various principles are generally accepted and which are not. It is the objective of this chapter to examine this important yardstick that the auditor uses in his work.

Standards of Reporting. It is only natural that members of a profession be expected to measure up to appropriate standards in the conduct of their work. Chapter 3 deals with auditing standards that guide the independent auditor in carrying out an audit engagement. These standards were adopted by the membership of the American Institute of Certified Public Accountants (AICPA), the national organization of independent public accountants. One of the standards, a standard of reporting, is that "the report shall state whether the financial statements are presented in accordance with generally accepted principles of accounting."

Nature of Accounting Principles. There has been much discussion on the part of people concerned with accounting as to the nature of accounting principles. Are they fundamental truths that are universally applicable or are they conventional rules developed by accountants and others for dealing with practical problems? If accounting principles are fundamental truths, they are of the order of natural laws, and one of the functions of the accounting profession is to discover these truths. Although a limited number of concepts appear to underlie accounting activities, such concepts are really basic assumptions rather than fundamental truths.

The view that accounting principles have been developed by man to deal with practical problems is held by most accountants. And these principles include concepts as well as procedures. As will become evident later in this chapter, most generally accepted principles of accounting are procedural in nature. The Accounting Principles Board of the AICPA construes the term "to include not only principles and practices, but also the methods of applying them." (APB Opinion No. 6, p. 39.) [1]

The accounting profession has found it desirable to distinguish between auditing standards and auditing procedures,[2] but it has not made a similar distinction between standards and procedures in the area of accounting principles. Such a distinction undoubtedly would be helpful in understanding accounting principles. Accounting standards, so conceived, would serve as a framework or guidepost for measuring the quality of financial reporting developed by the accounting process, while accounting procedures would constitute the specific means of meeting accounting standards.

[1] Accounting Principles Board Opinions, New York, AICPA.

[2] Statements on Auditing Procedure No. 33, *Auditing Standards and Procedures*, AICPA (Committee on Auditing Procedure), New York, 1963, p. 15.

General Acceptance. Despite the importance of accounting principles and the significance of generally accepted accounting principles in the auditor's work, one searches in vain for a concise list of such principles. Nevertheless, accounting is not without principles, and in some cases general acceptance of an accounting principle can be more easily determined than the truth or validity of what the principle asserts.

The recommendation that auditors state whether financial statements are in accordance with "generally accepted principles of accounting" grew out of correspondence during the early 1930s between an Institute committee and the Committee on Stock List of the New York Stock Exchange.[3]

Prior to 1964, pronouncements by the Committee on Accounting Procedure of the AICPA and of the Accounting Principles Board depended for their authority upon their general acceptance by independent auditors and their clients. Each Accounting Research Bulletin and Opinion concluded with a notation that incorporated the following points:

1. Except where formal adoption by the Council or the membership of the Institute has been asked and secured, the authority of the opinions rests upon their general acceptability.
2. The burden of justifying departures from the recommendations must be assumed by those who adopt other practices.

In 1964, the governing body of the Institute changed this policy by adopting the following resolution:

> RESOLVED: That it is the sense of this Council that reports of members should disclose material departures from opinions of the Accounting Principles Board, and that the President is hereby authorized to appoint a special committee to recommend to Council appropriate methods of implementing the substance of this resolution.

The recommendations of the special committee appointed by the Institute president were adopted with amendment by Council in October, 1964. Because of their importance, the first four of these recommendations are given below.

> 1. "Generally accepted accounting principles" are those principles which have substantial authoritative support.
> 2. Opinions of the Accounting Principles Board constitute "substantial authoritative support."
> 3. "Substantial authoritative support" can exist for accounting principles that differ from Opinions of the Accounting Principles Board.
> 4. No distinction should be made between the bulletins issued by the former Committee on Accounting Procedure on matters of accounting principles and the Opinions of the Accounting Principles Board. Accordingly, references in this report to Opinions of the Accounting Principles Board also apply to the Accounting Research Bulletins.[4, 5]

[3] See *Audits of Corporate Accounts,* New York, AICPA, 1934.

[4] This is in accord with the following resolution of the Accounting Principles Board at its first meeting on Sept. 11, 1959:

"The Accounting Principles Board has the authority, as did the predecessor committee, to review and revise any of these Bulletins (published by the predecessor committee) and it plans to take such action from time to time.

"Pending such action and in order to prevent any misunderstanding meanwhile as to the status of the existing accounting research and terminology bulletins, the Accounting Principles Board now makes public announcement that these bulletins should be considered as continuing in force with the same degree of authority as before."

[5] The Terminology Bulletins are not within the purview of the Council's resolution or of this report because they are not statements on accounting principles.

Accounting principles board. The Accounting Principles Board superseded the Committee on Accounting Procedure and the Committee on Terminology of the Institute on Sept. 1, 1959. As indicated above, the opinions of the Accounting Principles Board constitute "authoritative support" and hence are "generally accepted." The Board has incorporated in its opinions Accounting Research Bulletins issued on matters of accounting principles but not those dealing with terminology.

In 1964, the Board was asked to review prior to Dec. 31, 1965, all bulletins of the Committee on Accounting Procedure and to determine whether any of them should be revised or withdrawn.

Securities and exchange commission. The Securities Act of 1933 and the Securities Exchange Act of 1934 have as their purpose the full and fair disclosure of pertinent data by companies whose shares are publicly held. The SEC has authority over prospectuses for the sale of securities to the public and over annual reports required to be filed with the Commission. The Commission has the following specific authority over the form, content, and valuation of accounting data:

> to prescribe the form or forms in which required information shall be set forth, the items or details to be shown in the balance sheet and earnings statement, and the methods to be followed in the preparation of accounts, in the appraisal or valuation of assets and liabilities, in the determination of depreciation and depletion, in the differentiation of recurring and nonrecurring income, in the differentiation of investment and operating income, and in the preparation, where the Commission deems it necessary or desirable, of consolidated balance sheets or income accounts.

The SEC exercises its authority over accounting by the issuance of regulations and decisions and by the opinions of the Commission and its Chief Accountant. Accounting Series Release No. 4, issued Apr. 25, 1938, states the Commission's administrative policy on financial statements:

> In cases where financial statements filed with this Commission pursuant to its rules and regulations under the Securities Act of 1933 or the Securities Exchange Act of 1934 are prepared in accordance with accounting principles for which there is no substantial authoritative support, such financial statements will be presumed to be misleading or inaccurate despite disclosures contained in the certificate of the accountant or in footnotes to the statements provided the matters involved are material. In cases where there is a difference of opinion between the Commission and the registrant as to the proper principles of accounting to be followed, disclosure will be accepted in lieu of correction of the financial statements themselves only if the points involved are such that there is substantial authoritative support for the practices followed by the registrant and the position of the Commission has not previously been expressed in rules, regulations, or other official releases of the Commission, including the published opinions of its chief accountant.

Release No. 96, issued Jan. 10, 1963, contains a summary of the Commission's policy and indicates that its policy "is intended to support the development of accounting principles and methods of presentation by the profession but to leave the Commission free to obtain the information and disclosure contemplated by the securities laws and conformance with accounting principles which have gained general acceptance."

Trade practice. The Accounting Principles Board recognizes that "substantial authoritative support can exist for accounting principles that differ from the opinions of the Board." Trade practice is one source of differences, and accounting principles widely employed in a particular trade or type of business have authoritative support. Thus, "inventories representing agricultural, mineral, and other products, units of which are interchangeable and have an immediate marketability at quoted prices and for which appropriate costs may be difficult to obtain" are stated at selling prices less disposal costs. The effect of this practice may be to recognize profit before the time of sale, although the general practice is to account for inventories at cost.

Another example is found in certain mining activities where it is accepted practice to calculate income before a deduction for depletion. No attempt is made here to list practices that are limited to a particular trade; rather, the purpose is only to point out that the auditor must take cognizance of those practices that are unique for the particular trade of his client and decide whether their use is sufficiently widespread to constitute authoritative support.

Accounting principles applicable to hospitals, governmental units, and other nonprofit organizations may differ from those applicable to business firms.

Other authorities. Authoritative support for a particular principle or practice may come from other sources. The writings of practicing accountants and accounting teachers as well as others proficient in accounting matters can be found in periodicals such as *The Journal of Accountancy, The Accounting Review, Management Accounting,* and *Journal of Accounting Research.* The views of many professors can be found in textbooks and other published material.

The American Accounting Association, whose membership is made up largely of accounting teachers, has published from time to time statements of accounting principles. The National Association of Accountants, the membership of which is predominantly management accountants of business firms, undertakes research on specific accounting problems and publishes its findings in a series of Research Reports.

Other governmental bodies. Business firms that are under the supervision of governmental regulatory bodies will obviously be required to furnish financial information in a form prescribed by the governmental agency as essential to its function. In exercising whatever degree of control is deemed necessary or desirable, governments throughout the world find it necessary to establish rules for the accumulation and reporting of financial data. Thus, an electrical power firm may be under the jurisdiction of a state public utility commission as well as the Federal Power Commission. The firm may also be subject to the reporting requirements of the SEC. Occasionally, the requirements of two such agencies conflict, creating additional problems for the affected firms.

ACCOUNTING PRINCIPLES GENERALLY ACCEPTED

Basic Concepts. In discussing almost any accounting problem, certain underlying assumptions, concepts, or points of view become evident. Unfortunately, there is not complete agreement as to the specific concepts that are basic and belong in a list of underlying accounting concepts. However, it is desirable to identify the most common of these concepts before dealing with the superstructure built upon them.

Accounting entity. One of the observable facts of life is that economic activity is carried on by various types of units. These specifiable units are the accounting entities for which financial data may be accumulated, processed, and reported. Consequently, to account for an event necessitates identifying the entities affected. An entity consists of a quantity of economic resources under the control of a particular management which is devoted to certain planned activities. Thus, the accounting entity may be the entire estate of an individual, a portion of that estate devoted to a specific purpose, a venture involving the resources and efforts of more than one person, an association of individuals that qualify for recognition as a legal person as in the case of the business corporation, as well as groups of two or more legal units constituting a single business unit. The accounting unit may be a subdivision of a larger unit or a group of individual units, the important point being simply that the unit or entity which is being accounted for must be specified.

The significance of the entity concept may be noted in the following statement from Accounting Research Study No. 1:

> The function of accounting is (1) to measure the resources held by specific entities; (2) to reflect the claims against and the interests in those entities; (3) to measure the changes in those resources, claims, and interests; (4) to assign the changes to specifiable periods of time; and (5) to express the foregoing in terms of money as a common denominator.

The necessity for a clear indication of the entity is evidenced by the first sentence of Accounting Research Bulletin No. 51:

> The purpose of consolidated statements is to present, primarily for the benefit of the shareholders and creditors of the parent company, the results of operations and the financial position of a parent company and its subsidiaries essentially as if the group were a single company with one or more branches or divisions.

Monetary assumption. That the results of accounting are expressed in monetary terms was made clear in the excerpt from Accounting Research Study No. 1 given above. Accounting activities may begin with physical or intangible units, but such units must be stated eventually in terms of money.

The monetary assumption is subject to two conflicting interpretations. One view is simply that accounting results are stated in financial terms, that the monetary units in which economic events are expressed are expected to represent only purchasing power or value as of the date the events occur. This view conceives of accounting as historical in nature, whose function is limited to calculating results and position in terms of historical costs, as if the value of the monetary unit remained constant.

This point of view is frequently characterized as the "stable-money assumption." It is alleged that accountants assume that the purchasing power of the monetary unit remains constant or stable. In the face of fluctuating prices and inflation, such an assumption is clearly contrary to fact. Actually accountants do not assume that the purchasing power of money is constant; rather, they assume that small fluctuations can be ignored. Stated either way the result, of course, is the same: accounting in terms of historical costs.

The other interpretation of the monetary assumption emphasizes the mathematical deficiency in combining monetary units of different purchasing power and seeks as a common denominator a monetary unit of constant value. For example, this view of the assumption is the basis for Accounting Research Study No. 3 recommending adjusting historical costs for price-level changes.

This interpretation of the monetary assumption may have been one of the reasons that the Accounting Principles Board found the concepts in Accounting Research Studies No. 1 and No. 3 "too radically different from present generally accepted accounting principles for acceptance at this time."

Materiality. The concept of materiality applies to all opinions of the Accounting Principles Board, and a notation to that effect usually appears in each opinion. For example, beginning with Opinion No. 6, issued in October, 1965, each opinion contains the following statements relating to materiality:

> The Council action also requires that departures from Board Opinions be disclosed in footnotes to the financial statements or in independent auditors' reports when the effect of the departure on the financial statements is material.
>
> Unless otherwise stated, Opinions of the Board are not intended to be retroactive. They are not intended to be applicable to immaterial items.

However, the Board has never defined the term "material." The reason may well be that it is almost impossible to state precisely the meaning of the concept.

In Rule 1-02 of Regulation S-X, the SEC gives the following definition of the term:

> The term "material," when used to qualify a requirement for the furnishing of information as to any subject, limits the information required to those matters as to which an average prudent investor ought reasonably to be informed before purchasing the security registered.

The pervasiveness of the concept of materiality is indicated in the introduction to ARB No. 43:

> The committee contemplates that its opinions will have application only to items material and significant in the relative circumstances. It considers that items of little or no consequence may be dealt with as expediency may suggest. However, freedom to deal expediently with immaterial items should not extend to a group of items whose cumulative effect in any one financial statement may be material and significant.

The above statement is unsatisfactory in several respects:

1. The use of the phrase "material and significant" implies that materiality means something other than significance.
2. The statement implies that the accounting treatment appropriate for material items may be inappropriate for otherwise identical items which are not material.
3. Expediency rather than accounting logic appears to be the only guide for items not material.
4. The statement implies that a material item is one that is large; that materiality is only a matter of size.

Despite the implied emphasis on size in discussions of materiality, no quantitative criteria have been established for judging when an item is material. In fact, some recommendations of the Institute that have included quantitative criteria for distinguishing between alternative accounting procedures have been ignored in practice. (See APB Opinion 6, paragraph 22.)

The concept of materiality may be discussed in terms of the disclosure problem and in terms of the classification problem. The disclosure problem is essentially a question of whether a particular item should be disclosed separately in financial statements. If the item is material, separate disclosure is appropriate. In most disclosure problems materiality is a quantitative attribute of the item, a matter of relative size in the circumstances. However, in some disclosure problems, especially those dealing with innovations in business practices, materiality is a qualitative attribute to be found in the nature of the item itself rather than in its relative size.

The classification problem relates to the nature of an item and its classification into an appropriate accounting category. The quantitative aspect of materiality operates only in a negative fashion here because an item ought to be classified according to its nature whether it is large or small. However, if an immaterial item is misclassified, reclassification is not mandatory because the item is not material.

Going-concern assumption. The going-concern assumption may be stated briefly: In the absence of information to the contrary, it is assumed that the entity will continue its activities. This assumption does not mean that entities are never liquidated or that a particular entity will last forever; it means only that the termination of the entity's life cannot yet be seen on the horizon. The result of this assumption is to account for resources over their expected useful lives rather than to expense them on a cash outlay basis, to associate prepaid costs with the future periods that are benefited and precollected revenues with future periods of performance. More specifically, an investment in fixed assets should be spread over the future useful life of the asset to the firm. The useful life to the particular firm is the shorter of the firm's life or the asset's life.

It is implicit in the above discussion that when the end of a firm's life is in sight, the going-concern assumption is modified, and costs and benefits are allocated to the remaining life of the firm. When liquidation of the firm is contemplated or is underway, the assumption is abandoned altogether.

Accountants do not hesitate to invoke the going-concern assumption to justify deferring to future periods a proportionate part of the cost of a machine. They seem reluctant, however, to invoke the same concept when considering the tax-allocation problem.

Inasmuch as a business will usually not continue operations unless it is profitable, the going-concern concept assumes not only that the business enterprise will continue operations but also that its operations will be profitable.

Objectivity. Accountants have used the concept of objectivity to defend basing accounting recognition on exchange transactions between independent parties and to restrict its scope to historical costs. No one can object to establishing as a standard of performance measurements which have a high degree of objectivity, i.e., which are free of personal bias and are subject to verification. However, the problem is really concerned with the type of evidence needed to support accounting measurements. Even if current costs and market values are given accounting recognition, it is necessary that they be objectively determined.

Realization. The accounting concept of realization relates to the problem of periodic income determination, applying both to the revenue side as well as to the expense side of the problem.

This concept is closely related to objectivity and to historical costs as a basis of accounting. Its purpose is to assure objectivity. It accomplishes its purpose in the case of revenues by insisting on an exchange transaction involving the entity. In the meantime, fluctuations in prices are ignored and assets are stated at historical costs. The consequence of this concept is that gains or losses on the sale of assets are associated with the period of disposition rather than with the holding periods during which price changes actually occur.

Realization means simply that value changes are definite and will not be affected by subsequent price fluctuations. Thus increases should take the form of cash or claims to cash before recognition as revenues, and benefits (losses) should be consumed (sustained) before their costs are recognized as expenses. As consequences of exchange or use transactions, the effect of price changes is terminated and the amounts involved are made definite.

In the case of problems involving fluctuations in the monetary unit of measurement, realization has a similar meaning. For example, losses in purchasing power from holding cash during inflation are realized by spending the cash. Here, realization results from spending cash rather than from receiving cash.

Other concepts. There are undoubtedly other concepts that could be included in a list of basic accounting concepts.

Accounting Research Study No. 7 includes, in addition to the concepts discussed above, the following:

1. A society and government structure honoring private-property rights.
2. Diversity in accounting among independent entities.
3. Dependability of data through internal control.
4. Timeliness in financial reporting requires estimates.

The process of matching cost and revenue (effort and accomplishment) in determining periodic income is considered sufficiently fundamental by some accountants to be characterized as a basic concept.[6] The significance of the concept lies in associating revenues with a given period of time and in associating with the same period costs of services expired. The concept of matching in the sense of correctly selecting and relating to segments of revenue all costs of services used up in generating each segment is an ideal which is seldom attained in practice. The idea that "matching" means that reported expenses actually caused or were actually caused by the reported revenues must be rejected when one explores the practices necessarily employed in estimating periodic revenues and periodic expenses.

Accounting Research Study No. 1 contains three categories of basic concepts. The first category is derived from the environment of accounting; the second deals with those aspects of accounting which are considered valid in all circumstances, while the third group includes imperatives that have wide application but are not coextensive with accounting.

Postulate A-1. Quantification. Quantitative data are helpful in making rational economic decisions, i.e., in making choices among alternatives so that actions are correctly related to consequences.

Postulate A-2. Exchange. Most of the goods and services that are produced are distributed through exchange, and are not directly consumed by the producers.

Postulate A-3. Entities (including identification of the entity). Economic activity is carried on through specific units or entities. Any report on the activity must identify clearly the particular unit or entity involved.

Postulate A-4. Time period (including specification of the time period). Economic activity is carried on during specifiable periods of time. Any report on that activity must identify clearly the period of time involved.

Postulate A-5. Unit of measure (including identification of the monetary unit). Money is the common denominator in terms of which goods and services, including labor, natural resources, and capital are measured. Any report must clearly indicate which money (e.g., dollars, francs, pounds) is being used.

Postulate B-1. Financial statements. (Related to A-1.) The results of the accounting process are expressed in a set of fundamentally related financial statements which articulate with each other and rest upon the same underlying data.

Postulate B-2. Market prices. (Related to A-2.) Accounting data are based on prices generated by past, present or future exchanges which have actually taken place or are expected to.

[6] W. Paton and A. Littleton, *An Introduction to Corporate Accounting Standards*, Ann Arbor, Mich., American Accounting Association, 1940, chap. II; APB Opinion No. 11, p. 160.

Postulate B-3. Entities. (Related to A-3.) The results of the accounting process are expressed in terms of specific units or entities.

Postulate B-4. Tentativeness. (Related to A-4.) The results of operations for relatively short periods of time are tentative whenever allocations between past, present, and future periods are required.

Postulate C-1. Continuity (including the correlative concept of limited life). In the absence of evidence to the contrary, the entity should be viewed as remaining in operation indefinitely. In the presence of evidence that the entity has a limited life, it should not be viewed as remaining in operation indefinitely.

Postulate C-2. Objectivity. Changes in assets and liabilities, and the related effects (if any) on revenues, expenses, retained earnings, and the like, should not be given formal recognition in the accounts earlier than the point of time at which they can be measured in objective terms.

Postulate C-3. Consistency. The procedures used in accounting for a given entity should be appropriate for the measurement of its position and its activities and should be followed consistently from period to period.

Postulate C-4. Stable unit. Accounting reports should be based on a stable measuring unit.

Postulate C-5. Disclosure. Accounting reports should disclose that which is necessary to make them not misleading.

Accounting Research Study No. 1 also discusses uniformity, materiality, and conservatism, but it does not include these concepts in its lists of postulates.

DEFINITIONS

The Institute has issued a series of bulletins dealing with the terminology of accounting. (See Accounting Terminology Bulletins Nos. 1–4.) Definitions of the key terms given below are based on those bulletins.

Accounting

Accounting is the art of recording, classifying, and summarizing in a significant manner and in terms of money, transactions and events which are, in part at least, of a financial character, and interpreting the results thereof.

Accounting Principle. As used in accounting, a principle is "a general law or rule adopted or professed as a guide to action; a settled ground or basis of conduct or practice." The term is not understood to mean a rule from which there can be no deviation or to mean that there can be no conflict with other principles.

The process by which concepts become generally accepted accounting principles includes the following:

1. Initially, accounting postulates are derived from experience and reason.
2. After postulates so derived have proved useful, they become accepted as principles of accounting.
3. When this acceptance is sufficiently widespread, they become a part of generally accepted accounting principles.

Balance Sheet. The term "balance sheet" is considered more technical than "assets" and "liabilities" and is defined with reference to its origin in the accounts as follows:

A tabular statement or summary of balances (debit and credit) carried forward after an actual or constructive closing of books of account kept according to principles of accounting.

Asset (as used in balance sheets)

Something represented by a debit balance that is or would be properly carried forward upon a closing of books of account according to the rules or principles of accounting (provided such debit balance is not in effect a negative balance applicable to a liability), on the basis that it represents either a property right or value acquired, or an expenditure made which has created a property right or is properly applicable to the future. Thus, plant, accounts receivable, inventory, and a deferred charge are all assets in balance-sheet classification.

Liability (as used in balance sheets)

Something represented by a credit balance that is or would be properly carried forward upon a closing of books of account according to the rules or principles of accounting, provided such credit balance is not in effect a negative balance applicable to an asset. Thus the word is used broadly to comprise not only items which constitute liabilities in the popular sense of debts or obligations (including provision for those that are unascertained), but also credit balances to be accounted for which do not involve the debtor and creditor relation. For example, capital stock and related or similar elements of proprietorship are balance-sheet liabilities in that they represent balances to be accounted for, though these are not liabilities in the ordinary sense of debts owed to legal creditors.

Income Statement. This financial statement is characterized as "prepared from accounts and designed to show the several elements entering into the computation of net income for a given period."

Value

Value as used in accounts signifies the amount at which an item is stated, in accordance with the accounting principles related to that item. Using the word *value* in this sense, it may be said that balance-sheet values generally represent cost to the accounting unit or some modification thereof; but sometimes they are determined in other ways, as for instance on the basis of market values or cost of replacement, in which cases the basis should be indicated in financial statements.

Depreciation Accounting

Depreciation accounting is a system of accounting which aims to distribute the cost or other basic value of tangible capital assets, less salvage (if any), over the estimated useful life of the unit (which may be a group of assets) in a systematic and rational manner. It is a process of allocation, not of valuation. *Depreciation for the year* is the portion of the total charge under such a system that is allocated to the year. Although the allocation may properly take into account occurrences during the year, it is not intended to be a measurement of all such occurrences.

Revenue

Revenue results from the sale of goods and the rendering of services and is measured by the charge made to customers, clients, or tenants for goods and services furnished to them. It also includes gains from the sale or exchange of assets (other than stock in trade), interest and dividends earned on investments, and other increases in the owners' equity except those arising from capital contributions and capital adjustments.

Income and Profit

Income and *profit* involve net or partially net concepts and refer to amounts resulting from deduction from revenues, or from operating revenues, of cost of goods sold, other expenses, and losses, or some of them. The terms are often used interchangeably and are generally preceded by an appropriate qualifying adjective or term such as "gross," "operating," "net . . . before income taxes," and "net." The terms are also used in titles of statements showing results of operations, such as "income statement" or "statement of profit and loss," or, sometimes, "profit and loss account."

Cost

Cost is the amount, measured in money, of cash expended or other property transferred, capital stock issued, services performed, or a liability incurred, in consideration of goods or services received or to be received. Costs can be classified as unexpired or expired. Unexpired costs (assets) are those which are applicable to the production of future revenues. Examples of such unexpired costs are inventories, prepaid expenses, plant, investments, and deferred charges. Expired costs are those which are not applicable to the production of future revenues, and for that reason are treated as deductions from current revenues or are charged against retained earnings. Examples of such expired costs are costs of products or other assets sold or disposed of, and current expenses. Unexpired costs may be transferred from one classification to another before becoming expired costs as above defined, e.g., depreciation or insurance on plant may be included in unexpired costs ascribed to inventories.

Expense

Expense in its broadest sense includes all expired costs which are deductible from revenues. In income statements, distinctions are often made between various types of expired costs by captions or titles including such terms as cost, expense, or loss, e.g., cost of goods sold or services sold, operating expense, selling and administrative expenses, and loss on sale of property. These distinctions seem generally useful, and indicate that the narrower use of the term *expense* refers to such items as operating, selling or administrative expenses, interest and taxes.

Loss

Loss is (1) the excess of all expenses, in the broad sense of that word, over revenues for a period, or (2) the excess of all or the appropriate portion of the cost of assets over related proceeds, if any, when the items are sold, abandoned, or either wholly or partially destroyed by casualty or otherwise written off. When losses such as those described in (2) above are deducted from revenues, they are expenses in the broad sense of that term.

In developing accounting principles for business enterprises, Sprouse and Moonitz[7] offered the following definitions of key terms and concepts:

Financial statements are those which purport to show financial position and results of operations, including supporting schedules, elaborations of special aspects of business activity, rearrangements of underlying data, and supplementary statements.

Assets represent expected future economic benefits, rights to which have been acquired by the enterprise as a result of some current or past transaction.

Cost is a foregoing, a sacrifice made to secure benefits, and is measured by an exchange price.

Depreciation accounting is the process of allocating the cost or other basis of measurement of the services rendered by items of plant and equipment to the products or periods that used those services. *Depreciation for any given period* is the cost or other basis of the services used up in that period.

Liabilities are obligations to convey assets or perform services, obligations resulting from past or current transactions and requiring settlement in the future.

Owners' equity is represented by the amount of the residual interest in the assets of an enterprise.

Invested capital is that portion of stockholders' equity which arose from the commitment of assets to the corporation or from the conversion of retained earnings and which will not be withdrawn or reduced except as permitted by law. *Retained earnings (earned surplus)* is the portion which arose from operations and has not been converted into invested capital.

[7] R. Sprouse and M. Moonitz, Accounting Research Study No. 3, *A Tentative Set of Broad Accounting Principles for Business Enterprises,* New York, AICPA, 1962.

Net profit (earnings, income) or *net loss* for an accounting period is the increase (decrease) in owners' equity, assuming no changes in the amount of invested capital either from price-level changes or from additional investments and no distribution to the owners. *Revenue* is the increase in net assets of an enterprise as a result of the production or delivery of goods and the rendering of services. *Expense* is the decrease in net assets as a result of the use of economic services in the creation of revenues or of the imposition of taxes by governmental units. *Gains* are increases in net assets other than those resulting from additions to invested capital or from revenues. *Losses* are decreases in net assets other than those resulting from reductions in invested capital or from expenses.

GENERALLY ACCEPTED PRINCIPLES FOR BUSINESS ENTERPRISES

This section deals with the body of generally accepted accounting principles applicable to business enterprises and is based largely on the Opinions of the Accounting Principles Board (including Accounting Research Bulletins). The importance of business enterprises in society and in the development of accounting principles is recognized in the introduction to Accounting Research Bulletin No. 43. The Opinions of the Board are directed primarily to business enterprises organized for profit.

The following accounting principles are generally accepted for business enterprises. They are numbered and grouped solely for convenience in referring to them.

Financial Statements

1. *Comparative Statements.* Statements in comparative form are more useful than statements for a single period. (ARB No. 43, chap. 2A.)

2. *Comparability.* For statements of one period to be comparable with those of another, (*a*) there must be consistent application of accounting procedures or (*b*) the facts of any changes and effects of such change must be disclosed. (ARB No. 43, chap. 2A.)

3. *Valuation Allowances.* Asset valuation allowances should be shown contra to the assets to which they relate with appropriate disclosures. (APB Opinion No. 12.)

4. *Offsetting.* Assets and liabilities should not be offset in the balance sheet except where the right of setoff exists. (APB Opinion No. 10.)

5. *Special Receivables.* Notes or accounts receivable from officers, employees, or affiliated companies must be shown separately. (ARB No. 43, chap. 1A.)

6. *Working Capital.* Working capital (net working capital) is the excess of current assets over current liabilities. (ARB No. 43, chap. 3A.)

7. *Current Assets.* Current assets are cash and other resources which are expected to be realized in cash or sold or consumed during the normal operating cycle of the business or during a 1-year period if there are several operating cycles within a year. (ARB No. 43, chap. 3A.)

a. The following examples of current assets are given by ARB No. 43, chap. 3A:

(*a*) cash available for current operations and items which are the equivalent of cash;

(*b*) inventories of merchandise, raw materials, goods in process, finished goods, operating supplies, and ordinary maintenance material and parts;

(*c*) trade accounts, notes, and acceptances receivable;

(*d*) receivables from officers, employees, affiliates, and others, if collectible in the ordinary course of business within a year;

(*e*) installment or deferred accounts and notes receivable if they conform generally to normal trade practices and terms within the business;
(*f*) marketable securities representing the investment of cash available for current operations; and
(*g*) prepaid expenses such as insurance, interest, rents, taxes, unused royalties, current paid advertising service not yet received, and operating supplies.

b. The following examples of resources to be excluded from current assets are given by ARB No. 43, chap. 3A:

(*a*) cash and claims to cash which are restricted as to withdrawal or use for other than current operations, are designated for expenditure in the acquisition or construction of noncurrent assets, or are segregated for the liquidation of long-term debts;
(*b*) investments in securities (whether marketable or not) or advances which have been made for the purpose of control, affiliation, or other continuing business advantage;
(*c*) receivables arising from unusual transactions (such as the sale of capital assets, or loans or advances to affiliates, officers, or employees) which are not expected to be collected within twelve months;
(*d*) cash surrender value of life insurance policies;
(*e*) land and other natural resources;
(*f*) depreciable assets; and
(*g*) long-term prepayments which are fairly chargeable to the operations of several years, or deferred charges such as unamortized debt discount and expense, bonus payments under a long-term lease, costs of rearrangement of factory layout or removal to a new location, and certain types of research and development costs.

8. *Current Liabilities.* Current liabilities are obligations whose liquidation is reasonably expected to require the use of existing current assets, or the creation of other short-term obligations. (ARB No. 43, chap. 3A.)
a. Current liabilities include obligations for items which have entered the operating cycle, collections received in advance of delivery of goods or performance of services, debts which arise from operations, and other obligations whose ordinary liquidation is expected within 12 months.
b. Current liabilities include estimated or accrued amounts for known obligations: (1) the amount can be determined only approximately, or (2) the specific person to whom payment will be made is not yet known.
9. *Net Income.* Net income reflects all items of profit and loss recognized during the period with the sole exception of prior period adjustments. (APB Opinion No. 9.)
a. In the case of financial statements for a single period, adjustments for prior periods are made to the opening balance of retained earnings.
b. In the case of comparative statements, adjustments for prior periods are made to income and retained earnings of the proper period.
c. Adjustments for prior periods are expected to meet the following tests:

(*a*) specific identification with prior period
(*b*) attributable to economic events of prior period
(*c*) determination of amount made by other than management
(*d*) not susceptible to reasonable prior estimation

10. *Extraordinary Items.* Extraordinary items are to be segregated from the ordinary operations of a business. (APB Opinion No. 9.)
a. The following items should be reported as extraordinary (APB Opinion No. 9, APB Opinion No. 11):

(*a*) sale or abandonment of a plant or a segment of the business
(*b*) sale of an investment not acquired for resale

(*c*) write-off of goodwill due to unusual events during the period
(*d*) condemnation or expropriation of property
(*e*) major devaluation of foreign currency
(*f*) realized operating loss carryforwards from prior periods

b. The following items, regardless of size, are neither extraordinary nor prior period adjustments:

(*a*) write-down of receivables, inventories and research and development costs
(*b*) adjustments of accrued contract price
(*c*) foreign exchange fluctuations

11. *Earnings per Share.* Earnings per share or net loss per share data should be shown on the face of the income statement. (APB Opinion No. 15.) (See Appendix A of APB Opinion No. 15 for computational guidelines.)

a. Earnings per share amounts should be presented for (1) income before extraordinary items, (2) extraordinary items (less applicable income tax), and (3) net income.

b. "Earnings per common share" is the appropriate designation for corporations with relatively simple capital structures (common stock only or no potential dilution from convertible securities, options, warrants, or other rights).

c. Corporations with other than simple capital structures should present two types of earnings per share data with equal prominence on the face of the income statement: (1) primary earnings per share based on outstanding common shares and securities that are in substance the equivalent of common shares and have a dilutive effect of at least 3 percent, and (2) fully diluted earnings per share, a pro forma presentation reflecting the dilution that would occur if all contingent issuances of common stock that would individually reduce earnings per share had taken place at the beginning of the period.

d. Supplementary information should be furnished in a note for the latest period showing what primary earnings per share would have been (1) if conversions during the year had occurred at the beginning of the year, or (2) if common stock or common-stock equivalents issued for cash during the latest period presented, or shortly after its close but before completion of the financial report, to be used to retire preferred stock or debt had occurred at the beginning of the year.

e. The following types of securities are considered common-stock equivalents: (1) convertible securities if at time of issuance the cash yield is less than two-thirds of the current prime interest rate. (2) stock options and warrants (and their equivalents) and stock-purchase contracts. (3) participating securities and two-class common stock, if participation is on the same basis as common stock. (4) contingent shares, if the only contingency is passage of time or if the conditions for issuance have been met.

f. The designation of securities as common-stock equivalents is solely for the purpose of determining primary earnings per share.

g. The dilution reflected in earnings-per-share data by options and warrants should be determined by application of the treasury-stock method (i.e., as if exercised at the beginning of the period—or at time of issuance, if later—and the funds obtained were used to purchase common stock at the average market price during the period). (1) Application of the treasury-stock method is restricted to 20 percent of outstanding shares. (2) For amounts in excess of 20 percent of outstanding shares apply proceeds to reduce borrowings, with any remainder invested in U.S. government securities or commercial paper.

(3) In calculating fully diluted earnings, the number of treasury shares is determined by using market value at the close of the period.

h. Earnings-per-share data should be presented for all periods covered by the statement of income or summary of earnings; if prior periods' results are restated, earnings per share should be restated.

i. Financial statements should disclose rights and privileges of various securities outstanding and state the bases for making primary and fully diluted earnings-per-share calculations, together with any assumptions.

12. *Dividends per Share.* Dividends per share constitute historical facts but should be adjusted for stock dividends and splits or reverse splits. (APB Opinion No. 12.)

13. *Contingencies.* Material contingencies which are not sufficiently predictable to permit recording in the accounts but which have a reasonable possibility of affecting financial position or results of operations should be disclosed, while general-risk contingencies that are inherent in business operations need not be reflected in the accounts or disclosed. (ARB No. 50.)

14. *Consolidated Statements.* Consolidated statements are usually necessary for a fair presentation when one company in a group directly or indirectly has a controlling financial interest (over 50 percent of the outstanding voting shares) in the other companies. (ARB No. 51.)

15. *Intercompany Transactions.* All intercompany transactions and amounts should be eliminated in the preparation of consolidated statements. (ARB No. 51.)

16. *Cost in Excess of Equity.* Cost to the parent of an investment in a purchased subsidiary in excess of the parent's equity in the subsidiary's net assets at date of acquisition should be allocated to specific assets or appropriately disclosed in the consolidated balance sheet. (ARB No. 51.)

17. *Equity in Excess of Cost.* Except in unusual circumstances the amount at which net assets are carried in consolidated statements should not exceed the parent's cost. (ARB No. 51.)

18. *Amortization of Excess Credit.* The excess of net assets of a purchased subsidiary over cost to the parent which cannot be allocated as reductions to specific assets may, in unusual circumstances, be shown as a credit and taken into income in future periods on a reasonable and systematic basis. (ARB No. 51.)

19. *Elimination of Earnings.* The retained earnings or deficit of a purchased subsidiary at date of acquisition should not be included in consolidated retained earnings. (ARB No. 51.)

20. *Leasing Subsidiaries.* Subsidiaries whose main activity is leasing facilities to the parent should be consolidated. (APB Opinion No. 10.)

21. *Translation of Foreign Currencies.* In consolidating foreign subsidiaries, the following translation rules apply:

a. Cash, receivables, other current assets, and current liabilities should be translated at the exchange rate prevailing on the date of the balance sheet (current rate). (ARB No. 43, chap. 12.)

b. Inventory should be stated at the lower of cost or market, in domestic currency. (A departure from translation of inventory at current rate is in order when current net realizable value in domestic currency exceeds historical domestic cost. In such case, historical domestic cost may be considered the cost of inventory.) (ARB No. 43, chap. 12.)

c. Noncurrent assets should be translated at the exchange rates prevailing when acquired (historical rate), except that long-term receivables may be translated at the current rate in many circumstances. (ARB No. 43, chap. 12.)

d. In many circumstances long-term liabilities may be translated at the current rate, otherwise at the historical rate when incurred.

e. Capital stock should be translated at historical rates when the stock was issued.

f. Revenues and expenses (except depreciation) should be translated at the average rate for the period.

g. Depreciation should be translated at the same rates used for translating depreciable assets.

22. *Funds Statement.* The inclusion in financial reports of a statement of source and application of funds as supplementary information is recommended but is not mandatory. (APB Opinion No. 3.)

a. The "all financial resources" concept of funds should be used for annual reports in order to include all significant information.

b. Significant changes in noncurrent assets, in noncurrent liabilities, and in capital stock (except for stock dividends and splits) should be shown as separate sources or uses.

c. Funds derived from operations (cash flow) is not a substitute for or improvement upon net income as a measure of results of operations.

Assets, Liabilities, and Capital

23. *Accounts Receivable.* Accounts receivable should be stated at the amount of cash estimated as realizable, i.e., net of allowances for uncollectible accounts and for unearned discount, finance charges, and interest included in the face amount. (ARB No. 43, chap. 3A; APB Opinion No. 6.)

24. *Marketable Securities.* Marketable securities should be included as current assets at amounts not in excess of market value if the market value is not due to a mere temporary condition. (ARB No. 43, chap. 3A.)

25. *Inventory.* Inventory includes items of tangible personal property which (1) are held for sale in the ordinary course of business, (2) are in the process of production for sale, or (3) are to be currently consumed in the production of goods or services for sale. (ARB No. 43, chap. 4.)

26. *Inventory Valuation.* The primary basis of accounting for inventory is cost, the price paid or consideration given to acquire it. (ARB No. 43, chap. 4.)

27. *Inventory Cost.* Cost for inventory purposes may be determined under any one of several assumptions as to the flow of cost factors (such as first-in-first-out, average, and last-in-first-out). (ARB No. 43, chap. 4.)

28. *Lower of Cost or Market.* When the utility of inventory is less than cost, a current loss should be recognized and the inventory priced at the lower of cost or market. (ARB No. 43, chap. 4.)

a. Market means current replacement cost except that (1) market should not exceed the net realizable value (i.e., estimated selling price in the ordinary course of business less reasonably predictable costs of completion and disposal); and (2) market should not be less than net realizable value reduced by an allowance for an approximately normal profit margin.

b. The lower of cost or market rule may be applied either to each item in the inventory or to components or to the total depending on the character and composition of the inventory.

29. *Inventory above Cost.* Inventories may be priced above cost in exceptional cases where there is immediate marketability at quoted market prices with no substantial marketing costs. (ARB No. 43, chap. 4.)

30. *Consistent Valuation.* The basis of pricing inventories should be applied consistently and should be disclosed in financial statements.

31. *Purchase Commitments.* Losses on firm purchase commitments for in-

ventory should be determined in the same way as inventory losses and should be recognized in the accounts and separately disclosed in the income statement. (ARB No. 43, chap. 4.)

32. *Depreciable Assets.* The following disclosures of depreciable assets and depreciation should be made in financial statements: (*a*) depreciation expense for the period, (*b*) balances of major classes of depreciable assets, (*c*) accumulated depreciation, and (*d*) a general description of the methods used in computing depreciation. (APB Opinion No. 12.)

33. *Appraisals.* Property plant and equipment should not be written up to reflect appraisal, market, or current values which are above cost. (APB Opinion No. 6.)

34. *Intercompany Markup.* In the preparation of consolidated statements all intercompany profit or loss on assets remaining within the group should be eliminated. (ARB No. 51.)

35. *Unconsolidated Subsidiaries.* Investments in unconsolidated subsidiaries should be stated at equity in consolidated statements. (APB Opinion No. 10.)

36. *Leases.* The right under a long-term noncancelable lease to use property and the related obligation to pay rents are not considered assets and liabilities, unless the lease is clearly in substance an installment purchase. (APB Opinion No. 5.)

a. Disclosure rather than capitalization is the proper accounting treatment for such leases.

b. Leases which are clearly in substance installment purchases of property should be recorded as purchases.

c. If lessee and lessor are related, the lease should be treated as a purchase.

d. Gains or losses resulting from the sale of property which is leased back should be amortized over the life of the lease as an adjustment of rental cost.

37. *Financial Method.* Leases which pass to the lessee most of the usual ownership risks and rewards should be accounted for by the lessor in accordance with the financial method. (APB Opinion No. 7.)

38. *Operating Method.* Property under leases which retain the usual risks of ownership should be accounted for by the lessor in accordance with the operating method. (APB Opinion No. 7.)

39. *Intangibles.* The basis of accounting for intangibles is cost, which in the case of non-cash acquisitions may be measured by either the fair value of the consideration given or the fair value of the asset acquired, whichever is more clearly evident. (ARB No. 43, chap. 5.)

40. *Amortization of Intangibles.* Intangibles having useful lives limited by their nature or by law, regulation, or agreement should be amortized systematically over the periods benefited. (ARB No. 43, chap. 5.)

41. *Reclassification of Intangibles.* When it becomes known that the life of an intangible not having a limited life at acquisition becomes limited, its cost should be amortized systematically over its remaining useful life. (ARB No. 43, chap. 5.)

42. *Renegotiation.* Provision should be made for probable renegotiation refunds whenever the amount can be reasonably estimated. (ARB No. 43, chap. 11A.)

43. *Renegotiation Refund.* A renegotiation refund provision should be treated in the income statement as a deduction from sales and included in the balance sheet among the current liabilities.

44. *Deferred Taxes.* Deferred taxes should not be accounted for on a discounted basis. (APB Opinion No. 10.)

45. *Convertible Debt and Debt with Warrants. a.* No portion of the pro-

ceeds of debt convertible into common stock of the issuer or an affiliated company and which has a value at issuance not significantly in excess of the face amount should be attributable to the conversion feature. (APB Opinion No. 14.)

b. The proceeds of debt securities issued with detachable stock-purchase warrants which is allocable to the warrants should be accounted for as paid-in capital. (APB Opinion No. 14.)

46. *Stock Issued for Property.* The par value of stock issued for property is not necessarily the cost of the property. (ARB No. 43, chap. 1A.)

47. *Equity Changes.* Changes in all accounts comprising stockholders' equity should be disclosed. (APB Opinion No. 12.)

48. *Use of Capital Surplus.* Except by formal approval of shareholders, capital surplus should not be used to relieve current or future income of charges which would otherwise be made against it. (ARB No. 43, chap. 1A.)

a. If a corporation elects to restate its accounts by consent of shareholders (quasi-reorganization or readjustment), the balance sheet should be stated at fair but not unduly conservative amounts. (ARB No. 43, chap. 7A.)

b. Amounts written off in a readjustment should be charged first to the Retained Earnings account to its full extent before charges are made to other capital accounts.

c. A company's accounting, following a readjustment, should be similar to that appropriate for a new company, with a dated Retained Earnings account.

49. *Business Combination.* A business combination of two or more corporations in which an important part of the ownership interests is eliminated should be accounted for as a purchase and recorded at cost. (ARB No. 48.)

50. *Pooling.* A business combination of two or more corporations in which the holders of substantially all of the ownership interests in the constituents become owners of a single entity should be accounted for as a pooling of interests. (ARB No. 48.)

a. A new basis of accountability does not arise in a pooling.

b. The carrying amounts of assets, liabilities, and retained earnings should be carried forward.

51. *Pooling—Purchase.* A business combination which uses in part residual equities and in part cash or other property may be accounted for as a pooling to the extent of the use of residual equities and as a purchase for the balance. (Voided by APB Opinion No. 16, August, 1970.)

52. *Consolidated Retained Earnings.* Retained earnings of a subsidiary company accumulated prior to acquisition does not form a part of the consolidated retained earnings of the parent company and subsidiaries, nor are dividends from such earnings income to the parent company. (ARB No. 43, chap. 1A.)

53. *Stock Dividend.* A corporation issuing a stock dividend should transfer from Retained Earnings to permanent capital accounts an amount equal to the fair value of the shares issued. (ARB No. 43, chap. 7B.)

54. *Stock Split.* If the number of shares issued as a stock dividend is so great as to have the effect of a stock split, retained earnings should be capitalized to the extent of par or stated value of the shares issued. (ARB No. 43, chap. 7B.)

55. *Liquidation Preference.* The aggregate liquidation preference of preferred stock should be disclosed parenthetically or short in the equity section of the balance sheet. (APB Opinion No. 10.)

56. *Callable Price.* The aggregate or per share amounts at which preferred shares may be called should be disclosed. (APB Opinion No. 10.)

57. *Retirement of Stock.* When a corporation's stock is purchased for re-

tirement, the excess of purchase price over par or stated value may be allocated between capital surplus and retained earnings, while an excess of par or stated value over purchase price should be credited to capital surplus. (APB Opinion No. 6.)

58. *Treasury Stock.* When a corporation's stock is purchased for purposes other than retirement, the cost may be (1) reported separately as a reduction from capital, (2) allocated between capital accounts as when retired, or (3) in some cases reported as assets. (APB Opinion No. 6.)

59. *Treasury Shares in Pooling.* Treasury stock used to effect a pooling of interests should be accounted for as though retired and then newly issued. (APB Opinion No. 6.)

60. *Reciprocal Holdings.* Shares of the parent held by a subsidiary should not be treated as outstanding stock in the consolidated balance sheet. (ARB No. 51.)

Revenue, Expense, and Income

61. *Realization of Profit.* Although profit is attributable to the entire range of business activities, it is considered realized at the time of sale, unless collection is not reasonably assured. (ARB No. 43, chap. 1A.)

62. *Unrealized Profit.* Unrealized profit should not be taken into income directly or indirectly. (ARB No. 43, chap. 1A.)

63. *Long-term Contracts.* Income from long-term construction-type contracts may be reported using the percentage-of-completion method or the completed-contract method. (ARB No. 45.)

64. *Installment Method.* The installment method of recognizing revenue is not acceptable, unless collection is not reasonably assured. (APB Opinion No. 10.)

65. *Inventory Costs.* A major objective of accounting for inventory is the determination of income by matching appropriate costs against revenues. (ARB No. 43, chap. 4.) (See 26 to 32.)

66. *Depreciation.* The cost of a productive facility should be spread over the periods during which services are obtained from the use of the facility. (ARB No. 43, chap. 9C.)

67. *Alternative Depreciation Methods.* The declining-balance method of estimating periodic depreciation and the "sum-of-the-years'-digits" methods meet the requirements of being "systematic and rational" and are thus generally accepted methods. (ARB No. 44.)

68. *Depreciation on Appreciation.* If appreciation has already been recorded in the accounts, income should be charged with depreciation on the written-up amounts. (APB Opinion No. 6.)

69. *Property Taxes.* Real and personal property taxes should be accrued during the fiscal period of the taxing authority for which the taxes are levied. (ARB No. 43, chap. 10A.)

70. *CPFF Contracts.* Costs and fees under CPFF contracts should be taken up as revenue on the basis of performance if collection is reasonably assured. (ARB No. 43, chap. 11A.)

71. *Contract Termination.* Profit on a fixed-price contract terminated for the convenience of the government accrues as of the effective date of termination. (ARB No. 43, chap. 11C.)

72. *Foreign Earnings.* Earnings from foreign operations should be recognized to the extent funds have been received or unrestricted funds are available for transmission. (ARB No. 43, chap. 12.)

73. *Realized Translation Adjustments.* Realized losses or gains on foreign exchange should be charged or credited to operations. (ARB No. 43, chap. 12.) [See 10*a*(*e*) and *b*(*c*).]

74. *Unrealized Translation Adjustments.* Provisions should be made in determining income for unrealized translation losses on foreign net current assets, but unrealized gains should be deferred. (ARB No. 43, chap. 12.) [See 10*a*(*e*) and *b*(*c*).]

75. *Income Tax Allocation.* Income tax expense should include the tax effects of revenue and expense transactions included in the determination of pretax accounting income. (APB Opinion No. 11.)

76. *Deferred Method.* Tax allocation should follow the deferred method. (APB Opinion No. 11.)

77. *Carry-backs and Carry-forwards.* Operating-loss carry-backs should be allocated to the loss periods, while the tax effects of operating-loss carry-forwards usually should be recognized in the periods of realization and reported as extraordinary items. (APB Opinion No. 11.)

78. *Within Period Allocation.* Tax allocation should be applied within a period to obtain fair presentation of components of results of operations. (APB Opinion No. 11.)

79. *Disclosure of Income Taxes.* Financial statements should disclose (1) income tax expense currently payable and tax effects allocable to the period and (2) the current and noncurrent amounts of deferred taxes. (APB Opinion No. 11.)

80. *Guideline Lives.* Provision should be made for deferred income taxes if guideline lives for tax purposes are shorter than lives for financial accounting. (APB Opinion No. 1.)

81. *Investment Credit.* The investment credit may be accounted for (1) as a reduction in acquisition cost (directly, by use of a contra account, or by use of a deferred credit account) the effect of which is taken into income over the life of the depreciable asset or (2) as a reduction in income taxes of the year in which the credit arises. (APB Opinion No. 2, APB Opinion No. 4.)

82. *Reserves.* Reserves should not be used for the purpose of equalizing reported income. (ARB No. 43, chap. 6.)

a. The following examples are given by ARB No. 43, chap. 6, as reserves for which charges or credits should not enter into the determination of income:

(*a*) for general undetermined contingencies
(*b*) for possible future losses
(*c*) to reduce inventories below proper basis
(*d*) without regard to any specific loss related to current operations
(*e*) in amounts not based on reasonable estimates of cost or loss

b. Reserves of the type listed above (1) are appropriations of retained earnings, (2) should have no costs or losses charged to them, (3) should be restored to retained earnings when no longer considered necessary, and (4) should be reported in the balance sheet as part of shareholders' equity.

83. *Bond Discount.* Bond discount is a part of the cost of borrowed money and should be distributed systematically over the term of the issue. (ARB No. 43, chap. 15.)

84. *Interest Method of Amortization.* The interest method of amortization of debt discount and expense or premium is theoretically sound and is acceptable. (APB Opinion No. 12.)

85. *Refunding Adjustments.* Unamortized discount, issue cost, and redemption premium on bonds refunded may be either (*a*) charged against current income, (*b*) amortized over the remainder of the original life of the issue, or (*c*) amortized over the life of the new issue. (ARB No. 43, chap. 15; APB Opinion No. 6.)

86. *Stock Options as Compensation.* Compensation in the form of stock options is measured as the excess of fair value of the shares over option price at the date of grant. (ARB No. 43, chap. 13B.)

87. *Pension Cost.* Pension cost should be accounted for on the accrual basis whether the plan is funded or unfunded. (APB Opinion No. 8.)

a. The difference between the amount charged against income and the amount paid should be shown in the balance sheet as accrued or prepaid cost.

b. A legal obligation for pension cost in excess of amounts paid or accrued should be shown in the balance sheet as both a liability and a deferred charge.

c. Except to the extent indicated in (*a*) and (*b*) above, unfunded prior service cost is not a liability to be shown in the balance sheet.

88. *Pension Cost as Periodic Expense.* Pension cost should be charged against income subsequent to the adoption or amendment of a plan, with no portion charged directly to retained earnings. (APB Opinion No. 8.)

89. *Determining Pension Cost.* Annual provision for pension cost should be based on an accounting method that uses an acceptable actuarial cost method and should be consistently applied. (APB Opinion No. 8.)

a. To be acceptable, the actuarial cost method should be rational and systematic.

b. The annual provision should not be less than the total of (1) normal cost, (2) an amount equivalent to interest on any unfunded prior service cost, and (3) a provision for vested benefits.

c. The annual provision should not be greater than the total of (1) normal cost, (2) 10 percent of the past service cost (until fully amortized), (3) 10 percent of the amount of any changes in prior service costs arising from amendments of the plan (until fully amortized), and (4) interest equivalents on the difference between provisions and amounts funded.

90. *Actuarial Adjustments.* Actuarial gains and losses (including realized investment gains and losses) and unrealized appreciation and depreciation (except for debt securities expected to be redeemed at face at maturity) should be given effect in the provision for pension cost in a rational and systematic manner.

91. *Defined-contribution Plan.* The pension cost for a defined-contribution plan with benefits restricted to accumulated contributions is the contribution for a particular year.

92. *Disclosure of Pension Plans.* For pension plans financial statements should disclose (*a*) their existence and nature, (*b*) accounting and funding policies, (*c*) provision for pension cost for the period, (*d*) excess of actuarially determined value of vested benefits over total of the pension fund and accruals, less prepayments or deferred charges, (*e*) any other matters affecting comparability of the periods presented.

93. *Deferred Compensation.* Deferred compensation contracts with individual employees, which if taken together are equivalent to a pension plan, should be accounted for as pension cost; other deferred compensation contracts should be accounted for individually on an accrual basis. (APB Opinion No. 12.)

94. *Stock Dividends and Splits.* The receipt by a shareholder of additional shares of stock as a stock dividend or stock split does not constitute income. (ARB No. 43, chap. 7.)

95. *Dividends on Treasury Stock.* Dividends on treasury stock should not be treated as income to the company. (ARB No. 43, chap. 1A.)

96. *Treasury Stock Transactions.* The purchase and reissue of a corporation's own common stock are capital transactions and do not give rise to profits or losses. (ARB No. 43, chap. 1B.)

GENERALLY ACCEPTED ACCOUNTING PRINCIPLES FOR NONBUSINESS ENTITIES

Although the major focus of attention in this chapter has been on accounting principles applicable to business enterprises, it must be understood that other types of entities will require accounting principles which recognize their unique features. Thus, while some principles listed above as applicable to business enterprises may also apply to another type of organization, others will not, and additional accounting principles appropriate to that specific type will be required.

Governmental Units. Governmental units illustrate well the development of accounting principles tailored to their special needs. The National Committee on Governmental Accounting recommends the following principles: [8]

1. A governmental accounting system must make it possible: (a) to show that all applicable legal provisions have been complied with; and (b) to determine fairly and with full disclosure the financial position and results of financial operations of the constituent funds and self-balancing account groups of the governmental unit.

2. If there is a conflict between legal provisions and generally accepted accounting principles applicable to governmental units, legal provisions must take precedence. Insofar as possible, however, the governmental accounting system should make possible the full disclosure and fair presentation of financial position and operating results in accordance with generally accepted principles of accounting applicable to governmental units.

3. An annual budget should be adopted by every governmental unit, whether required by law or not, and the accounting system should provide budgetary control over general governmental revenues and expenditures.

4. Governmental accounting systems should be organized and operated on a fund basis. A fund is defined as an independent fiscal and accounting entity with a self-balancing set of accounts recording cash and/or other resources together with all related liabilities, obligations, reserves, and equities which are segregated for the purpose of carrying on specific activities or attaining certain objectives in accordance with special regulations, restrictions, or limitations.

5. The following types of funds are recognized and should be used in accounting for governmental financial operations as indicated.

(1) The General Fund to account for all financial transactions not properly accounted for in another fund;

(2) Special Revenue Funds to account for the proceeds of specific revenue sources (other than special assessments) or to finance specified activities as required by law or administrative regulation;

(3) Debt Service Funds to account for the payment of interest and principal on long-term debt other than special assessment and revenue bonds;

(4) Capital Projects Funds to account for the receipt and disbursement of moneys used for the acquisition of capital facilities other than those financed by special assessment and enterprise funds;

(5) Enterprise Funds to account for the financing of services to the general public where all or most of the costs involved are paid in the form of charges by users of such services;

(6) Trust and Agency Funds to account for assets held by a governmental unit as trustee or agent for individuals, private organizations, and other governmental units;

(7) Intragovernmental Service Funds to account for the financing of special activities and services performed by a designated organization unit within a governmental jurisdiction for other organization units within the same governmental jurisdiction;

(8) Special Assessment Funds to account for special assessments levied to finance public improvements or services deemed to benefit the properties against which the assessments are levied.

[8] *Governmental Accounting, Auditing, and Financial Reporting,* Chicago, 1968.

6. Every governmental unit should establish and maintain those funds required by law and sound financial administration. Since numerous funds make for inflexibility, undue complexity, and unnecessary expense in both the accounting system and the over-all financial administration, however, only the minimum number of funds consistent with legal and operating requirements should be established.

7. A complete self-balancing group of accounts should be established and maintained for each fund. This group should include all general ledger accounts and subsidiary records necessary to reflect compliance with legal provisions and to set forth the financial position and the results of financial operations of the fund. A clear distinction should be made between the accounts relating to current assets and liabilities and those relating to fixed assets and liabilities. With the exception of Intragovernmental Service Funds, Enterprise Funds, and certain Trust Funds, fixed assets should not be accounted for in the same fund with current assets, but should be set up in a separate, self-balancing group of accounts called the General Fixed Asset Group of Accounts. Similarly, except in Special Assessment, Enterprise, and certain Trust Funds, long-term liabilities should not be carried with the current liabilities of any fund, but should be set up in a separate, self-balancing group of accounts known as the General Long-term Debt Group of Accounts.

8. The fixed asset accounts should be maintained on the basis of original cost, or the estimated cost if the original cost is not available, or, in the case of gifts, the appraised value at the time received.

9. Depreciation on general fixed assets should not be recorded in the general accounting records. Depreciation charges on such assets may be computed for unit cost purposes, provided such charges are recorded only in memorandum form and do not appear in the fund accounts.

10. The accrual basis of accounting is recommended for Enterprise, Trust, Capital Projects, Special Assessment, and Intragovernmental Service Funds. For the General, Special Revenue, and Debt Service Funds, the modified accrual basis of accounting is recommended. The modified accrual basis of accounting is defined as that method of accounting in which expenditures other than accrued interest on general long-term debt are recorded at the time liabilities are incurred and revenues are recorded when received in cash, except for material or available revenues which should be accrued to reflect properly the taxes levied and the revenues earned.

11. Governmental revenues should be classified by fund and source. Expenditures should be classified by fund, function, organization unit, activity, character, and principal classes of objects in accordance with standard recognized classification.

12. A common terminology and classification should be used consistently throughout the budget, the accounts, and the financial reports.

13. Financial statements and reports showing the current condition of budgetary and proprietary accounts should be prepared periodically to control financial operations. At the close of each fiscal year, a comprehensive annual financial report covering all funds and financial operations of the governmental unit should be prepared and published.

Other Units. Other types of organizations will employ accounting principles which recognize their special features. For example, estates and trusts need principles (and rules) for distinguishing between corpus and income. The American Hospital Association recommends that hospitals follow principles of fund accounting and employ the accrual basis of accounting.[9]

PROBLEMS OF CONSISTENCY

Standards of Reporting. At the outset of this chapter reference was made to the first standard of reporting, which requires the auditor to state in his report whether financial statements are in accordance with generally accepted principles of accounting. The second standard of reporting requires the

[9] *Chart of Accounts for Hospitals,* Chicago, 1966.

auditor to "state whether such principles have been consistently observed in the current period in relation to the preceding period." (Statements on Auditing Procedure No. 33, p. 16.)

The Goal of Comparability. One of the basic accounting concepts discussed above was that of consistency and comparability. And in the list of principles applicable to business enterprises given above, No. 1 refers to the usefulness of comparative financial statements and No. 2 indicates the role of consistency in comparability. The objective of the standard of consistency is:

> (1) to give assurance that the comparability of financial statements as between periods has not been materially affected by changes in the accounting principles employed or in the method of their application; or (2) if comparability has been materially affected by such changes, to require a statement of the nature of the changes and their effects on the financial statements. [SAP No. 33, p. 42.]

SAP No. 33 lists three types of changes that affect comparability:

1. A change in accounting principles employed
2. Changed conditions which necessitate accounting changes but which do not involve changes in the accounting principles employed
3. Changed conditions unrelated to accounting

Because only the first of these types of changes relates to consistency, only changes of this class which have a material effect on financial statements require recognition as to consistency in the auditor's opinion. Such changes include (1) a change to an alternative generally accepted principle, (2) a change from a practice lacking general acceptance to a generally accepted one, and (3) a change to a practice lacking general acceptance. A change to a practice which is not generally accepted will require a qualified or an adverse opinion.

Financial statements may lack comparability for reasons unrelated to consistency or to accounting. Material changes of the second and third classes above are not ordinarily recognized in the auditor's report, although their disclosure in notes to the financial statements may be in order because they affect comparability.

Regulation S-X of the SEC requires the independent auditor to include in his report and to express his opinion on all material changes in accounting principles and methods which affect the comparability of financial statements filed with the Commission. (Rule 2-02.)

The purpose of the consistency requirement is to make reported financial data comparable between periods. If financial statements cover the current year only, consistency in the application of accounting principles will bring about comparability with the statements of the preceding year. Lack of consistency will result in lack of comparability.

The Problem of Changes. Current changes in accounting principles or methods of application which materially affect financial position or results of operation should be described adequately in notes and referred to in the opinion paragraph of the auditor's report:

> in conformity with generally accepted principles applied on a basis consistent with that of the preceding year, except that, etc.

Disclosure should indicate the amount by which the current year's income is affected. If a change has no material current effect but is likely to affect materially future years, it should be disclosed by footnote or in the auditor's report.

Financial data for two or more years may be placed on a comparable basis by giving retroactive effect to any changes in accounting principles. The auditor's opinion should mention in the restatement whether his report covers the current year only or both current and prior years:

in conformity with generally accepted accounting principles applied on a basis consistent with that of the preceding year after giving retroactive effect to a change, etc.

Obviously, the auditor's report on the first accounting period of a newly organized firm will make no reference to consistency. However, his first audit of an established company should include procedures which are reasonable and practicable in the circumstances to determine whether the accounting principles employed are consistent with the prior year.

1. If the client imposes limitations with respect to such procedures, his opinion will be appropriately modified.
2. If the accounting records of the prior year do not result in a fair presentation, comparison of current statements with those of the prior year will have no meaning. The auditor's report will be appropriately modified.
3. The accounting records of the prior year may be so inadequate that the auditor cannot form an opinion as to the consistent application of accounting principles. If he is unable to establish the reasonable accuracy of account balances at the beginning of the current year, he will be unable to express an opinion on the statement of income and retained earnings.

A problem involving consistency may arise in connection with a business combination accounted for as a pooling:

1. If statements for the current year only are presented, the auditor may express the usual opinion on consistency provided a note discloses the pooling and the incomes of the constituents for the preceding year.
2. Comparative financial statements which do not give retroactive effect to the pooling are not on a consistent basis. The inconsistency arises from the lack of application to prior years, not from a change in application during the current year. Appropriate disclosure must be made in the statements and in the auditor's report.

DEVELOPMENT OF ACCOUNTING PRINCIPLES

In a section above on general acceptance some indication was given of the historical development of accounting principles. An extensive discussion of this development is beyond the scope of this chapter. The efforts of the AICPA, of the American Accounting Association, and of individuals in formulating statements of accounting principles are related in an interesting fashion by Reed K. Storey.[10]

BIBLIOGRAPHY

Accounting Principles Board Opinions, Statements, Studies, etc., New York, AICPA, to date.

Accounting and Reporting Standards for Corporate Financial Statements and Preceding Statements and Supplements, Columbus, Ohio, American Accounting Association (Committee on Accounting Concepts and Standards), 1957.

Accounting Research and Terminology Bulletins, final ed., New York, AICPA (Committee on Accounting Procedure), 1961.

Accounting Trends and Techniques, New York, AICPA, annually.

[10] *The Search for Accounting Principles,* New York, AICPA, 1964.

Audits of Corporate Accounts, New York, AICPA, 1934.

Chart of Accounts for Hospitals, Chicago, American Hospital Association, 1966.

Regulation S-X, Securities and Exchange Commission, to date.

Statements on Auditing Procedure No. 33, *Auditing Standards and Procedures,* New York, AICPA (Committee on Auditing Procedure), 1963.

Grady, P.: *Inventory of Generally Accepted Accounting Principles for Business Enterprises,* Accounting Research Study No. 7, New York, AICPA, 1965.

Moonitz, M.: *The Basic Postulates of Accounting,* Accounting Research Study No. 1, New York, AICPA, 1965.

Paton, W., and A. Littleton: *An Introduction to Corporate Accounting Standards,* Ann Arbor, Mich., American Accounting Association, 1940.

Sprouse, R., and M. Moonitz: Accounting Research Study No. 3, *A Tentative Set of Broad Accounting Principles for Business Enterprises,* New York, AICPA, 1962.

Storey, Reed K.: *The Search for Accounting Principles,* New York, AICPA, 1964.

Wheeler, John T.: "Accounting Theory and Research in Perspective," *The Accounting Review,* January, 1970.

Gustafson, George A.: "Status of Accounting Research Study Nos. 1 and 3," *The Journal of Accountancy,* March, 1970.

Chapter **3**

Auditing Standards

PERCY B. YEARGAN

Professor and Head, Department of Accounting, University of Georgia

R. FRANK PAGE

Associate Professor of Accounting, University of Missouri, St. Louis

TYPES OF STANDARDS

Auditing is concerned with the verification of accounting data, with determining the accuracy and reliability of accounting statements and reports. The field of auditing consists of three major classifications best defined by descriptions of the auditors who perform the audit function in each area—independent auditing, internal auditing, and governmental auditing. The following definitions state the basic similarities and differences for each classification.

The Independent Auditor

Independent auditors, or independent public accountants as they are generally known, are not directly affiliated with the companies whose financial statements they examine. They are independent contractors who, after adequate examination and investigation, offer a professional opinion as to whether the concern's financial statements which they have examined present fairly the results of operations and the financial condition of the enterprise.[1]

The Internal Auditor

Internal auditing is an independent appraisal activity within an organization for the review of accounting, financial and other operations as a basis for service to management. It is a managerial control, which functions by measuring and evaluating the effectiveness of other controls.[2]

This definition is expanded by Brink and Cashin:

The internal auditing group thus exists as a special means by which management can more effectively direct and control the corporate affairs for the benefit of its owner—the stockholders. Existing as it does as a separate and independent group, it serves management both by making the accounting activities more efficient and by supplementing the regular accounting function. It serves by verifying previously reported facts, ascertaining compliance with rules and policies, protecting the company from losses—aspects which relate to the preservation of the current status of the company—and also through its appraisal of ways and means by which the company's methods, practices, or policies can be made more efficient. It is this latter type of appraisal or constructive analysis, which seeks the improvement of company welfare in every legitimate sense, that characterizes the highest type of internal auditing.[3]

The Governmental Auditor. In general, the standards, principles, and methods employed by governmental auditors, whether federal, state, or local, are similar to those employed by internal auditors in industry and independent auditors in public accounting. The principal differences relate to the responsibility of the audit unit and the scope of audit coverage. Stated another way, governmental auditing encompasses the following:

[1] R. K. Mautz, *Fundamentals of Auditing*, New York, John Wiley & Sons, Inc., 1964, p. 5.

[2] Statement of Responsibilities of the Internal Auditor, New York, The Institute of Internal Auditors, 1957.

[3] Victor Z. Brink and James A. Cashin, *Internal Auditing*, New York, The Ronald Press Company, 1958, p. 427.

Activities ranging from verification of a single document by a clerk in a remote accounting office to the comprehensive post-audit by independent auditors. The term as applied to government activities can apply to auditing of tax reports such as state income tax returns and sales tax returns, as well as to elaborate systems for pre-auditing and internal auditing of the governmental units' own financial transactions.[4]

The category more closely related to independent auditing includes "that type of post auditing of a governmental unit's own financial data and representations which leads to an expression of opinion as to the fairness of financial representations."[5]

In the federal government the General Accounting Office, the legislative audit branch, performs audits of all government agencies using standards comparable with those established by the American Institute of Certified Public Accountants (AICPA).

STANDARDS FOR ALL AUDITORS

In this section we will discuss the auditing standards that are applicable in varying degrees to all auditors. There are no published standards that automatically cover all auditors. Those standards relating to public accountants are included in the series of statements on auditing procedure issued by the Committee on Auditing Procedure of the AICPA. The standards are covered in considerable detail in Statements on Auditing Procedure No. 33. The standards pertaining to internal auditing are covered in the Statement of Responsibilities of the Internal Auditor issued by the Institute of Internal Auditors. The technical standards of the public accountant and the internal auditor apply to the governmental auditor depending on the particular agency. The GAO audits all government agencies, including those with their own internal audit staffs, and uses standards comparable with those of the independent auditor. The internal auditors of the various agencies use standards similar to those of the internal auditor. The standards described below apply generally to all auditors. Those which the public accountant must strictly observe are covered in the next section.

Influence of CPA Standards. When the independent auditor states in his short-form report that his examination "was made in accordance with generally accepted auditing standards," there must be no question as to what these standards are. Thus there was a direct need to spell out in considerable detail in Statements on Auditing Procedure No. 33, *Auditing Standards and Procedures,* the requirements for the independent auditor. As would be expected, some of these standards are applicable to internal auditing and governmental auditing as well as independent auditing. Thus all fields of auditing have been influenced by the "generally accepted auditing standards" developed by the AICPA, especially the general standards and the fieldwork standards. The standards relating to reports are not as applicable to all fields. In the following paragraphs we will discuss significant aspects which are applicable to all auditors. Those applicable only to the independent auditor are discussed later. Since many internal audits have an important bearing on the extent of the independent auditor's work, a comparable quality of performance is desirable. This comparable quality means maintaining standards equivalent to those of the CPA.

[4] Jerold J. Morgan, *Auditing for Alabama Governments,* pp. 6–7.
[5] *Ibid.,* p. 7.

Reliability of Statements and Records. The independent auditor is concerned with determining that the financial statements "present fairly the financial position of X Company at December 31, 19__, and the results of its operations." The internal auditor and governmental auditor also want to determine that the representations are reasonable. In addition, these two types of auditors also want to make sure that the records which underlie the statements are also reliable. Thus the standards will also relate to the records themselves.

Maintenance of Internal Control. Internal control is the foundation for the audit program for all auditors. It is important to the independent auditor, since he may restrict his auditing procedures where the degree of internal control permits. The evaluation of internal control is the second standard of fieldwork. In addition to evaluating the present system of internal control, the internal auditor must be constantly monitoring and improving the system. While the independent auditor will generally make his evaluation toward the year end, the internal auditor must be in constant touch with the controls throughout the year, and where control breakdowns occur or risk becomes evident he must take steps immediately to install new controls or make the necessary changes. In any company changes in procedures or activities occur daily and the controls must be changed correspondingly. The governmental auditor will also be charged with monitoring or evaluating controls.

Professional Integrity. A minimum qualification of any auditor is a high degree of professional integrity. The concept of professional integrity includes the quality of basic honesty and soundness of moral character. When the auditor has won the confidence and respect of those whom he has audited, he will usually receive the utmost cooperation. Local personnel will generally try in good faith to correct any deficiencies he encounters and to cooperate to improve the accounting structure.

Independence. This embraces the state or quality of being unimpaired, or free from the control or influence of interested parties. This will assure that all the benefits of objectivity are realized. Such objectivity or independence is essential to the effectiveness of all types of auditors. It is paramount in the case of the CPA, since third parties must know that the public accountant is not subordinate to the management. There should not be the slightest indication or appearance in any way that he has not been entirely objective. Further details with respect to the independence of the public accountant are given later in this chapter under "Generally Accepted Auditing Standards."

The internal auditor and the governmental auditor must be independent in a somewhat different way. They cannot be under the control or subordinate in the *organization structure* to the particular unit or individual they audit. For example, the internal auditor will audit functions under the control of the chief accountant but should not be subordinate to him. Generally both should report to a higher financial officer, such as the controller or vice-president—finance, who is far enough removed from routine accounting responsibility. This is clearly set forth in the Statement of Responsibilities of the Internal Auditor, as follows: "The head of the internal auditing department, therefore, should be responsible to an officer of sufficient rank in the organization as will assure a broad scope of activities and adequate consideration of and effective action on the findings and recommendations made by him."[6]

[6] Statement of Responsibilities of the Internal Auditor, New York, The Institute of Internal Auditors, 1957.

Collection and Evaluation of Evidence. The three types of auditors are involved in the basic auditing procedure of collection and evaluation of evidence to support findings and recommendations. This type of auditing procedure has not been delineated in as much detail for the internal auditor and governmental auditor as for the public accountant. This is understandable, particularly with respect to collecting audit evidence. The public accountant must secure the evidence for his audit file in case there may be a challenge to the report at a later date, such as a legal suit. However, in the case of the internal auditor and governmental auditor much of the evidence is an integral part of the company records and can be available later. Thus it does not have to be collected to the same degree that the public accountant has to collect and secure evidence.

Professional Image. A conceptual description of the qualities of an auditor indicates that he

> is conceived as a professional specialist, serving a useful function in a changing environment. To continue to do this successfully, he must understand the interacting forces of his environment, his role in the overall picture, and how he can best perform his functions. He must therefore understand the nature of accounting as a measurement process, its concepts and methodologies. His knowledge must be both general and specific: general in that his foundation must be conceptual in order that he may change as required; specific in that he must be familiar with the matters which comprise the real world of accounting.[7]

Range of Knowledge. The study quoted above also concludes that the auditor should possess varying degrees of knowledge in the following categories:

(1) *Thorough Knowledge*
- *a*) The functions of accounting: who uses accounting information and for what purposes
- *b*) The communication of accounting information: statement presentation for maximum utility and clarity
- *c*) Double entry structure: theoretical basis and application as an analytical tool
- *d*) Auditing standards: general standards, standards of field work, standards of reporting
- *e*) Internal control: principles and applications
- *f*) Professional ethics

(2) *Good Knowledge*
- *a*) Accounting theory and terminology, including income and asset measurement
- *b*) Cost classification and cost behavior
- *c*) Major categories of resources
- *d*) Major sources of capital
- *e*) Auditing methodology
- *f*) Sampling, statistical inference
- *g*) Income taxes
- *h*) Business law

(3) *Fair Knowledge*
- *a*) Computer: systems, functions of components, programming, internal control features
- *b*) Other accounting equipment and bookkeeping tools
- *c*) Quantitative techniques
- *d*) Types of formal organizations
- *e*) Organization design: authority, responsibility, information handling, retrieval and communication

[7] Robert H. Roy and James H. MacNeill, *Horizons for a Profession*, New York, AICPA, 1967, p. 214.

f) Taxes, other than income taxes
g) Governmental agencies: kinds, basic objectives, jurisdictions, requirements.[8]

GENERALLY ACCEPTED AUDITING STANDARDS

In the previous section we discussed the auditing standards common to all auditors. In this section, particularly with respect to the General Standards and Field Work Standards groups, there are certain standards that are applicable to a lesser degree to the internal auditor and the governmental auditor. However, it is preferable, from a reference viewpoint, to have the CPA requirements shown separately since the CPA must meet the "Generally Accepted Auditing Standards" specified by the AICPA. These standards are discussed below.

GENERAL STANDARDS

Training and Proficiency

The examination is to be performed by a person or persons having adequate technical training and proficiency as an auditor.[9]

Adequate technical training and proficiency as an auditor relates to the competence of the auditor. He must be a competent technician as well as one who can work with other professional people on an equal basis. The required competence is obtained by education, both formal and informal, and by experience.

The educational requirements for qualification as a certified public accountant are governed by state law and administered by the appropriate board in each of the states. The requirements vary from a high school diploma or its equivalent to a 4-year college degree with a major in accounting. However, the CPA certificate is not a requirement for entry into the public accounting profession, although the attainment of certificate status is definitely encouraged. In the areas of internal auditing and governmental auditing, the certificate is also not required but may be considered desirable and evaluated as objective evidence of auditing proficiency.

In 1969, a committee of the AICPA[10] recommended that five years of college study be made a requirement for the CPA certificate. In addition, the committee recommended that for those who meet this standard, no qualifying experience should be required.

The amount of experience which is required prior to receiving a certificate also varies from state to state. Some states require no experience; others require 3 years. Some states permit a person to sit for the examination before he has acquired his experience; others require the experience before sitting.

The amount of technical training and proficiency required by this standard is also flexible. More is required of the auditor who expresses an opinion on financial statements than is required for regular, routine write-up work.

[8] *Ibid.*, pp. 192–193.

[9] Statements on Auditing Procedure No. 33, *Auditing Standards and Procedures*, AICPA (Committee on Auditing Procedure), New York, 1963, p. 15.

[10] Report of the Committee on Education and Experience Requirements for CPAs, AICPA, New York, 1969.

More competence is required by an unusual or complex engagement than is required for a regular, routine engagement.

The standard is also flexible in this manner. More training and proficiency is required of the person who is responsible for the engagement than is required of those who work under supervision.

The auditor charged with final responsibility for the engagement must exercise a seasoned judgment in the varying degrees of his supervision and review of the work done and judgment exercised by his subordinates, who in turn must meet the responsibility attaching to the varying gradations and functions of their work.[11]

In deciding whether or not he should accept an engagement and in deciding who should be assigned to an engagement, a professional practitioner must keep in mind the requirements of this standard for adequate technical training and proficiency.

Independence

In all matters relating to the assignment an independence in mental attitude is to be maintained by the auditor or auditors.[12]

The second general standard requires that the auditor be mentally independent of his client. In Rule 1.01 the Code of Professional Ethics of the AICPA requires that he be in fact independent of his client. This rule states:

Independence is not susceptible of precise definition, but is an expression of the professional integrity of the individual. A member or associate, before expressing his opinion on financial statements, has the responsibility of assessing his relationships with the enterprise to determine whether, in the circumstances, he might expect his opinion to be considered independent, objective and unbiased by one who had knowledge of all the facts.[13]

The reasoning is well expressed by the following statement:

It is of utmost importance to the profession that the general public maintain confidence in the independence of independent auditors. Public confidence would be impaired by evidence that independence was actually lacking and it might also be impaired by the existence of circumstances which reasonable people might believe likely to influence independence. To *be* independent, the auditor must be intellectually honest; to be *recognized* as independent, he must be free from any obligation to or interest in the client, its management or its owners. For example, an independent auditor auditing a company of which he was also a director might be intellectually honest, but it is unlikely that the public would accept him as independent since he would be in effect auditing decisions which he had a part in making. Likewise, an auditor with a substantial financial interest in a company might be unbiased in expressing his opinion on the financial statements of the company, but the public would be reluctant to believe that he was unbiased. Independent auditors should not only be independent in fact; they should avoid situations that may lead outsiders to doubt their independence.[14]

The auditor is not expected to adopt the attitude of prosecutor or to be unreasonable in his demands. However, he is expected to guard his independence by being aware of a variety of factors which may affect it. Sharaf and Mautz have divided independence into three components and have listed guides for each of the components which will aid the auditor in avoiding both obvious and subtle influences.

[11] SAP No. 33, p. 19.
[12] SAP No. 33, p. 15.
[13] Code of Professional Ethics, AICPA (Committee on Professional Ethics), New York, 1967, p. 6.
[14] SAP No. 33, p. 20.

Programming Independence

1. Freedom from managerial interference or friction intended to eliminate, specify, or modify any portion of the audit.
2. Freedom from interference with or an uncooperative attitude respecting the application of selected procedures.
3. Freedom from any outside attempts to subject the audit work to review other than that provided for in the audit process.

Investigative Independence

1. Direct and free access to all company books, records, officers and employees, and other sources of information with respect to business activities, obligations, and resources.
2. Active co-operation from managerial personnel during the course of the auditor's examination.
3. Freedom from any managerial attempt to assign or specify the activities to be examined or to establish the acceptability of evidential matter.
4. Freedom from personal interests or relationships leading to exclusion from or limitation of the examination of any activity, record, or person that otherwise would have been included in the audit.

Reporting Independence

1. Freedom from any feeling of loyalty or obligation to modify the impact of reported facts on any party.
2. Avoidance of the practice of excluding significant matters from the formal report in favor of their inclusion in an informal report of any kind.
3. Avoidance of intentional or unintentional use of ambiguous language in the statement of facts, opinions, and recommendations, and in their interpretation.
4. Freedom from any attempt to overrule the auditor's judgment as to appropriate content of the audit report, either factual matter or his opinion.[15]

The Securities and Exchange Commission has issued Accounting Series Releases No. 47 and No. 81 dealing with the problems of independence. In these releases illustrations are given of situations in which auditors were considered not independent. In the latter one, some illustrations are given of situations in which a question arose concerning independence but the auditor was considered independent.

The independent auditor must be constantly aware of the vital part the concept of independence plays in the public's view of the profession, and he must guard his independence jealously.

Due Professional Care

Due professional care is to be exercised in the performance of the examination and in the preparation of the report.[16]

This standard requires that the auditor exercise that amount of care which a reasonably prudent auditor would exercise in the same or similar circumstances. Due care should be exercised concerning the procedures which are used in the examination and the diligence with which the procedures are carried out. For example, in the first engagement by a client, the auditor would usually be expected to do the following:

1. Visit the client's premises, acquaint himself with the client's accounting system, and review the client's internal control.
2. Prepare an audit program.
3. Instruct staff assistants who will be working on the engagement.

[15] Hussein A. Sharaf and R. K. Mautz, "An Operational Concept of Independence," *The Journal of Accountancy*, April, 1960, p. 53.

[16] SAP No. 33, p. 15.

4. Obtain evidence to warrant an opinion on the financial statements of the client, and prepare working papers to document the procedures employed. (Preparing working papers is usually a by-product of the process of obtaining evidence.)

5. Review the working papers prepared by assistants. (A partner or other competent person should do this, preferably at the location of the engagement.)

6. Prepare report based upon the evidence obtained during the examination.

7. Assign final review of the completed engagement to a partner or other competent person who has not been actively engaged in this examination, especially where unusual or troublesome problems were encountered during the engagement.

8. Prepare final draft of the report and provide for checking and proofreading before issuance.

In a subsequent engagement, the knowledge of the client obtained in the previous engagement would permit the auditor to change the order in which some of the items are listed above. However, the degree of internal control which has been exercised by the client during the period under examination has a definite effect on the extent of the tests and the timing of certain procedures. The auditor must keep in mind he is responsible for exercising due care in each engagement.

Due care permeates the entire auditing engagement. The proper care must be exercised in accepting the engagement and in planning it. Due care must also be exercised in assigning staff accountants to the job. The ones who are selected must have adequate technical training and must be properly supervised.

Due professional care must be exercised in the review of the client's internal control. Both the extent of procedures and the timing of certain procedures are directly affected by the degree of internal control which is in effect in the client's organization.

Throughout the engagement the accumulation of evidence must be done with due professional care. Evidence-gathering techniques such as inspections, observations, and inquiries must be applied diligently, and the evidence must be evaluated with care if the auditor is to be guided by this standard.

FIELDWORK STANDARDS

Planning and Supervision

The work is to be adequately planned and assistants, if any, are to be properly supervised.[17]

After the auditor has visited the client's premises, has acquainted himself with the client's accounting system, and has reviewed the client's internal control, he is in a position to plan the engagement in detail. This planning should be in the form of an audit program which consists of the various procedures to be followed during the course of the examination. During the preparation of the program, he should keep in mind the timeliness and orderliness of procedures.

Timeliness

The first standard of fieldwork concerns particularly the timeliness of the auditing procedures. The timeliness with which auditing procedures are undertaken involves the proper timing and synchronizing of their application and thus comprehends the possible need for simultaneous examination of, for example, cash on hand and in banks,

[17] SAP No. 33, p. 23.

securities owned, bank loans, and other related items. It may also require an element of surprise, establishment of audit control over assets readily negotiable, and establishment of a proper cutoff at a date other than the balance-sheet date. All of these matters are to be resolved in the light of the effectiveness of internal control in a particular situation.

Orderliness

The need for orderliness in carrying out audit procedures is apparent, for example, in the application of procedures for inventory observation. Review of proposed inventory count procedures, as planned by the client, is as essential for this purpose as is the review of the client's procedures for establishing a proper cutoff of sales and purchases in the books of account. Another example is found in the examination of negotiable securities. When the negotiable securities are of considerable volume, planning may be necessary to guard against the substitution of securities already counted for other securities which should be on hand but are not.[18]

The audit program may vary from a checklist of objectives and procedures to a very elaborate listing of objectives and procedures in minute detail. Whatever approach is taken in preparing an audit program, the preparer must keep in mind the objectives of the examination—the securing of sufficient, competent evidence to warrant the expression of an opinion. He should try to be specific enough in his program that no area will be ignored if it should be included and no unnecessary work will be done and no work will be a duplication of other work.

The instructions of assistants should be tailored to the individual and should take into consideration the individual assistant's experience and proficiency. Certainly the instructions should emphasize the necessity of modifying the program if internal control is not operating as it was originally thought. The assistant should also be encouraged to discuss unusual or unexpected items with his supervisor.

Proper supervision of assistants also includes review of the work papers prepared by the assistant in carrying out the various parts of the audit program. The auditor who is in charge of the examination should review the work of the assistants as they complete the work. The partner, principal, or manager responsible for the engagement should review the work papers at the end of the engagement. It is desirable for him to do his review before the report has been written and before the auditor in charge of the job and his assistants have left the client's premises.

Whether or not the review is made before the job has been completed, it is becoming more and more accepted by the profession that review is necessary as a part of the supervision required by the first standard of fieldwork.[19]

Evaluation of Internal Control

There is to be a proper study and evaluation of the existing internal control as a basis for reliance thereon and for the determination of the resultant extent of the tests to which auditing procedures are to be restricted.[20]

To meet the requirements of this standard, an auditor must make a proper study and evaluation of internal control and must base his audit program on the results of the study and evaluation.

In the broad sense, internal control includes, therefore, controls which may be characterized as either accounting or administrative, as follows:

[18] SAP No. 33, pp. 24, 25.
[19] See Statement on Auditing Procedure No. 39, pp. 62–63.
[20] SAP No. 33, p. 27.

a. Accounting controls comprise the plan of organization and all the methods and procedures that are concerned mainly with, and relate directly to, safeguarding of assets and the reliability of the financial records. They generally include such controls as the system of authorization and approval, separation of duties concerned with record keeping and accounting reports from those concerned with operations or asset custody, physical control over assets, and internal auditing.

b. Administrative controls comprise the plan of organization and all methods and procedures that are concerned mainly with operational efficiency and adherence to managerial policies and usually relate only indirectly to the financial records. They generally include such controls as statistical analyses, time and motion studies, performance reports, employee training programs, and quality controls.[21]

The extent to which particular organizational plans and control methods and procedures may be classified as accounting controls or administrative controls will, of course, vary in individual circumstances.

The characteristics of a satisfactory system of internal control would include:

a. A plan of organization which provides appropriate segregation of functional responsibilities,

b. A system of authorization and record procedures adequate to provide reasonable accounting control over assets, liabilities, revenues and expenses,

c. Sound practices to be followed in performance of duties and functions of each of the organizational departments, and

d. Personnel of a quality commensurate with responsibilities.[22]

The Committee on Auditing Procedure states that the auditor is primarily concerned with the accounting controls of his client; however, if the auditor believes that administrative controls are important to the reliability of the financial records, he should consider evaluating them also.[23] Mautz has expressed the same point of view in an article concerning supplementary standards for review of internal control.

The formal and informal organization of the company under examination is to be studied sufficiently to enable the auditor to conclude:

a. Whether authority for the performance of essential financial and accounting activities is clearly established and specifically prescribed.

b. Whether responsibility for the performance of financial and accounting activities is fixed.

c. Whether the authorization, recording, review, or approval of financial and custodial activities are accomplished by persons other than those who perform such activities.

The financial and accounting procedures in use by the company under examination are to be studied sufficiently to enable the auditor to conclude:

a. Whether completed transactions have been reviewed sufficiently to give reasonable assurance that financial transactions have been effected as authorized and that unauthorized and otherwise irregular transactions have been discovered.

b. Whether mechanical and other proof devices are utilized sufficiently to reduce errors and irregularities in operating and financial data to a reasonable minimum.

c. Whether reports are required and prepared to indicate responsibility for the authorization, performance, review, and approval of financial and accounting duties and transactions.

The work of the employees in the financial and accounting departments of the company under examination should be reviewed sufficiently to enable the auditor to conclude whether they discharge their assigned duties in a satisfactory manner.

The protection given valuable assets and records by the company under examination

[21] SAP No. 33, p. 28.
[22] SAP No. 33, pp. 28–29.
[23] SAP No. 33, p. 32.

should be studied sufficiently to permit the auditor to conclude whether the risks of destruction, theft, violation, or other loss have been reduced to a reasonable minimum.

If financial or accounting department procedures are considered unsatisfactory for internal control purposes, sufficient investigation should be made of related or supporting procedures outside those departments to enable the auditor to conclude whether the apparent weakness is offset by other procedures.[24]

A review of internal control should consist of interviews with responsible individuals in the client's organization and tests of the underlying records and documents to be sure that the system which has been described is being followed. The auditor may also prepare flow charts to use in the evaluation of the system of internal control. The auditor is not able to determine definitely the degree of reliance which may be placed on internal control at the beginning of an engagement because his subsequent tests may show the internal control is not functioning as it was described. For this reason, the auditor must be continually aware of the effect of the results of tests and procedures on his evaluation of internal control, the extent of his tests, and the timing of audit procedures.

Sufficient Evidence

Sufficient competent evidential matter is to be obtained through inspection, observation, inquiries and confirmations to afford a reasonable basis for an opinion regarding the financial statements under examination.[25]

This standard requires the auditor to have an understanding of evidence and how to evaluate it in forming an opinion on financial statements.

Auditing in its entirety is made up of two functions, both closely concerned with evidence. The first is the evidence-gathering function; the second is that of evidence evaluation. In many instances in practice, evidence is evaluated as it is gathered so these two functions appear to proceed simultaneously. There is little conscious separation of the two and for the examination as a whole they proceed as one. For judgment on any individual proposition, however, they must be undertaken one at a time and in the order stated. First, the auditor must turn his efforts to obtaining as much evidence as he feels he will need to judge satisfactorily the proposition before him. Having the evidence in hand, he must then examine it critically before he permits it to work on his mind and compel or persuade him to accept the truthfulness or falsity of the proposition.[26]

The auditor collects and evaluates evidence. This is a difficult task. The lawyer presents evidence to further the interest of his client in a case. The judge, however, rules on the question of whether or not the evidence is admissible. The auditor must be cautious in accepting evidence, even though he has gathered it, to be sure that he is arriving at a valid judgment. This idea is the main reason it is considered necessary to have a review of the work done by an auditor. It is extremely difficult, if not impossible, to be impartial concerning one's own work.

Audit evidence may be classified many ways. One such presentation follows:

1. Physical inspection
2. Written and/or oral statements of third parties
3. Authoritative documents prepared outside the client's organization
4. Calculations of the auditor

[24] R. K. Mautz, "Standards for the Review of Internal Control," *The Journal of Accountancy*, July, 1958, p. 30.

[25] SAP No. 33, p. 34.

[26] R. K. Mautz and Hussein A. Sharaf, *The Philosophy of Auditing*, Chicago, American Accounting Association, 1961, pp. 86–87.

5. Satisfactory internal control procedures of the client
6. Authoritative documents prepared inside the client's organization
7. Representations by officers and employees of the client
8. Satisfactory records underlying the financial statements
9. Satisfactory interrelationships with other data

As indicated by this standard, evidence may be obtained by inspection, observation, inquiry, or confirmation, or any combination of these methods.

Once evidence has been obtained by the auditor, he must evaluate the degree of pertinence and reliability of it and determine that he may or may not accept the proposition under examination. Once he has made this determination, proposition by proposition, he is then ready to make an overall determination that he may, or may not, attest to the fairness of the financial statements under examination.

REPORTING STANDARDS

These standards have been developed as general guides for the independent auditor who is expressing an opinion on the fairness of statement presentation. It should be recognized that this is not the purpose of most examinations performed by internal auditors and, with some few exceptions, governmental auditors. The internal auditor must write his report as indicated by the nature and purpose of his examination. The governmental auditor must do the same thing and at the same time be aware of the legal framework within which he is operating.

Principles of Accounting

The report shall state whether the financial statements are presented in accordance with generally accepted principles of accounting.[27]

This standard requires the auditor to know those principles and procedures, including the methods of applying them, which are generally accepted. This is done by keeping abreast of developments in business as well as the publications of authoritative organizations.

Consistency

The report shall state whether such principles have been consistently observed in the current period in relation to the preceding period.[28]

This standard requires the auditor to compare the principles and procedures, and the methods of applying them, used in current financial statements covered by the audit report with those utilized and applied in the preceding period in order to form an opinion as to whether or not appropriate principles and procedures have been consistently applied.

Disclosure

Informative disclosures in the financial statements are to be regarded as reasonably adequate unless otherwise stated in the report.[29]

Adequate disclosure relates to form, content, and descriptive material which is necessary to make the financial statements not misleading. The auditor must exercise his professional judgment to determine the proper presentation. If the significant information which he deems necessary is not properly included in the financial statements, he must give the appropriate effect to the item in his report.

[27] SAP No. 33, p. 40.
[28] SAP No. 33, p. 42.
[29] SAP No. 33, p. 54.

The report shall either contain an expression of opinion regarding the financial statements, taken as a whole, or an assertion to the effect that an opinion cannot be expressed. When an overall opinion cannot be expressed, the reasons therefor should be stated. In all cases where an auditor's name is associated with financial statements the report should contain a clear-cut indication of the character of the auditor's examination, if any, and the degree of responsibility he is taking.[30]

This standard requires the independent auditor to assume the responsibility of expressing an opinion or to state the reasons why he cannot express an opinion. He must, of course, keep in mind the other reporting standards as well as the previously discussed general standards and standards of fieldwork.

This standard is applicable when the independent auditor is associated with the financial statements in any manner. The conscientious auditor will write the appropriate report as dicated by the circumstances.

THE CPA OPINION

The issuance of a short-form report or opinion is usually the objective of the CPA's examination. Two examples of the standard short-form report, often referred to as the audit certificate, are provided below.

Standard Short-form Opinion

Date

To the Stockholders or Board of Directors
The ABC Corporation
Anywhere, U.S.A.

We have examined the balance sheet of the ABC Corporation as of December 31, 19__, and related statements of income and retained earnings for the year then ended. Our examination was made in accordance with generally accepted auditing standards, and accordingly included such tests of the accounting records and such other auditing procedures as we considered necessary in the circumstances.

In our opinion, the accompanying balance sheet and statements of income and retained earnings present fairly the financial position of the ABC Corporation at December 31, 19__, and the results of its operations for the year then ended, in conformity with generally accepted accounting principles applied on a basis consistent with that of the preceding year.

(Signed) C. P. Accountant and Co.

Modified Short-form Opinion

Date

To the Stockholders or Board of Directors
The ABC Corporation
Anywhere, U.S.A.

In our opinion, the accompanying balance sheet and statement of income and retained income present fairly the financial condition of the ABC Company at December 31, 19__, and the results of its operations for the year then ended, in conformity with generally accepted accounting principles applied on a basis consistent with that of the preceding year. Our examination of these statements was made in accordance with generally accepted auditing standards, and accordingly included such tests of the accounting records and such other auditing procedures as we considered necessary in the circumstances.

(Signed) C. P. Accountant and Co.

[30] SAP No. 33, p. 56.

Nature of the Auditor's Opinion. It should be noted that the short-form reports presented above imply that the company (client) must assume primary responsibility for the accuracy of the statements. The auditor's responsibility is secondary and arises with respect to his reporting on the company statements; essentially, the auditor renders a professional opinion as to the fairness with which the statements present the financial condition and operating results of the company.

To express an opinion, the auditor must first perform a satisfactory examination of the statements and underlying records and data. In performing his examination, the auditor is an independent and professional reviewer of the work of others, and his objective is to be satisfied as a matter of practical professional judgment that the financial data under examination, prepared and submitted by his client, result in a fair presentation unimpaired by serious inaccuracies. The basic routine may be summarized as follows:

1. The company (client) presents to the auditor statements and underlying data which are represented to be fair and accurate.
2. The auditor independently takes such steps as he considers necessary in his professional judgment to formulate his opinion that the statements are substantially accurate and fairly presented.
3. The auditor renders an impartial report reflecting his professional opinion.

BIBLIOGRAPHY

Accounting Research Study No. 1, *The Basic Postulates of Accounting* (Maurice Moonitz), AICPA, New York, 1961.

Code of Professional Ethics, AICPA (Committee on Professional Ethics), New York, 1967.

Statements on Auditing Procedure No. 33, *Auditing Standards and Procedures,* AICPA (Committee on Auditing Procedure), New York, 1963.

A Statement of Basic Accounting Theory, American Accounting Association (The Committee to Prepare a Statement of Basic Accounting Theory), 1966.

Statement of Responsibilities of the Internal Auditor, New York, The Institute of Internal Auditors, 1957.

Blough, Carman G.: *Practical Application of Accounting Standards,* New York, AICPA, 1957.

Carey, John L., and William O. Doherty: *Ethical Standards of the Accounting Profession,* New York, AICPA, 1966.

Cashin, James A., and Garland C. Owens: *Auditing,* New York, The Ronald Press Company, 1963.

Mautz, R. K., and Hussein A. Sharaf: *The Philosophy of Auditing,* Chicago, American Accounting Association, 1961.

Ray, J. C.: *Independent Auditing Standards,* New York, Holt, Rinehart and Winston, Inc., 1964.

Stettler, Howard F.: *Systems Based Independent Audits,* Englewood Cliffs, N.J., Prentice-Hall, Inc., 1967.

Chetkovich, Michael N.: "Standards of Disclosure and Their Development," *The Journal of Accountancy,* December, 1955.

Jackson, B. F.: "Reporting on 'Other Procedures' Used in Place of Confirmation or Observation," *The Journal of Accountancy,* June, 1956.

Skousen, K. Fred: "Standards for Reporting by Lines of Business," *The Journal of Accountancy,* February, 1970.

Gustafson, George A.: "Status of Accounting Research Study Nos. 1 and 3," *The Journal of Accountancy,* March, 1970.

Chapter 4

Professional Ethics

HOWARD J. BROWN

Assistant Professor of Accounting,
Hofstra University

ETHICS AND THE PUBLIC

Nature of Professional Ethics. Professional ethics represents an important part of the comprehensive system of discipline that is essential in any civilized society. Such a system of discipline is essential in order that the well-being of the group may be protected against the irresponsible acts of the individual. Thus responsibility is the price of group survival. If many individuals are permitted to act irresponsibly and are able to escape the consequences of their acts, the survival of the whole group is threatened. The more responsibility an individual accepts the more the community rewards him. Conversely the group rejects the individual who cannot be depended on to do a responsible job. There are three major levels of responsibility which make up our system of discipline. These are (1) legal responsibilities, (2) ethical responsibilities, and (3) moral responsibilities.

Legal responsibilities. These responsibilities are imposed by society as minimum requirements for those to whom it gives the honor of professional recognition. They are specified in state CPA laws and in federal government statutes such as the SEC laws.

Ethical responsibilities. These responsibilities are imposed by the profession upon its members. Legal responsibilities alone are not enough, and a profession must voluntarily assume responsibilities in the public interest. These are expressions of the profession's recognition of its social responsibility—what the profession stands for. They are usually stated in the profession's official code of ethics; thus a profession disciplines itself. In his *A Dictionary for Accountants*, second edition, Kohler defines professional ethics as "the rules imposed by a professional body on the behavior of its members." The rules of professional conduct for the auditor are primarily those promulgated by the American Institute of Certified Public Accountants (AICPA).[1] While other professional auditing organizations have developed general rules of responsibility, they are not as comprehensive as the Code of Professional Ethics issued by the AICPA. Though most of the rules in the Code relate to the relations of the public accountant with his client, the public, and other accountants, in general the Code is a guide for all auditors.

Moral responsibilities. These are imposed by individuals upon themselves. They call for a standard of conduct even higher than that required by ethical responsibilities.

Purpose of the Code of Ethics. The Code of Professional Ethics is more than a statement of responsibility. It is also a very practical working tool. It notifies the public that the profession will concern itself with protecting the public interest and the members will carry on the work in a way to benefit the public. The public has to trust the professional, must believe that he is competent and that his primary purpose is to help his patient or client. These are the factors which distinguish a profession from a business. Not only must the public be able to place faith in his technical skill but more importantly it must be able to rely on his integrity. He must be considered as a man of character who has earned the confidence reposed in him. The public, especially in the case of the auditor, must know that he can be trusted with the most private and important information. Confidence is even more important in the case of a certified public accountant than for members of some other professions. His professional service would have little value if the public did not have faith in his report. When he expresses an opinion in his certificate that the financial statements are fairly presented, the banker, the investor, and the government agency have no hesitancy in accepting the information as trustworthy. Without such third-party trust our complex financial structure would be in serious danger.

Development of Rules. The code of ethics for the accounting profession has evolved over the period of about 70 years, since the beginning of the accounting profession in this country. They are a dynamic, modern, realistic set of rules to keep pace with a constantly changing and expanding profession. They are the distillation of decades of experience of thousands of practitioners. Some rules were developed as specific events disclosed the need; others, such as those relating to management services, were developed as the profession took on new responsibilities. As the auditing profession becomes even more complex, new problems will arise and new rules will have to be developed. Ethical concepts in a society also change, which in turn affects the professional rules. Thus the present rules encompass a broad range of professional responsibility.

Ethics for All Auditors. There is no general code of ethics which is applicable to all auditors. The various professional organizations and government agencies have issued pronouncements, regulations, and rules of a general

[1] Code of Professional Ethics, as amended to December 30, 1969, and Interpretative Opinions, AICPA (Committee on Professional Ethics), New York, 1970.

nature relating to ethics, but no comprehensive code has yet been established. Following are the publications related to ethics for the principal branches of auditing.

Certified public accountants. For the certified public accountant the rules are primarily those set forth in the Code of Professional Ethics issued by the AICPA. However, CPAs are also subject to ethics rules issued by the state societies of CPAs and in many states by state regulations.

Internal auditors. For the internal auditor the general ethical requirements have been presented in the Code of Ethics issued by The Institute of Internal Auditors. Further information has been given in the Statement of Responsibilities of the Internal Auditor published by that organization. These are discussed later in the chapter.

Governmental auditors. For the federal government auditor the ethical standards have been established by the various units such as the Department of Defense, the Securities and Exchange Commission, the Internal Revenue Service, the General Accounting Office, and other agencies. Municipal auditors have been advised by their professional association, the Municipal Finance Officers Association of the United States and Canada, to observe the applicable provisions of the AICPA Code.

Enforcement of Rules. Unless there is effective enforcement, the established rules, no matter how good they may be, will have little effect on the profession. To date there has been a very effective enforcement of rules of ethics at both the national and state level. The enforcement procedures are described below.

Certified public accountants. The CPA who has been found guilty of a code violation may be admonished, suspended, or expelled from the AICPA. This would be possible only after a hearing by the established Trial Board of the Institute. The state societies also enforce state rules and also may admonish, suspend, or expel a member. While the CPA may be penalized by the AICPA or the state society of which he is a member, this is not effective in all cases. If a CPA is not a member of the AICPA or the state society, of course he could not be penalized by those organizations. Therefore, in most states the CPA's certificate may be suspended or revoked for violation of state rules. This is a far greater deterrent than expulsion from a society.

Internal auditors. Internal auditors may be admonished or expelled from the society for their actions, but this is a less formal procedure than would be expected in the case of the CPA. In the latter case there are very important investor and third-party responsibilities which are ordinarily not present in most of the work of the internal auditor.

Government auditors. The enforcement responsibilities of the government are twofold, that is, (1) it must determine that the auditors in the various agencies observe acceptable rules of conduct and (2) it must take action against auditors outside of the government who represent clients or practice before a particular government agency and who violate its rules of ethical practice.

Disciplinary action is carried out by the particular unit or agency involved with respect to its own auditors. The procedures, as in the case of internal auditors, are less formal than those applicable to the CPA. Various government agencies such as the Securities and Exchange Commission and the Internal Revenue Service have established high ethical standards. For example, the qualifications of the auditor for filing reports or for representing clients before the agency were established long ago by the SEC. Likewise the Internal Revenue Service may suspend or disbar an auditor from practicing before that agency. If he has been found guilty of failure to conduct his practice "in accordance with recognized ethical standards" or with violation of rules of conduct prescribed by the IRS.

ETHICS AND THE CPA

Contribution to Society. Our society has been described as "people's capitalism" and "regulated free enterprise." "People's capitalism" refers to the widespread ownership of corporate stock, a phenomenon which is possible only because of public faith in financial information. "Regulated free enterprise" refers to the network of laws and regulations which differentiate our system from the "laissez-faire" capitalism of the eighteenth century. A high degree of confidence in auditors by the regulatory and taxing authorities has made it possible to minimize governmental investigation and interference. To a great extent the CPA's usefulness to his client depends upon the credibility lent to published financial statements by the independent auditor's opinion. The client must use financial statements to communicate financial information to stockholders, bondholders, and potential investors, to banks and to trade creditors. Moreover, this information will help obtain capital and credit only because it is believed.

Professional Image. Experience has shown that adherence to high standards which place the client's interest above personal gain taken alone is not enough. The public must have an image of the public accountant which automatically places him above the "morality of the marketplace." For this reason he must not even seem to allow his personal interests to conflict with those of his clients or the public. He must not solicit, advertise, pay, or receive commissions. And he must not perform other acts which, while neither immoral nor illegal, would damage the prestige of the profession.

The Code of Ethics. The code of professional ethics is an enforceable guide to accountants' conduct both in fulfilling their professional obligations and in activities which affect the public's view of the profession. It consists of rules which have been codified by the AICPA in its Code of Professional Ethics. As need arises, the Code is interpreted officially in the numbered Opinions of the Division of Professional Ethics. The division will issue advisory opinions upon request. Summaries of significant advisory opinions are published in question and answer form from time to time. These are known as "informal opinions" or "Q and A's." The reader may be familiar with the opinions as those of the Committee on Professional Ethics since they were formerly issued by that body. Unless otherwise specified, opinions referred to will be those of the AICPA Division of Professional Ethics, which superseded the Committee.

The state societies of certified public accountants have also established codes, and in most states these rules, formulated by boards of accountancy, have the force of law. Generally they are patterned after the AICPA code.

While these codes are not identical, their basic tenets are the same. In this chapter the word "Code" will refer to the AICPA Code of Professional Ethics, the numbered Rules contained therein, and the numbered Opinions of the Division of Professional Ethics. The Code was developed to meet the needs of society and the accounting profession at a particular point in time and should not be viewed as a body of immutable laws. As the accounting profession continues to evolve along with our society, the code of ethics will inevitably grow and change.

Enforcement in States. In most states a license is required in order to practice as a public accountant. Unethical conduct in these states may result in loss of license and with it loss of the right to practice. Even where the ethical codes lack the force of law, the Trial Board of the AICPA may reprimand, suspend, or expel a member, as may the state societies.

ETHICS AND THE INTERNAL AUDITOR

General. Most of the guidelines for the internal auditor will be established by his particular company. In some cases the ethical aspects may be spelled out in company bulletins or pronouncements, and in many cases they may be understood but not formally published. Because of the wide diversity in the responsibilities and activities of the internal auditor it is not practicable to specify the ethics provisions to the same degree as in public accounting. However, many of the basic principles are similar in the codes of the American Institute of Certified Public Accountants and The Institute of Internal Auditors.

Independence. A special order of independence is required of the internal auditor if he is to serve management effectively. The requirements of independence with respect to the internal auditor are described in the Statement of Responsibilities of the Internal Auditor published by The Institute of Internal Auditors as follows:

Independence is essential to the effectiveness of the internal auditing program. This independence has two major aspects:

1. The organizational status of the internal auditor and the support accorded to him by management are major determinants of the range and value of the services which management will obtain from the internal auditing function. The head of the internal auditing department, therefore, should be responsible to an officer of sufficient rank in the organization as will assure a broad scope of activities, and adequate consideration of and effective action on the findings or recommendations made by him.

2. Since complete objectivity is essential to the audit function, internal auditors should not develop and install procedures, prepare records, or engage in any other activity which they normally would be expected to review and appraise.

The Code of Ethics. The Code of Ethics published by The Institute of Internal Auditors in 1968 contains 8 basic principles relating to internal auditing practice. There has not yet been a body of interpretive opinions accumulated for further guidance. That will come as the basic principles are further refined and tested in practice. The following is the Code of Ethics promulgated by The Institute of Internal Auditors.

INTRODUCTION:

Recognizing that ethics are an important consideration in the practice of internal auditing and that the moral principles followed by members of THE INSTITUTE OF INTERNAL AUDITORS, INC. should be formalized, the Board of Directors at its regular meeting in New Orleans on December 13, 1968, received and adopted the following resolution:

WHEREAS, the members of THE INSTITUTE OF INTERNAL AUDITORS, INC. represent the profession of internal auditing; and

WHEREAS, managements rely on the profession of internal auditing to assist in the fulfillment of their management stewardship; and

WHEREAS, said members must maintain high standards of conduct, honor and character in order to carry on proper and meaningful internal auditing practice;

THEREFORE BE IT RESOLVED that a Code of Ethics be now set forth outlining the standards of professional behavior for the guidance of each member of THE INSTITUTE OF INTERNAL AUDITORS, INC.

In accordance with this resolution, the Board of Directors further approved of the principles set forth.

INTERPRETATION OF PRINCIPLES:

The provisions of this Code of Ethics cover basic principles in the various disciplines of internal auditing practice. A member shall realize that individual judgment is required in the application of these principles. He has a responsibility to conduct himself so that his good faith and integrity should not be open to question. While having due regard for the limit of his technical skills, he will promote the highest possible internal auditing standards to the end of advancing the interest of his company or organization.

ARTICLES:

I. A member shall have an obligation to exercise honesty, objectivity and diligence in the performance of his duties and responsibilities.

II. A member, in holding the trust of his employer, shall exhibit loyalty in all matters pertaining to the affairs of the employer or to whomever he may be rendering a service. However, a member shall not knowingly be a party to any illegal or improper activity.

III. A member shall refrain from entering into any activity which may be in conflict with the interest of his employer or which would prejudice his ability to carry out objectively his duties and responsibilities.

IV. A member shall not accept a fee or a gift from an employee, a client, a customer or a business associate of his employer without the knowledge and consent of his senior management.

V. A member shall be prudent in the use of information acquired in the course of his duties. He shall not use confidential information for any personal gain or in a manner which would be detrimental to the welfare of his employer.

VI. A member, in expressing an opinion, shall use all reasonable care to obtain sufficient factual evidence to warrant such expression. In his reporting, a member shall reveal such material facts known to him which, if not revealed, could either distort the report of the results of operations under review or conceal unlawful practice.

VII. A member shall continually strive for improvement in the proficiency and effectiveness of his service.

VIII. A member shall abide by the Bylaws and uphold the objectives of THE INSTITUTE OF INTERNAL AUDITORS, INC. In the practice of his profession, he shall be ever mindful of his obligation to maintain the high standard of competence, morality and dignity which THE INSTITUTE OF INTERNAL AUDITORS, INC. and its members have established.

ETHICS AND THE GOVERNMENT AUDITOR

General. The Municipal Finance Officers Association of the United States and Canada has adopted the auditing standards of the AICPA for all governmental postaudits (audits made at the end of an accounting period or when transactions have been completed). The Association also advocates observance of the applicable provisions of the Code of Professional Ethics of the AICPA.[2] In support of the Code, the association is strongly opposed to the widespread employment of competitive bidding in arranging for independent audits and recommends that where audits are to be conducted by independent accountants "such post-audits should be performed by certified public accountants or, in states which have them, by registered municipal accountants."

Law vs. Principle. The National Committee on Governmental Accounting states,

[2] National Committee on Governmental Accounting, *Governmental Accounting, Auditing and Financial Reporting*, Chicago, Municipal Finance Officers Association of the United States and Canada, 1968, pp. 4, 128–130.

If there is a conflict between legal provisions and generally accepted accounting principles applicable to governmental units, legal provisions must take precedence. Insofar as possible, however, the governmental accounting system should make possible the full disclosure and fair presentation of financial position and operating results in accordance with generally accepted principles of accounting applicable to governmental units. [*Governmental Accounting, Auditing and Financial Reporting*, p. 4.]

Where compliance with the law produces financial statements which do not conform to generally accepted accounting principles, the Committee recommends that supplementary statements be prepared which do conform.

Public Disclosure. What of the CPA who, in the course of his audit of a governmental body, discovers fraud, embezzlement, or other wrongdoing on the part of an official? Certainly such discovery is one of the objectives of his engagement. But what if the person to whom he is to make his report is an official who might wish to suppress the information? The auditor would be caught between his moral obligation to the public to disclose his findings and the Code's stricture against violation of confidence. To avoid such a dilemma, the accountant accepting a governmental audit should see to it that the law under which he is engaged or the specific terms of his engagement provide for disclosure of any evidence of misconduct to an appropriate official.

Permits to Practice. Governmental agencies such as the SEC and the IRS prescribe rules and issue permits to practice before their respective agencies. Auditors permitted to practice before such an agency or representing clients before the agency are subject to the prescribed rules. Any violation of the established rules subjects the violator to suspension of his right to practice before the agency.

AUDITOR-CLIENT RELATIONSHIP

General. The certified public accountant's loyalty to his client, even under the most trying circumstances, is basic to the auditor-client relationship. The client must know that his accountant, like his physician or attorney, will treat him with fairness and frankness. He must be confident that the accountant will not take advantage of confidential knowledge for personal gain but will make every effort to assist him within the scope of his competence and, when an engagement appears to be beyond that scope, will not hesitate to suggest other assistance. Moreover the accountant is morally obligated to strive to attain and employ the highest degree of professional skill.

The various specific ethical problems of the auditor as they relate to confidential information, published financial statements, advertising, etc., will be discussed in this chapter. The responsibilities connected with legal requirements are treated in Chapter 5, "Legal Liability."

Confidential Information. Questions are often asked concerning the confidential nature of the auditor-client relationship and the auditor's position in the given situation. Following are representative questions and answers based on the informal opinions issued by the ethics committee.

Q. What does the rule concerning the confidential relationship (Rule 1.03) mean?

A. Confidential information obtained as a result of his engagement must not be revealed by the CPA voluntarily unless he has the consent of his client. Similarly, he must not use such knowledge for personal gain. (Opinion No. 3.) He should make every effort to assure that his employees also comply with this rule. Termination of his engagement does not free him from this obligation.

Q. May a CPA voluntarily testify against his client in a third-party litigation involving the client?
A. No. To do so would be a violation of his client's confidence.

Q. May a CPA under subpoena be forced to divulge confidential information concerning his client?
A. Yes. Communications between a client and his public accountant are *not* "privileged" as are those of attorneys, physicians, and clergymen. In some states this protection of confidentiality has been extended to CPAs. But even in these latter states the federal courts would probably not be bound by state law.

Q. Who may examine the accountant's working papers, tax returns, and other confidential documents?
A. No one may without the permission of the client unless this is required by a court of law. However, it is customary for clients to grant requests from governmental agencies such as the Internal Revenue Service.

Q. To whom do working papers belong?
A. They belong to the auditor, and he need not surrender them even to the client. When anyone is permitted to review them, a representative of the CPA should be present to prevent alteration or extraction without his knowledge.

Q. Do working papers, tax returns, and correspondence relating to an account become the property of the purchaser upon the sale of the account?
A. No. According to Opinion No. 3, the seller must obtain permission from his client to give the purchaser access to these documents.

Q. May a CPA who is defending a negligence action or suing for a fee reveal information concerning his engagement?
A. Yes, but only information necessary to his defense or to the proof of his claim.

Q. Would it be a breach of confidence to disclose the actions of officers or employees which might be financially injurious to the client?
A. On the contrary, it would be the auditor's duty to report these matters to higher authority.

Q. Must a CPA report a client's failure to comply with Federal Income Tax laws?
A. No. He need only "advise the client promptly of the fact." (*Treasury Department Circular* No. 230, Section 10.21.) This is discussed later in this chapter under Tax Practice.

Q. If a CPA learns of a client's intention to commit a crime, must he keep silent?
A. No. Not even the lawyer's right of privileged communication transcends his duty to prevent a criminal act. However, the accountant should consult his attorney and the AICPA Division of Professional Ethics before divulging his client's intention.

Independence. Significance. Among Webster's definitions of the word "independent" is "not subject to bias or influence." Rule 1.01 says independence "is an expression of the professional integrity of the individual," and the Council of the AICPA has referred to it as "an attitude of mind." However defined, it is public belief in the objectivity, the freedom from outside influence, the *independence* of the auditor which lends credibility to his opinions concerning financial statements.

Code requirements. Rule 1.01 forbids expression of an opinion with regard to financial statements of enterprises from which the auditor is not independent. But independence is a state of mind and is not subject to audit. For this reason the rule goes on to require that the circumstances of the auditor's relationship with an enterprise be such that one "might expect his opinion to be considered independent, objective and unbiased by one who has knowledge of all the facts. In short, his position with reference to his client should not be such that his objectivity might be impaired."

Conflict of interest. What circumstances might lead a reasonable man to question the independence of an auditor? They are those in which the substantial personal interests of the auditor conflict with his professional duty. Rule 1.01 itself cites examples in these words:

> A member or associate will be considered not independent for example, with respect to any enterprise if he, or one of his partners, (a) during the period of his professional engagement or at the time of expressing his opinion, had, or was committed to acquire, any direct financial interest or material indirect financial interest in the enterprise, or (b) during the period of his professional engagement, at the time of expressing his opinion, or during the period covered by the financial statements, was connected with the enterprise as a promoter, underwriter, voting trustee, director, officer or key employee.

In applying this rule, Opinion No. 16 views a retired partner who continues to be active in the firm as though he were still a partner.

The SEC. In Regulation S-X, Rule 2.01, the Securities and Exchange Commission establishes essentially the same criteria for independence as does the AICPA in Rule 1.01. The SEC regulation states:

> The Commission will not recognize any certified public accountant or public accountant as independent who is not in fact independent. For example, an accountant will be considered not independent with respect to any person or any of its parents or subsidiaries in whom he has, or had during the period of report, any direct financial interest or any material indirect financial interest; or with whom he is, or was during such period, connected as a promoter, underwriter, officer, or employee.
>
> In determining whether an accountant may in fact be not independent with respect to a particular person, the Commission will give appropriate consideration to all relevant circumstances, including evidence bearing on all relationships between the accountant and that person or any affiliate thereof, and will not confine itself to the relationships existing in connection with the filing of reports with the Commission.

It would appear that the SEC regulations goes somewhat beyond Rule 1.01 in specifying relationships which might impair an auditor's independence. However, judging from their decisions and opinions in actual cases, the AICPA and the SEC are in substantial agreement on the circumstances which destroy independence. In specifying the time during which the existence of certain relationships are deemed to conflict with independence, the Institute, unlike the SEC, differentiates between financial interest and the interest inherent in official positions. That is to say that, unlike Regulation S-X, Rule 1.01 leaves the door open for the CPA to establish financial independence by divesting himself of financial interest in an enterprise between the end of the period covered by the audit and the commencement of the audit itself.

Consideration of the Institute and the SEC views indicates that two general categories of circumstances are held to produce impairment of independence. These are (1) *conflict of financial interest* and (2) holding an *official position not compatible with objectivity.*

Conflict of financial interest. According to Rule 1.01, the auditor is not independent if during the time specified "he or one of his partners . . . had, or was committed to acquire any direct financial interest. . . ." The use of the term "any" clearly means that no direct financial interest, no matter how small, is to be tolerated. On the other hand, the rule prohibits only *material* indirect financial interests. Just how much is material? Materiality is a relative matter, and the Division of Professional Ethics has held that it is to be judged in relation to the total net worth of the client and that of the auditor or his firm.

Now how shall we distinguish between direct and indirect financial interest? Clearly, if accountant A owns stock in company B, he has a direct interest in B, and neither A nor his partners are independent with respect to B. But not every situation is so obvious, and there is no general formula for differentiation between direct and indirect financial interest. In the words of the SEC's Regulation S-X, one must "give appropriate consideration to all relevant circumstances, including evidence bearing on all relationships between the accountant and that person or any affiliate thereof. . . ."

The informal opinions relating to financial interest may serve as a guide to interpretation of these rules. Relevant opinions may be found in *Ethical Standards of the Accounting Profession* (John L. Carey and William O. Doherty, New York, AICPA, pp. 275–281). In addition Opinion No. 19 lists certain loan or deposit relationships with banks which might constitute conflicts of financial interest.

Official position not compatible with objectivity. "May a partner of an accounting firm serve on the board of directors of a country club without jeopardizing the firm's right to render an opinion on the club's statements? In short, does the country club come under the exception in Rule 1.01 which permits a member to serve as both auditor and director of charitable, religious, civic, and other types of nonprofit organizations?" The informal response expresses the essence of Rule 1.01's provisions regarding conflict of interest due to official position.

> If a member expressed an opinion on the financial statements of a country club of which he or one of his partners was a director, he would then be reporting on his own stewardship. The exception made for non-profit organizations was intended primarily to cover those situations in which a member was lending his name to a worthy cause without assuming administrative or financial responsibilities. The auditor may serve as director only "when the duties performed in such a capacity are such as to make it clear that the member or associate can express an independent opinion on the financial statements." This language of Rule 1.01 makes it clear that the objective test of independence should be applied in such cases.

The purpose of Rule 1.01, then, is to prohibit one who has served an organization in another capacity ("as a promoter, underwriter, voting trustee, director, officer or key employee") from standing as auditor in judgment of his own work. It also views the exception written into the rule as remaining in harmony with this concept. The exception reads:

> The word "director" is not intended to apply to a connection in such a capacity with a charitable, religious, civic, or other similar type of nonprofit organization when the duties performed in such a capacity are such as to make it clear that the member or associate can express an independent opinion on the financial statements.

In other words, to be exempt from the rule, such a titular directorship must not carry with it the performance of acts whose outcome will be the subject of audit.

The extension of the concept of Rule 1.01 to management advisory services is obvious. The consultant who makes a management decision or takes a position having a material effect on an organization's operations may place himself in a position analogous to that of a manager.

Time. Both the AICPA and the SEC agree that the official relationships listed impair independence if (in the words of Rule 1.01) they exist or existed "during the period of his professional engagement or at the time of expressing his opinion or during the period covered by the financial statements."

What of an auditor who has expressed an opinion on the financial statements of an enterprise and then ceases to be independent of that enterprise? May he re-express the opinion which he had rendered while he was independent? Rule 1.01 clearly answers that he may, for it says, "the phrase 'at the time of expressing his opionion' refers only to the time at which the member or associate first expressed his opinion."

When clients' interests conflict. Serving two or more clients whose interests conflict, for example, competitors, has never been viewed as impairing an auditor's independence. On the other hand, a client might not concur, especially if he were to learn from a third party that "his accountant" was working for a competitor. Therefore, it is generally wise to notify those concerned when accepting an engagement from a company whose interests do or might conflict with those of an existing client.

Moreover, accepting such an engagement does place an obligation upon the CPA to be especially careful about his own and his staff's observance of confidentiality.

The write-up. In "Special Reports—Application of Statement on Auditing Procedure No. 28," the Institute voices its position on "write-ups" as follows:

> *Writing Up Records.* Small businesses often have inadequate records. The independent auditor may be required to write up the books or make numerous adjusting entries and prepare the financial statements. The independent auditor is not necessarily lacking in independence simply because he has performed these services. Although he often does make disclosure of work he has performed, disclosure of these services is not necessary if in the circumstances of a particular engagement, the independent auditor considers himself to be, in fact, independent. If possible, the examination should be conducted by staff members who were not associated with the original accounting work.

The SEC takes the opposite position in Cases 44 and 45 of the Accounting Series Releases (compilation of Releases No. 78 to 79, inclusive, p. 36), holding that the auditor cannot be a truly independent reviewer of his own work. However, in certain emergencies such as the unexpected resignation of a registrant's comptroller or the death of a registrant's bookkeeper, the commission does accept the "certification" of the accounting firm whose personnel temporarily provide the necessary service.

Management services. Those professional services which an independent auditor provides beyond the scope of the audit and tax work he performs have come to be called "management services." These include services in areas such as systems design, data processing, budgeting, financial analysis, and pension plans. Many other services may be included, but on the whole CPAs have generally concentrated on data-oriented services. The AICPA's position on management services and the possible effect on the auditor's independence was summarized in Opinion No. 12 as follows:

> It is the opinion of the committee that there is no ethical reason why a member or associate may not properly perform professional services for clients in the areas of tax practice or management advisory services, and at the same time serve the same client as independent auditor, so long as he does not make management decisions or take positions which might impair that objectivity.

The first three opinions of the AICPA Management Services Committee continue to support this position as does the final report of the Institute's Ad Hoc Committee on Independence. However, these authorities stress the converse, that the auditor who *does* make management decisions or take positions which might impair his objectivity loses his independence. When a CPA is asked to perform such a service he must choose between complying and continuing to serve as an independent auditor. He may not do both.

What is the auditor to do if, in his judgment, performance of a particular service would not in fact impair his independence but might possibly lead others to doubt his objectivity? Before accepting such an engagement it might be advisable to consult the company's audit committee or board of directors. In fact, periodic reports to one of these bodies of all services being rendered may be advisable.

Joint occupations. May a CPA engage in another occupation while carrying on public practice, or would such engagement represent a conflict of interest? If by "another occupation" is meant an activity not related to public accounting, a conflict of interest would not normally be created. But if, for example, a client became a major customer of his auditor who was simultaneously the proprietor of a commercial enterprise, the auditor would lose his independence.

Is there no ethical restriction on the nature of the accountant's "moonlighting" activities? Rule 4.04 states:

> A member or associate shall not engage in any business or occupation conjointly with that of a public accountant, which is incompatible or inconsistent therewith.

Apparently this means that the public accountant's extra-professional activities must not be of a type which will, by reflection, degrade the profession.

And what restrictions are placed upon public-accounting-related activities such as data processing services? As to the ethical code, such work is not distinguished from general practice. Rule 4.05 stipulates:

> A member or associate engaged in an occupation in which he renders services of a type performed by public accountants or renders other professional services must observe the by-laws and Code of Professional Ethics of the Institute in the conduct of that occupation.

As was pointed out with respect to management services, independence is required only of those who would render an opinion upon financial statements and is not required of those concerned exclusively with nonpublished financial statements.

REPORTS

Introduction. The primary function of the public accountant is that of attestor to financial statements. As attestor, he voices a professional opinion upon the financial statements prepared and issued by his clients or others and thereby lends these statements greater credibility. The auditor's attestation takes the form of a signed opinion regarding the financial statements in question and is addressed to his client.

Short-form Report. Unqualified opinion. The AICPA recommends the following form for an unqualified opinion on the short form: [3]

> We have examined the balance sheet of X Company as of June 30, 19__, and the related statement(s) of income and retained earnings for the year then ended. Our examination was made in accordance with generally accepted auditing standards, and accordingly included such tests of the accounting records and such other auditing procedures as we considered necessary in the circumstances.
>
> In our opinion, the accompanying balance sheet and statement(s) of income and retained earnings present fairly the financial position of X Company at June 30, 19__,

[3] Statements on Auditing Procedure No. 33, *Auditing Standards and Procedures*, AICPA (Committee on Auditing Procedure), New York, 1963.

and the results of its operations for the year then ended, in conformity with generally accepted accounting principles applied on a basis consistent with that of the preceding year.

The usual short-form report consists of two paragraphs, (1) the scope paragraph and (2) the opinion paragraph. Where further explanation or description may be required, the appropriate paragraph is expanded as required.

SCOPE PARAGRAPH: This paragraph states that the auditor has *examined* the specified statements. He has searched out and evaluated the supporting data for the financial statements. Therefore, he did much more than "look at" or "review" the statements. The paragraph also states that the examination was made in accordance with generally accepted auditing standards and such other auditing procedures as required. There is no need to specify what procedures were carried out, as such procedures have been published by the AICPA and should be familiar to all auditors. The auditing standards are fully described in Statements on Auditing Procedure No. 33.

OPINION PARAGRAPH: Regarding this paragraph, Article I of the Code of Professional Ethics refers to the auditor's expression of opinion on financial statements but assiduously avoids mentioning certification. This latter term may lead the reader to the false conclusion that the auditor's report somehow guarantees the accuracy of the statements. The report states that the accountant, having performed an investigation whose scope is outlined in the first paragraph, voices an affirmative professional opinion regarding the fairness (but not the precise accuracy) of the financial statements.

The "generally accepted accounting principles" referred to in the opinion are basically the Opinions of the Accounting Principles Board, and while departure from these may be countenanced when supported by other authoritative opinion, such departures should be disclosed in the auditor's report. In forming his overall opinion, the CPA may rely in part on the audit work of another firm. According to Rule 2.01 he may rely on such work if the other firm has at least one member certified in the United States and is one "whose independence and professional reputation he has ascertained to his satisfaction." Special provisions in Rule 2.01 apply to foreign auditors.

When an unqualified opinion must be withheld. Thus far it has been assumed that the scope of the audit and the resultant findings permit the auditor to render an unqualified opinion concerning the fairness of the financial statements. In this case the short-form report just illustrated may be used. But frequently this is not the case. In Rule 2.03 and APB Opinion No. 8 we are given five alternatives to the unqualified report. They are (1) qualified opinion, (2) adverse opinion, (3) disclaimer, (4) disavowal, and (5) disassociation.

QUALIFIED OPINION: When any generally accepted auditing procedure is omitted, but the amount not verified is immaterial or is verified to the auditor's satisfaction by alternative means, the auditor may insert a full explanation, or "qualification," into his report and still render an affirmative opinion.

Similarly, if accepted auditing principles have not been adhered to or have not been employed in the same manner as in the previous period, an exception should be inserted in the report fully disclosing the deviation and its effect in financial terms. Full disclosure of material facts omitted from the report also must be rendered here. If these exceptions are not sufficient to make a meaningful opinion impossible, the auditor may then express such an opinion, but it should include references to all exceptions. Exceptions may sometimes be eliminated if the statement issued includes full disclosure in the form of footnotes.

ADVERSE OPINION: According to APB Opinion No. 8, if the audit has disclosed exceptions to fair and consistent reporting that are so material that an affirmative opinion must be withheld, the auditor is required to issue an adverse opinion disclosing all his reasons.

DISCLAIMER: An "adverse opinion" results not from a flaw in the scope of the audit but from the conclusion drawn from the audit. In contrast, when, because of limitation in the scope of the audit or for some other reason, the auditor lacks enough information to support an opinion, he must state this affirmatively in his report and give his reasons. Having made this "disclaimer," he may still express opinions on specific sections of the statements which have been subject to adequate audit. Another circumstance requiring a disclaimer arises when the auditor is not independent. In this latter case Statement No. 42 prohibits inclusion of the reason for lack of independence or recitation of auditing procedures performed. Inclusion of these matters might confuse the reader or appear to reduce the importance of the disclaimer.

When lack of independence calls for a disclaimer the following wording is recommended.

> We are not independent with respect to XYZ Company, and the accompanying balance sheet as of December 31, 19__ and the related statement(s) of income and retained earnings for the year then ended were not audited by us; accordingly, we do not express an opinion on them.

In addition, Statement No. 42 requires that, except for the page on which the disclaimer itself appears, each page of the financial statements must be conspicuously marked "Unaudited—see accompanying disclaimer of opinion."

DISAVOWAL: To repeat section (e) of Rule 2.03:

> When unaudited financial statements are presented on his stationery without his comments (the auditor must) disclose prominently on each page of the financial statements that they were not audited.

DISASSOCIATION: The second paragraph of APB Opinion No. 8 reads:

> In a circumstance where a member believes the financial statements are false or misleading as a whole or in any significant respect, it is the opinion of the committee that he should require adjustments of the accounts or adequate disclosure of the facts, as the case may be, and failing this the independent accountant should refuse to permit his name to be associated with the statements in any way.

Statement on Auditing Procedure No. 42 adds failure to conform to generally accepted accounting principles to the list of reasons for disassociation and calls for the auditor to withdraw from the case if necessary. SEC Accounting Series Release No. 115 precludes an opinion on statements prepared on a going concern basis if there is serious question whether the business will continue.

Long-form Report. An auditor's report which provides more information than the short form is known as a *long-form,* or *detailed,* report. Such a report generally is intended for a special audience, such as management or bankers. For example, it may include comments upon certain portions of the financial statements, or include additional ones, give details about some phase of audit procedure, or advise management upon an accounting matter. Statements of scope and procedure equivalent to the short-form report may be embodied in the detailed report, or a short-form report may be presented separately. In the latter case, the short-form report must be able to stand on its own without the assumption that the user will look to the detailed report.

Subsequent Events. When the CPA learns of events which occurred after the date of the financial statements but before he has released his report, full disclosure must be made if the events have a material effect on the financial statements. (Chapter 11 of Statements on Auditing Procedure No. 33.)

Subsequently Discovered Information. The auditor will sometimes have reason to believe that relevant facts of which he was previously unaware may have existed at the date of his report. If he believes that these facts might have required disclosure in the report had they been known in time it is his duty to investigate and to prevent users of the statements, including organizations such as the SEC and stock exchanges from reliance upon misleading information. This means that they must be notified promptly.

Notification by the client will normally take the form of revised financial statements or, if this will not cause delay, disclosure in subsequent financial statements. If a prolonged investigation will cause delay, prompt notice should be given that the financial statements are not to be relied upon pending completion of the investigation.

If the client refuses to cooperate either by declining to permit the necessary investigation or to issue the required notification, each member of the board of directors must be apprised of this refusal and of the steps the auditor will take. According to Statement on Auditing Procedure No. 41 (*Subsequent Discovery of Facts Existing at the Date of the Auditor's Report*) these measures may include:

1. Notification to the client that the auditor's report must no longer be associated with the financial statements.
2. Notification to regulatory agencies having jurisdiction over the client [and] to each person known by the auditor to be relying on the financial statements.

Because of problems related to confidentiality, legal liability to third parties and requirements of regulatory bodies, the auditor who faces any of the situations just discussed should consult an attorney.

SPECIAL STATEMENTS

A great variety of financial statements other than the balance sheet and income statement may be included with the report. Some of these are:

The Funds Statement. APB Opinion No. 3 states that the inclusion of a Statement of Source and Application of Funds is not mandatory. Its inclusion and reference to the statement is at the option of the CPA.

Forecasts. As to financial statements which reflect anticipated future events, Rule 2.04 holds:

> A member or associate shall not permit his name to be used in conjunction with any forecast of the results of future transactions, in a manner which may lead to the belief that the member or associate vouches for the accuracy of the forecast.

And APB Opinion No. 10 adds that "he must disclose the source of the information used and major assumptions made."

Cash Basis Statements. Since cash basis statements must not purport to reflect financial position or results of operations, the short-form report should be modified appropriately.

Statements of Nonprofit Organizations. If generally accepted auditing standards and procedures are applicable for the particular type of nonprofit organization, an opinion may be rendered in the same terms as for a profit-making enterprise.

Statements under Governmental Regulation. Special regulations of governmental bodies may call for specific procedures or information. They should be viewed as adding to the audit requirements and not as abrogating those which are generally accepted.

The SEC for one, in Rule 2.02 of Regulation S-X, calls for what is essentially the short-form report discussed above. It requires full and fair disclosure and holds the auditor guilty if he is negligent or his audit is of inadequate scope, even if the financial statements in question are in fact flawless.

The responsibilities which the law imposes on the auditor are dealt with in Chapter 5, "Legal Liability."

ADVERTISING, SOLICITATION, AND ENCROACHMENT

Advertising, solicitation, and encroachment are prohibited by Rules 3.01, 3.02, and 5.01, respectively. But what do the rules mean in terms of practical do's and don'ts for the practitioner?

Advertising Do's and Don'ts. The following paragraphs describe what actions are appropriate and what are not in a number of specific situations.

Announcements

SITUATION: A CPA wishes to announce to the community that he has opened an office, or has changed his address, his partners, or his supervisory staff. He also wishes to have it known that he is an expert prepared to render certain special services.

APPROPRIATE ACTION: Mail dignified announcements to friends, clients, and their attorneys and bankers, and to other professional acquaintances announcing the opening of the office or the change in personnel or address.

INADMISSIBLE BEHAVIOR: An announcement or the printing of a "card" in newspapers or in similar media would constitute advertising, which is forbidden by Rule 3.01 and Opinion No. 11.

Mailed announcements, which are sanctioned, must not hold the practitioner out as an expert or specialist in any given area such as "tax expert" or "management consultant." In fact, Opinion No. 5 does not permit him to advertise himself as an expert in any special branch of the profession by any means whatsoever.

Directory listing

SITUATION: A CPA is arranging for listing in a classified directory.

APPROPRIATE ACTION: He may enter a listing which, in the words of Rule 3.01, "is restricted to the name, title, address and telephone number of the the person or firm." The firm name and the names of each partner may be listed separately.

Classified telephone directory listings are permitted only in the areas where offices are located. Under Opinion No. 11, designation of areas is left to the state CPA societies.

INADMISSIBLE BEHAVIOR: Each name listed may not appear more than once in a given directory. It may not, for example, be listed under both "Certified Public Accountants" and "Public Accountants." However, when a trade association or similar directory includes a listing by location as well as the usual alphabetical listing, a name may appear in both places.

Directory listings may not be made to stand out from others in the directory by any means such as a printed border or by style or size of type. "Yellow Page" telephone directory listings outside of the office area are forbidden.

Listing in a membership directory which requires payment of a special fee is counter to Opinion No. 11, as is listing in a directory of CPAs who audit and perform other services for banks.

Stationery and business cards

SITUATION: A CPA is ordering letterheads and business cards and wishes to know what information may be printed on them.

APPROPRIATE ACTION: Opinion No. 11 of the Committee on Professional Ethics specifies that the stationery may include:

> (1) The firm name, names of partners, names of deceased partners and their years of service, and names of staff men when preceded by a line to separate them from the partners.
>
> (2) The letters "CPA" following the name, the use of the words "Certified Public Accountant," the address (or addresses) of officer(s), telephone number(s), cities in which other offices and correspondents are located, and membership in professional societies in which all partners are members.

When the firm cannot be designated "Certified Public Accountants" because of state law or the presence of a noncertified partner, the title "Accountants and Auditors" may be used instead.

Only the name of the person and his position, his firm's name, address, and telephone number, and the words "Certified Public Accountants" may appear on business cards.

A member of the AICPA employed in private practice may use the title "CPA" on his business card but not when engaged in non-accounting activities such as selling.

INADMISSIBLE BEHAVIOR: No specialty may be indicated on either letterheads or business cards.

When a firm has offices in other locations, listing them or the partners resident there is not actually prohibited, but the practice is frowned upon. It is suggested that some appropriate phrase such as "offices in other principal cities" be used instead.

Signs

SITUATION: A CPA plans to display his firm name in the lobby and outside the building where his office is located and on autos owned by the firm.

APPROPRIATE ACTION: Tasteful display of the firm name which by size, style, and location is clearly intended to assist persons seeking to find the office is approved. Appropriate locations for a sign might be on or near the office entrance doors or in a lobby directory. In the latter case, it should conform to other listings in the directory.

Listing the names of partners and staff members on the office door is acceptable. A line should separate the list of partners from that of the staff.

INADMISSIBLE BEHAVIOR: Large, conspicuous, or specially illuminated signs or those placed in inappropriate places such as in windows, on walls, building fronts, or vehicles (such as the firm's autos) are viewed as advertising and are therefore prohibited. Where there is a building directory, additional signs should not be displayed. According to Opinions No. 5 and 11, designation of a professional specialty is similarly banned.

CPA title

SITUATION: A newly licensed CPA wishes to know where it is appropriate for him to display his new title and where it is not.

APPROPRIATE ACTION: The propriety of using the title of CPA on public accounting firm letterheads, in directories, and in several other places is discussed in relation to a number of the specific situations included in this list. Some additional places where the CPA designation might appropriately follow the accountant's name are:

1. On the stationery of a charitable organization of which the CPA is an officer.
2. On a practicing accountant's business checks.
3. In advertising of lectures or courses to be given by a CPA or of his books, articles, or television appearances.
4. In connection with a campaign for public office.
5. In the letterhead of a nonpracticing accountant's employment agency for accountants.
6. On a bank's letterhead if the CPA is a director.

INADMISSIBLE BEHAVIOR: Some uses of the CPA title which are not appropriate are:

1. In advertisements of a bank of which a CPA is a director.
2. On license plates of firm-owned autos.
3. Imprinted on personal checks.
4. In a published listing of the states in which an accountant holds certificates. (While this practice may not actually be banned, it is felt that catalogs containing such listing might lead to the mistaken inference that the number of certificates held is a measure of an accountant's professional stature.)

Authorship, public speaking, and educational seminars

SITUATION: A public accountant wishes to write for publication. He has also been invited to speak publicly on a professional subject and contemplates sponsoring or participating in educational seminars.

APPROPRIATE ACTION: Authorship of authoritative books and articles is encouraged by Opinion No. 4, and appearances by CPAs before meetings and on radio and television to discuss topics related to their profession are quite customary. For example, accountants sometimes appear in tax information programs sponsored by professional societies. A CPA's participation in a televised stockholders' meeting would also be in order if he were actually the company's auditor. Publicity concerning these publications or appearances would not run counter to the rule against advertising. This publicity may properly include statements about the accountant's background such as his educational qualifications, the name of his firm, and the professional associations to which he belongs.

INADMISSIBLE BEHAVIOR: Opinion No. 4 reads, "a member of the Institute has the responsibility to ascertain that the publisher or others promoting distribution of his work keep within the bounds of professional dignity and do not make claims concerning the author or his writing that are not factual or in good taste."

Ethics Opinion No. 21 extends these basic rules to sponsorship or participation in educational seminars. In general it restricts those whom the accountant may invite to clients and professionals serving them. Solicitation of the opportunity to participate is prohibited when a seminar sponsored by others will be attended by non-clients. Nor, in the latter case, may the CPA distribute firm literature not closely related to the topic he is presenting.

In an informal opinion the Division of Professional Ethics has ruled against television appearances to verify statements which the accountant did not audit and on which he performed no technical work. This would seem to preclude attesting to such things as the secrecy of "quiz show" questions.

Distribution of literature

SITUATION: A firm is contemplating distribution of a newsletter, and other literature to persons outside the firm.

APPROPRIATE ACTION: Publications, such as booklets and manuals on tax problems and other professional topics and even the firm's house organ, which are prepared by the firm and bear the firm name, may be given to certain persons outside the firm. In the words of Opinion No. 9 they may be distributed "to clients and individuals with whom professional contacts are maintained . . . and to non-clients who specifically request them and universities if the material is of educational value."

This approval extends to material prepared by others when not imprinted with the firm name. Such printed matter ought to be accompanied by a letter disclaiming authorship.

INADMISSIBLE BEHAVIOR: Imprinting the firm name on literature prepared by others tends to imply authorship falsely and is forbidden by Opinion No. 1. The firm must not allow circulation of its publications to anyone not included in the list quoted above under "Appropriate Action." The firm is even responsible for circulation by others, so that when more than one copy is requested the firm must ascertain who is to receive each copy. Special care must be exercised to see that Rule 5.01 barring encroachment is observed.

News reports

SITUATION: A CPA who has done or said something newsworthy questions whether a press report concerning him or his firm would be construed as advertising.

APPROPRIATE ACTION: Publicity regarding actions which reflect well upon the accountant and his profession is certainly not to be discouraged. Opinion No. 9 specifically encourages the reporting of statements by CPAs which enhance the public's understanding of the profession. The accountant could therefore cooperate with reporters who wish to obtain an accurate account.

INADMISSIBLE BEHAVIOR: Opinion No. 9 warns that "Publicity deliberately cultivated either directly or indirectly by a member which advertises his firm's professional attainments or services is considered to be a violation of Rule 3.01."

Advertising for help

SITUATION: A public accounting firm is advertising for help.

APPROPRIATE ACTION: The firm may place the usual help wanted classified advertisements in newspapers, professional journals, and other publications and may even use display-type advertising. In the latter case, the firm's telephone number, address, or newspaper box number may appear.

INADMISSIBLE BEHAVIOR: The firm name or that of a partner or associate may not appear in display advertising. This stricture applies equally to advertisements entered in a client's behalf. In other classified advertisements the name should not be differentiated from the rest of the copy by any means such as size or style of type.

The advertisement must not imply an offer of services to the public.

Opinion No. 9 limits distribution of staff recruitment brochures to "college faculty and placement officials, students considering interviews and job applicants." In distributing these brochures special care should be exercised against infraction of Rule 5.03, which prohibits offers of employment to a member of another public accounting firm without prior notice to his employer.

Advertising for employment

SITUATION: A CPA wishes to seek either public or private practice through advertising. He is concerned about Rule 3.01, which states, "a member or associate shall not advertise his professional attainments or services."

APPROPRIATE ACTION: The usual "situation wanted" advertisments stating the accountant's qualifications and directing replies to a telephone number, address, or box would not violate Rule 3.01.

It is permissible to advertise for full-time employment by public accountants or by private industry, but per diem employment may be sought only from public accounting firms.

INADMISSIBLE BEHAVIOR: The accountant must not appear to or in fact attempt to attract public accounting engagements. Accordingly, advertisements under such headings as "Business Services" or "Professional Services" would violate Rule 3.01 and Opinion No. 11.

Display-type advertising and the use of such terms as "tax expert" and other self-glorifying phrases would also be violations.

Gaining New Clients. In light of the prohibition against advertising, how is the public accountant, especially one just going into practice, to gain clients? May he simply ask a potential client to engage his professional services? Such a request is certainly the very act meant by the word "solicitations" in Rule 3.02, which states, "A member or associate shall not endeavor, directly or indirectly, to obtain clients by solicitations."

What then may the accountant do? He may widen his sphere of acquaintance by active participation in social, religious, and service organizations. When his new acquaintances question him, as they surely will, he is free to discuss his profession. But direct or indirect solicitation must be avoided. This would still hold true if the accountant were to learn of a friend who was seeking a public accountant.

Other ethical avenues open to him such as the writing of books and articles, and public speaking, have been included in our discussion of advertising. An accountant is well advised to arrange his speaking engagements through accounting societies or in response to unsolicited invitations. Should he take the initiative in offering his services, this might be considered solicitation.

When someone interested in obtaining his services does approach the practitioner, the latter is free to discuss the matter and even estimate a fee (see "Remuneration"). Even if there is presently another engaged in the work, this is not viewed as encroachment because of a special provision in Rule 3.05. In this latter case courtesy requires that the client notify the incumbent accountant of his intentions before the new man accepts the engagement. At this point, it is well for the accountant to remember that there is no place in a profession for "special introductory offers" and that an inadequate fee may be considered evidence of solicitation, according to Opinion No. 18.

Communication with CPAs and Attorneys. Since they are not potential clients, the public accountant may communicate with fellow practitioners and lawyers with whom he is acquainted without quite the usual concern over solicitation or encroachment. For example, he is permitted to offer to act as a tax consultant or, if his practice is limited to that type of work, to announce that he is prepared to render systems installation or analysis service. He may also use his letterhead in soliciting contributions for charity from these professional men or to mail them tax charts and other useful publications. However, the public accountant must make sure that this material does not reach unauthorized persons, including even CPAs employed by private industry.

Retaining Clients. The rule against solicitation speaks of endeavoring "to obtain clients." Endeavoring to *retain* one's own clients is never solicitation. Therefore, if one's client is involved in a consolidation or merger, it is proper to seek to retain the engagement by approaching the corporation's officers.

Partnership Clients. In the absence of an agreement to the contrary, the clients of a partnership are the clients of all the partners. A partner who withdraws from a firm and the former members of a firm which has dissolved are free to solicit assignments from former clients. However, once a client has chosen his accountant, further solicitation by the others would be banned encroachment.

It has been suggested that when a partnership disbands, unseemly competition may be avoided if the partners send a joint letter to the firm's clients explaining the situation and asking them to indicate who is to continue the engagement.

PROFESSIONAL FEES

General. The businessman may charge "what the traffic will bear," and the giving and receiving of commissions and finder's fees are quite customary in the business world. Such practices by the CPA could not be reconciled with the accountant's duty never even to suggest by his actions that he is placing his personal interest above that of his client. This means that a public accountant may not take advantage of a client's naïveté to charge an exorbitant fee.

The Internal Revenue Service supports this view in Section 10.28 of *Treasury Department Circular* 230, revised November, 1966, where it states as follows:

> No attorney, certified public accountant, or enrolled agent shall charge an unconscionable fee for representation of a client in any matter before the Internal Revenue Service.

On the other hand, according to Opinion No. 18, "offering to perform services for an inadequate fee may be evidence of solicitation."

Contingent Fees. Rule 1.04 of the Code of Professional Ethics provides that "services shall not be rendered or offered for a fee which shall be contingent upon the findings or results of such services." Thus the auditor is prevented from compromising his independence by rendering an opinion upon financial statements when his fee may depend upon his findings.

Court-fixed Fees. Of course, where courts or other public authorities fix fees, there can be no question of compromising the auditor's independence, and the rule specifically excludes such fees from its prohibition.

Tax Cases. When the CPA moves from the role of independent auditor to that of advocate in a tax case, the rule points out the "findings are those of the taxing authority and not those of the accountant." Accordingly, Rule 1.04 also allows contingent fees in "cases involving federal, state or other taxes." But this does not remove the stricture against unreasonable fees. In the past *Circular* 230 restricted contingent fees in federal tax practice, but this has been dropped from the current edition.

Fee Splitting and Commissions. As to commissions and splitting of fees, Opinion No. 6, Rule 3.04, prohibits a member or associate from receiving or paying a commission or sharing fees or profits with any individual or firm not regularly engaged or employed in the practice of public accounting as a principal occupation. The rule does not prevent the payment or receipt of compensation for public accounting services rendered by an employee or consultant, whether such services are on a part- or full-time basis and whether the method of payment is an hourly or fixed basis or is measured by the fees or profits resulting from the engagement.

The rule does prevent the sharing of fees or profits or the payment or receipt of a commission in those cases where the recipient rendered no services, unless he was regularly engaged in public accounting as a principal occupation.

Forwarding Fees. A forwarding fee is a commission paid by one accountant to another for the latter's referral of a client. Forwarding fees are not commissions under Rule 3.04 and are *not* forbidden by the Code of Ethics, as is made clear in Opinion No. 6.

Estimating the Fee. Rule 3.03 prohibits competitive bidding for a professional engagement. However, the Code as amended declares that this rule is not to be enforced at present due to possible conflict with federal antitrust laws.

In any case, in selecting an auditor, a prospective client may quite properly request an estimate of the fee he is to be charged. Bearing in mind the ethical guides already discussed, the accountant may properly submit such an estimate. In the long run it will be best for both the auditor and client if some latitude can be left in the proposed fee for adjustment in the event the case requires more service than could be foreseen originally.

Collection. Nothing in the code prohibits suits for fees. But while the CPA may be justified in suing, he should first remember that neither he nor his profession can gain in stature as a result of such litigation and that the reverse may well be true. Would the retention of a clients' records to force payment of a fee be preferable to suing him? The ethics committee says "no," stating in an informal opinion that the "retention of clients' records is an act discreditable to the profession." (*The CPA*, September, 1968, p. 9.)

DEVELOPING THE FIRM

Building a Practice. The specific avenues open to the accountant who is building a practice and the limitations placed upon him are for the most part discussed under "Advertising" and "Solicitation." However, a possibility not considered elsewhere is the purchase of a practice.

Buying a Practice. Purchase of a practice is an ethical procedure. But according to Opinion No. 3, working papers and other documents must not be transferred without a client's consent.

FORM OF ORGANIZATION

Proprietorship or Partnership. A CPA may conduct a practice as a sole proprietorship or combine his capital and talents in a partnership with anyone (in the words of Rule 3.04) "regularly engaged or employed in the practice of public accounting as a principal occupation." But what does "regularly engaged in public accounting" mean? In determining whether one is so engaged, Opinion No. 6 states:

> The maintenance of an office or desk space, a listing in a directory, the possession of a license if one is required, and the availability for the performance of accounting services on a fee basis are all factors in making this determination.

Opinion No. 6 then goes on to declare that partnerships with non-CPA members are permitted. Of course, in states requiring licenses state laws must be observed.

The firm name. The profession's views concerning firm names are summed up in the following portion of an informal opinion:

> The title of a CPA firm should consist of the names of one or more present or former partners. Impersonal and fictitious titles are misleading and might endanger the personal element in a relationship between professional accountants and their clients. It is in the best interest of the profession and the public to continue the traditional use of firm titles which denote a personal association.[4]

In other words, "Door & Gish" or "Door & Co." would be appropriate titles. "The Excellent Audit Co." would not.

This opinion conforms to Rule 4.02, which in addition specifically permits "the remaining partner practicing as a sole proprietor after the withdrawal or death of one or more partners" to continue to use the partnership name for a reasonable period.

On the other hand, Rule 4.02 forbids practice in another's name except by partners and employees. Conversely, it requires that members not allow their names to be used by others.

Corporation or Professional Association. Until December 30, 1969, the Code prohibited both the corporation and the professional association. The latter is a hybrid organizational form having some of the characteristics of a partnership and some of a corporation.

Under Rule 4.06, the AICPA has now accepted these forms to provide a possible means for limiting the growing burden of the auditor's personal legal liability. To employ one of these forms, however, the firm must conform to specified "characteristics." Only when a professional corporation or association does conform may a CPA be its officer, director, stockholder, representative or agent.

Required characteristics. For a professional corporation or association to be acceptable under Rule 4.06 it must possess certain listed characteristics.

Broadly these restrict the name to those of present or former stockholders or partners of a predecessor firm, the purpose to those acceptable for other public accounting firms, and the ownership to CPAs certified in the United States. The same standards of conduct are required of those associated with these organizations as are required of the entire profession.

The unlimited liability normally imposed on partners is imposed on the stockholders unless adequate capitalization or insurance is maintained. According to the recommendation cited in the Code, capitalization or professional liability insurance "of $50,000 per shareholder/officer and professional employee to a maximum of $2,000,000 would offer adequate protection."

Applying the Code. Except for Rule 4.06 itself, acceptance of the two new organizational forms came too late to be reflected in the Code as amended December 30, 1969. The reader may generally assume that references to partners and partnerships in the Code and Opinions now apply to share-

[4] John L. Carey and William O. Doherty, *Ethical Standards of the Accounting Profession,* New York, AICPA, 1966, pp. 284, 285.

holders and professional associations or corporations as well. It is expected that an appropriately reworded code will be published soon.

Title and Affiliation. An individual who is a CPA, a partnership *all* of whose members are certified, and a professional association or corporation may use the CPA designation following the firm name if the individual or all the partners or shareholders are licensed in the state where the practice is conducted. As to firms having one or more partners who are certified public accountants of another state, local laws vary, and they, of course, govern.

As to the use of the designation "Members of the American Institute of Certified Public Accountants," Rule 4.01 states the following:

> A firm or partner, all the individual members of which are members of the Institute, may describe itself as "Members of the American Institute of Certified Public Accountants," but a firm or partnership, not all the individual members of which are members of the Institute, or an individual practicing under a style denoting a partnership when in fact there be no partner or partners, or a corporation, or an individual or individuals practicing under a style denoting a corporate organization shall not use the designation.

Of course the exception regarding corporations no longer applies to professional corporations.

An Institute member of a firm which cannot use the designation because not every partner or stockholder is a member may nevertheless use it after his own name.

Many problems arise with regard to designation. Answers sometimes depend upon state laws. Such a problem is the use of Institute membership designation in a state where the member is not certificated. Still other problems relate to such matters as advertising and solicitation and are considered in this chapter under appropriate headings.

Relationships within the Profession. The practitioner, having engaged a staff accountant, should remember that whether certified or not, the employee is a member of the accounting profession and should be accorded due courtesy and respect. He is also part of the accounting firm, and the firm has the obligation to concern itself with his training and professional advancement while not permitting him to perform services which the accountant may not perform himself.

Article 5 of the Code of Professional Ethics sets rules for members in their dealings with one another. Its aim is to reduce occasions for friction and thereby to promote the cooperation essential to the advancement of the profession. It consists of three rules, two of which deal with encroachment and one with pirating of staff.

Encroachment. Rule 5.01 prohibits the accountant from taking the initiative in seeking another's client but leaves the latter free to engage whomever he wishes. Rule 5.02 declares:

> A member or associate who receives an engagement for services by referral from another member or associate shall not discuss or accept an extension of his services beyond the specific engagement without first consulting with the referring member or associate.

Mutual clients. How are the rules on solicitation and encroachment to be applied when a client employs more than one CPA firm? Ethics Opinion No. 20 distinguishes "recurring" accountant-client relationships as those whose nature is such that the "relationship continues until affirmatively terminated." Any CPA having such a relationship may suggest performance of any service not already performed by another CPA.

On the other hand, a "nonrecurring" relationship exists when the practitioner is engaged for a specific purpose, whose nature is such that it is not expected to recur, so that the relationship will terminate upon completion of the assignment. A CPA having such a relationship, where another has a recurring relationship, may only endeavor to extend his own engagement to areas closely related to his own work, not presently performed by another and before termination of his engagement.

When an accountant is asked to perform services or sees the need for performance of additional services, courtesy dictates that he contact the CPA who has a recurring relationship with the client. If no relationship exists with any other CPA the accountant performing a nonrecurring assignment may seek extension of his services into any area, but only during the term of his engagement.

Pirating. Even in industry, pirating of an employee who may have been trained by another and upon whom that other relies is disdained. Rule 5.03 requires one who takes the initiative in attempting to hire another's employee to first notify the employer. Many, possibly most, accountants extend this courtesy of notice even to cases where they themselves are approached for employment. Notice allows the employer to try to retain his employee if he wishes to do so. The employee for his part is left completely free to discuss and accept employment from whomever he chooses.

Application of the rules set down in Article 5 is further discussed under "Advertising."

Association with other firms. Rule 4.02, which prohibits practice in the name of another, does not prevent firms or individual CPAs from sharing facilities or assisting one another for a fee.

Commissions and forwarding fees are discussed in the section dealing with compensation.

SPECIALIZATION

General. The growing complexity of the tax laws and of management problems and the emergence of new accounting-related fields such as data processing and systems analysis have created increasing needs for specialized expert services. Accountants feel ethically obliged to meet the needs of their clients. Certain partners and staff members of public accounting firms have specialized in specific areas. In other instances, firms have been organized which limit their activities to special management services or tax practice.

Management Services. Management services have already been defined and related ethical considerations having to do with independence, advertising, compensation, and other subjects discussed.

It remains to be said that Opinion No. 17 holds that non-CPA experts engaged with a CPA in providing management services are in fact engaged in public accounting and may therefore be partners or profit-sharing principals. Both Opinion No. 17 and Opinion No. 7 agree that a firm so engaged must observe the Code of Professional Ethics, but Opinion No. 7 contains special provisions for data processing firms.

It is well to note that specialists, including attorneys and licensed engineers, acting as part of a public accounting firm, may do only what accountants are permitted to do.

Tax Practice. Matters relating to tax practice have already been discussed in earlier sections dealing with government auditors, confidential information, advertising, and professional fees.

The Division of Professional Ethics' only official pronouncement regarding tax practice is Opinion No. 13, which holds that the Code does apply to such practice. But this opinion implies that tax returns are not financial statements. Accordingly, it excludes preparers of tax returns from Article 2 and all other sections such as that dealing with independence, "which relate only to examinations of financial statements requiring opinions or disclaimers."

The administrative regulations of the Treasury Department place upon the CPA a burden of due diligence in verifying the information presented in the tax returns which he prepares, but he may resolve doubtful issues in favor of his client. Moreover, he need not consider that an item was an error or an improper omission if valid grounds for the position taken exist or did exist at the time the return was filed.

Practice before the IRS. The Treasury Department's *Circular* 230 governs practice before the Internal Revenue Service. The circular specifies that attorneys, CPAs, certain former IRS employees, and those who pass special examinations are permitted to practice. Section 10.31 prohibits "persons not members of the bar to practice law" but does not indicate where the line between accounting and law lies.

Client errors and omissions. When the accountant learns a client has failed to file a required tax return or that there was a material error or omission in a previously filed return the CPA must promptly apprise the client of the situation and recommend a course of action. Generally, he would advise filing an amended return. However, rather than amend an erroneous return, a client *may* overstate a subsequent year's tax liability to compensate for an *inadvertent* prior understatement.

If the client refuses to take appropriate remedial action, the accountant must make a moral and ethical judgment as to whether to sever his professional relationship. But in no event may the accountant inform the Internal Revenue Service without the client's consent. If the CPA does continue his engagement and is to file a return for a subsequent period he must not permit a prior error or omission to be repeated or to materially reduce the current year's tax liability unless the permission of the Commissioner of Internal Revenue is required to change the method of reporting the item in question.

The problem of confidentiality may become especially difficult when the return found to be erroneous is already the subject of an administrative proceeding. While a client's refusal of timely disclosure might normally compel the CPA to withdraw from the case, in these circumstances the very act of withdrawal might constitute disclosure. In that event Statement on Responsibilities in Tax Practice No. 7 does not require the CPA to withdraw but directs him to "advise his client that the CPA's inability to answer questions may have a prejudicial effect on the client's case."

Advice to clients. The tax advice which a CPA renders his client must be professionally competent and designed to meet his needs. However, Statement on Responsibilities in Tax Practice No. 8 holds that unless there is a specific agreement to the contrary, after the accountant has finished assisting his client in taking the recommended action he need not keep the latter informed of related developments.

Other matters. Since *Circular* 230 contains many other rules governing the behavior of the tax practitioner, he would do well to familiarize himself with it. Similarly, the statements of the AICPA Division of Federal Taxation and the 23 rules governing members' activities in tax practice which was promulgated in 1966 by the Board of Governers of the National Society of Public Accountants should prove helpful.

BIBLIOGRAPHY

Accounting Series Releases, Compilation of Releases 1 to 112, and later releases, U.S. Securities and Exchange Commission, Washington, Government Printing Office.

Ad Hoc Committee on Independence, "Final Report of Ad Hoc Committee," *The Journal of Accountancy*, December, 1969.

Code of Professional Ethics and Interpretive Opinions, AICPA, New York, 1970.

Code of Ethics, The Institute of Internal Auditors, New York, 1968.

Regulation S-X, Form and Content of Financial Statements, U.S. Securities and Exchange Commission, Washington, Government Printing Office.

Rules Governing the Practice of Attorneys and Agents before the Internal Revenue Service, U.S. Treasury Department, Internal Revenue Service, *Circular* 230 revised, Washington, Government Printing Office, 1966.

Statement of Responsibilities of the Internal Auditor, New York, The Institute of Internal Auditors, 1957.

Carey, John L., and William O. Doherty: *Ethical Standards of the Accounting Profession,* New York, AICPA, 1966.

National Committee on Governmental Accounting, *Governmental Accounting, Auditing, and Financial Reporting,* Chicago, Municipal Finance Officers Association of the United States and Canada, 1968.

Trueblood, Robert M.: "Independence, Objectivity, Integrity," *The CPA,* September, 1966.

Schulte, Arthur A., Jr.: "CPA's Independence Affected by Management Services?" *The New York Certified Public Accountant,* January, 1967.

Roth, Joseph L.: "Breaking the Tablets—a New Look at the Old Opinion," *The Journal of Accountancy,* July, 1967.

Kaufman, Felix: "Professional Consulting by CPA's," *The Accounting Review,* October, 1967.

Stone, Marvin L.: "Specialization in the Accounting Profession," *The Journal of Accountancy,* February, 1968.

Barnes, William T.: "The CPA's Responsibilities in Tax Practice," *The Journal of Accountancy,* March, 1968.

Savoie, Leonard M.: "Ethics and APB Opinions," *The CPA,* September, 1968.

Chapter 5

Legal Liability

JOEL KAUFFMAN

Associate Professor of Economics, Hunter College, The City University of New York

NATURE OF LEGAL LIABILITY

New Developments. In recent years there has been an increasing number of malpractice and related cases involving auditors. This condition has been brought about by an enhanced awareness on the part of investors and lenders that such recoveries may be possible in some cases where loans or investments result in loss.

Resourceful claimants and their attorneys are attempting to increase the theories under which the auditor may be held liable. As a result, not only the number of parties to whom an auditor may have to answer are growing, but the period of time over which he may be held responsible is being extended.

This chapter will discuss the present status of the auditors' liability in a number of legal areas. Because of the changing nature of the liability, as well as the varying results in the different jurisdictions, it is strongly recommended that legal counsel be consulted at the earliest possible moment if a problem arises. In the event malpractice insurance is carried, the insurer should be notified as soon as it becomes evident that a claim may be pressed. Early notification and retention of counsel, should this become necessary, may aid materially in the preparation of a successful defense and will contribute immeasurably to peace of mind.

Liability for Malpractice. Malpractice is a broad term describing the failure of a professional person to render services up to the standards of his profession. The reasons for the failure may be unintentional, through ignorance, or as a result of negligence. The term usually implies that as a result of the complained act or failure some loss has been sustained.

Cooley on Torts (4th ed., vol. 3, p. 335) describes as follows the concept of professional responsibility:

> Every man who offers his services to another and is employed assumes the duty to exercise in the employment such skill as he possesses with reasonable care and diligence. In all those employments where peculiar skill is requisite, if one offers his services, he is understood as holding himself out to the public as possessing the degree of skill commonly possessed by others in the same employment, and, if his pretensions are unfounded, he commits a species of fraud upon every man who employs him in reliance on his public profession. But no man, whether skilled or unskilled, undertakes that the task he assumes shall be performed successfully, and without fault or error. He undertakes for good faith and integrity, but not for infallibility, and he is liable to his employer for negligence, bad faith or dishonesty, but not for losses consequent upon mere errors of judgment.

The dismay of finding oneself made a defendant in a malpractice suit may be all but disabling to one who considers himself a reputable practitioner, even where he was foresighted enough to have previously obtained malpractice insurance. However, some comfort may be taken in the fact that in the majority of such cases which are eventually tried, the defendant prevails, and further, the knowledge that virtually all the largest and most reputable firms have, at one time or another, been subjected to suits of this type may also be of some aid.

Responsibilities of Management and the Auditor. The Committee on Auditing Procedure of the American Institute of Certified Public Accountants (AICPA), Statements on Auditing Procedure No. 33 (*Auditing Standards and Procedures*) describes the objective of the independent auditor in examining financial statements as "the expression of an opinion on the fairness with which they present financial position and results of operations."

Through his report the independent auditor "expresses his opinion or, if circumstances require, disclaims an opinion. In either case, he states whether his examination has been made in accordance with generally accepted auditing standards. These standards require him to state whether, in his opinion, the financial statements are presented in conformity with generally accepted principles of accounting and whether such principles have been consistently applied . . ." in relation to the preceding accounting periods.

Statements on Auditing Procedure No. 33 goes on to distinguish between the responsibilities of management and the auditor. To management is assigned "the responsibility for adopting sound accounting policies, for maintaining an adequate and effective system of accounts, for the safeguarding of assets, and for devising a system of internal control that will, among other things, help assure the production of proper financial statements." Management has direct knowledge of transactions of the business, and the reflection of these transactions is within its control. Therefore, the fairness of the representations made in the statements is the responsibility of management.

While the auditor may make suggestions as to the form or content or aid in the drafting of the statement, "his responsibility for the statements he has examined is confined to the expression of his opinion on them. The financial statements remain the representations of the management."

LIABILITY TO CLIENTS AND THOSE IN PRIVITY

Fraud. The auditor is liable to his client for fraud or deceit by him or his subordinates. This may involve a situation where the auditor has, with knowledge, not disclosed a false item discovered in an audit. While the term "fraud" implies an intentional falsity, there are situations in which actual knowledge of the falsity is not required. The auditor owes a duty to make his examination with due care and with the requisite skill proper to his calling. A person who falsely represents that he has the requisite knowledge and skill to perform an audit properly may be held liable in fraud if he does not exhibit the necessary skill and possess the necessary education.

Where an auditor falsely represents that he has performed certain operations in connection with his audit, he may be held liable in fraud for damages resulting from such falsehood.

Negligence. The auditor undertakes to exercise the degree of care that the average prudent member of his profession would exert in performing the audit, and he may be held liable by a client who suffers damages as a result of his failure to exercise such care. Here, no wrongful knowledge or representation on the part of the auditor is required to establish liability; ordinary negligence is all that must be shown to hold an auditor liable to one in contractual privity.

Breach of Contract. A client who feels he has suffered damages as a result of an auditor's improperly conducted audit may attempt to hold the auditor liable on the theory of breach of contract. The particular theory of liability that the client proceeds under will have an important bearing on the length of the Statute of Limitations as well as the measure of damages.

Today, auditing contracts are usually to be performed "in accordance with generally accepted auditing standards." Where an auditor is making less than a complete audit, prudence dictates that he expressly state in a written contract precisely what acts usually associated with an audit are being omitted. Such a written contract may prove an invaluable aid should later litigation develop with the client.

Examples. As a rule litigation initiated by a client will be for one of two reasons. First, it may be alleged that the client has sustained a loss as a result of reliance on the audited statements. Dividends may have been paid out in reliance on incorrect profit figures, with the result that a company may be in such poor liquid position that a bankruptcy results. Likewise, a company may commit itself to some irrevocable course of action such as a major expansion or acquisition based on erroneous figures and seek later to hold the auditor liable should such decision prove improvident.

A second reason for a client to initiate litigation would be the auditor's failure to discover a defalcation. The theory generally advanced is that the client has sustained additional losses as a result of the auditor's failure to discover the defalcation.

1. In an early English case the auditors of a real estate company were held liable to a receiver for dividends paid out of capital for several years based on financial statements which erroneously showed a profit when the company was, in fact, running at a loss. [*Leed's Estates Building and Investment v. Shepard* (Eng.) L.R. 36 Ch. D. 787 (1887).]

2. On the other hand, in a California case where dividends were likewise based on an erroneous profit, the auditors were exonerated because it appeared that the directors had knowledge of the true facts. [*Flagg v. Seng,* 16 Cal. App. 2d 545, 60 P. 2d 1004 (1936).]

3. In a Florida case it was held that a firm of public auditors failed to discover early embezzlement by a bookkeeper because they had neglected to compare checks drawn by the bookkeeper with invoices and other supporting data. The court found that the auditors might be charged with gross negligence if not fraud. [*Dantzler Lumber & Export Co. v. Columbia Casualty Co.,* 115 Fla. 541, 156 So. 116, 96 A.L.R. 258 (1934).]

4. Public auditors hired by a city were held liable for negligence in failing to discover the defalcations of the city treasurer. The court pointed out that the auditors had been negligent in the following respects:

a. No attempt had been made by the auditors to investigate tax accounts shown on the books as delinquent.

b. The auditors failed to discover very crudely made alterations on the tax rolls.

c. The auditors failed to determine whether or not the balances of the delinquent subsidiary tax roll ledgers tied in with the balances in the control accounts.

d. After the auditors had discovered that several years of delinquent balances outstanding were out of balance with the control account for those years, they took no other action than to mention the fact to the director of finance. No attempt was made to balance the books or advise the city to do so.

e. The auditors failed to audit the separate control accounts maintained in the treasurer's office.

The court went on to state that the negligence of the auditors was the proximate cause of many of the shortages by reason of their failure to discover the frauds at an early date. [*Maryland Casualty v. Cook,* 35 Fed. Supp. 160 (1940).]

5. In a similar case, an auditor was held liable for breach of contract because of failure to exercise due diligence when, during the course of his audit, he made a bank reconciliation but failed to verify the actual cash balance in the bank. The auditor was found guilty despite the fact that the audit contract called for the performance of an audit of limited scope. [*National Surety Corp. v. Lybrand,* 256 App. Div. 226, 9 N.Y.S. 2d 554 (1939).]

Cases such as the previous two have been brought by clients' bonding or insurance companies by way of subrogation, and an interesting question may develop here: Where both the auditor and the client are insured, which company must ultimately bear the loss?

To help resolve this dilemma, the AICPA has worked out agreements with a number of bonding companies. In essence, these agreements provide that the companies will not attempt to recover against the accountant or his insurer unless a failure to discover a defalcation was the result of affirmative dishonesty or gross negligence.

Cases involving liability to clients for errors in inventory vary a great deal. Some cases have held that the auditor is not negligent where he accepted the certificate of a responsible official as to inventory values. Such cases, however, tend to be the older ones. The modern trend of decisions clearly indicates that an auditor may be held liable unless he has made a test check of inventory quantities and valuation, or clearly and unequivocally states that he has made no attempt to verify inventory.

In a Canadian case, the auditors were held liable for misconduct where they were aware that the corporation had given a check for bonds but had not received them from the broker. Despite this circumstance, the auditors stated in their certificate that "bonds, debentures and mortgages" had been subjected to physical examination. [*Canadian Woodmen of the World v. Hooper,* 41 Ont. Week N. 328, 1 D.L.R. 168, 521 A.L.R. 2d 337 (1933).]

Errors of Judgment. The fact that the auditor acted in good faith and that he conducted a proper audit, but made some error in judgment, may still result in liability to the client. The auditor represents that he has special skills which should enable him to exercise better judgment than a lay person. Therefore, when he makes errors through failure to exercise these skills properly, he may be held responsible. It is of interest to note, however, that there have been relatively few cases charging the auditor with incompetent judgment.

In order for the auditor to be held liable, it must be shown that the matter was within his special field of competence and that he failed to exercise the quality of judgment that might reasonably be expected from one in a skilled profession.

In *State St. Trust Co. v. Ernst* [278 N.Y. 104, 15 N.E. 2d 416 (1938)], which will be commented on more extensively later, the Court of Appeals of New York held that there was sufficient evidence to support a charge of gross negligence where the auditor reported receivables at their face amount even though he had uncovered extensive evidence of unsatisfactory collection. Despite the fact that the auditor had made an adequate investigation, he was guilty of a crucial error in judgment in failing to provide for an adequate reserve for uncollectible receivables.

In *C.I.T. v. Glover* (224 F. 2d 44), in a similar fact situation, the auditor was exonerated. In this instance, the auditor was charged with incompetent judgment for failure to reveal an overvaluation of receivables or to set up a sufficiently large reserve to cover them. The court found that the auditor had no special knowledge that would have enabled him to value the receivables. The evaluation was based, to a large extent, on the value of collateral which had been pledged to secure payment of said receivables. The valuation of the collateral was held to be outside the sphere of the auditor's special competence; he justifiably relied on an officer of the corporation to obtain the information relative to valuing the collateral.

The above two cases may be distinguished by the following observations. In the first situation, the auditor should have perceived that the accounts ought not to have been valued at their face amount since collections had been extremely slow over a period of time. In the second instance, valuation was based on the amount of collateral security for the accounts. The auditor's competence was not in the area of ascertaining market value of unique collateral, and he justifiably was forced to rely on the judgment of one of the corporate officers.

Contributory Negligence as a Defense. In most states, when the plaintiff in a negligence action has been found guilty of any act of negligence, no matter how minor, that was a contributing cause to the injury suffered, then the plaintiff will be barred from any recovery. Contributory negligence has been pleaded as a bar to recovery in some cases involving alleged negligence of auditors. These cases usually involve situations in which the client is attempting to recover for the auditor's failure to uncover a defalcation. The theory under which the suit is brought may be crucial. In a suit brought for breach of contract, contributory negligence would, of course, not be a bar to recovery. Furthermore, some writers have suggested that the defense of contributory negligence is not available in a malpractice suit.

Nevertheless, there have been cases where contributory negligence of the client has been successfully pleaded as a defense by the auditor, provided the client's negligence was such that it related to the auditor's failure to discover embezzlement. However, the fact that the client may have been negligent in allowing an employee to commit a defalcation will not be available as a defense to an auditor. An example of this is illustrated by the case of *National Surety Corp. v. Lybrand* [256 App. Div. 226, 9 N.Y.S. 2d 554 (1939)] in which an action was brought because of the failure of the auditor to discover a defalcation. The auditor maintained that the clerk who had committed the defalcation had total control of the funds of the corporation and that the client had been negligent in not setting up a proper system of internal control. The court held that the fact that a client conducts his business negligently will not make an auditor immune from liability.

In the past auditors were often employed to detect defalcations which may have been the result of the negligence of the client. Here, the alleged negligence could not be said to have contributed to the auditor's failure to discover the defalcation. In the New York case, *Craig v. Anyon* (212 A.D. 59, 208 N.Y.S. 262), the management advised the auditors that one of the employees was extremely trustworthy, going to some lengths to impress upon the auditors that this particular employee was virtually beyond suspicion. When the employee was subsequently found guilty of fraud, management brought an action against the auditors for negligence in failing to discover his defalcations earlier. The court held that the actions of management contributed to the auditor's failure to discover the defalcation. As a result, the auditor was able to defeat management's claim on the theory that management had been guilty of contributory negligence.

Another interesting case involving the successful defense of contributory negligence is *International Labs v. Dewar* [3 D.L.R. 665, 41 Manitoba R.

329 (1933), reversing 1 D.L.R. 34]. In this instance, a Canadian auditor advised his client to set up an improved system of internal control. The client did not comply and instead instructed the auditor to limit the scope of his subsequent audits. One of the employees of the client had been guilty of fraud, and the auditor failed to uncover the defalcations of the employee. As a result, the client sued the auditor for negligence. Based on the above facts, the auditor set up the defense of contributory negligence. The court held that the acts of the client here constituted a complete defense for the auditor, and he was exonerated.

Before leaving the question of special defenses available to an auditor, some comment should be made on the case of *Gammel v. Ernst & Ernst* [245 Minn. 249, 72 N.W. 2d 34, 54 A.L.R. 2d 316 (1955)]. In this case, the plaintiff sought damages from the defendant auditing firm on the grounds of fraud and negligence. It appeared that the plaintiffs had agreed to sell stock in a corporation at a price based on the net earnings of the corporation during a specified year. The defendants were retained to make an audit, and the plaintiff was compelled to sell his stock based on the erroneous earnings shown in the audited report. At the trial the auditors used the defense of immunity from liability on the grounds that they were quasi-arbitrators. They pointed out that the concept of immunity from civil liability in the discharge of official duties had been extended to quasi-judicial officers, such as tax assessors, prosecutors, arbitrators, and so-called quasi-arbitrators. In determining the earnings of the corporation and, in effect, determining the price that the stock was to be sold at, the auditors claimed that they were operating in the role of quasi-arbitrators and therefore should be entitled to this immunity.

Rejecting this argument, the court stated that a person who is selected to perform skilled professional services is not immune from charges of negligence and is required to work with the same degree of skill and care exercised by the average person engaged in the trade or profession involved. This is true even when the results of the work will be used, as they were in this case, in settlement between two parties. The court pointed out further that there was no agreement calling for the exercise of judicial authority or of independent judgment or discretion in this case.

While the defendants were unsuccessful in establishing the immunity from liability of the quasi-arbitrators concept in the *Gammel* case, it is conceivable that the defense might be valid in some similar situation, where the auditor is called in to settle a dispute between two dissident factions and a proper agreement is prepared and signed by all parties. Conceivably, the auditor, acting in the role of a quasi-arbitrator, might be able to use this defense successfully in a suit against him brought by one of the parties alleging negligence. Obviously, this defense would not be available in a situation involving fraud upon the part of the auditor.

Measure of Damage. The question of the amount of damages to be received by a successful plaintiff in a suit against an auditor has by no means been settled. The area that seems to be the most obscure is the one involving the auditor's failure to discover defalcations. The majority of courts have set the recovery at the amount of the defalcation taking place subsequent to the time of the audit in question. The theory here, of course, is that the auditor should have discovered the previous frauds by the same employee and his failure to do so resulted in the client's additional loss.

Other cases have limited the client's recovery to the amount of the auditor's fee, the theory that other factors prevent establishment of the negligence of the auditor as the proximate cause of the subsequent loss. Therefore, the action must be considered in the nature of breach of contract, and under this theory, the damages, with the exception of the auditor's fee, are too remote to have been within the contemplation of the parties.

In a Kansas case, *Board of County Commissioners of Allen County v. Baker* [102 P. 2d 1006 (1940)], the negligence of the auditors in failing to discover a series of discrepancies resulted in the auditor's having to return the amount received under the contract of audit. It had been argued that the auditor should be liable only for nominal damages since no actual loss was shown to have taken place after the time of the audit. However, the court reasoned that as a result of the auditor's negligence, no reliance could be placed on the auditor's report and, therefore, it was of no value. The court pointed out that the general rule in an action for breach of contract, where the performance furnished was not suitable or insufficient for the contemplated purposes, was that full recovery of the consideration paid was warranted.

Similarly, in the case of *Craig v. Anyon*, mentioned above, the liability of the auditors for negligence in failing to discover the defalcation of an employee was held limited to the compensation paid to the auditor and not to a loss of over $1 million resulting from the defalcation. Again, the court had reservations about the auditor's negligence being the sole proximate cause of the loss. Evidence had been introduced during the case that the company itself was negligent in failing to provide proper supervision of the employee and in the amount of authority which had been given to him.

Subsequent Events. A number of pronouncements of the Committee on Auditing Procedure have dealt with the auditor's responsibility for events subsequent to the date of the final statements.

Statement on Auditing Procedure No. 25 (1954), *Events Subsequent to the Date of Financial Statements.* This statement described the responsibility of the auditor for events subsequent to the date of the report but prior to the date of his certificate.

Statements on Auditing Procedure No. 33 (1963), *Auditing Standards and Procedures,* Chapter 10, described the auditor's reporting responsibility when the events or transactions known to have occurred prior to the balance sheet date are not reasonably determinable at the date of his report. Chapter 11 describes the auditor's reporting responsibility for events which occur after the balance sheet date but prior to the date of his report. This statement brought up to date the prior pronouncement and in paragraphs 11 through 14 of Chapter 11 stated the auditor's obligation "with respect to audited financial statements included in registration statements filed under the Securities Act of 1933 between the date of the auditor's report and the effective date of the registration statement."

Statement on Auditing Procedure No. 41 (1969), *Subsequent Discovery of Facts Existing at the Date of the Auditor's Report,* dealt with situations involving information which existed at the date of the auditor's report but of which the auditor then had no knowledge. The statement establishes procedures to be followed by the auditor who, subsequent to the date of his report, becomes aware of facts existing at that date which might have affected his report had he then been aware of such facts. The statement further outlines the action the auditor should take (1) when the client agrees to make appropriate disclosure and (2) when the client refuses to make appropriate disclosure.

LIABILITY TO THIRD PARTIES

The Ultramares Case. Under the common law, auditors have almost never been found liable to those not in privity on the theory of ordinary negligence. This is a result of the decision in the case of *Ultramares Corporation v. Touche* (255 N.Y. 170, 174 N.E. 441), which has been nominally followed in all American jurisdictions as well as in England and Canada. The plaintiffs in that case brought an action, in tort, for damages based on two causes of action against the defendant auditors. The first cause of action was based on misrepresentation due to negligence. The second cause of action was based upon misrepresentation as a result of fraud. The auditors certified the balance sheet of Fred Stern & Co. They were aware that, in the ordinary course of business, the balance sheet would be exhibited by the company to banks, creditors, stockholders, and other persons with whom the company had financial dealings. Accordingly, the defendants supplied Stern & Co. with 32 copies of their certified statement.

The statement was inaccurate in a number of different areas. However, in reliance upon this statement, the plaintiff made loans to Stern & Co. just before Stern went into bankruptcy. The plaintiff then brought suit against the auditors in an attempt to recover amounts lost by them in reliance upon the inaccurate statements.

The court said:

> The defendants owe to their employer the duties imposed by law to make their certificate without fraud; and a duty growing out of contract to make it with care and caution proper to their calling. Fraud includes the pretense of knowledge, when knowledge there is none. To the creditors and investors to whom the employer exhibited the certificate the defendants owed a like duty to make it without fraud since there was notice in the circumstances of its making that the employer did not intend to keep it to himself.

The court went on to dismiss the first cause of action based on negligence. In regard to the second cause of action, in finding that the defendants could be held liable for fraud, the court went on to say that

> negligence or blindness even when not equivalent to fraud is nonetheless evidence to sustain an inference of fraud. At least this is so if the negligence is gross. . . .
>
> We conclude . . . in certifying to the correspondence between balance sheets and accounts [that] the defendants made a statement that was true to their knowledge on the subject. If that is so, they may also be found to have acted without information leading to a sincere or genuine belief when they certified to an opinion that the balance sheet faithfully reflected the condition of the business.

Nothing in the *Ultramares* decision attempted to set up the test of different degrees of negligence under which an auditor might be liable. Instead the court suggested that where an auditor recklessly certifies to the truth of financial statements without taking the proper procedures to determine whether or not, in fact, the financial statements reflect the condition of the corporation, a jury might find that the auditor was guilty of fraud and therefore liable to third parties not in privity.

The State St. Trust Co. Case. The *Ultramares* doctrine was extended in the case of *State St. Trust Co. v. Ernst* [278 N.Y. 104, 15 N.E. 2d 416 (1938)]. In that case the plaintiff bank made a loan of $300,000 in reliance upon a certified balance sheet prepared by the defendants. The plaintiff had been repaid only a portion of the loan when the debtor went bankrupt. This action was brought on the theory that the balance sheet was incorrect in that inadequate reserves were set up for Accounts Receivable in light of the fact of a number of circumstances which were known or should have been known to the auditors who had been engaged to do the annual audit for the 3 years prior to the year in question.

In holding for the plaintiff, the New York Court of Appeals used some language which has sometimes been interpreted to mean that the liability of accountants to third parties will be extended to include situations involving gross negligence as well as fraud. "Accountants . . . may be liable to third parties even when there is lacking deliberate or active fraud. . . . Heedlessness and reckless disregard of consequences may take the place of deliberate intention."

The Duro Sportswear Case. In a case which relied entirely upon the previous decision, *Duro Sportswear, Inc. v. Cogan* (131 N.Y.S. 2d 20), an auditor who unqualifiedly certified financial statements as reflecting the true financial condition of a corporation was found guilty of gross negligence and, therefore, liable. It appeared that certain bills were not included on the books of the audited company that the auditor should have been aware of, based upon his past association with the corporation. The court specifically held that the evidence was insufficient to establish fraud on the part of the defendants. Nevertheless, the auditor was held guilty of malpractice.

The Fischer Case. The case of *Fischer v. Kletz* [266 F. Supp. 180 (1967)] presented several interesting questions concerning the auditor's liability to third parties. These questions involved liability under the common law as well as under the federal Securities statutes. The common law facet concerned the 1963 annual report of the Yale Express System, Inc. The auditor had certified statements showing a net profit. In reality the company had sustained a loss of almost $2 million. Employees of the Yale Co. had made spurious entries on the books which had not been uncovered by the auditors, hence the discrepancy in reported earnings.

The auditors continued their employment by Yale and sometime during the year 1964 became aware of the true state of affairs. However, it was not until May of 1965 that they "disclosed this finding to the exchange on which Yale securities were traded, to the SEC, or to the public at large."

A defendant's motion to dismiss was denied on the theory that the defendant's nondisclosure of the true state of affairs might be tantamount to fraud. The above decision relied heavily on Section 551 of the *Restatement of Torts,* which deals with nondisclosure. In essence this section imposes liability on a person who fails to disclose "subsequently acquired information which he recognizes as making untrue or misleading a previous representation which when made was true or believed to be so."

Summary. The exact state of the common law concerning liability of the accountant to third parties remains to be clarified. Most authorities state that the accountant will be held liable in a situation in which fraud or gross negligence is shown; others hold that the accountant will be held liable only where he is guilty of fraud. However, the accountant's gross negligence in ascertaining the true state of affairs may be relied upon by a jury in finding that the accountant had the requisite intention needed to prove fraud.

Still others suggest that where the auditor knows or should know that the statement is to be relied upon by a third party, such third party may hold the auditor liable for ordinary negligence. Where the third party is merely a member of a class which the auditor knows or should know may have occasion to rely upon the statement, the third party must show gross negligence on the auditor's part.

This last theory was elucidated in the English case *Hedley Byrne & Co. v. Heller & Partners* [2 All. E.R. 575 (House of Lords)]. The decision suggested that if the auditors "knew or ought to have known that the . . . financial statements in question were being prepared for the specific purpose or transaction which gave rise to the loss and that they would be shown to and relied upon by third parties in this connection," the auditors would be held liable for simple negligence.

In a 1966 Massachusetts case, *Blank et al. v. Kaitz* [216, N.E. 2d 110], the court refused to consider the question of whether or not an auditor would be liable to a third party in either gross or ordinary negligence, in the absence of an allegation that the auditor knew that the financial statements were being prepared for submission to a third party. The court did not state whether it would impose such a requirement if the auditor were being accused of fraud.

LIABILITY UNDER FEDERAL SECURITIES ACTS

Increased Liability. As a result of the passage of the Securities Act of 1933 and the Securities Exchange Act of 1934, the auditor's liability to third parties is substantially increased beyond the bounds set by the *Ultramares* decision and those decisions which followed it.

The 1933 act provides for the filing of a Registration Statement with the Securities and Exchange Commission before securities can be offered for sale to the public through the mails or interstate commerce. These filings must be accompanied by the financial statements of the corporation, certified by an independent public accountant. Section 11A of the Act provides:

> In case any part of the Registration Statement, when such part became effective, contained an untrue statement of a material fact or omitted to state a material fact required to be stated therein or necessary to make the statements therein not misleading, any person acquiring such security (unless it is proved that at the time of such acquisition, he knew of such untruth or omission) may, either at law or in equity, in any Court of competent jurisdiction, sue . . . every accountant . . . or any person whose profession gives authority to a statement made by him, who has, with his consent, been named as having prepared or certified any part of the Registration Statement or as having prepared or certified any report or valuation which is used in connection with the Registration Statement, with respect to the statement in such Registration Statement, report or evaluation, which purports to have been prepared or certified by him.

Auditor's Defense. The above quotation makes the liability of the accountant (as well as others) virtually absolute in the case of an untrue statement or in case of an omission. Only two possible defenses are suggested. First, the error or omission was immaterial, and second, the purchaser acquired the security after having learned of the error or omission. As yet there has been no litigation on the latter point, although several actions brought under the blue-sky laws of various states have touched on it.

The term "material" as used in the Federal security acts is not markedly different from its common law concept. It is defined identically in Rule 12(*b*) (2) of the 1934 act and rule 405 of the earlier act. "The term 'material' when used to qualify a requirement for the furnishing of information as to any subject, limits the information required to those matters as to which an average prudent investor ought reasonably to be informed before buying or selling the security registered."

The statute sets no requirement that the plaintiff in an action show that he relied on the statement or that such reliance was the proximate cause of any loss. Furthermore, there is no need to show fraudulent intent on the part of the accountant in making the misstatement or omission nor is there a need to show any "gross negligence" as a substitute for fraudulent intent.

The harsh rule set out above was somewhat ameliorated in an amendment to the section which was passed when the Federal Security Exchange Act of 1934 was adopted. This provided that where a

> person acquired the security after the issuer had made generally available to its security holders an earning statement covering a period of at least twelve months, beginning after the effective date of the registration statement, then the right of recovery under this subsection shall be conditioned on proof that such person acquired the securities relying on such untrue statement in the Registration Statement or relying upon the Registration Statement and not knowing of such omission, but such reliance may be established without proof of the reading of Registration Statement by such person.

This amendment seems to provide that if the plaintiff acquires the security after an earnings statement has been made generally available to security holders covering a period at least 12 months after the effective date of the Registration Statement, he must prove that he relied upon the error or omission in the Registration Statement when he acquired the securities. However, the reliance need not be established by showing that the plaintiff actually read the Registration Statement. Of course, this amendment would have no effect upon a person acquiring the security prior to the publication of the earnings statement referred to.

Section 11(*b*) provides that an auditor may employ two affirmative defenses in order to escape liability in a suit brought under Section 11(*a*). First, he may establish that, prior to the effective date of the Registration Statement or on his becoming aware of its effectiveness, appropriate steps to sever his relationship with the issuer had been taken by him. Furthermore, he had advised the Securities and Exchange Commission and the issuer that he had taken such steps and that he would not be responsible for that portion of the statement attributed to him and appropriate reasonable notice had been given to the public by him, but that a portion of the statement had become effective without his knowledge. Second, the auditor may show that "he had, after reasonable investigation, reasonable grounds to believe and did believe, at the time such part of the Registration Statement became effective, that the statements therein were true and that there was no omission to state a material fact required to be stated therein and necessary to make the statements therein not misleading."

Section 11(c) provides that "the standard of reasonableness" provided for in Section 11(b) is "that required of a prudent man in the management of his own property."

Measure of Damages. By Section 11(g), the damages which may be recovered under Section 11(a) are limited to the public offering price. This limitation, of course, would refer to a plaintiff who has purchased the securities in the open market rather than as a result of the initial public offering. Within this limitation, Section 11(e) generally sets the measure of damages of a plaintiff in a suit brought under this section to the price paid for the securities less market value at the time a suit is brought. However, where the security is disposed of prior to the time suit is brought, then the measure of damages will be the difference between the purchase price and the resale price.

Liability under the 1933 Act. The only case decided under Section 11 involving auditors was *Shonts v. Hirliman* [28 Fed. Sup. 478 (1939)]. This case involved the Registration Statement of a company organized to produce motion pictures. The statement failed to mention that the corporation was obligated to pay an annual rental of at least $35,000 for its studio lease. At the time of the statement the rental arrangements were being discussed and there had not been any definite agreement entered into. The auditors were exonerated since the court held that civil liability could not be imposed for the omission when the arrangement had not been made binding until after the auditors had certified the Registration Statement, although it was binding before the Registration Statement became effective.

The decision in this case has often been criticized for the very low accounting standards which the court seemed to feel would be adequate. In this respect, it seems that the court was in effect turning the clock back to the "gross negligence" required for third-party liability.

Liability under the 1934 Act. Under Section 18 of the Securities Exchange Act of 1934 an auditor may be held liable for a statement

> in any application, report or document filed pursuant to this title or any rule or regulation thereunder, or any undertaking contained in the registration statement . . . which statement was at the time and in the light of the circumstances under which it was made false or misleading with respect to any material fact.

The auditor may be held liable by

> any person (not knowing that such statement was false or misleading) who, in reliance upon such statement, shall have purchased or sold the security at a price which was affected by such statement, for damages caused by such reliance, unless the person sued shall prove that he acted in good faith and had no knowledge that such statement was false or misleading.

Section 18 seems to give third parties virtually the same protection that they have under the common law. The plaintiff must prove reliance on the statement which, of course, would be necessary in a case brought under the common law. Under Section 18, the auditor may show as a defense that he acted in good faith. In other words, the statute seems to imply that the auditor will be liable for fraud and not for ordinary negligence as under the terms of Section 11 of the 1933 act.

On the other hand, the number of possible plaintiffs is greatly increased under the 1934 statute, as compared with the earlier legislation. The 1933 act provides for recovery only in the case of a purchaser of a security. The 1934 act provides that a person who has sold the security, as well as a purchaser, may bring an action where the price of the security was affected by a false or misleading statement.

The 1933 act applies only to registration statements filed with the Securities and Exchange Commission. The 1934 act includes all statements filed in connection with any of the federal Securities acts. At least one court has held this to include all documents filed with a national security exchange even if the document is not filed with the Commission. (*Fischman v. Raytheon Mfg. Co.*, 188 F. 2d 783.)

Statutes of Limitations. Section 13 of the 1933 act provides:

> No action shall be maintained to enforce any liability created under Section 11 . . . unless brought within one year after the discovery of the untrue statement or the omission, or after such discovery should have been made by the exercise of reasonable diligence. . . . In no event shall any such action be brought to enforce a liability created under Section 11 . . . more than three years after the security was bona fide offered to public.

Undoubtedly, the phrase "reasonable diligence" will provide some difficulty in interpretation. It is not at all clear just what obligation is placed upon a stockholder in order to show that he acted with the necessary diligence in discovering the omission or error.

Louis Loss, in his authoritative work *Securities Regulation,* points out:

> One may doubt the propriety of going so far in saddling an investor with the burden of proclaiming his diligence as to demand of him the initiative—as well as the willingness and the ability to expend the time and money that would be necessary—to ferret out fraud upon the part of the management of a corporation, even though he may have legal "access to its books and records." Blind adherence to dogma must not be allowed to subvert the purpose of the particular statute.

Under Section 18(c) of the 1934 act, the period of limitation is 1 year after discovery of the error or omission and 3 years after the time when the cause of action shall have occurred.

Auditor's Fraud under the Acts. Where an auditor has participated in the use or preparation of false and misleading statements, he may be subject to suit under Section 10(b) of the 1934 act. This section provides:

> It shall be unlawful for any person, directly or indirectly, by the use of any means or instrumentality of interstate commerce or of the mails, or of any facilities of any national securities exchange . . . (b) to use or employ, in connection with the purchase or sale of any security registered, on a National Securities Exchange or any security not so registered, any manipulative or deceptive device or contrivance in contravention of such rules and regulations as the commission may prescribe as necessary or appropriate in the public interest or for the protection of investors.

This section has been supplemented by Rule 10(b)(5), which makes it unlawful:

> (a) to employ any device, scheme or artifice to defraud, (b) to make any untrue statement of a material fact or to omit to state a material fact necessary in order to make the statements made, in the light of the circumstances under which they are made, not misleading, or (c) to engage in any act, practice or course of business which operates or would operate as a fraud or deceit upon any person, in connection with the purchase or sale of any security,

over which the SEC has jurisdiction.

Only a few cases have been brought against auditors under this provision. However, its broad language indicates that it may be resorted to increasingly in the future.

One case brought under this section in which the defendants were auditors was *H. L. Green Co. v. Childree* [185 F. Sup. 95 (1960)]. The plaintiff was a corporation that had issued its stock in exchange for stock of another corporation. The defendants were auditors who, according to the complaint, prepared false financial statements to interest the plaintiff in the transaction.

The defendants moved to dismiss on the grounds that the transaction involved was a merger and not a "sale of securities" within the meaning of the statute. In denying the motion, the court pointed out that the term "merger" is not a term of fixed and definite meaning. A given transaction described by this term may or may not be within the meaning of Section 10(b). The court further pointed out that the defendants' role as auditors would not preclude civil suits against them for their alleged participation and activities contrary to the section.

A case which dealt with the section more fully was *Fischer v. Kletz,* one aspect of which has been discussed previously. In denying a motion to dismiss, the court pointed out that the defendants in other cases brought under Rule 10(b)(5) have generally fallen into four categories: (1) insiders, (2) broker-dealers, (3) corporations whose stock has been purchased or sold by those bringing suit, and (4) those who aid or abet or conspire with a party falling into one of the three previous categories.

The auditor in a typical case brought under Rule 10(b)(5) will not fit into any of the first three categories. The question, therefore, will be whether or not he will fit into the role of the aider or abettor. The trend of decisions seems to indicate that the courts are enlarging this category. Therefore, future suits in which auditors are held liable under Section 10(b) seem likely.

The benefit of the federal Securities acts is limited to those persons who have bought or sold securities covered by those acts. Ordinary creditors who do not hold evidence of indebtedness subject to the federal acts must proceed against an auditor on the theory of common law liability discussed previously. While most states have blue-sky laws regulating the sale of securities within the state, for the most part the question of auditor's liability is left to the common law in regard to securities not covered by the federal acts.

A notable exception to the above stated rule is the state of Florida, which attempts to incorporate by statute the federal laws governing situations in which auditors may be held liable. Despite the statute in a 1968 decision, *Investment Corporation of Florida v. Buchman,* it was held that purchasers of stock, who had relied on certified financial statements in acquiring the stock, were not entitled to recover losses resulting from the negligence of auditors in certifying the financial statements. The decision rested on the fact that there was no privity between the stock purchasers and the auditors and seemed to completely follow the *Ultramares* decision.

LIABILITY FOR UNAUDITED STATEMENTS

Due Care. From the point of view of the legal risks involved, auditors would undoubtedly be far better off if they could totally disassociate themselves from any unaudited statements. Unfortunately, the realities of life often make this impossible. However, under certain circumstances statements of this type may give rise to claims against auditors by both clients and those not in privity.

In a 1965 New York case (*Bloch v. Klein,* 43 Misc. 2d 1054, 258 N.Y.S. 2d 501), a company brought suit against its own auditors based on an unaudited statement issued by them without a disclaimer. Because of a largely inflated inventory figure, the company's profit had been grossly overstated. The client brought an action asking for $140,000 in damages resulting from the negligence of the auditors in failing to verify the inventory. The claim was that the company had stayed in business in reliance on the auditor's figures and, as a result, had suffered additional operating losses.

The auditors defended on the grounds that they had, over a period of years, always relied on the inventory figures supplied by the client and that the client knew or should have known of this. Furthermore, the auditors contended that even if they had been negligent, their maximum liability should be for $3,600, the amount received by them for one year's audit.

The court held that the auditors' failure to place a disclaimer on every page of the financial statements was enough to hold them guilty of negligence. However, the court limited the amount of the award to fees for one year, $3,600, plus the costs of hiring new auditors to prepare the statement correctly, which was an additional $2,500.

In arriving at its decision, the court stressed the fact that the auditors had not lived up to the requirement of due care in the performance of their work as defined by their profession. The court relied heavily on the Statements on Auditing Procedure No. 33 issued by the Committee on Auditing Procedure of the AICPA as well as the Code of Professional Ethics as setting forth the standards which should be maintained by the independent auditor.

In defining whether or not an auditor has lived up to the standards of due care required of him, courts frequently return to the standards set up by professional bodies of practitioners. In effect, these statements become the standard of due care which the courts seek to impose.

Statement on Auditing Procedure No. 38, issued by the Committee on Auditing Procedure of the AICPA, entitled *Unaudited Financial Statements,* sets forth the responsibility of the independent auditor in connection with statements for which he "(a) has not applied any auditing procedures . . . or (b) has not applied auditing procedures which are sufficient to permit him to express an opinion concerning them."

"Association" with Statements. Paragraph 3 of Statement No. 38 describes the circumstances under which an auditor may be said to be "associated" with an unaudited financial statement. This condition exists when the auditor "has consented to the use of his name in a report, document or written communication setting forth or containing the statements." Furthermore, if the auditor

> submits to his client or others, with or without a covering letter, unaudited financial statements which he has prepared or assisted in preparing, he is deemed to be associated with such statements. This association is deemed to exist even though the certified public accountant does not append his name to the financial statements or uses "plain paper" rather than his own stationery.

Paragraph 3 goes on to state that association will not arise if the auditor "as an accommodation to his client, merely types on 'plain paper' or reproduces unaudited financial statements *so long as he has not prepared or otherwise assisted in preparing the statements and so long as he submits them only to his client.*" [Italics added.] The Statement goes on to recommend that a "Disclaimer of Opinion" should accompany all unaudited financial statements. Disclaimers are the means by which the auditor "indicates the fact that he has not audited the financial statements and accordingly does not express an opinion on them." The disclaimer should accompany the unaudited financial statements or be placed directly on them. Furthermore, the fact that the statements are unaudited should be marked on each and every page of the document.

However, attaching a disclaimer does not relieve the auditor of all responsibility. If the auditor "concludes on the basis of facts known to him that unaudited financial statements with which he may become associated are not in conformity with generally accepted accounting principles, which includes adequate disclosure," he should insist (except under the conditions described in paragraph 5) upon appropriate revision; failing that, he should set forth clearly his reservations in his disclaimer of opinion. The disclaimer should refer specifically to the nature of his reservations and to the effect, if known to him, on the financial statements."

Disclaimer. If the client will not allow the auditor to make the appropriate revision or accept this disclaimer of opinion, then the auditor "should refuse to be associated with the financial statements and, if necessary, withdraw from the engagement." Of course, an auditor "should refuse to provide typing or reproduction services or to be associated in any way with unaudited financial statements which, on the basis of facts known to him, he concludes are false or intended to mislead."

The disclaimer of opinion should make clear that the financial statements, which it accompanies, have not been audited and that the auditor is not expressing any opinion in regard to them. The Committee on Auditing Procedure offers an example of such a disclaimer as follows:

> The accompanying balance sheet of X Company as of December 31, 19__ and the related statement(s) of income and retained earnings for the year then ended were not audited by us and accordingly we do not express an opinion on them.
>
> (Signature and date)

It is important to note that the use of a disclaimer will not protect the auditor in all situations. If the auditor has some knowledge or could have knowledge that the statements are false or misleading, or that the client intends to use them to mislead others, the auditor may well find himself the unsuccessful defendant in a lawsuit, despite the fact that his disclaimer of opinion is prominently displayed on each page of the audited statements.

DISCIPLINARY PROCEEDINGS

Where an auditor has been guilty of conduct which reflects unfavorably on his profession, he may be subject to disciplinary action. This penalty may be in addition to the civil liability discussed previously or entirely independent of it. For instance, a third party, who may be unable to prosecute a civil suit successfully because he is unable to show damages or because he is not protected under the federal Securities acts and can only show that the auditor was guilty of common law negligence, may bring a complaint before some relevant agency in the hope of having the auditor punished in some other way.

There are three types of organizations which have disciplinary power over auditors. The first of these are professional societies, such as the AICPA and the various state societies of certified public accountants. The second are the various state regulatory bodies, such as the Board of Regents of the State of New York, which have power over the issuance and revocation of certified public accounting certificates. Third are various government agencies before whom auditors practice, such as the Securities and Exchange Commission.

Professional Societies. Most state professional organizations have adopted codes of ethics patterned after the Code of Professional Ethics promulgated by the AICPA. Most codes state that when a provision of the code is violated by a member, he may be suspended, either temporarily or permanently, from membership. Provision is made for the protection of the rights of the individual member by requiring that suspension may take place only after a trial before an appropriate committee.

The Code of Professional Ethics of the AICPA deals with five general areas of responsibility. Article 1 deals with the member's relation with clients and public. It deals generally with the auditor's independence, the "confidential relationship" between the auditor and his client, and the charging of contingent fees by the auditor.

Article 2 deals with the technical standards to be maintained by the profession and will be covered here in some detail.

Article 2.01 provides that no member of the Institute shall sign a report purporting to "express his opinion on financial statements unless they have been examined by him, or by a member or employee of his firm." He may utilize, to the extent appropriate, the work done by another duly certified public accountant.

Article 2.02 states that a member who expresses an opinion as to financial statements may be held guilty of an act discreditable to the profession if

(*a*) he fails to disclose a material fact known to him which is not disclosed in the financial statements but disclosure of which is necessary to make the financial statements not misleading; or

(*b*) he fails to report any material misstatement known to him to appear in the financial statement; or

(*c*) he is materially negligent in the conduct of his examination or in making his report thereon; or

(*d*) he fails to acquire sufficient information to warrant expression of an opinion, or his exceptions are sufficiently material to negative the expression of an opinion; or

(*e*) he fails to direct attention to any material departure from generally accepted accounting principles or to disclose any material omission of generally accepted auditing procedure applicable in the circumstances.

Article 2.03 provides that

a member shall not permit his name to be associated with statements purporting to show financial position or results of operations in such a manner as to imply that he is acting as an independent public accountant unless he shall: (a) express an unqualified opinion; or (b) express a qualified opinion; or (c) express an adverse opinion; or (d) disclaim an opinion on the statements taken as a whole and indicate clearly his reasons therefor; or (e) when unaudited financial statements are presented, disclaim an opinion which will include disclosure of any material departures from generally accepted accounting principles of which he has knowledge, and disclose prominently on each page of the financial statements that they were not audited.

Article 2.04 prohibits members from allowing their names to be used in conjunction with forecasts of future transactions in a manner which may lead to the belief that the member vouches for the accuracy of the forecast.

Article 3 deals with promotional practices and is not relevant to this discussion.

Article 4 deals with operating practices of a member firm and sets forth generally the operating procedures which the Institute expects member firms to follow.

Article 5 deals with relations with fellow members. For further information on this topic see Chapter 4, "Professional Ethics."

State Regulatory Agencies. In each state there is an agency regulating the practice of public accountancy. In New York State this is done by the Board of Regents. Handbook 14, on Public Accountancy, issued by The University of the State of New York, provides "that all public accountants . . . are responsible for observing the prohibitions against unprofessional conduct and unprofessional advertising as set forth in Article 1, Section 94, of the Regulations of the Commissioner."

The handbook continues, "Failure to observe the rules against acts that the profession deems to be unprofessional, will subject the practitioner to disciplinary procedure in the manner prescribed . . ." in the education law.

The proceedings . . . are commenced by the filing of charges by any person with the Commissioner of Education. The division of professional conduct institutes an investigation of the charges, determines the facts and places the case before the Council on

Accountancy. If the Council determines that probable cause exists, it will refer the case to the Chairman of the Public Accountancy Committee on Grievances who, in turn, appoints a Trial Committee of 3 members to hear the charges. After the hearing, if the Committee finds the respondent guilty of the charges, the case record, recommendation and determination are forwarded to the Regents Committee on discipline. At this time the Regents Committee offers the respondent another opportunity to be heard. The Regents Committee renders a report to the Board of Regents who may, in their discretion, revoke, suspend for a fixed term the Certificate, endorsement or enrollment; or deliver a censure or reprimand to the accused.

Section 7406 of Article 149 of the Education Law sets forth the circumstances under which the Board of Regents shall have power to revoke or suspend a practitioner or to censure or reprimand him. These circumstances are where he has (*a*) . . . been found guilty of fraud, deceit or gross negligence in practice . . . , (*b*) has been found guilty of unprofessional conduct or unprofessional advertising as defined in rules established by the Regents upon being satisfied that such rules represent the consensus of opinion of the . . . profession in respect to such conduct or advertising, or (*c*) has been convicted of any crime in a Court of competent jurisdiction either within or without the State.

Federal Government Agencies. Various agencies of the federal government before whom auditors practice, such as the Interstate Commerce Commission, the Federal Communications Commission, the Internal Revenue Service, and the Securities and Exchange Commission, set up requirements regulating practice before the particular agency. For illustrative purposes, we can examine the rules of practice of the Securities and Exchange Commission.

Rule II(e) provides that the Commission may disqualify, and deny, temporarily or permanently, the privilege of appearing or practicing before it in any way to any person who is found by the Commission after a hearing in the matter "(1) not to possess the requisite qualifications to represent others; or (2) to be lacking in character or integrity or to have engaged in unethical or improper professional conduct." Where the work of an auditor is found substandard by the Commission, or the Commission totally criticizes an auditor's work, notification of this fact is sent to the AICPA, the relevant state society, and the relevant state agency for the initiation of disciplinary action.

In his book, *SEC Accounting Practice and Procedure,* Louis H. Rappaport summarizes the disciplinary proceedings under Rule II(e) brought against auditors which have been made public. Mr. Rappaport states that, as a result of these proceedings, some of the auditors involved were suspended from practice before the Commission. This means that they apparently could submit no documents whatsoever during the period of the suspension and, further, that after the suspension period was over, nothing could be filed with the Commission, which included an opinion dated during the suspension period. As Mr. Rappaport points out, "It will be readily seen that a suspension for even a short period—say, ten days—is a very serious thing indeed, since it punishes not only the accountant involved but also his clients."

BIBLIOGRAPHY

General Rules and Regulations under the Securities Exchange Act of 1933, Securities and Exchange Commission.

General Rules and Regulations under the Securities Exchange Act of 1934, Securities and Exchange Commission.

Public Accountancy, Handbook 14, The University of the State of New York, State Education Department, Albany, 1966.

Statements on Auditing Procedure No. 33, *Auditing Standards and Procedures,* AICPA (Committee on Auditing Procedure), New York, 1963.

Cashin, James A., and Garland C. Owens: *Auditing,* 2d ed., New York, The Ronald Press Company, 1963.

Dohr, J. L., E. L. Phillip, G. C. Thomson, and W. C. Warren: *Accounting and the Law,* 3d ed., Brooklyn, Foundation Press, 1964.

Levy, Saul: "Legal Responsibility and Civil Liability," *C.P.A. Handbook,* New York, American Institute of Accountants, 1952.

Loss, Louis: *Securities Regulation,* 2d ed., Boston, Little, Brown and Company, 1961.

Rappaport, Louis H.: *SEC Accounting Practice and Procedure,* 2d ed., New York, The Ronald Press Company, 1966.

Bradley, Edwin: "Auditors' Liability and the Need for Increased Accounting Uniformity," *Law and Contemporary Problems,* Autumn, 1965.

Hill, Thomas W., Jr.: "The Public Accountants' Legal Liability to Clients and Others," *The New York Certified Public Accountant,* January, 1968.

Cogliati, Norman: "Unaudited Financial Statements—Disclosure of Reservations," *The Journal of Accountancy,* April, 1968.

Bakay, Virginia Hicks: "A Review of Selected Claims against Public Accountants," *The Journal of Accountancy,* May, 1970.

Weyrich, Harry R.: "Exposure to Professional Liability," *The New York Certified Public Accountant,* July, 1970.

Reiling, Henry B., and Russell A. Taussig, "Recent Liability Cases—Implications for Accountants," *The Journal of Accountancy,* September, 1970.

Chapter **6**

Independent Auditing

EDWARD S. LYNN

Professor of Accounting, The University of Arizona

MARILYNN G. WINBORNE

Professor of Accounting, The University of Arizona

NATURE OF INDEPENDENT AUDITING

Introduction. Independent auditing has as its primary function the rendering of an opinion upon financial statements. Financial statements accompanied by an independent auditor's report are furnished to owners, creditors, unions, governmental agencies, and other interested parties. The independent auditor's report adds credibility to the financial representations of management. Because of the auditor's special skills and familiarity with business, he is called upon to render other services to his clients, such as tax return preparation and planning, informational system design, cost analysis, and budgeting.

The skills of the auditor are acquired through formal study and experience. Independence of attitude is the most important single ingredient and must be continually maintained. Without independence from the client, the auditor's opinion is suspect and does not serve the needs of the users of the financial statements.

An opinion may be rendered upon any financial statement. Unqualified, or "clean," opinions may be given for any financial statement which does what it purports to do. When an unqualified opinion is not appropriate, a qualified opinion or an adverse opinion will be issued. When the auditor has not performed an audit but he is "associated" with the statements, he should disclaim an opinion. The reasons for a qualified opinion, adverse opinion, or a disclaimer of an opinion should be stated within the report. The auditor's report should also state whether or not the financial statements are in accordance with generally accepted accounting principles consistently applied.

The corporate form of business organization is characterized by a legal existence separate from that of its owners. This form has made possible a longevity of life and a diversity of ownership interest that in turn have allowed a growth in size far beyond that achieved by any other form of private business enterprise. The size of corporations, individually and in the aggregate, has given them an economic importance far in excess of any other private institution. The diversity of ownership, the means of credit at their disposal, and the economic significance of the corporate form have increased the need for an independent opinion as to the fairness of the financial statements provided by management. The growth and development of independent auditing have followed closely that of the corporate form of business enterprise.

Public Aspects of Independent Auditing. The following statement from *Montgomery's Auditing* summarizes the utility of the independent opinion to the equity shareholders of a widely held corporation:

> Financing business expansion has required raising large amounts of capital, and the resulting diffusion of corporate ownership has created large numbers of relatively small shareholders who are not intimately connected with management. This diffusion emphasized the need for an independent appraisal of the fairness of reported results of management's stewardship as shown in annual financial statements made available to shareholders. Fairly stated financial statements result not only from dependable recording and summarization of financial transactions, but also from proper application of generally accepted principles of accounting. It is to be expected that the opinion of the public accountant, as a professional expert in such matters, should be sought. Thus the public accountant's independent, objective, and impartial report upon his examination of financial statements has become a major function.[1]

Though corporations accumulate vast contributions from owners, capital for growth and expansion may be acquired by the use of credit. The corporation is in a position to issue bonds to a large number of investors, private individuals, and institutions, who frequently require an independent auditor's opinion on the statements prior to the granting of credit. The larger the corporation and the more remote its creditors, the greater is the value of the independent opinion to credit grantors. Institutional credit grantors may require special reports or analyses prior to the granting or continuing of credit. Frequently the independent auditor is called upon to express his opinion upon the special reports as well as upon the standard reports made available to stockholders.

Labor unions have an interest in the financial well-being of corporations. It is not unusual for a union contract to require an opinion of an independent auditor upon statements and special reports furnished to the union. Because of the size and economic importance of corporations, governments and the public in general have an interest in corporate financial position and results of operations. The public makes its desires felt through laws and government agencies, many of which require that a corporation file information with an

[1] Norman J. Lenhart and Philip L. Defliese, *Montgomery's Auditing*, 8th ed., New York, The Ronald Press Company, 1957, p. 5.

agency and make available financial statements with the opinion of an independent auditor attached. The laws administered by the Securities and Exchange Commission are good examples of the demands made upon corporations for information by the public at large. The Committee on Accounting Procedure of the American Institute of Certified Public Accountants (AICPA) has expressed the government's and the public's objectives as follows:

> The test of the corporate system and of the special phase of it represented by corporate accounting ultimately lies in the results which are produced. These results must be judged from the standpoint of society as a whole—not merely from that of any one group of interested persons.[2]

To summarize, those factors that have directly affected the form of independent auditing as it is known today are (1) widespread ownership of enterprises (2) in a highly industrialized society (3) in which industry is mostly privately owned and mostly regulated by competition, and (4) in which the need for well-developed and well-applied accounting standards for reporting to stockholders and creditors is widely recognized.[3]

Role of the Independent Auditor. The objective of the independent auditor's examination of financial statements (the audit) is to enable him to express an opinion as to the fairness with which the statements present what they purport to present. The financial statements are the representations and the primary responsibility of management. In *In the Matter of Interstate Hosiery Mills, Inc.*,[4] the SEC held that the fundamental and primary responsibility for the accuracy of information filed with the Commission and disseminated among the investors rests upon management. Management does not discharge its obligations in this respect by the employment of independent public accountants, however reputable.

The independent auditor must clearly state the responsibility he is taking for any financial statements with which his name is associated. He may express his opinion on the financial statements taken as a whole or on specified portions of the statements. When the auditor is expressing his opinion on the financial statements taken as a whole, he may issue his report in a short form, a long form, or both. The opinion expressed by the independent auditor on the financial statements taken as a whole may take one of three forms: unqualified, qualified, or adverse. When the auditor does not have sufficient information upon which to base an opinion, he will issue a disclaimer of opinion and state his reasons for so doing. In connection with a qualified or an adverse opinion, the auditor will also state all the reasons for his opinion. If the auditor issues an adverse opinion or a disclaimer of opinion, he may give a piecemeal opinion covering those items that are, in his opinion, fairly stated. In the piecemeal opinion the auditor should clearly state the items that are included in or excluded from his opinion.

Independence. For the opinion of the auditor to add credibility to the financial statements presented by management, he must be independent of that management and therefore must not be an employee of management.

> His actions are not subject to supervision by the management of the business, and this situation alone creates considerable independence. Independence is also an attitude of mind, and independent thought and action are equally as important as the independent relationship between the accountant and his client. Unless the accountant is

[2] Accounting Research and Terminology Bulletins, final ed., AICPA (Committees on Accounting Procedure and Accounting Terminology), New York, 1961, p. 7.

[3] John L. Carey (ed.), *The Accounting Profession: Where Is It Headed?* New York, AICPA, 1962, p. 49.

[4] SEC 706, 721.

independent, his opinion is no more reliable than the statements which have been prepared by management.[5]

Independence is the focal point of the Code of Professional Ethics of the AICPA and the rules of ethical conduct adopted by the state boards of public accountancy. The rules of ethics prohibit financial as well as personal ties with the client or the affairs of the client; they promote the appearance of independence as well as the fact. It could be said that the rules of ethical conduct attempt to make the independent auditor, like Caesar's wife, "above suspicion."

CPA Designation. A certified public accountant is licensed by the various states to hold himself out as an expert in accounting and auditing.

The CPA has demonstrated the basic qualifications for assumption of the *professional* responsibility of attesting, or adding credibility to, financial representations—and this requires a comprehensive knowledge of the other underlying phases of the accounting function: record-keeping, internal accounting for management purposes, tax accounting, and external financial reporting.[6]

In 37 of the 54 jurisdictions only a CPA may render an opinion as to the fairness of financial statements. (In other jurisdictions no one may use the CPA designation unless he has been approved, but no attempt is made to restrict the attest function to CPAs.) State laws regulate the attest function only, leaving the other services that a CPA may render open to anyone who can sell his services.

To become a CPA, a candidate must meet the requirements set by his state as to character, citizenship, education, experience, etc., and must pass the Uniform CPA Examination. The education requirements vary from state to state, as do the experience requirements. There is a definite trend for the state laws to become more demanding as to education. Experience requirements vary from none to 6 years. The CPA requirements by states are described in detail in Chapter 44, "State Laws and Regulations."

The examination is prepared by the AICPA and is offered to the state accountancy boards, all of which currently avail themselves of the service as well as the AICPA's Advisory Grading Service. The nationwide use of the two services is the only uniform part of the process of becoming a CPA.

When the CPA signs his opinion in connection with financial statements, he does not do so lightly. He is placing on the line his license to practice, his livelihood. He has a major investment of time and energy in his license. Once licensed, the CPA is bound by the state board of accountancy's rules of ethical conduct and minimum audit standards. Violation of these professional standards may result in loss of the right to use the CPA designation.

To summarize, within the broad field of accounting the CPAs are the identified professionals.

They provide leadership in accounting research and education. In the practice of public accounting CPAs bring competence of professional quality, independence, and a strong concern for the usefulness of the information and advice they provide, but they do not make management decisions.

The professional quality of their services is based upon the requirements for the CPA certificate—education, experience and examination—and upon the ethical and technical standards established and enforced by their profession.[7]

[5] Howard F. Stettler, *Systems Based Independent Audits*, Englewood Cliffs, N.J., Prentice-Hall, Inc., 1967, p. 4.

[6] Carey, *op. cit.*, p. 28.

[7] A Description of the Professional Practice of Certified Public Accountants, AICPA (Council), New York, 1966.

PROFESSIONAL SERVICES

Attestation. The basis for accounting as a profession in the eyes of the several state governments is the attest function—the rendering of an opinion on the fairness of representations by management. The attest function originated with respect to financial statements of limited liability companies purporting to show financial position and results of operations. Attestation was adjudged desirable in that it afforded absentee owners a means of control over management. Distribution of corporate financial statements accompanied by an independent auditor's report has become increasingly prevalent. Audited corporate financial statements are required by stock exchanges and the Securities and Exchange Commission as well.

Attestation is used by owners of forms of business other than corporations, such as proprietorships and partnerships. The purposes of these audits may be to report upon management to absentee owners. More often, however, these audits will be directed toward the requirements of potential or existing creditors. In the course of an audit of a smaller business, the auditor may render valuable assistance in such areas as internal control, information systems, and tax planning.

The opinion of an independent auditor as to the fairness of financial statements, in whole or in part, may be required pursuant to a debt agreement. It is not uncommon for debt agreements to specify audited statements during the term of the debt. These statements may cover only those areas restricted by the loan indenture—such as working capital, sinking funds, dividends, or appropriations of retained earnings. Audited financial statements are also required under some lease agreements. The independent auditor is consulted in the establishment of budgeting procedures and in the analysis of variances from budget. He is consulted in connection with proposed mergers, pension plans, stock option plans, etc.

Since this is an auditing handbook, the emphasis is of course upon attestation. But as the independent accountant renders other services to clients and the public, some of these other fields are discussed briefly below.

Taxes. Most of the taxes levied by the various governmental units are based to some extent upon accounting information such as the amount of capital, total assets, or income. Because of his knowledge of accounting, the independent auditor has long been involved in the preparation of the various tax returns and in advising management on the tax consequence of various alternative courses of action. Tax planning is a valuable service to a business and to individuals.

Management Services. The knowledge the independent auditor possesses enables him to render many valuable services to management. His familiarity with accounting systems places him in a position to advise management on internal controls and the design and installation of information systems. His knowledge is called upon in analyzing costs of new products, financing alternatives, and the like. His counsel is sought in the highest of management circles because of his reputation of professionalism, his familiarity with business operations derived from experience with many businesses, his special knowledge of accounting, and his expertise acquired through continual study.

The independent accountant's familiarity with accounting and auditing has made many clients seek his services in the processing of financial and other data. When he offers data processing services to the public, the services are considered to be of the type offered by public accountants, and thus the rules of ethical conduct apply. For example, he must specify the responsibility that he is assuming for any financial statements with which he is associated. Opinion No. 7 of the Committee on Professional Ethics held that the offering of data processing services to other practicing public accountants is not within the definition of public accounting and so may be done by a corporation. Offering of block time is not included in the practice of public accounting so long "as it does not entail systems design, programming or service of any kind and what is being offered is the use of the equipment only."

The independent auditor must be independent in appearance as well as in fact. The question has been raised within the profession, "Does an auditor sacrifice his independence in regard to a client's financial position and results of operations when he performs other services for the client?" In Opinion No. 12 the Committee on Professional Ethics held that:

> The committee does not intend to suggest, however, that the rendering of professional services other than the independent audit itself would suggest to a reasonable observer a conflict of interest. For example, in the areas of management advisory services and tax practice, so long as the CPA's services consist of advice and technical assistance, the committee can discern no likelihood of a conflict of interest arising from such services. It is a rare instance for management to surrender its responsibility to make management decisions. However, should a member make such decisions on matters affecting the company's financial position or results of operations, it would appear that this objectivity as independent auditor of the company's financial statements might well be impaired. Consequently, such situations should be avoided.

THE REPORT OF THE INDEPENDENT AUDITOR

The purpose of the audit engagement is to enable the independent auditor to express an opinion upon the financial statements presented by management. He is required to state the responsibility he is assuming for the financial statements whenever his name is associated with such statements. The opinion will state whether or not in the auditor's judgment the statements present fairly that which they purport to present. The report issued by the auditor should designate the statements on which he is expressing an opinion and give his opinion as to their fairness. If the statements do not present fairly that which they purport to present, the auditor should express a qualified or adverse opinion and state the reasons he has reached such a conclusion. In the event the auditor did not perform sufficient work to form an opinion, a disclaimer should be issued and the reasons stated.

When the opinion is expressed upon the statements taken as a whole, the report issued by the independent auditor may be in a short form, a long form, or both. The independent auditor may also issue an opinion upon portions of the financial statements. Each of these facets of reporting will be dealt with separately; however, there are subjects that are generally applicable to all reports and are discussed below.

Date of the Report. The report should be dated as of the point in time when the auditor has completed all significant audit procedures. Usually this will be the date of the completion of work in the client's office. If the report is dated substantially later than completion of fieldwork, the auditor should indicate that the examination was made at an earlier date. The independent auditor has certain responsibilities for the reporting of subsequent events, as discussed more fully under that heading. In general the auditor should insist upon disclosure of those subsequent financial events that would affect a decision based upon the financial statements. When the independent auditor is engaged in the preparation of registration statements under the

Securities Act of 1933, his responsibility for reporting subsequent events extends to the registration date.

Address of the Report. The report should be addressed in a manner described in Statements on Auditing Procedure No. 33 as follows:

> The report should be addressed to the client, or to the board of directors or the stockholders of the client if the appointment is made by them or if such address is preferred. Where the appointment of the auditor is made by the directors and approved by the stockholders, the report may well be addressed to both.[8]

Generally Accepted Auditing Standards. Generally accepted auditing standards are the "measures of the quality of the performance of those acts and objectives to be attained by the use of the procedures undertaken."[9] The standards relate not only to the work performed but also to the judgment exercised by the independent auditor in the carrying out of the procedures and in rendering his report. The 10 standards adopted by the membership of the AICPA are:

General Standards

1. The examination is to be performed by a person or persons having adequate technical training and proficiency as an auditor.
2. In all matters relating to the assignment an independence in mental attitude is to be maintained by the auditor or auditors.
3. Due professional care is to be exercised in the performance of the examination and the preparation of the report.

Standards of Field Work

1. The work is to be adequately planned and assistants, if any, are to be properly supervised.
2. There is to be a proper study and evaluation of the existing internal control as a basis for reliance thereon and for the determination of the resultant extent of the tests to which auditing procedures are to be restricted.
3. Sufficient competent evidential matter is to be obtained through inspection, observation, inquiries and confirmations to afford a reasonable basis for an opinion regarding the financial statements under examination.

Standards of Reporting

1. The report shall state whether the financial statements are presented in accordance with generally accepted principles of accounting.
2. The report shall state whether such principles have been consistently observed in the current period in relation to the preceding period.
3. Informative disclosures in the financial statements are to be regarded as reasonably adequate unless otherwise stated in the report.
4. The report shall either contain an expression of opinion regarding the financial statements, taken as a whole, or an assertion to the effect that an opinion cannot be expressed. When an over-all opinion cannot be expressed, the reasons therefor should be stated. In all cases where an auditor's name is associated with financial statements, the report should contain a clear-cut indication of the character of the auditor's examination, if any, and the degree of responsibility he is taking.[10]

The application of standards is not meant to be an automatic process; proper application requires the exercise of mature judgment by the auditor as he evaluates the individual circumstances of the audit.

These standards to a great extent are interrelated and interdependent. Moreover, the circumstances which are germane to a determination of whether one standard is

[8] Statements on Auditing Procedure No. 33, *Auditing Standards and Procedures*, AICPA (Committee on Auditing Procedure), New York, 1963, pp. 57–58.

[9] SAP No. 33, p. 15.

[10] SAP No 33, pp. 15–16.

met may apply equally to another. The elements of "materiality" and "relative risk" underlie the application of all the standards, particularly the standards of field work and reporting.

The concept of materiality is inherent in the work of the independent auditor. There should be stronger grounds to sustain the independent auditor's opinion with respect to those items which are relatively more important and with respect to those of lesser importance or those in which the possibility of material error is remote. For example, in an enterprise with few, but large, accounts receivable, the accounts individually are more important, and the possibility of material error is greater than is another enterprise that has a great number of small accounts aggregating the same total. In industrial and merchandising enterprises, inventories are usually of great importance to both financial position and results of operations and accordingly may require relatively more attention by the auditor than would the inventories of a public utility company. Similarly, accounts receivable usually will receive more attention than prepaid insurance.

The degree of risk involved also has an important bearing on the nature of the examination. Cash transactions are more susceptible to irregularities than inventories, and the work undertaken on cash may therefore have to be carried out in a more conclusive manner, without, however, necessarily implying a greater expenditure of time. Arm's-length transactions with outside parties are usually subjected to less detailed scrutiny than intercompany transactions or transactions with officers and employees, where the same degree of disinterested dealing cannot be assumed. The effect of internal control on the scope of an examination is an outstanding example of the influence on auditing procedures of a greater or lesser degree of risk of error; i.e., the stronger the internal control, the less the degree of risk.[11]

Generally Accepted Accounting Principles. The term "generally accepted accounting principles" as used in the standard short-form report and the standards of reporting includes not only principles of accounting but the methods used in their application. "The first reporting standard is construed to require not a statement of fact by the auditor, but an opinion as to whether the financial statements are presented in conformity with such principles."[12] The auditor must have made an examination sufficient in scope to enable him to form an opinion as to the use of generally accepted accounting principles. The accounting procedures and techniques expressed in the Accounting Research Bulletins and the Opinions of the Accounting Principles Board are generally accepted and are usually followed. These pronouncements do not cover all contingencies, and where they are silent, other sources are to be drawn upon, of necessity. In Accounting Research Study No. 7, *Inventory of Generally Accepted Accounting Principles,* the following are listed as authoritative sources of support for accounting practices:

1. Trade practices, as they have demonstrated over time their ability to produce reliable results.
2. Opinions of leaders of the financial community such as stock exchanges, and commercial and investment bankers.
3. Accounting rulings and uniform systems of accounts for requested industries. Where there is a significant departure from generally accepted accounting in the accounting regulations, the auditor will have to qualify his opinion.
4. The Securities and Exchange Commission.
5. Affirmative opinions, written or oral, of practicing and academic CPAs.
6. Statements of the committees of the American Accounting Association and the AICPA.[13]

[11] SAP No. 33, p. 17.

[12] SAP No. 33, p. 40.

[13] Accounting Research Study No. 7 (Paul Grady), *Inventory of Generally Accepted Accounting Principles,* AICPA, New York, 1965, pp. 52–53.

In 1934, the membership of the AICPA adopted the following six rules of accounting practice:

1. Unrealized profit should not be credited to income account of the corporation either directly or indirectly, through the medium of charging against such unrealized profits amounts which would ordinarily fall to be charged against income account. Profit is deemed to be realized when a sale in the ordinary course of business is effected, unless the circumstances are such that the collection of the sale price is not reasonably assured. An exception to the general rule may be made in respect of inventories in industries (such as packing-house industry) in which owing to the impossibility of determining costs it is a trade custom to take inventories at net selling prices, which may exceed cost.

2. Capital surplus, however created, should not be used to relieve the income account of the current or future years of charges which would otherwise fall to be made thereagainst. This rule might be subject to the exception that where, upon reorganization, a reorganized company would be relieved of charges which would require to be made against income if the existing corporation were continued, it might be regarded as permissible to accomplish the same result without reorganization provided the facts were as fully revealed to and the action as formally approved by the shareholders as in reorganization.

3. Earned surplus of a subsidiary company created prior to acquisition does not form a part of the consolidated earned surplus of the parent company and subsidiaries; nor can any dividend declared out of such surplus properly be credited to the income account of the parent company.

4. While it is perhaps in some circumstances permissible to show stock of a corporation held in its own treasury as an asset, if adequately disclosed, the dividends on stock so held should not be treated as a credit to the income account of the company.

5. Notes or accounts receivable due from officers, employees, or affiliated companies must be shown separately and not included under a general heading such as notes receivable or accounts receivable.

6. If capital stock is issued nominally for the acquisition of property and it appears that at about the same time, and pursuant to a previous agreement or understanding, some portion of the stock so issued is donated to the corporation, it is not permissible to treat the par value of the stock nominally issued for the property as the cost of that property. If stock so donated is subsequently sold, it is not permissible to treat the proceeds as a credit to surplus of the corporation.[14]

This action is the only time that the full membership has acted on matters of accounting principle; in general the Institute has granted to a specific committee the sole right to speak for it.

If the auditor agrees to the use of a method that is contradictory to one that has been espoused by the Accounting Principles Board, in its opinions or in its endorsement of preexisting Accounting Research Bulletins, the following procedure is to be followed in conformity with disclosure requirements adopted by the Council of the AICPA:

If an accounting principle that differs materially in its effect from one accepted in an Opinion of the Accounting Principles Board is applied in financial statements, the reporting member must decide whether the principle has substantial authoritative support and is applicable in the circumstances.

a. If he concludes that it does not, he would either qualify his opinion, disclaim an opinion, or give an adverse opinion as appropriate. Requirements for handling these situations in the reports of members are set forth in generally accepted auditing standards and in the Code of Professional Ethics and need no further implementation.

b. If he concludes that it does have substantial authoritative support:

(1) he would give an unqualified opinion and

[14] Accounting Research and Terminology Bulletins, final ed., AICPA (Committee on Accounting Procedure), New York, 1961, pp. 11–12.

(2) disclose the fact of departure from the Opinion in a separate paragraph in his report or see that it is disclosed in a footnote to the financial statements and, where practicable, its effects on the financial statements.* Illustrative language for this purpose is as follows:

> The company's treatment of (describe) is at variance with Opinion No. __ of the Accounting Principles Board (Accounting Research Bulletin No. __ of the Committee on Accounting Procedure) of the American Institute of Certified Public Accountants. This Opinion (Bulletin) states that (describe the principle in question). If the Accounting Principles Board Opinion (Accounting Research Bulletin) had been followed, income for the year would have been increased (decreased) by $____ and the amount of retained earnings at (date) increased (decreased) by $____. In our opinion, the company's treatment has substantial authoritative support and is an acceptable practice.

If disclosure is made in a footnote, the last sentence might be changed to read: In the opinion of the independent auditors, ____________, the company's treatment has substantial authoritative support and is an acceptable practice.[15]

* In those cases in which it is not practicable to determine the approximate effect on the financial statements, this fact should be expressly stated.

Disclosure. The Securities and Exchange Commission has stated in Accounting Series Release No. 4, issued in 1938, that disclosures are not a substitute for use of generally accepted accounting principles.

> In cases where financial statements filed with this Commission pursuant to its rules and regulations under the Securities Act of 1933 or the Securities Exchange Act of 1934 are prepared in accordance with accounting principles for which there is no substantial authoritative support, such financial statements will be presumed to be misleading or inaccurate despite disclosures contained in the certificate of the accountant or in footnotes to the statements provided the matters involved are material. In cases where there is a difference of opinion between the Commission and the registrant as to the proper principles of accounting to be followed, disclosure will be accepted in lieu of correction of the financial statements themselves only if the points involved are such that there is substantial authoritative support for the practices followed by the registrant and the position of the Commission has not previously been expressed in rules, regulations, or other official releases of the Commission, including the published opinions of its chief accountant.

Consistency

> The objective of the consistency standard is: (1) to give assurance that the comparability of financial statements as between periods has not been materially affected by changes in the accounting principles employed or in the method of their application; or (2) if comparability has been materially affected by such changes, to require a statement of the nature of the changes and their effects on the financial statements.[16]

Changing conditions that require a change in accounting and changes in conditions unrelated to accounting do not require disclosure in the auditor's opinion, although disclosure of some type may be advisable for the sake of comparability. For example, if a majority-owned subsidiary is included in consolidated statements one year but excluded in the next because the parent company has divested itself of the majority ownership, no change in accounting principle has occurred. The change was in conditions that affected the accounting procedures; and if management does not call attention

[15] Disclosure of Departures from Opinions of Accounting Principles Board, Special Bulletin, AICPA (Council), New York, October, 1964.

[16] SAP No. 33, p. 42.

in the statements to the lack of comparability between the two years, the auditor may want to comment upon it in his report. If, on the other hand, management did not include the majority-owned subsidiary in the second year's statements, although the percentage of ownership did not change, the independent auditor would have to take exception in his opinion to the lack of consistency.

The consistency standard relates to the accounting procedures used in the preparation of the current financial statements and the immediately preceding year's financial statements, whether the prior year's statements are shown in comparative form with those of the current year or not. When the statements of several years are presented separately or in comparative form, then each year should be consistent with each other year. The auditor should point out any variations and their effects upon the financial statements. Consistency applies to classifications as well as procedures; however, if material changes in classifications are made and the changes are disclosed in the financial statements or notes thereto, it is usually not necessary to refer to the reclassifications in the auditor's report. When the report is made on the first year's operations of a newly organized company, no reference to consistency is necessary.

Present Fairly. The auditor expresses his opinion that the statements either do or do not present fairly the financial position and results of operations. The auditor is asseverating not that the statements are absolutely correct but that, in his opinion, based upon his audit work, the statements are free from material errors and are dependable representations of that which the statements purport to represent.

> Fairness in financial statements means two things: first, freedom from bias and dishonesty; and, second, completeness of information. This concept is applicable not only to the dollar amounts and descriptive titles but also to the propriety of classifications, as in the distinction drawn between current and noncurrent assets.[17]

Evidential Matter. The third standard of fieldwork states that the independent auditor will acquire sufficient competent evidential material to support his opinion on the financial statements taken as a whole, not upon individual items within the statements. The auditor works under time and cost pressures that require he satisfy himself with persuasive rather than conclusive evidence, even assuming that conclusive evidence were available in all instances. The degree of reliability the auditor will attach to the evidence collected depends upon the source of the evidence. Evidence collected outside the firm, such as a confirmation, is quite persuasive, as are the direct computations and findings of the auditor. The degree of reliance placed upon the records and documents originating within the firm under audit depends to a large extent upon the system of internal control and whether the documents have circulated outside the firm.

Evidence the auditor uses in the formation of his opinion may be classified as (1) the accounting records and (2) corroborating matter. The accounting records are the starting point of the examination, and the auditor will test to ascertain whether the information flowing into the firm has been properly recorded in the accounting records and whether all that should have been recorded was in fact recorded. Then the auditor will compare the records with the statements to see that the statements are in agreement with the underlying accounting records. The auditor will also use the informal

[17] Walter B. Meigs, *Principles of Auditing*, 3d ed., Homewood, Ill., Richard D. Irwin, Inc., 1964, p. 21.

accounting records, such as worksheets and cost allocations, to support his opinion.

Corroborating evidential matter may be classified by source: (1) internally originated documents, (2) externally originated documents, and (3) information generated by the auditor. External corroborating evidence is obtained through confirmations of receivables, payables, bank balances, debts, inventory in the hands of consignee's and public warehouses, etc. Cutoff bank statements and confirmations are completely outside the control of the client and are the most persuasive type of documentary evidence. Some externally originated documents have passed through the client firm, such as letters, bank statements, and vendors' invoices. Internally originated documents such as letters, contracts, and canceled checks have been treated by persons outside the firm, which adds to their credibility. Completely internal documents are such things as minutes of meetings of management committees and the board of directors. The auditor will generate corroborating evidence through his personal observations, inquiries, inspections, analytical tests, and evaluation of internal control.

Internal Control. Since it is not feasible to examine all the transactions of a large client for a year, the auditor must rely upon his evaluation of the client's system of internal control if he is to reach an opinion as to the fairness of the statements. His reliance necessarily involves a risk, but it is a risk that is minimized if his examination of the system of internal control reveals dependable records based upon the following:

a. A plan of organization which provides appropriate segregation of functional responsibilities;
b. A system of authorization and record procedures adequate to provide reasonable accounting control over assets, liabilities, revenues and expenses;
c. Sound practices to be followed in performance of duties and functions of each of the organizational departments; and
d. Personnel of a quality commensurate with responsibilities.[18]

The system includes both accounting and administrative controls. The auditor is particularly concerned with the financial controls, but he will investigate administrative controls if their presence and degree of effectiveness will assist him in arriving at an opinion as to the adequacy of the financial controls.

On the basis of his evaluation of internal control the auditor will determine the extent of his tests of transactions and documents. Observations made during the tests, in turn, may alter his evaluation. By this process of evaluation of internal control and confirmation of his evaluation, the auditor arrives at his opinion on the system. He is convinced by direct evidence or by his evaluation of the system that each significant item in the statements contributes to a fair presentation of financial position and results of operations.

First Audit of an Established Company. When the independent auditor's client is an established company and he is called in for the first audit, he has the problem of determining the fairness of the beginning balances, which affect the statement of operations and the consistency of application of generally accepted accounting principles. When the company has maintained adequate records in the prior years, the auditor should extend his procedures so that he can satisfy himself as to the fairness of the beginning balances. If he does satisfy himself, the standard short-form opinion is appropriate. If the client has released statements in the past that were in

[18] SAP No. 33, pp. 28–29.

conformity with generally accepted accounting principles, no qualification for consistency is necessary. However, if the client had released statements, say on the cash basis or modified cash basis, the auditor would qualify his opinion (if the current year's statements were on the accrual basis) because of a lack of consistency, and he would insert in his report a middle paragraph explaining the situation.

If the client had not maintained adequate records in the past, the auditor will not be able to satisfy himself as to the fairness of the beginning balances. Consequently, the auditor will not be able to express his opinion on the income statement and the statement of retained earnings; inability to satisfy himself regarding the fairness of the beginning balances will not, in and of itself, preclude expression of an opinion on the balance sheet.

First audits of established companies are frequently made to comply with registration requirements under the acts administered by the SEC. The Securities Act of 1933 requires a summary of earnings covering a reasonable period. In Accounting Series Release No. 62 (1947) the Commission held that the independent accountant could render an opinion on the summary of earnings in the event it was the first audit, although

> it would be necessary for (the independent auditor) to apply to the operations and transactions of each of the earlier periods with respect to which he is to express an opinion substantially the same auditing procedures as those employed with respect to (the periods immediately preceding the current period).

This position was explained in greater detail in Accounting Series Release No. 90 (1962). The observation of inventories, confirmation of receivables, and other such generally accepted auditing procedures cannot be applied to prior years and are thus not considered applicable in the circumstances. Alternative auditing procedures may be used; however, the "alternative procedures must be adequate to support an unqualified opinion as to the fairness of presentation of the income statement by years."

Pooling of Interests and Consistency. When companies have come together under the accounting concept of a pooling of interests, the comparative financial statements for prior years should be combined on the pooling basis. When they are not, the opinion should note that the statements are not prepared on a basis consistent with that of the previous year. "The inconsistency arises, in this case, not from a change in the application of an accounting principle in the current year but from the lack of such application to prior years." [19]

OPINION ON STATEMENTS AS A WHOLE

Forms of Reports. The purpose of the typical audit engagement is to enable the independent auditor to express his opinion as to the fairness of financial statements that purport to present financial position and results of operations. When the auditor is expressing his opinion upon the financial statements taken as a whole, he must state whether or not, in his opinion, the statements present fairly the financial position and results of operations in accordance with generally accepted accounting principles applied on a basis consistent with that of the preceding year. When the statements do not purport to have been prepared in accordance with generally accepted accounting principles, the independent auditor's report will so indicate. These and opinions on

[19] SAP No. 33, p. 52.

less than the financial statements taken as a whole are discussed in the section on special reports.

When the independent auditor is expressing his opinion upon the financial statements taken as a whole and the financial statements purport to be prepared in accordance with generally accepted accounting principles, the report issued may be the standard short form, long form, or both. The opinion may be that the financial statements are fair (a "clean" opinion), the opinion may be qualified, an adverse opinion may be issued (the statements do not present fairly), or the independent auditor may disclaim an opinion upon the financial statements taken as a whole. In the event an adverse opinion or disclaimer of opinion is issued, the independent auditor may render a piecemeal opinion, which is an opinion on less than the financial statements taken as a whole. Each of these forms of opinions is discussed in the following sections.

Standard Short-form Report. The standard short-form report applies to the financial statements taken as a whole. The wording recommended by the Committee on Auditing Procedure of the AICPA is as follows:

Date

To the Board of Directors,
ABC Company:

We have examined the balance sheet of ABC Company as of __________, and the related statements of income and retained earnings for the year then ended. Our examination was made in accordance with generally accepted auditing standards, and accordingly included such tests of the accounting records and such other auditing procedures as we considered necessary in the circumstances.

In our opinion, the accompanying balance sheet and statements of income and retained earnings present fairly the financial position of ABC Company at __________, and the results of its operations for the year then ended, in conformity with generally accepted accounting principles applied on a basis consistent with that of the preceding year.

(Signed) ____________________
Certified Public Accountant

This wording is recommended and does not have to be followed exactly. One national accounting firm uses the following form, which contains all the essential elements of the standard short-form report:

In our opinion, the accompanying (identify statements) present fairly the financial position of ABC Company at __________, and results of its operations for the year (then ended *), in conformity with generally accepted accounting principles applied on a basis consistent with that of the preceding year. Our examination of these statements was made in accordance with generally accepted auditing standards and accordingly included such tests of the accounting records and such other auditing procedures as we considered necessary in the circumstances.

* If a fiscal year.

Scope Paragraph. The first paragraph of the standard short-form report sets out the scope of the audit and the statements examined. This paragraph is a statement of fact, of what was examined and how. If less than the financial statements as a whole are to be covered by the opinion, the statements included in the opinion are to be specified in the scope paragraph. Limitations upon the audit scope are to be noted in the first paragraph and explained, perhaps in a middle paragraph.

Opinion Paragraph. The second paragraph of the standard short-form report expresses the independent auditor's opinion on the financial statements designated. The opinion covers the fairness of the statements, generally accepted accounting principles, and consistency, all of which have been discussed in preceding pages.

Long-form Report. A particular audit may yield a short-form report, a long-form report, or both. The long-form report usually contains the basic financial statements and other information, some of which may not be of an accounting nature. The audit procedures employed may be listed in greater detail than in the standard short-form report. The data generally included in long-form reports can be divided into the following categories:

1. Basic financial statements, usually a balance sheet and statements of income and surplus, which present the financial position and the results of operations, and on which the auditor has stated, or is in a position to state, his opinion in a short-form report.
2. Supplementary financial statements and other details of the basic financial statements which, in the auditor's opinion, are not necessary for a fair presentation of financial position and results of operations.
3. Statistical data which the auditor usually has not examined.
4. Financial statements and related financial data for prior periods, submitted for comparative purposes, all, part, or none of which may have been examined by the auditor.[20]

Thus, the long-form report is characterized by the expansion of the representations by both management and the auditor. The auditor must carefully delineate those parts of the report upon which he is expressing an opinion and those upon which he is not. For example, he may want to specify that

a. his examination has been made primarily for the purpose of formulating an opinion on the basic financial statements, taken as a whole, and
b. the other data included in the report, although not considered necessary for a fair presentation of the financial position and results of operations (whether or not cross-referenced in the basic financial statements), are presented for supplementary analysis purposes, and either (1) that they have been subjected to the audit procedures applied in the examination of the basic financial statements and are, in his opinion, fairly stated in all material respects in relation to the basic financial statements, taken as a whole, or (2) that they have not been subjected to the audit procedures applied in the examination of the basic financial statements, stating the source of the information and the extent of his examination and responsibility assumed, if any.[21]

The wording used by the auditor should clearly state that he is expressing his opinion upon management's representations and is not making factual representations on his own, as could be construed from the presence of the statistical and supplementary data in the absence of specific statements to the contrary.

When both long-form and short-form reports are issued as the result of a single examination, the auditor should use special care that:

a. the long-form report does not contain data which, if omitted from the short-form report, might support a contention that the short-form report was misleading because of inadequate disclosure of material facts known to the independent auditor; and
b. none of the comments or other data contained in the long-form report lend themselves to a contention that they constitute exceptions or reservations, as distinguished from mere explanations.[22]

[20] Lenhart and Defliese, *op. cit.*, p. 516.
[21] SAP No. 33, pp. 84–85.
[22] SAP No. 33, p. 85.

Types of Opinions. When the auditor is satisfied that the statements do present fairly what they purport to present and are consistent with the statements of the prior year, he will issue the kind of unqualified, or "clean," opinion found in the second paragraph of the standard short-form report. When either the scope or the findings of the audit are such that an unqualified opinion on the statements taken as a whole is not appropriate, the auditor will issue a qualified opinion, an adverse opinion, or a disclaimer of an opinion. The general circumstances which require a variation from the standard short-form are:

A. The scope of his examination is limited or affected:
   (1) By conditions which preclude the application of auditing procedures considered necessary in the circumstances
   (2) By restrictions imposed by clients
   (3) Because part of the examination has been made by other independent auditors
B. The financial statements do not present fairly financial position or results of operations because of:
   (1) Lack of conformity with generally accepted accounting principles
   (2) Inadequate disclosure
C. Accounting principles are not consistently applied.
D. Unusual uncertainties exist concerning future developments, the effects of which cannot be reasonably estimated or otherwise resolved satisfactorily.[23]

Any time a qualified opinion is issued, the nature of the qualification must be stated: the reasons for the qualification, the subject of the qualification, and the effect of the item(s). The nature of the qualification may be referred to in the opinion and referenced to notes within the statements unless the qualification is due to a limitation upon the scope of the audit.

An adverse opinion is issued when there is sufficient information for the auditor to form an opinion and the opinion is that the statements taken as a whole do not present fairly the financial position and the results of operations. A middle paragraph should be included stating all the reasons for the adverse opinion. When the auditor does not have sufficient information upon which to base an opinion, he will disclaim an opinion on the statements taken as a whole and include a paragraph stating all his reasons for the disclaimer. Statement on Auditing Procedure No. 38 (issued in 1967) requires that when an auditor is associated with financial statements and has not performed an audit, he must issue a disclaimer of opinion to accompany the unaudited statements. The disclaimer may be placed directly on the statements. Each page of the financial statements should be clearly marked as unaudited.

A certified public accountant is associated with unaudited financial statements when he has consented to the use of his name in a report, document or written communication setting forth or containing the statements. Further, when a certified public accountant submits to his client or others, with or without a covering letter, unaudited financial statements which he has prepared or assisted in preparing, he is deemed to exist even though the certified public accountant does not append his name to the financial statements or uses "plain paper" rather than his own stationery. However, association does not arise if the accountant, as an accommodation to his client, merely types on "plain paper" or reproduces unaudited financial statements so long as he has not prepared or otherwise assisted in preparing the statements and so long as he submits them only to his client.[24]

[23] SAP No. 33, p. 63.
[24] Statement on Auditing Procedure No. 38.

Limitations on Scope of Audit. When the scope of the examination is limited, the auditor may satisfy himself by the use of alternative auditing procedures; in this case no mention is necessary of the use of the alternative procedures nor is a qualification or disclaimer necessary, with two exceptions. If the auditor has not been able to satisfy himself as to the ending inventory by observation of the taking of the inventory or by physical contact with the inventory, or if receivables have not been confirmed, the auditor should refer to the omission of these customary procedures in the scope paragraph if the amount involved is material. If the auditor is able to satisfy himself through alternative procedures, an unqualified opinion is justified.[25]

If the auditor is unable to satisfy himself regarding the (material) statement item for which the procedure was omitted, he must mention the omission in the scope paragraph and then ask himself, "Is the amount of the statement so great that an exception would negate an opinion on the statements taken as a whole?" If the answer is "yes," he must give a disclaimer (perhaps accompanied by a piecemeal opinion). If the answer is "no," he may give a qualified opinion.

In either of the foregoing cases he would want to describe in a middle paragraph the factors that caused omission of the procedure and the possible effects of the item on the statements. References in the opinion paragraph should then be made to the statement item itself rather than to the factors that caused omission of the procedure.

Work of Another Auditor. When a part of the examination was made by another independent auditor, the primary auditor is usually willing to accept the report for use in his opinion but may be unwilling to accept the responsibility of the work done by the other independent accountant. The primary auditor should satisfy himself as to the independence and professional reputation of the secondary auditor. In such circumstances, the primary auditor should disclose in the scope paragraph the fact that the other reports were used as a basis for the overall opinion. In this case, alteration of the standard opinion paragraph to indicate that the work of other independent auditors is part of the basis for the primary auditor's opinion is not construed to be a qualification of the latter's opinion.

Audit Findings. If the auditor is of the opinion that the statements do not present fairly the financial condition and results of operation or they are inconsistent with the statements of the prior year, his opinion would be qualified or adverse in accordance with the materiality of the statement items involved. The amount of the disputed item and its effects upon the statements should be disclosed, usually in a middle paragraph, if it is reasonable to do so. Where the client is in a regulated industry and the accounting procedures are set by a regulatory agency or by statute, the client may not be able to use generally accepted accounting principles in the preparation of his statements. Even in this case, the independent auditor would have to note the departure from accepted principles, and again a qualified or an adverse opinion would

[25] The position of the Committee on Auditing Procedure when observation of inventory taking or confirmation of receivables has been omitted at the request of a client is rather different from the one it takes when such procedures are "impracticable or impossible." In the latter case, the Committee seems to feel (SAP No. 33, pp. 63–64) it is quite possible, in some cases, for the auditor to satisfy himself by other procedures. But if the restriction is imposed by the client, the Committee says (SAP No. 33, p. 65): "Generally, in such cases when inventories or receivables are material, the independent auditor should disclaim an opinion on the financial statements taken as a whole. Since the difficulty of obtaining satisfaction by other procedures would not seem to be made more or less by the source of the inability to perform the basic procedure, the Committee's position would seem to be based on moral or other similar grounds."

be required. If an adverse opinion is appropriate, the auditor may issue a piecemeal opinion on any data or supporting schedules that are presented in conformity with generally accepted accounting principles.

Future Developments. When future developments may have a material effect upon the financial position and the final outcome of these contingencies is dependent upon parties other than management, the auditor should qualify his opinion. The qualification may be a "subject to" phrase in the opinion paragraph calling attention to a note to the statements; this is the only type of case in which the "subject to" phrase should be used. In some cases the contingency may be so material as to require a disclaimer of an opinion.

Subsequent Events. The financial statements are historical in nature, yet events that occur subsequent to the date of the statements being examined may have a bearing upon the presentation and interpretation of the statements. Subsequent events may be grouped as to their effect on the financial statements as follows:

1. Those that have a direct effect on the current statements
2. Those that do not directly affect the current statements but should be disclosed
3. Those that have no effect on the statements and ordinarily do not require disclosure in financial statements of any period

The first kind of subsequent event affects the statements because the event furnishes information that would have been used in the statements if it had been available at the balance sheet date. An example is the collection of a receivable that had been written off. The second type of subsequent event is disclosed as required by the third reporting standard but has no dollar impact upon the statements because the event has its genesis in the new period, not the one under review. Examples of this type of event are the sales of a bond issue, material capital stock transactions, and casualty losses. These events are financial in nature and will directly affect the statements of subsequent periods. The third type of event is neither shown in the statements nor disclosed; it is not a "transaction" in the sense that transactions are the bases for accounting entries. The third type includes nonaccounting events such as management changes, legislation, and strikes. In rare cases the significance of the event is such that it should be disclosed; however, "disclosure of such conditions or events frequently creates doubt as to the reason therefor, and inferences drawn could be misleading as often as they are informative.[26]

General audit procedures such as follow-ups on receivables and payables, confirmations, cash cutoffs, and inventory cutoffs extend into the subsequent period. The auditor should also trace into the subsequent period the disposition of any item which was handled on the basis of incomplete information to ascertain if the original treatment is appropriate in light of any available additional data.

The Securities Act of 1933, in Section 11, specifies that the accountant, or other expert, has the burden of proof that he made a reasonable investigation and at the *time the registration statement becomes effective* has no reason to believe that any material facts were omitted. SAP No. 33 lists additional procedures which should be employed to disclose material subsequent events. Primarily the auditor should read the prospectus and other significant parts of the registration statement and the latest interim financial state-

[26] SAP No. 33, p. 77.

ments prepared by management; read the minutes of the stockholders' meetings, meetings of the board of directors, and meetings of any management committees; and obtain representations from responsible officers and directors as to material subsequent events.

SPECIAL REPORTS

Nature of Special Reports. A special report is one that is issued as the result of an examination other than an examination of financial statements that purport to show financial position and results of operations in conformity with generally accepted accounting principles. The wording of the standard short-form report, particularly that of the opinion paragraph, would not be appropriate for a special report. The following would ordinarily require that the auditor's report be "special" in the sense described below:

1. Statements prepared on a basis of accounting other than the accrual basis
2. Statements of not-for-profit organizations that do not follow the principles of accounting that are generally accepted for business enterprises
3. Statements that relate to specific matters or portions of the financial statements
4. Reports that are placed on forms prescribed by government or other agencies in an attempt to secure uniformity

When the auditor's name is associated with financial statements, he must state the responsibility he is assuming for the statements. When financial statements purport to show something other than financial position and results of operation, the independent auditor may express his opinion as to whether they present fairly that which the statements purport to represent. In such cases the auditor's report must specify that the statements are not in conformity with generally accepted accounting principles.

Applicability of Auditing Standards. The general standards, the standards of fieldwork, and the third and fourth reporting standards are applicable to special reports. The second reporting standard, dealing with consistency, may be appropriate. If the statements purport to show financial position and results of operations, even though they have not been prepared in accordance with generally accepted accounting principles, reference to consistency with the prior year should be made. In other cases, where a similar special report has been prepared in the previous year, the independent auditor's report should refer to consistency in the method of presentation.

A report may be characterized as a "special report" because of the absence of use of generally accepted accounting principles. When generally accepted accounting principles are not applied, the first reporting standard requires that the auditor's report so indicate. The independent auditor's opinion should specify what the statements purport to represent and whether they fairly do so.

Cash Basis Statements. Cash basis or modified cash basis statements may present fairly the summary of cash transactions or modified cash transactions. The independent auditor may express an opinion as to the fairness of these statements, but disclosure should be made of the basis upon which the statements were prepared. Since generally accepted principles of accounting include the accrual basis, cash basis statements are not in accord therewith. The statements and the auditor's report should avoid use of the words "Financial Position," "Balance Sheet," "Results of Operations," and "Income Statement."

The basis used in preparing the statements, together with the nature of any omissions or deviations from accrual accounting, should be disclosed, preferably in the statements or footnotes. However, the independent auditor should recognize that disclosures do not "make sick statements well," a point well made in Special Reports:

> Footnotes will not make an otherwise unacceptable statement acceptable since they lay upon the reader the burden of making revisions and adjustments requiring technical skill, knowledge and an informed judgment not presumptively attributable to the user of financial statements.[27]

The Securities and Exchange Commission expressed the same point in Accounting Series Release No. 4 (1938), which held that informative disclosures were not an acceptable substitute for the use of generally accepted principles of accounting.

Unincorporated Entities. Generally accepted accounting principles have been enunciated for the corporate form of business. The form of business organization should be identified on the financial statements and in the auditor's report because of differences in disclosure problems. For example, the business assets of proprietorships and partnerships are generally available for personal debts. Since income taxes are levied upon the owner or owners, not upon the business, the amount of taxes applicable to business income would depend in part upon the outside incomes of the owner(s). Similarly, the so-called "salaries" of the partners or proprietor may be withdrawals or may be business expenses. The independent auditor should make certain that the manner of treatment of these salaries is disclosed within the financial statements.

In expressing an opinion upon the financial statements of an unincorporated business entity, the independent auditor should state whether in his opinion the statements present fairly that which they purport to represent. They should clearly indicate that the business entity is not a corporation. By these means the reader of the financial statements will be put on notice that misleading inferences could be drawn if he compares these statements with those of a corporation.

Not-for-Profit Organizations. Generally accepted accounting principles apply to profit-oriented organizations, and the accounting principles for not-for-profit organizations may differ in significant aspects. In some cases the independent auditor may believe that the accounting principles for the particular type of not-for-profit organization (such as hospitals or schools) have been defined and accepted, and he may refer to them in his report. In such cases the report may (preferably) refer to generally accepted principles of accounting and to financial position and results of operations. Where the accounting principles have not been well defined, there should be no reference to financial position and results of operations and the auditor must carefully define in his opinion what the statements purport to represent.

Reports on Portions of Statements. The independent auditor may render an opinion on less than the financial statements as a whole. The piecemeal opinion should be accompanied by an adverse opinion or a disclaimer of opin-

[27] Application of Statement on Auditing Procedure No. 28, *Special Reports*, AICPA, New York, 1960, p. 12.

ion of the financial statement as a whole. "The auditor should realize that the expression of a piecemeal opinion with respect to individual items included in a financial statement may require a more extensive examination of such items than would be required if he were expressing an opinion on the financial statements taken as a whole."[28] The piecemeal opinion should not overshadow the opinion on the statements as a whole, and the report should clearly specify either the included or excluded items.

Reference to generally accepted accounting principles may be appropriate in limited examinations, such as those of working-capital position or stockholders' equity. Where appropriate, the independent auditor's report should state whether the accounts have been maintained in accordance with generally accepted accounting principles. References to consistency would also be made where appropriate.

Negative Assurance. A statement such as "However, nothing came to our attention which would indicate that these amounts (statements) are not fairly presented (stated)"[29] is inappropriate when the scope of the auditor's examination has been restricted so that he has had to give a qualified opinion or disclaim an opinion. Such negative assurance is

> permissible in letters required by security underwriters in which the independent auditor reports on limited procedures followed with respect to unaudited financial statements or other financial data pertinent to a registration statement filed with the Securities and Exchange Commission. These letters usually state specifically that no audit has been made of such statements and data, and distribution of the letters is restricted to parties to the underwriting agreement.[30]

Similarly, if an auditor has made an examination of data constituting less than a set of financial statements purporting to show financial position and results of operations, he may give negative assurances provided he has used appropriate procedures and describes the scope of the examination in his report.

Prescribed Forms. If financial statements are prepared on or in accordance with a prescribed form, the statements may not be in accordance with generally accepted accounting principles. The prescribed opinion form may be unacceptable to the independent auditor if it calls for him to assume responsibilities that are not his function as independent auditor.

> Some forms can be made acceptable by interpolating additional captions or wording; others can be made acceptable only by complete revision. Whenever the printed forms call upon the independent auditor to make an assertion which he believes he is not justified in making, he has no alternative but to reword them or to submit his separate report. Such revised or separate reports are generally accepted by the authorities with which they are filed.[31]

PROFESSIONAL RESPONSIBILITIES

Responsibility to Clients. At law, the independent auditor has a responsibility to the client based upon the contract, written or oral. The liability is the same as in any other contractual arrangement, namely, that both parties fulfill the conditions of the contract. The independent auditor is responsible to the client for ordinary negligence. He is holding himself out as an expert and

[28] SAP No. 33, p. 62.
[29] SAP No. 33, p. 61.
[30] SAP No. 33, p. 61.
[31] SAP No. 33, p. 91.

must exercise due care in the performance of his engagement. As an expert, the independent auditor cannot claim ignorance as a defense; knowledge must not be pretended when in fact none exists. He must prove that he employed skills that would reasonably be applied by any other independent auditor.

Responsibility to Third Parties. At common law the independent auditor is responsible to third parties only for fraud. For fraud to be found, there must be proof of intent and deceit. When fraud is found, anyone who relied upon the independent auditor's work may recover damages sustained as a result of such reliance. Gross negligence has been held to be constructive fraud; consequently third parties may recover damages incurred when gross negligence on the part of the auditor is found. The auditor must prove that he complied with generally accepted auditing standards to support his work against a charge of fraud.

The Securities Act of 1933 and the Securities Exchange Act of 1934 imposed statutory liabilities upon the auditor. The acts provide for recoveries by third parties for mere negligence as well as acts of fraud. Purchasers of debt and equity shares may recover damages sustained by reliance upon the independent auditor's report. Under the acts, the burden of proof is upon the independent auditor.

Responsibility for Detection of Fraud. In making an examination of financial statements, the independent auditor is necessarily aware of the possibility that fraud may be present. Nonetheless, the typical examination is performed to enable the independent accountant to express an opinion on the fairness of the presentation of financial position and results of operations and is not designed primarily to uncover fraud, nor should it be relied upon to do so. Fundamental responsibility for prevention and detection of fraud rests upon the client's management and is discharged through the client's system of internal control. The auditor evaluates the internal control system, in accordance with the second standard of fieldwork, and from this evaluation derives a basis for the exercise of his judgment as to the nature and timing of the examination he must make.

> The subsequent discovery that fraud existed during the period covered by the independent auditor's examination does not of itself indicate negligence on his part. He is not an insurer or guarantor; if his examination was made with due professional skill and care in accordance with generally accepted auditing standards, he has fulfilled all of the obligations implicit in his undertaking.[32]

If the auditor during the course of his examination uncovers a situation that makes him suspect the existence of fraud, and if in his opinion the amounts involved could be so material as to affect the fairness of the financial statements, he should contact the appropriate representative of the client for a decision as to who is to pursue the investigation of the possible fraud. If he is able to satisfy himself by his own investigation or a review of that by the client, his opinion is not affected. If he is unable to satisfy himself, he would qualify his opinion or disclaim an opinion, whichever is appropriate.

The basis for the auditor's legal responsibility in fraud detection as well as in other areas is explained by the following:

> In all those employments where peculiar skill is requisite, if one offers his services, he is understood as holding himself out to the public as possessing the degree of skill

[32] SAP No. 33, p. 12.

commonly possessed by others in the same employment, and if his pretensions are unfounded, this commits a species of fraud upon every man who employs him in reliance on his public profession. But no man, whether skilled or unskilled, undertakes that the task he assumes shall be performed successfully, and without fault or error; he undertakes for good faith and integrity, but not for infallibility, and he is liable to his employer for negligence, bad faith or dishonesty, but not for losses consequent upon mere errors of judgment.[33]

If a fraud would have been uncovered if an auditor had made his examination in conformity with generally accepted auditing standards, and if he fails to uncover it, his client may recover damages in an amount equal to the loss from the fraud from the date the auditor should have uncovered the fraud. The amount of recovery is usually limited to the amount of the fee on the grounds that the client is no worse off than if he had not had an audit.

PROFESSIONAL QUALIFICATIONS

Professional Characteristics. The following seven essential characteristics of members of a profession, taken from the pioneering work of Abraham Flexner in the evaluation of medical schools, serve to set the bench marks for all professionals:[34]

1. They possess a body of specialized knowledge.
2. They undergo a recognized, formal educational process.
3. They conform to a standard of professional qualifications governing admission.
4. They maintain certain standards of conduct.
5. They have a recognized status.
6. The work they perform is endowed with a public interest.
7. They belong to an organization devoted to the advancement of the social obligations of the profession.

These professional characteristics are possessed by certified public accountants in public practice.

Personal Characteristics. The personal qualifications of the independent auditor are competence, responsibility, and a professional attitude. The independent auditor must be competent to practice; he is holding himself out as an expert in accounting and auditing and is so licensed by the various states. The independent auditor has demonstrated his competence by passing the Uniform CPA Examination and meeting the standards of education and experience required by his state. The independent auditor does not claim competence in areas foreign to accounting and auditing; for example, when observing the taking of a physical inventory, the independent auditor does not claim to be an appraiser or expert in materials. By the same token, the independent auditor is informed in general about matters of commercial law, but "he does not purport to act in the capacity of a lawyer and may appropriately rely upon the advice of attorneys in all matters of law."[35]

The independent auditor must have a sense of responsibility to maintain the requisite degree of integrity necessary to promote public confidence. The auditor is offering a service—his opinion as to the fairness of management's representations. Unless the public has confidence in the integrity

[33] Thomas M. Cooley, *Cooley on Torts*, 4th ed., revised by D. Avery Haggard, Chicago, P. Callaghan, 1932, vol. III, p. 335.

[34] John L. Carey (ed.), *The Accounting Profession: Where Is It Headed?* New York, AICPA, 1962, pp. 26–27.

[35] SAP No. 33, p. 10.

and independence of the auditor, his opinion would add little to the credibility of the financial statements. Involved in the sense of responsibility is the auditor's acceptance of the challenge to continue learning throughout his professional life. He has the responsibility to stay current with the developments in accounting, auditing, and the business world in order to fulfill his obligation to the client and to third parties. This sense of responsibility is essential to the profession as a whole, because the work of one member reflects upon the entire profession. It behooves each member of the profession to encourage the highest of standards from each and every practitioner.

The professional auditor has the responsibility to adhere to the spirit as well as the letter of the rules of ethical conduct and the auditing standards. His professional responsibility manifests itself in his attitude and approach to each engagement, without regard to its size. The professional attitude is one of honesty and freedom from bias. Without such an attitude the public would lose confidence in the independent audit and the profession. A professional attitude is demonstrated by, among other things, respect for the confidential nature of the work the independent auditor performs, consideration of the many and varied users of the financial statements upon which he is expressing an opinion, and working with other professionals constantly to improve the profession in the aggregate.

Basis for the Code of Professional Ethics. The introduction to the Code of Professional Ethics of the AICPA states the reasons for the necessity of a code of ethics and the objectives of the Code:

> The reliance of the public and the business community on sound financial reporting and advice on business affairs imposes on the accounting profession an obligation to maintain high standards of technical competence, morality and integrity. To this end, a member or associate of the American Institute of Certified Public Accountants shall at all times maintain independence of thought and action, hold the affairs of his clients in strict confidence, strive continuously to improve his professional skills, observe generally accepted auditing standards, promote sound and informative financial reporting, uphold the dignity and honor of the accounting profession and maintain high standards of personal conduct.

The Code of Professional Ethics. The profession of accounting is dynamic, still growing and developing; thus the code of ethics is revised as conditions warrant. The Code, as amended Mar. 4, 1965, is divided into five articles. Article 1, "Relations with Clients and Public," deals with independence, confidential relationships with the client, and contingent fees. Article 2, "Technical Standards," holds that the professional will express an opinion on financial statements only when he or a member of his firm has a basis for an opinion. If there is not a sufficient basis for the opinion, he will disclaim an opinion and state his reasons therefor. The professional accountant should disclose all material facts known to him. Included in Article 2 is the injunction to follow generally accepted auditing standards. Article 3, "Promotional Practices," covers such activities as advertising, solicitation, competitive bidding, and fee splitting. Article 4, "Operating Practices," is designed to control a number of practices both within and without the profession. For example, the professional accountant should not permit an employee to perform any services for the client that the professional himself is not competent to perform, and the professional accountant should not engage in any activity that is incompatible or inconsistent with the practice of public accountancy. The last article deals with the relations among professional accountants.

These rules and the numbered opinions of the AICPA Committee on Professional Ethics cover most aspects of the professional's activities. Their objective is to foster public confidence in the independent auditors as a group. Malfeasance or misfeasance on the part of a single member of the profession tends to cause loss of public confidence in the entire profession.

Independence Requirement. The purpose of the independent auditor's opinion is to add credibility to the statements prepared by management. The auditor must be, in fact, independent of management and without direct and indirect financial interest in the enterprise. Independence is the keystone of the profession of auditing. In 1947, the Council of the AICPA in an official statement held that:

> Independence is an attitude of mind, much deeper than the surface display of visible standards.

It added:

> In the field of auditing, the certified public accountant is under a responsibility peculiar to his profession, and that is to maintain strict independence of attitude and judgment in planning and conducting his examinations, and in expressing his opinion on financial statements . . . . It has become of great value to those who rely on financial statements of business enterprises that they be reviewed by persons skilled in accounting whose judgment is uncolored by any interest in the enterprise, and upon whom the obligation has been imposed to disclose all material facts. . . .[36]

Rule 1.01 of the Code of Professional Ethics of the AICPA explains independence in the following manner:

> Independence is not susceptible of precise definition, but is an expression of the professional integrity of the individual. A member or associate, before expressing his opinion on financial statements, has the responsibility of assessing his relationships with an enterprise to determine whether, in the circumstances, he might expect his opinion to be considered independent, objective and unbiased by one who had knowledge of all the facts.

The auditor is not independent if he has direct or material indirect financial interest in the client during the period of the engagement or if, during the engagement, or during the period of time covered by the statements, he was connected with the client as a promoter, underwriter, director, officer, or key employee. However, in Opinion No. 12 the Committee on Professional Ethics held that an auditor does not lose his independence in relation to a particular client when he renders management advisory services or tax services unless he actually makes management decisions. In Opinion No. 15, the Committee stated that when an auditor is not independent he should disclaim an opinion and specify the circumstances that destroyed his independence.

ORGANIZATION OF PUBLIC ACCOUNTING FIRMS

Public accounting firms do not use uniform staff titles, but generally the professional staff is divided into four categories such as partner, manager, senior accountant, and staff accountant. In addition, a firm will also employ typists, clerks, secretaries, etc.

The partners of a firm have an ownership interest and have the authority to sign the firm's name to reports. They maintain contact with their clients and are responsible for contracts with new clients. Partners frequently

[36] Opinion No. 12 of the Committee on Professional Ethics.

specialize in tax, SEC practice, research, or other fields and supervise and render advisory services in their field of specialization. A managing or senior partner is elected by the partners and given the authority and responsibility for administering the operating policy of the firm and speaking for the firm on accounting and auditing matters.

Managers, or supervisors, work directly under a partner and have the responsibility for supervising the development of the audit program and supervising the fieldwork for each client. The senior accountant has the direct responsibility for planning and conducting the audit and for writing the audit report. He assigns staff accountants to particular tasks and reviews their working papers. During the audit the senior should be alert to audit findings which could alter the initial audit program. The beginning staff accountant usually performs tasks that are routine in nature. As he gains experience and judgment, the manager will curtail supervision of his work and assign him more challenging tasks.

SEC AND STOCK EXCHANGES

Requirements of the stock exchanges and of the acts administered by the Securities and Exchange Commission are significant influences upon current practices in public accounting.

Stock Exchanges. Since July 1, 1933, the New York Stock Exchange has required listed companies to provide audited financial statements to the Exchange with listing applications and to stockholders each year thereafter. The company also agrees to notify the Exchange immediately upon a change of auditors. Exemptions from the requirements are granted to railroads, banks, and insurance companies. To be listed on the New York Stock Exchange a company must be of national importance, have tangible assets of at least $10,000,000, income of $1,200,000, and a total market value of its common stock of $12,000,000. The completed application for listing is available to members and to the public upon request.

The American Stock Exchange deals in two classes of stock. Those that were listed prior to enactment of the Securities Exchange Act of 1934 enjoy all the privileges but do not have to submit financial reports. Securities listed subsequent to the 1934 act must comply with its provisions. To qualify for listing under the 1962 amendments of the American Exchange, a company must have tangible assets of $1,000,000, net earnings of $150,000 in the last year with a 3-year average of $100,000, and publicly held shares valued at $1,250,000. Current requirements of the American Stock Exchange as to submission of financial statements closely follow those of the New York Exchange.

The Commission. The Securities and Exchange Commission administers the following six acts:

Securities Act of 1933
Securities Exchange Act of 1934
Public Utility Holding Company Act of 1935
Trust Indenture Act of 1939
Investment Company Act of 1940
Investment Advisers Act of 1940

Of these, the public accountant most frequently comes into contact with the 1933 and 1934 acts; consequently these two will be discussed briefly in the following pages. Any accountant involved with these acts or desiring information on them may obtain copies from the Government Printing Office for a nominal price. By request any interested person may have his name put on the mailing list for the current SEC releases under any of the acts.

Securities Act of 1933. The 1933 act requires registration of any security issue (debt or equity) of over $300,000 which is publicly offered for sale in interstate commerce. All nonpublic offerings are exempt from the registration requirement. Definition of "nonpublic" is a thorny legal problem, one on which an accountant should seek the advice of an attorney. Offerings by any governmental unit within the United States or its territories are exempt as are common carriers under the jurisdiction of the Interstate Commerce Act. Other exemptions to the registration requirement are detailed in Section 3 of the act and in the General Rules.

A registration statement is required for all nonexempt public offerings. To complete a registration statement, the company must furnish the Commission with, among other things, a balance sheet and profit and loss statements certified by an independent public accountant. The act requires a prospectus to be furnished to prospective security buyers. The prospectus is to include the financial statements, with the independent opinion, and most of the information on the registration statement. In accordance with the 1933 act, the Commission does not pass on the merits of the issue but on the adequacy of disclosures.

Section 11 of the 1933 act provides for civil liabilities as follows:

> In case any part of the registration statement . . . contained an untrue statement of a material fact or omitted to state a material fact required to be stated therein or necessary to make the statements therein not misleading, any person acquiring such security . . . may . . . sue

any signers of the statement, directors, accountant, other expert, or underwriters.

Securities Exchange Act of 1934. The 1934 act created the Securities and Exchange Commission to administer that act and the 1933 act. The 1934 act sets requirements for trading activities. The act, as amended to Aug. 20, 1964, specifies that all issuers of securities (unless specifically exempt) engaged in or whose business affects interstate commerce, with total assets over $1,000,000 and equity securities held by 500 or more persons, are required to register with the Commission. The act also provides for the registration of national security exchanges and brokers and dealers trading in over-the-counter securities markets.

Section 2 of the act states its broad purpose:

> For the reasons hereinafter enumerated, transactions in securities as commonly conducted upon securities exchanges and over-the-counter markets are affected with a national public interest which makes it necessary to provide for regulation and control of such transactions and of practices and matters related thereto, including transactions by officers, directors, and principal security holders, to require appropriate reports, and to impose requirements necessary to make such regulation and control reasonably complete and effective, in order to protect interstate commerce, the national credit, the Federal taxing power, to protect and make more effective the national banking system and Federal Reserve System, and to insure the maintenance of fair and honest markets.

Applications for listing on any national exchange shall contain information as to organization of the business, financial interests of officers and directors, etc., and financial statements. The financial statements required are balance sheets and income statements for not more than the three preceding fiscal years, certified by an independent public accountant if so required by the rules of the Commission, and any other financial statements the Commission deems necessary or appropriate to protect investors. All companies required to register with the SEC must file certified annual financial reports and quarterly (unaudited) reports as specified in Section 13. The Commission may prescribe the forms, items or details shown, and the methods to be followed.

Section 18 provides for liability for misleading statements. It specifies that damages may be recovered when securities were purchased or sold at a price that is affected by such statements. Liability extends to "any person who shall make or cause to be made any statement in any application, report, or document" filed under the act which was at the time and under the circumstances "false and misleading with respect to any material fact."

Regulation S-X and Accounting Series Releases. Regulation S-X was adopted in 1940. It and the Accounting Series Release state the requirements of the independent accountant and the form and content of financial statements required to be filed under the 1933 act, the 1934 act, the Public Utility Holding Company Act of 1935, and the Investment Company Act of 1940.

Article 2 of Regulation S-X deals with certification. The Commission requires that the public accountant or the certified public accountant be entitled to practice under the laws of his place of residence. The public accountant or CPA must be in fact independent. To be independent the accountant must not have any direct or material indirect financial interest in the company. "The Commission will give appropriate consideration to all relevant circumstances, including evidence bearing on all relationships between the accountant and that person or any affiliate thereof, and will not confine itself to the relationships existing in connection with the filing of reports with the Commission." Accounting Series Release No. 2, released May 6, 1937, expressed the opinion of the Commission that a firm was not independent of a company when a partner in the firm had an investment in the company of more than 1 percent of the partner's personal fortune. In Accounting Series Release No. 22 (1941) the opinion was expressed that an auditor lost his independence when he entered into an agreement with the client the purpose of which was to indemnify the auditor against all losses and liabilities arising out of his certification, other than his own willful acts. Following this release, there were several on the definition of independence. Accounting Series Releases No. 47 (1944) and No. 81 (1958) are summaries of past releases and representative administrative rulings on independence of accountants. All accountants proposing to practice before the Commission must be familiar with the types of relations that have been found to destroy independence. Article 2 of Regulation S-X specifies the requirements for the accountants' certificate:

> The accountant's certificate (i) shall state whether the audit was made in accordance with generally accepted auditing standards; and (ii) shall designate any auditing procedures generally recognized as normal, or deemed necessary by the accountant under the circumstances of the particular case, which have been omitted, and the reasons for their omission. . . .
>
> The accountant's certificate shall state clearly: (i) the opinion of the accountant in respect of the financial statements covered by the certificate and the accounting principles and practices reflected therein; (ii) the opinion of the accountant as to any material changes in accounting principles or practices or method of applying the accounting principles or practices, or adjustments of the accounts, required to be set forth . . . ; and (iii) the nature of, and the opinion of the accountant as to, any material differences

between the accounting principles and practices reflected in the financial statements and those reflected in the accounts after the entry of adjustments for the period under review. . . .

Any matters to which the accountant takes exception shall be clearly identified, the exception thereto specifically and clearly stated, and, to the extent practicable, the effect of each such exception of the related financial statements given.

There have been 116 Accounting Series Releases to date. The topics covered include many accounting and auditing matters: reporting of federal income taxes, tax allocation, adjustments in a quasi-reorganization, presentation of rents and leases, treasury stock accounting, etc.; advantages of the natural business year in the staffing of public accounting firms; rounding to even dollars; audit requirements; and the auditor's independence.

BIBLIOGRAPHY

Accounting Principles Board Opinions and Statements to date, AICPA.

Accounting Research and Terminology Bulletins, final ed. (Committees on Accounting Procedure and Accounting Terminology), AICPA, New York, 1961.

Accounting Series Release No. 2, 1937; No. 4, 1938; No. 22, 1941; No. 47, 1944; No. 62, 1947; No. 81, 1958; and No. 90, Securities and Exchange Commission, 4.706, 721, 1962.

A Description of the Professional Practice of Certified Public Accountants, AICPA (Council), New York, 1966.

Disclosure of Departures from Opinions of Accounting Principles Board, Special Bulletin, AICPA (Council), New York, 1964.

Securities Act, 1933, Securities and Exchange Commission.

Securities Exchange Act, 1934, Securities and Exchange Commission.

Statement on Auditing Procedure No. 38, *Unaudited Financial Statements,* AICPA (Committee on Auditing Procedure), New York, 1967.

Statements on Auditing Procedure No. 33, *Auditing Standards and Procedures,* AICPA (Committee on Auditing Procedure), New York, 1963.

Carey, John L. (ed.): *The Accounting Profession: Where Is It Headed?* New York, AICPA, 1962.

Lenhart, Norman J., and Philip L. Defliese: *Montgomery's Auditing,* 8th ed., New York, The Ronald Press Company, 1957.

Davidson, Sidney: "Accounting and Financial Reporting in the Seventies," *The Journal of Accountancy,* December, 1969.

Norgaard, Corine T.: "The Professional Accountant's View of Operational Auditing," *The Journal of Accountancy,* December, 1969.

Chan, Stephen: "Reliance on the Reports of Other Auditors," *The New York Certified Public Accountant,* February, 1970.

Gustafson, George A.: "Status of Accounting Research Study Nos. 1 and 3," *The Journal of Accountancy,* March, 1970.

Chapter 7

Internal Auditing

THOMAS BURGESS, JR.

Auditor, Mutual of New York

CONCEPTS OF INTERNAL AUDITING

Introduction. The continued expansion of modern business has added to the problems of an already heavily burdened company management in maintaining control over widespread operations. The increase in regular activities, the trend toward decentralization and greater geographical dispersion have in themselves posed serious challenges to management control. When to these are added a new dimension of problems involved with mergers and acquisitions, diversification of products, computers and other technologies, and controlling and reporting for conglomerates, the degree of complexity calls for outstanding performance by all levels of management.

In the past it was possible for management to maintain control through constant personal contact with company operations, with other levels of management, and even with individual employees. The new problems have made it necessary to delegate responsibility and authority to many levels of supervision. However, management's responsibility does not end with this allocation of duties. *Management cannot delegate its overall responsibility or its accountability.* With such wide delegation of duties management had to turn to the control specialists, the internal auditors, for assistance in maintaining surveillance over the management control network. A systematic program of review and appraisal became necessary to determine that delegated responsibilities were being discharged and that established policies and procedures were being carried out as expected. Furthermore, if there could be a regular review by a qualified staff to determine that the system of control was adequate and through constant tests to determine that the system was operating effectively, then the integrity of the foundation for all control and reporting could be assured. Without such an assurance management could not rely on the financial statements as a guide in making many daily decisions. Without such an assurance the public accountant could not rely on the internal control system without increasing greatly the number of his tests and the extent of his auditing procedures. The special concern of the public accountant is expressed in the American Institute of Certified Public Accountants (AICPA) Statements on Auditing Procedure No. 33, as follows:

> The system of internal control must be under continuing supervision to determine whether (1) prescribed policies are being carried out, (2) changes in operating conditions have not made the procedures cumbersome, obsolete or inadequate, and (3) ef-

fective corrective measures are taken promptly where breakdowns in the system appear.

The statement further emphasizes the role of internal auditing in the control structure in the following words:

An internal audit staff is a strong factor in a system of internal control, since it provides a means of surveying the effectiveness of adherence to the prescribed procedures.

Responsibilities of Internal Auditing. The Institute of Internal Auditors, the professional society of internal auditors, has officially set forth the parameters of internal auditing in its Statement of Responsibilities of the Internal Auditor. The present edition is the second such release and was designed to emphasize the development of the profession and the continually broadening responsibilities that have been accorded to the function. A new statement giving effect to the current and probable future responsibilities is now under active consideration. The responsibilities in the current edition are classified as follows: (1) nature of internal auditing, (2) objective and scope of internal auditing, (3) authority and responsibility, and (4) independence.

Nature of internal auditing. Under this caption is presented the official definition of internal auditing as follows:

Internal auditing is an independent appraisal activity within an organization for the review of accounting, financial and other operations as a basis for service to management. It is a managerial control, which functions by measuring and evaluating the effectiveness of other controls.

The National Industrial Conference Board in *Internal Auditing*, Business Policy Study No. 111, 1963, gives a more detailed definition, which also emphasizes the management control aspects of internal auditing as follows:

Internal auditing is a series of processes and techniques through which an organization's own employees ascertain for the management, by means of first-hand, on-the-job observation, whether: established management controls are adequate and are effectively maintained; records and reports—financial, accounting and otherwise—reflect actual operations and results accurately and promptly; and each division, department or other unit is carrying out the plans, policies and procedures for which it is responsible.

The widening gap between management and action has made it necessary to develop a series of controls by means of which the business may be administered efficiently. The internal auditor perfects and completes each of these activities by providing on-the-scene appraisal of each form of control. There is no known substitute for this activity.[1]

Further discussion of the definition of internal auditing is given in Brink and Cashin, *Internal Auditing*, as follows:

Internal auditing thus emerges as a special segment of the broad field of accounting, utilizing the basic techniques and method of auditing. The fact that the public accountant and the internal auditor use many of the same techniques often leads to a mistaken assumption that there is little difference in the work or in ultimate objectives. The internal auditor, like any auditor, is concerned with the investigation of the validity of representations, but in his case the representations with which he is concerned cover a much wider range and have to do with many matters where the relationship to the accounts is often somewhat remote. In addition, the internal

[1] Francis J. Walsh, Jr., *Internal Auditing*, Business Policy Study No. 111, New York, National Industrial Conference Board, Inc., 1963.

auditor, being a company man, has a more vital interest in all types of company operations and is quite naturally more deeply interested in helping to make those operations as profitable as possible. Thus, to a greater extent, management services comes to influence his thinking and general approach.[2]

Objective and scope. The general approach and range of internal auditing are outlined in the Statement as follows:

The over-all objective of internal auditing is to assist all members of management in the effective discharge of their responsibilities, by furnishing them with objective analyses, appraisals, recommendations and pertinent comments concerning the activities reviewed. The internal auditor, therefore, should be concerned with any phase of business activity wherein he can be of service to management. The attainment of this over-all objective of service to management should involve such activities as:

Reviewing and appraising the soundness, adequacy and application of accounting, financial and operating controls.

Ascertaining the extent of compliance with established policies, plans and procedures.

Ascertaining the extent to which the company assets are accounted for, and safeguarded from, losses of all kinds.

Ascertaining the reliability of accounting and other data developed within the organization.

Appraising the quality of performance in carrying out assigned responsibilities.

Authority and responsibility. The nature of the function is spelled out as between staff and line responsibilities. It is pointed out that the internal auditor's review does not relieve those in executive or operating capacities of any assigned responsibilities. The Statement reads as follows:

Internal auditing is a staff function rather than a line function. Therefore, the internal auditor does not exercise direct authority over other persons in the organization, whose work he reviews. The internal auditor should be free to review and appraise policies, plans, procedures, and records; but his review and appraisal does not in any way relieve other persons in the organization of the responsibilities assigned to them.

Independence. In order to assure the degree of independence necessary for effective internal auditing, the Statement specifies that the department head should report to a high-echelon executive. Only this way can he be assured of an adequate scope of responsibility and the effective follow-up of recommendations. It is interesting to note that the Statement specifically prohibits the internal auditor from developing and installing procedures, from preparing records, and from engaging in any other activity that he would normally be expected to review and appraise. This view is somewhat at variance with that of the AICPA regarding the acceptability of the CPA's performing such work in connection with management services.

Independence is essential to the effectiveness of the internal auditing program. This independence has two major aspects:

1. The organizational status of the internal auditor and the support accorded to him by management are major determinants of the range and value of the services which management will obtain from the internal auditing function. The head of the internal auditing department, therefore, should be responsible to an officer of sufficient rank in the organization as will assure a broad scope of activities, and adequate consideration of and effective action on the findings or recommendations made by him.

[2] Victor Z. Brink and James A. Cashin, *Internal Auditing*, New York, The Ronald Press Company, 1958.

2. Since complete objectivity is essential to the audit function, internal auditors should not develop and install procedures, prepare records, or engage in any other activity which they normally would be expected to review and appraise.

Changing Role of the Internal Auditor. The modern concept of internal auditing, as indicated in the definitions, has moved some distance from the traditional concepts which limited the function not too many years ago. The extent of this move is well documented in the Survey of Internal Auditing, 1968.[3] The report points out that "internal auditing has not only retained its identity position since 1957, but has progressed in becoming an integral part of the management team." Since the previous survey in 1957, internal auditors have extended the scope of their work further into operational areas. In addition, they have gained increased stature in their companies and greater recognition by management. For those interested in further details, see the comparison between 1968 and 1957 for each of the questions included in the questionnaire, more than 50 in all. The conclusions of the 1968 survey are shown below:

Scope

1. More internal auditors are extending the scope of their work into nonfinancial (operational) audit areas.
2. The majority of internal auditors stated that they have unlimited scope of audit in their assignments.
3. Most companies utilize the internal audit staff to appraise systems rather than to develop and install the systems.
4. Many companies are also using internal auditing to appraise operating, as well as financial, systems.
5. Two-thirds of the respondents stated that the development of internal auditing in their companies has resulted in significant changes in their public accountants' audit programs.

Organization

1. About 30 percent of the respondents stated that their internal audit function was established since 1957.
2. More internal auditors are reporting to higher levels of management in their companies.
3. More companies emphasize formal training programs for continued education of the internal audit staff.

Methods and Reporting

1. Most internal audit staffs design flexible audit programs for each assignment with revisions made on the basis of need in individual audits.
2. About 60 percent of the respondents stated that they apply statistical sampling techniques wherever possible.
3. The great majority of internal auditors meet with the audited organization and discuss the findings and recommendations prior to release of the report, with the audit report indicating the corrective action to be taken.
4. Summaries of the audit findings are included with the report to highlight for management major items in the report.
5. Over 75 percent of the audit staffs include an overall opinion in their audit reports.
6. More audit staffs are regularly routing copies of audit reports to senior administrative executives.
7. About 70 percent of the respondents include audits of the EDP function in their audit programs.

[3] Survey of Internal Auditing, 1968, Research Committee Report No. 15, The Institute of Internal Auditors, New York, 1969.

Problems and Future Plans

1. The major problem of internal audit managers is obtaining qualified personnel.
2. The majority of the internal auditors have developed plans for changes in their internal audit function.
3. About 70 percent of the respondents stated that they were receiving more recognition from management.

Now internal auditors spend a greater part of their time in appraising operations in departments which are not under financial officers. For example, purchasing, traffic, advertising, production, etc., are now reviewed regularly by most auditors. This was especially significant in the 1968 Survey, page 5, which reported a number of operational audit activities that were not indicated in the 1957 Survey. These were inventory planning and control, insurance programs, electronic data processing, construction projects, management information systems, and organizational control.

Code of Ethics. The Institute of Internal Auditors has issued a Code of Ethics for the guidance of members of the Institute. The code applies to the various branches of internal auditing practice, those in government practice and in nonprofit organizations as well as those in private industry. It is pointed out that judgment is required in the application of the provisions of the code and that the auditor has a responsibility to conduct himself so that his good faith and integrity are not open to question.

CODE OF ETHICS

INTRODUCTION:

Recognizing that ethics are an important consideration in the practice of internal auditing and that the moral principles followed by members of THE INSTITUTE OF INTERNAL AUDITORS, INC. should be formalized, the Board of Directors at its regular meeting in New Orleans on December 13, 1968, received and adopted the following resolution:

Whereas, the members of THE INSTITUTE OF INTERNAL AUDITORS, INC. represent the profession of internal auditing; and

Whereas, managements rely on the profession of internal auditing to assist in the fulfillment of their management stewardship; and

Whereas, said members must maintain high standards of conduct, honor and character in order to carry on proper and meaningful internal auditing practice;

Therefore be it resolved that a Code of Ethics be now set forth outlining the standards of professional behavior for the guidance of each member of THE INSTITUTE OF INTERNAL AUDITORS, INC.

In accordance with this resolution, the Board of Directors further approved of the principles set forth.

INTERPRETATION OF PRINCIPLES:

The provisions of this Code of Ethics cover basic principles in the various disciplines of internal auditing practice. A member shall realize that individual judgment is required in the application of these principles. He has a responsibility to conduct himself so that his good faith and integrity should not be open to question. While having due regard for the limit of his technical skills, he will promote the highest possible internal auditing standards to the end of advancing the interest of his company or organization.

ARTICLES:

I. A member shall have an obligation to exercise honesty, objectivity and diligence in the performance of his duties and responsibilities.

II. A member, in holding the trust of his employer, shall exhibit loyalty in all matters pertaining to the affairs of the employer or to whomever he may be rendering a service. However, a member shall not knowingly be a party to any illegal or improper activity.

III. A member shall refrain from entering into any activity which may be in conflict with the interest of his employer or which would prejudice his ability to carry out objectively his duties and responsibilities.

IV. A member shall not accept a fee or a gift from an employee, a client, a customer or a business associate of his employer without the knowledge and consent of his senior management.

V. A member shall be prudent in the use of information acquired in the course of his duties. He shall not use confidential information for any personal gain or in a manner which would be detrimental to the welfare of his employer.

VI. A member, in expressing an opinion, shall use all reasonable care to obtain sufficient factual evidence to warrant such expression. In his reporting, a member shall reveal such material facts known to him which, if not revealed, could either distort the report of the results of operations under review or conceal unlawful practice.

VII. A member shall continually strive for improvement in the proficiency and effectiveness of his service.

VIII. A member shall abide by the Bylaws and uphold the objectives of THE INSTITUTE OF INTERNAL AUDITORS, INC. In the practice of his profession, he shall be ever mindful of his obligation to maintain the high standard of competence, morality and dignity which THE INSTITUTE OF INTERNAL AUDITORS, INC. and its members have established.

The Public Accountant's Role in Internal Auditing. One of the final and most important of the links in the chain of management control is that provided by the public accountant. According to the second standard of fieldwork, the public accountant is required to review the system of internal control in the company.

> There is to be a proper study and evaluation of the existing internal control as a basis for reliance thereon and for the determination of the resultant extent of the tests to which auditing procedures are to be restricted.[4]

The public accountant in his study and evaluation of internal control is primarily interested in two broad aspects, (1) determining that the established system is adequate and (2) determining that the system is operating as planned. The degree of reliability of the system of internal control will directly determine the extent of the auditing procedures. The public accountant may curtail some of his auditing procedures if he feels assured that errors and irregularities will be discovered with reasonable promptness. The work of the internal auditor should not be considered a substitute for that of the public accountant. The latter should survey the activities of the internal audit staff to determine its effectiveness and to consider this in determining the extent of his own tests.

ELEMENTS OF THE WORK

In the previous paragraphs have been outlined the philosophy and the responsibilities of the internal auditor. We will now review the fundamentals of his work, that is, just how he goes about doing his assigned job and what activities are covered. Other than for special assignments, the elements of internal auditing may be grouped under (1) compliance, (2) verification, and (3) evaluation.

[4] Statements on Auditing Procedure No. 33, *Auditing Standards and Procedures*, AICPA (Committee on Auditing Procedure), New York, 1963.

Compliance. The term "compliance" refers to the extent to which policies, rules, procedures, good business practices, generally accepted accounting principles, laws, governmental regulations, and even sound common sense are followed. It is an important part of his responsibilities to determine the degree of compliance in each area. For our purposes we may classify compliance activities of the internal auditor into (1) generally accepted accounting principles, (2) company policies and procedures, and (3) governmental requirements.

Generally accepted accounting principles. The internal auditor is expected to have a thorough knowledge of generally accepted accounting principles and to determine that such principles govern the accounting system. If he encounters violations of these principles, he would be expected to bring such violations to the attention of responsible parties immediately. The public accountant in his report states that the financial statements are in conformity "with generally accepted accounting principles." Since the public accountant cannot review every transaction, he relies on the system of internal control, of which internal auditing is a part, to assure him that generally accepted accounting principles have been applied in all operations throughout the year.

Company policies and procedures. Apart from the accounting principles that apply to all companies, there are certain policies and procedures that are peculiar to the particular company. In order for a company to achieve its desired goals, some general plan of action must be determined, and the policies and procedures necessary to reach the goals are formulated and made known to all levels of management. Where there are only a few levels of management, this is no great problem, but in a medium or large company this is an extremely difficult problem. There will be a large number of policies, some of which will not be known to all levels. Furthermore these policies and procedures will not be understood in every instance. Then there is the possibility of error, carelessness, or deliberate misrepresentation. The internal auditor performs an important service in reviewing all activities and ascertaining that all such policies and procedures have been received, that they are understood, and that they are being observed.

Governmental requirements. There are such a wide variety of governmental requirements in business today that constant attention must be exerted to avoid violations. In addition to the federal requirements for income tax, social security, security and exchange regulations, and regulatory requirements, there are many state and local requirements. In addition, many laws and regulations are issued or revised every day. Through this maze of requirements the internal auditor must find his way and make sure that the company is complying with all of them.

Verification. One of the important responsibilities of the internal auditor is the verification function. The size of modern enterprise has rendered the detailed verification by outside auditors impractical and uneconomical, and there has been a recognition on the part of both the public accountant and management that particular phases of the verification can be more advantageously accomplished by the organization's own internal auditing units. This is especially true because of the specialized knowledge that the internal auditor possesses of operations in the particular business. Also management requires verification of data on a continuous basis throughout the accounting period. That is, management must receive a more continuous assurance of the validity of current reports than is possible through the annual examination of the outside auditor. Generally, verification will include (1) records, (2) reports, and (3) assets and liabilities.

Records. In order to ascertain the reliability of the financial and operating reports prepared throughout the company, it is necessary that some unit undertake to examine the underlying records. For example, there is no assurance that a cost report prepared by a manufacturing location and forwarded to headquarters is correct until the underlying records are reviewed. Thus the internal auditor visits the location, evaluates the cost system and cost records, and determines that the results are proper and that the cost report agrees with the records.

Reports. The internal auditor will review all reports to determine their general reliability. In many cases the auditor has found that the presentation, arrangement, or grouping of data in reports has tended to obscure significant information. Often various external reports such as those for the SEC and other governmental agencies which are subject to specific requirements are either prepared or reviewed by the internal auditor. In addition, for a company which prepares consolidated financial statements, it is essential that the many separate underlying statements be uniform so that the consolidated total for each item is proper. The internal auditor will also determine that all statements are prepared in accordance with some uniform chart of accounts or other means of aiding proper account classifications.

Assets and liabilities. In addition to records and reports the internal auditor must verify that the assets and liabilities are properly stated. This verification function may be carried out at a decentralized location, at headquarters, or elsewhere. The verification of assets and liabilities is especially important in today's decentralized operations. Management must know whether an adequate return is being received on the investment. If not, a possible alternative use of funds may be decided. The internal auditor will determine that assets are being utilized efficiently and that they are being properly accounted for.

Evaluation. Evaluation is one of the most important responsibilities of the internal auditor. In connection with the verification function there are usually bases of comparison. For example, in reconciling the bank account there is the book amount to compare with the bank figure. In connection with evaluation the right result is not as clear. For example, in determining whether a particular policy is being observed, there may be a wide difference of opinion as to whether the practice conforms to the policy. In fact the practice in effect may be superior to that required by the policy. Evaluation requires the exercise of a very high degree of judgment.

Evaluation is especially important with respect to internal control. The internal auditor must continually review the system of internal control and make sure (1) that the system is adequate and (2) that it is operating as management expects. The manner in which the internal auditor carries out his evaluation of the system of internal control is also extremely important to the public accountant. The second standard of fieldwork applicable to CPAs, quoted previously, requires the public accountant to study and evaluate the internal control as a basis for restricting his audit procedures. Therefore, the public accountant will feel secure in restricting his program if he knows that the internal auditor is properly testing and evaluating the system of internal control.

PREVENTION AND DETECTION OF FRAUD

Prevention of Fraud. The objective of the internal auditor is to have the controls so effective that irregularities will not go undetected for a prolonged period. Normally, neither a supervisor nor the internal auditor is in a position to discover fraud at its inception, but they must always be alert to the possibilities. Since collusion of two or more employees might obscure fraud for a time, it is the internal auditor's responsibility to see that the internal controls are such that deviations in prescribed procedures or records will bring fraud to the attention of alert supervisors promptly.

Detection of Fraud. Any system, regardless of its fundamental soundness, may deteriorate if not reviewed periodically. Laxity becomes contagious and, if permitted to spread, may soon render any means of control useless. The internal auditor should emphasize to supervisory personnel their responsibility for maintaining proper controls and acting emphatically on abnormal conditions. Violations of controls should be called to the attention of the auditing department. In all cases of fraud, the internal auditor should control and guide the investigation and should cooperate with the legal, financial, and bonding company representatives. He may or may not do the actual investigation, depending upon the particular circumstances, but he should be responsible for proper coordination. At the conclusion of each investigation, a full report should be rendered including a review of the failures of the controls and recommendations for any appropriate improvements in controls and procedures.

The Problem of Errors. The primary responsibility of the internal auditor is to ascertain that an adequate system of internal control is established and maintained. The system must be adequate to disclose errors as well as defalcations. The auditor is expected to discover weaknesses in control and to suggest proper corrective action so as to limit the possibility of errors. There are many types of errors, but most can be grouped into those which are (1) errors of omission or (2) errors of commission.

1. Errors of omission. These are the unintentional human errors, which are by far the most numerous and costly in industry and undoubtedly contribute most to expense or the lack of profit. While very real, a great many of them are unknown and will never be found.
2. Errors of commission. These are intentional, the defalcations and the falsification of records. While often spectacular in nature and not to be condoned, they usually represent a smaller cost of doing business in comparison with the more numerous unintentional human errors.

The internal auditor must be alert to the pattern of errors. While a particular error standing alone may not be significant, it may actually be one of a pattern of many errors which indicate a greater underlying problem, such as poor training, poor supervision, or poor selection, which needs immediate correction.

DEVELOPMENT TO PRESENT TIME

Early View. In the early days most businesses were run by one man. In a one-man operation there is less of an internal control problem because the proprietor is constantly in contact with all phases of the operation. He makes sales, does the buying, signs all checks, and pays all taxes. In effect he is his own internal auditor. As the organization grows, additional people are required to assist with management, and the proprietor or operating head of necessity becomes further and further removed from firsthand knowledge of the detailed operations. At this point it is advisable that he have a continuing appraisal of the efficiency of the work as well as the honesty of his employees.

Internal auditing was first established as a separate function shortly after the turn of the century.

Initially, it was primarily concerned with protection against payroll fraud and loss of cash and other assets. Subsequently, its scope was extended to include the verification of practically all financial transactions. Today, it is a managerial control concerned not only with the protection and verification of the accuracy of recorded data but also with the review of policies and procedures covering all types of business activities. The ultimate objective is the making of constructive suggestions for increased profits (or reduced costs).

Present Approach. The advance in mechanization to full electronic data processing is bringing about a substantial change in emphasis in the work of the internal auditor. Emphasis on the detailed verification procedures will tend to decrease, and the testing, analytical and internal control procedures will assume greater importance. The auditor must keep an open mind to the present and to the future. He will have to develop new auditing concepts and learn how to make the computer work for him in his auditing procedures.

Impact of the Institute of Internal Auditors. The professional organization of internal auditors has had a fundamental impact on the growth and development of internal auditing in this country. Internal auditing as we know it is a new field. The first comprehensive book in this field was written in 1941 by Dr. Victor Z. Brink, who was on the faculty of Columbia University. At about the same period a number of internal auditors had been meeting in New York, and in the same year the Institute of Internal Auditors was founded, with 24 charter members.

This was quite unlike the start of public accounting here when, around the 1890s and the early 1900s, many British public accountants came to this country to establish the profession. They transplanted a profession that was well developed in Great Britain at that time. The function of performing auditing services for a company with the emphasis on the review and appraisal of internal control has no counterpart anywhere in the world. It is interesting to note that whereas the public accounting profession was brought to this country from overseas, internal auditing has been sent back overseas from this country. The Institute of Internal Auditors has chapters in practically every country of the world.

Types of Auditing. Very often internal auditing activities have been classified into (1) financial and (2) operational. However, the latter term is somewhat confusing, since it may have two meanings. At first it was generally understood to mean an audit of operations, that is, production, personnel, etc., which were not financial areas. Since the gauge for appraising these functions could not be based on dollars, somewhat different techniques were called for. They had to be matched against company policy, good business judgment, and common sense.

However, many progressive companies had been using the same approach for years, not only in audits relating to operations but in many so-called financial areas as well. For example, in what is known as a financial audit the cash receipts and disbursements may be reviewed and the bank account reconciled. However, from an operational viewpoint, is the company receiving a maximum return on the cash in the banks? If the turnover of cash at a location is once a month and the account can be reimbursed in 2 days, obviously there is idle cash in the account which is not earning interest.

The same holds true for payroll accounts. With wire service the reimbursement can be made the same day; therefore, there is little need to maintain a full payroll balance in the payroll account. In many cases this general approach has been described as "management auditing," that is, doing what the manager or owner would do if he were making the audit.

For our purposes, therefore, internal auditing will be discussed under three headings, although operational auditing and management auditing overlap in many respects.

Financial auditing. This activity resembles the work of the public accountant in many areas. This is particularly true where the internal auditor may assist in testing the physical inventory or confirming accounts receivable for the public accountant. However, generally the scope and objectives of the internal auditor will be different.

Many companies still insist that their internal audit department concentrate on financial auditing, that is, (1) fraud and error prevention and (2) asset protection. While these are understood to be necessary aspects of internal auditing, greater returns can be obtained from internal auditing if more time is spent on operational or management audits.

Operational auditing. Generally the term "operational auditing" means the extension of internal auditing to all operations of a company. At present there is a growing trend to attempt to reduce the amount of internal audit time spent on financial auditing and to do more operational auditing. In many cases this can be done in conjunction with the conventional audit procedures. For example, in connection with an audit of payroll the personnel department activities may be reviewed and evaluated.

Management auditing. The term "management auditing" has not been satisfactory either, as it may be thought to apply to the evaluation of management performance, that is, auditing *of* management rather than auditing *for* management. This is, in effect, being what is called the "eyes and ears of management." The internal auditor will approach every step in the light of management interest. The following illustrations are given for purchasing and accounts payable.

PURCHASING: In the case of purchasing there are few quantitative methods of evaluating purchasing efficiency such as are available in other areas. The auditor will want to determine, if he is examining a branch purchasing office, that general purchasing policies are being carried out. Are the required number of bids being received? Are orders placed without favor? Is the purchasing department cooperating with other departments such as engineering, research, and maintenance? Is the purchasing department keeping up with market trends? If so, how? Is value analysis being used to effect specification changes, design changes, etc., to lower costs? Is there a continuing study of "make or buy" considerations as conditions may have changed since the last review?

ACCOUNTS PAYABLE: In the financial audit of accounts payable the auditor is concerned with determining the correctness of the recorded amounts and the existence of material unrecorded amounts. From a management viewpoint the auditor would want to be sure that the company is receiving all the discounts to which it is entitled. In one case, an internal auditor compared discounts allowed at all plants and noticed that the same vendor was allowing a cash discount on shipments from the East Coast plants but none on shipments from the West Coast plants. When this was reported, the discounts were allowed, which aggregated $15,000 a year. In another case, in making an audit of accounts payable, the auditor noticed that many invoices under

$1, and many more under $10, were being forwarded to headquarters for payment. Many of these were being sent from distant plants. The internal auditor asked the data processing department for a distribution by dollar ranges of the number and dollar amount of the month's payments. The distribution showed that 21 percent of the number of invoices were for amounts less than $10. However, these items represented less than one-tenth of 1 percent of the total dollar amount. Items under $50 represented 55 percent of the items but only eight-tenths of 1 percent of the dollar amount. For items under $100, the number of items was 68 percent, but these represented only 1.6 percent of the dollar value. Looking at it from the other side, it means that for items under $100 headquarters could still control 98.4 percent of the dollar value and process only one-third of the number of items presently handled. It was the practice to place a copy of the paid invoice in the vendor's individual file. This required the services of a number of file clerks and a long battery of files for over 15,000 invoices a month. If invoices under $100 were paid at the plants, there would be 10,000 fewer invoices each month to be filed. If these invoices were paid at the plants, they would not be filed by vendor. Since the average invoice was less than $25, the dollar amount of purchases from individual vendors would not be greatly affected. The change was made without any significant transfers of funds out of headquarters. It was estimated that over $20,000 a year was saved by this suggestion.

PLACE IN THE COMPANY

Status of the Department. The status of the internal auditing department will depend to a large extent on its place in the organization and the support it receives. Top management determines the scope of its responsibilities and the basic policy governing the operation of the department. Support is given to the department when top management makes it known throughout the company that in order to derive full benefits from internal auditing full cooperation is expected.

Regardless of the particular place of the internal auditing department in the company organization it is essential that the department be independent of the functions and departments that it must review and evaluate. On this point The Institute of Internal Auditors, in its Statement of Responsibilities of the Internal Auditor, states, "The head of the department should report to an officer of sufficient rank in the organization as will assure a broad scope of activities and adequate consideration of and effective action on the findings and recommendations made by him."

In most companies the internal auditing department is set up as a separate department or unit at corporate headquarters. In addition to the corporate audit staff there may be a field audit staff, a divisional audit staff, a plant audit staff, and others depending on the organization and size of the overall activity. The degree of independence of the internal auditing department has a direct relationship to the reporting responsibilities of the internal auditing function.

Management's Role in Internal Auditing. Management's role and responsibilities with respect to financial statements have been clearly defined by various professional bodies. The penalties for filing misleading statements with the Securities and Exchange Commission have also been clearly set forth in publications of the SEC and other responsible organizations. One of the first publications to delineate management's role with respect to internal auditing was the AICPA release, *Internal Control,* the special report prepared by the Committee on Auditing Procedure, p. 17. There it was stated that:

> Management has the responsibility for devising, installing and currently supervising a system of internal control adequate to (1) safeguard the assets of an organization (2) check the accuracy and reliability of accounting data (3) promote operational efficiency and (4) to encourage adherence to prescribed managerial policies.

In recognition of these responsibilities the internal auditing objectives are stated in slightly different order from the above but are essentially the same. The principal objectives are to:

1. Review and appraise the system of internal control
2. Determine compliance with company policies and procedures
3. Safeguard assets
4. Prevent and discover fraud
5. Determine the reliability of the accounting and reporting system
6. Conduct systematic audits and report findings and recommendations to management

In addition to the primary objectives there are the additional objectives recognized by many companies, which are to:

1. Determine compliance with government requirements
2. Evaluate personnel performance
3. Cooperate with the public accountants
4. Participate in cost-reduction programs

From the overall viewpoint management generally establishes the level of internal auditing in the following ways: (1) establishes broad policy, (2) encourages support, and (3) follows up findings.

Establishes policy. In some companies the general direction of internal auditing may be determined by an auditing committee. However, in most companies the general direction will be established by the executive to whom the unit reports.

Encourages support. The company management that has a good understanding of internal auditing will find ways to encourage support for the internal audit program. When it is apparent to most personnel that management supports the program, the internal auditor's problems are greatly lessened. A management that is aware of the function understands that many of its benefits cannot be measured quantitatively. For example, how can the amount of losses prevented be measured? How is the reliability of reports measured?

Follows up findings. Probably the most important factor in any audit is a vigorous follow-up. Since internal auditing is a staff function, the follow-up of exceptions would be made by the executive branch of middle management. If local employees have received the message that top management will energetically follow up all exceptions, the exceptions will not remain open very long. In cases where the president is audit-minded, he or the vice-president may personally maintain a list of open exceptions.

Reporting Responsibilities. The 1968 Survey showed a definite trend for the chief internal auditor to report at a higher level than previously. The Survey shows that 47 percent of the chief internal auditors now report to a vice-president level or higher as compared with only 30 percent in 1957. Following is a summary of the data shown by the Survey:

Company Title	*Percentage*	
	1968	*1957*
Vice-president or higher		
Board of directors	6	7
President	10	7
Management committee	2	
Senior vice-president	5	
Vice-president	24	16
Subtotal	47	30
Others		
Treasurer	9	17
Others	12	11
	21	28
Controller (and assistant)	32	42
	100	100

Below are described the advantages and disadvantages of reporting to the various officers. These will be described under the general heading of (1) financial officers and (2) nonfinancial officers.

Financial officers. In many large manufacturing companies, such as the automobile companies, which are large enough to have a title such as vice-president—finance, the internal auditing department reports to that officer. In that case, the treasurer and the controller also report to him. Under each of the titles to whom the internal auditing department may report will be described the advantages and disadvantages of that practice.

THE FINANCIAL VICE-PRESIDENT: While it may be desirable to have internal auditing report to the top financial executive, not all companies have such a clearly defined title. Although there has been a decided trend over the past decade toward the use of such a title, the trend has been principally in the larger companies. This impact, however, was so pronounced that the Controllers Institute of America changed its name to Financial Executives Institute. The organization, founded in 1931 as the recognized professional organization of controllers, decided that as the range of responsibilities of controllers has so broadened the name was no longer appropriate. In 1962, the name was changed and the membership expanded to include financial vice-presidents, treasurers, etc.

From the internal auditing viewpoint there is an advantage in reporting to the vice-president or higher, as the scope of the activity would ordinarily then be considerably broader than otherwise. In addition, it is likely that more respect will be given to audit recommendations and follow-up will be easier. Often the audit head reports to the top financial officer, who might have a title of vice-president—finance, vice-president and treasurer, or vice-president and comptroller. Figure 1 illustrates the line of responsibility in reporting to the vice-president—finance.

THE TREASURER: Generally it is preferable that, where there are separate treasurer and controller functions, internal auditing be responsible to the controller rather than the treasurer. This is true particularly in manufacturing companies since the treasurer may not be as close to manufacturing as the controller. However, in some cases the title of treasurer may include much more than financial custody functions and may be close to financing and operating activities and be sympathetic to internal auditing objectives.

THE CONTROLLER: Generally the controller understands the internal audit function and can provide general direction and supervision. It is essential, however, that he be a true controller; that is, he should be far enough removed from detailed routine so that he can be objective. Therefore, there

Figure 1 REPORTING TO THE VICE-PRESIDENT—FINANCE

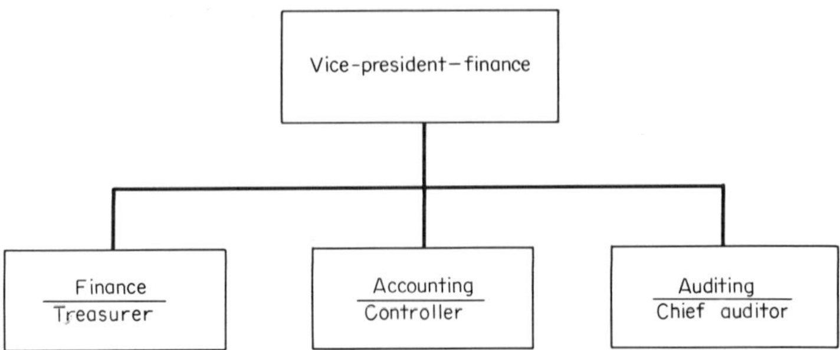

should be a chief accountant with direct responsibility for the accounting records and functions. The principal disadvantage may be the possible lack of independence where the internal auditor may be reluctant to make critical comments directed at his superiors. However, this has not proved to be a problem in most cases. For reporting responsibilities see Figure 2.

Nonfinancial officers. Those opposed to having the internal auditing function report to a financial officer feel that the internal auditor cannot be truly independent when he reports to an officer whose work he is auditing. These advocates of reporting to a nonfinancial officer usually name the president or a vice-president such as the vice-president—administration.

THE PRESIDENT: While the idea of reporting to the president may seem a good solution, it is sometimes difficult. Generally the president will have heavy executive and administrative duties and will have neither the time nor the inclination to give the necessary attention to the internal auditing function. Most often it is difficult to get a sympathetic hearing and to receive adequate support under this arrangement.

VICE-PRESIDENT—ADMINISTRATION: Those who advocate reporting to a nonmanufacturing officer often name a vice-president such as the vice-president—administration. They point out that to provide maximum benefits from internal auditing the function should be entirely independent of any department that may be audited. They wish to avoid any question of the auditor's right to make critical comments.

THE BOARD OF DIRECTORS: The advocates of this arrangement ask whether the primary purpose of internal auditing is to serve management or to serve the board of directors, who represent the stockholders. If it is to be the latter, then internal auditing can operate as a check on management. In some large companies the board of directors appoint an auditing committee to whom

Figure 2 REPORTING TO THE CONTROLLER

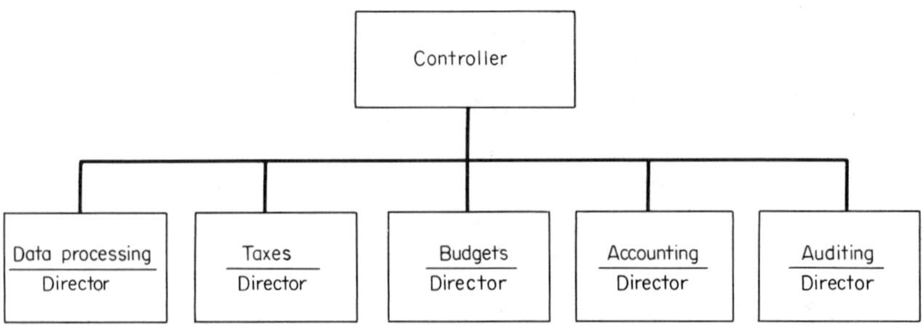

the internal auditing department reports. The auditing committee is also usually concerned with the activities of the independent auditors. In some industrial companies the chief internal auditor reports at intervals to the auditing committee but is administratively responsible to the controller. For reporting responsibilities see Figure 3.

Relationship to Other Functions. In order to clarify the responsibilities of the internal auditor with respect to other closely related activities, it may be well to discuss his relationship to internal control, internal check, and accounting routines.

Internal control. The internal auditor is responsible for reviewing and evaluating the system of internal control existing throughout the company. The nature of internal control is described well in the AICPA special report, *Internal Control.* In that report the following definition of internal control is given:

> Internal control comprises the plan of organization and all the coordinate methods and measures adopted within a business to safeguard its assets, check the accuracy and reliability of its accounting data, promote operational efficiency, and encourage adherence to prescribed managerial policies.

Internal check. This is a term which has taken on something of a different meaning over the years. Earlier the term was synonymous with internal control. For example, in 1936, in the bulletin *Examination of Financial Statements by Independent Public Accountants* issued by the AICPA it was referred to as "those measures and methods adopted within the organization itself to safeguard the cash and other assets of the company as well as to check the clerical accuracy of the bookkeeping." It was clear that internal control at that time was understood to be principally a device for the prevention and detection of irregularities. This is far different from what is given in the definition of internal control above. The earlier definition had three serious shortcomings. These were, first, the uncertain relation of the definition to assets other than cash, such as receivables, securities, and inventories. Second, the *safeguarding* feature was emphasized but little attention was given to efficiency. Third, the definition did not mention *operating* aspects such as those relating to purchasing, production, and other operating activities.

The need for a broader view of internal control was advanced in 1947 in the book *Internal Control Standards and Related Auditing Procedures,* where it was stated that:

Figure 3 REPORTING TO THE BOARD OF DIRECTORS

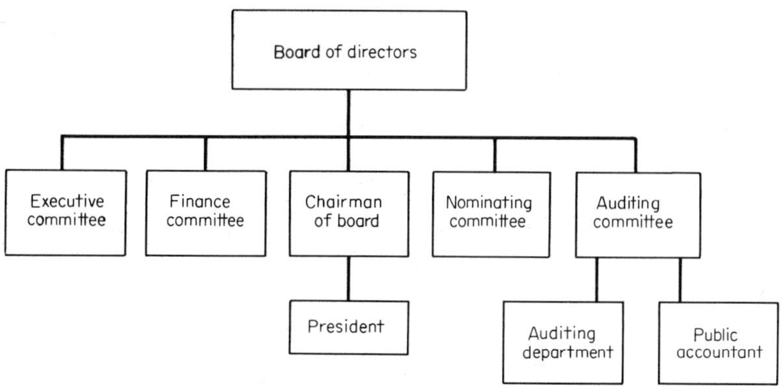

Too often internal control is thought of solely in terms of accounting practices and procedures. If, however, we enlarge our concept of internal control to include the basic policies laid down by executive management and provide the means whereby management can be assured that such policies are being carried out, it can readily be seen that effective internal control becomes one of the cornerstones of successful management. One of the essentials is organization planning coupled with well-defined statements of duties and responsibilities. The more one studies the subject of internal control, the more it becomes apparent that it is not the result of the application of abstract theories and principles, but rather a living, dynamic, and ever-changing condition resulting from a variety of decisions, some of which are accounting decisions, but many of which are the decisions of executive management itself.[5]

With the gradual recognition that internal control referred to the broad concept then, it was recognized that internal check referred to the more limited aspects. It is an integral part of the current routine operations and helps provide an automatic proof of clerical accuracy. For instance, the use of a control account and reconciliation with the subsidiary ledger is a type of internal check. It is a built-in part of the accounting system and is *mechanical.* This is contrasted with internal auditing, which is a review *after* the event and requires an *appraisal* or exercise of judgment as to whether the particular procedure is operating properly. Thus the present definition is: Internal check refers to those accounting and statistical procedures and the physical and other controls which safeguard assets against clerical errors, defalcations, and other irregularities.

Examples of internal check would be the following:

1. Controlling account (subsidiary detail controlled through an account in the general ledger), mentioned previously.
2. Perpetual inventory records (provide continuous accountability).
3. Use of mechanical equipment (cash registers, bookkeeping machines, calculators, check-signing machines, electronic computers).
4. Completeness of instructions (oral or written), e.g., written instructions, when expressed in a clear and competent manner, provide the basis for orderly and efficient operations.
5. Completeness of training and supervision.
6. Rotation of employees (provides insurance against fraud and broadens the training of personnel).
7. Required vacations.
8. Bonding of employees.

Accounting routines. Accounting routines refer to the system of processing accounting transactions. Generally there will be a large volume of transactions, and it is essential that an efficient and safe procedure be developed for this processing. Usually the efficiency aspects will be developed by those charged with systems and procedures. Generally the internal auditor will review the proposed accounting routines—preferably before they are installed. In many cases the public accountant may also review the proposed system. In both instances the auditors are looking for any violations of internal control. In many instances a routine or procedure is developed and after installation is found to have serious internal control shortcomings. Sometimes these shortcomings are discovered first by dishonest employees, to the chagrin of management.

[5] Walter H. Kamp and James A. Cashin, *Internal Control Standards and Related Auditing Procedures,* Stamford, Brock and Wallston, 1947.

Relationship to Other Departments. As pointed out in the Statement of Responsibilities, "Internal auditing is a staff function rather than a line function." Thus the auditor acts in an advisory rather than an executive capacity. He must be able to get his ideas accepted on the basis of logic and service to management. Where there may be a difference of opinion regarding the audit finding or conclusion, the matter in effect is referred to the next higher level of management when the auditor makes his report. Generally, the internal auditor's work requires the exercise of a high degree of tact in order to gain the cooperation and goodwill of persons being audited. This ability is one of the most important attributes of the internal auditor and requires a great deal of awareness and consideration of the points of view of others in order to earn their confidence and respect. He must remember, for example, that a department head is generally trying to do the best job he can. If the internal auditor can assure the department head that he is interested in helping him to do a better job, he will usually get a favorable response. One of the best approaches is for the auditor to offer to help the department head with his problems rather than to ask the department head to help him.

For example, in most organizations there is a problem in communicating top management's policies and procedures to the operating levels. Often policies are misunderstood or perhaps not even known. The internal auditor can perform an important service in making such policies easily available and perhaps helping to explain the reasoning behind the policies.

Regardless of the particular audit finding, the internal auditor must be fair in presenting the facts and giving both sides of the case. He must scrupulously try to recognize honest effort and to avoid criticism. Also under no conditions should he take credit for corrective efforts which may have been under way prior to his audit.

ORGANIZATION OF THE DEPARTMENT

Determining the Internal Auditing Role. There are a number of factors other than company size which have an important bearing on the internal auditing role in any company. The principal factors are (1) nature of the business, (2) management philosophy, (3) company organization, (4) size and dispersion, (5) training ground.

Nature of the business. The dominating factor in organizing the internal auditing department is the nature of the business. If it is a manufacturing company, the need for safeguards will be somewhat different from those in a nonmanufacturing organization such as a bank, finance company, or public utility. Various surveys undertaken have related the number of employees in the various industries to the number of auditors to develop a basis of comparison. In the National Industrial Conference Board survey released in 1963, which covered 157 companies, there were approximately 800 employees for each internal auditor. However, there were wide differences between manufacturing and nonmanufacturing companies. For manufacturing companies there were only about 400 employees per auditor.

Management philosophy. Another important factor in organizing the internal auditing department is management's philosophy as to the objectives and scope of the internal auditing program. The philosophy would apply to the type of auditing to be performed as well as the scope of the activities. For example, some managements require that the auditing program include an extensive examination of financial transactions. This orientation would generally require a large number of junior auditors and clerical workers to audit disbursements and reconcile bank statements. On the other hand some companies prefer to concentrate on operational or management-type audits. In such a case the department usually consists of a relatively small unit made up mostly of well-qualified senior auditors. The proponents of this type of audit feel that a small, active, high-level staff devoted to the review of all operations from a management viewpoint is more beneficial than a larger staff concerned with the detail checking of accounts. As a matter of fact, the reconciling of bank accounts is not an appropriate internal auditing activity, according to the definition of internal auditing.

Company organization. The particular type of company organization will of course affect the organization for internal auditing. If the company is organized along functional lines with separate sales, production, and management, there may be auditors assigned to the various divisions. If the company is organized along product lines, or product groups such as consumer products and industrial products, the auditing function will also be along that line. Again, the company may be set up along geographic lines, such as West Coast, Middle West, and East Coast, which will also affect the setup of internal auditing.

Size and dispersion. The size, of course, in most cases has an important bearing on the organization of the auditing department. As the company expands, more auditors will be needed. However, at some point the law of diminishing returns comes into play. For example, if a new plant is required, it will usually be located near the geographic center of distribution, which with expansion has probably moved away from the previous center. This dispersion will require more travel time and probably more auditors.

Training ground. Many companies use the internal auditing department as a training ground for future executives. In the internal auditing department the potential executive will have a better opportunity than in any other part of the company to study all operations of the company. This is helpful in balancing the internal audit staff, as it may include engineers, scientists, auditors, and other specialists. Where there are large numbers of technical evaluations to be made, such as in an oil refinery, an internal auditor with an engineering background would be most helpful. However, as would be expected, there is a period of training before such a staff man would be as useful as one with previous audit training. Therefore, this separate function would have a tendency to increase the size of the staff.

Department Head. The stature and experience of the head of the internal auditing department will have a decided influence on the organization of the department. If he is broad-gauged and cognizant of the potential of internal auditing, he probably will be able to convince management of the benefits of a wide scope of activities.

The title of the head of the internal auditing department varies. In most manufacturing companies the title would generally be "Chief Internal Auditor" or "General Auditor." In banks or insurance companies the title might simply be "Auditor." Where there is an established uniform designation for a department head in all departments, such as manager or director, the title may be "Manager—Internal Auditing Department" or "Director" or "Supervisor" followed by the particular department. If the particular unit is at headquarters, the title may be "Manager—Corporate Audit Staff." There may also be another auditor in charge of all field audits who would have the title of "Manager—Field Audit Staff."

The success or failure of the internal auditing activity could depend on the department head selected; thus he should be selected with great care.

Generally the job specifications require a bachelor's degree with a major in accounting. The trend is toward requiring an MBA, which is now desirable but not required. Very often a CPA certificate is mentioned as an additional requisite. Ordinarily, prior experience in auditing is required, which in many cases must be public accounting.

The department head must have, in addition to his technical ability, the ability to get along well with people throughout the company. He must have the ability to organize and manage an important organization. He must also have the ability to communicate effectively, both orally and in writing. He must be able to deal effectively with other department heads and must earn their confidence.

Figure 4 is a representative position description for manager—internal auditing, specifying the requirements of the job.

Staff Members. The staff members of the internal auditing department generally carry job titles similar to those of public accounting staff members such as junior, senior, and supervisor. It is important that a reasonable balance be maintained within the audit staff. Such a balance can be maintained in most cases by means of the recruiting procedures. Generally the sources of personnel will be (1) internal or (2) external.

Sources of personnel. INTERNAL SOURCES: The principal internal source of personnel for the audit staff would be the company accounting staff. Appointment to the audit staff is generally a reward for outstanding work. Usually the salary scale is somewhat higher than would be paid in the accounting department, which is also an incentive. One of the most important benefits of recruiting within the company is that the candidate is already familiar with company operations.

It is necessary generally to teach the new staff man auditing techniques and to provide more auditing instruction than if he had some prior auditing experience. However, it is likely that he was an accounting major in college and that he studied auditing, which should help him to learn quickly. Sometimes the recruit may be obtained from other than the accounting department, particularly if the company uses the internal auditing department to train future executives. In that case the recruit may come from the engineering department, the sales department, or even the research department.

EXTERNAL SOURCES: Training in public accounting is usually very helpful for internal auditing. Generally the recruit will be well trained in auditing practices and procedures. As would be expected, some orientation is required to acquaint the recruit with company operations and company personnel. There are three principal outside sources of recruits. One source would be employment agencies, the second would be the staff of the company's public accounting firm or another public accounting firm, and the third the college campus. Other sources might be professional societies, other companies, etc. The recruits from employment agencies would have had either public experience or internal auditing experience, and less training would be required. In some cases the public accounting firm may help out by releasing a staff man for the client's internal auditing staff if he is agreeable. Generally internal auditing visits to locations will not begin until the year-end work is out of the way and the public accountant's work is nearly finished. If the recruit has obtained the necessary public accounting experience to sit for the CPA examination, he may be interested in working on an internal audit staff. Additional problems are encountered when recruits are hired directly from the campus. They do not know the company operations and they do not have auditing experience. The usual procedure is for

Figure 4 POSITION DESCRIPTION, MANAGER—INTERNAL AUDITING

THE HAMBURG CORPORATION

DIVISION—Controllers
DEPARTMENT—Auditing
LOCATION—General Office

TITLE—MANAGER—INTERNAL AUDITING
APPROVED BY—Allen L. Johnson
DATE—May 24, 1970

PRIMARY FUNCTION

General supervision of all internal auditing performed within the Company and its subsidiaries. Monitoring the system of internal control; determining compliance with Company policies and procedures and external laws and regulations; and safeguarding assets.

RESPONSIBILITIES AND AUTHORITIES

1. Develop and maintain an internal audit program for all units.
2. Review and appraise the adequacy and application of accounting, financial and operating controls.
3. Report on audit findings and suggest means of correction.
4. Ascertain the extent of compliance with established Company policies and procedures.
5. Determine compliance with the applicable laws and regulations of all Governmental bodies.
6. Ascertain the reliability of accounting and other data.
7. Determine that assets are adequately safeguarded.
8. Coordinate the internal audit program with that of the public accountant.
9. Hire, train and replace audit staff members as required.

RELATIONSHIPS

1. Accountable to the Controller for interpretation of his responsibilities and authorities.
2. Supervise the corporate audit staff, the field audit staff and all departmental staff and clerical employees.
3. Responsible for providing advice, as requested by department heads and others in establishing and maintaining an effective system of internal controls.
4. Responsible for coordinating his audit efforts with those of the public accountant to provide maximum coverage without duplication.

PERSONAL QUALIFICATIONS

1. Baccalaureate degree with a major in accounting or its equivalent. Preferably a Certified Public Accountant's Certificate and further special courses or graduate study.
2. Minimum of ten years of diversified experience in public or private accounting, including five years in a supervisory audit position.
3. High degree of administrative and technical skill.
4. Demonstrated ability to get along with supervisors and others whose performance is being audited.
5. Ability to effectively organize the internal auditing department and to maintain good morale.
6. Must be able to communicate effectively both verbally and in writing.

LIMITATIONS OF AUTHORITY—(HIGHER APPROVAL REQUIRED)

1. Policies, objectives and department structure
2. Audit budgets and staff requirements
3. Major changes in programs or plans
4. Personnel changes
5. Property expenditures
6. Membership dues and contributions

the college graduate to join the accounting staff first, and if he can prove himself there he may win an appointment to the audit department after about 1½ or 2 years.

Staff Training. The type of staff training would depend on the past experience of the individual. If the recruit has come from the company accounting department, he would be given a training course in auditing procedures. It is likely that the program would be relatively brief, as he would already be familiar with company operations. Probably he would receive on-the-job training on an actual audit. Generally the auditor in charge of the particular audit would be expected to help him develop on the job.

If the recruit has already had auditing experience, he would be expected to spend some time at headquarters to become acquainted with the structure and operations of the company and with company personnel.

ADMINISTRATION OF THE PROGRAM

The Approach to Programming. There are important administrative responsibilities related to programming that must be carried out frequently and effectively whether the scope of the program is broad or limited. One of these basic responsibilities is the establishment of priorities for various audits. Where there are evident risks involved, of course, close auditing of such activities would be called for. The general objectives of auditing as established by management would also have an important bearing in scheduling the work. These and other factors would have to be considered by the department head in planning the overall program. The point at which the internal auditing department will meet the general objectives is usually some time in the future. Therefore, it is necessary to plan more than one year in advance for most companies. As in other types of scheduling or budgeting, the two broad classifications, (1) the long-range schedule and (2) the current schedule, have been found most satisfactory.

The Long-range Schedule. In most companies there are usually very practical considerations, such as the size of the staff, which do not permit as broad a scope as the department head may wish. Therefore, he will usually include new areas in a long-range schedule. Part of the new coverage may be attained by cutting back on the depth of present coverage, but the remaining part will have to be done by additional staff men. Since it takes some time for the recruiting and training of internal auditors, it is desirable to plan staff requirements on a long-term basis. Consideration should be given to broadening the areas of coverage. For example, a long-range schedule may include new audits of international operations. Additional desirable coverage may result from topical developments. For example, it may be desirable to emphasize the audit of management performance. These and similar considerations call for programming which extends far more than one year in advance.

The Current Schedule. The current, or short-range, schedule will usually be planned at least one year ahead. This schedule would include all the locations or areas of audit to be covered in the following year. When this list is coupled with the man-days needed for each audit, a total number of required man-days can be determined. When this amount is compared with the available man-days of the present staff, usually a problem arises. Either some of the proposed coverage must be cut back or one or two new staff members must be added. If the tentative program is made up in November and additional staff members are approved in December, the department head still has the problem to recruit, train, and have the new auditors ready for the current year. For detailed control purposes it is usually necessary to have a quarterly schedule for follow-up. Since a time estimate for a particular audit is subject to substantial fluctuation due to unforeseen circumstances, an up-to-date quarterly schedule is needed. Often changes are made between quarters, for example, where an audit may be deferred for a month or so.

Coordination with the Public Accountant. Another very important consideration is coordination with the public accountant to avoid audit duplication. A number of coordinated audit tasks may be scheduled with the public accountant. For example, the internal audit head will usually be able to minimize duplication by working closely with the in-charge public accountant on cash, receivables, inventory, payroll, and other work. At the year end, the internal audit staff may help in minimizing duplication in cash reconciliations and cutoff work. Prior to the year end, effective coordination can be worked out in confirming receivables and in observing inventories at various locations.

To be most effective, the internal auditing department should not be forced continually to "put out fires." Such crisis work, together with the usual number of special projects, may seriously disrupt the audit program. In many cases a crisis situation, such as a defalcation, may occur in a particular area where a known risk was involved. Often the probable amount involved is not enough to justify a special audit and would have been taken care of in a routine manner and the risk eliminated if the program had not been disrupted.

For example, where there is a small branch sales or engineering office some distance away from the audit base, it may not be practicable to send an auditor there for only a day or two. The cost involved may be almost as great as the risk. Therefore, this type of audit may be tied in with an audit of a manufacturing plant. That is, the same auditor may stop at the branch office on the way to or returning from plant audits. This requires good planning well in advance. Usually it is a good policy to visit the larger locations annually. However, there may be a number of borderline cases where good internal auditing management may dictate less attention. In some cases the internal auditing department head may be guilty of following a previous schedule without applying the same study and thought to his own operations that he applies to those which he audits. For example, if through repeated audits in some of the smaller locations the risk factors have been eliminated, then perhaps the visits could be scheduled on a 2-year basis. Another approach is to reduce the time and schedule such an audit in conjunction with a nearby audit to minimize travel costs. Of course, the internal auditing department head should be aware of possible returns or savings and should consider the greatest amount of savings possible with the available audit staff.

The Problem of Travel. One of the disadvantages of internal auditing positions generally is the traveling required. The amount of time away from home is usually specified as a principal cause of turnover of auditing personnel. A high percentage of travel is especially difficult for a staff member with young children. Auditing department heads are usually acutely aware of this problem and try to schedule accordingly wherever practicable. If the assignment extends beyond about 3 weeks the auditor often is permitted to return home at the end of 3 weeks. As a practical matter the cost of the trip home is usually no more costly than food and lodging costs for the weekend. In many cases the problem can be mitigated by holding most regular audits to 3 weeks. Instead of sending out one man for 6 weeks, two men are sent out for 3 weeks. There are other ways in which the problem can be made less burdensome if sufficient thought is given to it. For example, for the man with a family, being away from home over the weekend is much worse than being away during the week. By careful planning it is possible to limit all but a few audits to 3 weeks, with most audits lasting 2 weeks. By arranging to have the auditors fly out early Monday morning and fly back late Friday afternoon, they will be away only one weekend for 2-week audits and two weekends for 3-week audits. After completing the field audit, there is usually a week or more at the home office to follow up remaining items and to draft the report. By diversifying the jobs and periodic assignments to home office special projects, most of the problems can be minimized.

Auditing Manuals. The most important written internal auditing document is the internal auditing manual. While there may be statements of policy, statements of procedure, company bulletins, and various other published information affecting auditing, these are often incorporated where desirable as a part of the auditing manual. Generally the manual will state the auditing objectives, the standards of performance expected, and the procedure for time recording, audit report preparation, and other matters of a general nature. Generally the most important part of the manual is concerned with the detailed auditing procedures to be performed with respect to various audit tasks.

The contents of the manual will generally reflect the chief auditor's attitude toward manuals. If he feels that the auditor should have maximum flexibility, the manual will contain few detailed audit procedures. If he feels that the auditor should be guided by the manual, the procedures will be given in far greater detail. There are advantages and disadvantages to the use of an auditing manual. These considerations have to be weighed carefully by each internal auditing head for his own company.

Advantages and Disadvantages of a Manual. **The advantages**

1. It provides background data concerning company policies and procedures.
2. It specifies the minimum audit steps to be performed.
3. It aids the staff members by providing answers to routine questions.
4. It aids in the efficient distribution of staff work.
5. It is useful as a control on the progress of the job.
6. It fixes responsibility for the particular audit step.
7. It provides a useful guide for the following years.
8. It is a substantial help to the supervisor in his review of work done.
9. It provides evidence of the specific work done if litigation arises later.
10. It helps in accounting for staff time, reporting expenses, etc.

The disadvantages. Those opposed to the use of an auditing manual usually point out the following principal disadvantages:

1. There is a general tendency to limit the work to that specified.
2. Often the procedures become mechanical.
3. There is a tendency to discourage creative thinking.
4. The manuals are often not kept up to date.

Form of the Manual. There are various approaches to developing an audit manual. The following format is only one but has been found to be very effective:

Objectives. If the main objectives of the audit are listed, it will provide the auditor with an overall perspective of what is to be accomplished.

Illustrations. This is intended as desirable background. In the operation to be audited, where does the material come from and what is done with it? This should be very brief but complete enough to provide a mental flow chart of the important functions or operations.

Audit procedure. This will depend upon the complexity of the operation to be audited and the competency of the auditor assigned to the audit. A detailed step-by-step procedure may be outlined or simply suggestions made of areas to be reviewed.

REPORTS

Significance. The issuance of an audit report is one of the most important functions of internal auditing. It is one of the best means to help management measure its own performance, particularly with respect to the reliability of established controls. Equally important is the fact that the internal audit report is the yardstick by which management and others measure the performance of the internal auditing department. The working papers are the evidence of work performed and document audit findings, but it is the report that distills all the findings, conclusions, and recommendations in a manner that can be understood and intelligently acted upon by management. The prompt follow-up and necessary executive action on audit recommendations is one of the most important benefits of the internal auditing report. Therefore, the report must be presented in such a way as to generate prompt executive action.

Important Considerations. There are many types of reports, oral and written. Since there is no record provided through oral reports, they are normally regarded as relating to the preliminary aspects of matters which are later handled in more formal written reports. Important considerations to be included in written reports should include the following:

Brevity. It should be brief and to the point. A report should be complete but also as practical and concise as possible. Brevity encourages executives to give careful study to the report.

Constructive criticism. Criticism made without giving commendation for honest efforts is not constructive. Similarly, criticism without a reasonable suggested solution is also not constructive criticism and is usually of little or no value. To foster cooperation, a positive approach must be presented and suggestions made for improving the operation rather than the negative approach of condemning efforts made by the responsible personnel.

Support for all statements. It is almost axiomatic that every statement made in the report must be supported by documentary evidence, usually in the working papers related to the audit. It is often desirable to be conservative in reporting specific cases. For example, in stating instances of particular violations, one instance can be excluded so that if a particular item is contested another item can take its place.

Overall tone. Since the audit report will be concerned largely with exceptions, the auditor must be extremely careful to present the overall tone in proper perspective. This is usually done in a summary or introductory page at the beginning of the report. Here the auditor may state that there were no major violations of internal control or company policy found. He may then mention that the report cites instances where improvements could be made or possibly have been made since the previous audit. This creates an entirely different impression from that received when a recital is made of violations without putting these citations, many of which may be minor, in proper perspective.

Diplomacy. After the general tone has been set, the specific findings are reported. If at all possible, the report should be started in a complimentary vein. It is easy to find things to criticize, but criticism does not gain cooperation. No audit should ever be concluded until something is found that can elicit an honest compliment. As a general rule, it is a good policy to begin a report with a compliment and later launch into the exceptions.

Topical matters. The internal auditor is expected to be alert and always aware of top management's objectives. This is particularly true of established immediate objectives. For example, if top management has recently instituted a cost-reduction program, the internal auditor should of course make his contribution. In fact he may have a separate section in his report suggesting possible cost-reduction opportunities. Management's recognition of the potentialities of internal auditing and the help it provides in such endeavors will greatly enhance the status of internal auditing in the company.

Presentation sequence. The sequence in which the items are presented in the internal audit report will differ from the presentation sequence in the report of the public accountant. In the latter case the sequence would usually be according to the financial statement sequence such as cash, receivables, etc. However, the internal audit report will concern many operating personnel who are not familiar with or interested in financial statement sequence. Therefore, generally operating matters are most important and should be considered in determining the sequence. The most important matters should be presented first. They are the matters in which management is most interested and that will hold management attention. Putting them first also provides flexibility and helps to keep the report from appearing too structured and difficult to study.

Psychology in making recommendations. Where should recommendations be included in a report?

AT THE BEGINNING: In certain cases, it may be psychologically advantageous to include the recommendations near the beginning. Then, as the reader progresses through the supporting material, he is in a position to agree or disagree on the initial reading.

AT THE END: This is an approach often used. However, if the reader has to wait until the end, particularly if it is a long report, it may be necessary for him to review parts of the information a second time before he can reach a decision.

WITH THE FINDINGS: Unless the recommendations are of a general nature, it is usually better to include them immediately following the findings. In this way the reader can readily recognize the problem and then consider the proposed solution.

Promptness. The advantages of prompt reporting cannot be overemphasized. It is important to present a report at a time when it will be thoroughly reviewed and adequately considered; stale data are usually of little or no value. Normally, it is desirable to render a report as soon after the completion of the audit as possible, particularly where follow-up and prompt action may be needed.

Distribution. In most cases the distribution of reports is limited, usually not exceeding 10 recipients. The recipients would usually include the president, the chief financial officer, the chief accounting officer, and the chief operating officer. If an operating location or function is audited, the manager of the audited unit and the company's public accountants would receive copies.

If the chief internal auditor reports to the board of directors, the chairman of the board would receive a copy. Other recipients would be included in a particular company depending on the needs or desires of management.

Follow-up. The degree and type of follow-up is a good indicator of the support which management is giving to internal auditing. Where there is prompt and effective follow-up, the various units of the company will get the message very quickly and will in turn take prompt action to correct any reported deficiencies. On the other hand, if follow-up is not prompt and firm, the units audited will get the impression that management is not fully supporting the program, and the job of correcting deficiencies will be much more difficult.

Many chief auditors feel that a vigorous follow-up is the most important factor in a successful internal auditing program. The head of the auditing department is a keyman in this situation, and his stature in the company and the standing of the internal auditing department will have much to do with the follow-up carried out by management. The chief auditor can facilitate vigorous follow-up by designing his reports for easier follow-up and establishing his own follow-up with various levels of management to help ensure vigorous management follow-up.

BIBLIOGRAPHY

Bibliography of Internal Auditing 1950–1965, The Institute of Internal Auditors, New York, 1967.

Case Problems in Internal Auditing and Control, The Institute of Internal Auditors, New York.

A Guide to Organization and Administration of an Internal Auditing Department, The Institute of Internal Auditors, New York.

Internal Auditing, Review and Appraisal in the Federal Government, Research Bulletin No. 2, Federal Government Accountants Association, Washington, D.C., 1962.

Purposes and Objectives of Independent Audits by the General Accounting Office, General Accounting Office, Washington, 1961.

Research Reports, The Institute of Internal Auditors, New York, to date.

Statement of Responsibilities of the Internal Auditor, The Institute of Internal Auditors, New York, 1957.

Cadmus, Bradford: *Operational Auditing Handbook,* New York, The Institute of Internal Auditors, 1964.

Cadmus, Bradford, and Arthur J. E. Child: *Internal Control against Fraud and Waste,* Englewood Cliffs, N.J., Prentice-Hall, Inc., 1955.

Brink, Victor Z., and James A. Cashin: *Internal Auditing,* New York, The Ronald Press Company, 1958.

Kamp, Walter H., and James A. Cashin: *Internal Control Standards and Related Auditing Procedures,* Stamford, Brock and Wallston, 1947.

Mints, Frederic E., and Herbert Witt: "Internal Auditing," in *Financial Executive's Handbook,* New York, Dow Jones–Irwin, 1970.

Walsh, Francis J., Jr.: *Internal Auditing,* Business Policy Study No. 111, New York, National Industrial Conference Board, Inc., 1963.

The Internal Auditor, magazine, The Institute of Internal Auditors, New York.

McPhee, E. D.: "Scientific Management Control," *The Internal Auditor,* New York, March, 1953.

Mitchell, C. L.: "The Criteria of a Profession," *The Internal Auditor,* Summer, 1965.

Wilson, Duane E.: "Dynamic Auditing in a Changing World," *The Internal Auditor,* September–October, 1970.

Chapter **8**

Governmental Auditing

Part 1 Federal Government Auditing

SIDNEY S. BAURMASH

Deputy Director of Audits, U.S. Department of Commerce

Auditing by governmental units, whether federal, state, or local, is similar in standards, principles, and methods to internal auditing in industry and the audit function in public accounting. The essential differences relate to the responsibility of the audit organization and the scope of audit coverage. Since it is by far the largest and most complex of governmental entities, the following discussion concerns present-day practices in the United States government.

DEVELOPMENT OF AUDITING

Early Period. The audit function in the federal government goes back to United States beginnings. As early as Apr. 1, 1776, the Continental Congress passed a resolution establishing a Treasury Office of Accounts. Many later laws refer to the audit function within the federal government. Only brief reference can be made in this chapter to various laws relating to the historical development of auditing. Further details on this subject are included in *Research Bulletin* No. 2 of the Federal Government Accountants Association entitled "Internal Auditing, Review and Appraisal in the Federal Government." The act of Sept. 2, 1789, created the Treasury Department and established the auditor as one of its principal officers. The act of Mar. 3, 1817, added additional auditors for the Treasury Department, and the act of July 2, 1836, established the Office of Auditor of the Treasury for the Post Office Department.

Establishment of the GAO. In 1921, an important fundamental change was made in the audit function. The Budget and Accounting Act of 1921 removed the audit responsibility from the executive branch and placed it in the legislative branch of government. The General Accounting Office was created, and the duties of the former Comptroller of the Treasury, including those of the auditors of the Treasury, were transferred to the new unit. The new General Accounting Office was independent of executive control and responsible only to the legislative branch.[1] Headed by a Comptroller General, this independent unit began the audit of various government agencies. Audits were generally conducted at central locations and consisted mainly of the examination and settlement of financial transactions, accounts, and claims; decisions on legality of expenditures; and investigation of the receipt, disbursement, and application of public funds.

New Departure in Auditing. Shortly after World War I a new development in auditing was formalized. The Air Corps Act of 1926 placed with the Secretary of War the responsibility of auditing costs related to certain negotiated contracts and of developing cost data to be used in negotiating future contracts. Thus auditing was to be used as a management tool in an executive agency. The scope of auditing gradually expanded to include military property accounts and laundries.

With the beginning of World War II and the quick buildup of military strength, the War Department directed its audit effort to the procurement and audit of contracts. The use of auditing as a management tool in various executive agencies continued to expand and become a more important factor in government. While this new concept, called "internal auditing," became widely known in the early 1940s, it was not until 1949 that the term "internal audit" appeared in any legislation. In the 1949 amendments to the National Security Act of 1947 the Comptroller of the Department of Defense was to: "Establish, and supervise the execution of (a) Principles, policies and administrative matters relating to . . . internal audit."

Clarification of Responsibilities. As the auditing function continued to grow in the various executive agencies and in the legislative branch, the General Accounting Office, it became necessary to clarify the responsibilities and duties of auditing throughout the federal government. Accordingly, the Budget and Accounting Procedures Act of 1950 defined the responsibilities and duties of the Comptroller General and the head of each executive agency with respect to auditing. Section 113 of the act stated in part:

(a) the head of each executive agency shall establish and maintain systems of accounting and internal control designed to provide
  (3) effective control over and accountability for all funds, property, and other assets for which the agency is responsible, including appropriate internal audit.

Here, finally, was legislative recognition of the need for internal auditing within all agencies of the federal government. With the spread of internal auditing units throughout the various agencies it became necessary to establish some guidelines or standards.

Statement of Basic Principles and Concepts. To meet the growing need for uniformity in internal auditing activities the General Accounting Office issued in 1957 a statement of basic principles applicable to all federal agencies. The purpose of this statement was to stimulate the development of strong internal audit systems and to set forth general standards for all units. A complete revision of the statement was issued by the Comptroller General of the United States in 1968.

Joint Financial Management Improvement Program. Another important audit development was the creation of the Joint Financial Management Improvement Program. The program, originally established in 1948 for developing improved financial systems, has shown some impressive results in recent years. The program was endorsed by the Congress and is led by the Comptroller General, the Director, Office of Management and Budget, the Secretary of the Treasury, and the Chairman of the Civil Service Commission. One of the objectives of this program is to promote in all federal agencies the establishment of suitable internal control practices, including internal audit.

Government Operations Committee. Another legislative arm which has had a significant impact on auditing in the federal government is the Government Operations Committee of the House of Representatives. This continuing committee grew out of its original studies of economy and efficiencies in federal agencies in 1962–1963.

LEGISLATIVE BRANCH

General Accounting Office. Under the direction of the Comptroller General of the United States, the General Accounting Office assists the Congress in carrying out its constitutional responsibilities with respect to the expenditure of public funds. One of the major functions of this office is the independent audit of activities, financial transactions, and accounts of the federal government. In addition, it makes special audits, surveys, and investigations at the request of congressional committees and members of Congress. This responsibility and authority for audit extends also to records of contractors having government contracts negotiated without advertising, their subcontractors' records, and records of certain recipients of federal financial assistance such as loans, advances, grants, or contributions. The General Accounting Office is also responsible for determining the correctness of charges paid for freight and passenger transportation services furnished for the account of the United States, for the recovery of overcharges, and for the settlement of transportation claims both by and against the government. Details of General Accounting office audits are described beginning on page 8-11.

EXECUTIVE BRANCH

In the executive branch of the federal government there are 12 major departments which are at the cabinet level. In addition to these cabinet departments and the three military departments under the Department of Defense, there are over 40 independent agencies (e.g., National Aeronautics and Space Administration), and 8 other organizations under the Executive Office of the President (e.g., Office of Management and Budget, Office of Economic Opportunity).

The following description of the audit activities of some of the federal agencies will illustrate the types and scope of the audits involved. No attempt is made to describe the auditing activities in every executive department or agency. Representative auditing procedures in the most important departments or agencies are presented.

Department of Defense. In the Department of Defense are found both contract audit and internal audit functions.

Contract auditing. The greater portion of contract auditing activity in the federal government is centered in this department. In order to attain uniformity in this area, the Defense Contract Audit Agency (DCAA) was formed on July 1, 1965, and made responsible for all contract audit functions throughout the Defense establishment. Previously, this function was performed individually by the U.S. Army Audit Agency, the Auditor General, U.S. Air Force, and the Naval Audit Service.

DCAA has the primary responsibility for examining actual and proposed contract costs of defense contractors and expressing an informed and independent opinion on the fairness and propriety of these costs and related data. Reports and data are prepared for responsible government procurement and contract administration officials of the Department of Defense and other agencies such as the National Aeronautics and Space Administration, the Department of Health, Education, and Welfare, and the Atomic Energy Commission. DCAA performs much of the on-site auditing for other agencies on an "assist" basis. It is the largest auditing organization in the Executive Branch, with approximately 3,600 employees, of which about 3,000 are professional accountants.

Internal auditing. Each of the three military departments as well as the Defense Supply Agency and the Department of Defense itself have internal audit organizations. In the military departments, the audit responsibility has shifted over the years from a review of financial transactions and property accountability to an evaluation and appraisal of management operations. Audit emphasis is now placed on the managerial controls and reports concerning the basic mission of all functions or entities under review. The internal audit organizations are responsible for providing management at all levels with independent, objective, and constructive evaluations of the effectiveness and efficiency with which financial and mission responsibilities are executed. Audit activities are directed toward determining whether financial management controls at all levels are adequate and whether funds and other resources are effectively utilized.

Department of Health, Education, and Welfare. The audit activities in this department are centered in the HEW Audit Agency under the direction of the Assistant Secretary, Comptroller. The Audit Agency is responsible for conducting comprehensive internal audits of all departmental agencies and activities and also audits of grantees and contractors receiving funds from the department.

The audit workload, which is second in size to the Department of Defense among the executive departments, consists of over 1,000 department installations, about 550 state agencies, over 10,000 units of local governments, more than 4,000 universities and private organizations, and about 85 intermediaries and 10,000 hospitals and extended-care facilities under the Medicare program.

The scope of these audits extends beyond the review of individual transactions and contractual arrangements to the whole system of financial controls used by the audited organizations and to the functioning of their systems in relation to HEW programs. The extensiveness of the department's audit workload has resulted in using independent public accountants and state audit agencies to complement the auditing done by the Audit Agency.

Department of Agriculture. The audit and investigation activities of the 10 major agencies of the Department of Agriculture were transferred in 1962 to the Office of The Inspector General reporting directly to the Secretary of Agriculture. The responsibility of the centralized functions of audit and investigation is to provide management with effective evaluations of Agriculture programs. Emphasis is placed upon the understanding of the practices and concepts of management so as to enable the auditors to suggest management solutions to the inadequacies encountered.

Department of Commerce. The audit functions being performed under the jurisdiction of some of the major bureaus and offices within the Department of Commerce were centralized in 1967 in the Office of Audits, Office of the Secretary. The audit responsibility of the Office of Audits includes external audits of departmental contracts, grants, loans, and subsidies, and comprehensive internal auditing of the operating, administrative, and financial activities of all organizational units in the department.

Internal Revenue Service. There are two audit activities within the Internal Revenue Service in the U.S. Treasury Department. One is the examination and audit of the accounting books and records of individuals, partnerships, fiduciaries, and corporations to determine their correct federal tax liabilities. These examinations are performed by Internal Revenue agents. The other is the audit by internal auditors of the operations of the Internal Revenue Service. Their responsibility is to review and evaluate the performance of management at all levels and to determine the efficiency and effectiveness of internal policies, practices, procedures, and controls. In addition, the internal auditors analyze and verify the Service's financial transactions and reports to determine their propriety and accuracy, and assist in investigations to detect and resolve lapses in integrity of Service employees.

Federal Bureau of Investigation. The Federal Bureau of Investigation, as the chief investigative arm of the Department of Justice, has jurisdiction over matters which require the performance of audit work. Examples include violations of the National Bankruptcy Act, Federal Reserve Act, Fraud against the Government's Statutes, Labor Management Relations Act of 1947, as amended (Taft-Hartley Law), Labor Management Reporting and Disclosure Act of 1959 (Landrum-Griffin Act), Welfare and Pension Plans Disclosure Act, and investigation of civil suits in which the United States is a party in interest. These cases involve examinations of books and records of many different types of commercial organizations.

Examples of FBI audit work based on a description of accounting and auditing work by the Bureau, published in 1966, are as follows:

> A National Bankruptcy Act investigation may require detailed audits of the books and records of the bankrupt to prove or disprove an allegation that the bankrupt company violated a Federal criminal law. Many fraudulent bankruptcy schemes are planned in advance to avoid detection and transactions may be recorded falsely or omitted from the records. Such cases may require developing supplementary accounting information to bridge gaps resulting from missing or incomplete records. Sometimes it is necessary to examine records of companies which did business with a bankrupt company in order to reconstruct the financial transactions.
>
> Federal Reserve Act investigations usually result from an allegation that an officer or employee of a bank or a banking-type institution has embezzled funds, made false entries, or committed some other fraudulent act. Many embezzlement schemes are extremely complicated and have been in operation for many years, necessitating detailed examinations of records.
>
> Fraud Against the Government investigations are conducted when charges are made against contractors and others doing business with the Federal Government that they submitted false claims or made false representations to the Government. Detailed audits of books and records are often necessary to determine whether a fraud has been committed and the extent thereof.
>
> Labor Management Relations Act and related investigations are generally conducted for the purpose of detecting evidence of unlawful payments made by employers or associations of employers to labor organizations or to officers or employees of labor organizations. Allegations of embezzlement or unlawful conversion of funds, securities, or other assets of labor organizations including welfare and pension plan funds are also subject to investigation. These may involve detailed examinations of books and records of labor unions, financial institutions, and commercial enterprises.

Atomic Energy Commission. Primary responsibility for internal audit activities in this agency is assigned to the Controller. The basic audit policy, as prescribed[2] by the AEC General Manager, is as follows:

> It is the policy of AEC that internal auditing be an element in the administration of operations performed by AEC and its cost-type contractors, exclusive of technical operations. The internal audits, in addition to ascertaining the allowability of expenditures, realization of revenues, and compliance with AEC Manual and contractual provisions, are to include reviews of the business practices and procedures which have an impact upon the financial interests of AEC, including its appropriations, funds, obligations, costs, property, and other assets. Through an examination of these practices and procedures, including a review of internal controls and of compliance with AEC

[2] *AEC Manual*, chap. 1201, Atomic Energy Commission, Washington, October, 1959.

policy and practice, there will be provided the essential requirements for audit determination as to whether Government funds are properly used, adequately safeguarded and properly accounted for.

AEC's major production and research facilities are operated by private contractors, in addition to which numerous other contractors perform work for the agency either directly or as subcontractors under the operating contractors. With respect to AEC's contractors, the work of the agency's auditors includes the following attest functions:

1. After each fiscal year, operating contractors prepare a voucher form which provides a summary accounting for net expenditures accrued. The AEC auditor in charge of the audit of each such contract is required to approve this voucher as to correctness of the amounts of expenditures and compliance with contract provisions.
2. After completion of audit of each "nonoperating" cost-type contract, the auditor prepares a report which includes his audit opinion as to the validity of costs claimed by the contractor, their reasonableness, allowability, and applicability to contract work. Contractors are paid or disallowances of improper amounts are asserted on the basis of these attestations.

EXECUTIVE BRANCH AUDITS

Financial Audits. The principal objective of this type of audit is to examine accounts and financial transactions for the purpose of expressing an opinion whether the financial statements present fairly the financial position and results of operations. More limited objectives are often established which place primary emphasis on evaluation of the adequacy of an agency's prescribed policies and procedures, the adequacy of internal controls, and compliance with all prescribed requirements.

Operational Audits. Many audit organizations in the federal government have expanded the scope of their work beyond financial matters and into the operating activities they audit. Several types of such operational audits may be found; the procedures used are generally influenced by and tailored to the organization and mission of the department or agency in which the audit organization is located.

Installation audits. This type of audit is a simultaneous and coordinated examination of all of an installation's activities having financial significance, culminating in a single audit report on the effectiveness of its financial management operations.

In some areas, the scope of installations audits has been extended to the mission area. The U.S. Army Audit Agency, for example, describes the *mission-oriented audit* as one involving the performance of sufficient audit work "to evaluate the effectiveness and efficiency with which the installation or activity used its resources in accomplishing each of its assigned major missions."[3]

Under this approach, the major mission operations are made the starting and focal point of the audit. The extent and nature of the examination of other activities depends substantially on the manner in which they affect the conduct of the mission operations.

The audit objectives under the mission-oriented audit concept consist of determining or evaluating the

[3] *U.S. AAA Manual* 309-1, U.S. Army Audit Agency, Department of the Army, Washington, Jan. 15, 1966.

1. Effectiveness of major mission accomplishment
2. Efficiency of operations
3. Certainty of an efficient continuance of adequate mission performance
4. Effect and/or potential effect of deficiencies found on major mission accomplishment, both at the audited activity and at related activities
5. Basic cause of deficiencies found
6. Practical corrective actions that should be taken

Audit policies of the Army Audit Agency require the early identification of problem areas in these audits. The instructions specify the use of survey techniques which will serve as the key to identifying problems and channeling audit effort into the most essential areas. They further direct that the survey be used "to determine missions and related priorities and to identify specific policies, procedures, controls and apparent problem areas."

In general, a top-down approach is followed in applying the mission-oriented audit concept. The survey work is started at top management levels and proceeds to operations at all intermediate levels down to the lowest operating level. However, the nature of the examination or audit work at the intermediate and lower levels is dependent upon the results of audit at the higher levels. Thus, the audit at the lower levels of the organization and/or activity should provide only the amount of coverage necessary to evaluate effectiveness of accomplishment of the organization's major mission.

Vertical audits. Under this type of audit, a group of installations, each of which is a participant in a major program of the government department, is examined as an entity engaged in a specific mission. The vertical audit is concerned with the effectiveness of financial management operations pertinent to the program and less specifically to the operations of its component installations. This type of audit is most commonly used in the military departments.

Functional audits. A common practice of the larger audit organizations in recent years is to audit a specific function performed by several installations within a department. These audits usually cross organizational lines and are for the purpose of reviewing an area of interest common to all or most of the installations within a department. This type of audit, which is also referred to as a "lateral" audit by some organizations, will usually disclose some common cause for any breakdowns in management controls if they exist. In addition, it permits a comparison of efficiency in the performance of this function by the different installations, thereby enabling higher-level management to evaluate accomplishments and institute department-wide corrective action where required.

Other Types of Audits. Other types of audits performed by Executive Branch agencies in the federal government include contract audits, tax audits, bank audits, audits of private companies by regulatory agencies, Medicare program audits, and grant-in-aid audits.

Contract audits. The following description of contract auditing is based on a survey conducted of federal government contract auditing.[4] Audit groups in the military departments and in several of the civilian agencies provide contract audit services for their contracting and procurement officials. The work in the Defense Department has been centralized since July, 1965, in the Defense Contract Audit Agency, thus permitting Army, Navy, and Air Force audit organizations to spend full time on internal audit activities.

[4] Stancil M. Smith, "What's Going On in Government Auditing?" *U.S. Army Audit Agency Bulletin* (Department of the Army, Washington), December, 1965, p. 21.

Contract audit work usually breaks down into three general categories: (1) on-site reviews and audits at government contractors' plants to determine and recommend to contracting officers allowable costs under cost-type contracts, (2) on-site audits at contractors' plants, to determine the accuracy and acceptability of data appearing on pricing proposals submitted by contractors for use in negotiating fixed-price contracts, and (3) rendering advice and assistance to contracting officers and other management officials in the negotiation and administration of all types of procurement and contracting activity.

Contract audit principles are set forth in ASPR (Armed Services Procurement Regulations) for Department of Defense contracts and in FPR (Federal Procurement Regulations) for the civilian department and agency contracts. The two regulations are practically identical so far as cost principles are concerned.

Audits may be done on a continuing basis by resident audit staffs or by mobile teams, depending on the volume of work. Contract auditors approve or disapprove of vouchers claimed by contractors for reimbursable expenses. Periodic audit reports are submitted in which allowable and questioned costs are set forth. Audit reports, usually on a fiscal-year basis, are of value to contracting officers in negotiating overhead and general and administrative expense rates with cost-type contractors.

Tax audits. This type of examination performed by revenue agents may be conducted through either office interview or field examination. Field examination work is primarily concerned with income tax. Typical scope and objectives of the field audit are:

1. Determining the kind of audit to be made upon consideration of the adequacy and reasonableness of information given on the tax return and material developed during the course of the investigation, the sufficiency and accuracy of the accounting records involved, the complexity of the business activity concerned, the prior experience with the taxpayer involved, and other similar elements.
2. Analyzing accounting books and records to ensure that established accounting principles have been applied and related statutory provisions have been observed (e.g., items of income and expense are treated as such; amounts involved in expense items are reasonable; proper distinction between personal and business expenses has been made; methods of determining costs, expenses, and profits reflect the values involved; and similar elements).
3. Examining or investigating source documents, related financial transactions, operating methods, trade or industry practices, and business activities or conditions including such elements as the examination of correspondence, vouchers, leases, contracts, wills, and other documents or legal instruments. The securing of information from taxpayers, their representatives, or business associates in order to develop data regarding the nature of business transactions, the value of property or other assets involved, the degree of conformance in specific cases with operating or accounting methods practiced generally in the industry or business activity involved. And the extent to which bank accounts, the status of loans, the results of investments, and other records or transactions are accurately reflected in accounting records and tax returns.

Regulatory agency audits. There are a number of federal agencies which carry out regulatory functions pertaining to the operations of business enterprises.

The major federal regulatory agencies are:

Federal Power Commission
Federal Communications Commission
Federal Maritime Commission
Securities and Exchange Commission
Interstate Commerce Commission
Federal Trade Commission
Civil Aeronautics Board

In varying degree, the regulatory work of these agencies includes the making of audits for specified purposes. The auditing work of the Federal Power Commission illustrates the nature of such auditing.

The Commission has an auditing division composed of accountants and engineers who examine the books and records of public utilities, licensees, and natural gas companies. Audit work includes a study of the company's system of internal control utilizing the work papers of the company's certified public accountants. It also involves a study of selected areas of a company's books and records during the preliminary review stages to develop possible areas subject to more intensive audit.

Three types of audits are made:

1. *Licensed-project Audits.* The Commission is authorized by law to issue licenses to electric utilities for the construction and operation of hydroelectric power plants on navigable streams or other bodies of water over which the Congress has jurisdiction. Upon expiration of the license, usually for a limited period not to exceed 50 years, the federal government may acquire and operate the project by paying the licensee its net investment in the project.

One type of audit by Commission auditors, as described in a Commission release, is made

> to determine whether the claimed amounts are actual and legitimate costs applicable to the project property and to eliminate from the books all erroneous and improper items, such as intercompany profits between affiliates, write-ups of plant costs by appraisals, nonproject property costs, operating and maintenance costs improperly capitalized, improperly-priced and unrecorded retirements, excess interest and taxes during construction, gratuities, organization expenses of extinct corporations, preliminary exploration expenses not related to the project, lobbying expenses and political contributions, entertainment expenses, etc.

This type of audit work also includes examination of the accounting for additions and retirements of project property, and of depreciation and amortization reserves.

2. *Utility Plant Account Audits.* The Commission's auditors examine the books and records of electric and natural gas utilities to verify the amounts charged to plant accounts. These examinations are important in that the utilities are permitted to charge rates that will provide a fair return on the original cost less depreciation of their utility property.

3. *Compliance Audits.* Audits are also made to ascertain the company's compliance with the requirements of the Commission's uniform system of accounts for electric and natural gas utility companies and with good accounting principles and practices.

As described by the Commission, these audits are made to determine that

> operating expenses do not include extraneous items, that losses are not carried forward as deferred charges unless authorized; to ascertain whether allocations of cost between

departments of the utility or between the utility and subsidiary companies, or between the functions of the utility, are just and reasonable; to see that the consolidated income taxes of associated companies are properly allocated to the jurisdictional subsidiary; to see that the estimated accruals for income taxes as reflected by the books of the utility approximate actual taxes paid, and that proper accounts are maintained for deferred income taxes identified by years; to see that the utility is keeping its accounts in accordance with those prescribed by the Commission; to disclose irregular or unusual practices and transactions between the utility and its stockholders by analysis of surplus and the minutes of the stockholders' and directors' meetings; to see that the amounts reflected in the company's books conform to the amounts reported to the Commission by annual reports.

Medicare audits. This type of audit is carried out by the Audit Agency of the Department of Health, Education, and Welfare, internal auditors of the intermediaries (insurance companies), and providers (hospitals) under the Health Insurance for the Aged Act, and independent public accountants. With respect to the audit of providers (hospitals), the Social Security Administration in collaboration with the HEW Audit Agency developed an audit program[5] to be followed in the examination of the providers' financial and statistical records in determining reasonable costs of their services. This program was designed to meet the following audit objectives:

1. To ascertain that the hospital is conforming to the payment regulations under the act
2. To review, analyze, test, and verify the hospital's financial and statistical books and records and to determine that only proper items of costs applicable to hospital services have been included in reimbursable costs
3. To verify that expenses attributable to the health insurance program have been reasonably determined
4. To ascertain that records supporting statistical data and the adequacy of the methods used for accumulation are sufficient to properly develop valid and accurate statistical information
5. To make maximum utilization of hospital audits performed by others, where available, insofar as they reasonably further the audit objectives of the Bureau of Health Insurance

GENERAL ACCOUNTING OFFICE AUDITS

As described in broad outline earlier in this chapter, the General Accounting Office has broad responsibilities for auditing, on behalf of the Congress, the programs and activities of almost all federal agencies.

The published audit policies of this agency will be found in Title 3 of the *General Accounting Office Policy and Procedures Manual for Guidance of Federal Agencies,* from which the following is adapted.

Purpose of Audits. The primary purpose of General Accounting Office audits is to make for the Congress independent examinations into the manner in which the government agencies discharge their financial responsibilities. Financial responsibilities of government agencies include the administration of funds and the utilization of property and personnel only for authorized programs, activities, or purposes, and the conduct of programs or activities in an effective, efficient, and economical manner. Particular emphasis is placed on any aspects suspected or found to require correction or improvement and on the means of accomplishing it.

[5] Audit Program for Hospitals under the Health Insurance for Aged Act, Title XVIII, Social Security Administration, U.S. Department of Health, Education, and Welfare.

The audits also include examinations of the personal accountability of the certifying, collecting, and disbursing officers concerned and serve as a basis for making settlements with these officers, where required.

Audit Objectives. The general audit objectives of the General Accounting Office with respect to a government agency or an agency activity, program, function, or operation selected for audit, involve examination into:

1. Whether the agency is carrying out only those activities or programs authorized by the Congress and is conducting them in the manner contemplated to accomplish the objectives intended. Where appropriate, a review is also made for the purpose of considering whether the authorized activities or programs effectively continue to serve their originally intended purpose.
2. Whether the programs and activities are conducted and expenditures are made in an effective, efficient, and economical manner and in compliance with the requirements of applicable laws and regulations, including decisions of the Comptroller General.
3. Whether the resources of the agency, including funds, property, and personnel, are adequately controlled and utilized in an effective, efficient, and economical manner.
4. Whether all revenues and receipts arising from the operations under examination are collected and properly accounted for.
5. Whether the agency's accounting system complies with the principles, standards, and related requirements prescribed by the Comptroller General.
6. Whether reports by the Agency to the Congress and the central control agencies disclose properly the information required for the purposes of the reports.

The detection of fraud is not a primary reason for making audits. Agency managements are considered to be responsible for devising their organization structures, dividing responsibilities, and instituting appropriate control procedures so as to minimize the possibilities of fraud. The General Accounting Office investigates evidences of fraud, however, and gives full consideration to the possibilities of fraud, particularly where weaknesses in internal control procedures appear to exist.

Phases of Audit Work. A General Accounting Office audit includes the following broad phases of work:

Preliminary survey. Obtaining general working information on an agency or segment of agency activity selected for audit as a general basis for planning the specific work to be done and for use in making the audit.

Review and legislation. Studying the pertinent laws and legislative history to ascertain congressional intent as to:

1. The purpose, scope, and objectives of the activities or functions being examined
2. The manner in which activities are to be conducted and financed
3. The nature and extent of the agency's authority and responsibility

Review and testing of management control. Studying the policies established to govern agency activities under examination for conformity with applicable laws and the intent of the Congress and their appropriateness for carrying out the authorized activities in an effective, efficient, and economical manner.

Reviewing and testing the agency's operating and administrative procedures and practices, system of accounting, reporting, internal review, and other elements of the system of internal management control for effectiveness in promoting:

1. Adherence to prescribed policies
2. Accomplishment of intended purposes of activities conducted
3. Operational efficiency
4. Efficient and economical utilization of property and personnel
5. Effective control over expenditures, receipts, revenues, and assets
6. Proper accounting for resources and financial transaction
7. The production and reporting of accurate, reliable, and useful financial data
8. Compliance with requirements of applicable laws, regulations, and decisions

This phase of the audit also includes the exploration and development of all pertinent and significant information necessary to properly consider, support, and present any findings, conclusions, and recommendations made.

Reporting. Preparing and submitting appropriate reports on the results of the audit work to the Congress, to appropriate congressional committees, and to agency officials as a basis for appropriate action, where necessary, and for information purposes.

Relationship to Internal Auditing. The adequacy of the system of internal control, including internal audit, of each federal agency is of importance to the General Accounting Office in carrying out its statutory audit responsibilities.

Although there are numerous areas of common interest between the General Accounting Office and an agency's internal auditors, certain basic objectives and responsibilities differ. Internal auditing is an integral part of an agency's system of management control. In its audits, the General Accounting Office reviews the entire control mechanism within an agency, including the various arrangements made by the management for internal audits and other forms of inspection, appraisal, and evaluation. If warranted by its evaluations, the General Accounting Office will rely on such work and make full use of it in conducting its examinations.

The effectiveness of the internal auditing is given due weight in setting the scope of General Accounting Office audits. Where the internal audit work is capably carried out, the amount of work to be performed by the General Accounting Office can be substantially curtailed.

Relationship to Accounting Systems. The existence of good accounting records and sound accounting procedures facilitates the making of an audit. The accounting function is a management responsibility, the discharge of which is subject to audit review in the same manner as any other financial responsibility. The primary responsibility for establishing and maintaining adequate systems of accounting and internal control, including internal audit, is vested by the Budget and Accounting Procedures Act of 1950 in the heads of federal agencies themselves.

The accounting systems established, however, must conform to the principles, standards, and related requirements prescribed by the Comptroller General. In addition, the establishment of effective controls is required from the standpoint of sound fiscal management practice. Accordingly, it is the policy of the General Accounting Office to utilize audit processes based upon an evaluation of accounting systems and the effectiveness of related internal checks and controls in agencies at the site of operations, to the maximum extent practicable, as a basis for discharging its responsibilities to the Congress.

Identification of Causes of Deficiencies. The identification of the underlying causes of deficiencies in performance is an important part of the audit work.

Such identification is necessary in order to propose effective corrective actions, the objective being to improve the management systems, to save money, avoid improper payments or other losses, or promote greater efficiency or effectiveness in the future.

Significance of Matters Examined. In planning and conducting its audits, the General Accounting Office, with due regard to the significance and importance of the matters, places emphasis on those aspects of agency operations and activities in which opportunities for improvement appear to exist. This policy gives recognition to the need to examine into areas of known or anticipated congressional interest and, at the same time, provide for the most effective use of available audit manpower.

The General Accounting Office also gives recognition in reports to work resulting in favorable findings, to work sufficiently intensive to enable reporting no significant findings, and to general reviews which reveal no indications of weakness warranting closer examination.

Illegal Payments. While the General Accounting Office is not empowered to direct changes in agency policies, procedures, and functions, it does have the power to refuse credit to accountable officers for payments made illegally or improperly from appropriated funds. In substance, this means that the auditors have the responsibility to disallow credit for, and to enforce recovery of, money illegally or improperly paid out by action against the accountable certifying or disbursing officer or his surety.

Relation to Contracting Agency Auditing. In carrying out its audit work, the General Accounting Office gives full consideration to work done by the audit organizations of the contracting agencies concerned such as the Defense Contract Audit Agency described previously. Those organizations are an integral part of the government's administrative processes required to be reviewed. Moreover, the scope and effectiveness of the work of agency audit organizations on contracted and agency activities is an important consideration in determining the scope and nature of the audit work to be performed by the General Accounting Office. By reviewing and testing their work, the amount of direct General Accounting Office audit work may be curtailed. However, the fact that agency auditors have performed work in a particular area does not necessarily mean that additional work in that area by the General Accounting Office will not be determined to be needed.

Selection of Contracts for Audit. There are many reasons for deciding to make an audit in individual cases. Underlying all of them is the overall objective of testing the effectiveness of the federal agency management controls which should be operating to safeguard the government's interests.

Not all contracts or contractors are examined. In determining the work to be done, consideration is given to such matters as the size or type of contract, the basis for award, the nature of cost or pricing data furnished or the lack of such data, and a wide variety of other factors affecting the government's interest.

Right of Access to Contractor Records. The applicable laws require contract provisions giving the Comptroller General and his representatives the right to examine contractor records that are directly pertinent to, and involve transactions relating to, the contracts or subcontracts to be audited.

It is the position of the General Accounting Office with respect to this right that:

1. The clear intention of these laws is, among other things, "to afford a means whereby the Congress could be informed of any excessive or unrea-

sonable payments to contractors holding negotiated contracts and to serve as a deterrent to the making of contracts providing for unreasonable profits to Government contractors." (32 Comp. Gen. 278.)

2. All books, documents, papers, and other records relating to the pricing and cost of performance of negotiated contracts are directly pertinent records.

3. Such books, documents, records, etc., are not limited to the formal cost accounting records and their supporting data, but include all underlying data concerning contract activities and operations which afford the basis for contract pricing and the incurrence of costs by the contractor.

Reports on Contract Audits. Whether a report to the Congress is made as a result of a specific contract audit depends on the judgment made in the General Accounting Office as to the significance of the information obtained during the audit, the conclusions reached, and knowledge as to general or special interests of the Congress and its committees in procurement and contract matters.

In some cases, the findings and conclusions in a report may not be considered to be of sufficient significance to warrant reporting to the Congress but may still be of concern or interest to the contracting agency. In these cases, the reports are addressed to appropriate department or agency officials. In other cases, the audit work may have resulted in no significant findings, and a close-out letter to this effect is issued to the contractor.

Before a report is completed and submitted to the Congress, the contracting agency and the contractor are given the opportunity to review and comment on the draft of the report.

The purpose of this step is to give the agency and the contractor concerned an adequate opportunity to provide official written statements of their views on the matters included and to submit such additional factual information bearing on those matters as they believe may not have been considered in drafting the report.

In preparing the final report for submission to the Congress, the normal practice is to include the written comments of the contracting agency and the contractor in the appendix to the report.

INTERNAL AUDIT REPORTS

General. An important part of the audit process is the reporting of findings, observations, conditions, conclusions, and recommendations to the agency management. Although reporting methods vary widely in the audit organizations of the federal government, as a general practice, audit reports are prepared on the basis of the "management by exception" principle of reporting deficiencies only.

Types of reports prepared are influenced by the type of audit performed, the organizational structure of the department or agency, and the location and nature of the audience the report writer is trying to reach. The more complex reports result when authority for corrective action is vested in several levels of agency management.

Generally, audit reports reflect one or more of the following conditions:

1. Nonconformity with management or operating practices generally accepted as sound
2. Nonconformity with accepted or prescribed accounting principles and standards

3. Nonconformity with statutes, regulations, legal decisions, or other mandatory requirements
4. Inefficient, uneconomical, or ineffective performance

Standards. The following reporting standards for internal audit reports are suggested by the Comptroller General in the current GAO statement of basic principles and concepts of internal auditing for federal agencies:

> To be effective, audit reports must be carefully prepared in accordance with the following standards:
>
> 1. Factual matter must be accurately, completely, and fairly presented.
> 2. Findings must be presented objectively and in language as clear and simple as the subject matter permits. Findings must be adequately supported by the audit working papers.
> 3. Reports must be concise but complete enough to be readily understood by the users.
> 4. Information on underlying causes of deficiencies reported should be provided so as to assist in implementing proposals for or devising corrective action.
> 5. Reports should place primary emphasis on improvement of operations rather than on criticism of the past; critical comments should be placed in balanced perspective with any unusual difficulties or circumstances faced by the operating officials concerned.
> 6. Reports should point up issues and questions needing further study and consideration by the internal auditor or others.
> 7. Reports should recognize noteworthy accomplishments particularly where management improvements in one place may have applicability elsewhere in the agency.

The GAO statement also suggests that:

> Except where the possibility of fraud or other compelling reason may require a different treatment, the auditor's tentative findings should be discussed with the responsible operating officials whose activities are being reviewed. Their views should be obtained and given recognition so that the report can become a vehicle for constructive action in which the operating officials play an important role. Where possible without undue delay, operating officials' views should be obtained in writing.

Follow-up. One of the important ingredients in an agency's policy statement on auditing relates to the follow-up procedures on audit report recommendations. Most such statements in the federal government contain provisions requiring the addressees of audit report recommendations to submit written responses on a timely basis (usually 30 to 60 days) indicating concurrence or nonconcurrence with the recommendations and outlining corrective actions taken or planned. Most audit organizations keep control records on report responses and follow up in the next scheduled audit to confirm that corrections reported have actually been made.

The GAO release on internal auditing states that:

1. Primary responsibility for action and follow-up on audit recommendations rests with management.
2. A desirable procedure is to have regular status reports prepared for the information of management officials, and the internal auditors, as to actions taken on audit recommendations.
3. Provision should be made for regular inquiry into whether proposed corrective actions have in fact been taken and their effectiveness.
4. Where operating officials disagree with audit recommendations, a mechanism should be established to reconcile the differences or to call for a decision at a higher management level.

Chapter 8

Part 2 State Government Auditing

MARTIN IVES

Deputy Comptroller, State of New York

GENERAL

Types of Audits. Auditing in state government generally takes two forms, commonly referred to as "preaudit" and "postaudit." Preaudit is the examination of transactions before payment. It is the more traditional audit function, and is accomplished in a generally similar manner throughout the country. Postaudit represents an after-the-fact examination, is more recent in origin, and tends to differ in scope from state to state.

This section covers broadly the concepts and techniques of postaudit in state government. Preaudit is discussed primarily to provide the postauditor with information as to its values and limitations so that these factors may be considered in establishing the scope of postaudit.

Nature of Preaudit. Some form of preaudit of state revenues and expenditures is performed in all states, usually in a central office headed by the state comptroller. The preaudit, perhaps more accurately described as pre-encumbrance/prepayment audit, is generally an integral part of the central accounting and payment process. It tends to be clerical and routine in nature but can also make significant contributions to improved procedures and reductions in cost.

The basic objectives of preaudit are to provide assurance that (1) expenditures are not, upon their face, unreasonable or extravagant; (2) sufficient funds are available to enable encumbrance of the order or payment of the voucher; and (3) there has been compliance with budgetary, civil service, legislative, and legal requirements. It may include an examination of contracts prior to approval and encumbrance, scrutiny of all vouchers before payment, and review of all payrolls before payment. The preaudit objectives fall within the general concept of audit for "regularity." [1]

Contracts. Preaudit of contracts embraces the routine checking for legislative, budgetary, and agency authorization, sufficiency of funds, and mathematical accuracy. It may also include a deeper probing into the reasonableness of price, covering such matters as the review of bids for adequacy of competition, assurance of award to the lowest responsible bidder, and adequacy of documentation of price where competition was not obtained.

Payrolls. Payrolls will generally be reviewed by the central preaudit agency to assure that gross salaries are computed in accordance with governing statutes, that payroll changes (e.g., for new employments, promotions, or transfers) have been properly authorized by the employing department and other central control agencies, and that payrolls are submitted in accordance with line item or other controls established by the legislature or executive agencies. Vouchers for merchandise, construction payments, refund claims, state aid payments, travel allowances, etc., are examined for reasonableness, mathematical accuracy, compliance with statutory, contractual, or administrative rules and regulations, and departmental authorization.

Internal control. Since preaudit is a significant element of the state's internal control process, the postauditor should have a thorough understanding of the preaudit function within the state. An effectively functioning preaudit activity may provide the postauditor with information on weaknesses within specific agencies. For example, discussions with the preauditors or review of preaudit correspondence may disclose evidence of unusually high incidence of fund insufficiency, mathematical errors, delayed processing of invoices, and erroneous fund citations. Depending upon the nature and scope of the preaudit, the postauditor may be able to curtail the scope of his audit in certain areas, particularly in the more routine verification aspects.

Limitations. Even the most effective preaudit, however, has significant limitations which must be recognized by the postauditor in fixing the scope of his audit. For example, preaudit procedures may provide adequate assurance that prices shown on vouchers for supplies are in accordance with centrally negotiated contract prices, but they cannot provide assurance that the supplies were actually needed by the agency placing the order. Preaudit may be able to provide the postauditor with reasonable assurance of the effectiveness of central legislative and administrative controls over payrolls, but it

[1] E. L. Normanton, *The Accountability and Audit of Governments*, Manchester, England, The University Press, University of Manchester; and New York, Frederick A. Praeger, Inc., 1966, p. 22.

cannot provide assurance that the individuals on the payrolls are actually on duty, that they are performing the duties required, and that they are performing efficiently.

Finally, regardless of the effectiveness of preaudit, it must be recognized that the full implications of an agency's basic policy or procedure cannot be discovered through the preaudit piecemeal examination of individual isolated vouchers or transactions. Comprehensive audit for financial accountability, efficient performance, or effective program accomplishment must be done through the postaudit process.

Scope and Concept of Postaudit. The scope of postaudit in state government may be grouped into three general categories: (1) financial accountability and legality—the verification of accounting records and review of internal controls concerning revenues and expenditures; (2) performance efficiency—the examination of the efficiency and economy with which agency operations are carried out; and (3) program evaluation—the broad examination of the extent to which program goals are fulfilled. These classifications tend to overlap, but they are useful in demonstrating the changing concepts of auditing and in comparing them with parallel changes in the states' budgetary processes. The traditional control-oriented line-item budget is gradually giving way to the responsibility-oriented performance budget and to the planning-oriented program budget (planning-programming-budgeting system).

Many factors affect the scope of postaudit within a state. Some of these factors are the specific constitutional or statutory authority of the audit agency, the organizational position of the agency within the state, and the desire of the auditor to extend the audit scope beyond the traditional audit for financial accountability and legality. The general scope of postaudit and the differences in the manner in which postauditors take office may be illustrated by reference to state constitutions and published reports issued by state auditors.

The auditor general of the state of Michigan serves under an 8-year appointment by majority vote of each house of the legislature. Michigan's constitution requires that: "The auditor general shall conduct post audits of financial transactions and accounts of the state and of all branches, departments, offices, boards, commissions, agencies, authorities and institutions . . . , and performance post audits thereof."[2] The audits conducted by the Michigan auditor general endeavor:

> To determine whether the moneys which have been appropriated by the State Legislature to State agencies have been expended in accordance with the purposes for which they were appropriated;
>
> To determine whether the collections of State revenues and receipts are in accordance with applicable laws and that there is proper accounting and control of such revenues and receipts;
>
> To determine whether moneys handled by State agencies on behalf of the State or held in trust by them have been properly administered;
>
> To assist administrators of State agencies by indicating areas in their own organizations which could perform more efficiently and effectively.[3]

The state comptroller of New York, elected for a 4-year term by the people, performs both preaudit and postaudit functions. Under the constitution, the New York state comptroller is required "to audit all vouchers before pay-

[2] State of Michigan, Office of the Auditor General, *Report of Audits Completed during Fiscal Year Ending June 30, 1968*, Dec. 1, 1968, p. 1.

[3] *Ibid.*, pp. 1–2.

ment and all official accounts" and "to audit the accrual and collection of all revenues and receipts." His statutory responsibilities include the rendering of a report to the Legislature, "suggesting plans for the improvement and management of the public resources." He is also required by statute to examine the books and accounts of every public authority, including its receipts, disbursements, contracts, leases, sinking funds, investments and any other matters relating to its financial standing.[4]

The following excerpts from official reports of the New York state comptroller demonstrate the broad concept of postaudit within that state:

> The Legislature and the Executive need assurance that agency internal controls provide adequate financial accountability. They require independent appraisals of overall performance measured against established goals. Relevant data, scientifically and independently collated, are indispensable to program decisions. Modern "post-audit" fulfills this function.[5]
>
> Until recent years, post-audit was concerned primarily with the controls of cash and the verification of revenues. Today, its general scope involves the review and appraisal of the soundness, adequacy, and application of management's financial and operating controls and practices. Post-audit is directed to the basic programs of the agencies audited and to those financial and operating matters having an impact on the ability of the organizations to accomplish their programs effectively, efficiently and economically. The overall purpose of these audits is to provide those charged with the responsibility for policy decisions with objective analyses, appraisals, recommendations and comments concerning the activities reviewed.[6]

The state of Illinois auditor general is appointed by the governor with the advice and consent of the senate for a term of 6 years. The auditor general's "Instructions to Independent Certified Public Accountants Performing Audits of State Agencies" requires, in part, that audit reports should:

> include statements as to whether anything was observed . . . which would indicate that expenditures have not been made in accordance with legislative appropriations and other State fiscal requirements and restrictions and that revenues have not been properly accounted for . . .
>
> state whether the system of internal control including pre-audit of expenditures is adequate and whether it is functioning effectively, including personnel, payrolls, procurement and property . . .
>
> include a statement relative to compliance with statutes, laws, rules and regulations under which the agency was created and is functioning . . .
>
> disclose whether, in the course of the audit there were any indications of lack of efficiency in financial operations and management of the agency, it being recognized that the usual scope of an audit does not include a study of operating efficiency. . . .[7]

Audits for financial accountability and legality, efficiency of performance, and adherence to programmed goals are not mutually exclusive. Rather, they tend to overlap each other. The auditor examining for the accountability of cash in an agency might readily observe that available cash was not being invested so as to yield the maximum return. An auditor examining into the accountability for fixed assets might also observe, with relatively little extension of his audit procedures, that the items were excess to the agency's needs. Thus, some elements of performance auditing flow naturally from the financial accountability audit, particularly if the auditor is reasonably alert.

[4] State of New York, Office of the State Comptroller, Division of Audits and Accounts, *Audit of State Agencies and Authorities*, Feb. 18, 1969, p. 1.

[5] *Ibid.*, Transmittal letter to the Legislature of the State of New York.

[6] *Ibid.*, p. 3.

[7] State of Illinois, Office of the Auditor General, *Report of Department of Audits*, Jan. 31, 1967, p. 5.

But the "performance" or "program" audit will not be fully effective if it is left to chance or considered essentially as a by-product of the financial accountability audit. The audit program must instead make specific provision for audit steps leading to observations concerning the efficiency of agency performance and adherence to programmed goals. For example, the traditional payroll audit steps concerned with financial accountability are not likely to enable the auditor to express an opinion on the staffing of nurses in relation to patients at a teaching hospital. By supplementing these steps, however, with an analysis of the hospital's staffing in relation to its own nurse-patient standards and by comparing these standards with the nurse-patient ratio at similar hospitals, the auditor is in a position to comment on the efficiency of performance in this area.

In summary, postaudit in state government should be directed both to the financial and to the operating practices of an agency or a program. These are some of the questions that need to be considered in such an audit:

Financial accountability and legality. Are the internal control procedures, such as the separation of duties, adequate to safeguard against the loss of assets?

Are receipts properly accounted for? Do expenditures meet the requirements of the statutes and administrative procedures and are they adequately documented? Were the expenditures made in compliance with legislative intent?

Do financial reports fairly present the results of agency transactions for the period audited, and the agency's financial position as of a particular date?

Performance efficiency. Are men, materials, and capital so used as to enable the most efficient and economic marshalling of resources toward the achievement of a particular objective?

Have performance standards been established in terms of output for a given quantity of labor input? How do the established standards compare with similar operations inside and outside the state?

Have reporting systems been established to apprise management of deviations from standard? Was corrective action taken on deviations from standard?

Has the agency taken full advantage of the law in developing procedures and practices to maximize revenues?

Program evaluation. Have program goals been established by the agency? Were the program goals established after considering all available alternative courses of action?

Are the program goals established by the state legislature or the executive department being met? If not, what are the inhibiting factors?

One of the fundamental elements of managerial control is the establishment of standards, goals, or objectives, from which deviations may be measured so that corrective action may be taken. By the same token, audit for performance implies the existence of performance standards and program objectives—criteria against which the auditor can measure accomplishment.

Where such standards have been established, the auditor should compare actual performance with the standard and evaluate the actions taken by management to correct deviations from the standard. He should also evaluate the reasonableness of the standard by reviewing how it was established and, where feasible, comparing it with standards established by others. Where such standards have not been established, the auditor should recommend that the agency develop them. Even in these instances, it would be appropriate for the auditor to evaluate performance by reference to standards established or performance obtained by others in similar circumstances.

Program auditing will undoubtedly be influenced by the development and implementation of planning-programming-budgeting (PPB) systems. PPB attempts to rationalize policy making by providing (1) data on the costs and benefits of alternate means of attaining proposed program objectives and (2) output measurements to facilitate the attainment of chosen objectives.[8] Standards will thus be available to the auditor as a basis for evaluating performance.

AUDIT MANAGEMENT

Initiating Performance Audits. The performance audit represents a logical extension of the financial accountability audit. Because of this close relationship, the initial performance audits can be made most readily in those financially related matters with which the auditor has developed a general familiarity because of his training and experience. The areas of inventory control and procurement are suggested starting points. Such examinations might be made at the state's central purchasing agency if one exists, at highway maintenance or contracting activities, or at parks, colleges and institutions.

An auditor examining into physical inventories who makes observations concerning slow-moving stocks (a standard financial audit step) is, in effect, embarking upon the performance audit. When he takes the next step and examines into the causes of slow-moving stocks, reviews the controls concerning stockage levels, and audits the procedures for disposing of excesses, he is deeply involved in auditing for performance. Thus, performance audits can be undertaken by combining the standard financial audit of inventories with a review of supply control activities at an institution or a highway maintenance shop.

Before undertaking the performance aspect of the audit, the auditor should have a clear understanding of the audit objective. The traditional financial audit objective might be: "Are the inventory records reasonably accurate, and are the internal controls over the materials adequate to safeguard against loss?" To this, the auditor might add the following performance objective: "Do the managerial controls provide for maintaining inventories at a level which will assure sufficiency of quantities to meet current needs, without accumulating excesses?"

The same approach applies to procurement. When an auditor examines a purchase order supporting a payment voucher and raises a question concerning the reasonableness of the price, he is on the fringes of the performance audit even though his basic concern is that of financial accountability. When he goes behind the contractual documents and inquires into the agency's contracting procedures as a basic audit objective (e.g., in highway or building construction), he is making significant inroads into the performance audit.

Again, the audit objective must be clearly stated. The traditional financial audit objective might be: "Are payment vouchers supported by duly authorized purchase orders or contract documents, and by evidence of receipt of the merchandise or services?" To this, the auditor might add: "Are policies, procedures and practices so defined and carried out as to enable procurement of required materials and services in an economical manner and at the lowest available prices considering quality and delivery requirements?"

[8] Allen Schick, "The Road to PPB: The Stages of Budget Reform," *Public Administration Review*, December, 1966, pp. 250–251. For a detailed discussion of PPB, see series of articles in this issue of *Public Administration Review*.

By starting with those performance aspects which are clearly financially related, the audit staff can develop an approach which will be helpful in auditing other areas, such as personnel utilization and evaluation of program progress, where the financial relationship may be less apparent.

Preparing for the Audit. In undertaking a performance audit, it is particularly significant for the audit manager to "know the field"—to be generally aware of the management literature and significant recent developments affecting the agency audited. Many government agencies issue annual reports of accomplishment, which the auditor should review before undertaking the audit. He should also read the executive budget with regard to the agency, since it may contain a description of major agency activities and priorities, program objectives, and performance standards. The auditor should also be familiar with applicable statutes and areas of legislative interest, as evidenced by budget hearings, public hearings, and legislative committee reports.

The auditor should also familiarize himself with the results of prior audits of the agency as well as audits of similar agencies. He should review memoranda that may have been placed in the files between audits and should contact those responsible for preaudit for possible audit "leads." Early in the audit, he should review departmental policy and procedure manuals, scrutinize the agency's budget request, examine the organization chart, and review major internal management reports, including internal audit reports. Discussions should be held with key agency supervisors to determine those matters which they consider significant.

The foregoing general survey will provide the basis for establishing the major areas of audit concentration. While the survey is going on, some of the traditional financial accountability audit steps may be performed.

Making Comparative Analyses. From an operating viewpoint, state government is somewhat like a commercial conglomerate. A state is, in effect, a highly diversified service organization. Its activities may include educational services, social services, institutional care, recreation, highway construction and maintenance, and employment services, to name a few. Depending upon the size and organization of the state, many of the services may be performed through field offices in various locations, reporting to a central office. Furthermore, many other governmental agencies throughout the country and in foreign countries provide similar services, though not necessarily in competition.

The auditor may use this organizational structure to advantage in conducting audits. By scheduling simultaneous audits of similar agencies or by examining like functions at different types of agencies, the auditor has an excellent opportunity for making comparative analyses of costs, operating techniques, and managerial control systems among the agencies. For example, the auditor may compare prices paid for a particular commodity with prices paid by another level of government; he may compare staffing ratios (e.g., student-teacher ratios, nurse-patient ratios) with similar agencies in the state or in another state; he may compare operating standards (e.g., stockage levels) with a similar organization or for similar functions at another agency; he may make comparative analyses of cost per mile of highway maintained, cost per patient fed, etc. This type of comparative analysis provides the auditor with a frame of reference—a more objective means—for measuring the performance of the agency under audit.

This organizational structure also facilitates audit supervision and management. Two or more audit teams may examine similar agencies simultaneously, so that the talents of different individuals may be brought to bear upon a given situation. To add perspective to the audit observations, simultaneous audit may be undertaken at the departmental level. A single manager could be given responsibility for coordinating the audit results, through staff seminars and an exchange of findings. This approach also lends itself to the use of statistical sampling, enabling audit teams at different locations to make logical comparisons of audit results, such as error rates.

Reporting Audit Results. The auditor-in-charge should maintain liaison with agency operating officials throughout the audit, usually through a highly placed official on the staff of the agency director. As each segment of the audit is completed, the auditor should prepare a written memorandum to the agency's representative, setting forth the observations, conclusions, and recommendations. This procedure will help to keep agency officials informed, enable prompt corrective action, resolve questions of fact, and facilitate preparation of the final report. At the conclusion of the audit a final conference should be held to discuss the audit results. Some auditors have also found it useful to send a complete draft of the audit report to the agency for formal comment, which will then be incorporated in the final audit report.

Because the audit report will be of interest to officials at many levels of government, it should usually contain a summary of the more significant observations and conclusions. (Some auditors prefer to issue separate reports containing different levels of detail depending upon the recipient.) Each finding contained in the detail section of the report should consist of a description of the audit observation, sufficient background data to enable comprehension of the issue, a statement of the causes and effects of the condition, and appropriate recommendations. Comparisons of program objectives and performance standards with actual accomplishment may be incorporated in the finding, where appropriate, or placed in a separate section of the report. The audit report should also contain any other data which the auditor considers useful to the Legislature.

Audit reports should be forwarded to appropriate legislative officials (majority and minority leaders, finance committees, legislative committees interested in a particular program), executive officials (governor, lieutenant governor, budget director), and officials of the agency audited (department head, agency head). Annual audit reports summarizing the major audit findings during the year may also be issued.

AUDIT OBJECTIVES AND FINDINGS

The ensuing paragraphs illustrate some of the basic objectives of state government auditors. Each of the objectives is supplemented with a series of illustrations drawn from annual reports issued by various state auditors and comptrollers.[9] The concepts and techniques of state government auditing are rapidly changing. Hence, neither the statement of objectives nor the accompanying illustrations constitute an exhaustive study of the subject. They are intended instead to demonstrate the general trend in state auditing.

Defining Goals. Have program goals been established by the agency? Has performance been measured against these program goals? Have policies and procedures been adopted and directed toward the fulfillment of these goals?

[9] The illustrations are drawn from the author's experience in New York State, and from annual reports issued by the auditor general of Michigan (*Auditor General's Report of Audits,* fiscal year ending June 30, 1968) and the Legislative Audit Committee of the state of Colorado (*Third Annual Report,* Dec. 31, 1967).

Has the legislature adequately defined its intent with regard to program goals? Should the legislature reexamine the goals?

Industrial assistance. An agency made low-cost mortgage loans to private industry for the purpose of creating new jobs or retaining existing jobs in the state. However, the data necessary to measure the extent of new jobs created or existing jobs retained as a result of the agency's loans were inaccurate. Further, loans were made without specific criteria as to employment gains or other benefits to be achieved in relation to the dollar amount of loans made. The development of such criteria was recommended.

Correction. The basic objective of a youth camp program was to reorient the habits and attitudes of youthful offenders. Although the program had been in effect for almost 10 years, no formal studies of the rate of recidivism had been made. It was recommended that the department undertake cost-effectiveness studies evaluating the program in the light of available alternatives.

Student loans. An agency responsible for administering a student loan program delayed many years in establishing numerical guidelines for granting loans. Audit showed inconsistencies in granting and rejecting loans, relative to parental income. Because of the state's financial commitment to the program, it was recommended that loan eligibility criteria be established by the legislature.

Student scholarships. A higher education scholarship program provides for certain minimum awards to students, regardless of family income. The minimums do not appear to be significant factors in relation to the total cost of higher education. It was suggested that the Legislature study the statistical analysis presented in the report with a view toward restructuring the individual awards.

Youth rehabilitation. There was a need for closer departmental supervision of a youth rehabilitation program. Staffing shortages, lack of adequate data on program accomplishment, and time limitations on educational programs resulting from use of the public school calendar were suggested as matters requiring attention. It was noted, for example, that records were not maintained showing the status of social adjustment of children released from the school.

Mental hygiene. A state hospital had not established a procedure or record to serve as a reference to the plan prescribed for the treatment of individual patients. It was also found that ward treatment team meetings were not regularly scheduled to assure periodic case reviews of all patients, develop individual treatment programs, and plan ward activities for the patients. Recommendations were made for the development of individual patient treatment programs and improved teamwork among program personnel.

General. One state auditor inserts the following comment in all audit reports where it is appropriate: "We recommend that the department develop performance standards that would meaningfully measure accomplishments of predetermined program objectives and goals."

Establishing Performance Standards. Have performance standards been established with regard to major expenditure areas? Have reporting systems been established to show deviations from the standards? Has management taken action to correct deviations from the standards? Are the standards relevant and reasonable when compared with similar activities?

Mental hygiene. Standards or staffing patterns were not established for many categories of employee services. Audit showed wide variations among the various mental hygiene institutions in the relationship between number of employees and patient workload. Where standards were established, the hiring of staff was continued even though existing staff exceeded the authorized staffing patterns.

Social services. It was recommended that the department prescribe standards for the number of clerical personnel in relation to welfare district case load, in the same manner as staffing patterns were prescribed for case workers. Review of administrative staffing among similar welfare districts throughout the state showed wide differences in relation to the number of welfare cases processed.

Employment placement. Simultaneous audit of several employment placement offices within a large county showed relatively wide differences among the offices in the cost of accomplishing the same function. Audit analysis showed that the cost differences were related to the different methods used for making placements. Recommendations were made for the development of uniform work measurement and operating procedures, and for the consolidation of certain functions.

Institutional management-support services. Standards were established to measure the operating efficiency of power plants at a department's institutions. Audit of operating reports, however, showed that the plants were not performing at the standard level. It was recommended that the economics of making the necessary repairs be studied so that fuel costs might be reduced.

Social services. A social services agency was accomplishing part of its program through child foster care agencies. Audit showed that there was a wide range among the agencies in daily operating cost; e.g., the cost for management and administration was twice as much at one agency as at another. It was recommended that the causes of the cost differences be ascertained so that standards of reasonableness might be established.

Higher education. Audit reports on colleges were expanded to include observations and recommendations on faculty and classroom utilization. Analysis of the statistics showed a need for controls over the extent to which positions authorized for instructional purposes may be used for other functions. Recommendations were also made for improved classroom scheduling procedures.

Using Resources Efficiently. Do agency procedures and practices result in efficient utilization of available resources? Is there evidence of unnecessary duplications? Do procedures and practices result in accomplishing the agency's objectives at the least possible cost consistent with effective performance?

Institutional care. An agency operates several institutions within relatively close geographic proximity. Each institution maintains its own business office and storage facilities. Consolidation and centralization of accounting and storage operations was suggested.

Employee utilization. It was found that substantial savings could be made by reducing staffing requirements. For example, the cost of watchmen services could be reduced by better scheduling and location of employees, and by assigning automobiles to some of the watchmen.

Highway construction program. Statistical analysis of bidding results on highway construction contracts showed that a relatively large number of awards were being made on the basis of limited competition. To increase competition, it was suggested that the number of bid openings in the same geographical area on the same date be reduced and that projects be broken into smaller jobs to the extent feasible.

Highway policing. Based upon a comparison of policing costs at one highway with costs at similar highways, it was suggested that the staffing of this activity could be reduced without loss of service.

Accounting records. A department-level agency processes and records purchase documents, duplicating the record keeping at the institution level. It was suggested that the duplicate record keeping be eliminated and that controls be maintained through a reporting system.

Supply control. Analysis of supply control procedures at highway maintenance offices showed that the quantities of many items on hand were in excess of needs for the reasonably foreseeable future. Furthermore, some offices were purchasing items from outside suppliers even though neighboring offices had these items in excess supply.

Purchasing practices. Audit of a central purchasing agency showed that competition was not being obtained in acquiring the state's needs of a particular commodity. Since competition was not feasible with regard to this commodity, it was recommended that attempts be made to obtain lower prices through negotiation techniques.

Cash management. Cash in excess of current requirements should be transferred from checking accounts to savings and/or time deposit accounts so as to enable the earning of interest.

Providing Financial Controls. Are financial controls adequate to safeguard assets from loss? Do accounting procedures and reporting systems provide management with accurate, timely information for decision-making purposes?

Financial reporting. Management at one agency did not have data which would disclose accurately the income and expenses for each major revenue-producing activity. It was suggested that management could more effectively evaluate its operations through more accurate financial data by major activity.

Cash. Internal control over cash was not adequate because there was insufficient separation of employee duties. One employee handled the cash receipts and bank deposits for all funds, processed the cash disbursements for several funds, and reconciled bank statements for all funds.

Accounts receivable. Large amounts of accounts receivable have accumulated as a result of participating in federally supported highway programs. Audit showed that the agency responsible for making billings was not aware of all amounts due because of the lack of adequate control procedures.

Equipment. In many instances, minimum equipment accountability procedures (e.g., numbering and tagging of equipment, keeping control records) were lacking. In some instances, unused equipment was on hand even though it had been acquired several years earlier.

Accounting procedures. In order to increase the accuracy of the records and to render more meaningful operating reports, it was recommended that the state's agencies adopt accrual accounting and general ledgers supported by double-entry accounting systems.

Pricing practices. There is a need for establishing proper cost-price relationships for goods and services "sold" by one agency to another within the state.

Maximizing Revenues. Is the agency making efforts to maximize its revenues in accordance with federal statutes, state statutes, grants, and contracts? Are procedures adequate to assure contractor compliance with contracts and concession agreements?

Social services. Maximum federal funds were not being obtained under the Medicare and Medicaid programs. Patients in the state schools for the mentally retarded and in tuberculosis hospitals had not been enrolled in the program. In addition, certain institutions had not been accredited as "providers" of service, procedural weaknesses caused delay in enrolling patients, and billing rates were established below actual costs. Recommendations were made for the review of policies and the establishment of procedures for maximizing available funds.

Legislation authorized the federal government to match local expenditures for children removed from aid to dependent children households by judicial determination. The state was not obtaining the available funds, however, because the state social services agency had not submitted the required plan to federal authorities. It was recommended that such a plan be filed.

State laws require legally responsible relatives having the available resources to pay for the maintenance of children who are cared for at public expense. Delays in consummating repayment agreements with these relatives resulted in the loss of funds. More timely consummation of such agreements was recommended.

Pricing practices. With regard to a port authority which had not reviewed its tariffs in many years and which was suffering losses in its grain elevator operations, it was noted that the tariffs were substantially lower than those charged at other ports. It was suggested that a revised tariff structure be adopted.

Concession contracts. Comprehensive review of concession agreements showed a need for agencies to obtain adequate competition (consistent with the quality of services desired) or to undertake sufficient negotiations to assure maximum revenues to the state.

Billing procedures. A department operates power plants which sell excess energy to an electric company. Although the contract with the electric company contemplates recoupment by the state of the reasonable cost of operating the plants, the billings did not include charges for retirement expenses or administrative overhead. It was recommended that billings include all appropriate charges.

Assuring Legislative Review. Is there adequate control over the availability of funds? Is management aware of the amount of funds available for expenditure? Are all expenditures subject to legislative review?

Higher education. Student fees were being used to supplement administrative costs not approved in the budgetary process. The receipts and disbursements from these fees were not being reported in a manner which would adequately disclose their source and disposition. It was recommended that student fees be included in the budgetary process and that responsibility for increases and decreases be retained by the legislature.

Federally funded. All anticipated federal grants for state agencies should be included within the budgetary process and made subject to legislative review. Legislative review of federally sponsored programs was considered necessary because financial responsibility for some of the programs may be passed on to the state in subsequent years.

Special funds. Excessive subsidies from the general fund caused the needless accumulation of monies in a special restricted fund. It was recommended that minimum working capital requirements be established for the restricted fund, and that any excess monies be transferred to the treasury and made available for general operating expenditures.

Legislative intent—general. Where the legislature desires to restrict activities or the expenditure of funds, it should include in its appropriation statutes clear and precise language dealing with these restrictions. Such language is necessary to avoid repetition of questions as to whether legislative intent has been properly interpreted by the executive branch.

BIBLIOGRAPHY

Federal Government

Armed Services Procurement Regulations, Department of the Army, Washington.

Budget and Accounting Procedures Act of 1950.

Audit Program for Hospitals under the Health Insurance for Aged Act, Title XVIII, Social Security Administration, U.S. Department of Health, Education, and Welfare.

Internal Auditing in Federal Agencies, General Accounting Office, Washington, 1968.

AEC Manual, chap. 1201, Atomic Energy Commission, Washington, October, 1959.

General Accounting Office Policy and Procedures Manual for Guidance of Federal Agencies, Title 3, General Accounting Office, Washington, September, 1966.

Roy, Robert H., and James H. MacNeill: *Horizons for a Profession*, New York, AICPA, 1967.

U.S. AAA Manual 309-1, U.S. Army Audit Agency, Department of the Army, Washington, Jan. 15, 1966.

The Federal Accountant, published quarterly by the Federal Government Accountants Association, Washington.

U.S. Department of Agriculture, "Statement on Internal Audit," *The Internal Auditor*, September, 1959.

"Internal Auditing, Review and Appraisal in the Federal Government," *Research Bulletin* No. 2, Federal Government Accountants Association, Washington, 1962.

Jones, S. W.: "Army Audit Agency," *U.S. Army Information Digest*, Washington, January, 1962.

Witt, Herbert: "Management Audit of Government Contractors," *The Internal Auditor*, summer, 1964.

Lynn, B. B.: "Army Operational Auditing," *The Internal Auditor*, fall, 1965.

Smith, Stancil M.: "What's Going On in Government Auditing?" *U.S. Army Audit Agency Bulletin*, Department of the Army, Washington, December, 1965.

State Government

Municipal Finance Officers Association, National Committee on Governmental Accounting: *Governmental Accounting, Auditing and Financial Reporting*, Ann Arbor, Mich., Cushing Malloy, Inc., 1968.

Biennial Report of the Joint Legislative Audit Committee, State of California, Sacramento, Calif., November, 1969.

Report of Audits, State of Michigan, Office of the Auditor General, Lansing, Mich., January, 1970.

Audit of State Agencies and Public Authorities, State of New York, Office of the State Comptroller, Division of Audits and Accounts, Albany, N.Y., October, 1970.

Normanton, E. L.: *The Accountability and Audit of Governments*, Manchester, England, The University Press, University of Manchester, and New York, Frederick A. Praeger, Inc., 1966.

Knighton, Lennis M.: *The Performance Post Audit in State Government*, East Lansing, Mich., Bureau of Business and Economic Research, Michigan State University, 1967.

Chartock, Alan S., and Max Berking: *Strengthening the Wisconsin Legislature*, New Brunswick, N.J., Rutgers University Press, 1970.

Pinkelman, Franklin: "Michigan's Use of the Program Audit," *State Government*, Summer, 1967.

Ives, Martin: "Operational Auditing in State Government," *The Internal Auditor*, May/June, 1968.

Dittenhoffer, Mortimer A.: "The Case for Standards and Guidelines for State Audits," *The Internal Auditor*, July/August, 1970.

Part Two

Evaluation and Programming

Chapter **9**

Internal Control

FREDERICK E. HORN

Director of Personnel Education, Arthur Young & Company

NATURE OF INTERNAL CONTROL

Definition of Internal Control. The Special Report on Internal Control of the American Institute of Certified Public Accountants (AICPA) and its Statements on Auditing Procedure No. 33 define internal control as follows:

Internal control comprises the plan of organization and all of the coordinate methods and measures adopted within a business to safeguard its assets, check the accuracy and reliability of its accounting data, promote operational efficiency, and encourage adherence to prescribed managerial policies.[1]

If one studies this definition very carefully, it will become obvious that the term is somewhat broader than the meaning usually attributed to it. Normally the term "internal control" is associated with the procedures included in the accounting function of the organization. However, as used above, the term encompasses both accounting and administrative controls. On this subject Statements on Auditing Procedure No. 33 has this to say:

a. Accounting controls comprise the plan of organization and all methods and procedures that are concerned mainly with, and relate directly to, safeguarding of assets and the reliability of the financial records. They generally include such controls as the systems of authorization and approval, separation of duties concerned with record keeping and accounting reports from those concerned with operations or asset custody, physical controls over assets, and internal auditing.

b. Administrative controls comprise the plan of organization and all methods and procedures that are concerned mainly with operational efficiency and adherence to managerial policies and usually relate only indirectly to the financial records. They generally include such controls as statistical analyses, time and motion studies, performance reports, employee training programs, and quality controls.

The extent to which particular organizational plans and control methods and procedures may be classified as accounting controls or administrative controls will, of course, vary in individual circumstances.

Characteristics of Internal Control. Much has been written on this subject in all fields of accounting and auditing. However, Statements on Auditing Procedure No. 33, p. 28, summarizes the characteristics of a satisfactory system of internal control as follows:

1. A plan of organization which provides appropriate segregation of functional responsibilities.
2. A system of authorization and record procedures adequate to provide reasonable accounting control over assets, liabilities, revenues and expenses.
3. Sound practices to be followed in performance of duties and functions of each of the organizational departments, and
4. Personnel of a quality commensurate with responsibilities.

Skinner and Anderson, in *Analytical Auditing*, write in somewhat the same vein when they state:[2]

The characteristics of a satisfactory system of internal control include: (a) the delegation to specific individuals of powers of approval and the institution of checks to see that transactions are approved by authorized individuals; (b) a division of record keeping so that one record is checked by another record created independently; (*c*) proper physical control of assets, including dual custody of valuable negotiable assets; (d) separation of the custody of assets from the recording of the same assets and related transactions;

[1] Statements on Auditing Procedure No. 33, *Auditing Standards and Procedures*, AICPA (Committee on Auditing Procedure), New York, 1963, pp. 27 and 28.

[2] R. M. Skinner and R. J. Anderson, *Analytical Auditing, An Outline of the Flow Chart Approach to Audits*, New York, Pitman Publishing Corporation, 1966, p. 59.

(e) periodic verification of the existence of the recorded assets; and (f) employment of personnel having abilities and training commensurate with their responsibilities.

And Cashin and Owens, in *Auditing*, list the basic components or the elements which make up the concept of internal control as: [3]

1. Organization
2. Policies and procedures
3. Standards of performance
4. Reports and records
5. Internal auditing

The characteristics of Statements on Auditing Procedure No. 33 will be discussed in the comments which follow in order to give the reader the proper perspective regarding a satisfactory system of internal control before he undertakes the study of the procedures used by the auditor to make his review and evaluation thereof.

Plan of organization. The structure of the organization which will provide for appropriate segregation of functional responsibilities will vary because of the nature of the business, its method of operation, its size, the number of components—subsidiaries, divisions, departments—included in the organization, and their geographical distribution. However, what all managements of enterprises will strive to include in a satisfactory plan of organization are:

1. Organizational independence. In any plan of organization it is desirable to provide and maintain adequate separation of operating, custodial, accounting, and internal auditing functions. This means that there should be a separation of duties in such a way that records maintained outside of each department serve as controls over department activities. Furthermore, there also should be a separation of the custody of assets from the accounting for such assets or the recording of related transactions.

2. Lines of responsibility. In addition to the proper division of duties between departments, there also must be clear-cut definitions of responsibilities within the departments themselves in line with the overall policies and procedures adopted by management. Furthermore, there must be a proper delegation of authority to specific individuals in order for them to meet their assigned responsibilities efficiently and effectively.

One of the first steps, and probably the most important, in preparing a plan of organization is the creation of a very carefully developed and acceptable statement of company policies, objectives, and overall procedures. Without these basic tools no effective plan of organization can be established or installed by management. The next step in establishing the plan is the construction of an organization chart in which positions of responsibility are depicted and related functional duties are listed. Figure 1, taken from the AICPA's Special Report on Internal Control, illustrates the form of such a chart. The preparation of an organization chart is an effective device for:

1. Establishing executive relationships and defining areas of accountability
2. Fixing departmental, divisional, or individual responsibilities
3. Minimizing overlapping of responsibilities and duties, duplication of work, and inconsistencies in functions or activities

[3] James A. Cashin and Garland C. Owens, *Auditing*, 2nd ed., New York, The Ronald Press Company, 1963, p. 59.

Figure 1 ORGANIZATION CHART OF CONTROLLER'S DIVISION SHOWING FUNCTIONS INVOLVED IN INTERNAL CONTROL

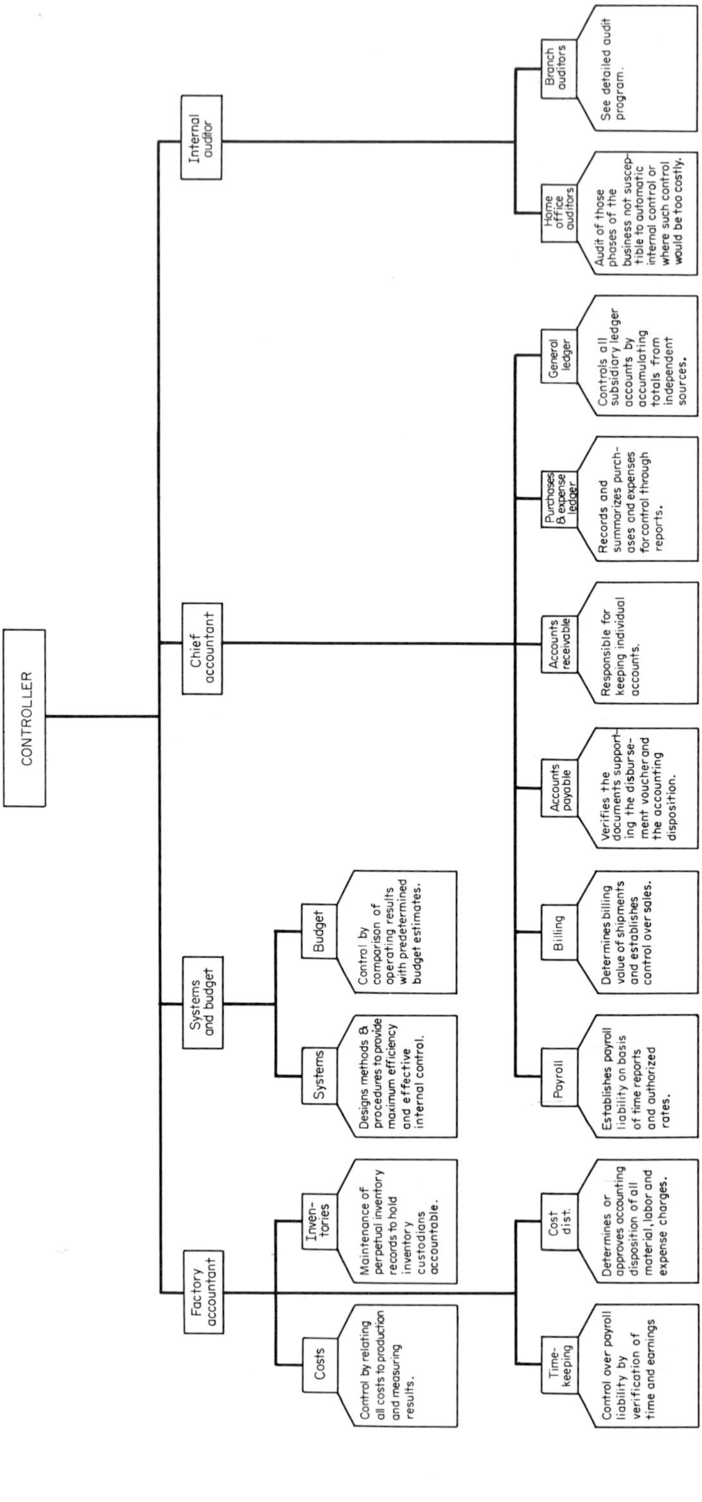

- CONTROLLER
  - Factory accountant
    - Costs: Control by relating all costs to production and measuring results.
    - Inventories: Maintenance of perpetual inventory records to hold inventory custodians accountable.
    - Time-keeping: Control over payroll liability by verification of time and earnings
    - Cost dist.: Determines or approves accounting disposition of all material, labor and expense charges.
  - Systems and budget
    - Systems: Designs methods & procedures to provide maximum efficiency and effective internal control.
    - Budget: Control by comparison of operating results with predetermined budget estimates.
  - Chief accountant
    - Payroll: Establishes payroll liability on basis of time reports and authorized rates.
    - Billing: Determines billing value of shipments and establishes control over sales.
    - Accounts payable: Verifies the documents supporting the disbursement voucher and the accounting disposition.
    - Accounts receivable: Responsible for keeping individual accounts.
    - Purchases & expense ledger: Records and summarizes purchases and expenses for control through reports.
    - General ledger: Controls all subsidiary ledger accounts by accumulating totals from independent sources.
  - Internal auditor
    - Home office auditors: Audit of those phases of the business not susceptible to automatic internal control or where such control would be too costly.
    - Branch auditors: See detailed audit program.

System of Authorization and Record Procedures. In the design of the system, it is important that the forms and procedures installed should provide for the review and authorization of all transactions before they are entered in the company's accounting records. The forms also should provide for a proper recording of such review and authorization, and this record – initials or signature – should establish full accountability for the actions taken by individuals responsible therefor. In addition, a carefully devised chart of accounts and an accounting manual are also necessary parts of the system. The accounts included in the chart are the framework of the entire accounting system, and they facilitate the gathering and classification of the various transactions. The accounting manual serves the purpose of delineating authority, responsibilities, and duties and blueprints the way in which the accounting work is to be performed in order to achieve the company's objectives most efficiently and economically. Together, the chart of accounts and the accounting manual provide the means for preparing periodic financial statements and operating reports for control purposes.

Sound practices. The concepts described above provide the procedures for authorizing and recording transactions and maintaining custody over the company's assets. However, these procedures must be supported by sound practices which assure management of the integrity of the transactions. In other words, sound practices should assure management (and its independent or internal auditors) that the procedures prescribed in the accounting manual are being followed and that no one person will handle a transaction completely from beginning to end. Sound practices also should assure management that the work of one person will, in the ordinary course, be checked by the subsequent work of another person or department. If this is achieved, the system will provide clerical accuracy, a built-in check on the reliability of the bookkeeping work, and a better opportunity for management to detect errors or fraud promptly.

Quality of personnel. Statements on Auditing Procedure No. 33, p. 31, deals with the quality of personnel very succinctly:

> 15. A properly functioning system of internal control depends not only on effective organization planning and the adequacy of the procedures and practices, but also on the competence of officers, department heads and other key employees to carry out prescribed procedures in an efficient and economical manner.

Obviously, the quality of the system installed by management is dependent not only upon the competency of officers, department heads, and other key employees but also upon the abilities of the people who perform the various designated routine tasks. Therefore, the plan of organization must include a systematic approach to the selection and training of these individuals to ensure good performance. However, these functions must be backed up with proper supervision so that the work of each employee is carefully reviewed to determine that the sound practices incorporated in the system are being followed. If they are not being followed, corrective action must be taken promptly by management to prevent deterioration in performance or the circumvention of prescribed procedures.

INTERNAL CONTROL AND MANAGEMENT

The Role of Management. At this point it must be clear, as Statements on Auditing Procedure No. 33, p. 31, points out, that "management has the responsibility for adopting sound accounting policies, for maintaining an adequate and effective system of accounts, for safeguarding of assets, and for devising a system of internal control that will, among other things, help assure the production of proper financial statements." It must also police the system to determine that prescribed procedures are being carried out, that changes in operating conditions are recognized, and that corrective action is taken when the system breaks down. However, part of the policing function can be delegated to the internal auditor. He, too, is concerned with the degree to which controls exist and how effectively they are being carried out.

The Role of the Internal Auditor. The internal auditor's role, as a part of the management team and as part of the control function, is clearly described in the Statement of Responsibilities of the Internal Auditor:

> Internal auditing is an independent appraisal activity within an organization for the review of accounting, financial and other operations as a basis for service to management. It is a managerial control, which functions by measuring and evaluating the effectiveness of other controls.[4]

It also describes the objectives and scope of internal auditing as follows:

> The over-all objective of internal auditing is to assist all members of management in the effective discharge of their responsibilities, by furnishing them with objective analyses, appraisals, recommendations and pertinent comments concerning the activities reviewed. The internal auditor therefore should be concerned with any phase of business activity wherein he can be of service to management. The attainment of this over-all objective of service to management should involve such activities as:
>
> Reviewing and appraising the soundness, adequacy and application of accounting, financial and operating controls.
>
> Ascertaining the extent of compliance with established policies, plans and procedures.
>
> Ascertaining the extent to which company assets are accounted for, and safeguarded from losses of all kinds.
>
> Ascertaining the reliability of accounting and other data developed within the organization.
>
> Appraising the quality of performance in carrying out assigned responsibilities.

At this point it is necessary to emphasize once again that the responsibility for preventing and detecting irregularities and fraud in the system rests with management and that the adoption and maintenance of an adequate and effective system of internal control is indispensable to a proper discharge of that responsibility.

INTERNAL CONTROL AND THE INDEPENDENT PUBLIC ACCOUNTANT

Reliance on Internal Control. Most opinions by independent public accountants on financial statements include a sentence which, in part, states that "Our examination was made in accordance with generally accepted auditing standards. . . ." One of the standards reads as follows:

> 2. There is to be a proper study and evaluation of the existing internal control as a basis for reliance thereon and for the determination of the resultant extent of the tests to which auditing procedures are to be restricted.

It should be noted that this standard stresses the "reliance" which can be placed on the system of internal control by the auditor and the "determination" by him of the extent and scope of his auditing tests and procedures.

[4] Statement of Responsibilities of the Internal Auditor, The Institute of Internal Auditors, New York, 1957.

Detection of Fraud. It is a primary responsibility of the independent auditor to review his client's system of internal control to determine the extent to which he can rely upon it. In making his review, the auditor must be aware that errors and fraud can exist or be introduced into the system, and if they are sufficiently material, they can affect his opinion on the financial statements. Therefore, in making his examination of the financial statements, he must be constantly aware of this possibility. However, his normal examination, in accordance with generally accepted auditing standards and directed to the expression of opinion on the financial statements, is not specifically designed to disclose all irregularities or defalcations, although in the normal course of the audit they might be uncovered. The detection of all instances of dishonesty or fraud by the auditor would require him to make a detailed examination of all transactions during the period under review, and this could be done only at a prohibitive cost to management. As an alternative, the auditor makes a review of the system of internal control and evaluates its effectiveness—in other words, he determines the reliance he can place on it. He next makes a selection of audit procedures, designs appropriate tests, and then determines the extent to which they are to be employed. In other words, based upon his conclusions, he either increases the number of documents or transactions he examines or reduces the degree of his detailed examination of these items. These procedures will be discussed at greater length in the comments which follow.

Scope and Timing of Review. Before undertaking the review of the system, the auditor should give consideration to the scope and the timing of the review. Obviously, both the size of the client and the quality of the controls involved have an important bearing on the scope of the review. In other words, the extent of the auditor's review of the system of a large publicly owned company with an efficient accounting organization and an effective system of internal control will vary greatly from the examination of a small closely held corporation lacking the degree of organization, system, and control of the large company. Furthermore, in the large company the existence of an internal auditing department, staffed with competent personnel and operating under a sound program, would contribute much to its system of control, and many opportunities would exist for close collaboration between the internal auditor and the external auditor to the benefit of each. On the other hand, in a very small company, because of the absence of any effective system of controls, it would be necessary for the auditor to make a more detailed examination of the transactions for the full period if he is to accept the product of the system or make suggestions for improvements.

The really troublesome cases in which the auditor might have the most difficulty in evaluating the system of internal control are in the medium-sized corporations which are not large enough to justify a wholly satisfactory system of internal control but which are large enough to have certain of its features. In such instances the problem of determining the reliance which might be placed on the system in determining the extent of his audit procedures is much more difficult than it is either in the case of the extremely small organization where he starts with a knowledge that no controls exist or, on the other extreme, in the cases of the large corporations where the needs of business require that the system be highly effective.

Insofar as timing is concerned, it would appear that, if a large company has effective controls, the review can be performed at an interim date provided the controls did not change during the intervening period. Furthermore, size and effective controls would make it possible to review company procedures and controls on a cycle basis, particularly if competent internal auditors reviewed the system in other areas or at the other locations. Thus, the major portion of any audit work could be accomplished at an interim date and the auditor could rely on accounting procedures and controls for mechanical accuracy of amounts in the accounts at the balance sheet date. Normal year-end auditing procedures, in the presence of satisfactory control, could be limited to a review of transactions subsequent to the interim examination, to the determination of the propriety of asset accounts, and to ascertaining that all liabilities had been recorded or considered.

For the small company the owner-manager may maintain good control. In this case the reliance on internal controls could be determined either at an interim date or at the year end. Review and evaluation of accounting procedures and controls would not be the greatest problem of the auditor; the most serious problem would be selecting the appropriate audit procedures and establishing the extent to which tests should be made.

The review of the controls of the medium-sized company which might not have a wholly satisfactory system of internal control could be a combination of the above-described approaches. At the interim date the strengths and weaknesses could be established and the extent to which reliance could be placed on a certain portion of the system could be determined. At year end the impact of the weaknesses on the financial statements would require a more detailed audit of the transactions.

Initial Audits. On an initial engagement the auditor's prior knowledge of the specific system will be limited; therefore, his tests will, of necessity, be more extensive in the first year than those employed in subsequent examinations. Particular attention must be given to the determination of the propriety of the amounts appearing in the accounts at the beginning of the period being examined. Where reports and working papers of reputable independent public accountants are available for examination, the auditor's review of internal control will be limited, to a great extent, to the current year. However, an examination of the reports and working papers of the prior accountants must be made to determine the extent of their reliance on internal controls and the impact of any weaknesses on the opening balances. Where there were no previous audits or the reports and working papers of the other accountants are not available to the auditor, the adequacy of the system of internal control must be considered for the years under consideration before the auditor can determine the extent of the audit procedures to be applied to those years and to the current year. Presumably the techniques will be the same; the only change in approach is that the auditor must cover more ground.

Continuing Engagements. When the company being audited has excellent internal control in certain functional areas, it may not be necessary to examine every such area each year. This is particularly true when internal auditors are employed. Similarly, if the company is organized on a multiple-entity basis with numerous divisions or subsidiaries and has decentralized or partially decentralized accounting, it may not be necessary to visit every division each year if the auditor's evaluation shows that internal controls are satisfactory. However, he should plan to cycle his examination so each division or unit is audited at least once in, say, 3 to 5 years.

If the company has internal auditors, their audit programs and reports should be reviewed, and their competence and their degree of independence should be considered in order that the public accountant can determine the areas in which he can rely upon their work to reduce or eliminate certain of his auditing procedures. A description of the work of the internal auditors should be made a part of the evaluation of internal control, and the extent to which he relied thereon and the reasons therefor also should be stated in the working papers.

Responsibility for Evaluation. While the review of the various parts of the system of internal control can be delegated to the staff assistants, the evaluation process requires the exercise of sound judgment and thus becomes a function which should be performed by the auditor in charge of the engagement. Also, the selection of auditing procedures on the basis of the evaluation is the responsibility of the auditor in charge since he is the person who is both close to the job and more professionally equipped to make the decisions that the initial or continuing review of internal control calls for. He is the one who should interpret the information collected, select areas for subsequent audit tests, and present management with recommendations for systems changes.

Before leaving the subject of the responsibility of the auditor in evaluating the system of internal control of the company, it should be pointed out that, if he—the auditor—delegates the review function to his assistants, he must be certain that the men who are doing the work understand what is expected of them. He must exercise close supervision; in other words, his instructions should be explicit, and by asking pertinent questions before the work is begun, he should ascertain whether the assistants understand the instructions. He also should maintain close day-to-day supervision in the early stages of the review to determine that they are proceeding as directed. Finally, he must be sure that the results of the review are being documented thoroughly so he can get the complete picture. Without properly prepared working papers his own supervisory review will be deficient and time-consuming.

It also may be desirable to let the internal auditors or other qualified company personnel participate in the review of the system. However, it still will be desirable for the auditor to "walk through" a number of documents to determine that the memoranda, questionnaires, or flow charts really depict the system.

Media Used in Evaluation. To facilitate the accumulation of the information necessary for the proper review and evaluation of internal controls, the auditor could use one of the following media to help him determine the system in use and to make the proper evaluation:

1. Narrative record
2. Checklist
3. Questionnaire
4. Flow chart

Narrative record. The narrative record is a complete description of the system as found in operation by the auditor. Cashin and Owens, p. 77, suggest that the auditor use the narrative technique as follows:

> The narrative record is well suited to an engagement relating to a small business where internal control may be weak. This method allows more flexibility than the questionnaire method and can be adapted readily to any type of enterprise. The extent of the narrative write-ups will vary with the requirements of the accounting firm. Some firms require a description of the basic features of internal control relating to broad functions such as sales, purchases, cash payments, etc. In other cases a firm may require comment only on the discovery of defects in internal control.

Checklist. A checklist is a series of instructions or questions which the auditor must follow or answer. When he completes an instruction, he initials the space opposite the instruction. If a question is asked, the answer—usually "yes," "no," or "not applicable"—is entered opposite the question. A portion of the checklist in Case Studies in Internal Control No. 2 AICPA, The Machine Manufacturing Company, is reproduced. The firm that prepared the case study described its use as follows:

> The audit program and scope of the audit work depend very largely on whether the client's accounting system and procedures provide good internal control. Therefore, it is our policy to determine the extent and effectiveness of the internal control at the beginning of the audit. Our study of internal control is based on our "Check List—Internal Control."
>
> Our first step in the use of this check list is to submit it to the chief accounting executive of the client company with a request that he answer each of the questions in the list with the word "yes" or the word "no" or "N.A." (not applicable). This is

CHECKLIST—INTERNAL CONTROL

(Each question must be answered "yes" or "no" or "N.A." (not applicable). If answer is qualified, key to a footnote).

Name of client *The Machine Manufacturing Company*

Period covered by examination *Calendar year* ____

CASH

ANSWER	
	RECEIPTS
	1. Are the duties or functions of all persons receiving or directly supervising the receiving of cash completely segregated from the following duties or functions?
	a. Performing work on customers' sales invoices or credit memos as to:
No	(1) Preparing
No	(2) Checking
No	(3) Recording
No	(4) Summarizing
	b. Performing work on customers' ledgers as to:
No	(1) Recording
No	(2) Balancing
Yes	c. Ageing accounts receivable
Yes	d. Following up delinquent receivables
No	e. Mailing or delivering statements to customers
Yes	f. Approving discounts or allowances
Yes	g. Preparing lists of bad accounts to be written off
Yes	h. Approving the write-off of bad accounts
No	i. Reconciling bank accounts
Yes	j. Opening incoming mail
No	k. Preparing vouchers for payment
No	l. Approving vouchers for payment
No	m. Preparing general or payroll checks
No	n. Signing general or payroll checks (or countersigning)
No	o. Mailing or delivering general checks or payroll checks
	p. Performing work on notes payable or any other evidences of indebtedness as to:
Yes	(1) Preparing
Yes	(2) Signing
No	q. Posting the general ledger
No	r. Recording entries in the purchase journal or invoice register

practically the first thing we do when we start the audit. If preliminary work is done before the close of the fiscal year, the check list is submitted at that time.

After the answers have been filled in by the client, the check list is divided among the members of our staff on the job, giving each staff member the part applicable to the division of the accounts that he is to examine. He is instructed to make tests, inquiries, and checks to determine that the procedures and practices actually in use are as indicated by the company accounting executive. Such tests can be accomplished in a large measure at the same time that he makes tests of transactions as part of the regular audit work. But each staff man is instructed to make this determination as to the procedures affecting the internal control as early as possible.

After satisfying himself as to what is actually being done as regards practices and procedures affecting internal control, the staff man reports to the senior in charge. The senior then decides what extensions of auditing procedures, if any, are required in view of the weaknesses in the internal control disclosed by this check list and investigation. The senior also makes notes regarding such internal control deficiencies for the purpose of making recommendations in his report.

Alternatively, the auditor could interrogate the personnel involved in the system and fill in the answers as received.

Questionnaire. *Montgomery's Auditing*, p. 64, suggests the auditor use the questionnaire as follows:[5]

A practical and useful device for investigating and recording the auditor's inquiries into a system of internal accounting control and internal check is the standard questionnaire, prepared for the use of staff members on all engagements. Such a questionnaire, designed by persons fully conversant with problems of internal control, makes available a large fund of accumulated experience and, perhaps more importantly, furnishes a basis for measuring the performance of the system under review. Questions can be framed so that a negative answer indicates a weakness in internal accounting control or internal check, which should be considered either for its possible effect on the audit program or for reporting to the client for consideration. . . . It is believed that the principles of internal accounting control and internal check are similar in all types of business; the nomenclature of some businesses may be specialized, but it is usually translatable into conventional accounting terms. Some types of business may require supplementary questions to bring out specialized situations, and if so they may readily be added.

Such questionnaires must not be used as a substitute for thinking, and they should always be susceptible to revision to fit the needs of the client. Properly used, they provide information upon which the public accountant can exercise judgment to determine whether the system of internal accounting control and internal check is reasonably designed to produce accurate summaries of the transactions and to minimize opportunities for fraud.

Cashin and Owens, p. 77, write as follows:

The internal control questionnaire is a comprehensive series of questions concerning internal control. Another variation of this approach is the check list or reminder list which is used as a guide for an auditor in his review of internal control. The questionnaire approach is favored by many large accounting firms, although some firms still prefer the narrative approach. The use of a questionnaire saves considerable time for the auditor as it eliminates the need for preparing a program for each engagement. The basic program can generally be modified to meet the needs of most regular audits. Another important advantage of the questionnaire approach is that oversights or omissions of significant internal control review procedures are less likely to occur with this method. With the questionnaire all internal control evaluations can be completed at one time or in sections. The review can more easily be made on an interim basis, thereby reducing the amount of work to be done at the year-end. The questionnaire form also provides an orderly means of disclosing internal control defects.

It is general practice to review the internal control system annually and record the

[5] Norman J. Lenhart and Philip L. Defliese, *Montgomery's Auditing*, 8th ed., New York, The Ronald Press Company, 1957.

review in detail. However, some firms provide for using the same questionnaire for a period of three years. The initial information may be answered with a black pencil, the second year amended with a blue pencil, and the third year with a green pencil. Questions are phrased so that a "Yes" answer denotes a satisfactory condition and a "No" answer denotes a weakness in internal control. Provision is made for an explanation or further details concerning the "No" answer. Where, because of the nature or size of the business, a question is not pertinent, the column "Not App." (not applicable) should be used. The preparation of the questionnaire is generally not intended to replace the write-up of the client's accounting and control procedures which should be reviewed and brought up to date each year. After the audit work has been completed, the accountant in charge should be able to state whether or not the company's system of internal control is adequate. The questionnaire is generally signed by the senior in charge and is reviewed and signed by the manager or partner. Generally the senior then prepares a report of deficiencies and his recommendations for improvement.

A typical page of an internal control questionnaire is illustrated in Figure 2. The illustration also shows how the form would be used by the auditor to describe the system.

Figure 2 INTERNAL CONTROL QUESTIONNAIRE

Questions	Not app.	Yes	No	Comments—(as to all "No" answers and further data as to "Yes" answers)
B1. CASH RECEIPTS				
1. Is the cashier without authority to sign checks and divorced from handling accounting records other than cash receipts and disbursements (particularly customers ledgers) and from custody of negotiable assets?			✓	No separate cashier. Cash handled by accounts receivable bookkeeper
2. Are receipts by mail opened by a person, other than the cashier, who prepares a listing thereof, sends checks and cash to the cashier for deposit and remittance advices to accounts receivable or accounting department, with a daily tie-in between receipts and total credits to customers ledgers?			✓	Mail clerk opens mail & sends checks to credit manager who in turn sends them to chief accountant.
3. Are receipts over the counter controlled by independent record of receivables with prenumbered receipt forms or customers stubs sent from cashier to accounts receivable department?	✓			
4. Are receipts in cash properly controlled through cash registers, vending machines, prenumbered locked receipt forms, etc. and are the readings on such registers or machines or the locked receipts used as an effective control over cash which should be recorded and deposited?	✓			
5. Is all cash which should be received recorded as a receivable prior to receipt, to the extent practicable?			✓	Only recorded after receipt
6. If checks are sent to other departments for investigation or for other reasons, does the cashier establish control by recording before they are so released?			✓	Mail clerk does not keep a record of checks sent to other departments
7. Are all receipts recorded promptly and deposited intact daily (or at other regular intervals—what interval?)			✓	Deposited by mail at end of week
8. Does the cashier prepare duplicate deposit tickets, one of which is signed by the bank and returned for checking to the cash receipts record by another person?		✓		
9. In the case of collections by branch offices, are those deposited in accounts on which the branch office may not draw, with duplicate deposit tickets forwarded to head office in support of receipts reported and bank statements mailed direct to the head office by the bank?	✓			

Flow chart. A flow chart is a graphic presentation of each part of the company's system of internal control. As stated in the AICPA's Special Report on Internal Control, the principal advantages of flow charts "are believed to be, first, visual assistance in developing a coordinated plan of organization and procedures and, second, their use permits simplification in the descriptive material included in procedures and practice manuals." The report also includes a number of illustrative flow charts which can be used for reference purposes by the auditor; however, the charts illustrated can be prepared in a more simplified form. For example, the preparation of the flow chart in Figure 3 does not require the touch of an artist. All that is required is a template, a ruler, and a piece of paper.

The Skinner and Anderson book previously referred to—which includes a template—is an excellent treatise on the subject of flow charting. It advocates, p. 12, the use of flow charts in these terms:

> A systems-oriented audit plan must include some method of recording systems information accurately and comprehensively. A narrative form, which might be the first thought, proves unduly cumbersome in practice. Narrative may be suitable for some purposes—company procedure manuals or clerical job descriptions—but for the auditor's needs it is too unwieldy. As soon as any degree of detail is attempted, narrative swells to too large a size. The large quantities are difficult to absorb, related points are hard to integrate mentally, and annual changes are awkward to record. In addition, some unique problems are usually posed by the handwriting.
>
> To these problems a standardized method of flow charting is the logical solution. First, this is the most concise way of recording the auditor's review of the system. The flow chart minimizes the amount of narrative explanation and thereby achieves a condensation of presentation not possible in any other form. It gives both a bird's-eye view of the system and an efficient documentation of the auditor's testing of it. Secondly, the flow chart is the most efficient tool for doing the actual *analyzing.* The charts clearly show what is taking place and provide an easy method of spotting weaknesses in the system or areas where improvements could be introduced. . . . This approach has the advantage of making it easy to visualize the relationship between different parts of the integrated system. Those internal control strengths or weaknesses which arise from the way in which duties are divided among the client's personnel can thus be readily seen on the flow charts themselves, where they would be hard to extract from many pages of narrative.

Steps in Evaluation. The auditor's approach to the review of the accounting practices and internal controls should be systematic. Basically the steps in the review and evaluation of a company's internal control and accounting procedures are as follows:

1. Determine by review of accounting manuals and/or inquiry what procedures and controls have been established.
2. Test by means of a "walkthrough" of a number of documents and by inquiry whether established procedures are being followed.
3. Evaluate the effectiveness of the procedures and controls to determine the reliance which may be placed upon them.
4. Confirm the evaluation of the procedures and controls by means of a limited test of transactions.
5. Select auditing procedures on the basis of either strong or weak controls.
6. Make recommendations to management for improvements in the system.
7. Follow up after recommendations have been made to determine if they have been accepted and put into practice.

Figure 3 FLOW CHART OF CASH RECEIVING FUNCTIONS (Symbols from R. M. Skinner and R. J. Anderson, Analytical Auditing – An Outline of the Flow Chart Approach to Audits, New York, Pitman Publishing Corporation, 1966.)

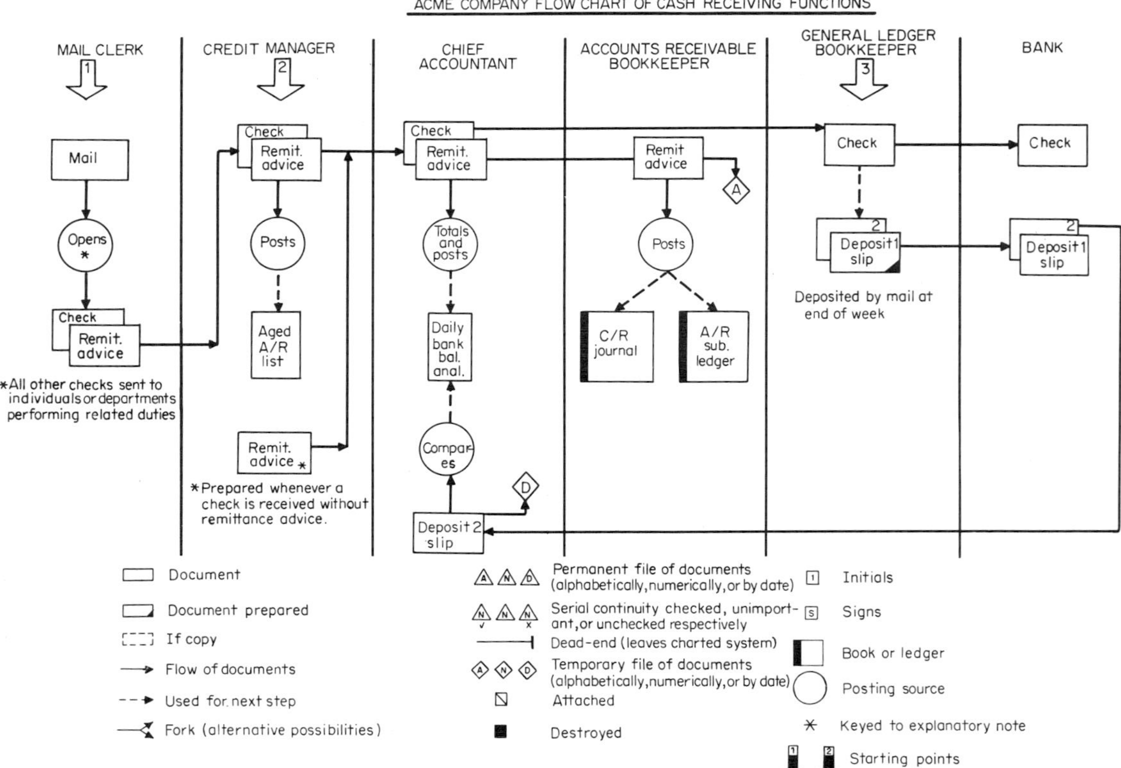

The logic which the auditor uses in his review and evaluation of the system of internal control is shown graphically in Figure 4.

Determination of established controls. In this initial phase of the review of the company's procedures and controls, the auditor should read all the existing literature of the company pertaining to its accounting system—accounting and auditing manuals, flow charts and block diagrams, accounting records and forms—to obtain a basic knowledge of the system as designed and installed by management. This search for facts should be supplemented by an interrogation of personnel who are involved with the system. In making the determination by inquiry, it might be desirable for the auditor to start with the individuals at the highest possible accounting organizational level. This is referred to as determination from the top down. In so doing, the auditor's subsequent detailed tests and audit steps perform a valuable service to management by verifying the controls which it believes exist at the operational level. However, this method is not always practical, and it may be necessary, in certain instances, to make the determination at the operating level. This may be referred to as determination from bottom up. In this latter case, the procedures and controls which the auditor observes should be reviewed with the company's top accounting people so that he can be certain of the completeness of the information obtained at the lower levels and also so that he can give management an opportunity to criticize its own operations. However, at this point it must be recognized that controls adequate for financial statement purposes may not be adequate for internal operating purposes. It must also be recognized that the literature may not

Figure 4 REVIEW AND EVALUATION OF INTERNAL CONTROL

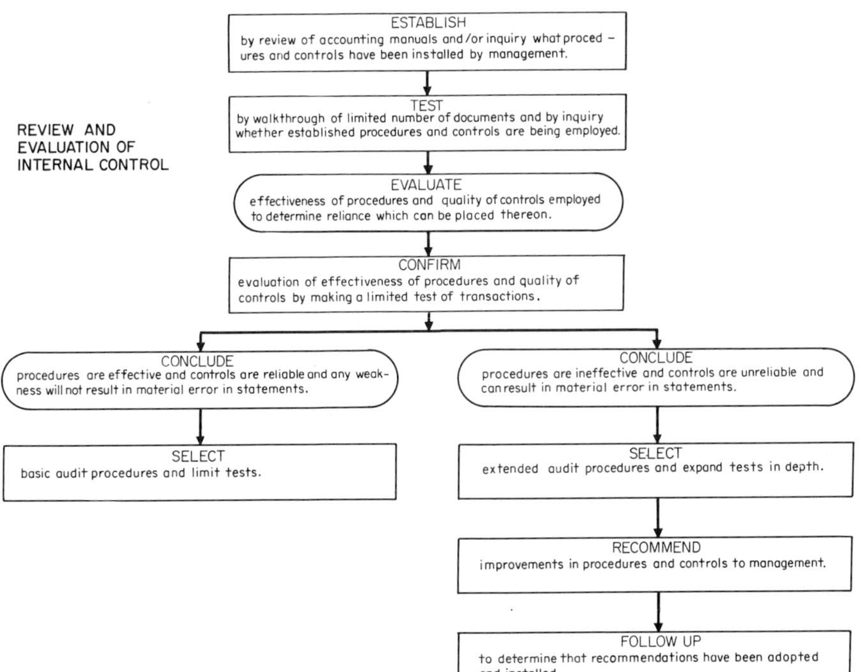

be up to date or that the system as described and executed may bear little resemblance to the one initially installed by management.

The documentation of this initial review of the company's system and procedures may take the form of an outline, a memorandum, a series of notes, the tentative draft of a flow chart, or if the company's written instructions or procedures are included in the auditor's working papers, reference may be made thereto with such supplemental comments as are necessary for a competent evaluation of the situation. However, at this stage of the review it is not important which medium is used; what is important is that the auditor should identify the records or documents examined and the procedures he followed in the review.

In an initial audit it also might be advisable for the auditor at this stage of his review to obtain copies of all accounting forms currently used by the company and to place them in the permanent files. On continuing audits, the forms placed in the permanent files should be updated as part of the walkthrough procedures described below.

"Walkthrough" of transactions. The next phase of the review is the "walkthrough" of a number of transactions. This step accomplishes the following:

1. Establishes the correctness of the procedures and controls previously determined
2. Confirms that the procedures and controls are functioning, thus providing a valid basis for a preliminary evaluation
3. Enables the auditor to obtain a better understanding of the detailed operations of the system with limited contact

The auditor, in making his "walkthrough" of the documents selected, must have a starting point. An excellent place to start is with the sample of the accounting forms which are to be placed in the permanent files. If each copy of the form includes a description of its flow through the organization, the auditor has a trail with which to begin his walkthrough procedures. Another technique, which can be used effectively by the auditor, is to "fan" out the forms and staple them to a 14-column work paper, say, the first 7 columns. The remaining 7 columns of the work paper would indicate the departments or the individuals where the particular copy flows, and a line drawn from each copy to the column would show the flow schematically. In fact, this presentation produces a simple flow chart. Any additional comments can be written along the "flow" line or in the column signifying a department or an individual.

The documents to be "walked through" should be selected with a definite purpose in mind in that they should be the typical product of the system to be tested. In other words, if the auditor wishes to test the fact that a check in an amount exceeding $1,000 requires two signatures after review and approval, he must select not only checks with only one signature but also checks with two signatures to determine that the system, as described to him, is functioning. If he plans to start his walkthrough by selecting several canceled checks from the files, he can review the procedures from the time the checks were filed back down to the point of their origin. Alternatively, and probably a better starting point after he has selected the canceled checks from the files, is to return to their point of origin and begin walking them up through the system until the checks ultimately are returned by the bank and filed.

As part of the process of gathering and recording the data during the walkthrough, the auditor should interrogate the personnel at each point where some action—such as a check of clerical accuracy, a review, or an approval—is taken. If the individual being queried initials or signs the document before it is passed along to another department, the auditor should ascertain that this is being done by verifying that the initials (or the signature) appearing on the documents being walked through are those of the particular employee. Furthermore, the auditor should observe how current documents flowing through the department are being handled by the individual being queried to be sure that what is being described to him is actually being done. One other effective check on the system is to ask each individual to describe the work which was done on the documents by the previous department and also the succeeding department. Last but not least, the alert auditor should always ask if there are any exceptions to the rule and then should follow their trails. For example, during the review of the mailroom procedures, the efficient auditor should always ask if anybody ever takes mail before it is opened and routed to the proper department.

Finally, the auditor should once again document his walkthrough procedures using any one of the media mentioned above. His documentation should identify the documents which he walked through and the individuals queried and include a brief description of his procedures and his findings. By doing this, the auditor leaves himself a clear audit trail.

Documentation of Review. After all information has been gathered by the auditor, he then can write his memorandum describing the system, or complete the pertinent sections of the checklist or internal control questionnaire or prepare a flow chart. If a flow chart is used and it is fairly complicated, the auditor should draft the chart on a 14-column work paper or similar size paper before making a final copy. By doing this, the auditor can establish the pattern of the flow of each document by departments and can avoid or minimize the crossing of the directional lines on the chart. Needless to say, all flow charts should be prepared in pencil.

If company personnel prepare the flow charts, it may be advisable for the auditor to work with duplicate copies as he walks documents through the various departments. Then any changes noted by him can be made on the copies and subsequently can be transferred to the original charts.

If the charts were prepared during a previous audit, the auditor may have photocopies made which should be placed in that year's work-paper binder. The original charts should be carried forward to the current work papers and any changes noted thereon. However, if a significant change in the system does occur, it may be more practical and efficient to prepare an overlay sheet which, when superimposed on the original chart, will show the new flow of documents. This technique has the advantage of showing both the old system in its original form and the change in the new system when the overlay sheet is superimposed on the original chart.

Evaluation Process. After the auditor completes his narrative description, checklists, questionnaires, or flow charts, he will then have some knowledge of where controls appear to be strong and where they seem to be weak. The evaluation of the effectiveness of the company's procedures and controls is undoubtedly one of the most difficult phases of an audit and requires the use of considerable judgment. Furthermore, there are varying degrees of effective control, none of them perfect but some stronger than others. Having determined the effectiveness of a specific control, it is then necessary for the auditor to come to a further conclusion as to the reliance which can be placed on it and the extent to which further auditing procedures are necessary. Strong controls presumably would result in the conclusion that:

1. Reliance can be placed on the controls found in the system.
2. A minimum of further audit tests are necessary. If the auditor can establish that the controls are reliable, he can limit the scope of any additional tests necessary to give an opinion on the financial statements.
3. Cycle tests could be made periodically in appropriate areas over a period of years in those areas of strong controls.

Ineffective or weak controls presumably would result in the conclusion that:

1. Reliance cannot be placed on the controls reviewed.
2. The audit program must be extended to include tests and procedures that do not rely on these controls, and the additional tests are necessary to enable a further evaluation regarding the effect of the weakness on the financial statements.
3. Cycle tests should not be made in those areas of weak controls.

Tests of Transactions. The extent of the additional tests or procedures selected by the auditor will depend on the circumstances. If the auditor is of the opinion that the client's controls are effective and are functioning on the basis of his walkthrough of a very limited number of recorded transactions, he should give himself added assurance by selecting additional documents scattered throughout the period under review to examine and confirm his preliminary conclusions that the system is functioning effectively and that it is producing clerical accuracy.

TESTING

Sampling Methods. The additional documents selected for examination could be selected haphazardly, systematically or at random. The number of items to be selected could be determined on a subjective or objective basis. If the documents are selected subjectively, the auditor must decide how many transaction documents are needed to be satisfied that the procedures and controls being tested are effective or ineffective. In other words, the number of items selected for examination is based upon the judgment of the auditor—a sort of "rule of thumb" approach.

Statistical Sampling. If the documents are selected objectively, the auditor will use a statistical sampling approach. A detailed description of this method is given in Chapter 15. However, the following steps illustrate the logic employed in this type of a test:

1. Define the objectives of the test.
2. Determine by experience, estimation, or sampling technique the frequency of occurrence of an error anticipated in the field or population.
3. Decide on sampling reliability (precision) desired.
4. Select a confidence level (the risk which the auditor is willing to take).
5. Determine the size and intactness of the universe from which a sample is to be drawn.
6. Define the errors which could occur in the field.
7. Calculate the size of sample by use of a formula or by reference to a table.

8. Draw the sample by use of systematic selection or random-numbers table.
9. From sample drawn, determine the frequency of the occurrence of the type of error of interest.
10. Interpret result and decide whether or not it is a satisfactory condition.

Case Study of Statistical Sampling. The following case study illustrates in concise form how statistical sampling is used by the auditor to test the effectiveness of a company's system of internal control.

Objectives of the test. The purpose of the test was to determine that the company's accounting procedures pertaining to sales resulted in clerical accuracy.

Frequency of occurrence of error. On the basis of previous year's tests and working-paper records the auditor anticipated that the rate of error generated by the system would be approximately 2 percent.

Sampling reliability. The auditor decided that he would be willing to accept a reliability or precision of ± 2 percent in the results of the sample.

Confidence level. He set his confidence level at 95 percent.

Size of universe. The universe was defined as every sales invoice entered in the sales journal for the year = 7,000.

Definition of errors. Among others, the following items were considered to be errors:

Invoice not in agreement with sales order with respect to:

Unit price
Quantity discount
Freight allowance

Size of sample. With a sampling reliability of 2 ± 2 percent, a confidence level of 95 percent, and a universe of 7,000 sales invoices, the auditor referred to a statistical table and, anticipating an error rate of 2 percent, ascertained that his sample size was 183 invoices.

Selection of sample. The auditor drew 183 sales invoices by using the random-numbers table.

Determined frequency of error from sample. From his audit of the items in the sample, the auditor determined that there was one invoice whose price did not agree with the sales order.

Interpret results. Since the frequency of error—1 ÷ 183 = 0.5 percent—was well below the anticipated rate of occurrence (2 ± 2 percent), the auditor concluded that the controls were satisfactory. The auditor could have referred to other tables to determine the upper limit of the error rate. At this point, if the auditor concluded that the weakness permitting the error did not cause a significant error in the financial statements, the audit could have proceeded on a sound basis and in accordance with generally accepted auditing standards. If the further evaluation had resulted in the conclusion that the weakness could have caused a significant error in the financial statements, the auditor would have used extended auditing procedures to determine the adjustments to be made. Also, the company's management would have been advised of the situation in order to take corrective action.

Combination of tests. If in the opinion of the auditor the system is weak and is not operating effectively, he may want to extend his test of transactions and combine this test with his application of extended audit procedures which are described below. Alternatively, he might decide to move directly into his extended audit procedures and omit the test of transactions entirely.

Figure 5 EVALUATION OF INTERNAL CONTROL

ACME COMPANY

DEFICIENCIES NOTED	AUDIT PROCEDURES TO BE PERFORMED	FINDINGS AND CONCLUSIONS REACHED	RECOMMENDATIONS FOR IMPROVEMENT
Cash receipts			
1. Checks and remittance advices received from customers are forwarded by the mail clerk to the credit manager, who forwards them to the chief accountant	1. Make a detail audit of cash receipts for the months of July and December, and check company's reconciliation at Dec. 31 in detail. *W/P C-1.1*	1. No discrepancies noted—cash recorded and deposited intact, except as noted below	1. Mail clerk should list cash receipts, sending list and remittance advices to credit manager and chief accountant and checks to general ledger bookkeeper
2. Credit manager prepares remittance advices for receipts when no remittance advices are received	2. See above; also trace all postings to customer accounts. *W/P D-4*	2. No discrepancies found	2. Mail clerk should prepare remittance advices where none are received and forward them with list
3. Deposits are made weekly by mail	3. See above; each cash receipt should be traced to authenticated deposit slip and into bank statement. *W/P C-2.2*	3. Some checks are not deposited promptly. Delays were explained and checks were included in next deposit. *W/P C-4*	3. In view of volume of receipts, deposit daily

STRENGTHS NOTED	LIMITATION OF AUDIT PROCEDURES	FINDINGS AND CONCLUSIONS REACHED	RECOMMENDATIONS TO MANAGEMENT
1. Credit manager ages and reviews customer accounts constantly	1. Obtain copy of age analysis at balance sheet date, test every 20th account to ledger for aging and investigate delinquent accounts. *W/P D-12.1*	1. No exceptions noted, except 6-months'-old account for $650.43 with J. Jones considered collectible by credit manager. *W/P D-12.3*	1. None required
2. Authenticated deposit slips are returned to chief accountant, who compares total cash deposited with his postings to daily bank balance analysis	2. See above	2. Details of receipts agree with details in daily bank balance analysis and cash receipts journal	2. Chief accountant should compare details in cash receipts journal periodically

Documentation. As strengths and weaknesses are discovered by the auditor, they should be summarized in a separate schedule. (A sample of the schedule is shown in Figure 5. It should be noted that the auditor could have inserted answers to each question listed in the internal control questionnaire or checklist or could have written a memorandum.) For each strength noted, the auditor should select and employ the basic audit procedures that are appropriate in the particular situation, with emphasis on what procedures could be eliminated or curtailed without affecting the quality of the audit or the results to be attained. For each weakness found in the company's system, the auditor should select those procedures which would explore each deficiency in depth. The results of the audit should also be summarized and entered on the schedule. Finally, the auditor should select those items which he will call to the attention of management and include his recommendations for improvement. At this point, his documentation of his review and evaluation of the company's system of internal control will present a complete picture of his findings and the actions taken with respect thereto.

SUGGESTED IMPROVEMENTS

Advantages of Letter. As indicated above, the first phase of the auditor's evaluation of controls should result in the selection of appropriate audit procedures. The second phase of evaluation should lead to the preparation of a letter or report to management suggesting improvements in the company's accounting system. A letter or report should be prepared on virtually every engagement even though it is possible that a company can have such strong controls and such a well-run business that the auditor can find nothing to say about them; however, even here it may be desirable to issue a letter or report and tell management that its system is effective and its controls are strong.

To put the form and content of the auditor's presentation to management in proper perspective, the following letter is an example of how one auditor piqued the interest of management. It also highlights what weaknesses the auditor was trying to communicate to the recipient of the letter in order to obtain the necessary corrective action. Case Studies in Internal Control No. 1 contains a different form of such a letter and is well worth studying for its form and content.

November __, 19__

Mr. M. C. Dunn
Financial Vice President
A Company

Dear Mr. Dunn:

Our recently concluded audit work included the flow charting of office procedures which indicated that some cost savings may be realized through the discontinuance of unnecessary clerical operations. In addition, our audit tests indicated that improvements in internal control and accounting procedures are possible without any increased cost. Our observations and suggestions are summarized below.

Sales and accounts receivable

The present sales and accounts receivable procedures do not adequately correlate shipping, billing and cost control. We believe the following suggested changes will correct these deficiencies:

1. The adoption of a five-part sales invoice to provide better control and eliminate recopying data.

2. Sales invoices should be prenumbered and accounted for.
3. All sales orders should be numbered and entered into a log by the order clerk by number and date. Data as to (1) amount of backlog and (2) any items shipped but not billed, can be readily obtained.
4. Credit approval should be given before shipments are made.
5. Provision should be made for shipping merchandise in less-than-order quantities.
6. The invoice numbers for goods released from finished inventory should be balanced to the numbers of the invoices posted to accounts receivable.

Cash disbursements and purchasing

The present system of purchasing and disbursing cash needs improvement in that it:

1. Concentrates purchasing and accounting functions in the purchasing department.
2. Does not provide adequate records of raw materials received to the inventory record keepers.
3. Concentrates payment functions in one person.

For better controls in this area, we recommend that:

1. Invoices and receiving documents be routed directly to the accounts payable unit.
2. The purchasing department should provide both the receiving department and the accounts payable unit with a copy of the purchase order showing prices and quantities.
3. The function of checking prices and calculations and of matching receivers to invoices be transferred to the accounts payable unit.
4. Signed checks should not be returned to the accounts payable unit, but to the mail clerk for mailing.
5. All invoices and supporting documents should be stamped "Paid" or perforated and the date paid at the time the check is signed. Alternatively, this may be done by the mail clerk before they are returned to the accounts payable bookkeeper for filing.

Cash receipts

Checks received from customers together with any remittance advices enclosed are presently forwarded by the mail clerk to the credit manager who in turn forwards them to the chief accountant. There is no listing or other control over these checks at this point. There is no reason why the credit manager or the chief accountant should have access to customers' checks. We recommend that the mail clerk forward all checks received directly to the cashier. For all remittances received without a remittance advice attached, the mail clerk should enter the remitter's name and the amount on the company's regular "Remittance Advice" form. All remittance advices should then be forwarded to the credit manager and the chief accountant for their use. Consideration should be given to making deposits at more frequent intervals than the present once a week.

Under the present scrap sales procedure the dealer picks up scrap once a month and takes it to the scrap yard for weighing. He returns the following day with a check which he gives to the chief accountant. Better control can be maintained by weighing the scrap before the dealer takes it or requiring that the dealer produce a certified weight slip. Also, obtaining bids from other dealers should be considered.

Since our examination did not include a detailed review of all systems and procedures, the above items should not be considered the only areas where clerical cost savings and improvements in internal control might be achieved. Copies of our flow charts of various office procedures have been given to plant management personnel. We will be happy to supply additional copies and discuss any of the foregoing comments with you.

Very truly yours,

Follow-up. The last step in the review and evaluation of a company's system of internal control is the investigation made by the auditor to determine if management has accepted his recommendations for improvements and incorporated them into the system. In subsequent reviews of the system, the changes in procedure will be examined to determine that they are now functioning properly. If management does not adopt the recommendations of the auditor, he must continue to call its attention to the weaknesses and deficiencies until corrective action has been taken.

Needless to say, the recommendations should deal only with significant items and be well documented in the auditor's workpapers and in his letter or report to management. In addition, the auditor should meet with management and discuss the recommended changes. He also should offer to help implement the changes so that the company will achieve the most effective system possible at a minimum of cost.

REVIEW AND EVALUATION OF CONTROLS IN AN EDP ENVIRONMENT

How does the auditor go about making a review and evaluation of the internal controls in an EDP environment? The answer is that he proceeds just as he would in a manual or simple mechanical system. The purpose of the review and its objectives remain unchanged and the steps taken to make the review and evaluation will continue to follow those outlined above. However, the methods or techniques employed by the auditor are subject to change; in other words, the auditor will have to devise new ways and means to measure the effectiveness of the EDP controls under review.

Chapter 16 describes the controls normally found in an EDP installation. Thus, the comments which follow will be limited to the description of those controls which are of particular importance to the auditor and to a discussion of the techniques which an auditor must employ to review and evaluate those controls.

Typical of the controls which an auditor must review and evaluate in an EDP system are the following:

1. Organization
2. Data movement and conversion
3. Program development and utilization
4. Processing procedures
5. Custodial procedures

Organization. The installation of a computer to process financial data usually has a significant impact on a company's organization and its accounting system and accounting procedures, including the related accounting controls. Quite frequently the installation of an EDP system results in major realignments in individual and departmental responsibilities, in job functions and in information flow. Responsibilities and work, which traditionally have been assigned to the accounting department, may be altered significantly or eliminated just as many clerical operations will be assumed by the more efficient EDP equipment. In short, the conversion from a non-EDP system to an EDP system will entail many changes in the organizational structure, in the system of authorization and record procedures and in sound business practices. Thus, one of the first things the auditor must determine is the relationship of the EDP function to the overall organization as well as the interrelationships between basic segments of the EDP internal organization. These relationships play an important part in the auditor's ultimate evaluation of the internal controls and accounting procedures because there is generally a greater concentration of responsibility for data processing lodged in the EDP organization than in any other single unit.

In considering the relationship of the EDP function to the overall organization, it is important to determine whether the EDP department is, in fact, functionally independent of the other operating departments in the organization. To be effective from a control viewpoint, this relationship must, as in a manual system, continue to provide for an adequate separation of duties which will result in a system of checks and balances throughout the organization and in the data flow.

Another consideration in reviewing the effectiveness of organizational control is that the EDP department should function completely as a service unit. It should not have any control over assets. For example, it is often possible for the EDP department to gain control over corporate funds and other resources of the company, such as allowing it to control blank checks, blank certificates, etc., by permitting it to circumvent prescribed processing controls.

The size of the company or the size of the installation can influence the internal organization of the EDP department. From an effective control viewpoint those individuals responsible for the design and development of the EDP system should be completely separate and independent of the programming function. In addition, there should be a separation of the personnel responsible for operating the equipment from the individuals responsible for controlling the data flowing into and out of the data processing installation and for handling the data files and output records. Again, the objective of the separation is to establish controls which will limit the opportunity for any one of these groups or subgroups to manipulate the data processed.

Another aspect of organizational control relates to the physical environment of the installation. Thus, a well-controlled installation will have procedures which limit admittance to the computer room to only those employees directly connected with the data processing operations. They also will limit admittance to the computer room to equipment operators and access to data records, files and programs to control unit personnel.

Thus, the auditor must begin his examination of the system by obtaining or preparing an organization chart of the overall organization and of the internal structure of the EDP department. With these documents in hand, he can then establish by queries and observation the responsibilities of the various functions and determine whether they operate as independent units or whether duties, responsibilities and operations overlap to create a weakness in the system.

Data Movement and Conversion. In reviewing the procedures used for data movement and data conversion, the auditor should determine that there are satisfactory controls in the following areas:

1. In originating departments supplying the input data to ensure its authenticity, accuracy and completeness.
2. In the transmission of data from the originating departments to ensure that all data transmitted is received intact by the processing unit.
3. In the conversion of source data into machine-readable form to ensure that all data received is processed.
4. In the use and handling of operating programs to ensure that they are processing the data and producing output in accordance with the system as designed.

5. In external checks and balances to ensure the reliability of the data processing output.

The failure of controls at any one point may very well lead to the loss of integrity of the system, the application, or the data.

In his review of controls over data movement, the auditor can use the "walkthrough" technique described above and by narrative memorandum, checklist, questionnaire or flow chart document his findings and conclusions. This can be done from the point of origin of the source data to the point where it enters the computer. Alternately, the auditor can use the charts and documentation of the systems analyst and follow the flow of data through these schematic presentations. At the point of conversion of source data into machine-readable form, the auditor can test the accuracy of this process by reviewing the efficiency of the keypunching and key verifying operation or other conversion procedures. He also can trace "live" transactions into and through the conversion process and ultimately into output data or files to determine the accuracy of the process or he can use test data to establish, to his satisfaction, that conversion is taking place properly.

Program Development and Utilization. A computer program is a series of instructions which the computer can interpret and execute. These instructions, or the program, guide the computer through each step in the processing of data. Controls over the programming process should include:

1. Complete documentation of all operating programs in use.
2. Procedures in effect for the approval of all modifications to programs.
3. Procedures in effect for the thorough testing of all programs and program modifications prior to their actual use.

Here the auditor should review the logic of the program, step by step, to determine the processing steps and the controls incorporated in the program. Where programs are in machine or other computer language and are difficult to follow, the auditor can create a test deck or adapt the EDP department's test decks to test the programs and subsequent modifications thereof. Obviously, the test deck should include both valid and invalid data in order to obtain evidence as to how the program handled the selected transactions. Alternatively, the auditor can acquire and apply one of several available systems which will read computer programs and prepare a flow chart or other schematic presentation of the program under review; he then can follow the logic of the procedures and controls through it. At this point in his review the auditor is trying to determine to what extent the output data is reliable. In other words, he is trying to determine whether there are any unknown instructions in the program which will divert, drop or manipulate the data being processed or create misleading information.

Processing Procedures. Typical of the controls over the operations of the computer itself are the following:

1. Written instructions—operating manual or run book—to cover each processing job
2. Controls established over all data received by the operating group
3. Procedures in effect for the issuance of only those programs and data record files required for a specific processing job
4. Procedures in effect for the recording and disposition of errors occurring as data is processed

5. Procedures for the retention and review of all console printouts or manual records of halts
6. Procedures for control and review of all computer running time

The objectives of these operating controls and procedures are to minimize the possibility of operator error and to limit his responsibilities to loading programs and data files and to operating the equipment in accordance with well-defined instructions. To be effective, these instructions must anticipate all of the operator's needs, yet at the same time limit his knowledge of and access to the programs and data files.

Obviously, the auditor should examine and evaluate the currency, applicability and completeness of the operating manual or run book and determine by observation, queries and other tests that the instructions included therein are being followed. He should test—by tracing transactions or other data from input to output—that the data received by the operating group is handled according to instructions. A very significant audit procedure requires that the auditor determine that errors occurring during the processing are all recorded and handled properly. He also should establish to his own satisfaction the reasons for computer halts and for any excess or unscheduled running time.

Custodial Procedures. Custodial procedures relate to the methods used by the data processing group to control access to data records, files and programs. These include:

1. A separate section in the EDP department which has custody of and control over all tape files, records and programs
2. A formal procedure for the issuance of data files, records and programs only as needed for a particular processing job
3. External and internal tape labels included in all data files identifying content, date created and earliest date upon which they may be erased for re-use
4. A formal time schedule for the retention and disposition of data files and records

The physical control over data records, files and programs should always be of concern to the auditor. In this facet of his review of controls, he will be interested in determining that custodial responsibility has been established and is enforced and that procedures which limit the access to such records, files and programs to only those individuals having the custodial responsibility are being followed. In addition, he should be concerned with insurance coverage and the company's ability to reproduce the data files, records and programs in the event they are destroyed.

BIBLIOGRAPHY

"Internal Auditing, Review and Appraisal in the Federal Government," *Research Bulletin* No. 2, Federal Government Accountants Association, Washington, 1962.

Internal Control, Elements of a Coordinated System and Its Importance to Management and the Independent Public Accountants, New York, AICPA, 1949.

Case Studies in Internal Control, AICPA, to date.

Statements on Auditing Procedure No. 33, *Auditing Standards and Procedures,* AICPA (Committee on Auditing Procedure), New York, 1963.

Statement of Responsibilities of the Internal Auditor, The Institute of Internal Auditors, New York, 1957.

Cadmus, Bradford: *Operational Auditing Handbook,* New York, The Institute of Internal Auditors, 1964.

Cashin, James A.: *Management Controls in a Growing Enterprise,* New York, Hofstra University, 1967.
Davis, Gordon B.: *Auditing and EDP,* New York, AICPA, 1968.
Jerome, William Travers III: *Executive Control—The Catalyst,* New York, John Wiley & Sons, Inc., 1961.
Kamp, Walter H., and James A. Cashin: *Internal Control Standards and Related Auditing Procedures,* Stamford, Brock and Wallston, 1947.
Skinner, R. M., and R. J. Anderson: *Analytical Auditing, An Outline of the Flow Chart Approach to Audits,* New York, Pitman Publishing Corporation, 1966.

Sawyer, L. B.: "The Anatomy of Control," *The Internal Auditor,* Spring, 1964.
Chippendale, Warren: "Evaluation of Internal Control," *The Canadian Chartered Accountant,* September, 1964.
John, Richard C., and Thomas J. Nissen: "Evaluating Internal Control in EDP Audits," *The Journal of Accountancy,* February, 1970.
Arnold, John F.: "The Dynamics of Internal Control," *The Internal Auditor,* May/June, 1970.

Chapter **10**

Planning the Audit

OSWALD NIELSEN

Professor of Accounting, Graduate School of Business, Stanford University

THE IMPORTANCE OF PLANNING

General. The process of planning an audit encompasses activities ranging all the way from making initial arrangements for access to data which are to be reviewed, to the procedures to be followed in examining them. Additionally, plans must be made to have adequate personnel available for the audit. Added to these major considerations are a number of minor matters that require attention, depending upon the specific nature of the audit that is to be made.

The planning function has now become one of the most important aspects of the audit. With the recent advances in generalized computer audit programs and the greater use of statistical sampling and greater importance of quantitative techniques, a new dimension has been added to the already complex problem of planning the present-day audit. Other factors that have an important bearing on planning are (1) the greater reliance on internal control, (2) the changing auditing approaches, such as flow charting, analytical review, and continuous audit, and (3) management services. With higher staff costs and the need for maximum utilization of staff time, better planning than ever before is required. In addition, the planning must provide, in the case of the independent auditor, the maximum practical utilization of the client's accounting and internal auditing staffs. In the case of a computer application the planning must take into account the client's system and needs, as printouts only for auditing purposes can be unnecessarily expensive.

The importance of planning was specifically recognized by the American Institute of Certified Public Accountants (AICPA) and was designated as the first standard among the Standards of Field Work. This standard states that

"The work is to be adequately planned and assistants, if any, are to be properly supervised."[1]

While the auditor must be careful to include all necessary procedures in his program, he must also make sure that only appropriate procedures are carried out. *The audit should be planned so that no audit procedures are performed which are not required.*

This chapter is organized to present first those procedures which are similar in the three branches of auditing, since it is difficult in many cases to determine where internal auditing or governmental auditing leaves off and public auditing begins, or vice versa. Procedures peculiar to the particular branch are described later in the chapter.

Responsibility for Planning. The audit is usually under the general supervision of a partner or resident manager. Where the auditor is practicing on his own account, he will maintain direct supervision of the jobs until his practice grows to such an extent that he may require a manager or supervisor and ultimately a partner. A partner will usually have the initial contact with the client and will usually visit the client's office and plant facilities. At this time he will usually make a determination as to whether he wishes to undertake the audit, and if so, he will obtain the preliminary data needed to estimate the fee. In the case of the internal auditor or governmental auditor the approach is usually somewhat different. Usually the determination has already been made as to whether the audit is to be undertaken and there is no need to obtain data to set the fee. In many cases the chief internal auditor or a supervisor may accompany the assigned auditors to a location and help set the general guidelines of the audit. The senior will then develop the audit program and submit it to the chief internal auditor for approval.

The Initial Audit. In making preliminary arrangements, there are some differences in procedure, depending upon whether or not the auditor is making his first audit of the company or whether he is serving on a repeat engagement. For the sake of simplicity preliminary arrangements are described as they apply in the case of the first audit. It is assumed that a new client, in the case of a CPA, approaches the auditor with respect to the proposed engagement. Under the Code of Professional Ethics as formulated by the AICPA the statement in reference to this made in Article 3.02 is that "A member or associate shall not endeavor, directly or indirectly, to obtain clients by solicitation."

A matter of primary importance is to determine just what constitutes the prospective client. The auditor needs to know if the prospective client is limited to a parent company only, or if it encompasses a definable series of subsidiary corporations as well. It also may be of importance in the case of either a corporation or a partnership to know if the unit being audited involves participation in some joint venture.

The Repeat Audit. Preliminary arrangements are less elaborate for the repeat audit. It is possible that fee structures are assumed to be continued and that arrangements for confirmations and access to files will continue as in the past, so that no specific memorandum need be prepared. Specific mention might be required for any new situations. They could apply to fee structure or to problems that demand specific attention.

For the repeat audit there are many papers and records from the previous

[1] Statements on Auditing Procedure No. 33, *Auditing Standards and Procedures,* AICPA (Committee on Auditing Procedure), New York, 1963, p. 23.

audits to help in planning the current audit. The audit program itself will ordinarily have to be modified on the basis of the previous year's experience. However, the time required for making any needed modification is usually far less than developing the initial program. Moreover, the working papers, the staff requirements, and the time budget for the previous year provide an excellent starting point for the current year after giving effect to changes since the previous year.

PRELIMINARY ARRANGEMENTS

The Initial Interview. The initial interview is one of the most important aspects in planning an audit. It is particularly critical in the case of the public accountant, since the essential facts concerning the audit have to be clear before the audit is begun. In the case of the internal auditor or governmental accountant the preliminary arrangements will be less formal than for the public accountant. All the following items will ordinarily apply to the public accountant's audit. Most of the items will also apply to the internal auditor and the governmental auditor.

Types of Arrangements. In the case of the first audit the auditor should obtain as much information as he can pertaining to the audit. First of all, he will want to make sure of the facts relating to the audit, such as the purpose of the audit and the type of audit. Second, he will want to know something about the nature of the business, the key personnel, etc. Third, he will need to obtain information relating to the program, such as when the report is due and when inventory is taken. Many of these points will be summarized in an "engagement letter" or "confirmation letter" which outlines the agreed arrangements. The senior accountant on the job is provided with a copy as a guide during the course of his audit. An example of an engagement letter is shown below.

The Board of Directors
Hamburg Manufacturing Company, Inc.
1125 South Michigan Avenue
Chicago, Illinois 60605

Gentlemen:

It was a pleasure meeting with Messrs. Harter, Knowles, and Smith of your company. We wish to thank the members of the Board of Directors for inviting us to visit your offices and plant and for asking us to present our qualifications for appointment as auditors of Hamburg Manufacturing Company, Inc. We found the visit to be interesting and informative. Responding to your request we are pleased to submit information concerning Woodlands & Heather, the scope of services rendered by our firm, our experience in the electronics industry, and certain specific details with respect to the work which you outlined.

BACKGROUND

Your company has expanded rapidly within the past few years. Recognizing the advantages of having one firm of accountants who are capable of providing on-the-spot services to your various divisions and subsidiaries, you have decided to retain the services of an international accounting firm. You have advised your present CPA's of your intent to change.

OBJECTIVES OF ENGAGEMENT

We are to make an examination of the consolidated balance sheet of Hamburg Manufacturing Company, Inc. and its wholly owned subsidiaries as of December 31, 1970 and the related statements of income and retained earnings for the year then ending.

SCOPE OF ENGAGEMENT

Our examination will be made in accordance with generally accepted auditing standards, and accordingly will include such tests of the accounting records and such other auditing procedures as we consider necessary in the circumstances for the purpose of expressing an opinion on the financial statements.

HOW WE WOULD CONDUCT THE ENGAGEMENT

Our examination will emphasize the following techniques which we consider to be of particular value:

1. Analytical review

In order to highlight meaningful data and trends, we make an analytical review of the financial statements and accounting records. We avoid an extensive examination of transactions having little or no importance to the financial statements as a whole.

2. Special industry audit programs and questionnaires

We have developed special industry audit programs and questionnaires, tailored to fit the circumstances of each client, as the basis of our audit of significant accounting transactions and balances and as a guide for our comprehensive review of the system of internal control. This practice tends to improve our efficiency and minimizes the time required to complete our examination.

3. Interim work

Preliminary work on audit engagements is started early in the year in order to complete as much of our work as possible prior to the year end. As a result, completion of the examination and issuance of our report after the year end are expedited and much of your accounting department's work with the auditors is completed well in advance of the other heavy requirements with which that department is normally faced at the end of the year.

4. Management letters

It is our practice to issue letters to management outlining comments and suggestions as to any weaknesses in internal control or accounting procedures which came to our attention during the course of our examination.

OUR QUALIFICATIONS

A recent study shows that Woodlands & Heather is one of the largest, fastest growing, and most diversified public accounting firms in the world. Our objective is to diversify our practice so as to serve a wide range of clientele and yet to have experts in the various industries and fields of business so as to render the best possible service available.

FEE

Our fees are based upon the amount of time required to complete an assignment and the level of the people assigned. We are also reimbursed for out-of-pocket costs which include travel subsistence, and report reproduction expenses. Based on the personnel to be assigned to this engagement, we estimate an over-all rate of $___ per hour. We will render interim billings as the work progresses and a final billing at the conclusion of the engagement.

* * *

Thank you for the opportunity to present this proposal. Will you kindly indicate your acceptance by signing and returning the enclosed copy of this letter or if you need additional information, please contact us.

Very truly yours,
Woodlands & Heather
A. C. Heather, Partner

Accepted:
Hamburg Manufacturing Company, Inc.
By__________
Date__________

The basic letter is usually very general. Additional material may be added to meet the needs of a particular client. For example, the estimated audit fee may be included. In other cases a certain client may require a long-form report for creditors. These and other provisions can be added to the basic letter.

General Data. **Purpose of the audit.** The audit may be needed for (1) credit purposes, that is, the bank may require an audited statement; (2) investment purposes, where the potential investor requests an audit; (3) purchase of a business, where valuations have to be established; (4) fraud, in which the nature and amount of fraud must be determined; and (5) special investigation undertaken for various purposes.

Change of auditors. In the case of the first audit it may be well to find out if possible why there was a change of auditors. In some cases the answer is simple—the company has a policy of changing auditors every 3 years. In some cases the new auditor may wish to contact the preceding auditor to find out if there was anything questionable about the client or the audit.

Nature of the examination. The nature of the examination will depend largely on the purpose. If it is for credit purposes, the usual type of opinion audit may be needed. If fraud is involved, an intensive audit of cash receipts and cash disbursements may be required. However, this may apply only to short periods, less than a year. If the purchase of a business is involved, it may be primarily the valuation of the business and may require only a short period of time.

Period covered. The period to be covered by the audit should be agreed upon at the first meeting. The client may wish an audit for a shorter period, or a special examination rather than a regular audit may be required. The period to be covered is essential in planning the staff requirements and the time budget.

Cost of the audit. The basis of compensation should be clearly understood. For the first audit, it is usually difficult to estimate the amount of time and the number of seniors and juniors needed. However, the client usually wants to have some estimate of what the audit will cost. Sometimes a top estimate may be given based on the understanding of what is to be done. If more is required than expected, an adjustment should be understood to be in order.

Business Data. **Nature of the business.** The auditor should obtain data concerning the history of the business, the headquarters, and various locations. He should also find out the various products manufactured, the raw material used, the labor skills required, and the general type of machinery required. Much of this information can be obtained during a tour of the facilities.

Organization structure. If an organization chart is available, the auditor should obtain a copy. If not, he should prepare his own chart. The chart should show reporting responsibilities by departments and individuals.

Key personnel. The auditor should meet the key personnel as soon as possible. He may wish to cross-reference any list or names of key personnel to those shown on the organization chart.

Condition of records. The client must understand that the books are to be in balance. Further, the subsidiary records and control accounts are to be in agreement. It should be clear that the auditor will be responsible for auditing, not bookkeeping.

Place to work. Since most of the audit work will be done in the client's office, the client should provide a place for the auditor. It should also be understood that some work will be done in the auditor's office as determined by the auditor.

Comments on internal control. An important part of an audit is a letter or list of comments on deficiencies in internal control. If the deficiencies are not significant enough to include in his formal report, he should protect himself by pointing these out to the client and giving recommendations for improvement.

Program Data. Due date of report. In order to plan the audit program, the first requirement is to know when the audit report is due. An early report may require overtime and weekend work.

Inventory observation. Where inventories are involved, especially at distant branches, the problem of timing and travel is critical. It may be necessary to get additional staff auditors to observe inventory taking. The auditor should point out to the client that the inventory must be observed by the auditor.

Confirmations. The auditor should point out that professional standards also require that confirmations of receivables, cash, securities, etc., be made. Assistance may be provided by the internal audit staff or accounting staff in following up minor differences.

Testing of records. The client should understand that not all transactions will be reviewed. Instead the internal control will be evaluated and selected tests made of transactions and records. If the tests indicate the figures are reliable, no further verification will be made.

Work by client's staff. The auditor should point out that a substantial amount of the auditor's time can be saved and the fee held to a fair size if the client's staff helps in preparing schedules and analyses. This can be done under control of the auditor. The amount of such help can have an important effect in determining the number and amount of time for staff members.

Interim work. It should be pointed out that certain audit work can be done prior to the year end. Make arrangements to do as much interim work as possible. This will help to prevent a bottleneck at the year end and reduces overtime.

Engagement memorandum. In order to avoid later misunderstandings, it is preferable to prepare a list of the points agreed upon and to forward a copy to the client. Any questions or differences can be resolved at the beginning rather than later after the audit has begun.

PREPARATORY PROGRAM WORK

General. After agreement has been reached with the client and the audit has been accepted, it is necessary to do some preparatory program work before the audit begins. While the partner or resident manager has discussed various points and outlined the broad parameters of the audit and estimated a fee, further details are needed in order to prepare the detailed audit program. Important in beginning any audit is acquiring familiarity with the physical surroundings and equipment. As the auditor gains experience in observing the physical environment of various audits, he develops ability to make overall appraisals of their nature and quality. He also gains the advantage of making comparisons and drawing contrasts where equipment or premises are used for the same or different purposes.

Plant and Storage Facilities. Inspection of plant and storage facilities is valuable in understanding inventory movements. A high degree of cleanliness and order suggests good reporting and managing of inventories.

Another thing to look for is the general state of repair. Much old, rundown machinery is suggestive of downtime on machines for repairs and maintenance. Lack of repair in storage facilities suggests they are subject to weather damage or pilferage. Nonoperating equipment may indicate several possible situations. Among these would be a lack of sufficient customers' orders for capacity utilization. Downtime on equipment sometimes indicates defective scheduling. An excessive amount of nonoperating equipment may indicate a low degree of morale and may be suggestive of unprofitable operation.

On the plant tour the auditor must observe the general transportation of goods, which indicates the sequencing of operations and is helpful in determining how goods in process are moved to various stages of production.

The auditor can determine inventory movements, from which he may appraise the stage of production of any work in process. Second, he gains knowledge of where the documentary evidence of the movements is generated. Third, he comes to know what movements might cause duplication in counting of inventory unless all movement can be stopped at the time of inventory taking.

The observation of general inventory movement often is a good indicator of what might be expected in the review of internal control for inventory. The auditor can ascertain the personnel responsible for the documentation and physical movement of inventory.

Receiving and Shipping Facilities. Inspection of receiving and shipping facilities reveals how documentation is generated for inflow and outflow of goods. It also enables the auditor to appraise how to measure cutoffs in that he learns how control of common-carrier containers provides evidence of inventory ownership or disposition.

Offices. General inspection of the client's offices contributes understanding of the degree of orderliness in the flow of paperwork, and gives evidence of employee morale. In addition, insight is gained into the physical working situation that the auditor will have. Unduly crowded and disorganized offices usually predict a difficult working environment for the auditor, which may hamper his effective and economical performance.

Examination of documentary systems and records. Inspection of the client's facilities encompasses the general documentary system and the records. Here the auditor observes the flow of information from point of generation to its input into the information system. This involves an understanding not only of the documents themselves but also of the various channels and repositories for the actual accumulation of data.

Documentary systems. There are two major classes of documentary systems. The first are those generated as individual events take place. Such documents include time tickets, production reports, receiving notices, shipping advices and bills of lading, sales invoices, vouchers (and the combination of the devices of documents that support them such as receiving notices, purchase orders, and suppliers' invoices), and production orders. This whole system of documentary information serves the dual purposes of actual recording of business events and, additionally, helps to assure that business procedures are adequate. To illustrate, a production order is designed to authorize production of goods ordered by the customer, and shipping instructions likewise authorize produced goods to be shipped to the customer. The billing procedure specifies the appropriate amounts to be collected for the goods shipped.

The second class are those that do not pace the individual events of the business but encompass more far-reaching activities. Among these are special contracts, the corporate charter, bylaws, minutes of stockholders' and directors' meetings, copies of tax returns, guarantees, and leases for real and personal property. Such documents evidence transactions and the terms governing their execution. These documents may be for single events (such as for purchasing a building) or may involve a series of events (such as the payment of monthly rentals for leases).

Ledger and journal voucher structure. Next the auditor wants to understand the general recording structure. This includes knowing the magnitude and detail of the account classification. It also involves determining whether or not the accounting system includes supporting ledgers or whether supporting information is in the form of file copies of documents. Also the journals, journal vouchers, or registers of documents need to be examined to determine their physical form. Sometimes documentary evidence is kept in a compressed form of storage such as microfilm. Likewise the auditor wants to know if the general ledger is in loose-leaf form, on cards for recording by means of bookkeeping equipment, or in the form of disk or computer-tape storage where only updated balances are kept to be taken off by computer runs. All such knowledge aids in determining means of access to the data.

Nature and extent of confidential records. If there are confidential records such as expense accounts of top executives which are not available for scrutiny, the partner or in-charge auditor will examine their contents to determine conformity with authorizations contained in the minutes of the board of directors. The same goes for private partnership ledgers, containing details on conformity with partnership agreements, which are needed for the preparation of partnership income tax returns.

Agreement on Dates for Audit. Two essential features are involved in planning the audit. One concerns the audit functions that must be done at certain times if they are to be done well at all. The other is that some dates must be arranged to minimize interference with the client's ongoing work and yet permit the auditor to conduct his work efficiently.

Generally the auditor will arrange for the needed days and hours to be present for inventory taking, so that he can be present with the necessary personnel. Details with respect to this and its significance are covered in Chapter 22.

Scheduling of Confirmations. For the most part the auditor specifies the dates for getting out confirmations. As far as receivables are concerned, this usually is timed with the preparation of end-period statements by the client. The auditor arranges for his firm personally to mail confirmation requests for direct confirmation to the auditor. Requests for confirmations of accounts payable are worked out for mailing at the end of the period. The dating of the bank and insurance company confirmations need not necessarily be scheduled for issuance precisely at the end of the client's fiscal year.

Date for Auditor's Report. Certain deadlines must be met for completion of the audit report. Controlling factors include scheduled dates for stockholders' or directors' meetings, dates for the filing of income tax returns, and filings with the Securities and Exchange Commission for security offerings. The client is sometimes impatient to obtain the auditor's report for submission to actual and prospective credit grantors. Clarification of the reporting date also informs the client when to have information ready so it can be reviewed in time for meeting the deadline for the auditor's report.

TIME BUDGET

Public Accounting Time Budget. In public accounting practice, the overall time budget is basic in efficient use of personnel. It extends to recruiting of sufficient personnel to handle contemplated assignments.

An overall time budget will be made preceding the actual operating year for the public accounting firm. Lionel Engelman has prepared an interesting unpublished manuscript as a required report for his master's degree at the University of California at Berkeley. This report, prepared under the title, "An Operations Research Model for the Scheduling of the Audit Staff," makes an interesting study into some of the qualities that are of significance in the long-time projection of the manpower requirements for a CPA firm. Because he knows that underprovision of manpower invites a loss of practice, whereas overprovision involves an undue amount of cost, he has developed a model to try to determine, within reasonable cost limits, the amount of manpower necessary to carry on the audit function. He also deals with a queuing model in arranging a reasonable time schedule for the handling of audits. Naturally such an attempt does not necessarily result in a good allocation of workers when one considers the immediate needs of various audit programs. However, the value of his study and its attendant viewpoint is its focus on the different types of problems incidental to the utilization of auditing personnel.

The time budget finally must condense to the amount of audit time which auditors apply to the various steps in the audit program. For a new engagement, it becomes an intelligent estimate based upon general experience, and is determined from two sources. One is the preliminary inspection of the facilities and accounting records; the other is discussion with the client's personnel, including top management, which may indicate areas requiring attention.

Internal Audit Time Budget. Since there is usually enough work for an imaginative internal audit department, the manpower question tends toward what should be done next. General duties consist of reviewing the operation of the accounting system itself, testing the capacity of the system to disclose significant facts relative to the management of the business, and appraising the effectiveness of company management at various levels. Long-term planning involves the assignment of personnel to perform these duties.

In an effective internal audit system review of the conceptual foundation of the accounting system is followed by subsequent reviews to ascertain its continued effectiveness, including capacity to change as managerial problems demand adaptations in the system. Beyond that the matter becomes one of analyzing the problems that are important in management. Problems involving the greatest cost or profitability are those which receive major initial attention. In addition there are special assignments made by management itself that supersede the regular plan for work within the internal audit department. Generally the program is designed by the head of the internal audit department in consultation with divisional and department heads, including the controller and vice-president of finance. Such advance planning simplifies working out manpower requirements. Major personnel problems then arise primarily from special assignments. Even so, if special assignments are made in advance, it is possible to include them in the regular program for the internal audit staff.

Governmental Audit Time Budget. In governmental auditing, classifications of personnel approximate the various grades in independent public accounting.

Regional assignments are generated from national headquarters in Washington by those governmental agencies which conduct audit functions. Once the general contours of the work are established, it becomes the responsibility of the regional auditor in charge to plan his own manpower assignments. Shortages are filled by recruiting through appropriate employment channels. Rush or special assignments receive precedence in sequence of work.

Here again, manpower tends to vary depending upon the nature of the audit. For example, in certain state governmental audit agencies such as for sales tax audits, the investigation tends to be detailed, with much of the work being done on a sampling basis, which can be planned at the local level. There may be some special audits in cases where assignments are probes into cases of suspected misunderstanding or avoidance of payment.

Further details concerning the various types of governmental audits are discussed in Chapter 8, "Governmental Auditing."

STAFF BUDGET

Planning Staff Needs. The planning of staff needs depends to a large extent on whether the job is an initial audit or a repeat audit. In the initial audit the staff needs will usually be prepared by the partner and the in-charge auditor for the job. After the job has been done at least once, the in-charge auditor is likely to develop the estimated staff needs subject to the partner's approval.

There are a number of factors which will have a bearing on staff needs. Some of the most important factors are:

Initial or repeat audit. On the initial audit the estimated staff needs may vary substantially from the actual. The estimate is likely to be much closer on subsequent audits.

Type of audit. The type of audit, whether for credit purposes, investor purposes, etc., will affect the staff requirements.

Nature of the business. While many of the financial functions such as cash and receivables may be fairly comparable among companies, a manufacturing company with inventories will vary substantially from other companies. Possibly another client in the same line of business may provide helpful data.

Size of the business. The size of the business may have an effect on planning, especially where there are branch locations. The auditor must be alert in the repeat audit for an increase or decrease in facilities, production, products, etc.

Period of the examination. The time span will have an effect on staff budgeting. A tight schedule may require overtime in the evening or weekends to meet the deadline. Possibly extra staff may be brought in to meet the deadline.

Degree of internal control. If the degree of internal control is good, the auditor may be able to plan a minimum of tests and audit procedures. However, this usually will have to await actual evaluation.

Flow of work. Work does not flow evenly during the course of the audit. Additional staff help may be needed for short periods to observe inventory at different locations simultaneously, or cash may have to be counted simultaneously.

Qualifications of staff. The qualifications of the staff will have a direct bearing on staff requirements. The ability of the staff members, of course, is most important. The senior will try to get juniors with good qualifications, especially if he has worked with them before. The ability of the in-charge auditor also is important. He must have proved himself on other jobs, usually smaller ones, in order to be given the present responsibility.

Staff training. An important responsibility is the training and development of the staff members. Even at the risk of using additional time there must be provision to train and develop all the auditors on the staff. This is a critical period in the careers of many young men, and the experienced auditors have a responsibility to help guide the new staff members.

Use of client's staff. The type of help and the amount of help to be given by the client will have a direct effect on the number and time of the audit staff.

Additional time on planning how to utilize the client's staff will pay handsome dividends in audit time saved. Since there will be some degree of flexibility, often it is advisable to begin with fewer assistants and take on more as the audit settles a little. That is better than having staff on the job but not using them to the maximum extent. Time can be saved by assigning staff to the work for which they are best qualified. For example, an experienced man should take charge of the audit of branches or subsidiaries in other locations. In the case of the internal auditor where considerable travel may be involved, the cost of travel for an extra auditor must be weighed against keeping the same staff a longer period.

Staff Ranks. The number of auditors in the various staff ranks must be balanced closely with the type and complexity of the work carried out. It is inefficient to have staff men doing work below their level of competence. However, in some cases it is more practicable to use the available man than to hire a new junior for the job who may not be needed later. The levels in a medium or large CPA firm are roughly comparable with those in a medium or large internal audit staff or government audit staff. Though the title may differ, there will be partners or directors, supervisors or managers, seniors, semiseniors, and juniors. There may also be specialists in taxes, management services, etc. The various titles are described below.

Partner or director. The partner has top responsibility in the CPA firm. The director or chief auditor would have top responsibility for the internal auditing function or the governmental function. In a CPA firm partners have responsibilities for various clients except where there may be specialties such as for tax or management services. The partners share in the profits of the firm.

Principal. The principal may have responsibility for a number of jobs or may be in a specialty such as data processing. However, the principal ordinarily is not a full partner. Frequently this is because he does not have a CPA certificate. The partnership wants to designate itself as a partnership of certified public accountants.

Manager. The manager is usually a young man on the way up and very possibly has a potentiality of becoming a partner. He is in charge of senior and staff accountants. He also oversees the progress of audits for a group of clients. In some firms the manager shares in part of the profits of the firm.

Senior. The senior accountant works directly under the manager or supervisor. In a small firm he may be directly responsible to a partner. It is his job to supervise juniors to see that their work conforms with the standards of the profession. Furthermore, he must be sure that they complete assignments given to them. He is concerned with the time schedule and with meeting the audit deadline. His success depends primarily on his capacity to train and to lead those assigned to work under his direction.

Junior or staff accountant. The junior is usually the lowest auditing rank. To help the junior's prestige, some firms designate the lowest rank as merely a staff accountant. His professional capacity ranges from that of a mere beginner to a person almost ready to assume duties as a senior. Some firms have the title of semisenior, but this title does not do much to enhance the image of the particular auditor. Generally the junior receives indoctrination in the firm's training school. The need for developing people of competence with a capacity for managing audits and assuming responsibility has forced many CPA firms and internal auditing units to give beginners a variety of training and move them into positions of responsibility as quickly as possible.

THE AUDIT PROGRAM

General. The audit program itself is a medium for having an organized auditing procedure. For an initial audit, it relates general arrangements with the client and the inspection of the client's operating situation and facilities with the type of work that is required. For audits on a continuing basis, the program describes innovations and improvements in past audit programs as previous experience dictates. It may serve special needs of the client, such as for management services, income tax, and property assessment problems.

Basic Approach. The basic approach for the preparation of the usual audit program varies in detail among auditing firms and from one client to another. Many of the large firms have preconstructed forms listing an array of audit operations. The senior in charge reviews these forms and selects the particular operations applicable in the audit which he is planning.

Generally, the senior in charge of an assignment drafts the program. He then reviews it with the manager in charge, and they will in most cases formulate the final audit program. Unusual problems or difficulties will be discussed with a partner for appropriate treatment. Although these problems may be discovered by the manager or the senior, awareness of them arises often from the partner's contact with the client.

The detailed steps in a program may cover many pages. Most such steps are covered in other chapters of this handbook. Hence, only the major contours of the program are covered here.

Relationship to Review of Internal Control. Any audit program must relate to the quality of the system of internal control. A first consideration in the audit is to appraise the conceptual soundness of the system of internal control. The auditor then determines the extent to which the system operates as intended. The auditor appraises the combination of conceptual soundness and operational conformity in deciding upon the required extent of testing.

Relationship to Previous Periods. One of the soundest approaches is to relate the audit program to those previously followed on the job. According to this view the following out of an audit program indicates several considerations of importance. One is a discovery of the extent to which there is a lack of operational conformity in following a system of internal control. It is contemplated, therefore, that an audit program for any given year will be designed to determine if the client has made the necessary corrections either in the system of internal control or in operational conformity with it. This may affect the extent of test checking or involve introduction of different audit steps because of what has been found.

Another situation that arises is that deviations from budgeted time for an audit may not reflect required time for various aspects of the audit. Therefore, a new audit program must incorporate changes actually needed in the time budget.

Still other adjustments may be needed to adapt to changes in the accounting system or in the actual operations of the client.

Content of the Program. Generally, the content of the program consists first of the various auditing steps to be performed. Second, it includes the contemplated audit time required to perform each of the audit steps. Third, when the audit is completed, it also shows the actual amount of time involved in carrying out the program.

Otherwise the content of the program is divided into the following main sections:

1. Review of the system of internal control

2. Audit of balance sheet accounts
3. Audit of income statement accounts
4. Preparation of the audit report
5. Preparation of income tax returns
6. Preparation of comments on the operation of the system of internal control

In each of these areas the various steps to be performed are listed, as is the time budget for carrying out the program. The various chapters dealing with audit of the specific items mentioned cover the detailed steps involved, and the reader is referred to these chapters.

Format of the Program. Some programs are predesigned formats that encompass all conceivable audit steps, and the auditor selects the appropriate steps for each specific audit. Steps that do not apply are marked as not applicable. If the reason for omission of any step is not obvious, it should be stated.

Some parts of audit programs are questionnaires. These apply particularly to the audit of the system of internal control. A questionnaire may be designed so that the "yes" answers indicate that any particular phase of the system of internal control is conceptually sound or possesses operational conformity. Then any "no" answers signify a deficiency either in the concept of internal control itself or in operational conformity. This approach is not applicable for review of the system of internal control by means of a flow diagram or a matrix.

Nature of Supporting Evidence. In order to express an unqualified opinion, the auditor must have competent evidential material to support the information contained in the client's financial statements. Competent evidential matter presumes documentary evidence of various business activities that is generated as business events occur.

Where evidential material applies to repetitive transactions, a sampling of evidence may demonstrate its reliability. In the event of major transactions such as leases, purchases of important material, or the letting of contracts for construction of buildings, the evidence is examined for each transaction.

Departures from a reliance on documentary evidence itself occur where confirmation from outsiders is sought. Here the attempt is to ascertain that outside information corroborates what has been generated by the client's own documentary evidence. In other cases departure involves appraisal of the soundness of the conceptual background for the generation of information. This becomes especially important where work is recorded in an online computer system without storage of the evidential material.

Detection of Fraud. The certified public accounting audit is not designed for detecting fraud. The principal objective is to make an examination in sufficient detail to determine that the client's financial statements are *fairly* stated. However, if any material amount of fraud exists, the generally accepted auditing procedures will usually bring it to the attention of the auditor. He should be aware that fraud may exist. One reason for being alert for fraud is that, if it exists, a comprehensive search for its nature and extent is likely to involve extensive change in the audit program and a consequent revision of arrangements with the client. If there is reason to suspect that fraud exists, the partner or manager in charge of the audit should discuss it with appropriate officials of the client and arrange for whatever additional auditing services are necessary and desired.

It might also be mentioned that there are other reasons why the auditor is on the alert for evidences of fraud. The first is that fraud often occurs in cases where the particular employee or the management are least suspected of wrongdoing. Then too, failure to detect fraud ranges all the way from a justifiable reason for nondetection to a case of gross negligence. If either the client or a third party can demonstrate gross negligence, the auditor might be held liable for nondetection.

INTERIM WORK

In order to reduce the amount of work at the year end, it is good modern practice to plan a maximum amount of work earlier. Much of this work, such as the review of agreements or the minutes of meetings, can readily be done before the year end. Following are details on various types of work that can be done on an interim basis.

Partnership Agreement. The partnership agreement deals with information of permanent quality. This encompasses information on respective required investments of the partners, how profits are to be divided, and how loans and related interest for loans will be handled. Allowances may be made for differences in the amount of investment or risk incurred. Furthermore, there should be information relative to the manner by which dissolution may be accomplished. Sometimes provisions specify what new venture or partnership arrangement will apply in the event of a partner's death or withdrawal for other reasons.

Corporate Charter and Bylaws. The auditor likewise examines and excerpts pertinent information from the corporate charter and bylaws. This includes date of incorporation, names of the initial incorporators, number of shares authorized, and procedures relating to control of corporate activities. Frequently, duplicated copies of these documents are made available so that detailed excerpting is eliminated. Such copies or excerpts go to the permanent file on the client.

Minutes of Meetings. Significant items to be abstracted about stockholders' meetings include, in addition to the appointment of the auditors themselves, any specific references to the auditing firm as to its duties, the authorization for issuing new shares or debentures, and approval of merger agreements.

From minutes of directors' meetings, items excerpted include dividend declarations (by classes of stock), authorizations for signatures for drawing funds from bank accounts and consummating contractual relationships, and authorizations for major acquisitions or disposals of property. Also excerpted are the approval of executives' salaries and fringe compensations in the way of stock options or bonuses and expense allowances. Similarly, approval of the amounts of insurance carried upon executives are made by the directors. Furthermore, the directors' minutes record election of corporate officers.

Here also, duplicated copies of the minutes of stockholders' and directors' meetings may be made available.

Contracts for Property, Employment, etc. Any major contracts should be excerpted or duplicated. These include contracts for sale and lease of property, employment arrangements with key personnel, and warranties and guarantees.

Tax Returns for Prior Years. In reviewing prior years' tax returns, information to be picked up includes the official name of the corporation, the corporation numbers (such as for social security taxation and other identification numbers), date of incorporation, and other specific matters called for on tax returns. Likewise any peculiar situations that arise in the preparation of the return can be anticipated, and provision can be made for handling them. Having such preliminary work done reduces year-end work and allows for closer review.

Reviews by Internal Revenue Service. If reviews of tax returns have been made by the Internal Revenue Service, it is important that the amount of any claims be checked out to determine their validity and propriety of recording.

Furthermore, matters of dispute between the client and the Internal Revenue Service should be clarified so that the auditors can prepare returns in conformity with final agreements between the two parties. If legal counsel has participated and prepared briefs or claims in connection with the client's position, excerpts or copies should be made part of the client's file.

Working-paper Plans and Procedures. Of special importance for a new senior staff accountant is the planning of working-paper format and arrangement in conformity with the audit program. Such consistency in working-paper structure expedites review, minimizes required time, and avoids confusion.

General Structure and Purpose. There are two principal formats of working papers. One may be used to the exclusion of the other, or both may be used simultaneously. There is the traditional form, which shows in columnar fashion, first the account balances at the close of the previous fiscal period, then the preliminary account balances for the close of the period under review, then columns for recording adjustments, and lastly columns for the final figures. Columns for final figures may be expanded to provide breakdowns of information for reports. Expanded columns tend to be more numerous as one comes to the top working papers.

A second format of considerable importance today is a simple narrative that indicates the nature of the review which was made of the client's own work or working papers. Such a narrative indicates the kind of work the auditor has done and the extent of his sampling, and concludes with his opinion of the matter with which the working paper deals. This format ties in especially well with working papers prepared by the client.

SPECIAL PLANNING DATA

General. In the preceding pages were discussed many phases of planning the audit that are common to the public accountant, the internal auditor, and the governmental auditor. However, there are specific differences among the three types of auditing, and these differences will be discussed in the following sections.

Public Accounting Audits. Who is the client? The public accounting audit differs from the internal audit or governmental audit in that the client may not be the enterprise that is being audited. For example, an audit might be initiated by a corporation or person interested in the possible purchase of another business or some portion of it. Again, a court may order an audit of a corporation because of certain matters that impinge on the public interest. It is important for the public accountant, at the outset, to determine just who the client is and what reports or other information are required by others besides the enterprise being audited.

Investigate prospective client. Again, when a new client is in prospect, there may be considerable inclination for the auditor to accept the client, perhaps without knowing too much about his affairs, sometimes with unfavorable consequences. He may become affiliated with a business of unsavory reputation, or there may be performance of an audit for a company lacking financial resources to pay for the work performed. It is best to learn about such matters before the client is accepted.

Furthermore, with respect to the investigation of the new client, the independent auditor should try to learn why arrangements with the previous auditor have been terminated. This contact serves the additional purpose of gaining access to the files of the previous auditor for working papers, communications, and other documentary information that might be helpful in the new engagement. Accepted courtesy in the profession is to make audit papers available to a successor. Of particular importance as far as routine audits are concerned are such data as beginning account balances and any information indicating how the predecessor determined the validity of information.

Becoming acquainted with the client. In planning for a new engagement, or a repeat engagement for that matter, one of the first steps is for the auditor to gain an understanding of the type of business being audited and an idea of its specific objectives and method of operation. This may involve considerable research for a client in a new industry and may include library research and study of material published by the client's trade association. The objective is better to understand the problems of the client, an increasingly difficult job as more clients become diversified. In such cases the auditor strives to obtain at least a knowledge of the overall managerial problems of the conglomerate and of specific problems relating to its segments.

Next the auditor must become familiar with the physical operation of the client's business. For manufacturers he should make inspection trips through factories, warehouses, shipping and receiving facilities, and general offices. For merchandisers the auditor inspects retail establishments, servicing warehouses, and offices for handling collections and other financial matters. Where marketing operations are on a large chain basis, he visits some of the outlets and obtains a listing of all the outlets.

What is expected in an audit. Preliminary arrangements include a determination of what is expected in the way of an audit. Is the audit needed for credit purposes, for registering securities, or for what other purpose? If the client himself does not understand just what the audit is to encompass, it is the responsibility of the auditor to review with him what can be expected from an audit and what is involved in arriving at the auditor's opinion for the usual opinion audit.

Along with this, the auditor must arrange with the client for working space and develop with him a schedule for access to relevant information.

There must be further understanding of the period to be covered by the audit, which is ordinarily the client's fiscal year. The auditor preferably has been elected at the beginning of that period to enhance his effectiveness on the engagement.

Other planning data. In addition to the matter included in the engagement memorandum, there are ordinarily many other matters that the auditor discussed with the potential client on his initial visit to the client's office. Many of these matters are helpful in planning the audit and are described in detail earlier in this chapter under "Preliminary Arrangements." However, some matters of this nature apply principally to the public accountant, or certain features may have special implications for the public accountant and should be discussed further. The principal points are:

UNDERSTANDING OF THE AUDIT: The auditor should make sure that the client understands that the audit will not extend to checking every transaction. It should be explained that test checks and a review of procedures will be made that will be sufficient for the ordinary audit requiring an expression of opinion as to the fairness of the financial statements. The client should know that the audit is not designed to detect fraud but that any material fraud is likely to be discovered. However, if the client thinks that fraud may exist, then a different type of audit should be undertaken.

RESTRICTIONS OF THE AUDIT: Any apprehension the auditor has about a possible qualified opinion should be discussed frankly with the client at this time, along with the nature and reasons for possible qualification. For example, it is possible that since the auditor was not present at inventory taking at the beginning of the period, he might find it necessary to give a qualified opinion on the statement of income for his first year, unless he can satisfy himself as to the reasonableness of the beginning inventory by reference to the previous auditors' working papers or other means. Such discussion of possible reasons for qualification might avoid later misunderstanding with the client.

There also should be a clear understanding as to the extent to which confirmations are to be requested from customers, creditors, banks, and insurance companies, as to receivables, payables, bank balances, loan balances, and cash values of insurance policies. Any restriction on confirmation of receivables would be serious, as would any restriction on observation of inventories.

REIMBURSEMENT OF EXPENSES: It should be clearly indicated to the client that the audit fees stated cover only professional services and do not include payments made or expenses incurred by the auditor during the course of the audit. For example, where inventory work is to be done at a distant location of the client, the auditor will incur travel and subsistence expenses while away from the home office. These and any other expenses incurred which are necessary to the audit should be reimbursed by the client.

CORPORATE DATA: The nature of the corporation and where the corporate charter and bylaws may be available for inspection.

MINUTES: The location of the minutes and arrangements made for access to them. Sometimes these are kept by an attorney and are to be reviewed in his office.

OFFICERS: The names, addresses, and places of availability of officers and others who may need to be contacted.

RESPONSIBILITIES AND DUTIES: The responsibilities and duties of financial vice-presidents and controllers.

CAPITALIZATION: The extent and structure of corporate equity and debt and any related reporting requirements.

LOCATIONS: The location of all offices, warehouses, branches, sales offices, and other outlets.

DISTRIBUTION: The nature and extent of market outlets and the market situation. The channels of distribution and the general percentage of the market held.

CONSOLIDATIONS: In the case of parent companies and subsidiaries where consolidations or poolings are involved, how and where the various divisional figures are brought together for the consolidation.

ACCOUNTING PRINCIPLES: Any changes in accounting principles or methods, or any problems which occurred in the current year or in past years that may have some impact on the current year.

PROBLEMS: What special problems did management bring out in the interview that need attention or require recommendations for improvement?

INVENTORIES: Any peculiarities as to the location and nature of inventories or their valuation.

TAX RETURNS: Questions relating to tax returns to be made by the auditor. What specific problems have arisen in dealing with the Internal Revenue Service or other taxing authorities?

OTHER REPORTS: Other government reports, tax reports, or other reports or forms to be prepared by the auditor.

INTERIM WORK: If auditors have been appointed early in the year, some indication should be made as to what agreement has been reached concerning interim work. For example, the auditor will be on the premises for inventory taking and other work previously agreed on to be done on certain dates.

CLIENT'S ASSISTANCE: Advanced planning for client assistance is very important to both the client and the auditor. Very often the client is glad to help with working papers, filing, etc., if he is notified in time and adequate instructions are given to the staff. It should be pointed out to the client that the cost of the audit can be held to a minimum and that the audit can be directed to matters more important to the client.

Determination of audit fee. For a new client, the fee structure is usually arranged before the audit work commences. The preferred arrangement is to use the firm's per diem rate for all professional levels, ranging from partners on down to beginning staff accountants. In most instances the arrangement is to charge on a per diem basis, with the proviso, however, that the fee does not exceed a certain maximum amount. In other cases, fees are set on a flat basis with an understanding that no unusual matters are included in the fee. There frequently is an arrangement that if some unusual matter arises that involves unexpected detailed investigation, adjustment of the fee will be made.

Certain governmental units such as municipalities or school districts often request audits by CPA firms. As a matter of cooperation with local governmental bodies, the auditor may accept the job.

In the case of repeat engagements, auditors who have been on a fixed fee and who believe that they have not been able to operate profitably on such a basis will usually ask for a rearrangement. Sometimes a client may feel that the audit fee might be reduced after the first year. If the engagement was on a fixed fee or maximum basis in the first year, it is possible that no profit has been made and the auditor is reluctant to reduce his fee.

Review of predecessor's work. Another step in making preliminary arrangements is to review the predecessor's work. It is one of the courtesies of the profession that a new auditor be given permission to review the working papers of his predecessor, which is usually done in the predecessor's office. Abstracts may be made of relevant items. With modern photocopying methods certain working papers, memoranda, and correspondence may be duplicated to save copying time. Such duplication should be made only with the specific permission of the predecessor firm. No public disclosure should be made of these copies without the specific permission of the predecessor except under court order.

Internal Audits. General. Planning for the internal audit differs somewhat from that for the outside audit. The outside auditor is independent in that he has the basic privilege of accepting or rejecting possible assignments. However, the internal auditor is part of an overall management team, and his duty is to engage in required activities including special assignments made by his supervisors. Such an assignment might be to audit a given store in a chain because of its specific problems. Additionally, the internal auditor makes his own determination of work requiring his attention.

Some believe that the internal auditor emphasizes managerial problems, whereas the outside auditor concentrates on the validity of figures per se. If this was true in the early years, it is less so today. Outside auditors naturally deal with the validity of data, but they are also concerned with what information reveals about management. Furthermore, the relative independence of the external auditor uniquely supports him in expressing his opinions on management.

The internal auditor likewise deals with the validity of information as well as with its managerial implications, and a well-established internal audit department generally is organized and selected to enhance its freedom in making suggestions to management.

In cases of both external and internal auditors, suggestions to management may be made from time to time. If they are disregarded, the reason should be ascertained. There are cases where these observations involve such serious matters that the external auditor may withdraw from the engagement. The internal auditor may feel that he does not have the support of management and may resign.

Responsibility on an internal audit engagement involves identification of the unit to which the internal audit applies. This, for example, could be a certain department in a factory, branch, merchandising outlet, or some function of the business where the audit will be conducted at all relevant managerial levels. For example, a review of research and development may be conducted all the way from the vice-president in charge of that function down to persons in charge of specific research projects.

Headquarters view of unit to be audited. In the sense used here headquarters refers to the top management, which is responsible for coordinating all the company's activities regardless of whether they are geographically centralized or decentralized, or if they function as divisions or subsidiaries manufacturing different lines of products. Top management must have some idea as to the soundness and harmony of operations of the entire company. The larger the company, the greater becomes the problem of having assurance that operations are effectively coordinated and optimized.

The headquarters' view generally is that the internal auditor's responsibility extends beyond providing quantitative information. He must supplement quantitative information with qualitative appraisals of business operations. Sometimes he recommends substitutions of material or improvements in plant technology and proposes other similar suggestions to save money or improve relations with customers. An article, "Company Watch Dogs," in the *Wall Street Journal* for Oct. 26, 1964, tells very interestingly how internal auditors serve the role of being "eyes and ears" for top management.

Level of operations. Top management is interested in information that reflects upon performance at any level of operations, for example, the effectiveness of a general wage policy. Top management wishes to avoid the details of wage administration as long as the policy works efficiently and harmoniously but wants to know promptly where problems arise or are likely to arise.

This same principle applies where there is a broad geographic distribution of operating units, such as in retail or service chains. Top management requires specific details about general coordination or about the operation of any given unit when it is in trouble.

Top management is also interested in management reviews which indicate how persons to whom they delegate responsibility are performing. Thus reports should indicate the general effectiveness of operations and pinpoint those which are especially effective or defective so that they may receive appropriate attention.

Generally, top management establishes the general policy under which the internal auditor operates, and the chief internal auditor implements this policy.

Effect of previous recommendations. The internal auditor generally will have made some previous recommendations for improvements in the operating system or more useful presentation of data. One of his most important functions is the follow-up of management to determine what steps have been taken to require compliance with recommendations. If the internal auditor determines that his recommendations have not been followed, the effect of ignoring them should be discussed with appropriate levels of management.

Planning data. In the case of the public accountant there is a need to make sure that there is full agreement with the client as to the nature of the audit, the fee, the date of the report, and similar matters. Therefore, there is a need to formalize the various points in an engagement memorandum. In the case of the internal auditor and the governmental auditor the nature of the audit is determined generally at headquarters rather than at the location. There is no audit fee to consider, and the date of the audit report is usually at the discretion of the audit department, generally as soon as practicable after completing the audit. Therefore, very often there is a tendency to have less formal procedures in the case of internal auditing and governmental auditing. Ordinarily all the required planning information is included in the prior year's working papers, but there may not be a particular place to look for the data in planning the audit for the following year. To save time, it is generally desirable to have a form for general data, a form to indicate the present level of activity, and a form to plan the staff requirements. Very often internal auditing will require a wider range of auditing services than the usual independent audit, which will ordinarily have a somewhat greater need to tailor the audit program to the particular job. The usual internal audit may have many of the requirements of both the public accountant's management services engagement and the attest audit.

General data. In order to plan the internal audit properly, it is desirable to have certain general information readily available for the particular location. In a company with many locations much of this data is likely to vary with the location. For example, it is desirable to know how many shifts the plant operates and the starting and finishing time of the shifts. Such data are needed in planning to observe the distribution of paychecks, also the pay period and day on which the payroll is distributed for both plant and office employees. Other data may be the number of employees and the names of company officials. To save time and to avoid the mistakes of the past, it is well to include data on transportation and accommodations. For example, what are the options on travel, by air, train, etc.—which is recommended? What are available hotel or motel accommodations and what is recommended? The type of information needed will vary by companies, but it can be easily determined and developed into a form. Figure 1 shows a representative form for general data.

Operating activity. In some cases the level of activity in a manufacturing plant varies considerably from year to year. Therefore, it is important in planning the internal audit for the auditor to know the level of activity before traveling to the location. Generally, all the information is available at headquarters

Figure 1 HENNESSY MANUFACTURING COMPANY—GENERAL DATA

Location ______________ Date ______________

Work Day

Plant Shifts

First, From ____ To ____
Second, From ____ To ____ Lunch Period ________
Third, From ____ To ____

Office Hours, From ____ To ____ Lunch Period ________

Pay Period and Payment Day

Plant ______________ Paid on ______________
Office ______________ Paid on ______________

Number of Employees	Total	Paid by N.Y.O.	Paid by Location
Plant			
Office			

Personnel

Plant Manager ______________
Office Manager ______________
Ass't Office Manager ______________
Personnel Manager ______________

Transportation	Air	Train	Other
Name			
Time			

Accommodations	Name	Address	Phone	Quality
Hotel or Motel				

and can be obtained and the form completed by the senior on the job. Where there has been a substantial reduction in sales, production, or number of employees, usually there would be a reduction in budgeted audit hours, though not necessarily in the same proportion. Information may be obtained for the current month and year to date, since a particular month may not be representative. Data as to sales and production in terms of quantity and price are significant, as also would be the level of inventories, the amount of payroll, and the level of construction at the location. An activity form that has been found useful in one company is shown in Figure 2.

Other data. In addition to the information shown on the general form it is desirable to develop additional information for the internal audit. There should be a budgeted time schedule prepared by the auditor in charge and approved by the chief internal auditor. This should show by particular sections of the program the prior year's actual time, the current year's estimated time, and the actual time for the current year. Since such current information is essential in managing the audit, the form is included in Chapter 11, "Managing the Audit," as Figure 2.

Figure 2 HENNESSY MANUFACTURING COMPANY—COMPARISON OF OPERATING ACTIVITY

Location ______ Date ______	Month			Year to Date		
	This Year	Prior Year	Percent Change	This Year	Prior Year	Percent Change
Gross sales – tons						
Net sales – tons						
Gross sales – dollars						
Net sales – dollars						
Cost of sales						
Sales price per ton						
Cost per ton						
Inventories – dollars						
Raw materials						
In process						
Finished goods						
Gross payroll						
Construction in progress						

There is a variety of other information the auditor should gather at headquarters before he travels to the location. Very often this has to do with understanding instructions at the branch. The auditor can help in interpreting instructions. Generally there will be correspondence, of which the auditor may photocopy sample letters, etc. Generally the internal auditor will visit the chief accountant to find out if he has any problems with the particular location or any suggestions for improving the work for his area. Many times the location may not be meeting the deadline for submitting financial statements or there may be a lack of understanding of the chart of accounts. Also the auditor will visit the chief cost accountant, the tax manager, or any area where problems may arise. The internal auditor or governmental auditor can perform a most valuable service by discussing the problem at headquarters and then discussing the problem at the location and interpreting any misunderstood instructions.

Making arrangements with the location. A few years ago it was fairly common to make surprise audits of locations. This may still be true in some cases, but generally it is better from a goodwill standpoint to contact the local operating manager and the accounting manager and notify them that an audit is to be made. Usually it is better not to make the notification too far ahead, in case records may be changed, etc., but just so these officers will not be surprised and perhaps annoyed by a visit at an inopportune time. These people are busy themselves and may have plans to be away on business for a few days. Perhaps the audit might be delayed a week or the officer's trip changed. While the auditor will be observing procedures in effect at the present time, he will be reviewing records for some time before; so in most cases records could not be effectively altered before the auditor's visit.

Credentials. In order that there will be no misunderstanding on the part of local management as to the auditor's right to inspect the records, usually it is desirable to have some form of credential. Some companies have a company auditing identification card such as a small wallet card which he carries. However, it is well to have a letter of introduction to the plant manager and the office manager. Generally the letter would be signed by the vice-president—finance or the controller and directed to the plant manager with a copy to the office manager. A copy would be provided for each auditor. Generally the letter might state that the visit is a routine audit and to see that all necessary records are made available to the auditors. Usually the names of the auditors will be given and the approximate date they will begin the audit. With such a letter there will be less misunderstanding as to the authority to conduct an audit.

Governmental Audits. The general nature of governmental audits hinges upon two major considerations. One of these is that the government is the largest purchaser and perhaps the single largest employer in the United States. It is not the avowed purpose of the government to support any industry in connection with its purchasing activities, and only in special circumstances does it subsidize an industry through purchasing activities.

The other consideration is that the government operates a number of businesses, mostly on a not-for-profit basis. In these cases, it is not the profitability of the operation itself that is a matter of concern. What does concern the public is that these service agencies are operated as economically as possible and that they give the maximum of service for the monies expended.

A third consideration, which is a corollary of the other two, relates to the expense accounts of government employees.

Audits of procurement contracts. When the government contracts work out to private firms, the purpose is to obtain goods and services needed for governmental activities. These range all the way from military work to actual conduct of those industries that are better handled by government than by private industry. Such contracts are let according to certain basic assumptions. One of these is that the contractor with the government should not realize an undue profit from his performance. However, he should be entitled to make a fair return. Consequently, many contracts are let, renegotiated, and reimbursed on the basis of government contract manuals which specifically set forth the types of expenditures for which payment will be made.

Some firms that contract with the government in turn subcontract work to other business firms. Subcontractors likewise are to provide goods and services for the government on the same basis as prime contractors.

Other audit agencies determine whether or not various individuals are paying the taxes which are required. The Internal Revenue Service, as well as the various state income tax departments, performs two general types of audits on tax returns. One type is what may be called a desk audit or review. In this review the internal consistency of the return is appraised to determine if revenue and deductions comply with the tax law or rate regulations. This job is facilitated materially by computers, by means of which information is analyzed for internal consistency and compared with what was reported on previous returns.

Additional sampling is done of other returns where actual investigation of the taxpayer's supporting documents is made. Auditors may request evidence to be brought to the office of the taxing authority, or the taxing authority actually may go to the taxpayer to examine records where they are kept.

Similarly, cases involving local and state taxing authorities involve audit of such items as sales taxes and property tax assessments. These audits are performed on a local basis and usually require on-the-premises access to the taxpayer's records.

Audits of agencies of the federal government. Many audits of agencies of the federal government are on an ad hoc basis. Some specific assignment is made in order to accomplish one particular investigation. Many assignments of the General Accounting Office are made on such a basis, for example, of a particular military installation. These audits involve reviews of financial transactions and related record keeping.

Even more important today are reviews of the general and specific qualities of the administration of the units' activities. Although the assignments are ad hoc, there may be a repeat assignment at a later time to determine progress made toward adopting earlier recommendations.

Another type of government audit involves continued surveillance. As such, the audit becomes a continuous part of internal control, and if carried out in great detail becomes less of a true audit function. Any mechanical review of vouchers for expense reimbursement which is a necessary condition for approval of the vouchers for payment is less of a true audit function and more of a paper-processing function.

Who audits governmental agencies? Outside independent auditors may be called in to audit various phases of governmental activity. Outside auditors do much of the auditing of municipalities and school districts. Within the federal government, however, much of the auditing is done by audit staffs attached to bureaus or departments, although independent auditors are used in some situations.

DATA PREPARED BY OTHERS

Advanced Planning. It is highly profitable to the auditor to do some advanced planning in connection with work to be done by others. This applies to the internal auditor and the governmental auditor. However, in the case of the public accountant he has even more of a stake in advanced planning. In addition to assistance from the bookkeeper and accounting staff, the public accountant can also plan for important help from the internal audit staff or governmental audit staff.

Type of Data. The greatest help that the client or the accounting department at a location can provide to the auditor comes from the preparation of various kinds of work papers and analyses. However, there are a number of other services that can be done by others that do not detract from the effectiveness of the audit and can save much time for the auditor. *It should be borne in mind that the auditor is being paid to do audit work, not accounting work.* Thus someone other than the auditor should pull vouchers from the files, return vouchers to the files, sort checks, prepare needed accounting schedules and analyses, and perform a wide variety of other time-consuming tasks.

Preparation of Schedules. In modern auditing procedure client personnel prepare many of the working papers. There are several advantages to this. First, much of the work is mechanical preparation which is time-consuming and hardest to charge to the client. Second, the audit is speeded up if the client prepares the papers ahead of time. Third, some of the information can be adapted from financial statements prepared each month. We must remember that the audit aspects of working papers are primarily the audit procedures and verification of the data by the auditor. The schedules and quantitative information are really *accounting data,* not *auditing data,* and can just as well be prepared by an accountant as by an auditor. A new aspect in this regard is the use of computer runs for audit purposes. Here the auditor may obtain copies of the computer runs that the client or location makes for internal purposes. The auditor's working papers in that case are the computer runs, and he can indicate his audit procedures performed in the legend on the last page of the run.

List of schedules. Following is a partial list of major schedules which can be prepared for the auditor.

Trial balances
Bank reconciliations
Recapitulation of cash
Schedule of notes receivable
Trial balance of subsidiary ledger
Aging of accounts receivable
Analysis of allowance account
Claims receivable list
Confirmation schedule
Inventory summaries and reconciliations
Analysis of inventory adjustments
Property schedules
Construction in progress
Gain or loss on disposal
Prepaid and accrual schedules
Schedule of notes payable
Accounts payable summary
Long-term debt analysis
Capital stock schedules
Surplus and retained earnings schedule
Income and expense analyses

The Internal Audit Department. Where there is an internal audit department the public accountant has a valuable objective check on accounting data. Many publications provide examples of the benefits of coordination between the public accountant and the internal auditor. One of the most effective uses is to have the internal audit department responsible for the follow-up, adequacy and accuracy of the various schedules prepared for the public accountant. When the internal auditor can perform such a preliminary screening the public accountant has additional assurance concerning the quality of the schedules prepared by the client.

BIBLIOGRAPHY

Industry Audit Guides, AICPA, New York, to date.
Martin, John C.: "Duties of the Senior Accountant," in *Duties of Junior and Senior Accountants*, ed. Robert L. Kane, Jr., AICPA, New York, 1953.
Statements on Auditing Procedure, AICPA, New York:
No. 33. *Auditing Standards and Procedures*, 1963.
No. 37. *Public Warehouses—Controls and Auditing Procedures for Goods Held*, 1966.
No. 39. *Working Papers*, 1967.
No. 41. *Subsequent Discovery of Facts Existing at the Date of the Auditor's Report*, 1969.
No. 43. *Confirmation of Receivables and Observation of Inventories*, 1970.

Cashin, James A., and Garland C. Owens: *Auditing*, New York, The Ronald Press Company, 1963.
Lenhart, Norman J., and Philip L. Defliese: *Montgomery's Auditing*, New York, The Ronald Press Company, 1957.

Meigs, Walter B., and E. John Larsen: *Principles of Auditing,* Homewood, Ill., Richard D. Irwin, Inc., 1969.

Stettler, Howard F.: *Systems Based Independent Audits,* Englewood Cliffs, N.J., Prentice-Hall, Inc., 1967.

Bergstein, Sol: "The Planning and Supervision of an Audit," *The New York Certified Public Accountant,* September, 1965.

Evans, E. R.: "Approach—The Key to Operational Auditing," *The Internal Auditor,* Spring, 1966.

Weyrich, Harry R.: "Exposure to Professional Liability," *The New York Certified Public Accountant,* July, 1970.

Isbell, David B.: "The Continental Vending Case: Lessons for the Profession," *The Journal of Accountancy,* August, 1970.

Chapter 11

Supervising the Audit

IRA M. LANDIS

Partner, Alexander Grant & Company

GENERAL

The Need for Supervision. The observance of generally accepted auditing standards by independent auditors, internal auditors, and governmental auditors requires the continuous exercise of judgment in all matters pertaining to each audit. Although various phases of the engagement may be delegated to assistants, responsibility for competent performance cannot be. The requirement for supervision and review of work performed is unequivocally set forth in the first standard of fieldwork, "The work is to be adequately planned and assistants, if any, are to be properly supervised."[1] Supervision is, therefore, mandatory at each stage of the engagement from the initial planning effort through the issuance of the audit report. In this chapter the term "supervisor" refers to the auditor who is directly in charge of the particular audit. In some cases he may have the title of "In-charge Auditor" or he may simply be a senior auditor. This is different from the official rank of the supervisor or manager, who may be in charge of several jobs simultaneously.

The emphasis in this chapter will be on the practical aspects of actually conducting the audit. This is one of the three closely related action chapters, "Planning the Audit," "Supervising the Audit," and "Concluding the Audit." Closely allied to these chapters are three chapters having to do with the methods and tools which the auditor uses in carrying on the actual audit functions. These are "Evidence and Testing," "Audit Procedures," and "Audit Working Papers." Detailed descriptions of various methods and tools are provided in the latter three chapters whereas the former three chapters are concerned primarily with the application of such methods and tools.

It is obvious that there is no one set of procedures and methods which may be equally applicable in every audit engagement; however, there are general guidelines which may serve as a reference for the major portion of situations that audit supervisors may encounter.

The Supervisor's Role. Primary responsibility for planning and supervising the audit, reviewing working papers, and making many of the required decisions rests with the supervisor, although certain problems of significance may have to be referred to his superiors for ultimate disposition. As a "professor without portfolio" he must initiate the "on-the-job training" of his

[1] Statements on Auditing Procedure No. 33, *Auditing Standards and Procedures,* AICPA, New York, 1963, p. 23.

assistants in order to enhance their knowledge, improve their technical skills, and increase their capacity to perform effectively. He is also responsible for objectively appraising the performance of his assistants and for advising them of their strengths and weaknesses in a timely, meaningful, and tactful manner.

Assigning tasks. The supervisor must provide day-to-day direction for the conduct of the audit. By word and deed he should encourage the highest standards of performance. In organizing and conducting the engagement, he will assign the tasks to be performed and define the duties and responsibilities attached to each task. He must establish that assistants are aware of the results he expects from them in each assignment. In certain circumstances, he will instruct them exactly how and when to perform their tasks. He will explain what it is they are to do, help them accomplish the assignment in a professional manner, determine how well the assigned tasks have been performed, and evaluate the progress being made toward completion of the overall assignment.

Controlling work. Because the audit must be comprehensive, constant supervision and control are required. Precise objectives and tasks must be crystallized and disciplined methods initiated for verifying proper performance. The supervisor must establish that the audit procedures are followed and that irregularities and problem areas are recognized and brought to his attention. It is essential that he be alerted to what is happening in order that he may initiate necessary changes or provide decisions as soon as problems develop. To ensure that the engagement is conducted in an efficient manner, the supervisor must work hard at narrowing any "communications gap." His ability to communicate with his staff and the personnel of the organization under audit will have a major effect upon the success of the engagement. Unless he is able to communicate to his assistants what it is he wants them to do, he certainly will be unable to get them to do it. He must develop a rapport with them in order to learn some of the things he must know. Each staff assistant should be encouraged to contribute as much as possible to the success of the engagement. Because the work performed by his different assistants will necessarily be interrelated, the supervisor must provide the coordinating link for their efforts.

Manner of operation. The manner in which a supervisor operates is determined by (1) the circumstances in which he finds himself, (2) the environment established by his organization, (3) the conditions in the industry and company under audit, and (4), to a very significant degree, his own nature. He is responsible for representing his organization in all dealings with the entity under audit, whether it be a governmental agency, a commercial organization, or a nonprofit enterprise. He must be thoroughly familiar with the organization under examination and with the strengths and weaknesses of his assistants, and must know how and when to delegate.

Qualifications of the Supervisor. The supervisor does not have the same level of duties in every audit. His responsibility varies with the size of the audit. In a small audit he may carry out the audit alone or may have only one assistant. In a medium-sized audit he may be the supervisor or senior-in-charge with several assistants. In a large audit he will have more assistants, which may include other seniors. On some very large jobs he may be in charge of only one phase of the job rather than of the whole job. Usually the supervisor will report to a principal or possibly to a partner.

Generally the supervisor will have the educational and experience qualifications comparable to the level of the Uniform CPA Examination. In some cases firms require auditors at this level to have a CPA certificate. Today, the supervisor is ordinarily a man who was recruited at college after earning a good academic record and who has moved up through the ranks of junior and semi-senior. Further information concerning the educational background for the auditor is discussed in Chapter 42, "Education and Experience," and in Chapter 46, "The Common Body of Auditing Knowledge."

Professional qualifications. The capable supervisor should have attained the following qualifications.

1. Auditing standards. Thorough knowledge of auditing standards and the application of those which are generally accepted in appropriate situations.
2. Accounting principles. Thorough knowledge of generally accepted accounting principles and ability to determine whether they have been properly applied.
3. Internal control. Thorough knowledge of the principles and application of internal control.
4. Auditing methodology. Thorough knowledge and skill in application of auditing procedure, sampling, and statistical inference.
5. Sound judgment. Must exercise sound judgment and use common sense in its application.
6. Leadership. Must possess the quality of leadership and the ability to organize and direct the work of others.
7. Professional ethics. Thorough knowledge of the professional code and its application to particular situations.
8. Accounting theory. Thorough knowledge of accounting theory and terminology, including income and asset measurement.
9. Specialized fields. Good knowledge of income taxes, cost, business law, etc.
10. Experience. Should have several years' experience in public accounting, internal auditing, or governmental auditing.
11. Business organization. Good knowledge of business organization design and administration.
12. Computer science. Good knowledge of the system and the internal controls, be able to prepare a basic flow chart, and understand programming language and instructions.
13. Resources. Good knowledge of the major groups of resources and the sources of capital.
14. Communication. Must be able to speak and write effectively.
15. Quantitative techniques. Good knowledge of principal quantitative techniques and their applicability in auditing situations.
16. Governmental agencies. Must know the kinds, requirements, and jurisdiction of various governmental agencies.

Personal qualities. The capable supervisor should possess the following personal characteristics.

1. General intelligence. Must possess better than average intelligence, which must be accompanied by common sense.
2. Integrity. Must possess moral soundness of character and personal integrity.
3. Self-reliance. Must be able, highly responsible, and able to accomplish the work satisfactorily with a minimum of supervision.
4. Ease of expression. Must be able to express himself easily and to lead others to an understanding of his views.

5. Analytical ability. Must be able to make a quick analysis and to distinguish the important from the unimportant.

6. Thoroughness. Must complete tasks in a thorough manner himself and see that others do so.

7. Working with people. Must be able to meet and work well with many different people.

8. Initiative. Must be able to know what is to be done and how it is to be done without needing to be told.

9. Orderliness. Must be able to approach his work in a systematic manner and must maintain a sense of orderliness.

10. Good personal habits. Must maintain good personal habits as an example to others.

11. Good appearance. Must be neat and reasonably groomed so as not to detract from his work.

Responsibilities. The supervisor will have a variety of responsibilities during the course of his work. How he meets these responsibilities will be an important factor in his success. His principal responsibilities are to (1) his firm or audit unit, (2) his associates, (3) the client or company, and (4) his profession.

Firm or audit unit. The supervisor is the direct representative of his employer. In the case of the public accountant, he represents to the client his CPA firm. For the internal auditor or governmental auditor, the supervisor generally represents the headquarters audit unit. In all cases the supervisor is expected to maintain high professional standards in his work and in his accomplishments. He is expected to be loyal to the firm or audit unit, to his superiors, and to the policies of his employer. He should have pride in his work and in his firm and should feel that he is an essential part of the organization. He should try to avoid idle time during lighter periods by looking ahead to coming audits, using such time to prepare any needed data and to seek other ways of improving the calibre of work. He should devote personal time to technical study and further education and should keep up to date in professional matters. He should also seek to broaden his understanding of cultural and social matters outside the technical field.

Associates. The supervisor, as the top representative in the field, is responsible for the work and conduct of all staff in the field. He must quickly learn the strengths and weaknesses of each member of his staff. He must know the technical ability of each staff member so that he can assign work in a way that will obtain maximum results. He should be interested in the professional progress of each staff member. He should be willing to help beyond the requirements of the work in the advancement of the staff. He should help promote cooperation among the staff for their mutual benefit and to further the work.

An important factor in rating the supervisor is the effect he has on his associates. The supervisor who brings out the best in his assistants, who earns their respect, and who works in harmony with them is a very valuable man. Generally advancement goes to the supervisor whose staff relations are as good as his technical ability.

Client or location. The supervisor for the CPA firm, the internal auditor, and the governmental auditor must maintain strict confidence concerning any information learned. Any information concerning business activities or operations or other data are not to be divulged to unauthorized persons. In the case of employees of the client, or of the location being audited, the auditor should be careful not to divulge any information which the employees do not already possess. Neither should the affairs of one client or location be discussed with another unless permission for such discussion has been obtained. The auditor is expected to provide the client with any helpful information developed during the audit that does not detract from his work.

Professional Standards. The auditor, and especially the supervisor as the top representative on the job, has a definite responsibility to his profession. As a professional man, he is expected to maintain the present standards of his profession and at the same time to strive to raise those standards. He should keep himself informed on the current issues in his field and should publish or help publish material which might be beneficial to his profession. He should maintain membership and actively participate in the activities of the professional societies as far as practicable.

Third Parties. Through his independence from management the supervisor is expected to conduct his audit according to professional standards and to make full disclosure in his report. Thus the third party—the creditor, the investor, or others—can rely on his work. The auditor may be held liable to third parties under the SEC acts for a loss caused by a misrepresentation in a financial statement filed with the Commission.

The auditor also has a moral obligation to carry out the work in accordance with high professional standards even though no legal liability may be involved.

ELEMENTS OF SUPERVISION

The supervision of an audit must include the elements of good managerial control that are generally accepted in all business undertakings. The supervisor must be able to understand the concepts of supervision so that he will be able to adapt his work to meet new conditions. The following elements are discussed below:

1. Setting objectives
2. Planning
3. Organizing
4. Directing
5. Controlling

Setting Objectives. The setting of objectives by the supervisor is comparable to establishing goals in any part of a business. The supervisor, as in all other similar cases, is limited by the parameters of the job. He knows the deadline date for the completion of the audit and he must be conscious of the supporting objectives needed to meet the general goal. In the case of the attest audit, the general objective is to make an examination in sufficient detail to determine that the financial statements of the client are fairly stated.

Planning. In the preceding chapter, "Planning the Audit," there were discussed a great many points concerned with carrying out an audit. It is essential that such planning be done as far as possible in advance, as that can contribute much toward a good audit. However, such planning, no matter how good, is planning *before* the audit is begun, and conditions may have changed. If the audit is being done for the first time, a large part of the planning must be done on the job as the needed information is built up. In the succeeding year more planning can be done before the audit. The audit working papers of the preceding year can be used as a guide. However, it must be borne in mind that conditions and people change, and often this is not known until the audit is well under way. Also, it may be well to change or improve on some parts of the previous audit.

Some of the important aspects of planning are (1) timing of procedures, (2) interim procedures, (3) testing, and (4) development of the audit program.

Timing of procedures. One of the most important features of planning concerns the timing of audit procedures. According to Statements on Auditing Procedure No. 33,

> The timeliness with which auditing procedures are undertaken involves the proper timing and synchronizing of their application and thus comprehends the possible need for simultaneous examination of, for example, cash on hand and in banks, securities owned, bank loans, and other related items. It may also require an element of surprise, establishment of audit control over assets readily negotiable, and establishment of a proper cutoff at a date other than the balance-sheet date.[2]

In addition, planning the audit procedures to be employed is essential for the orderly conduct of the audit. For example, advance review of physical inventory procedures is essential if confusion is to be avoided at the time of the inventory observation. The examination of negotiable securities provides another illustration of the need for advance planning as a defense against the shifting or substituting of securities. Proper planning will result in the application of audit procedures in an organized and coordinated manner.

Interim procedures. Closely allied to timing are interim procedures. When internal control is found to be effective, a substantial part of the audit work may be carried out during the year and the end-of-the-year work can be greatly reduced. In order to properly plan for interim work, certain key dates must be agreed upon, for example, the date as of which the accounts receivable will be confirmed and the date when the physical inventory taking will be observed. Various other kinds of interim work that can be undertaken during the year are the examination of the general records, examination of the minutes of meetings, evaluation of internal control, etc.

Testing. The tests of the records and procedures to be applied and the development of the audit program depend to a large extent on the reliability of internal control. Accordingly, it is necessary to make various tests to establish that the internal control system is operating as expected. Full details of the procedures for various types of testing are discussed in Chapter 12, "Evidence and Testing."

Developing the audit program. Generally, it is desirable to review and discuss the audit programs with the auditor who is to perform the particular part of the job. Although members of the audit team should be encouraged to develop audit programs for the specific areas to which they have been assigned, overall responsibility for accomplishing the audit objective rests with the supervisor. A desirable technique is to review the audit program with the assistant and jointly with him determine areas requiring modification, if any. By this approach, the need for various procedures will be fully understood by the assistant, and the supervisor can establish that the program is adequate and clearly comprehended by the man who will perform the procedures. The assistant will develop a better appreciation of the audit philosophy (what is to be accomplished by the procedures), which will prove beneficial not only in the specific task at issue but also on future tasks to which he is assigned. Frequently, audit procedures are applied by rote rather than by a full appreciation of what the audit objectives are and what will be accomplished by specific procedures. Every audit procedure employed must result in a

[2] *Ibid.*, p. 24.

specific contribution to the engagement. Audit staff members must be continually reminded of this philosophy if the audit is to be both effective and efficient. The relationship between various facets of the examination also must be highlighted. For example, the ramifications of matters developed in the course of the search for unrecorded liabilities must be brought to the attention of other members of the audit team for consideration. Frequently, to develop an adequate audit program it is necessary to gather additional operating data. Responses to questions such as the following can significantly affect the emphasis of the audit program.

1. What are the annual sales volume and profit contribution of each major product line? (Both unit and percentage details will be useful in highlighting trends.)
2. What are the annual sales for the last three years to each of the major customers by product category?
3. What is the percentage relationship of the costs of material, labor, and overhead to the total cost of the product for the past three years?
4. What factors enter into the determination of inventory levels?
5. How do the sales volume and profitability of the "client" compare with industry standards?
6. How does the company compare with industry leaders with respect to such important financial indicators as the current ratio, "acid" test, and receivables and inventories turnover rates?

How can responses to questions such as these aid in determining "what" should be audited? Inventory valuation and obsolescence problems may be highlighted by the awareness that the company is achieving a significantly lower rate of profit than its competitors. The relationships of material, labor, and overhead to total product cost will indicate whether audit emphasis is required in a manner which may significantly differ from what would normally be presumed. Responses to the above and similar questions could have a significant bearing on the auditor's decisions pertaining to various phases of the examination. A thorough awareness of the business factors and related risks will enable the auditor to critically assess his audit approach.

Organizing. The audit supervisor, no matter how competent, cannot operate well without some general plan of organization. In the preceding chapter were discussed the staff budget and the time projected for the audit. However, the supervisor must organize his team even a little further. For example, depending on the size of the job, he must organize the staff and delegate some responsibility to his top assistants. It is customary to have certain assistants handle specific components of the work. Thus, one assistant may be in charge of confirming accounts receivable, while another assistant may be in charge of inventories. Each assistant may have a number of juniors reporting to him. When inventories are maintained at a number of branches, it may be necessary for the assistant to arrange for observing inventory at a number of locations simultaneously and to arrange for the later audit of inventory pricing. If such work is undertaken by an assistant, it relieves the supervisor of much detail and helps the assistant to gain experience in organizing the work, as well as being useful to him when he becomes a supervisor. The way in which the supervisor "lays out" the work and the accuracy with which he estimates the individual capacity and ability of the assistants and juniors will have an important effect both on the particular audit and on his own advancement.

Staff. It is essential in allocating the various phases of the work to be performed that proper consideration be given to the experience of staff assistants. Certain assignments must be reserved for the more experienced staff members; however, every effort should be made to enrich the experience of the junior members of the audit team. Advance planning will lead to an organized approach whereby specific facets of the engagement are used to cultivate the individual's talents. In this respect, consideration should be given to the development of a well-rounded individual, one who has been exposed to as many aspects of the audit as is practicable. Accordingly, prudent planning would not automatically result in the cash work being performed by the junior. While there is an overwhelming tendency to perpetuate assigning what some consider to be the more menial tasks to the junior auditors, it is not a method which will challenge the man's initiative or other creative talents. The responsibility for staff training is well described below:

> Only a small part of the fund of knowledge necessary for auditing can be learned through classroom presentations. Most of an auditor's training, therefore, takes place on the job without receiving the benefit of instructors who are trained in the art of teaching. The job of instructor now falls upon the individuals who also have the primary responsibility for completing an audit.
>
> Understandably, the pressure of the immediate job requirements is often a cover for less than adequate time for staff development. Anyone who has had to meet the pressure of tight time deadlines or has tried to secure more effective or more timely performance from other auditors can appreciate that there is some merit to the above argument. In spite of the merits, however, . . . this is at best rather shortsighted thinking. Unless the audit staff is effectively developed today, there will be recurrences of the crises previously used to excuse less than required staff development. It is felt that additional effort by first-line supervisors in training activities will not only benefit the trainee but also serve to develop a better supervisor.[3]

The supervisor's role in assigning tasks may be summed up as follows:

> In all human endeavor the more people required to accomplish a purpose, the more exactly must the lines of responsibility and authority be defined.[4]

In the normal engagement the supervisor will have available as part of the audit team assistants with varying levels of audit experience. Every effort should be made to utilize to the maximum extent the experience of his assistants, both from the point of view of efficiency and from that of staff development. Senior assistants can be effectively utilized to direct and control the efforts of other members of the audit team, thereby enabling the supervisor to focus his attention upon problem areas and matters of unusual significance.

Directing. Delegation of duties. ". . . when delegating duties that involve initiative, judgment, and decision, it is important to assess realistically the nature of the duty to be delegated, the ability of the person to whom the duty is delegated, and your own ability to keep posted on your subordinate's progress in connection with that duty."[5] While relinquishing the day-to-day direction of each member of the audit team, the supervisor will be better able to control the overall effort, but must be extremely careful to avoid the impression that he is inaccessible to his assistants. He must continually be alert to

[3] Edward W. Dorcheus, "Staff Development," *The U.S. Army Audit Agency Bulletin* (Washington), Fall, 1966, p. 19.

[4] Norman J. Lenhart and Philip L. Defliese, *Montgomery's Auditing*, New York, The Ronald Press Company, 1957, p. 33.

[5] L. Lee Jones, "Delegation: Essential Tool of Audit Management," *The U.S. Army Audit Agency Bulletin* (Washington), Spring, 1968, p. 10.

means of generating feedback as to the progress of the various assignments in process. This can be accomplished by informally meeting with each member of the audit team at the beginning of the day to review what is to be accomplished that day; by spending some time during the lunch period to dwell upon pertinent aspects of the engagement; and, prior to "closing up" for the day, by specifically questioning what has been accomplished during the day, with leading questions as to possible problem matters. His assistants must be aware of his availability at all times to discuss unusual matters which may arise during the course of the daily activity. This point should not be taken for granted. In addition, the supervisor should periodically review the work as it is being performed. This is highly desirable when members of the audit team are scattered in different departments of the "client" organization.

Special delegation problems. Certain functions, such as "the power to discipline, the responsibility for maintaining morale, over-all control, the 'hot potato' that no one wants to handle, jobs that are too technical for one's subordinates,"[6] are best not delegated.

Controlling. Control of the engagement requires that the supervisor be constantly aware of what each of his assistants is encountering. What may appear to be problems or "roadblocks" to the assistant can generally be readily resolved by the supervisor. Frequently, problems can be resolved by the supervisor through discussion with the appropriate company personnel. On occasion, the matter may be of such importance that the supervisor will want to consult with his superiors. For example, a defalcation type of irregularity could justify such action. A major error having a material effect on the financial statements would also warrant prompt communication to a higher authority.

Minimizing inefficiencies. Supervisors should be concerned with minimizing the inefficiencies that tend to creep into engagements. Examples of such inefficiencies would include (1) spending excessive time on immaterial matters, (2) improper timing of various phases of the audit work, (3) manually preparing transcripts of accounts that neither interpret nor verify, when photocopies of the desired documents or records can provide the essential data in a more effective manner, (4) failure to utilize various records of the company to the maximum extent practicable, and (5) failure to utilize company employees on appropriate work when assistance is needed.

Communication. Auditors traditionally are weak in the art of communication, particularly with respect to writing, and must continually strive for self-improvement. Although auditors may possess all the technical tools to solve problems that may be encountered, their efforts may be in vain if the results of this expertise cannot be communicated to others. Supervisors must continually alert their assistants to the need for including essential information, and at the same time must stress the elimination of nonessential information.

Effective oral communication is an important tool for achieving the cooperation essential to the accomplishment of the audit. The supervisor must actively assist the audit team members in developing this facility. For example, the manner of phrasing questions to company personnel will significantly affect the information obtained. Quoting directly from an internal control questionnaire which requires "yes" or "no" responses obviously will not provide as meaningful responses as a carefully conceived question which requires a comprehensive response. Auditors with skills in interrogation will not be prone to accept glib answers and will be alert to pursue leads

[6] *Ibid.*, p. 11.

to matters requiring further consideration. Staff assistants should be continually encouraged to raise questions both of company personnel and of other members of the audit team; failure to raise one important question can adversely affect the entire engagement.

Problem areas. Assistants must be thoroughly advised beforehand as to the system and flow of documents to be encountered in the various areas of the examination for which they are responsible. In the absence of thorough communication in this regard, the various members of the audit team will be unable to make the maximum contribution to the engagement. Problem areas they may encounter should be stressed when instructions are communicated—e.g., the assistant responsible for bank reconciliation tests should be alerted to the symptoms of "kiting" and "lapping." Free and ready communication among the members of the audit team would envision ready access to both the current and the prior work papers in order that all members of the team may be thoroughly informed at all stages.

Flow charting. A technique receiving ever-increasing attention among auditors is the flow chart. (See Chapter 49, "Analytical Auditing—The Flow-chart Approach.") It is becoming apparent that the complexities of accounting systems can be more readily communicated and comprehended by means of this technique than by the narrative form of analysis. In addition to its significance as audit documentation, the flow chart can be utilized to focus upon the various aspects of the system which require further audit attention. The supervisor should encourage his assistants in using this technique as an objective approach to obtaining and evaluating information pertinent to the comprehension of the accounting system.

Supervisory characteristics. HANDLING ERRORS: A supervisor must know how and when to utilize his staff assistants. He should not hesitate to advise members of the audit team as to the significance of tasks delegated to them. He must continually employ tact in reviewing completed efforts, being careful to address himself to the job rather than to the personnel involved. He should be patient with assistants who are uncertain about instructions or problems they have encountered, and should continually encourage enthusiasm and initiative.

The supervisor should not hesitate to exercise his authority when required. However, he should be careful to point out in a positive manner how incorrect decisions may be corrected rather than dwell upon why errors have occurred, if he is to succeed in obtaining improvement in the performance of assistants without arousing a defensive reaction.

The supervision exercised on every engagement must be clearly demonstrated in the working papers supporting the audit conclusions, by a combination of memoranda, checklists, questionnaires, time analyses, specific audit comments and work papers, etc. Responsibility for the accurate and thorough conduct of the audit rests with the supervisor. He is responsible for ensuring that tasks are being done on time and that the audit objectives are being accomplished in accordance with the planned approach to the engagement. He must determine that all duties delegated to assistants have been performed in a satisfactory manner and should be alert to any developments which conceivably might affect the scope, objective, and value of the audit. To achieve such satisfaction, he must thoroughly review the nature and extent of the work performed and be satisfied that errors of principle or judgment have not occurred. This is not intended to imply that the competence of staff assistants is to be repeatedly reinvestigated, for the competent supervisor will quickly learn the extent of reliance that may be placed on various assistants.

DETERMINING RISK AREAS: Detecting deviations from expectations is essential if effective action is to be taken to correct problems and discrepancies. Through his understanding of such factors as the philosophy of management, the nature and sales volume of specific market areas, cost and profit relationships of various products, the significance of inventories, receivables, and related controls, etc., the supervisor will be in a position to determine the areas of risk and will be able to focus audit effort as required.

LEADERSHIP: It must be recognized that the supervisor will have a significant effect on the performance of the audit team. His intelligence, confidence, appearance, manner, and technical ability will be transmitted to assistants and will stimulate their productivity and desire for accomplishment and advancement.

In the final analysis, the supervisor's performance depends primarily upon his skill in handling people, communicating with them, and effectively administering the concurrent needs of several projects. Although the problems encountered will vary from engagement to engagement, the supervisor's responsibility is a serious one, as every effort must be made to have the audit findings correct and in accord with the established facts. High-quality supervision is the greatest safeguard for accomplishing this objective.

REVIEW OF INTERNAL CONTROL

Nature of Internal Control. Adequate supervision of an audit is closely interrelated with the evaluation of the system of internal control. As a matter of fact, the audit program should be based on the evaluation of internal control and *must* give full consideration to the strengths and weaknesses of internal control. The second standard of fieldwork reads, according to Statements on Auditing Procedure No. 33, p. 27, as follows: "There is to be a proper study and evaluation of the existing internal control as a basis for reliance thereon and for the determination of the resultant extent of the tests to which auditing procedures are to be restricted."

The review and evaluation of internal control can ordinarily be undertaken before the year end and can be planned along with other matters as part of the interim work. These points are discussed in some detail in Chapter 10, "Planning the Audit." As was stated before, it is desirable to do as much preaudit planning as practicable, particularly with regard to scheduling as much work as possible on an interim basis rather than at the year end. However, in most cases, as with internal control, certain planning can be done on the basis of the representations made as to how the system operates. Still, the auditor cannot rely on representations alone; *he must himself determine that the system is actually operating as represented to him.* The point is clearly set forth in Statements on Auditing Procedure No. 33, p. 32, as follows:

> The degree of reliance which may be placed on internal control in determining the extent of tests to which auditing procedures are to be restricted cannot be fully determined at the beginning of an audit engagement, as it may be predicated upon assumptions with regard to the system which the independent auditor's later tests may show not to be as represented to him.

Therefore, if tests of the system show that it is not operating as planned, a revision of the audit program or a shifting of emphasis or timing of the audit procedures may be required. Problems in the system often occur when employees take short cuts without notifying the accountant in charge. Often the steps eliminated are ones that may appear superfluous to the employee but are the very ones which include important internal control features of the system.

In this section we are concerned primarily with the relationship of internal control to the supervision of the audit. Thus we are emphasizing the application to a particular situation rather than discussing the nature, theory, and types of internal control. These and other aspects of internal control are discussed in Chapter 9.

Internal Control Features. In a small business internal control supplements and extends the personal supervision of the owner-manager. As a matter of fact the owner-manager performs many of the internal control features because he knows he should do so to protect his interest. In a large business internal control must take the place of much of this type of supervision since the business is too large for top management to follow up the thousands of details. A good system of internal control reduces the possibility that errors or fraud will remain long undetected. The various elements of internal control are discussed in detail in the internal control chapter and should be studied in conjunction with that phase of the audit. Internal control is defined in Statements on Auditing Procedure No. 33, page 27, as follows: "Internal control comprises the plan of organization and all the co-ordinate methods and measures adopted within a business to safeguard its assets, check the accuracy and reliability of its accounting data, promote operational efficiency, and encourage adherence to prescribed managerial policies." This definition is broader than the meaning sometimes attributed to internal control, and it has been broken down into (1) accounting controls and (2) administrative controls. Generally the independent auditor will be primarily concerned with accounting controls in the usual attest audit. However, the internal auditor and the governmental auditor will be concerned also with administrative controls. Following are the respective definitions given in Statements on Auditing Procedure No. 33, page 28.

Accounting controls

Accounting controls comprise the plan of organization and all methods and procedures that are concerned mainly with, and relate directly to, safeguarding of assets and the reliability of the financial records. They generally include such controls as the systems of authorization and approval, separation of duties concerned with record keeping and accounting reports from those concerned with operations or asset custody, physical controls over assets, and internal auditing.

Administrative controls

Administrative controls comprise the plan of organization and all methods and procedures that are concerned mainly with operational efficiency and adherence to managerial policies and usually relate only indirectly to the financial records. They generally include such controls as statistical analyses, time and motion studies, performance reports, employee training programs, and quality controls.

When Review Is Made. The review of internal control is normally made early in the field examination. It can be done as part of the interim work or as a special phase performed in an early stage of the fieldwork. In some cases it may be desirable to do some of the internal control work relating to general matters on an interim basis but hold the internal control work relating to cash, receivables, etc., until later when the audit procedures are being performed. Many of the subsequent audit procedures supplement the initial work already done and help in further understanding how the system operates and in establishing the degree of internal control present. An important phase of the audit is the submission to the client or the location of recommendations for strengthening its system of internal control. Generally such recommendations should be made in writing and followed by a conference between the client, or location representatives, and the principal and supervisor.

In the smaller unit, such as a small company or a small unit of a larger company, the review can be more informal. For the larger company, more formal procedures are desirable and an internal control questionnaire is ordinarily used. Generally the internal control review begins by inquiry as to features of the system, etc. Then a review is made of the chart of accounts and the accounting manual for determination of accounting procedures. A review is also made of any organization charts, if available, to ascertain the division of responsibility. The advantages and disadvantages of an internal control questionnaire are discussed in the internal control chapter.

Reliance on Internal Auditors. Where there is a competent internal audit staff, far greater reliance can be placed on the records and financial statements. The work of the internal auditor can be a valuable supplement but cannot be a substitute for the work of the independent auditor. The independent auditor must evaluate the work of the internal staff as he evaluates other aspects of the internal control system. On the basis of this evaluation he will select the appropriate auditing procedures and determine the extent of tests to be conducted.

It is usually desirable for the independent auditor to receive a copy of internal audit reports. Thus he can determine the type of examination and the calibre of performance. Advance planning for coordinating work with the internal auditor can pay very good dividends. For example, coordinating the inventory work at various locations, confirming receivables, and reconciling accounts, with the cutoff being done by the independent auditor, can save many hours of CPA time. Also, the internal audit staff can help substantially in getting working papers prepared and in following up and doing preliminary work to see that the papers are accurately and carefully prepared and that they are complete. For a description of how this follow-up can be initiated, see Cashin and Owens, *Auditing*, p. 108. By proper coordination a significant percentage of the independent auditor's hours may be saved on some jobs without impairing the quality or control of the job.

AUDIT PROGRAM MODIFICATION

Preplanning. The amount of preaudit work on the audit program depends on whether the job is a repeat audit and, if so, the extent of changes which may have to be considered. Since most jobs will be repeat audits, it is usually advisable to do some preliminary work by reviewing the working papers for the previous audit. It is a very good practice to require the auditor for the current year to suggest any needed modifications as a guide in planning the audit program for the succeeding year.

Regardless of what might have gone before, the supervisor is responsible for determining that the appropriate procedures are used. Therefore, he must review very carefully any audit program carried over from the previous year. He must make sure that changes are made for changed conditions. Unfortunately there is often a tendency to follow the previous program in many cases. A systematic way of determining the extent of operating changes is to use a form for comparing significant operating data for this year with the data for last year. If there has been a significant change in level of operations, this should be reflected in the audit program. For an illustration of such a form, see Chapter 10, Figure 2.

Types of Audit Programs. Audit programs are of two general types: (1) predetermined and (2) progressive. In the predetermined program all auditing procedures are included even though all procedures may not be required in a particular audit. The progressive type of program is an outline of the general scope, character, and limitations of the audit. Details are filled in as information is obtained and the reliability of records and internal control is determined. The progressive type of program gives far more discretion to the supervisor in developing the program. This type of program is especially applicable where conditions vary from year to year.

In the case of the predetermined audit program, the supervisor is usually allowed to make minor revisions, but must get the approval of the principal or partner to make major changes. In the case of a small business, there may be only a simple program or perhaps an outline or narrative description of the principal features of internal control.

Data for Modification. Most of the preparatory data can be obtained from the client for an initial audit, or from the previous year's working papers for a repeat audit. This has been fully discussed in Chapter 10, "Planning the Audit." In this section we are concerned with the changes which have occurred since the audit program was prepared. In the case of the initial audit, a large part of the program may have been constructed on a tentative basis from information obtained from the new client. If it is a repeat audit, the previous year's program may need to be modified. Some of the principal points to consider here are:

1. Legal data. Make absolutely sure that the corporate title has not changed. Examine corporate charter, bylaws, etc. Watch for any additional affiliates or sale of affiliates.
2. Organizational data. Obtain or prepare a new organization chart and compare it with previous chart. Watch for changes in personnel that may relate to the audit.
3. Previous working papers. Examine papers very carefully with a view of (1) eliminating those not needed, (2) substituting an internal report of the client, (3) combining data on another report, (4) photocopying client's data, (5) watching for duplication of papers with those for SEC and income tax. Consider combining some.
4. More client help. Examine each working paper carefully to determine if the paper could be prepared by client if enough preplanning is done.
5. Books and records. Determine any changes in books and records since previous audit. Evaluate effect on current audit program.
6. Accounting equipment. Determine if any new equipment has been obtained, leased, etc. For example, has punch-card equipment been changed to a computer? Has a later-model computer been obtained? How does this affect the program?
7. Accounting procedures. Have any changes in accounting procedures or accounting methods occurred which might affect the program?
8. Internal control. Have any significant changes occurred in internal control? An evaluation of the reliability of internal control would generally be undertaken regardless of previous data.
9. Change in business or products. Have any significant changes occurred in the business, such as going into new territories or opening new plants? Have any new products been added or old products dropped?

10. Type of report or due date. Were the previous report form and data satisfactory? Should changes be suggested?

The above points are only a guide, and there may be many others that should be considered by the supervisor in modifying the audit program. Any such changes should be carefully considered and made only with the approval of the principal, partner, or chief internal auditor.

Extent of Tests. The supervisor must give careful consideration to the extent of tests for the current year. In a repeat audit, the time spent previously and the degree of internal control relating to the audit data would have to be carefully weighed. If the previous tests showed that controls were good and if there have been no changes in related personnel, it is possible that the extent of tests may be reduced. This does not mean that there will necessarily be a reduction in total time, as there may be a need to spend time on new developments, such as new products, etc. Careful consideration should be given to the use of statistical sampling, which might permit a smaller sample and still give a satisfactory result. In any case *each previous test made should be studied very carefully before performing the same test in the same manner as before.*

CONDUCTING THE AUDIT

General. The supervisor is expected to conduct the field examination in accordance with professional auditing standards and in conformity with the policies of his firm or auditing unit. In the previous chapter we discussed planning of the work and in a later chapter we will discuss audit matters related to concluding the audit. If the supervisor was on the job the previous year, or if he participated in planning the audit for this year, he will have a good start toward acquiring the data he will need for his work in conducting the audit this year. In this section we are concerned primarily with carrying out the audit rather than with the theoretical aspects of the work.

Interim Work. As discussed previously, it is desirable to do as much interim work as possible to forestall any year-end bottleneck. Therefore it is likely that some work will ordinarily be done before the main audit work starts around the year end. For example, some work may have been done on the general records, the minutes, the accounting records, and internal control before the year end. The amount of year-end work will depend to an appreciable extent on what has been done on an interim basis. Wherever possible, no work should be done at the year end which could have been done before the year end when time was not at such a premium. Very often with proper planning more interim work could be done by using juniors and seniors who are between jobs.

Year-end Work. There will usually be some planned date for starting the full-scale year-end work. The supervisor will be assigned the crew of seniors and juniors who have been scheduled for the job. When the auditors arrive at the client's office or the location office, the supervisor will assign assistants to the various parts of the examination as planned. For example, one may be assigned to cash, another to receivables, etc. Also, juniors will be assigned to the various parts of the audit, depending on the time required and the complexity of the work.

Generally, experienced men will be assigned to work which will not require immediate supervision. This will permit the supervisor to instruct and orient the less experienced men. He can teach the junior how to approach his task and what he is expected to do. He can also point out what irregularities may be encountered and what to do about them. Generally it is desirable to have the junior check with the supervisor frequently until the supervisor is sure the junior understands the work. Also, the supervisor will be able to find out the ability and mode of approach the junior shows. The supervisor should satisfy himself by observation that his instructions are being carried out and that the audit is proceeding as planned.

Supervisor's Initial Work. Generally the supervisor will start his own work by reviewing the last trial balance and financial statements prepared by the client or location. He will find that additional insight can be brought to the audit by comparing the current trial balance with the trial balance from the previous year's working papers. The supervisor will find many advantages to this approach. Following are some of the principal advantages.

1. Fluctuations. By comparing the two trial balances the supervisor will note any fluctuation and may ask for an analysis or a precise reason for the fluctuation.
2. Opening balances. He will want to be sure that the opening balances agree and that last year's adjustments have been recorded in the proper year.
3. Closed accounts. He will follow up any closed accounts which may affect the audit.
4. New accounts. He may want to get information concerning any new accounts which have been opened since last year.
5. Special accounts. He may select special accounts which have special problems or need special attention.
6. Knowledge of accounts. If this is an initial audit for the supervisor, he will gain useful knowledge concerning the audit.
7. Overall ratios. Through comparative figures, changes in ratios or cost of sales components, and other data, he may want to discuss with the client or location the significance of changes observed.

Reviewing Work. As working papers are completed, it is desirable to have a prompt review by the supervisor from the viewpoint of both audit progress and auditor advancement. The principal features the supervisor will look for are (1) quality of presentation, (2) depth of investigation, (3) problems disclosed, and (4) resolution of problems. Other details on some of the points are discussed under "Directing" and "Controlling" in the section on elements of supervision.

Quality of Presentation. The supervisor will want to know first of all if the quality of the work is acceptable. Part of this he can determine by the quality of the working papers. He will want to be sure that an adequate examination was made and that the instructions and standards of the firm or auditing unit were observed. He will want to know specific details, such as the following:

Is the information clearly shown and appropriately organized? Is the working paper properly headed and signed? Is the source of information noted and oral information properly identified, along with the date received? Are the audit procedures clearly indicated? Are corrections indicated? Does the total agree with the trial balance? If it is based on an IBM or computer run, was it the final run and not a preliminary run? Are standards overlooked by the junior? Have the audit program steps been followed?

Depth of Investigation. The supervisor may likely wish to probe a little into the depth of the investigation. This might not be done with every working paper but should be done early in the job with every auditor. This will quickly put the junior auditor on notice that he must clearly understand the nature of the data he is supposed to be auditing. He will realize quickly that he may have to answer probing questions concerning the schedule, so that he must *think* about what he is putting into the working paper.

Problems Disclosed. In many cases problems will be disclosed by the audit procedures and may be indicated by questions or explanatory notes in the working paper. The supervisor should pay particular attention to these matters, as they may be indicative of serious problems. The fact that an explanation was given as to why an audit step was not done does not excuse the omission of that step. For example, the fact that an officer responsible for a particular function was away when the audit step was performed does not eliminate the requirement of a later follow-up or the need to get the information from the next higher officer or someone designated by him. Such fundamental matters should be discussed with each man so that he knows definitely that he is not to stop until he gets a satisfactory answer to his audit question or procedure. Some of the greatest frauds and other irregularities have been uncovered by an auditor who was not satisfied with an explanation for something which did not seem quite right. Often a junior's persistence, even after explanations by high officers, has paid off. Where the junior has communicated his concern to the supervisor and the latter has insisted on specific documentation, a serious fraud has been discovered. Sometimes the fraud has existed for some time but less stubborn juniors have not persisted enough.

Resolution of Problems. The manner of resolving a problem gives the supervisor good insight into the operations of the company and the ability of the junior. If an adjustment is required, the adjustments should be made to the trial balance in the working papers. If it is an important adjustment, it should ordinarily be taken up with the principal or the chief internal auditor. The supervisor or his superior should discuss the matter with the accounting executive, explaining the errors or principles involved. Since the financial statements are primarily the responsibility of the client or location, such adjustments are ordinarily entered on the books by the client or location accountants.

Work by Supervisor. In addition to overseeing the work of the juniors on the staff, the supervisor will personally do certain audit phases of the audit. This will include work that demands a high degree of technical knowledge or that is confidential or requires special judgment. Some may be delegated, under close supervision, to the more experienced auditors, such as semi-seniors or other seniors on the job. Following are the principal types of such work.

1. Corporate structure. Examination of articles of incorporation, bylaws, and minutes of stockholders' and directors' meetings.
2. Capital. The examination of the capital stock, paid-in capital, retained earnings, and other capital accounts.
3. Long-term debt. Determine the nature of the debt and that any restrictions are being observed, such as restrictions on working capital, dividend declarations, officers' salaries, amortization of premium or discount, sinking funds, etc.
4. Contracts, leases, indentures, etc. The terms and audit implications of various legal documents should be carefully reviewed by the supervisor.
5. Contingencies. The determination of contingent liabilities that may exist in any phase of the audit.
6. Conflicts of interest. The supervisor should be alert to any conflicts of interest whether it be in dealings of officers with affiliated companies, purchasing agents with suppliers, etc.

7. Accounts receivable. The collectibility of accounts receivable, adequacy of the allowance, propriety of charge-offs, and control exercised over those accounts written off should be reviewed.
8. Inventories. The valuation of inventories, accuracy of the physical count, possibilities of obsolescence, returned goods, etc.
9. Plant and equipment. The degree of control of and justification for acquisitions, the basis of valuation, and the propriety of depreciation.
10. Compensation arrangements. Review of employment agreements, bonus plans, deferred payments, and related liabilities.
11. Insurance. Survey of adequacy and extent of insurance coverage and the cost for particular coverage.
12. Important reconciliations. The preparation or close review of all important reconciliations.
13. Confidential data. Highly confidential data such as material relating to proposed mergers, acquisitions, sales, etc.
14. Income tax returns. The close review or preparation of working papers in connection with federal income tax returns.

Indexing. After the working papers have been examined by the supervisor, they should be indexed and filed according to the established plan. Supporting papers, such as bank confirmations, should be attached to the related schedules. There are various methods of indexing used for working papers. These are described in detail in Chapter 14, "Audit Working Papers." The index usually follows the sequence of the trial balance.

During the progress of the examination the working papers and supporting papers pertaining to a particular classification may be kept in folders. When the audit has been completed, the material can be filed and the folders may be used for subsequent engagements.

Material needed for the audit report, internal control letter, or other reports should be handled separately. Other useful information or background data may also be included in this file.

MONITORING PROGRESS

In addition to the superior technical knowledge which the supervisor must possess, there are many administrative details which he must follow up if a satisfactory audit is to be completed by the established date. An auditor may have superior technical knowledge and do an outstanding job himself; but he cannot do the whole job himself, and his success or failure will depend on how well he encourages and motivates the staff to do good work.

In the previous section we discussed the various responsibilities and the sequence of the work in conducting an audit. However, no time requirements or quantity of staff were covered. In this part we will be concerned with the actual manner of monitoring or continuously maintaining control over progress. For control purposes we may divide the problem into (1) time control and (2) staff control.

Time Control. "Time control" applies generally to the relationship of actual hours or days to budgeted hours or days. Of course, this must be related to the deadline date and the monitoring of progress toward the audit deadline. It would do little good to be able to meet the budgeted time but not finish the audit by the deadline date. Consideration must be given to any budgeted changes so that the audit deadline may really be the control date. Generally, this can be accomplished by a close control of component parts of the audit.

The supervisor will maintain the "feel" of the job as workpapers are completed for various parts of the audit. He may check off the figures on the trial balance or insert the number of the worksheet on his trial balance as each worksheet is completed. This will help him to see and evaluate the number of working papers yet to be completed. If he has had much experience, he can gauge roughly how much additional time may be needed. However, on most jobs it is preferable to have also a more specific time control. Generally, this will be some kind of summary sheet listing the component parts of the audit and the budgeted and actual time to date. For our purposes we may classify the requirements into (1) total time for the audit and (2) time for component part.

Total time for the audit. The supervisor must have the total picture readily available in order to monitor progress. This will include the total hours on the job and the summary of component parts so that he can see which particular part is deviating from the planned hours. Following are two representative forms: one is used in public accounting practice for various clients, the other by an internal audit department for field audits of manufacturing plants.

TIME ANALYSIS SHEET (FIGURE 1): This form shows the "Prior Year Actual Hours," the "Current Budget," and the present status. In the illustration the prior year actual hours were 472 and the current budget 500. The hours for

Figure 1 HENNESSY MANUFACTURING COMPANY—TIME ANALYSIS SHEET

Client Hennessy Manufacturing Company

Audit Date 12/31/70

Date	Staff Members: Jones	Ross	Smith	Hill			Daily Total	Estimate to Complete / Total to Date	Cash	--	--	--	Fixed Assets	--	Accounts Payable	--	--	Internal Control	--	--
Prior Year Actual								472	35	—	—	—	45	—	30	—	—	110	—	—
Current Budget								500	40	—	—	—	50	—	30	—	—	125	—	—
11/18	8	8	8				24	476 / 24	40 / 0	—	—	—	50 / 0		30 / 0	—	—	101 / 24	—	—
11/19	8	8	8				24	447 / 48	40 / 0	—	—	—	50 / 0		30 / 0	—	—	72 / 48	—	—
11/20	8	8	8				24	423 / 72	40 / 0	—	—	—	50 / 0		30 / 0	—	—	48 / 72	—	—
11/21	8	8	8				24	399 / 96	40 / 0	—	—	—	50 / 0		30 / 0	—	—	24 / 96	—	—
11/22	8	8	8				24	375 / 120	40 / 0	—	—	—	50 / 0		30 / 0	—	—	0 / 120	—	—
1/20	8	8	8	8			32	343 / 152	28 / 12	—	—	—	40 / 10		20 / 10	—	—	0 / 120	—	—
1/21	8	8	8	8			32	319 / 184	22 / 26	—	—	—	36 / 14		6 / 24	—	—	0 / 120	—	—
1/22	8	8	8	8			32	287 / 216	0 / 48	—	—	—	32 / 18		0 / 30	—	—	0 / 120	—	—
								—	—	—	—	—	—		—	—	—	—	—	—
								—	—	—	—	—	—		—	—	—	—	—	—
								—	—	—	—	—	—		—	—	—	—	—	—
								—	—	—	—	—	—		—	—	—	—	—	—
Total Actual																				
Total (over) under budget																				

Figure 2 HENNESSY MANUFACTURING COMPANY—SUMMARY OF AUDIT TIME

Location ______________________ Audit Period ______________________

PROGRAM SECTION	PREVIOUS YEAR	CURRENT YEAR		Aud				Aud.				
	Actual hrs	Est. hrs	Actual hrs	W/E				W/E				
FINANCIAL												
Cash												
Sundry Receivables												
Physical Inventory												
Fixed Assets												
Prepaid Expenses												
Deferred Charges												
Accounts Payable												
Accrued Liabilities												
OPERATING												
Sales & Billing												
Inventory Control												
Purchasing												
Payroll												
Production Costs												
GENERAL												
Construction												
Employee Funds												
Accounting Records and Journal Entries												
OTHER												
Review of Audit Comments												
Sundry (itemize)												
Mill Hours												
Travel Time												
TOTAL HOURS												

each day are deducted to arrive at the balance. For example, the time for three auditors, 24 hours, was deducted from the 500 current budget the first day to arrive at 476. An important part of this control is the separate "Component Control Sheet" for each audit activity, such as Cash, Receivables, etc., which must tie in with the total control sheet.

SUMMARY OF AUDIT TIME (FIGURE 2): This form may be more suitable for an internal or governmental audit, where a more limited number of separate parts are involved and fewer auditors are needed for a shorter period. In the case of a field audit of a manufacturing plant, the emphasis may be on operational auditing of production, inventory control, etc. Many times the general cash, accounts receivable, etc., records may be maintained at headquarters rather than at one of the manufacturing plants. The design can be modified to suit the particular company.

Time for component part. Where there are many different parts to be controlled, a separate form may be desirable for controlling each part.

Figure 3 HENNESSY MANUFACTURING COMPANY—COMPONENT CONTROL SHEET

Client *Hennessy Manufacturing Company* Audit Activity *Cash*

Audit Date *12/31 70* Current Budget *40*

Prior Year Actual Hours *35*

Date	Staff Members: Jones	Smith	Hill				Daily Total	Total to Date	Estimate to Complete	Estimated (over) under Budget	Explanatory Comments
1/20	*4*	*8*					*12*	*12*	*28*	*-0-*	
1/21	*2*	*8*	*4*				*14*	*26*	*22*	** (8)*	** Details re: outstanding checks inadvertently destroyed.*
1/22	*6*	*8*	*8*				*22*	*48*	*-0-*	** (8)*	*Client personnel unavailable to assist in reconstructing this information.*

The time expended on each facet of the engagement must be used to the best possible advantage. It is, therefore, essential that the supervisor receive the earliest possible warning if it becomes apparent that the time needed to complete the work is going to exceed the time budgeted.

This control can be accomplished by utilizing a "Component Control Sheet" (see Figure 3) for each facet of the engagement. This technique envisions a meeting of the minds as to the reasonableness of the budgeted hours required for completion of an audit task. For example: the assistant and supervisor, after agreeing upon the audit program required to satisfy the audit objectives pertaining to "Cash," should also agree upon the audit man-hours required to complete the specified audit procedures. The assistant should enter his time on a daily basis and concurrently update his estimate of the additional time required to complete the assigned task. The daily discipline of posting to the "Component Control Sheet" should alert the supervisor to potential problems which may result in "overruns," enabling him to initiate prompt action. In addition, he will be continuously informed as to who is doing what and will have an informed opinion as to how long the task will take. The "Time Analysis Sheet" summarizes the "Component Control Sheets."

Staff Control. In discussing staff control we are concerned primarily with the relationship to the operation of the audit rather than with general considerations relating to the personnel matters of the firm. In the previous chapter, "Planning the Audit," were discussed matters to be considered before the job is begun. In this chapter we will be concerned primarily with the activities after the audit work has started.

Relationship to preplanning. Prior to beginning the job it was necessary for the scheduling department of the firm or auditing department to plan how many auditors of each rank will be needed on each job and for how long. Such pre-audit estimates are understood to be subject to change as more detailed staff requirements are determined after the audit work is started.

Modification of staff needs. In many cases it is desirable to begin the audit with a minimum or skeleton staff and then to add staff as more specific information is available. Very often it is necessary to start a job on the date agreed upon with the client even though all the needed staff may still be tied up on other jobs. The client may object if it is started later, and also all the staff may not have sufficient work until the supervisor has had an opportunity to lay out a few days' work ahead.

Assistance from client. Proper utilization of the efforts of the personnel of the organization subject to audit requires careful coordination, detailed planning, and organizing. Various schedules the auditor will want to include as evidential matter in his working papers can be provided by the personnel if sufficient advance notice is provided. Members of the audit team can then focus upon verifying the data provided. Examination of invoices, purchase orders, shipping reports, etc., can be greatly facilitated by utilizing "client" personnel to obtain from the files the specific documents required. Common courtesy and good business judgment dictate that all such documents be returned in good condition and in an orderly manner. An illustrative form for control ensuring that (1) all documents requested are obtained, and (2) all documents obtained are returned, is presented in Figure 4.

Consideration also must be given to the nature of the work performed by "client" audit personnel whenever such a capability is present. This concept encompasses not only independent or governmental auditors accepting the work of internal auditors, but also corporate internal auditors utilizing the work of division audit personnel and division auditors utilizing the work performed by plant auditors. The efficiency of an audit can be significantly increased depending upon the extent of reliance the audit team is willing to place upon the work performed by the "client auditors." For maximum effectiveness, cooperative endeavors should be carefully planned and organized. Duplication of audit effort is difficult to rationalize and should be kept to a minimum, unless circumstances clearly dictate otherwise—e.g., where reliance cannot be placed on the efforts of other auditors, perhaps because of an obvious lack of independence or objectivity.

Key Staff Dates. There are certain key staff dates that have to be carefully planned. These would include confirmations of receivables and the observation of inventories. In the preaudit planning some estimate was probably made of the number and rank of any staff needed. However, that estimate is

Figure 4 HENNESSY MANUFACTURING COMPANY—DOCUMENT CONTROL SHEET

____
(client)

____
(audit date)

Documents Requested: ______________________
(insert document requested)

Date Requested:

Auditor Initiating Request:

Request Submitted To: ______________________
name and position of client personnel

Identify Documents Requested:

Date Received From Client ________ Date Returned To Client ________
Received by ________ Received by ________

subject to change based on changed conditions. Very often by careful planning some of the confirmation work can be done by the client or local staff. Also, in the case of inventory observation a coordinated program may be worked out with the internal audit department that could save substantial time. If a number of locations are involved, the independent auditor may elect to observe those representing a significant percentage of the dollar value. The internal audit department, where it is qualified, may observe the remainder. In certain situations inventory at some plants can be observed every other year or at the time an internal audit is made. A plan such as this can save a very substantial number of hours or days, especially where much traveling time may be involved. The particular plants can be alternated with the internal auditors so that practically every plant would be visited by the independent auditor every other year. Such a plan has proved highly satisfactory in some cases.

LEVELS OF REVIEW

The responsibility for an adequate audit review is much broader than determining that the work is done satisfactorily and on time. It must be remembered that the reliability of the audit report, whether of the CPA, the internal auditor, or the governmental auditor, rests largely on the thoroughness with which the various levels of review have been carried out during the course of the audit. Statements on Auditing Procedure No. 33, page 21, clearly points up the responsibility of the CPA for review in the following words: "Exercise of due care requires critical review at every level of supervision of the work done and the judgment exercised by those assisting in the examination."

A moment's reflection will bring to mind the broad scope of the variables included in almost any audit. First of all, there is a wide diversity in the type of business and the nature of the operations subject to audit. Second, there is a wide variety of auditing procedures and auditing tools that can be applied in a given circumstance. Third, there is usually a wide range of education, ability, and experience among those performing the audit. Regardless of the number of variables, however, there must be assurance that an established level or standard of quality is maintained for every job. This standard can be maintained by means of a comprehensive program of review.

The independent public accountant has an important additional factor which makes a program of review essential. This factor is the third-party interest in his audit. The third-party responsibility is ordinarily much greater for the public accountant than for the internal auditor or governmental auditor. Third parties include investors, bankers, creditors, security dealers, and others concerned with the company's financial affairs. A good review program has become even more necessary in view of the number of stockholder suits which have been brought against public accounting firms in recent years.

Generally there are three levels of review. The first two are carried out during the course of the fieldwork and the last level is carried out at the office, usually after the fieldwork is completed. The office review is included in Chapter 37, "Concluding the Audit," and will not be covered here. The two levels of field review are carried out by (1) the supervisor on the job and (2) the principal, a partner, or others.

Review by Supervisor. As discussed throughout the chapter, the supervisor is continuously carrying on an audit review. As each workpaper is completed and submitted to the supervisor on the job, he makes a review to determine whether it has been properly prepared and whether it adequately supports the pertinent data. In many cases there will be an additional review prior to the time the workpaper is turned in to the supervisor. Often a senior or semi-senior is placed in charge of a section of the audit, such as the cash section, the receivables section, etc. Two or three juniors may be assigned to help on the particular section. Weighing the quality of their performance and reviewing their working papers would be performed by the auditor responsible for that section. This permits additional review and relieves the supervisor of some detail. Other aspects of the audit are also reviewed by the supervisor as he follows up completed segments of the work to determine whether the job is proceeding as planned. For example, he will make sure that the applicable internal controls have been evaluated and that the audit program has given due consideration to the reliability of the internal controls. The supervisor will be reviewing daily the progress of the audit and perhaps checking off completed portions and studying the parts yet to be completed. He must also be alert for any modifications needed to the audit program and any problems involved up to this point. He will be in touch with his immediate superior to report on the progress of the job and to ask his concurrence or advice concerning action to resolve any problems.

Review by Principal, Partner, or Others. Ordinarily the principal, partner, or assistant general auditor, in the case of the internal audit or governmental audit, will be in charge of three or more jobs. He will be in contact with the work by telephone perhaps two or three times a week and may visit the job every other week, or more or less as required. He should be aware of the general progress of the job and the nature of the problems encountered to date. However, he must also visit the job to observe at first hand the progress of the work and the general level of supervision. He will have to provide an evaluation of the performance of the supervisor and he will have to review documents, workpapers, etc., and observe the morale of the staff and the type of leadership given by the supervisor. During the course of the audit there will usually be a number of such field visits by the principal. At the end of the job there will also be a summary review. Generally it is desirable to make a thorough review on the job of all aspects relating to the fieldwork. It is better not to have to go back to the job to check something after the fieldwork presumably has been completed.

AUDIT REVIEW CHECKLIST

In order not to overlook any of the many points to be reviewed, it is desirable to use some type of review checklist. The list can be as brief or as detailed as desired. Following is an example of each type. A comparable list in questionnaire form is shown in *Accounting Practice Management Handbook*, p. 894, which is a reprint from the *CPA Handbook*.

Audit Review Checklist—General. This list covers in brief terms the areas of internal control, audit programs, and working papers.

Audit Review Checklist—Detailed. This type of review form, taken from *The Journal of Accountancy*, November, 1968, covers the review points in considerable detail.

General

1. Review the problems that have been encountered on the engagement with the audit supervisor.

2. Review "Time Control Sheet" and related "Audit Control Sheets" to establish current status of the engagement. Be alert for significant budget variations which may be indicative of audit problems. This review also may be helpful in measuring the efficiency of the audit personnel.

3. Determine that the audit program is consistent with the conclusions developed in the evaluation of internal control. Be alert for modifications which may be required in light of deficiencies not adequately recognized.

4. Determine that the audit program is being followed and has been properly posted.

5. Establish that the working papers support the conclusions developed.

6. Determine that all questions in the working papers have been answered satisfactorily.

7. Determine that the working papers clearly indicate that the engagement has been adequately planned and that the work of assistants has been supervised and reviewed.

8. Determine that the working papers provide a record of the auditing procedures followed and tests performed.

9. Determine that the working papers provide a record of how exceptions and unusual matters, if any, have been resolved or treated.

10. Determine adherence to generally accepted accounting principles, company policies, and regulatory requirements, as may be appropriate to the nature of the engagement.

Detailed

PURPOSE OF REVIEW: Workpapers and report drafts prepared on audit engagements are subjected to review by staff members other than the staff member who prepared them in order to give assurance that the examination was conducted in accordance with generally accepted auditing standards, that our report and the company's financial statements conform to pronouncements of the American Institute of CPAs, the state society of CPAs, and all applicable regulatory bodies, and that our workpapers contain adequate evidence of our work.

FUNCTION OF REVIEW CHECKLIST: The following checklist contains many *but not necessarily all* review steps which should be performed on examinations where the firm expects to state in its report that our examination was made in accordance with generally accepted auditing standards. *It is the responsibility of the reviewer to perform all additional steps as may be required to satisfy himself that our work was properly done.*

HOW TO PROCEED: Insert a copy of this checklist in the front of the workpaper file at the start of field work. Where work done by a given assistant is reviewed in the field by another staff member, the reviewer should sign off on the checklist for review steps done and on the line provided, initial each schedule reviewed to eliminate the possibility of the same work being subjected to a second review. Where a review step is only partially done, the checklist should clearly indicate exactly what has been reviewed and the reviewer should not initial for the step. Review steps not signed off in the field will be done as part of the office review. Where a part of a review step is done in the field, the ultimate responsibility for the step lies in the person performing the office review. On audit engagements. reports and related workpapers are subjected to review in the office by staff members, other than those who prepared them. prior to submitting them to the partner. This procedure is known as office review.

FOOTING WORKPAPERS: Reviewers should not foot schedules or other documents contained in the file if they have already been footed by other personnel of the firm. It is sufficient if schedules prepared by our staff members are footed only by the preparer. However, any schedules prepared by our staff which result in an adjusting journal entry should be footed in review.

BLUE PENCIL: Reviewers should use only blue pencil.

Checklist

A. Workpapers

1. Review general ledger trial balance or working financial statements to see that:
   a. Necessary schedules in support of all significant accounts are included. ________
   b. Reasonable and complete explanations are included for all significant variations in account balances compared with prior year and for significant changes in gross profit percentages. ________
   c. Internal controls and procedures were tested in the following areas if transactions or balances are significant: general matters, cash, receivables and sales, inventories and cost of sales, payables and expenses, and payrolls. ________
   d. Accounts appearing on draft of the financial statements agree in amount and description with accounts on the trial balance or working financial statements. ________
   e. All accounts, particularly accruals, which are usual for this type of company have been included. ________
2. Adjusting and reclassifying journal entries:
   a. Review all of material amount for propriety of amount, accounts affected, and description. Review and test supporting schedules and computations. ________
   b. Satisfy yourself that they were properly posted to our general ledger trial balance or working financial statements. ________
3. See that the file contains the following documents and review them for propriety:
   a. Draft of client representation letter. ________
   b. Legal liability letters from all of client's attorneys. ________
   c. Draft of letter and memorandum to client on internal control. ________
4. Review internal control questionnaires or memorandums and related work programs to see that:
   a. All steps are signed off and all questions answered. ________
   b. Steps and questions appear proper in light of company's business. ________
   c. Scope of each step is adequately explained, specific items tested are adequately described and method of selecting items for testing is disclosed. ________
   d. Our conclusions on adequacy of system of internal control and results of our procedural tests appear proper. ________
   e. Scope of procedural tests appears proper in light of adequacy of internal control. ________
   f. All major internal control weaknesses are included in our memorandum to client. ________
5. Review each schedule and program in the file to see that it shows adequate tests were made and that it contains:
   a. No contradictory comments, "to do" notes, unanswered questions, unexplained tick marks, or other damaging items. ________
   b. Client's name, examination date, and initials of preparer. ________
   c. All needed indexing. ________
   d. Satisfactory explanations as to why possible adjusting entries were not made. ________
6. See that we did the following work where it was applicable and that we did all other work necessary under the circumstances. Review work for propriety:
   a. Confirmed all bank accounts at the examination date and made appropriate tests of reconciliations of all bank accounts at that date. ________
   b. Circularized receivables when they were material or, if we did not circularize, took required exceptions in our opinion. ________
   c. Performed adequate tests of sales and purchase cutoff at year-end and, if necessary, also at date of physical inventory. ________
   d. Observed the taking of the physical inventory, made appropriate tests thereof and of final priced inventory or, if we did not observe, took required exceptions in our opinion. ________

e. Reviewed adequacy of insurance coverage or obtained letter from client's insurance broker confirming adequacy of coverage. ______

f. Tested propriety of significant additions to and retirements from fixed assets and tested reasonableness of provision for depreciation. ______

g. Performed search for unrecorded liabilities. ______

h. Obtained confirmations on all significant liabilities evidenced by written agreements such as notes, contracts, etc. ______

i. Tested balances in all important prepaid and accrued expense accounts. ______

j. Tested provision for taxes on income for adequacy. ______

k. Reviewed minutes of directors' and stockholders' meetings held from date of last examination through our opinion date and determined that proper accounting treatment was accorded to items there where necessary. ______

l. Reviewed company's capital stock book and properly accounted for stock issued, outstanding or retired. ______

B. Draft of Financial Statements and Notes Thereto

1. Ascertain that we have fully disclosed all matters essential to a proper understanding of the statements such as:

a. Properly classified assets and liabilities as between current and noncurrent category. ______

b. Properly treated or disclosed amounts of cash restricted as to use. ______

c. Indicated basis at which assets are carried (generally, cost for noncurrent assets and whichever is lower, cost or market, for current assets). ______

d. Properly segregated items (e.g., fixed assets broken down into categories of land, buildings and equipment). ______

e. Disclosed basis for valuing inventories and of determining cost. ______

f. Showed amounts of assets gross and amounts of reserves separately, not just the net of the two amounts (parenthetical disclosure is acceptable). ______

g. Disclosed separately receivables from officers if they are material (material here means about $20,000 or 1 per cent of total assets—Securities and Exchange Commission definition). ______

h. Disclosed principles of consolidation. ______

i. Disclosed terms of stock options, pension and retirement plans, guarantees of debts, notes discounted, status of important lawsuits, minimum annual rentals under long-term leases of material amount (three years or more from balance sheet date is long-term, etc.). ______

j. Disclosed events subsequent to balance sheet date such as acquisition of other companies, sale of properties of large amounts, changes in capital stock, terms of additional financing and large casualty losses. ______

2. Review statements for use of modern terminology and presentation. Review notes for adequacy of disclosure, clarity, conciseness and writing quality. ______

C. Draft of Our Opinion

1. Do we have the right to say our examination was conducted in accordance with generally accepted auditing standards? If not, is our opinion properly worded in this respect? ______

2. Are the company's accounting principles generally accepted and were they consistently applied? If not, is our opinion properly worded in this respect? ______

3. Does our opinion contain all applicable informative disclosures such as:

a. Statements were prepared on a cash basis. ______

b. Opinion on balance sheet (income statement omitted) is based on examination of related income statement. ______

c. It was impracticable to extend our examination of contributions received from the general public beyond accounting for amounts recorded (charitable institutions).

D. Before Releasing Our Report

1. Ascertain that all adjusting journal entries are recorded in company's general ledger. ______

2. Obtained signed copy of client representation letter. ________

E. Miscellaneous Matters

1. Ascertain that extensions have been requested on tax returns if they appear necessary. ________
2. Ascertain that report covers have been ordered. ________
3. Ascertain that permanent file was brought up to date. ________
4. Upon completion of review prepare a brief schedule of suggestions for the next examination and submit to the partner for his approval. Give approved suggestions to the staff member in charge and *do not leave them in the workpaper file.* ________
5. See that memorandum on internal control and our report are mailed to client on time. ________

F. Review Was Performed by:

____
(In the Field)

____
(In the Office)

BIBLIOGRAPHY

Statements on Auditing Procedure No. 33, *Auditing Standards and Procedures,* AICPA (Committee on Auditing Procedure), New York, 1963.

Cashin, James A., and Garland C. Owens: *Auditing,* New York, The Ronald Press Company, 1963.

Cooper, Vivian R. V.: *Manual of Auditing,* London, Gee & Co., Ltd., 1966, pp. 34–36.

Editorial Board of Prentice-Hall, Inc.: *Accountants' Encyclopedia,* Englewood Cliffs, N.J., Prentice-Hall, Inc., 1962, pp. 806–823.

Hammond, Robert E., and William P. Stowe: *Complete Guide to a Profitable Accounting Practice,* Englewood Cliffs, N.J., Prentice-Hall, Inc., 1965, pp. 441–455.

Lenhart, Norman J., and Philip L. Defliese: *Montgomery's Auditing,* New York, The Ronald Press Company, 1957, pp. 33–52.

Martin, John C.: "Duties of the Senior Accountant," in *Duties of Junior and Senior Accountants,* ed. Robert L. Kane, Jr., New York, AICPA, 1953, pp. 77–117.

Stettler, Howard F.: *Systems-based Independent Audits,* Englewood Cliffs, N.J., Prentice-Hall, Inc., 1967, pp. 114–141.

Chan, Stephen: "The Supervision and Review of Accounting Engagements," *The New York Certified Public Accountant* (New York State Society of CPAs, New York), May, 1946.

Schermerhorn, Robert P.: "Supervision and Review of Accounting Engagements in a Small Firm," *The New York Certified Public Accountant* (New York State Society of CPAs, New York), January, 1948, p. 44.

Bergstein, Sol: "The Planning and Supervision of an Audit," *The New York Certified Public Accountant* (New York State Society of CPAs, New York), September, 1965, pp. 661–667.

Alexander, M. O., and D. S. Wells: "A New Look at the Extent of Audit Work," *Canadian Chartered Accountant* (Canadian Institute of Chartered Accountants, Toronto), May, 1968.

Dale-Harris, R. B.: *Quality Control in an Accounting Firm,* Toronto, Canadian Institute of Chartered Accountants, March, 1968, pp. 182–184.

Jones, L. Lee: "Delegation: Essential Tool of Audit Management," *The U.S. Army Audit Agency Bulletin* (U.S. Government Printing Office, Washington), Spring, 1968, pp. 6–14.

Reiling, Henry B., and Russell A. Taussig, "Recent Liability Cases—Implications for Accountants," *The Journal of Accountancy,* September, 1970.

Chapter 12

Evidence and Testing

HOWARD F. STETTLER

Professor of Business Administration, The University of Kansas

GENERAL

Relation of the System to Evidence. Auditing is essentially a review function. Internal auditors review accounting and operating systems for adequate control measures, and they review internal financial and operating reports for accuracy and adequacy. Independent auditors review clients' financial statements for the purpose of determining whether the statements present fairly the financial position of the client and the results of operations in accordance with generally accepted accounting principles applied on a basis consistent with that of the preceding year. In each situation the auditor makes his review critically for the purpose of forming an opinion on the compliance of the system and reports with appropriate standards. Sufficient competent evidential matter must be examined to support the auditor's opinion, and it is the question of evidence that is the subject of this chapter. Additionally, it is neither feasible nor necessary that every available item of evidence be examined. Hence, the examination of evidence is customarily limited to a test or sample of the total available evidence, and the subject of testing is likewise covered in this chapter.

Systems Orientation of Audit Examinations. An auditor's attention is directed to an entire system, including the inputs to the system, the processing of those inputs, and the outputs that result. The quality and reliability of the output are of major concern, and when evidence is available that directly supports output such as statements and reports, that evidence becomes a major basis for the opinion the auditor is seeking to form. Underlying assets, such as cash or goods and materials, are examples of this form of direct supporting evidence.

Also important to the quality of system output is the processing that produces the output, especially in situations where controls over the processing are important in themselves, as would be true for much internal auditing activity. System input must likewise be reviewed for the obvious reason that outputs can be no more accurate than the inputs on which they are based.

These, then, are the factors (evidence) on which an auditor's opinion must be based. But the auditor must also be able to present evidence showing how he arrived at his opinion. This evidence will be in the form of his working papers, which must be carefully preserved in the event the auditor is ever called upon to reconstruct the basis for his opinion. Thus an internal auditor will usually be expected to present evidence of his auditing activity for review by an independent auditor, as this review tells the independent auditor something about how the accounting and control system is functioning. Likewise, the independent auditor's opinion might be challenged at any time in a legal liability suit based on charges of negligence in the conduct of his examination. His working papers must then constitute sufficient evidence to refute the charge of negligence.

STEPS IN REVIEWING A SYSTEM

To review and evaluate a system, an auditor must first obtain a clear picture of how the system is supposed to operate. Next, he will gather evidence in the form of results of tests designed to show whether the system is operating in the manner that it is purported to operate. Finally, the system actually in effect is analyzed to ascertain whether it can be expected to produce reliable output and whether it meets standards for good internal control.

Description of the System. A variety of sources of information may be available about how a system has been designed to operate. Most important is the documentation that should have been prepared when the system was designed and for any subsequent modifications that may have been made. In addition, there should be instruction or operating manuals that specify the procedures to be followed by each employee involved in the system. With such a manual it should be possible to follow a transaction or resulting document through all processing steps that take place within the system.

Although documentation and operating manuals should be prepared in every instance, in reality they are seldom prepared in smaller businesses, where informality tends to be the rule and systems are likely to have "just growed." Under such circumstances an auditor has little alternative but to inquire of the people involved in the system in order to find out how the system operates. The best procedure will usually be to take a typical transaction and follow it through all the steps in the system. This activity is sometimes referred to as a "walkthrough" of a transaction; it will be referred to again in the section entitled "Tests of System Operation."

A remaining problem is how to summarize the garnered information in the working papers to provide evidence of how the system operates. A traditional method is to prepare a written commentary describing the inputs, outputs, and processing activities, but there is considerable current interest in recording the information in flow-chart form. Flow charting is a technique of long standing that has received a substantial boost from the field of computer programming. It has proved to be invaluable as a form of communication between systems analysts who interpret existing systems or develop new systems, and computer programmers who write the computer programs necessary to implement the systems on a computer. The major advantage of flow charting in this situation is the aid that a flow chart gives the reader in visualizing the operations that take place and the relationship between the various operations.

The two basic types of flow charts can both be used effectively in audit working papers. The first is an overall chart of the system, sometimes referred to as a "system flow chart." Such a chart gives considerable detail about the inputs and outputs of the system but describes the processing operations in very general, condensed form, such as, "Prepare and record customer invoices," or "Prepare reconciliation of balance per bank with balance per books." The operating details are then given in a "program flow chart" that specifies each individual step that must be performed, such as, "Account for all invoice numbers," or "Compare paid checks with cash disbursement book entries, as to number, date, payee, and amount." Examples of the two types of flow charts are given in Figures 1 and 2.

A variation of the typical direction flow in such charts from top to bottom and from left to right is especially useful in auditing, where there is considerable stress on the separation of responsibilities as a means of achieving good internal control. To clearly picture such separation, an individual column is provided for the processing activities carried out by each person

Figure 1 SYSTEM FLOW CHART

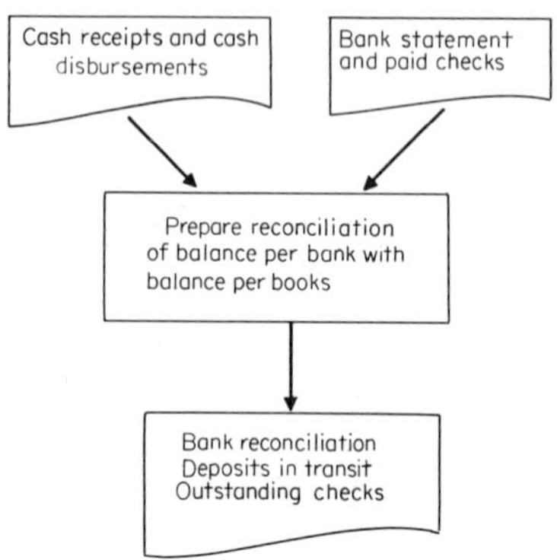

or department involved in the system. This arrangement facilitates determining whether a person is handling conflicting responsibilities that should be handled by different persons, such as preparing deposits of cash receipts and reconciling bank accounts. Another advantage of the columnar approach is that it readily discloses inefficiency in the form of "backtracking" that involves excessive reverse movement of documents between persons or departments and the attendant delays likely to result from such reverse movement.

Evaluation of the System. As has already been indicated, one of the important factors in the accuracy and credibility of accounting system output is the internal control present in the system. The internal control factor and the resulting reliance on system output in turn affect the selection of audit procedures designed to corroborate output figures, as well as the extent of samples to be taken and the timing of the application of the audit procedures relative to the close of the fiscal year. Methods of evaluating internal control and the factors that produce good internal control have already been discussed in the chapter on internal control. Among these are (1) an effective plan of organization that achieves proper delegation of responsibility and segregation of responsibility for operations and for accounting; (2) clear designation and segregation of responsibility for authorizing transactions, reviewing and approving transactions, and recording the transactions; (3) sound administrative practices, such as the development and use of procedures manuals, the use of budgets and standard costs as control techniques, and a program of internal auditing as a control over the effectiveness of all other controls; and (4) careful selection of competent and reliable employees coupled with effective training for the positions held.

An interesting quantitative approach to the evaluation of internal control is suggested by R. Gene Brown in "Objective Internal Control Evaluation," *The Journal of Accountancy*, November, 1962, pp. 50–56.

Tests of System Operation. After the accounting system has been fully described and the system evaluated in terms of internal control, tests must be made to obtain evidence that the purported system is being followed in actual practice. Of major importance in this connection is the "walkthrough" of representative transactions covering the various segments of the accounting system. Beginning at the point where the transaction itself is authorized and consummated, the procedures for creation of documents evidencing the transaction are compared with the procedures stated in the description of the system, and each subsequent operation in the system is similarly reviewed. Evidence of what is actually being done can be gained by observing employees in the act of performing their duties, by questioning employees about what they do and how they go about doing it, and by reviewing flow charts of computer systems to ascertain the controls incorporated in the systems. In the latter case, as a substitute for observing and questioning, a "test deck" of transactions can be processed. The hypothetical transactions should be devised to test the various limit and other controls purported to be incorporated in the system, and the output resulting from the introduction of the test-deck transactions should be compared with predetermined results of manually processing the test-deck transactions.

Figure 2 PROGRAM FLOW CHART

BANK RECONCILIATION PREPARATION
Reconciliation unit receives bank statement and paid checks directly from bank
List paid checks and prove total = beginning bank balance − ending bank balance + deposits
Sort paid checks into numerical sequence
Inspect paid checks for propriety of signature and endorsements; compare paid checks with cash disbursement as to number, date, payee, and amount
Did checks previously outstanding or written during past month clear the bank ?
Yes
Mark record "paid"
No
Prepare a list of current outstanding checks showing check number, amount, and total
Compare deposits per books and deposits per bank statement as to amount and credit by bank on next business day
Are deposits per books shown on current bank statement ?
Yes
Mark record to show received
No
Prepare list of deposits in transit showing date received and amount
Prepare list of any other differences between bank and book records
Reconcile balance per bank and balance per books using above reconciling items
Transmit reconciliation to treasurer for approval

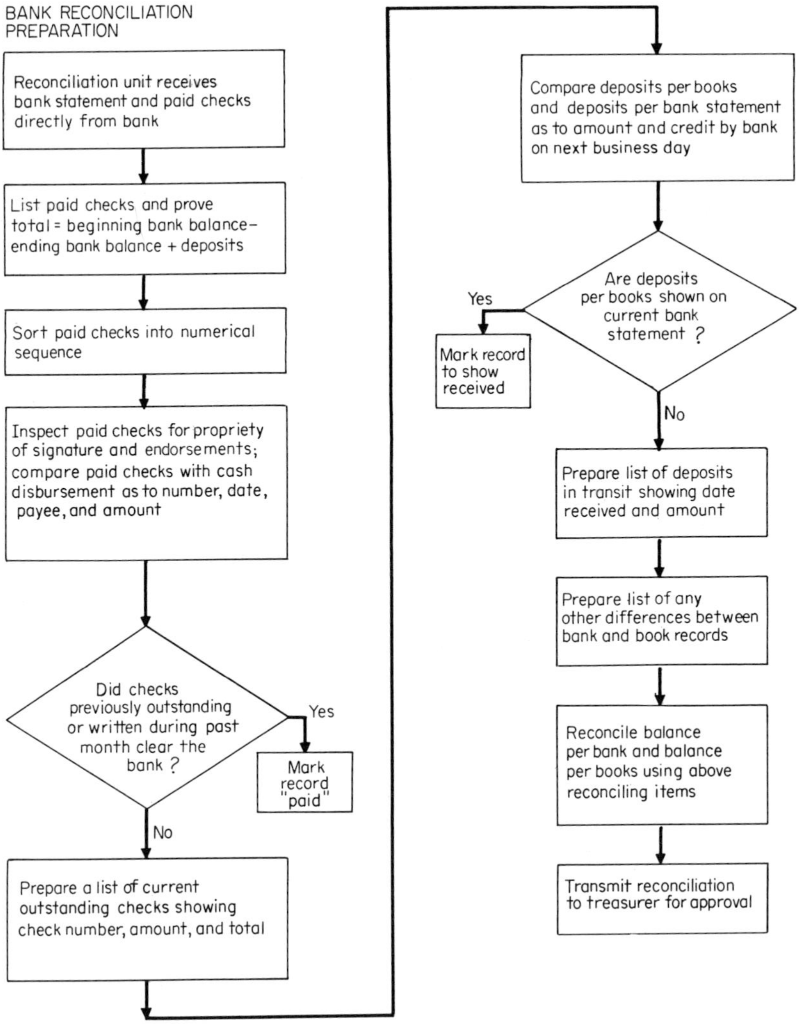

The Sample of One. The question of the number of transactions to be selected for a test of system operation is a moot one. Some argue that the number should be sufficient to meet reasonable standards of confidence and percentage defectives (errors or deviations from specified system procedures) for acceptance sampling. Others point out that the purpose of the sample is not to prove that the specified system is actually in effect and being followed. Rather, they say, the purpose is to ask questions of those operating the system, using an actual transaction as the basis for the questions so that there will be no misunderstanding concerning either the questions asked or the answers given. Those supporting this approach to testing the accounting system point out that it can be used only if good internal control is present, for internal control is relied upon to give assurance that only properly authorized transactions are processed, that accounting personnel recording the transactions have no operating responsibilities to tempt them to improperly record the authorized transactions, that procedure manuals are used to state unequivocally the procedures to be followed, that competent employees have been selected to carry out the specified procedures, and that internal auditors are engaged in a program of reviewing and testing all activities to provide assurance that prescribed procedures are being complied with. Under these circumstances, tests limited to single transactions of each type that normally occurs should give independent auditors sufficient basis for a conclusion about the accounting system and the attendant internal control measures.

It should be noted that regardless of the extent of sampling of the internal control over the accounting system, complete reliance is never placed solely on the accounting system to develop acceptable financial statement figures. Evidence that directly supports statement figures must also be examined to provide adequate support for the auditor's opinion on those statements.

The traditional approach to tests of the accounting system has generally been based on the independent auditor's judgment of what constitutes an adequate sample to test internal control. Such samples would tend to fall about midway between the two extremes just discussed. In other words, traditional sampling of internal control has been based on the notion that samples to fully support a conclusion about internal control are unnecessary because system outputs are also tested directly. Samples of single representative transactions are inadequate to support any meaningful conclusions about the system under consideration. Under these circumstances the usual solution has been to sample sufficient transactions to enable the auditor to feel "comfortable" in his evaluation of the system, but the number of transactions selected would tend to be arbitrary and less than the number that would be required by the relatively recently developed methods of acceptance sampling.

Internal auditors, on the other hand, are directly concerned with the problem of establishing compliance with the procedures specified for the accounting system as one of their objectives. It is they who must assume primary responsibility for assurance that the system is functioning as intended, and acceptance sampling is the technique best designed to achieve that result.

Tests in Support of Account Balances. Although careful study of the accounting system and tests of its operation provide important evidence about the reliability of system output, auditors invariably seek to "double-check" the output by also examining evidence in direct support of account balances. Balance sheet accounts that have a high turnover of the balance during the year are most efficiently verified by the "inventory" method. This involves reference to evidence of the underlying asset or equity, such as goods on hand, cash, or amounts owed to creditors.

For accounts that turn over less than once a year, the inventory method of verification would encompass many of the same items when an audit is made the following year. To avoid unnecessary reexamination of the same items, the auditor may simply concentrate on verifying the changes posted to the account as debits and credits. If the balance a year ago was determined to be fairly stated, and if the auditor is satisfied that changes in the account have been correctly reflected, then he can be satisfied that the ending balance is fairly stated. This method may be referred to as "analysis of transactions," and is equally applicable for income statement accounts as for low-turnover balance sheet accounts.

The examination of evidence using either the inventory or the analysis-of-transactions approach in the performance of an independent audit examination must be made in conformity with the third independent auditing standard of fieldwork, which states, "Sufficient competent evidential matter is to be obtained through inspection, observation, inquiries and confirmations to afford a reasonable basis for an opinion regarding the financial statements under examination." A key factor in reaching decisions on "sufficient competent evidential matter" is the internal control incorporated in a client's accounting and operating systems.

The amount of evidence to be obtained and the manner of obtaining it will vary with the internal control that the auditor has determined to be present. The scope of an examination involves the following variables, each of which has a direct relationship to the evidence that will be acquired:

1. Whether sampling is appropriate, and if so, the extent of the sample to be taken
2. The choice from among alternative auditing procedures
3. The timing of the application of the selected procedures; e.g., must they be applied to figures as of the balance sheet date, or may they be applied to figures at a preliminary date?

The balance of the discussion in this chapter will be devoted to problems of determining sample size and the competence of the forms of evidence that are available for use in the testing process.

THEORY OF TESTING

Testing and sampling are roughly identical in meaning, and involve selecting items from a population of items with the intention of arriving at an approximation of some characteristic present in the population. The characteristic may be an attribute, such as the presence or absence of an authorizer's initials, or whether inventory items have been correctly priced, or whether the extension of quantity and price has been correctly made. The characteristic may also be a variable, such as the individual amounts that collectively make up a total, as on a trial balance of accounts receivable or a list of outstanding checks.

Testing or sampling to arrive at an approximation of a characteristic present in a population is based on the theory of probability, which in effect says that a sample selected from a population of items will tend to evidence the same characteristics that are present in the population as a whole. The tendency of the sample to evidence the characteristics of the entire population increases as the absolute sample size is increased, reflecting a narrowing of the expected sample results relative to the true condition actually present in the population.

For instance, if 2 percent of the invoices in a population lack the proper approval, repeated samples of 100 invoices selected from the population may show percentages of invoices without approval ranging from 0 percent to as much as 5 percent. A distribution prepared from these sample results would show the bulk of the samples as containing 2 percent missing approvals and gradually decreasing numbers of samples in either direction from 2 percent. If 100 samples of 100 were taken, only about 14 samples would show 0 percent missing approvals, and only about 5 samples would show 4 percent or more missing approvals.

Doubling the sample size to 200 would still show a clustering of samples at the 2 percent figure, but there would be fewer samples at the extremes. In comparison with the sample size of 100, only about 2 samples (as against 14) would show 0 percent missing approvals, and only about 2 samples (as against 5) would show 4 percent or more missing approvals.

From this example, it can be seen that sampling cannot provide an accurate point estimate of a population characteristic. Rather, it can only provide an estimate of the characteristic within some range of possible values, with the breadth of the range decreasing as the sample size is increased. This range is referred to as the "precision" of the estimate of the characteristic for the entire population, and the fact that some specified percentage of the samples would tend to fall outside of a specified precision is referred to as the "risk" associated with the estimate. The complement of the risk figure, representing the proportion of samples falling within the range, is referred to as the "confidence" in the estimate.

The fact that there is always some risk of obtaining a "nontypical" sample that lies outside the precision limits that have been set is referred to as the risk of "sampling error." Such a sample will, of course, lead the person sampling to a false conclusion about the true characteristics of the population, but the risk of reaching such a false conclusion is under the control of the person devising the sample plan. The risk of sampling error varies inversely with the size of the sample taken, and also varies inversely with the precision that is specified. Thus, sampling error can be minimized by taking a large sample and by setting broad precision limits.

"Non-sampling error" presents another form of risk that may occur in sampling, but this risk is entirely within the control of the person taking the sample, for it involves the human element. Non-sampling error occurs when the value of a variable included in the sample is incorrectly used, as, for instance, an account balance of $87.65 is listed in the sample as $78.65. In attribute sampling, listing a sample item as possessing the specified attribute when in fact the sample item does not possess the attribute, or vice versa, would constitute a non-sampling error.

Factors Influencing Sample Size. As has been indicated above, the two factors affecting sample size are precision and risk. When sampling for a variable, precision is related to materiality. For instance, if positive confirmation requests are obtained for a sample of accounts receivable, the total amount of accounts receivable can be estimated from the sample of confirmation responses. But how much precision should be specified for the estimate? If the control account balance is $100,000, should the precision be ±$1,000, or could the precision be as broad as ±$10,000? The answer lies in the area of materiality, which may be defined for our immediate purposes as "any difference in reported financial statement figures that would be sufficient to affect a decision reached by a user of the financial statements." Thus, materiality deals with relative importance of figures. In the accounts receivable example, the $10,000 precision alternative would have to be considered relative to the total accounts receivable figure, total current assets, the current ratio, and net income before taxes. If a difference of as much as $10,000 in receivables would be unlikely to influence a statement user's investment or credit decision, then the difference would not be material.

Materiality is not ordinarily a factor in setting precision in sampling for attributes. In most instances, attribute sampling is utilized in systems tests intended to show the degree of compliance with established procedures. Lack of compliance has a bearing on the acceptability of the final figures produced by the system in question, but it is all but impossible to establish a quantitative relationship between the precision for attribute sampling and the effect on the accounting figures produced by the system. The precision to be set for attribute sampling must therefore be judged largely on the basis of at what point a process would be considered out of control as a result of the frequency of procedural errors or deviations from established procedures.

The risk to be accepted in devising a sampling plan is almost entirely a matter of a judgmental decision to be made by the sampler. In auditing, it is difficult to visualize accepting a risk of more than 10 percent, or of requiring a risk of less than 1 percent, but there is no generally accepted standard for a given risk percentage within this range. Relative risk is, however, a factor that may properly be taken into account in arriving at a decision on sampling risk. Relative risk involves the susceptibility of figures to irregularity or error. An asset such as cash is more susceptible to irregularity than property, plant, or equipment. Likewise, the risk of error in a figure is less if the figure has been developed under conditions of good internal control than if internal control is relatively weak. Another factor would be whether the transactions that enter into an account balance are the result of arm's-length transactions with third parties or are the result of intercompany transactions or transactions with officers or employees.

As a rule, the lower the relative risk that a figure being examined might be misstated, the greater the risk that the auditor would be justified in specifying in his statistical sampling activity. The chapter on statistical sampling discusses the use of tables and formulas for arriving at sample size based on specified precision and risk factors.

Responsibility for Detection of Fraud. In the usual examination of financial statements, it is generally accepted that the independent auditor has no responsibility to detect and disclose fraud in the accounts unless the fraud results in material misstatement of the financial statements. Nevertheless, in his verification activity the auditor should always be alert to any indication of fraud or embezzlement, the findings to be reported to an appropriate company official. Failure to recognize and report any evidence of fraud existing in documents or records selected in the process of sampling would subject the auditor to potential legal liability to the client on the basis of negligence in the conduct of the examination.

Relating the preceding assertions to the matter of determination of sample size, it may be stated that there is no necessity to specify a sample that will give some stated confidence that any fraudulent items in the population will appear in the resulting sample. On the other hand, precision of the sample should be sufficient to give adequate assurance that the sample will give clear indication if fraudulent items exist in the population to an extent that the financial statements would be materially misstated.

It should be noted that although almost all audits are conducted for the purpose of expressing an opinion on financial statements being examined, there may be other reasons that led to the audit engagement. For instance, the financial statements for a unit of government or an eleemosynary institution may be of relatively little interest to such third parties as taxpayers or contributors, although existing or potential creditors would have considerable interest. But those not interested in the financial statements would nevertheless have a strong interest in knowing whether the managers of such organizations have fully accounted for all receipts, and whether all disbursements were for the stated or described purposes. In other words, there would be an interest in assurance that no individual associated with the organization received any personal gain or income from the organization other than properly authorized payments. There would still be a question of materiality in such situations, but materiality should not be ascertained relative to the financial statements. Rather, it should be ascertained relative to the importance of any misappropriation to either the recipient of the funds or a typical contributor to the organization.

Selecting the Sample. If a sample is to give a good indication of a characteristic present in the population from which the sample is drawn, the sample must be representative of the population. Representativeness is best assured by drawing a probability sample, which is one that gives every item in the population an equal probability of being included in the sample. The most satisfactory means of accomplishing this result is an unrestricted random sample in which the items are selected on the basis of numbers from a random-number table tested for randomness. It may be quicker and more convenient, however, to take a systematic sample of every *N*th item, where *N* is calculated by dividing the population size by the size of the sample to be taken.

COMPETENCE OF EVIDENCE

The evidence gathered via the audit procedures will be of varying degrees of competence. The competence of the evidence in turn determines the amount of reliance to be placed on such supporting data. Obtaining sufficent basis for an opinion involves relating the quantity of evidence to be assembled (the extent of samples to be taken) to the competence or reliability of the particular evidence. In some cases additional evidence must be obtained to corroborate relatively weak forms of evidence. The principal types of evidence are as follows:

1. The system as primary evidence (internal control)
2. Physical supporting evidence
3. Documentary supporting evidence
   a. Evidence originating outside
   b. Originating outside but held by client
   c. Originating inside but circulating through third parties
   d. Inside evidence subject to good internal control
   e. Inside evidence subject to minimal internal control
4. Ledgers and journals
5. Overall analysis
6. Independent computations
7. Oral evidence
8. Subsequent events
9. Circumstantial evidence
10. Electronically processed records

The System as Primary Evidence (Internal Control). As has already been indicated, the accounting system and the output it produces in the form of account balances constitute the basic supporting evidence for the figures in the financial statements. The competence, or acceptability, of this evidence is largely a function of the internal control involved in the functioning of the accounting system. In no case, however, will the output of the accounting system stand alone as sufficient evidence to support an opinion on the fairness of the financial statements. The auditor must also gain some contact with the evidence of the real world that is purportedly reflected in the accounts maintained by the client. The amount of such contact, i.e., the amount of sampling of real-world evidence, will depend on the competence of the evidence available in the form of account balances, and such competence is in turn a function of internal control.

Physical Supporting Evidence. In the case of tangible assets, the best evidence is the actual physical assets, such as the inventory of goods or plant assets. However, it is not the physical assets themselves that are reflected on the balance sheet, but rather valuations expressed in money equivalents. The conversion from units to money equivalents must be scrutinized as carefully as the physical assets themselves in order for the auditor to arrive at an opinion on the fairness of the asset figures in the balance sheet. This process involves reference to documentary evidence such as is discussed in the following section.

There will be instances when the physical assets will not be available for inspection, as when the physical location of assets may be too distant to warrant travel to the site for inspection of the assets, or when there is no actual means of gaining contact with the asset or determining the quantity that is present, as in the case of natural gas that has been pumped into an underground natural reservoir. Similarly, if cash is classed as a physical asset, it may be in the form of a check or an amount deposited with a financial institution. In such instances, reference must be made to some form of documentary evidence.

Documentary Supporting Evidence. Evidence originating outside. Documentary evidence originating from sources outside the client's organization and transmitted directly to the auditor constitutes the most reliable form of documentary evidence. Written responses to confirmation requests are perhaps the best example of this type of evidence. Due care must be used in obtaining such evidence to assure its validity. The auditor must be satisfied that the requests are properly addressed, that the source of the addresses is reliable, and that requests have been prepared for all accounts selected for confirmation. The requests must be mailed with no opportunity for client employees to intercept the requests, and replies must be mailed to a location that is under control of the auditor.

Originating outside but held by client. Slightly less reliable is evidence originating outside the client's organization but held in the client's custody at the time the evidence is examined by the auditor. But there are variations even within this class of evidence. For example, certificates evidencing common stock investment or bonded indebtedness are printed under closely controlled conditions and equal care is exercised over their issuance or transfer between owners. Less reliable would be items such as bank statements or purchase invoices, which can be more readily forged or altered while in the client's possession.

Originating inside but circulating through third parties. Of roughly similar reliability are documents originating within the client's organization but gaining additional validity as a result of being circulated through the hands of third parties. Although there are relatively few examples of such evidence, one is especially common: bank checks drawn by the client and circulating through the hands of payees and the banking system.

Inside evidence subject to good internal control. Evidence that does not originate or circulate outside the client's organization is generally of lesser reliability, but if subjected to strong internal control within the client's organization it may nevertheless be quite reliable. An example of a document subject to strong internal control would be a time card, imprinted from an address plate prepared from an employment notification originating in the personnel department, clocked in and out by the employee under the observation of plant security guards, and subject to regular "floor checks" by a timekeeper.

Inside evidence subject to minimal internal control. Much less reliable would be a petty cash receipt for a travel advance bearing the purported signature of the recipient. If material amounts are involved in such an asset, reference to the petty cash receipt should be supplemented by confirmation from the recipient. The necessity for such supplemental verification indicates the limited reliability of the petty cash receipt resulting from the minimal internal control associated with the document. There would be little assurance that the receipt is valid and not merely a forgery prepared by the petty cashier to conceal a defalcation.

Ledgers and Journals. The financial statements are derived from the formal accounting books of record. These include the general ledger, the subsidiary ledgers, and the books of original entry. The general ledger is essentially the foundation of the audit work and an important source of gathering audit evidence, as it is the general ledger from which the financial statements are prepared. The subsidiary ledgers provide the detailed individual balances making up the general ledger total. They provide substantial audit support for the general ledger and also provide further breakdowns of financial statement totals where desired. The books of original entry provide the link between the source documents and the general ledger. Basic auditing procedures are applied to the books of original entry which form an important part of the total audit program.

Overall Analysis. An important source of evidence is the overall appraisal or analysis of an account or of the financial statements as a whole. Various types of ratio change and trend analyses have become recognized in recent years as important audit tools. Whether the data meet the tests of logic, reasonableness, and normality is just as significant as whether they are documentary evidence. Comparisons may be made of the elements of an item: Do the elements bear a reasonable relationship to each other and to the total? Comparisons can be made on a unit basis. Changes in unit data provide much good audit evidence. Various financial ratios between different periods for the same company and between the client company and other companies or between it and industry standards provide good audit evidence. Other helpful ratios are profitability ratios, utilization ratios, expense relationships, etc.

Independent Computations. An extremely important source of evidence is the independent computations made by the auditor. To be most effective, the basis for the computations should be interpreted independently by the auditor. In some cases misinterpretations or arithmetical errors have resulted in very substantial errors which have gone undetected for some time because no one studied carefully the stated terms. For example, very complex indenture restrictions have been improperly interpreted. Computations in connection with profit-sharing and bonus plans often are found by the auditor to be incorrect. The computations in connection with rental agreements based on a percentage of sales often are incorrect. For example, the auditor may question whether intercompany sales, resales, volume discount, etc., should be eliminated. Further clarification often provides substantial refunds.

Oral Evidence. During the course of the examination, the auditor will ask a great many questions of the officers and employees of the unit being audited. Many questions are essential, such as those attempting to locate the reason for certain procedures, or to determine the collectibility of a particular account as well as many other questions. Many of the questions develop an important type of evidence. While oral evidence often is not sufficient in itself, it is a very valuable form of corroborative evidence. In addition, it may disclose situations that require further investigation. Very often questions and particular responses elicit information pertaining to matters or ramifications of which the auditor was unaware when he asked his first question.

Subsequent Events. There are many audit situations where amounts in the financial statements can be supported by the effect of subsequent events reflected in documents evidencing such events. Examples are subsequent collection of an account receivable balance, subsequent payment liquidating a liability, and subsequent clearing of an outstanding check. Generally speaking, such a subsequent event gives relatively conclusive confirmation of the amount in question, but the auditor will have the usual problem of evaluating the documentary evidence supporting the transaction.

Circumstantial Evidence. The circumstances under which accounting figures are developed affect their credibility; hence circumstances are also a form of evidence. The most significant type of circumstantial evidence is internal control, and we have already stated that the assurance provided by the system of internal control has a direct bearing on the amount of additional evidence needed to support the accounting figures. Hence, internal control is circumstantial evidence that can serve as a substitute for other more direct evidence.

Other forms of circumstantial evidence would be the reliability of management representations in the past; general economic conditions and conditions within the client's industry, if they are consistent with reported operating and financial results; information about the plans and objectives of the management of the client; and finally, logical and consistent relationships between figures. For example, a gross margin percentage consistent with prior years and any known changes in conditions, plus an inventory shortage that bears a relationship to cost of sales that is consistent with prior years, would together lend substantial support to the reasonableness of figures for sales, cost of sales, inventory shortage, and the inventory figure in the balance sheet. Thus, reasonable and consistent relationships between figures can provide a major form of support for figures in the financial statements to which the auditor is to attest.

Electronically Processed Records. The introduction of the electronic computer for data processing has presented a host of new problems of evidence in the examination of financial statements. These are discussed extensively in the chapter on electronic data processing, but a brief reference to the topic is also included at this point. The substitution of electronic records for visible documents has necessitated a different approach in the examination of such records. The principal approach has been to place even greater reliance than in the past on the system that produces the output that appears in the financial statements. Internal control assumes even greater importance under these circumstances, and as a rule it will be stronger because the computer has no reason to deviate from prescribed procedures to conceal a defalcation, since greed is strictly a human characteristic.

Through "test deck" procedures the auditor can satisfy himself that stated controls are present in the computer program, and to further corroborate the resulting computer output, all of the customary forms of direct support for balance sheet amounts are available.

GUIDE TO AUDIT TESTING

General. Application of the preceding general comments and theoretical considerations is suggested by the Audit Procedure Guide (Figure 3), which shows for each major item on the financial statements the principal audit procedures customarily utilized, the forms of evidence consulted in executing those procedures, and the timing and extent of application of the procedures. Extent of application varies with internal control, of course, and the table treats with the two extremes: strong internal control and weak internal control. Actual situations are likely to vary between these extremes, and the suggested extent of tests would be varied accordingly. Following is a discussion of the principal factors used in determining the degree of testing in a particular circumstance:

1. Internal control
2. Materiality
3. Timing
4. Judgment
5. Purpose of the audit
6. Risk
7. Volume
8. Cost
9. Past experience
10. Questionable items
11. Unusual items

Internal Control. Under strong internal control, certain procedures may be unnecessary. In the table the extent of the tests in such circumstances is shown as "0%." For those instances where the extent of the test is shown as "50%," the auditor would be well advised to consider using statistical sampling techniques to arrive at the size of the sample results. When the table suggests a sample in excess of 50 percent of the dollar amount being verified, a judgmental sample would be appropriate and stratification can be used to build up the percentage of coverage by concentrating on the larger items in the population being tested. In these instances, with 100 percent coverage of larger items, the overall coverage of dollar amounts would range from 60 percent to 90 percent. The coverage would tend toward the lower end of the range when there is a large proportion of relatively homogeneous smaller items in the population.

Materiality. In addition to the degree of homogeneity, other factors that will have a bearing on the extent of tests to be conducted would be the materiality of the item relative to the client's financial position and results of operations. What is material is a matter of professional judgment based on experience and the requirements of the particular assignment. There are general considerations which are useful as guides. However, their application in any particular instance depends upon the context in which the matter falls. Following are the principal general considerations relating to materiality:

1. GENERAL OR PARTICULAR ITEMS: The materiality of an item would depend on whether it is of a general or particular nature. There is a distinction

between amounts arrived at on the basis of judgment and those subject to precise determination. For example, the amount of depreciation to be written off in one year is subject to value judgments. However, an error in the cash balance or a difference in a bank reconciliation might be small in amount and in total context but nevertheless may be material.

2. AMOUNT: The question of materiality of amount may relate to (*a*) the overall account, (*b*) the total of which it forms or should form a part, (*c*) associated items, or (*d*) the corresponding item in prior years.

3. RELATIONSHIP: In a small business an item of $1,000 may be material, whereas in a very large company an item of $50,000 may not be considered material. In this regard it might be pointed out that percentage guides can be useful but should not be applied without due regard to particular circumstances.

4. DISCLOSURE: There are instances in which the auditor will have to decide (*a*) whether an item should be disclosed, (*b*) if an error needs correction, or (*c*) whether the results of a computation or formula are reasonably close and fairly stated.

5. DESCRIPTION AND PRESENTATION: Materiality questions may arise in regard to the description of an item or its presentation in a particular context. Insufficient emphasis may be given to material items or excess emphasis may be given to immaterial items.

Timing. With respect to the question of when during the year under examination various tests should be carried out, it is assumed that when internal control is weak the tests must be carried out on or after the balance sheet date. There are many procedures that can be carried out at a date preliminary to the balance sheet date, and these are so indicated in the table. Always, of course, procedures that relate to testing activity throughout the year can be partially executed prior to the date of the financial statements, but activities in the succeeding interim period should then be reviewed at the end of the fiscal year.

Judgment. Finally, the reader should recognize that a satisfactory audit is never made on a "cookbook" basis. Professional judgment must be exercised at every point in the examination, including the application of procedures not listed in the following table, since the table is of necessity limited to only major procedures. Subsequent chapters of this handbook contain a thorough discussion of all procedures likely to be necessary in a typical audit.

Purpose of the Audit. The purpose of an audit will affect the extent of tests to a considerable degree. For example, an audit for special purposes, such as the purchase of a business, may require greater tests of inventory, closer review of fixed asset valuation, etc.

Risk. The degree of risk involved has an important bearing on the extent of tests. Certain accounts, such as payroll or cash receipts, which are more susceptible to irregularities, require more extended tests than some other accounts subject to less risk.

Volume. Where there is a large volume of items of small amount, the chance of material error is less than where the individual amount may be large. The internal controls would be reviewed carefully and only a representative sample verified. Statistical sampling may likely be suitable.

Cost. Very often the cost of tests may be greater than the potential benefits to be received. As in all audit procedures, the cost of the particular action is to be weighed against the applicable benefits.

Figure 3 AUDIT PROCEDURE GUIDE

Audit procedure	Evidence examined	Status of internal control: Strong — Approximate extent of tests	Strong — OK to do at preliminary date?	Weak — Approximate extent of tests
General Procedures:				
Trace recording of transactions	Original documents, journals, ledgers	<50% of 1 month	Yes	>50% of 1 month
Account for changes in balances	Previous balance, ratios, trends	Major accts.	.....	All accts.
Sales – Receivables:				
Test sales cutoff	Shipping records, sales journal	<50%, last 5 days	No	>50%, last 15 days
Tie in detail receivables/control	Subsidiary ledger, control account	<50%, of $	Yes	100%
Positive confirmation	Subsidiary ledger, customer reply	<50%, upper strata	Yes	>50% of $
Negative confirmation	Subsidiary ledger, customer reply	<50% of $	Yes	N.A.
Age receivables	Subsidiary ledger, client aging	<50% of $	Yes	>50% of $
Adequacy of loss provision	Uncollectible accounts, loss percentage	<50% of $	Yes	100%
Inspect notes	Promissory notes	<50% of $	No	100%
Purchases – Payables:				
Test purchase cutoff	Receiving records, invoices, purchase journal	<50%, last 5 days	No	>50%, last 15 days
Tie in detail payables/control	Subsidiary ledger, control account	<50% of $	No	100%
Confirm balances, major suppliers	Subsidiary ledger, supplier reply	0%	.....	>50%
Inspect supporting documents	Invoices, statements	<50% of $	No	>50% of $
Review subsequent transactions	Purchase journal, receiving records, invoices	<50%, next 30 days	No	>50%, next 30 days
Cost of Sales – Inventories:				
Test cost of sales cutoff	Shipping records, cost of sales entries	<50%, last 5 days	No	N.A.
Review client inventory plans	Printed instructions to employees	....	Yes	....
Observe inventory counting	Employee activities, records	<50% of crews	Yes	100% of crews
Test counts by auditor	Inventory items, count records	<50% of $	Yes	>50% of $
Confirm inventories not on premises	Subsidiary records, custodian reply	>50% of $	Yes	100%
Test inventory costing	Cost records, invoices, inventory record	<50% of $	Yes	>50% of $
Review for market declines	Invoices, price lists, condition of goods	<50% of $	No	>50% of $
Test clerical accuracy	Inventory sheets	<50% of $	Yes	>50% of $
Cash:				
Test cutoff of cash receipts	Receipts journal, cutoff bank stmt.	Deposits in transit	No	Deposits in transit
Test cutoff of cash disbursements	Disbursement journal, cutoff bank stmt.	<50% o/s checks	No	100% o/s checks
Count cash on hand	Cash items	Material amts. only	No	100%
Confirm bank balance	Standard bank confirmation form	100%	Yes	100%

Trace deposits in transit	Cutoff bank stmt., reconciliation	100%	Yes	100%
Trace o/s checks from cutoff stmt. to reconciliation	Cutoff bank stmt., reconciliation	<50%	Yes	100%
Prove reconciliation footings	Reconciliation	100%	Yes	100%
Account for o/s checks on previous audit not clearing cutoff	Reconciliations, paid checks	0%	.....	100%
Proof of cash transactions	Journals, bank statements	0%	.....	1 or 2 months
Payrolls:				
Verify year-end accrual	Payroll records	Overall calc.	No	Overall calc.
Test payroll details	Payroll journal, time cards, rate cards	<50% of 1 period	Yes	>50% 1 or 2 periods
Observe payoff	Payroll journal, checks, employees	0%	.....	100% of one payroll
Plant and Depreciation:				
Vouch plant additions	Plant accounts, repair accounts, invoices, paid checks	Major items, <50% of others	Yes	>50% of $
Inspect plant additions	Plant accounts, physical assets	<50% major items	Yes	>50% of $
Verify retirements	Plant accounts, gains & losses, proceeds	<50% of $	Yes	>50% of $
Verify depreciation	Plant accounts, depreciation schedules	Overall calc.	No	Overall calc.
Determine ownership	Paid checks, deeds, tax bills, ins. policies	Overall	Yes	Overall
Investments:				
Inspect certificates	Stock and bond certificates	>50% of $	No	100% of $
Confirm certificates not on hand	Reply from holder	100%	No	100%
Verify entries for purchases and sales to verify year-end valuations	Brokers' advices, investment account	<50% of $	Yes	100% of $
Account for income	Interest rates on certificates, dividend records	>50% of $	Yes	100% of $
Other Assets:				
Verify that debits are appropriate	Invoices, contracts, paid checks	>50% of $	Yes	>50% of $
Determine reasonable amortization	Estimates of life and remaining benefits	>50% of $	Yes	>50% of $
Review for losses not written off	Ascertain existence of remaining benefits	100%	Yes	100%
Other Liabilities:				
Verify accruals	Contracts	>50% of $	No	>50% of $
Trace loan proceeds	Cash receipts records, bank statement	Major items	Yes	Major items
Review subsequent transactions for unrecorded liabilities	Cash disbursement journal, voucher register, general journal, invoices	Major items, <50% others	No	>50% of $
Owners' Equity:				
Analyze all account entries	General ledger, general journal, charter	100%	Yes	100%
Verify income distributions	Directors' minutes, articles of incorporation or partnership	100%	Yes	100%
Determine proper treatment of extraordinary gains and losses	APB Opinion No. 9 *	100%	Yes	100%

* Accounting Principles Board Opinion No. 9.

Past Experience. The auditor may have past experience as a guide. His experience during the current or past year with certain accounts or transactions may help to determine the extent of future tests of particular items.

Questionable Items. Where an item may be questionable or may convey a suggestion of irregularity, additional tests should be made of that item.

Unusual Items. In general, unusual items are subject to less control and internal check than routine items. Therefore the auditor will ordinarily provide additional tests or will scrutinize unusual items more carefully.

BIBLIOGRAPHY

An Auditor's Approach to Statistical Sampling, AICPA, New York, 1967 to date.

Sampling Manual for Auditors and Supplement, The Institute of Internal Auditors, New York, 1967 to date.

Sampling Techniques and Regression Analysis for Accounting and Auditing Information, A Practical Approach, Federal Government Accountants Association, November, 1967.

Statements on Auditing Procedure No. 33, *Auditing Standards and Procedures,* AICPA, New York, 1969.

Statement on Auditing Procedure No. 41, *Subsequent Discovery of Facts Existing at the Date of the Auditor's Report,* AICPA, New York, 1969.

Statement on Auditing Procedure No. 43, *Confirmation of Receivables and Observation of Inventories,* AICPA, New York, 1970.

Arkin, Herbert: *Handbook of Sampling for Auditing and Accounting,* New York, McGraw-Hill Book Company, 1963.

Hill, Henry P., Joseph L. Roth, and Herbert Arkin: *Sampling in Auditing,* New York, The Ronald Press Company, 1962.

Murphy, Mary E.: *Advanced Public Accounting Practice,* Homewood, Ill., Richard D. Irwin, Inc., 1966.

Stettler, Howard F.: *Systems Based Independent Audits,* Englewood Cliffs, N.J., Prentice-Hall, Inc., 1967.

Stettler, Howard F.: "Some Observations on Statistical Sampling in Auditing," *The Journal of Accountancy,* April, 1966.

Mecimore, Charles D., and Thomas M. Collins: "Sufficient Competent Evidential Matter,"*Oklahoma CPA,* July, 1966.

Slaybaugh, C. Jay: "Pareto's Law and Modern Management," *Management Services,* March–April, 1967.

"Interpretation of Material in Relation to Accounts," *The Accountant,* July, 1968.

Feltham, Gerald A., and Joel S. Demski: "The Use of Models in Information Evaluation," *The Accounting Review,* October, 1970.

Chapter 13

Auditing Procedures

ROBERT W. VANASSE

Professor of Accounting, California State College, Fullerton

AUDITING PROCEDURES, TECHNIQUES, AND STANDARDS

Auditing Procedures Defined. Auditing procedures may be broadly defined as the acts performed by the auditor in the course of attaining the objectives of the examination.[1] In the usual case, the attainment of audit objectives requires the collection of evidence to support a decision. Therefore, auditing procedures may be considered as being primarily designed to obtain evi-

[1] Statements on Auditing Procedure No. 33, *Auditing Standards and Procedures,* AICPA (Committee on Auditing Procedure), New York, 1963, p. 15.

dence of one kind or another, even though some procedures also function as aids in supervising audits.

In this chapter, auditing procedures will be considered with respect to the various techniques which make up the procedures; the standards which govern applications of the procedures; and the relationships which exist between auditing procedures and the planning, organizing, and directing and controlling of audit engagements.

Auditing Techniques. Auditing procedures may be designed to incorporate the use of various auditing techniques to achieve a specific objective. The design and modification of different auditing procedures to fit different audit objectives and situations is largely dependent on the various circumstances of each audit engagement and the individual judgment of the auditor involved.

For example, the auditing procedures employed in carrying out an independent audit, where the primary objective is to form an opinion on the fairness of the financial statements based on tests of compliance with financial controls are likely to be quite different from those auditing procedures used in conjunction with an internal audit, where the principal objective is to evaluate the effectiveness of certain administrative controls based on tests of compliance with company policy.

Examples of some of the principal auditing techniques related to auditing procedures designed for use in an audit of financial statements may be listed as follows: [2]

1. Vouching
2. Confirming
3. Reconciling
4. Analyzing
5. Testing
6. Physically examining
7. Scanning
8. Posting verification
9. Footing
10. Extension verification

General applications of these techniques may be described briefly in the following manner:

Vouching. Examining the underlying written evidence such as a sales invoice or receiving report in support of a transaction, entry, or account balance

Confirming. Independently communicating with an outside party to establish the accuracy and validity of a recorded figure or fact

Reconciling. Identifying and explaining the items which cause two or more related amounts to be different

Analyzing. Describing in detail the composition of a total balance as to date, amount, and classification

Testing. Selecting and examining representative items from a large set of similar items for the purpose of drawing conclusions about the characteristics of the set

[2] James A. Cashin and Garland C. Owens, *Auditing,* 2d ed., New York, The Ronald Press Company, 1963, p. 149.

Physically Examining. Establishing the physical existence of items in support of recorded data concerning the items

Scanning. Appraising selected characteristics of data as a means of identifying specific items requiring additional examination

Posting Verification. Tracing selected items recorded in one source to another source to establish the propriety and consistency of the recording process

Footing. Adding a column of amounts to prove the accuracy of the total

Extension Verification. Multiplying two or more amounts to prove the accuracy of the total

A specific example of an auditing procedure incorporating some of the auditing techniques described above is the confirmation of Accounts Receivable as part of the examination of general financial records. This procedure is generally carried out by the independent auditor with the objective of obtaining evidence concerning the accuracy and validity of the customer account balances being examined. Examples of three specific auditing techniques which are normally employed in conjunction with the performance of this auditing procedure include scanning the Accounts Receivable trial balance for the purpose of selecting the specific accounts to be confirmed; reconciling the Accounts Receivable trial balance total with the general ledger balance; and test footing the Accounts Receivable trial balance total.

Auditing procedures are also employed in the process of examining nonfinancial records as well as general financial records. An example is the review of major contracts with suppliers or customers for the purpose of extracting significant and relevant data for inclusion in the audit permanent file. These data might then serve as a reference in the determination of compliance with the contract provisions.

The auditing procedures selected for a particular audit engagement or examination are generally combined in a written plan called an "audit program." An example of a page from a printed program is shown in Figure 1.

Auditing Standards. In the case of an ordinary examination of financial statements by an independent auditor where the principal objective is the expression of an opinion on the fairness of the statements, the quality of the auditing procedures performed by the independent auditor is normally measured in terms of the generally accepted auditing standards published by the American Institute of Certified Public Accountants.[3] Although these standards were prepared principally as a guide for members of the Institute, their comprehensiveness and clarity make them generally appropriate for most auditing services.

Six of the ten generally accepted auditing standards are related to the selection, timing, and proper implementation of auditing procedures and to the reporting of the examination's results.

General standards. The first general standard states that "the examination is to be performed by a person or persons having adequate technical training and proficiency as an auditor."[4] Since the element of judgment is such an important factor in terms of both the selection and application of proper auditing procedures, it is essential that the auditor be required to have the "informed judgment of a qualified professional person."[5]

[3] Statements on Auditing Procedure No. 33, pp. 9, 15.

[4] *Ibid.*, p. 15.

[5] *Ibid.*, p. 10.

Figure 1 AUDIT PROGRAM

PROGRAM FOR ACCOUNTS RECEIVABLE
AND ALLOWANCE FOR DOUBTFUL ACCOUNTS

Company ______________ Period Ended ______________

Item No.	Auditing Procedure	Done By	Remarks
1	Prepare related section of Questionnaire on Internal Control and ascertain by observation and test that the indicated procedures are being followed.		
2	On the basis of the evaluation of the system of internal control and the type of business, add below (or on a separate page) additional auditing procedures considered necessary in the circumstances. Delete procedures which are not applicable or are unnecessary in the circumstances.		
3	Obtain aged lists of accounts receivable balances and compare with detailed ledger accounts. Reconcile totals with general ledger control account.		
4	Classify balances on lists as to customers, officers and employees, parent and subsidiary companies and others. Exclude consignments.		
5	Select accounts for independent confirmation and communicate directly with debtors by positive request for confirmation and/or negative request for confirmation.		
6	Compare replies to requests for confirmation and investigate differences.		
7	Foot selected detailed ledger accounts.		
8	Trace postings in selected detailed ledger accounts back to original records.		
9	Determine propriety of material transactions in selected detailed accounts for two-week period including balance sheet date		
10	Scan general ledger control account for the period and thereafter to ascertain propriety of unusual transactions and material charge-offs.		
11	Discuss with responsible officials collectibility of accounts, consider review of applicable correspondence, and ascertain adequacy of allowance for doubtful accounts.		
12	If, as a result of your work on this section of the program, you have any suggestions for revising subsequent programs, indicate that fact and attach a memorandum setting forth in reasonable detail your suggestions.		
	No suggestions _ Suggestions attached _		

The third general standard states that "due professional care is to be exercised in the performance of the examination and the preparation of the report." [6] This third general standard complements the first general standard by giving formal recognition to the fact that the auditor must not only satisfy the requirement of adequate technical training but is also responsible for the proper use of this technical training through the exercise of due professional care in the selection, application, and coordination of the auditing procedures employed.

Standards of fieldwork. The first standard of fieldwork states that "the work is to be adequately planned and assistants, if any, are to be properly supervised." [7]

Apart from the phrase relating to the supervision of assistants, this standard is concerned with the timeliness of auditing procedures and the orderliness of their application.[8] In many audit situations it is essential that various audit procedures either be properly synchronized, applied simultaneously,

[6] *Ibid.*, p. 15.
[7] *Ibid.*, p. 16.
[8] *Ibid.*, p. 24.

or used on a surprise basis to ensure their effectiveness. For example, the examination of cash and other liquid assets as of a particular date often requires that several related audit procedures be executed at the same time or in a special sequence in order to obtain the desired control over the items being examined.[9]

The second and third standards of fieldwork provide more explicit guidance in regard to selecting the specific auditing procedures required to accomplish the objectives of an ordinary examination.

The second standard of fieldwork states that "there is to be a proper study and evaluation of the existing internal control as a basis for reliance thereon and for the determination of the resultant extent of the tests to which auditing procedures are to be restricted." [10]

The evaluation of internal control constitutes an auditing procedure by itself. However, the evaluation of the adequacy and effectiveness of internal control systems through tests of the accounting records and other related data is also one of the first and most important steps in selecting the other auditing procedures required for making an adequate examination.[11] "The effect of internal control on the scope of an examination is an outstanding example of the influence on auditing procedures of a greater or lesser degree of risk of error; i.e., the stronger the internal control, the less the degree of risk." [12]

The third standard of fieldwork states that "sufficient competent evidential matter is to be obtained through inspection, observation, inquiries and confirmations to afford a reasonable basis for an opinion regarding the financial statements under examination." [13]

This standard not only identifies the basic objectives of all generally accepted auditing procedures related to the independent examination of financial statements but also provides the necessary authority for the use of those special auditing procedures applicable to the examination of receivables and inventories.[14] The primary objective of these special procedures is to require confirmation of receivables and observation of inventories when the amounts are material and the auditing procedures are practicable and reasonable.

Standards of reporting. The fourth standard of reporting states: "The report shall either contain an expression of opinion regarding the financial statements, taken as a whole, or an assertion to the effect that an opinion cannot be expressed. When an over-all opinion cannot be expressed, the reasons therefor should be stated. In all cases where an auditor's name is associated with financial statements the report should contain a clear-cut indication of the character of the auditor's examination, if any, and the degree of responsibility he is taking." [15]

The standard audit report issued by an independent auditor in conjunction with an examination of financial statements consists of a "scope" paragraph containing a representation as to the work performed and an "opinion" paragraph containing a representation as to the auditor's conclusions.[16]

[9] *Ibid.*, p. 25.
[10] *Ibid.*, p. 16.
[11] *Ibid.*, p. 32.
[12] *Ibid.*, p. 17.
[13] *Ibid.*, p. 16.
[14] *Ibid.*, p. 38.
[15] *Ibid.*, p. 16.
[16] *Ibid.*, p. 57.

The scope paragraph usually reads as follows:

> We have examined the balance sheet of the X Company as of June 30, 19__, and the related statement(s) of income and retained earnings for the year then ended. Our examination was made in accordance with generally accepted auditing standards, and accordingly included such tests of the accounting records and such other auditing procedures as we considered necessary in the circumstances.[17]

In those situations where the auditor is able to employ all of the customary auditing procedures necessary, in his judgment, to provide a basis for an opinion on the financial statements, no departure from the standard wording of the scope paragraph is required. However, when the auditor is unable, for any reason, to carry out all of the auditing procedures customarily employed, generally accepted auditing standards may require disclosure of this fact in the audit report. In those circumstances in which it is impossible or impracticable for the auditor to follow certain customary auditing procedures, apart from confirming receivables or observing inventory, but in which the auditor is able to satisfy himself by the application of other auditing procedures, no reference to the use of alternative auditing procedures is required.[18] In those circumstances involving restrictions on the use of auditing procedures customarily followed in regard to the confirmation of receivables or the observation of inventories during the period under review, disclosure must be made of the restrictions and the use of alternative auditing procedures, even in those situations where the employment of alternative auditing procedures satisfies the auditor.[19]

An example of the pertinent phrase in a qualified scope paragraph reads as follows:

> Our examination was made in accordance with generally accepted auditing standards, and accordingly included such tests of the accounting records and such other auditing procedures as we considered necessary in the circumstances; however, it was not practicable to confirm accounts receivable from governmental agencies; by other auditing procedures, we have satisfied ourselves of the validity, amount, and collectibility of these receivables.[20]

In those circumstances where the auditor is unable to follow customary auditing procedures and where he is unable to satisfy himself by the application of alternative procedures, auditing standards require disclosure of this fact in the report. The limitations of the examination, as well as the effect, should be clearly indicated in the scope paragraph or in a separate middle paragraph of the report; depending on the materiality of the items involved, the opinion paragraph may have to be qualified or contain a disclaimer.[21]

The following report excerpts illustrate a situation in which both the restriction on an examination and the effect are fully disclosed and in which the auditor judges that a qualified opinion is warranted.

> [*Scope paragraph*]
> . . . and such other auditing procedures as we considered necessary in the circumstances, except as noted in the following paragraph.

[17] *Ibid.*, p. 57.
[18] *Ibid.*, p. 63.
[19] *Ibid.*, p. 64.
[20] Arthur W. Holmes, *Auditing: Principles and Procedures,* 6th ed., Homewood, Ill., Richard D. Irwin, Inc., 1964, p. 34.
[21] Statements on Auditing Procedure No. 33, p. 64.

[*Middle paragraph*]
In accordance with your instructions, we did not request any owners to confirm their balances or accumulated storage charges. Accordingly, we do not express an opinion as to accumulated storage charges, stated as $ . . . , which amount enters into the determination of financial position and results of operations.

[*Opinion paragraph*]
In our opinion, with the exception stated in the preceding paragraph, the accompanying . . .[22]

The SEC also requires that departures from normal or customary auditing procedures be disclosed in the auditor's report. Regulation S-X, Rule 2-02(b)(ii), states that the accountant's certificate "shall designate any auditing procedures generally recognized as normal, or deemed necessary by the accountant under the circumstances of the particular case, which have been omitted, and the reasons for their omission." [23]

AUDITING PROCEDURES AND PLANNING OF AUDITS

Preliminary planning for audit engagements includes the collection of information which can be used to assist in the planning of the various auditing procedures which are customarily employed in the course of a general audit examination. Since the preliminary planning process is likely to be influenced to a large extent by previous relationships between the client and the auditor, a distinction will be made between planning for new engagements and planning for repeat engagements.

New Engagements. The process of planning for a new audit engagement involves the collection and evaluation of many different kinds of information. In most cases, the required information is obtained through inquiry and visits to the place of business. A brief description of some of the principal items which would normally be covered as a part of the preliminary arrangements for a new engagement may be outlined as follows: [24]

1. Basic agreement
   a. Purpose of the audit
   b. Nature of the examination
   c. Fee basis
   d. Period covered
2. General data
   a. Nature of the business
   b. Organizational structure
   c. Key personnel
   d. Condition of records
   e. Where work is to be done
   f. Suggestions for system improvement
3. Program data
   a. When report is due
   b. Date of last audit
   c. Work by company staff
   d. Testing of records

[22] *Ibid.*, p. 65.
[23] Regulation S-X, Rule 2-02 (b) (ii), Securities and Exchange Commission, Washington [Legal citation: 17 CFR 210.2-02(b)(ii)].
[24] Cashin and Owens, *op. cit.*, pp. 104–106.

e. Inventory observation
f. Confirmation of receivables
g. Letter confirming agreement

Several items on this list are of major importance to the process of planning auditing procedures. These are the purpose of the audit, the nature of the business, the organizational structure of the firm, and certain items classified as program data which affect the scheduling of auditing fieldwork.

Purpose of the audit. In the case of the new engagement, as much information as possible should be obtained about the client's reasons for requesting an audit, since it is essential that both the auditor and the client agree on the purpose of the audit and the general nature of the work which must be done to accomplish this objective.

Examples of different audit purposes are: to provide information for creditors, to provide information for prospective purchasers of the business, and to provide information for management with respect to possible fraud losses. Since the nature of the audit for each of these special purposes would be quite different, the planning of the auditing procedures in each case would be influenced to a considerable extent by the purpose specified.

For example, the auditing procedures required to uncover fraud might involve extensive testing of liquid assets such as cash and the controls adopted for their protection. Auditing procedures followed for credit purposes or to establish the market value of a business, on the other hand, would require more extensive testing of the principles and procedures used in conjunction with the valuation of assets and the determination of earnings.

Nature of the business. The nature of the business influences the planning of auditing procedures principally in terms of establishing certain operational criteria governing the selection of applicable procedures. For example, business operations may be classified in terms of the nature of the activity, such as service, merchandising or manufacturing, and also in terms of the nature of the industry, such as banking, food, or steel.

As an illustration of the influence of the nature of business activity on the selection of auditing procedures, it may be noted that the use of standard procedures for the examination of inventories would normally be applicable only in conjunction with audits of merchandising and manufacturing firms and not in conjunction with audits of many kinds of service businesses not having inventories.

The nature of the industry also determines the applicability of auditing procedures in many instances. As an illustration, the AICPA industry audit guide entitled *Audits of Savings and Loan Associations* states that it "is intended to provide guidance as to proper and adequate procedure for independent audits of savings and loan associations to meet the needs of the investing public, the management of such associations, and the supervisory authorities."[25]

Other industry audit guides have also been published by the AICPA in recognition of the specialized nature of auditing procedures applicable to different types of industry. These include *Audits of Fire and Casualty Insurance Companies*, *Audits of Voluntary Health and Welfare Organizations*, *Audits of Construction Contractors*, *Audits of Brokers or Dealers in Securities*, and *Audits of Banks*.

[25] Industry Audit Guide: *Audits of Savings and Loan Associations*, AICPA (Committee on Savings and Loan Auditing), New York, 1962, p. 5.

Company organization structure. The organizational structure of a business firm may be considered both in terms of the managerial organization and in terms of the physical organization. The degree of internal control furnished by the pattern of authority and responsibility in the firm's managerial organization will have considerable influence on the planning of auditing procedures, primarily with respect to the extent of the testing considered necessary.

The physical organization will also influence the planning of auditing procedures, since the number, location, and relative sizes of the separate physical units must also be considered in determining which specific units are practicable and feasible to test.

Specific items of information which might be used to evaluate the organizational structure of the firm in regard to planning auditing procedures are organization charts, procedure manuals, charts of accounts, detailed descriptions of all units which are operated at separate locations, and prior years' financial statements. In situations in which the firm prepares consolidated financial statements, separate financial statements for each individual entity are normally obtained, together with information explaining the principles of consolidation and other accounting principles followed by the client, in order to assist in the planning process.

Scheduling of fieldwork. The client's schedule of certain accounting activities, such as closing the books, drafting the annual report to stockholders, and preparing other special information reports, must also be considered by the auditor in planning auditing procedures, principally in regard to timing. In order to complete the audit and all other special work on time and also to take advantage of the client's schedule of accounting activities, the auditor often has to arrange for some of the fieldwork to be done at an interim period, prior to the close of the fiscal period under review.

Two of the most important of the client's scheduled accounting activities which must be considered in planning auditing procedures are the taking of physical inventories, and, to a lesser extent, the preparation and mailing of periodic billing or statements of Accounts Receivable. Since generally accepted auditing standards require the physical examination of inventory and the direct confirmation of receivables on a test basis, it is essential that the auditor be present when the client takes inventory and when it is feasible to prepare and mail confirmations of account balances. Although receivables can be confirmed at any prearranged time, it is often more efficient to plan the necessary auditing procedures for the circularization of Accounts Receivable in conjunction with the client's normally scheduled billing activities than to attempt to carry out this required audit fieldwork at some other time.

In those situations in which the client does not take annual physical inventories but relies instead on other controls such as statistical sampling, the auditor may have to satisfy himself by evaluating the sampling methods used or by employing other alternative auditing procedures.[26]

Other activities may also occasionally influence the planning of auditing procedures. For example, a scheduled visit to a safe-deposit box near the end of the year or a scheduled payroll distribution by an internal auditor may also require the presence of an independent auditor and the implementation of selected auditing procedures in conjunction with the scheduled activity.

In recent years the study and evaluation of internal controls and accounting systems prior to the close of the fiscal period under review has become a

[26] Statement on Auditing Procedure No. 36, *Revision of "Extensions of Auditing Procedure" Relating to Inventories*, AICPA (Committee on Auditing Procedure), New York, 1966, p. 34.

relatively standard auditing procedure. This practice is especially desirable in the case of new engagements, since the use of systems information collected at a time when neither the client nor the auditor is under the pressures of year-end closing should help avoid unforeseen problems related to the scheduling of year-end auditing procedures.

Since the extent of audit testing is also dependent on the adequacy of the client's system of internal control, it is essential that basic information concerning internal control be available as early as possible to assist in the planning and designing of auditing procedures. The example of a printed page from an internal control questionnaire shown in Figure 2 is typical of the format used to accumulate data and evaluate the system of internal control as an aid to planning relevant auditing procedures.

Repeat Engagements. Planning auditing procedures for repeat engagements requires evaluation of the same factors considered earlier in regard to the planning of new engagements. However, if the purpose of the audit, the nature of the business, and the organizational structure of the firm remain relatively unchanged from the prior period, most of the auditing procedures applicable to the current period can be planned on the basis of data acquired during the previous audit.

Review of prior results. Basic information which is normally used to plan the repeat engagement is contained in the prior period's audit report, permanent file, internal control questionnaire, audit program, working papers, and time budget. The only new information which has to be obtained in regard to the preliminary planning for the repeat engagement is a current schedule of the client's accounting activities which affect the planning of fieldwork.

Revision of audit programs. The principal task in planning a repeat engagement is the review and revision of the audit program. If comments regarding proposed changes in auditing procedures applicable to future audits are listed in the audit program by staff members during the course of an audit, the process of revising the audit program is made much easier. Some printed audit programs provide space for such comments with respect to changes recommended both as a result of the evaluation of the system of internal control and the type of business and as a result of work done as directed by the existing program. The page from an audit program shown in Figure 1, specifically items 2 and 12, illustrates how suggestions for revising programs for repeat engagements may be accumulated for use in planning subsequent audits.

AUDITING PROCEDURES AND ORGANIZATION OF AUDITS

Certain basic auditing procedures can be directly related to the process of organizing audit engagements. These include the collection of data for permanent files, the evaluation of internal control systems, the design of audit programs, and the preparation of all other audit working papers.

Permanent File Information. The collection of data for a permanent file is a continuous operation. In a new engagement, the history of the business must be reviewed and all significant information regarding past and present business operations brought up to date. From that point on, assuming that there will be repeat engagements, the file should be maintained by recording all relevant information concerning the client's business operations as soon as the data become available.

In addition to providing assistance in the planning of subsequent audit engagements, the accumulated data contained in the permanent file are also very useful in terms of assisting in the organization of an audit. Examples of specific information which is normally used in this manner are the descriptions of accounting systems and business operations and the records of prior audit tests carried out on a rotating or random selection basis.

Accounting systems and business operations. The descriptions of accounting systems and business operations contained in a properly maintained permanent file should normally provide an auditor with a readily available source of reference material for organizing the fieldwork in an audit engagement. After considering both the type of data generated in a particular business operation and the type of system used to collect and summarize these data, an auditor should be able to effectively coordinate the tests of primary accounting records and other auditing procedures necessary to determine the reliability of the accounting information being examined.

In addition, if any changes in business operations or accounting systems are noted during the course of the examination, any required reorganization of the audit program can usually be made more effective by comparing the changes noted with the summary information of the entire system contained in the permanent file.

When the permanent file material relating to accounting systems and business operations is made required reading for all audit staff members participating in the engagement, the usefulness of this material as an aid to organizing and coordinating the audit is greatly enhanced.

Results of prior audit engagements. Permanent file information summarizing the results of prior audit engagements can be used as a basis of comparison for determining the extent of tests and procedures required under current operating conditions.

Since many audit decisions cannot be made in advance but must be made during the current engagement as test results become available, the permanent file data describing prior test results provide one of the best references for maintaining a consistent level of quality of the work being done. In addition, knowledge of the areas or periods selected for detailed testing in prior examinations permits the auditor to effectively utilize staff members to provide a well-balanced and representative series of audits over the long run.

Internal Control Information. The collection of internal control information, like the preparation of permanent files, is a continuous operation. The basic methods of gathering information concerning the internal control procedures in existence in a firm are through inquiry and tests.

Internal control questionnaires. The use of standardized internal control questionnaires permits an auditor to gather data related to basic internal controls in a form which can be used to evaluate the effectiveness of the controls at the time the answers are recorded. An illustration of a page from a standard internal control questionnaire is shown in Figure 2.

The use of such questionnaires is based on the assumptions that the procedures covered are essential to achieving adequate internal control and that the firm is large enough to permit extensive division of duties among employees.

It may be noted from the questionnaire page shown in Figure 2 that the answers have been organized for the purpose of identifying the areas where more extensive audit testing might be necessary. By comparing the current year's questionnaire answers with prior years' answers, the auditor should be able to organize the testing procedures to take into account any changes

Figure 2 **QUESTIONNAIRE ON INTERNAL CONTROL**

INTERNAL CONTROL QUESTIONNAIRE
FOR NOTES RECEIVABLE

Company ______

Period Covered ______

QUESTION	ANSWER			
	Not Appl.	Yes	No. (2) Secondary, (1) Primary, Weakness	Remarks
1. Are notes and related collateral in custody of persons not connected with accounting records?				
2. Are note details balanced with control account monthly?				
3. Are extensions, renewals and write-offs authorized by a responsible official?				
4. Is proper control maintained over notes charged off or not recorded in the accounts being examined?				
5. Is an adequate record of collateral maintained?				
6. Are notes physically safeguarded by adequate means?				

in the control system and also to coordinate the testing in different areas to maximize the efficiency of auditing procedures which are designed to obtain evidence about related areas.

If internal control questionnaires are not used, the auditor would generally prepare a written outline of the primary controls which are supposed to exist in the organization according to inquiry and observation. In many cases this would have to be done in smaller organizations and in those firms utilizing specialized types of accounting systems.

The widespread use of EDP systems requires that auditors be familiar with the controls involved in the operation of computers as well as manual systems. Typically, EDP systems should be evaluated in terms of their organizational, administrative, and procedural controls. A basic understanding of the controls and the flow of information through EDP systems is essential for the purpose of properly organizing and coordinating audit engagements of firms utilizing these systems.

Tests of internal control systems. Testing, the second method of collecting internal control information, can be used both to establish the validity of the questionnaire answers and to establish the extent of compliance with company procedures and policies described in company manuals and in the write-up of the accounting system and internal controls contained in the permanent file.

Comparisons of current questionnaire answers, current control descriptions, and current test results with similar information from prior periods provides a sound basis for the organization of the subsequent audit fieldwork. In most situations the collection of internal control data will take place in the interim phase or early final phase of the audit and will enable the auditor to utilize the information more effectively in conjunction with all other audit tests and procedures.

Audit Programs. Audit programs assist materially in organizing audit engagements. The organizational features are evident in the basic advantages often cited for programs and in the different kinds of programs generally in use.

Advantages of programs. The principal advantages of an audit program as an aid to organizing audit operations are described in the following list:

1. It identifies the essential work to be done.
2. It promotes the efficient distribution of work to all members of the audit staff.
3. It facilitates orderly and timesaving routines.
4. It places responsibility for the work performed.
5. It serves as a guide for succeeding years and as a basis for revising subsequent programs.

Essentially, the use of a printed audit program containing material such as that shown in Figure 1 provides a means for making sure that all of the auditing procedures called for in the original audit plan have been carried out. Since conditions, systems, and operations may change between engagements or during the course of an audit, the use of a program provides the auditor with a means of coordinating the standards originally set for the engagement with the work actually being done.

Certain disadvantages of audit programs have also been cited. These include the tendency to regard the program as establishing a limit for work and responsibility and also to view the program as a guide for implementing procedures automatically, without any need for independent thinking.

Kinds of programs. Two basically different forms of audit programs may be employed. One form contains general or standardized instructions and requires the auditor to edit the applicable procedures as the audit is carried out. An example of a page from a general program is shown in Figure 1. The other form, the special program, is prepared or tailored for a specific audit engagement and therefore contains only those instructions and procedures which are relevant to the engagement. Although the general program may be less efficient than the special program as a guide for specific procedures, both kinds of programs provide the organizational framework necessary to ensure that all significant audit procedures are considered during the course of the audit engagement.

Audit Working Papers. Purpose and contents. Technically, all of the written material prepared and collected in the course of an audit engagement might be considered as constituting audit working papers. Such items would include the permanent file, internal control questionnaire, and audit programs discussed above, as well as the accounting schedules, correspondence, copies of client's records, and all other documentary evidence collected in support of the procedural work done during the engagement. In addition, the audit working papers should contain statements regarding the conclusions reached as a result of the audit engagement.

Audit working papers assist in the process of organizing audit engagements by providing a means for evaluating the results of the audit tests and procedures called for by the audit program. This continuing evaluation provides the auditor with the information needed to confirm the adequacy of the audit procedures originally selected or to justify changes in the original audit plan to compensate for changing conditions uncovered during the course of the audit.

Additional benefits with respect to audit organization may be gained from the comparison of prior years' working papers with the current year's working papers. If the use of similar auditing procedures from year to year provides dissimilar results in any given year, then the need for change in auditing procedures or the extension of tests may be readily apparent.

Indexing and filing. In order to maximize the efficient use of audit working papers with respect to the organization of audit engagements, a basic plan of indexing the working papers should be adopted. By following the same indexing system from period to period, prior periods' working papers can be used quite effectively, both as a guide for organizing the current period's auditing procedures and as a source of comparative data. A completed file of audit working papers, properly indexed, also serves to organize the preparation of the audit reports and any other special reports which are required under the terms of the audit engagement.

AUDITING PROCEDURES AND CONTROL OF AUDITS

Some of the auditing procedures introduced earlier, such as the preparation of internal control questionnaires and the design of programs, also function as controls in carrying out audit engagements. In addition, other auditing procedures, such as the preparation of time budgets and working paper review, have been designed primarily for the purpose of maintaining control over the quantity and quality of the audit work done. In general, the auditing procedures which operate as controls may be classified in terms of supervision, mechanical checks, time budgets, and audit review.

Supervision. The preparation of permanent files, internal control questionnaires, audit programs, and all other working papers represents the use of auditing procedures to supervise audit operations to a considerable extent. By carefully assigning responsibility for the preparation of specific and related permanent file write-ups, internal control questionnaires, audit programs, and other necessary working papers, in-charge auditors are often able to delegate effectively the supervision of many routine activities. For example, if a specially tailored audit program is being used, the program will direct the staff member to undertake certain auditing procedures and accordingly employ certain auditing techniques to accomplish the stated objective. In those situations where the program and working papers can be completed as directed and the review of internal control and the write-up of the permanent file can be made without incurring any difficulty, the principle of "management by exception" can be employed. Where problems are encountered, the more experienced judgment of the auditor-in-charge can be sought to resolve the issues.

Other auditing procedures which are generally employed to supervise effectively the staff members performing the audit involve the assignment of duties and responsibilities to different levels of competence and experience in line with the auditing standards, introduced earlier, which require adequate technical training and supervision.

Mechanical Checks. One of the most effective methods of controlling audit performance involves the use of signatures, initials, and various other special identification marks. Signatures may be obtained from clients (e.g., in the case of liquid assets counted and returned to the client intact); audit staff (e.g., in the case of internal control questionnaire reviews as per Figure 2); and partners (e.g., in the case of the completed audit report).

Initials are usually entered on all completed audit working papers other than those requiring signatures. Both the person(s) preparing the working paper and the person(s) reviewing the working paper generally initial the completed form as evidence of completion and as an indication of responsibility.

The use of special "tick" marks provides an efficient method of indicating the work done on various working papers containing accounting schedules, correspondence, copies of client's records, and other documentary evidence collected during the audit engagement. When the meaning of all the "tick" marks used on each working paper is properly explained in a legend appearing on the working paper, this procedure will provide readily visible evidence that the various tests described in the audit program and other working papers have been accomplished.

Time Budgets. The use of itemized time budgets to record and compare estimated and actual time spent on each audit activity provides two different kinds of controls over audit engagements. The data provided by these detailed records can be used both as a basis for establishing or revising audit fees and as a means of evaluating the distribution of time among the various phases of an audit engagement.

The preparation of a time budget constitutes an auditing procedure which must be carried out on a continuing basis, since the recording of original time estimates must be made prior to commencement of the work, and the posting of the actual time required cannot be made until each identifiable activity has been completed. Comparisons of budgeted time and actual time for each activity can be made during the course of the audit, however, and this information can then be used to plan any changes required to maintain the original time schedule or to adjust the scope of the engagement. An illustration of a portion of a time budget is shown in Figure 3.

Audit Review. Perhaps the most effective auditing procedure for ensuring control over the quantity and quality of audit work done is the review of all working papers by individuals charged with responsibility for the audit engagement. When properly carried out, audit review is a continuous process. As each phase of an audit is completed, all related sections of the permanent file, internal control questionnaire, audit program, and other working papers are reviewed by an auditor in charge of the fieldwork. At other intervals, audit supervisors may be employed to review larger portions of the completed work. As a final control, the partner-in-charge, or other individual responsible for the audit report, generally reviews the entire set of working papers

Figure 3 TIME BUDGET

Client __________
Period __________ Partner __________

Date		Name-hours					Auditing Procedures												
Prior yr. actual	Interim ___ Final ___ Total ___						Reports	Audit program	Permanent file	Internal control	Trial balance	Working paper file	—	Cash	Securities	Notes receivable	Accounts receivable	Inventories	
Current yr. budget	Interim ___ Final ___ Total ___																		

with respect to their overall adequacy in support of the audit report. Through this process of continuous review at successively higher levels of authority, effective and timely control over the work being done is assured.

BIBLIOGRAPHY

Industry Audit Guides, AICPA, New York.

Statements on Auditing Procedure No. 33, *Auditing Standards and Procedures,* AICPA (Committee on Auditing Procedure), New York, 1963.

Statement on Auditing Procedure No. 34, *Long-term Investments,* AICPA (Committee on Auditing Procedure), New York, 1965.

Statement on Auditing Procedure No. 35, *Letters for Underwriters,* AICPA (Committee on Auditing Procedure), New York, 1965.

Statement on Auditing Procedure No. 36, *Revision of "Extensions of Auditing Procedures" Relating to Inventories,* AICPA (Committee on Auditing Procedure), New York, 1966.

Statement on Auditing Procedures No. 37, Special Report: *Public Warehouses—Controls and Audit Procedures,* AICPA (Committee on Auditing Procedure), New York, 1966.

Statement on Auditing Procedure No. 38, *Unaudited Financial Statements,* AICPA (Committee on Auditing Procedure), New York, 1967.

Statement on Auditing Procedure No. 39, *Working Papers,* AICPA (Committee on Auditing Procedure), New York, 1967.

Statement on Auditing Procedure No. 40, *Reports Following a Pooling of Interest,* AICPA (Committee on Auditing Procedure), New York, 1968.

Statement on Auditing Procedure No. 41, *Subsequent Discovery of Facts Existing at the Date of the Auditor's Report,* AICPA (Committee on Auditing Procedure), New York, 1969.

Statement on Auditing Procedure No. 42, *Reporting When a Certified Public Accountant Is Not Independent,* AICPA (Committee on Auditing Procedure), New York, 1970.

Cashin, James A., and Garland C. Owens: *Auditing,* 2d ed., New York, The Ronald Press Company, 1963.

Sorensen, James E.: "Bayesian Analysis in Auditing," *The Accounting Review,* July, 1969.

Langenderfer, Harold O., and Jack C. Robertson: "A Theoretical Structure for Independent Audits of Management," *The Accounting Review,* October, 1969.

Fox, Kenneth L., and Philip E. Fess: "Suggested Refinements of Procedures in Determining Earnings per Share," *The Journal of Accountancy,* January, 1970.

Chapter **14**

Audit Working Papers

JAMES W. PATTILLO

Professor of Accounting, Louisiana State University at Baton Rouge

INTRODUCTION

Importance of Working Papers. Working papers are a vital part of *every* audit engagement. Whether the auditor is a public, private, or governmental auditor; whether the audit is financial, procedural, or management; whether the end products are financial statements, reports, or special analyses, working papers are important tools of the profession.

Working papers translate into practice the auditor's technical knowledge of accounting principles and procedures and their application to business information and transactions. They are the bridge between the auditor's knowledge and its application in producing financial statements, reports, and special analyses.

The audit examination normally is for the purpose of expressing an opinion, and is largely a matter of gathering sufficient evidence to form and support this opinion. The examination may be concerned with the reliability of the accounting data or it may be concerned with other areas within a business—operational procedures or administrative and financial controls. To whatever purpose the examination is directed, the evidence the auditor gathers must be systematically accumulated for later reference. The device which accomplishes this is the audit working paper, which records the evidence gathered to support the conclusions reached by the auditor.

This chapter provides the auditor with procedures and techniques to enable him to make the best use of working papers. Although business activities are complex and diverse, the activities to a large extent ultimately appear in some form of working papers. Although working papers vary to reflect diverse business activities, many of their features may be standardized, as discussed in detail in this chapter.

Scope and Approach of the Chapter. Working papers are viewed first as a tool whereby the purpose of the audit is accomplished. Wherever possible, common elements or features of working papers are identified and explained. In other cases special working papers must be devised to meet the special purpose of the investigation. Several of these are also identified.

Working papers are viewed second as support for work accomplished. Therefore, their control and maintenance during and after the audit are likewise investigated and techniques suggested.

WORKING-PAPER CONCEPTS

The purpose of the audit is to arrive at informed opinions about the object of the investigation. Arriving at such an opinion is accomplished through selecting, examining, and organizing sufficient evidence for drawing logical and verifiable conclusions. The evidence may be physical or documentary, may be the books and records of the company, may be computational or verbal, or may be the financial and administrative controls established in the firm. Working papers describe the selection and examination of this evidence, help organize it, and record and support the conclusions reached.

Definition of Working Papers. Working papers, therefore, consist of the file of evidence obtained during the engagement, the details of the methods and procedures the auditor followed, and the conclusions he has reached concerning the object of the audit. Working papers are the records kept concerning the conduct of the audit engagement. The functions served by working papers fall into two categories: operational purposes and legal purposes.

Operational Purposes. The different types of audits necessitate working papers which are equally varied. They must generally include all the financial information for statements needed in reports to the different audiences. The statements are ordinarily used with slight modifications for reporting to stockholders, management, creditors, taxing authorities, and regulatory commissions. Therefore the working papers must also include reconciliations of these separate statements with the firm's underlying records. Following are the principal operating purposes served by working papers regardless of the type of audit being performed or report rendered.

1. PROVIDE SUPPORT FOR THE AUDITOR'S OPINION: The third generally accepted auditing standard of fieldwork specifies that sufficient competent evidential matter is to be obtained in order to afford a reasonable basis for an opinion regarding the financial statements under consideration. The evidence which is obtained to support the public accountant's opinion is detailed in the working papers. Likewise, any recommendations, assertions, or even implications must be fully supported by the working papers. Occasionally a question will arise as to the validity of the opinion or recommendation. Then it will be necessary to be able to support the opinion or recommendation as being based on sufficient examination and made by a competent person. The working papers become the vehicle to establish those facts.

2. ASSIST IN PREPARING THE REPORT: In providing support for the report, the working papers also facilitate the preparation of the report. During the audit engagement, many analyses, schedules, and notations are prepared. These may be the basis for similar items in the final report. Their skillful preparation and their inclusion in the working papers will facilitate the report, especially if it is for a special investigation or for a "long-form" report to management or for credit purposes.

3. ASSIST IN PERFORMING THE AUDIT: Working papers serve the accountant as a tool to help him in his work. They aid him in organizing and coordinating all phases of the audit engagement. As the work progresses, the working papers provide a record of the work already performed and that yet to be done. Verification procedures and analyses are made and retained in the working papers, later to be compared with other phases of the audit.

4. FACILITATE MANPOWER ASSIGNMENT: Manpower assignment is also facilitated. Different working papers or different phases of the audit may be assigned to assistants at one time. The senior auditor may then supervise the work of these assistants as their work progresses. As these various phases are completed, the working papers are systematically filed in the audit folder. Frequently all the work pertaining to one phase cannot be completed at one time. By carefully filing the work done and relating this to the audit program, the senior auditor is made aware of the additional work that must be completed at a later date or as a part of another phase of the audit.

5. COORDINATE LOCATIONS: Working papers coordinate the work where different locations of the client are involved. Separate parts of the audit program, or different audit programs, may be followed for different locations. Different staff men or even different firms may be assigned to the various locations. When the audit work at a particular location is completed, the finished working papers are returned to a central location for assembly, review, and final-report preparation. The finished working papers provide the senior with an overall view of the audit and of the work prescribed and performed. He will then determine whether the audit is complete and whether it meets the firm's professional standards.

6. PROVIDE A PERMANENT RECORD: Occasionally it is important that the records developed during the audit be available and accessible. The client may desire certain information that either does not exist as a part of its ordinary records or that may have been altered, lost, or destroyed since the audit. The working papers provide a permanent record of the auditing procedures used and the company data examined. If questions arise concerning the adequacy or the accuracy of the audit examination, the auditor is able, by referring to this record, to establish what tests and other procedures were employed.

7. GUIDE FOR SUBSEQUENT EXAMINATIONS: Probably one of the first things the auditor does when beginning a subsequent examination is to review the prior working papers. The program that was followed and the follow-up or change-in-procedure notes for the next audit will be particularly important both to the repeat auditor and to the replacement auditor. Modifications can be made where necessary in the planned program in light of the audit results of the previous examination. Parts of the previous audit may be applicable to the current audit, so those parts may be either photocopied or transferred to the current audit file. Also, certain of the schedules' formats will be repeated, so they may be copied and prepared at a more convenient time before the audit begins. Sources of data noted on the prior working papers and explanatory comments about unusual accounting system features will guide new or inexperienced auditors on subsequent examinations.

8. LINK ORIGINAL TRANSACTIONS TO FINANCIAL STATEMENTS: Much of the auditor's work consists of tracing, normally on a sample basis, the trail that an item follows from original recording to its final destination in the financial statements. Additionally, the auditor verifies, by examining the underlying evidence, that the transaction actually did take place and was originally recorded in the appropriate manner. The working papers that auditors prepare will include summaries and analyses of these transactions and recordings and will therefore provide a link between the original statements and the financial reports. Frequently the auditor is able to have these working papers prepared by the client's personnel. To these he will add his own comments, apply certain verification procedures, record the results, and make corrections or suggestions. The working papers also provide the first place for formulating any entries that will be necessary to correct or complete the company records. The latter may be incomplete because of errors in mechanics or as a result of applying accounting procedures, or just because they lack the final adjustments. The correcting or adjusting entries are formulated from the analyses in the working papers, listed, keyed to the appropriate items in the working trial balance, and then suggested to the company personnel as being appropriate in the circumstances. In some cases the auditor prepares parent-subsidiary consolidating working papers, a copy of which becomes a part of the company's permanent formal accounting records.

9. LINK TO RECOMMENDED PROCEDURES: Frequently in internal auditing a study is made of existing procedures within a department or function. These are studied and alternative procedures devised to improve the system. The working papers provide the link between the existing procedures and the final procedures that are recommended.

10. FACILITATE DETAILED REVIEW OF INTERNAL CONTROL: The second generally accepted auditing standard of fieldwork states that there is to be a proper study and evaluation of the existing control as a basis for determining the extent of the audit tests to be applied before expressing an opinion on the fairness of the financial statements. This is accomplished usually by completing an internal control questionnaire on the operations of the business. This questionnaire and any other papers showing the results of the tests of procedures become a part of the working papers. Other comments about the internal control existing within the various functions of the company would appear in the separate working papers pertaining to that function. The questionnaire, the other tests of procedues, and the supplementary comments provide evidence that this standard of fieldwork was met by a proper evaluation of internal control.

11. PROVIDE A PERSONNEL EVALUATION BASIS: Working papers provide an important basis for the evaluation of the auditing ability of the professional auditing staff by their supervisors. Usually the senior in charge of the audit prepares a report on each of his assistants. Some of the factors considered in judging the effectiveness of the working papers include completeness, clarity, arrangement, adequate cross-referencing, and the absence of unnecessary information. An auditor's progress in the organization will depend in large part upon his ability to prepare outstanding working papers. They are evidence that the auditor was able to decide what information he should accumulate, was able to understand the circumstances existing, and was able to determine the extent of the tests to be made and the information to be included in his working papers. Personality, ability to work with client personnel, appearance, and other factors are also evaluated, but the working papers provide a tangible starting point for the overall evaluation.

12. ASSIST IN STAFF TRAINING: Much on-the-job training is done with working papers. The senior may sit down with the assistant before beginning an engagement and review the prior year's working papers in some detail. This is then related to the proposed audit program for the current examination. This procedure affords the assistant an overall view of the job and helps him to anticipate problems he may encounter. The assistant may or may not have had the opportunity of studying the working papers before this session with the senior. Another training procedure used by some firms is to provide in formal training sessions an "audit practice case." Here the assistants prepare the working papers for a typical audit under close supervision for each step in the process. Later, on an actual job, if the assistant is assigned to only one phase of the audit, he is able to relate this phase to the whole examination.

13. PROVIDE BASIS FOR FURTHER WORK: During an audit, certain situations or conditions may come to the attention of the auditor. These usually involve changes in the system in some way and, if significant enough, usually find their way into the audit "management letter." Frequently these suggestions are outside the normal audit scope and come within the purview of the management services department of the firm. Some of the information accumulated in the audit working papers may prove helpful or even essential in doing this further work for the client. Although the purpose of the audit is not to do management services work, frequently the notes and analyses in

the working papers provide the basis for further work should the client consider it desirable. In addition to further work in the management services area, the working papers may provide analyses and data that are valuable for doing tax work and preparing other reports such as those to regulatory agencies or other special interests at the direction of management.

Legal Purposes. The working papers also serve important legal purposes. At some future time a question may arise as to the competence of the audit work performed. Third parties may bring suit against the auditor; other third parties probably would decide the case. The working papers should clearly show the nature and extent of the work done, the audit procedures followed, and the conclusions reached. If differences of opinion existed with management personnel of the client, the disposition of these points should be clearly detailed. Also, the parties should be named and the sides of the issue clearly shown. The auditor's working papers may be the principal basis upon which incompetency charges are made by third parties. It is important, therefore, that the working papers do not contain any unanswered questions, inconsistent statements, or unwarranted or unexplained changes in conclusions. The finished working papers must be complete, clear, consistent, and conclusive.

Confidential Nature of Working Papers. The AICPA Code of Professional Ethics Rule 1.03 states that a member shall not violate the confidential relationship between himself and his client. The relationship must be confidential. The nature of the auditor's work requires that the knowledge he gains of his client's private business affairs be kept to himself. If the auditor is asked to testify in lawsuits concerning his client, he should never comply voluntarily against his client. Accountants do not automatically enjoy the same status as lawyers and physicians in the matter of privileged communications. Several states have enacted statutes granting this right. However, in any event, if through performing his professional duties he learns of wrongdoing on the part of his client, he may not report this without the client's permission.

Client data are confidential to third parties. Whether oral or written, the data should be protected closely by the auditor. Client data are also confidential to the client's employees. Frequently analyses are made or questions asked during the audit which should be restricted to the client's top management. The auditor should take care that this information is not divulged either directly or indirectly.

Since many disclosures made to the auditor in the course of his engagement enter into his working papers, these too should be considered confidential. Both while the audit engagement is in process and after it is completed, the working papers should be protected from unauthorized use and disclosure.

Ownership of Working Papers. The working papers developed during the course of an audit are the property of the auditor. This precedent was established in the 1927 Massachusetts Supreme Court case of *Ipswich Mills v. Dillon and Son* (157 N.E. 604). Several states have since incorporated this right of ownership into statutory law. The AICPA Committee on Professional Ethics has in its Opinion No. 3 ruled that where an AICPA member sells his practice, he should not give the purchaser access to relevant working papers, income tax returns, and correspondence without first having obtained permission from the client. Frequently governmental agencies, especially the Internal Revenue Service, request the opportunity to review the audit working papers. Although these agencies have no right to direct access to the working papers, such requests are usually readily granted either by the accountant through his power of attorney or after obtaining permission from the client. Any review of working papers by third parties should be supervised to prevent the possibility of alterations being made.

Even though the working papers are the auditor's property, he may relinquish the right of ownership. In a 1967 ruling, the United States District Court, Connecticut, denied an order to enforce a summons to produce a CPA's working papers which were in the possession of the taxpayer (*U.S.A. and Brogan v. Levy, Weinberg and Silverstein,* Civil No. 11655).

The working papers should be kept under strict control at all times—in the client's office while the audit work is in progress and in the accountant's office after the audit is completed. While in the client's office, the papers should be placed in a locked file or briefcase overnight or when the auditor is away from his work place. This close control is necessary to prevent unauthorized use. There may be information in the working papers that the client wishes to keep from his employees. Or, client employees might attempt to alter or destroy certain information in the working papers in order to conceal some misdeed or to mislead the auditor. Lastly, the working papers contain information about the conduct of the audit itself, the scope or methods to be used, or items selected for testing. This information should not be available to the client or his employees. Moreover, working papers should be safeguarded merely because the data they contain may be impossible or impractical to reproduce.

WORKING-PAPER TECHNIQUES

Verification and investigation procedures are the essence of an audit. Each working paper, therefore, should provide for summarization and analysis of data and also indicate the investigation steps performed. Several common rules govern all working-paper preparation.

General Format. Practice differs, but a general standardized format should be established that will be followed for each working paper that is prepared.

Items Included in the Heading. Either centered at the top or over to the left margin of the working paper is the heading. This serves a number of purposes. It states the *company name, division* or *department,* and *location.* Frequently the company rubber stamp showing name and address is used by the auditor to save time. This may be done any time during the audit, but is more efficiently done all at one time, usually at the start of the fieldwork. Under the company identification is stated the *activity,* or the *account number* or *name.* A description or *subject matter* of the working paper is established next, either on the same line or on the line following the account number. Last, the heading should include either the *date* of the examination or the *period* covered by the examination.

Items Relating to Preparer. Either in the top right-hand corner or the lower left-hand corner of the working paper are usually placed the name or initials of the *preparer* and the date of preparation. Frequently space is provided here also for the *reviewer's* initials and the review date. If more than one staff man is involved with preparing a given working paper, each person should place his name or initials and the date adjacent to the symbol and an explanation of the symbol shown elsewhere on the working paper. In this way the individual work of each preparer can be evaluated. The symbols used, or "tick marks," are explained and illustrated in a later section. If the working paper was initially prepared by the client, department personnel, or outside parties, the auditor should initial and date this after reviewing and verifying the data. "PBC" ("prepared by client") is placed on the working paper, followed by the initials of the staff accountant who verified the data.

Items Relating to Preparation. On the lower left or lower right side of the working paper are stated items relating to its preparation. The *source* or records from which the information is drawn should be stated, identifying the ledger, account, invoice, or other documents and the place where these are found. This is especially important if the source has a bearing upon the reliability of the data (e.g., "Payroll change notices are obtained directly from Personnel Department files, not from the Payroll Department"). The function or *person* responsible for maintenance of and control over these records should also be named. This addition facilitates subsequent examinations. Since the evaluation of internal controls is a main part of many audits, the general *procedures underlying the accumulation of the information*, or other appropriate explanation of the significance of the source document, should be outlined on the working paper. A description of the *evidence examined* or persons interviewed is given, both to provide an "audit trail" and to help guide subsequent examinations. A brief outline of the verification or *testing procedures* used should follow, as well as an indication of the *extent of verification* employed. The subject matter of the working paper is placed in the heading, but frequently it is desirable to present along with other preparation details a fuller explanation of the objective or *purpose* of the working paper. Last usually is a legend of the auditor's tick marks which relates the items in the working paper to certain explanations or cross-references them to other figures elsewhere in the working papers.

If continuation sheets of a working paper are needed, they are frequently numbered sequentially, showing the total number of pages in the series ("1 of 3," "2 of 3," "3 of 3"). Some firms do not require that the continuation sheets be initialed, dated, or headed completely as described above. However, it is good practice to do these things for ready reference and so that no misunderstanding arises later should the sheets become separated.

WORKING-PAPER STANDARDS

In addition to the items in the general format described above, several other essentials of good working papers may be identified.

Completeness and Accuracy. Maximum usefulness should be the criterion for decisions in preparing working papers. The auditor's professional skill is reflected in the working papers he prepares. His working papers should be complete but free of unessential data and should be carefully organized for easy reference. Working papers are complete if they reflect several items: the composition of all significant data in the records or otherwise available and relevant; the testing and verification methods used; the extent to which these methods were applied; and any other evidence necessary for preparing an audit report or fulfilling the other audit objectives. Complete working papers should also reflect a distinction between factual statements and matters of judgment. A delineation is necessary when the auditor later prepares his report. He should fully explain procedures and analyses that are prepared, and should give the reasons for following certain auditing procedures while omitting others. He should record in his working papers his opinions about the quality of the data he has examined, the adequacy of internal controls, and, where desirable, the competency of persons in charge of the functions under his review.

His working papers must be accurate and technically correct. Crossfootings and additions of columns should be proved and all amounts tied in with other working papers where appropriate. The entire amount (even pennies) must tie in; if the difference is small or is of a nature not considered important, this should be noted on the working paper. Accuracy also covers grammar. Descriptions and other narratives should be reviewed to be sure that they are grammatically correct and have no misspellings of words or names, especially company names, officers, employees, etc.

Clarity and Understandability. The scope of the examination must be clearly defined and the facts that have been uncovered and the conclusions reached as a result must be clearly indicated. The form and content of each working paper should be constructed so that a person technically competent but unfamiliar with the work will understand it readily. The audit trail and significant stopping points should be clear to the reader. The arrangement of the various schedules and subschedules should be such as to indicate their importance and purpose. Totals should be easily understood and, where applicable, easily traceable to other working papers. The language of comments and other narratives should be accurate yet free of jargon or unduly complex grammatical construction. Reference symbols have already been commented upon; they add to the order, clarity, and understandability of the working papers. Much of the comment relating to completeness also applies to clarity; incomplete papers usually are also unclear.

Legibility and Neatness. The general appearance of the working papers should be neat. The two main elements contributing to neatness are a legible handwriting and evidence of orderly preparation. Legibility and neatness promote economy in the engagement and efficiency in its review. Although neatness is not all-important, it is a desirable quality. Many firms require that names of persons be printed out and that no abbreviations be used, so that no misunderstandings occur. Using a soft-lead pencil is preferable to writing with a pen, and colors should be used sparingly. "Pretty" working papers should be avoided. That is, avoid colorful underlining, excessively complex symbols, too perfect underlining, dollar signs, and other techniques which make the working papers a work of art but do not enhance their usefulness. Only one side of the paper should be used, since the papers are bound at the top or left side and writing on the back side of the paper may be overlooked or be inconvenient for reference. If only a small space is needed to complete the information, the length of the paper may be extended by pasting a part of another sheet to the bottom, later to be folded up to maintain the standard length for binding purposes. Full sheets are preferable, however, since this attached part could easily become separated with additional use.

Relevance and Detail. All items included in the final working papers should have a purpose related to the assignment. This purpose should be clear to the auditor and any reviewers or others who may have occasion to examine the papers. The more experienced the auditor, the greater is his ability to produce working papers containing essential but not superfluous information. No general rule may be stated; the amount of data needed may vary from a detailed listing of items or even photocopies of the original documents to an auditor's initials beside the program item or a notation indicating that certain supporting documents have been examined. Unnecessary analyses and narrative should not be prepared; if they exist but the detail was unneeded or the line of investigation pursued was found to be irrelevant, the working papers should not be retained. Including them only detracts from the overall quality and usefulness of the working papers. The working papers should be complete—they should contain that which is required, but no more.

If the auditor concludes that a certain analysis is required, some thought should be given to how to arrange the data most conveniently and economically. A summary is frequently preferable to a list of details; an analysis of several related accounts in one schedule is preferable to duplicated schedules. Preparing memorandums and narrative frequently can be overdone. Some preparation is essential, but the unnecessary and redundant should be avoided. Comments not serving any useful purpose should not be written at all.

Copies and excerpts from agreements and other records included in the permanent file should not be duplicated in the current file. Detail material such as adding-machine tapes, "tab" runs, inventory lists, and other miscellaneous papers should be retained in the working papers only as long as they serve their purpose. If they have a permanent value supplementary to the working papers, they should be filed separately, if bulky. Papers that have been superseded, including report rough drafts, should be discarded unless they have value separate from the new copy.

Attention to Design and Layout. Audit working papers must be designed and prepared so as to ensure that supervisors may efficiently and effectively review the work done. The design of the individual schedules and the other information included in the working papers must be directed to the purposes served by the audit, as stated above. No general invariable rules of layout and design may be set out, except that these should meet the standards outlined in this section. The schedules and analyses should be carefully planned before and during the course of the audit.

Other Preparation Standards. Each working paper should be self-explanatory. No questions, open points, incomplete notes, or other indications of unfinished work should remain on the working paper. Items on one working paper may tie into those on another working paper; both should be carefully *cross-referenced* and indexed. Special methods for indexing are explained later in this chapter. In any event, a separate sheet should be started for each topic, and the sheet (with continuation sheets if necessary) should be descriptively headed. After the separate phases of the audit program are completed, the working papers should be *filed systematically.* Preferably the filing during the audit should be in a binder in the order in which the papers will appear in the finished working-paper file.

A separate working-paper "*agenda sheet,*" "*audit notes,*" or "to do list" of points to be investigated later should be made as the audit develops. This will contain notes and reminders for points that cannot be settled as they arise. These notes may concern verifications, conversations with officers, unsettled items, and other matters. The auditor and reviewer go over this list before the audit is completed to be sure all items were satisfactorily settled. The items may or may not be cross-referenced to the corresponding audit program step and the appropriate working paper.

The auditor should also develop during the course of the audit a list of points to be covered in the "*management letter.*" These could be determined from the finished working papers and audit report, but it is more desirable to informally list these items as they develop so that they are sure to be covered in at least one of these places. This list of points calls attention to accounting (and sometimes administrative) matters deserving management's consideration. They may deal with internal control points, especially to point out weaknesses in the existing system and possibly to suggest improvements. The working papers should be clear in the steps taken to offset any weaknesses noted, and care must be taken that the comments do not contradict the opinion finally issued.

A list of the *supervisor's review points* should also be a part of the working papers. This list is prepared upon review of the auditor's work and relates to questions arising in the supervisor's mind about certain aspects of the working papers. There may be unanswered questions, unclear or illogical conclusions, unfinished schedules, imbalance or no tie-in of figures or any number of other items. The list serves the purpose of bringing these to the auditor's attention, for if the supervisor has these questions it is likely that other persons reviewing the working papers also would raise them. Usually the left half of the paper is used to list the reviewer's questions; the right side is left blank for the auditor's answer or explanation. When all questions are resolved to the reviewer's satisfaction, the report preparation can proceed.

Having to rewrite working papers should be considered as indicating inadequate planning and sloppy work. It is a mere waste of time to record audit data on a type of paper or in a form which necessitates rewriting. The auditor should *write it correctly the first time*, so that the record becomes a part of the finished working papers. The more experienced and foresighted the auditor, the easier this is.

CLASSIFICATION AND CONTENT

Depending upon the type of audit, the preferences of the auditor, and the policies of his employer, working papers differ widely in content and form. A considerable number of techniques and procedures are applied to a variety of different situations. No standard form or group of forms can be devised to cover all situations. The auditor must have the ability to devise new or modified forms to meet the situations as they arise. Typical working papers evolve for certain types of audits, and these are commented upon in this chapter. They are illustrated in more detail in other chapters of this handbook.

Standardizing the form of working papers does not imply rigidity in applying auditing or accounting procedures. Rather, this is a method of uniformly expressing the results of applying these procedures to various enterprises and similar situations. The greatest value in using standardized working papers to the maximum extent is that arising from the ability of several people to work on one project either concurrently or consecutively. For large firms this is generally important for continuity, and is important as well for audits involving several offices of the same firm. In this case the initiating office receives the working papers prepared at various locations by different personnel. It is imperative that the form be standardized and the content varied to meet the situation. It is desirable that any audit group develop standard working-paper forms to take care of similar situations and also to provide guidelines to working-paper form for nonrecurring situations.

Approach. The form the working papers finally take varies according to the approach taken to the audit engagement. This in turn reflects the approach of the auditor, which was explored in an earlier section.

Report captions. Report topics and headings frequently form the basis for the arrangement of materials in the working-paper file and the direction of the audit itself. This relates mostly to audits of an investigative or systems-inspection nature. The report would be planned in skeleton form before the audit begins, and this plan forms the basis for the audit procedures employed and the extent of the examination.

Working trial balance. Working papers may also be built around the trial balance. This is the case for almost all financial statement audits. The working trial balance serves the auditor as the main control device, and the program and the working-paper file reflect this. The working papers will present verification and support for each item appearing on the trial balance. Separate schedules are prepared for the individual items; combined schedules are prepared for certain analyses involving related accounts, such as Prepaid Insurance and Insurance Expense. These are appropriately cross-referenced to the trial balance. The finished working-paper current file is usually presented in the order of the trial balance items.

Procedural flow charts. Flow charts are adaptable as programs for both financial statement and procedure audits. In this approach detailed audit procedures are linked to internal and administrative control evaluation. The individual audit steps either confirm the systems information on which the auditor's evaluation of control was based or explore the possibility of errors permitted by specific weaknesses. Flow-charting technique is consistent with generally accepted auditing standards; it flows from the need for a proper study and evaluation of internal control. The focus, therefore, is upon the system which produces the account balances appearing in the trial balance, rather than upon the end product itself as the starting point.

Planning the Working Papers. Developing working papers which fulfill their purpose requires careful planning before and during the audit. The form and content of the working papers can be improved if sufficient planning is done by the auditor in charge of the audit. Substantial time savings also ultimately result from well-planned working papers.

Before the audit. The working papers reflect the basic patterns of investigation, evidence gathering, verification, and procedures. In perfecting these patterns, proficiency in working-paper preparation will develop with practice. The working papers should be planned according to the audit program and the report to be prepared. The information gathered should flow into the report form with a minimum of reclassification, recomputation, and rewriting. The lead schedule should be a summary picture, followed by details on supporting schedules.

The auditor should familiarize himself with the preliminary survey memorandum or last year's internal control questionnaire before planning the working papers, and should consider the prior examination's working papers, if this is a subsequent audit. He would decide if the format and content should be changed or if they should remain the same. Usually he would refer to suggestions developed at the time of the prior examination, and would also consider changed conditions in making his final decision. If the schedule remains unchanged from the previous engagement, it may be practical merely to carry the same schedule forward instead of preparing a new one. He would initial and date the schedule and include it in the current file; the removal from the prior file should be noted therein.

First-time or repeat audits. If the audit has been performed in previous years, some accountants at times follow the unfortunate practice of merely taking the prior working papers and in effect only changing the numbers. The prior working papers should be examined in order to determine coverage and particular difficulties encountered. But from this point on, the current examination should be independent of prior form and content. The auditor should decide what problems exist at this examination and what working papers will help him accumulate the evidence he needs to fulfill his current audit objectives.

First-time audits require substantially more planning than do repeat audits. Where the nature, history, organization, accounting control, and other features of the company have been set out as a result of previous examinations, these merely need to be updated. First-time audits require that these data, policies, and practices be initially determined and understood, and that they be incorporated into the working papers as the audit is planned and progresses. Much of the initial data accumulated as a result of this "spadework" will become the basis of a permanent file on this client. The contents of this file is explained in a later section of this chapter. During an initial examination, the auditor may be required to make extensive notes in the working papers explaining the extent of the work done. Notes in subsequent examinations should be limited to explaining the reasons for any important changes in audit procedures and the conditions necessitating the change.

Preparation by the client. Since many schedules and analyses can be prepared satisfactorily by the client, extensive thought should be given to this phase of working-paper planning. These schedules may be prepared by the company personnel as part of their regular duties or by special arrangement for purposes of the audit. The form and content of these analyses must be carefully spelled out so that they will be usable when completed. Care must be taken to ensure that the persons doing the work understand what is being required of them. A timetable should also be established so that the completed schedules will be available when the auditor needs them. These working papers should be tested by the auditor in a manner appropriate to the circumstances, and the nature and extent of the verification noted on the schedules.

Planning the working papers during the audit encompasses many of the concepts mentioned above. The main consideration is that the schedules and analyses be prepared in such a way that they will not have to be redone yet provide for a possible need for expansion of the working paper. New information may be discovered, or additional notes may be desired directly on the working paper, any time during the audit. Enough blank spaces should be provided for these eventualities. The working papers should be planned both for horizontal expansion without the need for pasting and for vertical expansion by adding continuation sheets to the schedule. The latter is desirable also from the viewpoint of readability. It is easier to read down than across.

Types of Working Papers. Since a working paper is any record that the auditor accumulates in the investigation which supports his opinion or report, it is apparent that working papers will vary widely in form and composition. However, most working papers fall into one or more common categories. These are modified in light of the nature of the engagement and of data needs. In addition to classifying types of working papers by their form and content, they may also be classified as permanent and current. This classification will be illustrated in a later section of this chapter.

List of accounts or items. Usually this listing of accounts or items is a summarizing device, although it may also be merely a restatement of certain information given elsewhere in its original form. An aging of receivables is an example; the auditor may obtain either a list of all open accounts or only category totals in his test of reasonableness of the bad debts provision. Similarly, inventory listings may be obtained and included in the working papers, or the auditor may summarize the inventory data and show in his working papers only these totals and the verification tests applied to the inventory items. Cash and property additions are other areas employing this form.

The trial balance is the best-known working paper consisting of a list of accounts and their balances. The techniques for its preparation are detailed in a later section.

Analytical working papers. In general, this type of working paper shows an analysis of a particular account or a particular item. It shows the composition and character of the item in sufficient detail so that the auditor may trace each component back to the basic document or other evidential matter. The analysis may be in vertical form or horizontal form. The vertical form is usually the easiest to work with and provides for continuation sheets without very much recopying of basic data being needed. However, the horizontal form is preferable when it is desirable to analyze two or more accounts simultaneously. Notes Receivable, Prepaid Insurance, Investments, and Notes Payable, together with their related nominal accounts, are examples of accounts lending themselves to horizontal analysis. The vertical form is similar to the account itself. The beginning balance is normally the opening figure, which is the basis for additions and subtractions of the transactions affecting the account and for adjustments and reclassifications to arrive at an ending balance. This is sometimes described as a "flow" schedule, because it reveals the movement in the account. This is opposed to the "position" schedule, which merely analyzes the composition of the ending balance, for example, detailing the component parts of insurance premiums applicable to future periods which comprise the year-end balance of Prepaid Insurance.

The majority of financial audit working papers are of this variety. Every material account will be analyzed and its components verified either completely or on a test basis.

Reconciliation working papers. Frequently the auditor must correlate the various kinds and sources of information available to him. This reconciliation of items is necessary to verify the record made. Differences are caused by the keeping of parts of the record in two or more places and by having the record kept by various individuals, as well as by lags in the record keeping. An analysis must be made of each balance, and likewise an analysis made of its components. Items are disclosed which are common to both balances and those which are included in one but not in the other; these are the reconciling items. Reconciling working papers should show that the unmatched items have been thoroughly explained and supported. Areas which frequently use this type of working papers include the cash accounts, confirmation of receivables by correspondence with the customer, and confirming perpetual inventory records by physically counting the item.

Computational working papers. These normally support the other types of working papers mentioned above and show the auditor's independent computation to verify computations inherent in certain types of accounts. The auditor compares his results with the amounts shown in the client's records. Differences are investigated further and explained. Computational verification is normal for bonuses, pensions, royalties, interest, taxes, and other payments based on estimated or agreed-upon terms.

Narrative and memorandum working papers. These are written working papers. They show that the auditor has adequately planned his examination and has followed through in his support work. Where a detailed audit program has been prepared, there is no need to cover all points in the narrative or memorandum working papers. Initialing that step in the program indicates the extent of the work done.

Procedural memorandums are usually prepared for each major area covered by the audit program. They are factual and answer the questions: What was done? What was found? and, What was done about what was found? Any exceptions found in the accounting procedures and policies, as well as weaknesses in internal control and the action taken thereon, should be noted. The working paper should be positive; if no exceptions are noted, this is disclosed, and conclusions should be worded positively. If the audit program does not describe the procedures to be followed, those that were applied should be detailed in the memorandum working paper.

The review process produces a number of other memorandum working papers and they are included in the file. The senior's memorandum ties together in summary form the numerical schedules and the narrative working papers. In it he points out problem areas and conclusions reached, his opinion on the completeness of the examination, and the propriety and consistency of the accounting principles followed. He states any exceptions necessary in the audit report, and the reasons for them. Special technical memorandums may also be prepared by various reviewers on any number of topics, ranging from special accounting or reporting problems, special tax situations, and internal control problems, to management services possibilities.

Abstract working papers. Not all the schedules the auditor prepares are numerical. Frequently purely expository material is gathered and is necessary to help support the audit report. Excerpts of contracts, minutes, and other records have accounting significance. Abstracts are usually prepared from these documents. The abstract should be brief unless the exact meaning is necessary, in which case a full copy is desirable. Frequently such documents must be the basis for a financial statement footnote; abstracts are likely to be incomplete for this purpose. Board minutes and abstracts of other very confidential company material may be placed in a special permanent file or binder for safekeeping. The auditor should be alert to indicated violations of the provisions of the contracts examined or of board resolutions. In nonfinancial audits, the majority of the working papers will consist of narrative explanations of procedures and other explanations of the system's operation.

Working Papers for Independent Audits. In this and the next section there are listed the contents of typical working papers relating to the independent audit engagement. Since these are explained and illustrated more fully in other chapters, only their relationship to the overall audit engagement and certain preparation techniques will be presented here.

Working trial balance. This is the key working paper for financial audits; it controls and summarizes all the supporting papers. It lists all the accounts and their balances as they appear in the general ledger and provides columns for audit adjustments and reclassifications and for the final adjusted amounts appearing in the financial statements. Variations on this minimum form exist. This last column may be expanded to provide debit and credit columns for balance sheet items and income statement items. Frequently columns are also provided for grouping related figures in order to report the total on the final published statements, and for narrative comments relative to specific items. Some accountants list the prior year's adjusted trial balance for reasonableness comparisons.

The column headings for the expanded working trial balance would be:

Figure 1 WORKING TRIAL BALANCE

Acct. No.	Acct. Title	Working Paper Reference	Prior Year Adjusted T.B.		Adjustments		Adjusted Book Balances		Current year				Groupings	Comments
									Income Statement		Balance Sheet			
			Dr.	Cr.	Dr.	Cr.	Dr.	Cr.	Dr.	Cr.	Dr.	Cr.		

In listing the accounts, a separate worksheet page may be used for the assets, liabilities, equity, revenue, expense, and totals. (If this is done, separate debit and credit columns are unnecessary.) In smaller audits, the accounts may be listed all on one or two pages. If the accounts are classified in report order, it is important that the groupings be similar to those used for the prior year so that meaningful comparisons are possible.

Grouping sheets. Related accounts may be combined into a single amount and listed in total on the working trial balance. If the accounts are quite detailed, even a summary grouping sheet may be necessary, showing the combination of several sections each of which has its own grouping sheet. The summary total is then carried to the trial balance. If this grouping procedure is followed, the "Groupings" column illustrated above would be unnecessary. Using grouping sheets facilitates the work and supervision of assistants and the working-paper review by other firm personnel.

Grouping sheets are also referred to as "lead schedules," "leading schedules," "top schedules," and "summary schedules." An underlying or supporting schedule will ordinarily be prepared for each item listed on the grouping sheet. If no grouping sheets are prepared, the underlying schedules support the individual items appearing in the working trial balance. If grouping sheets are prepared, they are the connecting link between the various related account analyses and the single summary-line item in the trial balance.

The supporting schedules show the work done in the verification and analysis of the account or item, the audit or investigation methods employed, the questions raised and answers thereto, and the conclusions reached and the reasons for those conclusions.

Adjusting and reclassification entries. As the audit progresses, the auditor determines whether adjustments or reclassifications are needed. The supporting schedules and analyses will show the necessary entry; it will then be carried to a listing of adjusting entries and reclassification entries. Separate sheets are preferable for this because reclassification entries do not require entry into the client's books. Using some number or letter cross-referencing system, the adjusting and reclassification entries are carried to the appropriate columns in the working trial balance. Exact account titles and numbers should be used to minimize errors, and explanations for all entries should be complete and understandable.

The adjusting entry or reclassification entry ordinarily should not be made if the item is immaterial, and should be made only after review by the supervisor and concurrence by the client. The working papers should show whether the journal entries have been booked. Frequently the client will also record the reclassification entries and reverse them at the beginning of the following year.

Other working papers. Other documents and evidential matter accumulated by the auditor, such as questionnaires, confirmations, time records, and programs, are noted in a later section of this chapter and illustrated in detail in other chapters.

Working Papers for Special Matters. Several situations arise that require some special recognition in the audit working papers. The more common of these are outlined here; other chapters contain more detailed discussion and illustrations.

Legal matters. In the event that the auditor's work and report are challenged. the working papers are likely to come under close scrutiny. They will be studied in detail by the opponents for indications supporting a charge of incompetence or negligence. All the working papers, correspondence, memorandums, and similar items would have to be introduced in support of the auditor's conclusions.

The auditor must avoid inconclusiveness and incompleteness in the working papers. Any indication that the auditor raised a question but did not follow through to a conclusion or that the point questioned was not otherwise adequately explained will be suspect. If tentative conclusions are made, based on incomplete information, they should be worded carefully so as to preclude any inference of finality. Any omission of audit procedures called for in the program should be explained carefully and fully. Any working papers prepared which serve no purpose in the record of work done should not be retained.

Resolved questions raised by various reviewers may or may not be retained, depending upon the circumstances. Normally such memorandums should be retained only if they contain a description of work performed or an explanation of the basis for a conclusion reached. Memorandums covering conferences with client employees should be preserved if they set forth the basis for certain conclusions or otherwise cover important matters concerning the engagement. Suggested modifications of audit procedures in future audits should be written on a separate paper and placed in a special folder for future attention. The suggestions should include the note that the current procedures applied were adequate, but that modifications are being suggested in the interest of increased efficiency or because of changing conditions.

The adequacy of audit work is measured in terms of both quality and quantity, in terms of both auditing procedures applied and the extent of testing done. The working papers must furnish a record which will support the conclusions expressed in the report, the indicated scope of work performed, and the examination standards applied.

Consolidated statements. The working papers should include consolidated statements where the accounts of several divisions of a company or of several separate but related companies are being combined. There are several items that should be specifically considered and covered.

The basis of consolidation should be determined and spelled out, for usually this information is disclosed in a footnote to the financial statements. The working papers should show data with respect to ownership percentage and/or control and a determination of any difference between the parent's investment account for consolidated subsidiaries and its equity in the subsidiaries' net assets. Unconsolidated and foreign subsidiaries need special consideration, and these should be detailed.

The working papers should give explanations of all interunit eliminations and consolidating adjustments. In connection with interunit transactions, analyses should cover a reconciliation of interunit accounts; the procedures covering sales and services and other controlled transactions; the interunit profit in inventories, properties, and other assets; and the extent of interunit stock and debt holdings. Minority interests in the net assets and net income of each subsidiary should be determined and scheduled.

If the auditor is to report on the financial statements of the individual subsidiary companies included in the consolidated financial statements, he must be sure that the scope of the audit of the particular subsidiary is extended to include all normal audit procedures. Frequently normal audit procedures are not applied because of the immateriality of the individual subsidiary relative to the whole entity, or because of the policy of examining the subsidiaries on a rotating basis. If separate statements of the subsidiary are prepared, evidence should be presented that they are complete in all respects.

The form of the consolidating statements depends upon the number of intercompany units involved and the complexity of their transactions. The auditor may obtain copies of the client's papers and use them or he may devise his own form suited to the circumstances.

SEC statements. Audited financial statements filed with the SEC are based upon examinations following normal auditing procedures. Certain supplementary notes and schedules must also be filed with the statements. It is important that these special requirements be known and developed during the course of the audit and included in the working papers. SEC Regulation S-X governs the certification, form, and content of financial statements filed with the Commission.

Statistical sampling. The working papers should show a clear record of the calculations made and references to tables used in determining the sample size and the values assigned to the factors of precision and confidence. For the latter, a statement should set out why these particular values were chosen; for the former, a statement should describe the method used in selecting the items for the sample. Identifying the exact random-number tables involved is desirable. It is usually easier to list the numbers used and to work from this list rather than directly from the table when selecting the sample items. Alongside the number may be shown the identifying information and other details about the items selected. The random numbers may be retained in the order of selection or they may be serially rearranged by using a matrix composed of column headings representing a range of numbers, for example, 100s, and a left-hand margin calibrated at another range, for example, 1,000 per line. The number 4,521 would then be written in the square formed by the intersection of the 4,000 line and the 500 column. After all numbers have been so placed, they may be easily listed serially.

EDP systems and records. The auditor should remember that, even in electronic systems, great importance is placed upon the evidence contained in the original entries. The accuracy of this recording is paramount from both the company's and the auditor's viewpoint. The dependable audit trail, backed by references and calculations, has been eliminated for the most part by EDP systems. Even though hard-copy reports are produced, only a duplicate run can ensure that accuracy was maintained. Since this is an impractical audit tool, other means must be employed to prove the accuracy and propriety of the system. The working papers should show the means supporting the review of the system. Examining the controls over the EDP system becomes the primary emphasis in the auditing situation. The working papers should show, as a minimum:

1. A record of the contacts made with the EDP and accounting personnel and of who is responsible for the job
2. Organization charts covering the systems, programming, operations, control, and internal auditing departments
3. The type of equipment used by the client and the applications to which it is put
4. Proper documentation of system and programming procedures by company personnel for all phases of data processing applications
5. Evidence of established controls over operations, including input and output controls, tabulating and computer operations, and personnel
6. A memorandum on the relationship of the internal auditors to data processing, covering their training and background, authority to determine control features of new or existing applications, and the audit functions and procedures they perform

TYPES OF FILES

In this section are listed the types of audit files usually associated with the various types of auditors, and the contents of those files. Depending upon the circumstances, other types of files may exist, and personal preference may dictate including other things than those which are listed below, or excluding some items, or rearranging them in a different order.

The Independent Auditor. The independent auditor's files relate to the audit engagement and may be expanded or contracted depending upon the size of the job.

Client master information file. Sometimes called the "client folder," this file shows general information on the client, mainly for local and national office coordination. Included are such items as client's name, address, and account number; parent company's name, address, account number, and percent of ownership; type of ownership; stock exchange; approximate gross sales; fiscal year-end date; Standard Industrial Classification code numbers; audit partner assigned to the client; and types of services rendered. This information may be on a separate sheet or may be printed on the front of the folder itself. Included in the folder also would be found information on client contracts, data on fees and billing, copies of financial statements, information on subjects that the client is likely to call about, and any other current data pertinent to the client's or auditor's interest.

A separate preaudit folder may also be maintained during the year to accumulate the correspondence, schedules, and other information directly related to the upcoming audit. Later all of this will be placed in the current audit working-paper file.

The prior audit's final reports and/or recommendations, with follow-up notes, may be placed in that year's file, in the preaudit folder, or in the master information file, according to the policy of the firm. The preaudit folder appears to be the most logical and convenient place for them.

Correspondence file. General correspondence with a client is usually kept in a separate file arranged by client, alphabetically, and chronologically. If the correspondence is pertinent to the upcoming audit, a copy is made for the audit file.

Tax file. This may be maintained in the audit file or in a separate file folder. The latter is preferable, and should be maintained by the tax department. Usually the auditor prepares the tax return and this is then reviewed by the tax department. All documents relating to the preparation and filing of the tax return should go into the tax file. The items that should be shown in this file include:

1. Pencil copy of tax return and copy of filed tax return
2. Record of company payments
3. Record and disposition of revenue agent reports
4. Special working papers relating to tax determinations, and reconciliations of book and tax figures
5. Correspondence between the firm, the client, and taxing authorities
6. Assessments, refund claims, and receipt records
7. Tax-filing policies and procedures

Permanent audit file. The permanent or carry-forward file includes those working papers that have current importance year after year. The information included has been accumulated in current and past audits and will be required in future audits. The permanent file permits a quick view of the financial history and operating facts of the business. It briefly summarizes recurring items that must be reviewed, thus avoiding the necessity of rereading lengthy client documents year after year. It also reduces the work involved in auditing accounts that have few changes; current items can be added to a continuing schedule.

The auditor takes the previous year's working-paper file and the permanent audit file to the engagement. Additions of new items and deletions of unessential items are made as the engagement progresses. Deleted items are either destroyed or put into a dead file.

The contents of the permanent file vary among firms, but generally included would be the following items.

1. Client's name and address. A hard cardboard binder is desirable for the permanent file. On the front of this cover are placed the name, address, and telephone number of the client and the name of the file. The name of the client should be exactly as it appears in the charter or articles of copartnership, or should be the business name if the client is a sole proprietorship.

2. Table of contents. Either on or inside the cover or on the first page of the file should be a table of contents. This may be preprinted with the items in this list and underlined or checked for the items included in the file. Dividers or the indexing system used by the firm keep the file contents in the order of the table of contents.

3. File contributors and reviewers. A separate page should be included in the permanent file for the names of persons contributing to or reviewing the file, the dates of their actions, and the action taken. The latter should be detailed and be cross-referenced by index number to the place of the change. A preprinted table of contents with vertical columns for the successive years may be most useful here for initialing items acted upon, this being cross-referenced to a yearly list of detailed changes.

4. Copies or excerpts of articles of incorporation and bylaws.

5. Meetings abstracts. Copies or abstracts pertaining to accounting matters of directors' and stockholders' meetings should be included.

6. Organization and authority structure. This section should include details about the organization and authority structure, usually in chart form,

supplemented by a memorandum on informal relationships existing. This is accompanied by lists of persons authorized to sign checks, contracts, leases, and other major documents. Signatures involved in other operations would normally be listed in the internal control questionnaire.

7. Financial and accounting matters. Under this section would be a chart of accounts of the client, procedure manuals covering all pertinent phases of operations, and a statement of the client's accounting principles and policies.

8. Special financing arrangements and other significant contracts. The client may have many of these outstanding, all of which will bear upon the financial statements. They include: outstanding leases; patents in force, and a statement of patents policy; pension, option, profit-sharing, and bonus plans and other labor-related contracts or policies; guarantee agreements; warranty agreements; indentures or other loan agreements; capital stock provisions or a sample stock certificate; royalty agreements; management contracts; agreements with stock exchanges; registration statements and other similar corporate documents; and other long-term contracts of any kind. Pertinent sections of these should be briefed or copied for inclusion in the permanent file.

9. Details of operations. Many items could be included under each of the following broad categories. Plant facilities: location and space devoted to plant, warehouse, and office; nature, age, and condition of buildings and machinery; appraisals; capital expenditures proposed or in process. Products: description of main and by-products; volumes; plants producing which products; service operations; demand for products. Production: nature of the processing operations; plant and storage capacities; engineering and research and development programs; production schedules and planning. Purchasing: volume; major items purchased and the main and secondary suppliers; receiving and inspection operations. Sales: methods of distribution; details on customers; sales by geographical areas and sales force; industry and competition comparisons; compensation methods; promotion and advertising; pricing methods and policies.

10. Auditors' analyses of "permanent" accounts and carry-forward schedules. Generally these schedules analyze changes in certain accounts that have little activity throughout the years. They include land, plant, and equipment and the related accumulated depreciation, long-term investments, intangibles, funded debt and related amortizations, capital stock and other capital items, long-term deferred charges and credits, sales by product per year, cost of sales by product per year, dividend declarations and payments, and any other similar account.

11. Other pertinent information. Personal preference governs whether other information is included in the permanent file. Copies of previous audit reports and letters or recommendations sent to the client are examples.

Current audit file. This file collects all the papers developed during the current audit. At the end of the audit the auditor should remove from the current file any items of continuing interest and place them in the permanent file.

The contents of the current file should be indexed, either on the front of the binder or on the first page. Indexing methods are described in a following section. Preprinted folders listing the items below may be used and the included items checked or underlined. The contents will vary according to the type of business being audited, but generally will include the following items. These have been explained and illustrated in other chapters, so here they are merely listed.

1. Engagement memorandums and correspondence, and instructions relating to the audit of other locations; an engagement control sheet may be devised to cover points to be completed prior to the report release and prior to filing the working papers; the completed control sheet, properly initialed and dated, would be included here
2. Internal control questionnaire
3. Audit program
4. Correspondence with debtors, customers, etc., and confirmations; letters of representation and other client "certificates"
5. Copies or excerpts of minutes of board of directors' and stockholders' meetings, new leases, new contracts, charter changes, etc.; these normally will be transferred to the permanent file at the conclusion of the audit
6. Agenda sheets
7. Audit report—both the manuscript copy and final copy
8. Management letter or letter of recommendations manuscript and final copies
9. Financial statements and tax return (unless a separate file is maintained)
10. Working trial balance
11. Audit adjustments and reclassifications, and closing and reversing entries suggested to the client
12. Leading schedules or grouping sheets
13. Supporting schedules following the appropriate leading schedule
14. Time and expense summary and budget, with variances analyzed
15. Memorandums pertaining to investigations into subsequent events
16. Notes for next audit

Special report or analysis file. Frequently examinations are undertaken with objectives other than the usual verification of financial condition and operating results. The objectives become the ascertaining of some specific information concerning a special phase of the business' activities. Detailed explanations and illustrations are given in later chapters covering fraud, special investigations, performance audits, and compliance audits. Most of these have the common thread of working-paper composition. The contents will vary with the type of analysis, naturally, but common items to be found in the working-paper file would include the following:

1. Engagement memorandums and correspondence
2. Report conclusions and/or recommendations summary
3. Detailed report manuscript and final copies
4. Investigation program
5. Correspondence and interview summaries
6. Copies or abstracts of relevant company documents
7. Leading schedules, keyed to investigation program
8. Supporting schedules following proper leading schedules
9. Time and expense summary, budget, and variances

The Internal Auditor. Requirements of the internal auditor vary only slightly from those of the independent auditor and the types of files the internal auditor maintains, therefore, are similar. Usually the investigations have a different objective; these things cause the variations that do exist in the working papers. General standards of working-paper preparation are the same as those set out in an earlier section of this chapter.

Financial investigations. These investigations vary widely in scope and purpose. The scope may be the examination of inventories or the confirmation of receivables, or may be as wide as a full balance sheet audit. The purpose generally is to report on departmental conditions and results, but may range to determining alleged fraud or verifying a certain fact. No specific working-paper contents may be prescribed in this situation; however, certain general items are included in this type of file:

1. Summary report, conclusions, and/or recommendations
2. Follow-up actions and replies on recommendations
3. Detailed report manuscript and final copies
4. Investigation memorandums
5. Internal audit program
6. Relevant information on operation or accounts being investigated
7. Internal control summary and questionnaire
8. Leading schedules, keyed either to audit program steps or to report captions or flow-charted to specific procedures
9. Supporting analysis and schedules
10. Time and expense summary, budget, and variations

Investigation of operations or procedures. The number of possible types of audits under this category is even broader than under financial investigations. Any function or department of the business or any procedure under which they operate may be the subject of the audit. The contents of the working-paper file for this type of investigation center around the objective of the audit. Usually included are the following items:

1. Replies to recommendations and other follow-up data
2. Report conclusions and/or recommendations summary
3. Detailed report manuscript and final copies
4. Investigation memorandums
5. Notes on verification that federal or other authorities' requirements have been complied with, if applicable
6. Investigation program
7. Review of company organization and policies
8. Review of departmental operations and procedures
9. Review of collateral operations
10. Review of records and reports
11. Flow charts, analyses, or other memorandums supporting recommendations

The Governmental Auditor. There are many phases of governmental agency operation and private business that are under the jurisdiction of or subject to examination by one or more governmental audit organizations. In some cases these governmental auditors act in an internal audit capacity and in other cases they operate as external independent auditors of the agency's or supplier's activities. At all times, however, they operate only within their prescribed legal limits as established by federal or other legislative bodies. The files these auditors maintain are similar in some respects to nongovernmental internal and external auditors' working-paper files. The preparation standards enumerated earlier are equally applicable here.

Governmental auditors' working papers serve as the basis for preparing work programs and reports. They are the evidence of work done, and they are the evidence of the fulfillment of specific audit and investigative responsibilities.

Working papers are generally classified into two categories, the permanent file and the current file. Determining what material goes into each file depends on the nature of the information. No set rules can be established; however, the following general guidelines may be set out.

Permanent file. This generally pertains to data on the audited entity, rather than to a particular audit. It should contain only material useful in planning and performing future audits. It would include the following categories of items in an audit primarily of an external audit nature:

1. Legislative history of the agency, its programs, and its activities
2. Statements of and excerpts from laws of continuing applicability to the agency
3. Relevant policies and procedures of the agency
4. Financing methods, and historical statistics on appropriations and expenditures
5. Organization-chart and responsibility relationships, and personnel
6. Accounting, reporting, and budgeting procedures and policies
7. Internal and administrative controls review
8. Location of activities
9. Record of disposition of current files no longer maintained at the audit site
10. Schedule of destruction dates

Permanent files of governmental auditors acting as external auditors of contractors will be similar to the independent auditor's file outlined above. It would, however, go more deeply into the contractor's accounting, cost estimating, and procurement procedures and practices.

The permanent file of governmental auditors acting as internal auditors will reflect the same type of material as is found in the corporate internal auditor's files outlined above. If the governmental auditor is not a continuing resident of the office or installation, he will also develop a file similar to the permanent file of the independent auditor. Included would be: general description of the activity; type of organization and mission; location of pertinent records and facilities; description of pertinent policies, procedures, controls, directives, organization charts, and functional manuals; names, titles, and areas of responsibility of key personnel; and audit history.

Current file of assignment. The material normally placed in the current file consists of information relevant to the present assignment and not considered to be useful in succeeding assignments. The working papers will be arranged according to the manner in which the audit is approached. On large audits, the working papers may be separated into a general-portion folder relating to the audit as a whole and other folders covering major audit segments. Within the segments' folders, items should be arranged in logical sequence to provide ready reference and review during and after the audit. Included in the current file, in general, would be the following:

1. Index to folders and to items in the folders
2. Request for or authority for audit statements
3. Audit assignment and work program
4. Report summary of findings and/or recommendations
5. Detailed report manuscript and final copies
6. Current correspondence
7. Agenda sheet and reviewer's notes
8. Current reviews of management controls
9. Analyses and other records of the auditors' examinations, verifications, conclusions, and action taken

10. Notes, letters, and memorandums of conferences with the agency, contractor, governmental personnel, or other officials

11. Accumulated supporting documents

12. Supporting schedules, keyed to work program or report findings and recommendations

13. Record of results of postaudit critique or other follow-up required by any parties to the audit

WORKING-PAPER CONTROL

All working papers must be protected and controlled during the audit and preserved for some time after the audit is completed. Both during and after the audit responsibility must be established for each working paper and for the files developed.

Safeguarding the Working Papers. Working papers, reports, and tax returns are confidential material. Necessarily, precaution should be taken to protect these documents from loss, destruction, or unauthorized use. There may be occasions when the auditor will permit the client access to the working papers. This should be done only when the user is fully acquainted with the financial details of the client's business and only when the user is an individual in whom the auditor has the highest confidence.

Arranging the Working Papers. The primary purposes of carefully indexing and filing the working papers are ready reference and report preparation. During the audit the working papers are arranged by subject matter in folders or binders. Heavy-paper separators or index tabs facilitate the division. The papers should be kept during the audit in the order in which they will be bound at the conclusion of the audit. Any logical order will suffice; the contents of various working-paper files outlined above constitute a logical order. Usually papers relating to general matters are placed first, then those relating to specific accounts or other details follow.

Indexing the Working Papers. There are any number of ways of indexing working papers. Regardless of what plan is used, the working papers should be arranged so that any item in the financial statements or report may be traced back to the trial balance and supporting schedules and any other analyses or underlying documents.

1. SEQUENTIAL NUMBERING OF ANALYSES: Perhaps the easiest method is to merely number the sheets sequentially after they have been assembled at the end of the audit. A variation on this would be to number the supporting schedules according to the working trial balance line number. Thus the schedule for accrued wages payable would be numbered 205 (2 for page 2 of the trial balance, and 05 for the line number on which this account appears). Items in the working papers that do not appear as trial balance accounts are each assigned a letter according to a supplemental index.

2. DIGIT SYSTEM: This method assigns a number to each main working paper and to each leading schedule. Supporting schedules carry the number of the leading schedule followed by a sequential subnumber. Continuation pages of the same analysis may be divided from the foregoing by a slash, hyphen, or fraction line. Thus, page 3 of the fixed asset (12) item of office equipment (6) would be written 12-6-3 or 12-6/3. This method is capable of indefinite expansion and easy standardization.

3. LETTER SYSTEM: This method uses a letter to designate each leading schedule, followed by numbers for supporting schedules. If leading schedules exhaust the alphabet, double letters may be used. Thus, page 3 of the fixed asset (J) item of office equipment (6) would be written J-6-3 or J-6/3.

4. COMBINATION SYSTEM: One form of this system uses double letters for all nonfinancial schedules. Financial schedules are numbered either on the basis of working trial balance line numbers or by using assigned numbers, say, in the 100s for assets, 200s for liabilities, etc. Single letters would be used for subschedules. Thus, BB-2 would signify page 2 of the abstracts of minutes. Page 3 of the fixed asset (135) item of office equipment (C) would be written 135-C-3 or 135C/3. A variation of the letter-digit system uses double letters for the nonfinancial schedules, single letters for the balance sheet line items appearing in the working trial balance, and number groups for the income statement items. Thus, page 3 of the fixed asset item of office equipment (F) would be written F-3 or F/3. Page 2 of the schedule of advertising expenses would be 44-2 (the 40-group would be reserved for selling expense items).

Many variations are possible on these basic methods, and the accountant must develop the one that best fits his situation and preferences. The method should be uniform for the audit and preferably the same in every audit. If the working papers are bound at the top, the index numbers should be written in color on the lower right-hand corner of each sheet; if bound on the left, either upper or lower right-hand notations may be used.

The accountants preparing the working papers have the primary responsibility for indexing as the audit progresses. In some cases it may be necessary to index them at the end of the audit. In any event, no working paper should be without an index number or letter (or be out of its normal order if no system is used for certain items). Cross-referencing is always necessary for items appearing on one working paper and related to or taken from other working papers. Cross-referencing is facilitated when the indexing method covers all items in the file.

Tick-mark Notations. Frequently the auditor uses a variety of symbols to indicate that certain work has been done, or as footnote references where the items are explained further. These symbols are commonly referred to as "check marks" or "tick marks." Since the symbols have no inherent meaning in themselves, they should be explained at the bottom of each schedule where they appear. In some firms, some marks become standardized to mean certain things; this is acceptable as long as there is universal understanding of their meanings. Geometric designs, letters, alphabetic letters, numbers, checks, arithmetic designations, and any of these circled, underlined, or in different colors may be used; personal preference usually governs. It is desirable not to be too elaborate. An easy system is to use standard symbols to signify different types of specific work done, and letters where further footnote explanations are necessary. The obvious advantage of standardizing tick-mark use is the time saving involved both for the auditor in writing the symbol and its explanation and for the reviewer in reading its meaning and making his interpretation.

BIBLIOGRAPHY

Accounting Practice Management Handbook, New York, AICPA, 1962.
CPA Handbook, New York, AICPA, 1953, chap. 15, "Audit Working Papers."
Statement on Auditing Procedure No. 39, *Working Papers,* AICPA, New York, 1967.

Accountant's Encyclopedia, vol. III, *Practical Audit Working Papers,* Englewood Cliffs, N.J., Prentice-Hall, Inc., 1964, chap. 26.
Brink, Victor Z., and James A. Cashin: *Internal Auditing,* 2d ed., New York, The Ronald Press Co., 1963.
Cashin, James A., and Garland C. Owens: *Auditing,* 2d ed., New York, The Ronald Press Co., 1963.

Handbook of Forms for Profitable Accounting Practice, Englewood Cliffs, N.J., Prentice-Hall, Inc., "Pre-Audit Forms and Check Lists," 1968.

Holmes, Arthur W.: *Auditing Principles and Procedures,* 6th ed., Homewood, Ill., Richard D. Irwin, Inc., 1964.

Meigs, Walter B., and E. John Larsen: *Principles of Auditing,* 4th ed., Homewood, Ill., Richard D. Irwin, Inc., 1969.

Silvoso, Joseph A., and Royal D. M. Bauer: *Auditing,* 2d ed., Cincinnati, South Western Publishing Co., 1965.

Staples, Frederick: *Standardized Audit Working Papers,* Thiensville, Wisc., The Counting House Publishing Company, 1957.

Stettler, Howard F.: *Systems-based Independent Audits,* Englewood Cliffs, N.J., Prentice-Hall, Inc., 1967.

Carroll, Richard: "Working Paper Techniques and Reviews," *The Internal Auditor* (The Institute of Internal Auditors, New York), 1957.

Pattillo, James W.: "Modernizing Audit Working Papers," *The Louisiana Certified Public Accountant,* Spring, 1969.

Hull, James C.: "A Guide to Better Workpapers," *The Journal of Accountancy,* February, 1969.

Chapter 15

Statistical Sampling

ALPHONSE L. NIGRA

Audit Manager, Allied Chemical Corporation

GENERAL

Introduction. Statistical sampling techniques have been used successfully for many years in industrial operations, particularly in product inspection and in similar areas. The techniques had also been successfully applied to internal accounting procedures and management control problems. However, until shortly before the beginning of the last decade statistical sampling techniques had not been generally applied to the more complex field of auditing. Further research in the field and the development of statistical techniques to meet the particular requirements of the auditor were essential. Intensive efforts toward refinement of statistical techniques and greater applicability to auditing were carried on by many groups around the early 1960s and shortly before. Advances were slow but definite on many fronts. Many of the large CPA firms, notably Price Waterhouse & Co., had study groups organized to consider the use of statistical sampling in audit tests. Some of the larger industrial firms such as Lockheed Aircraft Corporation began to study the applicability of statistical sampling to internal auditing. Various governmental agencies and organizations had also been making important advances in the field. The U.S. Department of the Air Force, the Interstate Commerce Commission, the Federal Government Accountants Association, and others had been making further advances in statistical techniques. Many universities were building on the earlier work of Vance and Neter, Herbert Arkin, and others. The professional organizations were also deeply involved with similar research.

The intensive research efforts of the various groups of auditors could not have come at a more appropriate time. With a new era of corporate integration and centralization of accounting records and the advent of the computer, it was recognized that new methods would have to be designed to make appropriate tests. With the greatly expanded volume of transactions it had become necessary to rely to a far greater extent on test checks, or in other words, sampling techniques. The detailed review of more than a fraction of a large company's transactions became extremely costly and the time involved so great that many of the benefits of the audit would have been lost by the time the work was completed.

It must be understood at the outset that a handbook is for reference purposes and practical application. It is not possible to cover the background, theory, and other aspects of a particular topic in one chapter. This is particularly true with technical subjects such as statistical sampling. Many volumes have been written on statistical sampling, and many more will be written as the field advances. Understanding of the concepts, background, etc., can be obtained from references in the footnotes and the bibliography.

Need for Improved Methods. With the great increase in testing there was always the question of whether the sample used was adequate in size, whether it was representative, and what were the chances that a major error might be included in the untested portion. This was a particular consideration in public accounting work, where much of the auditing effort may have been carried out at the year end. Interim work was being done as far as practicable, but still much of the transaction review was made of one or two months near the year end. There was the feeling on the part of many auditors that not enough review was being made of activities throughout the year. The internal auditing department, if one was available, usually reviewed some other portion of the year. Also the public accountant with sufficient experience and judgment scanned the records for unusual transactions in other months. At that time there was no systematic, reliable way to determine the amount of testing. It varied with the individual job, the individual auditor, and even the way the particular auditor felt that day. With the increasing use of testing there was the greater possibility that the selection of a particular sample might have to be explained or even defended in court. If so, a larger sample could be explained much more easily than a smaller sample which might indicate that insufficient work was done. This was understandable, *since there was no reliable way of determining how much sampling was enough.* This tendency toward oversampling increased the audit costs and required additional audit time. The determination of how much sampling is needed can be more easily determined through statistical sampling guided by the auditor's judgment. The degree of risk involved, the reliability of the sample, and other factors can be readily determined by means of statistical sampling. Thus a far more objective approach is generally possible by means of statistical sampling than through *intuitive sampling*, or what is sometimes called *judgment sampling.*

Nature of Statistical Sampling. Statistical sampling is a refinement of the *intuitive* or *judgment sampling* that auditors have been using for many years. It is a method for selecting items to be sampled and then arriving at an informed opinion of the whole population on the basis of mathematical concepts. It is a tool which permits the auditor to determine the reliability he wishes and the degree of risk he accepts with any given level. This is an important advantage; the auditor knows in advance the degree of risk he is taking. He does not know that in using the intuitive method.

It must be pointed out that statistical sampling techniques do not replace the auditor's judgment. He must use the same degree of judgment required in the traditional sampling method. There are several types of statistical techniques for selecting samples and several types of plans to measure the sample in relation to the population of the total with which the auditor may be concerned. Regardless of the particular technique or plan used, the following questions must be answered:

1. What are the objectives?
2. How are samples to be selected?
3. How much must be sampled?
4. How will the results be evaluated?

While the large CPA firms and industrial companies increasingly used statistical sampling, many of the smaller firms and companies were slow in adopting the technique. One of the principal problems was the difficulty of understanding the technique and relating it to auditing cases. Much of the difficulty has been overcome with the recent publication of the Individual Study Programs of "programmed instruction" by the American Institute of

Certified Public Accountants (AICPA)[1] and the Sampling Manuals for Auditors[2] published by The Institute of Internal Auditors.

The AICPA course, An Auditor's Approach to Statistical Sampling, includes four individual study programs with a coordinated supplementary section for each program. The material is arranged into a programmed text format for self-teaching purposes. The supplementary section includes primarily examples, worksheets, and tables. The individual volumes are:

1. *An Introduction to Statistical Concepts and Estimation of Dollar Values*
2. *Sampling for Attributes*
3. *Stratified Random Sampling*
4. *Discovery Sampling*

The Institute of Internal Auditors publications include a manual of instruction and a supplement. The material is primarily a tool for the working auditor rather than a treatise on sampling theory. The material was originally prepared by the general auditing department of Lockheed Aircraft Corporation for its own use. The first manual covers the development in the field up to 1967 and includes the various selection techniques and measurement plans. The supplement points out the advantages to be gained by extending the auditor's capabilities still further through a working knowledge of slightly more advanced techniques.

1. *Sampling Manual for Auditors*
2. *Supplement to the Sampling Manual for Auditors*

Advantages of Statistical Sampling. There are a number of advantages of using statistical sampling, and they increase as further research and refinements are made. The principal advantages are:

Objective method. A more objective method is provided in the determination of the sampling risks, the sample size, and the evaluation of the sample.

Justification for sampling. The auditor may be called on, possibly at some later date, to justify or explain the basis of his verification of an item. Statistical sampling provides an accepted objective justification for the sample used.

Greater exercise of judgment. Statistical sampling calls for greater rather than less use of judgment in the sampling process. These judgments are (1) what error rate is expected, (2) what reliability is required, and (3) the maximum limit of acceptable error. These are factors in determining sample size. Then he must judge (4) the best method of selection to avoid bias, (5) the best means of evaluating the sample, and (6) whether he tested all areas he should have.

Improved control of testing. Under the traditional or intuitive method each auditor determined generally his own sample, which resulted in much oversampling and some undersampling. With statistical sampling the risk, sample sizes, etc., can be established and controlled at a higher auditing level.

Improved planning. With statistical planning the sampling plans can be developed before the fieldwork begins. The documents and transactions to be reviewed can be determined and the working papers set up beforehand at the office, perhaps even using nonbillable time.

Smaller sample. The size of samples determined by statistical means may be smaller than previously used. A more effective evaluation of the samples is made than where a large amount is sampled in a less systematic way.

[1] *An Auditor's Approach to Statistical Sampling*, AICPA, New York, 1967 to date.
[2] *Sampling Manual for Auditors*, The Institute of Internal Auditors, New York, 1967 to date.

Training tool. Statistical sampling provides excellent training in mathematical techniques. It can be used in other quantitative applications and fosters greater familiarity with and use of quantitative techniques.

Relationship to Internal Control. In the following section we will discuss the relationship of statistical sampling to auditing standards. One aspect of auditing standards, the evaluation of internal control, relates to this section. However, the emphasis is on the evaluation of existing internal controls, for the purpose of expressing an opinion concerning the financial statements. In this section we are concerned with the relationship of statistical sampling to installation and maintenance of internal controls throughout the year in all areas of operations. For example, the internal auditor may test the accuracy of production records by means of statistical sampling. He may evaluate the effectiveness of the particular type of sampling controls or sampling charts used in the inspection department. Also the governmental auditor will be concerned with the installation and maintenance of various kinds of managerial controls. Both the internal auditor and the governmental auditor will be reviewing a wide range of company operations, such as manufacturing, personnel, purchasing, and other operating and managerial areas which are related to administrative internal controls or nonfinancial controls. The broad range of the internal auditor's duties is indicated in the Statement of Responsibilities of the Internal Auditor as follows:

> Internal auditing is an independent appraised activity within an organization for the review of accounting, financial and other operations as a basis for service to management. It is a managerial control, which functions by measuring and evaluating the effectiveness of other controls.[3]

It must be remembered that the dimensions of materiality and reliance assigned to internal control may differ considerably from what may be considered appropriate for internal auditors. The internal auditor will be concerned with accounting, financial, and *other operations* and will be reviewing the effectiveness of *other controls*. These other controls will, in many cases, be various managerial controls rather than accounting controls.

Relationship to Auditing Standards. The publications of the committee on statistical sampling and the committee on auditing procedures of the AICPA make it clear that statistical sampling is permitted under generally accepted auditing standards. In an article, "Relationship of Statistical Sampling to Generally Accepted Auditing Standards," it was pointed out that:

> Statistical sampling is not a fundamentally different audit approach, and that its use is permissive rather than mandatory under generally accepted auditing standards.[4]

The committee on statistical sampling mentions that, although statistical sampling furnishes the auditor with a measure of precision and reliability, it does not define the values of each required to provide audit satisfaction. Specification of the precision and reliability necessary in a given test is an auditing function and must be based upon judgment in the same way when any other method is used. The committee on auditing procedure reiterates this general point in Statements on Auditing Procedure No. 33, which points out, on page 37, that the use of sampling does not reduce the use of judgment by the auditor but permits statistical measurements relating to sampling that are not otherwise possible with any other method. The auditing standards to which statistical sampling is most related are the three standards of field-

[3] Statement of Responsibilities of the Internal Auditor, The Institute of Internal Auditors, New York, 1957.

[4] *The Journal of Accountancy* (AICPA, New York), July, 1964.

work, (1) planning and supervision, (2) evaluation of internal control, and (3) competent evidential matter.

Planning and supervision. A high level of planning and supervision is required in providing for the use of statistical sampling. This is consistent with the first standard of fieldwork. A generally uniform higher quality of sampling is possible where the sampling objectives are established and controlled by managers, partners, etc., rather than individual junior or senior auditors. The reliability and precision for each sample and the definition of errors can be better established and followed up. The working papers can be set up ahead of time in the office before fieldwork is started. Perhaps specialists may be used, and especially designed forms, tables, and other requirements can be more efficiently provided.

Internal control. The second standard of fieldwork requires an evaluation of internal control. The evaluation includes two phases, (1) the evaluation of prescribed procedures and (2) the extent of audit tests.

PRESCRIBED PROCEDURES: The auditor must gain a knowledge of company procedures by inquiry or through written instructions. On this basis he determines through a review of actual practices if there is satisfactory compliance with the procedures.

EXTENT OF TESTS: The testing of internal control will be by means of documentary evidence such as signatures and initials and working papers such as bank reconcilements and footings. Segregation of duties can be evaluated by observation of personnel and review of organization structure.

Evidential matter. The third standard relates to audit evidence. Statistical sampling aids the auditor's judgment with respect to materiality, reasonableness and sampling reliability, sufficiency of sample size, and competence of evidence.

With respect to materiality the auditor from his sampling will form an opinion as to the reliability of the records and the likelihood of errors having a material effect. In the case of monetary amounts if a sample indicates an asset is overstated by $10,000 it would involve the auditor's judgment as to the materiality of $10,000 in relation to the assets, etc. With regard to reasonableness the auditor relies on internal control to reduce the risk of material errors in the accounting process. He relies on his auditing procedures to reduce the risk that material errors in the financial statements will not be detected by his audit steps. When the auditor sets the precision and reliability desired, statistical tables or formulas can determine the sample of evidence that will be sufficient to meet the sampling objectives. With regard to competence of evidence the auditor may sample for certain characteristics in terms of errors, quantities, monetary amounts, or other features. He can determine by attribute sampling the competence of the evidential matter.

Computer Applications. The applications of the computer to statistical sampling are limited only by the computer time available and the imagination and ingenuity of the auditor. The computer is a natural companion to statistical sampling, and many of the detailed operations in the selection and measuring of samples can be readily done on the computer. There are presently the following areas where the computer has been successfully used with statistical sampling:

Selection of items. As much of the data used in statistical sampling is already available, only a simple program is needed to utilize the computer. This is particularly true with respect to selection techniques. The following techniques will be discussed: random number selection, interval selection, and stratified selection.

RANDOM NUMBER SELECTION: Tables of random numbers are available from many sources. These tables can be stored on tape. Random numbers can then be programmed for any subsequent tests. Random numbers can be generated for each sampling need by means of a random number generator program. After the numbers have been determined under either method, a computer program can select the particular sample items. A listing of the sample items can then be printed out in any form desired by the auditor.

INTERVAL SELECTION: The computer can select the sample items from magnetic tape under the systematic interval selection. Every *n*th item can be selected and a printout made as required. The possibility of selecting a biased sample can be avoided by having a random variation of the interval. That is, there could be a random interval rather than a fixed interval as in systematic sampling.

STRATIFICATION: Stratification can easily be accomplished with the computer, particularly stratification by dollar value. The stored information can be retrieved and a frequency distribution readily prepared.

Data made available. The computer can make available various kinds of data which can greatly assist the auditor, for example, tab runs of population, preferably stratified, count cards, ratio of audited to population values, the standard deviation, and sampling error.

Computer printouts. After calculations have been made as instructed by the auditor, a printout is available. In the case of inventory a listing in material code sequence may be produced. The final results in any form desired by the auditor may be available.

Charts and tabulations. Charts and tabulations for each stratum show the sample value and the projected or estimated total population, and the number of items in the sample and in the population. Also included may be various other statistical data as required.

Time-sharing computer programs. A great amount of flexibility is provided by means of time sharing. Terminals are made available in the user's office and are connected to a central computer. By time sharing it is possible for a number of people or organizations to use one computer simultaneously on entirely different programs. A wide variety of programs can be available to the auditor with a time-sharing arrangement.

A number of interesting and sophisticated examples of computer applications are given in Chapters 5 and 6 of the *Supplement to the Sampling Manual for Auditors.*

SAMPLING FUNDAMENTALS

Sampling is the process of obtaining information about an entire population by examining only a part of it. The principal consideration is that the sample must be truly representative of the whole; there must be no bias. Every item in the total under consideration must have an equal or known chance of being selected in the sample. Before sampling can be properly used, certain statistical fundamentals such as statistical concepts and principles must be clearly understood. The principal fundamentals and various terms used are discussed in this section. This part should be studied carefully before the application of these fundamentals is undertaken as discussed below under Selection Techniques and Measurement Plans.

Precision. This is the range within which the population average will lie, in accordance with the reliability specified in the confidence level as a percentage of the estimate ± or as a numerical quantity. Thus if the estimate is \$200,000 and the precision desired is ±3 percent, then the true value will be no less than \$194,000 and no more than \$206,000. This is the range within which the true answer should lie, \$194,000 to \$206,000. The auditor might have stipulated that his estimate should not deviate from the actual value by more than \$10,000 in either direction. Thus the precision rate would be \$190,000 to \$210,000.

Confidence Level. The confidence level or reliability is the expected percentage of times that the actual value will fall somewhere in the stated precision limits. Thus, if we refer to a confidence level of 90 percent, we mean that there are 90 chances in 100 that the sample results represent the true condition of the population (within a specified precision range), against 10 chances that it does not. Precision is the range within which the answer may vary and still be acceptable; the confidence level indicates the likelihood that the answer will fall within that range.

Population. The population is the total of the items or units about which information is desired. It is also called the universe or field. Thus the auditor must necessarily define this population precisely. For example, if the auditor's test objective is to select a number of accounts receivable balances for confirmation, the customer statements at the end of the period, or the balances in the customer's accounts at the end of this same period, would make up the sampling units—and the total number of such units would be the population. But if the auditor wishes to examine the individual sales or cash collections making up accounts receivable, then the sampling units would be the individual line items that make up the customer statements, or the cash remittance advices, or the individual sales invoices, depending on the particular result desired. Obviously, improper definition of the sampling units making up the population leads to eventual unsatisfactory results. A form for recording these specifications is shown in Figure 1.

Stratification. One of the principal reasons for the slow acceptance of statistical sampling by auditors was the lack of stratification of data. With further research in sampling and further attention to the particular needs of auditors this objection has been largely overcome. In the early days when the emphasis was on random sampling, the auditor had the fear that a large value or error might not be detected. For example, in observing inventory the auditor learns early that in most cases a few items make up much of the total dollar value of the inventory. In many cases 10 percent of the number of items make up about 80 percent of the total dollar value. Therefore, if the auditor makes careful test counts of the larger items and a few of the other items in each department, it is not likely that there could be any large discrepancy in the dollar value of inventory. Generally, the auditor receives a copy of

Figure 1 SAMPLING OBJECTIVES

DESIRED INFORMATION	
POPULATION	
DESIRED PRECISION	
DESIRED CONFIDENCE LEVEL	

the inventory listing or tag and from the previous inventory value and present quantity he can determine the items of larger value. This method has worked remarkably well, and in the history of accounting there are very few cases where the results were substantially incorrect. During all this time the auditor did not call the method stratification, but that is what he was doing in the case of inventory and what he does in many other areas when he is making test counts or sampling. The bad part of it is that he was probably sampling much more than he needed to do under statistical sampling techniques. In statistical sampling means are provided for measuring the degrees of variability in each sample, class, or population. In any population there will be *normal variability.* However, *extreme values* at either end should not be confused with normal variability. By stratifying the data, we segregate the extreme values. Separate samplings are made for the separate strata. In many cases high-value items will be isolated, or segregated into suitable groupings from which appropriate samples can be taken. For example, a frequency distribution by dollar value may be set up with about five or more classes depending on the particular need. The highest class may be verified or sampled 100 percent, that is, all items may be counted. The next class will be sampled less, etc. Different methods of selection may be used for each class. In the highest-value class there would be few items of high value; in the lowest class there may be a very large number with very small unit value. An error in one item in the latter class would have little effect on the total amount.

Sample Size. In order to determine the size of the sample the auditor must stipulate the precision range, the confidence level, and the occurrence rate. A change in any of these factors may substantially change the size of the sample required. The auditor should become familiar with the effect on sample size when he makes the judgment decisions for precision, confidence level, and occurrence rate. Various types of tables are now readily available, and it is not necessary for the auditor to study the formulas to determine sample size.

The closer the precision or the greater the sample reliability required, for example, ±2 percent compared with 4 percent, the larger the required sample. The higher the confidence level, the larger the required sample. The sample size increases as the expected occurrence rate becomes larger. The effect of the occurrence rate, however, is not as great as that of the precision rate or confidence level. In using the table, if the auditor finds that the results of his review confirm his estimate of the occurrence rate, he may stop. However, if the occurrence rate shown in the sample is larger than the acceptable rate, he may decide that his estimate of the sample size was too low and that he has to draw a larger sample.

In statistical estimation the first step is usually to select a preliminary random sample. The number of items in this preliminary sample may vary, but in most cases it will be 50 items or less. In the AICPA programmed course, volume 1, *An Introduction to Statistical Concepts and Estimation of Dollar Values,* it is pointed out that a preliminary random sample of 30 items is sufficient. "It has been proved mathematically that this number of elements generally suffices to give us a reasonable estimate of the variability of a population." [5]

In discussing the sample size, it should be mentioned that the size or number of items does not increase proportionately with the increase in popu-

[5] *An Auditor's Approach to Statistical Sampling,* AICPA, New York, 1967, vol. 1, p. 59.

lation. The sample size, of course, will increase but not as much as the population. For example, as Arkin points out,[6] "An examination of these tables indicates that the sample size required for a reliability of ±.10 times the standard deviation (±$10.00, if the standard deviation equals $100.00) at the 99% confidence level for a field size of 2,000 is 500, whereas for a field size of 5,000 it is only 588. Thus with a field size 2½ times as great, the sample size rose only 18%."

Sample Replacement. If the auditor, in using the random number table, happens to draw a duplicate number, he has the option of using the number again or ignoring it. If he uses the number for a second time or more, he is "sampling with replacement." That is, the numbers drawn are then replaced and have an equal chance of being drawn again. If he ignores the duplicate number, he is "sampling without replacement." For practical considerations the duplicate numbers are ignored. However, that is not strictly proper from a theoretical viewpoint, and certain compensating adjustments should be made for interfering with the chance factor.

Acceptance Sampling. Acceptance sampling has long been used in industry for accepting or rejecting certain lots of products. Its application to the general field of auditing has been slow. The method has been adapted to internal auditing needs and used widely in industry. A variation is the stop-or-go method discussed later in the chapter. As more research is done, further uses will probably be made of acceptance sampling in auditing.

Estimation Sampling. Estimation sampling, or what is sometimes called survey sampling, is probably the most widely used technique in auditing. It is particularly useful in public accounting and in the financial auditing phases of internal auditing and governmental auditing. It is a method used to estimate or project the total of the population based on an examination of a sample of that universe. For example, it can be used in estimating the dollar valuation of an inventory based on counting and pricing only a required sample. The figure thus estimated can be compared with a physical inventory or book inventory dollar value. This is variables estimation.

If the examination is concerned with a certain characteristic or attribute such as number of errors or violations of internal control, that would be attribute estimation. These two methods are discussed separately under Measurement Plans because the means used to determine the final results are quite different.

Means. The principal types of means or averages that the auditor will be dealing with in statistical sampling are the arithmetic means and the standard error of mean. There are references to sample mean or population mean, but these are usually arithmetic means of the respective data. This is the sum of the population or sample divided by the number of items. The mean is a measure of the central tendency of a frequency distribution. It is the arithmetic average of the data. However, the average alone is not sufficient, since many of the items may depart considerably from the average. It is useful to know the range of the items. For example, the average or mean may be $207.15, but the values may range from $11.75 to $517.61. The latter two items indicate the extremes at either end. A better measure of dispersion is the standard deviation. The standard error of the mean or standard error of the estimate refers to the variability of the mean of the sample from a population from the mean of other similar samples of the same size. It is possible

[6] Herbert Arkin, *Handbook of Sampling for Auditing and Accounting*, New York, McGraw-Hill Book Company, 1963, p. 112.

to measure the variability among all the possible samples of the same size in a population. We can determine the reliability of the estimate by determining the maximum difference between the sample mean and true means that will meet our established precision, then computing its equivalent and referring to the table. The formula for the standard is generally built into the tables, and no special computations are required.

Standard Deviation. The standard deviation is the most frequently used measure of variation. We estimate the variability of the population by determining the standard deviation of the sample. The quantity is the square root of the sum of the squared deviation from the mean divided by n-1 (n = the number of items in the sample).

Normal Curve. The normal curve or normal distribution is symmetrical; that is, the curve is the same on both sides of the average. When it is shown graphically, it resembles closely a cross section of a bell. Hence it is often called a bell-shaped curve. Where there is a cluster or concentration of items away from the average or center, it is described as the skewness of the distribution.

SELECTION TECHNIQUES

There are two distinct phases in statistical sampling: statistical selection and statistical measurement. Statistical selection concerns the technique or method of drawing the sample, while statistical measurement concerns the sample size and the particular measurement plan for evaluation of the sample. The various measurement plans will be described in the next part of the chapter. In this part we will be concerned with the various selection techniques. The principal selection techniques used in auditing are random number selection, systematic selection, stratified selection, and cluster selection.

Random Number Selection. In normal auditing situations the random number technique is the most widely used. Often called simple or unrestricted random sampling, it is the easiest method of selecting items to be tested. The items included in the sample must be drawn completely at random from the entire population so that each item in the population has an equal or known chance of being selected. Unless the sampling is free from bias, that is, each item has an equal chance of being selected, the results will not be reliable.

Random number tables. There are a number of published random number tables which are easily available and have been used in statistical sampling for some years. Table 1 (page 15-28) is one type of random number table. Other tables are listed in the bibliography. The easiest method of selecting items to be tested on a random basis is generally by the use of the random number table. However, where there are 300 or more sample items to be drawn from a large population, either by using a table of random numbers or by using every *n*th item, it can be a time-consuming job. If computer time is available, the statistical samples can be selected more quickly and perhaps more accurately by computer. Random numbers can be stored on tape, or they can be separately created for each specific application. However, the program used for generating random numbers should be reviewed for true randomness. For example, in a properly randomized table there are about equal numbers of digits 0 through 9 with the order of digits completely random. Computer programs are now available which have been certified for randomness, such as the Lehmer method, in which large numbers of random numbers can be produced without repeating a sequence.

USING THE TABLE: Before the auditor can begin to use the random number table, he must make certain decisions concerning the relationship of the data to be sampled to the table. These are (1) the *correspondence* of the numbers, (2) the direction he will proceed in selecting the samples, the *route,* and (3) the method of picking the first number, the *starting point.*

CORRESPONDENCE: The first step in preparing to use the random number table is to establish correspondence between the elements of the population and the digits in the table. Generally the correspondence basis should be stated in writing before the sample is selected. This can readily be accomplished by using a worksheet somewhat similar to that used in *An Introduction to Statistical Concepts and Estimation of Dollar Values*[7] and shown in Figure 1. The auditor may wish to select a sample from a group of items numbered from 3,501 to 10,099 which will require five-digit numbers. Again the items may be identified by lot number and he may assign numbers, for example, from 1 to 500. It may be well at this point to discuss some of the principal considerations in matching various kinds of data to be sampled with the numbers in unbroken series, broken series, lettered series, block series, duplicate numbers, unnumbered items, inapplicable numbers, and other problems.

UNBROKEN SERIES: A large part of the auditor's work with statistical sampling will be concerned with numbers of documents, transactions, or inventory which is already numbered in sequence. These ordinarily would be in unbroken sequence, and it is only necessary to draw the required number of samples, perhaps 200 from about 3,000 items, depending on the precision and confidence level, from numbers 5,115 through 8,256. The necessary four-digit items could be easily matched with the numbers in the table.

BROKEN SERIES: Sometimes the auditor may find that the series of numbers may be broken. For example, in the inventory he is examining, one class of inventory may have numbers from 1,001 to 2,000, the next class may have numbers from 4,001 to 5,000, the next 7,001 to 8,000, etc. Once the auditor has selected the starting point and the route, he selects only the numbers from the table that correspond with numbers in the group of items he is examining. If a number comes up in any other series, he should ignore it and go on to the next number. Thus if number 2,781 would ordinarily be included in a sample but is not in any of the series now included, it would be ignored.

LETTERED SERIES: In many cases, particularly in a manufacturing plant, the auditor may find that a part number in an inventory has a letter of the alphabet as a prefix or a suffix. One method is to assign 1 through 26 as numbers in place of letters. For example, M1517 would be considered 131517 and D2615 would become 042615. Another way would be to select separately the digits for the letters and the numbers.

BLOCK SERIES: The auditor is used to working with numbers in a block series, particularly in reviewing transactions. For example, it is common practice to number vouchers in block series with a different block for each month. Thus the first voucher in January would be 1-1, going up to as many as needed, such as 1-915. February would consist of 2-1 up to as many as needed, perhaps 2-866, and March from 3-1 to 3-1176. One method of selection would have the first numbers to designate the month of the year and the remaining digits to designate the transaction number. The number of digits

[7] *An Auditor's Approach to Statistical Sampling,* AICPA, New York, 1967, p. 25.

needed would depend on whether only a few months were included with a small number of transactions or all months would be included with perhaps a large number of transactions in each month. In another method the auditor would assign numbers in sequence according to the number of transactions. For example, for January the numbers would be 1 to 915, for February 916 to 1,781 and for March 1,782 to 2,957. If number 615 is drawn, it would be translated to voucher 1-615. If number 919 is drawn, it would be the fourth voucher in February and thus 2-4.

DUPLICATE NUMBERS: The auditor will find in using the random number tables that he may sometimes draw the same number more than once. If he examines the same number two or more times, he is "sampling with replacement." If the duplicate number is ignored, he is "sampling without replacement." Very often the procedure is to ignore duplicate numbers.

UNNUMBERED ITEMS: In many cases the items to be reviewed are not serially numbered and it is not worthwhile to assign numbers. For example, the auditor may have a tabulated or manual listing of inventory items. In such a case he may use both the page number and the line number. Assume that there are 200 inventory pages each containing 25 lines, and that a sample of 150 items is required. One method often used to select the sample is to have the first three numbers represent the page number and the last two numbers represent the line number. For example, 14725 would be page 147 and the 25th item on that page. It is possible to select the page number and the line number separately, but the matching process is an extra operation.

INAPPLICABLE NUMBERS: In selecting the sample items, the auditor is concerned only with the numbers in the group of items he is examining. If a number comes up which is not in such a group, he will ignore it and select the next number according to the route he has decided on.

OTHER PROBLEMS: There are various other kinds of problems connected with matching the numbers in the data to the random number table. Only a limited amount of material on a topic, particularly a specialized topic, can be included in one chapter of a handbook. Specific references on particular points are given in the footnotes; general references are listed in the bibliography at the end of the chapter.

ROUTE: After the correspondence basis has been established, the next step to be decided is the route to be taken through the table. Various directions are acceptable if they are consistently followed. Generally the simplest method is to move from starting point to the bottom. At this point there are several choices. The auditor may move to the first column of the next page or to the top of the second column on the same page. More complex routes are possible; for example, the last two digits in one column and the first three digits in the next column could be used. However, it is best to have as simple a route as possible.

STARTING POINT: The third step in using a random number table is to select a starting point randomly. It is not essential to have the steps in this same order; that is, on an informal basis the starting point could be selected before the route was decided. However, on an audit where these steps would be in writing and a part of the working papers, it would be better to proceed in the order shown in Figure 2. The auditor may start his selection from the table at any point. For example, he may start at the top left side of the table, assuming it is by manual selection. He might also begin at the top right side just as well. However, the starting point should be selected randomly rather than on any fixed basis. There is a general tendency to begin such a process at the upper left side, and a bias in selection is thus introduced since the

Figure 2 SAMPLING PLAN DATA

TYPE OF PLAN	
CORRESPONDENCE	
ROUTE	
STARTING POINT	

numbers on the upper left side would have a greater chance of being selected than numbers in the middle of the table. One of the most frequent ways to help assure a random selection is the "blind stab" method. In using this method, the auditor closes his eyes and makes a blind stab at the random numbers table with his pencil. The starting number will consist of the one closest to the mark made by the pencil point.

Systematic or Interval Selection. Systematic selection or interval sampling provides for the selection of items in such a way that there is a uniform interval between sample items. In other words it provides for the selection of every "*n*th" item. The auditor has often used this method in the past in selecting items to be counted in inventory or vouchers to be examined. If there were 300 items in the inventory, the auditor might elect to count every twentieth item. The auditor must be careful that he begins with a random start. If proper care is taken, the systematic technique can be as reliable as the random number technique. Where a computer is available, the selection of items by machine can save considerable time. Various kinds of reports are produced from which every "*n*th" item can be readily selected by the computer.

Stratified Selection. This is a technique in which items in a population are segregated into groupings or strata. It has been devised to deal most effectively with populations containing items with substantially different characteristics or with great ranges of values. The primary objective of this stratification process is to obtain the smallest sample possible by dividing the total population into groupings reasonably similar in characteristics and values. The auditor has used stratified sampling in his testing procedures with good success for many years. He has had more confidence in the test if he was able to have a 100 percent examination of the items of highest value, and a slightly lower percentage of examination of items of lower cost. Under his traditional method the auditor was able to satisfy himself as to about 80 percent of the dollar value by examining about 10 percent of the items. Any errors in the part not counted would generally not have too much effect on the final figure, if the internal controls were adequate.

In many cases stratification provides a natural segregation since the characteristics of the groups vary. For example, one group of accounts receivable may be industrial accounts, another wholesale accounts, another chain stores, government accounts, etc.

The basic purpose of stratification is to reduce variability. The auditor cannot change the variability, but he can break it up into smaller groups each of which will have less variability than the whole population. The lower the variability the smaller the sample size needed to meet the given precision and confidence requirements. Some of the factors to consider in deciding to use a stratified sample are the range, the curve, and distribution.

Range. The range of the population is the interval between the highest and lowest value. A stratified sample is more efficient when the range of the whole population is relatively large and can be divided into subgroups or strata which have a smaller range.

Curve. The graphic shape or curve of the population is also an important factor to be considered. Generally a "bell-shaped" or "normal curve" is preferable, since there are approximately equal numbers of high-value and low-value items. Most of the remaining values tend to group toward the middle.

Distribution. In a normal distribution there would be about an equal number of very high and very low value items. A symmetrical distribution can be graphically shown by a bell or normal curve. The numbers would be arrayed approximately equally on each side of the mean. A skewed distribution or curve would be one which extends further in one direction than in another.

Other considerations in stratifying the data may be the reliability of the internal control applicable to each stratum. Generally there is more likelihood of poor internal control in the processing of low-volume transactions. The auditor would therefore sample this group or stratum with a greater precision and confidence level than in other areas. Thus the auditor can determine the materiality, turnover, or other characteristic of each stratum and apply appropriate auditing and statistical sampling procedures to each group.

For a comprehensive step-by-step study of this plan, see the AICPA programmed text, volume 3, *Stratified Random Sampling*, which is part of *An Auditor's Approach to Statistical Sampling*. Also see the *Sampling Manual for Auditors* and its supplement published by The Institute of Internal Auditors.

Cluster Selection. In this technique of sampling, the items making up the population may be divided into subgroups or clusters. These clusters may be located within reasonable proximity of each other, such as records in file drawers or bundles of documents. The clusters to be examined are then selected in a random manner—and each cluster is examined in its entirety. The number of clusters to be selected will be dictated by the nature and size of the population. It is recommended that whenever possible at least 20 clusters be selected for examination.

A variation of cluster sampling is known as "multistage sampling." In this sample selection technique, the selected clusters are *sampled*, instead of being entirely examined.

Assume that an auditor wishes to examine items filed on long shelves—with very little variability in the characteristic being tested. The total population of the items is about 80,000, located on about 8,000 linear feet of shelving. Dividing 8,000 into 80,000 shows that the population averages about 10 items per linear foot. The auditor decides on a sample size of 400 items that will be included in an examination of 20 clusters. Each cluster, therefore, should contain 20 items (400 divided by 20), and the population will be divided into 4,000 clusters (80,000 divided by 20). Each cluster of 20 items represents 2 linear feet—and 20 clusters 40 linear feet. If the auditor now desires to select 40 linear feet from a total of 8,000, he could use interval sampling with a random start and an interval of 200 feet (8,000 divided by 40) to select his sample. Each of the 20 clusters the auditor eventually selects, of course, would then be examined 100 percent. It has been found that in most auditing situations there will be a definite loss in sample reliability when cluster sampling is used instead of sample techniques such as interval or random number sampling. This condition arises because the variability among clusters is often greater than the variability within the clusters. In order to compensate for possible loss in sample reliability, the auditor, by applying experience and

Figure 3 SELECTION WORK PAPER

Minor series	Major series							
	100	200	300	400	500	600	700	800
0–9								
10–19								
20–29								
30–39								
40–49								
50–59								
60–69								
70–79								
80–89								
90–99								

judgment, should either increase his required reliability or reduce his precision requirements in order to obtain a larger sample.

In this method the auditor must evaluate the cluster as if it were a single item. With a large number of items this can be a substantial task. In any case he must use this method with caution and if possible review the proposed sampling with a statistical specialist.

Where random number selection is used, it is desirable to design an appropriate work paper for the individual items in the sample. Since the selected items are to be examined, it facilitates pulling vouchers or other documents if the items are shown in convenient sequence. A form for this purpose is shown in Figure 3. Where computer time is available, a printout in proper sequence serves this purpose.

MEASUREMENT PLANS

The measurement of the sample is distinct from the processes used in selecting the sample. In fact in some cases auditors may select the sampling by statistical means and measure the sample by traditional means. However, for auditing purposes it is preferable to document fully the selection of the sample and the means used in measuring the sample. Wherever practicable, statistical means should be used to the greatest extent in both the selection and the measurement of samples.

Viewed broadly the two basic methods of measuring the sample selected are by estimation sampling and acceptance sampling. Estimation is the most widely used type in auditing operations. It is separated into two general methods, variables sampling and attribute sampling. Variables sampling provides the answer to "how much"; attribute sampling answers the question of "how many." Discovery sampling is another variation of estimation sampling and is concerned with the probability of uncovering at least one item of a certain characteristic in a random sample. Acceptance sampling is used to determine the acceptability of a particular population. It requires a "yes" or "no" decision. The method has long been used in industry in the inspection process in determining whether to accept or reject certain production based on the number of defective products. This method is used in connection with accounting functions and is now widely used in internal auditing as stop-or-go sampling. These various plans will be discussed under Variables Sampling, Attribute Sampling, Discovery Sampling, and Stop-or-Go Sampling.

Variables Sampling. Auditors use variables sampling to provide the answer to "how much," for example, to estimate how much is the inventory total, stated in dollars, pounds, etc. Variables are the *quantitative* characteristics of a population, while attributes are usually *qualitative*. The total dollar value of invoices in a particular period would be an example of a variable. The percentage of invoices containing errors would be an example of an attribute.

To provide a better understanding of variables sampling, we will use an example. However, first it will be well to delineate the steps in appraising the reliability of an average value computed from a random sample. The steps are listed in Hill, Roth, and Arkin as follows: [8]

1. From the sample at hand, compute the average value.
2. Specify the sample size used and the field size from which it was obtained.
3. Select a confidence level (degree of assurance) which will satisfy the auditor (95, 99, or 99.9 percent if these tables are used).
4. Group the values which comprise the sample (or at least 100 of them) into groups of six or seven using the original order of their occurrence in the random number table or their systematic selection. The arrangement will be facilitated if the slips on which the random numbers are entered also contain the original sequence number of each random number used. Entry of the values for each entry on the slip with its random number and sorting back into original sequence according to this number will provide the required grouping.
5. Obtain the range of each group of six or seven. The range is the difference between the largest and smallest value in each group.

[8] Henry P. Hill, Joseph L. Roth, and Herbert Arkin, *Sampling in Auditing*, New York, The Ronald Press Company, 1962, p. 41.

6. Obtain the average range for all groups.
7. Divide this average range by the factor obtained from Fig. 3. The factor will be dependent upon the number of items included in each group. The result will be an estimate of the standard deviation.
8. In Table 2 find the section for the appropriate field size and the line for the sample size.
9. Select the column for the previously selected confidence level (95, 99, or 99.9 percent). On that line in this column the sampling reliability is expressed as a decimal of the estimated standard deviation. By multiplying the estimate of the standard deviation as obtained in 7 above by this decimal value, the sampling reliability (in terms of dollars or other units used) will result.

Where there are a small number of very high-value items, it is desirable that these items be grouped separately. For such high-value items the auditor may examine 100 percent or in any case, a much larger proportion than the low-value items. Such is the case in the example described below. The auditor wishes to estimate the amount of unreasonable travel expense charges in a given department. During the year 1970, the auditor finds that 10,400 weekly travel expense reports were paid in the particular department. This total can be readily obtained by computer or by count. The next consideration is the variability of the population, that is, the range between the lowest and highest values. He finds relatively few reports over $200, most being nearer $100. The auditor decides to stratify the population and to make a 100 percent examination of all items over $200. For the remainder he will use random selection. He finds there are 400 expense reports over $200 to be examined 100 percent, the balance of 10,000 reports to be sampled. In selecting the sample, of course, he can employ an unrestricted random selection using employee code numbers and tabulating cards of random digits, if a computer is available, or a table may be used. He may make a systematic selection with a random start, where every "*n*th" item is selected. The next consideration is the sample size for the items under $200. The sample size will depend on the precision and confidence levels the auditor judges to be desirable. To help in understanding the process, we might follow the steps previously stated.

1. *Average value.* The average value per report as shown by the sample is $183.54. With 10,000 reports the total value of the population would be about $1,835,400.
2. *Sample size.* The auditor then draws a preliminary random sample of about 50 items. These are listed in 8 groups of 6 items each. It is important that the items are grouped in the order they were randomly drawn from the population. Following are the numbers in the sample.

Group Number

1	2	3	4	5	6	7	8
$190	$196	$169	$170	$199	$190	$192	$181
177	188	171	172	192	184	180	184
180	185	181	174	186	187	179	176
186	180	174	178	180	185	178	179
179	193	179	176	184	186	189	173
189	195	170	179	181	185	191	181

3. *Range.* The next step is to determine the range between the highest and lowest values in each group. In the first group the highest value is $190 and the lowest $177, or a range of $13. The total of the ranges in these eight groups is $100, or an average of $12.50. The formula for determining the standard deviation is

$$\text{Standard deviation} = \frac{\text{average range}}{d_2 \text{ factor}}$$

The d_2 factor equals 2,534 for groups containing 6 items and 2,704 for groups containing 7 items (see Figure 4). Then

$$\text{Standard deviation} = \frac{12.50}{2.534} \text{ or } \$4.93$$

For simplicity, the auditor can use an estimated standard deviation of $5. Overstating the standard deviation slightly results in a larger sample size, is conservative, and simplifies the subsequent computations.

4. *Precision degree and confidence level.* The auditor now exercises his judgment in setting the precision degree and confidence level he desires. Assume that the auditor specifies a precision degree or range of ±0.4 percent (4/10 of 1 percent).

5. *Sampling error.* At this point the auditor is in a position to compute the stipulated error. By dividing the sampling error per expense report of 40 cents by the estimated standard deviation of $5, the auditor obtains the figure of 0.09. Table 2 shows that for a ratio sampling error to standard deviation of 0.08 for a confidence level of 95 percent and a population or field size of 10,000, the sample size should be 567.

6. *Complete sample.* To complete the sample it is necessary to select randomly an additional 519 items.

7. *Evaluation.* After the auditor has drawn the 567 reports required in the sample, he is ready to make his evaluation or measurement of his selection. After he has audited the reports, he can tabulate the unreasonable or excessive charges. It is important that the supervisors or approvers of the expense reports agree that the amounts are excessive. Assume that the total excessive charges were $500, or 88 cents per report. He can project the total amount of excessive charges in the population to be $8,800—and that the true amount of excessive charges should fall between $5,600 and $12,000, 95 times out of 100. This relates to an estimated total expense amount of $1,835,400.

There are three principal methods of projecting the sample results to arrive at the population total: (1) simple projection or blow-up method, (2) difference estimate, and (3) ratio estimate.

Simple projection or blow-up. This is the simplest method and the one most commonly used. After appropriate review and computations the sample mean is

Figure 4 FACTORS FOR ESTIMATING THE STANDARD DEVIATION

$$\text{Estimated standard deviation} = \frac{\text{average range}}{d_2 \text{ factor}}$$

Group Size	d_2 *Factor*
5	2.326
6	2.534
7	2.704
8	2.847

projected, or blown up, to provide the estimate for the population. This method has given way in many cases to the more advanced methods of difference estimation or ratio estimation.

Difference estimation. In the single projection method all items in the audited sample are included in the computations to project the sample to the entire population. However, in difference estimation only the amounts of the items with differences are used in the computation. Therefore, it is possible to deal with a much smaller sample size and attain the same reliability. Looked at another way, it is possible to attain greater reliability with the same sample size.

The amounts dealt with in difference estimation are generally smaller, and the standard deviations are likewise smaller. A simple example relates to an inventory population of 50 items, from which the following sample was taken. The precision rate is ±2 percent with a confidence level of 95 percent.

Item No.	Book value	Audit count	Difference
1	$1,250	$1,190	$ 60
2	1,010	970	40
3	780	780	0
4	260	240	20
5	530	480	50
	$3,830	$3,660	$170

The range of the book values is $990 ($1,250 − $260), and the range of the audit counts is $950 ($1,190 − $240). However, the range of the differences is $34 (170 ÷ 5). The difference of the total population is $1,700 (50 × $34). A number of examples of this method together with detailed computations and tables are given in Chapter 2 of the *Supplement to the Sampling Manual for Auditors.*

Ratio estimation. Ratio estimation is similar to difference estimation and also provides good reliability with smaller sample sizes. Ratio estimates have smaller sampling errors than difference estimates when the differences or errors have a consistent relationship to book values. However, more computations are required with the ratio method, and they are best handled by the computer.

If we use the previous example and assume the total book value is $38,000, we have the following data available:

Sample: $\dfrac{\text{audit count}}{\text{book value}} = \dfrac{3{,}830}{3{,}660} = 95.56\%$

Population: $\$38{,}000 \times 95.56\% = \$36.313$

Examples, computations, and tables for this method are given in Chapter 3 of the *Supplement to the Sampling Manual for Auditors.*

Attribute Sampling. Attribute sampling generally relates to the rate of occurrence or *qualitative* characteristics of a population. For example, the percentage of vouchers containing errors would refer to an attribute. It is also termed survey or estimation sampling for attributes and is probably the most versatile plan. It answers the question "how many?"

The objective of this method usually is to estimate how often an occurrence has taken place based on a sample. An auditor may wish to determine the frequency of coding errors in disbursement vouchers. The auditor may stipulate that he will be satisfied with an error rate of ±2 percent. He will then draw a preliminary sample and determine if the occurrence rate is close to the estimate.

To evaluate the reliability of the computation from a preliminary random sample, the following steps are suggested:

1. Determine the population to be sampled and the approximate size of the population. The data may be stratified at this time and different procedures applied to each stratum.
2. The expected occurrence rate should be set by the auditor based on his knowledge of the business, the type of transaction, and the system of internal control.
3. The precision limit and confidence level should be set in accordance with the auditors' judgment.
4. Determine the preliminary sample size from the table.
5. Draw the sample required using random selection techniques.
6. Examine the sample by means of appropriate auditing procedures.
7. Evaluate the results of the sample review. The auditor may be satisfied, or he may draw additional items to improve the results. If he is not satisfied, he may decide to change the precision and confidence levels.

To help in understanding this plan, we may provide an example and relate it to the above steps.

Assume that an auditor wishes to ascertain the correctness of coding on a certain type of document (accounts payable invoices, punching media, etc.). There exists a population of 50,000 such documents, and each document contains only one code of the type to be tested. We may now proceed with the suggested steps.

1. *Population.* The population size is 50,000. We will assume that stratification is not necessary in this case.
2. *Occurrence rate.* The occurrence rate or error rate expected by the auditor is to be no more than 5 percent.
3. *Precision and confidence level.* The auditor wants the precision rate to be ±3 percent and the confidence level 95 percent.
4. *Preliminary sample size.* From Table 3*b* we see that with an error rate of 5 percent, a precision rate of 3 percent, and a confidence level of 95 percent for a population of 50,000 the preliminary sample size would be 202 items.
5. *Sample selection.* The auditor will draw the samples by random selection either manually or by computer.
6. *Sample audit.* The auditor will audit the sampled items, keeping in mind the nature of the item and the degree of internal control present.
7. *Sample evaluation.* As the auditor is evaluating the sampled items, he must take into consideration the nature of the exceptions as well as the percentage of the exceptions. The auditing process is not mechanical, and there are many variations in the nature of the exception and the degree of error of the exception. There are four possibilities that the auditor has to consider: (1) the actual occurrence rate is approximately equal to that expected, (2) the actual rate is higher, (3) the actual rate is lower, and (4) internal controls have been violated.

ACTUAL RATE EQUALS EXPECTED RATE: Where the actual occurrence rate is equal to that expected and there is no evidence of violation of internal controls, the auditor may stop at this point. There is statistical support that if he continues sampling, further tests will also be around the expected rate of 5 percent. According to Table 3*a*, the rate of occurrence (error rate) of 5 percent in a sample size of 200 reflects a range of precision that has a lower limit of 2.4 percent and an upper limit of 9 percent. The auditor knows that the true error rate is closer to 5 percent than to 2.4 or 9 percent. He also knows that there are 95 chances out of 100 that the sample is representative of the population. Whether or not at this point the auditor is satisfied becomes a question of personal judgment. If he wants more conclusive results, he can obtain them by increasing the confidence level or reducing the precision limits. This would mean, of course, an increase in the sample size to a figure higher than the 202 items the auditor already has examined.

ACTUAL RATE IS HIGHER: Suppose instead of 10 errors the auditor found 20 errors, or 10 percent of 202, with no evidence of internal control violations. According to Table 3*d*, he would need to sample a total of 179 more items to maintain the same precision and confidence levels. Looking at it another way, this error rate means, according to Table 3*d*, that the precision range is now 6.2 to 15 percent for 202 items. The auditor has the following options: draw more samples, change the precision and confidence levels, or undertake other auditing procedures. The next course of action must be based on the judgment of the auditor.

ACTUAL RATE IS LOWER: If the auditor found errors of less than expected or if he found no errors, he may stop at this point. However, this does not mean he can safely assume there are no errors in the population. It is quite possible for a number of errors to exist and for the auditor by some chance to select 202 items without any errors. For this reason special tables have been devised, such as Table 3*e*, to indicate the precision ranges when there are no errors in the auditor's sample. In this regard Table 3*e* indicates for the 202 items selected from a population of 50,000 a precision range of 0 to 1.5 percent.

Those wishing comprehensive, step-by-step instruction in this measurement plan are referred to the AICPA programmed text, volume 2, *Sampling for Attributes,* also the *Sampling Manual for Auditors* and its supplement published by The Institute of Internal Auditors.

Discovery Sampling. This measurement plan, sometimes called exploratory sampling, is suitable for determining whether at least one particular characteristic exists in a population. It is more limited in its application than attribute sampling. Attribute sampling permits the auditor to estimate a particular population from the examination of a sample. Discovery sampling is used to show evidence that certain characteristics exist in a population when they occur at a specified minimum rate. Since discovery sampling involves the occurrence rate of a characteristic, it is in effect a special form of attribute sampling. The plan is used where the auditor's initial estimate of the occurrence rate is near 0 percent. He is looking for a type of characteristic which might indicate more widespread irregularities such as a serious internal control weakness or a significant discrepancy. For example, it may be used to detect a fictitious employee on the payroll, unauthorized shipment of goods, or duplicate payments.

To fix the sample size in discovery sampling, the following steps are necessary: (1) determine the population, (2) set the occurrence rate, (3) set the confidence level, (4) find the sample size, (5) select the sample, (6) audit the sample, and (7) evaluate the sample.

To help in understanding the plan, the following example is given:

Assume that an auditor wants to determine whether or not a commercial bank has granted loans to customers without obtaining proper collateral. The bank presumably has 15,000 loans outstanding, and the auditor wishes to find at least one loan without proper collateral, assuming that there are not more than ½ of 1 percent, or 75 such loans in the total population. (See Table 4, page 15-36.)

1. *Population.* In this example the population size is 15,000. For our purposes we will not stratify the population. However, if there is significant variability in the data, it should be considered.

2. *Occurrence rate.* According to the facts given, the occurrence rate is not more than ½ of 1 percent or 0.5 percent.

3. *Confidence level.* The auditor wants the confidence level to be at 95 percent. After this has been established, the size of the required sample can be found.

4. *Sample size.* The field size for Table 4 is already 15,000; so this factor is set. Under the occurrence rate columns are shown the probability levels (confidence levels) and on the comparable line the required sample size. Under the occurrence rate of 0.5 percent the nearest to a confidence level of 95 percent is 95.4 percent, the fourth line down. On the same line in the left column is shown 600, the sample size required.

5. *Sample selection.* The auditor will select the sample by random selection either manually or by computer. Where there are many numbers to be drawn, such as 600 in this case, the selection could be done much faster by computer.

6. *Sample audit.* The items in the sample will be carefully audited for the particular characteristic. Since the sample size is a maximum, the auditor may find one such loan at any point in his audit of the sample. Once the auditor has detected such a loan, he can stop the test and investigate the reason for the irregularity.

7. *Sample evaluation.* If the auditor finds no such loan in the sample of 600, he can state there is a 95.4 percent probability that there are no more than 0.05 percent, or 75 such loans in the entire population. Should the sample actually disclose one loan without proper collateral, the auditor can switch from discovery sampling to estimation sampling in order to determine how large a sample is needed to provide a proper estimate of either the rate, or the amount, or both, of this occurrence. As the sample already used in discovery sampling was selected by a random method, the auditor can use the data already examined as part of the sample needed in any other plan.

The AICPA programmed text, volume 4, *Discovery Sampling,* provides detailed instruction in this measurement plan. The Institute of Internal Auditors publication, *Sampling Manual for Auditors,* and its supplement also provide helpful material.

Stop-or-Go Sampling. This measurement plan is a variation of acceptance sampling that has been used in the quality control of manufactured products for many years. This plan requires the auditor to make a "yes" or "no" decision as to the population. It has been used widely in industry in sampling various accounting transactions and has been refined by internal auditors and found very useful in many phases of internal auditing.

Stop-or-go sampling permits the auditor to reduce the extent of his testing when preliminary samples disclose a small number of errors or none at all. He can begin with smaller samples than those called for by the tables for attribute sampling. Where stop-or-go sampling results are inconclusive, the auditor can switch to attribute sampling and add to the sample already selected. Stop-or-go sampling permits the auditor to stop sampling as soon as he has arrived at results that are acceptable. If not acceptable, he can go on sampling with the attribute concept. Tables for stop-or-go sampling have been prepared by the U.S. Air Force for populations ranging in size from 200 to over 2,000. Populations over 2,000 are considered "infinity," and the maximum figure can be used. This plan has the greatest applicability in situations where the auditor has reason to believe that the population he intends to test has a low rate of error. Thus the auditor will wish to use a sampling plan that permits him to reach a conclusion with the smallest possible sample size.

In proceeding with this plan, the principal steps as discussed below should be followed. These relate to (1) population, (2) occurrence rate, (3) sample size, (4) sample selection, (5) sample audit, and (6) sample evaluation. An example of stop-or-go sampling is given as follows: Assume that an auditor is examining the inventory of a manufacturing plant with a maintenance storeroom containing 3,385 items. He decides to use a sample size of 220 items for his physical check of this stock. Following is a discussion of the principal steps.

1. *Population.* The population as given in the example is 3,385 items of inventory.

2. *Occurrence rate.* The auditor expects a low occurrence rate and then tests the samples drawn to verify that fact.

3. *Sample size.* According to Table 5*b*, the size of the sample required to be drawn for populations of over 2,000 is 220. This would include all populations in excess of 2,000 regardless of how great the excess is.

4. *Sample selection.* The auditor will draw the sample by random selection, either manually or by computer. Where a small sample is involved such as this one, probably manual selection would be satisfactory. The desirability of stratification will be discussed after the sample has been examined.

5. *Sample audit.* In examining samples drawn under statistical sampling techniques, the auditor will apply the same standard of audit procedures as he does in any other case. He will consider the degree of internal control over all items in the storeroom. If prior physical inventories have varying error rates in the classes of stockroom items, he would consider this point. He would also consider the nature of each class of inventory.

6. *Sample evaluation.* The auditor is now ready to make his evaluation of the population based on the sample. During his examination of the sample the auditor finds 14 errors. These errors are distributed among the inventory classes as follows:

Code	Description	Total No. of items in the inventory	No. of items tested	No. of errors found
14711	Spare parts	1,580	104	1
14713	Rough castings	200	13	0
14731	Metals, bars, etc.	210	14	1
14741	Pipes, fittings, etc.	330	21	1
14742	Valves	100	6	0
14743	Tubes	35	2	0
14751	Electrical supplies	430	27	4
14761	Bricks and concrete materials	10	1	1
14762	Other building materials	12	1	1
14771	Gasoline and lubricants	3	1	0
14772	Packing supplies	55	4	1
14779	Other supplies	420	26	4
		3,385	220	14

The auditor is now ready to use his stop-or-go sampling tables to determine the reliability. In Table 5*b* the auditor finds that the probability rates for 14 errors in a sample size of 220 are:

Less than 8% = 77.53% (or 77.53 chances out of 100)
Less than 9% = 89.82% (or 89.82 chances out of 100)
Less than 10% = 96.02% (or 96.02 chances out of 100)
Less than 12% = 99.59% (or 99.59 chances out of 100)
Less than 14% = 99.97% (or 99.97 chances out of 100)

This indicates that there is a very good probability that the error rate in this storeroom is less than 10 percent and a good probability that it is even less than 8 percent. Should the auditor now be willing to classify his findings as satisfactory? Or does he need some additional information before he can safely come to this conclusion? Suppose the auditor had already made the following observations:

1. Spare parts, rough castings, and valves are large, slow-moving items that are well identified and under good physical control by the storekeeper. Prior physical inventories of these items disclosed very low error rates.
2. Bricks, concrete, and other building materials are stored in an area not under good physical control by the storekeeper. These items, plus gasoline and lubricants, have always shown high error rates during physical inventories.
3. All other items appear under good physical control by the storekeeper. Prior physical inventories taken by the plant and by the auditors have disclosed satisfactory error rates of less than 10 percent.

Based on these three observations alone, the auditor is in a better position to devise a sampling plan flexible enough to take into account existing conditions within the storeroom.

He knows the storeroom universe consists of three groups of materials that are homogeneous in certain respects. Based on past physical inventory results, the auditor can decide what error rates he can expect to find if conditions have not changed. Suppose the auditor now reclassifies this universe into three homogeneous groups and attempts to select the *smallest* sample sizes as indicated in the tables. He would now have a more flexible plan. Assume that when he employs this plan with another sample he comes up with the following results:

Code	Description	Total No. of items in the inventory	No. of items tested	No. of errors found
Group 1:				
14711	Spare parts	1,580	42	0
14713	Rough castings	200	5	0
14742	Valves	100	3	0
	Total group 1	1,880	50	0
Group 2:				
14761	Brick and concrete materials	10	10	5
14762	Other building materials	12	12	5
14771	Gasoline and lubricants	3	3	2
	Total group 2 (100% test)	25	25	12
Group 3:				
14731	Metals, bars, etc.	210	10	1
14741	Pipes, fittings, etc.	330	14	1
14743	Tubes	35	1	0
14651	Electrical supplies	430	21	3
14772	Packing supplies	55	3	1
14779	Other supplies	420	21	3
	Total group 3	1,480	70	9
	Grand totals	3,385	145	21

An inspection of Table 5*a* indicates that for group 1, where the auditor sampled 50 items and found no errors, there are:

78.19 chances out of 100 that the error rate is less than 3%
87.01 chances out of 100 that the error rate is less than 4%
92.31 chances out of 100 that the error rate is less than 5%

Based on his knowledge of storeroom operations, he is now in a position to decide satisfactorily that this group of homogeneous stored materials is under proper control—provided that all other necessary audit observations taken in conjunction with this test also support this conclusion. After examining the results with group 2, the auditor would take a 100 percent test, coming up with proof that his conclusions were correct.

For group 3, Table 5*a* indicates that for a sample of 70 items with 9 errors there are:

15.86 chances out of 100 that the error rate is less than 10%
32.88 chances out of 100 that the error rate is less than 12%
52.46 chances out of 100 that the error rate is less than 14%
70.10 chances out of 100 that the error rate is less than 16%
83.23 chances out of 100 that the error rate is less than 18%
91.55 chances out of 100 that the error rate is less than 20%

Complete physical inventories of this group of items in the past have resulted in error rates of less than 10 percent. The above test indicates that something has indeed gone wrong with this phase of the storeroom operation. There is no question that this second sampling plan has highlighted situations that need attention.

A well-thought-out sampling plan will reveal deficiencies not necessarily disclosed by other kinds of plans. Nor does a good plan necessarily require using a larger sample size or counting more items. In the previous examples, the second plan employed by the auditor readily revealed a deficiency not obviously noticeable in the first plan. By stratifying the material in the storeroom into three homogeneous groupings, the auditor was able to pinpoint the errors turned up in the sample.

The stop-or-go sampling plan is discussed in some detail in the *Sampling Manual for Auditors* published by The Institute of Internal Auditors.

BIBLIOGRAPHY

American Institute of Certified Public Accountants: *An Auditor's Approach to Statistical Sampling*, New York, AICPA, 1967 to date.

Auditor General, Comptroller of the Air Force: *Table of Probabilities for Use in Exploratory Sampling*, Attachment No. 5 to AG1 50-5, Aug. 5, 1959.

The Institute of Internal Auditors: *Sampling Manual for Auditors* and *Supplement*, New York, The Institute, 1967 to date.

Interstate Commerce Commission, Bureau of Transport Economics and Statistics: *Table of 105,000 Random Decimal Digits*, Statement No. 4914, File No. 261-A-1, Washington, 1949.

U.S. Department of the Air Force, Auditor General: *Table of Probabilities for Use in Stop-or-Go Sampling*, 1961.

Arkin, Herbert: *Handbook of Sampling for Auditing and Accounting*, New York, McGraw-Hill Book Company, 1963.

Hill, Henry P., Joseph L. Roth, and Herbert Arkin: *Sampling in Auditing*, New York, The Ronald Press Company, 1962.

Rand Corporation: *A Million Random Digits*, Glencoe, Ill., The Free Press, 1955.

Vance, Lawrence L., and John Neter: *Statistical Sampling for Auditors and Accountants*, New York, John Wiley & Sons, 1956.

Cashin, James A., and Garland C. Owens: *Auditing*, 2d ed., New York, The Ronald Press Company, 1963.

Healy, Robert E.: "Sampling in Auditing—The Whole Story," *The Price Waterhouse Review*, Winter, 1964.

Stettler, Howard F.: "Some Observations of Statistical Sampling in Auditing," *The Journal of Accountancy*, April, 1966.

Kraft, William H., Jr.: "Statistical Sampling for Auditors—A New Look," *The Journal of Accountancy*, August, 1968.

Nigra, Alphonse L.: "Statistical Sampling with EDP Equipment," *The Internal Auditor*, March/April, 1969.

Tummins, Marvin, and Earl F. Davis: "Block or Random Sampling," *The Internal Auditor*, May/June, 1970.

TABLE 1 Random Numbers

Line \ Col.	(1)	(2)	(3)	(4)	(5)	(6)	(7)	(8)	(9)	(10)	(11)	(12)	(13)	(14)
1	10480	15011	01536	02011	81647	91646	69179	14194	62590	36207	20969	99570	91291	90700
2	22368	46573	25595	85393	30995	89198	27982	53402	93965	34095	52666	19174	39615	99505
3	24130	48360	22527	97265	76393	64809	15179	24830	49340	32081	30680	19655	63348	58629
4	42167	93093	06243	61680	07856	16376	39440	53537	71341	57004	00849	74917	97758	16379
5	37570	39975	81837	16656	06121	91782	60468	81305	49684	60672	14110	06927	01263	54613
6	77921	06907	11008	42751	27756	53498	18602	70659	90655	15053	21916	81825	44394	42880
7	99562	72905	56420	69994	98872	31016	71194	18738	44013	48840	63213	21069	10634	12952
8	96301	91977	05463	07972	18876	20922	94595	56869	69014	60045	18425	84903	42508	32307
9	89579	14342	63661	10281	17453	18103	57740	84378	25331	12566	58678	44947	05585	56941
10	85475	36857	53342	53988	53060	59533	38867	62300	08158	17983	16439	11458	18593	64952
11	28918	69578	88231	33276	70997	79936	56865	05859	90106	31595	01547	85590	91610	78188
12	63553	40961	48235	03427	49626	69445	18663	72695	52180	20847	12234	90511	33703	90322
13	09429	93969	52636	92737	88974	33488	36320	17617	30015	08272	84115	27156	30613	74952
14	10365	61129	87529	85689	48237	52267	67689	93394	01511	26358	85104	20285	29975	89868
15	07119	97336	71048	08178	77233	13916	47564	81056	97735	85977	29372	74461	28551	90707
16	51085	12765	51821	51259	77452	16308	60756	92144	49442	53900	70960	63990	75601	40719
17	02368	21382	52404	60268	89368	19885	55322	44819	01188	63255	64835	44919	05944	55157
18	01011	54092	33362	94904	31273	04146	18594	29852	71585	85030	51132	01915	92747	64951
19	52162	53916	46369	58586	23216	14513	83149	98736	23495	64350	94738	17752	35156	35749
20	07056	97628	33787	09998	42698	06691	76988	13602	51851	46104	88916	19509	25625	58104
21	48663	91245	85828	14346	09172	30168	90229	04734	59193	22178	30421	61666	99904	32812
22	54164	58492	22421	74103	47070	25306	76468	26384	58151	06646	21524	15227	96909	44592
23	32639	32363	05597	24200	13363	38005	94342	28728	35806	06912	17012	64161	18296	22851
24	29334	27001	87637	87308	58731	00256	45834	15398	46557	41135	10367	07684	36188	18510
25	02488	33062	28834	07351	19731	92420	60952	61280	50001	67658	32586	86679	50720	94953
26	81525	72295	04839	96423	24878	82651	66566	14778	76797	14780	13300	87074	79666	95725
27	29676	20591	68086	26432	46901	20849	89768	81536	86645	12659	92259	57102	80428	25280
28	00742	57392	39064	66432	84673	40027	32832	61362	98947	96067	64760	64584	96096	98253
29	05366	04213	25669	26422	44407	44048	37937	63904	45766	66134	75470	66520	34693	90449
30	91921	26418	64117	94305	26766	25940	39972	22209	71500	64568	91402	42416	07844	69618

31	00582	04711	87917	77341	42206	35126	74087	99547	81817	42607	43808	76655	62028	76630
32	00725	69884	62797	56170	86324	88072	76222	36086	84637	93161	76038	65855	77919	88006
33	69011	65795	95876	55293	18988	27354	26575	08625	40801	59920	29841	80150	12777	48501
34	25976	57948	29888	88604	67917	48708	18912	82271	65424	69774	33611	54262	85963	03547
35	09763	83473	73577	12908	30883	18317	28290	35797	05998	41688	34952	37888	38917	88050
36	91567	42595	27958	30134	04024	86385	29880	99730	55536	84855	29080	09250	79656	74211
37	17955	56349	90999	49127	20044	59931	06115	20542	18059	02008	73708	83517	36103	42791
38	46503	18584	18845	49618	02304	51038	20655	58727	28168	15475	56942	53389	20562	87338
39	92157	89634	94824	78171	84610	82834	09922	25417	44137	48413	25555	21246	35509	20468
40	14577	62765	35605	81263	39667	47358	56873	56307	61607	49518	89656	20103	77490	18062
41	98427	07523	33362	64270	01638	92477	66969	98420	04880	45585	46565	04102	46880	45709
42	34914	63976	88720	82765	34476	17032	87589	40836	32427	70002	70663	88863	77775	69348
43	70060	28277	39475	46473	23219	53416	94970	25832	69975	94884	19661	72828	00102	66794
44	53976	54914	06990	67245	68350	82948	11398	42878	80287	88267	47363	46634	06541	97809
45	76072	29515	40980	07391	50745	85774	22987	80059	39911	96189	41151	14222	60697	59583
46	90788	52310	83974	89992	65831	38857	50490	83765	55687	14361	31780	57375	56228	41546
47	64364	67418	33339	31926	14883	24413	59744	92351	97473	89286	35931	04110	23726	51900
48	08962	00358	31662	25308	61642	34072	81249	35648	56891	69532	48373	45578	78547	81788
49	95012	68379	93526	70765	10592	04542	76463	54328	02349	17247	28865	14777	62730	92277
50	15664	10493	20498	38391	91132	21999	59516	81652	27195	48223	46751	22923	32261	65633

SOURCE: Interstate Commerce Commission, *Table of 105,000 Random Decimal Digits*, Washington, D.C., Bureau of Transport, Economics and Statistics, 1949.

TABLE 2 Variables Sampling—Sample Sizes for Estimating Average Values

Ratio of sampling error to standard deviation (sampling error/standard deviation)	Sample size required with confidence levels of			
	90%	95%	99%	99.9%
Field size is 9,000				
.02	3,862			
.03	2,254	2,896	4,060	
0.4	1,424	1,896	2,846	3,876
.05	966	1,313	2,055	2,936
.06	694	954	1,534	2,265
.07	520	722	1,181	1,783
.08	404	563	933	1,432
.09	322	451	754	1,170
.10	263	369	620	972
.11	218	307	519	819
.12	184	260	440	698
.13	157	222	378	602
.14	136	192	328	524
.15	119	168	287	460
.16	105	148	253	407
.17	93	131	225	362
.18	83	118	201	325
.19	75	106	181	292
.20	68	96	164	265
.21	61	87	149	241
.22	56	79	136	219
.23	51	73	125	202
.24	47	67	115	186
.25	44	62	106	171
.30		43	74	120
.35			55	89
.40			42	68
Field size is 10,000				
.02	4,035	4,900		
.03	2,312	2,991	4,252	
.04	1,447	1,936	2,938	4,050
.05	977	1,332	2,103	3,034
.06	699	965	1,561	2,323
.07	523	728	1,196	1,819
.08	406	567	943	1,455
.09	323	453	760	1,186
.10	263	370	624	982
.11	219	308	522	826
.12	184	260	442	704
.13	158	223	379	606
.14	136	193	329	527
.15	119	168	287	462
.16	105	148	254	409
.17	93	132	226	364
.18	83	118	202	326
.19	75	106	182	293

SOURCE: Herbert Arkin, *Handbook of Sampling for Auditing and Accounting*, New York, McGraw-Hill Book Company, 1963, pp. 542, 543.

TABLE 3a Attribute Sampling—Revised Precision Limits Based on Error Rate Found in Sample Audited

Confidence level 95%, sample error rate 5%

	For field size of													
	500		1,000		1,500		2,000		10,000		50,000		100,000 and over	
And sample size is	Lower limit, %	Upper limit, %	Lower limit, %	Upper limit, %	Lower limit, %	Upper limit, %	Lower limit, %	Upper limit, %	Lower limit, %	Upper limit, %	Lower limit, %	Upper limit, %	Lower limit, %	Upper limit, %
80	1.7	11.7	1.5	12.0	1.5	12.1	1.5	12.2	1.4	12.3	1.4	12.3	1.4	12.3
90	1.8	11.1	1.7	11.4	1.6	11.5	1.6	11.6	1.5	11.7	1.5	11.7	1.5	11.8
100	2.0	10.6	1.8	11.0	1.8	11.1	1.7	11.1	1.7	11.3	1.6	11.3	1.6	11.3
120	2.3	9.8	2.1	10.2	2.0	10.3	2.0	10.4	1.9	10.5	1.9	10.6	1.9	10.6
140	2.5	9.4	2.3	9.8	2.2	9.9	2.2	10.0	2.1	10.1	2.1	10.1	2.1	10.1
150	2.6	9.0	2.3	9.4	2.3	9.6	2.2	9.6	2.1	9.8	2.1	9.8	2.1	9.8
160	2.7	8.8	2.4	9.2	2.3	9.4	2.3	9.4	2.2	9.6	2.2	9.6	2.2	9.6
180	2.8	8.4	2.6	8.9	2.5	9.0	2.4	9.1	2.3	9.2	2.3	9.3	2.3	9.3
200	3.0	8.1	2.7	8.6	2.6	8.7	2.6	8.8	2.5	9.0	2.4	9.0	2.4	9.0
250	3.3	7.5	3.0	8.0	2.9	8.2	2.8	8.3	2.7	8.4	2.7	8.5	2.6	8.5
300			3.2	7.6	3.1	7.8	3.0	7.9	2.9	8.1	2.8	8.1	2.8	8.1
400			3.5	7.0	3.4	7.2	3.3	7.3	3.1	7.6	3.1	7.6	3.1	7.6
500					3.6	6.9	3.5	7.0	3.3	7.2	3.3	7.3	3.3	7.3
600					3.8	6.6	3.7	6.7	3.4	7.0	3.4	7.0	3.4	7.1
700					3.9	6.4	3.8	6.5	3.6	6.8	3.5	6.9	3.5	6.9
800							3.9	6.4	3.7	6.7	3.6	6.7	3.6	6.7
900							4.0	6.2	3.7	6.6	3.7	6.6	3.7	6.6
1,000									3.8	6.5	3.8	6.5	3.7	6.5
1,500									4.0	6.1	4.0	6.2	4.0	6.2
2,000									4.2	5.9	4.1	6.0	4.1	6.0
3,000									4.4	5.7	4.3	5.8	4.2	5.8

SOURCE: Herbert Arkin, *Handbook of Sampling for Auditing and Accounting*, New York, McGraw-Hill Book Company, 1963, p. 439.

TABLE 3b Attribute Sampling—For Determining Sample Sizes When Expected Rate of Occurrence Is Not over 5 Percent

Confidence level 95%

Population size	Sample size for reliability of						
	±.5%	±1%	±1.5%	±2%	±2.5%	±3%	±4%
3,000		1,135	639	396	267	190	110
3,100		1,149	643	398	267	190	110
3,300		1,175	652	401	269	191	110
3,500		1,200	659	404	270	192	110
3,700		1,222	666	406	271	192	111
3,900		1,243	672	409	272	193	111
4,000		1,253	675	410	273	193	111
4,500		1,299	688	414	275	194	111
4,700		1,315	692	416	275	194	111
5,000		1,337	698	418	276	195	112
5,500		1,370	707	421	278	196	112
6,000		1,400	715	424	279	196	112
6,500		1,425	722	426	280	197	112
7,000		1,448	727	428	281	197	112
7,500	3,700	1,468	732	430	282	197	112
8,000	3,817	1,486	737	432	282	198	112
8,500	3,932	1,503	741	433	283	198	113
9,000	4,031	1,517	744	434	283	198	113
9,500	4,128	1,531	748	435	284	199	113
10,000	4,220	1,543	751	436	284	199	113
10,500	4,306	1,555	753	437	285	199	113
11,500	4,465	1,575	758	439	285	199	113
13,000	4,675	1,600	764	441	286	200	113
14,500	4,856	1,621	769	442	287	200	113
15,000	4,851	1,627	770	443	287	200	113
16,500	5,061	1,643	774	443	287	200	113
19,000	5,274	1,665	778	446	288	201	113
20,000	5,348	1,672	780	446	288	201	113
22,000	5,482	1,685	783	447	289	201	113
24,000	5,595	1,696	785	448	289	201	114
26,000	5,699	1,705	787	448	289	201	114
28,000	5,790	1,713	789	449	289	201	114
30,000	5,871	1,720	790	449	290	201	114
32,000	5.944	1,727	791	450	290	202	114
34,000	6,010	1,732	793	450	290	202	114
36,000	6,069	1,737	794	451	290	202	114
38,000	6,123	1,741	795	451	290	202	114
40,000	6,173	1,745	795	451	290	202	114
45,000	6,282	1,754	797	452	291	202	114
50,000	6,370	1,761	799	452	291	202	114
60,000	6,508	1,771	801	453	291	202	114
70,000	6,610	1,779	802	453	291	202	114
80,000	6,689	1,784	803	454	291	202	114
90,000	6,752	1,789	804	454	291	202	114
100,000	6,803	1,792	805	454	292	202	114
150,000	6,961	1,803	807	455	292	203	114
200,000	7,043	1,809	808	455	292	203	114
250,000	7,092	1,812	809	455	292	203	114
300,000	7,126	1,814	809	456	292	203	114
400,000	7,169	1,817	810	456	292	203	114
500,000	7,196	1,818	810	456	292	203	114

SOURCE: Herbert Arkin, *Handbook of Sampling for Auditing and Accounting,* New York, McGraw-Hill Book Company, 1963, pp. 350, 351.

TABLE 3c Attribute Sampling—Revised Precision Limits Based on Error Rate Found in Sample Audited

Confidence level 99%, sample error rate 5%

	For field size of													
	500		1,000		1,500		2,000		10,000		50,000		100,000 and over	
And sample size is	Lower limit, %	Upper limit, %	Lower limit, %	Upper limit, %	Lower limit, %	Upper limit, %	Lower limit, %	Upper limit, %	Lower limit, %	Upper limit, %	Lower limit, %	Upper limit, %	Lower limit, %	Upper limit, %
80	1.2	14.1	1.0	14.5	1.0	14.7	0.9	14.7	0.9	14.9	0.9	14.9	0.9	14.9
90	1.4	13.3	1.2	13.7	1.1	13.9	1.1	14.0	1.0	14.1	1.0	14.2	1.0	14.2
100	1.5	12.6	1.3	13.1	1.2	13.2	1.2	13.3	1.1	13.5	1.1	13.5	1.1	13.5
120	1.8	11.6	1.5	12.1	1.5	12.2	1.4	12.3	1.3	12.5	1.3	12.5	1.3	12.5
140	2.0	10.9	1.8	11.4	1.7	11.6	1.6	11.7	1.5	11.9	1.5	11.9	1.5	11.9
150	2.1	10.4	1.8	11.0	1.7	11.2	1.7	11.3	1.6	11.5	1.6	11.5	1.6	11.5
160	2.2	10.1	1.9	10.7	1.8	10.9	1.8	11.0	1.7	11.2	1.6	11.2	1.6	11.2
180	2.4	9.6	2.1	10.2	2.0	10.4	1.9	10.5	1.8	10.7	1.8	10.8	1.8	10.8
200	2.6	9.2	2.2	9.8	2.1	10.0	2.0	10.1	1.9	10.4	1.9	10.4	1.9	10.4
250	3.0	8.3	2.5	9.1	2.4	9.3	2.3	9.4	2.2	9.6	2.1	9.7	2.1	9.7
300			2.8	8.5	2.6	8.7	2.5	8.9	2.4	9.1	2.3	9.2	2.3	9.2
400			3.2	7.7	3.0	8.0	2.9	8.1	2.7	8.4	2.6	8.5	2.6	8.5
500					3.2	7.5	3.1	7.7	2.9	8.0	2.8	8.1	2.8	8.1
600					3.4	7.1	3.3	7.3	3.1	7.7	3.0	7.7	3.0	7.8
700					3.6	6.8	3.5	7.0	3.2	7.4	3.1	7.5	3.1	7.5
800							3.6	6.8	3.3	7.2	3.2	7.3	3.2	7.3
900							3.7	6.6	3.4	7.1	3.3	7.2	3.3	7.2
1,000									3.5	6.9	3.4	7.0	3.4	7.0
1,500									3.8	8.5	3.7	6.6	3.7	6.6
2,000									4.0	6.2	3.9	6.4	3.8	6.4
3,000									4.2	5.9	4.1	6.1	4.0	6.1

SOURCE: Herbert Arkin, *Handbook of Sampling for Auditing and Accounting*, New York, McGraw-Hill Book Company, 1963, p. 440.

TABLE 3d Attribute Sampling—Revised Precision Limits Based on Error Rate Found in Sample Audited

Confidence level 95%, sample error rate 10%

	For field size of													
	500		1,000		1,500		2,000		10,000		50,000		100,000 and over	
And sample size is	Lower limit, %	Upper limit, %	Lower limit, %	Upper limit, %	Lower limit, %	Upper limit, %	Lower limit, %	Upper limit, %	Lower limit, %	Upper limit, %	Lower limit, %	Upper limit, %	Lower limit, %	Upper limit, %
50	3.7	21.2	3.5	21.5	3.4	21.6	3.4	21.7	3.3	21.8	3.3	21.8	3.3	21.8
80	4.9	18.0	4.6	18.4	4.6	18.5	4.5	18.6	4.4	18.7	4.4	18.8	4.4	18.8
90	5.2	17.4	4.9	17.8	4.8	17.9	4.8	17.9	4.7	18.1	4.7	18.1	4.7	18.1
100	5.4	16.8	5.2	17.3	5.1	17.4	5.0	17.4	4.9	17.6	4.9	17.6	4.9	17.6
120	5.9	15.9	5.6	16.4	5.5	16.5	5.4	16.6	5.3	16.8	5.3	16.8	5.3	16.8
140	6.2	15.3	5.9	15.8	5.8	15.9	5.7	16.0	5.6	16.2	5.6	16.2	5.6	16.2
150	6.4	15.0	6.0	15.5	5.9	15.6	5.9	15.7	5.7	15.9	5.7	15.9	5.7	16.0
160	6.6	14.7	6.2	15.3	6.1	15.4	6.0	15.5	5.9	15.7	5.8	15.7	5.8	15.7
180	6.8	14.3	6.4	14.8	6.3	15.0	6.2	15.1	6.1	15.3	6.0	15.3	6.0	15.3
200	7.1	13.9	6.6	14.5	6.5	14.7	6.4	14.8	6.3	15.0	6.2	15.0	6.2	15.0
250	7.6	13.1	7.0	13.8	6.9	14.0	6.8	14.1	6.6	14.4	6.6	14.4	6.6	14.4
300			7.4	13.3	7.2	13.6	7.1	13.7	6.9	13.9	6.9	14.0	6.9	14.0
400			7.9	12.6	7.6	12.9	7.5	13.0	7.3	13.3	7.3	13.4	7.2	13.4
500					8.0	12.4	7.9	12.6	7.6	12.9	7.5	13.0	7.5	13.0
600					8.2	12.1	8.1	12.2	7.8	12.6	7.7	12.7	7.7	12.7
700					8.5	11.8	8.3	12.0	8.0	12.4	7.9	12.5	7.9	12.5
800							8.5	11.8	8.1	12.2	8.0	12.3	8.0	12.3
900							8.6	11.6	8.2	12.1	8.1	12.1	8.1	12.2
1,000									8.3	11.9	8.2	12.0	8.2	12.0
1,500									8.6	11.5	8.6	11.6	8.5	11.6
2,000									8.9	11.3	8.7	11.4	8.7	11.4
3,000									9.1	10.9	9.0	11.1	9.0	11.1

SOURCE: Herbert Arkin, *Handbook of Sampling for Auditing and Accounting*, New York, McGraw-Hill Book Company, 1963, p. 454.

TABLE 3e Attribute Sampling—Revised Precision Limits Based on Error Rate Found in Sample Audited

Confidence level 95%, sample error rate 0%

And sample size is	For field size of 500 upper limit, %	1,000 upper limit, %	1,500 upper limit, %	2,000 upper limit, %	10,000 upper limit, %	50,000 upper limit, %	100,000 and over upper limit, %
30	9.2	9.4	9.4	9.4	9.5	9.5	9.5
40	6.9	7.1	7.1	7.1	7.2	7.2	7.2
50	5.5	5.7	5.7	5.7	5.8	5.8	5.8
60	4.6	4.7	4.8	4.8	4.9	4.9	4.9
70	3.9	4.0	4.1	4.1	4.2	4.2	4.2
80	3.4	3.5	3.6	3.6	3.7	3.7	3.7
90	3.0	3.1	3.2	3.2	3.3	3.3	3.3
100	2.6	2.8	2.9	2.9	2.9	3.0	3.0
150	1.7	1.8	1.9	1.9	2.0	2.0	2.0
200	1.2	1.3	1.4	1.4	1.5	1.5	1.5
300		0.8	0.9	0.9	1.0	1.0	1.0
400		0.6	0.6	0.7	0.7	0.7	0.8
500			0.5	0.5	0.6	0.6	0.6
1,000					0.3	0.3	0.3
2,000					0.1	0.2	0.2

SOURCE: Herbert Arkin, *Handbook of Sampling for Auditing and Accounting*, New York, McGraw-Hill Book Company, 1963, p. 505.

TABLE 4 Discovery Sampling

Probabilities of including at least one occurrence in a sample (field size is 15,000)

When sample size is	When occurrence rate is			
	0.1%	0.2%	0.3%	0.4%
	Probability, %, of finding at least one occurrence is			
100	9.6	18.2	26.1	33.1
200	18.2	33.2	45.3	55.3
500	39.9	63.9	78.2	86.9
600	45.8	70.6	84.1	91.4
700	51.2	76.2	88.4	94.3
800	56.1	80.7	91.5	96.3
900	60.5	84.4	93.8	97.6
1,000	64.5	87.4	95.5	98.4
1,500	79.4	95.8	99.1	99.8
2,000	88.3	98.6	99.8	99.9+
3,000	96.5	99.9	99.9+	99.9+
	When occurrence rate is			
	0.5%	1%	1.5%	2%
	Probability, %, of finding at least one occurrence is			
100	39.5	63.6	78.1	86.8
200	63.6	86.9	95.2	98.3
500	92.3	99.4	99.9+	99.9+
600	95.4	99.8	99.9+	99.9+
700	97.2	99.9	99.9+	99.9+
800	98.4	99.9+	99.9+	99.9+
900	99.0	99.9+	99.9+	99.9+
1,000	99.5	99.9+	99.9+	99.9+
1,500	99.9+	99.9+	99.9+	99.9+
2,000	99.9+	99.9+	99.9+	99.9+
3,000	99.9+	99.9+	99.9+	99.9+

SOURCE: Herbert Arkin, *Handbook of Sampling for Auditing and Accounting,* New York, McGraw-Hill Book Company, 1963, pp. 542, 543.

TABLE 5a Stop-or-Go Sampling

Size of sample examined	No. of errors found	Probability that error rate in universe size of over 2,000 is less than														
		1%	2%	3%	4%	5%	6%	7%	8%	9%	10%	12%	14%	16%	18%	20%
50	0	39.50	63.58	78.19	87.01	92.31	95.47	97.34	98.45	99.10	99.49	99.83	99.95	99.98	100.00	100.00
	1	8.94	26.42	44.47	59.95	72.06	81.00	87.35	91.73	94.68	96.62	98.69	99.52	99.83	99.94	99.98
	2	1.38	7.84	18.92	32.33	45.95	58.38	68.92	77.40	83.95	88.83	94.87	97.79	99.10	99.65	99.87
	3	0.16	1.78	6.28	13.91	23.96	35.27	46.73	57.47	66.97	74.97	86.55	93.30	96.88	98.64	99.43
	4	0.02	0.32	1.68	4.90	10.36	17.94	27.10	37.11	47.23	56.88	73.21	84.72	91.92	96.01	98.15
	5		0.05	0.37	1.44	3.78	7.76	13.51	20.81	29.28	38.39	56.47	71.86	83.23	90.71	95.20
	6		0.01	0.07	0.36	1.18	2.89	5.83	10.19	15.96	22.98	39.35	56.18	70.81	81.99	89.66
70	0	50.52	75.69	88.14	94.26	97.24	98.69	99.38	99.71	99.86	99.94	99.99	100.00	100.00	100.00	100.00
	1	15.53	40.96	62.47	77.51	87.03	92.81	96.10	97.93	98.92	99.45	99.86	99.97	99.99	100.00	100.00
	2	3.34	16.50	35.08	53.44	68.63	79.87	87.59	92.60	95.72	97.58	99.28	99.80	99.95	99.99	100.00
	3	0.54	5.19	15.87	30.71	46.61	61.15	73.07	82.10	88.53	92.88	97.48	99.19	99.76	99.93	99.98
	4	0.07	1.32	5.93	14.85	27.21	41.13	54.77	66.80	76.61	84.12	93.36	97.51	99.16	99.74	99.92
	5		0.28	1.86	6.12	13.72	24.27	36.58	49.24	61.06	71.28	85.94	93.92	97.64	99.17	99.73
	6		0.05	0.50	2.18	6.04	12.61	21.75	32.70	44.40	55.82	74.98	87.57	94.50	97.81	99.20
	7			0.12	0.68	2.34	5.80	11.54	19.54	29.33	40.12	61.33	78.13	89.04	95.08	98.00
	8			0.02	0.19	0.80	2.38	5.49	10.54	17.59	26.37	46.66	66.03	80.85	90.36	95.63
	9				0.05	0.25	0.88	2.36	5.14	9.60	15.86	32.88	52.46	70.10	83.23	91.55
100	0	63.40	86.74	95.25	98.31	99.41	99.80	99.93	99.98	99.99	100.00	100.00	100.00	100.00	100.00	100.00
	1	26.42	59.67	80.54	91.28	96.29	98.48	99.40	99.77	99.91	99.97	100.00	100.00	100.00	100.00	100.00
	2	7.94	32.33	58.02	76.79	88.17	94.34	97.42	98.87	99.52	99.81	99.97	100.00	100.00	100.00	100.00
	3	1.84	14.10	35.28	57.05	74.22	85.70	92.56	96.33	98.27	99.22	99.86	99.98	100.00	100.00	100.00
	4	0.34	5.08	18.22	37.11	56.40	72.32	83.68	90.97	95.26	97.63	99.47	99.90	99.98	100.00	100.00
	5	0.05	1.55	8.08	21.16	38.40	55.93	70.86	82.01	89.55	94.24	98.48	99.66	99.93	99.99	100.00
	6	0.01	0.41	3.12	10.64	23.40	39.37	55.57	69.68	80.60	88.28	96.33	99.03	99.78	99.96	99.99
	7		0.09	1.06	4.75	12.80	25.17	40.12	55.29	68.72	79.40	92.39	97.67	99.39	99.86	99.97
	8		0.02	0.32	1.90	6.31	14.63	26.60	40.74	55.06	67.91	86.14	95.08	98.53	99.62	99.91
	9			0.09	0.68	2.82	7.75	16.20	27.80	41.25	54.87	77.44	90.78	96.84	99.08	99.77
	10			0.02	0.22	1.15	3.76	9.08	17.57	28.82	41.68	66.63	84.40	93.93	98.00	99.43
	11				0.07	0.43	1.68	4.69	10.29	18.76	29.70	54.58	75.91	89.39	96.05	98.74
	12				0.02	0.15	0.69	2.24	5.59	11.38	19.82	42.39	65.66	82.97	92.89	97.47
	13					0.05	0.26	0.99	2.82	6.45	12.39	31.14	54.36	74.69	88.19	95.31
	14					0.01	0.09	0.41	1.33	3.41	7.26	21.60	42.94	64.90	81.77	91.96
	15						0.03	0.16	0.59	1.69	3.99	14.15	32.27	54.20	73.70	87.15

SOURCE: U.S. Department of the Air Force, Auditor General, "Table of Probabilities for Use in Stop-or-Go Sampling," p. 65.

TABLE 5b Stop-or-Go Sampling

Size of sample examined	No. of errors found	Probability that error rate in universe size of over 2,000 is less than														
		1%	2%	3%	4%	5%	6%	7%	8%	9%	10%	12%	14%	16%	18%	20%
220	0	89.04	98.83	99.88	99.99	100.00	100.00	100.00	100.00	100.00	100.00	100.00	100.00	100.00	100.00	100.00
	1	64.69	93.55	99.04	99.87	99.98	100.00	100.00	100.00	100.00	100.00	100.00	100.00	100.00	100.00	100.00
	2	37.76	81.77	96.21	99.35	99.90	99.99	100.00	100.00	100.00	100.00	100.00	100.00	100.00	100.00	100.00
	3	17.99	64.30	89.84	97.75	99.58	99.93	99.99	100.00	100.00	100.00	100.00	100.00	100.00	100.00	100.00
	4	7.15	44.96	79.15	94.15	98.66	99.74	99.95	99.99	100.00	100.00	100.00	100.00	100.00	100.00	100.00
	5	2.42	27.91	64.88	87.67	96.58	99.21	99.84	99.97	99.99	100.00	100.00	100.00	100.00	100.00	100.00
	6	0.71	15.43	49.06	77.99	92.66	97.99	99.53	99.90	99.98	100.00	100.00	100.00	100.00	100.00	100.00
	7	0.19	7.65	34.10	65.67	86.34	95.61	98.81	99.72	90.94	99.99	100.00	100.00	100.00	100.00	100.00
	8	0.04	3.43	21.78	51.99	77.48	91.57	97.38	99.30	99.83	99.67	100.00	100.00	100.00	100.00	100.00
	9	0.01	1.39	12.81	38.57	66.51	85.50	94.83	98.43	99.59	99.90	100.00	100.00	100.00	100.00	100.00
	10		0.52	6.95	26.77	54.32	77.32	90.79	96.85	99.07	99.76	99.99	100.00	100.00	100.00	100.00
	11		0.18	3.50	17.38	42.07	67.35	84.98	94.21	98.09	99.45	99.98	100.00	100.00	100.00	100.00
	12		0.06	1.63	10.57	30.84	56.27	77.36	90.22	96.40	98.85	99.92	100.00	100.00	100.00	100.00
	13		0.02	0.71	6.03	21.39	44.96	68.19	84.67	93.72	97.78	99.81	99.99	100.00	100.00	100.00
	14			0.29	3.23	14.03	34.28	57.98	77.53	89.82	96.02	99.59	99.97	100.00	100.00	100.00
	15			0.11	1.63	8.71	24.92	47.43	69.00	84.51	93.35	99.18	99.94	100.00	100.00	100.00
	16			0.04	0.78	5.13	17.26	37.25	59.50	77.78	89.54	98.46	99.86	99.99	100.00	100.00
	17			0.01	0.35	2.86	11.40	28.06	49.59	69.80	84.46	97.28	99.71	99.98	100.00	100.00
	18				0.15	1.52	7.18	20.26	39.87	60.89	78.09	95.47	99.43	99.95	100.00	100.00
	19				0.06	0.77	4.31	14.02	30.89	51.53	70.57	92.85	98.94	99.90	99.99	100.00
	20				0.02	0.37	2.48	9.29	23.04	42.22	62.17	89.25	98.15	99.80	99.98	100.00
	21				0.01	0.17	1.36	5.91	16.53	33.46	53.29	84.58	96.93	99.61	99.97	100.00
	22					0.07	0.71	3.60	11.42	25.61	44.36	78.82	95.12	99.29	99.93	100.00
	23					0.03	0.36	2.11	7.59	18.94	35.81	72.06	92.59	98.76	99.86	99.99
	24					0.01	0.17	1.19	4.85	13.52	28.02	64.49	89.21	97.93	99.74	99.98
	25						0.08	0.64	2.99	9.31	21.23	56.40	84.90	96.69	99.52	99.95
	26						0.04	0.33	1.78	6.20	15.58	48.12	79.63	94.93	99.17	99.91
	27						0.02	0.17	1.02	3.98	11.06	40.01	73.47	92.51	98.62	99.83
	28						0.01	0.08	0.56	2.47	7.60	32.39	66.56	89.34	97.78	99.69
	29							0.04	0.30	1.48	5.06	25.51	59.11	85.34	96.56	99.45
	30							0.02	0.15	0.86	3.26	19.54	51.39	80.49	94.85	99.09
	31							0.01	0.08	0.48	2.03	14.54	43.69	74.83	92.56	98.52
	32								0.04	0.26	1.23	10.52	36.28	68.46	89.58	97.69
	33								0.02	0.14	0.72	7.40	29.41	61.54	85.86	96.50
	34								0.01	0.07	0.41	5.05	23.26	54.30	81.37	94.86
	35									0.04	0.23	3.36	17.94	46.97	76.13	92.69
	36									0.02	0.12	2.17	13.49	39.80	70.21	89.20

SOURCE: U.S. Department of the Air Force, Auditor General, "Table of Probabilities for Use in Stop-or-Go Sampling," p. 65.

Chapter **16**

Computerized Systems

GORDON B. DAVIS

Professor and Director of the Management Information Systems Research Center, University of Minnesota

Auditing of records maintained on a computer system rests on the same concepts as auditing of noncomputerized records. However, computer processing presents unique control problems and the auditor may need to use special audit techniques. The chapter is oriented toward these problems and therefore assumes that the reader has an elementary understanding of the basic elements of computer hardware, software, and programming.

PROCEDURAL OBJECTIVES

The auditing approach to be described has three procedural objectives:

1. To gather information on how the computer data processing system is purported to operate
2. To accumulate evidence which demonstrates how the data processing system actually does operate (tests of compliance)
3. To accumulate evidence as to whether or not the computer-based records are reasonably correct.

The auditor obtains information on the way the system is purported to operate from organization charts, documentation, inquiries of responsible data processing personnel, and inquiries of accounting and other personnel. Methods for obtaining and recording the information include questionnaires, checklists, flow charts, and narrative memoranda.

The information obtained by the auditor can be verified by supplemental inquiries and discussion with data processing personnel, by personal observation of activities, and by examination of evidence of compliance. In addition, both manual and computer-based tests can be used to acquire evidence on how the system actually does operate. From the system description and evidence of compliance the auditor can evaluate the reliance to be placed on the processing system in producing reliable output.

Evidence regarding the quality and correctness of computer-based records can be obtained by testing extensions and footings, selecting and printing confirmation requests, examining records for quality, performing analyses, comparing duplicate data maintained on separate files for correctness and consistency, and comparing audit data with company records. Many of these can be performed manually, but the use of the computer should be considered for those applications involving large volumes and for those where manual procedures are difficult or impossible to use.

In the conduct of the audit of computer-based records, the computer records may exist in a larger control framework. For example, the payroll application has both computer and non-computer controls, and the total application should be evaluated with the computer portion being evaluated in the context of the whole application.

APPROACH TO AUDITING

The approach to auditing of computer data processing involves three general steps that will be outlined in this section. The sections to follow will explain in more detail the elements to be examined, desirable control practices which should be used by the company, and audit techniques to be applied.

Step 1: Examine the control framework.

1. The organizational control framework
2. The management and control practices of the data processing organization

3. The control function

Step 2: Identify the key applications from an audit standpoint and review their controls.

1. Control over input and output
2. Processing controls
3. Adequacy of processing (audit) trail
4. Handling of errors detected in processing

Step 3: Identify appropriate audit techniques and use them for testing each selected application.

1. Tests of the computer processing system
2. Tests for quality of computer records

The approach may need to be modified, especially with respect to step 3, if the computer system is an online realtime system with an integrated file and other advanced features. Some special techniques for this purpose are discussed in a later section of the chapter.

FRAMEWORK OF CONTROL

The general elements of internal control—plan of organization, system of authorization and accounting, sound practices in performance of duties, and quality of personnel—are applicable to the computer-based data processing system. The control framework may in fact be more critical because the system concentrates in a small staff, functions which in other systems are widely dispersed. There is a hierarchy of control in a computer data processing system. The outer level of control is provided by the company organization, management, and procedures. Within this framework operate the organization and management of the data processing activity. A component part of this activity is the control function which monitors the quality of processing. The computer processing operations are subject to departmental control activities. This hierarchy of control is illustrated in Figure 1. Although not of primary interest for the audit, the hardware control features are also surveyed in this chapter because the auditor needs to understand the general applicability and availability of such hardware controls.

Organizational Control Framework. A computer installation is significant in the overall organization not only because of the expense of the equipment and personnel but also because of its role as a service department which accepts input data, performs processing and storage, and provides information. If the function is not well managed, it can seriously impair the activities of the entire organization. There must be proper authorization of computer activities by top management and adequate review of its performance.

Top management authorization and review. Top management responsibility for data processing consists of:

Authorization of major systems additions or changes
Post-installation review of actual cost and effectiveness of systems projects
Review of organization and control practices of the data processing function
Monitoring of performance

Top management responsibility for authorizing major systems work means that each such major addition or change must be presented to management as a proposal to be evaluated in terms of its cost and the benefits to be derived from it. A new or improved data processing system is similar to a large expenditure for an addition to the plant or equipment and should receive

Figure 1 THE CONTROL FRAMEWORK FOR A COMPUTER DATA PROCESSING SYSTEM (From Davis, Auditing and EDP, New York, AICPA, 1968.)

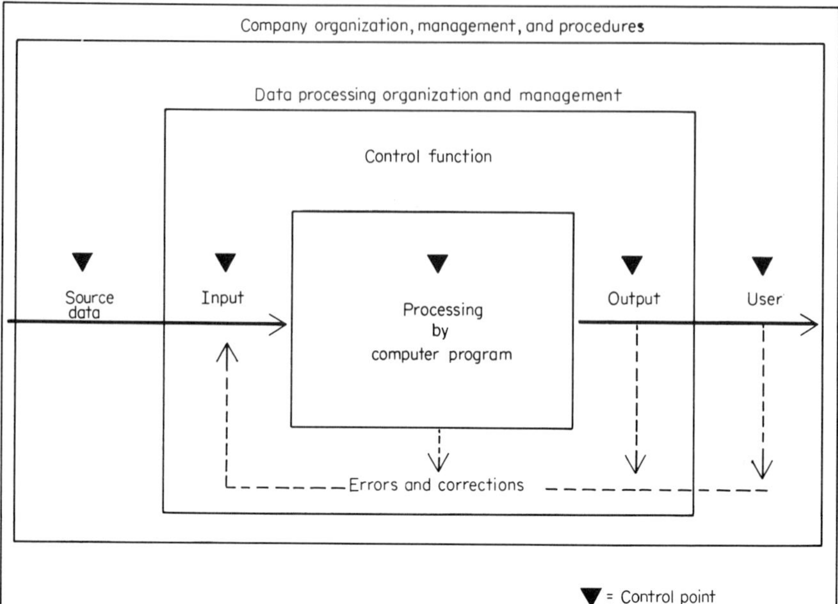

careful scrutiny before resources are committed to the project. Also, since data processing systems work will affect both the data-handling requirements of other departments and the information available to them, top management understanding of the addition or change and top management approval are necessary for adequate control over data processing. Requiring top management approval also enforces adequate preplanning by data processing management.

There is a tendency among data processing personnel to underestimate both the cost and the difficulty of implementing new or improved data processing systems. It is a part of the responsibility of management to follow up on project proposals and to evaluate the reasons for deviations from planned cost, planned schedule, and estimated benefit. The assessment of performance on the post-installation review will aid in evaluating future systems requests.

Top management has the responsibility for employing competent, adequately trained data processing management personnel and for reviewing the organization and control practices of the data processing function. Day-to-day control is the responsibility of the data processing management, so that poor organization and inadequate control procedures indicate a weakness at this level of management.

The monitoring of performance requires a performance plan or standard and the reporting of deviations from this expected level of performance. The plan and variation reporting should cover three types of performance:

1. Cost of data processing activities compared with planned cost
2. Frequency and duration of delays in meeting processing schedules
3. Error rates for errors detected at various control points

Plan of organization. A data processing installation should be organized and managed using the same methods which have proved effective in other segments of the organization. There should be a plan of organization and clear assignments of responsibilities. Although titles vary among installations, the following abbreviated, general job descriptions cover the most common data processing positions other than the managerial level.

Title	*Description*
Systems analyst	Analyzes the requirements for information, evaluates the existing system, and designs new or improved data processing procedures. Outlines the system and prepares specifications which guide the programmer.
Programmer	Flow-charts the logic of the computer programs specified by the system designed by the system analyst. Codes the logic in the language of the computer. Debugs the resulting program. Prepares documentation.
Computer operator	Operates the computer according to the operating procedures for the installation and the detailed procedures for each program described in the computer operator instructions. Also called a "console operator."
Keypunch operator	Prepares data for machine processing by keypunching into cards. Operates a card punch (also called a "keypunch").
Unit record equipment operator	Also called a "tabulating equipment operator." Operates the non-computer punched-card equipment, such as sorter, collator, reproducer, accounting machine, etc.

Figure 2 is a generalized organization chart for a data processing operation. It does not show the location of the computer data processing in the overall organization plan. The most common approach is to have data processing report to the chief financial or accounting officer, such as financial vice-president, treasurer, or controller. There is a growing tendency, however, to move the data processing executive to a higher position in the organization. In cases where the computer acts as a service center for many departments, the possible conflicts over the scheduling of the computer and the design of common files require that the data processing executive be on the same level organizationally as the department heads of the units being serviced.

The plan of organization and operating procedures should provide for a control function. The control function can be divided into two types:

Figure 2 ORGANIZATION OF THE DATA PROCESSING FUNCTION

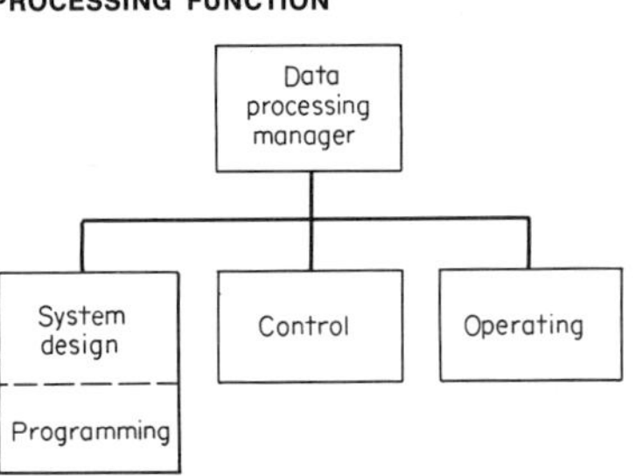

1. Control – internal to data processing
2. Control – external to data processing

Internal processing control is a function of the data processing department and is concerned with ensuring that processing is performed correctly and that no data are lost or mishandled within the department.

Management and Control Practices. The management practices of the data processing installation affect the reliance that can be placed on the system and on the resulting records. The use of good administrative procedures for scheduling and supervising personnel improves not only the efficiency but also the quality of data processing. This section will concentrate on control of programs, protection of records and files, insurance, security, and division of duties.

Control over computer programs. Computer programs are a valuable product of the data processing programming staff. Copies should be protected from fire or other destruction. There should also be controls to prevent unauthorized changes. Controls include those based on organization of duties and approval and documentation of program changes.

It is feasible in most installations to segregate the systems and programming responsibility from the computer operating responsibility. Access to the complete documentation of the run manual should be restricted, where possible, and the operators given only the operator instructions. Under these circumstances, the operator is less likely to attempt unauthorized changes (whether desirable or not) than when he is also a programmer and has access to the complete documentation.

Before a program is put into use, it should be reviewed by a supervisor to check whether or not it performs as specified and to check for adequacy of testing and completeness of documentation. After being approved and put in use, there will be a need for program changes. These should be approved by the program manager or data processing manager and a record of the change should be made and filed with the run manual for the program.

The program change record is useful in keeping documentation current. It is very time-consuming to correct all documentation each time a program change is made. Instead, a change record is included with the documentation, and unless there is a rather substantial rewrite of the program, the flow charts are not redrawn. The original documentation plus the change records form the current documentation.

Protection of computer records and files. A data processing installation should establish and follow procedures to safeguard the program and data files from loss or accidental destruction. If loss or destruction does occur, advance provisions should have been made for reconstruction of the records. The protection of computer records and files involves physical safeguards, procedural controls, and a retention and reconstruction plan.

Physical safeguards include fire protection and off-premises storage. Tape files, card files, disk packs, etc., are more subject to fire damage than the printed or written records available with manual or tabulating systems. A small fire which may char only the edges of paper or books can melt a magnetic tape or warp a disk. The National Fire Protection Association has made extensive recommendations with respect to computer installations.[1] These call for housing of the computer in a noncombustible environment, storage of vital records in storage cabinets having a class C rating (one hour at 1700°F),

[1] *Standard for the Protection of Electronic Computer Systems,* Bulletin No. 75, National Fire Protection Association, 60 Batterymarch Street, Boston, Mass., 1964.

Figure 3 EXTERNAL MAGNETIC TAPE LABEL

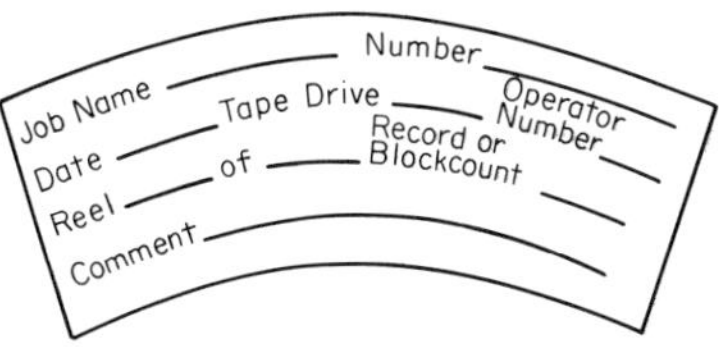

separate air-conditioning and power controls, carbon dioxide fire extinguishers, etc.

Off-premises storage is used to provide a further safeguard for essential data processing records. Space can be rented in a secure, fireproof location, or another storage location in the same company can be used.

Procedural controls can be used in the management of a computer center in order to minimize the possibility that an operator error will result in the destruction of a data or program file. Some common methods are external labels, magnetic tape file protection rings, and tape library procedures.

Files should be clearly labeled so that the operator will know the file contents. Punched-card files are usually labeled on the top of the deck with a felt marking pen. File name, identification, and date are commonly written. The first and last cards are also labeled. A paper label should be attached to magnetic tape reels and disk packs (Figure 3).

A physical safeguard used to prevent writing on a magnetic tape and destroying information prior to the release date for the tape is a removable plastic or metal ring, the presence or absence (depending on the computer manufacturer) of which will prevent writing on the tape. The most common method is the insertion of the ring to allow writing and its removal to inhibit writing (Figure 4). The ring is used in conjunction with the external label as an added protection. The procedure for writing a file will include instructions as to the external label and a reminder to remove the file protection ring.

Tape library procedures provide a log of the use to which tape reels have been put and for systematic methods of storage of reels to allow the tapes to be easily located or replaced in the storage racks. Similar provisions apply to disk packs.

The retention plan of a data processing department provides a means for record or file reconstruction. Source documents are retained at least until the computer file has been proved and balanced with its controls. However, other considerations may require a longer storage period for these documents. Copies of important master files or cards should be produced and a copy maintained in secure storage, preferably off the premises.

Figure 4 MAGNETIC TAPE FILE PROTECTION (OR WRITE ENABLE) RING

File protection ring

A retention plan for magnetic tape is usually accomplished by the use of the son-father-grandfather concept (Figure 5). The files retained under this concept on a Wednesday (assuming daily processing) would be:

Wednesday's file (son)
Tuesday's file (father)
Monday's file (grandfather)

If, during processing on Thursday, the Wednesday tape was destroyed, Tuesday's tape would be processed again with Wednesday's transactions to recreate Wednesday's master tape. If no other processing or retention considerations require keeping the tape longer, the old grandfather can be released when a new tape is produced.

Disk file processing, unlike magnetic tape, does not automatically produce a duplicate, updated copy of the file. To provide for reconstruction, the disk must be duplicated to provide a reference point and all transactions saved until the next reference file copy is made. The reference copy can be put onto another disk or magnetic tape. The "dump" to another disk or magnetic tape provides good reconstruction capabilities. If a second disk or magnetic tape is not available, the disk may be copied onto punched cards or even printed out. These are the least satisfactory methods because of the difficulty of reloading the file from punched cards or of having to re-punch the entire file from a printout.

The file protection plan requires not only a retention plan but also a plan for reconstruction in the event of loss of a file or of destruction of equipment. The plan will include backup facilities, either through the manufacturer, a service center, or another user, and special programs, if required, to facilitate reconstructing of files.

Insurance. Insurance should be part of the protection plan of a data processing installation. The major risk is fire, unless work is performed for others, in which case there should be liability insurance for errors or omissions in doing the work. The ordinary fire insurance policy is limited in its coverage of risks associated with losses connected with data processing. Therefore, many organizations take special data processing insurance coverage.

Although the number of losses arising from the dishonesty of data processing employees is apparently quite small, the risks associated with the

Figure 5 SON-FATHER-GRANDFATHER CONCEPT FOR RETENTION OF MAGNETIC TAPE FILES

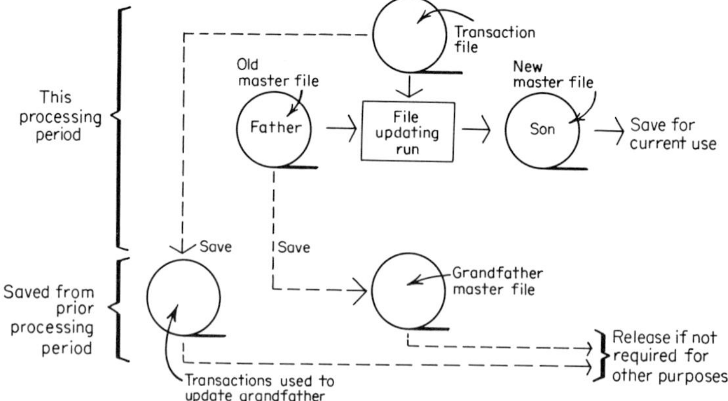

concentration of the data processing function on a relatively small number of people suggest that bonding (fidelity insurance) of data processing employees is a desirable practice.

Security. A computer installation will have equipment valued at between $100,000 and several million dollars, with an average installation being in the half-million-dollar range. The equipment is concentrated in a small area and is easily damaged. In civil commotion or riot, the computer facility is a likely target for destruction.

The magnetic tape and magnetic disk files have a modest intrinsic value, but when they contain data files they have a high value to the organization. In many cases, the data on the tapes, etc., have a value to outsiders—for example, prospect lists, employee lists, and mailing lists.

Because of the risk of damage from unauthorized access and the potential loss from the theft or destruction of tapes and disks, access to the computer facility should be controlled and security should be maintained over computer tapes and disks containing the data files for the organization.

Division of duties. In the organization of the data processing activity, it is desirable both from an operating standpoint and from a control standpoint to separate the three functions of (1) system design and programming, (2) operating, and (3) control. If possible, it is frequently advantageous also to separate system design and programming; in larger installations control over data files and programs may be increased by the use of a separate file librarian. Figure 2 shows this division of functions. A suitable plan of organization and the resulting division of duties are internal control features which protect the organization against the consequences of incompetence or fraud. The small number of people in computer processing as compared with manual processing exposes the system to manipulation if a single person is given both programming and operating responsibility. As an example, a programmer for a company servicing a bank sometimes acted as an operator. One of the applications he had programmed was a listing of accounts which were overdrawn. While serving as computer operator, he inserted a "patch" in the program to cause it to ignore overdrafts in his account when printing the overdraft report. The fraud was discovered when, because of a computer breakdown, the report was prepared manually.

Control Function. The plan of organization and the operating procedures should provide for a control function. The control function can be divided into two types: (1) processing control internal to data processing and (2) independent, outside checks. The internal processing control, a function of the data processing department, is concerned with monitoring accuracy of processing and ensuring that no data are lost or mishandled within the department during processing. For example, if a detail transaction file is processed with the current master file to produce an updated master file, the sum of the transaction file and the related master file records should equal the total of the records on the updated master file. The person charged with the processing control function is responsible for making or reviewing the results of such a comparison. In very small installations, the data processing manager may perform the control activities; in others, a control clerk will perform this task.

The activities of the control clerk or control group are specified both in the systems and procedures manual and in the description of control activities for each computer application. The control function will include duties such as the following:

1. Logging of input data and recording of control information
2. Recording progress of work through the department

3. Reconciling computer controls with other control information
4. Supervising distribution of output
5. Scrutiny of console logs and control information in accordance with control instructions
6. Liaison with users regarding errors, logging of correction requests, and recording corrections made
7. Scrutiny of error listings and maintenance of error log or error report

Independent, outside checks can take several forms, but they are basically concerned with an independent check of the functioning of the data processing department. This check may be performed by a user department. If the general ledger, for instance, is maintained on the computer, the accounting department may keep a control total of all debits and credits to be posted by the computer. This control can be checked against the debits and credits from the computer run. Another possibility is an independent quality-control evaluation group in a user department where the volume of data to be controlled is large. As an example, a large corporation has a payroll-processing control group responsible for evaluating the payroll data produced by the computer.

Control over Equipment Malfunctions. A computer system consists of both electronic elements and mechanical parts. The central processing unit, for example, consists almost entirely of electronic elements, such as transistors, resistors, and diodes, whereas most input/output equipment and file storage devices contain both electronic components and parts which move mechanically. Failure in the system can therefore result from the malfunction of one of the mechanical parts or through the failure of an electronic element.

The electronic portion of the computer system operates with electrical pulses which are created, counted, delayed, transmitted, etc. The electronic circuitry of the computer is designed to control the timing, shape, strength, and frequency of these pulses. Failure of an electronic element such as a transistor, resistor, diode, etc., may cause a change in the timing, shape, strength, or frequency of the pulses and lead to an error. Some of the reasons for deterioration of an electronic element are extremes of heat or humidity, power disturbances, mishandling, and normal wear.

Quality control in manufacture, built-in equipment checks, and programs of periodic preventive maintenance have made the electronic portion of the computer system very reliable. Preventive maintenance procedures usually detect elements which are getting out of adjustment or are close to failure, and allow adjustments or replacements to be made. Preventive maintenance is performed daily on complex computer systems and less frequently on simple configurations.

Mechanical operation is required in almost all input/output and file storage equipment. Two mechanisms with mechanical actions are generally used:

1. A transport mechanism to move the media (input/output or file storage) past the reading or writing mechanism
2. Mechanism to read or write

These actions occur at high rates of speed. For example, a card reader must transport, say, 1,100 cards a minute past the read mechanisms (brushes or photoelectric cells) at a precise speed and in a precise position. A printer which turns out 1,000 lines of 136 characters per minute requires as many as 136,000 individual print-mechanism movements per minute.

A machine error can be caused by a failure in the timing, speed, and movement of a transport mechanism or through a malfunction of the read/write units. This can result from the devices getting out of adjustment, operator mishandling, wear, etc. Failures can also be traced to faulty media, such as warped cards, magnetic tape with surface defects, and poor-quality paper stock.

Equipment controls are usually based on the concept of redundancy. This concept has received much attention in communication theory but is also applicable elsewhere as a general basis for error control. Redundancy, with respect to error control, means that an element is added to a process or the code for an item for the sole purpose of detecting any error which may occur. If there were no possibility of error, the redundancy would usually be eliminated.

Equipment controls can be divided into five types: a redundant or parity character, a duplicate process, an echo check, a validity check, and an equipment check. Each of these involves a separate operation which provides a check on the results of the main operation.

Redundant or parity character. A redundant character is one attached to a data item for the purpose of providing for error detection. The most common is the parity bit. A separate parity bit or check bit, when used, is associated with each separately identified group of bits which is moved as a separate unit through the computer. This unit may be a large, fixed set of bits, as in a computer word, a smaller set which can encode a single alphanumeric character, or a byte which is a separately identified part of a larger fixed word. The parity of the binary word, character set, or byte is made even or odd when the data are first converted to binary from input items or when data are formed from a computation or other manipulation. The number of bits is summed, and a 1-bit or a 0-bit is placed in the parity bit position to make the total number of bits odd if an odd-parity check is used or even for an even-parity check. Figure 6 illustrates the parity bit in a 6-bit binary coded character bit set. Each time this basic group of bits is moved in the computer, the parity of the group is checked. If the parity bit, as newly computed, is different from the parity bit previously computed, a bit has been destroyed. This test is not infallible in the sense that the alteration of two bits might leave the parity bit unchanged, but the probability of this happening is very low.

Duplicate process. Another type of equipment control is to have the same process performed twice and then to compare the results of the two operations. Any difference between the first operation and the second will signal an error. This is used by most card readers which have two "read" stations. The

Figure 6 ILLUSTRATION OF ODD PARITY BIT FOR A COMPUTER USING A SIX-BIT BINARY CODED CHARACTER BIT SET

	The number 2			The number 3	
C →	0	Check bit	C →	1	Check bit
B	0		B	0	
A	0		A	0	
8	0		8	0	
4	0		4	0	
2	1		2	1	
1	0		1	1	

duplicate process may also be a complementary action, such as reading after writing to check what was written.

Echo check. In an echo check the central processor sends a command to an input or output device to perform an operation. The device returns a signal which verifies that the proper mechanisms for performing the actions have been activated. This verifies that the equipment was activated, but does not check the results obtained. This check is frequently used for verifying the printer and the card punch.

Validity check. Since on many operations only certain results (e.g., data character codes) can be considered correct, one method of checking is for the computer-system circuitry to compare the results attained with all valid results. Any results not fitting into this set of valid results are considered incorrect. This is used with some card readers and in data communications.

Equipment check. In this control, the computer checks the equipment to see if it is functioning properly, rather than checking the results from the operation. It is not a positive check, since the equipment may be working properly with defective media or other factors nevertheless giving an improper result. An example is a card reader using photoelectric sensing, which tests the photoelectric cells to make sure they are on and working.

CONTROLS FOR AN EDP APPLICATION

In addition to the control framework of the organization, the processing management, the control function, and the hardware controls, each data processing application (payroll, accounts receivable, order entry, billing, etc.) has specific controls associated with it. These are controls established for input and over output, program controls over processing, and the processing or audit trail. A related topic, the handling of errors detected in processing, is also discussed in this section.

Control over Input and Output. Input data are the weakest link in the chain of data processing events. A study of 100 computer installations showed input errors to be the major operating problem. Good system design should therefore make provisions to assure the quality of the input into the system.

The input data for a program may be in error for one of four general reasons: (1) they may be incorrectly recorded at the point of inception; (2) they may be incorrectly converted to machine-readable form; (3) they may be incorrectly read or otherwise entered into the computer; or (4) they may be lost in handling. Input controls should therefore be established at the point of data creation and conversion to machine-readable form, at the point where the data enter the computer, and at points when the data are handled, moved, or transmitted in the organization. Table 1 presents an inventory of methods from which the system designer selects in order to achieve the level of error control required for an application. Each of these will be discussed in this chapter.

Before data are used in updating files or other processing, they are usually tested for errors to the extent possible or appropriate in the light of the consequences of input errors. A separate input validation run or input editing run is usually performed in systems where the data are batched and transferred to a file medium such as magnetic tape before processing.

If errors are detected by this run or during subsequent processing, the erroneous transaction or record found to contain an error is shunted aside rather than stopping the computer to make corrections. It will usually be written on a temporary file to be examined later, and information will be written on the console typewriter or printer explaining why the item was re-

TABLE 1 Methods for Input-data Error Control

At point data are created and converted to machine-readable form	At point data are first put into the computer	At points data are handled, moved, or transmitted

Procedural controls
Data review
Verification
Check digit
	File label (internal)
	Tests for validity:
	  Code
	  Character
	  Field
	  Transaction
	  Combination of fields
	  Missing data
	  Check digit
	  Sequence
	  Limit or reasonableness test
	Control total
		Transmittal controls
		Route slip
		Control total
		External file labels

jected. There will thus usually be a file of rejects and an error listing indicating the reason for rejection (Figure 7). Items which are rejected by the input editing run should be carefully controlled to make sure they are corrected and reentered at a later run.

Procedural controls and data review. Standard clerical practices and well-designed data forms impose procedural controls on the creation of data. For example, if a part number is to be written on a document, boxes may be printed which contain the exact number of spaces required for the part number. Any clerk writing a part number containing fewer or more digits than the required number of characters will notice the error. Where direct input devices are used, templates over the keys, identification cards, and other procedural aids help to reduce input errors.

Some installations make a review examination of input data (especially codes which identify part number, product, etc.) before they are converted to machine-readable form. This checking may be performed in connection with the addition of information, or it may be an entirely separate step.

Verification of data conversion. When data are punched into cards, the accuracy of the data conversion can be tested by mechanically verifying the keypunching operation. Two separate keydriven machines are used—a card punch and a verifier. The data are first punched by a keypunch operator. The punched cards and original data are then given to a verifier operator,

Figure 7 SAMPLE OUTPUT FROM INPUT VALIDATION RUN (From Davis, Auditing and EDP, New York, AICPA, 1968.)

```
BG // JOB BETTY
BG 00.00.06
BG BEGIN UNEARNED INCOME REPORT
BG ALLSTORES CORP.
BG OP111   1   DATA CHECK SYS001=181
           CCSW=02100031680E000000 SNS=085203C00000 CCB=003128
BG NO MATCH CARD 026102R3
BG NON NUMERIC FIELD 02980452
BG DUP 03110004
BG TERMS NOT  EQUAL ACCOUNT 03200024 TB 48 CARD 36
BG NON NUMERIC FIELD 03910053
BG DUP 03910087
BG TERMS NOT EQUAL ACCOUNT   04610200   TB 08  CARD 36
BG TERM NOT GREATER THAN ZERO OR REMAINING PAYMENT   IS NEGATIVE 04610200
BG NON NUMERIC FIELD  04660002
BG DUP 06510011
BG TRIAL-BALANCE READ ERRORS 000001
BG END UNEARNED INCOME REPORT
BG EOJ BETTY
BG 00.07.25
```

who inserts the punched card in the verifier and rekeys the punches, using the original source documents. The verifier does not punch but instead compares the data keyed into it with the punches already in the card. If they are the same, the punched card is presumed to be correct. A common indication that this check has been performed is for the verifier to notch over the column containing a difference. The incorrect cards are returned to the keypunch operator for repunching and reverification.

Similar verification is used with a magnetic tape encoder, where data are keypunched and recorded directly on a magnetic tape. The same device is used (at separate times) both to record data and to verify them. The verification process includes the correction of errors.

Verification is a duplicate operation and therefore doubles the cost of data conversion. Various methods are used to reduce the amount of verifying. One method is to verify only part of the data. Some data fields are not critical, and an error will not affect further processing. Examples are descriptive fields containing vendor name, part description, etc., which, under most circumstances, are not critical. The use of prepunched cards and prepunched stubs and the duplication of constant data during keypunching may allow verification to be restricted to the variable information added by the card punch. A second approach used with statistical data is to verify only if the card-punching error rate is above an acceptable level. Each operator's work is checked on a sample basis. If her error rate is acceptable, no verification is made; if not acceptable, there is complete verification.

Verification can also be conducted by visual inspection of the printing on the card or by a visual review of a listing of the cards. Other control procedures to be explained may be substituted for verification, e.g., a check digit on an account number or a batch control total.

Other techniques for data conversion produce a punched card or a punched paper tape as a by-product of another operation. For example, the typing of an invoice may, by the use of a device hooked up to the typewriter, automatically produce a punched card or punched paper tape for inventory control, sales analysis, etc. Proofreading of the invoice serves also to verify the punched-card by-product, although not to the same extent as mechanical verification.

Check digit. In most applications involving an identification number, the identification number may be verified for accuracy by a check digit. A check digit is determined by performing some arithmetic operation on the number. The arithmetic operation is performed in such a way that the typical errors encountered in transcribing a number will be detected. There are many possible procedures. For example, a simple check-digit procedure might be as follows:

57648 ↙ ↓ ↘ 10 12 16	1. Start with a number without the check digit. 2. Take every other digit and multiply these by two.
$1+0+7+1+2+4+1+6=22$	3. Sum the digits in the resulting numbers plus the digits not multiplied.
$30-22=8$	4. Subtract sum from next higher number ending in zero.
576488	5. Add check digit to number (at end or elsewhere).

Note that a check-digit procedure is not completely error-proof. For this example method, 57846 or 54678 gives the same check digit. It is unlikely, however, that transpositions of this form will occur. The check digit does not guard against assignment of an incorrect but valid code, such as the assignment of the wrong but valid identification code to a customer.

The checking of the code number for the check digit may either be performed by the input device, such as a keypunch or a paper-tape punch, or be programmed into the computer. The use of the check digit as part of the input device has the advantage that an incorrect code is detected before it enters the computer process and a field checked by a check digit does not need to be verified. Examples of uses are charge account numbers, employee pay numbers, and bank account numbers.

Internal file label. A file label is a record at the beginning and also possibly the end of the file which records identification and control information. It is used to ensure that the proper transaction or master file is used and that the entire file has been processed. At the beginning is the header label, which identifies the file. Typical contents are:

Name of file
Creation date
Purge date
Identification number
Reel number (for magnetic tape)

The trailer label is the last record and summarizes the file. Contents normally include:

Record count
Control totals for one or more fields
End-of-file or end-of-reel code

Tests for valid data. The data, once read by the computer, can be subjected to programmed tests to establish that it is within the limits established for valid data. Some examples of checking which can be done are:

1. VALID CODE: If there is only a limited number of valid codes, say for coding expenses, the code being read may be checked to see if it is one of the valid codes.
2. VALID CHARACTER: If only certain characters are allowed in a data field, the computer can test the field to determine that no invalid characters are used.
3. VALID FIELD SIZE, SIGN, AND COMPOSITION: If a code number should be a specified number of digits in length, the computer may be programmed to test that the field size is as specified. If the sign of the field must always be positive or always negative, a test may be made to ensure that there is not an incorrect sign. If the field should contain only numerics or only alphabetics, a test may be made to determine that the field does indeed contain a proper composition of characters.
4. VALID TRANSACTION: There is typically a relatively small number of valid transactions which are processed with a particular file. There is a limited number, for example, of transaction codes which can apply to accounts receivable file updating. As part of input error control, the transaction code can be tested for validity.
5. VALID COMBINATIONS OF FIELD: In addition to each of the individual fields being tested, combinations may be tested for validity. For example, if a salesman code may be associated with only a few territory codes, this can be checked.

6. MISSING-DATA TEST: The program may check the data fields to make sure that all data fields necessary to code a transaction have data in them.

7. CHECK DIGIT: The check digit is verified with identification fields having this control feature.

8. SEQUENCE TEST: In batch processing, the data to be processed must be arranged in a sequence which is the same as the sequence of the file. Both the master file and the transaction file may be tested to ensure that they are in a proper sequence, ascending or descending as the case may be. The sequence check can also be used to account for all documents, if these are numbered sequentially.

9. LIMIT OR REASONABLENESS TEST: This is a basic test for data processing accuracy. Input data should usually fall within certain limits. For example, hours worked should not be less than zero and should not be more than, say, 50. The upper limit may be established from the experience of the particular firm. Input data may be compared against this limit to ensure that no input error has occurred or at least that there has been no input error exceeding certain preestablished limits. Examples are:

The total amount of a customer order may be compared with his average-order amount. If this order exceeds, say, three times the amount of his average order, then an exception notice may be printed.

A material receipt which exceeds two times the economic order quantity established for the particular item might be subject to question.

A receiving report amount may be compared with the amount requested on the purchase order. If there is more than a small percentage variance, then there is an assumption of an error in the input data.

In a utility billing, consumption is checked against prior periods to detect possible errors or trouble in the customer's installation.

Control totals. Control totals are a basic method of error control to determine whether or not all items in a batch have been received and processed. The control total procedure requires that a control figure be developed by some previous processing and that the current data processing recompute this amount, comparing the resultant total with the previous total. Control totals are normally obtained for batches of data. The batches are kept to a reasonable size so that errors can be easily isolated. For example, the sales slips to be processed by computer are first added on an adding machine to arrive at a control total for the sales in the batch. A control total for payroll might be the number of employees for whom checks should be prepared. Control figures may be financial totals, hash totals, or document or record counts.

FINANCIAL TOTALS: Financial totals are totals such as sales, payroll amounts, inventory dollar amounts, etc., which are normally added together in order to provide financial summaries.

HASH TOTALS: Hash totals are totals of data fields which are typically not added. The total has meaning only as a control and is not used in any other way in data processing. To determine that all inventory items are processed, a control total might be developed of the inventory item numbers, and this would be compared with the sum of the item numbers obtained during the processing run.

DOCUMENT OR RECORD COUNT: In many cases, rather than obtaining a financial total or hash total, it may be sufficient merely to obtain a count to ensure that all documents or records have been received and processed.

Control totals prepared prior to computer processing are furnished to computer processing as an input data item. The computer is then pro-

Figure 8 USE OF CONTROL TOTALS

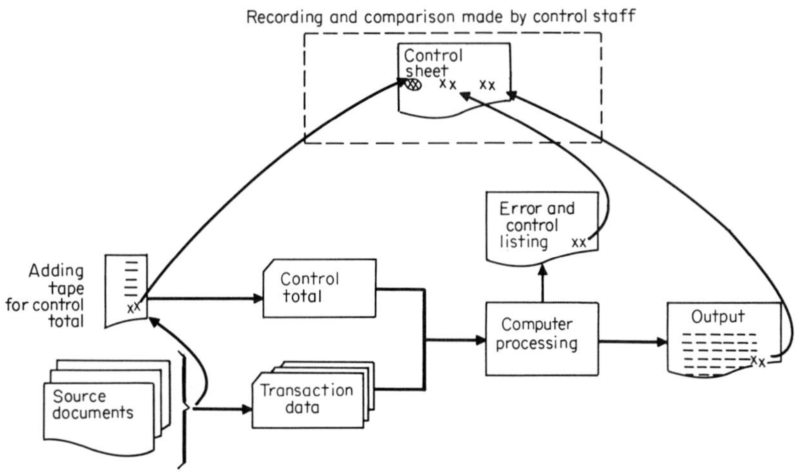

grammed to accumulate control totals internally and make a comparison. A message confirming the comparison should be printed out even if the comparison did not disclose an error. These messages are then subject to review by the control clerk (Figure 8).

Movement and handling controls. Transmittal controls, route slips, control totals, and external file labels are examples of controls over the internal handling and movement of input data. Control totals have already been explained and external file labels are described in connection with file safeguards. The transmittal controls and route slips are discussed in this section.

When data are moved about through an organization, there is always a possibility that they may be lost or otherwise diverted from the proper processing channels. To ensure proper identification of data as they move through the company, and more especially as they move through the data processing steps, it is customary to use some form of status identification. As they enter the data processing center, batches of data may be logged on a listing showing the data received. As each batch passes a data processing station, it is registered, recording the fact that the batch has been processed. The batch itself usually carries a route slip which indicates the path of processing which it should follow and a record of processing performed (Figure 9).

Output controls. The distribution of output should be controlled to ensure that only those persons authorized to receive reports do so. The output should

Figure 9 BATCH CONTROL TICKET TO ACCOMPANY SOURCE DOCUMENTS

Batch no.	To	
Date	From	
No. of documents	Numbered From	To
Control totals		
Date rec'd	Rec'd by	

be reviewed for completeness and agreement with controls and screened for obvious errors. Persons receiving the output are an important error-detection control point, and provisions should be made in the system design for error feedback from recipients of output.

Programmed Control over Processing. Assuming that there are proper input controls so that the input data are considered to be correct, and that there are proper equipment controls to detect equipment errors, what is the need for programmed control over internal processing? A program will perform exactly as written. If properly debugged and tested, there should be no program-based errors. However, large programs are sufficiently complex to harbor latent errors which may not show up for weeks, months, or even years after the program has been accepted. For example, a large payroll program worked well for several years but failed when required to process name changes for two newly married female employees whose names were on adjacent records in the master file. The program was not able to handle this somewhat unusual situation. Another reason for programmed controls over processing is the possibility of improper modification of a program, intentional or accidental, while the data are being processed. It therefore makes sense to put various error-control features into the program.

The types of program controls which test computer processing are the limit and reasonableness test, the crossfooting or crosstesting check, and control figures.

Limit and reasonableness test. As with input data, a control over processing can be exercised by program steps testing the results of processing by comparing them with predetermined limits or by comparison with flexible limits testing the reasonableness of the results. In a payroll application, the net pay can be checked against an upper limit. The upper limit is an amount such that any paycheck exceeding the limit is probably in error. In a billing operation for a relatively homogeneous product, such as steel bars and plates, the weight of the shipment may be divided into the billing in order to develop a price per pound. If the price per pound exceeds the average by more than a predetermined percentage, a message will be written for subsequent follow-up to determine if the billing is in error.

Crossfooting test. It is frequently possible to check computer data processing in a manner similar to the manual method of crossfooting. Individual items are totaled independently and then a crossfooting total is developed from the totals. For example, in a payroll application the totals are developed for gross pay, for each of the deduction items, and for net pay. The total for net pay is then obtained independently by taking the total for gross pay and deducting the totals for each of the deduction items. If this crossfooting does not yield identical figures, there has been some error in the program of processing.

Control figures. Control figures developed in a manner similar to the input control totals can be used for testing the data processing within the machine. For example, the number of items to be invoiced in a billing run may be used as a control total and compared with the number of items billed on invoices.

The Processing or Audit Trail. The term "audit trail" refers to the documents, journals, ledgers, worksheets, etc., by which an original transaction can be traced forward to a summarized total or a summarized total can be exploded backward to the original transaction. In other words, the trail documents the processing. It is necessary for internal inquiry purposes as well as for audit examinations.

The auditor has become accustomed to certain facilities in tracing source documents to specific journal entries and in tracing general ledger postings back to selected source documents. These are:

1. Source documents. These records of originating transactions contain information relative to authorization, preparer, etc.
2. Detailed chronological journal. A record of all events is provided as a regular step in the accounting cycle.
3. Ledger summaries. These give not only the current balance but also a record of the accumulation of amounts leading to the balance.

The traditional audit trail is summarized in Figure 10. In manual and most punched-card systems, the records have been accessible without special arrangements for the use of machines and without disturbing normal processing activities. Moreover, the auditor can observe transactions being recorded, listings being prepared, etc. The non-EDP audit trail does not impose special requirements because its elements are an integral part of the processing system.

The use of EDP equipment can affect the audit trail. It is possible to eliminate source documents by the use of direct input devices, to eliminate processing references in master files, to eliminate transaction listings, and to file source documents so that they are difficult to retrieve. However, good system design requires some form of audit trail for internal operating purposes as well as for the use of audit personnel.

The general principles governing the design of proper processing (audit) trails are as follows:

1. For all transactions affecting the financial statements, there must be a means for establishing the account to which the transaction is posted.
2. For all accounts reflected in the financial statements there must be a means for tracing the summary amount back to the individual transaction elements.
3. For all transactions and accounts drawing a large number of inquiries, regular provision should be made to supply the records necessary for answering the inquiries.
4. For all transactions and accounts not typically subject to inquiries there must be a means for tracing, even though regular provisions are not made.

These principles will normally satisfy regulatory agencies. The Internal Revenue Service guidelines (Revenue Procedure 64.12) emphasize the need for the capacity for tracing transactions forward to summary total and back from summaries to individual source documents. There is a specific requirement for a printout of the general ledger and subsidiary ledgers coincident with the date of the financial report. Documents can be filed in any way as

Figure 10 THE TRADITIONAL AUDIT TRAIL

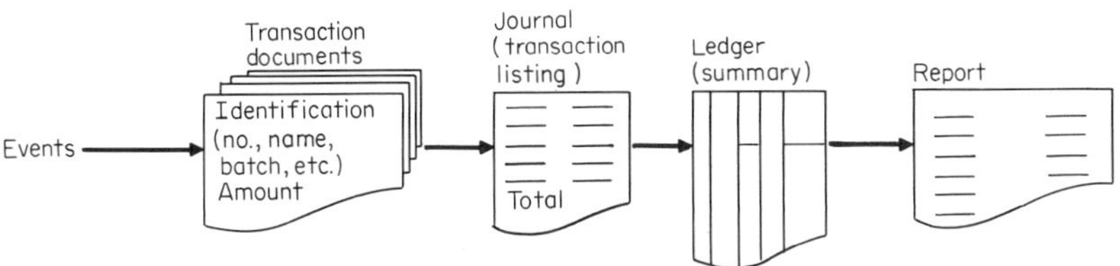

long as they can be made available to the examiner within a reasonable period of time.

Perhaps a more serious impact for the auditor of EDP records is the fact that the sequence of records and processing activities is difficult to observe because much of the data and many of the activities are contained within the computer system. The auditor cannot read computer files except by use of the computer and a computer program.

In most cases, auditors have found sufficient printed records, listings, etc., to provide a fairly traditional audit trail. The trend, however, is to include more of the audit trail in the computer system, making the auditor more dependent on the computer equipment to obtain audit data and perform audit tests.

Handling of Errors Detected in Processing. Computer installations normally try to have programs written so that errors will not halt processing. An error procedure written into the program usually provides for a temporary halt—for error identification and listing to facilitate subsequent follow-up—and then a continuation of processing. The procedure following error identification in any particular case depends on the nature of the errors detected, but it is not considered good practice to have the operator initiate data corrections.

If there are errors in input data, an input error listing or report which explains the reason for each rejected item should be prepared. The rejected data and the error report should be returned to the originator for correction and resubmission. Personnel receiving the error reports should be instructed in the handling of them. The data processing organization should log out or prepare an error listing to establish a control over follow-up and to make sure corrections are made.

When faulty records are detected, one method of ensuring correction is to write the faulty records on a suspense file for subsequent analysis. Another method is to flag the faulty items but leave them in the file. An error in control totals may be handled through a suspense entry which temporarily corrects imbalances between debits and credits or between control totals. If there are dummy or suspense records maintained in the file to hold balancing entries or unmatched items, such records should be identified clearly and the purpose of each should be investigated promptly.

Master file changes, such as changes in employee pay rates, customer credit limits, etc., should be closely controlled. All master file changes or changes in program data factors should be authorized in writing by the departments initiating the changes. A notice or register of all the changes should be furnished to the initiating department to verify that the changes were made and to subject the changes to their review.

AUDIT TECHNIQUES FOR TESTING DATA PROCESSING

The information obtained by the auditor with respect to segregation of duties or other organizational and operational aspects of the EDP system ordinarily can be tested by supplemental inquiries and discussion with data processing personnel and by personal observation of their activities during the course of his examination. In addition the auditor needs to obtain evidence on the performance of control procedures by the data processing organization and on the existence and satisfactory operation of computer-based controls for specific applications included in the scope of the audit. In other words, the auditor needs evidence on the actual operation of the data processing system. In addition to obtaining evidence on the performance of the processing system, the auditor needs to obtain evidence with which to evaluate computer-prepared records.

Tests of the Processing System. Tests to obtain evidence of the performance of specific control procedures in non-computer systems are made by examining some form of documentary evidence such as signatures or initials indicating authorization and approval and by the verification and reconciliation of details with control totals. Such forms of visible evidence are also available with respect to many control procedures in computer data processing. Examples of compliance tests using such evidence are:

- Examination of cards for end notch if the cards are supposed to be key-verified
- Examination of machine room log book for proper recording of control information
- Examination of documentation for completeness and evidence of proper authorization of program changes
- Examination of control and error listings for evidence of control totals said to be used

The testing of controls contained in the computer programs requires evidence that the controls exist in the program and were operative during the period of the examination. Two approaches are used in obtaining this evidence—one which does not use the computer and one which does. The specific audit techniques involve tracing of transactions, test data, controlled processings, and controlled reprocessing. These may be used separately or in combination, as appropriate.

Note that the chapter does not emphasize auditing "around" or "through" the computer. These terms are somewhat misleading because the auditor should be able to use any technique that is appropriate. Some of these will use the computer; others will not.

Tracing transactions. Tracing of transactions makes use of computer printouts and error listings to obtain evidence as to the processing actually performed. Transactions are traced from input to either regular output or error listing. Conducted on a sample of items processed during the period, this testing procedure does not attempt to test the computer program directly but instead infers the processing and control steps contained in the program by obtaining evidence as to how the program handled selected transactions, both correct and erroneous.

Test data. The use of test data involves the preparation of transactions which illustrate all valid and invalid conditions the auditor wishes to test. The data for each application are run under audit control on the client's computer with the client's programs for an application.

The use of test data (sometimes referred to as "test decks") is somewhat analogous to the audit procedure of tracing of actual transactions. However, the rationale underlying the two tests and the scope of the tests are different.

In tracing transactions, the tracing activity involves looking at the source documents, processing, and output for a sample of transactions processed during the period being audited. The items traced provide evidence on what took place because they are a sample of the activity of the period.

In using test data, the programs for an application are tested at a single point in time (during or after the period in question), and performance during the period under audit is inferred from this test. To make this a valid inference, the auditor must have evidence about the condition of the program during this time.

Note that the test data are a test of procedures contained in the program and are not a test of input data processed by the program. In order to comply with auditing standards, the use of test data must be coupled with an examination of source documents and other source evidence supporting the records being produced.

The use of test data requires a fair amount of expertise on the part of the auditor. It also requires computer time to process the transactions. Test data have been frequently mentioned as a desirable technique, but they have been used only infrequently.

The applicability of the test-data method should be considered under the following circumstances:

1. A significant part of a system of internal control is embodied in the computer program.
2. There are gaps in the audit trail, making it difficult or impractical to trace input to output and to verify calculations. This can be the situation in a simple application as well as in complex integrated systems.
3. The volume of records is large, so that it may be more economical and more effective to use testing of the program (and related procedures) than to use manual testing methods.

As an example, an insurance company maintained a master file of insurance policies in force. Each month end, the file was processed to calculate unearned premiums for each policy and the total for all policies. Only the total was printed out, and the general ledger was adjusted to this amount. The auditing firm used test data to satisfy themselves that the program provided an accurate calculation and summarization of the unearned premium. The auditors also performed tests to satisfy themselves that source data were properly prepared and entered the system without loss or non-processing and that the tested program was the one used in the processing.

Given the same program and the same data, the computer will consistently produce identical results. A test of the processing performed by a program can be used as a valid basis for inference as to actual processing performed by the client only if the independent auditor can assure himself that the program tested was the one used. If changes were made in the program during the period, the auditor must be able to ascertain their impact on the processing performed before and after the changes.

Two approaches to obtaining assurance about the program are possible. The feasibility and applicability of the different approaches depend on the type of application and the type of processing performed.

1. Controlled processing or reprocessing. The auditor checks the program using test data, and then has the tested program run under his control. This approach will be explained later in the chapter.
2. Repeated use of test data during the period. This is practical for the outside auditor under very limited circumstances. One of these is an online system with remote terminals.

The general steps in developing and using test data are:

1. Decide on the type of master records to be used (if required).
2. Determine the types of transactions to be included in the test data.

3. Develop appropriate working papers.
4. Obtain the master records to process with the test transactions and precompute the results for comparison with the output resulting from the test processing.
5. Investigate the effects that the processing of the test transactions will have on the results of the system if transactions are run with regular master files or with the regular processing run.
6. Make arrangements to get the test transactions prepared and to obtain output in a useful form.
7. Obtain the programs to be tested and verify that these programs are used in processing the test transactions.

Many of the problems of implementing the test-data method relate to the master records. These are the ledger-type permanent records which are updated by transaction records. For example, the processing of a test transaction representing a payment received from a customer will need to update the master file of accounts receivable records. The different alternatives for obtaining master records are:

1. Use current master records.
2. Use special audit records maintained in the master file.
3. Use obsolete master records or copy of current master records.
4. Use simulated master records.

In the first two approaches, the auditor performs his tests by including his transactions in the client's normal processing run. In the latter two, the auditor obtains a master file for later use.

Controlled processing and reprocessing. A second method for gaining assurance about the operation of a data processing system is for the auditor to control the processing run using a program which has been tested. The procedures can take two forms: (1) control over the processing run which prepares data for the financial statements and (2) reprocessing of a sample of data from the period being audited.

In the first case, the auditor controls either the original processing run or a subsequent reprocessing run. The run uses a program which has been tested and then maintained under auditor control. This procedure provides assurance that the processing results are based on the authorized tested program. As an example of this procedure, the case of the insurance company mentioned previously is relevant. The auditing firm proved the client's computer program for computing unearned premiums at month end by the use of test data. The client was then requested to prepare a duplicate copy of the tested program for the auditor. At year end, the client was requested to use, under audit control, the auditor's duplicate copy of the program to calculate the unearned premium figure for the balance sheet.

The second use of reprocessing involves the reprocessing of transactions for a selected period or periods. An auditor's copy of the program is used for the reprocessing. The results obtained by the client are compared with the results of the reprocessing run.

The use of controlled processing or reprocessing does not require that a new program be written. The program used is the regular client program which the auditor has tested to satisfy himself that the program is performing the processing satisfactorily.

This method requires a knowledge of computer data processing on the part of the auditor sufficient to test the program and to control the processing or reprocessing. It requires advance planning to obtain, test, and control a copy of the program and to obtain computer facilities, files, and transactions for reprocessing.

In the case of controlled processing or reprocessing at the end of the period being audited, the client will normally have the data on hand in the proper form. Advance arrangements must be made for computer time, operators, etc. In using reprocessing to test processing performed during the period, the reprocessing may be performed by obtaining copies of transaction files before they are released. The tests can be performed for as many periods as the auditor deems necessary in order to obtain sufficient audit evidence.

Controlled processing or reprocessing represents a substantial use of the computer in performing audit procedures. Because it requires a testing of the program and control over the running of the program, the method is best suited for situations which justify using the computer rather than using manual procedures based on visible audit trail printouts. The method should therefore be considered for a year-end processing run if the volume of data to be processed (and tested) is large or the processing to be verified is complex or otherwise difficult to follow by means of visible printouts.

The reprocessing of samples of transactions during the period is, from a logical standpoint, a very effective procedure. However, it is difficult and costly to implement, and therefore alternative procedures are often preferred. The procedure can be carried out quite successfully by an internal auditing group. If so, the outside auditor can follow usual audit practice with regard to the extent of reliance on the work of internal auditors.

Tests for Quality of Records. Records may be tested by using regular manual examination of computer printouts or by using the computer in the testing process. Keeping in mind the fact that computer records can always be dumped or listed and the records to be tested taken from this printout, the decision to utilize the computer in testing and evaluating the records will depend on the economics of using the computer versus performing the tests by hand, and also on non-cost factors such as increased assurance from audit procedures.

A computer program can be used in the audit for any computational or comparison task for which quantitative criteria can be established. Examples of these types of tasks are:

1. Testing extensions and footings
2. Selecting and printing confirmation requests
3. Examining records for quality—completeness, consistency, invalid conditions, etc.
4. Summarizing data and performing analyses useful to the auditor
5. Selecting and printing audit samples
6. Comparing the same data maintained in separate files for correctness and consistency
7. Comparing audit data with company records

A common characteristic of these applications is the fact that the auditor can define clearly and precisely what is to be computed, compared, summed, printed, etc.

The programs for use in evaluation of computerized records come from three sources. These are:

1. Programs written by the client
2. Generalized audit programs
3. Programs written by or for the auditor

Client programs. Much of the analysis desired by the auditor is equally useful to the client. Therefore, the client will frequently write the programs for his own use, or he will prepare the program for his installation if the auditor requests the analysis and there is also an internal use for it. Examples of programs needed by both the client and the auditor are programs to age accounts receivable and programs to analyze inventory turnover and obsolescence.

If an auditor is to use the output of a client's analysis program, he must be able to assure himself that the program is performing what he wishes and is doing it correctly. He may obtain this assurance by manually testing samples of the analysis, by tracing totals to controls, and by similar audit procedures. Or he may test the program by methods such as the use of test data.

Generalized audit software. Two general approaches to generalized audit software have been used. The first is the use of an industry program which is applicable to all clients in an industry. A good example is the brokerage field, where generalized audit programs have been used to perform standard audit procedures having to do with confirmations, margin computations, etc. The client's files are transferred to a standard format on magnetic tape by a conversion program which is unique for each client having a different computer. The data file, in standard form, is processed by an audit program used for all clients. The client computer is used only if it fits the model and configuration specifications for which the audit processing program was written. It should be noted that, even though two computer systems are not program-compatible, they are probably data-compatible if the data are put on magnetic tape. In some cases, it requires a processing run to adjust the data codes to make them compatible.

The second approach is a generalized set of computerized audit routines [2] which can be used with a specified computer configuration (and others compatible with it). The set of routines usually includes programs to select samples for confirmation, foot and crossfoot selected items, select and print out items meeting exception criteria defined by the auditor, etc. The auditor can use the audit routines without extensive expertise in computers since the routines are for testing and analyzing the client computer records and not the client computer programs. This software is explained in more detail later in the chapter.

Auditor programs. The writing of a special computer program for audit use only is an extension of the case of using a tested and controlled copy of a client program. The auditor must, in both cases, assure himself that the program does what he wishes it to do; but in the case of a special program written specifically for the auditor, the auditor has additional responsibilities in the preparation of the program. This is summarized in Table 2.

GENERALIZED COMPUTER AUDIT SOFTWARE SYSTEMS

A generalized computer audit software system consists of a set of prewritten computer routines which an auditor may use to test the computerized records of an organization. The generalized computer audit software systems represent a significant development in the use of the computer in testing records maintained by the computer. They are also useful for nonaudit tasks such as special analyses.

[2] An example is the Haskins & Sells Auditape, the first of this type. A number of these systems are now available.

TABLE 2 Steps in Preparing an Audit Computer Program and the Auditor's Role

Steps	Resulting in:	Auditor's role
1. Analysis of problem............	Statement of objective	Preparation
2. Design of a system to perform the processing and provide the information	System flow charts Report layouts File designs Record layouts	Preparation or supervision of preparation
3. Planning of the computer logic	Program flow charts and/or decision tables	Review
4. Program preparation		
a. Coding in a computer language	Coding sheets in source language. Input deck keypunched from coding sheets	General cognizance
b. Translation (assembly or compilation)	Source and object code listings plus the machine language program	General cognizance
c. Debugging....................	Test data and test results	Preparation of test data and supervision of use
d. Documenting.................	Run manual and computer operator instruction manual	Supervision and review
5. Input data preparation	Input data cards Master file Transaction file	Supervision or review
6. Running of program............	Report or other output Error messages	Supervision and control

Development of Computer Audit Software Systems. The first generalized computer audit software system was Haskins & Sells Auditape which was publicly announced in 1967. Operating on an IBM 1401 or an IBM System/360 in IBM 1401 emulation mode, this version can be viewed as the first generation of computer audit software. Subsequent Auditape versions were for the IBM System/360 and other equipment. Auditape was made available to industry and to other CPAs under a licensing arrangement.

Subsequently, all major CPA firms have developed generalized audit software packages to assist their auditors in testing records maintained on the computer. Some of the firms have made their systems generally available through licensing agreement; other systems have remained completely proprietary. Non-CPA firms have also developed audit software systems or software packages which can be readily adapted to satisfy audit purposes. By early 1971, about 18 audit software systems could be identified, but only about half were of major interest.

The American Institute of Certified Public Accountants has not endorsed or otherwise supported any computer audit system. However, in recognition of the need for training by CPAs who wished to learn about and possibly lease Auditape (when it was the only readily available alternative), the AICPA sponsored professional development seminars in 1967 and 1968 on the nature and use of Auditape. In 1970, the AICPA agreed to act as a facilitating organization for CPA firms desiring to use a computer audit system (AUDASSIT) which was offered by the developers as a service to the profession. This audit service included running the audit programs on data files sent to a CPA operated computer facility. The offering of the service and the related seminars were a recognition by the AICPA of the difficulty experienced by small CPA firms in auditing computerized records and their need for assistance in applying computer audit software.

Types of Design and Operation. The generalized computer audit software systems can be classified according to the approach to program design and the approach to operation:

Program Design	*Operation*
Specific to only one computer system	Used by the auditor with minimal help from experts and usually run on client computer
Routines in COBOL (or other language) to be run on different computers	Run by computer specialists using a CPA operated computer

The most common approach is for the software to run on a specified computer system and to be used by auditors who have received training but who are not computer experts. Each of the design and operational approaches will however be explained.

Audit software specific to a single computer has the advantage of being able to use the characteristics of that computer to advantage. Coding of the computer audit routines may be in machine-oriented code which generally provides faster running time with less memory required than coding in higher-order language. Audit software specific to a single computer system has generally been written for the IBM System/360. The audit system has specified memory size and peripheral requirements. For example, one audit system requires an IBM System/360 model 30 with 32,000 bytes of core storage and one disk drive. All larger System/360s and 370s are also acceptable. However, the software will not run on the smaller System/360 model 20 or the specialized model 44. There have also been audit systems written for the IBM 1401, Honeywell 200 and others.

Audit software may also be written in a higher order language such as COBOL. This means that the program can, with minor modification, be run on any computer which has a COBOL compiler. This design has the advantage that the specific computer need not be specified in advance, but it requires some work by a trained computer programmer to get the programs operational on a given computer. Another advantage is the fact that the audit system may be modular and only the selected modules are used on an application. This reduces storage requirements and allows more versatility of design option. It also allows rather rapid modification of the programs, but with a need for programmer assistance.

A major operational objective of most computer audit software systems is to allow an auditor with relatively little EDP training to use the computer in testing computer-maintained records. The major audit systems require very little training if the auditor is reasonably knowledgeable in EDP. Two to three days training is sufficient. For the untrained auditor, at least one week training period appears to be a bare minimum. It is true that with very little training, the untrained auditor may use the audit systems. The difficulty arises in handling unusual situations. These tend to require an auditor with some general EDP understanding. The most effective use of the audit software systems appears to require the availability of trained staff to support and supervise field use of the system. A major problem is obtaining time on the client computer to run the application. If necessary, the file to be audited may be copied and the audit work performed at a data processing service center.

An alternative to field operation of the audit software is to have the field auditor obtain copies of files to be examined plus necessary specifications for the data files and to send the files and specifications to a data processing center together with a description of the work to be performed. The file is then processed by data processing personnel employed by the auditing firm. The advantage of this approach is the fact that the field auditor need not be concerned with running the audit tests, only with obtaining file audit copies and file description and in writing up specifications for the program to be run. Time need not be obtained on the client computer. On the other hand, it may sometimes be advisable to use the client computer for the audit runs and this approach does not provide for it.

Functions Performed by Audit Software Systems. The functions which are usually performed by the audit software systems are:

Interpret audit specifications for processing the file, examine for errors, and print out instructions and error messages.

Create a working audit file by copying all or part of the client file. The audit working file is put into an audit specified format. All processing is with the audit working file; the client file is released back to the client. If processing is done other than at the client center, a copy of the client file is obtained for audit use.

Update the audit working file with data from a second client file.

Select and print records which meet criteria specified by the auditor. Examples of criteria are:

1. All records with gross pay greater than $8,000
2. A record with a key equal to 94761
3. Records which are zero or negative in rate field
4. Records which are blank in name field

Summarize data on the audit file producing totals for numeric fields. Examples are totals for gross-pay-to-date, item inventory valuations, etc. Data can be stratified by category.

Calculate additional values from the data on the audit file. For example, the client inventory file could be updated with market prices and calculations then could be made to obtain a "lower of cost or market" inventory value.

In addition to the above functions, most of the software systems include the following:

Sort the audit working file into a specified order.

Select a systematic or random sample based on sampling criteria provided by the auditor.

Print audit confirmations and prepare all necessary confirmation data for analysis and followup. It is possible by the use of special forms to print the confirmation already in the envelope ready for mailing plus printing of the followup request (for positive confirmations).

These functions may be performed in a series of one or more runs using the audit working file or other audit files generated during the processing. The audit functions usually print out data describing the functions performed and control information necessary to determine that processing has been completed properly. The printout provides complete documentation for audit papers.

Using an Audit Software System. The auditor uses an audit software system by a sequence of steps. A typical sequence is:

1. The auditor selects the files and records to be tested and decides the tests and processing to be performed.

2. The auditor fills out specification using preprinted forms such as the following:
   - *a.* General system specification describing the computer system
   - *b.* Description of client file and the data records in it
   - *c.* Description of audit working file
   - *d.* Specification of fields to be summarized
   - *e.* Specification of calculation to be performed and stratification criteria to be used
   - *f.* Sort specifications to sort the audit working file
   - *g.* Specifications on selection of records and printing of a report
3. The specifications are punched into cards.
4. The computer operator mounts (*a*) the client data file on a tape or disk, (*b*) a device for the working file, and (*c*) the audit software package which is usually on a magnetic tape or magnetic disk.
5. The computer operator loads the audit software system executive program which reads the specification cards and then takes control and executes the functions specified by the auditor on the specification sheets. The audit software routines copy specified data from client files. Thereafter, the software operates on the audit working file rather than the client file.

The use of preprinted forms guides the auditor in preparing the necessary specifications. The specification of client files and record layouts is based on client documentation. The auditor should be able to read the documentation and extract the necessary information. This documentation may be a record layout, a COBOL DATA DIVISION description or both. Input file specifications such as blocking, recording mode, density, and labels can be obtained from data processing personnel.

The audit working file usually contains only part of the data fields from the client records, because many data items are not of interest to the audit. Having extracted the data fields relevant to the audit, the auditor can perform a variety of analyses by filling out fairly simple processing specification sheets. Typical operations the user may specify are:

Mathematical	*Comparison of Two Fields*	*Other*
Add	Less	Sample selection
Subtract	Less than or equal	Analyze field for limits
Multiply	Greater than	Stratify
Divide	Greater than or equal	
Foot	Equal	
	Not equal	

The output specifications allow the auditor to prepare a report with useful headings. The auditor usually specifies the criteria for output, the headings, the column order in which data is to be printed, and the totals and subtotals to be printed.

One problem is the use of a software system written to run on say an IBM System/360 or System/370 to process files prepared by the equipment of other manufacturers. In general, the programs for one computer will not run on another, but it is frequently possible to process data files on magnetic tape written by one computer using another make computer. This means that a CPA having an audit software system which runs on an IBM System/360 and a client with another manufacturer's equipment may get a copy of the files on magnetic tape and process them using the IBM computer at a service center, CPA office, etc. There are usually certain technical problems in using magnetic tapes in this way, but these can generally be solved without serious difficulty.

Applications for Audit Software Systems. The following are examples of applications which have been run using audit software:

Confirmation selection and printing
Test of accruals
Aging of receivables
Test of payroll transactions
Test of depreciation calculations and selection of items for vouching
Selection and analysis of inactive depositor accounts
Pricing of inventory (lower of cost or market)
Inventory price tests
Search of voucher register for unrecorded items and selection of items for examination
Computation of unearned finance charges
Test of adequacy of maintenance reserve

The uses are not limited to audit applications. The audit software systems are essentially limited-purpose information retrieval and analysis systems, so that the systems have a general applicability for use in extracting data from a file and performing fairly simple operations on the data.

AUDITING ONLINE REALTIME SYSTEMS

Changes and improvements in computer hardware and software have allowed the implementation of new, advanced systems concepts. Two of these concepts important in business data processing are online realtime response and integrated processing.

"Online" pertains to peripheral equipment or devices connected to and in direct communication with the central processing unit of the computer. The term is also used to describe the connection of terminal equipment to a transmission line in a data communications system.

"Realtime" refers to the time required for an action, an activity, or a decision to take place. Data processing which is performed concurrently with the activity and can therefore influence the course of the action being taken or the decision being made is said to be "realtime" processing. In business applications, the term is used to refer to fast response systems in which files are updated at the time the transactions are recorded and in which outputs are provided immediately when they are requested. By the nature of the requirements, realtime systems are always online.

An integrated data processing system is a system designed to minimize duplicate operations and duplicated records. The concept of an integrated data processing system recognizes the interrelationship and dependence of the economic functions of a business. Rather than performing processing and maintaining records based on organizational functions (purchasing, accounts payable, sales, etc.), the integrated system is designed so that records for different functions with similar information are combined into a single comprehensive record. Some important characteristics of an integrated system for data processing are:

1. A single source document describing a transaction or providing other data, once entered into the system, initiates the updating of all records associated with the transaction or data item.

2. The parts of the system are interrelated and duplicate records are eliminated.

Problems of Auditing Online Realtime Systems. The characteristics (integrated, online, realtime) of the systems suggest four problem areas:

1. Source documents
2. Authorizations
3. Audit trail
4. Control totals

The source documents will not be found in traditional form if there is direct input from point-of-origin devices. However, good control dictates for most systems that all system inputs should be logged in, so that a substitute for the source documents will usually be found.

When there is direct input, transactions should still be authorized. This can be done by providing users with key words, passwords, etc., to establish the authority of the user. Also, a listing of inputs may subsequently be returned to the supervisor of the originator for review and ex post approval.

Since a characteristic of an integrated system is the updating of all related files from a single data input, the system will have less printed output documentation of processing steps taken than one which requires separate documents for each step in processing. The intermediate authorization documents are not prepared, since the system is designed to proceed automatically to do all processing required by the input or by the results occasioned by the input. For example, when an inventory requisition is processed against the inventory file and the expense file, the transaction may automatically trigger a reorder purchase order and associated processing without human intervention. Although a system designer could design a system without an audit trail, the various needs of management normally require an adequate method of tracing the results of processing.

Control totals are a feature of batch processing which can also be used in online realtime systems to establish controls for remote input stations, certain types of transactions, etc.

Procedures for Auditing Online Realtime Systems. One of the audit possibilities with an online realtime system is the use of some form of continuous monitoring by the audit staff. Whereas normal audit procedure typically includes tests of a sample of the processing performed during the period being audited, it may be more effective in an advanced system employing remote input devices and integrated processing to arrange for continuous monitoring of the system either by a monitoring audit routine designed for this purpose or by tests performed at irregular intervals during the period.

The use of a monitoring audit program is a sophisticated technique perhaps best suited for internal audit use but indicative of the range of available techniques. An audit routine is added to the set of programs controlling the data processing. Transactions entering the system are sampled at random intervals and the sampled transaction is written on an audit tape or at an audit output terminal for use in testing. The system may be designed to automatically record control information on an input/output device under auditor control.

The use of online input/output devices may make it feasible for the auditor to introduce test transactions into the system randomly during the period in order to trace the system response. This is similar to the use of test data; but since it is a "live" testing of the system, it should be used under strict control.

QUESTIONNAIRE FOR EVALUATION OF INTERNAL CONTROL IN ELECTRONIC DATA PROCESSING [3]

This is a model questionnaire for obtaining information on internal control in an electronic data processing installation.

The questionnaire is divided into two major parts:

1. Questions relating to the operation of the electronic data processing installation
2. Questions relating to an individual data processing application.

This division reflects the fact that the organization, the policies and the procedures of the installation provide an environment in which individual applications are run. This environment must be understood before the controls associated with individual applications can be evaluated.

The review of a computer processing application should be carried out in the context of the entire processing cycle, including both computer and non-computer processing and controls. The firm's internal review questionnaire (or other method used to obtain information) should cover the non-computer procedures and controls; the application questionnaire is structured to provide only the added questions related to computer processing.

The number of questions to be included in a review questionnaire depends somewhat on how broadly the auditor views his audit assignment—whether he looks at items affecting operational efficiency as well as items directly affecting the audit. The control significance of the response to a particular question often, however, depends on the characteristics of the system being evaluated and the total picture of internal control. Each question in the model is coded A, B or C according to its general control significance. This code is only an indicator to aid the auditor; he must evaluate the significance in each particular case.

Code	*In General, Question Relates to:*
A	Control element which may affect the auditor's evaluation of internal control
B	Control element which tends to affect data processing safeguards but is, however, not likely to affect audit procedures
C	Element affecting operational effectiveness or efficiency

All yes-or-no questions are worded so that "yes" is a favorable response and "no" indicates that further investigation or evaluation is required. The auditor may also wish to expand and clarify his answers by adding comments.

PART I: QUESTIONNAIRE FOR OPERATION OF THE ELECTRONIC DATA PROCESSING INSTALLATION

1. *Background*
   - 1-1. Where is the computer located? ____________________
   - 1-2. Give a brief description of equipment ____________________
     ____
     - (*a*) Manufacturer and model number of computer (this can be obtained from a copy of the manufacturer's invoice)
       ____
     - (*b*) Internal memory size ____________________
     - (*c*) File storage devices
       - Magnetic tape (no. units ______) ☐
       - Disk (no. drives ______) ☐
       - Other (describe) ☐
         ____
         ____
         ____

[3] SOURCE: Gordon B. Davis, *Auditing and EDP*, New York, AICPA, 1968, pp. 325–340.

(*d*) Input/output devices
- Card reader ☐
- Card punch ☐
- Printer ☐
- Other (list) ☐

____

____

____

1-3. Applications
- Cash ☐
- Receivables ☐
- Inventory ☐
- Property, plant and equipment ☐
- Payables ☐
- Sales ☐
- Payroll ☐
- Cost and expenses ☐
- Other (list major ones below) ☐

____

____

____

2. *Organization*

2-1. Prepare or obtain an organization chart of the EDP organization. Determine position titles, job descriptions and names of persons in these positions.

	Yes	*No*	
2-2. Is there a segregation of duties such that:			
(*a*) The functions and duties of system design and programming are separate from computer operation?	☐	☐	A
(*b*) Programmers do not operate the computer for regular processing runs?	☐	☐	A
(*c*) Computer operators are restricted from access to data and program information not necessary for performing their assigned task?	☐	☐	B
(*d*) The employees in data processing are separated from all duties relating to the initiation of transactions and initiation of requests for changes to the master files?	☐	☐	A
2-3. Are the operators assigned to individual application runs rotated periodically?	☐	☐	A
2-4. Are the computer operators required to take vacations?	☐	☐	B
2-5. Is supervision of operators sufficient to verify operator's adherence to prescribed operating procedures?	☐	☐	B

3. *The Control Function*

3-1. Is there a person or group charged with responsibility for the control function in the data processing department? Obtain description of duties. These duties will normally include:			
(*a*) Control over receipt of input data and recording of control information?	☐	☐	
(*b*) Reconciliation of control information (batch control with computer control totals, run-to-run controls, etc.)?	☐	☐	

Yes *No*

(*c*) Control over distribution of output? ☐ ☐

(*d*) Control over errors to ensure that they are reported, corrected and reprocessed? ☐ ☐

(*e*) Review of console logs, error listings and other evidence of error detection and control? ☐ ☐

3-2. Is the person or group responsible for control over processing by the data processing department independent from the person or group responsible for the operation of the equipment? ☐ ☐ A

3-3. If there is an internal auditing group, does it perform EDP control activities related to:

(*a*) Review or audit? ☐ ☐ A

(*b*) Day-to-day control activities? ☐ ☐ A

If "yes" note the nature and extent of these activities.

3-4. Are master file changes or changes in program data factors authorized in writing by initiating departments? ☐ ☐ A

3-5. Are departments that initiate changes in master file data or program data factors furnished with notices or a register showing changes actually made? (Examples of such changes are changes in pay rates, selling prices, credit limits and commission tables.) ☐ ☐ A

4. *Control over the Console*

4-1. Are provisions adequate to prevent unauthorized entry of program changes and/or data through the console? The following questions reflect the types of controls which may be used.

(*a*) Are adequate machine operation logs being maintained? For each run, these should include information covering the run identification, operator, start and stop time, error halts and delays, and details of reruns. Idle time, down time, program testing, etc., should also be logged. ☐ ☐ B

(*b*) Is there an independent examination of computer logs to check the operator performance and machine efficiency? If "yes," ☐ ☐ B

(1) How often ______

(2) By whom ______

(3) How carried out ______

______

______

______

(*c*) If the computer has a typewriter console, is there an independent examination of the console printouts to detect operator problems and unauthorized intervention? ☐ ☐ B

(1) How often ______

(2) By whom ______

(3) How performed ______

______

______

______

5. *Management Practices*

	Yes	No	
5-1. Is there a written plan for future changes to be made to the system?	☐	☐	C
5-2. Is approval for each application supported by a study of cost and benefit?	☐	☐	C
5-3. Is a schedule of implementation prepared showing actual versus planned progress?	☐	☐	C
5-4. Is there a systems and procedures manual for the activities of the installation?	☐	☐	C

6. *Documentation*

6-1. Is a run manual prepared for each computer run?	☐	☐	C
6-2. Are operator instructions prepared for each run?	☐	☐	C
6-3. Are documentation practices adequate?	☐	☐	C

Does the normal documentation for an application include the following?

	Yes	No
Problem statement	☐	☐
System flowchart	☐	☐
Record layouts	☐	☐
Program flowcharts	☐	☐
Program listing	☐	☐
Test data	☐	☐
Operator instructions	☐	☐
Summary of controls	☐	☐
Approval and change record	☐	☐

6-4. Is there supervisory review of documentation to ensure that it is adequate?	☐	☐	B
6-5. Is documentation kept up to date?	☐	☐	C

7. *Program Revisions*

7-1. Is each program revision authorized by a request for change properly approved by management or supervisory personnel?	☐	☐	B

(*a*) Who authorizes? ______________________

(*b*) How evidenced? ______________________

7-2. Are program changes, together with their effective dates, documented in a manner which preserves an accurate chronological record of the system?	☐	☐	C
7-3. Are program revisions tested in the same manner as new programs?	☐	☐	B

8. *Hardware Controls*

Unless there is evidence of hardware-based processing difficulties, the auditor can usually rely on the hardware. No review is ordinarily required for audit purposes.

9. *Control over Input and Output Data*

Although the control over input and output data must be exercised for each application, general questions regarding these controls may be used to ascertain policy regarding the use of control procedures.

9-1. Are initiating departments required to establish independent control over data submitted for processing (through the use of batch totals, document counts, or otherwise)?	☐	☐	A

	Yes	No	
9-2. Is a schedule maintained of the reports and documents to be produced by the EDP system?	☐	☐	B
9-3. Are output reports and documents reviewed before distribution to ascertain the reasonableness of the output?	☐	☐	A
9-4. Are there adequate procedures for control over the distribution of reports?	☐	☐	B
10. *Programmed Control over Processing* Programmed controls must be evaluated in terms of each application.			
11. *Controlling Error Investigations*			
11-1. Are all error corrections reviewed and approved by persons who are independent of the data processing department?	☐	☐	A
11-2. Are records maintained of errors occurring in the EDP system?	☐	☐	C
11-3. Are these error records periodically reviewed by someone independent of data processing?	☐	☐	C
12. *Physical Safeguards over Files*			
12-1. Are important computer programs, essential documentation, records and files kept in fireproof storage?	☐	☐	C
12-2. Are copies of important programs, essential documentation, records and files stored in off-premises locations?	☐	☐	C
13. *Procedural Controls for Safeguarding Files*			
13-1. Are external labels used on all files?	☐	☐	B
13-2. Are internal labels used on all magnetic tape files?	☐	☐	B
13-3. Are file header labels checked by programs using the files?	☐	☐	B
13-4. Are file protection rings used on all magnetic tape files to be preserved?	☐	☐	B
13-5. Is the responsibility for issuing and storing magnetic tape or portable disk packs assigned to a tape librarian, either as a full-time or part-time duty?	☐	☐	C
14. *Capability for File Reconstruction*			
14-1. Are there provisions for the use of alternative facilities in the event of fire or other lengthy interruption?	☐	☐	C
14-2. Is there adequate data processing insurance (other than fire coverage)?	☐	☐	B
14-3. Are data processing personnel covered by fidelity insurance?	☐	☐	B

Part II. Questionnaire for Individual Applications

The questions in this section are expected to supplement an internal review questionnaire or any other information-obtaining method. They should enable the auditor to obtain information on whether or not various control techniques have been used in the computer processing phase of a particular application.

The questionnaire is organized around the following control points:

1. Adequacy of control over input data
   (*a*) Verification of correctness of input data
   (*b*) Control over transmittal of data for processing
   (*c*) Validity tests and other tests of input data

2. Adequacy of control over processing
   (*a*) Control for completeness of processing
   (*b*) Checks for correctness of processing
   (*c*) Handling of rejects
   (*d*) Management trail or audit trail
3. Adequacy of control over programs and data files
   (*a*) Documentation
   (*b*) Control over changes to master files
   (*c*) Back-up procedures

The questions are numbered from 101 to distinguish them from questions in the general questionnaire. In cases where a control can be implemented by two or more methods, the related question is followed by a check-list of common control procedures. For each application (or run) related to the audit, the auditor should obtain information sufficient for answering all the relevant questions.

A data processing control review sheet [Figure 11] may be used as a means of describing the input, processing and output controls for a particular application. It may be used in place of or in addition to questions 101 and 102.

101. *Control over Input and Output for an Application*

	Yes	*No*	
101-1. Are there adequate controls over the creation of data and its conversion to machine-readable form?	☐	☐	A
(*a*) Procedural controls ☐			
(*b*) Mechanical or visual verification ☐			
(*c*) Check digit ☐			
101-2. Is there adequate control over transmittal and input of data to detect loss or nonprocessing? Note data field controlled.	☐	☐	A
Field			
(*a*) Financial control totals ______			
(*b*) Hash control totals ______			
(*c*) Document counts ______			
(*d*) Sequential numbering of input documents ______			
(*e*) Other ______			
101-3. Are the input control totals and run-to-run control totals for each application checked by someone other than the equipment operator?	☐	☐	A
By whom? ______			
101-4. If data transmission is used, are controls adequate to determine that transmission is correct and no messages are lost?	☐	☐	B
(*a*) Message counts ☐			
(*b*) Character counts ☐			
(*c*) Dual transmission ☐			
(*d*) Other ______			
101-5. Is input data adequately tested for validity, correctness and sequence?	☐	☐	B
Note: Questions may have to be applied to each important data field of the input being reviewed by the auditor.			
Fields Tested			
(*a*) Validity tests:			
(1) Valid code ______			
(2) Valid character ______			

Figure 11 CONTROL REVIEW SHEET

DATA PROCESSING CONTROL REVIEW SHEET

Application ______________________ Prepared by ______________ Date ________

Reviewed by ______________ Date ________

Run No. and Run Name	Description of Control Field or Control Item	Type of Control	Controls Established by				Controls Verified by			
							Computer Program			
			Department Sending Data	Data Processing Department Control Section	Computer Program	Preceding Run (Run-to-Run)	Control Information Output	Exception Output Only	Data Processing Department Control Section	User or Other Outside Department

(3) Valid field ______
(4) Valid transaction ______
(5) Valid combinations ______
(6) Missing data ______
(*b*) Sequence ______
(*c*) Limit ______
(*d*) Reasonableness ______
(*e*) Other ______

	Yes	*No*	
101-6. Is control over distribution of output adequate? Describe.	☐	☐	B
101-7. Describe the control function, if any, for evaluating quality of output.			
102. *Programmed Control over Processing*			
102-1. Are control totals used to check for completeness of processing? These may include trailer file labels, run-to-run totals, etc.	☐	☐	B
102-2. Are programmed controls used to test processing of significant items?	☐	☐	B

Item applied to

(*a*) Limit and reasonableness test ______
(*b*) Crossfooting test ______

102-3. Does the program check for improper switch settings (if sense switches are used)?	☐	☐	C
103. *Control over Handling of Errors*			
103-1. Does the program provide an adequate console printout of control information (switch settings, control violations, operator intervention, etc.)?	☐	☐	B
103-2. When a program is interrupted, are there adequate provisions for re-start?	☐	☐	C
103-3. Are there adequate controls over the process of identifying, correcting and reprocessing data rejected by the program?	☐	☐	B
103-4. Inquire into handling of unmatched transactions (no master record corresponding to transaction record). Is it adequate?	☐	☐	A

(*a*) Reject and note on error log ☐
(*b*) Reject and write on suspense record ☐
(*c*) Other ______

104. *Control over Program and Data Files*			
104-1. Is there adequate up-to-date documentation for the application?	☐	☐	C

	Yes	*No*
(*a*) Application summary	☐	☐
(*b*) Run manuals	☐	☐
(*c*) Operator instructions	☐	☐

104-2. Is test data documented and kept up to date?	☐	☐	C
104-3. Are controls over master file changes adequate?	☐	☐	B

	Yes	*No*
(*a*) Written request for change from outside data processing	☐	☐

	Yes	No	
(*b*) Register of all changes reviewed by initiating department	☐	☐	
(*c*) Supervisory or other review of changes	☐	☐	

	Yes	No	
104-4. Are there adequate provisions for periodically checking master file contents?	☐	☐	B

	Yes	No
(*a*) Periodic printout and review	☐	☐
(*b*) Periodic test against physical count	☐	☐
(*c*) Other ______		

104-5. Are the back-up and reconstruction provisions adequate? Describe ______	☐	☐	B
105. *Management or Audit Trail*			
105-1. Do the records or references provide the means to adequately:			
(*a*) Trace any transaction forward to a final total?	☐	☐	A
(*b*) Trace any transaction back to the original source document or input?	☐	☐	A
(*c*) Trace any final total back to the component transactions?	☐	☐	A
105-2. When ledgers (general or subsidiary) are maintained on computer media, does the system of processing provide:			
(*a*) An historical record of activity in the accounts?	☐	☐	B
(*b*) A periodic trial balance of the accounts?	☐	☐	B
105-3. Are source documents retained for an adequate period of time in a manner which allows identification with related output records and documents?	☐	☐	C

BIBLIOGRAPHY

Computer Research Studies, AICPA, New York, to date.

Internal Auditing of Electronic Data Processing Systems, The Institute of Internal Auditors, New York, to date.

Boutell, Wayne S.: *Auditing with the Computer*, Berkeley, Calif., University of California Press, 1965.

Computer Auditing in the Seventies, New York, Arthur Young & Company, 1970.

Davis, Gordon B.: *Auditing and EDP*, New York, AICPA, 1968.

Davis, Gordon B.: *Computer Data Processing*, New York, McGraw-Hill Book Company, 1969.

Haskins & Sells Auditape System Manual, New York, Haskins and Sells, 1967.

Sanders, Donald H.: *Computers in Business: An Introduction*, New York, McGraw-Hill Book Company, 1968.

STRATA Users Guide, New York, Touche Ross & Co., 1970.

Davis, Gordon B.: "Standards for Computers and Information Processing," *The Journal of Accountancy*, September, 1967.

Freed, Roy N.: "Computer Fraud—A Management Trap," *Business Horizons*, June, 1969.

Wasserman, Joseph J.: "Plugging the Leaks in Computer Security," *Harvard Business Review*, September–October, 1969.

AUDASSIST, Alexander Grant & Company, March, 1970.

Harlan, Stephen D., Jr., and Thomas J. Donahue: "System 2170," *World* (Peat, Marwick, Mitchell & Co., New York), Fall, 1970.

Webb, Richard: "AUDASSIST," *The Journal of Accountancy*, November, 1970.

Chapter 17

Fraud and the Auditor

NEALE KURLANDER

Associate Professor of Business Administration and Director,
Accounting Program, Adelphi University

GENERAL

Introduction. In order to properly deal with the auditor and his responsibility concerning fraud, this chapter has been divided into four areas. First, we examine and define the various crimes related to fraud; second, we evaluate the auditor's responsibility for the discovery of fraud and the American Institute of Certified Public Accountants' position relative to this problem; third, we examine selected specific areas of fraud and defalcations; and fourth, we suggest certain specific conduct and procedures that an auditor should pursue when he discovers fraud during the course of his audit.

Legal Liability. In this chapter we are concerned with fraud on the part of employees and officers, not fraud on the part of the auditor. However, in recent years in some of the well-publicized cases where false financial statements were issued as described in this chapter, the auditor has also been charged with fraud. In one case two partners and a senior associate in one of the large national firms were convicted of mail fraud and conspiracy after the auditor's opinion represented that the financial statements "present fairly the consolidated financial position of X Company—in conformity with generally accepted accounting principles." The court held that in fact the balance sheet did not fairly present X Company's financial position because of inadequate disclosure of loans. The matter of legal liability of the auditor in the above situation as well as other instances of such legal liability is discussed in Chapter 5, "Legal Liability."

Federal Securities Acts. With the passage of the Securities Act of 1933 and the Securities Act of 1934, the auditor's liability to third parties is substantially extended beyond the bounds set by the court in the *Ultramares* decision. Section 11 of the 1933 act makes the liability of the auditor as well as others very definite in the case of an untrue statement or an omission. A number of the recent court cases concerned with the issuance of false statements have been brought under the federal securities acts. As the filing of financial statements with the SEC is after the completion of the audit and the expression of the opinion which is usually included in the report to stockholders, serious problems have arisen when the auditor has become aware of unfavorable information of which he had no knowledge at the year end. Had he so known, the information probably would have affected the financial statements. To clarify the auditor's responsibility with respect to the subsequent information the Committee on Auditing Procedure of the AICPA issued in 1969 Statement on Auditing Procedure No. 41 *Subsequent Discovery of Facts Existing at the Date of the Auditor's Report.* Where the auditor discovers such information he should undertake to determine whether the information is reliable and whether the facts existed at the date of his report. If the information is reliable and did exist at the date of his report he should advise his client to make prompt disclosure to persons who are relying on the financial statements. If the client refuses to make adequate disclosures then the auditor should notify each member of the board of directors of such refusal and the fact that the auditor will take steps to prevent future reliance upon his report.

Definitions. Let us examine some of the legal definitions of embezzlement, fraud, and negligence. The auditor should be familiar with the basic definitions of these crimes.

Embezzlement. Embezzlement, in general, is the fraudulent appropriation of another's property by one to whom it has been entrusted or into whose hands it has lawfully come.

Negligence. When we discuss negligence, we refer to the degree of care, or lack of proper diligence, exercised by the auditor. Perhaps one of the best definitions of negligence is: the failure to observe that degree of care which the circumstances demand, whereby another person suffers injury.

Whether negligence exists in a particular case must be determined by a consideration of all the attendant or surrounding facts and circumstances.

In a legal sense, negligence means nothing more or less than substandard care.

Fraud. Generally, fraud embraces any cunning, deception, or trick employed to deceive or cheat another. It includes all the means which human ingenuity can devise that are employed to gain an advantage by false suggestion or by suppression of the truth.

A civil legal action based on fraud should have the following elements:

1. The defendant made a false material representation.
2. He knew it was false when he made it, or he made the statement without any knowledge of the truth.
3. He intended the plaintiff to act upon the statement.
4. The plaintiff, having no knowledge of its falsity, relied and acted upon the statement.
5. As a result thereof, the plaintiff suffered injury.

It should be noted that there can be no legally actionable fraud unless all of the elements are present. For example, if elements (1) through (4) are present, but the plaintiff has suffered no damages, he cannot recover a money award in a court of law.

CRIMES RELATED TO FRAUD

Under the New York Penal Law effective September 1, 1967, new statutes defining financial statement crimes were enacted. The purpose was to clarify and specify crimes involving fraudulent financial statements.

Offenses Involving Falsifying of Business Records. A person is guilty of falsifying business records in the second degree when, with intent to defraud, he:

1. Makes or causes a false entry in the business records of an enterprise; or
2. Alters, erases, obliterates, deletes, removes, or destroys a true entry in the business records of an enterprise; or
3. Omits to make a true entry in the business records of an enterprise in violation of a duty to do so, which he knows to be imposed upon him by law or by the nature of his position; or
4. Prevents the making of a true entry or causes the omission thereof in the business records of an enterprise.

A person is guilty of falsifying business records in the first degree when he commits the crime of falsifying business records and when his intent to defraud includes an intent to commit another crime or to aid or conceal the commission thereof.

Issuing False Financial Statements. A person is guilty of issuing a false financial statement when, with the intent to defraud:

1. He knowingly makes or utters a written instrument which purports to describe the financial condition or ability to pay of some person and which is inaccurate in some material respect; or

2. He represents in writing that a written instrument purporting to describe a person's financial condition or ability to pay as of a prior date is accurate with respect to such person's current financial condition or ability to pay, whereas he knows it is materially inaccurate in that respect.

We have already examined some of the legal definitions of fraud and defalcations. The accountant generally delineates the two as follows:

Defalcation is considered to be the misappropriation of business assets by officers and employees. The meaning is usually restricted to confiscation of physical properties or cash. Fraud is a more inclusive term. What is important to remember in distinguishing these two definitions is that the actual theft of business assets is defalcation or employee fraud, but the issuance of financial statements which present false account valuations by management is fraud as it concerns the creditor, the stockholder, the government, and the public in general.

The Auditor and Liability. Accountants have long been plagued with the problem of legal liability. The exposure of the accountant falls generally into two categories, namely, liability to his client and liability to third parties. These groupings are primarily based on deficiencies in the audit procedure or faulty reporting. The accountant is liable to the client for negligence in performance of the audit, as well as for the breach of contract. The existence of liability because of privity of contract between the auditor and the client has long been established.[1]

Discussion of third-party liability necessitates mentioning the landmark *Ultramares* decision of the New York Court of Appeals. This decision made it clear that accountants owe creditors and investors a duty to offer their opinions without *gross* negligence. In the *Ultramares* case, the auditors did not sufficiently investigate to acquire complete knowledge. This is fraud by circumstantial construction (neither deliberate nor active).[2]

Insofar as his liability to the public at large is concerned, the third party must still prove gross negligence on the part of the auditor. The current trend indicates that the general public is relying more and more upon the auditor, especially in the case of publicly held corporations.

Recently, there has been a marked increase in the number of lawsuits against public accountants as a result of their failure to detect fraud during the course of the ordinary audit. The dollar value of these lawsuits is fast approaching the 50-million-dollar mark. Obviously, the accountant does have cause for concern. This is particularly true since there is, at present, no clear-cut legal definition of the accountant's liability. Perhaps a practical step might be for the practitioner to examine the adequacy of his own liability insurance.

Responsibility for Discovery of Fraud. The layman is generally under the impression that an auditor is primarily in search of errors, theft, defalcations, and frauds of all types. However, the AICPA, together with various other accounting societies, has tried to educate both the general public and the business community in order to dispel this incorrect impression. The purpose of the usual audit is not primarily to uncover fraud (unless the audit is so designed). In the normal course of an audit, fraud may be discovered, but this would be a by-product and not the main purpose.

The auditor should not be held responsible for ferreting out carefully con-

[1] Edward J. Davis, "Accountants' Liability Today," *The New York Certified Public Accountant*, November, 1967, pp. 835–844.

[2] *Ibid.*

trived fraudulent schemes—unless his suspicions are aroused during the routine audit. Under ordinary conditions, the auditor is entitled to rely upon the trustworthiness of the officers and employees of the company. Despite the foregoing, the auditor must nevertheless be alert to the possibility of the existence of fraud.

Obviously there is uncertainty regarding the accountant's duty to discover fraud. Furthermore, is the auditor responsible for every type of fraud, or only for material defalcations which would affect his opinion regarding the client's financial statements when taken as a whole? If the auditor complies with proper auditing standards and procedures and fails to discover fraud, is he liable?

In order to help clarify these problems, the AICPA published Statement on Auditing Procedure No. 30, entitled *Responsibilities and Functions of the Independent Auditor in the Examination of Financial Statements.* This statement is set forth at length in the following paragraphs.

Responsibilities of the Auditor. The objective of the ordinary examination of financial statements by the independent auditor is the expression of an opinion on the fairness with which they present the client's financial position and results of operations. The auditor's report is the medium through which he expresses his opinion or, if circumstances require, disclaims an opinion. In either case, he states whether his examination has been made in accordance with generally accepted auditing standards. These standards require him to state if, in his opinion, the financial statements are presented in conformity with generally accepted principles of accounting and if such principles have been consistently applied in the preparation of the financial statements of the current period in relation to those of the preceding period.

Responsibilities of auditor and management. Management has the responsibility for adopting sound accounting policies, for maintaining an adequate and effective system of accounts, for safeguarding the assets, and for devising a system of internal control that will, among other things, help assure the production of proper financial statements. The transactions, which should be reflected in the accounts and in the financial statements, are matters within the direct knowledge and control of management. The auditor's knowledge of such transactions is limited to that acquired through his examination. Accordingly, the fairness of the representations made through financial statements is an implicit and integral part of management's responsibility. The independent auditor may make suggestions as to the form or content of the financial statements or he may draft them in whole or in part, based on management's accounts and records. However, his responsibility for the statements he has examined is confined to the expression of his opinion on them. The financial statements remain the representations of the management.

Professional qualifications of the auditor. The professional qualifications required of the independent auditor are those of a person with the education and experience to practice as such. They do not include those of a person trained for or qualified to engage in another profession or occupation. For example, the independent auditor, in observing the taking of a physical inventory, does not purport to act as an appraiser, a valuer, or an expert in materials. Similarly, although the independent auditor is informed in a general manner about matters of commercial law, he does not purport to act in the capacity of a lawyer and may appropriately rely upon the advice of attorneys in all matters of law.

Judgment. In the observance of generally accepted auditing standards, the independent auditor must exercise his judgment in determining which auditing procedures are necessary in the circumstances to afford a reasonable basis for his opinion. His judgment is required to be the informed judgment of a qualified professional person.

Detection of fraud. In making the ordinary examination, the auditor is aware of the possibility that fraud may exist. Financial statements may be misstated as a result of defalcations and similar irregularities, or of deliberate misrepresentation by management, or both. The auditor recognizes that fraud, if sufficiently material, may affect the financial statements, and his examination, made in accordance with generally accepted auditing standards, gives consideration to this possibility. However, the ordinary examination is not primarily or specifically designed, and cannot be relied upon, to disclose defalcations and other similar irregularities, although their discovery may result. Similarly, although the discovery of deliberate misrepresentation by management is usually more closely associated with the objective of the ordinary examination, such examination cannot be relied upon to assure its discovery. The responsibility of the independent auditor for failure to detect fraud (which responsibility differs as to clients and others) arises only when such failure clearly results from failure to comply with generally accepted auditing standards.

The accounting system. Reliance for the prevention and detection of fraud should be placed principally upon an adequate accounting system with appropriate internal control. The well-established practice of the independent auditor of evaluating the adequacy and effectiveness of the system of internal control by testing the accounting records and related data and by relying on such evaluation for the selection and timing of his auditing procedures has generally proved sufficient for making an adequate examination. If the objective of an independent auditor's examination were the discovery of all fraud, he would have to extend his work to a point where its cost would be prohibitive. Even then he could not give assurance that all types of fraud had been detected, or that none existed, because such items as unrecorded transactions, forgeries, and collusive fraud would not necessarily be uncovered. Accordingly, it is generally recognized that good internal control and fidelity bonds provide protection more economically and effectively. In the case of fidelity bonds, protection is afforded not only by the indemnification for discovered defalcations, but also by the possible deterrent effect upon employees; the presence of fidelity bonds, however, should not affect the scope of the auditor's examination.

Suspicion of fraud. When an independent auditor's examination leading to an opinion on financial statements discloses a situation that makes him suspect that fraud may exist, he should decide whether the fraud, if in fact it should exist, might be of such magnitude as to affect his opinion on the financial statements. If the independent auditor believes that fraud so material as to affect his opinion may have occurred, he should reach an understanding with the proper representatives of the client as to whether the auditor or the client, subject to the auditor's review, is to make the investigation that would be necessary to determine whether fraud has in fact occurred and, if so, the amount thereof. If, on the other hand, the independent auditor concludes that any such fraud could not be so material as to affect his opinion, he should refer the matter to the proper representatives of the client with the recommendation that it be pursued to a conclusion. For example, frauds involving "lapping" accounts receivable collections or frauds involving over-statements of inventory could be material, while those involving peculations from a small imprest fund would normally be of little significance because the operation and size of the fund tend to establish a limitation.

Subsequent discovery of fraud. The subsequent discovery that fraud existed during the period covered by the independent auditor's examination does not of itself indicate negligence on his part. He is not an insurer or guarantor.

Responsibility to the profession. The independent auditor also has a responsibility to his profession: the responsibility to comply with the standards accepted by his fellow practitioners. In recognition of the importance of such compliance, the Institute has adopted, as part of its Code of Professional Ethics, rules which support the standards and provide a basis for enforcement of them.

Official pronouncements. It is noted that paragraph 2 of the AICPA statement clearly places responsibility for the financial records and statements upon management, whereas the auditor's responsibility is confined to his opinion of the statements. Paragraph 4 defines his qualifications (and therefore the degree of care required) as the informed judgment of a qualified professional person.

Paragraph 5 specifically delves into the responsibility for the detection of fraud. The ordinary examination is not primarily or specifically designed, and cannot be relied upon, to disclose defalcations and other similar irregularities. This pronouncement is the guide. However, it does not mean that the auditor can ignore the possibility of fraud or that he can ignore the discovery of fraud. Furthermore, his responsibility arises only when he fails to observe and comply with general auditing standards. The famous *BarChris* decision supports these guidelines in that the court stated, "Accountants should not be held to a standard higher than that recognized in their profession. His review did not come up to that standard."[3] Paragraph 5 also indicates that the auditor's responsibility differs as to clients and other third parties.

If an auditor were to attempt to seek out and uncover all defalcations and other irregularities, he would have to extend his work to a point where its cost would be prohibitive. An adequate system of internal control, coupled with fidelity bonds, provides protection much more cheaply. The client is responsible for the prevention of fraud through his system of controls. The auditor must be so explicit in preaudit meetings with the client as to have the client understand exactly what the audit is to entail. Sometimes, the auditor is engaged to conduct a special investigation for the specific purpose of uncovering fraud. This we shall examine and discuss later. In Statement on Auditing Procedure No. 30, it was felt that fraud should be looked at two ways:

1. The type wherein a deliberate attempt at misrepresentation by management is made (obviously directed at stockholders, credit grantors, and other interested outsiders).
2. Employee defalcation, which constitutes a diversion of the company's assets. Paragraph 5 in this statement makes it clear that the auditor must be aware that fraud can possibly exist and that, if it went undiscovered, it might be material enough to cause his opinion concerning fairness to be faulty.

The auditor has responsibilities with regard to himself and the client. These can be summarized:

1. The auditor must make sure he is financially independent of and has no business connection with the client at any time during the report period.
2. Before starting, the auditor should make an investigation of the company

[3] *Escott v. BarChris Construction Corporation* (D.C., S.D. N.Y. 1968, 283).

and its officers, especially if it is a new client. This will provide valuable background for interpreting conditions revealed during the audit.

3. He should make an intensive check of the company's system of internal checks and controls, so that his testing and sampling procedures will be unassailable.

4. All verifications should be made by himself or his representative.

5. If there are items which cannot be verified to his satisfaction, he must make a disclaimer in his certification.

6. If the financial statements depart from generally accepted accounting procedures, he must state so, and why.

7. If the auditor takes exception to any item in the financial report, he must make the exception clear and disclose the effect, if any, that the exception has on related financial statements.

8. He should give a comprehensive description of the scope of the audit.[4]

Paragraph 7 of Statement No. 30 states that auditing procedures should be extended when the auditor's suspicions are aroused. A business may suffer losses in many ways: management may make wrong decisions, costs may be higher than they should be, operating losses may be incurred, and employee defalcations may be hidden. The additional audit tests that might be required could make the cost prohibitive. The auditor must not be expected to verify and investigate such losses if they will not affect his opinion as to fairness. However, he should report his findings to management so that they can determine whether further procedures are desirable. If the auditor actually has discovered facts indicating fraud which are so *material* as to affect his opinion, he must notify management, and management must decide who is to do any further investigation.

Circumstances of fraud. There are many circumstances which could arouse the auditor's suspicions. Some of the more common circumstances are set forth below. Usually, where two or more items occur simultaneously, they are accompanied by poor or weak internal control.

1. Control accounts do not agree with subsidiary ledgers.
2. Missing checks, vouchers, invoices, contracts, minutes, etc., are not accounted for.
3. Confirmations disclose differences with account balances which are unexplainable.
4. Trial balance differences cannot be located.
5. Differences between physical count and perpetual inventory records cannot be explained.
6. Marked fluctuations occur in the gross profit ratio.

INTERNAL CONTROL

General. Internal control is extremely important, especially in relation to fraud deterrence. "Internal control" as defined by the AICPA in its Statements on Auditing Procedure No. 33 ". . . comprises the plan of organization and all of the coordinate methods and measures adopted within a business to safeguard its assets, check the accuracy and reliability of its accounting data, promote operational efficiency, and encourage adherence to prescribed managerial policies." One factor in considering the proper elements for a system of internal control is the size of the business. Larger firms would re-

[4] Regulation S-X, Rule 2-02, *P-H Securities Regulation,* 8602.2.

quire more elaborate controls, while a small firm may require quite different and less sophisticated controls. In any case, a good internal control system should include most of the following: statement analyses, common-size and and comparative statements, operating reports, ratio comparisons, prenumbered invoices, checks, and petty cash vouchers, and rotation of employees. Important general controls are segregation of duties and adequate internal auditing. Management must also take human factors into account when designing internal controls. They have a responsibility to maintain important moral values in business. Some specific guidelines in this area are:

1. Setting realistic performance goals
2. Maintaining good communications
3. Following through on employee performance
4. Maintaining uniform policies—dilemmas are often created by favoritism, double standards, or procedural violations.[5]

Responsibility for Internal Control. The origination, installation, and effective supervision of a proper system of internal control is the responsibility of management. Responsibility for the authorization and approval of purchases, payments, sales, returns, discounts, and allowances must be defined and adhered to. The auditor should suggest internal controls such as the following:

1. A plan of organization clearly establishing lines of authority and responsibility.
2. Clear division of duties, so that no one person handles transactions from beginning to end.
3. Careful personnel selection and training which will tend to eliminate unqualified applicants.
4. Easily understood records and forms.
5. Supervision and enforcement of the plan. It should be reviewed periodically for possible improvement.[6]

What about the role of the internal auditor with regard to controls? First of all, internal auditing is a review-and-appraisal activity. Its function is to assess present safeguards and make recommendations for strengthening or improving controls. Fraud prevention is not its primary responsibility. To repeat, the internal auditor's role is one of review and appraisal—management has the responsibility for action.

Public accountants also are not charged with the responsibility of detecting fraud. An independent public accountant does the ordinary audit solely to express an opinion on management's actions for a certain period of time. However, he is interested in internal controls. He relies on controls as a basis for expressing his opinion on the financial statements. If during his testing he finds that the controls are weak and/or that fraud exists, he has a responsibility to report his findings to management. But he is not responsible for the internal controls of the organization.

The conclusion is thus formed that management must be responsible for internal controls. They may delegate the actual installation of such controls to a specific group, but they are still accountable for the success or failure of the controls.[7]

[5] Norman Jaspan, "Management Responsibility for Preventing Fraud," *Preventing and Detecting Fraud in Business,* American Management Association Bulletin 43, 1963, p. 6.

[6] Surety Association of America, *Safeguards Against Employee Dishonesty in Business,* New York, Surety Association of America, 1954, p. 3.

[7] *Ibid.*, p. 2.

It is important to remember that a potential embezzler will take a risk only if he feels that he will not be apprehended. Internal controls act as a psychological deterrent to defalcation. They can make fraud difficult, though not impossible. A good system of internal controls offers the following benefits:

1. The data used in making business decisions will be more reliable.[8]
2. Fraud is much more likely to be detected in its early stages.
3. Fraud is discouraged because the potential embezzler is aware of greater odds against indefinitely concealing his acts.
4. The cost of dishonesty insurance is kept at a minimum through an overall low loss level.

Internal Control and Fraud. Reliance for the prevention and detection of fraud should be placed principally upon an adequate accounting system with appropriate internal control. Through his review and verification of the operation of internal controls the auditor aids in discouraging and preventing fraud. In performing the audit, no step is so insignificant that it can be performed in a perfunctory manner. The standard audit procedures should and do disclose irregularities due to fraud if proper reviews and tests are carried out.[9]

The auditor must constantly be alert to the proper function and operation of the internal control system. He must be on guard to see that the controls are not circumvented, or rendered useless by careless employees. An internal control system that is not properly supervised and enforced is tantamount to no control system at all.

MAJOR FRAUD CLASSIFICATIONS

A fraud committed by the company officers for the purpose of presenting false or misleading financial statements usually does not involve actual thefts of assets. In fact, very often the assets are deliberately understated to reduce the impact of income taxes. However, where a good financial presentation is desired, the officers may overstate assets and/or understate liabilities.

Sometimes, the two types are combined, that is, theft of assets may be combined with overstatement of the assets in an attempt to conceal the defalcation.

The last major type of employee defalcation is theft of assets charged off to the income account. The result is that while the net income for the period may be correctly stated, the various account classifications are improperly reflected on the income statement. Another effect is that comparative operating ratios are misstated and the net profit percentage would be unfavorable when compared with prior years.

Falsification of Financial Statements. There are other types of frauds which we have not yet discussed. One of these is the falsification of financial statements. When management wishes to present a good financial picture for credit purposes, it may deceive the auditor by means of inventory manipulations, false invoices and receiving and shipping documents, false entries, unrecorded loans, capitalization of expenses, and other deliberate misleading acts. Thus, we have to contend not only with frauds (defalcations) where assets are actually taken out of the corporation, but also with frauds

[8] J. J. Schornack and R. E. Burt, "Responsibilities of Internal and External Auditors in Internal Control," American Management Association Bulletin 43, 1963, p. 13.

[9] Charles A. Stewart, "The Nature and Prevention of Fraud," *The Journal of Accountancy,* February, 1959, p. 45.

simply involving misstatements with the intent to defraud the auditor and, consequently, the public at large. This second type of fraud is also of major concern to the auditor.

The courts have decided that it does not matter whether deceptions are intentional or not. In the *BarChris Construction* case, contract backlogs were stated as $6.9 million when they were actually only $2.4 million. Also, it was found that gross profit was overstated by 90 percent. In this suit, the auditors were not accused of trying to intentionally deceive anyone, but they were held liable for the incorrect facts because they had not made a *reasonable effort* to verify the information given to them by management.[10]

There are many areas that offer temptation to employees and that are susceptible to fraud; some of those areas are cash receipts, cash disbursements, inventory and supplies, payrolls, scrap and damaged merchandise, sales, promotion expenses, deliveries, and branch and chain store operations. In short, almost every area, including fictitious payables, is subject to fraudulent schemes.

No attempt will be made to cover every possible area of fraud and defalcation. Certain main areas, such as cash, accounts receivable, inventories, etc., will be covered, and some of the highlights will be pointed out.

Areas of Fraud. The various methods and devices by which fraud can be committed are almost limitless, being restricted only by the imagination of the employees, coupled with the opportunity to put their plans into operation. However, there are certain main areas which lend themselves to theft and defalcation more readily than others.

Historically the greatest known dollar loss through fraud occurs in cash disbursements, and is closely followed by frauds involving cash receipts. Of course, many other types of larcenies and embezzlements concerning inventories, marketable securities, and even fixed assets have occurred. However, cash is the easiest thing for a dishonest employee to steal and conceal. It is for this reason that the auditor must carefully investigate the system of internal control for cash and cash-related functions.

Cash receipts. A favorite source of employee theft is cash receipts. Internal control is strengthened if:

1. All receipts are deposited daily and intact.
2. All sales slips are prenumbered and accounted for.
3. Different employees handle cash receipts and cash disbursements.
4. Someone other than the cashier prepares the bank reconciliations.

When cash is being audited, the auditor must maintain control over all negotiable items to prevent substitution for cash shortages. Such items as marketable securities, collateral, and cash held by the client as custodian must be accounted for in addition to the cash.

Another practice of defalcators in this area deals with accounts receivable and is known as "lapping." This occurs when receipts from customer A are misappropriated and then replaced at a later date by receipts from customer B, and so on. This procedure continues until the money is replaced by the employee or until his methods are discovered. If the employee has access to the general ledger or can issue sales allowances or discounts he can conceal the shortage. Independent confirmation by the auditor aids in the detection of this pattern of defalcation.

[10] "The Law: Trouble for the Top," *Forbes*, Sept. 1, 1968, p. 25.

Cash disbursements. The auditor must use particular care in this area, as cash disbursements are frequently targets of defalcators. The following matters are appropriate to any system of disbursement control:

1. Checks must be supported by properly approved vouchers.
2. Individuals authorized to sign checks should be divorced from all routine cash operations and transactions.
3. Checks must not be made payable to cash or bearer.
4. Checks should be prenumbered.
5. Voided checks should be so marked and retained as evidence.
6. All checks should be accounted for.

In reconciling the cash account, endorsements on checks should be examined; those drawn to "Cash" or "Petty Cash" should be questioned; those for loans to employees should be examined for authority and authenticity.

Negotiable securities. Proper internal controls suggest that:

1. Securities should be registered in the company name.
2. Separate records should be maintained by someone other than the custodian.
3. The auditor must be alert to possible substitution made in order to temporarily hide a defalcation.
4. At least two authorized officers should be present when securities are removed from the safe or safe deposit box.

Fraud in this area often receives a great deal of publicity because of the large amounts of money which may be involved. In cases where fake stock certificates are issued, innocent buyers of the shares become the victims. This situation raises serious problems for the company in the area of public confidence.

Inventory. Another favorite target for theft is inventory. Sometimes the employee may consider his peculations of small items to be a "fringe benefit." Internal control suggests that perpetual inventory records should be maintained and compared with actual physical counts. Frequent comparison of these book records and the physical inventories should be made by someone other than the inventory custodian. The auditor should be alert to changes and alterations made on inventory records. Consigned merchandise and borrowed goods or goods stored or on loan must be excluded from the inventory.

Accounts payable. One common method of employee theft is to pay for nonexistent liabilities. Invoice forms can easily be printed, compiled, and presented for payment. The auditor should verify actual receipt of goods; invoices should be compared with purchase orders; prices of certain merchandise should be compared with similar products purchased from other suppliers; and total quantity purchased should be compared with the quantity actually put into production. In addition, accounts payable should be independently confirmed by the auditor and compared with the ledger account.

AUDIT PROCEDURES

After Discovering Fraud. If, during the course of an audit, the auditor's suspicions are aroused concerning the possibility of fraud, he should inform his supervisor. The supervisor or partner will then discuss the matter with company officials. If the peculation is small in amount, the auditor is not precluded from rendering an opinion, since his responsibility is primarily to express an opinion as to the fairness of the financial statements and not as to their exactness. However, if the amount is determined to be material when considered in relationship to the whole, or if a company official may be involved, the auditing firm partner will insist that the nature and extent of the fraud be determined before an unqualified opinion is given.

Disclosure of Fraud. Irregularities and frauds should be reported promptly to the proper official. With which official should the auditor discuss his suspicions? That depends upon the level at which the fraud is believed to have occurred. The report should be made to responsible officers at least one level above that of the suspected perpetrator of the fraud.

Management must then make a decision either to expand the scope of the audit or to conduct an investigation of their own. If the company chooses not to authorize further investigation, the auditor may withdraw from the engagement, in order to prevent future legal liability.

Usually, management will ask the auditor to extend his audit and to investigate the fraud. If this occurs, the auditor must apprise the company of the estimated increase in audit fees which will result from the proposed extended audit.

Notifying the Bonding Company. Today most company employees are bonded. Therefore, the next step is to notify the fidelity bonding company in accordance with the usual insurance company requirements.

Commencing the Investigation. Having received management's approval to investigate, and after obtaining legal counsel and guidance as to the suspect's rights, the auditor is now ready to commence his investigation. The company's records should be carefully reviewed to determine the *modus operandi* of the perpetrators. Documentation should be made of each suspected transaction.

Many defalcations are uncovered through fortuitous circumstances. These include absence of the defaulter through illness or vacation, a chance observation by another employee, a tip, or a rumor. The important point to remember is that in any suspicious situation nothing should be ignored by internal auditors, accountants, or management.

The steps you now take depend on the facts and circumstances. At the outset, *before* the perpetrators suspect that they may have been discovered, it may be wise to transfer them to other duties. This would stop the thefts and prevent those employees from destroying necessary evidential material.

This type of audit must proceed with all possible speed and yet must be extremely thorough. Speed is essential in order to prevent collaborators from altering or destroying records.

Outline of Investigation. Once it has been ascertained that a fraud is being perpetrated, the investigation must begin promptly. An investigation plan might include the following.

1. Question and get all information possible while those being questioned are still employees. As long as the employer-employee relationship exists, the employer has a legal right to demand explanations. Once the employee leaves or is fired, the company no longer enjoys any immunity and its risk increases.
2. Obtain the aid of the internal auditors, as they can be valuable in documenting particulars about work operations, etc. They can also help in determining the extent of the fraud and in pinpointing those responsible.

3. If necessary, management may enlist the aid of an outside detective agency or police authorities. Otherwise, the auditor could become involved in a damage claim suit if the investigation proves inconclusive.

Considerable work is involved and much time is needed as suspected or related transactions must be reviewed in detail and entries and postings examined for accuracy and amount. Deliberate errors in extensions, footings, additions, subtractions, etc., are to be carefully sought out. The auditor must be alert for forced totals, incorrect schedules, and erroneous trial balances. The auditor must determine what has been stolen: cash, merchandise, securities, or all three; how much the total shortage amounts to; over what period of time the theft was committed; and the person or persons involved.

Legal Pitfalls. The accountant must be ever mindful of the legal pitfalls that surround him in the course of an employee fraud investigation. An attorney's advice should be sought repeatedly during the course of the investigation. Among the legal dangers that the auditor must be alert to are libel, slander, false arrest or imprisonment, and perhaps even compounding a felony.

This chapter does not allow for extensive discussion of each of the above. Suffice it to say that extreme caution is to be used at all times. Don't accuse the employee, for this may be libel or slander, depending upon whether the accusation is in the form of a written or oral statement and upon its publication. False imprisonment requires only that you illegally restrain another's freedom of movement; and this does not have to be physical, nor does it mean that he is actually confined to a jail or house of detention. The agreement by the employer not to prosecute, coupled with the promise of the employee to repay the theft, may constitute compounding a felony.

In order to substantiate the charge of fraud, all facts, amounts, dates, times, places, and other key information must be specified in detail. All invoices, receipts, checks, and other original evidence must be carefully documented and preserved. All worksheets must be carefully prepared and arranged for future reference. A program for the investigation should be prepared. Consultation with the company's attorney is vital in view of recent court decisions regarding the rights of the accused. Remember that you are the auditor and not the lawyer. Should this extremely important point be overlooked, the auditor may infringe upon the civil or constitutional rights of the accused; he may subject himself to charges of false arrest, illegal search and seizure, defamation of character, libel, and slander. The auditor must remember that he is an auditor and not a policeman, detective, judge, or jury. His job is to audit and record pertinent data in order to substantiate the suspected fraud.

The Special Report. Once the auditor determines the time or period involved, the type of fraud, and the parties involved, he then will pursue his fraud audit program, gather all possible evidence, and prepare a special report. This report should include such specifics as: particulars as to method of the fraud; names of persons involved; list of all records and transactions involved in the fraud; specific dates and amounts of each defalcation; and the total loss sustained.

Effect of Defalcations on the Auditor's Opinion. Once the theft has been established, the amount substantiated, and the malfeasor discharged and possibly brought to trial, there still remains the question of the auditor's opinion regarding the financial statements.

The amount of loss (net of insurance recovery) should be shown separately. This would maintain consistency of reporting and might otherwise be misleading. The net earnings previously shown may not be affected greatly where the fraud was the result of amounts charged off to various expense accounts and no recovery can be made. Any invalid expense charges would be offset by receivables, such as restitution or insurance received. The expense accounts should of course be changed to the correct amount.

The auditor must reappraise the system of internal control with the intent of eliminating the weakness that permitted the fraud to occur and also with a view to eliminating other weak areas. Management will generally cooperate in maintaining a strong internal control system.

The auditor's knowledge and expertise, joined with an imaginative management program of internal control, has proved to be the most effective and economical means of fraud defense.

BIBLIOGRAPHY

AICPA: *Embezzlement—Its Prevention and Control,* New York, AICPA, 1968.

AICPA (Committee on Auditing Procedures): Statements on Auditing Procedure No. 30, 33, 38, and 41.

American Mutual Liability Insurance Company: *Crime Loss Control,* Boston, American Mutual Liability Insurance Company, 1950.

Cardwell, H.: *The Principles of Audit Surveillance,* Princeton, N.J., D. Van Nostrand Company, Inc., 1960.

Jaspan, Norman: "Management Responsibility for Preventing Fraud," *Preventing and Detecting Fraud in Business,* New York, American Management Association, 1964.

Meigs, W. B., and E. J. Larsen: *Principles of Auditing,* 4th ed., Homewood, Ill., Richard D. Irwin, Inc., 1969.

Prentice-Hall Editorial Staff: *How to Guard against the New Dangers that Face Corporate Officers, Directors, Accountants, Lawyers, and Others under BarChris and Related Cases,* Englewood Cliffs, N.J., Prentice-Hall, Inc., 1969.

Queenan, John: *Selected Papers 1968,* ed. Haskins and Sells, New York, Haskins & Sells, 1969.

Stewart, C. A.: "Frauds," *The Price Waterhouse Review,* September, 1958.

Davis, E. J.: "Accountant's Liability Today," *The New York Certified Public Accountant,* November, 1967.

Hill, T. W.: "The Public Accountant's Legal Liability," *The New York Certified Public Accountant,* January, 1968.

"The Law: Trouble for the Top," *Forbes,* Sept. 1, 1968.

Igleski, Thomas R.: "Legal Considerations when Employee Fraud is Evident," *The Independent Auditor,* January/February, 1969.

Weyrich, Harry R.: "Exposure to Professional Liability," *The New York Certified Public Accountant,* July, 1970.

Isbell, David B.: "The Continental Vending Case: Lessons for the Profession," *The Journal of Accountancy,* August, 1970.

Chapter **18**

Special Investigations

L. H. TOLER

Department Head, Accounting Department,
Mississippi State University

W. C. FLEWELLEN, JR.

Dean, College of Business Administration, University of Georgia

GENERAL

The auditor is frequently called upon to perform special services of an auditing nature which do not conform to the usual "generally accepted auditing procedures." These services are generally referred to as *special investigations*. In the public accounting field many of these special investigations would be undertaken by the management services department of the firm.

Literature on these fringe services is extremely limited, particularly with reference to any general auditing programs on procedures to be employed in conducting these special investigations. This chapter covers some of the factors that are pertinent to special investigations in general and illustrates the approach to two specific types of special investigations. It should be noted that many elements of any special investigation will be conducted in accordance with the procedures discussed in earlier chapters of this book in relation to auditing specific segments of a firm.

Definition. A special investigation may be defined as any examination which requires extraordinary or extended audit procedures; or one which is limited in scope, or which is limited in the procedures which the auditor may utilize. Any audit which requires an "exception" or a "subject to" clause in the opinion may also be categorized as a special investigation.

General Auditing Criteria. The precise nature and procedures of a special investigation will depend on the purpose of the investigation and the terms of the engagement. The auditor will normally discuss in broad terms with the client the course he intends to adopt, but he must maintain control of the specific procedures undertaken to ensure his professional independence. This independence, of course, is essential whether the auditor is an internal auditor, a governmental auditor, or a public accountant.

Audit Program. It is not usually possible to provide a generalized audit program for special investigations. In most instances, the auditor will be unable to write a detailed program even for the specific engagement at hand. The program will depend to a great extent on the availability of the required information, and this can normally be determined only as the audit proceeds.

It is essential that the auditor be flexible in carrying out the broad plan of the audit and that he be prepared to amend his plan if necessary. Great attention should be paid to the preparation of detailed working papers as the auditor proceeds so that he can frequently review the logic of his approach. These working papers will also provide the justification for the judgments and conclusions that he must make at the end of the audit.

Auditing Standards. While it is not possible to provide a detailed program for special investigations, there are certain criteria that the auditor should bear in mind. All of the normal criteria for an audit engagement must be followed. That is, the auditor must be proficient and independent; he must exercise due professional care; and he must gather sufficient evidential matter to support his opinion. The CPA auditor is required to follow the general standards and the standards of fieldwork on engagements involving special reports "to the extent appropriate in view of the character of the engagement."[1]

Critical Analysis. The special investigation usually entails more skill and responsibility than the opinion audit. The auditor must be very critical and analytical, and in certain types of cases he must approach the engagement with a great deal of caution. Often, it is not sufficient to confirm what has taken place, and the auditor may need to examine whether or not an alternate

[1] Statements on Auditing Procedure No. 33, *Auditing Standards and Procedures*, AICPA (Committee on Auditing Procedure), New York, 1963, p. 88.

line of action would have been more appropriate. For example, in an examination of purchasing procedures, the auditor may determine the savings that would have been achieved if a different order size had been utilized or if a different supplier had been used. In brief, the special investigator generally must be more knowledgeable about business and economic affairs, be more skillful in analyzing data and reaching conclusions, and have a broader-based approach than the auditor on a routine audit.

APPROACH TO THE WORK

In the usual attest audit, the auditor is ordinarily examining data and reviewing financial statements and records which have been developed by the client. That is generally not the case with most special investigations. In the usual case the auditor will have to develop new data or provide support for a particular viewpoint. For example, he may be employed by a prospective buyer or a prospective seller or even may be acting for both sides. In many cases he will be acting in an advocate capacity; that is, he will be primarily interested in developing data to support the interests of the buyer, or the seller, as the case may be. He must, of course, be independent and perform professional services in a professional manner, but his approach will be considerably different for such a special investigation from the approach for the attest audit.

To illustrate the significant points in one type of special investigation, we might consider the approach of the auditor when he is (1) acting for the buyer, (2) acting for the seller, and (3) acting for both sides. For our purposes we will use as an example a purchase investigation, since that type may easily have one or more of the above aspects. In some cases there will be more than one auditor involved, that is, the prospective buyer may have his auditor and the prospective seller may have his auditor. This is analogous to the situation where both sides have legal representatives.

Purchase investigations undertaken in connection with the purchase or sale of a business usually have one or more of the following objectives.

Basis of Exchange. To determine the most advantageous basis of exchange for either the buyer or the seller. Which particular items or types of assets should be exchanged? For example, should the exchange include one or more of the following:

a. Capital stock
b. All assets
c. Net assets
d. Inventory
e. Fixed assets

Computation of Price. In some cases the purchase price may be set within broad limits and the exact amount may await the auditor's valuation. In other cases the auditor's computation of price or value may be the starting point for negotiations. Particular items may or may not be included in the final transfer depending on the negotiations. In some cases the valuation of particular items, such as plant assets, may be subject to negotiation or may be based on a subsequent valuation by a professional appraiser.

Form of Transfer. The nature of the investigation of course depends on the services to be performed. In some cases the form in which the transfer is to be made has already been determined. For example, the acquiring company may have already obtained legal and tax advice and have determined that it wants to purchase only certain assets, not the whole business. Therefore the seller may still have the corporate structure and be responsible for the settlement of any liabilities. In other cases the form of transfer will be the quiet acquisition of the capital stock, generally enough to assure control. In such a case the auditor may have only the responsibility of installing the financial records for the new unit. In some cases, as in a pooling of interests, the corporate status may remain for a period. In other cases the corporate status is eliminated and the new unit becomes a division of the parent corporation. Following is a discussion of the auditor's activities depending on whether he is acting for the buyer, acting for the seller, or acting for both sides.

Interest Represented. **Acting for the buyer.** Naturally a prospective buyer wants to know as much as possible about the company he is proposing to buy. In such a case the auditor is in a position to provide much valuable information. Such information may relate not only to financial and accounting matters but to other aspects of the business as well. Such an assignment provides a business-oriented auditor an excellent opportunity to study what has occurred and to suggest approaches the buyer may not have considered. For example, information may be available showing that a particular course of action which seemed favorable was tried some time ago without success. Perhaps conditions have changed and the course of action or an adaptation of it may now have a good chance of success. In some cases certain leases or contracts may not be in the best interests of the new owners. Usually the auditor in his review will evaluate the benefits to be obtained or not obtained. Perhaps the lease or contract may be renegotiated or canceled where possible.

Acting for the seller. The accountant's role on behalf of the company being acquired is to advise management of all of the factors that can affect the interests of the company. He may also be the channel through which much of the information required by the acquiring company may be obtained. He will seek to assure that the favorable aspects of the company are made clear to the prospective acquirer during negotiations. Very often there are assets or additional values not included in the financial statements. Documentation might be obtained of comparable assets or an appraisal may be used to show additional value. Also, new developments or processes might be evaluated by the auditor and found to be useful to the seller in negotiations.

Acting for both sides. When acting as an independent expert advising both sides to the purchase, the auditor's investigation must be thorough enough to ensure that all relevant aspects of the affairs of the company are included in his report. In the case of a merger, he may need to investigate both companies to find out if they are compatible. That is, would the businesses fit in with each other, with regard to type of trade markets, manufacturing facilities, location, compatibility of outlook of top managements, etc.? Other questions of particular interest would be: Are there any unique factors about either company that would particularly affect the price? and, What facts are necessary to arrive at a fair price? In such a case the investigation must be broad enough and deep enough to encompass many aspects of the business besides the financial and accounting aspects. In a specific case additional areas may need investigation and some of the areas previously scheduled for investigation may be changed, depending on the findings.

TYPES OF SPECIAL INVESTIGATIONS

As has been indicated earlier, there is a very wide range of services that may be classified as special investigations. Rather than give a long list of specific investigations it will be better to group them into broad classes and describe the special characteristics common to each principal group. On this basis the following classifications are presented and discussed:

Compliance reviews
Special audits
Surveys
Evaluations
Analyses
Attest audits
Special reports

Compliance Reviews. One of the largest groups of special investigation jobs has to do with compliance in some form. While there are a large number of kinds of compliance investigations, they may be grouped into two broad classes: (1) those involved with interpretation of terms and (2) those involved with determining the reliability of data.

Interpretation of terms. This type of special investigation can involve some very complex and very important matters. For example, the auditor may be called on by bondholders to determine that the terms of the indenture are being strictly observed. There may be restrictions on the payment of dividends, the amount of officers' salaries, or the maintenance of working capital. Sometimes very complex factors are involved and require an extremely careful study of the terms of the indenture and the computation of the amounts subject to restriction. Very often interpretations may differ widely on the amount subject to restriction. Other interpretations concern the terms of a contract or the terminology used in a contract or agreement. For example, the contract may refer to cost without identification as to average cost, FIFO, or LIFO. There may be need to determine the interpretation of financial terms in a lease, or of certain aspects of a partnership agreement.

Reliability of data. This type concerns not the interpretation but the reliability of the data under the contract. Are the parties complying with the terms or payments? Often this includes the investigation of royalty payments. For example, the holder of the patent may question whether all required payments on the production of a patented machine are being received. The auditor will not only review the financial data submitted by the company using the machine but will determine if all payments due are reflected in the reports. For example, the production of the machine under license may be determined by various shipments made and the inventory of the output on hand at any time. Another type of investigation might be that of data in disputed claims of various kinds. In other cases a minority stockholder may want to be sure that his proper interest is recognized.

Special Audits. Generally this work involves a special or limited investigation of a particular account or type of transaction. Following are the principal kinds of items which make up this category.

Cash, payroll, inventory, etc. In this case irregularities may be suspected or certain data may be desired relating to cash, payroll, inventory, or other accounts or transactions. Usually an intensive examination is made for a three-month or six-month period rather than an annual period. In most cases such investigations pertain to fraud in the records or outright theft of property.

Fire losses. Often the auditor is called on to determine the amount of a fire loss sustained. This usually includes building up or carrying forward the book figure for inventory to the date of the fire and computing the loss sustained. Of course, the fire loss may include assets other than inventory.

Casualty losses. Many other types of special audits relate to various kinds of casualty losses. For example, a breakdown of a large machine may cause substantial damage to nearby property. A large insurance claim often is involved, including the computation of profits lost while the machine is down or the handling of the cost of building a new foundation for the machine or of moving out the factory wall to accommodate the new machine. Sometimes very large amounts are involved. In some cases the claim date is initially developed by a company accountant without prior experience in audit or claims work. Often the result is a serious understatement of the amount and the failure to include many perfectly valid items in the claimed amount.

Surveys. This type of investigation is becoming more important and makes up a significant part of the work of the management services department in some accounting firms. This could include a wide range of jobs, from a personnel survey to a feasibility study for the installation of a computer. Such a study is usually undertaken by a high-level auditor with experience and knowledge in the particular field. It is ordinarily extensive rather than intensive and covers a wide range of matters. Often a questionnaire type of approach or program is most suitable.

General accounting system. A large number of survey jobs have to do with the review of the accounting system. Often the work is a follow-up of the audit where certain deficiencies were noted. It may also be related to the development of new budget controls. For example, the accounting system may need to be realigned to conform with the responsibility accounting concepts of the budget. Where individuals are responsible for particular functions, the accounting system should provide accounting data to help control such functions. Generally the accounts have to be rearranged to provide for this type of responsibility accounting.

Cost system. Somewhat akin to the general accounting system survey is the survey of the cost system. Often, but not always, this is an outgrowth of the audit work. In many cases the audit of inventory pricing discloses that the cost system is not providing reliable data for inventory pricing. Perhaps the cost system was established some years before and is not adequate for present conditions. Perhaps the overhead distribution is being made on the basis of direct labor whereas new machines may have made a distribution of overhead on a machine-hour basis more equitable. Again, a standard cost system rather than an actual cost system may be more economical and more accurate. These various factors can be readily determined on the basis of audit data available plus additional survey work performed.

Personnel. There are a great number of surveys being performed in connection with personnel. Some surveys measure or categorize personnel attitudes or characteristics. Other surveys may measure employee performance. This might include surveys made in connection with installing an incentive or bonus plan or with measuring departmental performance. Another type of measurement may be the determination or evaluation of divisional performance in a large company. Certain criteria may be developed for computing the return on invested capital in the various divisions of the business.

Evaluations. Usually in this type of investigation the emphasis is on the measurement or appraisal as of a particular time rather than on establishing criteria for continued measurement.

Purchase or sale of a business. As described earlier in this chapter, the auditor may be asked to evaluate the assets or earning power of a business by a person interested in buying the business. In another case the auditor may be working for the one interested in selling the business. In any case the principal purpose is evaluation rather than an audit of financial data. In many cases the financial statements available will not provide the current or replacement cost of fixed assets or of various other asset items.

Personnel evaluation. In many cases the special investigation or management service will entail a personnel evaluation, or a determination of the ability of the employee to perform the services for which he is responsible. Usually this is not a repetitive job and often it is needed to determine a specific course of action as opposed to a periodic evaluation of employees made by a company personnel department.

Equipment efficiency. In many cases the investigation may relate to the determination of the efficiency of a machine or piece of equipment. The auditor may be called to evaluate the performance of a machine in comparison with its projected performance. This is a rather common type of evaluation for the internal auditor. On the basis of engineering and other estimates of performance, management has approved the purchase of a costly machine. However, the actual performance of the machine may fall far below expectations. The auditor will review actual results and try to evaluate what is the cause of the disparity between expected and actual performance. For example, does the machine operate at the expected speed? Did the saving in labor cost actually come about?

Analyses. Very often the auditor, particularly the public accountant, is called in to develop information in connection with public organizations such as public utilities. In a growing number of cases the government auditor, particularly in the GAO, has been called on by Congress to develop objective data in connection with various government functions.

Rate-making factors in public utilities. In a number of cases an auditor may be called in by an interested agency or governmental unit to analyze the rate-making factors in a public utility such as a gas or electric company. This ordinarily requires a great deal of analysis and development of different factors to show earnings—either excess or substandard earnings based on various bases.

Cost for decision making. In some cases the auditor may be asked to develop analyses as a basis for a management decision. This may relate to almost any kind of data. It may relate to the detailed analysis required to determine whether a new plant should be built in a particular location or whether a new product should be launched.

Attest Audits. Very often the auditor, particularly the public accountant, will be called on to act as a judge or to objectively determine the outcome of an event.

In some cases auditors have been called on to attest the outcome or to verify the ballots cast in a contest or an election. This has been the case in a number of radio or television programs in recent years.

In some cases auditors have been called on to attest the contributions to charitable organizations such as the Red Cross, etc.

Special Reports. With the increase in special reports being required by governmental agencies and others in recent years, the auditor is often called on to prepare these reports. Usually the accounting staff in a company is continuously employed in developing its own financial reports and often there is not enough qualified personnel available to do substantial special reports.

Very often information has to be prepared, usually in great detail and on special forms supplied by the requesting unit. Generally this entails reading voluminous instructions and interpreting what is required. These would include SEC reports, census reports, and other kinds of required financial data.

Reports to the SEC. For companies listed on a stock exchange various kinds of reports must be filed. For example, an annual report must be submitted to the SEC, a registration statement submitted when additional shares are issued, a report on officer transactions submitted, etc. These reports have to be prepared in accordance with detailed instructions and regulations. In many companies the internal auditor or the public accountant is called on to perform this task.

Reports to other regulatory agencies. For certain kinds of industries, such as public utilities, periodic reports on prescribed forms are required. In other cases, such as for the Federal Trade Commission, certain specific requests would be made for information pertaining to certain matters during a particular period. Very often the auditor will be called in to prepare the data and to present the information and answer questions concerning the development of the data.

ASSEMBLING DATA

In most types of special investigations it is necessary to assemble a great deal of information pertaining to the company and its operations. This will not apply in all cases, but such data are ordinarily needed during the course of the work or in the report. Following is an illustration of the information to be assembled in the usual purchase investigation. The illustration can also serve as a general program for such an investigation. The material may be expanded or cut back to serve the purposes of various other kinds of investigations where applicable.

- I. Introduction
  - *A.* Instructions and scope of work to be carried out
  - *B.* Sources of information to be used; e.g., officers, board of directors, records of the company, etc.
  - *C.* Statement of the proposed transaction
- II. Company Background
  - *A.* General description of the business
    - 1. Main products
    - 2. Principal markets and customers
    - 3. Marketing methods
  - *B.* History of business
    - 1. Formation of business
      - *a.* Date
      - *b.* By whom
      - *c.* Predecessor companies
    - 2. Subsidiaries
      - *a.* Dates
      - *b.* Former association, if any
  - *C.* Number and location of plants
  - *D.* Number and location of sales offices
  - *E.* List of officers and directors
  - *F.* Stock ownership
  - *G.* Credit reports
  - *H.* Analysis of business territory: population trends, growth potential, condition of industry, competition
  - *I.* Sources of supply
    - 1. Raw materials or goods bought for resale
    - 2. Labor
  - *J.* Description of company's organizational structure
    - 1. Organization chart
      - *a.* Board of directors
        - (1) Qualifications, experience, potential
      - *b.* Top management
        - (1) Qualifications, experience, potential
        - (2) Salary brackets

2. Subsidiaries' organization
   a. Description
   b. Personnel
   c. Products
   d. Location
3. Departmental organization

III. Financial Position

A. Most recent financial statements
B. Comparative summary statements for a period of years (5 to 10 years)
   1. Audited statements
   2. Common dollar analyses
   3. Ratio analyses
   4. Funds statements
C. Projected operating and financial statements
D. Summary of tax situation
   1. State and local taxation
   2. Current tax status
   3. Tax status of proposed transaction

IV. Detailed Analysis

The outline below indicates some of the major financial factors normally discussed in the accountant's report. The outline is general and should not be considered all-inclusive.

A. Assets
   1. Cash
      a. List bank accounts and purpose of each.
      b. Review the internal control and accounting procedures of the company.
      c. Review generally the cash requirements and ascertain whether or not the cash balances are adequate or in excess of normal requirements.
   2. Receivables
      a. Summarize by type.
      b. Review aged trial balances.
      c. Review procedures for balancing and tie-ins to general ledger control account.
      d. If installment receivables are present, review method of computing income deferred for income tax purposes.
      e. Indicate most significant customers and comment on collectibility.
      f. Indicate credit terms, discount policies, and credit insurance coverage.
      g. Analyze experience with returns and allowances.
      h. Indicate receivables of officers and other affiliated interests.
      i. List notes receivable and comment on adequacy of collateral.
      j. Indicate adequacy of reserves for bad debts, discounts, returns, freight allowances, etc.
      k. Indicate if receivables are pledged or assigned as collateral on loans of the company.
   3. Inventories
      a. Summarize inventories by type.
      b. Indicate date of last physical inventory and if quantities were previously adjusted to the physical count.
      c. Indicate method of determining inventory value and cost of sales.
      d. Note types of inventory records and controls.
      e. Note status of purchase commitments.
      f. Note existing sales commitments and adequacy of inventory to meet the commitments at normal profit margins.
      g. Note company policy relating to valuation of obsolete items.
      h. Note approximate value of supply items which may be expensed when purchased.

   i. Note company's inventory turnover as compared with the industry average.
   j. Determine market value of inventories.

4. Investments
   a. Summary of advances and investments (if significant, a special section of the report probably should be prepared).
   b. Indicate type of business and principal products of the concerns in which investment is held.
   c. Compare investment at cost with underlying book value and market values.
   d. Determine existence of investments.
   e. Determine the percentage of ownership interest (if significant) that the company holds in the corporations in which it has investments.
5. Fixed assets
   a. Summarize by type of asset.
   b. Indicate basis of valuation, accumulated depreciation, date acquired, purpose, location, etc.
   c. Compare valuation, recent appraisals, insurance values.
   d. Indicate depreciation methods and policies used.
   e. Indicate obsolete or scrapped equipment not retired from accounts, and any fully depreciated equipment which has been written off but may have residual value when considered in light of a potential merger or purchase.
   f. Comment on maintenance of property records and on policy regarding physical inventory of property items.
   g. Note any long-term leases, indicating expiration date, renewal options, payment provisions, assignment privileges, etc.
   h. Note any commitments for capital expenditures, sales of property, or additional leases.
   i. Comment on idle facilities (if any).
   j. Comment on overall condition and adequacy of the property.
   k. Tie-in property, reserves, and depreciation with income and property tax returns.
6. Prepaid and other assets
   a. Summarize prepaid items and indicate if bona fide prepayments.
   b. Indicate methods of recording and expensing items.
   c. Indicate amounts and types of insurance coverage and comment on adequacy of coverage.
   d. Note if all prepaid and deferred items are recorded.

B. Liabilities

1. Accounts and notes payable, and accrued liabilities
   a. Summarize major balances.
   b. Confirm amounts with creditors.
   c. Pinpoint unusual items and overaccruals or underaccruals.
   d. Determine proper accrual of interest on notes, executive bonuses, vacation pay, royalties, etc.
   e. Determine if there are any unrecorded liabilities such as for warranties, guarantees, non-funded pension plans, renegotiation liabilities, etc.
   f. Note any liabilities in default and related penalties.
   g. Note relation of current liabilities to current assets and adequacy of working capital.
   h. Note any restrictions or liens on liabilities because of loan agreements or other causes.
   i. Review status of tax liabilities, deferred taxes, and adequacy of reserves for open years.
   j. Note any loss carried forward.
   k. Note revenue agent's reviews:

(1) Latest year reviewed;
(2) Nature of agent's adjustments and deficiencies (if any).

2. Long-term debt and other liabilities
   a. Summarize major categories.
   b. Note specific provisions of:
      (1) Bond indentures;
      (2) Mortgage agreements;
      (3) Pension plans;
      (4) Profit-sharing agreements.
   c. Comment on compliance with restrictions noted.
   d. Note and comment on any commitments on forward contracts and contingent liabilities.
   e. Confirm accounts with holders.
   f. Obtain statements from directors and attorneys with regard to pending lawsuits, liabilities, and contingent liabilities.
   g. Note liabilities of company on any long-term leases, the value of equipment leased, any provisions for purchases of the equipment upon expiration of the lease, and any potential tax liability which may accrue from the disallowance of rents under the lease.

C. Capital
1. Summarize ownership of stock shares issued and outstanding.
2. Note classes of stock and number of shares outstanding.
3. Note any special restrictions relating to any class of stock or repurchase agreements.
4. Indicate provisions for unpaid cumulative dividends or stock options.
5. Analyze paid-in surplus accounts and describe charges and credits to the account.
6. Analyze Retained Earnings for extraordinary charges or credits.
7. Comment on dividend policies.
8. Note and comment on any appropriations of retained earnings.

D. Review of operations
1. Prepare summary of earnings for a period of years (5 to 10) and obtain explanation of major variations.
2. Compute profit ratios by product, locations, or other breakdowns and compare with industry averages.
3. Review major expense categories and determine if charges are reasonable.
4. Compute cash flow for a period of years (5 to 10).
5. Review financial statements for extraordinary charges and credits and determine effect on reported income.

LIMITED INVESTIGATIONS

General. Many special investigations are of the type in which the auditor is engaged for a limited, or specific business segment, audit. In such cases, the auditor will generally confine his activities to the specific procedures requested or to such procedures as are necessary for him to reach a conclusion. Two such engagements are discussed briefly.

Observation of Physical Inventory. An auditor was engaged to observe the physical inventory in order to establish the quantities on hand. The engagement did not call for comparing the physical count with recorded book quantities, nor for tracing test counts beyond the company's count sheets.

The auditor followed the usual procedures in observing a physical inventory. He established control over tags, count sheets, and the organization for the inventory. During the inventory, the count procedures were observed and test counts were made and recorded. Where the tests showed differences, they were reviewed and the tally sheets were adjusted to the correct amount.

At the conclusion of the inventory, the counts were reviewed with company personnel, but no effort was made to determine if adjustments were made to the company books. A letter was drafted to the client enumerating the procedures employed and noting the significant differences found during test counts. The conclusion contained in the letter was that except for the differences noted in the letter, there were no inaccuracies in counting or accumulating inventory quantities on hand.

Repricing Inventory. Computing amounts of understatement of prior years' inventories. An auditor was engaged to reprice the inventory for the past three years. The client assured the auditor that the inventories had all been counted and that inventory count sheets and tags were available for inspection. It was determined that the firm had no costing system for valuing in-process and finished goods and that the inventories had been priced at an amount derived from selling prices.

Because of the lack of any method of valuing in-process and finished goods inventories and of the inability to segregate the physical count sheets relating to the specific inventories taken in the past, the following scope was adopted:

1. An estimated cost system was set up for use in valuing the in-process and finished goods inventories. Material, direct labor, and overhead costs were determined based on actual production figures for the most recent year.
2. Using actual quantities on hand currently, the inventories were computed by reconciling back, using the quantities sold, the amount of raw materials consumed based on quantities sold (using an overall average), and the total raw material purchased.

During the inventory work, it was discovered that certain sales in December had been reported as sales in January. The effect of the inventory and sales adjustments on reported income for the relevant years was computed. The findings were discussed with the client and it was decided that the audit would be extended to include an examination of the financial statements at the end of the current year in order to ascertain that the inventories and other balance sheet accounts were properly stated at that time.

These examples of special investigations indicate the scope of audits the auditor may have to perform. As discussed, each special investigation must be approached with an open mind as to the audit program or procedures that must be employed. In most cases, the audit program must be written as the investigation proceeds.

REPORTING RESULTS

Upon the completion of a special investigation, the auditor must make a report of his findings to the client. This report may take many forms, depending on the purpose of the investigation, the type of auditor involved, and the nature of the findings. The auditor should take into consideration some of the following report criteria.

Standards of Reporting. In reporting the results of special investigations, the CPA auditor is bound by generally accepted reporting standards applicable to the usual short-form or long-form report. He is required to include an expression of opinion, or an assertion to the effect that an opinion cannot be expressed and the reasons therefor. In addition, the CPA must state the scope of his examination and the degree of responsibility he is assuming.[2] In short, the AICPA requires the CPA to state clearly what he does do and what he does not do in a special investigation. Ethical standards of reporting included in the Code of Professional Ethics also apply to special reports.

Auditors who are not bound by the reporting standards required of the CPA, such as internal auditors or governmental auditors, should clearly and explicitly delineate the nature of the special investigation, the stated objectives of the investigation, any specific instructions received, and any limitations imposed. The report should include a description of the scope of the investigation, including the major areas examined and any unusual investigative or audit procedures employed. For example, in a special investigation to determine that the total cost of work, as determined by the company, is properly stated pursuant to the provisions of an agreement, the following description of the examination might be included in a letter report:

> Our examination included direct confirmation of amounts due to contractor and engineers, review of vouchers for the purchase of pipe and reconciliation of quantities purchased to quantities installed, the review of right-of-way payments included and excluded from the fee base, and a review of the accounting records and discussion with Company personnel to determine whether all costs incurred have been accounted for in the fee base. Our review does not preclude the possibility of additional minor charges or credits subsequent to our examination.

The findings of the investigation should be summarized and, depending on the type of investigation, supported with schedules and adequate evidential matter. Any limitations on the findings, such as inadequate evidence, areas not included in the investigation, or other items that would indicate an incomplete study of the situation, should be detailed in the report. The auditor should be fully cognizant that most special investigations are undertaken to provide specific information for some special purpose or decision. Any material information bearing on that purpose or decision should be included in the report.

The auditor may or may not be expected to express an opinion about the results of his investigation. If an opinion is required, the auditor should make certain that the opinion expressed is supported by evidential information noted completely and concisely in his working papers and in his findings, as noted in his report.

Examples of Opinions. The following are examples of opinions (or conclusions) that might be expressed in special investigations that fall outside the normal audit; they may be in the form of a letter or a longer type of report. These opinions are for illustrative purposes and should not be taken as recommended formats.

1. Commenting on review of financial forecast:

   > Our review of these assumptions and estimates indicated no material items of cash income or expense that had been excluded from them and we have no reason to question their reasonableness. However, since they are subject to audit verification, we cannot express an opinion as to how closely actual operations may approximate these estimates. This forecast can be considered a fair representation of the prospective operations and cash flow of the Company during the year ended December 31, 19__, only in the event these assumptions and estimates can be realized.

[2] *Ibid.*

2. Commenting on the cost accounting principles and methods used in a study by a company on the cost of distribution of a product:

   On the basis of the foregoing review, in our opinion the cost accounting methods set forth in this report, and the methods of cost determination and allocation as set forth under that heading for each of the functions, conform to sound cost accounting principles and should result in equitable allocation of the costs of distribution as between products sold and, in the case of (this product's) sales, as between customer groups classified according to purchase volume brackets. Further, in our opinion, the study was sufficiently comprehensive in point of time and extent of sales areas covered in the list as to constitute an acceptable sampling of costs.

3. Opinion in which certain assets were omitted from consideration at request of client and not included in the accompanying statement (in connection with a proposed purchase):

   In our opinion, the accompanying statement of certain assets and liabilities presents fairly (excluding cash and receivable balances as explained in the preceding paragraph) the assets and liabilities of (X Company) as of June 15, 19__, in conformity with generally accepted accounting principles.

BIBLIOGRAPHY

Audits of Voluntary Health and Welfare Organizations, New York, AICPA, 1967.
Statements on Auditing Procedure No. 33, *Auditing Standards and Procedures,* AICPA, New York, 1963, chap. 13, Special Reports, pp. 87–91.

Cadmus, Bradford, and Arthur J. E. Child: *Internal Control Against Fraud and Waste,* Englewood Cliffs, N. J., Prentice-Hall, Inc. 1962.
Glendening, Frank S.: "Special Investigations," in *CPA Handbook,* ed. Robert C. Kane, Jr., New York, AICPA, 1953.
Grinaker, Robert, and Ben B. Barr: *Auditing: The Examination of Financial Statements,* Homewood, Ill., Richard D. Irwin, Inc., 1965.
Ingalls, Edward F.: *Practical Accounting and Auditing Procedures,* New York, AICPA, 1966.
Johnson, James T., and Herman J. Brasseaux: *Readings in Auditing,* 2d ed., Cincinnati, South-Western Publishing Company, 1965.

Weinstein, Edward A.: "Examining a Company in Bankruptcy," *Credit and Financial Management,* April, 1964.
Weinstein, Edward A.: "Let the Buyer Beware," *The Journal of Accountancy,* June, 1965.
Rachel, Nolan N.: "Auditing Fund-Raising Campaigns," *Management Accounting,* vol. 47, October, 1965.
Williams, Doyle Z.: "Reporting Standards for Cash Basis Statements of Non-profit Organizations," *The New York Certified Public Accountant,* December, 1965.
Ballard, J. R.: "Approaches to Operational Auditing," *The Internal Auditor,* Summer, 1966.
Caron, C. W.: "Procurement Audit," *The Internal Auditor,* Summer, 1967.
Burton, John C.: "Management Auditing," *The Journal of Accountancy,* May, 1968.
Steinwurtzel, Samuel L.: "Nonprofit Organizations under the 1969 Tax Reform Act," *The New York Certified Public Accountant,* September, 1970.

Chapter 19

Auditing International Operations

IRVING L. FANTL

Associate Professor of Accounting, Seton Hall University

INTRODUCTION

The growing importance of international trade and the emergence of multinational business organizations have compelled accountants to become familiar with the special problems connected with international operations. As smaller companies follow the financial leaders into the international arena, their auditors will be obliged to become familiar with intricacies not met by purely domestic firms. Until the present, international trade consisted largely of importing or exporting, dealing with unaffiliated customers and suppliers. Today the trend is toward branch offices and subsidiary companies at points around the world where the parent company desires representation.

Structure for Foreign Operations. The structure of this representation can take a number of forms, each of which is appropriate to a specific set of circumstances. The conditions which dictate the most advantageous form for the foreign operation fall into two categories: (1) the purpose and aims of the operation and (2) the environment and country in which the operation is located.

If the primary goal of a foreign operation is to sell in a foreign market products which are made at home, no formal organization in the market is required. An agency to represent the seller is all that would be needed. The same arrangement would be appropriate for the purchase of foreign products for import. Under these circumstances, the primary problem would be fluctuations of foreign currencies in relation to the dollar. The determination of whether the transactions would be conducted in dollars or in foreign monies is important. If dollars are the specified currency, then the foreign businessman would lose or benefit from exchange fluctuations. If transactions are conducted in the foreign currency, then the American assumes the risks of exchange variation.

Branch Office. Should activity expand so that greater control becomes desirable, the next stage is to establish a branch office abroad. This step creates a host of complex problems which must be carefully evaluated and understood if the venture is to succeed. These same problems confront any international business operation, and it is important that the auditor understand them in order to serve his client adequately and in order for the accountant to conduct his own foreign operations effectively. These problems fall into four categories, each of which will be examined further. They are:

1. Customs, traditions, temperament, and economic structure of the country
2. Legal regulation of the business community, including limitations on foreign capital and control of the flow of money
3. U.S. taxes and taxes levied by foreign countries which affect U.S. foreign operations
4. Accounting practices, especially the comparability with American practices, the reliability of audit procedures and certification standards, and the influences which custom, law, and taxation bear on accounting methods

The branch office located in a foreign country involves all the above problems to a degree. If the home office accountants are responsible for the audit of the branch, they must first determine that bookkeeping procedures follow those established for domestic branches and that the office is staffed with personnel capable of following such procedures. It might be necessary to train personnel before the system can function efficiently. Such education, because it must overcome established attitudes, is a serious consideration in such a branch operation. If the foreign branch business is conducted in terms of local currency, which will generally be the case, foreign exchange fluctuations assume a much larger role than when an agency is being dealt with. Such fluctuations will cause profits or losses of a special nature which will be discussed in the section on foreign exchange.

Domestic Corporation. A second step which might be advisable is the organization of a domestic corporation to operate exclusively in foreign markets. Thus a Western Hemisphere Trade Corporation established for this purpose is advisable and tax advantages can be gained. If such a corporation qualifies under Section 921 of the Internal Revenue Code, the maximum federal income tax will be 34 percent instead of 48 percent. Or, if such a corporation qualifies under Section 931 operating in certain U.S. possessions, it will not be liable for any U.S. tax. In addition, a domestic subsidiary operating overseas can transfer property tax-free under Section 351 and is not restricted by the provisions of Section 332 upon liquidation.

Other than in the special cases listed above, U.S. subsidiaries listed above are subject to full U.S. taxes. However, losses also can offer some tax advantages.

Foreign Subsidiary. The final step into international operations is the acquisition of foreign subsidiaries, either wholly or partly owned. In this situation, the full impact of international accounting problems is brought to bear. A corporation is controlled by the legal and tax statutes of its country of incorporation. Its personnel is drawn largely from local talent. If it caters to a local market or draws supplies from local vendors, it must adhere to the business customs of the area. Such laws and customs generally differ markedly from their American counterparts. To operate successfully in a foreign environment it is essential that such differences be understood fully and be complied with.

In addition, certain elements of American taxation become involved which must be considered relative to their effect on foreign operations. The auditor of foreign subsidiaries must be familiar with certain sections of the Internal Revenue Code and their regulations, with tax treaties between the United States and foreign nations, and with agreements among foreign nations if trade crosses national boundaries.

Consolidation of Foreign Subsidiaries. Finally, the decision of whether to consolidate the report of the foreign subsidiary's activity with the report of the domestic parent company is of great importance and requires a knowledge of conditions governing operations. The American Institute of Certified Public Accountants advises that consolidation of foreign subsidiaries should be carefully weighed in the light of possible losses through exchange restrictions and possible seizure of assets. There is great diversity in consolidation practices, and the consequences must be fully examined.

Each of these aspects bearing on foreign operations must be understood by the American auditor who is involved in protecting the interests of his domestic client abroad. The large accounting firms, as their clients' foreign interests expanded, found it advisable to open offices in strategic foreign business centers. But as smaller corporations also branch out, smaller accounting firms are faced with the unique problem of either following these operations or developing relations with local practitioners. This gives rise to the most serious problem of international auditing, the appraisal of the reliability of audit reports and auditing standards of other countries.

Reliability of Audit Reports. The title of "Registered Accountant" or "Chartered Accountant" is no assurance that audit standards and treatment of accounts are comparable to American standards or that they can be relied upon. Even certifications, although worded exactly according to the suggestions of the AICPA, do not give any assurance that "auditing standards" or "accounting principles" are the standards and principles recognized by the American accounting profession. The independence of the public accountant also varies. In the United Kingdom the auditor has greater independence than in the United States, being responsible directly to stockholders. In certain other countries the audit is prepared by a company employee. Reliance on such statements might lead to false conclusions and distorted reporting.

To complicate the problems, each nation has its own standards and is at a different stage in its accounting development. Having mastered the situation in France, for example, is no assurance that the same formula can be applied in Italy or Argentina. The accountant who is involved with international accounting must study every aspect of the situation in order to present an adequate financial report comparable to that which he has been accustomed to presenting for domestic operations.

Grouping of Countries. It would be impossible and unnecessary to detail the above conditions for every country in the world. Since accounting and law have been evolved through spheres of influence, the nations will be grouped here according to the similarity of their practices rather than on a geographic basis. Thus, the British influence is evident in many nations of Africa and Asia, while the effects of Spanish culture predominates in Latin America. Under each heading, the discussion will be divided into systems of operation, with further differentiation between the problems of developed countries and those of less developed countries. The basic systems, which will be compared with the U.S. counterpart, will be:

1. Britain and the sterling-influence areas following British methods
2. Germany (West) and its areas of influence
3. France and French-influenced areas
4. Spain and Latin America
5. Italy
6. Those other countries, such as Japan, India, Australia, Israel, and various other nations, which are developing independent or mixed systems

The accountant must realize that similarity and a common heritage do not mean that any two countries have identical business methods. If an organization is to optimize its chances for success, complete understanding of the environment in which it must function is necessary. It cannot be assumed that American practices are universal or would even work in a foreign country. The practitioner must examine the factors which influence auditing practices in each. In this way, although the circumstances may differ, the U.S. accountant will be prepared for the general situation he is liable to meet in a specific foreign country.

Caveat. This study cannot anticipate changes that will inevitably occur in legal, tax, and accounting requirements both in the United States and abroad. The accountant must not only acquaint himself with conditions existing at the start of his engagement but must keep abreast of new developments which will affect the conduct of his continuing engagement. Even while this section is being written, France and the Netherlands are contemplating major revisions of their accounting requirements.

Because of this dynamic situation, the following discussion is meant to alert the auditor to areas which should be investigated for an adequate appraisal of existing conditions. Sources of current information are limited. Periodicals from the country concerned generally contain important releases and government sources will provide much information.

CUSTOMS AND TRADITIONS

In order to gain a proper appreciation of any activity peculiar to a society, the customs of its people and the laws which formalize those customs must be understood. Since accounting is a service function to the business community, the laws which govern this function are, in each instance, a reflection of the particular business environment. Europe, including the United Kingdom, is the cultural and legal center of most of the world's developed and developing economies. Additionally, a great proportion of American foreign business is gravitating toward Europe. Therefore, it is important to understand the attitudes which have given rise to different accounting approaches.

Legal Philosophies. First, the sharp distinction between legal philosophies has greatly influenced accounting practices. The British common law system has dominated attitudes in Northern Europe, which includes the Scandinavian countries, Germany, and the Netherlands. Under this system, a person is assumed innocent until proven guilty; basic statutes constitute a series of prohibitions, specifying what is not to be done. In France and the Mediterranean area, the civil code is prevalent. Under these laws the accused is assumed guilty until proven innocent. The laws function through a list of directives specifying what one must do to remain within the law.

Accounting Practices. Applying these contrasting approaches to accounting has resulted in highly developed auditing standards throughout Northern Europe. Holland, the United Kingdom, Scandinavia, and Germany have developed highly skilled accounting professionals whose audits and reports continue to grow more reliable and revealing as these individuals actively work toward reform and improvement. Certain national variations must be recognized in order to be able to interpret reports, and the American auditor must become familiar with these variations in order to compare or consolidate foreign operations with domestic accounts. These same national differences can be traced to other countries where colonial dominance or trade relations have carried with them European influences. Former British colonies in Africa and Asia retain much of the British accounting system; Japan shows the strong effects of German contacts; and the Dutch point of view persists in the former colonies of the Netherlands.

In those countries bordering the Mediterranean, including Switzerland, accounting practices have been much slower in developing, largely because of the legal structure. But the temperament of the inhabitants is also pertinent. Business is organized on a family basis, and distrust of anyone outside the family circle is common. This situation has limited the size of business operations and hampered the effectiveness and reliability of accounting reporting in these countries. The main functions of the public accountant in these nations are the performance of statutory audit procedures, which have become largely stereotyped, and contending with tax collectors in the protection of his client's interests. Such motivation creates accounting procedures deliberately conceived to confuse the tax collector and conceal the true financial picture in the process.

Against this background, the American auditor is presented with the difficult task of determining the reliability of reports prepared by foreign auditors, how those reports might differ in treatment of specific accounts, and to what extent terminology might be confusing.

The best approach to this complex situation is to segregate the accounting world into spheres of influence and to examine the dominant characteristics of each group. To a large extent the nature of the culture, its historic background, the customs of its people, and the evolution of its economy will determine its laws and its business environment.

Because they are important to a proper understanding of the accounting environment of various countries, the following brief sketches of pertinent historical and cultural factors are included.

Great Britain. The United Kingdom and its area of influence form one of the greatest economic spheres in the world. Colonial activities over the past 500 years have carried British customs and methods around the earth. This does not imply that these traditions foster maximum efficiency.

British education has been established on the Oxford-Cambridge tradition. The most qualified brains, ideally, went to these seats of higher learning and from thence into government, the clergy, the military, or such learned professions as law and medicine. The less adept student went to trade school to study engineering or other technical pursuits. From this stratum come the businessman and accountant.

Similar cultural strata will be found in many countries which have come under British influence. The exceptions are those nations to which Britons came to escape some unpleasant aspect of the home culture. Among these last would be the United States, Canada, Australia, and New Zealand. These four nations have developed a more democratic approach to business.

The instability of many African governments makes for difficult situations. With tribal and national customs superimposed on basically British law, a familiarity with the local situation becomes essential for success. Local personnel must be understood and the limitations of their knowledge or their emphasis on other values must be accepted if we are to function within their environment. We cannot expect men raised in a culture with a more leisurely tempo to work at the same pace as we are accustomed to at home.

Germany. On the European continent, the culture which is nearest to the British is that of Germany. Although the industrial revolution reached Central Europe later than England, the Germans adapted to it readily and have turned their culture to its demands much more readily than has Britain. Perhaps because Britain, oriented to the sea, was more a trading country and Germany, being largely landlocked, was essentially a producing country, the German temperament is more scientific in its approach. Mass production and engineering skills are prevalent. A fondness for exactness has evolved some unique accounting concepts. Germany's influence is felt most strongly in Scandinavian countries and to some extent in Japan.

The large, integrated organization has been highly developed in Germany, together with the managerial skills requisite to such firms. Because of the nature of German history, engineering skills are highly regarded and efficiency at all levels of work is respected.

France. France and her areas of influence, especially in North Africa, have a cultural heritage that differs sharply from that of either Britain or Germany. The French, except for the Parisians, are of peasant stock. They are frugal and conservative with extremely close family ties. French business enterprises are still largely family operations despite government efforts at encouraging mergers and expansion.

The reason for this is subtle. The Frenchman considers anyone outside his family circle as a stranger, and, in business, a stranger is a potential enemy. Thus, the business is limited to members of the family and its capital expansion is controlled by the extent of the family's resources. To obtain managerial or technical skills from strangers or to borrow from a banker who would pry into family conditions would be to court danger. Those with greatest ability were restless and, as in Britain, joined the government, the military, or a profession. The less adventuresome stayed at home. Current income was of less concern than the preservation of wealth.

The influence of Napoleon and the legal structure he imposed are an important influence on French thinking and customs. It is a rigid code, implying guilt until the accused is proven innocent. Its effect has been docile compliance with orders from higher authority. This subservience becomes unbearable to the American manager. But to be successful it is necessary to understand and adjust to national customs.

The French government has been the most active and possibly the most successful in economic planning. Where firms would not merge, the government has stepped in, as with the Renault organization. Concessions in the form of tax abatement, low interest rates, and subsidies have succeeded in inducing development of industry in areas plagued with unemployment. Government approval is required for all capital expansion, and capital is channeled into those activities which the government desires. Under these rigid controls, France has experienced economic expansion since World War II.

There is a strong movement in Europe advocating the adoption of a uniform chart of accounts. This group is especially active in the Common Market countries. France, through governmental insistence, has gone farthest in this direction, although the concept originated in Germany. Of course, this type of accounting classification has been used widely by totalitarian countries since their beginnings. The U.E.C. (Union Européenne des Experts Comptables) is seriously considering giving its approval to uniform charts of accounts.

Spain. More than Spain herself, the vast continent of Latin and South America bears the stamp of Spanish culture. Like France, the legal foundation of this group is the civil code. But the domination of a landed aristocracy has persisted much longer than in France. This society, both in Europe and in America, has developed an economic structure which retains the old social distinctions while adapting to modern industrial growth. This requires the continued dominance of the aristocracy with the emergence of a strong middle class. But at the base of the structure remains the peon living at the starvation level. In Latin America this group consists of the Indians and mestizos. Industrial expansion, rather than bringing improvement to the majority, has worsened their lot. The middle class is becoming increasingly affluent. But the balance-of-payments conditions indicate that imports of capital goods and manufactured luxury items far exceed exports, which are largely primary minerals, crude oil, and agricultural products. The economic well-being of the middle class must come from somewhere. Part of it is drawn from loans and investments flowing in from the United States and Europe. But a great portion is provided by the lower class, whose living standard is worsening.

A rigid class distinction persists throughout Spanish cultures. This has given rise to many customs which are alien to the U.S. businessman. In particular, the role of the accountant is far beneath that which we assume. As in Italy and France, the accountant's purpose is twofold: to comply with legal requirements and to manipulate accounts so as to confuse and thwart the efforts of tax collectors. Neither of these occupations would give rise to a respected profession. The accountant is looked upon as a mixture of clerk and charlatan. The profession has only recently gained a measure of recognition through the demands of U.S. corporations for adequate reporting and control.

Italy. The Italian business environment is a strange mixture of rapidly growing industrialization and an archaic regulatory system. To further confuse the situation, Italy has what is known as a "dual" economy. An expanding industrialized segment exists in the north, with a backward agrarian economy eking out a precarious existence in the barren Mezzogiorno to the south. Although income per capita has increased phenomenally during the last 15 years, the relative improvement of the south has not been any greater than in the north. The peasant in the south is still as far behind his northern countryman as he ever was.

Various inducements, in the form of tax abatement, low interest rates, and subsidies offered by the government, have drawn some industry into the Mezzogiorno. But poor transportation, even poorer communication, and a lack of skilled labor have deterred any great influx of business into the area. Another plan introduced by the government was to induce emigration away from the south, which also has been only partly successful.

Because of the tax structure, most business establishments are very small or very large. Taxes and labor regulations fall most heavily on the medium-size firm, while the very small business operates under government subsidy. Such a practice has stunted the growth of enterprises which would otherwise have expanded. This situation is most acute in the Mezzogiorno. For example, if there are more than four employees, the income tax rate is sharply increased. If there are between 10 and 20 employees, termination pay, family allowances, and labor rates are sharply increased. And if profits are below 9 percent, a regressive capital tax becomes effective.

Because of these labor regulations, even the largest firms do not operate at optimum capacity. They must either hold their labor force below capacity needs and curtail production or retain an excess of workers during slack seasons, giving them high labor costs. Therefore, as in France, most companies are not operating at an efficiency level.

A summary of the policies of the foregoing nations would not be complete without some reference to the European Economic Community. Much as the unity of this organization has been shaken by nationalistic attitudes, the EEC remains a strong progressive force which must be considered by the American venturing abroad. Growing cohesion of this group and its expansion throughout Western Europe appear inevitable. The attitude of this bloc toward intrusion of U.S. capital is not predictable. At present, anything we can do to benefit their progress is welcomed. But future conditions will depend on new leaders who will establish those policies most advantageous to internal growth.

We must, therefore, expect tariff protection from U.S. imports and regulations regarding local control of industries rather than foreign control. As the EEC becomes stronger, some restrictions may be relaxed, but this is a look far into the future.

Asia. Accounting in Asia is in its infancy, but great strides are being made to improve the profession and to provide educational facilities for it. There are many difficult problems to be overcome. But determined efforts in Japan, Thailand, India, and Pakistan are showing results in ever-improving auditing and reporting standards.

There are many other important trading nations having traditions and customs strikingly different from our own whose business environment requires understanding for successful operation. Some of these nations are far advanced industrially and have well-organized business sectors. Each of these countries has evolved its own distinct culture and traditions. Japan, recognized only since 1948 as a partner in the Western community of nations, has grown rapidly and continues to strive for a greater proportion of Free World trade. Ambitious and aggressive, the Japanese welcome any assistance that will improve their economy.

Developing countries. The greater portion of the earth is occupied by nations which have been called "less developed," "underdeveloped," and "developing," depending on the source used. Characteristic of many of these countries is an unstable government. This element, which does not breed confidence in the economy or in the safety of private property, is a deterrent to investment and business expansion. In this category can be grouped most of Asia, Africa, and South America, as well as Greece and Turkey on the European continent.

The traditions of these countries are deeply rooted in agriculture, and the transition to a business or industrial economy often requires the abolition of religious as well as cultural values that contradict such progress. The foreigner is at a distinct disadvantage in these whirlpools of religious, tribal, political, and cultural ferment. Not only his property but his physical safety may be in jeopardy. And yet there are rewards, both economic and moral, in contributing to the improvement of these peoples. A knowledge of their customs and business procedures is of the utmost importance.

The most pressing problem in both government and private business in less developed countries is the need for good administrative leadership. With the attainment of nationhood, the new countries have ousted those foreign officials who did not leave voluntarily. The organizations which had functioned smoothly in a colonial system, when left to inept and untrained leadership soon broke down.

This is the current situation in much of the world today. Industrialization will not work without better-trained people and more stable administrations. The U.S. investor must be aware of these circumstances. The future growth of the countries depends as much on the development of "human capital" in the form of education as on economic capital in the form of machinery and public works.

LEGAL CONSIDERATIONS

In addition to the basic philosophy behind the legal structure of a country, certain specific laws are passed to encourage, discourage, or limit the activities of foreign investors. Also, the forms under which a business enterprise can be organized differ among countries.

However, there exists a similarity in the legal structure of countries with similar cultural background. One peculiarity exists, however, in developing countries. Whereas more advanced nations will modify their basic law when required, the developing country which adopts the basic law from a developed country rarely makes any changes. For example, the United Kingdom revises its Companies Act periodically as a result of the findings of special committees. But developing countries which pattern their business structure on the United Kingdom do not make periodic modifications once the law is adopted, nor do they modify it to meet the changing needs of their growing economies. Such rigid laws ultimately become a deterrent to progress.

U.S. Laws Affecting Foreign Operations. Very few legal restrictions upon foreign operations of U.S. corporations are imposed by the United States government. The only major restriction at present is the Foreign Direct Investment Law. This law, enacted as a measure to reduce the U.S. unfavorable balance of payments, is an attempt to limit the amount of direct investment by U.S. corporations in foreign operations. It also tries to recapture investments already made. Since it is supposedly a temporary measure (with no stated time limit), its constitutionality has not been established and, as the methods for administering its provisions have been challenged, the impact of this statute is questionable. If upheld, it will become a barrier to foreign operations and a step toward isolation.

Foreign Laws Governing Business Enterprises. The British Companies Acts (1948 and 1967). The public company corresponds closely to the U.S. corporation having the same essential legal status and organization. It is designated by having "Ltd." in its name, indicative of the limited liability of its shareholders, of which there must be at least seven.

The private company (or proprietary company in Australia and South Africa) is limited in the number of its members to no more than 50 (excluding employees and former employees). The British Companies Act of 1967 requires that private companies as well as public companies file an annual report with the authorities, removing one of the advantages of this type of organization, at least in the United Kingdom. Such companies must have at least two shareholders.

Exempt private companies, which are generally closely held family firms with no corporations as stockholders, were exempt from many of the reporting requirements of other companies. Although an audit is required, the auditor need not be a qualified person under the Companies Act. The exemption from filing reports was abolished under the British Companies Act of 1967 but continues to be effective in other countries.

Branches of foreign corporations doing business in the country must first obtain approval from some official body and must generally abide by the provisions of the Companies Act applying to similar domestic corporations.

Partnerships and individual enterprises are provided for, except that a partnership with more than 10 partners must register. In Australia having more than 20 partners is prohibited.

The Companies Acts generally control company formation, issuance of shares and debentures, acts of management such as shareholders' meetings, duties of directors, dissolution procedures, prospectuses, filing of reports, voting processes, and the audit and disclosures in financial statements. These regulations are set forth in great detail.

German Corporation Law. In Germany the Stock Corporation Law (Aktiengesetz) of 1965 controls the activities of corporations and other forms of business organization. These forms are similar to those recognized in British-type companies acts.

The corporation (Aktiengesellschaft—A.G.) closely resembles the U.S. corporation. One peculiarity is that all shares must be subscribed for when the corporation is founded and at least 25 percent must be paid for in cash on each share. The corporation must be entered in the Trade Register of Commerce.

The limited liability company (G.m.b.H), similar to the private company, must also be entered in the Trade Register of Commerce. A separate Limited Liability Company Law governs these organizations. Their stock cannot be traded on an exchange.

The general commercial partnership (O.H.G.) has no maximum limit as to the number of partners. Each partner has unlimited liability for the debts of the organization. The O.H.G. must also be entered in the local Trade Register of Commerce. The general provisions for regulation of partnerships are contained in the commercial code (Handelsgesetzbuch). Specific provision is made that:

1. Each partner is entitled to a voice in management of the operation.
2. Each partner is entitled to 4 percent of his investment out of profits and the remaining profits are to be divided equally among the partners.
3. The limited commercial partnership (K.G.) must have at least one unlimited partner to accept liability for debts.
4. Branches of foreign enterprises doing business in Germany are subject to varying controls depending on the form of organization. If the firm is a limited company or corporation, the requirements are more burdensome than for other types of organization.

The commercial codes. The nations functioning under the civil code, including France, Italy, Spain, Latin America, and some areas of Africa and the Near East, have very similar laws related to business. However, France enacted a new company law in 1966 which contains some departures from the traditional regulations. The new law became completely operative on October 1, 1968.

This group of laws provides for a form of organization similar to that of the U.S. corporation. The Société Anonyme (S.A.) in France, the Società per Azioni in Italy, and the Sociedad Anónima in the Spanish-speaking countries generally require that all capital must be fully subscribed and issued at the time of organization. This makes the use of debentures for expansion a necessary element. It also limits the growth potential of the corporation. A 25 percent initial payment and a limited time for payment of the balance are required generally for the issuance of shares.

In some countries, a one-man company is not permitted. Companies are considered dissolved automatically if one person owns all the shares for a specified length of time. The form of corporate organization is generally dictated by the commercial code, and is most commonly a board of directors with certain other officials, such as the statutory auditors. France's new law also permits a supervisory council which controls a directorate of not more than five individuals.

The code generally limits the life of a business firm. In France this limit is 99 years for all types of companies. Corporations, as well as most other forms of business firms, must be entered in some form of trade registry at the time of organization. Methods of keeping records vary widely, although all these countries require that statutory financial reports be published in an official gazette.

The forms of legal entities permitted are:

1. The corporation or S.A.
2. The private company or Société à Responsabilité Limitée (S.A.R.L.), with between 2 and 50 shareholders, which enjoys the privilege of limited liability and the lack of restrictions. As in Britain, the new French law places more severe requirements on this form of organization than is traditional.
3. Single proprietorships, general partnerships, limited partnerships, cooperatives, and joint ventures all are employed in business and closely resemble similar organizations in the United States.

Labor laws and social legislation. The business environment in many foreign countries is strongly affected by the type of labor legislation existing and its restrictions on management. Some of these laws are burdensome and have varying accounting implications.

The United Kingdom has two types of contributions to its social security program. The first is a flat rate levied against the employer on the basis of age and sex of the employee. Out of the fund so generated are paid the workmen's compensation awards or industrial injuries insurance.

In addition, employer and employee each contribute about 4½ percent of wages to the State pension fund. Benefits from this fund are payable for sickness, unemployment, pregnancy, and widowhood and for death benefits. In addition, there is a national assistance program for hardship cases.

The government also requires that a pension plan be maintained by the employer with benefits starting at age 65.

Since Germany was the first country to introduce social security legislation, an advanced program is to be expected here. Workers must be appointed to the corporate board of directors, are protected against unjustified dismissal, and have many other safeguards to their position.

There is a 48-hour maximum work week, overtime being one and one-fourth times the regular rate. A legal vacation of a minimum of 15 days is required, with between 10 and 13 legal holidays in addition. Pension funds are common among German firms.

Problems. Certain aspects of business law practiced in many developing countries are worth mentioning. These legal and quasi-legal restrictions should be investigated carefully before entering into agreements with foreign governments or collaborations with foreign private organizations. Most of these requirements stem from two views. The first is suspicion and fear of the strong industrialized power. This feeling may have its origins in suppression by colonial rulers. It shows itself in a strong national pride and provisions to protect the rights of nationals against foreign exploitation. The second motivation is a desire to replace foreign assistance with local self-sufficiency as quickly as possible.

These restrictions take several forms, depending on the stage of development of the country and on the background of its experience with Western nations.

1. Restrictions as to industries in which foreigners are permitted to invest.
2. Restrictions as to percentage of ownership foreigners are permitted to hold in a collaboration.
3. Restrictions regarding voting control of an enterprise. In many instances, there must be no greater than a 50 percent interest by foreigners in a private venture and less than a 50 percent interest where the government is the other partner.
4. Management control of operations by foreign managers is permitted in countries which admit to a lack of management skills and personnel. In Japan, management must be in the hands of Japanese nationals.
5. Restrictions of imports of materials used in manufacture. Such imports are limited to those items which cannot be obtained locally. This restriction is often administered inequitably and can cause hardship.
6. Limitation of time during which foreign technicians are expected to train their local replacements.

These are a few of the pitfalls an investor must avoid in dealing with developing countries. In addition, the force of a contract under law should be understood. In Japan, certain contracts can be broken without any recourse available to the injured party.

Another warning must be given regarding negotiation of agreements. In many countries the national government is a party to all arrangements with foreigners. Because of this, negotiations may drag on interminably. It is also important to know with whom you should deal. Too often Americans think they have done enough when a departmental minister approves a plan, only to find that some minor bureaucrat has the power to withhold final approval indefinitely.

TAX CONSIDERATIONS

U.S. Taxes Affecting Foreign Operations. Under the Revenue Act of 1962 many changes were made in connection with foreign operations, most of them designed to plug loopholes in the existing law and to remove the tax shelter afforded by operating in low-tax countries. The U.S. company has the choice of operating abroad in three ways, each of which involves different tax implications. In order to serve his client adequately, the accountant must be familiar with the tax implications of the method of operation chosen by the client. A U.S.-based organization is subject to both U.S. taxes and taxes levied in the foreign country in which operations will be located.

The three choices of organization are:

1. ESTABLISHING A BRANCH OFFICE OF THE AMERICAN CORPORATION: This has certain immediate advantages in charging off against U.S. revenue the expenses of setting up the branch and losses that can be expected from its operations during the first year.

The rising income tax rates in many foreign countries have reduced the advantage of the overseas income deferral—the advantage that income taxes paid to foreign governments may be deductible for U.S. income tax purposes from income earned abroad.

2. ORGANIZING AN AMERICAN CORPORATION TO FUNCTION WHOLLY IN FOREIGN ACTIVITIES: Such a subsidiary is advisable if it qualifies as a Western Hemisphere Trading Corporation under Section 921 of the Revenue Act or under Section 931, which deals with corporations operating in U.S. territories, essentially in Puerto Rico. Under Section 921, the tax advantage is a 34 percent rate instead of the 48 percent income tax on corporate profits. If the company qualifies under Section 931, it is not subject to any U.S. income tax.

In addition, such corporations, being domestic subsidiaries, are exempt under Section 951 from taxes on transfer of property. Certain other reporting requirements applicable to controlled foreign corporations do not apply.

3. A FOREIGN SUBSIDIARY EITHER WHOLLY OWNED BY THE U.S. PARENT OR WITH A CONTROLLING INTEREST VESTED IN THE PARENT: The auditor of an organization with such an arrangement must become familiar with a number of sections of the Internal Revenue Code to assure his clients' compliance and to take advantage of tax relief afforded. Neglect of certain of these regulations may result in severe penalties. It is important to check the appropriate regulations for changes and decisions, since many of these regulations are being contested.

Under all three methods of operation, the host country will have jurisdiction and taxing powers over activities within its borders. Familiarity with the tax structure of the country is essential before establishing a foreign operation and for the tax costs that might be incurred.

U.S. tax regulations concerning foreign operations are being changed constantly as new methods of foreign operation are devised. Most of the present changes are aimed at plugging loopholes in the law. Certain outstanding provisions must be considered, but familiarity with all sections of the code bearing on foreign operations is advisable. A list of those that were in force in 1970 will be found at the end of this section.

Gross-up provision. Under Section 78 of the Internal Revenue Code dividends reported as being received from a controlled foreign corporation must be reported in gross, that is, including the foreign taxes withheld from the payment. These are included in the "deemed" paid credits when calculating the foreign tax credit.

Foreign tax credit. Sections 901 through 905 of the code permit citizens of the United States, domestic corporations, certain aliens resident in the United States or Puerto Rico to claim a credit for taxes paid or accrued to foreign countries subject to conditions of this section. In Section 902, a corporation organized in a less developed country is defined and the special tax relief afforded is set forth.

The U.S. taxpayer may offset foreign income taxes or other taxes paid in lieu of income tax against his U.S. obligations instead of taking them as a deduction. However, such offset can be taken only to the extent he would have been liable for U.S. income tax on the same income. In other words, if the foreign income tax is greater because the rate is higher or the method of arriving at taxable income differs from U.S. calculation of taxable income, then the amount of foreign tax paid that can be offset is only that which would have been paid at the U.S. rate or by U.S. methods of calculation. If the foreign tax credit is to be applied where taxes of more than one foreign country are involved, an overall basis for calculation can be used or, alternately, a country-by-country basis. The overall basis is more advantageous where tax rates are involved from some countries having rates exceeding the U.S. rate which can be offset by rates in other countries which are lower than the U.S. rate.

An additional provision is the right to carry back for two years or forward for five years foreign income taxes which are in excess of current allowable deductions because of the above ruling.

Foreign tax credit is allowed on an "indirect credit" if a domestic corporation owns at least 10 percent of the controlling stock of a foreign company; also if this foreign company owns at least 50 percent of the voting stock of a subsidiary of the foreign company. However, such consideration does not extend below the second tier of ownership.

In order to encourage investment in less developed countries, a more liberal method of calculating the deemed paid tax is permitted and the gross-up provision is relaxed. The following example illustrates how the U.S. tax on dividends is calculated for a developed country as contrasted with the calculation for a less developed country.

EXAMPLES OF EFFECTS OF FOREIGN TAX CREDIT AS APPLIED FOR LESS DEVELOPED COUNTRIES' INCOME AND FOR DEVELOPED COUNTRIES' INCOME

	Less Developed Country	*Developed Country*
	$	$
Earnings before tax	1,000	1,000
Foreign income tax at 30%	300	300
Earnings after foreign taxes	700	700
Dividend paid	500	500
Less: Foreign withholding tax of 15%	75	75
Net dividend received in U.S.	425	425
Foreign tax credit:		
a. Direct withholding	75	75
b. "Deemed" paid for subsidiary's tax:		
$\frac{\text{(dividend) } 500}{\text{(earnings before tax) } 1000} \times \text{(foreign tax) } 300 =$	150	
$\frac{\text{(dividend) } 500}{\text{(earnings and profits) } 700} \times \text{(foreign tax) } 300$		217
Foreign tax credit	225	292
Calculation of U.S. tax:		
Gross dividends received	500	500
Plus deemed tax paid		217
	500	717
U.S. tax at 48%	240	344
Less: Foreign tax credit	225	292
U.S. tax payable	15	52

Discretionary powers of the director. Several sections of the code presently grant the Director of Internal Revenue broad discretionary powers. The first of these, Section 269, is concerned with acquisitions made to evade or avoid income taxes. If, in the opinion of the Treasury Department, one corporation acquires either directly or indirectly property or control of another company in order to receive some tax benefit it would not otherwise enjoy, such deduction, credit, or allowance may be disallowed.

If either tangible or intangible property is to be transferred to a foreign subsidiary at a value which exceeds basis or if a foreign subsidiary liquidation realizes a gain, under Section 367 a ruling must be obtained in advance in order for the transaction to receive tax-free treatment. If the Treasury Department is satisfied that such a transaction does not have as a principal purpose the avoidance of income tax, it will grant tax-free status. If such permission is not obtained or if request for permission is not submitted prior to the transaction, such gains are taxable.

One of the most powerful tools of the Treasury Department is Section 482. Under its provisions the Director has the right to determine whether allocations of expenses and revenues among related corporations are equitable or have been manipulated to avoid tax. Specific items which come under scrutiny most often are:

1. Sales to affiliates; whether they are at fair market price or at an arbitrary price which causes distortions of profits.
2. Interest-free advances to affiliates; the Treasury Department may require that interest be imputed.

3. Charges for home office, management, and technical services; determination of a sound basis for these charges may be at the discretion of the Director.
4. Licensing and royalty franchises where no fees or excessive fees are charged.

The agent will generally measure such items on the basis of arm's-length prices. Adequate records should be kept in case it is necessary to justify the company's policy.

Western Hemisphere Trading Corporations. Sections 921 and 922 specify that a Western Hemisphere Trading Corporation signifies a corporation doing all its business within the Western Hemisphere, that 95 percent of its income for the last three years is derived from sources outside the United States, and 90 percent of its gross income is from active trade or business. Such corporations are subject to a special reduction in income taxes.

Possessions of the United States. Special tax provisions apply to business organizations which meet certain conditions if they have income from Puerto Rico (Sec. 933) or the Virgin Islands (Sec. 934). Income from other possessions (including Guam, American Samoa, Panama Canal Zone, and Wake and Midway Islands) can be excluded for tax purposes if certain conditions are met.

China Trade Act corporations. Income from sources within Hong Kong and Formosa of a corporation organized under the China Trade Act of 1922, when distributed as dividends, may, under certain conditions, be tax-exempt.

Subpart F. The Revenue Act of 1962 contained certain provisions designed to eliminate the use of artificial arrangements between operating companies and base companies located in tax-haven countries as a means of deferring or avoiding U.S. taxes. These provisions are found in Sections 951 through 964 of the code. The rules apply to the "controlled foreign corporation," which is defined as a foreign corporation with 50 percent or more of its voting stock owned directly or indirectly by U.S. shareholders each of whom holds at least 10 percent of such voting stock.

The following kinds of income of controlled foreign corporations are taxable under Subpart F:

1. Subpart F income, consisting of:
   a. Foreign-base company income
   b. Income from insurance of U.S. risks
2. Previously excluded Subpart F income withdrawn from investment in less developed countries
3. Increase in earnings invested in U.S. property

A foreign-base company, usually incorporated in a tax-haven country, is interposed in an artificial arrangement between the purchaser and seller of a product or service one of whom, either the purchaser or the seller, is an affiliated company. For example, a Swiss (tax-haven) company selling goods manufactured by an affiliate in France to a customer in Germany would generate Subpart F income to the Swiss affiliate if it realized a profit from the transaction. If the transaction were handled between the French affiliate and the German customer directly, no Subpart F income would arise.

There are certain exceptions to the general rule.

1. If Subpart F gross income is less than 30 percent of the total gross income of the controlled foreign corporation, no part of the income is treated as Subpart F income for that year. If gross foreign-base income exceeds

70 percent of total gross income, the entire gross income will fall under Subpart F.

2. Foreign-base company income does not include dividends, interest, and capital gains from *less-developed-country corporations* to the extent that such income is reinvested in less developed countries.

3. If the District Director is satisfied that there is *no substantial reduction of income tax* because of the creation of such foreign-base company, its income will not fall under Subpart F.

4. Foreign-base company income excludes certain income from *shipping* and *aircraft* operations.

5. All *appropriate expenses* incurred by the foreign-base company may be deducted in arriving at net foreign-base-company income taxable under Subpart F.

6. Special relief is being given to corporations which qualify as *export trade corporations.*

The regulations under Subpart F have been subject to many changes and have not yet been fully tested by the Treasury Department. New interpretations will be added in the future.

The minimum-distribution provision of the law affords relief from Subpart F. Under this arrangement the U.S. corporation will not be subject to U.S. tax on Subpart F income if the combined rate of (1) foreign tax and (2) U.S. tax on income distributed is not substantially below the U.S. corporate tax rate. Tables are provided to show the amount of minimum distribution required to avoid being taxed under Subpart F.

If foreign income is blocked because of foreign currency restrictions, it is excluded from profits of a controlled foreign corporation for Subpart F purposes.

One of the tax abuses which Subpart F is aimed at eliminating is the case of liquidation of a controlled foreign corporation. Formerly, if profits of such a corporation were not distributed and the company was finally liquidated, these profits would appear as gains on liquidation and would be subject to treatment as capital gains. Under the 1962 law such gains would be treated as ordinary income. Dividend treatment under this provision does not apply where advance ruling has been obtained under Section 367.

Tax treaties. The United States has negotiated bilateral tax treaties with some 28 foreign governments primarily for the purpose of avoiding double taxation of income of nationals involved. In addition these treaties allocate certain types of income to a particular country. The question of whether a company maintains a permanent establishment within a nation's boundaries is important to tax considerations. If no such condition exists, the tax treaty might exempt the U.S. company from local taxes.

Payments such as dividends to nonresidents are usually subject to a withholding tax which generally is at a reduced rate where a tax treaty exists. Such treaties also may exempt foreign nationals who are visiting on a temporary basis, such as technicians, teachers, and students. Also, provision for appeal of special cases may be provided where the treaty does not prevent double taxation.

Some treaties with less developed countries contain tax incentives for U.S. investors. Since these treaties are constantly being revised and new treaties are being negotiated, it is necessary to study the agreement with the country where business dealings are being contemplated. Seemingly standard provisions often have slight but important variations of wording.

Reporting requirements. At present, three forms are required of shareholders of certain foreign corporations.

1. Form 959 must be filed by U.S. shareholders who own or acquire 5 percent or more in value of the stock of a foreign corporation. The form must also be filed by U.S. citizens or residents who are officers or directors of a foreign corporation owned to the extent of 5 percent by a U.S. person. This form must be filed within 90 days after the transaction giving rise to the requirement. Failure to file can result in penalties up to $1,000 in addition to criminal prosecution where appropriate.
2. Form 2952 is an annual return to be filed by U.S. shareholders owning over 50 percent of the stock of a foreign corporation. This form contains details of relations between affiliated companies and of certain transactions among the foreign corporation and related persons. Failure to file can result in reduction of foreign tax credit and other criminal penalties where appropriate.
3. Form 3646 is required of U.S. shareholders of controlled foreign corporations and gives details of income and deductions for determination of any Subpart F income.

Interest equalization tax. In September, 1964 an act was passed to help reduce the balance-of-payments deficit of the United States. It tried to discourage purchases by U.S. persons of foreign securities which bear higher interest rates than those carried by domestic securities. The bill has been extended numerous times and appears to be a permanent feature. Maximum rates have been set at 18.75 percent on stock acquisitions and from 1.31 percent to 18.75 percent on debt obligations, depending on maturity date. However, investments by U.S. corporations in at least 10-percent owned foreign operating companies are exempt from this tax, permitting U.S. corporations to organize and finance foreign subsidiaries without liability thereunder. Also exempted are securities of less developed countries and less-developed-country corporations.

The Foreign Investors Tax Act (P.L. 89-809). The Foreign Investors Tax Act of 1966 is the first major revision in more than 20 years in U.S. treatment of nonresident aliens. Its purpose is to encourage foreign investment in the United States. It also removes certain inequities that formerly existed. Essentially, it distinguishes between business income and investment income. Business income is taxed at the rate generally applicable to U.S. citizens or corporations. Investment income is taxed at 30 percent unless lower treaty rates apply.

Caveat. Since interpretations of the Internal Revenue Code are constantly being changed by regulations and court decisions, it is important, for proper understanding of tax aspects, to refer to the Internal Revenue Service or some reliable tax service for changes which might affect any particular country or any corporate arrangement.

At present, the following sections of the Code are concerned with foreign operations:

Section		
	78:	"Gross-up" provision
	164:	Deduction for foreign taxes
	245:	Dividends from foreign corporations
	269:	Acquisitions made to evade or avoid tax
	275:	Restriction of deductions for foreign taxes
	301:	Distribution by foreign corporations

Section		
	367:	Foreign corporations defined
	482:	Allocation of income and deductions
	551–558:	Foreign personal holding companies
	861–864:	Income from sources within and without the U.S.
	881–884:	Tax on foreign corporations
	894:	Tax treaties
	901–905:	Foreign tax credit
	921–922:	Western Hemisphere Trade Corporations
	931:	Possessions corporations
	951–964:	Controlled foreign corporations (Subpart "F")
	970–972:	Export trade corporations
	1221–1231:	Capital assets
	1246–1247:	Foreign investment companies
	1248:	Sale or exchange of stock in certain foreign corporations
	1249:	Sale or exchange of patents
	1441–1442:	Withholding of tax on foreign corporations
	1491–1494:	Foreign transfers of stock to avoid tax
	6038:	Annual information return form 2952
	6046:	Form 959 return on acquisition or disposition of foreign stock
	6511:	Special rules on foreign credit against income tax
	7701:	Definition of "domestic" and "foreign"

Foreign Taxes. Most foreign countries levy taxes against branches of U.S. companies, U.S. corporations, and foreign subsidiaries of U.S. corporations which operate within their borders in the same manner as they tax local income or operations of their own nationals.

One exception is the tax on dividends distributed outside the country. A withholding tax on such dividends of 30 percent has been common except where tax treaties reduce the amount.

Types of taxes. The types of taxes levied differ widely from country to country. Although most countries have an income tax at present, there is a shift to a value-added tax as the basis in many countries. This is especially true in the Common Market countries (EEC), where a deadline of 1971 has been set for uniform value-added tax treatment in all six countries. Those nations which hope to join the Common Market can be expected to adopt similar measures.

Methods of enforcement. Although an understanding of the tax laws of the country in which the corporation operates is important, of even greater importance is an understanding of the methods of enforcement. Whereas in England the accountant's certification on a tax return is relied on implicitly by the Department of Inland Revenue, in Italy the final levy is the result of bargaining. The handling of tax matters is usually left to nationals who are familiar with local customs.

The latter procedure is especially the case in less developed countries where there is prejudice against foreign investors. The American investor often finds that regulations are applied much more rigidly in his case than in the case of indigenous organizations.

There are other tax areas to be watched. First among these are the social security taxes. In Italy the payroll taxes can be between 50 percent and 100 percent of the payroll itself. Other countries also levy heavy taxes for social welfare purposes which are based on payroll. Social legislation in many countries might have requirements which are concealed taxes. Heavy separation pay, statutory bonuses, and maternity pay are found. A comparison of tax rates of different countries cannot be made without also considering the differences in allowable deductions.

A tax on net worth or total assets is not uncommon in addition to the income tax. A turnover tax or its more modern counterpart, a value-added tax, may also be levied.

AUDITING AND ACCOUNTING PRACTICES

Although accountants may regard their profession as an independent body of knowledge, a study of the many uses and applications of accounting indicates that it is also a service function. Its purpose is to supply interested parties with financial information they require in accordance with customs and legal requirements of their particular society. No two countries use accounting in exactly the same way. And what "fairly" represents financial information in one nation may be considered a gross distortion of facts in another.

Three major areas of difference will be discussed: (1) differences in auditing practices, (2) differences in accounting and reporting methods, and (3) differences in professional education and ethics. As in previous discussions of foreign practices, it would be impossible to enumerate the variations found in each country. Broad areas will be mentioned, with the warning that each country must be examined separately by the accountant involved because of changes over time as well as differences of geography.

Auditing Practices. The U.S. accountant who receives a financial report of his client's foreign subsidiary audited and certified by a local certified accountant must review it carefully. Most countries have adopted the AICPA short-form certification letter and state that the audit was conducted according to generally accepted standards and fairly presents the financial information in accordance with generally accepted accounting principles. But auditing standards which are generally accepted in one country might be considered wholly inadequate elsewhere. The accountant should be familiar with the auditing standards of the country where the report originated.

Independence. Most crucial to the reliability of an audited report is the independence of the auditor. This is not always easy to determine. The codes of ethics of most countries mention independence, but adherence to the code often is lax.

In Britain the corporate auditor is elected by the stockholders and may appeal to the stockholders if a disagreement arises with the board of directors. This assures even more independence than in the United States, where the board of directors selects the auditor. Custom in some countries dictates the degree of independence. In Japan and in Italy the auditor is practically an employee, developing financial data to suit the desires of management. In countries where very few accountants are certified as compared to the work to be done, the audit either will be performed by an inferior accountant or will be a cursory examination.

Competence. It is difficult to separate the reliability of the audit from the ability of the auditor. Educational facilities and requirements differ from the Netherlands, where there is great emphasis on academic accomplishment, to countries where a college degree is not required. In many countries, especially in Latin America, the mere possession of a degree and the taking of an accounting course entitles one to a certificate.

But most countries are in the process of improving their accounting education programs. A static conclusion is out of order where growth and change are so prevalent. The next few years may witness vast improvements in the qualifications of auditors in many countries.

Types of audit. There are three distinct types of audit which might result in reports of varying degrees of reliability. These are:

1. A STATUTORY AUDIT CONDUCTED STRICTLY IN ACCORDANCE WITH LEGAL REQUIREMENTS: It is often conducted by persons with no accounting background who are appointed as a gesture of honor or respect. Its requirements are to ascertain that the financial report reflects the book figures and that the books are kept in conformity with the law. Since lawyers and legislators are not accountants, these laws seldom reflect good accounting principles and are often loosely interpreted.

The audit fee is often a good indicator of the extent of the work done. If it is nominal, a statutory audit is usually the case.

2. A TAX AUDIT CONDUCTED FOR THE PURPOSE OF MINIMIZING THE CLIENT'S INCOME TAX: The lack of a code of ethics is one of the factors preventing local accountants from attaining professional status and a position of respect in the community. Reports prepared for tax purposes in many countries are often not comparable with U.S. standards and cannot be consolidated without a review of the work done.

3. A COMMERCIAL AUDIT, WHICH IS GENERALLY REQUIRED BY CREDITORS, BANKS, AND STOCKHOLDERS: It should be the most reliable reflection of corporate activity available. However, in many countries tax treatment of reserves and other adjustments must be booked, distorting the commercial audit.

Also, in many countries, especially where issuance of capital stock is limited, borrowing is extremely important. The urge to show the most profitable picture is strong. Where the accountant's independence is questionable, commercial audits may be no more reliable than tax audits.

Consistency. In many countries, even those with highly developed economies, the need for consistency in financial reporting is often ignored. There is generally little assurance that depreciation, bad debt provision, or inventory values are calculated on the same basis from year to year. Such inconsistencies may make various analyses, comparisons, or consolidations misleading.

Disclosure. Related to the lack of consistency in audit reports in many countries is a lack of adequate disclosure. However, there are instances of fuller disclosure than will be found in the United States. It will also be found that the methods of disclosing information vary. Some countries consider the accompanying letter of the company president as part of the report and disclose pertinent information that way. Several countries effect disclosure in the body of the report itself. For example, contingent liability for notes discounted may appear in short form directly under the note category in the balance sheet. Awareness of these practices can avoid embarrassing conclusions.

In many countries reports of operations contain very scant information, generally disclosing total sales and net operating profit with no indication of the types or amounts of operating costs. The nations with more advanced accounting methods, such as Germany and the United Kingdom, have improved their expense disclosure, but many countries cling to the scant form. Behind this practice lies a cultural situation. Until recently, business was a family-oriented unit—and even today in some areas it still is. The firm, whether incorporated or not, remained small because its growth was limited to its internal resources. It did not resort to borrowing or any arrangement that might permit "strangers" to gain any control.

Methods of operation and costs were not revealed to competitors as a measure of good business practice. Many foreign executives still feel that the amount of disclosure practiced in the United States is dangerous and could give unfair advantage to competitors.

Auditing procedures. Emphasis on auditing procedures has a wide variation throughout the world. The audit practices of confirmation of receivables and observation of inventory taking are not widely accepted as necessary in other countries.

On the other hand, frequent counting of cash and other current assets is considered essential in most Latin American countries. Concern for accurate detail is often emphasized above the analytical approach. Especially in countries where junior accountants are plentiful and accounting fees are lower than in the United States, much more audit time is spent verifying bookkeeping records.

Counteracting this, many countries neglect an investigation of internal controls. In fact, there may be very little in the way of internal controls to investigate. This may give rise to the need for a detailed audit.

Adherence to commercial code regulations often determines the scope of the audit. If a great deal of time is consumed on detailed cash counts and complete audit of transactions, without using sampling techniques, additional audit procedures would make the engagement too costly and would tax the capacity of available practitioners.

On the other hand, where only a statutory audit is required, the tendency is to do nothing more than is absolutely necessary. Such audit procedures become routine and lose their effectiveness.

Accounting and Reporting Methods. It sometimes happens that the same basic principles will be used to obtain different results. Such fundamental differences as arranging the balance sheet with assets on the right or on the left; or changing the format to $A - L = E$, instead of $A = L + E$, is easy to understand. But there are other variations more subtle and more deeply involved with the philosophies of the society.

Hidden reserves. The use of hidden reserves to defer reporting of high profits might be considered a universal practice. But the practice is more common in some countries than in others, and in some it is actually encouraged by the government. The result is that the pattern of profits is stable because reserves hidden in good years are disclosed in poor years, showing a level of reported profit over the long range. Preferential tax treatment is accorded such reserves to encourage their use. Although this might be an admirable procedure in stabilizing the economy and bolstering morale, it cannot be accepted as sound accounting for consolidation purposes in the United States.

Similar practices but without government sanction are found in many other countries. Here the actual amount of the reserves is more difficult to discern.

Generally such reserves arise from inventory valuation. Most countries prescribe maximum limits for inventory values, but few establish minimums. Under Swedish law the inventory could actually be a negative figure. Another common practice is to greatly vary the amount of depreciation taken, thus correcting for profit variations from year to year. Pension fund and retirement provisions are also adjusted in the same manner.

Revaluation of assets. In those countries where excessive inflation is common, we often find legal provisions for revaluing assets in order to have the books more accurately reflect the true status of the business. Such revaluations may be voluntary or mandatory, and the increase in equity which results may be taxable or not. The allowable increase seldom reflects the total inflationary effect.

Of course, in the United States we have had inflation while rigidly adhering to the historical basis of asset valuation. The change, however, has been small from year to year.

Generally, the effect of revaluation is carried in a reserve account, but it might be buried in capital, where it is difficult to distinguish it. In some countries it is customary to value assets on the basis of an appraisal of replacement value. This might be commendable except where the appraisers are officers of the company.

Language differences. Special emphasis must be placed on the language differences to be found in accounting terminology. For example, the word "stock" means inventory in Britain and ownership shares in America. It can be realized that although Spanish is the common language of Latin America, each country has its own idioms in accounting terminology. Inept translation can make matters worse.

It must be remembered that technical accounting terminology is new to many of the languages of developing countries. Old terms are adapted to new usages and only one familiar with subtle language nuances should be trusted to translate a report.

Retained earnings. The reports of many countries contain no account equivalent to "Retained Earnings." All profits are either assigned to specific reserves or distributed as dividends unless they are appropriated.

Inventory valuation. Most countries do not permit LIFO inventory valuation. However, actual inventory values are so loosely controlled as to give great latitude. The stipulation generally found is that the value should not exceed the lower of cost or market. This sets a ceiling but no floor. In addition, actual methods used in inventory valuation are seldom disclosed in financial reports.

Rubrication. The practice of having books of account bound and of having each page signed (rubricated) by a local official is common in countries dominated by the civil code. This includes Italy, Spain, France, and Latin America. The charge for this service constitutes a form of tax. Any audit purpose of this practice has long since been lost.

Legal reserves. Many countries require that a legal reserve of 5 percent of net profits be set aside each year until this reserve aggregates 20 percent of invested capital. Such reserve can be applied against losses but must be reinstated in the same manner out of subsequent profits. The percentages may differ from the above example.

Consolidations. Many countries do not permit consolidated reports. This leads to possible distortions where the parent company may bury losses in subsidiaries which do not report.

Germany recently revised its commercial code to require consolidated reports and it is expected that many other countries shortly will follow suit.

Uniform chart of accounts. France has adopted a uniform chart of accounts which is functioning successfully. This concept was first advocated in Germany, but that country did not pursue the matter after the overthrow of the Nazi regime. Such uniform systems of accounts are used in communist countries to control economic activities. Although government-required uniformity is not acceptable in most free countries, it does aid where national government planning is in force.

Accounting Education. It is important to recognize the educational qualifications of an accountant in order to judge the reliability of the reports he produces. Throughout most of the world the British apprenticeship system of education is most common. This condition exists not only because the British Empire exerted a strong influence in developing business practices around the world, but also because this system does not require establishment of college curricula to teach accounting. It also is popular because in many countries the accounting profession has not reached the stature it has attained in the United States.

Under the United Kingdom system, the responsibility for accounting rests with the Institute of Chartered Accountants. The aspiring youth becomes an "articled" or apprenticed clerk for a number of years, taking an approved correspondence course while gaining experience. His entire background is technical with little or no liberal arts education. What has been called the "common body of knowledge" involving broad concepts is completely ignored. This education is augmented by several examinations as the student advances until he has completed his clerkship and passed his final examination.

The new trend in the United Kingdom is toward a broader cultural background for accountants, and more emphasis is being placed on acquiring a university degree.

This system is adopted in varying forms by most countries of the world which have established an accounting profession. Many of the smaller countries even use the British test material and subscribe to the Institute's correspondence course.

In some less advanced countries, especially in Latin America, the universities do offer courses in accounting, and the mere acquiring of a degree at such a university with courses in accounting entitles one to become a member of the national accounting organization. These organizations are not recognized by the government and the accounting title has no official significance.

Only in the United States, the Netherlands, Germany, and Sweden are a college degree plus a state-controlled examination required. In the United Kingdom and many other countries, a college degree serves to reduce the time of clerkship.

Translation of Local Currencies. In a group of related corporations functioning in more than one country, it generally becomes necessary to express the consolidated statements in a specific language using one currency. It would be impossible to evaluate a report containing U.S. dollars, British pounds, and French francs in the same statements. But the translation of monetary information is generally much more complex than the translation of languages. For, where the meanings of words change very slowly through usage, the relative values of money often change rapidly because of different rates of inflation and governmental revaluation of currency.

For example, if the U.S. parent's investment in a British subsidiary was $2,800,000 at cost before revaluation, it represented £1,000,000 on the books of the British subsidiary. If historical cost was the basis for expressing value, then a report after revaluation would be distorted. For the £1,000,000 now represents only $2,400,000, so a consolidated statement must show either a decrease of $400,000 in the investment of the U.S. parent, an increase of

£166,667 on the subsidiary's books, or some reconcilable figure between the two.

The reconciliation of contra accounts is not the only problem involved. In a country, such as Brazil, where inflation is a way of life, the value of inventories changes from the time the merchandise is purchased until it is sold. It is necessary to divide balance sheet accounts into those affected by inflation and those not affected. Generally, so-called financial assets, including cash and current receivables and payables, should be converted at the current rate of exchange, not at any rate at which the cash or receivable was acquired or the debt incurred, The current exchange rate is the best estimate of the true value of these items.

But a different problem arises concerning physical assets. It can be assumed that inventory items are acquired at different times when exchange rates differ. If the monetary value of the merchandise increases with inflation, then there is neither gain nor loss, and the asset value is properly translated at the exchange rate existing when it is acquired. Suppose when the local currency is LC 4.00 = $1.00, machinery costing $500,000 is purchased. On the subsidiary records this would be valued at LC 2,000,000. Now, assume that the exchange rate changes to LC 6.00 = $1.00, showing a 50 percent inflation. It would be improper to translate the LC 2,000,000 at the new rate, giving a dollar value of $333,333 to the machine. The machine is still worth $500,000 (ignoring depreciation), so that the rate at time of acquisition should be used.

The problem of revaluing fixed liabilities is more complex. The AICPA has advocated that the rate at the time the debt was incurred should be used, based on the premise that this liability was assumed to acquire fixed assets which are similarly treated. But the liability will be paid in the future and, assuming continuing inflation, the best basis would be the present exchange rate, since it is impossible to guess what the rate will be when the debt matures.

Capital stock and accumulated earnings are generally translated at the rate existing when the stock was acquired or the earnings recorded.

It can be readily understood that a statement which had been in balance in the original records will no longer have this relationship when different rates are used to translate various accounts. If we go one step further and translate the income statement at some appropriate average rate for the period, with the exception of inventory and depreciation accounts, it can readily be understood that an "exchange" profit or loss for the period will be created to bring the accounts into balance. There are several different points of view on how these foreign exchange translation gains and losses should be handled.

For tax purposes, realized gains or losses must be separated from unrealized gains or losses. Basically, realized gains or losses occur when a conversion of currency is made to liquidate a liability payable at an exchange rate which is different from that prevailing when the debt was incurred. Unrealized exchange gains or losses are those arising from translation of accounts. How these gains and losses should be reported is a subject of much controversy.

If a foreign corporation wishes to translate its financial statement in its entirety to another currency, no such problems as described above will exist. Since there is no matching of currencies or intercompany accounts, it is only necessary to establish the rate of exchange and apply it to all amounts, retaining the element of balance in the report. Some foreign corporations merely translate the wording, leaving the figures of the report in their original currency.

Several excellent discussions on foreign exchange translation techniques have been written. Among them are:

Gerhard G. Mueller, *International Accounting,* New York, The Macmillan Company, 1967, pp. 167–204.

Samuel R. Hepworth, *Reporting Foreign Operations,* Ann Arbor, Mich., University of Michigan, 1956, pp. 1–101.

Finney and Miller, *Principles of Accounting, Advanced,* 5th ed., Englewood Cliffs, N.J., Prentice-Hall, Inc., 1960, pp. 498–522.

Management Accounting Problems in Foreign Operations, N.A.A. Research Report 36, New York, National Association of Accountants, 1960, pp. 13–60.

Sidney Davidson, *Handbook of Modern Accounting,* New York, McGraw-Hill Book Company, 1970.

BIBLIOGRAPHY

Department of Commerce: pamphlets on establishing a business, foreign trade regulations, selling to and other aspects of nearly every country in the world.

Department of the Treasury: tax guides. Available from U.S. Government Printing Office, Washington.

National Association of Accountants: *Management Accounting Problems in Foreign Operations,* New York, 1960.

Professional Accounting in 25 Countries, AICPA (Committee on International Relations), New York, 1964.

United Nations (Department of Economic and Social Affairs): *National Accounting Problems in Foreign Operations,* New York, 1960.

Hepworth, Samuel R.: *Reporting Foreign Operations,* Ann Arbor, Mich., University of Michigan, 1956.

Bureau of National Affairs, Inc., Foreign Income Portfolio series of pamphlets, Washington.

Business International Corporation: *Accounting Practices in Fluctuating-currency Countries,* Management Monograph no. 4, New York, 1963.

Center for International Education and Research in Accounting: The International Journal of Accounting, University of Illinois, Urbana, Ill.

Columbia University Graduate School of Business: *Columbia Journal of World Business,* New York.

Dunn & Bradstreet Publications Corp.: *Business Abroad,* New York.

Harvard University Law School: *World Tax Series,* Chicago, Commerce Clearing House, Inc.

International Bureau of Fiscal Documentation: European taxation supplementary service, Amsterdam, Mees & Hope, Bankers.

Martindale-Hubbell, Inc.: law directory, *Foreign Digest,* Summit, N.J.

National Industrial Conference Board, Inc.: *Studies in Business Policy,* New York.

Part Three

Objectives and Audit Procedures

Chapter 20

Cash

EDWARD DARCEY

Partner, Haskins & Sells

GENERAL

Scope of Chapter. This chapter deals with the audit of cash, that is, with the examination of cash receipts and disbursements (cash transactions) and of cash on hand and on deposit (cash balances). It is concerned mainly with the auditing procedures for testing the accuracy and validity of the cash transactions and the resulting cash balances, and, except to the extent necessary to accomplish that purpose, it is not concerned with the effect of the cash transactions on other accounts.

The discussion in this chapter is written in terms of a commercial organization whose principal revenues are from sales, but it is also generally applicable to other organizations, including those not organized for profit.

Auditor's Objectives. The auditor's objectives will vary to some extent depending upon his role and the purpose of his examination. This variation may affect the matters and the magnitude of the amounts with which he is concerned, and may affect the nature of his auditing procedures and the extent and timing of their application.

The objective of the independent auditor in auditing cash transactions and cash balances as a part of an examination of financial statements is to obtain a reasonable degree of assurance as to the accuracy and validity of the cash transactions and as to the cash balances that will be consistent with the overall objective of his examination, which is the expression of his opinion on the financial statements. Unless the engagement involves some special purpose, he should be interested no more and no less in cash transactions and balances than in any other transactions or balances reflected in the financial statements. The degree of assurance that the independent auditor obtains in an engagement for some special purpose will be consistent with the objective agreed upon with his client, that is, with the terms of his engagement.

The objective of the internal auditor in auditing cash transactions and cash balances is to obtain a degree of assurance as to the accuracy and validity of the cash transactions and balances that will be consistent with his role as an important part of the managerial controls of an organization.

The objective of the governmental auditor may be much like that of the independent auditor in the case of a separate auditing agency of a governmental body, or much like that of the internal auditor in the case of an auditing branch of a governmental agency. In either case the governmental auditor's objectives will be to obtain a degree of assurance consistent with his role, whether as an independent agency or as a managerial branch of an agency.

Auditing Standards. Auditing standards provide the general guidelines by which the auditor accomplishes his objectives. For the independent auditor, these are set forth in a set of standards formally adopted by the American Institute of Certified Public Accountants and included, among other pronouncements, in Statements on Auditing Procedure No. 33 entitled *Auditing Standards and Procedures.* The standards that are most directly involved in determining the nature, extent, and timing of auditing procedures for particular classes of transactions or account balances are the second and third standards of fieldwork, which are quoted below:

> 2. There is to be a proper study and evaluation of the existing internal control as a basis for reliance thereon and for the determination of the resultant extent of the tests to which auditing procedures are to be restricted.
>
> 3. Sufficient competent evidential matter is to be obtained through inspection, observation, inquiries and confirmations to afford a reasonable basis for an opinion regarding the financial statements under examination.

The foregoing standards for independent auditors, of course, are not directly applicable to internal or governmental auditors but are likely to influence their work indirectly because of its interrelationship with the work of independent auditors. The following definitions and additional excerpts from Chapter 5 of Statements No. 33 are relevant in considering the respective purposes and roles of independent and internal auditors with respect to internal control.

5. In the broad sense, internal control includes, therefore, controls which may be characterized as either accounting or administrative, as follows:

a. Accounting controls comprise the plan of organization and all methods and procedures that are concerned mainly with, and relate directly to, safeguarding of assets and the reliability of the financial records. They generally include such controls as the systems of authorization and approval, separation of duties concerned with record keeping and accounting reports from those concerned with operations or asset custody, physical controls over assets, and internal auditing.

b. Administrative controls comprise the plan of organization and all methods and procedures that are concerned mainly with operational efficiency and adherence to managerial policies and usually relate only indirectly to the financial records. They generally include such controls as statistical analyses, time and motion studies, performance reports, employee training programs, and quality controls. [Italics added.]

. . .

16. Management has the responsibility for devising, installing and supervising an adequate system of internal control. . . . An internal audit staff is a strong factor in a system of internal control, since it provides a means of surveying the effectiveness of and adherence to the prescribed procedures.

. . .

18. A function of internal control, from the viewpoint of the independent auditor, is to provide assurance that errors and irregularities may be discovered with reasonable promptness, thus assuring the reliability and integrity of the financial records.

. . .

21. The independent auditor is primarily concerned with the accounting controls. . . . If the independent auditor believes, however, that certain administrative controls may have an important bearing on the reliability of the financial records, he should consider the need for evaluating such controls.

The foregoing reference to errors and irregularities should also be considered by independent auditors in the context of the following excerpt from Chapter 1 of Statements No. 33:

5. In making the ordinary examination, the independent auditor is aware of the possibility that fraud may exist. Financial statements may be misstated as a result of defalcations and similar irregularities, or deliberate misrepresentation by management, or both. The auditor recognizes that fraud, if sufficiently material, may affect his opinion on the financial statements, and his examination, made in accordance with generally accepted auditing standards, gives consideration to this possibility. However, the ordinary examination directed to the expression of an opinion on financial statements is not primarily or specifically designed, and cannot be relied upon, to disclose defalcations and other similar irregularities, although their discovery may result. Similarly, although the discovery of deliberate misrepresentation by management is usually more closely associated with the objective of the ordinary examination, such examination cannot be relied upon to assure its discovery. The responsibility of the independent auditor for failure to detect fraud (which responsibility differs as to clients and others) arises only when such failure clearly results from failure to comply with generally accepted auditing standards.

The roles assigned to internal auditors and governmental auditors in their own organizations will determine their responsibilities for detection of errors and irregularities.

The independent auditor's evaluation of internal control should, of course, be related to the primary objective of his examination, which is the expression of his opinion on the financial statements. A secondary but nevertheless important objective is also recognized in Chapter 5 of Statements No. 33 as follows:

> 23. As a by-product of this study and evaluation, the independent auditor is frequently able to offer constructive suggestions to his client on ways in which internal control may be improved.

The distinction between accounting and administrative controls will vary from organization to organization and even between segments of the same organization. This distinction is more important to the independent auditor, who is primarily concerned with the accounting controls, than to the internal auditor and the governmental auditor, who as part of the managerial system are more directly concerned with the efficacy of all the managerial controls, whether accounting or administrative.

Since the primary purpose of the independent auditor's study and evaluation of internal control, as previously quoted from the second standard of fieldwork, is to provide a basis "for the determination of the resultant extent of the tests to which auditing procedures are to be restricted," it is clear that its ultimate purpose is to contribute to the "reasonable basis for an opinion" comprehended in the third standard.

In this context, the second standard does not seem to contemplate that the auditor should place complete reliance on study and evaluation of internal control to the exclusion of other auditing procedures. The connotation of "restricted" in the second standard does not seem to imply "eliminated," and the third standard includes no language suggesting complete reliance on internal control. This view is supported further by the comment in Chapter 5 of Statements No. 33 that "The work of an internal auditor [which is an element of internal control] should be considered by the independent auditor as a supplement to, not as a substitute for, the work of the independent auditor." Finally, the most fundamental reason underlying this view is the recognition that there are certain inherent limitations on the effectiveness of internal control that should be recognized in making evaluations and determining the extent of audit reliance thereon. In the performance of most internal control procedures, there are possibilities for unintentional errors arising from such causes as misunderstanding of instructions, mistakes of judgment, and personal carelessness, distraction, or fatigue. Furthermore, internal control procedures designed to assure the processing of and accountability for transactions in accordance with management's authorizations may be ineffective against intentional errors or irregularities perpetrated by management.

For the foregoing reasons, it appears that there should be a certain minimum level of testing transactions and balances, even when good internal control apparently exists. This minimum level of testing should be less than that appropriate in the absence of internal control. The particular levels of tests for good and bad internal control situations must be determined by each auditor on the basis of his judgment in the circumstances. Statistical sampling provides a useful means for expressing this judgment in quantitative terms and for designing, selecting, and evaluating audit samples on this basis.

Errors and Irregularities. The fairness of presentation of financial statements depends on several factors, including the application of generally accepted accounting principles, the exercise of appropriate judgment in making necessary estimates in areas involving uncertainties, and the adequacy of disclosure of significant matters, in addition to the basic accuracy and validity of transactions and balances. Insofar as cash is concerned, however, questions concerning principles, judgment, or disclosure usually are less significant than with respect to other important items in the financial statements. Consequently, the audit of cash ordinarily is concerned primarily with the accuracy and validity of cash transactions and balances. Since accuracy and validity describe the condition that results from the absence of errors or irregularities, it may also be said that the audit of cash ordinarily is concerned primarily with possible errors and irregularities. Therefore, a classification of the possible types of errors and irregularities involving cash should be useful in considering the related possibilities for internal control and auditing procedures.

As used in this chapter, errors are regarded as being unintentional and irregularities as intentional. Since it is more difficult to prevent or detect irregularities than errors, consideration of internal control and auditing procedures in relation to possibilities for irregularities also encompasses the possibilities for errors. Therefore the remainder of this section is applicable both to errors and to irregularities, although it is presented primarily in terms of the latter.

The possible irregularities involving cash transactions and balances may be classified, in terms of the type of perpetration, as follows:

A. Defalcations:
  1. Interception—taking cash receipts before accountability for the cash has been recorded (for example, unrecorded cash sales or collections on receivables)
  2. Abstractions—taking cash after the accountability has been recorded (for example, taking cash from recorded but undeposited receipts, imprest funds, or bank accounts)
  3. Diversions—causing an otherwise legitimate disbursement to be diverted from its proper destination

B. Distortions—misstating the financial statements without taking any assets

Irregularities in cash transactions and balances may also be classified in terms of the possibilities for concealment and the resulting condition of related records, as follows:

A. Unconcealed or open—the cash counts or reconcilements are less than the recorded accountability.

B. Concealed:
  1. Temporarily—the cash counts or reconcilements are overstated to cause spurious agreement with the recorded accountability.
  2. Permanently—the accountability has not been recorded or has been reduced after being recorded.

"Temporary" and "permanent" concealment as used in this chapter do not refer to the likelihood or timing of possible detection, but to the frequency of the action required to attempt the concealment. In this sense, permanent concealment requires action only once, while temporary concealment requires repetition each time that reconcilement of bank accounts or other forms of agreement of recorded accountability with actual assets is undertaken.

The foregoing classifications of possibilities for perpetration and concealment may be combined in a useful way to focus attention on the purposes of internal control and auditing procedures for cash transactions and balances and to show their interrelation with other accounts. This is done in the next few paragraphs.

Interceptions result in permanent concealment insofar as cash transactions and balances are concerned, since the accountability for the cash received is not recorded. If the unrecorded cash is received as a payment for some other asset for which the accountability has previously been recorded, the interception results in a shortage in the other asset account, and this in turn may be either open or concealed, as previously indicated. A common example of this situation is the interception and subsequent "lapping" of collections on receivables. If the unrecorded cash is received for sales or other income for which no accountability has been recorded, the permanent concealment is in the form of understatement of such income accounts.

Abstractions involve improper disposition of cash for which the accountability has been recorded. The disposition of the cash may be either recorded or unrecorded. If it is unrecorded, a shortage will be created, which may be either unconcealed or temporarily concealed by overstatement of cash counts or bank reconcilements. If the disposition of the cash is recorded, the related accountability will be reduced and permanent concealment effected. The recording may be accomplished either directly, through an entry purporting to be a proper disbursement, or indirectly, through reducing accountability for cash by falsifying related records, totals, postings, or balances.

Diversions result in permanent concealment insofar as cash accountability is concerned, since the disbursement is recorded. However, they result in an understatement of liabilities which may be either open or temporarily concealed, depending on the procedures followed in recording and reconciling accounts payable.

Distortions could relate either to the time of recording legitimate entries or to improper entries. Examples of the former would include the practice of "window dressing" accomplished by "holding the books open" beyond the end of a reporting period in order to improve either the working capital ratio or the relationship between cash and receivables or payables. In this event, the distortion would either be open or would result in a form of temporary concealment, since the actual cash at the end of the period would differ from the purported accountability. Distortion attempted by improper entries increasing or decreasing cash would create a discrepancy that might be either unconcealed or temporarily concealed.

From the foregoing analysis it is evident that internal control and auditing procedures relating to cash transactions are concerned with possibilities for permanent concealment of errors and irregularities, and that those relating to cash balances are concerned with temporary concealment and open shortages. Similarly, internal control relating to transactions is concerned with establishing and maintaining records of the accountability for cash, while that relating to balances is concerned with determining that the actual cash available satisfies the recorded accountability.

An example of the distinction between errors and irregularities and also between perpetration and concealment of irregularities should be helpful in considering the nature and extent of auditing procedures related to cash transactions. If the auditor were not concerned with intentional irregularities but were interested only in unintentional errors, there would be little, if any, need for the auditor to test the footings of the records of cash transactions.

If a single column in a multicolumn cash record were inadvertently misfooted, the record would not crossfoot and the general ledger would not balance. If this misfooting affected the cash debit or credit column, the accountability for the cash would change without a corresponding change in the actual cash on hand or on deposit. In this event, the cash counts or reconcilements would reveal the unintentional error.

If a cash record were intentionally misfooted, it would be obvious that the purpose was to conceal a defalcation, and the shortage would not be detected by cash counts or bank reconcilements, since these would agree with the reduced accountability. Thus, it is evident that cash counts and bank reconcilements should reveal errors but not irregularities in footings of cash records.

INTERNAL CONTROL

General. The auditor's study of internal control covers three phases: a preliminary survey to determine the prescribed procedures, tests of compliance with those procedures, and evaluation of the system based on his survey and test.

The survey of the internal control over cash balances and cash transactions will focus on the handling and custody of funds (including withdrawals from bank accounts), preparation, footing, and posting of records, and the controls exercised over all of these functions by way of independent observation, check, or test. The data obtained in the auditor's preliminary survey and his initial conclusions should be reduced to writing, in a questionnaire, flow chart, or memorandum. Any change in the auditor's initial conclusions that may result from his audit tests of compliance with the system should also be documented.

The preliminary survey of the internal control should include careful inquiry of appropriate supervisory employees and reference to organization charts, procedures manuals, job specification sheets, and similar sources of information. The survey may include inspection of documents, observation of procedures, and similar steps and thus, to some extent, may result in some audit tests being made during the preliminary survey; this, however, is not always the case, and the audit tests may be made quite apart from the preliminary survey of internal control.

Although compliance with the internal control procedures will be tested by the auditor, the preliminary survey should reflect the auditor's best judgment of the potential effectiveness of the internal control procedures, and, accordingly, the auditor should consider the possible effect of any apparent lack of alertness, competence, independence, or integrity of employees and the possible effect of any changes in procedures or duties, including temporary changes during lunch hours, vacations, periods of illness, and similar circumstances.

In any system of internal control there often exist other collateral procedures or circumstances that may mitigate weaknesses in the system of internal control, such as the use of cash forecasts, budgets, or standards and the independent investigation of deviations from such criteria; and rotation and vacation policies. On the other hand, the lack of collateral controls or the existence of potential conflicts of interest or other unusual circumstances may result in impairment of what otherwise appears to be a well-designed system of internal control.

The financial condition and other aspects of the organization should also be considered. In a prospering, fast-growing organization the management may not see the need for, or have the capability of, expanding its personnel to meet increasing demands on its employees. Conversely, an organization in less sound financial condition may be tempted to false economies by dispensing with or short-cutting essential controls.

While these collateral circumstances are usually difficult to evaluate, application of auditing procedures requires consideration of their possible impact upon the internal control.

As previously indicated, internal controls over cash transactions and balances should be evaluated in terms of their potential to prevent or detect possible errors or irregularities. Since the requirements as to the latter are more stringent, the evaluation should be primarily in terms of segregation of duties to determine whether any one person who has access to cash and therefore can perpetrate an irregularity can also affect the accountability for cash and thereby conceal an irregularity.

Records and Functions. Definitions of the records and certain functions referred to hereinafter are given below to facilitate the reader's understanding of the discussion that follows.

"Initial records" are the first records prepared by the organization or its agents that are used directly or, through intermediate records, as a basis for entry in the general ledger. Such initial records include copies of documents (such as duplicates of checks), tapes (such as cash-register tapes), or other listings. "Final records" are the journal entries or other sources used as general ledger posting media. "Intermediate records" are any records, in detail or summary form, between the initial records and the final records. These definitions apply whether the respective records are prepared manually or by use of mechanical or electronic data processing equipment.

These distinctions are significant for two reasons. First, the internal control objectives and requirements differ somewhat as between the initial and subsequent records. Second, procedures and segregation of duties may afford satisfactory control over some of the records but not over others, and any such differences should be recognized in evaluating the controls and correlating them with the auditing procedures to be applied.

In considering the assignment of functions to individuals, it is necessary to include all persons who are in a position to alter, insert, or suppress data in the process of performing the function being considered. Persons who prepare or post records should include not only those who make entries directly, but also those who do so indirectly by preparing or handling any documents or other media from which the entries are made. Persons who prepare, foot, or post records should include those who program or operate mechanical or electronic data processing equipment for these purposes. Persons who prepare, foot, or post records or who handle cash receipts, signed checks, or documents usually should include only those who do so in the normal course of their duties and their immediate superiors.

In the following sections possibilities for perpetration and concealment of irregularities involving cash receipts, disbursements, and balances and related internal control procedures are discussed. This discussion is intended to focus the reader's attention on the principal possibilities and to indicate the general nature of the analysis that should be applied to the circumstances in particular cases; it is not intended to be all-inclusive or a substitute for such analysis.

Cash Receipts. Cash receipts are susceptible to unintentional errors and to either interception or abstraction, as those terms were previously defined. Obviously, anyone who handles cash receipts is in a position to perpetrate either type of irregularity. This possibility may be reduced in varying degree by the following practices:

Instructing customers to mail all remittances directly to a lock-box under the control of a depository bank.

Instructing depository banks in writing not to cash any checks payable to the organization.

Endorsing immediately all checks received "For Deposit Only" to the credit of the organization.

Depositing receipts of each day intact before receipts of the next day become available.

Aside from the foregoing or other practices designed to deter perpetration, the remaining possibilities for internal control over cash necessarily focus on limiting possibilities for concealment. This, in turn, is concerned basically with establishing and maintaining records of accountability and comparing actual cash available with the recorded accountability at timely intervals.

Since interceptions refer to unrecorded receipts, the obvious objective of internal control against this risk is to assure prompt recording of all receipts. The degree to which it is feasible to achieve this assurance depends on the nature of the receipts and a variety of circumstances, and consequently only a few general concepts and distinctions in this respect are discussed in this chapter.

Where the nature of the receipts is such that recording can be accomplished practicably as an integral step in the transaction, this procedure offers the most direct means of control against interceptions. Examples of this procedure include automatic recording by locked mechanical devices (such as cash registers, turnstiles, meters, etc.) and physically restricting access to copies of receipt forms issued directly to the remitters. The common element of control in these examples is that recording is simultaneous with the receipt of cash and is observable by the remitters.

Where the recording cannot be observed by the remitter, dual participation in opening mail or emptying collection boxes or similar containers that produce no automatic record and in the initial recording of such receipts is a second possible means for control against interception.

The third class of possible controls against interceptions depends on some independent source for determining or estimating the accountability for receipts. Within this class there are a range of variations with respect to timeliness and effectiveness.

An example of this possibility is the determination of the receipts for which route salesmen or ticket agents are accountable by frequent inventories of products or unsold tickets. Another example is the independent preparation and control of sales checks or invoices by retail sales personnel to predetermine amounts to be collected by a cashier. Both of these examples are similar to the possibilities discussed earlier in that the accountability can be established for receipts for particular days or periods.

In contrast, the ultimate accountability for collections of recorded receivables can be established from such records but the daily accountability ordinarily cannot. Consequently, the effectiveness of recorded receivables as an indirect means for establishing accountability for related receipts turns largely on the possibility for concealment of interceptions by the practice of "lapping" or by non-cash credits to customer accounts.

Where "lapping" is practiced, the accounts of customers whose remittances have been intercepted are credited later for recorded receipts from other customers. This results in a form of temporary concealment, since the cumulative amount of such interceptions at any time is represented by improper balances in the accounts of one or more customers. The most apparent requirement for control against lapping of credits for collections of receivables is segregation of the functions of handling cash before initial recording from the posting of credits to receivable accounts.

Improper non-cash credits to customer accounts to effect permanent concealment of interceptions may be recorded either through the cash receipts records as discounts or other deductions taken by customers, or through other records as allowances or write-offs by the organization. In either event the most apparent requirement for control in this respect is to require approval of non-cash credits by persons who do not handle cash receipts before initial recording.

Possibilities for alternative or counter controls over other forms of concealment that relate primarily to records and procedures with respect to receivables, inventories, or other accounts are beyond the scope of this chapter.

Additional illustrations of independent sources that may provide some indication of accountability for receipts include a wide variety of ratios and trends concerning results, such as cash forecasts, sales volume, gross profit ratios, and accounts receivable turnover; rental, royalty, or other contracts; equipment or scrap disposal reports; established interest or dividend rates on investment securities; membership records of clubs or similar organizations; and attendance or registration records for meetings. The internal control requirements and effectiveness with respect to these and similar sources of data vary widely with the circumstances in particular cases, and therefore no further discussion is included in this chapter.

Since abstractions of cash receipts occur after the initial recording of accountability, anyone who handles receipts thereafter is in a position to perpetrate this type of irregularity. The practices mentioned earlier in this section as deterrents to perpetration apply to abstractions as well as to interceptions.

Unless permanent concealment of abstractions is effected by reduction of the recorded accountability, the cash shortage will be either open or temporarily concealed through falsification of cash counts or bank reconcilements. Procedures for control against the latter two possibilities are discussed in the section relating to cash balances.

Reduction of the recorded accountability for cash receipts can be accomplished by falsifying the footing of initial cash receipts records or the preparation, footing, or posting of intermediate or final cash receipts records or the computation of balances of general ledger cash accounts. Further possibilities for improper reduction through journal entries or other records affecting such accounts should be recognized, but these are outside the scope of this chapter. One approach to control against falsification at any stage in the summarization process described above is to assign this function to persons who do not handle cash receipts after the initial recording. Another approach is to require that initial records not susceptible to manipulation be compared in total with daily bank deposits by someone who does not handle recorded receipts. If the initially recorded receipts are deposited intact on a timely basis, it is evident that no abstraction has occurred.

Cash Disbursements. Abstractions through cash disbursements can be perpetrated by anyone who is in a position to issue checks singly or to disburse currency. Since the same internal control considerations apply generally to both forms of disbursements and the latter usually are minor, the discussion in this section is in terms of disbursements by checks.

Persons to be considered as issuing checks singly should include single check signers, dual signers if supporting documents are not examined by both, and others who are in a position to cause checks to be issued without approval by anyone else. The latter should include persons who prepare checks if supporting documents are not examined by at least one check signer, persons who have custody of required signature plates, and persons who operate signing equipment without independent control over the number and details of the checks signed.

Restricting access to the supply of blank checks and using protected paper for them are desirable practices to deter perpetration of abstractions, but the effectiveness of these practices probably should be considered limited.

Improper checks may be either recorded or unrecorded. If such checks are recorded, this accomplishes the necessary reduction in accountability and permanent concealment will result unless the absence or impropriety of supporting documents is detected. Consequently, internal control against this form of abstraction requires either (1) that no one be in a position to issue checks singly or (2) that supporting documents be examined subsequently by someone who does not issue checks singly. The first of these approaches focuses on possibilities for perpetration and the second on those for concealment.

If improper checks are unrecorded and permanent concealment is not attempted, the resulting shortage will be either open or temporarily concealed through falsification of cash counts or bank reconcilements. Control against the latter possibilities is discussed in the next section.

Permanent concealment of unrecorded checks requires reduction of the accountability for cash by some other means. This can be accomplished by falsifying the footing of initial cash disbursements records or the preparation, footing, or posting of other cash disbursements records or the computation of balances of general ledger cash accounts. The reduction of recorded accountability for cash can also be accomplished through falsification of journal entries or other records affecting such accounts, but these possibilities are beyond the scope of this chapter. One approach to control against these possibilities is to assign all of the summarization functions mentioned above to persons who do not issue checks singly. Another is to require comparison of all paid checks returned by banks with the initial cash disbursement records by someone who does not issue checks singly.

Persons who handle signed checks are in a position to divert a legitimate check from its proper destination and convert it to their own use. Such conversion ordinarily would require alteration of the payee or forgery of the payee's endorsement, followed by the diverter's endorsement, but experience indicates that even these requirements do not prevent perpetration of diversions.

Since diversions involve payments intended for legitimate vendors, the immediate result is a form of temporary concealment in that the actual accounts payable exceed those shown by the related records, and complaints from the vendors would be expected in due course. Consequently, permanent concealment of diversions requires that the perpetrator be in a position to cause proper payments to be made to the vendor either concurrently or within a reasonable period. The payments to the vendors could be made by duplicate checks or possibly from funds obtained by the diverter through raising the amount of the diverted check and retaining the excess. In the latter event, the excess constitutes an abstraction. Duplicate checks might be supported either by copies of the documents used to support the diverted checks or by uncanceled documents used to support other checks. The most direct procedure for control against perpetration of diversions is to restrict the handling of signed checks to persons who do not participate in the preparation of vouchers or other documents supporting disbursements. Possible controls against concealment include examination of paid checks for any evidence of alteration or irregular endorsements and examination of supporting documents by persons who have no incompatible duties.

Cash Balances. The objectives of internal control over cash balances are to provide assurance that the actual cash available (1) agrees with the accountability resulting from the recorded transactions and (2) is adequate but not excessive for the needs of the organization. The latter objective is an aspect of administrative control and is discussed later in the chapter.

The cash available will agree, of course, with the recorded accountability if no errors or irregularities have occurred in recording the transactions. The first requirement for determining whether there is such agreement obviously is to require periodic cash counts and bank reconcilements. This procedure alone should be adequate to disclose errors, but not to disclose irregularities. To disclose irregularities it is necessary that the counts and reconcilements be performed (1) by persons who are not in a position to perpetrate abstractions or diversions, as discussed earlier, and (2) in a way that should disclose any attempted temporary concealment.

Temporary concealment of shortages in bank balances may be attempted by (1) falsification of cash counts or bank reconcilements, (2) inclusion of invalid items in cash counts or bank deposits, or (3) substitution of valid items from other funds of the organization.

"Falsification of cash counts or bank reconcilements," as used in this chapter, refers to erroneous listing of items counted, balances shown by the books or bank statements, outstanding checks, or other reconciling items, or erroneous footing of the counts or reconcilements. Performance of the counts and reconcilements by independent persons, as mentioned earlier, is the most direct means of control against this possibility. The remaining two possibilities mentioned above would involve actions by the custodians of the funds being counted or reconciled and therefore should be considered by independent persons in performing these functions.

"Invalid items," as used above, refer to improper checks, vouchers, or other documents included in cash counts under the pretense of being held for subsequent deposit, collection, or reimbursement, and to improper checks that have been deposited but will be rejected by the bank in due course. Procedures to disclose the inclusion of invalid items in cash counts and bank reconcilements include examination of checks, vouchers, or similar documents included in cash counts, obtaining independent approval of questionable items, depositing checks under control of the person making the count, and investigating checks deposited but rejected by banks for a reasonable period following the cash count.

"Substitution of valid items" refers to the use of currency or checks obtained from other funds of the organization to conceal a shortage in the fund being counted or reconciled. The sources from which substitution can be made include undeposited receipts, working funds, and bank accounts. A common example of substitution is the use of receipts of a subsequent day or days to make the bank deposit required by the recorded receipts of a preceding day. Another is the deposit into one bank account of a check or proceeds thereof drawn on another bank account, which is commonly called "kiting." Simultaneous counts of all funds from which substitution would be feasible, considering the custody and location of the respective funds, constitute the principal procedure for control against substitution into cash counts. As to undeposited receipts, this requires that the accountability be recorded for all receipts up to the time of the count. Performing simultaneous reconcilements of all bank accounts is also a means for control against "kiting." However, since "kiting" also requires an unrecorded deposit into the bank account from which the substituted check was drawn, a comparison of actual deposits with recorded receipts since the date of the latest reconcilement of other bank accounts is an alternative procedure for control against substitution.

In addition to the errors and irregularities previously discussed, cash balances are also susceptible to the form of distortion sometimes referred to as "window dressing." As indicated earlier, this practice does not involve defalcations, but is intended to improve the apparent financial position, working capital ratio, or the relationship between cash balances and other accounts such as receivables or payables. It may be accomplished either by "holding the books open" to affect the time of recording the proper entries or by improper entries. Timely cutoff dates and the controls previously discussed for cash counts and bank reconcilements should disclose this form of distortion; however, such distortion is not likely to occur without overt instructions from management to override the prescribed internal control procedures. Consequently, independent audits provide the most effective deterrent to this practice.

AUDITING PROCEDURES

General. The usual auditing procedures for cash transactions and balances are discussed generally in this section. They are not, however, set forth in the degree of detail necessary to constitute a complete cash audit program, since this handbook is intended as a reference for experienced auditors rather than as an elementary textbook.

The foregoing analysis of possibilities for errors and irregularities was intended to make clear the purposes of the auditing procedures discussed in this section, and the related analysis of internal control requirements was intended to provide guidance as to the extent of their application. As indicated earlier, the author believes these procedures should be performed at some minimum level regardless of the internal control, and should be extended where the necessary control procedures are not in effect. If such procedures are in effect for certain functions or records but not for others, this distinction should be recognized in applying the auditing procedures to the respective functions and records.

Cash Receipts. Cash discounts, allowances, or other customer deductions recorded in the cash receipts records should be tested by examining supporting documents for approval or other independent indications of validity.

Cash sales should be tested by selecting from any available independent records (such as sales, delivery, shipping, or timely inventory records) and comparing them with cash receipts records.

Miscellaneous cash receipts (those other than collections on receivables and cash sales) should be tested by selecting from any available independent sources of information and comparing them with cash receipts records or with related accounts.

The preparation of intermediate and final cash receipts records should be tested by tracing cash amounts from the initial records to the final records.

The footings and postings of cash receipts records should be tested.

Cash Disbursements. Entries in initial cash disbursements records should be tested by comparing amounts and other pertinent details with paid checks and by examining such checks for unusual features such as alternate payees, alterations, unauthorized signatures, or questionable endorsements (especially checks not endorsed directly into a bank for deposit).

Entries in initial cash disbursements records should also be tested by examination of supporting documents unless such documents have been or will be examined as a part of the audit of purchases and accounts payable. The examination of supporting documents should be concerned with approvals and with the propriety of payments and of account distributions.

The preparation of intermediate and final cash disbursements records should be tested by tracing cash amounts from the final records to the initial records.

The footings and postings of cash disbursements records should be tested.

Cash Balances. Consideration of auditing procedures for cash balances involves questions as to what funds are to be audited and when, as well as how.

Cash balances frequently include a number of imprest or other working funds and sometimes depository bank accounts with relatively small recorded balances. Both independent and other auditors should consider the materiality of such balances in relation to their respective roles and audit objectives in determining whether and with what frequency they require audit.

For the independent auditor's purposes it is preferable that any material recorded balances of cash on hand and in banks be audited at a date as near to the balance sheet date as is practicable in the circumstances, which in most cases is the balance sheet date. For internal and other auditors, the date of audit of cash balances may be of less significance. In any event, simultaneous examination or equivalent procedures, as explained earlier, should be applied to accounts from which concealment of a material shortage by substitution might be practicable. Similarly, simultaneous examination or equivalent procedures should be applied to the audit of securities, receivables, or other accounts from which funds might practicably be derived for substitution into cash balances.

The remaining paragraphs in this section describe generally the auditing procedures to be applied to the balances selected, assuming simultaneous examination if such is necessary in the circumstances.

Currency, checks, vouchers, etc., comprising imprest and other working funds and undeposited receipts should be counted and listed as necessary for subsequent investigation.

Checks represented to be undeposited receipts should be traced to entries in the initial cash receipts records as of the date and time of the count.

Checks represented to have been cashed should be considered as to their propriety and, if necessary, should be deposited at the bank or approved by a responsible person other than the fund custodian.

Checks drawn on other bank accounts of the organization should be traced to the related cash disbursements records or, in the event of simultaneous examination, to the related list of outstanding checks.

Vouchers for advances or expenses and any other documents included in the cash count should be examined for whatever indications of propriety are considered necessary in the circumstances. If such items are significant in amount, it may be necessary for them to be recorded as disbursements for the period being audited.

Bank reconcilements should be prepared or independently checked by the auditor, and confirmations of balances should be obtained directly from the banks by him. Although not an integral part of the audit of cash balances, bank confirmations usually cover additional matters such as direct and contingent liabilities, collateral held, assets pledged, and other relations with the banks.

Deposits shown by bank statements should be compared with recorded cash receipts for a sufficient period prior to the reconcilement to permit any unrecorded transfer checks on other bank accounts to reach those banks for payment prior to the reconcilement date.

Deposits in transit shown on the reconcilements should be identified with recorded receipts prior to the reconcilement date and traced to credits by the banks within an appropriate period thereafter.

Bank statements and paid checks for a reasonable period after the reconcilement date should be obtained directly from the banks by the auditor. Check numbers and dates and bank endorsement dates on the returned checks should be examined to determine those that were issued prior to the reconcilement date, and such checks should be traced to the list of outstanding checks used in the reconcilement.

Any other reconciling items would be unusual and therefore should be investigated thoroughly.

ADMINISTRATIVE CONTROLS

The preceding sections of this chapter described the accounting control aspects of cash, that is, the internal control considerations and the pertinent auditing procedures. The independent auditor as well as the internal auditor and the governmental auditor are vitally interested in those matters of accounting control.

The independent auditor is not primarily concerned with *administrative controls* since they relate only indirectly to the financial records and do not require evaluation. However, if the independent auditor believes that certain administrative controls "may have an important bearing on the reliability of financial records, he should consider the need for evaluating such controls." This point is fully described in Chapter 5 of Statements on Auditing Procedure No. 33 and discussed in this chapter under "Auditing Standards."

Emphasis on Operations. While the independent auditor is primarily concerned with *accounting* controls and secondarily with *administrative controls,* the reverse is true for the internal auditor and the governmental auditor. They are primarily interested in administrative controls, that is, those controls concerned with operations. Their work is "concerned mainly with operational efficiency and adherence to managerial policies and usually relates only indirectly to the financial records." This was also discussed previously under "Auditing Standards." Since this handbook is intended to be useful to all auditors we will also discuss matters pertaining to administrative controls. As indicated previously, these matters will not be set forth as an audit program. The book is intended as a reference source rather than as an elementary text. Further information may be found in standard internal auditing textbooks.

Internal Auditing Responsibility. The responsibility of the internal auditor and the governmental auditor performing internal audits of administrative controls is described in the Statement of Responsibilities of the Internal Auditor, issued by The Institute of Internal Auditors, as follows:

"Internal auditing is an independent appraisal activity within an organization for the review of accounting, financial and other operations as a basis for service to management. It is a managerial control, which functions by measuring and evaluating the effectiveness of other controls." The statement goes on to specify in what way the internal auditor can assist management.

> The over-all objective of internal auditing is to assist all members of management in the effective discharge of their responsibilities, by furnishing them with objective analyses, appraisals, recommendations and pertinent comments concerning the activities reviewed. The internal auditor therefore should be concerned with any phase of business activity wherein he can be of service to management. The attainment of this over-all objective of service to management should involve such activities as:
>
> —Reviewing and appraising the soundness, adequacy and application of accounting, financial and operating controls.
>
> —Ascertaining the extent of compliance with established policies, plans and procedures.
>
> —Ascertaining the extent to which company assets are accounted for, and safeguarded from losses of all kinds.
>
> —Ascertaining the reliability of accounting and other data developed within the organization.
>
> —Appraising the quality of performance in carrying out assigned responsibilities.

Areas of Administrative Control. In connection with his attest function the independent auditor will be concerned more with the financial aspects of the enterprise. However, when he performs management services he will generally be concerned with the operational aspects, in much the same way as is the internal auditor.

Following are illustrations of administrative controls relating to cash:

Cash forecasting. One of the most important administrative controls for cash is cash forecasting of receipts and disbursements. By careful cash planning many companies have kept cash needs constant while sales volume has increased many times. The auditor can review the underlying data and the estimates of shortages or excesses. He may suggest a change in timing of receipts and disbursements to reduce cash requirements.

Evaluating risks. While in general it is desirable to maintain tight controls, sometimes the control is too costly for the risk. Instead of having continuous control it may be better to reasonably increase the audit work. In a small office it may be difficult to have the best separation of duties and additional audit work is needed. However, certain important functions, such as signing checks and reconciling bank accounts can usually be segregated.

Procedural efficiency. The auditor during his review of cash should consider the efficiency of the procedures. Often cash procedures can be streamlined and cost reduced but still be effective for the risks involved. For example, increased efficiency in processing remittance checks will help in speeding deposits in the bank. The auditor may investigate the need for verification of invoices of small amount. The cost often exceeds the possible saving. To maintain tight control companies with numerous locations may have all payments made at the head office, even invoices of small amount. The extra processing and mailing may be costly. The auditor may review the operation and suggest a minimum dollar value for invoices that are sent to the head office. It has been shown that with such a minimum the number of payments can be reduced as much as 33% and the head office can still control 98% of the dollar value of payments.

Flow-charting. A useful analytical technique that is being used more frequently by auditors is flow-charting. It is especially helpful in reviewing the internal controls in effect for cash receipts and cash disbursements. It is helpful in depicting the company relationships in the form of an organization chart. It is also a basic technique in computer auditing.

Utilizing cash funds. The auditor should be aware of cash funds that are not being utilized. For example, in a company with a number of locations there may be a substantial amount of excess funds at various locations. The auditor may compute average disbursements and determine the number of weeks' supply of cash in the particular fund, which often far exceeds the need. He may weigh the cost of keeping a balance equivalent to the net amount of payroll in the payroll bank account against the cost of cabling funds the same day payment is made. Some special restrictive funds such as escrow funds may not be earning interest. The auditor should review pertinent documents to make sure the full amount being held is presently required. Perhaps changes have occurred that may warrant a reduction in the fund.

Accelerating cash inflow. Accelerating cash inflow is equivalent to increasing the total amount of cash. The auditor should therefore be aware of the means by which the cash inflow can be accelerated. For example, if a lock-box is used for remittances the cash "float" can be greatly reduced, especially where a lock-box may be available on the West Coast while the head office may be on the East Coast. Another way to accelerate cash flow is to require prompt billing to customers. As part of his procedure the auditor may determine that all billings are made the next working day after shipment. Means of reducing inventory levels and receivable levels also accelerate cash inflow.

Decelerating cash outflow. The amount of cash available can be maximized by decelerating cash outflow. Payments to vendors may be set at the last day of the discount period. The auditor may determine the company's period of peak receipts and suggest that vendors set payment dates to coincide with the peak period of receipts.

Distributing cash funds. The auditor may suggest a change in the distribution of bank accounts after reviewing various service charges. For example, if a payroll account is maintained in one bank and the revolving fund in another there may be a service charge for the payroll account with no interest on the revolving fund balance. If both accounts are maintained in the same bank there may be an offset and no bank services charge made.

BIBLIOGRAPHY

Accounting Principles Board, Opinion No. 3, *The Statement of Source and Application of Funds*, New York, AICPA, 1963.

Accounting Research and Terminology Bulletins, final edition, New York, AICPA, 1961.

American Institute of Certified Public Accountants: *Embezzlement—Its Prevention and Control*, New York, AICPA, 1968.

Cash Management in Retail Businesses, National Retail Merchants Association, New York, Controllers Congress, 1968.

Research Study No. 38, *Cash Flow Analysis for Managerial Control*, New York, National Association of Accountants, 1961.

Cardwell, Harvey: *The Principles of Audit Surveillance*, Princeton, N.J., D. Van Nostrand Company, Inc., 1960.

Cashin, James A., and Garland C. Owens: *Auditing*, 2d ed., New York, The Ronald Press Company, 1963.

Helfert, Erich A.: *Techniques of Financial Analysis*, rev. ed., Homewood, Ill., Richard D. Irwin, 1967.

Wright, Maurice Gordon: *Discounted Cash Flow*, New York, McGraw-Hill Book Company, 1967.

Fess, Philip E., and Jerry Weygandt: "The Funds Statement: Trends and Recommendations," *The New York Certified Public Accountant*, February, 1967.

Radler, Irving: "Embezzlements and the Independent Auditor," *The New York Certified Public Accountant*, April, 1969.

Jones, Reginald H.: "Face to Face With Cash Management: How One Company Does It," *Financial Executive*, September, 1969.

Barton, L. Marvin: "Discounted Net Cash Flow—Measure of Economic Worth and Aid to Decision-making," *The GAO Review*, Fall, 1969.

Chapter 21

Receivables

CORNELL G. WRIGHT

Partner, Ernst & Ernst

DAVID M. SCHOEN

Senior Accountant, Ernst & Ernst

NATURE OF RECEIVABLES

Broadly defined, the term "receivables" refers to all claims against others collectible in money, goods (i.e., deposits on purchases), and services (i.e., prepaid expenses such as insurance). "Receivables" are, however, more commonly defined as only those claims collectible in money. Accounts receivable, particularly trade accounts receivable and notes receivable, are the most common types of receivables.

Importance of Receivables. Receivables generally represent one of a company's most important assets. Trade accounts receivable due from customers for goods sold or for services provided are the most significant receivables. It is not unusual for trade accounts receivable to represent from 35 to 50 percent of a company's current assets. Of all assets, only cash has greater liquidity than accounts receivable. It is thus not surprising that independent accountants must devote a considerable portion of their audit to receivables. To the auditor, both internal and independent, receivables represent a constant challenge, not only because of their significance and liquidity, but also because of the continual change in their underlying composition.

The major portion of this chapter is devoted to a discussion of audit objectives, internal control, and auditing procedures applicable to accounts receivable. Most of such material is also applicable to notes receivable. Aspects of audit objectives, internal control, and auditing procedures specifically applicable to notes receivable are presented separately.

Overall Audit Responsibilities. In the area of receivables, as in many other audit areas, there are overlapping responsibilities between the work of the internal auditor and that of the independent auditor. The independent auditor, however, always retains the overall responsibility for satisfying himself as to the reliability of the client's records, the fairness of the amounts set forth as assets on the balance sheet, and the adequacy of the reserves for doubtful accounts. The extent to which he may make use of and rely upon procedures performed by the internal auditor depends upon the characteristics of the particular situation.

The internal auditor has two major concerns in his examination of receivables. His first concern is with verification of the receivables. Here he has the same objectives as the independent auditor:

1. To establish accuracy of amounts
2. To establish their validity as claims
3. To establish collectibility and determine realizable value
4. To determine the fairness of financial statement presentation

These objectives are developed more fully in the section on objectives of the examination. To fulfill these objectives the internal auditor performs procedures similar to those used by the independent auditor, generally in greater detail than the independent auditor.

The second major concern of the internal auditor is with the receivable processes and procedures (see *Internal Auditing*, by Brink and Cashin):

1. Procedures resulting in a receivable which is a valid claim
2. Procedures for handling the receivable within the bookkeeping framework
3. Procedures for disposition of the receivable through payment, adjustment, or write-off

In studying these procedures the internal auditor desires to know if company rules and policies are being followed, if general company interests are being furthered, and if the accounting procedures being used are of maximum efficiency. The independent auditor should have similar objectives in order to offer practical suggestions to management; however, those objectives must be secondary to the asset verification function. See the section on operational auditing below.

Coordination of internal and independent auditors. Both the internal auditor and the independent auditor will, as discussed in *Internal Auditing*, by Brink and Cashin, find it beneficial to coordinate their interim audit work in the receivables area. The confirmation of receivables requires a considerable amount of work, especially in the case of companies which have subsidiaries that keep their own receivables records. Much duplication and wasted time can be eliminated by having the internal auditor confirm the accounts receivable for one group of subsidiaries while the independent auditor confirms the accounts receivable for a different group. The procedure is usually done on a rotating basis and results obtained are shared by both sets of auditors. The independent auditor generally determines the extent and basis of the confirmations to be sent out and the internal auditor has the confirmations prepared.

Coordination also extends to the year-end audit work. Generally the independent auditor has the client prepare various year-end schedules and analyses, such as a trial balance of the accounts receivable and an aging schedule. Frequently such client-prepared schedules are not properly prepared and much time is wasted in correcting the errors. The internal auditor can be of assistance here by setting up procedures to insure that these schedules are properly prepared.

Description. Broadly defined, accounts receivable represent all money claims against debtors on open account—those claims not supported by a signed promise to pay. Frequently the use of the term "accounts receivable" is limited to trade accounts receivable—amounts owed by customers as the result of sales of goods or services in the ordinary course of business. The broad definition is used here. Various industries have their own terminology for trade accounts receivable. "Revenues Receivable" is used by municipalities, "Rentals Receivable" by real estate agencies, and "Subscriptions Receivable" by publishers. Trade accounts receivable represent, by far, the largest single portion of accounts receivable.

Objectives of Examination. The auditor is concerned with four principal objectives, as follows:

1. To establish the substantial accuracy of the balance sheet amount relative to supporting accounting records.
2. To establish the validity of the accounts receivable as claims against the recorded debtors. The auditor must satisfy himself that the receivables are bona fide obligations of existing businesses or individuals, as the case may be. This is accomplished basically through correspondence with the debtors—confirming or circularizing the accounts.
3. To establish the collectibility and determine the realizable value of the receivables. This objective involves determining the adequacy of the provision for doubtful accounts.
4. To determine that the receivable balances are properly shown on the financial statements. The presentation must be consistent with the first three objectives.

The following sections deal with the analysis of internal control and the auditing procedures performed by the auditor in order to attain the above objectives.

Systems for Control. Frank H. Moeller, Jr. (in "Accounts Receivable Records" in *Handbook of Successful Operating Systems and Procedures with Forms*) discusses four types of systems used to carry out the function of recording and controlling the amounts due from customers: manual systems, bookkeeping machine systems, punched-card systems, and computer systems.

There are two basic types of manual systems: the ledger card system and the open-invoice file system; their concepts are also applicable to automated systems.

The ledger card system is the most commonly used manual system and involves the maintenance of a ledger card for each customer, usually with a running balance resulting from sales debits and payment credits. Posting sources are indicated in a reference column. At the end of each accounting period a trial balance is taken of the individual accounts to prove against the general ledger control account.

Under the open-invoice file system, accounts receivable are represented by a file of copies of all unpaid invoices, generally grouped by customer, sometimes by date of sale or due date. At the end of a period the unpaid-invoice amounts in the file are totaled to agree with the general ledger balance.

Although the use of an open invoice file system can reduce clerical costs, it should not be used unless adequate physical control can be established over the file. Access to the file should be limited to as few individuals as possible. Credit personnel, salesmen, and other individuals requiring information from invoices should obtain it from invoice copies other than those in the open invoice file. Strict control is also required over invoices added to the file and over those removed because of payment and adjustment.[1]

Accounting control of the file is obtained by using a form that provides a record of daily changes in the file. Control is provided through the fact that records of daily changes must agree with the entries made in the books of account. Partial payments present a major problem when using an open invoice system.

The clerical work involved in recording and controlling accounts receivable transactions is reduced considerably through the use of bookkeeping machines. Accounting control is maintained in a way similar to that for manual systems.

Punched-card systems, as compared with bookkeeping machine systems, provide greater accuracy in recording transactions and greater processing speed. Customer debit cards and customer credit cards are created at the same time that invoices are prepared and cash receipts recorded, respectively.

There are two punched-card methods that can be used: the "tub file" method, which is similar to the open-invoice file and which requires cards for charges and adjustments, and the "all card" method, which requires cards for both remittances and adjustments. "The all card method allows for better physical control over the accounts receivable records. Under an all card method, access to the records is limited to personnel familiar with punched cards. The tub file method has the disadvantage of exposing 'live' current balance cards to all personnel interested in accounts receivable information and extreme care must be taken that no cards are removed by unauthorized personnel."[2]

A computer system provides the greatest accuracy because many operations required in other systems are eliminated. In a typical system information is transcribed from the source documents for sales, merchandise returns, cash discounts, and cash receipts to punch cards, which are sorted by customer identification number. The information is then machine-posted to the customers' accounts, which are usually stored on magnetic tape. Reports are periodically produced, summarizing the information on the tape. Data entering the system can be automatically checked by the computer to determine if it is prepared correctly and if it compares with data already in the system. A computer can automatically make decisions concerning the application of receipts and adjustments—a procedure which in other systems requires the decision of a clerk. A properly programmed computer can also provide an aging analysis and can indicate the status of accounts with regard to past-due amounts.

Accounting control of computer input data may be maintained by preparing adding-machine tapes of invoices, collections, journal charges, and journal credits and reconciling the totals with the totals maintained in the data processing center.

Most computerized accounts receivable processing systems do not provide complete automation. A major bottleneck is the application of cash receipts when, because insufficient information is enclosed with the payment, the computer cannot determine what bill is being paid. Thus, each open item

[1] Frank H. Moeller, Jr., "Accounts Receivable Records," *Prentice-Hall Editorial Staff Handbook of Successful Operating Systems and Procedures with Forms*, Englewood Cliffs, N.J., Prentice-Hall, Inc., 1964.

[2] *Ibid.*

being paid must be manually identified before being processed by the computer. Some companies have put into operation a fully automatic cash application program (see Solomon, "Making Accounts Receivable Processing More Automatic"). By analyzing customer paying habits and making use of the computer's logical abilities, it is possible to match cash receipts to open items on their magnetic tape accounts receivable file. Eighty-five percent of the checks received are processed on a totally automatic basis (the remaining 15 percent are printed out as exceptions). Advantages of this system include the following:

1. Cost savings
2. Increased accuracy
3. Quicker mailing of customer statements
4. Quicker application of remittances
5. Impartial application of cash (especially as to discounts)
6. Production of clearer and more precise statements
7. Production of aged trial balances on accounts of over set dollar amounts

Internal Control. The extent to which audit procedures are to be applied is dependent upon the evaluation of the internal controls in effect.

Separation of duties. The separation of duties is a key element of all internal control. The list below provides a good indication of the duties relative to accounts receivable which should be separated:

1. The cashier should be denied access to the accounts receivable ledgers.
2. Management of the credit and sales departments should be completely separated.
3. Statements to customers should be mailed by a person having no access to cash and who is also independent of accounts receivable bookkeepers and billing clerks.
4. The employees keeping the customers' ledgers should have no access to cash receipts.
5. Adjustments should be handled by someone outside the bookkeeping department.
6. Additional duties that should be handled separately are billing, reconciliation of subsidiary ledger accounts with the control account, approval of non-cash credits, the maintenance of records for accounts written off, and collection follow-up.

Proper authorization procedures. Accounts receivable transactions requiring proper authorization include:

1. All sales orders should be approved by the credit department before they are accepted. This is to guarantee that all accepted orders meet company requirements (i.e., to make sure that the credit limit is not being exceeded).
2. Bad debt write-offs and other non-cash credits, and payments to customers to clear up credit balances, should be approved by an executive who has no other primary responsibilities in the accounts receivable area.
3. All new accounts should be approved by the credit department.

Additional internal control standards. There are a number of other internal control standards relating to accounts receivable.

1. The accounts receivable should be periodically verified by the company, preferably by the internal audit staff. The book records should be

examined and the account balances should be confirmed directly with the customers.

2. Monthly statements should be mailed to all customers. These statements must accurately reflect the subsidiary ledger accounts and thus should be prepared by employees who have no other responsibilities with respect to accounts receivable. No other employees should be allowed access to the statements before they are mailed. These statements give the customers a chance to report any differences directly to someone independent of the record keeping functions, a strong deterrent to manipulation of the accounts.

3. The individual subsidiary ledger accounts should periodically be reconciled with the general ledger control account.

4. Entries should be posted to the individual accounts from the original documents. All receivable documents (i.e., invoices and remittance advices) should be numbered—this provides a check as to whether all documents have been posted.

5. The company should periodically prepare aging schedules for the accounts receivable balances. This provides a check on the adequacy of the work performed by the credit and collection departments.

These internal control standards, and additional ones not discussed above, are embodied in the sample internal control questionnaire for accounts receivable discussed below.

Internal Control Questionnaire. An internal control questionnaire, such as the one shown in Figure 1, can, if used properly, be quite useful to the auditor in determining the adequacy of the system of internal control for accounts receivable. The questionnaire included here is a sample only—the circumstances of the particular audit engagement will determine which questions are to be used and if additional questions are necessary. The questionnaire should be supplemented by a description of the system and appropriate comments, particularly with respect to negative answers. The internal control review is not accomplished solely by answering all the questions; the auditor must also satisfy himself, by observation and test-checking as described below, that the procedures indicated by the questionnaire answers are, in fact, being carried out.

Inquiry, Observation, and Testing. The internal control questionnaire discussed above should make provision for the auditor to indicate how he obtained the answers to the various questions, namely, by: (1) inquiry; (2) observation; or (3) testing.

The auditor can obtain answers to many of the questions by inquiring of the various personnel with accounts receivable responsibilities (i.e., credit manager, sales manager, accounts receivable bookkeeper, and cashier). It is possible that some of the answers may represent not what is actually being done, but rather what should be done. To support the answers, the auditor should observe the performance of receivables duties and how receivables activities are organized. He should review procedures manuals and job descriptions relevant to receivables. Finally, the various tests of the bookkeeping records that are a part of the regular audit procedures for receivables will provide indications as to the extent and effectiveness of internal control and may indicate the need for extending the audit procedures. As indicated here, there is no clear dividing line between tests of internal control and the regular audit tests. For example, receipt of a number of confirmation replies showing differences would probably both be an indication of unsatisfactory

Figure 1 SAMPLE INTERNAL CONTROL QUESTIONNAIRE*

ACCOUNTS RECEIVABLE

1. Are customer ledgers kept by employees having no access to cash receipts?
2. Are customer ledgers balanced at least monthly with the general ledger control account?
3. Are monthly statements of open items mailed to all customers?
4. Are the statements prepared by someone who has no access to cash and who is independent of accounts receivable bookkeepers and billing clerks?
5. Does the above employee retain control of the statements until mailed?
6. Are disputed items and differences reported by customers routed to the above employee for investigation?
7. Are delinquent accounts periodically reviewed by an official other than the credit manager?
8. Are write-offs of uncollectible accounts approved by a proper official—one other than the credit manager?
9. Are charged-off accounts kept under proper control and followed up?
10. Are credit memos approved by a proper official?
11. Are credit memos sequentially numbered and accounted for?
12. Do discounts allowed after the discount date or in excess of normal credit terms require the approval of a proper official?
13. Are credits for returned goods checked against receiving reports?
14. Does the client periodically obtain direct confirmation by:
    a. Internal auditors?
    b. Other designated employees?
15. Is management of the credit department entirely separate from the sales department?
16. Is the cashier denied access to the accounts receivable ledgers?
17. Are the duties of the accounts receivable bookkeeper completely separated from all cash receipts and disbursements functions?
18. Do journal entries affecting accounts receivable require the approval of someone senior to the accounts receivable bookkeeper?
19. Are goods out on consignment recorded in a memorandum accounts receivable ledger?
20. Are accounts receivable periodically aged by the client?

* Affirmative answers indicate a satisfactory degree of internal control.

internal control and make it advisable to confirm a greater number of accounts.

Extent of Internal Control. A prime determinant of audit procedures and time of examination. It is frequently desirable to perform the receivables portion of the annual audit as of a date prior to the balance sheet date. This provides additional time in which to investigate any differences that are found and to record resulting adjustments prior to year end. In addition, the volume of clerical work associated with the confirmation procedure is best done prior to other demands (such as inventory) at year end. Provided sufficient controls exist, it is considered acceptable procedure to confirm the receivables and reconcile the individual subsidiary ledger accounts with the control account at a date one, two, or three months prior to year end, and then, at the balance sheet date, to review the collectibility of the receivables and perform various test checks. (Although not usually done, receivables may also be confirmed subsequent to year end.) Tests of the data supporting the entries to the control account (sales, cash receipts, credits, etc.) for the interim period are usually considered necessary.

The effectiveness of internal control is a prime determinant not only of the time of the audit examination but also of the extent of the examination. As explained in the following pages, many of the audit procedures for receivables involve tests. As would be expected, these tests must be more extensive in situations of weak internal control than in situations of satisfactory internal control.

Operational Auditing. The independent accountant can, as indicated in *Management Services Handbook,* published by the AICPA, provide special services to management by extending some portions of his usual receivables audit work. The auditor should briefly review the credit and collection system while he is reviewing bad-debt write-offs or aging the accounts. Frequently such a review will reveal control deficiencies that have contributed to losses. Another deficiency that the independent auditor may find is that of a too tight credit policy. The auditor can be of assistance here by reviewing the credit administration of a business that takes pride in a low bad-debts-to-sales ratio. The auditor may find that not only are profits being lost because sales are restricted as a result of a tight credit policy, but also too much is being spent on credit administration.

One of the audit procedures mentioned at a later point in this chapter is the computation of a turnover ratio. The auditor is in a position to make suggestions for improving an unsatisfactory ratio by expediting the transmittal of invoices or by revising the credit and collection procedures.

The internal auditor's work is similar to the operational auditing work of the independent accountant. The areas mentioned above are likely to be covered by the internal auditor as part of his regular work. Additional aspects of operational auditing are indicated in Figure 2 (reproduced from the AICPA's *Management Services Handbook*). This table provides a sample of the orders, billing, and receivables portion of a questionnaire sometimes used by independent accountants in reviewing management controls.

AUDITING PROCEDURES

The auditing procedures discussed in this chapter are of general applicability. No attempt is made to discuss the peculiarities involved in the audit of specific types of business. Many other sources are available for auditing procedures applicable to a specific type of business.

Figure 2 SAMPLE QUESTIONNAIRE FOR REVIEW OF MANAGEMENT CONTROLS[3]

Orders, billing, and receivables:

A. Attach key forms used to acknowledge sales, authorize shipment or manufacture, and bill customers.

B. Are sales and receivables records handled
1. Manually?
2. By pegboard system?
3. By machine? Type?

C. Are accounts receivable records maintained in
1. Book ledgers?
2. Ledger cards?
3. Open invoice system?

D. How are sales data analyzed for ledger entry and statistical purposes?

E. Are unfilled and back order records efficiently maintained for production and sales department use?

F. Evidence of good credit and collection follow-up system?

[3] Henry De Vos, ed., *Management Services Handbook,* New York, AICPA, 1964.

Obtain Trial Balance. The first step in the audit of accounts receivable is to prepare or obtain a trial balance of the subsidiary accounts receivable ledgers. This trial balance may be prepared as of the balance sheet date or as of the confirmation date, and should preferably be prepared by the client's personnel. In the case of a punch-card or computer system, it will be the result of a machine printout.

Where the trial balance is prepared by the client, the auditor should foot and crossfoot it, generally on a test basis, and reconcile the total with the general ledger control account. The extent of the test depends on the adequacy of internal control over accounts receivable. If there is a difference between the control account and the total of the individual accounts, it should be brought to the client's attention and the client's employees—not the auditor—should locate the difference (the work involved is basically of a bookkeeping, not auditing, nature). When there is a difference and internal control is weak, the auditor should consider the possibility of fraud, especially if the control account is greater than the total of the individual accounts.

The auditor should check the accuracy of the amounts and aging on the trial balance by tracing, on a test basis, the names, addresses, and amounts to the appropriate source data. Again the adequacy of internal control determines the extent of the test. Where there is a large number of accounts and internal control is good, it is generally adequate to check all accounts with balances in excess of a specified amount and a percentage of the accounts with smaller balances. In reviewing the subsidiary ledger accounts or other source documents the auditor should be alert for unusual debits, credits, or balances and note such items for later investigation. In testing the trial balance amounts it is important that the auditor work from the trial balance to the individual ledger accounts or other source documents, for two reasons:

1. The purpose of the test is to prove that all trial balance amounts are represented by actual subsidiary ledger accounts.
2. It is more likely for the receivable control account to be overstated than understated.

As part of the auditor's work with the trial balance, he should obtain information for segregation, if significant, of accounts with credit balances, accounts resulting from non-trade transactions, receivables from officers, employees, directors, principal shareholders, and affiliated companies, deposits or advances, and accounts that are secured or have been pledged.

Confirmation of Receivables. The confirmation or circularization of receivables is probably the most important accounts receivable audit procedure. The confirmation procedure provides a test of both internal control effectiveness and the existence and dollar amount of the receivables.

AICPA and SEC requirements. The confirmation of receivables is a generally accepted auditing procedure, as is indicated by the following excerpt from Statements on Auditing Procedures No. 33 of the AICPA:

> 16. By vote of the Institute's membership in 1939, confirmation of receivables and observation of inventories were established as generally accepted auditing procedures, where they are practicable and reasonable and the assets concerned are material to financial position or results of operations. The procedures must be both practicable and reasonable. In auditing, practicable means "capable of being done with the available means" or "with reason or prudence"; reasonable means "sensible in the light of the surrounding circumstances."
>
> 17. In the rare situation in which these procedures are practicable and reasonable and are not used, and other procedures can be and are employed, the independent

auditor must bear in mind that he has the burden of justifying the opinion expressed.

18. Confirmation of receivables requires direct communication with debtors; the method and time of requesting such confirmations and the number to be requested are determined by the auditor. Such matters as the degree of internal control to which accounts receivable are subject, the apparent possibility of disputes, inaccuracies, or irregularities in the accounts, the probability that requests will fail to receive consideration and the materiality of the amounts involved are factors to be considered by the auditor in selecting the method, extent, and timing of his confirmation procedures.

In September 1970, the Committee on Auditing Procedure of the AICPA issued Statement on Auditing Procedure No. 43, *Confirmation of Receivables and Observation of Inventories.* The Committee reaffirms the importance of the well-established auditing procedures concerning the confirmation of receivables. The purpose of Statement No. 43 is to provide additional guidelines and to modify existing reporting requirements. The most significant change is that the independent auditor no longer has to comment in his report when he was unable to confirm receivables because it was impractical or impossible to do so, as long as he is able to satisfy himself by use of other auditing procedures. (See section on "Accountant's Reports" for current treatment.)

The particular concern of the accounting profession with respect to accounts receivables originated largely as a result of the McKesson and Robbins case of the late 1930s. (See Rappaport's *SEC Accounting Practice and Procedure* for a description of the case.[4]) The Securities and Exchange Commission made the following recommendations regarding confirmation of receivables (Accounting Series Release No. 19):

> Viewed as a whole the audit program for accounts receivable as used by (the certifying accountants) conformed to then generally accepted procedures for an examination of financial statements although confirmation of the accounts was not included in the program. The facts of this case, however, demonstrate the utility of circularization and the wisdom of the profession in subsequently adopting confirmation of accounts and notes receivable as a required procedure . . . wherever practicable and reasonable, and where the aggregate amount of notes and accounts receivable represents a significant proportion of the current assets or of the total assets of a concern. . . .
>
> . . . Particularly, it is our opinion that auditing procedures relating to . . . confirmation of receivables, which, prior to our hearings, had been considered optional steps, should, in accordance with the resolutions already adopted by the various accounting societies, be accepted as normal auditing procedures in connection with the presentation of comprehensive and dependable financial statements to investors.

The action of "the various accounting societies" referred to by the SEC with respect to accounts receivable (as well as inventories) was principally the adoption of a special report entitled "Extension of Auditing Procedures" by the American Institute of Accountants (now AICPA). The report became the first of a series of Statements on Auditing Procedures which were consolidated in the aforementioned Statements No. 33.

Rule X-17A-5 of the SEC Act of 1934 requires the circularization of accounts receivable on a 100 percent basis for brokers' customer accounts. The positive form of confirmation is generally used for stock brokerage houses in conformity with this rule and the identical rule 417 (formerly 532) of the New York Stock Exchange Board of Governors.

Extent. Based on his review of internal control the auditor decides whether to confirm all the accounts or only a portion of them. All the accounts should

[4] Louis H. Rappaport, *Accounting Practice and Procedures,* New York, The Ronald Press Company, 1966.

be confirmed if internal control is unsatisfactory or if fraud is suspected. If the accounts are few in number and they make up a material portion of the company's assets, they should, again, all be confirmed. When internal control is satisfactory and there is a large number of accounts receivable, a representative sample of the accounts may be selected for confirmation. The auditor should consider the use of statistical sampling (see the section on statistical sampling) in selecting the accounts to be confirmed. In selecting the sample the auditor must be sure that he has access to the entire population (all the accounts from which the sample is to be selected). In addition to the representative sample, confirmations should be requested for the following types of accounts:

1. Accounts with large balances
2. Past-due accounts
3. Accounts with zero or credit balance
4. Accounts written off during the current period
5. Accounts whose collection is considered questionable
6. Other accounts of an unusual nature

When a sizable portion of a company's sales are to a few customers, positive confirmation requests should be sent to all of these customers. If the company requests that certain receivables not be confirmed, the auditor should obtain an adequate reason and, if he feels it desirable, apply alternative procedures to these accounts.

Form. There are two basic types of confirmation requests: the positive and the negative (illustrated in Figures 3 and 4, respectively). The positive form

Figure 3 POSITIVE CONFIRMATION REQUEST

CONFIRMATION REQUEST

Gentlemen:

Our auditors are making an examination of our financial statements and wish to obtain direct confirmation of the correctness of the amount owed us as of the date indicated. Please compare the balance shown below with your records, noting details of any exceptions on the reverse side. Then sign this letter in the space provided and return it direct to our auditors, Black & White. A reply envelope which requires no postage is enclosed for your convenience.

This is not a request for payment and remittances should not be made to our auditors.

Very truly yours,

Audit date __________

Account balance $__________

Black & White:

The balance shown above was correct on the date named. (If not correct, check here ☐ and indicate difference on reverse.)

____
Company

____
Signed by

No. __________

Return this confirmation to the __________ Office of Black & White

Figure 4 NEGATIVE CONFIRMATION REQUEST

> **Please Examine This Statement Carefully**
>
> If it does not agree with your records, report any differences in writing to our auditors
>
> BLACK & WHITE
> 100 BROADWAY
> NEW YORK, N.Y. 10010
>
> who are making an examination of our financial statements. If no differences are reported to them, this statement will be considered correct. This is not a request for payment and remittances should not be made to our auditors.

requests the debtor to directly notify the auditor as to whether or not the information is correct, while the negative form requests a reply only if the information is incorrect. For the positive form, second and third requests should be sent if necessary; while for the negative form, a failure to reply may be assumed to indicate that the information is correct.

Use of the positive form is preferable when there are a small number of accounts of relatively major importance, or when there appears to be a greater than usual possibility of disputes, inaccuracies, or irregularities in the accounts. The negative form is acceptable in the majority of cases and is the more widely used of the two. The negative form should not, however, be used in cases where it is not likely to be given any consideration, i.e., with respect to receivables from the United States government and from many retail sales organizations.

Procedure. Once the accounts to be confirmed have been selected, the procedures listed below should be followed. These procedures are important and failure to adhere to them may invalidate the confirmation work. Unless noted otherwise, these procedures apply equally well to the use of the positive and negative forms of confirmation.

1. Confirmation requests and statements to be mailed must be compared with the individual ledger accounts (or with the accounts receivable trial balance, if it contains all necessary information and if it has already been compared with the ledger accounts) as to name and address of debtor and the amount receivable.
2. The auditor must maintain control over the accounts and the statements from the time the accounts are selected for confirmation until the confirmation requests and statements are mailed.
3. A record should be made of the accounts selected for confirmation. For positive requests, the auditor may retain duplicate copies of the confirmation requests, indicate which accounts have been chosen for confirmation on the aged trial balance, or prepare a worksheet showing the customer's name, address, and account balance (additional columns may be included for

Figure 5 BLOCK-OUT STAMP

differences and disposition of differences). For negative requests, a copy of the trial balance or an adding-machine tape is adequate.

4. Confirmation requests, if numerous, should be sequentially numbered and the same numbers used on the record described above. This practice facilitates tracing in the replies.

5. The auditor's return address should appear on the envelopes used to mail the confirmation requests. This can be accomplished by use either of the auditor's envelope or of the client's envelope with the application of a "block-out stamp" (Figure 5) to line out the client's name and address and add on the auditor's name and address. This procedure assures that any undeliverable requests will be returned to the auditor. When the internal auditor confirms receivables, it is advisable to use as the return address a post office box to which only the internal auditor has access.

6. If receivables are confirmed prior to the balance sheet date, it is necessary to review transactions in the control accounts between the confirmation and balance sheet dates. In this connection, the accounts at the balance sheet date should be reviewed for particularly large balances or significant changes in the balance since the confirmation date, for which accounts the auditor may wish to consider confirmation or other forms of support as of the balance sheet date.

Alternate auditing procedures are necessary when responses to positive confirmation requests are not received. Because such procedures consume more time and are less conclusive than confirmation replies, every effort should be made to encourage confirmation replies. Listed below are a number of ways of encouraging replies (W. H. Broadhurst, "Follow-up of Accounts Receivable Circularization"[5]):

1. Prepare positive requests on the client's letterhead if possible, otherwise on standard forms.

2. Include company's statement of account showing all open items in detail with confirmation request.

3. Mail requests as soon as possible after confirmation date.

4. Enclose stamped, self-addressed return envelopes with confirmation requests.

5. If requests are going to foreign countries, they should be in bilingual form.

[5] *The Canadian Chartered Accountant*, February, 1965, pp. 145–147.

6. Send second requests if replies are not received after a reasonable length of time.

The confirmation replies received by the auditor may be divided into three general categories: confirmations affirmatively signed, confirmations indicating disputes or discrepancies, and confirmations which are returned as undeliverable. No further work is required on signed confirmations. The auditor does not assume responsibility for the genuineness or authenticity of the confirmation signatures; however, if the auditor has reason to question the authenticity of a confirmation reply he should consider remailing the request to an executive of the customer. Confirmations returned because of incorrect addresses should be investigated by the auditor and remailed to the correct addresses. A large number of such replies would warrant special procedures. The auditor should be aware that such return confirmations may be indicative of fictitious accounts.

All exceptions, whether in response to positive or negative requests, should be investigated. The client may be asked to follow up the exceptions unless a serious weakness in internal control is indicated or the exception is material in amount. The auditor should follow up any differences that indicate the possibility of irregularities (e.g., a claim that no credit has been given for merchandise returned or for a payment made prior to the confirmation date). The client should provide the auditor with copies of all follow-up correspondence, and responses thereto should be directed to the auditor.

A schedule summarizing the extent of and responses to the confirmation requests should be part of the audit working papers. The schedule should show both amounts (in dollars and as percentages) and number of confirmations for the following confirmation categories: affirmative confirmations, confirmations with unresolved differences, confirmations with resolved differences, and confirmations for which no replies have been received.

Reliability of Confirmations. Case study of a midwest bank. Although the use of confirmations is considered to be a standard auditing procedure, there has been very little research as to the reliability of confirmations. One study ("An Experimental Study of Audit Confirmations," by Gordon B. Davis, John Neter, and Roger R. Palmer[6]), reported in 1967, made use of a statistically designed and controlled field experiment to determine the probability that confirmation replies are correct. The experiment used as its basis a bank's confirmation procedures. After the monthly bank statements were sent out, duplicate audit statements were sent to a sample of demand deposit customers. The customers were asked to compare the two statements and notify the auditor of any differences. Because it was not practical to provide incorrect account balances, a code number was put on each of the two statements and the customer was asked to compare both the account balance and the code number. The experiment involved putting a different code number on the audit statement. Both positive and negative confirmations were used. With the positive form, 36 percent of those who replied failed to report an actual difference in the code numbers. The detection rate was significantly lower with the negative form. A major reason for the higher detection rate with the positive form would seem to be the use of second requests (for the positive form only). The confirmation procedure was more reliable for large accounts than for small accounts. A follow-up questionnaire revealed that a small proportion of the customers had noted the difference but had failed to report it.

[6] *The Journal of Accountancy*, June, 1967, pp. 36–41.

Problems of Non-response. In recent years failure to obtain responses to confirmation requests has become a serious problem. Three of the more important reasons for this growing problem are discussed here: the policy of governmental agencies, the use of the voucher system, and the use of mechanized data processing. A partial solution to the problem follows.

In general, federal governmental agencies do not respond to confirmation requests, and many auditors now feel it is not practical to request such confirmations. SAP No. 43 (see page 21-11) has relaxed disclosure requirements in such cases.

Another source of difficulty in obtaining confirmation responses is the use of the voucher system by customers. Under this system no running account balance is maintained; instead, individual vouchers provide evidence of indebtedness and are used as subsidiary ledger accounts for creditors. The customer can usually reply only as to the unpaid vouchers as of the date of receipt of request and cannot reconstruct amounts at earlier dates without considerable effort.

A fairly recent development has been the return of confirmation requests by some large companies unconfirmed, with the explanation that their mechanized data processing systems do not provide the needed information. There are two reasons for the growing volume of "non-replies": the elimination of individual vendor accounts in the mechanized accounting systems, and the desire to eliminate the clerical cost of replying. The problem is likely to increase in seriousness until such time as machine programs are arranged to provide the necessary data. There have already been situations where the number of "non-replies" has been great enough to necessitate the use of alternate procedures.

The use of confirmation requests which show all open items, rather than a single balance, may result in a higher percentage of confirmation replies. The future growth of mechanical data processing may lead to the practice of sending requests to customers prior to the confirmation date asking them to provide a listing of open items as of the confirmation date. This listing would then be compared with the client's records. A computer properly programmed could provide such listings at relatively small cost.

Alternative Procedures. It is necessary to use alternative auditing procedures when it is not practicable and reasonable to confirm accounts receivable or when replies cannot be obtained for material amounts. Alternative procedures should be used when experience indicates that confirmation requests may fail to receive consideration (e.g., United States government and chain stores). As the number of companies not replying to confirmation requests has increased, the problem of finding adequate alternative procedures has become more serious.

Some accountants believe that the alternative procedure of applying cash receipts for periods subsequent to the confirmation date to accounts receivable is by itself adequate. This procedure involves inspecting incoming checks or remittance advices; tracing invoice numbers to the customer's account; and tracing amounts collected to the customer's account, the cash receipts record, and the bank deposit.

Other accountants feel that reliance solely on cash realization may be risky because it does not sufficiently substantiate the accounts receivable balance. It is possible that payment has been made for merchandise shipped after the confirmation date or that a recorded payment is not genuine. Further, the fact that a payment has been made does not provide proof that the debtor had no claims against the company (i.e., for defective goods) at the confirmation date.

Although realization is the most widely used alternative procedure, it is valid only if, in addition to there being evidence of remittances, the remittances can be identified with the balances outstanding at the confirmation date. Remittance advices which identify the related invoices by number or date are particularly good evidence to the auditor because they originate outside the client's control. Complete reliance upon them is dangerous, however, because if not received directly by the auditor, they are subject to alteration.

A second alternative audit procedure involves the examination of internal evidence such as copies of the customer purchase orders, shipping records and documents, sales invoices, and sales contracts and correspondence.

A third procedure involves taking reasonable steps to establish the debtor's existence if there is any question as to that fact. This can be done by referring to the Dun and Bradstreet *Reference Book*, a business or city directory, or a credit report, if available. Direct telephone calls to the debtor are also feasible.

The above procedures assume a situation in which there is good internal control. If internal control is weak, it may be necessary to control receipts from the balance sheet date until the receivables have been largely collected.

Special Procedures for Factored Accounts. There are three types of accounts receivable factoring: the sale of receivables at a discount with no recourse to the seller, the sale of specified receivables with recourse to the seller if they are not paid, and the pledge of specified receivables as collateral with title remaining with the borrower. The latter two methods, in which the borrower takes the credit risk, are more common than the first method, and audit procedures applicable to them are discussed here (see D. J. Griff, "Accounting for Accounts Receivable Factoring,"[7] for a full discussion).

Auditing procedures can become quite complex when accounts receivable are taken by a factor as collateral only and on a nonnotification basis (the ultimate debtor is not notified that his account has been factored). The auditor of the factor may wish to confirm directly with the ultimate debtor the debt due to obtain assurance that the debts factored by the borrower are not fictitious. The auditor is faced with the problem of how to confirm the amount due with the ultimate debtor without at the same time disclosing to him that his account has been factored. The debtor may find himself faced with the confusing situation of receiving two confirmation requests—one from the factor's auditor and one from the borrower's auditor—for the same debt. Such confusion can be avoided through cooperation between the two auditing firms involved. Three possible solutions, assuming that the confirmation dates are different, are:

1. The borrower's auditor acts as agent for the factor's auditor in sending out confirmation requests.
2. The factor's auditor uses the name of the borrower's auditor (after obtaining his approval) on the confirmation requests.
3. The factor's auditor sends out confirmations without any auditor's name, indicating that the request is in connection with an internal audit.

[7] *The Canadian Chartered Accountant*, March, 1965, pp. 205–208.

Confirmation of the receivable with the ultimate debtor does not relieve the factor's auditor of his responsibility to confirm the debt due directly with the borrower.

The audit procedures followed by the borrower's auditor vary according to whether the receivable is sold or pledged as collateral to the factor. When the account receivable is sold on a recourse basis, the auditor is interested in verifying the receipt of funds from the factor, the disposition of the funds, the resulting reduction of the accounts receivable account, the interest charged, and the contingent liability on the receivables sold. When the receivable is pledged as collateral, the auditor must verify many more transactions, such as the receipt of funds from the debtors. The auditor's work will be easier if the factor sends advice notices to the borrower when payments are received from debtors. Partial, independent verification of amounts received is provided by such notices.

Test for Proper Cutoff of Sales Records. The accounts receivable balance should include all sales transactions up to the balance sheet date but should exclude any transactions completed after the balance sheet date. The auditor should make a careful examination of the sales cutoff for two reasons: unintentional errors in the cutoff can easily occur and intentional manipulation of the cutoff is a convenient method of presenting a more desirable financial condition and increased sales. The sales cutoff should be tested by examining invoices and shipping documents for several days before and after the balance sheet date. Invoices should be traced to sales and receivable records to determine that sales are recorded in the proper accounting period (the goods should be shipped in the same period in which the sale is recorded). The adequacy of the client's internal control determines the number of days to be tested and the number of transactions to be examined.

Test of Discounts, Returns and Allowances, and Related Credit Memoranda. Discounts taken by customers should be tested by the auditor. This may be done when the audit of cash transactions is performed. The auditor should investigate trade and client practices as to discounts. Credit memoranda for sales returns and allowances should be sequentially numbered and accounted for. The auditor should particularly check the memoranda for proper authorization. A more complete discussion of this area will be found in the chapter on sales.

More directly related to the examination of receivables is an investigation of the adequacy of allowances for cash discounts on unpaid balances created during the discount period, for merchandise returns after the balance sheet date, for disputed charges, and for other losses. Such allowances affect the accounts receivable balance. Credit memorandums issued after the balance sheet date, but not entered in the accounts at that date, should be reviewed. It should be determined if additional credit memorandums are to be issued that would affect the period being audited. It is often informative to inquire as to the status of processing returned goods. A heavy backlog of unprocessed returns is indicative of future credits for which adequate provision may not have been made. Such inquiry may best be directed to people outside the accounts receivable or accounting areas, perhaps during observation of the physical inventory.

Collectibility of Accounts Receivable. **Collectibility objectives.** The primary concern of auditors in auditing accounts receivables is to determine that the receivables exist. They are concerned also as to whether or not the accounts will actually be collected. The auditor must determine the collectibility of the accounts in order to be satisfied that the reserve for potential bad debt losses is sufficient. Satisfactory confirmation of receivables does not provide proof that the accounts will actually be collected. To determine collectibility other auditing procedures must be used. The auditor has two primary concerns:

1. That all accounts considered uncollectible at year end have been charged off or specifically reserved against.
2. That the allowance for doubtful accounts is adequate to reduce receivables on the balance sheet to the amount expected to be collected.

Before attempting to estimate what the allowance for doubtful accounts should be, the auditor should have a clear understanding of credit management and should be familiar with all sources of credit information.

Use of aging analysis and turnover ratio. Probably the best-known of the techniques for estimating the bad debt allowance is the aging schedule. This schedule analyzes receivables by their age (i.e., those under 30 days old, those 30 to 60 days old, those 60 to 90 days old, and those over 90 days old). It is assumed that the older the receivable, the less likely it is that it will be collected. This is a valid assumption, but it is difficult to determine what percentage of the receivables in a particular aging class should be considered uncollectible.

The receivables may be aged on the basis of either due date or billing date. The aging schedule should preferably be, and usually is, prepared by the client. It is frequently prepared as part of the trial balance to provide what is called an "aged trial balance." The accounts may be aged on a specific-invoice or first-in, first-out basis. The specific-invoice basis is more exact, but also more time-consuming. The first-in, first-out basis will generally provide an accurate enough picture when there are many small accounts. When there are a few large accounts, the specific-invoice method should be used. When the client prepares the schedule, and there are many small accounts and good internal control, it is not necessary for the auditor to check the aging of every account. Rather, he can use statistical sampling techniques, making sure to test both accounts shown as delinquent and those shown as current (see the section in this chapter on statistical sampling). The test involves checking the schedule figures against the ledger detail. To provide an indication as to whether or not the receivables are improving in collectibility, the current year's aging schedule should be compared with schedules of prior years. A schedule of dollar and percentage amounts running for several years is particularly useful in disclosing trends or significant differences that should be further investigated.

The auditor then considers the allowance for doubtful accounts on the basis of his review of the aging schedule, his discussion with the credit manager, and prior years' experience. As mentioned above, it is difficult to determine what percentage of the receivables in each aging class should be considered uncollectible. It is possible to determine experience rates for each class by reviewing bad-debt write-offs and aged trial balances for prior years. The reader is referred to *Practical Accounting and Auditing Problems,* published by the AICPA, for a discussion of how this procedure is used. Basically it involves taking a prior year's aged trial balance and determining the amounts that were either written off as uncollectible during or still open at the end of the following year. This information is then used to arrive at current percentages. Such a procedure is quite time-consuming and it is questionable whether the additional accuracy obtained from determining a percentage for each age classification (rather than one overall percentage) warrants the cost involved.

When there is a large number of small accounts, J. B. Galvin (in "Estimating Bad Debt Losses" [8]) suggests that the auditor will find it useful to prepare an estimate of bad debt losses expressed as a percentage of sales. This technique is valid for a company whose credit and collection practices do not change significantly from year to year.

The auditor can obtain additional information that will be of use to him in estimating the allowance for bad debts by computing the turnover ratio or number of days' sales outstanding. The turnover ratio represents the number of times receivables have been replaced during the year, and is found by dividing the sales for the year by the average receivables balance during the year. The number of days' sales outstanding is found by dividing the average receivables by the average daily sales. For example:

Given: Receivables at beginning of year = \$ 90,000
Receivables at end of year = \$110,000
Sales for year = \$730,000
Average receivables = (\$90,000 + \$110,000) ÷ 2 = \$100,000
Turnover ratio = \$730,000 ÷ \$100,000 = 7.3
Average daily sales = \$730,000 ÷ 365 = \$2,000
Days' sales outstanding = \$100,000 ÷ \$2,000 = 50 days

All other things being the same, a higher turnover ratio (or fewer days' sales outstanding) is indicative of improvements in credit and collection procedures. The figures for the current year should be compared with those for prior years to see if there has been an unusual change this year. A graphic presentation, such as the one in Figure 6, provides a good indication of the trend over a period of years. The graph indicates that the number of days' sales outstanding has tended to increase over the period covered. The technique may be more significant to the independent auditor when actual receivables at year end and average sales based on the most recent three months then ended are used.

The mean collection period is considered by Haskel Benishay (in "Managerial Controls of Accounts Receivable: A Deterministic Approach" [9]) to be a more meaningful and relevant concept than the accounts receivable turnover ratio for evaluating a company's credit policies.

Discussion of Collectibility with Client. Another procedure involves discussing the collectibility of individual accounts with the company's credit manager. In preparation for such discussion the auditor should scan the individual accounts and the aged trial balance looking for indications of doubtful or uncollectible accounts of sufficient amount to warrant individual discussion (see the section on indications of doubtful and uncollectible accounts). The auditor should then review such accounts with the credit manager, paying particular attention to the accounts which may be uncollectible (i.e., accounts containing past-due items). If the auditor is not satisfied by his discussion with the credit manager, he should examine correspondence with the debtors and any collection agencies involved. As an alternative, the accounts may be scanned on a test basis, and this may be supplemented by reviewing an aging analysis prepared for at least a portion of the accounts. It should be noted that a complete scanning of the accounts is less important when there

[8] *The Canadian Chartered Accountant,* April, 1966, pp. 305–307.
[9] *Journal of Accounting Research,* Spring, 1965.

Figure 6 GRAPH OF DAYS SALES OUTSTANDING

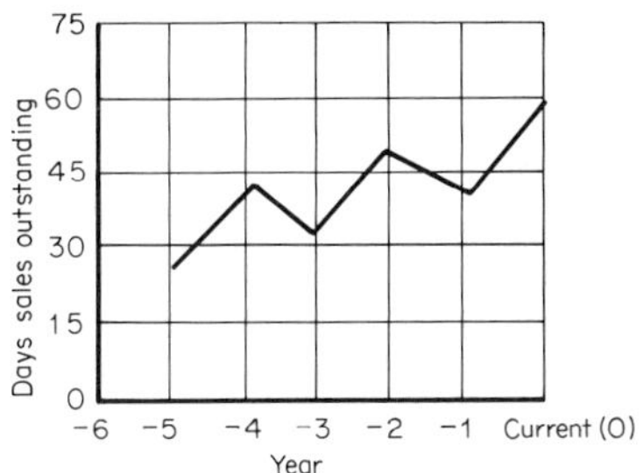

are many open accounts than when there are only a few—the uncollectibility of an individual account is likely to be more significant when there are only a few large accounts rather than many small accounts. As the number of accounts increases, the auditor tends to rely more on statistical analyses and the procedures followed in the granting of credit.

Additional procedures. There are a number of additional procedures involved in determining the collectibility of accounts receivable:

1. The auditor should examine amounts charged off to the allowance account or directly to expense during the year to determine whether these actions have been properly authorized.
2. It may be advisable to send out positive confirmation requests for some of the larger amounts that have been charged off as uncollectible.
3. The collectibility of accounts discounted or sold with recourse should be reviewed to determine if any allowance is required.
4. It may be advisable to obtain independent credit information (i.e., Dun & Bradstreet reports) for customers whose receivables represent a significant portion of total assets.
5. The auditor should prepare an analysis of the account Allowance for Doubtful Accounts. The calculation of the current year's allowance should be reviewed and the allowance should be compared with that of prior years.
6. Receivables transactions occurring after the balance sheet date should be examined, as they may provide indications of collectibility of amounts stated as receivables at the balance sheet date.

Statistical analysis. The methods normally used to appraise liquidity and collectibility are the aging schedule and the turnover ratio or average number of days' sales outstanding. These methods have been criticized as not measuring fund flows. It is argued that use of the turnover ratio is limited to cases where sales are constant, and that the aging schedule fails to relate the balances due in each age classification to the sales during the month in which the balances originated. According to Leroy A. Hewitt (in "Appraising the Firm's Collection Policy"[10]), evaluation of collection policy should be based on an analysis of cash flows. He proposes the use of elementary statistical methods to determine collection patterns and to set control limits. His method relates the flow of cash to sales.

Goran Schroderheim (in "Using Mathematical Probability to Estimate the Allowance for Doubtful Accounts"[11]) suggests the use of mathematical probability calculations involving the application of the principles of bino-

[10] *NAA Management Accounting*, March, 1966, pp. 34–38.
[11] *The Accounting Review*, July, 1964, pp. 679–684.

mial probabilities and the use of matrix algebra in estimating the allowance for doubtful accounts.

Indications of doubtful and uncollectible accounts. There are a number of indications that an account may be doubtful or uncollectible. Among them are the following:

1. The terms of credit have been continuously ignored.
2. Payments are being made on account but the balance is continuously increasing.
3. An old item has been only partly paid while newer items have been fully paid.
4. Credit has been stopped and there have been no collections recently.
5. A customer who formerly paid cash is now giving notes.
6. An old account has been assigned to a collection agency.
7. Amounts are due from former employees.
8. Notes have been accepted for an open account.
9. A customer has either become deceased, disappeared, gone out of business, been discharged from bankruptcy, or gone into receivership.
10. Collection is barred by the statute of limitations.
11. The presence of discouraging correspondence.

FINANCIAL STATEMENT DISCLOSURE

Receivables are commonly described in balance sheets as "Accounts Receivable," "Accounts and Notes Receivable," and "Accounts Receivable less Allowance for Doubtful Accounts." If no additional information is provided, the financial statement user is entitled to make the following assumptions (*Auditing Principles*, 2d ed., by Howard F. Stettler)[12]:

1. That all the receivables resulted from arms-length transactions with third parties, and not from transactions with officers, employees, or subsidiary companies.
2. That only receivables resulting from normal trade transactions with customers are included.
3. That any potential losses have been provided for, and that therefore the full amount shown is expected to be realized in cash. (Notation should be made if a provision for doubtful accounts has been deducted from the gross receivables, with only the net amount shown in the balance sheet.)
4. That the amount of cash to be realized will be received within one year, or within one complete operating cycle if the cycle is longer than a year.
5. That the business has full ownership of the receivables, with no liens outstanding against them and no contingent liability for discounted receivables.
6. That no liabilities have been offset against the receivables.

If any of the above captions are to be used, the auditor should be satisfied that all of these assumptions are in fact true. Any *material* amounts of receivables that cannot properly be included with trade accounts receivable must be shown separately on the balance sheet. Examples of receivables that should be shown separately if material or significant in amount are:

1. Trade notes and acceptances receivable
2. Installment notes and accounts receivable
3. Receivables from subsidiaries and affiliates
4. Receivables from officers, directors, or principal stockholders

[12] Howard F. Stettler, *Auditing Principles—Objectives, Procedures, Working Papers*, 2d ed., Englewood Cliffs, N.J., Prentice-Hall, Inc., 1961.

5. Credit balances in accounts receivable
6. Receivables resulting from transactions not in the ordinary course of business (i.e., sale of fixed assets)

Trade notes receivable are generally not significant in amount and can therefore be combined with trade accounts receivable. (See the section on notes receivable for further discussion of the statement presentation for notes receivable.) Receivables from employees, officers, and directors for purchases (i.e., department stores) may be included with the trade accounts if the accounts are paid regularly and the granting of credit is properly controlled.

Those receivables that are expected to be collected during the normal operating cycle are classified on the balance sheet as current assets, in accordance with AICPA Accounting Research Bulletin No. 43, and appear on the balance sheet directly after cash and marketable securities. Those receivables not expected to be collected during the normal operating cycle should be classified as noncurrent assets. The following excerpts are taken from Bulletin No. 43 (Chapter 3, Section A):

> 4. For accounting purposes, the term *current assets* is used to designate cash and other assets or resources commonly identified as those which are reasonably expected to be realized in cash or sold or consumed during the normal operating cycle of the business. Thus the term comprehends in general such resources as . . . (*c*) trade accounts, notes and acceptances receivable; (*d*) receivables from officers, employees, affiliates, and others, if collectible in the ordinary course of business within a year; (*e*) installment or deferred accounts and notes receivable if they conform generally to normal trade practices and terms within the business. . . .
>
> 6. This concept of the nature of current assets contemplates the exclusion from that classification of such resources as . . . (*c*) receivables arising from unusual transactions (such as the sale of capital assets, or loans or advances to affiliates, officers, or employees) which are not expected to be collected within twelve months. . . .

Receivables should be shown on the balance sheet at their estimated realizable value—the allowance for doubtful accounts should be deducted from the receivables. Opinion No. 12 of the Accounting Principles Board refers to the classification of asset valuation allowances for losses: "*It is the Board's opinion that such allowances should be deducted from the assets or groups of assets to which the allowances relate, with appropriate disclosure.*" The following are possible presentations:

1. The receivables may be shown on the balance sheet gross with the allowance shown as a deduction (see example (3) below).
2. The receivables may be shown on the balance sheet net with the amount of the allowance in the caption (examples (1) and (2)).

Other allowances (i.e., those for cash discounts, collection costs, and merchandise returns) should be shown in a similar fashion. They may be combined with the allowance for doubtful receivables if properly indicated in the statement caption. Accounting Terminology Bulletin Number 1, *Review and Resume,* issued in 1953 by the Committee on Terminology of the AICPA, recommends that the term "reserve" not be used in the balance sheet to describe deductions from assets. More appropriate terms would be "allowance" and "provision."

Opinion Number 6 of the Institute's Accounting Principles Board, issued in October 1965, revised Accounting Research Bulletin Number 43, Chapter 3A, "Current Assets and Current Liabilities," by adding the following paragraph.

10. Unearned discounts (other than cash or quantity discounts and the like), finance charges and interest included in the face amount of receivables should be shown as a deduction from the related receivables.

Balance Sheet Presentation. The following are suggested balance sheet presentations for receivables:

(1)

Trade notes ($XXX,XXX) and accounts, less allowance of $XX,XXX for doubtful accounts	$XXX,XXX

(2)

		1970	1969
Trade receivables, less allowance (1970 – $XX,XXX, 1969 – $XX,XXX)	$	XXX,XXX	$XXX,XXX

(3)

Trade receivables:		
Notes	$ XXX,XXX	
Accounts	X,XXX,XXX	
Allowances (deduction)	(XX,XXX)	$ X,XXX,XXX

For governmental units, taxes and assessments receivable should be shown separately in the balance sheet rather than in combination with other accounts receivable. Likewise, amounts due from other governmental units should also be shown separately.

Financed Notes and Accounts Receivable. The balance sheet treatment of financed notes and accounts receivable has become more complex with the increase in the variety of financing methods. Receivables may be sold, assigned, pledged, discounted, factored, or hypothecated, and the balance sheet treatment varies accordingly.

Albert L. Schaps (in "Balance Sheet Treatment of Financed Notes and Accounts Receivable"[13]) lists four basic categories of financed receivables: those sold or assigned outright without recourse, those sold with guarantee of repurchase, those assigned with recourse, and those pledged in connection with a loan.

When receivables are sold or assigned without recourse, the receiver thereof assumes all credit risks and the company gives up its entire interest in the receivable. These accounts therefore should be eliminated from the balance sheet and no contingent liability should be shown.

Extreme care must be taken with such transactions because outright sale without recourse may be indicated by an underlying agreement, but in actual practice the seller may substitute receivables for those found to be uncollectible. The independent auditor should review carefully the related post-balance sheet events and insist on disclosure of any which indicate intent of the parties at variance with the form of the agreement. Audit procedure should include confirmation with the purchaser as to the absence of recourse, and representation thereto in the client's letter of representation.

When a company guarantees repurchase of uncollectible accounts, the amounts should be eliminated from the balance sheet but a contingent liability should be indicated for those accounts subject to repurchase. Such contingent liability may be indicated on the balance sheet either by parenthetic disclosure or as a "short" figure not included in columnar totals, or it may be disclosed by a footnote. Such indications are also common for dis-

[13] *The New York Certified Public Accountant,* October, 1966, pp. 773–774.

closure as to the amount of such accounts which has been realized to a date subsequent to the date of the balance sheet. Consideration should be given to the need for a reserve to cover estimated losses related to accounts reasonably expected to be repurchased.

Those receivables assigned with recourse should be shown on the balance sheet as a deduction from the gross amount of receivables and the contingent liability disclosed as with the guarantee of repurchase. The amount of receivables pledged in connection with a loan must be disclosed, shown either parenthetically next to the receivable caption or by footnote.

Survey of Current Practice. An excellent source of information concerning current financial statement practice and terminology is *Accounting Trends and Techniques,* published annually by the AICPA. This publication provides a survey of industrial and commercial corporation annual reports and includes detailed tables showing the financial statement terminology used by the surveyed companies for describing current trade receivables, noncurrent receivables, uncollectible accounts, and special features related to accounts receivable found in the annual reports. The survey usually includes a table of cases in which the auditor's report disclosed the omission of confirmation procedures. This publication is indispensable for any auditor who wants to determine the current acceptability of a particular way of presenting receivables in the financial statements.

The material presented in a recent survey is summarized here. The most common descriptions for trade receivables included in the current asset section of the balance sheet were "Accounts Receivable" and "Accounts and Notes Receivable." Most of the companies presented all of their receivables under a single caption only.

Approximately ten percent of the companies disclosed the use of receivables for financing. The four most often noted presentations were:

1. Pledged
2. Discounted
3. Sold with contingent liability
4. Used as collateral for debt

Considerably fewer companies presented noncurrent receivables in their annual reports than presented current receivables. The four most common presentations for noncurrent receivables were:

1. Notes receivable
2. Accounts receivable or receivables
3. Long-term receivables
4. Notes and accounts receivable

The most popular descriptions for the balance sheet caption related to uncollectible accounts in the survey reports were:

1. Allowance for doubtful accounts
2. Allowance
3. Reserve
4. Allowance for losses
5. Reserve for doubtful accounts

The use of the term "reserve" has steadily decreased. In the survey "allowance" was used more than three times as frequently as "reserve," as recommended by the AICPA.

Of the annual reports surveyed, 46 accountants' reports disclosed the omission of normal auditing procedures as to accounts receivable, of which 37 indicated satisfactory alternative procedures; however, SAP No. 43 (see page 21-11) was not then in effect.

ACCOUNTANTS' REPORTS

Required Disclosure. Mention has already been made of the proper financial statement treatment for accounts receivable. Additional material on statement presentation is found in the sections of this chapter dealing with installment receivables and notes receivable. In accordance with Statements on Auditing Procedure No. 33 of the AICPA, if the client declines to disclose data considered essential to a fair presentation of receivables (i.e., fails to show separately material amounts of receivables from officers, directors, or principal stockholders), "the independent auditor should provide the necessary supplemental information in his report, usually in a middle paragraph, and appropriately qualify his opinion."

Supplemental Disclosure. The independent auditor may provide supplemental information to the financial statements, additional explanatory material which is not required for adequate disclosure. Examples of such material are:

1. List of notes receivable
2. List of important debtors by name and balance
3. Summary of trade accounts and contracts classified as to age or due date
4. Realization to a specified date
5. Bad debt experience, collection ratios, and changes in allowance for doubtful accounts
6. Terms of sale
7. Concentration of receivables in a small number of accounts

Such material is not referred to in or covered by the standard short-form auditor's report as it is usually not necessary for a fair presentation of the financial position or results of operations. The independent auditor usually directs his separate report on such material to its fair presentation in relation to the financial statements taken as a whole. In instances when the long-form auditor's report is used, the supplemental material should not be referred to in the opinion paragraph.

Qualifications and Exceptions. When confirmation of accounts receivable has been omitted and it is not considered impractical or impossible to perform such procedures, the scope paragraph of the auditor's report should disclose such omission even if the auditor has satisfied himself by alternative procedures. (See page 21-11 with regard to SAP 43.) When the auditor has satisfied himself through the use of alternative procedures, he should so state in the scope paragraph but make no reference to them in the opinion paragraph. If the auditor has not been able to satisfy himself, he should indicate the limitations on his work in the scope or middle paragraph and then either qualify his opinion or disclaim an opinion on the financial statements taken as a whole, depending on the materiality of the amounts involved. When an auditor gives a qualified opinion because the scope of the examination was restricted by the client (i.e., at the client's request the confirmation of receivables by direct communication was omitted), the qualification should refer not to the restriction but to the item (i.e., receivables) on which an opinion cannot be expressed. When the receivables are material, the auditor should, in general, disclaim an opinion on the financial statements.

Illustrated below are examples of the various types of opinions discussed above.

1. Conditions which preclude necessary auditing procedures—satisfaction through other auditing procedures—scope paragraph

We have examined . . . . Our examination was made . . . . We were unable to obtain replies to our requests for confirmation of accounts receivable from certain customers, but we satisfied ourselves as to such accounts by means of other auditing procedures.

(Normal opinion paragraph follows.)

2. Restrictions imposed by client—qualified opinion

. . . and such other auditing procedures as we considered necessary in the circumstances, except as set forth in the following paragraph. In accordance with your instructions, we did not request confirmation of certain past-due accounts receivable from customers. Accordingly, we were unable to satisfy ourselves as to these receivables stated in the balance sheet at $205,000, which amount enters into the determination of financial position and results of operations.

In our opinion, with the exception stated in the preceding paragraph, the accompanying . . .

Client's Representations. The auditor may request the client to provide written representations as to receivables. The representations should include the following:

1. All receivables shown on the company's books are valid.
2. Non-trade receivables and notes receivable discounted are properly shown in the balance sheet. There is no recourse to the company for accounts receivable sold.
3. Goods shipped on consignment, on approval, or under repurchase agreements and charges for merchandise shipped subsequent to the balance sheet date are excluded from receivables.
4. Assigned receivables are properly indicated.
5. The allowance for doubtful accounts is adequate, and all known uncollectible receivables have been charged off, at the balance sheet date.
6. If receivables were not confirmed at the client's request, even though it was practicable and reasonable, the client should indicate that he made such a request and that he understands that a qualified opinion (disclaimer of opinion in situations involving material amounts) will be issued.

The representations as to receivables may be included in a separate letter or as a section of a letter covering many areas.

STATISTICAL SAMPLING OF ACCOUNTS RECEIVABLE

General. The application of statistical sampling to the audit of receivables is primarily in the area of validation testing such as:

1. Confirmation of accounts receivable
2. Testing the client's aged trial balance of accounts
3. Testing sales and shipments for proper cutoff (usually done in conjunction with the sales test)
4. Selecting items for testing when confirmation of accounts receivable is not practical and alternate procedures such as cash realization, tracing to original documents, etc. are being utilized

Auditor's Judgment. The Committee on Statistical Sampling for the AICPA suggests that the basis for statistical decisions, i.e., the "reliability level" and the "precision limit," should be the auditor's reliance on internal controls, other audit procedures, and materiality. (See "Relationship of Statistical Sampling to Generally Accepted Auditing Standards," *The Journal of Accountancy*, July, 1964, pp. 56–58.) This applies to statistical sampling in the audit of accounts receivable as well as to the other financial areas of concern to the auditor.

In general, the use of statistical sampling may help reduce the amount of audit work required while still permitting the auditor to express positive conclusions about the accounts receivable population.

Types of Approaches. Normally, one of two types of statistical approaches is found in the audit of accounts receivable. They are "estimation" sampling and "attribute" sampling. Estimation sampling allows the auditor to state that he is $R\%$ confident that the true value of the accounts receivable population is between $\pm P\%$ dollar limits. Attribute sampling, on the other hand, allows the auditor to state that he is $R\%$ confident that the actual frequency of errors in the population (e.g., sales or shipments recorded incorrectly, etc.) is no greater than $P\%$. (R = reliability level and P = precision limits selected.)

For more detailed information on the techniques of applying statistical sampling and its general value to the auditor, the reader is referred to the chapters in this handbook dealing with statistical sampling and quantitative methods.

SPECIAL PROBLEMS

Cycle Billing. Businesses that have many customers (e.g., public utilities and department stores) frequently use a cycle billing plan to avoid the cost of sending out all statements at the end of the month. To put a cycle billing plan into operation, the customers' accounts are divided into a number of groups—generally on an alphabetical basis. Each group of accounts is balanced on a particular day of the month (the same day is used each month) and bills or statements are sent out as of that day. Such a procedure spreads the billing work out over the whole month. At the end of any given month, the receivables balance represents amounts billed on the various billing dates but not yet paid plus charges that have arisen after the billing dates. It is not possible to confirm the receivables at month end—rather, the receivables must be confirmed by groups at their respective billing dates and then reconciled with the month-end controlling account balances. So long as the accounts are homogeneous, the auditor may perform his examination of these receivables before the balance sheet date and then review the transactions that have occurred between the date of his examination and the balance sheet date.

Receivables from Officers, Directors, Stockholders, and Employees. These receivables, because of the relationship between the debtor and creditor, should be carefully investigated by the independent and internal auditors. The independent auditor must analyze these accounts to find out why they exist, to determine if the entries to the accounts have been properly made, and to determine the balance sheet presentation. Receivables from employees frequently arise from transactions in the ordinary course of business (i.e., sale of merchandise). Such receivables do not have to be segregated from trade receivables unless they represent a sizable portion of trade receivables or unless there are special circumstances. Receivables from officers, directors, and principal stockholders should be shown separately, regardless of how they arise, if they are significant in amount, because the relationship between the debtor and creditor may affect collection of the receivable.

The internal auditor is concerned with these receivables for several reasons. For control purposes it is desirable that these receivables be segregated if significant in amount. The internal auditor must determine if the extension of credit to these people has been properly approved—the approval procedure in these cases is generally different from that for regular trade receivables. Finally, because of the personal relationships involved, the internal auditor must determine the program in effect and the extent of effort for collection of these receivables.

The SEC has a number of requirements concerning the disclosure of these receivables in financial statements. According to Regulation S-X, the total of current amounts, other than trade accounts, due from directors, officers, and principal stockholders should be stated separately on the balance sheet. Accounting Series Release No. 41 states that amounts due from officers and directors should, because of their origin and nature, be shown separately even if the amounts involved are relatively small. The significance of this item is, according to the Commission, independent of the amount. Regulation S-X (Rule 5-04) prescribes the filing of Schedule II, "Amounts due from directors, officers, and principal holders of equity securities other than affiliates" (Figure 7), in support of the balance sheet caption, as follows:

The schedule prescribed by Rule 12-03 shall be filed with respect to each person among the directors, officers and principal holders of equity securities other than affiliates from whom an aggregate indebtedness of more than $20,000 or 1 percent of total assets, whichever is less, is owed, or at any time during the period for which related profit and loss statements are filed, was owed. For the purposes of this schedule, exclude in the determination of the amount of indebtedness all amounts due from such persons for purchases subject to usual trade terms, for ordinary travel and expense advances and for other such items arising in the ordinary course of business.

Consignment Sales. A consignment arises when one company (the consignor) ships merchandise to another company (the consignee), payment for which is required only when the consignee actually sells the merchandise. The auditor must check to see if the consignor is creating a sale and a corresponding receivable on his books at the time of consignment. This treatment is common for control purposes, but improper for financial statements. Consigned goods are owned by the consignor and are part of the consignor's inventory until sold by the consignee. Consignment accounts should be created for merchandise out on consignment, but these accounts should not

Figure 7 SCHEDULE II

Rule 12-03 Amounts due from directors, officers and principal holders of equity securities other than affiliates.

Col. A	Col. B	Col. C	Col. D		Col. E	
			Deductions		Balance receivable at close of period	
			(1)	(2)	(1)	(2)
Name of debtor	Balance receivable at beginning of period[1]	Additions	Amounts written off	Collections[2]	Current	Not Current

[1] The balance at the beginning of the period of report may be as per the accounts.

[2] If collection was other than in cash, explain.

be included in accounts receivable. To satisfy himself that consignment accounts are being treated properly, the auditor should examine consignment contracts, records, and correspondence, including consignment reports from consignees, should confirm the accounts, and should check the accounts receivable for indications of consignments (large debits and small credits). Any receivables for goods not yet sold by the consignee should be reclassified as inventory. An account receivable should be created for goods that the consignee has sold but not yet paid for.

Claims. A claim arises when an outside party fails to properly provide services or merchandise which he has agreed to provide. Examples are claims against transportation companies and insurance companies. The independent auditor must satisfy himself as to such claims through examination of correspondence, including proofs of loss and approved copies of claims. Confirmation of material amounts is a normal procedure. The internal auditor is concerned with seeing that all legitimate claims are recognized, properly calculated, recorded, and collected for benefit of the company.

Claims should be classified on the balance sheet separately from trade accounts receivable if material in amount and should be treated as current assets unless an extended delay in collection is indicated.

Installment Receivables. Installment accounts receivable arise from the sale of merchandise on a deferred payment plan—the customer will pay the amount owed in a series of payments over a specified time period. The auditing procedures for installment receivables are generally quite similar to those for accounts receivable in the areas of trial balancing, confirmation, and evaluation. The validity and balances of the accounts are determined in much the same way as for regular trade accounts receivable; however, certain additional procedures are required.

The auditor must inspect and be familiar with the various installment documents, such as conditional sales agreements, chattel mortgages, installment notes, and installment sales contracts. Familiarity with the installment documents helps the auditor determine whether or not payment agreements are being met, whether or not there are any special discounts, and what the billing and payment procedures are.

The installment receivables should be aged—preferably by the client's personnel. The aging schedule should be set up with time intervals according to either the number of installments past due or months of the current and subsequent years. The schedule should show the month in which the most recent payment was received, installments past due under the terms of the contract, and the unpaid balances on contracts with delinquent installments. A separate aging schedule should be prepared for each payment plan used by the client. Where the client prepares the schedule, the auditor should test the agings by referring to the ledger accounts, and should also compare the totals with agings at prior dates.

The client's procedures as to charge-offs, foreclosures, and repossessions should be reviewed by the auditor. The auditor should devote particular attention to observing the control and approval of repossessions. Additionally the auditor must verify the method used to price repossessed goods and must ascertain that receivable balances are being reduced when goods are repossessed. Request for confirmation of installment receivables should provide information as to the last payment date, the amount of each installment, and, possibly, the number of unpaid installments. Because the payment books used by installment buyers often do not show the total unpaid balance at any date, such information should not be provided on the confirmation request. Installment receivables that have been discounted, sold, or assigned and amounts that have been withheld or retained by the purchaser or other transferee should be confirmed.

Opinion No. 10 of the AICPA Accounting Principles Board states the following concerning the installment method of accounting:

> 12. Chapter 1A of ARB No. 43, paragraph 1, states that "Profit is deemed to be realized when a sale in the ordinary course of business is effected, unless the circumstances are such that the collection of the sale price is not reasonably assured." The Board reaffirms this statement; it believes that revenues should ordinarily be accounted for at the time a transaction is completed, with appropriate provision for uncollectible accounts. Accordingly, it concludes that, in the absence of the circumstances[8] referred to above, the installment method of recognizing revenue is not acceptable.
>
> [8] The Board recognizes that there are exceptional cases where receivables are collectible over an extended period of time and, because of the terms of the transactions or other conditions, there is no reasonable basis for estimating the degree of collectibility. When such circumstances exist, and as long as they exist, either the installment method or the cost recovery method of accounting may be used. (Under the cost recovery method, equal amounts of revenue and expense are recognized as collections are made until all costs have been recovered, postponing any recognition of profit until that time.)

When installment income is recognized at time of sale, adequate allowances should be provided for doubtful accounts, collection expenses, and repossession losses. A separate allowance may be set up for each year's sales. In such cases the auditor must assure himself that the proper year's allowance is charged when an account proves uncollectible, that the remaining allowances for each year are adequate, and that no allowance remains after all accounts from a particular year have been collected.

There is no set balance sheet treatment for installment receivables. They may or may not be shown as a separate item on the balance sheet, depending on whether or not the amounts are significant. Receivables are classified as current assets if there is a reasonable expectation that they will be collected during the normal operating cycle—usually a year. The operating cycle as to installment receivables is frequently longer than a year because of long credit terms. Such receivables are properly classified as current assets. Regulation S-X, Rule 3.13, of the SEC relates to this classification:

> Items classed as current assets shall be generally realizable within one year. However, generally recognized trade practices may be followed with respect to the inclusion of items such as installment receivables or inventories long in process, provided an appropriate explanation of the circumstances is made and, if practicable, an estimate is given of the amount not realizable within one year.

Consideration must be given to deferred federal income taxes related to installment accounts receivable. SEC Accounting Series Release No. 102 prescribes current liability treatment of such taxes to the extent that related accounts receivable are classified as current assets.

EDP AND RECEIVABLES—A COMPUTER AUDIT PROGRAM

General. One of the national accounting firms has published a series of case studies of computer audit programs. In one case (Christopher and Richards, "Case Study of a Computer Audit Program—No. 5"[14]), a study was made of the procedures and controls in those areas chosen for detailed review, one of

[14] *The Price Waterhouse Review,* Spring, 1966, pp. 24–29.

which was accounts receivable. The client's computer programs and the checks built into the computers were reviewed as part of the internal control evaluation.

Case I. In the area of accounts receivable, the accounting firm had as its goal the design of a computer audit program that would check the accounts receivable total, select by random and stratified sampling the accounts to be confirmed, and prepare the confirmation requests and statements. The program for accounts receivable confirmation involved choosing certain accounts from the accounts receivable file and entering them into a statement preparation run. A tape was prepared of all accounts which either had a balance greater than a predetermined amount or contained open items originating prior to a predetermined date, and of a randomly selected sample of all other accounts. The accounts receivable audit program was processed on the computer as soon as the receivables trial balance was ready. In less than an hour the console typewriter provided a printout which indicated the total accounts receivable balance and the number and amount of each category selected for confirmation. The confirmations and detailed statements were then produced, ready for review, stuffing, and mailing. The total elapsed time from when the program was started was three hours.

Case II. The same accounting firm designed a computer-based accounts receivable audit program for another client (Connolly "Case Study of a Computer Audit Program—No. 6"[15]) designed to assist the auditor in making a random selection of accounts receivable for confirmation and at the same time to determine that the field agreed with subsidiary ledger control accounts. The program was also designed to check all accounts for unusual balances and to foot and check the aging of all accounts. Two additional procedures that were to be added to the program when the client's magnetic tape record provided for them were a comparison of the customer's account balance with his history of purchases to test for reasonableness, and a check to determine that the credit limit had not been exceeded.

There were several benefits achieved in the accounts receivable area from the use of the computer. The accounting firm was able to select accounts receivable for confirmations which included certain specified past-due charges. This would have been impracticable with manual procedures. The client's time required for typing confirmation forms was eliminated, as was the auditor's time required for footing the accounts receivable trial balance. Another one of the national accounting firms has also found the use of electronic data processing in this area to be beneficial (see John B. Irvin, "Case Study on Use of Computer and Statistical Techniques,"[16] for a description of the procedures used). Both the selection time and the sample size required were somewhat less than with traditional auditing procedures.

NOTES RECEIVABLE

Description. "Notes receivable" is descriptive of a broad category of formal documents of indebtedness, including both notes and acceptances receivable. A note represents an unconditional promise in writing to pay a specified sum of money on demand or at a future date. It must be signed by the maker and may be payable to bearer or the order of a particular person. An acceptance also represents a promise to pay a specified sum of money made by the

[15] *The Price Waterhouse Review*, Summer, 1966, pp. 34–45.
[16] *The Journal of Accountancy*, April, 1964, pp. 67–68.

drawer, and becomes the equivalent of a note when the drawee indicates on its face that he has agreed to accept it. Notes receivable are probably more negotiable than accounts receivable but are not necessarily more collectible.

Objectives of Examination. The auditor usually has the same four objectives in his examination of notes receivable as he has in his examination of accounts receivable, namely, to establish the accuracy of amounts, the validity of the notes as claims, and their collectibility and realizable value and to determine their proper financial statement treatment. The reader is referred to the accounts receivable section of this chapter for a discussion of these objectives.

Internal Control. The key factors involved in good internal control for notes receivable are the same as for accounts receivable, namely, separation of duties and proper authorization procedures. The elements of these two standards discussed in the section on accounts receivable are, in general, also applicable to notes receivable. The review of internal control is also performed in much the same way as for accounts receivable. An internal control questionnaire, a sample of which is shown in Figure 8, is used, and the auditor also makes use of observation and test checking.

Additional standards to maintain good control over notes receivable are as follows:

1. New or renewed notes should be properly approved before acceptance.
2. A detailed record should be maintained of notes receivable and notes receivable discounted.
3. The notes and any collateral should be periodically examined and interest and maturity dates checked.
4. Partial payments should be shown on the note itself.
5. The various functions mentioned in the sample questionnaire (Figure 8) should be performed by different individuals.
6. Notes should be kept in a safe place.

Figure 8 INTERNAL CONTROL QUESTIONNAIRE*

NOTES RECEIVABLE

1. Are notes authorized by a responsible official before being accepted?
2. Are renewals and changes in terms of notes authorized by a responsible official?
3. Is the notes receivable custodian independent of the cashier or bookkeepers?
4. Is the custodian of negotiable collateral held against notes receivable independent of the cashier or bookkeepers?
5. Is the negotiable collateral inspected regularly?
6. Are the individual notes regularly totaled to agree with the general ledger control account?
7. Is a detailed record maintained of
   a. Notes receivable?
   b. Notes receivable discounted?
8. Are partial payments recorded on the backs of the notes?
9. Are direct confirmations of unpaid note balances obtained periodically:
   a. By internal auditors?
   b. By other designated employees?
10. Are notes receivable reviewed by a proper official to determine delinquent amounts?
11. Is the write-off of uncollectible amounts approved by a responsible official?
12. Are charged-off notes and future recoveries properly controlled?
13. Are more than one person required to be present for obtaining access to the actual notes?

* Affirmative answers indicate a satisfactory degree of internal control.

Auditing Procedures. The auditing procedures used for accounts receivable are generally also applicable to notes receivable. The auditors should obtain a listing of notes and acceptances receivable from the client (this listing represents the notes receivable trial balance). The listing should provide detailed information for each note. As with accounts receivable, the auditor proves the footings of the list and reconciles the totals with the general ledger control account or accounts. He also must check the listing against the individual accounts or other detail records and against the actual notes. In checking the list, the auditor should indicate the following types of notes:

1. Renewed notes
2. Past-due notes
3. Notes not from trade debtors: i.e., notes from employees, officers, directors, stockholders, and affiliated companies

This segregation is similar to the procedure followed for accounts receivable.

Other accounts receivable procedures are also applicable. If the audit procedures are performed prior to the balance sheet date, the auditor should review the intervening transactions. In such cases he should also review the balance sheet date listings to determine if any notes should be reclassified and if there are any new notes of sizable amount that should be confirmed. The notes receivable transactions should be examined to verify the genuineness of the notes. As with accounts receivable, the collectibility of the notes must be determined and confirmation procedures must be performed. These last two procedures are discussed in more detail below.

Inspection and confirmation. It is of primary importance to inspect or otherwise account for the notes and any collateral involved. It is generally not sufficient to confirm a note receivable with the maker of the note because a note may be negotiated to a third party without notifying the maker. Through physical inspection of the notes, the auditor can determine if any notes have been sold, discounted, or pledged. Notes and any related collateral should preferably be inspected at the same time that cash is counted and securities are inspected. Such a procedure removes the possibility of converting notes, after they have been counted, into cash in order to cover up a cash shortage. The actual notes should be compared with the client's records (i.e., note register) for payee's and maker's names, endorsers, principal amount and interest rate, date made, and maturity date. Endorsements on the note may indicate a temporary conversion and should be investigated. Maturity dates should be examined to determine proper classification of the notes (as to current and noncurrent).

Confirmations should be requested from the makers of the notes, including those notes discounted, assigned with recourse, or otherwise pledged. For those notes in the custody of others at the time of inspection, confirmation requests should be sent not only to the maker but also to the present holder. The auditor should determine why notes are in the custody of others (i.e., whether for collection or as collateral for a loan). Alternate procedures, such as examining evidence of subsequent payment, must be applied to notes for which no replies are received to positive confirmation requests.

Any collateral securing the notes should be confirmed with the debtor as to description and amount. The auditor should determine that the collateral is properly segregated from the client's assets. The value of the collateral should be determined by the auditor in order to see if there is adequate security for the note.

Determine collectibility. The auditor must review the collectibility of notes receivable for the same reasons that he reviews the collectibility of accounts receivable:

1. To determine that notes considered uncollectible have been charged off
2. To determine that an adequate allowance has been set up for losses on doubtful items

Some of the procedures are the same as for accounts receivable and thus are not discussed in detail here. The auditor should check the client's aging of notes and obtain a summary of the aging for the working papers. As with accounts receivable, information should be obtained as to amounts due more than one year from the balance sheet date.

The auditor should investigate the origin of the notes receivable and should determine the client's policies as to accepting notes for past-due accounts and as to note renewals. He should discuss the collectibility of the notes with the client and should review the credit files for large notes, renewed notes, and past-due notes. The credit standing of the debtors should be investigated on an appropriate test basis. The auditor should ascertain that note renewals are being satisfactorily indicated. He should also ascertain whether there have been any collections or write-offs of notes receivable during the period from the balance sheet date to the report date. Control over notes that have been written off as uncollectible should be considered and a review made of notes written off in prior periods.

There are a number of situations which indicate that a note may be uncollectible:

1. A note is past-due.
2. It is not the trade custom to accept notes.
3. A note has been renewed a number of times.
4. A note has been taken in settlement of an overdue account receivable.
5. The debtor is in financial difficulty.
6. Payments have not been made regularly.

Verify interest items. Trade notes receivable are generally interest-bearing. There are four interest items relating to notes receivable that should be verified through test calculations:

1. Interest income on notes receivable
2. Interest expense on notes receivable discounted
3. Accrued interest receivable
4. Unearned (prepaid) interest

The entries in the various interest accounts should be reconciled, on a test basis, to the notes. The verification of interest items is particularly important in bank audits because of the large volume of notes and the much greater than usual significance of interest income.

Determine contingent liability for notes receivable discounted. The auditor must determine the contingent liability for notes receivable discounted. Such a liability arises when a company sells or transfers a note receivable not yet due to a third party (generally a bank). The company becomes contingently liable as a result of this transaction—it will be required to pay the face amount of the note to the bank if the maker of the note fails to make payment when the note falls due. The best indication of the existence of notes receivable discounted is item 3 of the Standard Bank Confirmation form used in connection with the cash phase of the audit. The client's bank (or banks) in completing the confirmation is requested to list the contingent liability for all notes that have been discounted with it:

3. The customer was contingently liable as endorser of notes discounted and/or as guarantor at the close of business on that date in the total amount of $________, as below:

Amount	Name of maker	Date of note	Due date	Remarks
$				

The bank confirmation is not the only source of information concerning notes receivable discounted. When reviewing the notes receivable accounts, the auditor should be alert for any indications that a particular credit represents the discounting of a note as opposed to the collection of the note (when a note is discounted, a Notes Receivable Discounted account and not Notes Receivable should be credited).

Balance Sheet Classification. Trade notes and acceptances (those arising in the ordinary course of business) are frequently combined with accounts receivable for financial statement purposes, with a single caption such as "Accounts and Notes Receivable" being used. This practice is acceptable so long as the notes and acceptances are not significant in amount, as is generally the case. If the notes are significant in amount, either they should be shown in a separate caption or their amount should be disclosed parenthetically. Examples of these three forms of presentation may be found in the section on financial statement presentation of accounts receivable. If not combined with accounts receivable, notes receivable and acceptances receivable may be shown either separately or together. Non-trade notes if significant in amount should be shown separately from trade notes. The SEC requires notes receivable to be shown separately from accounts receivable for statements prepared according to Regulation S-X.

Careful consideration should be given to the classification of notes as current or noncurrent. Notes are generally treated as current if they are to become due within the company's normal operating cycle. However, not all such notes are properly classified as current, as in the case of a company that is in the midst of severe financial difficulties and is thus not likely to pay its notes when due.

The nature of any collateral for notes of a significant amount should be disclosed. Notes should not be represented as "secured" unless it is known that the realizable value of the collateral is at least equal to the amount of the note. Disclosures such as "mortgage on real estate held as collateral" or "500 shares of X Company stock held as collateral" permit the reader of the financial statement to decide for himself the extent of security represented by the collateral.

Allowances and accrued interest. Most companies do not show a separate allowance for uncollectible notes and acceptances. Rather, they use a combined allowance for both notes and accounts receivable. It is acceptable to show a combined allowance in the balance sheet so long as the allowance is deducted from the total of all the receivables to which it relates. Any accrued interest on notes receivable may be combined on the balance sheet with the face amount of the notes. It is, however, preferable that the caption indicate that the amounts have been combined.

Notes Receivable Discounted. Notes receivable discounted are described above in the section on audit procedures. A contingent liability must be shown for the total amount of notes receivable discounted. There are several ways of showing this contingent liability:

1. The contingent liability may be indicated in a footnote to the balance sheet.
2. The contingent liability may be shown parenthetically.
3. The contingent liability may be shown "short" (the amount is not extended into the money columns).
4. Notes receivable discounted may be included with other notes in the asset section of the balance sheet with a contra account for the discounted notes in the liability section.
5. Notes receivable discounted may be shown as a deduction from the total notes receivable.

For the first three methods the amount shown for notes receivable is a net amount (total notes receivable less notes receivable discounted). The footnote method is probably the most widely used.

The presentation of notes receivable discounted is sometimes affected by events that occur after the balance sheet date but before the date of the auditor's report. If a discounted note is dishonored during this period, an actual current liability, rather than a contingent liability, should be shown on the balance sheet. A contingent liability should still be shown for discounted notes that are paid during this period, but it is acceptable to indicate that such notes have since been paid.

Government Entities. There are four types of governmental receivables: taxes receivable, special assessments receivable, accounts receivable, and notes receivable. For a discussion of the auditing procedures for taxes receivable and special assessments receivable, the reader is referred to *Municipal Accounting and Auditing*, prepared by the National Committee of Governmental Accounting. The verification procedures to be used for accounts and notes receivable are the same as those used for a private business.

"Accounts receivable" and "notes receivable" have the same meaning for governmental units as they do for private business. "Accounts receivable" do not include amounts due from other funds within the same governmental unit. "Taxes receivable" represent taxes levied but not yet collected. "Special assessments receivable" represent the amounts levied against, but not yet collected from, certain properties or persons who will particularly benefit from a specific improvement or service provided by the governmental unit (the improvement or service is often to some extent beneficial to the general public).

The Accounting and Auditing Act of 1950, Section 117(a), requires the Comptroller General of the United States to give due regard to generally accepted auditing standards in determining what auditing procedures are to be followed. This requirement applies to receivables as it does to all other accounts. Effective June 30, 1965, the General Accounting Office issued a restatement of accounting principles and standards to be followed by federal agencies. The section on receivables is reproduced here:

12.4 RECEIVABLES

Under the accrual basis of accounting, receivables representing amounts due from others are accounted for as assets from the time the acts giving rise to such claims are completed until they are collected, converted into other resources, or determined to be uncollectible. Accounting for receivables is an important form of control over agency resources in that it results in a systematic record of amounts due that must be accounted for.

Specific principles and standards to be observed in accounting for receivables follow:

(1) Amounts receivable shall be recorded accurately and promptly on completion of the acts which entitle an agency to collect amounts owing to it (billing for performance of service or sales of materials, loans or advances made, etc.).

(2) Amounts to be accounted for as receivables shall consist of the amounts actually due under contractual or other arrangements governing the transactions which result in receivables.

(3) Separate accounts for major categories of receivables should be maintained to facilitate clear and full disclosure of the nature of an agency's resources in its financial reports.

(4) Loans to others shall be accounted for as receivables only after the funds have been disbursed. Loans authorized but not disbursed are a form of commitment to be disclosed in explanatory notes to financial reports, but they should not be reported as assets with related liabilities representing obligations to make loans.

(5) Accounting records for receivables shall be maintained so that all transactions affecting the receivables for each period for which reports are to be prepared, and only such transactions, are included.

(6) Regular estimates shall be made from time to time of the portion of amounts receivable that may not be collectible. Such estimates shall be accounted for and disclosed separately in financial reports. (Specific procedures for handling and accounting for receivables determined to be uncollectible are prescribed by the Comptroller General in Title 4 of this Manual.)

(7) Receivables that are collectible in the form of foreign currency that is not freely convertible to U.S. currency are subject to the same financial reporting standard as restricted foreign currency (see section 12.3).

BIBLIOGRAPHY

Accounting Principles Board, Opinions of the Accounting Principles Board, AICPA, New York:
APB No. 6, *Status of Accounting Research Bulletins*, 1965.
APB No. 10, *Omnibus Opinion*, 1966.
APB No. 12, *Omnibus Opinion*, 1967.

Accounting Trends and Techniques, AICPA, New York, issued annually.

Committee on Auditing Procedure, Statements on Auditing Procedure No. 33, *Auditing Standards and Procedures*, AICPA, New York, 1963.

The Comptroller General of the United States, *Accounting Principles and Standards for Federal Agencies*, U.S. General Accounting Office, Washington, 1965.

Brink, Victor A., and James A. Cashin: *Internal Auditing*, 2d ed., New York, The Ronald Press Company, 1958.

DeVos, Henry, ed.: *Management Services Handbook*, New York, AICPA, 1964.

Ingalls, Edmund F.: *Practical Accounting and Auditing Problems*, New York, AICPA, 1966.

Palen, Jennie M., and the Prentice-Hall Editorial Board: *Encyclopedia of Auditing Techniques*, Englewood Cliffs, N J., Prentice-Hall, Inc., 1966.

Solomon, Sid J.: "Making Accounts Receivable Processing More Automatic," *Management Services*, October, 1966.

Davis, Gordon B., John Neter, and Roger R. Palmer: "An Experimental Study of Audit Confirmations," *The Journal of Accountancy*, June, 1967.

Colt, Donald G.: "Management Information Systems for Cash Management," *Management Accounting*, June, 1969.

Radin, Arthur J.: "Auditing Computerized Retail Receivables—A Case Study," *The New York Certified Public Accountant*, August, 1969.

Denning, W. Edwards, and T. Nelson Grice: "An Efficient Procedure for Audit of Accounts Receivable," *Management Accounting*, March, 1970.

Chapter 22

Inventories

WYMAN G. PATTEN

Partner, Price Waterhouse & Co.

GENERAL

In this chapter will be discussed the principal problems an auditor may encounter in examining inventories. Under each heading the subject will be discussed at sufficient length to outline the accepted auditing standards and procedures. References will be given to texts and articles which cover the accounting aspects, history, etc., of the subject. Related auditing material touching on inventory may be found in other handbook chapters.

Importance of Inventories. The one asset appearing on the balance sheet of a company which is usually more characteristic of the company's business than any other is inventories. Almost all companies, even those engaged in service activities, carry inventories. In the case of manufacturing companies, inventories present very complex problems of a management and accounting nature. Success or failure of the business depends on the manner in which the problems are met. The largest swings in the income may derive from the estimation and valuation process connected with inventories. The most complex and important problems in an entire audit frequently relate to the inventory.

Inventories generally are the lifeblood of business. They are the center of all productive effort and the principal source of company revenues. They supply the cash to meet payrolls, taxes, and other business expenses. They are, however, susceptible to accumulations of errors in judgment in such vital areas as: What will sell? What will the cost be? How much inventory must be carried to meet sales deliveries, at how much risk of obsolescence and high carrying charges?

Inventories present problems to the independent auditor from the point of view of frauds of peculation and manipulation. Inventories present problems to the governmental contract auditor and cost inspector concerning allowable costs for reimbursement purposes. They present problems to the internal auditor, who must make certain that inventories are efficiently managed and that internal controls are adequate.

Broad Classes of Inventories. Inventories range in nature from the simplest case of purchased items—tangible and easily identifiable—to highly complex manufactured inventories which start with raw materials and purchased parts and go through many stages of manufacture and assembly with substantial value added in the process.

An illustration is the simple case of lead pencils carried in a wholesale supply house inventory. The auditing problems here are relatively straightforward. Quantities are easily determined, and so is cost, which is taken directly from vendors' invoices. There is not likely to be any serious problem of deterioration or spoilage or obsolescence from change in style or customer preferences. The turnover rate is probably good. Except that lead pencils may be part of an inventory which is comprised of thousands and thousands of items, none of which is very important to the overall picture, it is hard to visualize any important audit problems having to do with such an inventory. Such a situation would, however, present problems to the management from the point of view of what detail records need to be kept and how often physical inventory counts need to be taken in order to keep the stock records reliable.

By contrast, one might turn to the problem presented in the inventories of an aerospace equipment company or a sophisticated electronics manufacturer. In these cases, the items in the inventory are difficult for the auditor to identify. Also, a high degree of obsolescence is present because the products change rapidly. In either case, many manufacturing operations and stages of assembly are encountered, bringing up problems of identification of costs with the manufactured and assembled items.

Inventories may be long-term in nature—a construction contract on a power dam or a government contract to develop and test an entirely new defensive weapon, for example. In such cases as these, the inventory amounts are not determinable by taking quantity counts and multiplying the quantities counted times the prices shown by vendors' invoices or developed by a cost system. The inventory may really be an inventory of dollars and the auditing problem may be a matter of substantiating the dollars which have been put into the contract. Where the contract is for a fixed price, the matter of measuring how far along the contract has progressed, and the matter of whether or not it can be completed within an amount of expenditure which will produce a profit, are sometimes very difficult audit problems.

Government contract inventories may present problems to the independent auditor and to the government contract auditor. The government, in attempting to foster efficiency on the part of contractors, has developed some very complex forms of contracting and some highly sophisticated methods for measuring performance. The ordinary cost-plus-a-fixed-fee contract carries with it difficult problems of determining what costs may properly be charged and what amount of overhead may be attributable to the contract. In price-incentive contracts, difficult accounting and auditing ramifications become involved.

Audit Objectives. Accounting has been likened to a continuing process recording change and movement throughout the year—with a snapshot picture taken at intervals. If this is a fair picture, it is the inventories which are the most difficult to get into focus. Several things contribute to the clearness and accuracy of the inventory picture: (1) the controls should be good (good controls minimize confusion, and it is in confusion that inaccuracies and misstatements often build up); (2) accurate counts must be made and summarized; and (3) reliable and consistent means of determining values must be used.

There are, of course, operational audit objectives which are of interest to auditors. Are the inventories well managed as to size of investment? Are carrying cost and handling costs held to a minimum? For the governmental auditor, there are technical criteria relating to contract performance, determination of taxes, etc. But primarily the objectives of all auditors relate to the fair statement of the inventories for balance sheet and income determination purposes.

AUDIT RELATIONSHIPS

Role of the Independent Auditor. All auditors, whether they are independent auditors, internal auditors, or auditors in the employment of governmental agencies, have many interests in common in determining the accuracy and fairness of the amount at which inventories are carried. It is difficult to ascribe a particular role to one group without seeming to deny it to the others. The fact is that all auditors have much the same interests but in somewhat different and varying degrees.

The independent auditor has a primary responsibility to ascertain, insofar as practical, that the amount shown for inventories is represented by physical goods and that reasonable care has been taken in determining the physical quantities and their condition. He must ascertain that the quantities have been fairly and consistently priced in accordance with accepted accounting principles and that they have been carefully extended and summarized. He must satisfy himself that they include no obsolete or defective goods except at fair values, and that due provision has been made for probable losses on slow-moving goods, that the company owns the goods, and that liens upon pledging or assignment are disclosed in the financial statements.

In expressing an opinion on financial statements, the independent auditor should require that the inventories be fairly stated and that the basis of pricing be disclosed. If there has been a change during the year in the basis or methods used to value the inventories, he should see to it that the change and the effect thereof on income for the year are clearly disclosed.

Role of the Internal Auditor. As stated in The Institute of Internal Auditors' Research Committee Report No. 11: "Coordination of actual auditing work between an internal auditing staff and a company's independent public accountants is usually designed (1) to minimize duplication of work and (2) to take advantage of the specialized knowledge that the internal auditor has of his company's operations. A typical example of such coordination is in joint work in observation of the taking of inventory."

The role of the internal auditors with regard to inventories tends more in the direction of searching out and disclosing weaknesses and inefficiencies in the controls over the management of inventories. The internal auditor is extensively interested in inventories from their inception in the purchasing department through the receiving, inspection, and storing departments. He may carry out examination programs designed to appraise the overall effectiveness of the functioning of these departments in the handling of inventories. (See Bradford Cadmus, *Operational Auditing Handbook*, chapter VI.)

Role of the Governmental Auditor. Auditors representing various branches of federal, state, and local government have rights established by law and regulations which empower them to examine a company's or individual's accounting and related records. The Comptroller General, who heads the General Accounting Office, has a large and active staff of auditors who make independent examinations into the manner in which government agencies discharge their financial responsibilities, including the administration of funds. These auditors frequently examine the costs of contractors included in inventories for defense contracts. The GAO is responsible to Congress rather than to any of the agencies of the executive branch of government.

The Department of Defense carries a large audit staff. It has now consolidated its audit efforts into a single Defense Contract Audit Agency, which is under the direction, authority, and control of the Secretary of Defense. This agency is empowered to examine into the acceptability of costs incurred under cost-type, redeterminable, incentive, and similar contracts. The DCAA also may examine into the adequacy of accounting and financial management systems of contractors to the Department of Defense.

The examining agents of the Internal Revenue Service have long had the power to examine, and indeed have often examined, taxpayer records. Taxpayers on an accrual basis must report inventories if such are used in the business, since, according to the Internal Revenue Code:

> Whenever in the opinion of the Secretary (of the Treasury) or his delegate the use of inventories is necessary in order clearly to determine the income of any taxpayer, inventories shall be taken by such taxpayers on such basis as the Secretary or his delegate may prescribe as conforming as nearly as may be to the best accounting practice in the trade or business and as most clearly reflecting the income.

State tax commissioners also employ auditors and examiners to look into state income and franchise taxes reported by taxpayers, and local taxing authorities have need at times to ascertain the fairness of inventories where personal property is included as part of the base against which a rate is applied for local taxing purposes.

Cooperation between Auditors. The independent auditor views the functioning of an effective internal auditing group as an important part of a company's internal control. Physical inventory observation presents an excellent opportunity for the independent auditor and the internal auditor to coordinate their work. On these occasions, the staff of the independent auditor would often be stretched too thin to give adequate observation if there were not full coordination with the company's internal audit staff. These occasions provide the internal auditor with the opportunity for gaining useful contact and experience with the company's manufacturing and inventory operations, and provide the independent auditor with an opportunity for appraising the quality of the company's internal auditing organization.

In situations where inventories are not physically counted at one time and the annual inventory is based on a "draw-off" of quantity records (test-counted throughout the year), the internal auditor often makes test counts at various locations and dates throughout the year. Where this is done, the outside auditor may restrict his own test counts in reliance on the strengthened internal control thus provided.

INTERNAL CONTROL

Nature of Internal Control. The concept of internal control as applied to inventories requires segregation of responsibilities for custody and accounting. Good business management and housekeeping methods must be brought to bear to prevent overstocking, spoilage and obsolescence, loss of sales from downtime or shortages, and fraudulent loss through theft or embezzlement.

Controls to prevent fraud involving a company's inventories lie in the overall segregation of purchasing, receiving, storing, and treasury and accounting functions. They consist in exercising physical protection measures and in maintaining effective accountability. These controls may not prevent all frauds, but should usually disclose them before too great a loss has been incurred.

It may be well, however, to recognize realistically that, except for those companies which deal in a relatively small number of high-value, easily marketable items, sound business judgment may conclude that it is too costly to maintain precise and strictly controlled inventory quantity and dollar records. Furthermore, it is costly and impracticable to make frequent physical counts of the inventory items and to check them against the quantity records. In many businesses the only formal record of inventories is the general ledger account. This account may be brought into line with physical reality only once a year when a complete count is taken.

It is well for the auditor to recognize that it is difficult to maintain accurate and reliable quantity records unless they are tied into the general ledger. Where a business has thousands of items in inventory, this is tedious and expensive to accomplish, although with the speed of the electronic computer it is becoming feasible in more and more instances. However, various records and internal reports within the area of production and inventories provide controls and add to the difficulties of would-be defrauders. Production and yield reports, shrinkage reports, turnover ratios, etc., may give clues to inventories which have been forced out of line by frauds concealed within them. The auditor should be familiar with all the management reports of this nature and should investigate any unusual variations or trends.

One area where controls are often lacking is scrap. Whether because management fails to regard scrap as important or for other reasons, its handling is often insufficiently controlled. Rarely are figures developed to indicate the quantities and classes of scrap which should be generated in a manufacturing operation. In most cases control over scrap starts only at the point of independent weighing and billing. The auditor would do well to give close attention to the controls designed to protect the company against lost revenue from the sale of scrap. The value of scrap frequently reaches sizable proportions, particularly if it is compared with the company's net income.

Testing Internal Controls. Following are pertinent internal control questions which the auditor should carefully consider in his examination of inventory:

1. Is there a central receiving point established, and do all receipts clear through this point?
2. Are receiving, shipping, and storing responsibilities clearly separated?
3. Are all receipts evidenced by a receiving record, preferably prenumbered?
4. Are all receipts counted, weighed, or measured promptly?
5. Are company premises adequately surrounded by appropriate protective devices, such as fences, guards, etc., to prevent unauthorized shipments or removal of finished goods, materials, and equipment?
6. Are inventory items of significant value which would be susceptible to pilferage kept under adequate controls inside the plant by designated personnel who are the only ones authorized to enter such controlled areas?
7. Are perpetual records maintained wherever practicable?
8. Are employees who maintain perpetual stock records independent of storekeeping, purchasing, and shipping?
9. Are physical units counted at least once a year, and are the counts reconciled with the perpetual records by someone other than the custodian?

10. Are substantial variations between perpetual records and physical counts investigated? By whom? Are adjustments of perpetual inventory records to physical inventory quantities approved in writing? Are adjustments priced and accumulated and periodically reported to management?

11. Are cycle counts utilized wherever practicable?

12. Are withdrawals from stores made only on the basis of properly approved requisitions, shipping notices, bills of lading, etc.?

13. Do all shipments go through the shipping department?

14. Are requisitions and shipping notices prenumbered to assure that all are recorded in the general ledger and the perpetual records? Is one copy sent directly to the accounting department so that no opportunity is presented to the storekeeper to increase the quantity issued?

15. Are all shipments, including goods returned to vendors, properly accounted for?

16. Have inventory valuation policies been set by established authority, and are they being observed?

17. Are vendors' invoices matched in the accounting department with receiving reports and purchase orders prior to being passed for payment?

18. Are the amounts posted to the general ledger control accounts computed and passed to the general ledger bookkeeper by someone other than those employees engaged in keeping the stockroom?

19. Does the company have an established procedure for the identification of excess, surplus, obsolete, and slow-moving inventories?

20. Are all inventories, including inventories stored at warehouses, in transit, and with others, adequately covered by insurance? In Figure 1 is shown a schedule of "Interim Test Counts of Perpetual Records." This is an important procedure in testing the reliability of inventory controls.

Receiving Procedures. For our purposes we will begin with receiving functions, since purchasing functions are discussed in another chapter. The receiving department should be independent of departments connected with purchasing, storage, and disbursement.

It should count, weigh, or otherwise measure all items received. To facilitate this function it is often furnished with a copy of the purchase order. The receiving copy usually has all quantity areas blocked out to encourage independent counts. Statistical sampling should be used, if practicable.

The receiving report form should be prenumbered and should provide copies for the purchasing department, to follow up partial receipts under open purchase orders; copies for the voucher audit group in accounts payable, to support disbursement vouchers; copies for inspection, for stores, or for other needs. One copy should be retained in the receiving department and bound with others in numerical order. The auditor should visit the receiving department early in his examination and review its operation as an effective part of the internal control over disbursements and inventories.

Proper functioning of the receiving department is sometimes circumvented in instances where costly items are hand-delivered by salesmen and expeditors who seek to get early inspection and clearance for payment. Good procedure should require that purchasing and inspection personnel redirect such deliveries to the receiving department for proper receipt and processing. (See Bradford Cadmus, *Operational Auditing Handbook*, page 64.)

Issuing Procedures. Another link in the chain of controls over inventories is found in tight issuing procedures. The basis of accounting for the issuance of materials and supplies is the materials requisition. To the degree that

Figure 1 INTERIM COUNTS

Downtown Manufacturing Company
Gun Division
Interim Test Counts of Perpetual Records
Finished Parts

SCH: E 114 Cont.
DATE: 12/31/70

Product Code	Part No.	Description	Balance Per Perpetual Card	Auditor's Count	Count Over (Under) Perpetual Card	Standard Cost Per Hundred	Amount of Difference
Card to Floor						$	$
161	20555	Magazine Tube Cap	13,996	14,051	55	22.72	12.50
168	11300	Firing Pin	7,984	7,916	(68)	25.83	⟨17.56⟩
273	10110	Ejector Latch Housing	21,505	21,481	(24)	13.33	⟨3.20⟩
272	7523	Ejector Rod	16,887	16,900	13	17.74	2.31
166	2409	Forehand Cap	17,020	17,041	21	28.57	6.00
185	3053	Action Spring	4,906	5,067	161	21.60	34.78
187	2254	Cylinder	4,186	4,200	14	32.19	4.51
266	8411	Handle Pin	3,896	3,896	–	161.93	–
171	10067	Grip Assembly	2,500	2,500	–	117.45	–
Floor to Card							
165	7666	4" Handle	3,000	2,996	(4)	112.14	⟨4.49⟩
162	8990	51/64" Barrel	491	489	(2)	267.82	⟨5.36⟩
261	20563	Forehand Slide	5,500	5,500	–	20.59	–
84	25405	Underbody	15,710	15,710	–	6.90	–
162	3458	Guard Assembly	392	391	(1)	492.67	⟨4.93⟩
161	8749	Control Element	4,690	4,870	120	100.84	121.01
172	7652	Ejector Assembly	109	109	–	262.66	–
						Over	541.02
						Under	⟨415.04⟩
							125.98
						Total Tested	$261,056.62
						Total Inventory	$1,309,610.00
						Tested	Approx 20%

10/24/70 RWC

All differences appear to be minor and insignificant in total – perpetual card records give good evidence of being reliable.

materials or supplies are not permitted to leave the stores area except through properly approved requisitions, the reliability of the perpetual quantity records is enhanced. The materials requisition form supplies the source for credit posting to the stores. A priced counterpart of the requisition supplies the debit posting to work in process inventories, fixed assets, expense, etc., as the case may require. The forms should be prenumbered and the numerical sequence of the forms accounted for as the issues are processed. This sometimes presents a problem where forms are available throughout the plant. Good procedure requires that the number of pads in use be limited and that a record be kept of their location.

The auditor should satisfy himself, by appropriate tests, that the issuance of materials is being properly controlled and that the appearance of charge via an approved materials requisition represents a genuine materials movement.

PHYSICAL INVENTORY

Inventory Date. Where a company's accounting system is so elementary that the amount of the inventory is known only at such times as counts are made and priced, there is very little alternative to having the physical inventory counts taken near the year end. Companies with good accounting systems facilitate the year-end account closing by having the count or a "draw-off" made several months in advance, relying for the intervening period to the year end on charging input at cost and relieving for sales via standard or other established costs. Unless the inventory costing and accounting can produce reliable results and the intervening transactions can be adequately tested, the auditor should insist that the physical counting or "draw-off" be done near the year end.

Physical Inventory Instructions. If reliable results are to be achieved, much time and thought must be given by a company and its auditors to formulating plans for taking the annual inventory. It is in the auditors' interest to take care in advance to see that planning is adequately done, for if the counting is poorly controlled and the item descriptions are indistinct and inconclusive, the auditor may not be able to rely on the results.

The inventory taking logically should fall under the general supervision of the controller, who is most vitally interested in the accuracy of the company's financial statements. Plant personnel are familiar with the stock and can best identify the items in counting. Therefore, an ideal procedure would coordinate the work of the plant and accounting departments. In the counting of stores it is mandatory that the storekeeper not play a role in the counts made in his own area. Similarly, counts which cover piecework items or those on which departmental bonuses are paid should not be made by persons who benefit from such payments. The auditor should be vigilant to note any substantial lack of independence or any basic conflict of purpose in the count assignments.

Good housekeeping methods in the plant, warehouse, storeroom, or whatever, aid in making the inventory counts proceed smoothly. If stacks are squared up, like items brought together, and aisles and shipping and receiving areas cleared, counting is more quickly done and mistakes and recounts are more easily avoided. In a neatly arranged inventory area the auditor can quickly make test counts and can sight-check to see that all items have been counted. Spoiled work and obsolete and inferior materials and parts should be labeled and segregated prior to the commencing of the count.

Movement while counting. To facilitate accurate count, all substantial movement of inventories should be stopped. Vendors should be requested not to make deliveries during the count period, and customers should be asked to order sufficient quantities in advance to tide them over the period of the count shutdown. However, it is not uncommon to find that the company will use the inventory shutdown period to catch up on shortages and unbalanced inventories and will have machines running while the counting is being done. Also, emergency shipments and receipts inevitably take place. The auditor must expect that variations in inventory plans will occur and must be prepared to cope with them. It usually helps to have an extra assistant assigned to the job during the count to cover unforeseen changes in plans and to follow through on unscheduled movements in inventories.

Tag control. It is most important that plans be made for the adequate control of count tags. They should be serially numbered and have identifying colors and stripes for various types of counts. One person should be in charge of the tag control and should keep a record of the series of tags handed out to the various count teams. Unused tags should be returned to tag control and retained for the auditors' inspection. Since the auditor and his assistants cannot accompany each of the count teams, the tag control is all-important to the validity of his testing of inventory counts.

Using tags or sheets. In doing the planning for the physical inventory, the relative advantages of count tags and count sheets should be considered. The count tag (a two- or three-part tag is customarily used) has marked advantages over count sheets for recording physical inventory counts. The stub end may be tied to the stack or batch of items counted, thus facilitating inspection to make certain that all items have been counted. The detached portions of the tags may be arranged in a number of different ways to group like items, on the one hand, or to present the count tags in serial-number sequence, on the other. Where punched cards are used, the card number and inventory item number may be prepunched and the item description preprinted on the card. The count can be inserted by "mark-sensing." Also, the punched count cards can be merged with a pricing deck and extensions and footings accomplished mechanically.

The inventory should be summarized two ways, once in tag-number sequence (this is important to the auditor, who must make tests of the tag control and false-inclusion tests) and a second time with like items grouped and totaled (important to the company for correcting perpetual quantity records and important to the auditor, who must make certain that items which are important in the aggregate come within the purview of his tests). Furthermore, the two-way recapping of the count tags provides a double check on the mathematical accuracy of the inventory total.

Planning the Physical Inventory. Following is a list to guide the auditor in ascertaining whether sufficient precautions have been taken in planning the physical inventory counts.

1. Are the physical counts to be supervised by persons independent of purchasing, storekeeping, and maintenance of perpetual inventory records?

2. Are counts and identification of part number and last operation to be adequately rechecked by a second employee who has a knowledge of the product?

3. Are inventory tags or count sheets to be prenumbered and controlled and accounted for satisfactorily to ensure proper recording in final inventory sheets?

4. Have written instructions been prepared for the guidance of company employees participating in physical inventories pertaining to:

   a. Counting and listing?
   b. Use of scales for scale counts, and accuracy of scales?
   c. Part number, description, and last-operation verification by foreman or other qualified person?
   d. Issue and control of tags or count sheets by department heads?
   e. Sorting and tabulation of count tags by office personnel?
   f. Pricing by office personnel?

5. Has care been taken to limit and control inventory movements during physical inventory taking, and do proper cutoff procedures exist?

6. Have vendors been advised to stop shipments several days beforehand to alleviate receipts?

7. Have arrangements been made to stop all shipments other than emergency orders?

8. Are all interdepartment and interplant transfers to be suspended several days beforehand?

9. Do company procedures provide for liabilities to be taken up for all items included in inventory?

10. Do company procedures provide for exclusion from inventory count of items sold and billed but not shipped?

11. Does the company have a procedure for identifying excess or surplus materials and obsolete and slow-moving inventories?

12. Have careful arrangements been made for identifying complex inventories of in-process items and for determining the stage of completion or last completed operation? Operation sheets or "travelers" frequently accompany the batches of items through the plant and may be referred to for identification purposes.

Inventory Count. Following is a list of important matters to be attended to by the auditor and his staff in observing the company's counts and counting methods while the physical inventory work is in progress.

1. Obtain a copy of the company's physical inventory instructions sufficiently in advance of the inventory date to study and make recommendations.

2. Obtain copies of physical layouts of all plants showing department numbers and descriptions and the names of department heads. Sketch on the plant layout sheets approximate values as shown by the last inventory or more up-to-date records, if available, so that the relative more important areas may receive the attention they warrant.

3. Assign audit staff to determine that all important areas are covered. Arrange to facilitate communication between the assistants and the in-charge person through the "auto-call" and like systems. In large plants much important time may be lost through failure to establish such communication, particularly when inventory movement is found to be taking place and there is an immediate need to accompany and check it in at its destination.

4. Make certain that all assistants are properly instructed in what they are supposed to do, how they should select items for test-counting, approximately how many they should select, and how they should list the counts. The usual experience is that assistants list far more test counts than can be verified.

5. Follow up to make certain that tight control is exercised over count tags. A sufficient stock of prenumbered two- or three-part tags should be obtained by the company for the inventory counts. This stock should be in the complete control of one of the company's supervisory personnel, who will issue an appropriate series to the various count teams in accordance with their needs and maintain a proper record. The tag control center is a focal point in any large inventory count, and the auditors' control and communications point should be near by.

6. Ascertain in advance of the start of the count whether arrangements have been made by the company to compare the physical tag counts or listing sheets with quantities shown by perpetual inventory records. It is important that this be done promptly so that significant differences can be investigated. A difference may indicate a miscount, an error in the perpetual record, or a shortage, or there may be postings not yet made. Accordingly, time and care must be taken to find the reason for a difference. Too often the record is simply adjusted to the count without spending time to find out where the fault lies. If the fault should be in unposted paper work for an inventory movement which has already taken place, the inventory, even though adjusted to the true count, will become "wrong" just as soon as the paper work is posted.

7. Arrange to cover the receiving and shipping areas. These areas should be visited at the beginning of the inventory count and again at the end. Any materials or products in the receiving and shipping areas and which have not already been tagged or marked "before inventory" or "after inventory" should be listed, with reference given to any paper work which may accompany them. At the same time, a note should be made of the last receiving report number and the last shipping order number used. This information will be needed in checking the accuracy of the receiving and shipping cutoff at the inventory compilation. Areas outside the plant should be toured, including railroad sidings, and the contents of loaded railroad cars should be noted and tagged. The car numbers and seal numbers of sealed cars should be listed for future reference. It should also be borne in mind that rough forgings and other materials which are not easily harmed by the weather may be stored in the open and should not be overlooked. At the same time, the adequacy of the physical security precautions should be noted.

8. Inquire regarding goods held on consignment or consigned to others, and make certain that care is taken during the counts to note items which give evidence of being held on a consignment basis but which may nonetheless have been tagged as having been counted. Note: This problem has been somewhat simplified with the advent of the Uniform Commercial Code. The Code provides that most shipments which prior to the Code were on a consignment basis now by law become sales. Consignments now are limited to those situations in which the receiving company is one which deals primarily in consigned goods or in which proper notice is given to third parties through identifying tags being attached to the merchandise.

9. Require assistants assigned to observe counts and make test counts to read company inventory instructions carefully and become acquainted with any special features. They must bear in mind that the purpose of their observation is to make certain that counts are being carefully and accurately made by the count teams. It is more important that they concentrate their attention on this than on making numerous test counts, since most of the counting will be done by the count teams and the auditors cannot expect to count more than a small percentage of the whole stock.

10. Instruct assistants to be alert for errors in counts and to bring any errors to the attention of those in charge for correction. Common count errors arise from recording wrong units: hundreds or dozens instead of units, or hundredweight (cwt) instead of pounds, and from erroneous scale weight conversions. Sometimes count teams make the mistake of trying to include quantities stored in two or more locations on one tag. The best plan is to use a separate tag for each location. The assistant when making his test counts will need to rely to some extent on company factory personnel to help him in identifying part numbers and stage of completion. He will usually find that the manufacturing order or "traveler" form which accompanies the work will greatly simplify the identification. Where the inventory is packaged in sealed cartons and containers, the company personnel should be requested to open some selected by the auditor for testing. The opening should be made by company personnel since it may be necessary to have the container reinspected and resealed for shipment.

11. Arrange to tour departments where the count is completed with a company supervisor so that both may be satisfied that nothing has been missed. On the tour raise questions regarding any materials which appear to be obsolete or damaged or slow-moving but not marked as such on the count tag. The presence of accumulated dust or rust is indicative, though not neces-

sarily conclusive. Though it may seem obvious and should not require mentioning, it is not unusual that count teams will count without questioning items which still have last year's count tag attached. So that these instances will stand out clearly, each year's count tags should be of a different and distinctive color.

12. Arrange to have a "false-inclusion" test made in departments which have been cleared and the count tags pulled and brought into tag control. This may be done by noting the item description and count for a number of randomly selected tags and for some selected on the judgment basis. The auditor then should proceed to locate the material and check the count as shown. The purpose of the "false-inclusion" test is to guard against the possibility that tags may have been surreptitiously prepared. The same kind of test should be carried out when perpetual inventory records are being test-checked by physical counts. The tests should be made in two directions: from records to stock and from stock to records.

13. At the conclusion of the count, review test-count schedules for completeness and prepare a brief summary notation of the work done and note any questions for review.

14. Where bulk inventories, such as ore, coal, pulpwood, etc., are involved, specialized estimating techniques may be required. Engineering plats and profiles and density tests are examples. Where there is sufficient space for "turnaround," piles may be exhausted in rotation which fixes the input quantities in the remaining piles. Oil and petroleum products, chemicals, grain, etc., in storage tanks may be determined by means of a gauge and conversion tables. The auditor must take care to ascertain that the tanks are solid, i.e., that they do not have merely a layer of production on top with a false bottom. Oil floats on top of water, and devices have been used down through the years to load in water to inflate quantities. Samples of the bulk items should be taken and sent out for independent testing.

Instructions to audit assistants. Following is a checklist of instructions to guide audit assistants in observing counts and making test counts:

1. Select certain pallets, bins, piles, or stacks of material and check count description, last operation, and other data on completed tags. Make certain that stacks counted are solid, i.e., that there is not a hollow square inside.

2. Make sight-test comparisons of other pallets, bins, etc., of the same or similar products. The latter step will often provide a good estimate of the quantity without a detail count.

3. Determine that the part number, description, and last-operation number of manufactured parts selected for count are correct by referring to part numbers stamped in the material or through requesting identification by client personnel.

4. Open some sealed cartons or containers to determine the quantity and type of contents.

5. Ascertain that the company compares counts with perpetual records and investigates immediately any large differences.

6. Investigate any movements of material during inventory taking to avoid the possibility of duplicate inclusion in or exclusion from the count.

7. After completion of the count, make a final tour of the area, preferably with a department head, and make sure that: (*a*) all inventory is tagged or listed; (*b*) any significant amount of obsolete, slow-moving, excess, damaged, or inferior inventory has been recorded for later investigation; (*c*) any scrap materials have been counted according to written instructions.

8. Release the area to the person designated in the written instructions to pull the inventory tags or the completed count sheets, and accompany him on his rounds made to pull the tags.

9. Prepare or obtain a summary of the tags or sheets assigned to each department, showing tags or sheets originally assigned, used, unused, and voided.

10. For some departments, the working papers should include time and day that tags were authorized to be pulled. Note serial numbers of blocks of unused tags or count sheets for later test to make sure that they remained unused, as a test for *false inclusion.*

11. Test the summary of tags by selecting a sequence of originally issued tags or count sheets and account for all serial numbers, ascertaining that they have been recorded properly as used, unused, or voided. Record the test for later comparison with the final tabulation.

12. As a precaution against improper inclusion of tags or lines on count sheets at the departmental head level, select several of the "used" tag numbers and locate and count the corresponding material. When count sheets are used, see that an inked line has been run through all unused spaces before making this test. Record these on your count sheet as "counts after department completed."

Inventory Cutoffs. Proper cutoffs are as important as accurate inventory counts, if not more so, in arriving at reliable inventory valuations. Planning should provide for (*a*) the proper cutoff of receipts, shipments, and inventory transfers and (*b*) the clearance of all unprocessed receiving reports, requisitions, shipping reports, and other documents relating to inventory movements. This may call for an effort approaching in size and importance the counting work itself.

The timing of the paper work cutoff is of prime importance. If meaningful comparisons are to be made of count figures with perpetual quantity records, the quantity records must first have been brought down to date for the ins and outs to the point where operations were shut down. If meaningful comparisons are to be made between the ledger dollar amount and the priced-up counts, all movement up to the cutoff point must have been priced out and reflected in entries posted to the general ledger account. If accurate cutoffs have not been made, the worth of the count may be nullified, as values may be incorrectly switched between the current and the succeeding period.

The auditor should visit locations where inventory movement paper originates to record the serial number of the last ticket used before the the counts began. He should also follow up to see that all such used tickets are included in the summaries from which the inventory records are posted and adjusted in the closing.

Testing inventory cutoff. Following is a list of audit steps designed to show whether an accurate cutoff has been achieved in receipts, shipments, and transfers of inventories:

1. Ascertain by the use of receiving report workpapers that goods received before and after the inventory count date are recorded in inventories and accounts payable in the proper period.

2. Ascertain that shipping reports or bills of lading before and after the inventory count date are recorded in sales and out of inventories in the proper period.

3. Select transactions from accounts payable or cash disbursement records

(before and after the inventory date) and examine vendors' invoices and related receiving reports to ascertain whether both inventory and accounts payable are entered in the proper period.

4. Select transactions from the sales journal and shipping documents and sales invoices to ascertain whether sales, accounts receivable, cost of goods sold, and inventory disposition are entered in the proper period.

5. Agree intercompany, interdivision, and interplant transfers of inventory listed during the observation with counterpart information listed at other locations.

Following are illustrations of two cutoff schedules. These are Figure 2, "Receiving Cutoff," and Figure 3, "Shipping Cutoff." This type of schedule is essential in determining whether proper inventory cutoffs have been made.

Inventories in Transit. This caption most commonly relates to purchases which have been shipped from the vendors' premises on an f.o.b. basis prior to the year end but have not been received by the company until the new year. The amount is ordinarily determined by scheduling the shipments which span the year end. If the physical inventory is taken at the year-end date, care must be taken to make certain that in-transit items are not doubled by being included in the count of items on the premises.

Inventories may be in transit between plants and warehouses within the company. However, accounting for such items is usually so arranged that accountability at the shipping point is not dropped until the item is picked up at the receiving point, and vice versa. Movements within a plant or warehouse are usually cleared directly and not through an inventories in transit account. The auditor in examining inventories must take care to see that inventories in transit are properly substantiated and documented.

Pricing and Clerical Accuracy. Following is a list of audit steps applicable to the testing of the pricing and the clerical accuracy of inventories valued on a FIFO or average-cost basis, although not to inventories valued on a retail method or on LIFO (see the subsequent sections on these subjects). Such

Figure 2 RECEIVING CUTOFF

Downtown Manufacturing Company
Chemical Division

SCH: D56
DATE: 10/31/70

Receiving Cut Off 9/30/70

Date Received	Purchase Order No.	Vendor	Description	Quantity
Received prior to inventory and included in inventory:				
9/30/70	K 100806	American Hoist	US 1002 7½ m 17½ wide	340 # ✓
9/25/70	K 101165	Marcus Bickwell	100 ml Cylinder	10,154 ea. ✓
9/30/70	K 101049	Central Chemical	50 cc Oval Printed Bottles	1500 ea. ✓
9/26/70	K 101070	Bucka rite	9" x 12" Tiles	40 css. ✓
9/25/70	K 100814	Howe Chemical	Ethyl Alcohol	1206 gal. ✓
9/30/70	K 100796	Plastic Mold	Plastic Granules	46 bbls. ✓

✓ Traced to accounts payable as at 9/30/70/RWK

Figure 3 SHIPPING CUTOFF

Dountown Manufacturing Company
Chemical Division
9/30/70
Shipping Cut Off

SCH: D55
DATE: 12/31/70

Shipped prior to Inventory:

Date	Sales Order No.	Means	Customer	Description		
9/30/70	39138	Truck	Squire & Co.	5 pkgs.	#7 Adhesive	✓
	39337		York City Mfg	1 ctn.	Glutinous Adhesive	✓
	39207		Bermdr Inc	8 ctns.	#3 Adhesive	✓
	39204		C.L. Smith Co	4 ctns.	Lacquer No1 Primer	✓
	37390	PP	Curtis Industries	10 cc	Methanate	✓
✓	39147	PP	Henry & Hobbs Co.	100 lb	Methyl Cyanonylate	✓

Shipped after Inventory:

Date	Sales Order No.	Means	Customer	Description	
after 9/30/70	39349	Truck	Atlantic Ball Co.	See A/R File for details	✓°
	39350	"	" " "	See A/R File for details	✓°

✓° Traced to accounts receivable and the relief of inventory before 9/30/70 / RWA

✓° Traced to accounts receivable after 9/30/70 and to the inclusion in the inventory counts / RWA

steps apply to tabulations prepared from perpetual quantity records and to tabulations prepared from a completed physical inventory count.

1. Select items for price testing, indicate basis for selection, and identify items. Selections should be made from all categories of inventories.

2. Agree unit prices (material, labor, and overhead) with unit costs per cost records tested elsewhere in connection with the audit of inventories. In the case of work in process, note that incomplete parts are correctly priced according to the last operation completed.

3. Screen the inventory tabulation for the purpose of noting whether unit prices appear reasonable in relation to description, quantities, and other information presented.

4. List exceptions for discussion. Consider the materiality thereof to total inventory before proposing adjustment of physical inventory amount. If errors are numerous, consider the necessity of extending the scope of tests made.

5. Trace all information relating to test counts—i.e., tag number, quantity, part number, last operation, etc.—from test-count schedules to the final priced inventory. Select a number of items from the final priced inventory tabulation and agree quantity, part number, last operation, etc., with the actual inventory tag or count sheet. The basis of selection of the items used in these tests should be stated and the items should be identified.

6. Ascertain that tag number or count sheet reference per final inventory agrees with control information already developed.

7. Check extensions of the company's priced inventory tabulation, identifying the items tested by the easiest method possible. Stratified sampling techniques should be considered for these tests.

8. Sight-test extensions generally, and on common-sense basis look for obvious errors due to misplaced decimals or use of wrong unit (dozens instead of hundreds, etc.).

9. Check the footing of the inventory tabulation. This, too, may be done on a test basis if page or section subtotals are provided. Indicate the basis of the test.

10. List the clerical errors found and, if material in amount, advise the company in order that the inventory summary may be corrected.

In Figure 4, "Test of Prices," is shown a typical schedule used by the auditor to verify pricing. As indicated, 41 percent of the total work in process inventory was verified.

Obsolescence. Apart from a deliberate and fraudulent attempt to overstate inventories by including nonexistent items, overpricing, etc., the greatest risk to the auditor in examining inventories lies in the possibility that obsolete and unsalable items may have accumulated in quantities reaching far beyond

Figure 4 TEST OF PRICES

Downtown Manufacturing Company
Handtool Division
Price Testing of Work in Process

SCH: E 200 (Cont.)
DATE: 12/31/70

Product Code	Part No	Operation Number	Quantity	Standard Costs: Material	Labor	Overhead	Total	Inventory Amount
61	1 116	—	1,510	$20.43	—	267%	$20.43	$30,834
|	947	—	2,950	11.05	—	}	11.05	32,597
|	2 326	99	552	70.48	$21.95	}	149.93	82,761
62	178	57	950	99.97	12.57	}	145.47	138,196
}	3 420	36	4,235	81.08	31.45	310	210.02	259,374
}	3 457	201	993	38.54	18.24	250	102.38	101,663
65	4 100	54	1,385	20.13	21.11	}	94.01	130,203
66	6 614	21	6,998	11.39	—		11.39	79,707
67	629	13	4,470	56.50	2.52	300	66.58	297,612
69	813	107	9,669	12.92	12.81	}	64.16	620,363
—	—	—	—	—	—	—	—	—
—	—	—	—	—	—	—	—	—
				Amount of prices tested				$3,231,233
				Total Work in Process Inventory				$7,881,052
				Percent price tested				41%

See Sch. E 400–450 for work done in testing standard costs + overhead

10/27/70 RWA

what anyone in top management suspects. Such accumulations may result from mistakes in production records, faulty work in the manufacturing departments, and various other causes. Unless controls for policing production and inventories are effective, employees responsible may place spoiled items aside rather than face the blame for their poor performance. This possibility becomes particularly important where incentive plans are in effect and the reporting of spoilage would reduce the bonus.

The auditor should be aware of any obsolete and slow-moving stock when observing inventory. After the counts have been summarized, audit tests should be made to see how inventory quantities compare with sales prospects and whether they are badly out of balance with the sales backlog. This may be done by aggregating all materials, components, work-in-process parts, subassemblies, final assemblies, and finished items, plus outstanding purchase orders for a particular product, and measuring them in the aggregate against sales orders for that product on the books, plus the sales forecast for a reasonable future period. Such a test will show up accumulations of inventory in excess of the company's reasonable requirements. It will show up instances, if such exist, where the assembly department is having trouble getting enough good parts together to complete the finished product even though large numbers of unfinished parts and subassemblies exist at the earlier stages. The test will also bring to light situations where the market for a particular item has fallen off but management has not acted in time to curtail purchases and production orders.

Common Errors in Compilation. Following are some of the common errors the auditor should guard against in physical inventory compilation.

1. Improper name, size, or part number listed on the count tag.
2. Improper identification, or failure to note stage of completion on the tag (item is likely to be priced at completed cost if not identified as partially complete).
3. Wrong unit of measure listed on the tag. Inventory planning should set rules for units of measure to be used for particular items; otherwise the counters may use the unit shown on the box or can whereas the inventory records use another unit. Example: dozens versus gross; grams versus ounces.
4. Omission of distinguishing prefix or subnumber for assemblies and subassemblies. Partially complete assemblies usually bear completed assembly number but with an identifying prefix or subnumber.
5. Erroneous application of unit prices—the price may be per unit, per 100, per 1,000, per pound, per cwt, etc.
6. Nonstandard parts. Where a standard pricing deck is used for mechanical pricing and extension work, care must be taken lest items be present for which no cost standards have been set. Such a situation will result in a "no value" extension.
7. Insufficient fields allowed in tab setup. If only five digits are allowed for extended quantities, a $105,000 item, for example, comes out as $5,000.
8. Footing errors. All inventories, longhand or machine processed, should be double-footed, once in parts number sequence and the second time in tag number sequence. The first is important to management so they may know how much inventory value is in particular parts and series of parts. The second is important to the auditor so he may check test counts into the inventory summary and test the summary for "false inclusion."

Control of the inventory tags or sheets is a critical control point in determining whether all goods are included in inventory. In the following illustration,

Figure 5, "Tag Control," the method of accounting for all tag numbers is indicated. As part of the inventory count procedures the auditor must (1) determine that all inventory is tagged and (2) that all tags are accounted for.

Adjustment of Books to Physical Inventory. Following are audit steps to be taken care of after the physical inventory has been priced and summarized in

Figure 5 TAG CONTROL

Pountown Manufacturing Company
Can Division
9/30/70
Tag Control

SCH: D58
DATE: 12/31/70

Inventory Tags Issued From	Inventory Tags Issued To	Supervisor Assigned To	Inventory Tags Used From	Inventory Tags Used To	Voided Tags	Unused Tags
13,001	13,400 ✗	N. Benoit	13,001 13,351	13,250 T 13,400 T		13,251–13,350 ⸸
14,401	14,600 ✗	N. Benoit	14,401 14,493	14,491 T 14,600 T	14,492 ⸸	
12,001	12,397 ✗	W. Ouellette	12,001 12,296	12,294 T 12,397 T	12,295 ⸸	
12,401	13,000 ✗	W. Ouellette	12,401	13,000 T		
14,201	14,400 ✗	R. Valetsky	14,201 14,301	14,250 T 14,400 T		14,251–14,300 ⸸
14,601	15,000 ✗	R. De Pionto	14,601 14,701 14,713	14,698 T 14,711 T 15,000 T	① 14,712 ⸸	14,699–14,700 ⸸

① Note that tickets # 14709, 14710, 14747 were used, yet they were not on the inventory. Subsequently we traced these tickets to the Mixer Cup Division's inventory /RWA

✗ Accounted for all numbers in sequence issued /RWA

T Traced tag sequence to inventory tab run and accounted for all tags /RWA

⸸ For void tags traced to inventory run and determined that tags were not used in the final priced run /RWA

⸸ Determined that these tickets were not used in the valuation of the inventory /RWA

9/30/70
RWA

order that the auditor may satisfy himself that the general books have been properly adjusted on the basis of the physical counts.

1. Ascertain that all debits and credits of material amounts in the inventory control account in the month before and after the physical inventory have come under audit scrutiny and that all adjustments to the account as a result of cutoff tests have been posted.
2. Discuss and clear all proposed adjustments to the physical inventory as a result of counts, pricing, extension tests, etc.
3. Compute adjustment required to bring book balance into agreement with final adjusted physical inventory and ascertain that the company prepares and records such entries in the general ledger where they are material in amount.
4. Where the adjustment of books to the physical inventory is material in amount, seek to obtain an explanation for the difference in terms of price difference and quantity difference, and determine whether such differences indicate errors of principle or of clerical inaccuracy in the cost system and/or weaknesses in the physical control of assets. Reference to the last prior inventory tabulation is often helpful in disclosing errors and the reason for variances.

INVENTORY VALUATION

Tests of the Cost System. In approaching inventory valuation, the auditor should ascertain whether the company has an adequate system for determining the cost of inventories and for computing the cost of goods sold. In arriving at a decision on this point, the auditor should seek answers to the following questions:

1. Does the cost system tie into the general books? If not, how does the company know whether all costs are included and whether all charges to inventory control accounts are relieved?
2. Are the cost records revised currently to establish recent-cost prices?
3. Are engineering changes in the product reported to the cost accountant so that he may revise the related costs where necessary?
4. Have costs that are not properly includible in inventories, such as interplant or intercompany profits, advertising, etc., been excluded?
5. Do the costs include all items properly includible in valuing inventories?
6. Does the cost system pinpoint specific cost variances, such as material price and usage variances, labor rate and hour variances, and overhead absorption variances?
7. Are make-or-buy cost studies prepared regularly?

Following are tests of documents and other evidence to be carried out in support of the auditor's inquiries and investigations into the cost accounting system and the perpetual records and the controls surrounding them. These tests should be coordinated with the examination of vendors' invoices in connection with accounts payable and with payroll work, etc.

1. Select and list from the perpetual card records and cost records a number of representative items of raw materials, purchased parts, work in process, and finished goods. Note the approximate percentage of inventory so selected for test and the basis for the selection.

2. Agree the unit material prices of items selected with vendors' invoices, published catalogs, freight bills, etc.

3. Test the reasonableness of standard costs of materials and purchased parts by computing the ratio of overall actual purchase costs to overall standard costs. If price levels have changed or standards have been revised recently, a shorter period than "year to date" may have to be analyzed for variance information.

4. Inquire of engineering and production departments as to whether there have been any recent changes in material or labor content or in production processes for which the cost standards may not have been revised.

5. Trace items selected in "1" above to monthly details developing credit entries to raw materials, work in process, or finished goods accounts, as the case may be, and check for transfers between inventory accounts and cost of goods sold.

6. Using variance accounts and reports for the year to date, compute the overall ratio of current year's actual costs to standard costs in order to appraise the reasonableness of the unit costs established for purposes of determining cost of inventory and cost of goods sold. If product unit or standards have changed recently, a shorter period than "year to date" may need to be used for analyzing variance information.

7. In the case of process unit cost records, compare the total material, labor, and overhead costs with the prior year's comparable amounts and obtain explanations for major fluctuations.

Absorption of Overhead. Regardless of the method used for absorbing manufacturing overhead—whether a percent of direct labor, or a rate per machine hour or labor dollar, or whatever—the auditor must examine the method and its application carefully to see that the application results in a fair allocation and that it properly reflects current conditions. The overhead allocated should include all items relating to the production effort which the company has consistently included in inventory costs—depreciation, insurance, taxes, supervision, materials handling maintenance, payroll department, etc.—and should exclude general and administrative expenses and costs which come after the production stage, such as packaging and shipping costs. Borderline expenses include plant protection costs, guards, plant accounting, purchasing, spare parts handling, and the like.

With the advent of large-scale automation in industry, direct labor has come to represent a narrower and narrower base for allocating overhead. As the amount of direct labor needed on automatic machines becomes smaller, the amounts of depreciation, taxes, and maintenance and other overhead expenses relating to the expensive automated machinery become larger. A more accurate base in such cases is provided by machine-hour rates. All direct and indirect costs relating to a particular machine are assigned or allocated to it and absorbed into production on the basis of that machine's usage.

It sometimes happens that overhead costs are incurred for items purchased and carried in inventory with very little or no direct labor or machine time being expended on them. As a consequence, those items never bear any of the indirect costs they cause, unless bases of allocation other than the two mentioned above are used. Purchased replacement parts and components are examples. These entail costs of procurement, receiving, inspection, and handling, but no part of such costs gets allocated to them when direct labor dollars or machine-hour rates are used as the basis for absorbing overhead, since these items do not incur machining operations. In such situations a separate overhead pool of costs relating to purchased parts and assemblies may need to be set up and the pool distributed on the basis of purchase cost of receipts into inventory.

Companies frequently construct and install their own machinery and equipment. In such cases, the question often arises as to how much overhead should be relieved from inventory and capitalized into fixed assets for such items. A reasonable basis is provided by the direct costing theory. Since company-made machinery is usually constructed or installed during periods when the plant is not operating at its full capacity, a "rump" overhead rate, sufficient to cover variable overhead incurred on the work, should be applied.

The auditor should include tests of overhead expense accounts in his testing of cash disbursements and in his examination of insurance, taxes, etc. Furthermore, he should satisfy himself that the bases used for distributing overhead pools to production are acceptable. Unusual and extraordinary items of expense should be excluded from the overhead absorption process.

Where substantial amounts of overabsorbed or underabsorbed overhead exist, the auditor will need to consider whether the ending inventory needs to be adjusted to a more nearly actual rate. Overabsorption of overhead frequently gives rise to the need for adjustment because investigation indicates that the accounting method is in error. Underabsorption, on the other hand, may relate to inefficiencies in plant operation, situations where the plant is operating at less than normal capacity, and other conditions which do not warrant adjusting the absorption rate. Where a plant is operating below capacity, there may be good reason for setting the absorption rate lower than would be needed for full absorption. (See Robert I. Dickey, *Accountants' Cost Handbook,* Chapter 7.)

LIFO Inventories. The subject of LIFO inventories is dealt with extensively in Chapters 8 through 11 of *Inventories, a Guide to Their Control, Costing, and Effect on Income and Taxes,* by R. A. Hoffman (Ronald Press Company). Following is a program for audit testing of LIFO inventory cost calculations:

1. Record in carry-forward working papers the various layers of LIFO inventory cost; also, the quantity and unit cost where the dollar-value principle is not used, and the base-year cost and the indices for conversion to current-year cost where the dollar-value principle is used.

2. Where unit LIFO is used, review the company's schedules of inventory quantities at year end. If inventory was counted at year end, the auditor will have tested the clerical accuracy of the pricing schedules. If the inventory was counted at an interim date, agree the year-end quantities with perpetual records. Agree unit costs per the company's schedules with carry-forward working papers by layers for those quantities not in excess of preceding-year quantities.

3. Check the computation of LIFO cost of increases in quantity during the current year in accordance with company's election against price increases in quantities at FIFO, LIFO, or average cost of acquisitions during the year.

4. Where dollar-value LIFO is used, price all or a portion of the closing inventory at current-year cost (first acquisition, last acquisition, or average cost for the year) and at base-year cost, and compute an index of aggregate current-year cost to base-year cost. Test prices and clerical accuracy of the final inventory tabulation at current-year cost. Check computation of index used for conversion from current-year cost to base-year cost.

5. Agree base-year unit costs with carry-forward LIFO working papers. If the scope of this step requires additional tests, agree base-year unit cost with prior-year schedules previously tested. Agree quantities with the final inventory tabulation. Test the clerical accuracy of extensions and footings.

6. Obtain or include in carry-forward working papers a statement describing the method used in computing the index and indicate whether, and in what manner, the method has been approved by the Internal Revenue Service. Note: The income tax regulations require that a taxpayer using either an index—one based upon a partial double extension or a statistical industry index—or the link-chain method must attach to his income tax return for the first taxable year for which the index or link-chain method is used a statement describing the particular link-chain method or the method used in computing the index. In addition, a copy of the statement is required to be filed with the office of the Commissioner of Internal Revenue in Washington.

7. State the closing inventory in terms of base-year cost for each LIFO pool; where there has not been a 100 percent extension at base-year costs, this may be done by applying the index to inventory totals at current-year cost.

8. Check the computation of LIFO cost of any increase in inventory at base-year cost in accordance with the company's election against price increases at first or last acquisition or average cost during the current year.

9. Ascertain that the aggregate inventory at LIFO cost is recorded in the general ledger and that no other inventory procedure has been used to ascertain the income or loss of the year for purposes of a report to shareholders, creditors, etc.

10. Where items are voluminous, the preceding procedures may be carried out by tests. The tests may need to be modified in certain special situations such as where the retail inventory method is used.

Retail Method. The retail method of pricing and carrying inventories is commonly used in department stores, chain stores, supermarkets, etc. From the management point of view, the system permits a check on persons in charge of single departments or separate stores, much as follows: (1) the store or department begins an accounting period with a known value of merchandise at selling prices; (2) shipments received during the period are charged at retail prices; (3) sales are credited at retail prices; (4) regularly scheduled or surprise inventory counts are taken by the internal auditors or store supervisors and priced at retail prices. If a significant shortage is found to exist between the book inventory and the physical inventory, an immediate investigation is made and possibly the inventory is retaken. The following description of the retail inventory method is adapted from the Internal Revenue Service Regulations:

> Under the retail method, the total of the retail selling prices of the goods on hand at the end of the year is reduced to approximate cost by deducting therefrom an amount which bears the same ratio to such total as (1) the total of the retail selling prices of the goods purchased during the year, with proper adjustment to such selling prices for all markups and markdowns, less (2) the cost of goods included in the opening inventory plus the cost of goods purchased during the year, bears to (1).

Market Value and Replacement Cost. The description "at lower of cost or market" has long been used to describe the basis on which inventories are valued in financial statements. Modern practice requires that "cost" be further defined as FIFO, LIFO, average, etc. The word "market" was originally applied to raw materials and commodities for which price quotations could be obtained. If the quoted price was lower than the cost amount at which the items were carried, they would be written down to the lower amount.

The term "lower of cost or market" acquired early acceptance for income tax purposes and thus remains in broad usage, being applied even to many situations where no market quotations are obtainable. It is common practice to use "market" as meaning current replacement cost by purchase or reproduction.

The Accounting Research and Terminology Bulletins, final edition, 1961, as restated, point out that: "(1) Market should not exceed the net realizable value (i.e., estimated selling price in the ordinary course of business less reasonably predictable costs of completion and disposal); and (2) Market should not be less than the net realizable value reduced by an allowance for an approximately normal profit margin." Thus the concept of reducing inventories to "lower of cost or market" means the recognition of loss of carrying value whether from change of style, shifting of market, deterioration, or spoilage, or for any number of reasons which may have no direct relation to a market quotation. The auditor in his work on inventories must be careful to detect loss of value and to see that it is taken into account in determining inventories.

Inventories of Replacement Parts. How large a stock of replacement parts a company should carry is always problematic, and whether parts should be priced at full value is troublesome to the auditor. To begin with, ordinary measures of turnover and realization through sale within one year cannot be applied in determining price validity for replacement parts. Generally, in the final production runs the manufacturer provides for a supply of parts to last as long as the models are likely to be in operation. The carrying cost and obsolescence loss are far less than the subsequent high setup and short-run costs.

Experience tables assist in estimating how large a stock of replacement parts to carry for discontinued models. Experience tables are kept and adjusted from time to time to take into account the ability of a particular model or part to withstand wear and breakage. Where the models are currently in production, the problem is a simple one of "max and min"—to have enough inventories to fill sales orders and permit scheduled production.

At some point, the calls for a part on an old model become so infrequent as to warrant writing off any cost assigned to parts still in stock, since the handling charges and paper work tend to equal or exceed the sales price.

Some companies solve the valuation problem of replacement parts by carrying two or three or four years' sales requirements at full-cost value and the balance at no value. There may be little means available for ascertaining the validity of the number of years' requirements on an across-the-board basis, but usually a conservative number is chosen. Finally, it may be noted that the parts inventory usually does not represent a significant portion of a company's total inventory.

Construction Contract Inventories. When inventories involve long-term construction contracts—for bridges, highways, tunnels, buildings, ships, etc.—special problems are encountered. Two bases of accounting are common: (1) the percentage-of-completion basis, and (2) the completed-contract basis. In either case the costs for materials, labor, overhead, machine and equipment rentals, etc., are charged in, and progress payments are deducted and shown parenthetically in the balance sheet. The difference between the two bases lies in the method of accounting for profit.

Under the percentage-of-completion basis, estimates are made of how far the work has progressed toward completion. That portion of the estimated profit which relates to the percent of work completed is added to the contract inventory and taken into income. The completion percentage may be determined in one of several ways or by a combination of ways—dollars or man-days of labor expended, cubic yards of material moved, tons of concrete poured, etc.—all in relation to the estimated total of each. If the work is being done under a cost-plus-a-fee contract, the percent is applied to the total fee to be earned when the contract has been completed. If the contract is a fixed-price contract, the percent is applied to the estimated profit. In the latter case, an estimate must be made of the cost to complete the contract in order to determine whether a profit or loss is to be expected and how much. If the costs already incurred plus the estimates of costs to be incurred exceed the amount recoverable under the contract, a loss provision will need to be made and subtracted from the inventory.

The completed-contract basis is the easiest and safest of the two, since estimates of completion are not required, although estimates of completion costs are still needed in order to ascertain whether a loss will be sustained and, if so, to provide a reserve for the lesser value likely to be realized. However, the completed-contract basis is less desirable than the percentage-of-completion basis in that it is likely to produce income distortion as between years as a result of the incidence of taking in the former basis all profit in the year in which completion occurs, whereas the productive effort which produced the profit may have been spread out over several years.

The estimate of cost to complete presents difficulty for the auditor since it may depend very largely on the knowledge and judgment of persons who have a stake in the outcome of the project. A project engineer or supervisor faced with unforeseen problems, such as difficult rock removal, heavy water seepage, etc., may tend to hope for the best and delay reporting the worst. On the other hand, a new supervisor brought in to replace a supervisor who is being relieved may tend to exaggerate the difficulties in order to set the stage in a manner which will make his own performance appear good. These elements present difficulties to the auditor, since he must weigh the objectivity with which the estimates have been made. (See AICPA, *Audits of Construction Contractors.*)

Government Contract Inventories. Unbilled costs on government contracts are usually shown in the balance sheet as inventories, as they represent costs for which requests for reimbursement have not been assembled in time for billing.

To the extent that fixed-price contracts are involved, the audit of inventories carried for government contracts will not vary from the audit of ordinary contract inventories, and the items may be accounted for by any of the various inventory costing systems described elsewhere in this manual. If a cost-plus-a-fee contract or one of a number of incentive-type contracts is involved, questions concerning the proper basis of allocating manufacturing and general overheads may arise. (See Armed Services Procurement Regulations (ASPR) for rules, definitions, and discussion of this subject.)

The auditor, in examining inventories relating to government contracts, should:

1. Determine that the basis for stating inventories is in accordance with generally accepted accounting principles consistently applied.
2. Determine that there are no significant unrecorded losses on government contracts in progress.

3. Determine whether there are any significant contingent liabilities or uncertainties relating to pending contract price redeterminations, cost disallowances, penalties under incentive-type contracts, renegotiation, etc.

All government procurement is carried out in accordance with prescribed regulations. Uniform policies and procedures relating to the procurement of property, supplies, and service have been set out in separate regulations for each of the procuring activities. These are as follows:

Armed Services Procurement Regulations (ASPR)
Air Force Procurement Instructions (AFPI)
Navy Procurement Directives (NPD)
Army Procurement Procedures (APP)
Defense Supply Procurement Regulations (DSPR)
National Aeronautics and Space Administration Regulations (NASAPR)
Atomic Energy Commission Procurement Regulations (AECPR)
Federal Procurement Regulations of the General Services Administration (FPR)

Most of these regulations follow a fairly uniform numbering system with regard to subject matter. Probably the most important section in any one of them, as far as audit activity is concerned, is entitled "Contract Cost Principles," which is Section 15 in ASPR. It is extremely important that the auditor familiarize himself with this section, since it contains general cost principles and procedures for the determination and allowance of costs in connection with the negotiation and administration of cost-reimbursement-type contracts and in connection with such contracts when terminated for the convenience of the government. Under a recent revision, Section 15 of ASPR has been made to apply generally to negotiated fixed-price-type contracts as well and to such contracts when terminated for the convenience of the government.

In addition to Section 15 there are other segments of the regulations with which the auditor should be familiar because of their impact on contract income. Among the more important of these contained in the ASPR (and other procurement regulations) are the following:

Section 1, Part 17, "Value Engineering"
Section 3, Par. 807.4, "Certificate of Current Cost or Pricing Data"
Section 3, Par. 808.2 to 808.7, "Weighted Guidelines Method"
Section 7, Par. 104.29, "Clause for Price Reduction for Defective Cost or Pricing Data"

The Armed Services Procurement Regulations, Section 15-201.1, defines the total cost of a contract as "the sum of the allowable direct and indirect costs allocable to the contract incurred or to be incurred, less any allocable credits." In determining the allowability of costs, ASPR Section 15-201.2 states: "Factors to be considered in determining the allowability of individual items of cost include (i) reasonableness, (ii) allocability, (iii) application of those generally accepted accounting principles and practices appropriate to the particular circumstances, and (iv) any limitations or exclusions set forth in this Part 2, or otherwise included in the contract as to types or amounts of cost items."

With regard to cost limitation or exclusion of specific items of cost incurred by contractors, ASPR, Section 15-205, entitled "Selected Costs," details 47 specific cost items commonly incurred by most business enterprises. It sets forth for each item the allowability of such cost. Failure of the regulation to specifically cite a cost item is not intended to imply that the item is allowable or nonallowable.

It will be noted that the above explanation covers only contracts issued by the Department of Defense, or any of its prime contractors or higher-tier subcontractors. However, with the lone exception of the Atomic Energy Commission (AEC), almost every other government agency has patterned its "Cost Principles" along the lines set forth in Section 15 of ASPR and no significant differences have been noted. The AEC "Cost Principles" are substantially different from those stated in ASPR, and direct reference to that manual should be made by the auditor in determining the extent of allowability of costs.

The auditor should determine whether company procedures provide for segregation in the accounts or in worksheet analyses of costs that are stated in ASPR, Section 15, to be unallowable. If they do not, he should determine that contract accounts receivable and inventories do not include costs that may be subject to disallowance as a result of audit by representatives of a governmental agency, a prime contractor, or a higher-tier subcontractor. The auditor should also determine whether the company utilizes provisional overhead rates in billings to the government or in the accumulation of unbilled cost, and, if so, whether adequate procedures have been provided for adjusting the provisional rate or rates to actual at interim periods or year end.

OTHER CONSIDERATIONS

Inventories in Public Warehouses. Following the exposure of the Allied Crude Vegetable Oil Company fraud, the AICPA Committee on Auditing Procedure issued Statement No. 37 entitled *Special Report—Public Warehouses—Controls and Auditing Procedures for Goods Held.* Statement No. 37 deals with the problems presented to the auditor in making an examination of the records of the warehouseman. It makes clear that direct confirmation on a test basis from the custodians is still acceptable procedure to be followed, and that the supplemental inquiries to be made in cases where such inventories represent a significant portion of the owner's current assets or total assets should include the following steps, to the extent that the auditor considers them meaningful in the circumstances:

1. Discussion with the owner as to the owner's control procedures in investigating the warehouseman, and tests of related evidential matter.
2. Review of the owner's control procedures concerning performance of the warehouseman and tests of related evidential matter.
3. Observation of physical counts of the goods, wherever practicable and reasonable.
4. Where warehouse receipts have been pledged as collateral, confirmation (on a test basis, where appropriate) from lenders as to pertinent details of the pledged receipts.

Following is a form-letter request for confirmation of inventories in public warehouses.

Dear Sirs:

Please prepare in duplicate an inventory signed by an official of your company of all goods held for our account at (*inventory date*). We would appreciate your sending the original directly to our independent public accountant, E. E. Jones and Co., (address) and sending the copy to us.

Please include in your reply:

(1) Description of items, including catalog numbers, size, color, quality, and other pertinent features
(2) Quantities
(3) Special earmarkings or packing
(4) Indication of any damaged, spoiled, or deteriorated goods
(5) The amount of any lien against the inventory of which you have knowledge
(6) Whether any negotiable warehouse receipts have been issued

In addition, please include a statement of storage and other charges, if any, owing to you as of (date of examination or inventory).

Envelopes are enclosed for your reply.

Yours very truly,

____
Name of Client
By______________

Note: It may be advisable to request the warehouse to count the inventory being confirmed, and to base the reply upon such physical count rather than upon the records it maintains of the goods in its custody.

Consignment Inventories. Earlier auditing texts deal extensively with the accounting requirements for consignments in or consignments out. The advent of the Uniform Commercial Code (now formally adopted by most states), however, has changed the legal status of shipments which heretofore have been considered as consignment inventories. Under the Code, title is deemed to pass in all instances except those in which the merchandise is shipped to persons engaged primarily in the handling of consigned goods and where proper notice can be given to lenders and others through ownership plates attached to merchandise. With this change in the legal status of merchandise so transferred, the accounting for shipments on a contingent basis may shift from inventories to accounts receivable. The auditor still must take care (if the sale is not final) to make certain that the profits, if any are recorded thereon, are reversed in the year-end closing.

Purchase Commitments. The auditor should inquire into the nature and amount of the company's commitments to purchase materials. In the event that commitments exist at prices in excess of current market as of the date of the balance sheet, disclosure may be required in a note to the financial statements. It is not customary to record losses until the items are received, at which time the application of the lower-of-cost-or-market principle would require their recognition.

Commodity Futures and Hedging. Manufacturers who use commodity raw materials for which an open market exists in futures contracts frequently make use of the market to "hedge" their inventory and sales commitments against fluctuations in market value. If they are "long" on inventory, they may sell futures contracts to hedge against a fall in the market which would cause an inventory loss. At the same time, they would, of course, forego the chance of a gain from a rise in prices. If the manufacturer sells a quantity of manufactured goods for future delivery but does not have the required raw material on hand, he may buy futures contracts in order to guard against an interim rise in the cost of the materials. If it is the manufacturer's policy to avoid speculation in the commodity market and to make only a manufacturing profit, he will try to maintain a balanced position so that he has neither a "long" position (or unsold inventory) nor a "short" position (where contracts have not been signed for the required material).

Processors of wheat, cotton, soybeans, lard, potatoes, pork products, sugar, coffee, cocoa, etc., frequently engage in hedging operations. In the examination of the accounts of such companies, the auditor must verify the "long" and "short" positions and see that unrealized losses (sometimes offset by unrealized gains) on open contracts are taken into account in valuing inventories.

AICPA Case Study in Auditing Procedures No. 7 deals with the audit of a grain company. Hedging operations and auditing procedures to be applied in such instances are clearly set forth in this case study.

Insurance Coverage. The following insurance matters should be considered by the auditor:

1. *Type of merchandise.* This will indicate the kind of insurance to be carried. For instance, the average manufacturer of heavy or bulky, combustible goods may carry only fire insurance. Manufacturers, wholesalers, and retailers of jewelry are interested chiefly in theft insurance, their stock in trade usually being kept in fireproof vaults and safes. Manufacturers or dealers in lightweight and expensive goods or materials, such as furs and silks, are interested in both fire and theft insurance.
2. *The value of the inventory at each location.* Except in the case of small concerns, the inventory is seldom housed in one warehouse, factory, store, or office.
3. *Insurance policies.* These should be examined with respect to:
   a. The name and address of the insuring company and the face amount of the policy.
   b. The location of the inventory covered.
   c. The coinsurance clause and the effect of its operation in relation to the value of the inventory involved.
   d. The name of the beneficiary. Where a name other than the client's is given, the auditor should determine ownership, or the reason for the lien or other assignment.
   e. The expiration date of the policy.
   f. Waivers of premiums in cases of minor losses.
   g. Recoveries noted on "waiver of premium" slips should be traced to the cash records.
4. *Inventory fluctuations.* Many inventory fluctuations are seasonal, and the amount of insurance coverage should correspondingly be increased or decreased unless covered by a so-called "blanket" policy. The fluctuating factor should not escape the auditor's attention. He should not judge the year-round coverage by the value shown at the balance sheet date, since the latter may be at its maximum or minimum figure.

For the purpose of the present brief reference to insurance of inventories, attention need be called only to the fact that inventories, wherever located, should be covered by the proper type of insurance and for the period that they are exposed to risk of loss.

If the facts and amounts relating to insurance coverage of inventories vary substantially from those shown in the company's books of account, the auditor should make suitable inquiry as to the reasons therefor from two points of view:

1. Does lack of coverage raise any questions as to the bona fides of the company's inventory accounts?
2. Should the lack of coverage be reported to the company's officers? (See Institute of Internal Auditors, Research Committee Report No. 9, "Internal Audit of Insurance Programs.")

Frauds Involving Inventories. In examining inventories, auditors should be aware of the possibilities of fraud. Frauds involving inventories may range in size from minor thefts to large sums. Where the charges created by a defalcation cannot be "washed down the drain" of expenses, or concealed through unreported income, or disposed of by cash shortage or padded accounts receivable, they may wind up in overstated inventories.

Because of the close scrutiny that cash and receivables get at fairly frequent intervals, inventories present a relatively safer resting place for the concealment of fraud than do cash and receivables. In many companies complete inventories are taken only once a year. Therefore, a full year's errors and variations may accumulate before they are brought together and disposed of all in one figure as the year-end difference between book and physical inventories. Not infrequently is a company unable to track down the causes of the difference. The difference can represent a conglomeration of unreported spoilage, overshipments, pilferage losses, bookkeeping errors, count errors, etc., and, of course, the uncleared debits resulting from a fraud which has been buried in the inventory account. Case studies on fraud show that the larger frauds are contrived by embezzlers who learned that they can inflate such accounts as merchandise purchases, raw materials, freight expense, etc., without immediate detection. For further details, see the chapter, "Fraud and the Auditor."

Management Representation Letters. In order to avoid misunderstandings with clients, the independent auditor at the conclusion of his examination should obtain a written representation covering the company's year-end inventories. Such a representation letter does not relieve the independent auditor of any of his audit functions or responsibilities. It complements, rather than substitutes for, a proper examination, and he should use every practicable means to substantiate the information developed by the inquiries in the letter. Following is a skeleton form of representation letter covering inventories, together with explanatory notes thereon appearing in AICPA's *Codification of Statements on Auditing Procedures.*

Certified Public Accountants
Blank Street, City

Dear Sirs:

In connection with your examination of the accounts of (Blank Company) and more particularly in connection with your examination of the (Blank Company or Department) as at (blank date), we hereby make the following statements and representations concerning inventories of (Blank Company):

A. Quantities and amounts
B. Title and ownership
C. Prices and calculations
D. Commitments
E. Condition

The foregoing constitutes a fair statement of quantities and valuations of the respective inventories as at (date as of which audit is made) to the best of the knowledge and belief of the undersigned.

(Signature)

(Date signed)

OVERALL VIEW

Analytical Review of Inventories. Use of the analytical review approach will help the auditor to avoid meaningless and unproductive detailed testing. In carrying out an analytical review, the auditor will discuss business trends and problems with the client's financial and operating personnel. He should study the industry in general and all recent material on developments in auditing techniques applicable to it. He should seek information on other companies in the industry and make comparisons. He should become familiar with the company's statistical records, budgets, and internal reports.

Analytical review program

1. Compare sales (as to amounts and units) with prior periods, sales department forecasts, reports to government agencies, etc.
2. Compare sales and profit trends with industry averages available from sources such as the Federal Reserve Board, trade associations, and Dun & Bradstreet, Inc.
3. Study the ratio of inventory quantities to sales and cost of products sold.
4. Relate inventory quantities to capacity of storage facilities and to recent production quantities and rated capacity of production facilities.
5. Compare statistical data from operating departments with results recorded in the accounting records.
6. Compare pounds in opening inventory, plus pounds purchased (from disbursement records), less pounds sold (from sales recaps and scrap proceeds), less percentage allowance for loss in process (usually an industry-known figure), with the ending inventory which the auditor observed.

Other analytical review steps will come to the auditor's mind as he relates the reasonableness and reliability of the inventories to the economic facts of the company and the industry.

An important step in the analytical review of inventory is illustrated in Figure 6, "Month's Supply of Inventory." Selected larger items are related to cost of sales to determine the number of months' supply on hand. An excessive number of months' supply will indicate slow-moving items or possibly obsolete material.

Efficiency Recommendations. The auditor should be alert to areas in which the accounting records may be improved and the company's overall performance and profitability increased. He need not be an engineer to recognize areas of inefficiency. Following are some points on inventories which auditors may consider for recommendations to management.

1. Does the company use tamper-proof mechanical counting devices or other overall means to establish that production counts are accurate and independent of workmen? (This is important in the case of piecework or incentive labor rates.)
2. Does the company utilize one master set of perpetual inventory records to furnish information for purchasing, sales, production control, cost accounting, and stores departments, thus eliminating costly duplication?
3. Does the company use scientific, mathematical, and statistical techniques for determining economic lot sizes for production, purchases, and inventory levels? For determining quality of product produced? For inspection of purchased materials and parts?
4. In the case of multiplant operations, has a study been made to determine whether warehousing and shipping are being supplied from the proper plant to minimize transportation and handling costs?
5. Does adequate use appear to be made (to you as a non-engineer) of material handling devices such as forklifts, pallets, conveyors and conveyor belts, and gravity flow in the movement of materials?
6. Could the company avoid the cost and disruption of annual physical

Figure 6 MONTH'S SUPPLY OF INVENTORY

Downtown Manufacturing Company
Wire Division
Test of Quantities against Sales
Finished Goods – Work in Process – and
Raw Material plus Commitments – In feet

SCH:- E 261
DATE: 12/31/70

Product Code	Description	Yearend Inventory	1970 Sales Forecast	Months Supply on hand *	January Sales to 1/25/70	
A 335	Treated Wire	$8,617,500 ✓✗	$98,100,000 ✗	1.05 ¢	$4,701,000 ✓	
336	Magnetic thread	12,225,500	25,925,000	5.80	12,342,000	
337	Cloverleaf Mesh	298,000	600,000	6.00	—	⊛
338	White Mesh	4,087,000	7,000,000	7.01	602,000	⊛
B 135	Waxed Cord	11,212,000	80,450,000	1.67	3,358,000	
136	Plastic Coated	2,439,600	7,450,000	3.93	150,000	Φ
138	Hi Cor.	4,178,000	8,700,000	5.76	160,000	Φ
142	Cuprinal	2,613,000	6,600,000	4.75	900,000	
XR 4	Taped Capictors	2,077	9,100	2.74	517	⊖
81-12	004 Reels	2,777	30,000	1.11	2,278	
06	Furnster of 5°	1,394	31,000	.54	1,971	
048	Coated Coils	434	4,500	1.16	545	
041	Black Seam	835	7,000	1.43	770	✓

* Selected larger quantity and value items for comparison with activity in sales

Turnover – entire inventory – 1968 4.5 times
Cost of sales ÷ closing inventory – 1969 4.4 "

⊛ Item is just coming out of experimental stages –

⊖ Sales are seasonal

Φ More than normal inventory on hand – Obsolescence not indicated however.

✓ Per January stock status report
✗ Per forecast submitted by sales dept
✓✗ Per year end inventory summary.
¢ Calculated

9/30/70
RWA

inventory counts completed simultaneously? If the perpetual quantity records are adequate and are properly tested by counts throughout the year, the annual simultaneous counts may be eliminated.

7. Does the cost system permit reasonable estimates to be made of new-product costs? Does it enable the sales department to make price quotations promptly?

8. Has the cost system been simplified to reduce excessive clerical work by eliminating excessively detailed overhead distributions? Handling of small charges as overhead instead of as direct costs? Grouping items of substantially similar nature into classes?

9. Does the company utilize modern machine accounting methods in its cost accounting system?

10. Are purchases and manufacturing orders well coordinated with sales requirements? Evidence of poor coordination are: an excessive number of out-of-stock notices to customers; emergency production orders; out-of-balance inventory levels; high obsolescence.

11. Is there effective budgetary control? Does it cover manufacturing and other expenses, and is it integrated with the cost system? Does it provide for a segregation of fixed and variable costs?

12. Are manufacturing expenses reported simply and concisely by departments, cost centers, plants, etc., and compared with budgets in a manner useful to top management, department heads, and others responsible for incurring and controlling expenses?

13. Are reports to management on costs and manufacturing expenses simple and concise? Do they highlight results by areas of responsibility? Are results compared with predetermined objectives? Is gross profit by products or product lines reported? Is the "return on investment" concept used?

14. Does the company have a plan for scheduling the most effective use of its productive facilities so that machines and employees are generally kept busy and long production runs are the general case?

STATISTICAL SAMPLING

Value Estimation Method. The "value estimation" method of statistical sampling may be used for quantifying an entire inventory by counting only a small part thereof. This method may be applied where there are sufficiently large numbers of items suitably segregated and identified so that a statistical cross section (without bias) sample may be taken as truly representative of the whole. The "value estimation" method is too complex for describing in a chapter such as this; however, a good exposition on the subject is to be found in "Physical Inventories by Statistical Sampling Methods," by Herbert Arkin, *The New York Certified Public Accountant,* October, 1959. Further details are given in the chapter, "Statistical Sampling."

AICPA Recognition. The Auditing Committee of the AICPA has issued Statement on Auditing Procedure No. 36, entitled *Revision of Extensions of Auditing Procedure Relating to Inventories,* in which it is stated:

> In recent years some companies have developed inventory controls or methods of determining inventories, including statistical sampling, of sufficient reliability to make an annual physical count of each item of inventory unnecessary in certain instances. The purpose of this statement is to recognize this development. Where a client's inventory control procedures or methods of determining inventories are highly effective, an accurate determination of inventory quantities may be made without a count of all items once each year. In such circumstances the independent auditor must satisfy himself that the client's procedures or methods are sufficiently reliable to produce results comparable to those which would be obtained by a complete physical inventory each year. If statistical sampling methods are used by the client in the taking of the physical inventory, the auditor must be satisfied that the sampling plan has statistical validity, that it has been properly applied and that the resulting precision and reliability, as defined statistically, are reasonable in the circumstances.

COMPUTER APPLICATIONS

Test of Counts. Up to this point auditors have not made extensive use of EDP equipment in carrying out their audits. An example of what can be done is the use of the computer in comparing audit test counts with those on the perpetual inventory on tape and in summarizing the results. A taped program can be developed which provides as output a tabulation showing:

1. Part number
2. The auditor's count
3. The perpetual inventory quantity
4. The quantity difference
5. Unit cost
6. Dollar amount of the variance
7. Percent variance: (4) ÷ (3).

In addition, the tabulation can be summarized as to the aggregate dollar amount of count variances in excess of book amounts and the aggregate dollar amounts of count variances less than book amounts.

Test of Pricing. A test of pricing may also be put into the taped audit program where the company maintains a "master" cost tape for parts, assemblies, and completed devices. This record can be tested by the auditor against vendors' invoices for materials and parts and against cost records showing the compilation of labor and burden. Tests of payrolls and cash disbursements can be coordinated with the inventory tests. By comparing the cost shown by the master cost tape with the perpetual inventory record, the auditor can establish an audit trail from source documents to the inventory.

Computer Case. In an actual case the auditor used the computer to trace some 700 test counts (there were over 100,000 individual count cards) into the final inventory tabulation. This would have been a most time-consuming job had it been done manually, since the count cards were summarized by department, of which there were more than 100. The taped program for this audit function contains the following steps:

1. Transfer the complete inventory from punched card to tape.
2. Sort the inventory to count-card sequence.
3. Compare test counts with the inventory in count-card sequence. Prepare an exception list of all differences.
4. Search the complete inventory for serial numbers of all unused count cards to determine whether they appear in the inventory. Prepare a list of all such serial numbers.
5. Print out the complete inventory in count-card serial-number sequence with subtotals printed for every 100 unit records.

Once the program has been run on the computer, the auditor's work can be limited to analyzing the results, investigating exceptions, and satisfying himself that the program has been run as requested.

Tests carried out by the computer can save many hours of audit assistants' time, while making it possible to perform more effective tests and to concentrate on following up exceptions. The computer processing cost for these programs is usually small and programming time reasonable. The programs, of course, should be usable for a number of years.

Electronic data processing equipment may be used in a variety of other ways to eliminate many of the routine auditing procedures required in the examination of inventories. In planning his audit program, the auditor should consider using the computer to the greatest practicable extent.

BIBLIOGRAPHY

Accounting Research and Terminology Bulletins, final ed., AICPA, New York, 1961.

Statements on Auditing Procedure, AICPA, New York:

- No. 33. *Auditing Standards and Procedures,* 1963.
- No. 36. *Revisions of "Extensions of Auditing Procedure" Relating to Inventories,* 1966.
- No. 37. *Public Warehouses—Controls and Auditing Procedures for Goods Held,* 1966.
- No. 43. *Confirmation of Receivables and Observation of Inventories,* 1970.

Cadmus, Bradford: *Operational Auditing Handbook,* New York, The Institute of Internal Auditors, 1964.

Cashin, James A., and Garland C. Owens: *Auditing,* 3d ed., New York, The Ronald Press Company, 1963.

Hill, H. P., J. L. Roth, and H. Arkin: *Sampling in Auditing,* New York, The Ronald Press Company, 1962.

Hoffman, Raymond A.: *Inventories—A Guide to Their Control, Costing, and Effect upon Income and Taxes,* New York, The Ronald Press Company, 1962.

Lenhart, N. J., and P. L. Defliese: *Montgomery's Auditing,* 8th ed., New York, The Ronald Press Company, 1957.

Trueger, Paul M.: *Accounting Guide for Defense Contracts,* 5th ed., New York, Commerce Clearing House, Inc., 1966.

Current, Kathryn: "Hedging as an Aid in Inventory Cost Control," *NAA Management Accounting,* October, 1966.

Hoffman, Raymond A.: "Inventory Frauds," *The Price Waterhouse Review,* vol. 12, no. 2, Summer, 1967.

Wright, F. K.: "Dual Variables in Inventory Measurement," *The Accounting Review,* January, 1970.

Trueger, Paul M.: "Terminations—Cost Principles and Costing Procedures," *The Journal of Accountancy,* June, 1970.

Chapter 23

Investments

ROBERT L. MAY

Partner, Arthur Andersen & Co.

GENERAL CONSIDERATIONS

Areas of Emphasis. The material presented herein is divided into discussions of two general aspects of the auditor's assignment.

Nature of investments. First, the nature of the investments to be audited, the objectives of the audit, and the routines necessary to develop all pertinent and relevant data concerning the investments are explored. As indicated by the reference material listed at the conclusion of the chapter, the reader may find additional detailed explanations of audit techniques and supplementary material on this basic background information. Comments herein on these matters are limited to the fundamental thinking about, and organization of, the work to be performed.

Evaluation of investments. The second aspect of the auditor's assignment deals with problems of evaluation of investments beyond routine vouching of purchases and sales, security counts, and the like. This aspect of the material concerns itself with the utilization of data bearing on the credibility of carrying values, possibilities for misstatements and irregularities, extension of auditing procedures beyond the audit date, and, finally, ways in which the audit results and observations may be put to good use.

Types of Investments. This chapter will deal only with the audit of securities held by industrial and similar organizations. Enterprises such as banks, insurance companies, investment companies, leasing companies, and funds have distinct operating problems that involve audit procedures and problems peculiar to their businesses which require specialized audit programs and planning.

For the purpose of this discussion, it is useful to distinguish between marketable securities and long-term investments. The former are readily salable while the latter are held with no probable intent to sell, or are not readily salable.

Marketable securities. These consist of:

1. Corporate stocks, bonds, and notes
2. Government obligations

Long-term investments. These include:

1. Marketable securities which are intended to be held on a long-term basis
2. Stock of, and advances to, subsidiaries or affiliates
3. Bonds, notes, mortgages, etc., not traded in open markets
4. Cash surrender value of life insurance
5. Nonoperating real estate
6. Other interests held for income or appreciation in value, such as joint ventures, mineral interests, etc.

Methods of Acquisition. The most common form of acquisition of an investment is cash; however, it should also be noted that investments may arise by exchanges of other forms of property, including stock for stock, stock for assets, property received in cancellation of indebtedness, and possibly some others. It is important to know the method of acquisition, for, as we shall discuss later, it is a consideration in the determination of carrying values.

Importance in Company Operations. Prior to the development of the program for the audit of investments, it is important to determine the significance of the investment to the company and its form. The greater the significance and the "why" behind the investment help the auditor to direct his attention to the operational aspects of the investment and to tailor his program, reports, and recommendations to the needs of the organization. Investment objectives may range from the temporary investment of idle cash, through such corporate objectives as diversification of risk, stabilization of income, and access to marketing know-how and technological data, to ultimate take-over or merger or other legitimate corporate objectives, such as legal qualifications in foreign states or countries, minimization of taxes, or segregation of activities unrelated to the primary operations.

Audit Objective. The broad audit objective is to form an opinion on each of the following:

1. Evidence of ownership and safeguarding of custody
2. Carrying value, in accordance with generally accepted accounting principles, consistently applied
3. Proper accounting for income from investments
4. Proper classification in financial statements as current or noncurrent assets
5. Adequacy of disclosure of any pledging, hypothecation, collateral, or other matters bearing on the carrying value or the company's unilateral right to dispose of the investment

Special or Limited Examinations. From time to time special or limited examinations may be required. Before undertaking such assignments, care must be exercised to determine the precise objectives to be achieved so that time will not be wasted, irrelevant material will be excluded from the report, and steps not necessary to accomplish the limited objectives will be avoided.

OVERALL REVIEW

Review of Internal Controls. Controls over investments must be carefully evaluated if the proper scope of examination is to be set and the audit objectives achieved. The review should determine that:

1. Proper accounting records are maintained identifying each investment, its origin (date), cost or other carrying value, location of physical evidence of ownership, disposition, gains or losses, worthless securities, and income from investments.
2. There is a proper segregation of duties between the custody of securities, accounting for income, and the handling of receipts of proceeds relating to disposition or income from securities.
3. Physical custody is adequate, either by use of a safe deposit box or in safekeeping with a trustee. Access to securities should be under dual control.
4. Securities are in the name of the company or properly endorsed and income assigned to the company.
5. Investment policies have been approved by the board of directors in the minutes and authorization for acquisition or disposition of investments has been approved in writing by the designated committee or officers of the company.
6. Adequate fidelity bonds cover all personnel handling investments.
7. Periodic reports are made to management on investments held, with such related information as may be useful to management.
8. Internal procedures require that follow-up be made to ensure prompt and proper receipt of all income.

Weaknesses in one or more of these areas may necessitate modification of the audit program to cover the deficiencies and most certainly would call for recommendations to eliminate the weakness noted and safeguard the assets and income of the company.

Review of Audit Programs. The review of the sample audit programs indicates the importance of advance planning and the many details that must be anticipated if the work is to proceed efficiently. It should be obvious that each program should be tailored to fit the company, the audit objectives, and the company's procedures, and that even the most carefully prepared program will be modified during the course of the examination as the actual facts and circumstances are compared with the purported controls and procedures set forth in company manuals.

Review of Workpapers. In addition to providing an orderly means of accomplishing the primary audit objectives, the workpapers should be reviewed to determine that they serve the following purposes:

1. Documentation of work performed
2. Documentation of weaknesses, deviations from policy, or other matters for management disposition
3. Facilitation of review by superiors

Special attention should be paid to the disposition of all matters not immediately resolved. For this purpose special "point" sheets should be prepared for follow-up. The audit cannot be considered complete and the report and recommendations conclusive until all matters of substance have been satisfactorily resolved or reported to appropriate authority for further action.

THE AUDIT PROGRAM

Responsibilities. The company attempts to invest all excess funds to the fullest possible extent. Decisions to buy or sell are recommended by Blank Trust Co., investment consultants, and when circumstances are deemed compelling, verbal approval of two members of the Finance Committee permit immediate buy or sell authority, subsequently confirmed in writing. Blank Trust Co. maintains custody over the securities and submits detailed statements monthly. Transactions are approved by the Finance Committee monthly, at which time recommendations are considered and acted upon. (See Permanent File for policy limits regarding types of investments authorized and limitations on percentage ranges of common and preferred stocks in relation to total portfolio holdings.) Blank Trust Co. has authority to redeem maturing securities.

The company maintains a detailed ledger, which is reconciled monthly to the statements from Blank Trust Co. Recording of transactions is based upon the receipt of advices from Blank Trust Co. Gains and losses are computed on a first-in, first-out basis.

Strong Points of Internal Control:

1. Detailed ledger maintained and reconciled monthly to report from custodian/managers.
2. Transactions approved by Finance Committee.
3. Internal auditors compare all advices of transactions to detail ledger and reconcile this ledger to general ledger.
4. Internal auditors verify income on all securities against published sources.

Weak Points of Internal Control:

1. Custody *and* management of fund vest in Blank Trust Co.
2. Internal audit workpapers do not reveal adequate follow-up on reasons why certain securities do not reflect income.

The mere fact that securities are held by an outside custodian may not be deemed to be satisfactory in terms of internal control in all cases. Appropriate inquiry may be made as to the safeguards maintained by the custodian over the release of securities to assure that adequate controls exist.

Illustrated Programs. In most cases audit work can be set up to perform many audit steps at a preliminary date. Circumstances will dictate the practicality of such division or spreading of work and the extent thereof. The following steps are set forth to cover all pertinent procedures rather than to reflect how the division of work might be accomplished in a given instance. It should also be noted that all of these steps are susceptible to sampling or testing techniques rather than 100 percent verification, depending upon the degree of internal control, volume and size of transactions, and relative significance to the company.

Stocks, bonds, and notes:

1. Obtain investment schedules analyzing the activity for the year and tie in to general ledger.
2. Obtain directly from Blank Trust Co. confirmation of balances as of audit date.
3. Trace beginning balances for all securities to prior-year workpapers.
4. Trace purchases and sales transactions to broker's advices and check commissions and transfer taxes.
5. Trace transactions to market quotations on date of transaction. (See weakness in internal control re custody/manager role of Blank Trust Co.)
6. Trace transactions to approval in minutes of Finance Committee.
7. Ascertain that all securities yield income or explain reasons for holding non-income-producing securities. Check dividend income against published sources and compute interest on bonds.
8. Have comptometer operator foot and crossfoot all schedules.
9. Check calculations of gains and losses on first-in, first-out basis.
10. Check calculations of amortization of premium or discount on bonds.
11. Cross-reference income from interest and dividends, net of amortization/premium, to income workpapers and gains/losses on sales to income workpapers.
12. Check market prices of all securities on hand at audit date in quoted sources and compare with carrying values.

Real estate and mortgages:

13. Obtain or prepare analysis of activity for the year (see 1 above).
14. Vouch transactions by tracing to invoices or contracts and trace to minutes for approval by Finance Committee. Examine mortgages.
15. Cross-reference depreciation to expense schedules.
16. Confirm balances, terms, etc., of any mortgages held with mortgagee.
17. Cross-reference real estate holdings to appropriate liability workpapers and confirmations therein.
18. Work to be performed on audit of income from income-producing real estate is included in income section of workpapers. Calculate income from mortgages and cross-reference such income to income workpapers.
19. Write overall investment conclusion that is directly responsive to audit objectives.
20. In-charge man review workpapers.
21. Staff man dispose of in-charge man's review points.
22. Senior review and approve disposition of all points raised, including review points.

Physical Counts. If it is deemed necessary to physically count securities, for whatever reason, the count may be made as of the audit date or at any prior or subsequent date provided that control is maintained over the securities between the audit date and the time of count.

General points

1. Proper planning should be made to determine that all locations, types, and volumes are known in order to properly schedule the manpower requirements.

2. Provision should be made for the simultaneous count of cash and securities or physical control should be secured by the auditor of locations of such assets until all counts are completed and reconciled to company records.

3. Detailed lists of securities to be counted are prepared in advance of the count, company representatives are present at all times, and ink-written receipts are obtained for the return of all items inspected or counted.

Details of the count

1. Worksheets should be signed and dated to indicate who performed count and company representative present.

2. Proper descriptions of securities should be checked off as to name, description, maturity, and interest rate and dates. Evidence of authenticity should be considered, but responsibility for uncovering forged securities is not normally the auditor's responsibility.

3. Note whether all interest coupons due subsequent to the date of count are attached and that bonds, notes, and mortgages are either payable to bearer or in the company name or that of an authorized nominee.

4. Because of weaknesses in internal control and the possibility of substitution of securities, consideration should be given to accounting for security numbers.

5. Bonds, notes, and mortgages should be examined for evidence of principal payments as indicated by terms.

6. Insurance policies should be examined as to coverage of officers or key employees.

7. Mortgage indentures and related notes receivable, recorded trust deeds, and deeds to or leases covering mineral interests should be examined.

8. The listing of the vault or safe deposit box contents should be complete and all included items satisfactorily explained or accounted for.

Problems of Valuation. In other sections of this chapter the subject of marketability has been briefly discussed and guidelines cited as to the distinction between marketable securities and long-term investments; also, some of the fundamentals of auditing used to gather the data required for valuation of the investments were discussed.

The general premise in reflecting carrying values of investments is historical cost, with some understandable departures. Increases or decreases may be reflected by recording the parent's share in the net earnings or losses of subsidiaries, the so-called "equity" method, or "one-line consolidation" method. Permanent impairments in investments may require a write-down of the carrying values. At times, mere disclosure of the facts surrounding the uncertainties involved, together with appropriate qualifying language in the report, will suffice.

Care should be exercised in comparisons of market values of quoted securities with carrying values. Securities infrequently traded or held in controlling blocks by very few stockholders may not be representative of the disposition value of the stock held by the company if significant in terms of normal trading volumes of the security held. Broadly traded securities do not ordinarily pose this particular problem.

ILLUSTRATIVE CASES

The following cases are illustrative, but not all-inclusive, of the valuation problems frequently faced by the auditor and the treatment of the matter that is recommended by the author.

Case I: Dividends before Acquisition. Problem. Dividends from earnings before acquisition credited to earned surplus.

Facts. Company A has a 50 percent interest in company B and received a 20 percent cash dividend within six months of acquisition, which it credited directly to earned surplus. Company B had breakeven operations during the six months' holding period but had accumulated substantial earned surplus prior to A's acquisition of it.

Conclusion and reasoning. Dividend should have been credited to the investment account, since it represented a return of capital invested and not earnings generated during the period of A's investment. The auditors should describe the circumstances in their report and take exception in their opinion.

Case II: Unaudited Statements. Problem. Unable to evaluate investment—audited statements not available.

Facts. Company A had investments in several other companies, principally banks, which aggregated more than the net worth of A, with the remainder of the financing represented by a bank loan. The stock of these companies is closely held, and, accordingly, market quotations were not available. The banks all had good reputations, were located in good economic areas, and had stable reported earnings and a good dividend record. However, these companies had never been audited by independent public accountants.

Conclusion. Disclosure should be made of the known facts regarding the inability of the auditor to satisfy himself on the carrying values and an exception should be taken in the opinion.

Reasoning. The auditor was not able to support the carrying values of these investments, and the circumstantial evidence of stability and dividend payout is insufficient to overcome this limitation, particularly when the statements of the companies invested in were not audited.

Case III: Unconsolidated Subsidiary. Problem. Realization of investment in unconsolidated subsidiary dependent on successful future operations.

Facts. Company A holds a 54 percent equity interest in a foreign company B and has advanced monies to B, representing about 75 percent of A's net worth. Company B is in the development stage and has capitalized research and development costs to be amortized over a three-year period. Operating losses of B from inception have required additional cash advances by A.

Conclusion. Company A's statements should reflect a provision for possible loss on the investment in B. The auditor's opinion might be worded, "In our opinion, except that no provision has been made for possible loss, etc. . . ."

Reasoning. Company B has not demonstrated the ability to attain profitable operations, rendering A's investment at cost a questionable carrying value. In line with the principle of anticipating losses, but not profits, a provision for possible loss is indicated in this instance.

Case IV: Disclosure of Investment Data. Problem. Investment in affiliate, at cost, is substantially below market but less than underlying book value.

Facts. Company A owned approximately 40 percent of company B, which, in turn, owned substantial real estate for development and sale. Company B was audited by the independent public accountants of company A and an unqualified opinion rendered thereon. Management of A made its investment as a long-term one and expects recoveries in excess of its investment.

Conclusion. Disclosure of facts desirable in a footnote.

Reasoning. Since company A acquired its interest in B as a long-term investment, the short-term market swing of B's stock cannot be of significance unless other factors lead to or cause a need to divest. The fact that the auditors of B rendered an unqualified opinion indicates that they found satisfactory evidence of the underlying value of B's investment in the real estate. Disclosure, however, is required for a fair presentation of the significance of the investment to A and its present and prospective stockholders.

Case V: Market Decline after Year End. Problem. Market decline in quoted value of common stocks subsequent to balance sheet date.

Facts. XYZ Company had disposed of its operating properties and invested the proceeds in marketable securities while considering entering other fields. These securities, at cost, represented 85 percent of total assets and 95 percent of net worth. At year end the quoted market prices of these investments slightly exceeded cost, but, prior to the issuance of the auditor's report, market declines reduced the quoted prices by almost 18 percent of carrying value.

Conclusion. A "subject to the future realization of the investment in marketable securities, in our opinion . . ." report was clearly indicated.

Reasoning. A significant and present impairment of the value of these investments had occurred, and it was not possible to ascertain whether the market would recover. Because the company had no present plans to liquidate the securities and only future events would determine whether the impairment in value would be permanent, there was no need to take an "Except for . . ." opinion.

Case VI: Recorded Amount in Excess of Book Value. Problem. Investment acquired for stock recorded at amount approved by directors. Amount recorded in excess of book value per share.

Facts. Company A acquired an interest in company B by purchase of shares from the president and sole stockholder of A. The investment represented 100 percent of the net worth of company A. Audited financial statements of B revealed a book value equal to only one-fifth of the assigned value, with breakeven operations. The stock of B is not subject to an established market and quoted prices.

Conclusion. An overall opinion on the fairness of presentation of this investment, and consequently the overall fairness of presentation of the financial statements, should probably be denied because of the significance of the carrying value of this investment to company A's financial position.

Reasoning. There is lack of evidence of an arm's-length transaction and no substantive evidence to support the appraised value. B is not generating profits and its book value is only one-fifth of carrying value. A could offer no support for the assigned value that was subject to audit verification.

Appendix to Cases. In some instances, where the auditor is unable to obtain reasonable evidence that an investment will be recovered, it may be appropriate to render a "piecemeal" opinion. Let us assume that the recovery of the investment and advances to a subsidiary are dependent upon the subsidiary's ability to attain profitable operations, and that there is sufficient evidence to indicate that the cause might be hopeless. In such a case of uncertainty the auditor might state, after a middle paragraph explaining the uncertainty involved:

In view of the significance of the matters discussed in the preceding paragraph, we are unable to express an overall opinion on the fairness of presentation of the financial statements of XYZ Co., Inc., as of December 31, 19____. However, in our opinion, the amounts reflected in the accompanying financial statements for cash, accounts receivable, plant and equipment, and current liabilities as of December 31, 19__, and income and selling and general and administrative expenses are fairly stated, in conformity with generally accepted accounting principles applied on a basis consistent with that of the preceding year.

OTHER CONSIDERATIONS

Potential Misstatements and Irregularities

Misstatements

1. Marketable securities carried at cost where significant market declines have occurred
2. Long-term investments carried at cost where permanent declines in carrying value have occurred because foreign exchange fluctuations have impaired value or where significant operating losses are not recognized, etc.
3. Misclassification as current assets of long-term or nonmarketable investments

Irregularities

1. Misappropriation and either sale or use as collateral for loans (personal rather than company loans)
2. Write-off of securities as worthless and proceeds diverted
3. Collusion with broker/seller on purchase/sale with split of illicit proceeds
4. Improper recording of securities purchased, received as dividends, or exchanged for other securities or assets and illicit proceeds diverted
5. Coverage of shortages of securities held by substitution of like securities borrowed, temporarily purchased, or forged
6. Misappropriation of income from bearer-type interest coupons or by nominee of dividends on stock

Tax Considerations. In the course of the examination the auditor should be alert to tax considerations and bring to the attention of the appropriate persons responsible for filing tax returns questions and information which may assist in the proper handling of such matters. Areas commonly giving rise to matters for such attention include the following:

1. Formation, acquisition, sale, or liquidation of subsidiaries
2. Intercompany transactions, including loans and advances, rendering of services, use of property, and transfer or sale of property
3. Liquidating dividends received or securities (sometimes included with regular dividends but separately stated or indicated in published sources)
4. Nature and source of all dividends
5. Complete details, including holding period of securities sold and gain or loss reflected
6. Identification of investments as to domestic or foreign at any time during the year
7. Indication of whether foreign-source income has been booked net of taxes withheld
8. Schedules of amortization of bond premiums or discounts

Reports and Recommendations. The results of the work performed should be communicated to the appropriate authorities in the company. These reports serve either as confirmation that all is in good order, no weakness in procedure noted, no policy deviations noted, etc., or they can direct the attention of management to areas requiring action. Before citing some examples of the type of points which might arise from the auditor's observations, it should be emphasized that the effectiveness of the report is frequently determined by the attention given to its presentation. The report should be as brief as possible, cite the deficiencies in the matter reported upon, explain the benefits to be achieved by improvement, and conclude with a sound recommendation to overcome the deficiency and achieve the desired benefits. Ordinarily no important purpose is served by a recitation of the audit procedures employed unless they have a definite influence on evaluating the report. Limitations in scope, unavailability of data, use of assumptions or calculations based upon unverified data should, of course, be incorporated in the report.

The following list of matters which might be brought to the attention of appropriate company personnel are indicative only of the inherent opportunities to assist management in conducting company affairs on a sound business basis. Obvious care must be exercised in the manner of presentation to avoid misunderstanding or implying criticism where none is intended.

1. Weaknesses in internal control. Many matters may be noted during the review of internal control and procedures and testing thereof.

2. Valuation problems. Such points could relate to data that were late, incomplete, or nonreceived relating to the underlying value of investments or to problems requiring further inquiry into the soundness of the carrying value of the investments.

3. Declines in value. Recommendations might be made to reserve for losses or to write down investments to sound carrying values.

4. Policy deviations relating to circumventing established procedures, or deviations from authorized investment policies on proportions of common stock held relative to total portfolio, etc.

5. Income tax considerations. Recommendations regarding possible tax savings by use of such vehicles, where appropriate, as subchapter S treatment, Western Hemisphere Trade Corporations, and a host of other matters.

6. Investment of idle funds. Comments regarding proper reporting of and immediate application of idle funds, utilization of cash flow forecasting techniques, etc.

7. Significant changes during the year. Pertinent comments or observations on investment matters which might include, but not be limited to, details of return on investment, yield based on cost and yield based on market value for marketable securities, and significant changes since the date of audit which may modify the significance of the historical data for the year under review.

Subsequent Events. The auditor should always bear in mind that while his examination is directed toward a specific balance sheet date and a period ending thereon, the findings and consequent reports are only as useful as they are current. Therefore, it is imperative that he carefully review events subsequent to the balance sheet date up to the rendering of his report to avoid misleading the user of the information developed because circumstances have been materially altered since the examination.

BIBLIOGRAPHY

Accounting Research Studies Nos. 3, 5, 6, 7, and 10, AICPA, New York.
APB Accounting Principles, Accounting Principles Board, AICPA, New York.
Statements on Auditing Procedure, AICPA, New York:
No. 33. *Auditing Standards and Procedures*, 1963.

No. 34. *Long-term Investments,* 1965.
No. 41. *Subsequent Discovery of Facts Existing at the Date of the Auditor's Report,* 1969.
Practical Accounting and Auditing Problems, AICPA, New York, 1966.

Baker, Ray E.: *Cases in Auditing,* Englewood Cliffs, N.J., Prentice-Hall, Inc., 1969.
Cashin, James A., and Garland C. Owens: *Auditing,* New York, The Ronald Press Company, 1963.
Meigs, Walter B., and E. John Larsen: *Principles of Auditing,* Homewood, Ill., Richard D. Irwin, Inc., 1969.
Palen, Jennie M.: *Encyclopedia of Auditing Techniques,* Englewood Cliffs, N.J., Prentice-Hall, Inc., 1967.

Olson, Irving J.: "Valuation of a Closely-held Corporation," *The Journal of Accountancy,* August, 1969.
Duncan, F. P., and P. Y. Southam: "A Simplified Rate of Return Analysis," *Canadian Chartered Accountant,* April, 1970.
Anderson, Jay H.: "Some University Investment and Accounting Concepts," *The Journal of Accountancy,* June, 1970.
Mandich, Donald R.: "Devaluation, Revaluation, Re-Evaluation," *NAA Management Accounting,* August, 1970.
Backer, Morton: "Financial Reporting for Security Investment and Credit Decisions," *The New York Certified Public Accountant,* November, 1970.

Chapter 24

Property, Plant, and Equipment

DANIEL A. SCHAEFFER

Partner, Richard A. Eisner & Company

GENERAL

Property, plant, and equipment consists of all tangible assets used in the operation of a business. These assets have a service life of more than one year and in the ordinary course of business are not expected to be sold. They may be classified as follows:

1. Property not subject to depreciation or depletion, such as land.
2. Property subject to depreciation, such as buildings, machinery, equipment, and tools.
3. Property subject to depletion, such as oil wells, mines, and timber.

A group of assets which are closely related to property, plant and equipment are the intangible assets. These may be identifiable assets such as franchises, patents, leaseholds, etc. They may also include items not individually identifiable (unspecified intangible values) such as goodwill, as stated in APB Opinion No. 16, paragraph 87. For auditing purposes these intangibles can more conveniently be grouped with prepaid expenses and deferred charges and discussed in Chapter 26.

Basis of Valuation. Generally, the basis of valuation of property, plant, and equipment is cost, which includes all incidental payments necessary to put the asset in condition and location for use.[1] Thus, cost of purchase or construction includes the invoice or contract price plus freight, the cost of materials, supplies, labor, and services used in construction and installation, and title examination and recording fees.

APB Opinions. Recent Accounting Principles Board Opinions have an important bearing on property, plant and equipment and the related intangible assets. Two opinions, No. 16, *Business Combinations* (August, 1970), and No. 17, *Intangible Assets* (August, 1970), may have an especially important effect in valuing the assets of an acquired or merged company. The two methods of business combination, the *purchase method*, and the *pooling of interests method* are discussed in detail in Opinion No. 16 and summarized under the section "Business Combinations," later in this chapter. The related intangibles such as goodwill, franchises, patents, and leaseholds are discussed in detail in APB Opinion No. 17 but for auditing purposes are covered in Chapter 26, along with other intangibles.

Audit Objectives. The auditor's objectives with respect to property accounts in connection with the examination of financial statements may be summarized as follows:

1. To determine that property, plant, and equipment is properly recorded on a basis in accordance with generally accepted principles consistently applied
2. To establish existence of the assets
3. To determine ownership of the assets and whether there are any liens against them
4. To ascertain that depreciation charges for the period are reasonable and that accumulated depreciation is adequate
5. To determine whether internal controls over the acquisition, utilization, and retirement of property, plant, and equipment are adequate and operating effectively

Examination of property, plant, and equipment should include a study of accounting principles and procedures, a review of internal control, and an examination of transactions in the accounts during the period. In the case of a first audit, it will be necessary to extend the examination to cover prior years.

An understanding of property accounts and transactions requires a knowledge of the property layout and the nature of operations. Actual inspection of the plant is necessary for such an understanding as well as to aid in the evaluation of internal control.

Internal Control. In most companies the investment in property, plant, and equipment represents a sizable portion of the organization's total assets. Therefore a company's procedures in connection with the acquisition, control, and retirement of property, plant, and equipment should be of great interest to the auditor in most examinations. While cases of fraud involving companies' properties can undoubtedly be cited, the prevention of fraud is

[1] Paul Grady, *Inventory of Generally Accepted Accounting Principles for Business Enterprises*, Accounting Research Study No. 7, New York, AICPA, 1965, p. 254.

not the primary objective for maintaining good internal control over plant assets. Of more importance are the securing of close control over plant expenditures and obtaining maximum utilization of existing equipment.

As a part of his examination of the property accounts, the auditor should evaluate the effectiveness of the client's system of internal control by observation, inquiry of company employees and officials, review of records, and tests of transactions. Before undertaking this evaluation, the auditor should be aware of the procedures essential to providing adequate internal control over an organization's properties and the transactions affecting the accounts.

Internal control procedures. A system which encompasses the procedures outlined below, as warranted by the circumstances, would generally provide adequate internal control over property, plant, and equipment.

1. Preparation and use of a budget of capital expenditures for the year approved by the board of directors.

2. Requiring approval in advance by authorized officials of the company for actual expenditures authorized in the budget. Minor expenditures not over a stated amount might be approved by an official such as a plant superintendent, while larger expenditures might need the approval of a committee of top officials or even the board of directors. In cases where authorized expenditures for construction projects are likely to be exceeded, the procedures should call for prompt reporting of such a situation to designated officials so that appropriate action may be taken.

3. Formulation of a written statement of policy distinguishing between those expenditures to be capitalized and those to be charged to repairs and maintenance. Frequently a minimum amount is established calling for the automatic charge to repairs and maintenance of items costing the stated minimum or less.

4. Approval of all sales and retirements by a designated official or officials, and the immediate forwarding of notification of such action to the accounting department by the party approving the transaction.

5. Purchasing of property items through a centralized purchasing department with payment subject to the normal routines of receiving, approval, and disbursing. Buildings and heavy machinery not going through the receiving department would have to be approved by the engineering department or other designated officials.

6. Maintenance of adequate property records in the accounting department. These records should include separate control accounts in the general ledger for each asset classification, as Land, Buildings, Machinery and Equipment, Furniture and Fixtures, etc., as well as separate control accounts for the related accumulated depreciation. There should also be a subsidiary plant ledger with a card or sheet for each unit of property, showing details such as description, number (for identification), location in plant, cost, date of purchase or installation, estimated scrap value, rate and method of depreciation, amount of annual or other periodic depreciation, depreciation accumulated to date, and repairs. At least once a year, cost and accumulated depreciation totals for each classification should be tied in with the general ledger balances; differences, if any, should be investigated and the accounts adjusted as necessary. A small company which considers that the maintenance of a plant ledger is not warranted may obtain similar information and objectives by use of a "lapsing schedule" similar to the one shown in Figure 3.

7. Establishing control and accountability of small tools, possibly including storage under lock and key and issuance only on requisition.

8. Periodic physical inventories of plant items to verify the existence of property carried in the accounts and to permit possible disclosure of unrecorded items. Where differences are found between the physical inventories and book records, the records should be adjusted accordingly. Significant discrepancies should be reported to management for appropriate action.

9. Periodic appraisals of property, plant, and equipment for insurance purposes.

10. Examination by internal auditors to ascertain that company policies and procedures with respect to property accounts are being followed and that transactions are being accurately recorded.

The auditor must evaluate the effects of omissions of procedures, under the existing circumstances, which he considers to be important for adequate internal control of property, plant, and equipment, and must alter the scope of his examination accordingly. Where he finds that major weaknesses in the system of internal control exist, he should discuss these with company management and recommend appropriate improvements in accounting and control procedures.

Internal control questionnaire. An example of a questionnaire which the auditor may use to assist him in his evaluation of a company's system of internal control of property, plant, and equipment is presented below.

1. Are detailed plant ledgers maintained in support of general ledger control accounts?
2. Are such ledgers maintained by persons other than those who are responsible for the properties?
3. Are they balanced at least annually with general ledger controls?
4. Are capital expenditures authorized or approved by the board of directors or some authoritative management group?
5. If so, are actual expenditures later compared with amounts authorized and additional approvals required if authorization is exceeded?
6. Does client have a well-defined policy to govern accounting for capital additions as opposed to maintenance and repairs?
7. Do company procedures provide for establishing that the materials are delivered or the services performed?
8. Is formal approval necessary for the sale, retirement, or scrapping of capital assets?
9. Do authorizations for the purchase of new plant assets indicate the items to be replaced?
10. Are retirements reported in a routine manner directly to the accounting department so as to provide reasonable assurance that they will be treated properly in the accounts?
11. Is control of scrapped items maintained to ensure reporting of sales thereof?
12. Is a satisfactory system in effect for the safeguarding of small tools, dies, and fixtures?
13. *a.* Does the client take periodic inventory of plant items?
    b. Are significant differences between such physical inventories and book records reported to management?
14. Are periodic appraisals made for insurance purposes?

Initial Audit. On a first examination, the auditor must satisfy himself as to the property account balances at the beginning of the period under examination. He must, therefore, review the property accounts and accumulated depreciation from inception. The extent of this review will depend on whether satisfactory examinations of prior years' financial statements have been made, upon the property records available, and the existence of other supporting documentation. If financial statements of prior years have been examined by public accountants considered to be competent and reliable, a limited review of the past history of the accounts will suffice. Otherwise, the auditor must undertake a more detailed examination of the opening balances.

He should obtain from the client or prepare schedules by classes of property, summarizing by years additions and retirements of property and changes in the related accumulated depreciation accounts. The extent of the testing of the details in these schedules will depend on internal control and the factors mentioned in the preceding paragraph. A review should be made of the accounting principles and procedures used by the company with regard to additions and retirements and the consistency of their application throughout the years. The basis of valuation of property acquired other than for cash, such as in exchange for securities or other assets, should be investigated. Sufficient information should be obtained regarding intercompany acquisitions to determine if any profits are reflected in the accounts. Major property acquisitions in a merger or consolidation should be studied by reference to agreements, corporate minutes, etc. Write-ups, write-downs, and appraisal reports should be examined.

The auditor generally assumes no responsibility for title to real estate and liens thereon, but he should examine documents which are indications of ownership, such as tax receipts and insurance policies, recorded deeds, and title policies, and should physically inspect plant facilities. If any legal question of title arises, the matter should be cleared by an attorney or title company.

Data accumulated in the initial audit should be incorporated in the permanent file and kept up to date in future periods.

PLANNING THE AUDIT

For the current period a schedule summarizing the changes in property, plant, and equipment by category (see Figure 1) should be obtained from the client, preferably, or prepared by the auditor, as a basis for review. Beginning balances of this schedule should agree with the prior year's ending balances.

Under a Work Order System. Where a work order system is used, a summary of work orders, by number, should be obtained from the client or prepared by the auditor to show the following information (where there is a large volume of work orders, the listing may be limited to those over a minimum amount):

Work order number
Description
Amount authorized
Expenditures to beginning of audit period
Expenditures during audit period
Total expenditures to date
Amount of transfers and accounts to which transferred, or other deductions with reasons therefor.
Work order balance remaining at end of period

Work orders completed during the period may be scheduled separately from construction still in progress, to facilitate tying in with amounts capitalized and recorded by account classification in the general ledger. It should be

Figure 1 ABC CORPORATION, SUMMARY OF PROPERTY, PLANT, AND EQUIPMENT, YEAR ENDED DECEMBER 31, 1970

	Assets				Accumulated depreciation			
	Balance, 12/31/69	Additions	Deductions	Balance, 12/31/70	Balance, 12/31/69	Depreciation 1970	Deductions	Balance, 12/31/70
Land	$ 25,400.00	....	....	$ 25,400.00	....	....	....	....
Buildings	181,500.00	....	....	181,500.00	$26,301.10	$ 4,362.05	....	$ 30,663.15
Machinery and equipment	87,568.32	$ 8,642.28	....	96,210.60	30,590.92	7,120.26	....	37,711.18
Furniture, fixtures, and office equipment	32,557.54	6,835.67	$ 534.37	38,858.84	6,803.50	3,501.26	$ 438.91	9,865.85
Automobiles and trucks	45,211.26	11,354.00	9,710.00	46,855.26	18,383.70	10,621.20	8,845.00	20,159.90
Leasehold improvements	15,658.54	2,314.19	....	17,972.73	5,394.61	1,831.43	....	7,226.04
Total	$387,895.66	$29,146.14	$10,244.37	$406,797.43	$87,473.83	$27,436.20	$9,283.91	$105,626.12

The 12/31/69 balances should agree with the corresponding final balances of the 12/31/69 workpapers. The 12/31/70 balances should agree with amounts shown in the trial balance. Additions and deductions should be scheduled (see Figures 2 and 4) and checked against supporting data. Depreciation calculations should be examined.

noted that among those companies which use work orders, the procedures vary. Some companies use work orders only for construction undertaken and/or contracted by the companies themselves, while others assign work order numbers also to items of additions which will be completed by purchase alone.

Descriptions of jobs should be reviewed to determine that all items are proper capital charges (in this connection, it may be helpful to physically inspect major additions). Questionable items should be discussed with the plant superintendent or another person who is familiar with the work done. Expenditures for extensive alterations of buildings or machinery are often difficult to classify; in some cases the expenditures should be allocated between capital items and maintenance on the basis of the judgment of architects, engineers, or the plant superintendent. When replacements of plant facilities or equipment are involved, the recorded values of items replaced should be deducted from the accounts.

Charges to work orders generally involve the following categories:

1. Materials from stores
2. Labor
3. Direct purchases
4. Contracts
5. Overhead allocations
6. Miscellaneous

The work orders listed should be supported by schedules of additions which show the above information detailed accordingly (where volume is large, the schedules may be limited to items over a minimum amount). These schedules will then serve as the basis for selection for detailed examination.

The auditor must determine that the selected work orders are properly authorized. Materials from stores should be tested for one or two months that show significant charges by reference to requisitions to determine the nature of the materials charged. Payroll records, including time tickets, should be checked to determine that such charges represent the time of men actually working on the project. Invoices supporting direct purchases and billings for work done under contracts, as well as the contracts themselves, must be examined to determine that such charges are appropriate. Frequently there are changes in specifications resulting in extra charges. It should be determined that these are properly approved and are justifiable additions to construction cost.

Capitalization of overhead directly attributable to construction projects is acceptable practice. Supervisory or indirect expenses of construction, drafting, tool, or maintenance departments, which are found in some companies, are usually considered overhead, and allocations may be made to construction jobs to the extent reasonably applicable to such work.

Other than a Work Order System. When a work order system is not in use, the charges for additions and the credits for retirements are made directly to the various property, plant, and equipment accounts in the general ledger.

Schedules of the details of property additions and retirements, by account classification (such as shown in Figures 2 and 4), should be prepared or obtained from the client, as a basis for review and selection of items for testing. The cost and accumulated depreciation totals in these schedules should agree with the amounts shown in the schedule summarizing the changes in the property accounts for the period (Figure 1).

Timing of the Examination. Substantial portions of the current year's exami-

Figure 2 ABC CORPORATION—FURNITURE, FIXTURES, AND OFFICE EQUIPMENT—ADDITIONS, YEAR ENDED DECEMBER 31, 1970

Date	Reference	Description	Amount
Jan. 27	Vo. 1–58	1 16″ pica IBM electric typewriter, IBM Corp.	$ 520.00
March 18	Vo. 3–37	1 Monroe calculating machine, Model CSA 10, Monroe Calculating Machine Co.	791.78
April 1	Vo. 4–6	4 Pedestal cabinet units and standard parts, Esbet Supply Co.	951.00
May 10	Vo. 5–19	2 60″ secretarial desks 2 posture chairs Janbob Office Equipment Co.	787.20
Oct. 17	Vo. 10–35	Conference room furniture: 1 table 8 chairs Standard Furniture Co.	3,171.52
		Total of items under $200 not scheduled	614.17
		Total	$6,835.67

Supporting data such as vouchers, invoices, etc., should be examined.

The total, $6,835.67, should agree with the corresponding amount in the Summary of Property, Plant, and Equipment (Figure 1).

nation of property, plant, and equipment may be undertaken during interim periods in advance of rather than subsequent to the balance sheet date. These include the following audit procedures:

1. Evaluation of internal control surrounding property, plant, and equipment and related transactions
2. Analysis of general ledger accounts to a cutoff date, and examination of additions and retirements to that date
3. Tests of charges to construction in progress (which can be substantially completed during a preliminary audit period)
4. Physical inspections of plant additions

After the close of the year, transactions recorded between the interim and the year-end dates should be reviewed carefully as a part of the year-end examination.

In connection with first-year examinations, virtually all of the investigation to substantiate the opening book balances of the property accounts may be completed well in advance of the year-end date. This would include review of principles and procedures followed in prior years, preparation by client or auditor of summaries of changes in property accounts by years, testing of major additions and retirements, investigation of upward or downward adjustments, and physical inspections if desired.

Relationship to Other Accounts. In connection with the auditing of property, plant, and equipment accounts, the auditor should be aware of the relationships with other accounts. Capital additions can be related to tests of purchases, payrolls, materials and supplies issued from inventories, etc. Examination of contracts and other documents in support of property acquisitions may disclose the existence of liens and liabilities which might otherwise be overlooked. Inspection of deeds, insurance policies, and real estate tax receipts may disclose important omissions from the property accounts. Study of leases may reveal expenditures which properly should be capitalized rather than recorded as lease expenses. Vouching maintenance and repairs expense accounts may disclose expenditures properly chargeable to property accounts; examination of property accounts may disclose items which should have been charged to maintenance and repair accounts.

CLASSES OF PROPERTY, PLANT, AND EQUIPMENT

Ownership of real estate may be indicated by the absence of rent expense or by the receipt of rental income. Other indications of ownership are expenditures for real estate taxes, building repairs, and interest on mortgages payable; these items are not conclusive, however, as they are also sometimes paid by lessees of real property in accordance with lease provisions.

Land. The cost of land includes the purchase price, cost of options, unpaid taxes assumed, broker's commissions, title examination and recording fees, title insurance, legal fees, and also clearing, grading, draining, and other conditioning. Where costs are incurred for sidewalks, streets, water mains, or sewers, which may arise from special assessments by a municipality or expenditures by the owner, such costs may be added to the land account or carried separately in a land improvements account. The use of a separate account is preferable, because these items are often subject to depreciation. If special assessments are payable in installments with interest, the interest should be charged to expense.

When land and buildings are purchased as a package, the auditor should review the data supporting the apportionment of costs between land and buildings. Appraisals, tax assessment valuations, and amounts of insurance coverage may be used for this purpose.

If buildings are located on land purchased with the intention of demolishing the buildings, the costs of demolishing less realized salvage are includable with the original purchase price as land costs. When the decision to demolish the buildings is made after the purchase because of structural defects or for other reasons, the cost of demolition less salvage plus the undepreciated cost of the purchased buildings is usually charged to expense.

When land is being held for sale as a speculation or for development and sale, taxes and other reasonable carrying charges may be capitalized so long as the investment is not carried to a point in excess of a reasonable valuation of the property. While it is conservative to charge off such expenditures, such procedure understates the income from current operations and overstates the profit from sale of the asset. If the land is being held for future use as a plant site rather than for sale, market values are not an important consideration and all costs up to the time a plant is constructed and occupied may properly be capitalized.

Regarding land under development for subsequent resale, either with or without houses or other commercial buildings on it, as development proceeds additional expenditures incurred for such items as grading, paving of streets and sidewalks, water installations, and sewers should be added to the property costs. Related administrative, promotion, and advertising expenses should be recorded as expenses or deferred charges. The total capitalized cost should be allocated to the salable lots in accordance with sales prices based on location within the developed area or other reasons. While the improvement expenditures may or may not vary by lot or location, the original purchase price of the land will undoubtedly have been determined on the basis of the desirability of distinctive land features and factors. For example, property for homesites which has frontage on water suitable for swimming or boating is considered very desirable and is higher priced than property without this feature. Thus in the developed area, the selling price of homesites fronting on the water will be higher; accordingly, the proportionate share of costs allocated to such sites should be higher.

Buildings. A building is a relatively permanent structure designed for use as a dwelling, shelter, storehouse, factory, or for another commercial or private purpose. If a building is purchased, cost includes the contract purchase price, expenditures for repairs to place the building into serviceable condition, the cost of alterations, improvements and remodeling to suit the purposes of the new owner, unpaid taxes assumed, and legal and closing fees. When a building is constructed, costs which may be capitalized are the following: architects' and engineers' fees, cost of materials, labor, temporary buildings used for construction offices and sheds for materials and tools, fees for permits and licenses, premiums for workmen's compensation and casualty insurance, easements, and allocable overhead.

Fixtures and equipment permanently affixed to the building, such as heating, refrigerating and air-conditioning equipment, elevators, lighting fixtures, plumbing, and other improvements, are also proper additions to building cost but may be carried separately in one or more other accounts. Since the useful life of these improvements is usually less than that of the building and varies according to the type of equipment, segregation in separate accounts facilitates the use of varying depreciation rates.

Audit procedures for land and buildings. The auditor should ascertain that real estate acquisitions as discussed above are properly authorized by the board of directors or other appropriate officials of the company. If expenditures for purchase or construction exceed the amounts authorized, this should be discussed with company executives concerned with such matters, to determine the reasons for the excess and to obtain approval. Documentation, such as purchase contracts, closing papers, deeds, vouchers, invoices, special assessment notices, and tax bills, should be examined or tested to support additions to land or buildings accounts. When construction is involved (other than under a work order system), auditing procedures similar to those explained previously to be followed under a work order system are appropriate, except that vouchers and invoices may have to be scrutinized more closely to determine the exact nature thereof when this is not clearly indicated or evident.

All liabilities for construction work completed to date must be reflected in the accounts. Information regarding significant purchase and construction commitments should be obtained for disclosure in the financial statements.

Machinery and Equipment. All expenditures relating to the purchase or construction of machinery and equipment should be capitalized. For purchased items, this includes invoice price, freight, duty, and unloading charges. When machinery and equipment are constructed by the company, the same general principles relating to materials, labor, overhead, and other costs apply as in the case of buildings. For either purchased or constructed items, installation costs and any other charges necessary to place the asset in condition for use should also be capitalized. Costs of testing or breaking in are proper additions to machinery and equipment, but any proceeds during this period from the sale of scrap or production should be credited to the asset.

Both large and small tools may be carried in a separate tools account, but large tools such as lathes, looms, and motors, sometimes referred to as "machine tools," are more frequently included with machinery and equipment and are recorded, depreciated, and retired in a manner similar to that used for machinery. Small tools, on the other hand, are generally handled in a different manner, as described in a subsequent section of this chapter.

Purchase on a deferred payment plan. When machinery or equipment is purchased on a deferred payment plan, the gross purchase price usually includes interest and finance charges, but only the net cash purchase price may be recorded as the asset cost. The charges for financing the installment purchase are not proper asset costs and should be charged to expense or deferred over the payment period. The auditor should ascertain that the total purchase price less any down payment has been set up as a liability at the time of acquisition and that depreciation is being calculated on the entire asset cost rather than on the paid amounts only. Unless such purchases are not significant, the sales contract, chattel mortgage if any, and invoices should be examined to determine the method of payment, when title passes, and liens, and that the total cost and expense charges have been properly recorded.

Purchase under royalty agreement. If machines are purchased under a royalty agreement which provides for the payment of royalties on units of production or some other basis, it is incorrect to add the royalty payments to the cost of the asset. The royalties should be charged to operations as they accrue according to the terms of the agreement.

Machinery on rental. Machinery being used under a rental agreement should not be included in the company's asset accounts, as the lessee does not have title to the equipment. However, under certain conditions the transaction is considered to be a purchase rather than a rental, and the asset should be capitalized, a liability set up for the calculated cost, and depreciation taken on the amount so recorded. The various factors to be considered in this connection are explained in another section of this chapter on lease arrangements and commitments.

Rearrangement and reinstallation costs. Sometimes machinery in a factory is rearranged and reinstalled to improve routing or flow of work with a view to reducing time and production cost. Since the cost of one installation has already been capitalized, it would be an inflation of asset values to capitalize the rearrangement expenses. The mere relocation of the equipment does not increase its value even though it may result in production improvements. The preferred procedure would be to charge the costs of rearrangement and reinstallation to expense regardless of amount. However, if such expenditures are large and would distort the results of operations for the period in which incurred, they may be set up as a deferred charge and amortized over a reasonable period not in excess of future periods to be benefited. This may apply particularly in situations where machinery or equipment has been transferred from one factory to another or where an entire plant has been moved to a new location for valid production, cost, or efficiency reasons. Forced removal because of the expiration of a lease would not ordinarily be considered a valid reason for deferral.

In general, the above discussion applies as well to major relocations of equipment other than that used in the factory.

Detailed records. Companies frequently maintain a detailed record of machinery and equipment, with a page or card allotted to each piece of equipment. The record is often kept in considerable detail to provide information for depreciation, retirement, and insurance purposes as well as for control. Where such records are kept, all or part of the following data will be provided:

Name or description of machine
Number (for identification purposes)
Location in plant

From whom purchased
Date of installation
Purchase price
Cost of installation and other elements of capitalized cost
Estimated life
Estimated scrap value
Depreciation rate and method (i.e., straight-line, declining-balance, etc.)
Amount in dollars of periodic depreciation provision
Depreciation amount accumulated to date
Repair information—date, cost, and nature
Other information affecting the equipment

If this record is maintained accurately, the total asset costs should agree with the amount shown in the general ledger control account.

Audit procedures for machinery and equipment. Additions to the machinery and equipment account (as well as to the other equipment accounts) must be analyzed to determine that amounts capitalized during the period represent actual additions rather than items which should have been charged to maintenance, repairs, or other expense accounts. Documents and records which provided the needed information and served as the basis for the entries, such as purchase orders, vendors' invoices, contracts, requisitions, construction reports, etc., should be examined in support of large additions and selected smaller ones. Particular attention should be directed to amounts capitalized over and above invoice purchase costs, such as freight, installation costs, labor, and other items.

Construction in Progress. The balance in this account represents the charges accumulated to date on uncompleted construction projects. Under a work order system, this balance should be in agreement with the total of the open work orders balances. Construction in progress is a temporary classification; as projects are completed, the costs are transferred to the appropriate permanent account classification, such as Buildings, Machinery and Equipment, etc. In some companies all capital additions pass through this account, whether representing costs for items entirely purchased or charges relating to construction.

All liabilities for construction work completed to date must be reflected in the accounts. Information regarding significant purchase and construction commitments should be obtained for disclosure in the financial statements. Examination of contracts, of minutes of meetings of the board of directors and discussion with company officials, and confirmation requests of such matters from vendors and contractors with whom the company has been doing business may disclose such data.

Interest during construction. It is permissible to charge construction costs with interest paid during the construction period on money borrowed to finance the construction, but this practice is mainly confined to public utility companies. Public utility commissions permit utility companies to follow this practice, as well as the capitalization of a reasonable rate on other funds of the utility used for construction, because the rates which may be charged by such companies are fixed on the basis of capital investment. Since new construction does not become a part of the rate base until the equipment is placed into service, and there is no income against which to offset the interest, the utility is permitted to recover the interest by including it in the investment on which rates will be based. Although industrial companies have no similar justification for the capitalization of interest during the construction period because their earnings are not controlled and they can set their own prices, the capitalization of interest during construction has carried over into industrial accounting and the auditor will sometimes encounter this practice.

Furniture, Fixtures, and Office Equipment. Included in this category are desks, chairs, bookcases and showcases, counters, shelving, partitions, display fixtures, carpeting, safes, typewriters, accounting machines, computers, and various other items of office equipment. If the account gets burdened with a myriad of items having little value, accounting for them may result in the expenditure of time, effort, and money unwarranted by the relatively minor value of the equipment. Where the auditor finds such a situation, he should recommend the capitalization only of units having a cost over a set minimum amount.

To facilitate the allocation of depreciation charges among various categories of expenses, such as selling, administrative, store (for retail establishments), etc., the account may be subdivided or the items recorded in appropriate separate accounts. Also, the cost of items attached to walls, ceilings, or floors of leased premises, such as the aforementioned shelving and partitions, floor covering, and electrical fixtures, may sometimes be found in a leasehold improvements account. Whether the items enumerated in the preceding paragraph are included in one or more accounts, the audit procedures are the same; in general, these procedures are similar to those for machinery and equipment.

Transportation Equipment. For most companies (excluding motor carriers and bus companies), depending on the size and needs of the business, this classification includes:

1. Trucks of various sizes, truck tractors, and trailers—used for pickup and delivery purposes:
   a. From vendors, piers, and terminals
   b. To customers
   c. Intracompany
2. Sedans, station wagons, and small buses—used for transporting company personnel

Companies maintaining their own vehicle repair and maintenance shops have, in addition, suitable equipment for carrying out this function, such as gasoline and air pumps, battery chargers, motor-testing machines, grease racks, hydraulic jacks, and tow trucks, all of which should be capitalized. The initial purchase of parts and accessories for use in the shop should be set up as supplies inventory, or as an asset with replacements charged to expense.

In recent years there has been a marked increase in the tendency of companies whose plants or operations are spread over wide areas to own and operate their own airplanes. Boats and freight cars are also sometimes owned by industrial companies, and a noted example of a type of transportation equipment used for advertising and promotion purposes is the Goodyear blimp.

It is desirable to classify transportation equipment by function, so that depreciation, maintenance, and operating expenses may be more easily allocated to production, selling, or administration.

The auditing procedures relating to examination of the transportation equipment accounts are substantially the same as the procedures for machinery and other equipment. Where motor vehicles are concerned, the auditor should relate the number owned to the overall operation. For example, where the auditor notes a major increase in the number of vehicles from the prior period, he may reasonably expect to find that this occurred because of an increase in operations; a major decrease may have stemmed from reduced overall operations, or it may have resulted because of a change in company policy to replacement of retired equipment by leasing rather than by purchase. In either case, satisfactory explanation should be obtained for large variations between periods in number of vehicles and their dollar value.

A factor relating almost exclusively to transportation equipment, which can be used by the auditor to substantiate ownership, is registration. Motorized equipment which moves on the highways, on railroad tracks, in the water, and in the air must be registered for a fee (usually based on type of equipment and weight) by state or federal government authorities, such as state motor vehicle bureaus and other state and federal commissions and agencies. The registration certificates, containing information as to ownership and detailed identification of the equipment, are on file at the issuing agencies and they should be available for examination at the offices of the company being audited. Where equipment is "on the road" or at remote locations and the certificates are with the equipment, a "renewal" stub may be on file. The auditor should be able to tie in the registration payments with the number of pieces of equipment owned, or to test-check the recorded individual items against the disbursement record.

Transportation equipment is usually insured against theft, damage, and liability. The insurance policies will also contain information regarding ownership and identification of the equipment.

In connection with truck usage, some states require the payment of a truck mileage tax, which is based on mileage traveled in a state by trucks operated by the company. When a company has trucks in operation, the auditor should ascertain whether the mileage tax applies and the status of payment, to determine that liability for such taxes has been correctly calculated and properly reflected in the books of the company.

Transportation companies. Railroads, airlines, motor carriers, bus companies, and steamship lines of necessity have a large proportion of their capital invested in transportation equipment. Therefore a greater proportion of the auditor's time may be spent in the examination of property, plant, and equipment in companies whose main business is transportation than in manufacturing companies.

The operations of transportation companies are in great measure controlled by federal and state regulatory agencies, such as the Interstate Commerce Commission, the Federal Aviation Agency, the Federal Maritime Commission, and state public service commissions. These agencies also prescribe regulations covering record keeping and reporting. Consequently, while the auditing procedures described in other parts of this chapter will in general also apply to transportation companies, before undertaking an audit of a transportation company the auditor should familiarize himself with the requirements of the regulatory agencies by reference to rules, regulations, instructions, and forms published by the appropriate agency.

Trades. Because of the relatively high rate of wear and tear of transportation equipment, generally resulting in rising maintenance and operating costs as the equipment becomes older, such equipment is frequently traded for new equipment before or after the used equipment has been fully depreciated on the books. In such trades, equipment is purchased for a stated price less an amount allowed for the old equipment given in exchange, and there is usually a difference between the net book value of the old equipment and the amount of the allowance. Some companies record this difference as a gain or loss on disposal of equipment, but most companies follow the procedure acceptable for federal income tax purposes: no recognition is given to gains or losses from such exchanges, and the basis of the asset acquired is the net book value of the asset exchanged plus the net amount paid.

An example of a purchase involving a trade and the preferred method of recording the transaction is as follows: an automobile originally purchased for $3,500 and having accumulated depreciation of $2,500 is given in exchange, plus cash of $2,800, for a new automobile with a market price of $4,000. The proper entry is:

Automobile B (new)	$3,800	
Accumulated depreciation, Automobile A (old)	2,500	
Automobile A (old)		$3,500
Cash		2,800

Depreciation is then calculated over the useful life of automobile B, based on the recorded value of $3,800 less estimated salvage. The auditor should check the calculations by reference to the purchase price, trade-in allowance, and net amount paid shown on the vendor's invoice, and should ascertain that depreciation on the automobile exchanged has been taken to date of trade. Machinery and other equipment is also traded in a similar manner, and the above illustration applies to such trades as well.

Small Tools. This classification includes hand tools and portable machine units which are small in size and therefore easily lost, mislaid, or stolen. Because of this most companies do not account for small tools in the same manner as other equipment. The three most generally used methods of accounting for this type of asset are the following:

1. Establish a fixed total base amount for small tools and charge to expense upon acquisition all additions and replacements. This may result in large variations in such expense charges from year to year, but in most companies the total charges falling in this classification will usually be relatively minor compared with other production costs.
2. Charge such items to an asset account when acquired, take a physical inventory at the end of the year, and value the assets at cost less an estimated amount for wear and tear. Charge to expense the difference between the unadjusted book amount and the inventory value. This results in the operations of the period absorbing the charges of items worn out, lost, or stolen since the last inventory, as well as the dollar increase or decrease of those on hand. The disadvantage of this method for the company lies in the expense of taking and pricing the inventory.
3. Treat the tools in the same manner as supplies and charge them to expense as they are issued, so that only new tools not yet placed in service remain on the books as an asset.

In some companies where the small tools have a somewhat longer useful life than most such items, say two or more years, additions are capitalized and depreciation taken each year.

Control of small tools can best be maintained by keeping them in storerooms under inventory control with detailed records in the nature of a perpetual inventory reflecting quantities and costs.

Where these tools are accounted for by the base asset amount, the auditor should determine that the amount is not in excess of the value that would be shown if an inventory were taken. If an inventory is taken, the auditor should test the quantities, prices, extensions, and footings. Since the total value of such assets is usually not material, the scope of such tests should be limited. Where an allowance for depreciation is provided, the auditor should satisfy himself that the rates are realistic and that the net book value of these assets is reasonable.

Patterns, Drawings, and Dies. Patterns, drawings, and dies are frequently large in number, involving large expenditures, and generally present difficult problems of valuation. If purchased or constructed to be used for regular or stock production, a problem arises in estimating their useful life and the probability of repeated future use. If acquired for special jobs, their residual value is usually negligible and the cost should be charged to the special jobs; this should be done even when there is a possibility that there may be repeat orders for the special job, as such expectations frequently do not materialize.

When there is no longer demand for a model, or when production of a model ceases for other reasons, such as obsolescence or improvement, the patterns, drawings, and dies become worthless and should be written off. Accounts containing these assets should be reviewed frequently to prevent their overstatement.

Two methods frequently used for valuation of patterns, drawings, and dies acquired for continuing production are described below:

1. At the end of a period, a physical inventory is taken of those items remaining in the account and they are valued at cost less an amount for estimated wear and tear.

2. Items in the account are depreciated on the basis of a composite rate or of an individual rate for each item. In either case, because of the limited useful life expectancy of such assets, a rapid rate of depreciation should be used, say three years. Where depreciation is calculated on individual assets, a lapsing schedule (such as is shown in Figure 3) is often used as a record of cost and accumulated depreciation.

If a lapsing schedule is not maintained by the company, the auditor may find it useful to prepare such a schedule for his permanent file and keep it

Figure 3 LAPSING SCHEDULE

(1)	(2)	(3)	(4)	(5)					
			Depre-	Annual depreciation					
Date acquired	Description	Cost	ciation period	1968	1969	1970	1971	1972	1973
5/1/68	Item A	$ 2,700	3 yrs.	$450	$ 900	$ 900	$ 450		
8/4/68	Item B	2,400	3 yrs.	400	800	800	400		
3/15/69	Item C	6,000	3 yrs.	....	1,000	2,000	2,000	$1,000	
10/12/69	Sold Item B	(2,400)	....	....	(400)	(800)	(400)		
1/5/70	Item D	8,100	3 yrs.	....	....	1,350	2,700	2,700	$1,350
6/20/70	Item E	3,900	3 yrs.	....	....	650	1,300	1,300	650
	Total	$20,700		$850	$2,300	$4,900	$6,450	$5,000	$2,000

It is assumed above that all of the assets in the account are depreciated over a three-year life, and one-half year's depreciation is taken in the year of acquisition and in the year of retirement. The Cost column total should be in agreement with the asset control account balance in the general ledger; the total for each year shown in column 5 provides the amount to be recorded as the annual depreciation charge for that year.

current for each examination. He should ascertain that additions are supported by vouchers and other satisfactory evidence, as explained in the discussion of machinery and equipment. The items capitalized should be reviewed for current and future use, and the auditor must satisfy himself that consistent practice is being followed in the recording, depreciation, and retirement of these assets.

Returnable Containers. Returnable containers include bottles, cartons, sacks, kegs, drums, barrels, baskets, and other containers which companies engaging in certain businesses, such as beverages, oil, and chemicals, use for the shipment of products. In some cases, such as beverage companies, these containers represent a sizable investment.

To encourage the return of such containers, refundable deposits may be required by vendors. The deposit amount received in cash or charged to the purchaser's account represents a liability and must be set up as such in the accounts; correspondingly, upon return of the containers the applicable deposit amount is returned or credited to the customer's account and the liability is debited. Where no charge is made at the time of delivery, a memorandum or some other appropriate record must be maintained and a cash settlement is later made for containers which are not returned.

Returnable containers on hand and those in the hands of customers are usually carried in a supplies inventory account, but those of sturdy construction not easily broken or damaged by normal usage are frequently carried as depreciable assets. The rate of depreciation, as is the case with other depreciable assets, is based on the estimated useful life.

There is little difficulty in substantiating the existence of containers on hand, but a considerable problem arises in connection with containers in the hands of customers. Even where the company maintains accurate records of containers charged out to customers, it is known that a portion of these containers will never be returned and therefore they cannot continue to be shown as assets. The company should estimate the percentage of containers which are not likely to be returned and periodically remove them from the asset account, depreciation (if applicable) from the accumulated depreciation account, and the deposits (if any) from the liability account. The net effect of these entries for the cost, accumulated depreciation, and deposits on the containers which are not returned will be a gain or loss to be recognized in income. The estimate of the percentage of those containers which will not be returned should be based on the past experience of the company. Where the company does not develop such information from its own records, or where the company is in the first year or early stages of operation, industry or trade associations usually have available such statistics appropriate for use by the company.

Examination of returnable containers should include the following procedures:

1. Test-count containers on hand.
2. Examine the details of the records supporting the quantities of containers held by customers. Such details may be in the form of a separate memorandum record or of entries in the accounts receivable ledger showing quantities shipped and returned for each customer.
3. Review the basis and calculation of the percentage of containers held by customers estimated to be nonreturns, and ascertain that these containers have been properly removed from the accounts.

4. Test the pricing of the containers by reference to suppliers' invoices.
5. If depreciated, check the rate and computations.

It may be possible to confirm the deposits paid or the quantities held by customers, particularly when the containers are larger and more valuable. Whether confirmed or not, the aggregate deposit amount may be divided by the deposit per container to determine the quantity out on deposit. It may also be possible to count the containers held by customers, and this should be done where feasible. This does not have to be done each year. In a continuing audit, every two or three years may be appropriate, or a procedure may be followed of rotating these counts among customers so that each customer is covered at least once over a predetermined time period.

Leasehold Improvements. Improvements to leased property made by the lessee revert to the lessor at the expiration of the lease. This pertains to buildings erected on leased land and alterations, additions, and other improvements made to real estate. Leasehold improvements may be carried in a separate account under property, plant, and equipment. However, since the lessee has the right to the benefits of the improvements only during the life of the lease, the auditor may find leasehold improvements classified as an intangible asset. In either case, leasehold improvements should be amortized over the life of the lease or the useful life of the improvements, whichever is less. In the determination of the number of years to be used for amortization purposes, only the original life of the lease is used without consideration of options for renewal unless such options are actually exercised. When an option is exercised or it is reasonably certain that it will be, the unamortized portion of the leasehold improvements should be spread over the period starting with the date the option is exercised to the new expiration date of the lease or the remaining useful life of the improvements, whichever is less.

When a lease calls for a payment to the lessee as compensation for improvements (such as a building) which revert to the owner of the property, or the restoration of leased property to its original condition (except for normal wear and tear), the amount of the payment to be received or the estimated costs of restoration should be taken into consideration in determining the amount required to be amortized over the life of the lease.

Wasting Assets. An apt definition of "wasting assets" is found in Kohler's *A Dictionary for Accountants*, 4th ed., p. 452, as follows: "An asset that diminishes in value by reason of and commensurably with the extraction or removal of a natural product such as ores, oil, and timber, which it contains."[2] Thus, in the examination of wasting assets, we must establish the value (cost) of the tangible asset, the amount by which it diminishes in value (depletion) for a given period, and the amount of accumulated diminution (depletion) to a given date.

The verification of cost and ownership of wasting assets involves procedures similar to those outlined for the auditing of real estate, and includes examination of purchase contracts, deeds, vouchers, leases, tax bills, and other documents. Capitalized costs may include, in addition to the original cost of land, title costs and exploration, development, and carrying charges to such time as commercial production begins. After that date additional development charges are frequently treated as expense, although they may also be

[2] E. K. Kohler, *A Dictionary for Accountants*, 4th ed., Englewood Cliffs, N.J., Prentice-Hall, Inc., 1970, p. 452.

capitalized. In Holmes' *Auditing: Principles and Procedure* this is stated as follows:

> All cost of exploitation and original development should be capitalized, and these costs should be amortized on the basis of commercially recoverable units of product. Subsequent additional costs for shaft extensions, additional trackage and cars, and other equipment, incurred after production has begun and made for the purpose of maintaining output, frequently are charged to expense at incurrence; in most cases, they should be charged to asset accounts and depreciated.[3]

The calculation of depletion is usually based on the relationship established between the total cost of the wasting asset and the number of recoverable units. To accomplish this the total number of units of product to be extracted must be determined. Dividing the total cost by the total number of units will provide the cost of one unit. (Methods and calculation of depletion are discussed in detail in Chapter 25.) The total number of units to be recovered can only be estimated, and frequently these estimates must be revised as operations progress because of the discovery of new resources or processes, improvements in extraction or reduction methods, or changes in product value which may make it worthwhile to extract ores previously considered to be of no value. For the estimates of the total number of units to be recovered, companies usually rely on surveys and reports of engineers and geologists; the quantity of timber available may be established by cruising. In his examination, the auditor should inspect the engineers' and geologists' reports and other data on which the company based its original estimates of quantities and any changes in estimates. Regarding the number of units extracted during the period, the auditor should check production records and reconcile these with records of shipments and sales.

PROPERTY ACQUIRED FOR CONSIDERATION OTHER THAN CASH

When property is acquired for consideration other than cash, the criteria used in determining its value should be based on a sound method, reasonable in the circumstances. Land, buildings, or equipment may be acquired in exchange for the company's capital stock or bonds or by donation.

In Exchange for Company's Securities. When property is acquired in exchange for securities, cost may be considered to be either the fair value of the consideration given or the fair value of the property or right acquired, whichever is the more clearly evident. Thus, when the company's capital stock is issued, the property should be capitalized at the fair market value of the stock if a fair market price is available; usually such a price will be available for a publicly held corporation. If a market price for the stock is not available, as will probably be the case when the stock of a corporation is closely held, the asset should be recorded at the amount at which it may be purchased on the basis of a cash offer. If the cash cost amount is not available, an appraisal of the property should be made, preferably by independent appraisers, to establish a reasonable valuation.

When bonds are issued at a yield fairly representative of existing rates of interest for similarly rated borrowers, the principal amount of the bonds exchanged would be an adequate measure of the value of the property

[3] A. W. Holmes, *Auditing: Principles and Procedure*, 6th ed., Homewood, Ill., Richard D. Irwin, Inc., 1964, p. 530.

acquired. Where this condition does not exist—for example, if the company issued 3 percent bonds when the interest rate for bonds issued by similar corporations was 6 percent—the bonds cannot be presumed to be worth their principal amount. Under the latter circumstances, fair value of the property should be determined by assessing a realistic interest rate as a basis for determination of a reasonable value of the bonds. The difference between the principal amount of the bonds and the fair value of the property can be treated as bond discount.

Acquired by Donation. Property acquired by donation should be recorded at the current market value determined on the basis of a reliable appraisal, with a corresponding credit to a paid-in capital account. The donation may be unconditional or it may be contingent upon the fulfillment of certain requirements stipulated by the donor. If it is contingent, the entries should be made in temporary or contingent accounts until the conditions are met, at which time these accounts will be closed out to conventional asset and paid-in capital accounts. Any expenditures which must be made in connection with the donated property, such as charges for moving or dismantling of an old building, should be capitalized or offset against the paid-in capital account.

In connection with such assets, the auditor should examine the appraiser's report where this was the basis for valuation, ascertain whether the property was free of encumbrances, such as mortgages, judgments, or taxes, and determine the status of title with respect to the requirements of the donor.

Acquired from Officers or Affiliates. Assets acquired from officers or affiliates may fall within the category of transactions not involving arm's-length bargaining between buyer and seller. Consequently, the recorded amounts for property so acquired may reflect inflated values. Such acquisitions should be reviewed by the auditor to ascertain the basis upon which the sales price was settled, the cost of the property to the vendor, and the period of ownership, as well as any other available evidence to determine whether there are any irregular gains to the seller or any intercompany profits that should be eliminated in consolidation. Regarding property acquired from officers, as with any transfer of property where the problem of placing a fair value arises, reference may have to be made to independent appraisal if no other satisfactory basis of valuation is available.

Acquired in Merger. A corporation which distributes assets or incurs liabilities to obtain the capital stock of another company is the acquiring company. APB Opinion No. 16, paragraph 70, states that "presumptive evidence of the acquiring corporation in combinations effected by an exchange of stock is obtained by identifying the former common stockholder interests of a combining company which either retain or receive the larger portion of the voting rights in the combined corporation. That corporation should be treated as the acquirer unless other evidence clearly indicates that another corporation is the acquirer."

The proper basis for recording property acquired in a merger or other business combination depends on whether the combination is deemed to be a *purchase* or a *pooling of interests.* The various other aspects of business combinations are described in the following section.

When properties are acquired in a merger, the auditor should examine the merger agreement, corporate minutes, and other documents to ascertain whether the combination is considered to be a purchase or a pooling of interests and to determine that under either basis the assets have been properly carried forward in accordance with generally accepted accounting principles.

BUSINESS COMBINATIONS

According to APB Opinion No. 16, *Business Combinations,* paragraph 1, a business combination occurs "when a corporation and one or more incorporated or unincorporated businesses are brought together into one accounting entity. The single entity carries on the activities of the previously separate, independent enterprises."

The conclusions in this Opinion modify the previous views of the APB and its predecessor committee. Therefore, this opinion supersedes the related paragraphs in existing Accounting Research Bulletins or Accounting Principles Board Opinions. Two methods of accounting for business combinations are accepted in Opinion No. 16, "pooling of interests" and "purchase." The two methods are not alternatives in accounting for the same business combination. A business combination which meets the specified conditions *must* use the pooling of interests method. All other business combinations are to be accounted for as a purchase. The practice of part-purchase, part-pooling is not acceptable. The particular method selected may significantly affect the financial position and net income of the combined corporation.

The background and the development of the two methods, their respective advantages and disadvantages, and other aspects are covered in detail in Opinion No. 16 and need not be repeated in the limited confines of this chapter. The principal auditing features are described below.

Pooling of Interests Method. The pooling of interests method "accounts for a business combination as the uniting of the ownership interests of two or more companies by exchange of equity." No acquisition is recognized since no resources are disbursed. Ownership interests continue and the recorded assets and liabilities of the constituents are carried forward at their recorded amounts. Income of the combined corporation includes income of the constituents for the entire fiscal period in which the combination occurs. The circumstances which require pooling of interests method are described in APB Opinion No. 16, paragraphs 45 to 48.

Conditions for pooling of interests. The two essential attributes of combining companies are:

1. "Each of the combining companies is autonomous and has not been a subsidiary or division of another corporation within two years before the plan of combination is initiated."
2. "Each of the combining companies is independent of the other combining companies."

The seven conditions following relate to the exchange of stock:

[1.] The combination is effected in a single transaction or is completed in accordance with a specific plan within one year after the plan is initiated.

[2.] A corporation offers and issues only common stock with rights identical to those of the majority of its outstanding voting common stock in exchange for substantially all of the voting common stock interest of another company at the date the plan of combination is consummated.

[3.] None of the combining companies changes the equity interest of the voting common stock in contemplation of effecting the combination either within two years before the plan of combination is initiated or between the dates the combination is initiated and consummated; changes in contemplation of effecting the combination may include distributions to stockholders and additional issuances, exchanges, and retirements of securities.

[4.] Each of the combining companies reacquires shares of voting common stock only for purposes other than business combinations, and no company reacquires more than a normal number of shares between the dates the plan of combination is initiated and consummated.

[5.] The ratio of the interest of an individual common stockholder to those of other common stockholders in a combining company remains the same as a result of the exchange of stock to effect the combination.

[6.] The voting rights to which the common stock ownership interests in the resulting combined corporation are entitled are exercisable by the stockholders; the stockholders are neither deprived of nor restricted in exercising those rights for a period.

[7.] The combination is resolved at the date the plan is consummated and no provisions of the plan relating to the issue of securities or other consideration are pending.

There are three conditions which relate to future transactions. They are:

[1.] The combined corporation does not agree directly or indirectly to retire or reacquire all or part of the common stock issued to effect the combination.

[2.] The combined corporation does not enter into other financial arrangements for the benefit of the former stockholders of a combining company, such as a guaranty of loans secured by stock issued in the combination, which in effect negates the exchange of equity securities.

[3.] The combined corporation does not intend or plan to dispose of a significant part of the assets of the combining companies within two years after the combination other than disposals in the ordinary course of business of the formerly separate companies and to eliminate duplicate facilities or excess capacity.

Application of pooling of interests method. A business combination which meets all of the required conditions for a pooling of interests should use the following procedures, prescribed in APB Opinion No. 16, paragraphs 50 to 65:

Assets and liabilities. The recorded assets and liabilities of the separate companies become the recorded assets and liabilities of the combined corporation. If the separate companies used different methods of accounting the accounts may be adjusted to the same basis of accounting, if appropriate. Any such change should be applied retroactively and prior-period statements should be restated.

Stockholders' equity. The stockholders' equities of the separate companies are also combined. The amount of outstanding shares of the combined corporation at par or stated value may exceed the capital stock of the separate companies: the excess should be deducted first from the combined retained earnings. Any treasury stock should be considered as though retired.

Combined operations. Results of operations should be reported as though the companies had been combined as of the beginning of the period. The effects of intercompany transactions should be eliminated from operations before the date of combination on the same basis as after the combination. The effects of intercompany transactions on current assets, current liabilities, revenue and cost of sales should be eliminated. Financial statements and financial information of the separate companies for prior years should be restated on a combined basis.

Expenses related to combination. Costs incurred in a pooling of interests are expenses of the combined corporation rather than additions to assets or direct reduction of stockholders' equity. Thus registration fees, stockholder information, finders' fees and consultants, salaries and other expenses, and costs and losses of combining the operations should be deducted in determining the net income of the combined corporation for the period in which the expenses were incurred.

Disposition of assets after combination. Duplicate facilities or excess capacity after combination may be disposed of and any losses deducted from the combined income for ordinary disposals. Separate disclosure should be made of disposal of a significant part of the assets of one of the companies. A profit or loss resulting from such a disposal should be disclosed separately provided the amount is material in relation to combined net income or if the disposition was made within two years after the combination.

Date of recording combination. The combination should be recorded as of the date the combination is consummated. The substance of the consummation agreement should be disclosed in notes to financial statements. Comparative financial statements should disclose earlier adjusted financial statements on a combined basis. In some cases a business combination may have been initiated but not consummated at the date of the financial statements. The corporation should record as an investment the common stock of the other combining company acquired before the statement date. Stock acquired in exchange should be recorded at the proportionate share of the underlying net assets at the date acquired as recorded by the other company. Until the pooling of interests method is known to be appropriate, the investment and net income of the investor corporation should include the proportionate share of earnings or losses of the other company after the date of acquisition of the stock.

Disclosure of a combination. Disclosure that a pooling of interests combination has occurred should be made in the financial statements of the current period. Notes to the financial statements should disclose the following:

1. Name and a brief description of the acquired company
2. Method of accounting for the combination—that is, by the pooling of interests method
3. Period for which results of operations of the acquired company are included in the income statement of the acquiring corporation
4. Cost of the acquired company and, if applicable, the number of shares of stock issued or issuable and the amount assigned to the issued and issuable shares
5. Description of the plan for amortization of acquired goodwill, the amortization method, and period (APB Opinion No. 17, paragraphs 27 to 31)
6. Contingent payments, options, or commitments specified in the acquisition agreement and their proposed accounting treatment

Purchase Method. The purchase method accounts for a business combination as the acquisition of one company by another. The acquiring company records at its cost the acquired assets less liabilities assumed. According to APB Opinion No. 17, paragraph 11, "a difference between the cost of an acquired company and the sum of the fair values of tangible and identifiable intangible assets less liabilities is recorded as goodwill."

Application of purchase method. The general principles in applying the purchase method depend on the nature of the transaction as discussed in APB Opinion No. 16, paragraph 67, as follows:

1. An asset acquired by exchanging cash or other assets is recorded at cost—that is, at the amount of cash disbursed or the fair value of other assets distributed.
2. An asset acquired by incurring liabilities is recorded at cost—that is, at the present value of the amounts to be paid.
3. An asset acquired by issuing shares of stock of the acquiring corporation is recorded at the fair value of the asset—that is, shares of stock issued are recorded at the fair value of the consideration received for the stock.

Assets acquired in groups require the determination of the cost of the group as well as the individual assets in the group. A difference between the assigned costs of the tangible and *identifiable intangible assets* acquired less liabilities assumed is evidence of *unspecified intangible values*.

The acquiring corporation normally issues the stock and commonly is the larger company. However, in some cases the smaller company acquires the larger company. The presumptive evidence of the acquiring corporation is the stockholder interests which receive the larger portion of the rights. That corporation should be considered the acquirer unless evidence indicates otherwise. If a new corporation is formed to issue stock to effect a business combination one of the existing companies should be considered the acquirer.

In some cases additional consideration may be contingent on maintaining specified earnings levels or on the market price on a specified date. When the contingency is resolved the acquiring corporation should record the current value of the consideration issued as additional cost of acquired company.

Recording assets acquired and liabilities assumed. An acquiring corporation should allocate the cost of an acquired company to the assets acquired and liabilities assumed. The allocation should be made according to the principles stated above. Specifically these are:

1. All identifiable assets acquired should be assigned a cost equal to their fair values at the date of acquisition. This would include both tangible and intangible items.

2. The excess of the cost over the sum assigned to identifiable assets less liabilities should be recorded as goodwill. If the identifiable assets acquired less liabilities assumed exceeds the cost, then the values assigned to *noncurrent* assets should be reduced by a proportionate part of the excess. No negative goodwill or deferred credit should be recorded unless those assets are reduced to zero value. Independent appraisals may be used in determining fair value of some assets and liabilities. Subsequent sales also provide evidence of value.

General guides for assigning amounts to the individual assets are as follows:

1. *Marketable securities.* At current net realizable values.

2. *Receivables.* At present values of amounts to be received determined at appropriate current interest rates, less allowances for uncollectibility and collection costs, if necessary.

3. *Inventories.* (1) *Finished goods and merchandise.* At estimated selling prices less the sum of (*a*) costs of disposal and (*b*) a reasonable profit allowance for the selling effort of the acquiring corporation. (2) *Work in process.* At estimated selling prices of finished goods less the sum of (*a*) costs to complete, (*b*) costs of disposal, and (*c*) a reasonable profit for the completing and selling effort of the acquiring corporation based on profit for similar finished goods. (3) *Raw materials.* At current replacement costs.

4. *Plant and equipment.* (1) *To be used.* At current replacement costs for similar capacity unless the expected future use of the assets indicates a lower value to the acquirer. (2) *To be sold.* At net current realizable value. (3) *To be used temporarily.* At current net realizable value recognizing future depreciation for the expected period of use.

5. *Intangible assets* (*identifiable*). At appraised values, such as contracts, patents, franchises, etc.

6. *Other assets.* At appraised values, such as land, natural resources, and nonmarketable securities.

7. *Accounts and notes payable, long-term debt and other claims.* At present values of amounts to be paid determined at appropriate current interest rates.

8. *Liabilities and accruals.* At present values of amounts to be paid determined at appropriate current interest rates, such as accruals for pension cost, warranties, vacation pay, deferred compensation.

9. *Other liabilities and commitments.* At present values of amounts to be paid determined at appropriate current interest rates, such as leases, contracts, commitments, and plant closing expense incident to the acquisition.

REPAIRS, REPLACEMENTS, ETC.

Repairs and Maintenance. Repairs may be classified as ordinary or extraordinary. Ordinary repairs, including minor replacements of parts, should be charged to expense, as they merely serve to maintain an asset in good operating condition. Regarding extraordinary repairs, Holmes, in *Auditing: Principles and Procedure*, states, "although they do not make the asset more valuable or more efficient than it was when originally acquired, (they) may have the effect of lengthening the useful business life of an asset over normal expectations and therefore may be chargeable to the allowance for depreciation."[4] Expenditures which result in improvements to an asset and added value should be capitalized by adding the charges to the cost of the asset. It will not always be easy to distinguish between ordinary repairs, extraordinary repairs, and improvements; the auditor will have to use his best judgment and evaluate each case according to the existing circumstances.

To save record keeping and reduce time and expense in accounting for numerous small items, some companies follow the acceptable practice of setting a minimum amount under which no additions are capitalized. For example, the policy may state that no expenditure under $75 will be capitalized regardless of the useful life of the item purchased. Where this is in effect, the auditor should review the charges to the repairs and maintenance account to ascertain that the policy is being consistently followed, as well as to determine whether the account includes items over the minimum amount of a capital nature which should have been capitalized rather than charged to expense.

Comparison with amounts charged to repairs and maintenance in prior years will be useful to the auditor in his analysis of the current year's account. Of course, variations are to be expected, but major variations will require explanation and possibly closer scrutiny. When examination of the repairs and maintenance account discloses items which should be capitalized, audit procedures similar to those in the case of other additions to property accounts should be followed to substantiate the charges.

Replacements, Improvements, and Rehabilitations. Replacements may be classified into three categories and treated as follows:

1. Replacements of minor parts should be considered as ordinary repairs and charged to expense.

2. Extensive replacements of parts will usually be treated as extraordinary repairs and charged to accumulated depreciation. Unless complete units are replaced, it is acceptable to charge accumulated depreciation rather than capitalize the expenditures by adding them to asset costs and retiring the replaced items, the cost of which may be difficult to ascertain. For example,

[4] *Ibid.*, p. 523.

replacement of a roof or floor of a building would fall into this category.

3. Replacements of whole units should be capitalized, and the costs and accumulated depreciation of the replaced units should be removed from the accounts.

In addition to the cost of replacements of entire units of an asset, amounts spent for improvements which increase capacity, efficiency, or the useful life of an asset should be capitalized by increasing the cost of the item on the books. As a general rule, expenditures which do not benefit future operations should not be capitalized.

"Rehabilitation" involves a complete overhauling and reconditioning, and may include charges for repairs, replacements, and other improvements. Rehabilitation of property originally purchased new or in sound operating condition, while it may not result in increased capacity or efficiency over that of the asset when originally acquired, should substantially extend the useful life of the asset and assure its continued productivity.

To the extent that expenditures for the various segments of the rehabilitation project are considered to be repairs, replacements, or other improvements, the amounts should be treated as explained above. That is, amounts allocated as ordinary repairs should be charged to expense, extraordinary repairs and extensive replacements of parts may be charged to accumulated depreciation, and replacements of whole units and other improvements which will benefit future periods may be capitalized by adding them to asset costs and retiring the items replaced.

In connection with rehabilitation of plants in poor condition when acquired, *Montgomery's Auditing* states:

> When partly worn-out or run-down plants are purchased with the intention of rehabilitating them so that they can be operated efficiently, it may be assumed that the purchase price takes into consideration the poor condition of the plant. Under these circumstances, the entire cost of repairs and renewals required to bring the plant to a satisfactory operating condition, including applicable overhead expense, should be capitalized.[5]

VALUATION PROBLEMS

Appraisals. As stated at the opening of this chapter, generally the basis of valuation of property, plant, and equipment is cost, but under certain circumstances cost may not be readily determinable when assets are acquired. In such cases it is necessary to determine fair value, and frequently the best method for determining this is by appraisal. In earlier sections of this chapter several such circumstances were described, as when property is acquired:

1. In exchange for company's stock or bonds
2. By donation
3. From officers or affiliates
4. In a merger deemed to be a purchase

Other purposes for which appraisals may be made are:

1. Determining values to be used in reorganization or quasi-reorganization
2. Determining the amounts to be used in recording retirements of plant when such information is not otherwise available

[5] N. J. Lenhart and P. L. Defliese, *Montgomery's Auditing*, 8th ed., New York, The Ronald Press Company, 1957, p. 244.

3. Judging the adequacy of insurance coverage
4. Providing a basis for the sale of property
5. Determining fair values for tax evaluation
6. Determining values for credit purposes

Of the situations mentioned above where appraisals may be used for determining costs and fair value, six (all four in the first group and the first two in the second group) are important from the standpoint of determining "balance sheet" amounts to be used in financial statements which the independent auditor examines and reports upon. Valuations determined for the remaining listed purposes are for the particular uses of management and other interested parties and do not appear in balance sheets.

Write-ups of Property, Plant, and Equipment. In connection with the valuation of property, plant, and equipment in financial statements, the auditor should be guided by the latest pronouncement on the subject issued by the Accounting Principles Board in 1965, Opinion No. 6 (paragraph 17), which states:

1. Property, plant and equipment should not be written up by a company to reflect appraisal, market or current values which are in excess of cost to the entity.
2. Exceptions are reorganizations, quasi-reorganizations, and foreign operations under certain conditions such as serious inflation or currency devaluation. However, in the case of companies with foreign operations, when the accounts are translated into United States currency for consolidation, the write-ups should normally be eliminated.
3. When appreciation has been recorded on the books, income should be charged with depreciation expense computed on the written up amounts.

During World War II and in the years following, in the wake of inflation and the attendant rapid rises in price levels, there has been advocacy by some managerial personnel of companies, as well as by some members of the accounting profession, that financial statements should reflect the changes in price levels and replacement values of property, plant, and equipment, and that depreciation should be based on replacement cost rather than historical cost. A discussion of the pros and cons of this issue will not be undertaken here, but throughout the years this theory has not gained wide acceptance and it has not been adopted by the profession.

Write-downs of Property, Plant, and Equipment. Appraisals may also indicate that the sound value of property, plant, and equipment is less than net book value. This may result because of insufficient depreciation taken in prior years, obsolescence, incorrect recording of retirements, or the insufficient consideration of such factors as excessive production capacity of the company or the entire industry, idle plant, and anticipated future useful value.

It will be noted that APB Opinion No. 6 (cited earlier in this section) makes no mention of write-downs of property, plant, and equipment. Thus there appears to be no objection to write-downs for valid reasons such as those in the preceding paragraph. However, changes in price levels would not be considered an acceptable reason, as the AICPA concluded in Accounting Research Bulletin No. 43: "The committee disapproves immediate write-downs of plant cost by charges against current income in amounts believed to represent excessive or abnormal costs occasioned by current price levels. . . ." (Chapter 9A, paragraph 9.)

Assets should not be written down too far merely because this reflects conservatism in the balance sheet. Reduced values of depreciable assets result in smaller depreciation charges, which lead to overstatement of future profits.

Examination of Valuation Reports. When amounts based on appraisals have been recorded, a condition which the auditor may find in first-year audits, in cases of reorganization or quasi-reorganization, or under the various circumstances described elsewhere in this section, the report of the appraiser should be examined. The auditor should ascertain whether the appraisal was made by reputable appraisers, inquire as to the basis on which the appraisal was made, and ascertain that the amounts recorded reflect the values shown in the appraisal report. Since appraisals involve a careful physical inspection and inventorying of property, plant, and equipment, they can be used by the auditor to compare the properties on hand with the accounting records.

Disclosure in Financial Statements. When amounts are stated in financial statements on the basis of appraisal, this should be disclosed. There should also be disclosure of whether the appraisal was made by independent appraisers or by management, and of the date and basis of the appraisal. If there is a departure from generally accepted accounting principles, as "where write-ups of assets to appraisal values have been made, the auditor should disclose the effect on the financial statements and should qualify his opinion, or, if the effect is sufficiently material, express an adverse opinion." [6]

LEASE ARRANGEMENTS AND COMMITMENTS

A lease is an agreement between a lessor and a lessee for the use of real or personal property. In connection with the agreement, certain factors must be considered in accounting for the transaction on the records of the contractual parties to reflect properly the substance of the agreement and the related circumstances.

These factors involve the proper accounting of assets and liabilities and income and expenses with respect to leases and sale and leasebacks. In recent years, the Accounting Principles Board has issued two opinions dealing with the treatment of leases from the standpoint of lessees (APB Opinion No. 5) and lessors (APB Opinion No. 7).

Transactions of Lessees. APB Opinion No. 5, *Reporting of Leases in Financial Statements of Lessee,* issued in September, 1964, stated that lease agreements which are essentially equivalent to purchases of property should be capitalized. Also enumerated in some detail were the criteria for determining when a lease agreement may be considered to be an installment purchase of property. In Opinion No. 5 the APB rejected the contention that the acquiring of property rights alone under a lease qualified the property for capitalization on the books of the lessee. Instead the APB maintained that the important factor necessary for capitalization of leased property was evidence that an equity in the property was being built up as rental payments were made, making the transaction essentially equivalent to a purchase.

In discussion paragraphs 9 and 10 of Opinion No. 5, the APB included two conditions which will tend to indicate that an equity in the property was being built up. This was stated as follows:

[6] *Departures from Generally Accepted Standards and Accounting Principles,* AICPA (Committee on Practice Review), 1966, p. 14.

> . . . some lease agreements are essentially equivalent to installment purchases of property. In such cases, the substance of the arrangement, rather than its legal form should determine the accounting treatment. . . .
>
> The property and the related obligation should be included as an asset and a liability in the balance sheet if the terms of the lease result in the creation of a material equity in the property. It is unlikely that such an equity can be created under a lease which either party may cancel unilaterally for reasons other than the occurrence of some remote contingency. The presence, in a noncancelable lease or in a lease cancelable only upon the occurrence of some remote contingency, of either of the two following conditions will usually establish that a lease should be considered to be in substance a purchase:
>
> 1. The initial term is materially less than the useful life of the property, and the lessee has the option to renew the lease for the remaining useful life of the property at substantially less than the fair rental value; or
> 2. The lessee has the right, during or at the expiration of the lease, to acquire the property at a price which at the inception of the lease appears to be substantially less than the probable fair value of the property at the time or times of permitted acquisition by the lessee.

In paragraph 12, Opinion No. 5 provides criteria for the capitalization of leases between related parties.

> In cases in which the lessee and the lessor are related, leases should often be treated as purchases even though they do not meet the criteria set forth in paragraphs 10 and 11, i.e., even though no direct equity is being built up by the lessee. In these cases a lease should be recorded as a purchase if a primary purpose of ownership of the property by the lessor is to lease it to the lessee and (1) the lease payments are pledged to secure the debts of the lessor or (2) the lessee is able, directly or indirectly, to control or influence significantly the actions of the lessor with respect to the lease. The following illustrate situations in which these conditions are frequently present:
>
> 1. The lessor is an unconsolidated subsidiary of the lessee, or the lessee and the lessor are subsidiaries of the same parent and either is unconsolidated.
> 2. The lessee and the lessor have common officers, directors, or shareholders to a significant degree.
> 3. The lessor has been created, directly or indirectly, by the lessee and is substantially dependent on the lessee for its operations.
> 4. The lessee (or its parent) has the right, through options or otherwise, to acquire control of the lessor.

It should be noted that paragraph 4 of 1966 Omnibus Opinion No. 10 of the APB in effect supersedes the requirements of paragraph 12, above, of Opinion No. 5, calling for lease capitalization when a parent company leases property from a real estate subsidiary, except where unconsolidated parent company statements are presented. Opinion No. 10 requires that the accounts of all subsidiaries whose principal business activity is leasing property or facilities to their parents or other affiliates be consolidated.

Sale and Leaseback. In connection with such transactions, the same conclusions covering leases apply to an agreement covering the leaseback as though no concurrent sale were involved. Also, the principal details of any material sale-and-leaseback arrangements should be disclosed in the year in which the transaction originates.

Transactions of Lessors. Lessors may engage in leasing activities to accomplish one or more objectives, such as investing funds; facilitating the sale or use of the lessor's own products; and retaining control of locations when it is desirable that property be operated by others.

In Opinion No. 7, issued in May, 1966, the APB discusses the two predominant methods in general use for allocating rental revenue and expenses over the accounting periods covered by a lease: the "financing" and the "operating" methods. Under the financing method, the excess of aggregate rentals over cost of the leased property is considered to be in the nature of interest, and should be recognized as revenue during the term of the lease in decreasing amounts related to the declining balance of the unrecovered investment. Under the operating method, aggregate rentals are reported as revenue over the life of the lease as rentals accrue.

These methods and the basis of selection, which are amply discussed in Opinion No. 7, will not be discussed in detail in this chapter, except for brief references relating to reporting in the balance sheet under the two methods. As stated in Opinion No. 7 (paragraphs 14 and 15):

> When the financing method is used, the aggregate rentals called for in the lease should be classified with or near receivables and a description used along the lines of "receivables under contracts for equipment rentals" or "contracts receivable for equipment rentals." When a company is predominantly engaged in leasing activities for which the financing method is appropriate, information should be disclosed regarding future maturities of the rentals receivable. Unearned finance charges or interest . . . included in the aggregate rentals should be shown as a deduction therefrom. Estimated residual value should be classified separately with or near property, plant, and equipment unless the residual value represents an amount expected to be collected from the lessee (e.g., when a favorable purchase option exists), in which case it should be classified with or near notes and accounts receivable. Thus, the investment is represented by the net rentals receivable plus the residual value. . . .
>
> When the operating method is used, the investment should be classified with or near property, plant, and equipment and a description used along the lines of "investment in leased property," "property held for or under lease," or "property (equipment, buildings, machines, etc.) leased to others"; accumulated allowances for depreciation and obsolescence should be shown as a deduction from the investment.

Disclosure in Financial Statements. Various disclosures must be made in financial statements of companies engaged in leasing activities. In financial statements of lessees it is required to disclose sufficient information regarding material, noncancelable leases which are not recorded as assets and liabilities, to enable the reader to assess the effect of lease commitments upon the financial position and results of operations of the lessee. Such disclosure should include:

1. Minimum rentals under such leases
2. The period over which the payments will be made
3. Current year's rentals if significantly different from minimum rentals
4. Types of property leased
5. Obligations assumed or guarantees made
6. Provisions of lease agreements imposing restrictions on dividends debt, or further leasing

Financial statements of lessors require disclosure of the principal accounting methods used in accounting for leasing activities as well as disclosure of pledges of leased property and leases as security for loans.

Auditing of Leases. In order to ascertain that lease transactions and leasing activities have been accorded proper treatment in the accounts and financial statements, the auditor should:

1. Review internal control procedures in connection with lease agreements, including authorizations.

2. Review the lease agreements and available additional information and evidential matter relating to the leases, to establish the true nature of leasing arrangements.
3. Make inquiry to ascertain the relationships of the parties to leases.
4. Examine lease documents to verify the amounts of valuation (where capitalized) and of recorded income and expenses, and to ascertain that information disclosed in footnotes is accurate and complete.
5. Check receipts, payments, income, and expenses against related records as considered necessary.

Under certain conditions, the auditor may consider it desirable to request direct confirmation of leases from lessees or lessors.

The auditor should familiarize himself with the provisions of APB Opinions Nos. 5 and 7. In addition, AICPA Accounting Research Study No. 4 should be read for an in-depth study of the subject of leases, including accounting questions raised and recommended treatment.

RETIREMENTS

Objectives. The main objectives of the examination of retirements of property, plant, and equipment are:

1. To determine that no property has been physically retired without having been recognized in the accounts, and
2. To ascertain that the retirements have been properly recorded.

Retirements generally arise as a result of replacements, sales, trades, or abandonments. When property is retired, depreciation should be provided to the date of disposal in accordance with the company's depreciation policy, the asset account should be relieved of the cost of the asset, accumulated depreciation should be reduced by the related amount of depreciation accumulated, and the gain or loss (less salvage value plus cost of removal) on disposal should be charged or credited to income. (Note that when a company calculates depreciation on a composite rate basis as described in the standard accounting texts, the retirement of an asset is recorded somewhat differently from that described above, and no gain or loss is recognized in the accounts in connection with normal retirements.)

When detailed property records are not maintained, the cost and accumulated depreciation to date for the particular property units may not be available. In such cases, in order to determine or estimate the amounts to be used in recording retirements, the company may have to resort to prices furnished by vendors, estimates of cost and accumulated depreciation, averages of cost and accumulated depreciation for similar property, or appraisals. It must be remembered that all components of cost, including freight, installation, and other costs capitalized, must be considered when recording retirements.

Schedules of items retired should be prepared, preferably by the client, classified by accounts with columns showing amounts of cost, accumulated depreciation, proceeds, and gain or loss. One schedule may be prepared, as shown in Figure 4, or a separate schedule made for each property classification. Where applicable, separate amounts should be shown for removal costs and salvage.

To ascertain that retirements have been correctly recorded, amounts representing proceeds of sale of the asset or scrap, or amounts allowed in trade, should be checked against the cash receipts book, accounts receivable records, notes and mortages received in settlement, and contracts, and against

Figure 4 ABC CORPORATION, PROPERTY, PLANT, AND EQUIPMENT RETIREMENTS, YEAR ENDED DECEMBER 31, 1970

(a)	(b)	(c)	(d)	(e)		(f)	(g)
				Depreciation		Proceeds of sale	
Date	Description	Year acquired	Cost	Rate	Total to 12/31/69	or salvage	Gain or (loss)
	Office equipment:						
March 18	Typewriter..............	1963	$ 318.27	10%	$ 222.81	$ 60.00	$ (35.46)
May 10	Adding machine	1958	216.10	10%	216.10	45.00	45.00
			$ 534.37		$ 438.91	$ 105.00	$ 9.54
	Automobiles and trucks:						
April 1	Chevrolet sedan	1967	$3,460.00	25%	$2,595.00	$1,300.00	$ 435.00
Oct. 17	Mack truck..............	1965	6,250.00	25%	6,250.00	1,800.00	1,800.00
			$9,710.00		$8,845.00	$3,100.00	$2,235.00

Note: 50% of year's depreciation is taken in year of acquisition and in year of disposal.

The totals in columns (*d*) and (*e*), above, should agree with the corresponding amounts in the schedule summarizing changes in property, plant, and equipment (Figure 1).

purchase invoices for new equipment. Costs of removal should be checked against contracts, vouchers, and invoices. Amounts of cost and accumulated depreciation recorded to relieve the applicable accounts should be checked against plant ledgers or other records. Amounts of gains or losses arising from disposal (see Figure 4) should be checked against the appropriate income account.

When a company uses a work order system for plant retirements, the same general principles and procedures are involved in the examination of entries as in the examination of charges for additions under a work order system (described earlier in this chapter).

Unrecorded Retirements. Sometimes companies retire property without the knowledge of those responsible for maintaining the records (as when machinery is scrapped in the factory and the accounting department is not informed), or there may be a deliberate attempt to inflate the amounts shown for assets by neglecting to reduce capitalized costs of property when retirements are made. In an endeavor to detect omissions of proper recording for any reason, the auditor should carry out procedures such as the following in a search for unrecorded retirements.

Audit Procedures

1. Ascertain whether major property additions made during the year represent replacement of old assets.
2. Review miscellaneous income accounts for possible proceeds of the sale of plant assets or scrap.
3. Make inquiry of plant superintendents, engineers, management, and other supervisory personnel regarding retirements of property during the year.
4. Review retirement work orders and ascertain that the retirements have been recorded.
5. Investigate the possibility that changes in product, machinery, or equipment or discontinuance of products during the year may have resulted in the retirement of plant assets.

6. Investigate any reduction in insurance coverage to determine whether this results from retirement of property.

7. Consider physical inspection on a test basis of property shown in the plant ledger, appraisal listings, or other records.

OTHER CONSIDERATIONS

Foreign Exchange. Many U.S. companies have subsidiaries or branches operating in foreign countries and are faced with the problem of translation into U.S. dollars of asset, liability, equity, income, and expense accounts expressed in foreign currencies. In order to ascertain that such translations are done in accordance with accepted practice, the auditor must familiarize himself with the acceptable methods and rules governing translation. Only the translation of property, plant, and equipment accounts will be covered in this chapter.

Property, plant, and equipment asset accounts should be translated into U.S. dollars at the rates prevailing when such assets were acquired or constructed. When such assets are purchased for U.S. dollars, the U.S. dollar cost will, of course, be used. If the property is purchased with a foreign currency, the cost of the assets should be stated at the equivalent amount of foreign currency in U.S. dollars, at the rate prevailing when payment is made.

The related accumulated depreciation should be translated on the same basis as that used for translation of the cost. If the foreign subsidiary or branch has correctly applied appropriate rates of depreciation, the same result may be attained by expressing the accumulated depreciation in U.S. dollars in the same ratio to the U.S. dollar cost as the foreign-currency accumulated depreciation bears to the foreign-currency cost.

Depreciation expense for the period in dollars should be computed by applying appropriate depreciation rates to the property, plant, and equipment amounts as expressed in U.S. dollars.

There are two situations, however, meriting mention which justify departure from the methods outlined above. The first such situation exists when property, plant, and equipment have been acquired with funds obtained in a foreign country shortly before a substantial change in the exchange rate of its foreign currency. As expressed in AICPA Accounting Research Bulletin No. 43, chapter 12 (paragraph 12):

> . . . An exception to the foregoing general principle might be made where fixed assets . . . were acquired shortly before a substantial and presumably permanent change in the exchange rate with funds obtained in the country concerned, in which case it may be appropriate to restate the dollar equivalents of such assets to the extent of the change in related debt.

The second situation occurs when a U.S. corporation acquires all or a substantial part of the voting shares of a foreign company on a date subsequent to that on which the foreign company was organized and began operations. A problem arises as to the appropriate exchange rate to use in the translation of property, plant, and equipment. In his book *Reporting Foreign Operations,* Hepworth covers this situation and gives what appear to be valid reasons to support his preferred solution, i.e., use of the exchange rate on the date of acquisition of the foreign company, rather than on the date of the foreign subsidiary's original acquisition of the assets.[7]

[7] S. R. Hepworth, *Reporting Foreign Operations,* Ann Arbor, Mich., Bureau of Business Research, University of Michigan, 1956, pp. 27 and 28.

Insurance Coverage. The auditor should investigate insurance coverage on buildings and equipment to ascertain that coverage is adequate to compensate the company for loss resulting from fire, hurricane, or earthquake. In some areas the latter two are extremely important, and insurance against these risks should not be overlooked.

Insurance policies should be examined or coverage confirmed with insurance brokers who may be holding the policies. The auditor should compare the coverage with appraisal values, if available, as the latter are frequently greater than book values because of rising prices or excessive depreciation. Where appraisals are not available, it may be advisable to recommend that the company obtain them.

If the auditor concludes that insurance coverage of plant assets is not adequate, he should convey this information to the client and recommend that coverage be appropriately increased. If insurance coverage remains inadequate, it may be necessary to disclose this in the auditor's report and issue a qualified opinion.

SEC Requirements. In connection with the examination of property, plant, and equipment accounts of a company filing with the SEC, the auditor should be familiar with the SEC rules and regulations dealing with the reporting and disclosure requirements.

Regulation S-X, the principal accounting regulation of the SEC, contains the form and content for reporting of property, plant, and equipment. The major reporting requirements are summarized as follows:

1. The basis of carrying value must be stated (e.g., cost).
2. Each major class must be shown, such as land, buildings, machinery and equipment, and leasehold improvements. The detailed classification may be shown in the balance sheet or in a footnote thereto.
3. The provision for depreciation, depletion, and obsolescence of physical properties, including the methods and, if practicable, the rates used in computing the annual amounts, is required to be stated.
4. The accounting treatment for maintenance, repairs, renewals, and betterments, and the methods of handling disposals of property, plant, and equipment, must be stated.
5. Supplementary schedules must generally be furnished to the SEC showing the changes in property, plant, and equipment and related allowances for depreciation, depletion, and amortization for the period or periods under audit. Examples of the required schedules are shown in Figures 5 and 6.

Figure 5 ABC CORPORATION AND SUBSIDIARIES, SCHEDULE V—PROPERTY, PLANT, AND EQUIPMENT, YEAR ENDED DECEMBER 31, 1970

(A) Classification	(B) Balance at beginning of period	(C) Additions at cost	(D) Retirements or sales	(E) Other debits (Other credits)	(F) Balance at close of period
Land	$ 2,800,000	$ 200,000	$ 100,000	$ 300,000(*a*)	$ 3,200,000
Buildings	2,000,000	300,000	400,000	1,500,000(*a*)	3,400,000
Machinery and equipment	6,500,000	800,000	500,000	2,800,000(*a*)	9,600,000
Leasehold improvements	600,000	100,000	100,000	200,000(*a*)	800,000
Construction in progress	600,000	100,000	....	....	700,000
Total	$12,500,000	$1,500,000	$1,100,000	$4,800,000(*a*)	$17,700,000

(*a*) Includes assets of acquired companies at dates of acquisition.

Figure 6 ABC CORPORATION AND SUBSIDIARIES, SCHEDULE VI—RESERVES FOR DEPRECIATION AND AMORTIZATION OF PROPERTY, PLANT, AND EQUIPMENT, YEAR ENDED DECEMBER 31, 1970

(A)	(B)	(C) Additions		(D)	(E)
Classification	Balance at beginning of period	Charged to Profit and Loss or Income	Charged to other accounts	Retirements, renewals, and replacements	Balance at close of period
Buildings...................................	$ 400,000	$100,000	$ 200,000(*a*)	$100,000	$ 600,000
Machinery and equipment...........	2,600,000	600,000	1,200,000(*a*)	300,000	4,100,000
Leasehold improvements.............	300,000	100,000	100,000(*a*)	100,000	400,000
Total..	$3,300,000	$800,000	$1,500,000(*a*)	$500,000	$5,100,000

(*a*) Includes reserves of acquired companies at dates of acquisition.

The SEC has taken a strong position against write-ups of property, plant, and equipment. The Commission holds strongly to the cost valuation concept and generally disapproves of deviations.

Management Representation Letters. Auditors usually obtain written representations from clients covering certain matters relating to an examination, but many firms limit these representations to inventories and liabilities. However, where the property accounts and related accumulated depreciation are significant, it will generally be desirable to obtain representations covering these accounts. The representations may be made in a single comprehensive letter covering practically all items in the balance sheet or in separate letters for inventories, liabilities, receivables, etc. Generally when representations concerning property, plant, and equipment are obtained, these will more often be part of a comprehensive letter.

A detailed discussion of clients' written representations and examples of matters covered in such letters can be found in the AICPA *Codification of Statements on Auditing Procedure* issued in 1951 (pages 55 and 56). The codification lists the following items which may be included in representations concerning property, plant, and equipment.

Property, Plant, and Equipment:

1. The company has title to property included in plant, machinery, and equipment accounts.
2. Sales, dismantlements and abandonments have been properly accounted for.
3. There are no liens or encumbrances on properties except as recorded on the books.
4. All charges to property accounts represent actual additions.
5. The basis on which property is carried is properly described in the statements.
6. All property, plant, and equipment are being utilized in current operations or exceptions are noted.
7. The property is maintained in an efficient working condition.
8. No obsolete machinery or equipment is included in the asset accounts.

9. All property, plant, and equipment have been paid for or liability therefore taken up on the books.
10. If properties are appraised, the results of the appraisal in relation to the book value are fully and fairly set forth.

Accumulated Depreciation and Provision:

1. The annual provision for depreciation and depletion is adequate.
2. The total accumulated depreciation is adequate at the date of balance sheet.
3. The basis for providing depreciation is consistent with that used the previous year or exceptions are noted.

COMPUTER APPLICATIONS

Nature of the System. A general discussion of auditing and the computer will be found in Chapter 16 of this Handbook, but certain considerations having application in the auditing of property, plant, and equipment will be discussed in this section. Although the auditor may not be an expert in electronic data processing, he will need to have an understanding of the client's computer processing of transactions relating to the property accounts to evaluate controls and to facilitate the obtaining of desired audit evidential matter. The availability of usable input material and auditor-readable printouts will vary with the complexity of the electronic data processing installation, but the auditor is still faced with the same problem as with manually prepared records, namely, of satisfying himself as to the existence and ownership of the assets and the determination of proper costs and depreciation. Fortunately, contrary to the spate of publicity regarding the instant EDP updating of accounts leaving little or nothing in the way of audit trails, most companies' EDP systems are designed so that significant transactions can be identified and traced back to their origins. This serves their own informational needs and internal auditing purposes, and complies with the requirements of governmental agencies.

Audit Approach. The computer usage for property, plant, and equipment records may include the recording of all additions, retirements, and transfers, updating the accounts, calculating depreciation and maintenance of a plant ledger, or only one or two of these functions. In auditing the records processed by computer, there are four general approaches, as outlined in AICPA Computer Research Study No. 3:

1. Conventional audit trail procedures using printed listings produced by the computer
2. Use of test data having predetermined solutions to check the output of a client's computer programs
3. Modification of the client's computer program to assist the auditor
4. Writing of original computer programs to assist the auditor [8]

Which of these approaches the auditor uses in his audit tests will generally depend on his own familiarity with computers, the property records processed by the computer, the tests he wishes to make, the adaptability of the computer, and the feasibility of each approach as to time and cost.

[8] *Computer Applications to Accounting Operations*, AICPA, Computer Research Studies No. 3, 1966, p. 9.

Examples of computer printouts which the auditor may be able to obtain (approach 1, above) are the following:

a. Schedule summarizing the changes during the period in the property accounts, by account classification, showing opening balance, additions, retirements, and closing balance.

b. Selection and listing, with sufficient identifying data, of transactions over a designated amount and a sample of smaller items; these transactions can then be traced to vouchers and other supporting documentation in the same manner as with manually prepared records.

c. Schedule summarizing the transactions for the period in the Construction in Progress account by work order number, showing expenditures to the beginning of the audit period, expenditures during the audit period, total expenditures to date, transfers, and balance at the end of the period.

A procedure which may be followed for testing the computer program by use of test data (approach 2 above) is as follows:

If the plant ledger is maintained by the computer, in order to check the total or totals by account classification, the auditor has a test deck with a predetermined total prepared. The test deck is footed by using the client's operating computer program; the program used to foot the test deck is then used to foot the computer-maintained plant ledger. This procedure may also be carried out by using other input test data, such as a test tape or a test disk.

Examples of approaches 3 and 4, above, are not included in this chapter since modification of the client's computer program or the writing of original computer programs will depend on and vary with the specific situations encountered for each client and in each computer installation.

If the auditor decides to use statistical sampling for the selection of items in his testing of charges representing property additions, the computer may be employed to select the items. Statistical sampling may be used effectively in the examination of property, plant, and equipment accounts when there are a large number of separate charges for additions, which will often be the case where companies do their own construction work.

For literature supplying more comprehensive and detailed information regarding guidance and techniques to follow in the auditing of computer-processed records, the auditor may refer to three publications of the AICPA, listed below:

1. *Auditing and EDP*, by Gordon B. Davis, AICPA, 1968.
2. *Computer Applications to Accounting Operations*, Computer Research Study No. 3, AICPA, 1966.
3. *Accounting and the Computer* (a selection of articles from *The Journal of Accountancy and Management Services*).

INTERNAL AUDITING

Internal auditing and the public accountant. The functions and objectives of the internal auditor and the public accountant overlap to some extent. Therefore, the public accountant should review the property, plant, and equipment internal audit program and the related reports to ascertain the extent of checking being done by the internal auditors and to obtain the benefits of their findings.

The public accountant should endeavor to coordinate his work with that of the internal auditors with a view to reducing the scope or details of the public accountant's testing. This may be done effectively in connection with the vouching of purchased additions, the testing of charges to construction work orders, physical examination of plant assets, preparation of summary and detail schedules, and the entire examination of property, plant, and equipment at some subsidiaries and divisions.

Internal auditing objectives. In connection with property, plant, and equipment, the objectives of the internal auditor are to determine that:

1. Policies, procedures, and instructions with respect to additions to, and deductions from, property, plant, and equipment are being followed.
2. Proper distinction is being made between capital and revenue charges.
3. Property, plant, and equipment transactions and depreciation are recorded correctly and are accurately reflected in the records and reports of the company.
4. Plant assets are properly cared for, accounted for, and safeguarded from losses of all kinds.
5. Maximum utilization and efficiency are being obtained from existing plant assets.

Internal auditing procedures. The internal auditor should review the policies and procedures regarding the acquisition, care, depreciation, and disposal of plant assets and check details thereof to the extent considered necessary in order to carry out the objectives listed in the preceding paragraph.

Organizations maintaining an internal audit staff can be expected to be among those using a budget to forecast and control expenditures for property, plant, and equipment. Budgeted and actual expenditures should be compared, and variances from the budgeted amounts should be analyzed and investigated.

Expenditures for purchased items should be checked by examination of vouchers, invoices, and other supporting data to ascertain that the charges are properly and accurately recorded and that established procedures concerning authorization, ordering, receipt, and payment approval are being followed. For construction projects, charges for labor, materials, subcontracting, and overhead should be checked against supporting data to ascertain proper recording and to determine that established procedures concerning approvals, supervision, progress reports, transfers, and reporting of variances are being followed. In the course of this checking, the internal auditor should satisfy himself that proper distinction is being made between items which should be capitalized and those which should be charged to current expenses. In connection with cost-plus contracts with subcontractors, such contracts should provide that the purchaser's internal auditors have access to job sites and subcontractor's records, so that it can be determined that the charges are proper and are accurately supported in bills submitted for payment.

The procedures and processes in connection with retirements should be reviewed to determine that assets are not sold, abandoned, or otherwise disposed of without proper authorization and immediate routine reporting of the details to the accounting department. Any deductions from the asset accounts and debits to accumulated depreciation should be checked for accuracy. The controls over scrap and the proceeds of scrap sale should be checked at each installation visited by the internal auditor.

The plant ledger should be balanced at regular intervals with the related general ledger accounts. Physical examination of plant assets should be made periodically to check the existence of the items included in the property accounts and to determine that assets owned have not been omitted from the property inventories.

The internal auditor should also satisfy himself that equipment is maintained in good working order, that maximum use is being made of plant assets, and that company property is safeguarded by adequate fencing, guards, or both. He should ascertain that idle plant and equipment have been reported to management.

AUDIT PROGRAM

The following is an example of an audit program which may be used in the examination of property, plant, and equipment:

1. Obtain or prepare schedules as follows:
   a. A summary of changes in property, plant, and equipment assets and accumulated depreciation accounts
   b. For construction in progress, a schedule showing for each project the description, amount authorized, opening balance, charges during the year, total charges to date, transfers, and balance at end of year
   c. Schedules, by account classification, of significant additions during the year
   d. For selected construction projects, schedules of charges for additions during the year
   e. Schedules, by account classification, of the major retirements during the year, showing asset cost, accumulated depreciation to date of disposition, proceeds from sale or salvage, and gain or loss on disposition
2. For schedules 1*a* and *b*, above, compare opening balances with the prior year's closing balances.
3. Foot and crossfoot schedules as necessary.
4. Ascertain that major additions, including purchases and construction, were properly authorized.
5. For items purchased, examine vouchers, invoices, and other data supporting the year's principal additions.
6. For construction projects, verify charges by reviewing payroll distributions, test-checking time cards and requisitions for materials, and examining invoices and contracts for subcontracting, supplies, and services. Review allocations of overhead.
7. Review repairs and maintenance accounts to ascertain that these accounts do not contain items which should have been capitalized.
8. Examine leases to determine if any lease commitments are in substance installment purchases and should have been capitalized.
9. If practicable, inspect major additions made during the year.
10. Check title to property by reference to deeds, motor vehicle or other registrations, tax bills, insurance policies, and correspondence with attorneys.
11. Regarding retirements:
    a. Examine approval for principal items.
    b. Trace deductions to property accounts and determine that the credits were recorded at cost or other appropriate amount.

c. Ascertain that accumulated depreciation has been properly relieved.
d. Determine that proceeds of sales or salvage have been satisfactorily accounted for.
e. Review property additions to determine whether retirements should have resulted therefrom.

12. *a.* If there are detail property records, ascertain that the total of each asset classification agrees with the control account balance in the general ledger.
b. Foot trial balances and make tests of the detail as considered necessary.

13. Determine whether insurance coverage is adequate.

14. Determine whether there are any liens or whether property has been pledged. If so, obtain appropriate details for disclosure in the statements.

The existence of liens on various units of property will usually be disclosed in connection with the examination of liabilities, but the auditor should also be on the alert for liens during other phases of his examination. For example:

1. Examination of contracts for the purchase of machinery or equipment may disclose the existence of a conditional sales contract. Contracts for the purchase of real estate may disclose the existence of a purchase money mortgage or a second mortgage.
2. Examination of insurance policies may disclose that property has been mortgaged because:
   a. The policy may not be available since some mortgagees insist on possession of such policies to assure protection of their interests.
   b. Invoices or premium-due notices may not be available because such premiums are sometimes billed to and paid by the mortgagee, whose reimbursement for the insurance payments is included with undisclosed mortgage installment payments.
   c. The insurance policy may reveal an endorsement requiring payment of any proceeds of claims to a mortgagee.
3. In connection with real estate taxes,
   a. Tax bills may not be available because, as with insurance premium-due notices, the bills may be sent directly to and paid by the mortgagee (with reimbursement included with mortgage installment payments).
   b. Where the tax bills are available, they should be scrutinized to determine that there are no liens because of unpaid taxes or assessments.

Public records may be examined to ascertain whether there are any liens on a company's property, but most auditors do not follow this procedure. Questions which arise concerning liens on property may require discussion with an attorney.

The amount of property mortgaged, pledged, or otherwise subject to lien should be disclosed in the financial statements or notes thereto.

STATEMENT PRESENTATION

Disclosure Requirements. Accounting Principles Board Opinion No. 12 requires the following disclosures to be made in financial statements.

1. Amount of depreciation expense for the period

2. Balances of major classes of depreciable assets at the balance sheet date
3. Accumulated depreciation, either by major classes or in total
4. A general description of the method or methods used in computing depreciation with respect to the major classes of depreciable assets

Other Disclosure Matters. Other points to be considered in the presentation of property, plant, and equipment in financial statements are the following:

1. The basis of valuation should be stated in the balance sheet. While cost is the preferable basis and the one used in the great majority of cases, the auditor may encounter other bases of valuation which may be acceptable under certain circumstances, such as a quasi-reorganization or reorganization. When appraisal values are used (see the section in this chapter on appraisals), this should be indicated. There should also be disclosure of whether the appraisal was made by independent appraisers or by management and the date and basis of the appraisal. Valuation reflecting write-up based on appraisal, market, or current values is not acceptable; this was stated definitively in APB Opinion No. 6, issued in 1965.
2. Accumulated depreciation, depletion, and amortization should be shown as a deduction or deductions from the related property accounts, and not shown under liabilities.
3. Construction in progress should be shown separately in the property, plant, and equipment section.
4. Property not being used currently should be classified separately or with "Other Assets," but not under "Property, Plant, and Equipment." Differentiation should be made between standby or temporarily idle equipment and obsolete, abandoned, or dismantled equipment. Obsolete, abandoned, or dismantled equipment should be carried at estimated salvage value.
5. Property purchased under an installment plan should be carried at gross cost, with unpaid installments shown among the liabilities.
6. Disclosure should normally be made of property acquired in exchange for securities, and the basis of valuation.
7. Property being held for sale should be classified separately, not under "Property, Plant, and Equipment," at an amount not in excess of its estimated sales price. If property has been purchased for resale, it should be carried as an investment.
8. If plant assets are fully depreciated and still in use, the cost and related accumulated depreciation should remain in the accounts and disclosure should be made in a footnote, parenthetically, or by showing the assets separately in the property accounts group.
9. Carrying property, plant, and equipment at nominal value is not acceptable practice for commercial enterprises.
10. Full disclosure should be made of property pledged or of liens; in connection with the related liability, the nature of the security should be indicated.
11. Leased property which is considered to be in substance a purchase should be capitalized and included with the property, plant, and equipment accounts (see the section in this chapter on lease arrangements and commitments for additional details).

BIBLIOGRAPHY

American Institute of Certified Public Accountants, New York:
Opinions of the Accounting Principles Board
No. 7. *Accounting for Leases in Financial Statements of Lessors,* 1966.
No. 16. *Business Combinations,* 1970.
Statements of the Accounting Principles Board
No. 4. *Basic Concepts and Accounting Principles Underlying Financial Statements of Business Enterprises,* 1970.
Statements on Auditing Procedure, AICPA, New York:
No. 33. *Auditing Standards and Procedures,* 1963.
No. 44. *Reports Following a Pooling of Interests,* 1971.
Ingalls, E. F.: *Practical Accounting and Auditing Problems,* New York, American Institute of Certified Public Accountants, 1966.

Cashin, J. A., and Garland C. Owens: *Auditing,* New York, The Ronald Press Company, 1963.
Lenhart, N. J., and P. L. Defliese: *Montgomery's Auditing,* New York, The Ronald Press Company, 1957.
Stettler, H. F.: *Auditing Principles,* 2nd ed., Englewood Cliffs, N.J., Prentice-Hall, Inc., 1961.
Rappaport, L. H.: *SEC Accounting Practice and Procedure,* 2nd ed., New York, The Ronald Press Company, 1966.

Greiner, Sydney C.: "Audit of a Construction Program," *The Internal Auditor,* November/December, 1969.
Alvin, Gerald: "Resolving the Inconsistencies in Accounting for Leases," *The New York Certified Public Accountant,* March, 1970.
Jenkins, David O.: "Internal Audit of the Capital Expenditure Decision Process," *The Internal Auditor,* May/June, 1970.
Hawkins, David F.: "Objectives, Not Rules, for Lease Accountings," *Financial Executive,* November, 1970.
Gunther, Samuel P.: "Poolings – Purchases – Goodwill," *The New York Certified Public Accountant,* January, 1971.

Chapter 25

Depreciation, Depletion, and Amortization

E. J. DE MARIS

Professor and Head, Department of Accountancy, University of Illinois

FREDERICK L. NEUMANN

Associate Professor, Department of Accountancy, University of Illinois

INTRODUCTION

Definition of Terms. Since certain long-lived assets relinquish their potential service over several periods of time, accountants charge the cost of such assets against the revenue earned during the periods of the asset's expected useful life. The accounting process of allocating this depreciation to the periods affected is described below. The accounting processes relating to depletion and amortization are similarly described in the following paragraphs. Also included are accepted definitions of depreciation, depletion, and amortization.

Depreciation. Land, as such, and under normal conditions, is not expected by the accountant to diminish in value. As a result, its cost is generally not allocated to expense. Plant and equipment, however, do diminish in value over time as a result of wear and tear, obsolescence, and exhaustion. Such assets used in the operation of a trade or business, not intended for sale and with an estimated useful life in excess of one year, are termed "depreciable assets." Examples include buildings, other structures, machinery, equipment, furniture, fixtures, etc.

"Depreciation," for accounting purposes, is the allocation of the cost of depreciable assets over the useful life of the unit. *It is thus a process of allocation, not valuation.* As depreciation is charged against the revenue of each period, the total is accumulated in a separate account, Accumulated Depreciation. The balance in the allowance account is offset on the balance sheet against the related asset amount.

Depletion. Other long-lived assets, particularly of the natural resource type, have their value diminished by the removal of that resource. This feature contrasts with depreciable assets, which usually retain their physical characteristics over their lifetime. Depletion represents the portion of cost allocated to the natural resources removed from the property. Depletion is charged against revenue at a rate proportional to the estimated exhaustion of the wasting asset. Depletable assets include mines, oil and gas deposits, and timberlands.

The general procedure in allocating the cost of long-lived assets is not to reduce the cost of the asset. Generally, separate offsetting accounts, called "Accumulated Depletion" or "Allowance for Depletion," are used.

Amortization. The allocation of cost due to the decrease in value of intangible assets, such as patents, leaseholds, organization costs, etc., and purchased goodwill, is called amortization. "Amortization" also refers to the allocation of bond premiums and discount and various issuing expenses connected with debt securities. Certain tangible assets, such as defense facilities, may also be amortized. In APB Opinion No. 17, paragraph 9, the Board concludes that a company should record as assets the cost of intangible assets acquired from others, including goodwill. The costs to develop assets not specifically identifiable should be expressed. The cost of each type of intangible asset, including goodwill, should be amortized over the periods to be benefited. The period of amortization should not exceed forty years.

DEPRECIATION

The objectives of the audit of depreciation are to determine:

1. That the accumulated cost allocation has been accurately computed and made in accordance with generally accepted accounting principles, and that, as a deduction from the asset account, it produces a reasonable estimate of the proportion of service potential remaining.
2. That the provision for the current period is accurately computed and made in accordance with generally accepted accounting principles applied on a consistent basis. Such a provision should be both adequate and equitable.
3. That retirements, replacements, and adjustments are reflected in the accounts by the proper application, on a consistent basis, of generally accepted accounting principles.
4. That adequate disclosure is made of the methods employed, the resulting amounts, and any changes made from prior-year data.

For the external independent auditor, this is just one more group of accounts in his audit of the fairness of the financial statements taken as a whole. The internal and governmental auditor's concern may have a more procedural emphasis. As a result, the latter auditor's focus may be more on adherence to established policies, internal control, and overall business significance. His tests of decisions and practices may be more extensive and in greater detail. But many of the objectives and procedures are basically the same for both types of auditors.

Generally Accepted Accounting Principles. Generally accepted accounting principles require that the cost or other basic value of a tangible capital asset, less salvage (if any), must be allocated as equitably as possible to the periods during which the asset is expected to render its services. This means that the asset's cost must be depreciated by an acceptable method applied on a consistent basis over a reasonable life. Depreciation should be charged regularly as established, regardless of whether an operating loss results.

Depreciation Methods. **Financial accounting.** The American Institute of Certified Public Accountants (AICPA) states only that the means of allocating the cost or other basic value of tangible capital assets (net of salvage) shall be "in a systematic and rational manner."[1] Many methods have been used. Grant and Norton (in *Depreciation*) list the following in addition to the straight-line method.[2]

1. Consistent Methods Based on Time
    a. Methods giving smaller write-off than straight-line in early years of life
        (1) Sinking-fund or present-worth method
        (2) Retirement method
        (3) Replacement method

[1] Accounting Research and Terminology Bulletins, final ed., New York, AICPA, 1961, p. 76.

[2] Eugene L. Grant and Paul T. Norton, *Depreciation*, New York, The Ronald Press Company, 1955, p. 185.

- *b.* Methods giving larger write-off than straight-line in early years of life
  - (1) Declining-balance method
  - (2) Sum-of-the-years'-digits method
  - (3) Multiple straight-line methods
2. Consistent Methods Based on Use
   - *a.* Production method
   - *b.* Combination of production and straight-line method

Most of the methods have been found in practice, with varying degrees of approval. The most commonly used methods are:

STRAIGHT-LINE: The annual provision is computed by multiplying the cost of the asset (net of salvage, if any) times the reciprocal of the estimated life. The annual provision thus remains the same over the asset's life.

DECLINING-BALANCE: The annual provision is computed by multiplying the undepreciated base of the asset (disregarding salvage) by a uniform rate. This rate may be computed by the formula $1 - \sqrt[n]{\frac{s}{c}}$, where $n =$ the expected life of the asset (in the number of periods), $s =$ the anticipated salvage value, and $c =$ the asset cost. The annual provision thus decreases over time.

SUM-OF-THE-YEARS'-DIGITS: The annual provision is computed by multiplying the cost of the asset (net of salvage value, if any) by a fraction. The denominator of this fraction is composed of the sum of the numbers representing the years making up the life of the asset (e.g., for an asset with a five-year life, it would be 15). The numerator of the fraction is the remaining life of the asset. The annual provision thus declines over time.

UNITS OF OUTPUT: The annual provision is computed by multiplying the period's output (in hours of operation, units of product, mileage etc.) times a cost per unit. This cost per unit is established by dividing the cost of the asset (net of salvage value, if any) by the output (however measured) expected during the asset's life. The annual provision will therefore be directly related to output activity. Where production falls off substantially, it may be necessary to institute a minimum charge for depreciation.

A single company may use more than one method on its different classes of assets.

Tax accounting. The straight-line, the declining-balance, and the sum-of-the-years'-digits methods are acceptable for the computation of depreciation for tax purposes. The second method may employ a rate not to exceed twice the annual allowance determined under the straight-line method. Unless agreement is made with the Internal Revenue Service (IRS) to the contrary, a taxpayer may switch from the declining-balance method to the straight-line method at any time. Other changes in the methods used for tax purposes, however, require the permission of the Commissioner. Any change for financial accounting purposes may require a qualified opinion.

Other consistent methods may also be employed to the extent that the depreciation accumulated during the first two-thirds of the useful life of the property (beginning with the period of the taxpayer's use thereof) does not exceed the total of such depreciation that would be accumulated under the declining-balance method. The taxpayer may use different methods for different assets or groups of assets.

The sum-of-the-years'-digits method, the declining-balance method, and equivalent methods may be used for tax purposes only by the original user and may be applied only to assets which were acquired after December 31, 1953, with a useful life of three years or more.

The methods used for tax purposes need not be the methods used for financial statement purposes, although the general rule for methods of accounting in Section 446 of the Internal Revenue Code states, "Taxable income shall be computed under the method of accounting on the basis of which the taxpayer regularly computes his income in keeping his books." The section continues, "To the extent that the two are different, tax allocation may result."

Useful Lives. The depreciable life of a fixed asset is based on its expected period of usefulness, not its inherent life. The auditor is an expert neither in evaluating the worth of fixed assets nor in estimating their useful lives. He must depend on the experience of the industry and the company itself to help him appraise the estimates prepared by knowledgeable company personnel. Disproportionately large amounts of fully depreciated assets or large and consistent gains on fixed asset disposals would indicate excessive depreciation from underestimated lives. Excessive and consistent losses could be indicative of overestimating the useful lives of assets. The company's maintenance policies, as well as its experience with similar assets, also need to be considered. The auditor should carefully review any conditions, such as design changes and estimates of future operating conditions, for changes required in the estimated lives of assets newly procured which are similar to those already on hand.

Revenue Procedure 62-21, issued by the Bureau of Internal Revenue, provides the current guideline lives for tax purposes. It may be a helpful reference for comparison with estimates of asset lives made by the client. Conformance with these guideline lives, if reasonable, has been suggested by the Accounting Principles Board.[3]

In addition to physical causes of depreciation, the auditor should consider other possible reasons, such as inadequacy and obsolescence, for decline in service potential in appraising the estimated useful life. "Inadequacy" refers to changes in economic and legal conditions, while "obsolescence" encompasses changes in the state of the arts, such as inventions and technological innovation. Accounting Terminology Bulletin No. 1 states that the depreciation charges adopted assume a given standard of maintenance and, as a rule, are not adjusted for fluctuations in maintenance costs. The Bulletin concludes that depreciation provisions are generally limited to ". . . costs and losses which are not restored by current maintenance and are (*a*) gradual in their nature, (*b*) due to physical or functional causes, and (*c*) reasonably foreseeable."[4]

Improvements made to leased property should be amortized over the shorter of their own useful lives or the life of the lease. Options for lease renewal are generally ignored unless it becomes apparent that such options will be exercised. The unamortized costs may then be spread over the shorter of their own useful lives or the life of the extended lease.

Depreciable Base. Depreciation under normal conditions is to be based on cost, less expected salvage or other recoverable value. The term "salvage" refers to any proceeds expected from the disposal of retired assets whether for the asset itself or for its parts or components. Salvage need not be deducted in establishing the base for the declining-balance method, but it must be explicitly recognized if a change is subsequently made to the straight-line method. In any event, an asset should not be depreciated below its net salvage value, if material. The term "net salvage value" is used because

[3] Accounting Principles Board, APB Opinion No. 1, *New Depreciation Guidelines and Rules*, New York, AICPA, 1962, pp. 1–2.

[4] Accounting Terminology Bulletins, in Accounting Research and Terminology Bulletins, final ed., New York, AICPA, 1961, p. 24.

costs of removal should be used to reduce expected proceeds on disposal. If salvage value is estimated at a standard percentage of cost, the auditor should satisfy himself that the cost base used for this calculation relates to invoiced cost only and does not include freight or installation charges.

Many assets are depreciated individually. Some fixed assets, however, are depreciated in groups. Assets grouped for depreciation may be of a similar type with approximately the same useful lives (group depreciation), or used for the same or different purposes but with different lives (composite depreciation). The disparity in lives, however, should not be too great. In the latter case the assets are depreciated over the weighted-average useful life of all the assets in the group. Thus, there will be assets with expected lives which both exceed and are exceeded by the group average. The main implication of assets depreciated as a group is that on retirement of an individual asset, there will be no gain or loss recognized. The assumption is that since short-lived and long-lived assets are averaged together, a normal retirement thus represents the disposal of a fully depreciated asset.

Determination of depreciable cost by the auditor is discussed in Chapter 24. Sometimes it is not an easy matter, such as for assets constructed by the company itself. During the period of construction, depreciation is generally not considered except on assets which may actively be used in the construction, even though part or all of this depreciation may in turn be capitalized as part of the cost of the asset under construction. The auditor must also be careful about the cost of assets not established in an arm's-length transaction, such as those obtained through intracompany transfers.

Companies which have assets that periodically may require extraordinary repairs may capitalize an annual provision to provide for such costs. These accumulated provisions are then charged when the repairs are actually made. The auditor must satisfy himself of the justification for this practice and the reasonableness of the amount. If material, the amount and explanation should be disclosed. Such accumulations should appear on the liability side of the balance sheet and not combined with accumulated depreciation. Normalization of expenses is not looked upon with favor by some accountants who feel that income should reflect changes in expenditures as they occur even if they could be reasonably estimated.

Where it has been determined that certain of the fixed assets have been written up in value, the auditor must determine whether such appreciation is acceptable. Cost is the generally accepted basis for depreciation, so such increases should be carefully examined and generally should be supported by reasonably expected earning power. If satisfied with the appreciated basis of the asset and its recording, the auditor must ascertain that depreciation is calculated on the appreciated basis and the entire amount charged to income.

The issue of whether depreciation should be taken by nonprofit institutions is not clear. In *Practical Accounting and Auditing Problems*, the issue is related to the financial and fund-raising policy, depending upon

> whether rates charged for certain services are to be on a *self-sustaining* basis and whether total costs of such activities are to be accumulated as *supportive* of such rates; whether operations of the year of replacement are to be saddled with the entire cost of replacement or replacement costs spread over a number of fiscal periods; and whether the cost of plant in use is to be reflected in the balance sheet of the particular organization.[5]

[5] Edmund F. Ingalls, *Practical Accounting and Auditing Problems*, vol. II, New York, AICPA, 1966, p. 1568.

The discussion goes on to state: "If depreciation is not employed by a nonprofit organization, we believe expenditures should be reflected on its income statement as a special charge . . . ."[6]

If the funds to acquire property, or the property itself, are acquired with no commitment to maintain the property intact, no periodic depreciation is required. If there is a stipulation that the property shall remain intact, and there is no promise of funds for replacement, depreciation should be recognized and probably should be coupled with funding.

Because of the difference in the nature of operating and wasting assets, depreciation and depletion will be discussed separately.

AUDIT OF DEPRECIATION

Internal Control Evaluation. The quality of the general accounting policies and performance, plus the nature and extent of the accounting records dealing specifically with depreciation, will form the major basis for the internal control evaluation of depreciation. Internal control for depreciation purposes is directly related to internal control over fixed assets. The policies and their implementation in control over, and accounting for, additions, maintenance, and retirement of such assets, plus distinguishing between capital and revenue charges, will have a very direct effect on depreciation.

Supporting Records. For companies with extensive investments in fixed assets, property ledgers usually provide detailed information not only on the assets but on accumulated depreciation as well. There is no standard format for such a record, and the amount of detail varies. But these records should provide an adequate description of the assets and be periodically reconciled to the controlling accounts in the general ledger and to the assets themselves by physical inventory. A sample hand-posted record might include the following section:

Depreciation record	Annual provision		Book value
	Year	Amount	
Method Straight-line	1965	$ 600.00	$11,400
Estimated life 10 years	1966	1,200.00	10,200
Cost $12,380	1967	1,200.00	9,000
Salvage value $380	1968	1,200.00	7,800
Depreciable balance $12,000	1969	1,200.00	6,600

Such records may, of course, be on tab cards or tape and be electronically maintained.

Companies which have fewer fixed assets may simply maintain a lapsing schedule such as the following:

Asset	Cost	1968	1969	1970

Asset retirements result in credits in the Cost column and in any annual columns in which depreciation will not be taken. Thus, the total of each annual column will equal the provision for depreciation for that year.

[6] *Ibid.*, p. 1570.

The extent of the fixed asset records may be only the detail in the general ledger. Whatever the form of the records, they should not be under the control of the asset custodian. Somewhere, the auditor needs to find a record of the individual additions and disposals for the period. The absence of adequate supporting records may be indicative of weak internal control and may even require an inventory of such assets.

The mere existence of such records is no guarantee of their accuracy. Until adequately tested, such records offer relatively weak evidence of the existence and ownership of such assets or of their proper depreciation. Most of the testing of these records, such as footing and reconciling with the general ledger control accounts, is performed as part of the audit of the fixed assets themselves. To save time and duplication of effort, the depreciation tests should be done at the same time, preferably by the same auditor.

The review of the internal control over fixed assets will also have established the reliability of the system for properly recording fixed assets, consistently distinguishing between capital and revenue charges on an acceptable basis, and ensuring that retired assets are completely removed.

Companies should be encouraged to retain on the books all fixed assets on hand, even though some may be fully depreciated or considered useless. These latter categories should be accounted for separately but accounted for, nevertheless, for control purposes.

Special Provisions. Because of the nature of many fixed assets, physical security may be given less attention when considering "safeguarding assets." But some fixed assets are highly pilferable and may warrant a physical inventory. Adequate protection from the elements may be another aspect of "safeguarding assets" which should be considered in physical observation of the assets themselves. Assets exposed to, and unprotected from, the elements may warrant accelerated depreciation to provide for weather damage. Inadequate maintenance may also cause premature exhaustion. Consideration of the insurance coverage of fixed assets, both in type and in amount, should be part of the general appraisal of the client's insurance program.

Preliminary Work. If satisfactory internal control exists, fixed assets and their related depreciation are readily adaptable to interim examination. Both policies and internal control can be reviewed and a substantial amount of testing accomplished as of a preliminary date. Such timing would provide greater flexibility in scheduling, more time to adequately appraise the area, and a reduction in the amount of work required at final time.

Audit approach. Because of the long-lived nature of fixed assets and their relatively high cost per unit, there are usually fewer transactions in such assets. As a result, the audit approach is to examine the changes, rather than the ending balance, as with the more active current assets. The auditor establishes the propriety of the beginning balance, satisfies himself as to the acceptability of the changes, and accepts the ending balance resulting.

Also, unlike current assets, there is less concern about market values of fixed assets. If the business is a going concern, then cost is the primary basis for depreciation, and the auditor must verify the cost basis of the assets. The related audit procedures for this are discussed in Chapter 24. In addition, errors are likely to be less serious than among current assets. Intentional misstatements are probably also less likely, thereby reducing relative risk.

As part of his review of operations, before beginning the audit, the auditor should discuss depreciation and related fixed asset policies. He should satisfy himself that these policies are sufficiently sound and specific to provide a reasonable and regular allocation of cost over the lives of the assets by the consistent application of acceptable methods.

During this discussion, the auditor should determine whether any changes have been made. The inquiry should determine whether extra work or abnormal conditions may have upset established patterns. If appropriate, the auditor should discuss the need to recognize obsolescence or inadequacy. The reason for, and the effect of, any changes should be considered in preparing the audit program, and noted for possible disclosure.

The procedures adopted by the auditor are meant to satisfy himself as to the propriety of basis of the asset, its estimated life, and the method used to depreciate it. In addition, he will check the calculations, recording, and disclosure.

Opening Balance. Repeat audits. If the auditor performed the prior year's audit, then all that needs to be done to establish the propriety of the opening balance is to foot the opening balance and compare it with the preceding period's closing balance, as adjusted.

First-time audits. If the auditor did not perform the prior-period audit, then he must examine the prior years' activity in much the same manner that he will test the current year's transactions, though probably in much less detail. He must go back far enough to account for the major portion of the assets and satisfy himself as to the acquisitions, adjustments, and retirements of fixed assets and the company policies used in recording them. The scope of his examination of prior years' depreciation will depend on the materiality of the fixed assets, the quality of the internal control, and whether the client had been previously audited by a CPA. In any event, the client should be made aware that (insofar as this present auditor is concerned) this extra work will be required for the first year's audit only.

If the client has been previously audited by a CPA, then the new auditor should make arrangements to discuss the prior audits with the former auditor and, if possible, get permission to examine the workpapers. One of the areas for review should be fixed assets and related depreciation. From this examination, the auditor should try to determine the scope of the audit and the nature of any adjustments or exceptions. The results of such a conference may significantly influence the extent of tests of prior years' activity.

The actual work performed will be much the same as for an annual examination described below. The auditor must go back into the accounts, perhaps even to inception, and examine a sufficient number of transactions to determine that the fixed asset amounts are proper capital items, that they exist, and that they are stated at cost, with depreciation accurately computed thereon by acceptable methods. His review of past years' repairs and maintenance and related accounts should reveal whether any fixed assets were expensed. As benchmarks in this process, the auditor may want to compare year-end figures with company statements and tax returns. Prior-year tax returns and filings with the SEC and similar agencies may provide some assistance in determining the activity during earlier years. In addition to establishing the substantial accuracy of the beginning balance, he must also satisfy himself that the remaining book value represents a reasonable apportionment of the asset costs, in the light of existing conditions. Recent insurance appraisals may be one source of information which will be helpful in this determination.

Provision for Depreciation. (1) Assets on hand at the start of the year. For assets on hand at the beginning of the year, the auditor must determine whether any changes have been made affecting depreciation, or whether any should be.

Changes may be made in depreciable lives or in the method of computation. The former, if made for good and sufficient reasons, should be disclosed in the notes to the financial statements, if material in their effect on the financial statements. The latter change requires a qualification by the auditor for lack of consistency and is discussed in greater detail in the section on disclosure later in this chapter.

Changes in the depreciation of existing assets may be recommended because of changed conditions. Accelerated use of certain assets may justify shortened depreciable life. Plant and equipment which has been idled for various reasons may have to be written down to realizable value if its future uselessness appears permanent. This latter comment does not apply to facilities retained on a standby basis for emergency needs. It applies, rather, to assets no longer needed. Separate offset accounts for estimated losses on disposal may be used for such purposes. The provision for such write-downs should be disclosed if material, but not generally as an extraordinary item.

In addition to discussion of these issues with the company official, it may be helpful to review reports by revenue agents who have examined prior years' tax returns, both to determine any changes recommended and to see if these have been properly reflected in subsequent returns. The financial records are not required to be kept on the same basis as tax records, but the auditor should be aware of the differences and be able to satisfy himself as to their justification.

The auditor will want to be sure that records of assets fully depreciated (i.e., decreased to salvage value), or which will be fully depreciated by the current provision, are suitably segregated so that they will not be erroneously depreciated beyond that point.

There are two ways of reflecting a change from a depreciation method which has proved to be excessive or inadequate to one which is more appropriate. A way which has found favor with practitioners and tax authorities is to adjust the depreciation rate to absorb the undepreciated balance over the new estimate of the remaining life. This approach, which accepts the past calculations, is in keeping with the reluctance to go back and attempt to make adjustments based on subsequent information regarding prior estimates made in good faith after considered judgment and competent review. Opponents of this method, however, recommend that the rate adjustments be made retroactive to prevent misstating the expense of both the past and the future. Materiality may be a deciding factor.

(2) Current additions. Companies vary in the amount of depreciation taken in the year of acquisition. Some commence depreciation calculations the month after acquisition; others take an arbitrary half-year of depreciation for all assets acquired during the year and do the same in the year of retirement. An alternative method is to begin depreciation the first of the year after acquisition. For the auditor, the important consideration is that, whatever the basis used (so long as it is reasonable), it be applied consistently. In reviewing rates and methods for current additions, the auditor should be mindful of the treatment of related types of assets already on hand and whatever was learned during the review of them.

Acquisition of used property in arm's-length transactions should be recorded at cost. It should not be reflected at a net book value by recording a prior cost and accumulated depreciation even if the net effect is the cost. On intracompany transfers, the auditor must satisfy himself concerning the cost basis as well as determine whether the existing depreciation procedure is still applicable. Changed conditions may warrant adjustment in the estimated life.

Depreciation expense. The scope of the accuracy test adopted for appraising the provision may be determined on a statistical or judgmental sampling basis. It may include a test of the detailed calculations or just an overall test of certain or all of the categories. If the company maintains a property ledger which has been reconciled to the general ledger control accounts as to asset cost, provision for depreciation, and accumulated depreciation, then the work may be simplified. Tests can be made from the depreciation calculation for specific assets or groups of assets (if depreciated on such a base), traced to a footing of that group, and checked against the control account total in the general ledger. If the auditor's lapsing schedule is the basis for his test of the provision, and if discussion with the client and related audit work disclose no reasons for adjustment, the provision for the year can be taken directly from that schedule.

Improvements, additions, or betterments of assets, if material, may be capitalized. If so, they should be accounted for separately. Assuming no change has been made in the life of the existing asset, the depreciation rate on the improvement will be greater than that on the basic asset.

Once the annual provision for depreciation has been ascertained, it must be traced into the related expense accounts. In addition to accounting for all depreciation expense, the auditor should determine whether the classification is reasonable and on a basis consistent with prior years. If the provision has not been classified on a reasonable basis, or if a change has been made which has a material effect, disclosure may be warranted.

The auditor should also satisfy himself as to any difference between the book and tax provision and explain it in his working papers.

Retirements and Replacements. Retirements. Part of the audit of fixed assets is the determination that all retirements have been recorded. Failure to establish this may result in an overstatement of assets and of depreciation expense and may allow a gain or loss to go unrecognized. In addition, the auditor must ascertain whether these retirements have been recorded correctly. For depreciation, this means the determination that depreciation has been charged to the date of disposal and that the accumulated balance has been completely removed from the books of account.

Accounting for retirements calls for the determination of gain or loss based on the comparison of the net book value (cost, less accumulated depreciation) of the individual asset with the proceeds received. This holds true whether the new assets are obtained by purchase or in whole or in part by a trade-in. Tax authorities do not permit the recognition of gain or loss where trade-ins of fixed assets are involved. The net book value of the retired asset serves as the basis for the new asset. This is increased by any money paid out and decreased by any money received. Thus, any gain reduces the basis of the new asset and any loss adds to it. The same method may be employed on financial records if no major distortion results.

No gains or losses will be recognized under normal conditions for those assets depreciated on a group basis. The asset retired is presumed to have been fully depreciated and therefore has its full cost charged to the accumulated depreciation account. If the retirement occurs under other than normal conditions, however, such as in the case of a casualty loss or unexpected obsolescence, then gain or loss should be recognized. In such cases, it is the asset's own life which should be used as a basis, not that of the group. Gain or loss must also be recognized on the final disposal of an entire group. If the composition of the group should radically change over time, its depreciation rate may have to be recomputed.

Replacements. Expenditures which increase the services or life of an asset may be charged to the accumulated depreciation account. This method is prescribed for tax purposes. The difficulty is that the cost of the item replaced remains in the base and the cost of the replacement applied to the accumulated depreciation may have little or no relation. A new depreciation rate may have to be calculated.

The auditor, by examining documentary evidence and by discussion with appropriate executives, must satisfy himself that the replacement has in fact increased the life of the asset. If the cost of the replacement is materially different from the cost of the item replaced and is material itself, then the item replaced should be removed from the asset account, with a proportional share of the accumulated depreciation, and the replacement cost added to the cost of the asset. Consistency in the application of this procedure should be checked. The new depreciation rate and calculation should then be reviewed.

Other Charges. Debits to accumulated depreciation accounts for any other reasons should be carefully investigated and appraised on the basis of generally accepted accounting principles. The treatment of the corresponding credit should also be examined.

Ending Balance. By the above procedures, all charges and credits to the accumulated balances during the year should have been accounted for. The various classifications should then be crossfooted to the ending balance. The latter, in turn, should be downfooted and checked against the trial balance and the applicable controlling accounts in the general ledger. Care should be taken to be sure that all recommended adjustments are properly reflected on the books.

As a final review of depreciation, the auditor should compare the percentage relationship between the cost of fixed assets and the related accumulated depreciation by major classification for the current period with that of prior periods and with industry averages, if available. He should investigate any significant variations and discuss them with appropriate members of management. Comparison of these percentages with those of other companies in the industry may also be helpful in highlighting areas of concern.

Working Papers. **Lead schedule.** The audit workpapers for depreciation reflect the basic procedure of testing the changes in the account rather than the ending balance. Schedule VI, prescribed by Rule 12-07 of Regulation S-X of the SEC, provides a rather comprehensive format for the analysis of depreciation, depletion, and amortization. Its organization is as follows:

<table>
<tr><th rowspan="2">Column A</th><th rowspan="2">Column B</th><th colspan="2">Column C</th><th colspan="2">Column D</th><th rowspan="2">Column E</th></tr>
<tr><th colspan="2">Additions</th><th colspan="2">Deductions</th></tr>
<tr><td>Description</td><td>Balance at beginning of period</td><td>(1) Charged to profit and loss or income</td><td>(2) Charged to other accounts</td><td>(1) Retirements, renewals, and replacements</td><td>(2) Other—describe</td><td>Balance at close of period</td></tr>
</table>

If the client must file with the SEC, the depreciation lead schedule, properly prepared, can provide an adequate basis for such a schedule. If possible, depreciation should be summarized in the same classifications used on the schedule of property, plant, and equipment. Depending on the activity and classification detail, both schedules may be combined on one workpaper.

The lead schedule for fixed assets is the type of working paper which the company can conveniently prepare and have the auditor check. Footing and crossfooting the schedule and checking it against prior-year working papers, the trial balance, and the general ledger should establish its acceptability for this purpose.

Where the fixed asset account is relatively minor, the auditor may use his own lapsing schedule. Such a schedule, kept in the continuing or permanent audit file, provides a control on annual depreciation with a minimum of effort. With suitable safeguards, the schedule could even be updated by company personnel and subsequently reviewed and tested by the auditor.

Supporting schedules. The necessary detail to test recorded retirements can be obtained from the following type of schedule:

Asset	Cost	Depreciation start of year	Depreciation this year	Book value at disposal	Proceeds	Gain	Loss

FINANCIAL STATEMENT DISCLOSURE

Classification and Detail. Accumulated depreciation should not be netted against related assets. It should be reported for meaningful classifications of fixed assets disclosed either on the balance sheet or in notes thereto. The classifications should not be excessive but should provide a reasonable idea of the types of assets owned. Depreciable assets and their related offset accounts should be reported separately from depletable assets and nondepreciable assets. If there is a material amount of fully depreciated assets, these should be classified separately or reported, by classification, either parenthetically or in a footnote. Idle assets should also be disclosed if material in amount. Fixed assets held for sale or investment should be separately classified.

Methods and Extent of Disclosure. The provision for depreciation will appear in various parts of the income statement, depending on the use of the assets involved. If it is not elsewhere disclosed, a footnote should reveal the total provision for the year. This figure, a non-cash charge, is important in determining the cash flow of a business and in appraising the rate of property utilization. Such a footnote would be more complete if it disclosed the methods of depreciation, the asset classes to which they are applied, and the related portions of the annual provision.

If there is a difference between the procedures used to determine depreciation for book purposes and for tax purposes, this too should be disclosed, perhaps in a footnote about tax allocation.

Disclosure of Changes. Change of depreciation method. Changes in the depreciation method, if material in their effect on the financial statements, require qualification of the auditor's opinion. If adequately described in a footnote, the auditor may simply conclude his opinion,

> . . . on a basis consistent with the prior year except for the change, which we approve, explained in note __.

Such a note should identify the procedure previously used, the newly adopted procedure, and the effect on net income before and after taxes. If the statements are comparative in nature, the effect on net income should be given for both years if practicable. This is true even if the prior year is restated. It would be helpful to readers if the company disclosed why the change was made. Such a footnote might read as follows:

> Because of the rapid obsolescence caused by technological advances, which makes the estimated useful lives of assets difficult to forecast, the company has decided to change from the straight-line method of providing for depreciation to the declining-balance method at double the straight-line rate. The effect of this change was to decrease net income $5,000 before taxes and $2,500 after taxes. If the change had been made in the previous year, net income would have been decreased $4,000 before taxes and $2,000 after taxes. The company has been using the declining-balance method for tax purposes since 1955 and will continue to do so.

If there is no note, or if the content of the note is inadequate, then the auditor must provide the necessary detail in his opinion, either at the conclusion of the opinion or in a paragraph inserted between the scope and opinion sections.

Change of depreciation rate. Changes of depreciation rates, if justified, do not require opinion qualification. Nevertheless, they should be disclosed if they are material in their effect on the financial statements. Such a note might read as follows:

> The company has decided to contract for much of the delivery service rather than continue to provide it itself. As a result, the company has decided to decrease the rate of depreciation on the remaining lives of its delivery vehicles. The change this year had the effect of increasing net income $2,000 before taxes and $1,000 after taxes. Had this change been made last year, the effect would have been to increase net income $2,200 before taxes and $1,100 after taxes.

If the accumulated allowances or the current provision appear unreasonable or inappropriate, the auditor should see that the facts are adequately disclosed. If these result from the application of methods not generally accepted, or do not result in a fair presentation of the financial statements, the auditor may have to qualify his opinion.

TAX ISSUES

In addition to the tax elements discussed above, there are two other provisions which directly affect depreciation: emergency facilities and the investment credit.

Emergency Facilities. Because certain facilities may be suitable only for defense purposes, the government may permit all or a part of such items to be amortized over a 60-month period for income tax purposes. The AICPA is quite specific in pointing out that such arrangements should not govern financial accounting if they do not conform to generally accepted accounting principles.[7] The Institute does acknowledge that where the results from applying such rules do not differ materially from those of following the income tax procedures, there are practical advantages in keeping the accounts in agreement with the income tax returns.

If the 60-month amortization is being used in the financial accounts, the auditor must determine that such assets are indeed covered by certificates of necessity. He must then determine whether this is a reasonable life for the assets. The AICPA has listed as possible considerations in this determination, "their adaptability to post-emergency use, the effect of their use

[7] Accounting Research and Terminology Bulletins, final ed., New York, AICPA, 1961, pp. 76, 77.

upon economic utilization of other facilities, the possibility of excessive costs due to expedited construction or emergency conditions, and the fact that no deductions for the certified portion will be allowable for income tax purposes in the post-amortization years if the company elects to claim the amortization deduction."[8] If the amount allowed for tax purposes is materially different from that estimated, then the latter should be used for financial accounting purposes. This may result in income tax allocation.

If the rapid amortization is justified and used for financial accounting purposes, it should be disclosed separately from the amount of regular depreciation. The cost of the facilities so amortized should also be disclosed, together with the years of the facilities' acquisition, or their remaining life. Such a note might read as follows:

> The equipment classification includes $500,000 of machinery which is being amortized over a five-year period under certificates of necessity issued in 1967. One hundred thousand dollars was amortized this year and is included in cost of sales.

If an asset so amortized is subsequently assigned a longer life, the accumulated amortization may be reduced to what it would have been if the new longer life had been used, with a credit adjustment to the tax liability to show that the tax benefit is no longer available, and the balance going to Retained Earnings.

Price Level Changes. Changes in money value affect fixed assets and their depreciation probably more than any other area of accounting. There are many who recommend that fixed asset costs and their depreciation should at least reflect changes in general price levels, and some would advocate a current- or replacement-cost basis for depreciation. The most likely possibility is a supplementary statement in which all assets are adjusted by a general price index for changes in purchasing power.

If this practice is adopted, the auditor will probably not be required to render an opinion on them, other than perhaps in regard to the correct application of the respective index. More extensive adjustments, such as valuation at current or replacement costs, could involve only the use of more specialized indices or the reference to evidences of market values.

DEPLETION

Introduction. Depletion, and the audit thereof, is in many respects similar to depreciation. Both relate to the decline in service potential of long-lived assets. The former relates to physically extracted products from natural resources, while the latter refers to the effects of use and the passage of time on productive assets. Both represent an attempt to allocate equitably the respective investment costs over the estimated economic lives of the assets. For depletion, this means charging of the cost against expected output of the resource until exhausted, or the limit of what can be economically produced and sold.

Depletion Methods. The most common accounting method of allocating depletion is the unit-of-production method. The cost of the resource is divided by the estimated production to get a per-unit depletion factor. This factor is then applied to the output to determine the charge for that period. The estimated production may represent assured reserves or only estimated recoveries. If the former basis is used, then estimated production represents the production for the year plus what is in sight at the end of the year. With

[8] *Ibid.*, p. 77.

successful operations, this approach will usually result in an approximation of a diminishing-balance type of allocation, with higher charges in the earlier years.

The use of total estimated recoveries makes estimation more hazardous and tentative. The auditor should be reluctant to accept this basis unless he can determine from acceptable geological authority or other competent evidence that there is a high degree of probability of realizing expectations. If such evidence or written representation is not available, the auditor may wish to consider a qualification to his opinion. Estimates of recoverable units, even by the most experienced experts, may be in error. Where substantial changes are made in estimates, the current year's provision must be based on the latest revision. If prior estimates were made on the best evidence then available, no adjustment need be made of depletion based thereon and taken in prior periods. A change in the depletion provision may also affect depreciation on related assets.

In appraising estimates of the useful economic lives of deposits of natural resources, the auditor must consider external conditions similar to those used in reviewing lives of depreciable assets. However, obsolescence is less likely to be an issue in depletion estimates. Also, a temporary halt in activity seldom has any effect on depletion, though it may even increase the rate of depreciation of related fixed assets.

Depletion is a generally accepted accounting practice. There are instances, however, in which depletion is not taken. The auditor should carefully review such a policy in terms of the legal implications and industry practices to determine whether to qualify his opinion.

The auditor's procedures, as with depreciation, are to satisfy himself that the depletion is accurately calculated on an acceptable base by a generally accepted method which is consistently applied. He must also determine that adequate disclosure has been made. Such disclosure should distinguish between depletion and depreciation.

The auditor must establish the proper unit of property, the nature of his client's interest in this property, his cost, and the elements thereof. There should be detailed records supporting the general ledger controlling accounts providing just such information. Usually producing properties are accounted for separately from nonproducing property. The auditor would verify and vouch such data as part of the audit of the natural resources. He would also examine appraisals of the resource that are commercially available. These reports should be reviewed for reasonableness and propriety. Using such estimates and current production records (previously compared with inventories and sales records), the auditor should test the current charge to operations for depletion. This charge should be compared with prior years' data and information on comparable properties, if such exist. Changes in the method of determining depletion should be considered for opinion qualification. Changes in estimated reserves should be considered for disclosure.

As in a first audit of fixed assets and depreciation, first audits of natural resources require verification of ownership, costs, and depletion computations from the start of operations.

Timber. The production of lumber and other wood products provides an interesting example of depletion. The process begins with the acquisition of timberlands by outright purchase or by acquiring the right to remove the timber from a certain acreage. Then begins the harvesting of the timber. If the tract is large enough, a sawmill may be established on it. More probably, the logs will be taken to a railroad siding or to water, where they will be chained together and towed to the permanent mill site, or they may simply be loaded on large trucks and hauled to the mill. The following hypothetical situation provides for an identification of some of the elements of depletion problems:

Cascade Lumber purchases stumpage rights to tracts A and B. The standing-lumber estimate for tract A is 1,000,000 log feet; for tract B, 1,500,000. Cascade Lumber plans to bring the logs to boom grounds on tract B, where they will be hauled by tugboat over a water course to the mill.

If, for example, the decision is made to log tract A first but access to tract A is only through tract B, and if the boom grounds, which must be prepared, are on tract B, then we begin to see the need for cost allocations that the auditor must eventually review. The key element in the depletion charge is, of course, the estimate of the amount of standing timber by a professional estimator called a "timber cruiser." His estimate is the basis for the contract to sell the stumpage and also the basis for allocating not only the stumpage costs but other "sunk costs"—outlays for logging roads, boom grounds, spur track and sidings, and any other production aids—that determine the cost per thousand feet, log scale, of the timber moved to the mill.

If we now add some assumed outlays to the hypothetical case stated above, we can illustrate certain of the calculations that will be necessary. Let us assume that the following costs were incurred:

Road through B to A	$ 11,000
Roads in tract A	7,000
Boom ground and access road, tract B	14,000
Stumpage cost, tract A	75,000
Stumpage cost, tract B	120,000

During the current year 400,000 log feet of timber were felled, hauled to the boom ground, and towed to the mill.

With the facts given, the auditor could expect the following cost assignments to the timber sent to the mill:

Tract A

	Cost	*Cost per 1,000 ft*
Background:		
Road through B to A	$11,000	
Boom ground and access road (B)	14,000	
	$25,000	
Timber cruise estimate (A and B)	2,500,000 ft	
Depletion unit		$10.00
Roads:		
Cost	$ 7,000	
Timber cruise estimate (A)	1,000,000 ft	
Depletion unit		7.00
Stumpage:		
Cost	$75,000	
Depletion unit		75.00
		$92.00

At the mill we would expect to find a cost assignment of $36,800 (400,000 × $92.00 per 1,000) to the 400,000 feet of timber cut. This, of course, represents the depletion cost only. The towing costs and all of the other applicable product costs need not be considered here.

The auditor's approach is to determine the cost of the timber from authoritative reports. From a review of current reports, discussion, and observation, the auditor should then determine the condition, extent, and amount of the timber removed during the period and the amount still remaining (in physical units and dollar value). The annual depletion would be computed by multiplying the number of the units removed times the established cost for such units. The auditor must be sure to allocate a fair portion of the cost to the remaining cutover land if the land is owned.

Accretion based on the growth of trees is generally not recognized in the accounts. To the extent that such growth affects estimates of recoverable timber, the depletion rate should be adjusted. For this reason, comparisons with estimates of the actual output of various sections should be made periodically. The auditor should also consider the effect of fire, disease, and other casualties, as well as the use of dead and falling trees, in appraising estimates. Costs incurred in clearing and reseeding cutover land may be capitalized and charged to subsequent logging.

Minerals. Mine depletion would be based on estimates by competent engineers and geologists of the condition and extent of the holdings. Authoritative reports of the quantity and quality of the resources removed furnish the bases for the computation of annual depletion. The actual unit of output on which depletion is based may vary. It may be applied to the tonnage mined or to the mineral at some other stage of processing. Similarly, it may be based on the raw ore or the metal content thereof. The latter would appear to provide a more equitable basis.

Oil and gas. The costs of drilling and completing productive oil and gas wells (except the cost of tangible equipment) are called "intangible drilling or development costs" (IDC). The taxpayer may elect to expense such costs for income tax purposes, and many do for financial accounting purposes, as well. Alternatively, for financial accounting purposes the company may capitalize the recoverable IDC, gross or net of the related income tax deduction, and amortize the balance over the estimated productive life of the wells. The auditor's responsibility is to assure himself that the method used is applied accurately on a consistent basis and given adequate disclosure.

Costs incurred in exploring and developing productive oil and gas properties are also often expensed as incurred. These "finding" costs, which are in addition to IDC costs, include such costs as geological survey and tests, dry holes, rentals on undeveloped leases which expire or are abandoned, and related operating expenses. Reference to company "well logs" may provide important information in this regard. Some companies do capitalize a portion of these costs for financial accounting purposes. It is reasonable to expect that such capitalized costs should not be permitted to exceed the expected recovery value of estimated reserves. Though this may be acceptable for new companies in the field if proper disclosure is given, such a condition may require a qualified opinion by the auditor. Accurate and consistent application of the method chosen plus adequate disclosure are again the auditor's major concerns.

Basis and Alternative Methods. Cost is the only basis generally accepted for depletion in financial accounting. Wasting assets are recorded at the cost of locating, acquiring, and developing them, offset by depletion to date. The general rules distinguishing capital charges from revenue charges hold for wasting assets as well as for other assets. However, the federal government allows a percentage depletion allowance based on gross income from the property. Currently such allowances range up to 22 percent of such income, not to exceed 50 percent of the taxable income from the property before the depletion deduction. This method is generally not acceptable for accounting purposes. Where such allowance exceeds the amount available from cost depletion, the auditor should be aware that there is a very strong incentive to expense costs otherwise capitalizable.

Depreciable assets used in connection with the recovery of wasting assets may have estimated useful lives which vary from those otherwise expected. If these assets cannot be economically moved from the site of the resource, they should not be given an estimated life in excess of that of the natural resource. Depreciation should be computed separately for each lease or depletable unit of property. Salvage values may also be affected. Also, operating conditions around resource recovery areas are often more rugged than in other areas, which may justify shorter lives for some depreciable assets than might otherwise be expected.

Depreciation usually occurs with the passage of time, whether there is production or not. Thus, some oil companies take depreciation on the equipment of shut-in wells, though computed at a lesser rate than that computed on producing wells. Such a provision should be made even if another method of depreciation is expected to be used when the well becomes productive. For tax purposes, an election to that effect should be filed with the initial return.

Disclosure. Disclosure of wasting assets and their related accumulated depletion should be classified on the balance sheet among the fixed tangible assets but separately from depreciable and nondepreciable items. The provision for depletion should also be disclosed separately from depreciation expense, either in the income statements or in a footnote. The method of depletion, as well as the basis on which depletion is determined, should also be mentioned.

AMORTIZATION

Introduction. Amortization, like depreciation and depletion, involves the allocation to operations of the cost of long-lived assets. The term "amortization" is usually applied to the allocation of the cost of intangible assets. It is also applied to the systematic reduction of accounts related to debt security transactions. The term "amortization" is also used to describe the accelerated write-off of defense facilities, discussed above.

Amortization of Intangible Assets. Intangible assets are those which reflect privileges, rights, and competitive advantages enjoyed by their possessor. While they give promise of potential service and thus qualify as accounting assets, they lack physical substance (though documents may provide evidence of their existence). Nevertheless, the special advantages these rights confer may be extremely valuable. Formerly, the designation "fixed assets" was used to denote long-lived assets, both tangible and intangible in nature. Despite the decline in use of this general designation, the term "intangible assets" has continued to refer only to long-lived, nonphysical assets intended for use in the business.

The Accounting Principles Board in its Opinion No. 17, provides for the following with regard to the acquisition of intangible assets

> . . . a company should record as assets the cost of intangible assets acquired from other enterprises or individuals. Costs of developing, maintaining, or restoring intangible assets which are not specifically identifiable, have indeterminate lives, or are inherent in a continuing business and are related to an enterprise as a whole—such as goodwill—should be deducted from income when incurred.[9]

[9] Accounting Principles Board, APB Opinion No. 17, *Intangible Assets,* New York, AICPA, 1970, p. 339.

The Board describes the determination of cost in terms similar to those for long-lived assets, that is, the amount of cash disbursed, the fair value of other assets distributed, the present value of amounts to be paid for liabilities incurred, or the fair value of stock issued as described in paragraph 67 of APB Opinion No. 16.[10]

It is the Board's opinion that all intangible assets should be amortized on the basis of the specific asset's estimated life. Such assets should not be written off at the time of acquisition. The Board believes that an analysis of all factors should result in a reasonable estimate of the useful lives of most intangible assets, even those whose period of existence is not precisely determinable. In any event, the Board has ruled that the period of amortization should not exceed forty years.

The Board concludes that, "the straight line method of amortization—equal annual amounts—should be applied unless a company demonstrates that another systematic method is more appropriate. The financial statements should disclose the method and period of amortization." [11]

The Committee prescribed the following principles for amortizing intangible assets:

> The cost of type (*a*) intangibles should be amortized by systematic charges in the income statement over the period benefited, as in the case of other assets having a limited period of usefulness. . . .
>
> When it becomes reasonably evident that the term of existence of a type (*b*) intangible has become limited and that it has therefore, become a type (*a*) intangible, its cost should be amortized by systematic charges in the income statemeet over the estimated remaining period of usefulness.[12]

The period benefited may be shorter than the legal life. Problems of obsolescence and supersession may limit the economically useful life of patents to less than 17 years. Many literary and artistic pieces of work diminish in value quite rapidly and require amortization over a briefer period than the 28-year legal life of copyrights (with an option for one renewal of equal term). Thus, costs of copyrights on such items are usually absorbed in the first, or the first few, printings or pressings. Where intangible assets, such as franchises, contracts, and leaseholds, possess a renewal option, amortization is generally confined to the life of the original agreement because of the uncertainty of the lease extension. Leasehold improvements, such as buildings, should be amortized over the shorter of their own economic life or the life of the lease, allowing for any value to be recovered according to the terms of the contract. The tax law gives similar treatment. In addition to amortization of assets with limited legal lives, such as patents and copyrights, the tax law now permits amortization of such items as organization costs, trademarks, and trade names over a period of not less than 60 months. Amortization of goodwill, however, is not deductible for tax purposes.

The Committee on Accounting Procedure also provided for adjustments in rates, partial write-downs, or lump-sum write-offs when expected future benefits become impaired or disappear. It discouraged, however, any write-offs without evidence of impaired value. The amortization charge to expense is to be classified according to the primary use of the asset. The corresponding credit may be made directly to the related asset or, preferably,

[10] Accounting Principles Board, Opinion No. 16, *Business Combinations,* New York, AICPA, 1970, p. 311.

[11] Accounting Principles Board, Opinion No. 17, *Intangible Assets,* New York, AICPA, 1970, p. 340.

[12] Accounting Research and Terminology Bulletins, final ed., New York, AICPA, 1961, p. 38.

to a contra account. Amortization of intangible assets is generally computed by the straight-line method (the only one allowed for tax purposes).

Auditing the Amortization of Intangibles. Auditing intangible assets and their amortization is quite similar to auditing their tangible counterparts except that physical examination is not possible. The auditor should obtain a complete schedule, listing all intangible assets and their amortization. Whether the client must file with the SEC or not, the latter's Schedule VII (and VIII, if required) provides a suitable format.

SCHEDULE VII

Description	Balance at beginning of period	Additions at cost	Deductions		Other changes	Balance at close of period
			Charged to income	Charged to other accounts		

Schedule VIII follows a similar format for the accumulated amortization account if the periodic credits are not made directly to the asset itself. The auditor should recommend that separate accounts be maintained for each kind and class of intangible, where material.

The auditor, by examining supporting documents and correspondence, and by discussion with company officials and attorneys and others, must ascertain the nature and substance of the expected benefits of an intangible asset and any related details which require disclosure. The auditor must satisfy himself as to the probability that future benefits will accrue and the fact that the client is the owner and will be the direct beneficiary of these benefits. If the continuous existence of the intangible requires any specific actions on the part of the client, the auditor must obtain evidence of satisfactory compliance. This may require discussions with the company attorney.

For additions (and on a first audit for all major intangible assets), the auditor must ascertain their origin and the cost or other valuation basis used, and must judge whether the resulting accounting conforms to generally accepted accounting principles. He must examine approval of the incurrence of such costs and appraise their propriety. Because of the difficulty in objectively determining the value of intangible items, accounting has tended to countenance, in addition to capitalizing, the expensing (perhaps over an arbitrary period) of some types of intangibles such as research and development costs. Consistency in recording such items may therefore be an important consideration for the auditor. Ascertaining the reasonableness of an allocation of a lump-sum purchase price between tangibles and intangibles as well as among intangibles may require obtaining estimates from experts. The cost of intangible assets acquired for non-cash consideration may be considered as the fair value of the consideration given or the fair value of the property right acquired, whichever is more clearly evident.

Having satisfied himself as to the validity and propriety of the intangible and its cost, the auditor must determine what life and method of amortization are appropriate. Such an appraisal must be made of all intangible assets at each audit and appropriate adjustments made where there has been a significant change in the estimated period of usefulness. Write-downs and write-offs are permitted where impairment of value is established.[13] The auditor

[13] Accounting Principles Board, Opinion No. 17, *Intangible Assets*, New York, AICPA, 1970, p. 341.

should determine that proper executive approval has been given for any such action. Lump-sum write-offs of intangibles, however, should not be made arbitrarily immediately after acquisition, nor should they be charged to capital surplus under any circumstances. The amortization charge for the period should be traced to the income accounts to assure the propriety and consistency of the treatment.

On the balance sheet, intangibles should appear below tangible long-lived assets (often as the last items on the asset side, as being the most illiquid) and be described in sufficient detail so a reader will be aware of their nature, the basis of determining cost, and the method of amortization used. If amortization is credited directly to the intangible assets rather than to an offset or contra account, the disclosure of the current basis of the individual intangible assets as cost or amortized cost would be appropriate. Assets of type (*b*) should be classified separately from those considered type (*a*) in nature. In the income statement, amortization of intangibles may be combined with depreciation (with perhaps parenthetical or footnote disclosure of its separate amount) to report in one amount the major non-cash charges against income.

Amortization of Bond Premium and Discount. Purchase or sale of bonds at other than face value (disregarding accrued interest) results in a premium (if the price exceeds face value) or discount (if the price is less than face value). Bond premium or discount thus represents the adjustment between the face or par value and the market price of the security. These adjustments may be reflected as part of the security account or as separate accounts. (The former treatment appears to be more common for security investments, the latter for the debt liability.)

Bond investments. Three alternative treatments by the investor have been suggested for amortization of a premium paid on a security investment: to leave it untouched, to revalue the security from time to time at market, or to systematically allocate the amount as a charge to income. Except for temporary investments, investments of questionable value, and investments held by companies that deal in securities, the third alternative is probably the preferred choice, especially if a long-term commitment is contemplated. A fourth alternative, to immediately write off any premium, relieves income of subsequent periods of charges which should be made to them. Such a practice should be avoided.

For tax purposes, bondholders may be able to deduct premium amortization. On bonds for which the interest is tax-exempt, amortization of premium is required (but nondeductible); for partially tax-exempt bonds, it is required for corporations but optional for other taxpayers. Amortization is optional on fully taxable bonds for all taxpayers. If premium amortization takes place, it reduces the basis. Discount realized on disposal of a bond is taxable as profit at that time and not as accruing over the period the bond is held.

Strictly speaking, the term "amortization" is applied to the systematic reduction of a premium, and "accumulation," to the systematic elimination of a discount. For security investors, premiums are generally amortized but discounts are seldom accumulated except on high-grade bonds, where a discount more clearly represents an adjustment to the interest rate and does not reflect an uncertainty about the ultimate realizability of the bond. Both discount and premiums should be systematically allocated to income by the bond security issuer. The term "amortization" is also applied to the systematic allocation to operations of costs incurred in issuing long-term debt securities.

Amortization of premium and accumulation of discount may be computed by the straight-line method or the compound-interest method. Under the former method the premium or discount is adjusted in equal installments or operations until maturity. The latter method establishes a uniform rate which, applied to the decreasing base, results in diminishing amounts being absorbed by operations with the passage of time. The latter method better reflects the circumstances, but the straight-line method is simpler and produces only minor distortion if the amount involved is small and the period relatively short.

Conservatism dictates the amortization of the premium to the date of call rather than maturity if the security purchased possesses such a feature. Serial bonds bearing different maturities and rates should be accounted for separately if possible; otherwise, the average length of time the securities will be outstanding may be established and used.

Amortization on Bond Retirements. Accounting Research Bulletins Nos. 2 and 18 deal with unamortized discount and redemption premiums on bonds refunded. Three alternatives are considered:

1. Direct write-off to income
2. Amortization over the remainder of the original life of the issue retired
3. Amortization over the life of the new issue

The first alternative was accepted, but the second was preferred. The third was unacceptable. The Accounting Principles Board (in its Opinion No. 6) has subsequently stated, however, that this method is appropriate under circumstances where refunding takes place because of currently lower interest rates or anticipation of higher interest rates in the future. An accelerated amortization period of less than the life of the old issue is also acceptable. If the term of the new issue is less than that of the old issue, then the shorter life should govern. Whatever the method adopted, it should be clearly disclosed and, if material in its effect, the amount should be reported separately from other charges for discount amortization.

If debt is discharged, other than by refunding, before the original maturity date of the issue, any balance of discount and other issue costs remaining on the books should be written off to income.

Auditing the Amortization of Premium and Discount. By examining related authoritative documents and discussions with management, the auditor must establish the cost of the security transaction and ascertain whether proper recognition has been given to any applicable premium or discount and related costs. Where the bonds were exchanged for non-cash consideration, the price may be either the fair market value of the security (perhaps as evidenced by subsequent sale for cash) or that of the property or right given in exchange, whichever is the more clearly evident. Except in those unusual cases where premium and discount amortization and accumulation are not warranted, the auditor must determine that an acceptable method of allocation is used and that it is accurately and consistently applied. The period's adjustment should be traced to the interest account or to a construction account if capitalized. The auditor should determine that capitalization, amortization, and any write-offs have received the proper executive approval.

Premiums and discounts on bond investments may be included as part of the investment account. Premiums and discounts on bond liabilities should preferably be shown separately, as adjunct and contra accounts, respectively, to the bonds payable account.

BIBLIOGRAPHY

Accounting Principles Board, Opinions, AICPA, New York.
No. 1. *New Depreciation Guidelines and Rules.*
No. 17. *Intangible Assets.*

Accounting Research and Terminology Bulletins, final ed., New York, AICPA, 1961.

American Accounting Association: *Accounting and Reporting Standards for Corporate Financial Statements and Preceding Statements and Supplements,* Report of the Committee on Concepts and Standards underlying Corporate Financial Statements, American Accounting Association, Evanston, Ill.

Brink, Victor Z., and James A. Cashin: *Internal Auditing,* 2d ed., New York, The Ronald Press Company, 1958.

Davidson, Sidney: *The Meaning of Depreciation,* Chicago, Ill., The University of Chicago Press, 1962.

Grant, Eugene L., and Paul T. Norton: *Depreciation,* New York, The Ronald Press Company, 1955.

Ingalls, Edmund F.: *Practical Accounting and Auditing Problems,* 3 vols., New York, AICPA, 1966.

Lenhart, Norman J., and Philip L. Defliese: *Montgomery's Auditing,* 8th ed., New York, The Ronald Press Company, 1957.

Meij, Jacob L.: *Depreciation and Replacement Policy,* Chicago, Quadrangle Books, 1961.

Morrissey, Leonard E.: *The Many Sides of Depreciation,* Hanover, N.H., The Amos Tuck School of Business Administration, 1960.

Terborgh, George: *Realistic Depreciation Policy,* Chicago, Machinery and Allied Products Institute, 1954.

Wright, F. K.: "Towards a General Theory of Depreciation," *Journal of Accounting Research,* Spring, 1964.

Van Horn, Lawrence G.: "Accelerated Depreciation—A Tax Benefit, but Harmful Accounting," *The New York Certified Public Accountant,* May, 1967.

Pick, John: "Concepts of Depreciation—Business Enterprises," *The New York Certified Public Accountant,* May, 1970.

Chapter **26**

The Intangible Assets: Prepaid Expenses and Deferred Charges

M. TABIBIAN

Partner, Touche Ross & Co.

SCOPE OF THIS CHAPTER

This chapter deals with accounts that would normally be considered a part of the "intangible asset" phase of the audit. Accordingly, it includes a discussion of some liability accounts where they relate closely to an account normally considered as an intangible asset account. For example, the discussion of prepaid insurance includes a discussion of accrued insurance; the discussion of prepaid rent includes a discussion of accrued rent. By the same token, some intangible assets are closely related to accounts which are examined in other phases of an audit, and, accordingly, are not specifically discussed in this chapter. For example, prepaid or deferred income tax charges resulting from interperiod allocations of taxable income are covered in Chapter 39, "Review of Taxes," and prepaid or deferred pension-plan costs and deferred debt costs are discussed in Chapter 28, "Long-term Liabilities." Nevertheless, the concepts outlined in this chapter will generally apply to all such intangibles.

GENERAL DESCRIPTION

In a literal sense, virtually all assets appearing in a balance sheet are intangible assets, except perhaps cash on hand. Some could argue that within present accounting concepts, even the inventory and fixed assets captions portray intangibles since they represent merely the deferral of costs from one period to another, rather than the assignment of real values to any underlying physical asset. In a more conventional sense, however, the term "intangible assets" has been confined to prepaid expenses and deferred charges, excluding cash accounts, rights to receive cash, investments, and physical properties. Although there are definable differences between prepaid expenses and deferred charges, these differences are not of very great auditing or accounting significance. If there is any broad categorizing to be done, it is far more useful to draw a distinction between those which would be considered current assets as opposed to those to be classified as noncurrent assets. A few concrete examples will suffice to illustrate these classifications:

	Prepaid Expenses	Deferred Charges
Current Assets	Rent, taxes, insurance, subscriptions	Advertising and catalog costs
Noncurrent Assets	Franchise fees	Debt expense, plant rearrangements, formulas, and processes

Prepaid Expenses. "Prepaid expenses" represent items for which a payment has been made in advance for services or rights to be received over some future period of time. The nature of the services or rights and the period of time over which they are to extend are firmly established by a contractual arrangement. In some cases, a premature termination of the contractual arrangement may result in a refund of a portion of the prepayment.

Deferred Charges. "Deferred charges" represent costs incurred for a service or activity *that has already been completed* but which is expected to benefit future periods. They differ from prepaid expenses in that no further services are expected for the expenditures made.

Characteristics. For the various types of intangible assets, prepaid expenses, and deferred charges, it will be found that most prepaid expenses are of a current asset nature, with relatively few deferred charges in that category; conversely, most deferred charges will be of a noncurrent nature, with relatively few prepaid expenses as noncurrent assets. In any event, the prime audit approach to intangible assets will consider their characteristics as current or noncurrent assets, rather than the academic distinction between prepaid expenses and deferred charges. The main characteristics of intangibles that influence the audit approach are as follows:

CURRENT ASSETS:

1. They are usually individually small in dollar amount.
2. There are relatively few different kinds of items, and most will be found in each audit situation.
3. They are typically common items found in most companies.
4. They are usually closely related to the day-to-day operations of the enterprise.
5. They are usually recurring or repetitive items.
6. They are relatively short-lived.

NONCURRENT ASSETS:

1. The individual items are relatively large in dollar amount.
2. There is a wide range of different kinds of items that may be encountered, although only a few will be encountered in any given audit situation.
3. Each individual item is a relative rarity among various companies (although some items may be common to all companies in a given type of industry).
4. They usually arise from unique or relatively infrequent occurrences.
5. The creation of the item is not usually related directly to the day-to-day operations of the enterprise.
6. The items are usually relatively long-lived.

Thus, it can be seen that the audit problem that emerges from these characteristics is very different for the current intangible as compared with the noncurrent intangible. The exact nature of a current intangible can be rather easily perceived, and the question of existence of a future benefit can be satisfied without undue difficulty; furthermore, verification of dollar amounts is not critical in view of the relatively minor amounts involved. On the other hand, for the noncurrent intangibles, considerable study of background and underlying transactions may be required to establish the nature and existence of a future benefit and to substantiate the dollar amounts that have been assigned to them.

Audit Objectives. There is a twofold objective in the examination of intangible assets. First, there is the usual objective of coming to an informed opinion as to whether or not the item in question is fairly stated on the balance sheet. This objective can often be satisfied rather easily, especially for those items in current assets, which are rarely large in dollar balance or complicated in nature. Because of this, there is often a tendency to minimize the importance of the examination of these assets. However, the very small amounts involved often belie the very significant information that is to be obtained from an appropriate examination of them.

The second objective of auditing intangible assets, therefore, is more important than merely obtaining satisfaction that the item is fairly presented. It contemplates the discovery or gathering of certain information which may support or contradict conclusions reached in other phases of the audit. For example, a review of insurance coverage and comparison with recorded properties may disclose the existence of insurance coverage on property which was not otherwise accounted for. Insurance coverage on inventories which varies materially from the recorded amount of inventories should generate questions not only into the insurance practices of the company, but also into the valuation of the recorded inventories. Comparison of real estate taxes with the property accounts may similarly reveal the ownership of properties not otherwise recorded; the absence of real estate tax on a recorded property should also arouse the auditor's curiosity.

Furthermore, the items which find their way into intangible assets may be the only available indication of very major activities or developments affecting the company. A thousand-dollar item among miscellaneous assets may not concern the auditor very much in view of the nominal amount involved. However, this could be the only available clue to the fact that the company had placed a deposit and committed itself to, say, a very large property acquisition.

A proper examination of intangibles may also serve to alert the auditor to an underlying attempt on the part of the company to influence the reporting of profits or financial condition. As mentioned, many intangible assets are relatively minor in amount. Most companies will not go to the trouble of recording every such item as an asset, even though such procedure is theoretically justified, but rather will charge many of them off directly to expense as soon as they are incurred. Where the company has been very meticulous about recording every possible prepaid or deferred asset—especially in the absence of equal fastidiousness on the liability side—there is reason to suspect a scraping for profits. Conversely, a desire to restrain the reporting of profits might manifest itself in a very liberal write-off of other assets and scrupulous accrual of liabilities. Any impressions gained in the examination of intangibles should alert the auditor in his examination of other sections where such influences may not be as readily apparent.

For these reasons, determining the scope of the examination of intangibles can be particularly challenging. The extent of audit penetration in the examination of intangible assets may vary over a very wide range. The auditor is faced with the dilemma of devoting an inordinate amount of attention to relatively minor items on the one hand, or the risk of missing important revelations by too light an examination on the other hand. The auditor must carefully consider all aspects of his examination, the reliance he can place on his other procedures, the candor and frankness with which management receives him, and the reliability of the information being submitted to him. From these considerations and the exercise of seasoned judgment, and by orchestrating the relative risks, available procedures, time allowances, and experience levels of the assistants assigned to the examination, the auditor must establish a program to meet the specific circumstances encountered.

Internal Control. Intangible assets are not ordinarily subject to misappropriation, nor are they likely to be the source from which major errors in the accounting records originate. The critical point in controlling these assets is in their creation and initial recording. An important peculiarity of intangibles is that they usually originate and enter the accounting records through sources other than the routine channels for purchases, cost controls, and cash disbursements. Their creation and administration are ordinarily under the jurisdiction of individual executives, with little opportunity being afforded for review and challenge of their activities. These circumstances create a situation which is vulnerable to inefficient procurement practices as well as fraudulent activities (for example, authorization of a payment for a nonexistent purpose).

Effective internal control must therefore be imposed at the point of origin. Authorization for the making of a disbursement is often in the form of a "check request," which should be supported by some externally generated document—a rent bill, insurance invoice, lawyer's invoice, etc. (too often, executives responsible for these disbursements prefer to retain the bills in their own office files). Once drawn, the check should be signed by some other executive and then mailed directly to the payee; it should not be returned to the party who initially authorized the disbursement.

Refund checks or other forms of incoming cash should be processed through normal procedures for recording, controlling, and depositing receipts and should not be diverted to other channels merely because they represent nonroutine receipts. Journal entries creating, writing off, or amortizing the intangible assets should be governed by the usual rules requiring proper authorization and supporting data. The important thing to guard against in an otherwise effective system of internal control is the sanctioning of exceptions or circumventions when accounting for intangible assets.

The administering practices of the individuals responsible for these assets should be reviewed from time to time by someone in a position to make an effective challenge. The internal audit department may be particularly well suited for this purpose. Periodic reports detailing the costs of the various activities (insurance, research and development, legal and other costs related to a major acquisition, etc.), prepared by the accounting department and distributed to the management group, are also an effective means for challenge. Management should not overlook the danger of collusive practices—say, between the executive responsible for insurance matters and the insurance broker.

CURRENT INTANGIBLE ASSETS

The usual time test for current assets is applied in classifying intangibles (i.e., realizable within one year, or within the normal operating cycle of the company), but some exceptions are tolerated because of the immateriality of the individual items involved. For example, prepaid insurance is commonly included in current assets but may include, or consist entirely of, premiums on policies of three to five years' duration.

Some of the broad considerations in auditing the current intangibles have been described previously. The principal items of current intangibles will be individually discussed in this section.

Prepaid Insurance. The examination of prepaid insurance is a case in point of the varying degrees of audit penetration that may be applied, depending upon the materiality of the amounts involved, the degree of assurance or precision required by the auditor, and the extent to which the auditor tends to use the examination of prepaid insurance to corroborate the results of his examinations in other areas.

Regardless of the extent of audit procedures to be applied, it is desirable for the auditor to have prepared a worksheet showing all policies in force during the year. The worksheet should provide four money columns to show (1) the prepaid balance at the beginning of the year, (2) premium payments or refunds during the year, (3) the write-off of insurance expense, and (4) the prepaid balance at the end of the year. (See Figure 1*a*.) The amount of the expense write-off should be tied in to the related profit and loss accounts. The purpose of this tie-in is to see that the insurance expense has been properly classified in the profit and loss accounts, and also to see that all policies in force have been listed on the schedule; i.e., that policies had not been purchased and charged off directly to expense without appearing before the auditor's scrutiny.

Lightest penetration procedures. Having obtained such an insurance schedule, the auditor may feel justified in making only a very light review if the amounts are relatively small and he feels there is nothing to be gained by a more extensive examination in this area. The review then would entail comparing the prepaid balance at the beginning of the year with the prepaid balance at the end of the year, and comparing the expense for the year with that for the prior year. Where it is the company's practice to purchase insurance on an annual basis, this kind of comparison can be limited to a review of totals only. However, where the company purchases policies for longer periods, say three to five years, a comparison of opening and closing balances may have to be made for each policy. In any event, major variations should be accounted for.

Moderate penetration procedures. Where the amounts involved are of some consequence and the auditor feels that some degree of additional verification is desirable, he can extend the procedures in some circumstances by confirming the insurance with the broker. He should request a list of all policies in force, together with the amount of unearned premiums thereon. The information furnished by the broker can then be compared with the auditor's worksheet. Although the amount of unearned premium reported by the broker would rarely coincide exactly with the amount of prepaid insurance recorded by the company, this comparison should suffice to disclose any major discrepancies.

Full-scope procedures. Where the previously described methods are not deemed adequate for one reason or another, a more complete examination is called for, which would entail the following steps:

1. Agree beginning balance of prepaid insurance with the ending balance shown in the prior year's workpapers.
2. Vouch the larger payments appearing on the schedule.
3. Check the computation of the ending balances for the major policies (in most cases, a fair approximation of the calculation can be made visually, without requiring a detailed computation).
4. Foot and crossfoot the schedule, and tie it in to the ledger accounts.
5. Examine the major insurance policies listed. Bear in mind that the absence of any policy or the naming of a loss payee may indicate hypothecation of the insured assets.

The foregoing procedures will apply where policies are of the fixed-premium type. However, where premiums are subject to retrospective adjustment based on experience, or where the amount of the premium is determined on some reporting basis geared to exposure, additional procedures will be required.

Retrospective adjustments. Premiums on certain policies, usually casualty or liability protection, are based on loss experience factors. Such policies usually operate as follows:

Figure 1 FOUR-MONEY-COLUMN WORKSHEET: (a) PREPAID INSURANCE, (b) PREPAID TAXES, (c) PREPAID (OR ACCRUED) RENT

(a)

Policy number	Insurance company	Type of coverage	Insurance limits	Premium	Term	Prepaid beginning of year (1)	Payments made: Voucher No.	Payments made: Amount (2)	Insurance expense (3)	Prepaid end of year (4)

(b)

Description of tax	Property	Annual period: From	Annual period: To	Payable	Prepaid beginning of year (1)	Payments made: Voucher No.	Payments made: Amount (2)	Tax expense (3)	Prepaid end of year (4)

(c)

Property	Landlord	Term of lease: From	Term of lease: To	Monthly rent	Date payable	Prepaid/(accrued) beginning of year (1)	Payments: Last monthly Voucher No.	Payments: Total amounts paid during year (2)	Rent expense (3)	Prepaid/(accrued) end of year (4)

1. An initial premium deposit is made, either in a fixed amount at the beginning of the policy year or by payments on some reporting basis during the year.

2. All claims arising during the policy year are tabulated by the insurance company and a loss reserve representing the estimated amount to be paid under each claim is established. From this the total estimated loss for that year is determined and the premium is then adjusted based on prenegotiated premium rates. To the extent that this calculated premium differs from the initial deposit, there will be either an additional billing or a refund to the insured. However, this adjustment is subject to further annual adjustments as long as any of the claims remain open and unsettled.

3. In each succeeding year after the first, the loss estimate for that policy year is recomputed by taking actual losses for all settled claims and the reserves (adjusted for new information, where necessary) for all remaining open claims. The amount of premium as determined at the last previous annual computation is then recomputed on the basis of the latest loss estimate. If, after a number of years, a few small claims still remain open, it may be possible for the insured and the insurance company to agree to consider such claims as closed at the amounts of reserve then established. Otherwise, the policy year will remain open as long as the claims have not been settled. Ordinarily, it can be expected that the first premium adjustment may be large, but that subsequent ones will be relatively small refinements.

As is to be expected, these computations cannot be made until some time after the end of each policy year. If the policy year coincides with the company's fiscal year, it is unlikely that the latest year's computations will be available for the auditor until after the audit report is required. If the latest full policy year does not coincide with the company's fiscal year but ends several months before, then the auditor will probably have the computations for the latest completed year; however, in such cases, the fiscal year will contain several months of a new policy year which are not included in the computations.

In either event there will be a period of several months to a year, or more, for which a retrospective premium adjustment is likely, but for which the amount has not been determined. Furthermore, at any point in time there may be as many as three or four open years to be considered (although, as previously stated, the adjustments applicable to years other than the most recent are generally quite small).

Policies of this kind are usually taken by companies that have relatively high risks and high insurance costs. Accordingly, the amount of potential adjustments that may arise must be carefully weighed by the auditor to determine whether an accrual is required for potential premium adjustments for periods subsequent to the latest available computation. The determination is based on a review of past experience and a comparison of current experience with that of the past.

The auditor should perform the following:

1. Read the policy and discuss its terms with people knowledgeable in the company's insurance affairs.

2. Review the past history of adjustments to determine if they have been substantial in size.

3. Contact the agent or carrier and determine the years which were open at the last previous adjustment, the amount of loss reserves applicable to each such year at that time, and the present status of such loss reserves.

4. Determine the amount and nature of claims filed for periods subsequent to the last policy year included in the previous adjustment, and whether or not there have been any significant insured losses for which the claims have not yet been filed. Consider whether such claims appear materially greater or less than for comparable periods of prior years.
5. Considering the amount of previous annual premium adjustments and the likelihood that the more recent experience may differ significantly from the prior experience, conclude as to whether or not a pro rata accrual is necessary for the potential retrospective premium adjustment.

Reporting-basis policies. For certain policies, the premium is not based on a fixed amount determined at the beginning of the policy year, but rather on some variable factors of exposure which the insured reports to the insurance company from time to time, generally monthly or quarterly. Some common applications of this type of insurance are workmen's compensation policies where the premium is based on gross covered payrolls, and fire insurance (on building contents) where the premium is based on inventory levels.

For such policies, the following audit procedures should be applied to see that proper insurance costs have been recorded:

1. Read the policy and make note of the coverage, premium rates, reporting requirements, and other significant terms.
2. Review the company's method of accumulating the data to be reported. Select at least one of the periodic reports filed for detailed checking. Trace data appearing on the report to the sources from which obtained and consider the reliability and appropriateness of such sources. See that data reported correspond to the coverages provided in the policy, i.e., that appropriate adjustment has been made for exclusions, etc. Check the accuracy of computations.
3. Scan the reports of other periods and see that variations from period to period are reasonable in view of seasonal fluctuations in the business.
4. Such policies usually provide for an audit by the insurance company from time to time. Review the results of the last completed audit and consider whether any adjustments made at that time affect the current year or any open prior years.

Review of adequacy of coverage. Although the auditor is not an insurance expert, the coverage provided by the company's insurance program is, nevertheless, a proper area of inquiry for the auditor. He should compare existing coverage with the recorded values of the applicable assets, bearing in mind that insurable values will differ from recorded values, and should also take into account the effect of any coinsurance provisions of the policies. Any apparent condition of overinsurance or underinsurance revealed by this comparison should be called to the company's attention. These conditions should also alert the auditor to the possibility that the related assets may be misstated in the records.

Where the company uses the services of a reputable and attentive insurance broker, or has developed a competent internal insurance department, these circumstances themselves may suffice to satisfy the auditor as to the adequacy of coverage. More often, however, the auditor will want to make some review himself, even where these conditions exist. Because of his familiarity with the operations of the company, he may be aware of special situations affecting insurance coverage which have not come to the attention of the insurance experts. Some examples of situations requiring modification of insurance coverage, which the auditor might be aware of, are:

1. New property acquired, or existing property expanded
2. New methods or locations for storage of goods
3. Changed shipping or packing procedures
4. Changes in sales terms
5. Changed production processes, methods, or materials
6. Installation or removal of protective features such as sprinklers, guards, etc.
7. Where property is in the custody of others, inadvertent duplication of coverage by the company and the custodian—or, conversely, absence of coverage by either party
8. Existence of assets, such as dies, jigs, molds, etc., that, under the company's accounting practices, are written off or carried at nominal amounts, but with real value that should be covered by insurance

Prepaid Taxes, Licenses, etc. Real estate and personal property taxes are generally paid in advance and amortized over the fiscal period of the taxing authority. Permits, licenses, and similar items are also paid at the beginning of some privilege period and are amortized over that privilege period. Certain franchise taxes are treated similarly to income taxes because the amount of tax is based on the income or gross receipts of a previous period; although for a future privilege period, the tax is usually charged to the operations of the period upon which it is measured.

Audit procedures. The standard four money-column schedule (see Figure 1*b*) should be obtained for all taxes. The worksheet should be footed, cross-footed, and tied in to the general ledger. Profit and loss accounts should be scanned to identify any other taxes which may have been paid and charged directly to expense.

Where the amounts of prepaid tax are not very large, a review can be made comparing beginning and ending balances with the prior year's balances and the expense for the year with the prior year's expense, to account for any major variations. More extensive procedures would entail the vouching of major payments, including an examination of receipted tax bills and checking visually the computation of the prepaid portion at the end of the year. In vouching the payments, bear in mind that the absence of a tax bill or the presence of a bill in a name other than the company's may indicate sale, assignment, or hypothecation of the taxed property or privilege.

The auditor should account for any new property taxes or the discontinuance of any previous property taxes. Conversely, if property has been acquired or sold during the past year, he should see that an appropriate change appears on the tax schedule. For first audits, he should relate all property taxes to the property accounts.

Prepaid Rent. Since rent is usually paid on a monthly basis, the amount carried as prepaid is unlikely to be very large under any circumstances. As with many other prepaid expenses, verification of the prepaid balance is a secondary objective, the principal objective being to examine the subject matter itself. In the case of rents, the auditor is concerned with all leases, whether or not they produce a prepaid (or accrued) balance, in order to account for properties in use and to see that the leases are appropriately disclosed in the notes to the financial statements, or that they are capitalized, where required, in conformity with the requirements of Opinion No. 5 of the Accounting Principles Board. In the typical audit, the entire subject of renting is treated as a single phase of the audit and accordingly brings under scrutiny any accrued rents as well as prepaid rents. The amount of accrued rent may be far more important than the amount of prepaid rent, especially where the lease provides for percentage rentals or requires the payment of certain expenses, such as taxes, maintenance costs, or insurance, in addition to a base rent.

Audit procedures. Two basic types of worksheet are required for the examination of rentals:

1. A permanent-file worksheet to be carried forward from year to year, listing all leases and their essential provisions. Where practicable, this worksheet should be designed in such a manner that the information required for the lease footnote, including projected minimum annual rent commitments, may be readily drawn off. (See Figure 2.)
2. An annual worksheet in the four money-column format listing each lease and showing the prepaid or accrued rent balance at the beginning of the year, payments made, expense for the year, and the prepaid or accrued balance at year end. The prepaid and accrued balances should be totaled separately, since they cannot be offset in the financial statements. (See Figure 1*c*.)

The aggregate minimum annual rental for the year under examination, as shown on the permanent-file worksheet, should be reconciled with the payments column of the annual worksheet, and the expense column of the annual worksheet should be tied in to rent expense charged to profit and loss. In this way, the auditor is assured that all leases are accounted for on both worksheets; the tie-in will also give reasonable assurance that payments have been made in accordance with the terms of the leases.

The auditor should review the permanent-file worksheet each year, bearing in mind that leases sometimes contain special terms that become operative only after the passage of several years or upon the occurrence of some designated event. He should also watch for any leases which are due to expire in the near future and should determine what, if anything, the company intends to do about them.

Where the terms of the leases call for the payment of taxes, insurance, maintenance costs, or other similar items, the auditor should see that these terms are being met.

In a first audit, the auditor should account for all major properties in use by reference to the fixed assets records or lease schedules. Thereafter, he need only account for the changes from year to year.

The annual worksheet is used to document the verification of money balances for the year.

1. Beginning and ending prepaid balances are compared with the closing balance of the previous year, and rent expense is compared with the prior year's rent expense. Significant variations should be accounted for.
2. Computation of the ending prepaid or accrued balance should be checked. In most cases, reasonable satisfaction can be achieved by a visual check without requiring actual recomputation.
3. Some of the indicated payments should be vouched. Where the leases are numerous, this can be limited to the major ones and, perhaps, a sampling of some of the less important leases. It is rarely necessary to vouch all 12 monthly payments. Generally, it will suffice to vouch only one monthly payment—preferably, the last required payment in the fiscal year.

Figure 2 SUMMARY OF LEASES

Property	Landlord	Expiration of present term	Annual rental: Amount	Annual rental: Special provisions	Renewal options	Other significant terms	Projected approximate minimum annual rentals: To 1970	1971-1975	1976-1980	1981-1990
Plant:										
Main building	Tina Realties, Inc.	12/31/90	127000	net lease (insurance, taxes, repairs)		$50,000 security deposit	127000	127000	127000	127000
Annex	1127 Corporation	11/30/70	70000	plus excess taxes over base period	10 year option at $80,000	Option to buy after 1970 - see copy of lease	70000	-	-	-
Garage	Sample Company, Inc.	5/31/75	20000 30000	to 5/31/70 6/1/70 to 5/31/75	10 year option at $35,000	$5,000 security deposit	20000	30000	-	-
Retail stores:										
White Plains	Blue Corporation	8/31/80	36360	5% of sales - minimum $36,360		Quarterly reports - annual certified	36360	36360	36360	-
Mount Vernon	Blue Corporation	9/30/79	29000	5% of sales - minimum $29,000		Quarterly report - annual certified	29000	29000	29000	-
Newark	Herjo, Incorporated	2/28/76	45000	plus 4% of sales over $1,000,000		Annual certified report	45000	45000	-	-
Administrative offices	Hermoline Bldg. Corp.	12/31/75	10000		2 five year options		10000	10000	-	-
		Aggregate minimum annual rentals (approximate)					337360	277360	192360	127000

Percentage rentals. Where a lease calls for percentage rentals, usually based on sales, the expense shown on the above-mentioned annual worksheet should be cross-referenced to a supporting schedule on which the computation of the percentage rental is presented. The auditor should see that the rates, definition of terms, and methods of computation conform to the lease provisions. It is particularly important to see that the sales base used in the computations conforms to the definition in the lease. Very often, certain items are considered as sales under a lease which are not recorded as sales in the company's accounts. Typical examples are vending-machine commissions, gross sales of subtenants or leased departments, and mail or phone orders filled from another location. Conversely, the lease may exclude certain kinds of sales or sales of certain merchandise.

Leases of this type usually contain certain reporting requirements, often including special reports required of the auditors. The auditors should see that the necessary reports are being filed as required.

Where the lease year does not correspond to the company's fiscal year, there is an additional matter of providing for the partial lease year that spans the fiscal year end. This provision may result in either an accrual or a prepayment at the fiscal year end, depending on the seasonal pattern of the company's sales and the effect of required minimum rent payments. While there are many ways of dealing with this provision, one such method is described below.

1. In the first fiscal year in which the lease becomes operative (fiscal year 1), the sales for the entire lease year are estimated on whatever basis is available and the rent is computed on such sales. The estimated rent is allocated to the fiscal year in the proportion of reportable sales included in the fiscal year to estimated sales for the entire lease year.
2. In fiscal year 2, the first lease year will have been completed and the actual rent for that year will have been established. From this information, the amount of estimation error introduced in fiscal year 1 can be determined. As a second step, the rent for the entire fiscal year 2 is computed as if it were a lease year. The amount so computed, plus an adjustment for the estimation error introduced in fiscal year 1, should be charged as rent expense for fiscal year 2.
3. In fiscal year 3 and thereafter, the rent expense for the year will be computed as if the fiscal year were a lease year. In each year, rent *payments* will be made in accordance with the terms of the lease (the auditor should see that this is the case). The difference between payments made and rent expense charged to operations will automatically produce an appropriate accrual or prepayment at the end of the fiscal year for the partial lease year.

In the foregoing computations, there is no need to scorn debit balances (prepayments) at the end of the year, if the company is subject to wide seasonal fluctuations and the minimum monthly rent payments exceed the allocable rent expense for the uncompleted lease year, provided there is reasonable assurance that the volume in the later months of the lease year will make up for the deficiency. Where there is any significant doubt that the minimum rental will be exceeded by the percentage rental at the completion of the lease year, the accrual should be based on minimum rentals rather than percentage rentals.

Deferred Advertising and Catalog Costs. Because advertising is a recurring cost without a fixed or determinable benefit period, advertising costs are ordinarily written off as period expenses when incurred. However, where the costs are for an advertising project that is in preparation or has not yet been released, deferral of costs to a subsequent period may be appropriate. Catalog costs are likewise written off as period costs unless the catalog has not yet been released or was released so close to the year end that it is practically still new.

Audit procedures. The auditor should inquire into the nature of the programs for which the costs are being deferred and consider whether there is reasonable assurance of future benefits to justify the deferral. Where the programs being deferred have not yet been completed, an estimate of the total cost at completion should be obtained. If his review reveals that the company has embarked on a major untried and costly new program, he should be alert to the effects of this program on other sections of his audit as well, such as the examination of inventories, property commitments, etc. For the items being deferred, he should see that similar items were consistently treated in the past.

The auditor should vouch the major payments included in the deferral and perhaps some of the smaller payments if they represent a substantial amount in the aggregate. He should be alert to the inclusion of any charges which are not directly related to the programs which are the subject of deferral.

Prepaid Subscriptions; Membership Dues. The auditor should obtain or prepare a listing of the items included in this caption and scan it for items unusual to the company's business. He should compare the listing with the prior year's and account for major variations, if any. If the amount is substantial in the aggregate, he should vouch a limited number of the items and eye-check the reasonableness of the prepaid portion.

Deposits; Down Payments; Option Payments. Although the amounts appearing under this caption are usually small, they are often the forerunner of transactions that can be very significant, and therefore they must be examined with great care. The examination is frequently complicated by the fact that complete information concerning the transaction is not readily available to the auditor. The people with whom the auditor normally comes in contact may not be fully aware of the transactions or negotiations in progress. Such negotiations may be highly sensitive and, for that reason, are being handled on a discreet and confidential basis, with little information being disseminated beyond the small group of people actually involved in the negotiations. Nevertheless, the auditor has a legitimate interest in these activities and must pursue his examination to the point where he is satisfied that he has been apprised of all facts relevant to his examination.

Audit procedures. The auditor should obtain or prepare an analysis of the ledger account showing all transactions for the year.

1. Items which existed in the prior year and had been covered in a previous examination should be traced to the prior year's working papers; the likelihood of their remaining valid should be considered.
2. The disposition of all closed items should be determined.
3. All additions during the year should be vouched unless they are clearly of a minor, routine, and insignificant nature. The objective here is discovery. The auditor should examine any agreement to which the deposit relates and conclusively identify the deposit with the agreement. The vouching of additions is not complete if it is confined merely to the examination of a canceled check.
4. Deposits of significant amount should be confirmed.

5. In his examination in other areas, he should be alert to the possibility that deposits or option payments may have been made and charged to other accounts, such as miscellaneous expenses, accounts receivable, or legal expense (if, for example, the payment was made through an attorney's billing for fees and costs).

Prepaid Postage. The amounts of prepaid postage are rarely significant, and extensive auditing is usually not warranted. The auditor can generally satisfy himself as to the reasonableness of the recorded amount by his general familiarity with the company and by inquiry as to how the amount was determined. He can also perform some or all of the following additional procedures:

1. He may review the pattern of purchases immediately before and after the year end; considering the lapse of time, he may come to a fair conclusion as to the reasonableness of the amount stated.
2. At some time during his audit, he may count the postage stamps and take meter readings, and may see that the amounts at that time are generally in line with the amounts recorded at the year end. If he is present at the company's premises on the last day of the fiscal year for any other purpose, he may make his counts then, if time permits. However, a special trip just for this purpose is hardly ever necessary.
3. Where postage meters are in use, a log book of daily usage is often maintained, and this can be used to corroborate the amounts stated.

Employee Advances; Prepaid Commissions. Employee advances represent funds made available to employees for expenditures to be made on behalf of the company. The expenditures made by the employees are recorded by the company on the basis of periodic reports submitted. Some companies will request employees to render an expense report as of the close of the fiscal year in order to obtain a clean cutoff. In other situations, the company will have decided that the amounts involved do not warrant this procedure; it will carry the expense advance at the full amount over the balance sheet date, even though some unknown portion of it may have already been expended.

Prepaid commissions represent advances made against future commission earnings. Such advances may or may not be recoverable if unearned, depending upon the arrangements the company has with its salesmen.

An important characteristic of these accounts is that they are usually made up of a great many individually small balances which represent important amounts in the aggregate. Because of the mass of detail and because internal control typically is weak over the originating of an advance and the related record keeping, this area is somewhat sensitive to misappropriations. Occasionally, the advances and prepaid commissions will also include outright loans to the employees, which of course should be reclassified or segregated in a separate loan account.

Audit procedures. The auditor should prepare or obtain a trial balance of the individual items. If he does not prepare the trial balance himself, he should trace the trial balance to the detailed records; or, if it is excessively lengthy, he may select portions of the trial balance for tracing to the detailed records. Footings should be checked and tied in to the control balance.

1. The trial balance should be scanned for any large balances which appear to be uncharacteristic. The auditor should consider the reasonableness of the total, perhaps by comparison with the prior year's total, and should also consider the reasonableness of the number of individual items listed. If the

trial balance provides subtotals by sales districts or other similar groupings, then such comparisons can be even more meaningful.

2. The auditor should check or verify some of the details. Although this can be accomplished by vouching the advance and examining subsequent reports, the simplest and most positive approach is by direct confirmation from the employee. Where the confirmation approach is adopted, the auditor must be on guard to maintain the integrity of his confirmation procedures. There is a strong temptation in these situations to hand over the confirmation requests to the company for distribution through its normal channels for communication with employees. These channels are not appropriate for audit verification, since the request or the response may be subject to interception by unauthorized persons.

3. The auditor should consider whether or not any portion of the balance should be written off. Where the company has not adopted the practice of making a clean cutoff of expense reports at the fiscal year end, the auditor may select a small but representative sample of subsequent expense reports and determine what portion of the amount shown as an advance at the fiscal year end had already been expended by the employees at that date. From this sampling he can then project an approximation of the total amount of advances which should be charged off to expense for the fiscal year. A similar procedure may be adopted with prepaid commissions, although commissions are usually accounted for on the basis of periods which coincide with the company's fiscal periods. The auditor should also consider whether or not the prepaid commissions account includes any amounts of minimum commissions which will not be recovered.

Miscellaneous Other Assets. Unless clearly trivial in amount, any accounts with vague or catch-all titles should be explored fully to the extent necessary to assure the auditor that he has a clear understanding of their contents. This would apply not only to miscellaneous other assets but also to miscellaneous liabilities, miscellaneous income, and miscellaneous expense. It is prudent to adopt the attitude that any transaction which cannot be accommodated by the established descriptive accounts may have some unusual circumstances attached to it that could be of audit significance. Even where the balance of an account is very small, the ledger record should be scanned to see that the balance does not represent the net result of several more substantial offsetting, but unrelated, debits and credits.

NONCURRENT INTANGIBLE ASSETS INCLUDING GOODWILL

Earlier in this chapter, the principal characteristics that distinguish the noncurrent intangibles from the current intangibles were set forth. Briefly restated, the characteristics are as follows:

1. The noncurrent intangible assets are obviously longer-lived than the current assets.
2. They usually originate from extraordinary or infrequent transactions, rather than from the normal day-to-day operations of the business.
3. They are more often in the nature of deferred charges rather than prepaid expenses; thus, their useful lives are not as readily determinable.
4. The individual items usually represent rather sizable dollar amounts (otherwise, the company would not bother to defer them).

These characteristics have an unmistakable influence on the auditor's approach. While a few simple comparisons and spot checks may satisfy the auditor as to the cost of the current intangibles, a much more direct and positive verification is necessary for the larger dollar amounts in the noncurrent intangibles. Furthermore, the elements of cost are likely to be considerably more complex, and thus their verification will be more difficult. Once the verification of cost has been accomplished, it need not be repeated again year after year, but the long duration of these assets presents another major problem, which is of only slight concern with current assets.

For the items in current assets, the existence of a future benefit can usually be assumed without undue risk of a misstatement. In fact, in the case of prepaid expenses, which constitute most of the current asset items, the future benefit can be directly related to a formal arrangement which confers the benefit, such as an insurance policy, a lease, a tax law, etc. This is not the case with respect to the noncurrent intangibles. Many of the items in the latter category do not have any assured benefits over a determinable life, and, therefore, the benefits and the life of the items must be estimated on whatever bases may be available. Even where a fixed and determinable formal life is present, as in the case of a patent or copyright, the actual benefit period rarely coincides with the formal life. Patent and copyright costs are written off over the estimated benefit period, which may be of only a few years' duration rather than over the full 17 or 28 years stipulated in the engraved documents. Even where the benefit period had been established initially on what was thought to be a conservative basis, that period may be abruptly curtailed by new inventions or shifts in taste. Therefore, at the outset, and at each examination thereafter, the auditor must evaluate and reassess the existence of a future benefit period that will justify continuing the deferral and maintaining the amortization policies, if any, with respect to the costs under examination.

The audit of noncurrent intangibles therefore entails, initially, the verification of recorded costs, and thereafter the gathering of data to demonstrate the existence of a future benefit sufficient to justify the deferral of such costs.

There are a great number of different kinds of items that may be found in the noncurrent intangibles, and the auditor is likely to encounter relatively few items in each audit situation. This is another distinguishing feature of the noncurrent intangibles. In the current assets, there are relatively few kinds of items, most of which are usually present in every audit situation.

Regardless of the variety of items that may be encountered, the procedures for verifying costs are directed to the sources from which the costs originated, and they can be classified into two broad categories:

1. Costs originating from a direct purchase, either of a specific item or a group of items, i.e., a "basket purchase."
2. Costs internally generated, which may include some direct purchases.

Procedures for establishing the existence of a future benefit are not directly related to the form in which the deferred cost originated. These procedures will generally be common to all forms of origin and therefore will be discussed separately herein.

Opinions of the Accounting Principles Board. In August, 1970, the Accounting Principles Board of the American Institute of Certified Public Accountants released two opinions of far reaching impact on the accounting for intangible assets. Opinion No. 16, *Business Combinations*, deals with acquisition of intangibles, including goodwill, through a business combination and measuring and allocating costs of the acquisition. Opinion No. 17, *Intangible Assets,* deals with the accounting for intangible assets including amortization policies. Both opinions became effective for transactions occurring after October 31, 1970, and are not to be applied retroactively for prior transactions; however, special rules provide for prospective application to prior transactions in certain cases, and for the treatment of transactions in process at the time the opinions became effective. These opinions will be referred to in more detail in the following discussion.

Purchased Items. Following are typical examples of noncurrent intangible assets arising from a purchase:

Franchises
Royalty or license contracts
Water rights
Mining, timber, or fishing rights
Copyrights
Patents
Name lists
Trade routes
Scripts, scenarios, story or film rights
Formulas and processes
Brand or trade names
Goodwill (or excess of cost over value of assets acquired)

Any of the foregoing items, except goodwill, may have been acquired by a specific purchase, or it may have been acquired together with other assets as part of a "basket purchase." Goodwill can arise only from the latter type of transaction, since it cannot be severed and sold separately.

Specific purchases. Specific purchases are, of course, the easiest to verify. Ordinarily, examination of the purchase documents and some evidence of payment (or obligation to pay) will establish the existence of the purchase and the cost of the item.

Before leaving the matter at that point, however, the auditor must first consider the possibility that the transaction may not, in fact, be a specific purchase of substance, but merely a sham to obscure the true nature of the underlying transactions between the parties. Because the value of intangibles cannot usually be established with any degree of certainty, their ostensible purchase or sale sometimes becomes a convenient vehicle for masking some other transaction. One typical example is the segmenting of what is, in reality, a "basket purchase" in order to influence the allocation of purchase price among the various assets acquired (see under the heading "Basket Purchases" below). The device might also be used to conceal the making of a confidential investment in another business. Many other examples, sinister and otherwise, could be offered. While no specific audit tests can be applied to reveal these situations, the auditor should be watchful for any other relationship between the parties, any significant change in the company's activities at about the time of the transaction or following thereafter which cannot otherwise be accounted for, and a purchase price assigned to the transaction which appears to be radically inconsistent with the value of the benefits to be derived.

Basket purchases. "Basket purchase" refers to the acquisition of a group of assets in a single transaction (or in a series of related transactions) for a lump-sum price. The most typical example is the purchase of an entire business by one party from another. ("Poolings of interest" are excluded, by definition, from a discussion of purchases.)

In these purchases, the total price must be allocated among the various assets on some rational basis, since the costs assigned to the various assets will be charged off to operations at varying rates and may also have differing income tax attributes. The assets acquired may be both tangible and intangible assets, and, in the allocation process, costs may be allocated for the first time to certain intangible assets which had not previously been articulated (such as brand names, franchises, private formulas, etc., and goodwill). There is a valid presumption that the existence of these intangibles influenced the negotiation of a purchase price between the parties even though the seller had not previously recorded the intangibles on his books.

ALLOCATION OF PRICE: Occasionally, the purchase documents drawn up between the parties will stipulate a price for each of the various assets acquired. The auditor should be wary of accepting these documents at face value. Once the parties have completed their negotiations and arrived at an acceptable total purchase price, the subsequent dissection of that agreed price in the purchase documents may be self-serving and need not necessarily follow the actual agreements that were reached on an item-by-item basis. In any basket purchase, the auditor is obliged to view the transaction in its entirety and consider whether the allocation of the total has been made on a fair and rational basis.

The total negotiated purchase price represents the aggregate cost of the acquisition to the purchaser, and the objective is to dissect this total cost so that each of the individual assets acquired may also be stated at cost. Assuming that a fair price in total was negotiated by the parties, it follows then that each of the individual elements was also priced at its fair value. Since the fair value of noncurrent intangible assets cannot usually be determined with any great degree of assurance, the purchase price is allocated first to those assets exclusive of the noncurrent intangible assets. The remainder, if any, is then allocated to whatever noncurrent intangible assets were acquired, other than goodwill. If a balance still remains after the foregoing allocations, that balance is presumed to apply to purchased goodwill (often labeled in financial statements by the more cautious caption, "excess of cost over fair value of assets acquired").

NEGATIVE GOODWILL: Some form of "negative goodwill" may arise where the fair value of the acquired assets exceeds the total purchase price. In such cases, the values assigned should be reexamined to see if they have been determined on a sufficiently conservative basis. Sometimes the negative goodwill arises from the greater negotiating skill of the purchaser to produce a true bargain purchase. More often, however, the negative goodwill is merely illusory and the depressed purchase price represents a recognition by the parties of some inherent defect in the assets acquired.

The true nature of the apparent negative goodwill must be identified in order to give it the proper treatment. When it arises from some impairment of specific assets, it should, of course, be applied in reduction of the value assigned to those assets. Where an operating business was acquired in which extensive rehabilitation will be required (such as eliminating ineffective personnel and hiring and training new employees, revitalizing marketing programs, revising inefficient production techniques, etc.), the negative goodwill probably arose from a recognition of these conditions and may be carried as a deferred credit to which the purchaser's necessary rehabilitation expenses are charged as incurred. In these situations, it would appear at first blush that the acquired assets are stated at amounts which exceed cost to the extent of the deferred credit. This is not the case, however, since the deferred credit is in reality a provision for additional costs still to be incurred in connection with the acquisition.

In those cases where a careful evaluation indicates that the fair value of the net assets acquired does, in fact, exceed the cost of the acquisition, then the resultant negative goodwill must be dealt with. APB Opinion No. 16 specifies that the negative goodwill must first be applied proportionately to reduce noncurrent assets (other than long-term investments in marketable securities). Negative goodwill may not be carried as a deferred credit unless a balance survives after the foregoing allocations have reduced those noncurrent assets to zero value. The remainder, then, may be carried as a deferred credit and amortized in the same way as positive goodwill. (See "Amortization and Future Benefits" below.) Prior to the adoption of APB Opinion No. 16, application of negative goodwill to noncurrent assets was not required.

DETERMINING FAIR VALUE: As previously indicated, the cost of the individual assets acquired in a basket purchase is determined by allocating the total cost in proportion to the fair values of the individual assets. Furthermore, in this process, the allocation is made first to those assets for which the fair value is most readily demonstrable. Thus, the allocation would first be made to the various current assets, noncurrent receivables and investments, and fixed assets before the remainder of purchase price, if any, is allocated to the noncurrent intangibles.

For the current assets, book values of the seller are useful, but not necessarily conclusive, indicators of fair value—the amounts assigned to bad debt reserves and the inventory valuations would require particular scrutiny. The book values are not quite as useful for the noncurrent assets, since they are stated at cost (or amortized cost) to the predecessor, which rarely reflects the current market conditions. In valuing long-term receivables, interest rates as well as collection risks must be considered. Long-term investments, even if represented by marketable securities, must take into consideration the size of the investment and the price that would prevail for the purchase of an investment of that size in a single transaction. Long-term investments and fixed assets may require a qualified expert's appraisal if the market value cannot be reasonably ascertained by other means.

Because the value of the noncurrent intangible assets is usually more obscure than that of the assets mentioned above, the foregoing allocations are made before any excess purchase price is deemed to exist for allocation to the noncurrent intangible assets. The basket purchase must be scrutinized to identify the intangibles which may have been acquired, such as trade names, circulation lists, patents, or any of the other items previously listed in this section. The allocation of the excess purchase price to these assets must be made on some viable and rational basis. These values cannot be determined with any degree of certainty, but, among other things, the auditor might consider the potential future benefits to be derived from assets as such potential benefits appeared to exist at the time of negotiation. (Changed conditions or circumstances subsequent to the negotiations should not affect any of the allocations unless they also changed the outcome of the negotiations; the changed conditions should be considered only in the determination of write-off or amortization requirements after the allocations have been made.)

Determining Purchase Price, or "Cost." "Cost" has been defined as the fair value of consideration given or consideration received, whichever is the more readily determinable. All of the foregoing discussion has dealt with the problems of establishing the fair value of consideration received, as if the fair value of the consideration given (and, consequently, the "cost") had already been unquestionably established. However, purchases frequently involve complexities in valuing the consideration given, as well as the consideration received. These complexities arise whenever the consideration given entails anything other than a lump-sum immediate cash payment. Some examples of these complexities are presented below.

1. When the payment is to be made over a period of time, the reasonableness of the stipulated interest rate must be considered in light of current money market conditions; and if no interest is stipulated, an interest factor may nevertheless have to be imputed.
2. Where the purchaser has agreed to assume certain obligations of the seller, these liabilities must be evaluated and added to the cost of the purchase.
3. The cost may also include expenditures necessary to cure a substandard condition inherent in the consideration received, as was mentioned under the heading "Negative Goodwill."
4. The acquisition may be coupled with other agreements between the parties, such as employment agreements, service or merchandise purchase contracts, leases for properties retained by the seller, etc., at contract amounts inconsistent with the subject matter of the contract which, in effect, represent adjustments to the purchase price of the acquisition.
5. Frequently, the purchase will be made partly or entirely with stock of the purchaser being given in payment. The value of such stock should ordinarily be taken at the time the negotiations were settled. Determining that value may be complicated by the fact that the traded market value may have been influenced by publicity concerning the proposed acquisition. This is not necessarily an unfair influence (doesn't it reflect an independent appraisal of the situation by the public?), but it can be subject to severe distortions from situation to situation, depending on the amount and reliability of information being circulated.
6. The purchase price often includes a contingent pay-out, especially where significant intangibles are involved in the purchase. The parties themselves may have encountered the same kind of difficulty in valuing the intangibles as has previously been described, and accordingly may set the price, contingently, on the basis of demonstrated benefits to be received—for example, on the basis of profits or sales to be derived over a fixed future period from the acquired assets. Sometimes the terms of these arrangements are tantamount to a profit-sharing agreement between the parties. More often, however, the contingent payments represent bona fide additions to the asset purchase price and should be added to the cost of the acquisition from time to time as the contingencies are eliminated (for example, when the specified profits have been achieved).

Paragraphs 67 and 72 to 86 of APB Opinion No. 16 deal in detail with various complexities in determining cost. The auditor should have a clear understanding of these provisions at the time of his examination.

Deferred Charges Internally Developed. The following are typical examples of other assets arising from the deferral of internally developed costs:

Research and development
Patent development and perfecting costs (including costs to defend or pursue infringement suits)

Pre-operating, pre-opening, or start-up costs
Moving expense
Plant rearrangement or relocation expenses

The costs for items of this kind have passed through the normal accounting structure of the company and are not readily distinguishable on the records from any other costs, except that they have been separately accumulated, segregated, and reclassified to a special category. Labor and material costs pass through the normal payroll and materials requisition procedures of the company. Expenditures for special purchases of materials or services pass through the normal cash disbursement operations of the company.

These systems will have been tested by the auditor in other phases of his examination. If any important costs originate in sources which have not been previously tested, these sources must, of course, be tested for the deferral. For example, if an experimental laboratory ordinarily charges all of its payroll costs directly to expense but during the past year worked at times on a special project the costs of which are to be deferred, it may be that the timekeeping functions within that department had never before been tested by the auditor to see that costs were properly allocated between programs. The auditor then must extend his scrutiny into the procedures of this department to see that proper charges are being added to the program which is being deferred. Similarly, if special purchases are being made which bypass the normal purchasing activities and the purchasing department of the company, these special purchasing procedures must also be scrutinized. The auditor should obtain or prepare an analysis of the costs entering into the program, showing in full detail their nature and origin in order that he may vouch or trace the items to their source and assess their reasonableness.

Occasionally, the auditor is confronted with the situation in which the company has come to a decision to defer certain costs long after the costs have been incurred. For example, some months after a plant rearrangement has been completed, the company management may decide that the costs of the rearrangement should have been accumulated for a deferral over a future benefit period. It may then find, however, that steps had not been taken, at the time the rearrangement was actually going on, in order to capture the necessary cost information for accumulation as a deferred charge. Much of the rearrangement may have been performed by the maintenance department, which did not keep job records of any kind. The costs relating to this kind of item can usually be estimated with sufficient support and basis for the estimates to satisfy the auditor. Where outside purchases of materials and services were an important element in the cost of the item, such costs can usually be reconstructed by a search of the disbursement records. Labor costs can be approximated by identifying the individuals who worked on the program and the approximate period of time they were so occupied. As an alternative approach, or as additional corroboration, the various tasks that had to be accomplished can be listed, and approximate time and material requirements can be estimated for each task. Perhaps even the individuals occupied in these tasks may be identifiable. Production records which show dips or interruptions in production may further serve to pinpoint the period of time during which the rearrangement took place. With sufficient corroborating indications from several different sources, the auditor should be in a position to satisfy himself as to the reasonableness of the amounts estimated.

Amortization and Future Benefits. The existence of a deferred charge carries with it a presumption that there is some future benefit to be derived from the intangible asset and that such future benefit will equal or exceed the amount of the costs deferred. This presumption must be tested by the auditor.

The auditor must satisfy himself that the future benefit exists to an extent sufficient to justify the amount of the deferred charge. When it appears that a future benefit does not exist, the related deferred charge should be written off. Where the auditor is in doubt as to its existence, he may have to qualify his report or deny an opinion if the related deferred charge is material. If he is satisfied that a future benefit exists, he must further consider the duration of the benefit period since amortization policies are based on that period.

APB Opinion No. 17 establishes amortization policies for intangibles acquired after November 1, 1970. Briefly, it provides that all intangibles are to be amortized over the period expected to be benefited, but in no case may that period be deemed to exceed forty years from date of acquisition. Intangibles may not be amortized over a period *shorter* than the expected benefit period, except, of course, for the forty-year limitation. Amortization should be on the straight-line method unless some other systematic method is demonstrated to be more appropriate in the given circumstances.

The opinion also deals with intangibles acquired prior to its effective date, November 1, 1970. It states that such assets may be amortized (prospectively only) in accordance with its provisions, or in accordance with standards existing prior to its adoption. The forty-year limitation and attendant mandatory amortization did not exist prior to APB Opinion No. 17 with respect to intangibles of perpetual or indefinite duration.

Deferred charges with a limited benefit period should be systematically amortized over that period. For example, product development costs, patents, or copyrights should be amortized over the period of expected substantial sales of the product or copyrighted materials. On this basis, a copyright on a highly topical book would be amortized over the relatively short period during which sales of the book are expected to be active, rather than over the full 28-year legal life of the copyright. Even though a reasonable amortization period has been established at the outset, that period may have to be abruptly curtailed or shortened if it becomes clear that the future benefit has been reduced because of obsolescence or other factors. Paragraph 27 of APB Opinion No. 17 cites some of the factors that will affect the duration of the expected benefit period.

Goodwill and trademarks are typical examples of deferred charges with indefinite or perpetual benefit periods. These items, if acquired prior to November 1, 1970, need not have been amortized, although some companies had adopted amortization policies for them without being required to do so. Where they were not being amortized prior to November 1, 1970, APB Opinion No. 17 encourages, but does not require, the adoption of amortization prospectively for the remainder of the period ending forty years from date of acquisition.

Establishing the existence of a future benefit thus becomes a major concern to the auditor in evaluating the deferred charges and the amortization policies applicable to them. In making his evaluation, the auditor may take into consideration the following:

1. The expressed intentions and expectations of management. Where the deferred charge was recently acquired through a purchase, he may also consider the expressed representations of the seller.

2. Past history of productiveness of the deferred charge or, if recently created, of similar items.

3. The results of market studies, sales forecasts, or profit projections, if available. These, in turn, must also be challenged for credibility. The absence of any of these might indicate that management itself has not made an adequate appraisal of future benefits.

4. Observation of a course of action or activity within the company which corroborates or negates the expressed intentions and expectations of management. For example, the validity of deferred product development cost might be supported by the initiation of an extensive advertising campaign or the setting up of production facilities.

No one of the foregoing considerations is necessarily conclusive by itself, nor are the foregoing the only available indicators. However, they suggest the kinds of things the auditor should look for in making his evaluation. Needless to say, the results of the evaluation should be well documented in the auditor's workpapers. Comparison of these results from year to year will serve as a further indicator as to whether or not the potential for future benefits seems to be changing.

BIBLIOGRAPHY

Accounting Research Bulletin No. 43, Chapter 5, AICPA, June, 1953.

APB Opinion No. 16, *Business Combinations,* AICPA, August, 1970.

APB Opinion No. 17, *Intangible Assets,* AICPA, August, 1970.

Catlett, George R., and Norman O. Olson: Accounting Research Study No. 10, *Accounting for Goodwill,* AICPA, 1968.

Wyatt, Arthur R.: Accounting Research Study No. 5, *A Critical Study of Accounting for Business Combinations,* AICPA, 1963.

Backer, Morton, ed.: *Modern Accounting Theory,* Englewood Cliffs, N.J., Prentice-Hall, Inc., 1968.

Cashin, James A., and G. C. Owens: *Auditing,* 2d ed., New York, The Ronald Press Company, 1963.

Lenhart, Norman J., and Philip L. Defliese: *Montgomery's Auditing,* 8th ed., New York, The Ronald Press Company, 1957.

Stettler, Howard F.: *Auditing Principles: Objectives, Procedures, Working Papers,* Englewood Cliffs, N.J., Prentice-Hall, Inc., 1967.

Wixon, Rufus, et al.: *Accountants' Handbook,* 5th ed., New York, The Ronald Press Company, 1970.

New York State Society of Certified Public Accountants, Committee on Accounting and Auditing Procedures: "Valuation of Intangible Inventory," *The New York Certified Public Accountant,* February, 1968.

Kelly, Daniel J.: "Accounting for Start-up Costs," *The New York Certified Public Accountant,* November, 1968.

Burns, Arthur E.: "Profits, Net Worth and the Tax Court: Precedents in Renegotiation," *Federal Accountant,* March, 1969.

Lall, R. M.: "Tangibility in Asset Accounting—A Plea for a New Approach," *Accountancy* (England), May, 1969.

Copeland, Ronald M., and Joseph J. Wojdak: "Valuation of Unrecorded Goodwill in Merger-minded Firms," *Financial Analysts Journal,* September–October, 1969.

Moore, Carl L.: "Deferred Income Tax—Is It a Liability?" *The New York Certified Public Accountant,* February, 1970.

Chapter 27

Current Liabilities

SAUL FELDMAN

Assistant Professor of Accounting, Hofstra University

GENERAL

In the examination of current liabilities, the auditor is faced with two distinct, but related, problems. The first deals with the valuation of liabilities; the second, with the discovery of those liabilities which, for one reason or another, have not been reflected in the accounts. An invoice from a supplier is, after all, stated at a given amount and, unless there is some dispute with respect to one or several of the items on the bill, will be entered as a payable in the normal course of operations and be paid. Unentered invoices, and liabilities which may arise from a variety of sources and of which the company has no knowledge, require even more attention from the auditor than the former.

Disclosure of Data. Auditing, after all, is concerned to a very large extent with the protection of those who read financial statements. A balance sheet, for example, asserts that the enterprise has certain assets and that there are claims against those assets as stated. It further asserts that those items are appropriately disclosed and described. But a balance sheet also asserts the nonexistence of all items not so listed. In other words, a balance sheet not only makes positive statements concerning the listed items but says, in effect, that there are no other items in any category of a material nature which are not listed or otherwise disclosed.

Stating Current Liabilities. Stating current liabilities correctly, therefore, is of paramount importance. Credit grantors, for example, depend to some extent on both the current asset and the current liability figures to give them an approximation of the working capital position of the firm—one of the chief indicators of ability to pay maturing obligations. It is, therefore, one of the factors in determining whether the debtor is worthy of having his credit extended, maintained, or, possibly, curtailed. Knowledgeable investors and their financial analysts use the current asset–current liability picture as a means of estimating the firm's needs for working capital in the near future. Management, with its more intimate knowledge of the firm's operational requirements for the future, will also use this as a starting point for assessing the firm's needs for additional working capital by drawing up a cash-flow budget. In evaluating the ability of contractors to perform according to schedule, or in deciding whether to accept a delayed-payment schedule for back taxes, the federal government is also interested in this relationship between current assets and current liabilities. In fact, the proper reporting of current liabilities can be of such overriding importance that a great deal of attention and time may have to be paid to this phase of the audit examination.

What Are Current Liabilities? The American Institute of Certified Public Accountants, in its Accounting Research Bulletin, final edition, defines "current liabilities" as follows:

> The term *current liabilities* is used primarily to designate obligations whose liquidation is reasonably expected to require the use of existing resources properly classifiable as current assets, or the creation of other current liabilities. As a balance sheet category, the classification is intended to include obligations for items which have entered into the operating cycle, such as payables incurred in the acquisition of materials and supplies to be used in the production of goods or in providing services to be offered for sale; collections received in advance of the delivery of goods or performance of services; and debts which arise from operations directly related to the operating cycle, such as accruals for wages, salaries, commissions, rentals, royalties, and income or other taxes. . . .

Furthermore,

> this concept of current liabilities would include estimated or accrued amounts which are expected to be required to cover expenditures within the year for known obligations (*a*) the amount of which can be determined only approximately (as in the case of provisions for accruing bonus payments) or (*b*) where the specific person to whom payment will be made cannot as yet be designated (as in the case of estimated costs to be incurred in connection with guaranteed servicing or repair of products already sold). The current liability classification however is not intended to include a contractual obligation falling due at an early date which is expected to be refunded, or debts to be liquidated by funds which have been accumulated in accounts of a type not properly classified as current assets, or long-term obligations incurred to provide increased amounts of working capital for long periods. . . .

Based on the above definition, the following would be included within the current liability category:

1. Trade liabilities resulting from the acquisition of materials and supplies. This category would include not only trade accounts payable but also trade acceptances and notes payable.
2. Deposits received from customers, or advances received for magazine or newspaper subscriptions, tickets to all kinds of events, or any other types of deposits where the performance of services will be made in the near future in the ordinary course of business.
3. Accruals for obligations arising from operations during the operating

cycle under review such as salaries and wages, taxes, all other operating expenses, royalties, rentals, etc.

4. Deposits made to the client to guarantee the performance of contracts or the payment of bills, or to ensure the return of containers.
5. All other obligations which are expected to be liquidated within a relatively short period of time, such as loans and notes payable, serial maturities of long-term obligations, etc.
6. Accruals resulting from operations, even though:
   a. The amount of such accrual must be approximated, e.g., bonus payments.
   b. The specific individuals and/or organizations are not known, e.g., guaranteed service costs or repairs under warranties.
   c. They must be measured by current transactions such as:
      (1) Rents or revenues received.
      (2) Property obligations measured by depletion of natural resources.

AUDIT OBJECTIVES

The Public Accountant. The objectives of the audit of current liabilities may be stated as to make certain:

1. That all liabilities already on the books are properly valued.
2. That all liabilities of a material nature are properly disclosed.
3. That all current liabilities are properly classified and presented on the balance sheet so as to disclose significant relationships and amounts.
4. That all internal control and internal check procedures with respect to the incurrence, recording, and payment of current liabilities are being observed.

The first two objectives deal with the proper evaluation and discovery of all current liabilities and represent, therefore, the basic problems confronting the auditor. The third objective deals with the presentation of current liabilities on the balance sheet in a manner to disclose, for example, all current liabilities secured by company assets, the segregation of specific liabilities representing such items as federal income taxes, current maturities of serial or other bonded indebtedness, and any other significant items. The fourth objective, the evaluation of existing internal control and internal check procedures, represents the means by which the auditor can determine the extent to which actual audit procedures and tests will have to be made during the course of the audit engagement. As such, it represents one of the key elements not only in the audit of current liabilities but in all other sections of the financial statements. This aspect of the audit of current liabilities will be discussed in greater detail in a subsequent portion of this chapter.

It might be well, at this point, to mention one of the matters involved in any audit engagement which may arise subsequently to plague the auditor unless he is aware of its importance. It is vitally important that the auditor be continually aware of the necessity of keeping adequate workpapers to disclose not only those items which will eventually appear on the balance sheet, but also those items which will not appear, the basis upon which the various decisions were made, and other matters that disclose the extent and nature of the auditor's work in this area. A more complete discussion of audit workpapers and their importance appears in Chapter 14.

The Internal Auditor. The objectives of the internal auditor in the audit of current liabilities are not really different from those of the CPA. However, there can be said to be a difference in emphasis. Where the independent auditor will tend to concentrate on the first two objectives, utilizing the fourth to determine the extent of his actual audit procedures, the internal auditor will tend to concentrate on the internal control aspects of current liabilities. The reason is that he will be more concerned than his CPA counterpart with the day-to-day operations of his company, and, therefore, he will be more keenly alive to the possibilities inherent in the operational characteristics of the organization.

However, of more concern to management in its day-to-day operations are the possibilities of effecting economies in the handling of the paper work surrounding the receipt of goods and/or services, the process of recording suppliers' invoices, and finally, their payment. Through his observations and analyses of these procedures the internal auditor can, by using his imagination and analytical abilities, make a real contribution to the operational efficiency of the organization.

PLANNING THE AUDIT OF CURRENT LIABILITIES

In any engagement it is important that the auditor plan his audit work carefully so that he covers the details of his audit program as efficiently as possible and with the least amount of inconvenience to himself and to his client. Furthermore, it is generally possible to perform certain types of work on an interim basis. Thus the auditor need not schedule all of his work into a relatively short time period toward the end of the engagement.

Prior to Year End. The basic interim work to be performed in any engagement is the examination of internal control and the review of the client's procedures for handling various types of transactions. The purpose, of course, is to satisfy the auditor that the client's system of recording transactions and safeguarding company assets actually accomplishes its intended purpose. This serves as a guide toward the actual testing of transactions during the course of the subsequent examination. It is as the result of this internal control examination that the auditor must reach a decision as to whether he should make any modifications in his audit program or should allow that program to remain as originally conceived.

Generally speaking, therefore, the examination of internal control should take place prior to the beginning of the actual audit, for the aforementioned reasons. As a part of this internal control examination in the area of current liabilities, the auditor should examine the extent and kind of work performed in this area by the internal audit staff so as to reach a judgment on how much work he should do.

In the area of current liabilities, however, the possibilities of doing some actual audit work prior to the beginning of the engagement are limited only by the amount of staff the outside auditor is willing to commit at that time, the extent and kind of cooperation the client is able and willing to give him, and the requirements of the program itself. In general, however, the following steps should be considered as areas in which some actual audit work can be performed prior to the end of the fiscal year:

1. Footing the books of original entry and tracing those totals to the general ledger
2. Examination of receiving records and suppliers' invoices

3. Analyses of notes payable accounts with suppliers, banks, and other creditors, and their related aspects
4. Analyses of payroll and other tax liability accounts and their related matters
5. Examination of contracts, loan agreements, etc., entered into during the year, in an effort to determine their effect on the year-end statements
6. Examination of minutes of board of directors' meetings near the end of the fiscal year to determine any dividend liability or other matters which may affect the current liability picture
7. Observation of client's practices in the handling, recording, and payment of suppliers' invoices in order to gauge the amount of work needed for the discovery of unrecorded liabilities at year end
8. The retention of attorneys for the handling of lawsuits which might give rise to contingent or actual liabilities

The above, of course, does not exhaust all of the possibilities in this area. The auditor must be continuously aware of the possibility of doing as much of the work on current liabilities as possible prior to the end of the year in order to have an opportunity to investigate significant and important items while they may still be fresh in the minds of company officials.

Year-end Work. As part of his year-end procedures the auditor will do some of the work on liabilities at the same time. The following represents the principal audit procedures in this area which can or should be considered at this time:

1. Selection of trade creditors to whom requests for confirmation of balances will be mailed, and the mailing of such requests.
2. Circularization of banks and other financial institutions with respect to outstanding loans, discounted notes, etc., plus a listing of company assets either held or pledged as security for such loans and advances.
3. The drafting and mailing of letters to bond indenture trustees with respect to outstanding bond issues, unpaid interest thereon, and other matters which may affect current liabilities.
4. Letters to company attorneys requesting information as to the status of any suits brought against the client company and the amounts involved, plus the liability for any legal fees to date.
5. In connection with the observation of inventory, a visit to the receiving platform and/or storeroom will disclose incoming shipments which have not been processed as yet. These should be listed by vendor and receiving-ticket number for consideration for inclusion in or exclusion from both the inventory and/or accounts payable. At the same time, the final receiving-ticket number for the fiscal year should be noted for the workpapers for later use.
6. Again, in connection with the inventory observation, a visit to the shipping department and/or platform will disclose vendors' returns awaiting shipment. A list of those should be made and the shipping documents in connection therewith examined and pertinent extracts made for the work-papers.
7. The auditor should consider the nature and extent of the client's outstanding purchase commitments at this time, particularly with respect to items of raw materials, supplies, and finished goods which tend to fluctuate rather widely in price and which are consumed in large quantities.

Again it must be pointed out that the above procedures for year-end work are not intended to be all-inclusive but represent the principal matters which might normally be accomplished prior to the beginning of the year-end work. Here, as elsewhere, the work to be performed will ultimately be the result of the auditor's judgment based upon the conditions he finds at a particular time.

During the Engagement. At this point the auditor must plan to complete all the steps in his program on current liabilities which he has been unable to complete up to now. In general the work to be performed will consist of the following:

1. Examination of vendors' invoices for a few days prior to and a few days after the close of the fiscal year to determine if all liabilities for merchandise received have been recorded
2. Checking confirmations received against the trial balance of accounts payable and the reconciliation of any differences
3. Bringing the analyses of liability accounts up to the end of the fiscal period
4. Examination of correspondence with those vendors whose confirmations indicate significant and material differences in amounts due as of the close of the fiscal year
5. Analyses of tax payment liability accounts. The problem at this point is not so much the liability for payroll taxes but for federal, state, and local income taxes
6. Checking client's computation of the liability for accruals for wages, salaries, commissions, rentals, royalties, bonuses, etc.
7. Determination of amounts due during the coming operating cycle under bond indenture agreements and other deferred installment contracts, and any accrued interest thereon
8. Determination of the actual or contingent liabilities arising from contracts, lawsuits, etc.
9. Segregation of amounts received in advance from customers for the delivery of goods or the performance of services
10. An examination of transactions for the subsequent period for the disclosure of liabilities not taken into account as of the close of the fiscal period
11. The obtaining of a liability letter from the client

Internal Control. If financial transactions have been properly controlled from their inception and recorded in accordance with generally accepted accounting principles, the end result will be a set of financial statements which present fairly the financial position of the enterprise and the results of operations for the period under review. If the above is true for the financial statements as a whole, then it must also be true for the current liability section of the balance sheet.

As an example of poor internal control, consider the situation where no systematic review is made of account classifications to which purchase invoices for raw materials and other expenses have been charged. In this area the auditor must now enlarge the extent of his tests, since he is not at all certain that account totals accurately reflect what has happened during the year, with the result that any ratio or other analysis may very will result in misleading conclusions. If the auditor's tests indicate significant errors in account classification, he will have to extend his audit procedures in order to produce meaningful results, particularly where comparative profit and loss statements are to be presented.

The examination of internal control should normally precede the audit in order for the auditor to estimate the extent of the testing he will have to conduct. This internal control phase of the engagement will consist of not only what is called "internal accounting control," but also that portion called "internal check." The distinction between these two has been pointed out in Chapter 9.

Data for Permanent File. This phase of the internal control examination is designed to assure the auditor that the accounting records relating to current liabilities are what they appear to be and that account totals for purchases, expenses, etc., are accurately stated.

On an initial engagement the auditor should build up his internal control file in this area by outlining for the workpapers the following matters:

1. A listing of the books of original entry involving liabilities
2. A copy of the chart of accounts, indicating the accounts to be charged and credited for various types of transactions
3. Copies of vouchers or other documents to be used in connection with the receipt, recording, and subsequent payment of invoices
4. The frequency with which outstanding obligations are balanced against the general ledger control account
5. Procedures for the handling of duplicate invoices from suppliers and others, particularly freight invoices
6. Procedures for the adjustment of vendors' accounts, especially where returned merchandise may be involved
7. The frequency with which vendors' statements are compared with recorded liabilities and reconciled
8. Procedures for checking the mathematical accuracy of vendors' invoices before entry and/or payment
9. The existence of numerical controls over vouchers, checks, drafts, receiving and shipping documents, etc.
10. The system used to assure that payments are made on or before due dates of vendors' invoices, to make certain that all discounts are taken to which the organization may be entitled
11. Procedures for the prompt recording of transactions in order to minimize the search for unrecorded liabilities at the end of any one period
12. Procedures for the handling of disputed items on vendors' invoices to minimize the possibility of lost invoices and their subsequent payment more than once

On subsequent audits, this permanent internal control file is brought up to date by investigating any departures therefrom and noting those changes in the papers. In addition, the auditor will also assure himself, by testing a representative selection of transactions, that the procedures outlined by the client, and which are designed to provide adequate internal accounting control, are in fact being adhered to by the client's employees.

TRADE PAYABLES

Definition. For purposes of discussion, the term "trade payables" means the following:

1. Obligations to vendors on "open account"
2. Notes and trade acceptances payable arising from the purchase of goods and services for consumption by the firm

"Open account" balances arise from the normal, everyday operations of the organization characterized by the order, receipt, and consumption of goods and services. In the normal course of business operations, these will be paid within the credit terms set by the vendor and/or by mutual agreement between the firm and its vendors. Generally speaking, these obligations are unsecured.

Notes and trade acceptances payable also arise from the purchase of goods and services, but the use of these negotiable instruments as evidence of indebtedness to vendors is not at all widespread when compared with "open account" balances. These instruments, however, may arise from any one of the following conditions:

1. Some industries use these negotiable instruments quite extensively and as a matter of normal, everyday business practice, e.g., the "hard goods" industries.
2. Some firms may be temporarily hard pressed for cash with which to pay maturing obligations and, therefore, may resort to the use of these negotiable instruments to permit the seller to obtain cash by discounting them.
3. Because of the seasonal nature of some industries, e.g., furs, where the buying season is long and the selling season short, creditors may make extensive use of these instruments to enable the vendor to secure cash.

These obligations may or may not be secured, again depending upon such factors as industry practice, vendor relationships, and the nature of the transaction, and other factors. Generally speaking, short-term (less than three months) obligations are not secured, but here too the ability of the firm to pay may be the deciding factor. Sometimes the vendor may require that the officers and stockholders of a closely held corporation endorse the note personally in order to protect himself.

Internal Control Problems. The internal control problems that arise in dealing with vendors may be classified into two broad categories:

1. Authorization for the incurrence of the expenditure
2. The documentation, recording, and ultimate disposition of the vendor's invoice

The problem of internal check and internal accounting control begins with the decision to purchase those goods and services which the firm may need in order to operate. Authorization to buy, therefore, is the key initial problem to be solved.

Generally speaking, the authority to buy goods and services for the use of the company is centered in a purchasing department, although the purchase of certain types of goods (such as machinery and equipment, real estate, etc.) may be, and generally is, specifically reserved for certain key management individuals or groups of individuals. The function of the purchasing department, therefore, is to act in the firm's name for the purchase of those goods and services needed for daily operations. In most cases this will be the department which will have the authority to initiate purchase orders to vendors and will be the department which will be responsible for incurring the bulk of the trade liabilities.

It is important, therefore, that the purchasing agent who will have the responsibility of dealing with the company's vendors have a clear set of guidelines in the form of company policy and procedures to assist him in his function. For example, it is generally essential for the purchasing agent to know the quality standards relating to the goods he is to purchase, the price range within which he may be allowed to move, the number of quotations he is expected to get before writing his purchase order, and many other matters relating to his function.

Of prime importance, however, in this area is the quantity of goods the purchasing agent may buy at any one time, thus committing the organization to tie up funds (cash) for fairly long periods of time until those same goods are consumed and reconverted to cash. Here it becomes the responsibility of management to properly gauge its needs for raw materials and/or finished goods so that there is a fairly uniform flow from cash to inventory and back to cash once more.

It should suffice to say, therefore, that while the very nature of the purchasing function implies the creation of liabilities in its exercise, that function should and must be spelled out in such a way as to minimize the possibility of its misuse. It is to those established guidelines and the exercise of the authority of the purchasing function thereunder that the auditor must address himself in this area.

A part of the internal control examination in this area will revolve, therefore, about the controls imposed by management on the purchasing function. If, however, the independent CPA cannot examine these areas as a part of his annual audit, he should request that the internal audit group examine the purchasing area at least once every two or three years and make their report available to him. In the absence of such a group within the organization, the CPA must discuss this with his client and attempt to elicit from him, and without further checking, the procedures that have been set up for the guidance of purchasing agents.

Of equal importance, however, is the handling of incoming shipments and the handling of vendors' invoices from the time the shipment is received until the time when the invoices are processed, paid, and filed. Here we are dealing with the system of internal check, and it is here that the responsibility of the independent auditor is primary.

Incoming Shipments. All incoming shipments of raw material and/or finished goods should be received at a specified point. At the time of receipt, the receiving clerk should prepare a receiving ticket indicating the nature of the incoming shipment, the number of cartons or other containers involved, the method of shipment, the name of the vendor, the date of the incoming shipment, and other pertinent data. In addition there should be available at this point a copy of the vendor's shipping document which should be attached to the receiving ticket. All cartons and other containers should now be marked with the number of the receiving document and the number of cartons involved.

If at all possible, all incoming shipments should be cleared from the receiving department premises the same day they are received and the goods forwarded to their destination. It may also be necessary to advise various departments and/or individuals within the organization of the arrival and availability of newly arrived raw materials, finished goods, or parts. The receiving ticket, therefore, if properly designed and used, can serve a variety of purposes.

Internal Control of Vendors' Invoices. Upon the receipt of vendors' invoices through the mail, the mail department should stamp all copies of each invoice with the date and time of receipt. If the incoming invoice has more than one copy, each copy other than the original should also be stamped with the words "Duplicate Copy" across its face in large, bold letters. The purpose here is to establish a control to prevent the payment of other than original invoices. All copies should now be sent to the accounts payable (or vouchers payable) unit within the accounting department for further processing.

The handling of vendors' invoices within the accounting department now revolves about the following matters:

1. The separation of original invoices from duplicates. If there is no need for any of the duplicate copies, those should be destroyed as quickly as possible. If there is a need for a copy of the invoice elsewhere within the organization, one of the duplicates can be used. With modern duplicating equipment, however, copies of any invoices can be made almost instantly and those copies used for any internal purposes for which they may be needed.

2. All vendors' invoices should now be matched with a copy of the receiving ticket, the purchase order, or any other document indicating that the goods have been ordered and received. At this point the invoice should be scrutinized and compared with both the receiving ticket and/or a copy of the purchase order to determine whether the quantity received agrees with the amount billed and whether the unit price agrees with the purchase order.

3. If there is any discrepancy between the amount billed and the amount shown as received, or in the unit price of the item, the invoice should now be processed with the corrected information and correspondence initiated with the vendor seeking to rectify the apparent error. The purpose of processing the invoice at the corrected amount is twofold: (1) to enter all liabilities immediately, and (2) to take advantage of discount terms, if offered.

4. All invoices should now be checked for mathematical accuracy and coded as to the account or accounts to be charged.

5. All invoices should now be recorded in the purchase journal or vouchered for payment. At the same time, these invoices should be filed by due date in order to avoid the possibility of losing valuable discounts. (As an illustration of the importance of this step, consider the case where an organization purchases merchandise from a vendor at terms of 2/10, N/30. The effective rate of interest equivalent to the cash discount can be measured as follows:

$$I = 0.02 \times \frac{360}{30 - 10} = 36\%$$

Based on the net amount the rate is 36.7%.)

6. All invoices other than those for goods that are not exactly correct should be sent to the individual or department utilizing the service and authorizing the expenditure, for their approval for final payment.

7. After payment, all invoices should be properly canceled and filed. For cancellation a "paid" stamp may be used on each or a perforator may be used to perforate a group of invoices simultaneously.

Audit of Payables. The initial step in the audit of payables, including notes and trade acceptances, is the preparation of a list of outstanding obligations as of the end of the fiscal period. At this point the totals of the various schedules should now be compared with their respective general ledger account balances, any differences discovered, and schedules and general ledger reconciled. If there are too many individual accounts for listing, various groups can be selected and the total of those groups compared with the totals of the subcontrols generally maintained for that purpose. Usually, in the latter case, the groups selected for individual listing will correspond to those selected for confirmation.

The listing of the individual accounts accomplishes several audit objectives:

1. Provides the detail to tie in with the general ledger account balance.

2. Facilitates the comparison of balances per books with replies received to confirmation requests.

3. Segregates those payables with debit balances from those which have balances due. For balance sheet purposes, accounts payable with debit balances should be reclassified as "Due from Vendors" under the Current Asset category. It is possible, of course, that the existence of a debit balance in some cases may indicate the absence of a purchase entry for the year under review. In the latter situation, an adjusting entry may be needed.

4. The listing of open balances facilitates the preparation of an aging schedule for payables. Generally speaking, the purpose of such a schedule is the detection of trade payables which may have problems connected with them plus the detection of those accounts in which contra errors may have been made and which have remained undetected and unadjusted for various periods of time.

5. In the case of notes and trade acceptances payable, the listing will also facilitate the computation of accrued interest charges thereon, if any.

Confirmation of Trade Payables. The selection of trade payables for circularization of confirmation requests concerning balances due as of the end of the fiscal year is one of those areas which requires the use of judgment by the auditor. Unless the selection of those accounts is done statistically (a subject covered elsewhere in this handbook), this part of the audit program will require that the auditor be keenly aware of the pitfalls of an improper selection of accounts. The selection of those accounts to be confirmed should accomplish the following objectives:

1. Confirm the existence of *all* trade payables with individual balances in excess of 2 to 3 percent of the total trade payables, plus a representative selection of all those under said amount.

2. The detection of any unrecorded liabilities for goods and/or services received prior to the end of the current year, especially those where the merchandise may have been taken into inventory and the liability not recorded.

3. The existence of disputes with company vendors concerning prices, quantities, etc., which may require adjustment for balance sheet purposes.

4. The detection of any irregularities which may have arisen through the collusion of two or more employees within the organization who are in a position to influence the expenditure of funds for nonexistent goods or services. In this connection the auditor should send out confirmation requests to either all or a representative selection of those accounts with whom the firm began doing business during the year under review.

Utilizing the Cutoff. As a result of his observation of the taking of year-end physical inventories, the auditor now has in his workpapers a series of "cutoff" points indicating the precise point at which the year under review has ended. These cutoff points consist of a series of document numbers from various parts of the organization. For purposes of indicating the cutoff point for trade payables, these final numbers will come from both the receiving department (for goods received) and the shipping department (for goods to be returned).

Once having established that point where all transactions for the year under review cease, an examination of vendors' invoices for a few days prior to the end of the fiscal year and for a period of time subsequent to the end of the fiscal year will accomplish the following:

1. Determine which invoices, entered prior to the end of the fiscal year, may belong to the subsequent period.

2. Determine which invoices, entered subsequent to the end of the fiscal period under review, belong in that period. In this connection it should be noted that the auditor will have to secure from the accounts payable department a list of receiving tickets, by name of vendor and number, awaiting matching with vendors' invoices. This step, generally done at the time of establishing the cutoff points, will greatly facilitate the examination of payables to determine whether all trade liabilities belonging to the period under review have, in fact, been properly reflected.

NOTES AND LOANS PAYABLE

This section of the chapter is devoted to the internal control and audit problems associated with borrowings from financial institutions and individuals other than normal trade sources.

Internal Control. The chief internal control problem in this area is the question of what individual, or group of individuals, within the organization is authorized to borrow funds in the name of the corporation, the extent to which such authority may be exercised, and the limitations, if any, surrounding such authority.

Generally speaking, the authority to borrow funds should be spelled out in detail in the minutes of the board of directors or in the bylaws of the company, especially in those sections dealing with the powers of board members and/or officers. This is especially true of large organizations, where, by the very nature of the operation, one of the officers, usually the treasurer, may have been given specific authority to borrow funds from banks and other financial institutions for short-term operating needs. Long-term borrowings in the form of loans or bonded indebtedness may, and generally does, require the approval of the board of directors and possibly even of the stockholders. All of these details should be made a part of the auditor's permanent internal control file for future reference and should be revised and brought up to date periodically.

Due to Banks. The notes and loans payable to banks should be confirmed directly with those institutions as part of the normal cash confirmation procedure. This confirmation request will usually ask for the details as to any collateral held as security for the loans.

For those loans negotiated with banks and/or other financial institutions with which the firm does not have the usual banking arrangements, it will be necessary to send out individual specific confirmation requests asking for the details of the notes or loans, including details as to collateral, if any. Loans made by banks with whom the corporation does not have normal banking relationships may sometimes have other stipulations and conditions attached to them which may affect the credit standing of the borrower. The confirmation request, therefore, should be spelled out in sufficient detail so that the auditors may be apprised of the existence of those other conditions in order to weigh them properly.

Due to Directors, Officers, and Other Employees. All loans from individuals connected with the corporation should be confirmed directly with the individual involved. At the same time, those individuals should be requested to disclose the details surrounding their loans to the company. These details, including authorization for the borrowing, should also be found in the minutes of the board of directors' meeting.

It is entirely possible that some of these items may not only represent advances to the company, but relate to bonus or extra-pay agreements. If that is the case, it will be necessary for the auditor to examine those agreements and check the mathematical computations to determine the accuracy of the amounts shown.

Maturing Long-term Obligations. Long-term obligations which fall due within the next accounting period are properly classified as current liabilities unless the redemption of those obligations will be accomplished by means of a sinking fund held by the bond trustee. In that event they should be excluded from the current liability classification.

When a trustee is employed, the confirmation request should contain the following:

1. The face amount of bonds to be redeemed during the coming year plus the details as to any past-due interest.
2. The amount of any cash and/or other assets held for the redemption of the securities.
3. The details as to any premium to be paid for bonds called for redemption by the corporation in advance of the due date, or for bonds being redeemed serially. In this connection, an examination of the minutes of board of directors' meetings should also be made to verify the information supplied by the trustee.

Where a bond trustee was not used and the bonds were sold directly to their holders, it may be impracticable to determine the face amount of bonds outstanding by direct correspondence with the bondholders, unless the securities are registered. In those cases, a review of the company's records should suffice to enable the auditor to "state fairly" the amount of bonds outstanding to be redeemed during the coming year by summarizing the transactions in the Bonds Payable account in the general ledger and tracing through any cash receipts and disbursements shown therein, and by reference to minutes of board of directors' meetings.

INCOME RECEIVED IN ADVANCE

In many cases, and in many industries, it is usual to collect income in advance for services to be performed or goods to be delivered in the future. When such an amount is collected in advance and recorded before it is actually earned, any unearned portion not applicable to the period under review should be deferred to the period(s) in which it is or will be earned. Where that period falls within the next accounting cycle, it will be classified as a current liability. Where it falls outside of the next accounting period, it will be properly classified otherwise.

Magazine and Newspaper Subscriptions. Magazine and newspaper subscriptions received in advance should be credited to an "Unearned Subscriptions" account. Each month a journal entry is made reducing the balance of such account as a result of revenue earned resulting from the delivery of newspapers and/or magazines to subscribers. The auditor, therefore, must first acquaint himself with the client's mode of operation with respect to the manner in which such advance income is recorded; then, at the end of the period under review, he must examine the client's method of calculating that portion of the revenue which has been earned.

Advance Sales of Tickets. Tickets for sporting events, concerts, plays, and other performances are usually sold months in advance. When the event is held, that portion of the unearned revenue is removed from the account and credited to an "earned revenue" classification. For example, in the legitimate theatre, an accounting is rendered after each performance of the show, based upon an actual examination of the tickets remaining unsold and of the ticket stubs collected from the patrons at that performance. On the basis of that accounting, which must be agreed to by all parties concerned—i.e., a representative of the producer and a representative of the theatre owner—the income for that performance is divided in accordance with the agreement between the respective parties. This accounting now also furnishes the basis for the removal of the unearned revenue to an actual revenue account, or to an actual liability account for that portion which does not belong to the party keeping the records (generally, the theatre owner). Any unsold tickets for performances held are put aside and safeguarded until such time as the show finally closes, at which point a final accounting generally takes place.

Other Revenue Received in Advance. To attempt, at this point, to detail all of the numerous types of income collected in advance would be an almost impossible task. Interest, rents, and insurance premiums are some of the other types of income that normally come to mind at this point. But obviously there are others, depending upon the nature of the activity being audited. This means, in effect, that it is up to the auditor himself to be constantly alert in this area and to recognize those situations which may give rise to unearned income and to adopt those methods of satisfying himself with respect to what has been done in terms of accounting records.

Deferred Income on Sales of Merchandise. Before leaving this part of the chapter, however, it should be pointed out now that what has been discussed up to this point has been income arising from the rendering of services. What has been omitted is any mention of "unearned income" arising from the sale of goods, particularly in those situations in which the installment method of payment may be used.

When merchandise, or other tangible property, is sold on an installment or other deferred payment plan, the profit on the sale may be deferred and taken into income as collections are made on the receivable. In other words, a portion of every dollar collected on installment accounts receivable is treated as "realized" income. Gross profit in proportion to the installments still uncollected is then deferred and is treated for balance sheet purposes as a "deferred credit."

The usual method of accounting for deferred profit on installment sales is to compute the gross profit percentage on total installment sales for an accounting period and to apply that percentage to all installment contracts for that period as collections are made. Since gross profit percentages may vary from year to year, it is important that the auditor apply the proper percentage to the collections for that year.

INCOME TAXES

Federal Corporate Income Taxes. As part of his examination of current liabilities, the auditor must determine the client's liability, if any, for federal income taxes for the year under review and must reflect that liability in the balance sheet for the current year. This means that the auditor must be thoroughly familiar with the effects of the tax law upon business transactions. In order to do that, he must also be aware of those transactions or situations which may require specified tax treatment even though for book purposes they may have been handled in some other way.

Where there are material differences between book and taxable income, it may be necessary for the auditor to keep a record of those items listed on Schedule M-1, "Reconciliation of Income Per Books with Income Per Return," of federal income tax Form 1120, in order to properly carry forward items of income and/or expense which affect future periods, so that the tax liability for those future periods may be properly set forth.

Where agents of the Internal Revenue Service have examined the client's returns for past years, the auditor should now obtain copies of the revenue agent's reports for the years examined. The objectives of such a step are:

1. To determine that all liabilities for back federal income taxes are properly reflected, if not already paid
2. To judge the effect of adjustments made by the agent on the present year's and future years' returns

It is important, therefore, that the auditor review all correspondence with the Internal Revenue Service resulting from such audits, especially where it is still possible for the government to make additional assessments or for the taxpayer to file claims for refunds.

State and Local Income Taxes. With an ever-increasing number of states and municipalities imposing income taxes on business enterprises, today's auditor is required to keep up with and be knowledgeable about a great variety of income tax laws and regulations in addition to those of the federal government. If, for example, a client corporation is doing business in a dozen states, the auditor will have to be familiar with not only the income tax laws of those states, but also the laws of the specific localities in which the enterprise is located.

The first problem confronting the auditor, therefore, is to determine the precise locations in which his client may be considered to be doing business. It must also be pointed out that the definition of what constitutes "doing business" within a particular state or locality is very much open to legal question and interpretation and is, therefore, one which the auditor may be unable to cope with. In that event he may have to seek a legal opinion when there is a question in his own mind as to whether or not his client is liable for taxes in that particular state or locality.

Generally speaking, many of the states and localities imposing taxes based in part on net income utilize federal net income as a starting point. The reason is an attempt to simplify the computational and reporting problems of the businessman and to cut the costs of administering the local laws. This does not mean, however, that there will not be differences between federal and state laws in this area, differences which the auditor will now have to be aware of if he is to either check the client's computation or prepare the return himself.

The auditor must also be aware of the fact that most, if not all, of these state and local income tax laws require that any adjustments made to federal taxable net income by agents of the Internal Revenue Service must be reported to them within a specified time period. In effect, therefore, a change in federal taxable net income may give rise to an additional liability not only to the United States but also to the various other taxing jurisdictions and authorities.

ACCRUED EXPENSES AND TAXES

This section of the chapter will deal with the problem of the evaluation and disclosure of expenses which have been incurred during the period under review but for which no invoices have been received; taxes other than those based on income; and taxes withheld from employees under the various laws and regulations governing the withholding of taxes of all kinds. It must be pointed out, of course, that no attempt is being made to be exhaustive in this discussion. The particular items which an auditor may encounter during the course of his examination are too numerous to be detailed here. What is suggested, however, is that the auditor must utilize his judgment and ingenuity in uncovering those items which fall in this category.

Salaries and Wages. One of the more common accruals is the amount of salaries, wages, commissions, and other remuneration which has been earned by employees but which will not be paid until some time in the next accounting period. The end of a company's fiscal period may fall during the week before salaries and wages for that period are paid; commissions may be paid after the end of the month; or profit-sharing bonuses may be paid after the books for the year have been closed and the profit determined. All of these require the creation of an accrued liability account for unpaid wages, salaries, commissions, bonuses, etc.

The audit problems for this particular area revolve about the discovery and evaluation of earned but unpaid remuneration to employees. As a starter, therefore, the auditor should examine the payroll for the period encompassing the end of the fiscal year and determine that portion within the year under review. To test the accrual for salesmen's commissions, the auditor must first learn the method of computing commissions by reference to agreements with the sales force or with independent commission men. At this point the auditor can proceed to verify the details of the existing computation or to undertake the gathering of the necessary data with which to make his own computation.

Profit-sharing and bonus arrangements should generally be spelled out in the minutes of the board of directors' meetings. By reference to these the auditor can proceed to verify the client's computation for such an accrual or to make his own calculation by first gathering the required information upon which such a computation is based.

Taxes (Other than Income Taxes). There are several types of taxes involved in the operation of almost any business, each of which presents its own peculiar auditing problems. The principal types are: (1) payroll taxes; (2) property taxes; and (3) sales and excise taxes.

Payroll taxes. Generally speaking, the liability for taxes based on payroll will be unpaid as of the close of the fiscal year under review and will, therefore, automatically require an accrual. This accrual must include not only those amounts required to be withheld from employees by the various taxing jurisdictions, but also any employer's share for contributions required to be made. All of these are current liabilities since, generally, the organization will be required to remit payment for these taxes within a month or two.

Federal, state, and local withholding requirements also impose penalties and interest charges for failure to file timely returns, to pay amounts due with returns, or to pay over-amounts withheld if such amounts exceed a stipulated sum. It is up to the auditor to acquaint himself with federal, state, and local laws in this area and to ascertain, during the course of his audit, whether the various laws and regulations have been observed. It is also the duty of the auditor to check computations of taxes due and accrued as of the end of the fiscal year, to examine the employment tax payments and the quarterly returns submitted to the various taxing authorities subsequent to the audit, and to compare the totals of such returns with the accrued liabilities set up at the close of the year.

As a by-product of this part of the examination, the auditor should be in a position to tie in directly or be able to reconcile total salaries and wages expense for the year with the total salaries and wages reported on these returns. Any differences, if material, should be investigated.

Property taxes. Property taxes are generally assessed upon the real or personal property of a business enterprise within a particular taxing jurisdiction. The assessment may be based on real property values, as in the case of land and buildings, or upon valuations placed on personal property by the business organization in the case of machinery and/or inventory.

State and local laws may vary widely in their provisions as to the assessment and collection of property taxes, and the auditor must familiarize himself with all such local laws and regulations before he can even hope to perform his audit function properly in this area. Any accruals of property taxes should be compared with current tax bills, after taking into account actual or estimated changes in either valuations, rates, or both. In examining these tax bills, the auditor must be constantly alert to the possibility that the tax bills he is examining actually are not those of his client and that material changes may have taken place since the last bill was submitted and paid.

Sales, excise, and other taxes. State and local sales and use taxes are fast becoming universal, and it is the rare business organization that is still doing business in any jurisdiction which does not impose such a tax upon at least some of the transactions. Here, as elsewhere, the auditor must acquaint himself with all provisions of these laws in order to do his job properly.

In general, the sales tax is imposed on sales to the ultimate consumer of a list of items which may be specifically enumerated in the law and regulations or may be part of a general category of sales subject to tax. The "use" tax portion of these laws is imposed upon the corporation itself on those items purchased outside the taxing jurisdiction which would be normally subject to tax if the purchase had originated within that jurisdiction.

In the case of the sales and use tax liability, the auditor may check the accuracy of the accrual by an examination of the return filed subsequent to the end of the period under review and by verifying the basis upon which the tax liability computation was made. The auditor must also bear in mind that these returns are subject to independent verification by the taxing authorities involved and that there may be additional liabilities involved not only for the tax itself but for interest and penalty charges.

In computing or checking the liability for excise taxes, the auditor should first ascertain the basis on which the tax is computed. Utilizing this information, the auditor may then proceed to verify the liability by reference to sales made since the last excise tax return was filed and multiplying this figure by the excise tax rate. As a by-product of this examination, the sales figures for those items subject to tax for any particular period may be checked out or reconciled. Needless to say, any material discrepancy in this area should be thoroughly investigated and satisfactorily explained.

In addition to these two types of taxes, there has also developed a host of others, all of which may be small in themselves but which in total may become material. Here the problem may be more of a large variety of such taxes rather than of complexity.

Rentals. Not all corporations own the premises they occupy. In fact, it would be the rare organization that did not rent at least a portion of the premises it occupies. The contractual obligations of the lessee for rental payments, therefore, would be specified in the lease agreement, as would the amount required of the organization as security for the faithful performance of the lease agreement.

In the case of retail establishments, it is not unusual to find that the lease agreement provides for additional rental payments to be made based upon sales, net earnings, or some other basis. If an amount has been accrued, the auditor must check the computation of such accrual and trace that amount to subsequent payments. If no accrual has been set up and the agreement calls for such additional payments, the auditor must compute the amount due and consider an adjusting entry.

Generally, also, the auditor may wish to confirm the continued existence of the security deposited with the landlord. As a part of such confirmation the auditor should also request the landlord to inform him whether the corporation is indebted to him for any items under said agreement as of the end of the fiscal year.

Other Operating Expenses. The accrual method of accounting demands, of course, that there be offset against recorded revenue all expenses incurred in earning that revenue. In effect it places a burden upon the auditor in that he must now use his ingenuity and resourcefulness in seeking out and recording those items of expense which have been incurred but which have not been either recorded or paid in the year under review.

Generally speaking, there are some items of expense which are common to all companies—insurance premiums, utilities, advertising (especially dealers' advertising), vacation pay, and others. The requirement here, as elsewhere, is that the auditor familiarize himself with the methods of calculation, dates of payment, and other relevant facts and check the accruals made by the client against the information he has obtained through other means.

DEPOSITS

The liabilities arising in this area originate as the result of moneys deposited with the company for a variety of reasons. The chief categories are:

1. Returnable containers
2. Building construction deposits
3. Security deposits
4. Advance payments for merchandise

Returnable Containers. In certain industries deposits are required to cover the cost of containers in which the product is shipped. When these containers are returned, the deposits are refunded. The charges for these containers are usually included on the invoice for the merchandise shipped. If these charges to customers are settled by credits for their return, the container liability account can be offset against the receivables. If, on the other hand, it is customary for customers to pay these container charges, no segregation is needed.

Where customers do not ordinarily return containers, the deposit liability account should be adjusted periodically to reflect the estimated refunds to be made during the next period. This estimate, of course, can either be based on past experience projected into the future, or the company may simply assume that any containers held for sale will produce future income.

Building Construction Deposits. Construction industry practice usually requires that, upon the signing of a contract for construction work to be performed over a period of time, there be deposited with the general contractor a sum computed as a percentage of the total contract. These deposits are a current liability on the books of the general contractor unless actual construction is scheduled for more than a year after the end of the fiscal period.

Some states require that construction deposits on residential homes be physically segregated from the contractor's regular funds. If that is the case, the deposits may not be considered a current liability unless the cash in escrow is considered a current asset.

In any event, the auditor should also consider the necessity and advisability of confirming these deposits and including in such confirmation request questions which he may consider pertinent and relative to the contract itself.

Security Deposits. Many types of industries require deposits from customers for various reasons. For example, public utilities generally require their customers to make deposits with them to secure payment of bills. Landlords generally require a deposit from the tenant to be applied either as payment of rent for the final period of the lease or to secure substantial performance within the terms and conditions of the lease.

The deposits required by utility companies bear interest under regulations promulgated by some of the state utility commissions. This interest may be paid periodically either in cash or by credit to the customer's account. Or, in some cases, interest may not be paid until the deposit is returned. Some of these deposits may never be claimed and may eventually be paid over to the state after the lapse of the required statutory period.

Confirmation of these deposits is generally not undertaken except on a very limited basis. But the auditor may satisfy himself as to the reliability and accuracy of the accounts controlling these deposits in the general ledger by testing the transactions charged or credited to these accounts against current customer billings, or by some other means. Under uniform systems of accounts as prescribed by various state regulatory bodies, these deposits are considered to be current liabilities at all times.

Advance Payments for Merchandise. Advance payments for merchandise are most prevalent in the retail trade under so-called "layaway" or "will-call" sales. In this type of transaction the customer selects the merchandise, which is then set aside, or "laid away," awaiting the completion of payments before actual delivery is made. In a sense, of course, these plans are similar to installment selling except for the fact that under the installment method, the goods are actually delivered to the buyer at the time of selection, thus enabling the buyer to enjoy use and possession even though he may have to make a series of payments before title is actually passed.

Advance payments may have to be made also in cases where a large order has been placed and the credit standing of the buyer may be open to serious question. It is not unusual, for example, to require of firms just going into business that they make a substantial deposit, or down payment, against the delivery of large quantities of raw materials or finished goods they require to commence operations.

MISCELLANEOUS PAYABLES

This section of the chapter will be devoted to an exposition of the remaining items generally considered to be of a current nature. Although the list can be expanded to include a large variety of accounts and transactions, the discussion will be limited to the following more important categories:

1. Unclaimed obligations
2. Bonuses and other profit-sharing agreements
3. Pensions
4. Product warranties
5. Dividends

Unclaimed Obligations. It is not at all unusual to find many individuals and even some business organizations not claiming what is rightfully theirs. This may involve not only utility deposits (mentioned previously) but also such items as bank deposits, salaries and wages, interest, dividends, and others. Each year, for example, one can find in the daily newspapers lists of people who, for one reason or another, have unclaimed bank deposits to their credit. Under state law, the financial institution holding these unclaimed deposits must attempt to find these depositors and, failing that, must turn these deposits over to the state. Generally, good internal control requires that these bank deposits be segregated from the active ones to avoid the possibility of unauthorized transactions taking place in them except insofar as those transactions may involve the actual owners. The auditor's responsibility in this area is to ascertain periodically whether any unauthorized transactions have in fact taken place and whether proper procedures have been set up to guard against such an eventuality.

Industrial and commercial concerns, on the other hand, are faced with the safekeeping of unclaimed salaries awaiting the appearance of former employees, or their heirs, who, for reasons best known to themselves, have neglected to pick up their final salary check. The responsibility of the auditor is to determine that unclaimed salaries at the end of any pay period are promptly redeposited and a liability account set up. Payments thereafter should be made only upon proper identification.

Sometimes checks to vendors or other individuals may be outstanding for long periods of time. In that event the company should stop payment on that particular check, remove the check from the list of outstanding ones, and set up a miscellaneous liability to the payee. Payment should then be made only upon the written authorization of a responsible company official.

The key problem in this area revolves about the installation of a proper system of internal control over these unclaimed obligations. All accounting entries involving these accounts should be scrutinized very carefully and proper explanations obtained from responsible company officials for any items which may appear to be out of the ordinary.

Bonuses and Other Profit-sharing Agreements. Generally speaking, the details as to bonuses and other profit-sharing agreements can be found in the minutes of board of directors' meetings. The chief problem of the auditor, therefore, is to determine that these agreements are observed and to test the amount set up as a liability. Amounts due to officers and other employees under these agreements become liabilities in the period to which they relate. If the amount cannot be definitely fixed, the auditor may have to estimate the liability as closely as he can.

Pensions. Except for pension plans covering an entire industry and administered by either a trade union or a combined union-management association, the details as to individual pension plans will vary considerably. A plan, for example, may be funded, i.e., through insurance, or it may be non-funded and administered through a trustee. It may provide for benefits based on past service as well as present and future service. It may be tied in with payments to be made to the employee under FICA or it may not, and even the amounts to be paid to employees will vary considerably from company to company. The plan may be contributory or non-contributory; that is, it may or may not require contributions from the employee as well as from the employer. All of these factors, as well as others, will require recognition by the auditor, for each will undoubtedly have some effect upon the amount of contribution required at the end of the fiscal year and, therefore, upon the liability.

Under the terms of many pension plans, the employer may be required to make a lump-sum deposit at the plan's inception where past service on the part of the employee is to be recognized, in addition to meeting the obligation for current contributions. Ordinarily this past-service cost may be amortized, in accordance with Accounting Research Bulletin No. 43, over current and future periods, on the grounds that such past-service costs relate to present and future services of the organization as a whole. The amount of past-service cost, as well as current-service costs, should be disclosed by a note to the financial statements which should also indicate the period, if any, over which such cost is to be amortized.

At the institution of such a pension plan, or upon the initial audit, the auditor should secure a copy of the agreement for his permanent file. In subsequent audits this agreement should be kept up to date by obtaining any modifications or extensions thereto. By confirmation request the auditor may also obtain from the actuary the amount of required contributions for the year and the past-service liability at year end. From the trustee of the plan he should also obtain confirmation of fund transactions and the balance in the fund at year end.

Product Warranties. As part of the inducement to prospective purchasers, a company may warrant trouble-free service of its products in the hands of consumers for some period of time depending upon a variety of factors. Under the terms of such agreements, the company guarantees to repair or replace defective products within the meaning of the guarantee if such defect takes place within the period specified. These agreements, therefore, give rise to estimated liabilities.

In determining the extent to which sales of the company's products may bind the company to provide this free service, the auditor can only be guided by the company's experience in servicing its products. The auditor will, therefore, merely review the contract and the company's statistics on service to determine whether the charge to expense and the amount of the estimated liability shown are indicative of the actual experience of the organization.

Dividends Declared but Unpaid. Details of this liability will generally be found in the minutes of board of directors' meetings. The liability for dividends occurs at the date of declaration, which would have to be prior to the end of the fiscal year under review. The computation of this liability will be supported by the shares outstanding, as indicated by the capital stock records, multiplied by the dividend rate.

Where there exists a cumulative preferred stock, the auditor may have to consider the advisability of disclosing the arrearages of past dividends if such have not been declared and paid, and especially if the amount of such cumulated dividends owing to the senior securities has a significant bearing on Retained Earnings available to the common stock. Certainly the residual owners, the common stockholders, are entitled to know of any situation that may affect their interests adversely.

UNDISCLOSED AND CONTINGENT LIABILITIES

This section of the chapter is devoted to the problems confronting the auditor in his attempt to uncover liabilities to which no direct reference appears in the records and those for which the organization may have no direct liability, except as an endorser or guarantor, or except as the result of the operation of law. In a sense these two go together since, quite frequently, undisclosed liabilities may be of a contingent nature. Contingent liabilities are, therefore, a subgrouping of the general category "undisclosed liabilities."

Undisclosed Liabilities. During the course of his examination the auditor must be constantly alert to the possibility that any of the current liability categories mentioned previously may contain hidden liabilities. Audit techniques and procedures, therefore, should be so designed that these hidden claims against the company can be discovered as a matter of routine audit. But there are other areas which may be examined and other procedures which may be utilized even if normal, routine procedures have not disclosed the existence of these "hidden" claims. These are:

1. Responses to bank confirmations may disclose the existence of liens against company property or the existence of collateral assets or securities which do not appear on the records.
2. An examination of fire insurance policies on merchandise, materials, or machinery may disclose the hypothecation of such items even though the liability may not be recorded.
3. An examination of agreements entered into between the company and sales agents or franchised dealers may disclose the company's obligation to supply those people with advertising and/or demonstration material.
4. Canceled purchase commitments frequently involve some kind of penalty to the buyer, especially where these cancellations may have occurred during a period of falling prices. In order to establish the extent of such liability, the auditor may have to correspond with the particular creditor involved.
5. Some manufacturers of machinery and equipment sell their product at a price which includes installation costs. If this is the case, the auditor will have to review billings made toward the end of the period under review to determine whether the contract has, in fact, been completed, since the profit was recorded in the year under examination.

An auditor must have an active imagination and an inquiring mind when auditing in this area of current liabilities. Misrepresentation of accounts can usually be accomplished more simply through an understatement of liabilities than through an overstatement of assets.

Contingent Liabilities. Contingent liabilities may arise from a number of sources. They may arise from the endorsement of notes, proposed assessment of additional taxes, merchandise guarantees, lawsuits, etc., or any other prior act or circumstance that may result in an actual obligation at some future date. Unless they are negligible, their existence should be disclosed by an appropriate footnote or shown on the balance sheet.

If notes receivable have been discounted, the answers to bank confirmation requests should disclose that fact. Endorsement of notes of other organizations or of affiliated companies may be more difficult to discover, particularly where the officers of a corporation may have obligated their company for the benefit of another company whose credit standing may not be good enough. Confirmation requests to attorneys may disclose the existence of suits against the company which may threaten its financial stability, if maintained successfully. Property upon which there is a mortgage may be sold subject to the mortgage, thereby creating a contingent liability until the mortgage is satisfied. Additional assessments for taxes may be made by various taxing authorities, which assessments the organization may be contesting for one reason or another. Liabilities for these may be contingent until such time as agreement is reached between the organization and the taxing authority fixing the exact amount of such liability.

Sometimes the organization may appropriate a portion of its retained earnings to a "reserve for contingencies." Through an examination of the minutes of board of directors' meetings and through judicious questioning of company officers, the auditor should be in a position to determine the purpose for which such an appropriation was made. The purpose of such a segregation should, of course, be disclosed in an appropriate footnote.

Liability Letter. At the conclusion of his audit of current liabilities, the auditor should obtain from responsible company officials written assurance that all known liabilities have been recorded in the accounts and that contingent liabilities of all types have been properly disclosed. This liability letter, or certificate, should be signed by the chief executive of the corporation and countersigned by the officer responsible for accounting.

The auditor, of course, can really never be certain of the accuracy of the balance of Accounts Payable or of any other liability account, as he can, for instance, in the case of Cash, Investments, and some others, basically because management may have inadvertently or intentionally omitted some liabilities from the financial accounts. The letter in no way actually relieves the auditor of any responsibility for applying adequate verification procedures. It is, however, evidence of the precaution taken by the auditor in asking management some rather important questions in this area. It does, therefore, serve a very important function and should not be omitted.

The liability letter should be comprehensive in scope in that it should specifically enumerate any and all types of liabilities applicable to the operation of the organization under examination. Generally it should be dated as of the date on which the auditors leave the client's premises and return to their office to prepare the necessary statements. There may be several types of letters which the auditor should be able to secure—one to fit most any type of audit engagement. But care should be taken when using these standard form letters in that particular situations may arise during the course of the examination of current liabilities which may require some alteration of the wording or the insertion of additional paragraphs to cover special situations. Here the auditor must use his best judgment in determining when to use standard liability letters. The eighth edition of *Montgomery's Auditing* (Ronald Press Company, pages 347 and 348) contains a liability letter covering a wide variety of matters.

BALANCE SHEET PRESENTATION

Criteria for Balance Sheet Presentation. All current liabilities appear as the first grouping on the liability side of the balance sheet, with subgroupings of liabilities listed in the order in which they will become due. In some industries, such as public utilities, current liabilities may be listed after the corporation's capital section and long-term obligations.

Disclosure. It is important, of course, that all liabilities be disclosed. Disclosure may take the form of a specific subgrouping such as "Accounts and Notes Payable—Trade" or "Current Portion of Mortgage Payable," or it may take the form of a footnote for contingent liabilities. Adequate disclosure should also be made for federal, state, and local taxes based on income. Generally this amount will be quite substantial in and of itself, especially where there may exist liabilities not only for income taxes for current operations but for back income taxes as well.

Secured Liabilities. The existence of secured obligations should be emphasized by disclosing the specific liability so secured plus the assets so pledged. This may be accomplished by a general note in parentheses or by a footnote listing the actual collateral. Footnotes should be used rather sparingly and only when the auditor feels that adequate information cannot be otherwise presented to the reader.

Similar Items. Wherever possible, current liabilities of a similar nature, i.e., accrued expenses and taxes, should be grouped into one figure unless there may be specific items of a material amount requiring disclosure by themselves. Obviously it would be impractical to list all liabilities individually on the balance sheet.

BIBLIOGRAPHY

ARB No. 47, *Accounting for Costs of Pension Plans,* AICPA, 1956.
ARB No. 50, *Contingencies,* AICPA, 1958.
ARB No. 43, *Accounting Research and Terminology Bulletins,* final edition, New York, AICPA (Committee on Accounting Procedure), 1961, Chaps. 3, 6, 10, and 13.
APB Opinion No. 7, *Accounting for Leases in Financial Statements of Lessors,* AICPA, 1966.
APB Opinion No. 11, *Accounting for Income Taxes,* AICPA, 1967.
Cashin, James A., and Garland C. Owens: *Auditing,* 2d ed., New York, The Ronald Press Company, 1963.
Johnson, James T., and J. Herman Brasseaux: "Events Subsequent to the Date of Financial Statements," in *Readings in Auditing,* 2d ed., Cincinnati, Ohio, South-Western Publishing Company, 1965.
Lenhart, Norman J., and Philip L. Defliese: *Montgomery's Auditing,* 8th ed., New York, The Ronald Press Company, 1957.
Mautz, R. K.: *Fundamentals of Auditing,* 2d ed., New York, John Wiley & Sons, Inc., 1964.
Stettler, Howard F.: *Auditing Principles,* 3d ed., Englewood Cliffs, N.J., Prentice-Hall, Inc., 1970.
Hirschman, Robert W.: "A Look at 'Current' Classifications," *The Journal of Accountancy,* November, 1967.
Phillip, G. Edward: "Pension Liabilities and Assets," *The Accounting Review,* January, 1968.
Bevis, Herman W.: "Contingencies and Probabilities in Financial Statements," *The Journal of Accountancy,* October, 1968.
Weinstein, E. A.: "The Achilles Heel of Retailing: Accounts Payable," *The Journal of Accountancy,* July, 1969.
Crumbly, D. Larry, and Joseph M. Crews: "The Use of the Installment Tax Method for Revolving Accounts," *The Journal of Accountancy,* July, 1969.

Chapter 28

Long-term Liabilities

GERALD P. ROONEY

Partner, Peat, Marwick, Mitchell & Co.

NATURE OF LONG-TERM LIABILITIES

Introduction. A general definition for liabilities is given in APB Statement No. 4, *Basic Concepts and Accounting Principles Underlying Financial Statements of Business Enterprises,* as follows:

Liabilities—economic obligations of an enterprise that are recognized and measured in conformity with generally accepted accounting principles. Liabilities also include certain deferred credits that are not obligations but are recognized and measured in conformity with generally accepted accounting principles.

Obligations due more than one year from the balance-sheet date are long-term. Thus long-term liabilities are those *which are not expected to be settled by* (1) the use of current assets, (2) the creation of other current liabilities, or (3) within a relatively short period of time, usually one year. Current liabilities are defined in Chapter 27, "Current Liabilities."

The principal examples of long-term liabilities are bonds, notes, mortgages, and long-term obligations under pension plans and long-term leases. The incurrence of long-term liabilities is a formal commitment for the future of the organization. These obligations are usually based on written agreements which describe in considerable detail the rights of the lender and the obligations of the debtor. The points customarily covered in such agreements are due dates for principal and interest repayments, collateral, and restrictions on the debtor while the debt is outstanding. Such obligations must be accorded responsible attention at time of issuance, during their term, and upon satisfaction or termination. In addition to responsibilities to review authorizations, recording, accountability, etc., the auditor must determine that the company has satisfied all significant requirements and restrictions imposed by the debt and that the obligations and restrictions are adequately disclosed.

Characteristics of Liabilities. Before discussing audit and control objectives, it is appropriate to review the characteristics of liabilities in order not to exclude audit and control consideration of any particular liability, no matter how labeled. For this purpose the following characteristics are pertinent:

1. A liability involves a future outlay of money or an equivalent acceptable to the recipient;
2. A liability is the result of an external transaction of the past—not the future; and
3. The amount of the liability must be the subject of calculation or of close estimation.

Types of Long-term Obligations. Long-term obligations are most often issued in accordance with terms specified on the face of the obligation or in attached indentures or agreements. The provisions of these agreements vary generally in relation to the business of the issuer, the purpose of the issue, conditions of the money market, and the particular needs of the lender. Included in this category is a wide range of bonds, notes, and other long-term obligations. For example, an obligation may be *secured* by a lien on business property or may be a *debenture bond* backed by the general credit of the company. Following are some of the principal types of long-term obligations and their pertinent characteristics. For better presentation, a broad grouping into bonds, notes, and other long-term obligations is used.

Bonds

SENIOR, JUNIOR, OR SUBORDINATED BONDS: These may be secured or unsecured and designate a relationship with other obligations, principally as to priority of payment in liquidation.

DEBENTURE BONDS: These are unsecured and issued under the general credit of the corporation.

CONVERTIBLE BONDS: This type has been used extensively in recent years and provides the right to convert the security into shares of common stock at stated conversion rates.

REGISTERED BONDS: These are registered as to owner in the records of a trustee and may include registration as to principal and interest or as to principal only.

SERIAL BONDS: These mature in installments, as opposed to *term bonds,* which mature on a fixed maturity date.

COUPON BONDS: These have attached negotiable interest coupons for each interest due date that must be detached and submitted to a paying agent for payment.

REVENUE OR INCOME BONDS: These are unsecured bonds with principal and interest payments contingent on specific revenues or income generated by a specific operation, such as parking tolls, ship charter fees, etc.

Notes

MORTGAGE NOTES: These are secured by real or personal (chattel) property, and the interest in the property is usually recorded with designated governmental courts or agencies.

DEBENTURE NOTES: These are unsecured and are issued under the general credit of the corporation.

INSTALLMENT NOTES: These notes require repayment of principal and interest in series or installments extending more than one year.

Other long-term obligations

PENSION PLANS: These plans provide for retirement payments at a future date based on current and/or past service.

DEFERRED COMPENSATION AGREEMENTS: These provide for compensation payments at a future date based on current and/or past service.

EQUIPMENT TRUST CERTIFICATES: A part ownership of a trust created for the purpose of purchasing equipment and selling or leasing it to the user.

RECEIVER'S CERTIFICATES: Evidence of indebtedness issued by a receiver for funds necessary to preserve or operate the property in his charge. It ranks ahead of other secured liabilities.

LONG-TERM LEASES: Obligations for the payment of rent for the use of property covering extended periods.

PRODUCT WARRANTIES: The guarantee by a seller to make good on a product deficiency or less than specified performance over extended periods.

DEFERRED INCOME TAXES: These represent the interperiod allocations of income taxes to future periods.

INTERNAL CONTROL AND AUDIT FUNCTIONS

With all business transactions there must necessarily be a logical order in completing the full cycle of the transaction. The function of internal control is to provide controls at each phase of the transaction and independent checks to ensure that this order is being properly followed. The audit has as its function the testing of the effectiveness of the internal check and control procedures over the transactions, and, correspondingly, of the reliability of the accounting records. Because of the significance of amounts of long-term obligations, a summary of the significant provisions of each agreement should be maintained in both the accounting and the administrative departments. In addition, a tickler of required due dates, reports, and compliance provision computations should be maintained by an appropriate officer.

The following sequence in the full cycle of a long-term obligation transaction is applicable to all types of long-term liabilities:

1. Initial authorization
2. Issuance of obligation
3. Consideration received
4. Activity during term
5. Compliance with terms

Initial Authorization. **Internal control.** Because of their nature—future and obligatory—there should be specific authorization procedures for incurring long-term liabilities. These procedures may be described in the laws of the state of incorporation, in the corporate charter, or in the bylaws of the company or organization. Since long-term obligations are usually material in amount, the authorization should require approval of stockholders, trustees, or directors. In some organizations, specific authorization provisions usually are not made for many obligations that are incurred in the normal course of business, such as purchase commitments and lease obligations. However, since the amounts of these obligations can be significant, good internal control dictates that appropriate authorization procedures be established.

The authority for the issuance of all long-term liabilities should be appropriately documented. The authority should conform to legal requirements or to established internal procedures equal to the magnitude of the obligation. In some instances, the opinion of legal counsel may be necessary to document the legality of incurring the obligation.

Audit program. Audit steps should establish both the existence of documentation for authorization and the appropriateness of that authority in the light of legal requirements and established internal procedures.

Issuance of Obligation. **Internal control.** When a long-term obligation transaction is initiated, some form of documentation is usually issued. In those instances in which specific acknowledgments of indebtedness (notes, bonds, etc.) are issued in series, or in units, they should be prenumbered, accounted for by such serial number, and maintained, until issued, in the custody of an independent trustee or authorized corporate officer not involved in the approval of or accounting for the obligations.

In the absence of an independent trustee, registrar, or transfer agent, detailed records must be maintained of the serial numbers (also the names and addresses, in the case of registered obligations), by date issued, exchanged, redeemed, and canceled. These records should be maintained currently and balanced with general ledger control accounts on a regular basis. The use of an independent trustee satisfies internal control over the detailed record keeping of the issued and unissued obligations. However, periodic reports should be required from the trustee, and such reports should be reconciled with the corporate records.

Audit program. If independent trustees are used, verification of the issued, redeemed, and unissued obligations should be made by direct communication with the trustee. In addition, the trustee reports should be reviewed and the reported activity compared with that recorded in the accounting records. In the absence of an independent trustee, obligations should be verified by direct communication with the holder. Internal accounting records should be verified for accuracy with underlying data.

Consideration Received. **Internal control.** Whether the issue is for cash, real or personal property, rights, or in exchange for other liabilities, control of the receipt of such consideration must be maintained. In addition, expenses connected directly with the transaction should be properly budgeted, approved, and segregated in order that they may be charged to operations in accordance with generally accepted accounting principles.

Cash should be deposited in the bank immediately upon receipt.

Real or personal property received should be listed in detail, showing its type, valuation, location, and useful life in order that it may be physically identified and properly accounted for. Any additional information required for internal purposes should be obtained at this time. It may also be necessary to ensure that the company has authority to own such property.

Rights to the use of property (under lease agreements, for example) should be treated in the same manner as indicated for property in the preceding paragraph.

Other rights, such as rights to pension or other benefits, should be specifically detailed to ensure receipt as provided.

Other liabilities received in exchange should by their terms permit the exchange, and provision should be made to ensure that the original obligation is canceled, recorded, or documented as to its satisfaction in order to avoid future claims thereunder.

Audit program. Review should be made of the type, amount, existence, and propriety of the recording in the accounts of the consideration received for obligations issued.

The appropriateness of the recording of interest, discount, and other expenses incurred in connection with the issuance should also be verified.

Activity during Term. During the term of an obligation or agreement, activity —generally in compliance with the terms of the obligation—occurs regularly. Such activity includes the payments of principal and interest, sinking fund payments, redemptions, and conversions.

Internal control. Control during the term of an obligation is necessary in order to avoid penalties established by the provisions of the obligation and to provide appropriate safeguards to ensure that all provisions are being satisfied.

Internal control procedures dictate that there should be independence of responsibility between those performing functions of record keeping, those making cash disbursements, and those reconciling detail records or trustee reports to general ledger accounts. As indicated previously, the use of an independent trustee should include provisions for the receipt of periodic reports which should be reviewed and reconciled with the corporate accounts.

There should be procedures to ensure that interest payments are properly computed and that the accrual of, or amortization of, interest or discount to or from payment dates is recorded in the accounting records in accordance with generally accepted accounting principles.

In situations in which the company has undertaken responsibility for maintaining a sinking fund, control should be provided to ensure that the use of the fund complies with sinking fund provisions and that disbursements from the fund require an authorized signature.

Bonds or notes that have been redeemed should be effectively canceled to prevent their reissuance and should be safely stored to provide the documentation of their payment.

In addition to the usual controls over the timeliness of payments of principal and interest made under the agreement, there should exist procedures to verify that required performances, compliance ratios, and periodic reports are being met.

Audit program. Audit of activity during the term of the obligation should include verification that required payments have been made on a timely basis, that such payments were computed properly, and that all significant provisions of the agreement have been complied with.

In addition, any or all of the activities can be verified, as considered necessary, by direct communication with the lenders.

Compliance with Provisions. Internal control. Close control must be exercised over the terms of loan agreements. Auditors must be aware of the major provisions which are contained within the indenture, trust agreement, or note itself. The agreement defines the nature of, and limitations on, performance of the borrower.

Following are a number of the more common provisions:

1. Amount of loan, payment due dates, and interest rates
2. Prepayment privileges and restrictions, and related penalty amounts
3. Sinking fund requirements and their application
4. Collateral security requirements
5. Redemption dates and rates
6. Conversion periods and the security into which conversion is permitted and the conversion rate
7. The effect of dilution on conversion rates
8. The type of reports and letters that are required to be issued by the company or its independent certified public accountants, and their due dates
9. The type and amount of insurance coverages to be maintained
10. The ratios that must be maintained, such as:
    a. Quick-asset ratio
    b. Working capital ratio
    c. Net worth amount
    d. Debt-to-equity ratio
11. The limitation on cash expenditures for:
    a. Property, plant, and equipment
    b. Investments, advances, and loans to third parties
    c. Lease obligations and rental payments
    d. Amounts of executive compensation
    e. Amounts of drawings or borrowings by owner-stockholders
    f. Amounts of dividends, distributions, or repurchase of company equity securities
12. Other limitations, such as:
    a. Creation of liens
    b. Incurrence of additional indebtedness
    c. Sales of assets, mergers, or dissolution
13. Description of events that constitute events of default
14. Definitions of terms that are necessary for interpretation of the agreement are usually included. These include net earnings, current assets, current liabilities, net worth, tangible assets, and such other descriptive definitions as are appropriate to the agreement

Audit program. The auditor's objectives over such a wide range of agreement provisions are to determine that internal controls are adequate and that all significant requirements and restrictions have been met. The auditor should carefully read the agreement and review the company's compliance with each significant requirement and restriction. Often important differences in interpretation of complex agreements arise at inception or as the company business changes and substantial dollar amounts may be involved. It may be necessary to obtain legal opinions supporting the company's interpretation of provisions.

SPECIAL AUDIT CONSIDERATIONS

Amortization of Premium or Discount. To the extent that an obligation is issued for more or less than its face value, a premium or discount is created. In connection with an audit of long-term obligations, it is convenient to review the method of accounting for this addition or reduction of the cost of money and to verify the calculations of the amounts charged or credited to operations.

If payment for property is in the form of long-term liabilities they should provide for the payment of interest at realistic rates. It may be necessary to restate the face amount of the obligations (and the cost basis of the asset received) to reflect a realistic interest rate. The repayments of the debt must be allocated between principal and interest.

Recently, considerable attention has been directed to the assignment of a portion of the proceeds received for convertible long-term debt or debt issued with stock purchase warrants. To the extent that an assignment is made, debt discount (or a reduction in premium) is created. To determine the appropriateness of the accountability of such discount, special attention should be given to current pronouncements of the Accounting Principles Board. See APB Opinion No. 14, *Accounting for Convertible Debt and Debt Issued with Stock Purchase Warrants.*

Pension Plan Obligations. The variety of business and social needs and philosophies has caused a large number of pension plans to develop and, correspondingly, a variety of actuarial methods and accounting practices for determining their cost.

While a company may limit its legal obligation under pension plans, experience shows that with rare exception pension plans continue indefinitely and that limitation of liability is not invoked while the company continues in business. Accordingly, an examination of the obligations of any business requires a review of its pension agreements, and a determination that its terms are being fulfilled, that liabilities are properly recorded, and appropriate disclosures are made in notes to its financial statements. See APB No. 8, *Accounting for the Cost of Pension Plans.*

Lease Obligations. Long-term lease obligations have generated considerable interest in the accounting profession, principally with respect to the method by which they are reported. Accounting Research Study No. 4, *Reporting of Leases in Financial Statements*, and APB Opinion No. 5, *Accounting for Leases in Financial Statements of Lessee* provide extensive background on lease transactions and their accountability. The substance of a lease agreement may require either that the obligation be recorded in financial statements or that it be disclosed in notes to such statements. In addition to the control and audit procedures for any long-term obligation, the agreement must be read and interpreted specifically in the light of the provisions of APB No. 5.

Deferred Income Taxes. A deferred income tax liability exists when accounting income is larger than taxable income for either of the following reasons: (1) income is recognized in the accounting records but is not taxed until later periods; (2) expenses are deductible for tax purposes in one period but are not recognized as accounting expenses until later periods. These differences in timing between financial statements and income tax reports are more fully discussed in Chapter 39, "Review of Taxes," and in APB No. 11, *Accounting for Income Taxes*. To the extent that these timing differences arise from noncurrent assets transactions, they should be classified as noncurrent liabilities. The more common examples of these are the deferred taxes arising from timing differences relating to the accumulated depreciation on plant and equipment and deferred research and development costs. In reviewing the computation of deferred taxes, the auditor should be familiar with APB No. 11, *Accounting for Income Taxes*, and the Study on Interpretations.

Service Guarantees. It is common practice in some industries to offer free product service or replacement over an extended period. In the automobile industry, for example, such warranty may cover five years or 50,000 miles, whichever comes first. In order to match income and expense, the estimated future costs to fulfill the warranty should be anticipated in the year in which the product is sold. Generally there will be some experience upon which to base the estimated future expense. The auditor should review the computation of the current provision and evaluate the balance at the end of the period. In addition, he must review the underlying experience documentation and test the actual charges to ascertain that only proper charges are included.

PROGRAM

Internal Control Questionnaire

A. General
1. Does the company have internal auditors?
2. Does the internal auditor's program include periodic review of long-term debt records for:
   a. Authorizations?
   b. Issuance of obligations?
   c. Principal payments?
   d. Interest payments?
   e. Compliance with terms?
3. Is a copy of the obligation agreement maintained on file?
4. Are key officials kept abreast of the terms and conditions of existing agreements, including status of compliance-provision computations?
5. Is a summary of the obligation agreement provisions, including a tickler file of required due dates, reports, computations, etc., maintained by appropriate officers?
6. Are amendments to agreements given the same attention as though they were original documents?

B. Authorization
1. Have all long-term obligations been approved by the board of directors?
2. If not, is the approval commensurate with the requirements of the charter bylaws or state law?
3. Indicate authority for approval of:
   a. Long-term bonds or notes
   b. Pension agreements
   c. Deferred compensation
   d. Leases
   e. Long-term purchase commitments

C. Issuance of obligations
1. Are notes pre-numbered?
2. Is a record maintained by number of all unissued, issued, voided, and redeemed notes?
3. Is custody of the records in "2" above maintained by:
   a. Someone not involved in the cash or accounting functions?
   b. Trustee, registrar, or transfer agent?
4. Are the records of the custodian compared regularly with the general ledger control accounts?
5. On newly issued obligations, is a record maintained with respect to:
   a. Consideration received?
   b. Expenses of the issue?
   c. Accounting treatment accorded to the obligation, consideration, expenses incurred, and premium or discount?
6. Is such record approved by a responsible officer?

D. Accounting records
1. Are the accounting records adequate to permit:
   a. Ready balancing of details with controls?
   b. Determination of amounts held by each creditor?
   c. Determination of maturity dates?
   d. Computation of interest paid or accrued on each issue or note?
2. Are the personnel handling the note records independent of:
   a. Cash disbursements personnel?
   b. Personnel reconciling note records with general ledger accounts?
3. Are proper authorizations received for:
   a. Principal payments?
   b. Interest payments?
   c. Redemptions?
   d. Sinking fund payments?
   e. Conversions?
   f. Prepayments?
4. Are records for the sinking fund properly segregated and adequately detailed to conform with the sinking fund provisions of loan agreements?

E. Agreement provisions
1. Are determinations made monthly of:
   a. Ratios that are to be maintained, such as working capital, debt to equity, etc.?
   b. Limitations on cash expenditures?
   c. Other limitations specified in agreement?

Audit Program

1. Prepare related section of questionnaire on internal control and ascertain by observation and test that the indicated procedures are being followed.

2. In the light of (*a*) the evaluation of the system of internal control, (*b*) the audit program performed by the internal auditor, and (*c*) the type of industry, add below (or on a separate page) additional audit operations considered necessary in the circumstances. Likewise, delete inapplicable operations considered unnecessary in the circumstances.

3. Obtain and check or prepare a schedule of all long-term liabilities. The schedule should provide for description of debt, balance at the beginning of period, additions and/or reductions, balance at the end of period, amounts held in treasury and/or sinking funds, amounts due currently, interest expense for the period and amounts of interest accrued or prepaid at the end of the period, and reference to audit permanent file for computation of compliance provisions.

4. For each new obligation or revision to existing obligations during the period:

A. Obtain a copy of the indenture or agreement for the permanent file.

B. Prepare a permanent-file record for each new issue (update for revisions) to show the following:

(1) Description of debt
(2) Authorized and issued amount and rate of interest
(3) Authority for issuance
(4) Consideration received
(5) Repayment schedule of principal and interest
(6) Holders or obligees
(7) Special provisions or options for repayment, such as prepayment clauses, etc.
(8) Summary of other major provisions of agreement
(9) Schedule for computation of all required compliance provisions

C. Ascertain the appropriateness of, and the documentation of, the authority for issuance.

D. Verify the receipt of the consideration received as to its type, amount, existence, propriety, and appropriateness of the recording in the accounts.

E. Review the authorization for, and the computation of, interest and expenses incurred in connection with issuance, including such expenses as finder's or broker's fees, legal and accounting fees, printing costs, and valuation amounts assigned to warrants, conversion, or other rights granted or issued.

F. Perform audit steps indicated under 5 below.

5. For existing obligations:

A. Verify that all payments, prepayments, sinking fund payments, redemptions, and interest payments required during the period have been made.

B. Verify that the amount of each payment is properly computed.

C. Examine paid checks and other applicable documentation as considered necessary in the circumstances.

D. Verify the computation of all compliance provisions and include the computations in the permanent file. Note the effect, if any, on such computations of new obligations issued during the period.

E. Verify by direct communication to each holder or trustee:

(1) Balances outstanding at the end of the period (including security pledged thereto, as applicable);
(2) Payments of principal or interest or other significant events occurring during the period as considered necessary in the circumstances.

BIBLIOGRAPHY

Accounting Research Study No. 1, *The Basic Postulates of Accounting*, by Maurice Moonitz, AICPA, New York, 1965.

Accounting Trends and Techniques, AICPA, New York, published annually.

APB Statement No. 4, *Basic Concepts and Accounting Principles Underlying Financial Statements of Business Enterprises*, AICPA, New York, 1970.

APB Statement No. 47, *Accounting for Costs of Pension Plans*, AICPA, New York, 1956.

Opinions and Statements of the Accounting Principles Board, AICPA, New York, to date.

Cashin, James A., and Garland C. Owens: *Auditing*, New York, The Ronald Press Company, 1963.

Johnson, James T., and J. Herman Brosseaux: "Events Subsequent to the Date of Financial Statements," in *Readings in Auditing*, 2d ed., Cincinnati, Ohio, South-Western Publishing Company, 1965.

Meigs, W. B., and E. John Larsen: *Principles of Auditing*, 4th ed., Homewood, Ill., Richard D. Irwin, Inc., 1969.

Meigs, W. B., C. E. Johnson, and T. F. Keller: *Advanced Accounting,* New York, McGraw-Hill Book Company, 1963.
Simons, H., and W. E. Karrenbrock: *Intermediate Accounting,* Cincinnati, Ohio, South-Western Publishing Company, 1964.

Bevis, Herman W.: "Contingencies and Probabilities in Financial Statements," *The Journal of Accountancy,* October, 1968.
Davidson, Sidney: "Accounting and Financial Reporting in the Seventies," *The Journal of Accountancy,* December, 1969.
Abrams, Reuben W.: "Accounting for the Cost of Pension Plans and Deferred Compensation Contracts," *The New York Certified Public Accountant,* April, 1970.
Beechy, Thomas H.: "The Cost of Leasing: Comment and Correction," *The Accounting Review,* October, 1970.
Hawkins, David F.: "Objectives, Not Rules, for Lease Accounting," *Financial Executive,* 1970.

Chapter **29**

Owners' Equity

FRANK W. KOLMIN

Professor of Accounting and Finance and Director of Accounting Programs, School of Business, State University of New York at Albany

NATURE AND TYPES OF OWNERS' EQUITY

Nature of Equity. By comparison, the verification of a firm's owners' equity accounts usually takes less time than the completion of most other phases of an auditing program. This fact is due primarily to two reasons:

1. The comparatively insignificant number of transactions involving proprietorship accounts.
2. The reliance on the indisputable correctness of the equation of accounting. Once the correctness and accuracy of asset and liability accounts are assured, the excess of total assets over total liabilities, the total net worth, is also considered correct.

With respect to item 1 above, little can be said except that the relatively small number of transactions which are directly recorded in net worth accounts is very often more than offset by the size and importance of the individual items. This fact justifies very careful analysis of each entry. Another point to be borne in mind is the need for strict adherence to legal requirements and contractual obligations.

Concerning item 2 above, it is evident that proprietorship *in total* must be correct if all assets and liabilities have been assigned their correct values. This fact does not, however, exclude the possibility of misstatements in individual net worth accounts in the case of an individual proprietorship or a partnership or the wrong classification of transactions so far as various corporate net worth accounts are concerned. Such errors of classification could seriously affect the respective financial interests of different classes of stockholders which may vary considerably from each other. Of equal importance is the observance of legal requirements and provisions concerning transactions involving retained earnings, authorizations by the board of directors, the control of outstanding subscriptions receivable, the price at which new capital stock is sold, and many others. With respect to partnerships, the adherence to or the violation of the partnership agreement must be established beyond doubt so far as interest on partners' investments, partners' salaries and drawings, profit-sharing ratio, etc., are affected.

In view of the aforesaid, the *responsibility of the auditor* when reviewing net worth accounts is clearly established. Taking for granted the mathematical accuracy of the overall amount of proprietorship, each transaction appearing in the various capital accounts must be verified as to its correct classification as well as to its adherence to legal and contractual requirements. Good accounting practice and generally accepted principles must be preserved and authorization for all transactions must be proved. Beyond signing a certificate of audit the accountant must be aware of income tax implications, particularly so far as partnerships and corporate entities are concerned, because it is customary that the accountant performing the audit also prepares the client's income tax returns. Attention is drawn in this connection to the reconciliation statements required on partnership and corporation tax returns which, in turn, require the thoroughgoing analysis of asset, liability, and proprietorship accounts.

Internal Control and Internal Auditing. As in all other phases of an auditing program, the rigor and depth of the independent accountant's examination of net worth accounts depends on the degree of internal control and audit practiced in each individual firm. The evaluation of such practices is of particular importance in the case of larger partnerships and corporate entities where a more or less unified interest in owners' equity is lacking and where the rights and privileges of different parties (partners, stockholders, creditors) must be preserved and guarded. The accountant should establish the following facts:

1. That the internal control practiced in a firm under review does indeed exist and is not, in reality, a mere "illusion" of control without actual substance.
2. That the expense of establishing and operating certain controls does not exceed to a considerable measure the benefits one can justly expect to be derived from such practices.

Sole Proprietorships. When auditing the capital accounts of a single proprietorship, documentation of original or subsequent capital investments is sometimes not available. Another difficulty frequently encountered, particularly in the case of smaller firms, is the intermingling of personal transactions with business transactions. A third point to be taken into account is the usual lack of sufficient internal control; this deficiency is particularly serious if the owner customarily makes small withdrawals in cash, thus opening the door to employees' dishonesty.

Auditing considerations and procedures

1. In the case of an initial audit, a complete analysis of the *owner's capital account* from the inception of the business is recommended. Should this be too long ago to be practicable, the auditor should at least go back a number of years to establish the comparative correctness of this year's opening balance. In the case of a repeat audit, changes in the capital account between audit dates should be analyzed fully and substantiated.

2. The genuine *character of personal drawings* as opposed to business expenses must be established. This is sometimes a problematic task without actually reviewing all expense items, but spot checks of expense accounts might at least offer some insight into the accounting and business practices followed. Expenses of the business charged to drawings should be reclassified and entered in expense accounts. On the other hand, personal expenses paid from business funds should be reclassified as personal drawings.

Such lack of separation may well be coincidental; in many cases however, it is specifically aimed at tax savings. The auditor should turn his attention primarily to certain borderline items which might fall between business expenses and those of a private and social nature. Accounts with titles like "Maintenance and Repairs," "Travel Expenses," "Entertainment," "Advertising and Promotion," and others should be scrutinized to establish the correct classification of entries.

3. The *owner's drawing account* must be analyzed with care, examining original vouchers for each entry. Where clear evidence of the owner's receipt of alleged drawings is available, they are accepted at face value. Where, however, frequent small cash withdrawals are booked, it is advisable to establish the fact that these alleged drawings were actually received by the proper person.

4. A *summary of capital changes* is recommended, explaining differences of capital balances between audit dates. Thus, actual results from operations can be clearly separated from capital contributions or capital withdrawals.

5. It might be advisable in some cases to ask the firm's owner to *confirm the final net worth amount* as shown on the audited balance sheet.

Partnerships. The accountant is confronted with the same basic problems in the audit of partnerships' net worth accounts as in the case of an individual proprietorship, but on a larger scale. The following equity accounts are usually found in the ledger of a partnership: partners' capital accounts; partners' drawing accounts; partners' salary accounts; interest on investment accounts; partners' loan accounts; interest on partners' loan accounts.

Internal control. Following is a brief summary of the more important points which an internal control system should cover, so far as partnership net worth accounts are concerned. It is advisable to ascertain the presence or absence of such controls before actually reviewing the capital accounts in order to establish the probable scope and depth of the review work to be performed.

1. Strict adherence to contractual agreements among partners
2. Active control over partners' drawings
3. Accurate computation of interest on partners' capital and correct determination of residual profits and their distribution
4. Strict separation of authority for and recording of transactions affecting net worth accounts and related items which determine the extent of residual profits available for distribution
5. Handling and recording of partners' loans to and from the firm
6. Valuation of contributed assets reflected directly in proprietorship accounts

Auditing considerations and procedures

1. *The articles of copartnership* are the legal basis for a partnership's operation from which the auditor must determine the true intent of the partners. In case of doubt, discussion with the partners should clarify matters. *In the absence of a written partnership agreement,* the auditor must satisfy himself that all partners fully understand and agree to the method of keeping the accounts, particularly so far as profit distribution, partners' salaries, loan agreements, interest provisions, etc., are concerned. The auditor should reduce to writing all the salient points of the verbal agreement and ask the partners to initial the document. This should be done for the auditor's own protection. Under no condition should the auditor prepare a document which could be interpreted as a partnership agreement; this should be done by the firm's attorney.

2. *Excerpts* of the pertinent parts *of the partnership agreement* should be prepared for inclusion in the client's permanent file. The following facts should be noted: names and types (classes) of partners; period to be covered by the financial statements; duties of each partner and time devoted to the business; capital contribution requirements; interest provisions as they apply to partners' loans, capital contributions, and excess contributions or capital deficiencies; provisions and limitations for partners drawings and/or salaries; profit and loss distribution ratio; provisions concerning the death or the withdrawal of partners; procedures in case of liquidation of the firm; reciprocal life insurance arrangements; any additions to and deletions from the contract during the year under audit.

3. *Intermingling of partners' private affairs* with those of the firm must be disclosed and correcting entries must be made. This problem has already been mentioned in the discussion of the sole proprietorship; in the case of a partnership, however, it is of much greater consequence because the actions of one partner eventually affect the capital accounts of all other partners.

4. In an initial audit, the *original opening entries* should be traced to their respective sources and must be verified. Attention is directed to details such as:

a. Partners' contributions in assets other than cash; the auditor must establish the basis and adequacy of asset valuation.

b. Liabilities assumed by the firm.

c. Adherence to contractual provisions as they apply to partners' initial contributions.

5. In a repeat audit, all *changes in partners' capital accounts* between audit dates must be traced to original entries and available documentation. The maintenance of the contractually established levels of capital accounts must be checked, and deficiencies and overages should be brought to partners' attention. Overages in capital accounts could indicate that a loan to the firm rather than additional investment was intended.

6. *Partners' salary accounts* should be checked as to compliance with contractual provisions. No items of drawing should appear on this account because the distribution of residual profits would thus be distorted. Partners' salaries reduce profits available for final distribution, while drawings do not; the latter are made against anticipated profits.

In the absence of a partnership agreement, salaries and drawings must be clearly distinguished from each other after the intent of the partners has been determined. In case of doubt, items marked "salaries" should be included among drawings.

7. *Partners' drawing accounts* must be analyzed and each item vouched. Drawings of individual amounts as well as amounts in total must comply with contractual provisions. If frequent small withdrawals in cash are evident for which no written proof exists, they should be confirmed with the partners concerned to avoid possible misappropriation of funds by employees and to detect any fictitious charges to drawing accounts. Expense accounts should be analyzed as extensively as possible within the framework of the audit to ensure that personal drawings have not been booked as expense items. Any appropriate adjustments should be discussed with the principals of the firm.

8. If partners take *firm merchandise for personal use,* the individual drawings account should be debited. The accountant must determine the correct valuation as agreed upon by the partners. Consistency in this practice is important in order to avoid undue advantages or disadvantages to the several partners.

9. *Interest charged or credited* to the various partners should be checked for compliance with the partnership agreement and for mathematical correctness. As in the case of salaries, errors in interest items would necessarily affect the firm's profit. Items to consider are interest on capital contributions, interest on loans, interest on capital deficiencies, and interest on additional contributions.

10. The *division of profit or loss* should be carefully checked and recomputed in accordance with contractual arrangements. Unless otherwise stated, profits are considered for final distribution *after* allowing for partners' salaries and interest.

11. If this is the first audit since the inception of the firm, the auditor should pay considerable attention to possible *changes of a legal nature* which might have taken place since the firm was first established, such as partner's death, withdrawals from the firm, admission of new partners, etc. These occurrences are legal dissolutions of a partnership (without partnership termination) followed by the immediate reestablishment of a new partnership. Related accounting entries must be checked for compliance with the partnership agreement and for correctness of the mathematical computation.

Anything dubious or erroneous should be brought to the partners' attention in order to avoid possible difficulties in later years.

12. *Partner's loan accounts* should undergo careful analysis to establish the following facts:
    a. Timely repayment of loans.
    b. Correct classification; if the partner has made a loan to the firm and, at the same time, is deficient as to his capital contribution, this fact should be brought into the open and a reclassification of the loan (or part thereof) as capital should be recommended.

13. A *Statement of capital changes* should either be incorporated in the net worth section of the balance sheet or presented in an appendix thereto. This can be done in any form convenient to the accountant, so long as it shows clearly the development of the various capital accounts from one audit period to the next.

14. Without going into details, the problem of *liquidation of a partnership* is mentioned here because the auditor's services are sought frequently when this problem arises. As liquidation of a partnership proceeds and funds become available, the accountant must make sure that:
    a. Partnership liabilities are discharged before payments to partners are made.
    b. Partners do not receive payments which could, at a later date, prove in excess of their just share of liquidation proceeds.
    c. The "right of offset" is enforced whenever applicable.
    d. Partners' loans to the firm are repaid before partners' capital investments are refunded.

For details concerning partnership liquidation procedures and accounting, reference may be made to any one of the many accounting textbooks available.

Corporations. Specific objectives. Because of the materiality of the amounts involved and because all the rights and privileges of the various groups of stockholders must be observed and secured, the audit of corporate proprietorship accounts should be comprehensive in scope and detailed in practical application. It is important to remember that certain restrictions imposed by law or by contract are frequently beneficial to one group of stockholders to the disadvantage of another.

The principal purposes of reviewing corporate proprietorship accounts can be grouped as follows: (1) auditing objectives, and (2) statement presentation.

1. *Auditing objectives:*
    a. All stock issues must be *authorized* by charter and must be *approved* by the board of directors. No overissue of stock must take place.
    b. *Cash and other assets* acquired through the issuance of stock must have been received, properly classified and valued, and correctly recorded.
    c. *Internal control* and the *scope of internal auditing* must be evaluated to ascertain the degree of reliability of the accounting system and the extent of the audit required.
    d. *Distributions to stockholders* of any kind as well as all reservations of retained earnings must be approved by the board of directors and sometimes by the stockholders.
    e. *All rights and privileges* of creditors and the various groups of stockholders must be preserved, and all restrictions must be observed and disclosed.

f. Account balances must be stated correctly, and *generally accepted accounting principles* must be followed.

2. *Statement presentation:*

The disclosure of the true capital structure of the firm so that present stockholders and creditors, as well as prospective investors, may be given a clear and unbiased picture. To achieve this objective the following details must be observed:

a. Ownership—the respective equities of the various groups must be shown separately and should not be intermingled.

b. Sources—the origin of each item of capital should be established and noted as clearly and expediently as possible; each source should be shown separately.

c. Commitments which may eventually affect stockholders' interests must be disclosed. Among these are shares of stock reserved for issuance under stock purchase and option plans, outstanding stock purchase warrants, outstanding convertible securities (preferred stock or bonds) which may be exchanged into common stock at holders' option, and merger plans either fully consummated or contingent upon future developments.

d. Amounts shown on financial statements must be proved by supporting records.

e. Restrictions on the use of retained earnings and the conditions under which such restrictions are to take effect should be disclosed in some detail.

f. Appropriations of retained earnings, either voluntary or contractual in nature, must be shown separately and should be adequately explained.

Internal control. In order to review a corporation's system of internal control as it affects net worth accounts, the following pertinent points should be kept in mind:

1. Adherence to state corporate laws and to provisions of the charter and the bylaws.
2. Proper authorization for capital transactions and related accounting entries by the board of directors (and possibly by stockholders).
3. Proper delegation and division of duties and decision making, separated from the recording of capital transactions.
4. Complete control over the number of shares issued, their sale price, and the method of payment.
5. The transfer (and reclassification) of items from one proprietorship account to another.
6. Capital contributed in assets other than cash, control of the valuation of such assets, and the amount of equity created by property thus received.
7. The procedure of physically signing and issuing stock certificates either when fully paid-up or when replacing previously returned certificates.
8. Control over the computing, recording, and actual paying of dividends.
9. Transactions involving treasury stock.
10. The proper handling of federal and state tax stamps.
11. The employment of an outside registrar and transfer agent. This by itself is an important part of internal control, which reduces the scope of the independent auditor's examination to requesting confirmatory reports from these independent agents.

Terminology. In connection with the statement presentation of corporate net worth, attention is drawn to the Accounting Terminology Bulletin No. 1 of the American Institute of Certified Public Accountants. Without going into details, it is suggested that auditors attempt to adhere to the Committee's suggestions as closely as possible in order to prepare more meaningful and more uniform financial reports. The words "Surplus" and "Reserve" as used in the past by many accountants have contributed to the confusion of nonprofessional readers of financial statements. In summary, it is recommended that the use of the term Surplus on financial statements be discontinued and that it be replaced by words more descriptive of the source of the portion of net worth concerned. Instead of "Earned Surplus," for instance, "Retained Earnings" might be used. Instead of "Capital Surplus" or "Paid-in Surplus," some description like "Excess of Contributed Capital over Par or Stated Value," or simply "Premium on Capital Stock" is recommended.

The term "Reserve" should be used with discretion and applied only to appropriations from Retained Earnings. Such use makes unnecessary the troublesome distinction between valuation reserves, capital reserves, and surplus reserves.

Corporate documents. Before actually starting the audit of corporate net worth accounts, the nonfinancial records must be surveyed. These include: the corporate charter (including amendments), the bylaws, and the minute books of directors' and stockholders' meetings. The auditor must develop a thorough understanding of the provisions contained therein because the operations of the corporate client and, indeed, its very existence, are based on these provisions.

In an *initial audit* these nonfinancial records should be excerpted and included in the client's permanent file. Legal counsel for the client should provide the auditor with a representation letter indicating total authorized shares of stock, par or stated value, and whether or not all outstanding shares are fully paid and nonassessable. During *subsequent audits,* only additions to these documents must be reviewed and brought up to date. Following are the most important details to be included in the auditor's excerpts of nonfinancial records.

THE CORPORATE CHARTER (ARTICLES OF INCORPORATION):

1. The number of shares authorized with respect to each class of stock
2. Par values or stated values
3. Rights, privileges, and restrictions with respect to each class of stock together with possible call or redemption features and the pertinent prices and dates for each
4. Voting power (or the lack of it) for each class of stock
5. Dividend rates for preferred issues, cumulative or participating features, etc.
6. Preferences in liquidation of preferred stock
7. Powers and authority vested in stockholders and in the board of directors
8. Special reserve requirements directed toward preserving paid-in capital
9. Any other matter of importance to the operation of the corporation

THE CORPORATE BYLAWS:

1. How directors are to be elected
2. What constitutes a quorum for stockholders' general and special meetings

3. Duties and policies of the directors
4. Dividend policy (if any)
5. The method of stockholders' voting
6. The method to be used in amending the charter and the bylaws

THE MINUTES OF BOARD OF DIRECTORS' MEETINGS:

1. Compensation of officers and directors
2. Bonus and profit-sharing plans, pension and retirement plans, etc.
3. Actual declarations of dividends
4. Authorization (by stockholders) for capital stock increases and decreases
5. Contracts with executives and unions
6. Purchase and sale of treasury shares

THE MINUTES OF STOCKHOLDERS' MEETINGS:

1. Authorization for sale and merger
2. Authorization for stock issuance and retirement
3. Changes in par or stated values of stock and in other actions including quasi-reorganizations

Although not absolutely necessary, some accountants request responsible officers or directors to confirm the completeness of stockholders' and directors' minutes as of the date of the audit. In the case of actions taken by either the stockholders or the directors of which no record appears in the minutes, the auditor should request that these documents be brought up to date before the conclusion of the audit engagement.

CAPITAL STOCK

Auditing Considerations and Procedures

1. Establish legal authority for all stock issues.
2. Verify all outstanding stock.
3. Schedule and analyze capital stock accounts; verify and vouch all entries.
4. Ascertain and note possible commitments of future issuance of stock.
5. Review statement presentation of capital stock accounts.

Legal authority. A review of the excerpts prepared from the original nonfinancial records in the client corporation's permanent file will familiarize the auditor with all legally possible stock issues. As one class of stock after the other is verified and scheduled in the working papers, the main points of interest with respect to each individual issue should be shown on each respective schedule. This will facilitate the final preparation of the net worth section of the balance sheet.

Outstanding stock. As mentioned earlier, the employment of an independent registrar (and possibly also a transfer agent) to handle the stock transactions of the corporation constitutes a strong element of internal control. The employment of a registrar is mandatory for corporations with stock issues listed on one of the security exchanges, and these corporations usually employ a transfer agent as well. While the former is charged with the responsibility of ensuring that no overissue of stock takes place, the latter is employed to handle the corporation's stock records including the transfer of ownership of shares.

If a registrar and a transfer agent are employed, a considerable amount of detail work in auditing is obviated. It is sufficient to confirm with each of the two independent agents the following points with respect to each of the several stock issues:

1. The number of authorized shares
2. The number of issued and outstanding shares
3. The number of treasury shares held for the client corporation

The requests for confirmation should be made by the client, with answers to be addressed directly to the independent auditor by the registrar and the transfer agent. The information supplied in these reports must substantiate the number of shares shown as issued on the various capital stock accounts in the client's ledger.

If no independent agents are employed and the corporation issues its own stock and keeps its own stockholders' records, the accountant must satisfy himself that stock certificates and related records are being handled in a proper and safe manner. Following are the most important of these safeguards:

1. An officer authorized by the board of directors, usually the secretary of the corporation, should be the custodian of unissued stock certificates which must be prenumbered by the printer. This officer should supervise the actual issuance of stock, the transfer of ownership, and the handling of the stockholders' records.

2. The officer authorized to sign stock certificates must do so only if stock has been fully paid for or if certificates are issued in replacement of canceled ones.

3. Upon the issuance of certificates, the corresponding stubs in the certificate book must be filled in completely and have affixed the required amount of federal (and sometimes also state) tax stamps.

4. Canceled stock certificates should show the proper endorsements on the back; they should be mutilated to prevent reissue and must be attached to the corresponding stubs.

5. If the corporation has more than just a few stockholders, a stockholders' ledger should be kept.

Once the accountant has reviewed these procedures, *actual verification of outstanding stock* necessitates only a few, rather simple steps:

6. Make sure that all unissued stock certificate blanks are accounted for.

7. Secure a trial balance of the stockholders' ledger showing the total number of shares issued and outstanding.

8. Stock certificate stubs, filled in and without canceled certificates attached, represent outstanding stock. Ascertain the total number of issued shares from this source.

9. The total of the trial balance from the stockholders' ledger, the total from adding together the number of shares shown on "active" certificate stubs, and the total number of shares shown on the appropriate capital stock account in the general ledger must agree.

10. Ensure that no overissue has taken place in any class of stock by comparing the total number of outstanding stocks with the respective authorization in the charter.

Capital stock accounts. The capital stock account for each class of stock should be scheduled separately, mentioning the more important characteristics of that stock, such as dividend rates, redemption values, restrictions, etc. Starting with the opening balance for the period under audit and ending with the year-end balance as per ledger account, all debits and credits should be scheduled. It may be convenient to arrange each of these working papers in the form of a "running analysis" for inclusion in the client's permanent file, to be brought up to date during each subsequent audit.

If this is an *initial audit engagement,* the correct balance of each capital stock account as of the beginning of the year under audit must be established. If at all possible, this should be done by reviewing all entries since the inception of the corporation. Should this prove impracticable, the auditor must at least go back far enough to be reasonably convinced of the correctness of this year's opening balance. In a *follow-up audit,* the last audited balance on each capital stock account is taken as the starting point. For the year under audit, each change, debit or credit, must be analyzed and verified as to authority, propriety, and accuracy of amount. This phase of the audit requires the accountant's attention to the following details:

1. All stock transactions must be checked for *proper authority* and conformity with applicable *state laws.* It is recommended that the accountant familiarize himself with the most important points of the corporation law of the state of incorporation.

2. In the case of *par value stock,* no problem of apportionment arises. Amounts received in excess of par value must appear on a separate Premium on Capital Stock account (or Contributed Capital in Excess of Par Value account) for each class of stock. A Discount on Capital Stock account will absorb amounts received below par value. In this connection it is essential to ascertain whether applicable state laws permit the original issuance of stock at a price below par value.

3. *If no par value stock* is sold, and a minimum stated value is either fixed by state law or prescribed in the corporate charter or by decision of the board of directors, the statement in 2 above also holds true. If no provision for stated value exists, the proceeds from stock sales can either be credited in total to the Capital Stock account or divided between the Capital Stock account and the related Premium account in any proportion, following the board of directors' decision.

4. *Cash proceeds* from stock sales should be traced through the cash receipts records to bank deposits. Prices at which stock sales were completed must be checked for the board's approval.

5. If stock is sold for *assets other than cash,* the debit entries must be traced to the appropriate asset accounts in the general ledger. Valuation of assets received must conform with the board's decision as contained in the minutes. It is important to remember that, in the absence of fraud, the board's valuation is considered valid even though it may appear unrealistic. This fact, however, should not deter the accountant from bringing drastic overvaluations to the board's attention; he might even consider qualifying his opinion. The SEC will also object to any overvaluation of assets received in exchange for the corporation's stock that it detects.

6. The *capitalization of retained earnings* through the declaration of stock dividends must be checked for conformity with the board's decision. This transaction results in a debit to Retained Earnings and a credit to the appropriate Capital Stock account.

Although mentioned in a later section of this chapter, the differences between a *stock dividend* and a *stock split* might be discussed here, cautioning the auditor that such differentiation must properly be made. Beyond the fact that a stock dividend entails a reduction of retained earnings while a stock split-up does not, both actions appear similar in their effect upon the recipient and neither involves the distribution of corporate assets. The main difference lies in the *intent* of the issuing corporation, which the auditor must establish. According to the definitions contained in the Accounting Research and Terminology Bulletins, final edition, 1961, Chap. 7, a *stock dividend* is "motivated by the desire to give shareholders some ostensibly separate evidence of a part of their respective interests in accumulated corporate earnings." A stock split-up, on the other hand, "is prompted by a desire to increase the number of outstanding shares for the purpose of effecting a reduction in their unit market price."

The difference between a stock dividend and a stock split-up, then, lies in the number of shares additionally issued and their effect upon the stock's market price. Issuance of shares in a quantity of less than 20 or 25 percent of previously outstanding shares, which are expected to have no effect or only minor effects on the market price, should be treated as stock dividends in the corporation's records. Issuance of an additional quantity of stock in excess of about 25 percent of outstanding shares should be recorded as a stock split-up, regardless of the name originally used by the corporation. (Accounting Research and Terminology Bulletins, final edition, 1961, Chap. 7.) In any event, legal requirements must be observed in each instance.

7. Any *reduction of outstanding capital stock* either through direct purchase, the payment of liquidating dividends, or the cancellation of treasury stock must be checked against the authorization contained in the minutes of stockholders' and/or board of directors' meetings.

Future stock commitments. Such contingent commitments must be examined by reference to contracts and other nonfinancial records:

1. Examine *underwriting agreements* and marketing contracts showing past and future selling prices, underwriters' commissions, etc. For past transactions trace the amount of net cash received to accounting records and bank statements.
2. Review *stock option agreements* with employees and other parties. The total number of shares authorized for issuance under a stock option plan must be reserved, and this fact should be noted on the balance sheet. Option rights exercised during the period under audit must be checked for strict adherence to the original agreement.

Attention is drawn to the problem of valuation of stock option rights. The Accounting Research and Terminology Bulletins, final edition, 1961, Chap. 13, B, recommends that the value of stock options as of the date of issue of the rights be considered compensation. On the other hand, the Internal Revenue Code provides that stock options without a readily ascertainable market price be valued as of the date of their being exercised, at the earliest. The assigned (and taxable) value is the excess of the fair market price of the stock issued over the amount the option holder actually paid for the stock.

Statement presentation. Financial statements must be self-explanatory; reference to underlying records should not be necessary. It is essential, therefore, that each stock issue be adequately described on the balance sheet as to number of shares authorized; number of shares issued and outstanding; stock held in the treasury; par or stated value; preference, conversion, and liquidation rights; call features and call prices; dividend rates; etc. This information should be readily available from the working papers mentioned earlier. With respect to statement presentation of capital stock issues, the following particulars should be noted:

1. *Each class of stock should be shown separately* on the balance sheet in order of priority as to liquidation rights (and/or preference as to earnings), starting with the senior preferred issue. Related paid-in capital in excess of par or stated value should immediately follow each class of stock described.

2. *Preferred shares should not be shown at liquidation (redemption) values* but at par or stated values. Some accountants, however, prefer to enter no-par preferred issues at liquidation values rather than at stated values, debiting the difference to the related Contributed Capital in Excess of Stated Value Account so far as it can be absorbed; the unabsorbed difference is then shown as a debit to Retained Earnings. This kind of statement presentation has the advantage of creating a clear impression of the residual values left for holders of junior (common) stock. At the same time the retained earnings available for dividend payments are reduced.

In spite of this advantage, the use of the latter method is not recommended. The use of redemption values on the balance sheet creates the illusion of a stock liquidation which did not really take place. The APB Opinion No. 10, page 148, points out the need of establishing the relationship between the preference in liquidation and the par or stated value of preferred issues on the balance sheet. This may be done either parenthetically or "in short." The Board also recommends the disclosure, on the face of the balance sheet or in related notes, of the aggregate or per share amounts at which preferred shares may be called or otherwise redeemed. The same applies to aggregate or per share amounts of cumulative preferred dividends in arrears. It should also be noted that SEC Regulation S-X, Rule 3-19, provides that disclosure must be made to show:

a. The excess of redemption values over par or stated values

b. The amount by which such preference plus preferred dividends in arrears exceeds the net worth left for junior securities, if such be the case

c. Possible restrictions of retained earnings due to preferential liquidation or redemption treatment attached to one or more classes of preferred stock

3. *Agreement affecting stockholders' interests* in any way must be disclosed either within the net worth section proper or in the form of footnotes. Thus, reserved shares of stock must be mentioned, giving specific reasons for the reservation, quantities to be reserved, and prescribed purchase prices. The most common of these reservations are due to:

a. Outstanding options or purchase warrants

b. Conversion rights of preferred stock or bondholders

c. Capital stock subscribed but as yet unissued

4. *Unexchanged "old" stock, following a recapitalization,* sometimes creates a problem so far as statement presentation is concerned. It is customary to show the "new" stock issued and replacing old shares called in as if all old shares had been properly exchanged. The amount of unexchanged old stock must be disclosed either within the net worth section or by footnote.

This procedure should not be applied, however, if old shares are being held by a known group of dissenting stockholders. Such shares cannot be considered exchanged because the dissenting group may have applied to the courts for an evaluation and appraisal of the stock they hold.

5. If a plan exists for the *installment redemption of preferred stock,* the amount of money needed for the redemption of next year's lot should be deducted from the Capital Stock account and the related Premium account in the net worth section and shown as current liability.

Stock Subscriptions. To start, the auditor must familiarize himself with the essential provisions of the subscription contracts in effect. Such contracts may vary not only from corporation to corporation but also from one class of stock to another within the same firm.

Auditing considerations and procedures

1. All contracts must follow the basic rules laid down by the board of directors and must have been approved.
2. *Installment payments* on stock subscribed should be received as scheduled. Any installments in arrears should be noted and brought to the attention of the board.
3. *Stock certificates* should be issued only after full payment has been received or, if approved, after the subscriber has signed notes in the appropriate amounts.
4. *Cancellation of subscriptions* is to be handled as prescribed by state laws and/or as provided by contracts in force.
5. Any *unusual subscription contracts* should have the board's specific authorization.

The auditor should prepare a list of outstanding subscriptions, the total of which must match the balance on the subscriptions receivable control account. If a comparatively small number of subscriptions are outstanding, all individual items may be confirmed by correspondence with the subscribers. If the number of unpaid subscriptions is rather large, confirmations on a test basis are acceptable.

Statement presentation. Subscriptions receivable may be shown in three different ways on the balance sheet, depending upon when collection can reasonably be expected. This account should appear among investments as a *long-term receivable* if collection is not foreseen within the near future. If collection is expected within a year following the date of the audit, the subscriptions receivable account should appear among *current assets.* Should collection not be expected at all or if it is delayed for an indefinite period of time, subscriptions receivable should be *deducted from the balance of the Subscriptions account,* showing only the difference as paid-in capital.

The account "Capital Stock Subscribed" usually appears in the capital section of the balance sheet as a separate item; it represents the corporation's obligation to issue a certain number of shares once the contract price is fully paid. Some accountants prefer to credit the Capital Stock Issued account for the whole subscription amount, even though full payment was not received and no stock certificates were issued. This type of statement presentation, however, has not found wide acceptance in the accounting profession.

Stock Options and Warrants. *Stock options* differ from *stock warrants* in that the latter are transferable, enabling the holder to derive income from them without actually taking title to any shares of stock; the former must be exercised to create income.

Employee stock options present the auditor with two basic problems: (1) determining the value of option rights, and (2) determining the date of valuation. Both problems are, of course, interrelated.

1. It is not possible to arrive at an *objective valuation* of nontransferable stock options as the Accounting Research and Terminology Bulletins (final edition), 1961, Chap. 13, B, states. Yet, since there is a value to the grantee and a cost to the grantor corporation if the option price of the stock is below its fair market value, the auditor might suggest that the excess of the market price over the option price be considered the corporation's cost of the option and hence income to the employee. Accountingwise, at the time the option is granted, this should be expressed by a debit to the Salary (or Bonus) account and a credit to a *temporary capital account* like "Capital Through Stock Options." This account is, in essence, similar to a Subscription to Capital Stock account. As the option is exercised, a transfer to a permanent paid-in capital account should take place.

2. Deciding on a *date of valuation for stock options* is even more uncertain than determining its reasonable and acceptable compensation value.
   a. The APB Opinion No. 6 recommends the selection of the *date of granting the option* for valuation purposes.
   b. Many accountants feel that options should be valued as of the *date when the option right becomes unconditionally vested* in the holder.
   c. The auditor's attention is directed to the income tax aspects of employees' stock option plans generally. Whether such plans can be considered "qualified," "nonqualified," or "restricted" within the definitions of the Internal Revenue Code determines the amount and the time both of a deductible expense for the grantor corporation and of taxable income received by the grantee employee. Generally speaking, the corporation will experience a deductible expense (salary, bonus, etc.) at the time the employee realizes taxable income. (For details refer to Sec. 421 through 424 of the Internal Revenue Code.)
   d. The lack of uniformity of opinion as to the valuation date for stock options has been recognized by the SEC Accounting Series Release No. 76, which leaves the choice of method to the individual corporation.

Statement presentation of stock options. The reader of corporate financial statements must be enabled to gain a clear impression of the magnitude of possible stock purchases through options, with respect to stock issued which would otherwise be available for outright sale. The importance of this fact is evidenced by statements in the Accounting Research and Terminology Bulletins, final edition, 1961, Chap. 13, B, in SEC Regulation S-X, Rule 3-20, and in the New York Stock Exchange requirements for the listing of stock issues.

1. Disclosure must be made as to:
   a. The terms of the option plan (or plans) including the time during which it may be exercised and the lapse of time required before the option vests unconditionally in the holder
   b. The number and value of shares under option at balance sheet date and the number and value of shares which could have been, and actually were, opted during the year ended at balance sheet date
   c. The basis of accounting for any option arrangement in effect

2. Options accorded to employees as compensation, for which no shares have as yet been issued, should appear in the Capital section of the balance sheet at the amount of compensation (excess of market value over option price), in the same manner as proceeds from stock subscriptions.

3. After options have been exercised, appropriate amounts should be transferred to the credit of paid-in capital accounts.

Treasury Stock. Legal aspects. A corporation's transactions in its own stock are regulated by state laws in varying degrees. It is essential, therefore, that the auditor review the legal provisions governing treasury stock in the client's state of incorporation. Although some states have almost no such restrictive laws, the following regulations are most commonly found:

1. The cost of treasury stock acquired may not exceed the amount of retained earnings of the corporation at the time of acquisition.
2. The amount of retained earnings available for the payment of dividends is restricted to the excess over the cost of treasury stock acquired.

These restrictions, designed to prevent impairment of contributed capital, are of importance for the protection of creditors' interest.

Acquisition and valuation. Treasury stock may be acquired by purchase, by exchange for other assets, by donations from stockholders, in settlement of debts due the corporation, or through forfeiture of subscriptions. A difference of opinion exists because some accountants do not consider that shares which were forfeited by nonpayment of subscriptions are properly includable as treasury stock.

Treasury shares are commonly valued at acquisition cost and are so shown in the Treasury Stock account. A different method of valuation which is found sometimes records treasury shares at par or stated value in the Treasury Stock account, with any excess of cost over par or stated value absorbed by a related Capital Contributed in Excess of Par or Stated Value account. (See also "Statement Presentation," below.) It appears that the former method has gained considerable popularity over the latter, although both approaches are theoretically defensible. (Compare also AAA Accounting Concepts and Standards Underlying Corporate Financial Statements and APB Opinion No. 6, 12b.)

Auditing considerations and procedures

1. If treasury shares are held by a custodian (the corporation's own transfer agent) or deposited as collateral, the number of shares as well as the certificate numbers should be confirmed by correspondence with the custodian.
2. If treasury shares are available for inspection, the auditor should view the certificates to make sure that they are not attached to the related stubs (indicating cancellation) and that they are *properly endorsed* to the corporation or have a power of attorney endorsement attached.
3. Besides conforming to applicable state laws, each treasury stock transaction must have the *board of directors' express authorization* as stated in the minutes. The board's direction as to purchasing or selling prices must be followed; if available, correspondence and/or brokers' advice should be inspected.
4. *List all certificates representing treasury shares* showing certificate numbers and the quantity of shares involved. If such a list is available from the preceding audit, compare all certificates to that list and note any changes. This step may be useful in disclosing any unauthorized transactions which might possibly have taken place.
5. With the ledger account as a basis, prepare a schedule of changes for the year under audit and *trace each cash disbursement* (for acquisitions) *and each cash receipt* (for sales) to the cash records. If noncash assets were received or given up in treasury stock transactions, the board of directors' valuation

must be reviewed. *Non-cash assets acquired* by the corporation must not appear in the asset accounts at values exceeding the realizable cash value of the treasury shares given up in exchange. Any overvaluation of assets received in transactions of this kind should be brought to the board's attention with a request for a revaluation to realistic figures.

6. Whether treasury stock is carried in the accounts at cost or at par or stated value, the auditor must satisfy himself that accounting entries are consistent and are theoretically correct.

7. Sales of treasury stock directly to employees should be vouched, and related contracts should be reviewed.

Gain or loss. To avoid the misstatement of financial conditions the auditor must review the recording of gain or loss resulting from the sale of treasury stock. Basically, such gain or loss necessitates an adjustment of paid-in capital. *Gain* resulting from the resale of treasury shares at a price in excess of cost must be credited to a contributed capital account. A *loss* sustained should first be applied to prior gains from similar transactions; any loss not so absorbed may be debited to a paid-in capital account (premium account) relative to a class of stock which is no longer outstanding, with any residual loss reducing retained earnings.

The treatment of gain or loss due to treasury stock transactions, as described above, follows generally accepted accounting practices and is also approved by the SEC. It is essential to make sure that gains are not included either in the periodic income statement or in the credit of the retained earnings account.

Retirement of treasury stock. If treasury stock is *retired and canceled* pursuant to the board of directors' authority, the number of authorized shares of the specific class of stock is usually reduced. Should treasury stock be *retired without legal cancellation,* no reduction of the number of authorized shares is required. In either case, state laws may require the reservation from retained earnings of an amount equal to the cost of the retired treasury stock. The auditor should make certain that the balances of the appropriate capital accounts have been reduced by the par or stated value of the retired treasury stock and that any paid-in capital in excess of par or stated value pertaining to the treasury shares retired be eliminated. A *gain on retirement* should be credited to a special paid-in capital account. Any *excess of cost* of treasury shares retired over par or stated value should first reduce any Premium account related to that class of stock in proportion to the number of shares retired. Further unabsorbed cost may be debited to a paid-in capital account of an issue no longer outstanding, with any residual excess cost debited to the Retained Earnings account.

The APB Opinion No. 6, paragraph 12, clarifies this issue and, in addition, suggests that "alternatively, the excess may be charged entirely to retained earnings in recognition of the fact that a corporation can always capitalize or allocate retained earnings for such purposes."

Statement presentation. Under ordinary circumstances, *treasury stock should not appear among the assets on a corporate balance sheet* on the theory that a corporation cannot own part of itself and that assets and net worth should not be presented in inflated amounts. Some accountants consider the classification of treasury shares as assets acceptable if such shares were acquired for the specific purpose of resale to employees or others, following a definite plan. If a corporation speculates in its own stock as it would in the stock of other firms, the inclusion of the cost of such shares may be found sometimes among the corporation's "Investments." While not really objectionable, such treatment has not gained wide acceptance in the accounting profession. In any event, the reason for including treasury shares among the assets must be clearly stated. (Accounting Research and Terminology Bulletins, final edition, 1961, page 12.) Because treasury stock is not considered capital stock outstanding and because it is usually not considered an asset, it is logically excluded from dividend declarations.

Treasury stock is usually shown in the net worth section of a corporate balance sheet in one of two ways:

1. Following the *par value method*, the proper category of outstanding capital stock is reduced by the par or stated value of the treasury shares while the related Premium account is debited with an amount proportionate to the number of treasury shares held.
2. Following the *cost method*, the actual cost of acquisition is shown as a deduction from the total stockholders' equity.

The laws of many states provide that earned surplus must be restricted to the extent of the cost of treasury shares, regardless of the method of statement presentation. Where the establishment of such a reserve is not legally required, the board of directors may voluntarily order that this procedure be followed to avoid the payment of dividends which could possibly jeopardize creditors' rights.

Because of its simplicity and clarity, the cost method has gained in popularity over the par value method and is used widely today. The following illustration will exemplify the two alternative methods.

Par Value Method

Capital stock preferred; noncumulative 5%, $100 par value. 10,000 shares authorized, 6,000 shares outstanding		$ 600,000
Capital in excess of par value, preferred		420,000
Capital stock common; no par value, $5 stated value. 50,000 shares authorized, 40,000 shares outstanding	$200,000	
Less: 2,000 treasury shares	10,000	190,000
Capital in excess of stated value, common	$440,000	
Less: paid-in excess attributable to treasury shares (1/20)	22,000	418,000
Retained earnings:		
Unrestricted	$292,000	
Restricted * by actual cost of treasury stock	40,000	332,000
Total stockholders' equity		$1,960,000

Cost Method

Capital stock preferred; noncumulative 5%, $100 par value. 10,000 shares authorized, 6,000 shares outstanding		$ 600,000
Capital in excess of par value, preferred		420,000
Capital stock common; no par value, $5 stated value. 50,000 shares authorized, 40,000 shares outstanding of which 2,000 shares are held in the treasury		200,000
Capital in excess of stated value, common		440,000
Retained earnings:		
Unrestricted	$300,000	
Restricted * by actual cost of treasury stock	40,000	340,000
Total		$2,000,000
Less: Cost of 2,000 treasury shares, common		40,000
Total stockholders' equity		$1,960,000

* State laws requiring the restriction of retained earnings by the amount of the cost of treasury stock are presumed. This fact could also be shown by means of a parenthetical remark or by footnote.

PAID-IN CAPITAL

Nature of Paid-in Capital. The auditor must determine and fully understand the various *sources of paid-in capital* for each individual corporation whose books he audits. Such sources may vary from firm to firm, and the auditor should insist on the use of headings which are sufficiently descriptive and meaningful to both the professional and the nonprofessional reader of corporate records and statements.

With a view to efficiency and to avoid duplication of effort, *paid-in capital accounts* and *capital stock accounts* should be audited simultaneously, because many transactions affect both sets of accounts. Assuming that stock has been issued at a value above par or stated value, the following are some examples of transactions affecting paid-in capital accounts and capital stock accounts at the same time:

1. The exercise of stock options and warrants
2. The conversion of convertible securities
3. The issuance of stock in the case of corporate combinations accounted for as pooling of interests
4. Writing off unamortized debt discounts and expenses relating to the conversion of convertible securities
5. Stock splits

Sources of Paid-in Capital. Paid-in capital in excess of par or stated value is invariably the result of transactions between a corporation and its stockholders, and it may arise through:

1. *The original issue of stock at a premium.* What constitutes a premium is clear in the cases of par value stock or no par value stock with an established stated value. If, however, no par or stated value is established, the decision of the board of directors rules as to the amounts credited to the Capital Stock and the Premium accounts respectively. The same is true if stock dividends are declared and the market value of the shares distributed exceeds the established par or stated value.
2. *Gain on disposition or retirement of treasury stock* at prices above the cost of acquisition.
3. *Donations* received in the corporation's own stock or in the form of other assets.
4. Receipts from *assessments* levied on capital stock either before or after the contract price has been received by the corporation, provided such assessment brings the total received in exchange for the stock above par or stated value.
5. *Conversion of preferred stock into common stock.* The excess of par or stated value of the converted preferred issue over that of the common stock represents paid-in capital.
6. *Reduction of par or stated value* of an outstanding stock issue or the change from par value stock to no-par value stock with a lower stated value (quasi-reorganization).
7. *Forfeited stock subscriptions,* if the applicable state laws provide that money received from subscribers prior to their default need not be returned and becomes the property of the corporation. It is important to note that many states provide for the return to the subscriber of any surplus funds received through the public or private resale of the defaulted stock.

Auditing considerations and procedures

1. Once the auditor has determined the various sources of paid-in capital, he should satisfy himself that each is shown on a *separate paid-in capital account.* Subsequent retirement or sale of treasury stock or the retirement of a complete stock issue may make such separation of accounts consequential. If the auditor encounters combined or mixed paid-in capital accounts, he should attempt proper classification and segregation to the greatest extent possible. Any part of premium on a preferred stock issue can become part of common stock equity only after the preferred issue is eliminated through conversion or redemption.

2. Each paid-in capital account should be completely scheduled, and *each entry must be verified and vouched* for authority, source, reason for existence, and correctness of amount. Original documents and minutes should be inspected. In the case of an initial audit this verification should be extended to the inception of the corporation, if possible.

3. *Operating deficits* and *extraordinary losses* must not be covered from paid-in capital in any manner, except in the case of a properly planned and authorized quasi-reorganization. Should the auditor find violations of this basic principle, appropriate adjustments must be made.

4. *Expenses of organization and of stock issue* may be charged against paid-in capital in excess of par or stated value of the specific class of stock if this is possible, if state laws so permit, and if the board of directors so authorizes. Frequently, however, such expenses are amortized and charged against earnings over a short period of time. The Internal Revenue Code provides for a write-off of such expenses over a minimum period of sixty months.

5. Regarding *paid-in capital arising from donations,* the auditor must make sure that such donations were genuine and unconditional, properly authorized, and entered at approved values. Any overvaluation should be brought to the attention of the board of directors, and an appropriate adjustment should be requested. Should any conditions be attached to a gift of stock or other assets, the item might best be transferred to a "Contingent Donation" account until the conditions are removed.

If a donation consists of the corporation's own stock, some accountants recommend that no paid-in capital account be established until the donated stock has been resold. (Lenhart and Defliese, *Montgomery's Auditing,* and Holmes' *Auditing: Principles and Procedures.*)

While it is an established fact that paid-in capital in excess of par or stated value must be considered part of a corporation's permanent capital, a difference of opinion should be mentioned here:

1. The majority of accountants maintain that before it can absorb charges attributable to other classes of stock, all paid-in capital must remain intact until the class of stock to which it pertains is fully retired or redeemed.

2. Other accountants believe that *any* paid-in capital in excess of par or stated value can absorb premiums, call expenses, expenses of issue, etc., of *any* class of stock.

Discount on Capital Stock. The auditor must satisfy himself that each transaction involving the original sale of stock below par value meets with applicable state laws and has the approval of the board of directors. In a number of states the sale of stock at a discount is prohibited, while the laws of other states permit such action. But even then, conflicting decisions regarding the subsequent liability of stockholders who acquired shares at a price below par value create some uncertainty, and the accountant might advise the client to seek legal advice.

When finding stock issues at a discount, the auditor should consider the following:

1. Discount accounts should be clearly marked as such and *should not be amortized against income;* neither should unpaid subscriptions be written off, because such action would create the same effect.

2. Although discounts may be deducted on the balance sheet from premiums pertaining to the same class of stock, *discount accounts and premium accounts in the ledger should not be merged* even if they attach to the same class of stock. Although some accountants approve of such offset, it is recommended that these accounts be retained independently in the ledger.

Statement presentation

1. Each of the various types of capital contributed in excess of par or stated value should be *shown separately* on the balance sheet, even though two or more may apply to the same class of stock.

2. When a number of paid-in capital accounts have only quite insignificant balances, they may be lumped together on the balance sheet. Capital from sources other than contributions received must not, however, be included.

3. Discount on *common stock* may be shown as a deduction from:
   a. Premiums at which part of the same stock issue may have been sold
   b. The capital stock account to which it relates
   c. Total corporate net worth

4. Discount on *preferred stock* may be shown as a deduction from:
   a. Premiums applicable to the same class of preferred stock
   b. Paid-in capital in excess of par value of another issue no longer outstanding at that time
   c. Retained earnings

5. *Paid-in capital created through donation with an unfulfilled condition pending* is not yet part of the corporation's net worth. The item should therefore be removed from the capital section of the balance sheet or adequately explained in the form of a footnote.

Revaluation of Plant and Equipment. The restatement of assets, frequently at values higher than book values, may be due either to excessive depreciation charged in prior years or to a price level increase. If the former is the reason, the auditor should treat the revaluation as a prior years' adjustment affecting retained earnings. In the latter case, a Revaluation of Plant and Equipment account (previously called "Revaluation Surplus") should be set up. This increase of corporate net worth should remain separate from either paid-in sources of capital or from retained earnings because such appreciation is actually unrealized and not available for dividend payments.

Auditing considerations and procedures

1. "Revaluation Surplus" *must not be used to charge off any existing deficit or other current losses* in order to free retained earnings for the payment of dividends. Such practices, if they exist, must be disclosed.

2. The auditor should decide whether reappraisals were made by qualified experts and whether their inclusion *fairly represents the client's financial position.* A negative answer to these questions could induce the auditor to withhold an opinion.

3. There are two possible methods for the *computation of depreciation* subsequent to the write-up of assets:

a. Depreciation charged against income may be based on original cost.

b. Depreciation may be based on the full reappraisal value. Although the former method is approved for income tax purposes while the latter is not, convincing arguments for either method may be advanced.

Statement presentation. It is usually considered acceptable to retain the Appreciation of Fixed Assets account as a permanent item of corporate net worth on the balance sheet. It is advisable, however, to decrease this account periodically by an amount equal to the depreciation of the appreciation. (Compare also Wixon and Kell, *Accountants' Handbook,* page 18.31.)

Not very frequently used, but theoretically defensible, is the thought of using the Appreciation of Fixed Assets account for the coverage of stock dividends.

RETAINED EARNINGS

Type of Income Reporting. The volume of debit and credit entries in a Retained Earnings account depends primarily on the type of income reporting favored by corporate management, either (1) the "all-inclusive" concept of income reporting, (2) the "clean" (or "current") income statement theory, or (3) a combination of the two. If the *all-inclusive concept* is favored, only the following few entries would normally appear on the Retained Earnings account each year: net gain or loss per income statement for the year; the declaration of dividends; appropriations from retained earnings and the restoration of such appropriations after they have served their purposes. Following the *current income theory,* a considerably greater number of entries may appear on the Retained Earnings account, in addition to the ones mentioned above: adjustments to prior years' income; gains and losses from unusual sales of assets; losses of an uninsured nature; the write-off of intangibles; the write-off of unamortized bond premium or discount; etc.

The AICPA Accounting Principles Board Opinion No. 9 concluded that "net income should reflect all items of profit or loss recognized during the period with the sole exception of prior period adjustments. *Extraordinary items* should, however, be segregated from the results of ordinary operations and shown separately on the income statement, with disclosure of the nature and amounts thereof."

The APB Opinion No. 9 also specifies the criteria for determining which items may be considered either as pertaining to prior periods' operations or as pertaining to the current period but of an extraordinary nature.

Auditing considerations and procedures

1. *In an initial audit of corporate records,* the Retained Earnings account should be reviewed since the organization of the firm. Besides ascertaining the correct beginning balance for the period under audit, the auditor will learn of past practices and trends. These records may be placed in the client's permanent file and brought up to date from year to year so that a complete history of the development of retained earnings will be available.

2. For the year audited, *all changes in the account* should be scheduled, vouched, and traced to basic financial and nonfinancial records and documents to establish proper authority, theoretical correctness so far as accepted

accounting principles are concerned, and accuracy of amounts. The auditor must make sure that he understands the reason for each entry he encounters.

3. Whether the current or the all-inclusive income statement is preferred, the auditor should not approve of "mixed surplus accounts" as they are occasionally found. Items which represent paid-in capital or those which are due to an unearned increase of net worth (revaluation of assets) must be analyzed, eliminated from retained earnings, and shown on separate accounts of appropriate classification. Any item of current income and expense which may have found its way into the Retained Earnings account must be eliminated, as must be any intercompany profits, when consolidating financial reports. Attention is drawn to SEC Regulation S-X, Rule 5-02 which provides for the separation of net worth items into their proper categories. This distinction is of great importance because only pure retained earnings should be made available for dividend distributions.

4. *Dated retained earnings* indicate that a *quasi-reorganization* has taken place. The auditor should ascertain the reason for such action, which is frequently either to permit income for subsequent periods to be shown fairly or to eliminate from the Retained Earnings account an operating deficit. Following a quasi-reorganization, the retained earnings should remain "dated" for a "reasonable number of years" (usually five to ten). SEC regulations require that the *amount* of the eliminated deficit be disclosed for three years following the reorganization.

5. *Losses on capital transactions* sometimes appear on the Retained Earnings account when other proper means of absorbing them are exhausted. The auditor must trace such transactions beyond their effect on retained earnings to satisfy himself of the correctness and propriety of all entries involved. Expenses of stock issue, underwriting discounts, SEC filing fees, etc., may be charged to retained earnings only after any premiums received on the particular stock issue have been exhausted and if there exists no paid-in capital account relative to previously retired stock issues against which such expenses can be charged.

6. *Undistributed earnings of unconsolidated subsidiaries* may have been included in the retained earnings of the corporation under review. If this is the case, such amounts should be removed or at least disclosed parenthetically or by footnote.

Appropriations (Retained Earnings Reserves). The auditor must be thoroughly conversant with the reasons for and the complete background of all restrictions on retained earnings he may find on the books of his client, and he must also satisfy himself that all restrictions have been put into effect if and when required. Appropriations from retained earnings may be of three basic types:

1. *Those required by state laws;* the most common example is the establishment of a reserve equal to the cost of acquiring treasury shares.

2. *Reserves created in observance of contractual obligations* as, for instance, reserves for bond sinking funds or for the retirement of preferred stock issues, based on contracts with bondholders or holders of preferred stock.

3. *Voluntary appropriations from retained earnings* to provide for future developments, such as the expected future decline of inventory values, reserves for working capital, or reserves for possible payments following the unknown outcome of legal actions; a virtually unlimited number of voluntary reserves is possible.

The auditor must remember that such appropriations assume only that an unidentified portion of assets has been earmarked and that these reserves have really nothing to do with future costs and expenses. Their purpose is solely to preserve certain asset values, making them unavailable for dividends, and to put stockholders on notice that some assets might be needed for specific future uses. Although separated technically from the Retained Earnings account, appropriations always remain part of retained earnings.

Auditing considerations and procedures

1. *The review of excerpts from nonfinancial records and documents* should reassure the auditor that all legal, contractual, and voluntary restrictions of retained earnings have been observed and that all required appropriations were allotted following proper authorization by the board of directors. Particular attention should be paid to contracts into which the corporation may have entered with creditors and stockholders.

2. Each Retained Earnings Reserve account should be *scheduled separately.* In the event of an initial audit, such schedules and subsequent analyses should go back to the inception of the corporation, if possible. These work sheets, placed in the client's permanent file, may be used and brought up to date in subsequent years. *All changes on each reserve account must be vouched and checked* for authority, legal or contractual basis, and the theoretical and mathematical correctness of accounting.

3. Appropriations from retained earnings *must not be considered liabilities.* If a liability materializes due to a loss or an expense for which a reserve account had been created, a charge against current income or against retained earnings directly (if the theory of current income reporting is followed) must be made.

4. *No operating expenses or losses* should ever be charged to retained earnings appropriation, because this would result in an understatement of current year's expenses. Should a reserve account show any debit entry other than the one affecting its dissolution and return to retained earnings, the auditor should insist that an appropriate adjustment be authorized.

5. The auditor should discourage the maintenance of a sizable "general purpose contingency reserve" for which there is no definite or specific reason. The Accounting Research and Terminology Bulletins, final edition, 1961, page 41, mentions

> two types of reserves whose misuse may be the means of either arbitrarily reducing income or shifting income from one period to another:
> (a) General contingency reserves whose purposes are not specific;
> (b) Reserves designed to set aside a part of current profits to absorb losses feared or expected in connection with inventories on hand or future purchases of inventory.

6. *Once the usefulness of a reserve is ended,* either after the event for which it was created has occurred or when the emergency no longer exists, the reserve account should be closed into the Retained Earnings account without undue delay. To continue an obsolete appropriation on the books and on financial reports tends to impair the clarity of presentation.

7. Some accountants feel that a *Bond Sinking Fund Reserve* or a *Reserve for the Redemption of Preferred Stock* should be closed into a contributed capital account because it represents permanently invested assets not available for dividends.

This thesis is not widely accepted in the profession. One could, however, achieve the same result by closing the reserve into the Retained Earnings account with the subsequent declaration and distribution of a stock dividend of equal amount.

8. *"Secret" (hidden) reserves* should not be approved by the auditor. Secret reserves are created by the undervaluation of assets or through the overstatement of liabilities. This practice violates the theory of "full disclosure" and should be discontinued.

Statement presentation. When preparing the net worth section of a corporate balance sheet, the auditor should keep the following points in mind:

1. A clear and concise *analysis of retained earnings* may be presented in three different ways:
   a. Within the net worth section of the balance sheet. This approach is quite satisfactory if only few changes in retained earnings took place during the year under audit.
   b. By means of a separate "Schedule of Retained Earnings" attached to the balance sheet. This type of reporting is commonly found when the "clean" income statement theory is followed. Fitting a comparatively large number of retained earnings items into the net worth section might well detract from its clarity. Only the final balance of retained earnings should then appear in the balance sheet.
   c. Following the "all-inclusive" method of income reporting, certain changes in retained earnings would be shown as appendixes to the income statement, following the subheading "Net Income from Operations." This would leave only very few entries for inclusion in the net worth section.

2. *Appropriations (reserves) are still part of retained earnings* and should be shown in a subsection under the heading of Retained Earnings. They should be described properly to express the rights of creditors and others, and the reason for the existence of each appropriation should be disclosed at the same time.

3. *Any limitation of the use of retained earnings* (primarily to declare dividends), if not already expressed in the form of appropriations, must be disclosed on the balance sheet parenthetically or by footnote. Such restrictions are most frequently due to preferred dividends in arrears, or they may be based on borrowing agreements restricting common dividends to earnings subsequent to the date of the indenture.

4. Dated retained earnings subsequent to a quasi-reorganization must be indicated clearly and consistently for a "reasonable number of years" (usually five to ten years following the reorganization).

The reader is referred to standard auditing texts for illustrations of different statement presentations exemplifying the various considerations mentioned above.

Dividends. The declaration and payment of dividends is not an automatic occurrence but is based on the decision and express authorization of the board of directors as documented in the minutes of the meetings. This authorization, in turn, must conform to the legal requirements of the state of incorporation, which the auditor must review and understand. The most important of these legal considerations, which vary from state to state, pertains to the source from which dividends (other than liquidating distributions) may be paid.

1. Most states provide that payments from sources other than retained earnings are quite legal and proper, provided the source of the dividend is clearly stated.
2. Many states permit the declaration of dividends from retained earnings as well as from any paid-in source.
3. Some states do not permit the declaration of dividends from a Paid-in Capital in Excess of Stated Value account as it applies to no-par stock.

The most common types of dividends the auditor is likely to encounter are the following: cash dividends; dividends paid in assets other than cash; scrip dividends (evidenced by the corporation's promissory notes); and stock dividends (representing the capitalization of earnings).

Auditing considerations and procedures

1. Check the *authority and legality* of dividend declarations against the minutes of the board of directors' meetings and against the ruling state laws. The minutes will also reveal the date of declaration, the date of record, and the date of payment; these should be compared to the dates in the accounts and cash disbursements to ensure the timely execution of the board's orders. Any dividend payment and/or declaration for which no proper authorization can be found in the board's minutes should be ratified promptly.

2. Check the *amount of dividends* declared for each class of stock outstanding by multiplying the number of outstanding shares at date of record by the dividend rate. This amount must agree with the total of the dividend list taken from the trial balance of the stockholders' record or with the transfer agent's confirmation. If an independent agent acts as the corporation's dividend-paying intermediary, the amount of the total dividend check sent to the agent must be verified and vouched. Any special dividend checking account used should be audited with some care, and some of the canceled dividend checks may be viewed. Amounts paid to individual stockholders should be test checked and traced to the related accounts in the stockholders' ledger.

3. *The sources of dividends* declared must be reviewed carefully. If all or part of the dividends are paid from sources other than retained earnings, this should be stated clearly and the stockholders must be so informed. Dividends debited to a paid-in capital account while the Retained Earnings account shows a credit balance should be discussed with responsible officers.

Attention is drawn to the declaration of "mixed dividends" found frequently in the case of *extractive industries*. As operations of part of a mine are discontinued due to the exhaustion of deposits, part of the stockholders' investment may be returned together with dividends declared out of retained earnings. Besides making sure that this fact was properly communicated to the stockholders, the auditor must review the accounting procedure followed. The amount of income distribution is debited to the Retained Earnings account, while the portion representing a return of capital usually appears on the debit of a "Capital Depletion" account. The auditor should satisfy himself that no capital repayment jeopardizes creditors' rights.

4. *Unclaimed dividends* should be controlled and noted. After a reasonable time they can be written off to a "Miscellaneous Income" account. In some states this may not be done because unclaimed dividends escheat to the state treasury after expiration of the legal holding period.

5. *Restrictions on dividend payments* must be strictly observed. The auditor must be satisfied that no dividends were declared or paid in violation

of any legal or contractual restriction or in excess of limitations voluntarily imposed by the board of directors. (Check against state laws, contracts, and minutes of board meetings.) In any event, dividend payments may not reduce the capital stock accounts below par or stated value of the stock outstanding, except in the case of planned liquidating dividends.

6. *Dividends payable in assets other than cash* may present a problem of valuation. The auditor can do no more than compare the *amount* of dividends thus declared with the valuation decided upon by the board of directors and ensure that proper accounting procedures were followed.

Stock dividends. In contrast to all other corporate profit distributions, stock dividends do not reduce the aggregate total of proprietorship but represent merely the capitalization of earnings—the reclassification of a portion of retained income as permanent corporate capital. In his review the auditor must pay attention to the following details:

1. *The valuation of stock dividends,* i.e., the amount transferred from retained earnings to paid-in capital, is not based on a uniformly accepted theory but depends on the directors' decision, so long as the distributed stock is not valued below its legal minimum issue price. Many accountants suggest that the valuation should come as close as possible to the fair market value of the stock at the time of distribution. (See also Accounting Research and Terminology Bulletins, final edition, 1961, page 51.) The auditor's attention is directed to the fact that this can be done much more efficiently and correctly in the case of a small stock dividend which has only a very limited effect upon the market price of the particular class of stock. When the market price is changed radically because of a relatively large stock dividend, valuation at fair market value may prove problematic.
2. *Original authorization for the stock issue* as a whole must not be exceeded because of the declaration and payment of a stock dividend.
3. When a stock dividend on one class of stock is *distributed in shares of another class of stock,* the auditor must make sure that the rights of the holders of all classes of stocks are being respected and preserved.
4. *Stock splits,* while having the same effect as have stock dividends so far as the stockholders and the stock's market price are concerned, are theoretically quite different from pure stock dividends. No capitalization of earnings is effected and the Retained Earnings account plays no part in the procedure.

Statement presentation of dividends. Although dividends declared are not really part of corporate net worth they must appear in the detailed retained earnings statement, whether this be done within the net worth section or in an accompanying schedule. Following are some of the salient points:

1. *Dividends declared but unpaid at year end* generally reduce retained earnings and become current liabilities on the balance sheet. *Stock dividends declared but unpaid,* however, should not be shown among the liabilities; the amount to be capitalized can be introduced as a separate classification in the net worth section of the balance sheet, and the number of shares to be issued can be mentioned. These shares must be reserved from the time of declaration of a stock dividend. *Liquidating dividends* declared after all legal formalities have been satisfied, but unpaid at year end, reduce the value and quantity of outstanding stock on the balance sheet and must be shown among the current liabilities.

2. Care must be taken that dividend declarations of any type do not cause a *debit balance (deficit) on the Retained Earnings account.*

3. Unpaid and undeclared cumulative preferred dividends do not reduce retained earnings, nor do they constitute a liability. The amount of such arrearages should be disclosed parenthetically or by footnote because they restrict future dividend declarations on common stock.

4. SEC Regulation S-X, Rule 11-62, requires that the medium of dividend payments and the rate per share be clearly disclosed.

CORPORATE COMBINATIONS

Introduction. Once a business combination of two or more corporate entities has been consummated and properly recorded either through the *purchase method* or the *pooling of interests method* of accounting, the audit of the single successor corporation, subsequent to the period in which the combination took place, is generally no different from that of any other corporate entity. It is, therefore, the period in which the combination took place that requires the auditor's special attention. He must clearly determine whether a *de facto pooling of interests* or an *acquisition through purchase* has taken place because of the different accounting treatment required. This decision does not rest on the conventional legal distinction applied to mergers, consolidations, exchanges of securities, etc., but depends on circumstances surrounding the combination. For further details refer to AICPA Accounting Research Bulletin No. 48 and to APB Opinions No. 10, December, 1966, and No. 16, August, 1970. APB Opinion No. 16 supersedes all previous pronouncements concerned with the recording of business combinations, without having, however, any retroactive effects.

Any of the legal steps taken to effect a business combination may result in either a purchase or a pooling of interests, depending upon the attending circumstances. Theoretically, neither method must be accepted to the exclusion of the other, but each case of a business combination should be recorded in the manner that reflects the intent and actions of the constituent parties. If cash or other assets are distributed to achieve a combination or if liabilities are incurred toward this goal, the purchase method of accounting should be used. On the other hand, if only voting common stock is issued to effect a business combination, the pooling of interests method is usually favored. The Accounting Principles Board does not approve, however, of applying both principles of accounting to the same combination. In each individual case one method must be selected to the exclusion of the other. (See APB Opinion No. 16, pars. 42 and 43.)

The Pooling of Interests Method. Business combinations which satisfy *all conditions* mentioned below should be accounted for through the *pooling of interests method.*[1] All other combinations should be properly recorded following the *conventional purchase method.*

1. The constituent companies were autonomous (not subsidiaries or divisions of another corporation) for not less than 2 years prior to the initiation of the plan of combination.
2. At the time of combination, the combining companies are independent of each other by not holding more than 10% of the total outstanding voting common stock of any of the participants in the combination.

[1] These conditions are excerpted from the APB Opinion No. 16. Refer to this original document for a full discussion and explanation of the various points mentioned.

3. The combination, to meet the pooling of interests theory, should result from a single transaction or should be based on a specific plan to be put into practice within one year of its initiation.

4. Only common stock which has the identical rights and features as the majority of common stock already outstanding, is being offered by a corporation in exchange for substantially all of the voting common shares of another corporation.

5. The equity interest of the voting common stock of any of the participants in a combination has not been changed within two years before the initiation of the plan of combination, or between such initiation date and the actual consummation of the plan. This restriction applies primarily to equity interest changes made in contemplation of an expected combination.

6. No reacquisition by constituent companies of their own voting common stock has occurred solely for the purpose of the expected business combination.

7. The ratio of an individual common stockholder's interest as compared to that of other common stockholders in the same constituent company has not been changed through the exchange of stock resulting in the combination.

8. The voting rights of common stockholders in the combined corporation are exercisable and are not subject to restrictions or abolishment, even temporarily.

9. After the business combination is consummated, there exists no further provision or commitment for any additional issue of securities or for the payment of any further consideration.

10. There exists no direct or indirect understanding that the combined corporation will retire or reacquire all or part of the common stock issued as the basis for the combination.

11. The combined corporation does not enter into any financial arrangement which would, in effect, destroy the original exchange of equity securities.

12. There is no intent on the part of the combined corporation to dispose of a significant part of the assets of a constituent company within two years following the combination. Dispositions made in the ordinary course of business are, of course, excluded from this restriction.

Accounting and Auditing Considerations. For a detailed discussion and explanation of the application of the pooling of interests method and of the purchase method of accounting for business combinations, reference is made again to APB Opinion No. 16, August, 1970 (pars. 50–95). Following are some of the most important points to be considered by the auditor.

1. ACCOUNTABILITY BASIS: If a combination is recorded by use of the *purchase method,* a *new accountability basis for assets* acquired from constituent corporations necessarily arises. Such assets must appear on the successor-corporation's books at acquisition cost or at their fair market values at the time of acquisition. If the *pooling of interests method* of accounting is properly employed, *no new accountability* basis arises. The assets (and liabilities) of constituent companies are shown on the successor corporation's books at the same values as appeared in the records of the predecessor corporations.

2. STOCKHOLDER'S EQUITY: In the case of *pooling of interests* it is logical that the stockholder's equities of the constituent corporations are combined, as were the assets and liabilities, to result in the successor corporation's *capital stock* and *capital in excess of par or stated value.* The same is true

with respect to the *retained earnings* of the constituent companies which are carried forward to the books of the combined corporation, representing the total retained earnings of the single successor corporation. This procedure follows the thesis of continuance of the businesses of the constituent companies. The auditor must make sure that *deficits* which might exist for one or more of these participating corporations *are not used to reduce the total paid-in capital* while other retained earnings continue unchanged. Such deficits must be offset against the retained earnings of the other constituents in arriving at the overall balance of retained earnings for the successor-corporation. It should be pointed out, however, that the carrying forward of retained earnings is optional. The successor-corporation may consider all or part of the retained earnings of the constituent companies as paid-in capital on its books. This procedure is no different from an ordinary capitalization of earnings. If an *acquisition through purchase* is deemed to have taken place, the retained earnings balances of acquired corporations must not continue in existence, because the net acquisition value of all assets received becomes the paid-in capital of the successor-corporation.

3. UNIFORMITY: The auditor must satisfy himself that accepted accounting principles were followed by all predecessor-corporations so far as they affect book values of assets and retained earnings. In the absence of such uniformity, the auditor should make appropriate adjustments to place the accounts of all constituent companies on a reasonably uniform and comparable basis.

4. PARENT-SUBSIDIARY RELATIONS: If, subsequent to a pooling of interests, one or more of the constituent corporations retain their identity in the form of a subsidiary company, the summation of retained earnings in the consolidated balance sheet is quite proper. However, this is true only if the parent-subsidiary relationship is new, and did not exist prior to planning the pooling of interests.

Statement presentation. When a business combination meets the requirements of a pooling of interests, financial statements should express the results of *combined operations for the entire reporting period* in which the combination took place. If comparative financial statements are to be prepared involving periods prior to the one in which the pooling of interests has occurred, such prior periods' statements should be restated on a combined basis to make meaningful comparison possible. (APB Opinion No. 16, August, 1970.)

BIBLIOGRAPHY

Accounting Research and Terminology Bulletins, final edition, AICPA, New York, 1961.

Opinions of the Accounting Principles Board, AICPA, New York, to date.

SEC Accounting Series Releases, Securities and Exchange Commission. Statements on Auditing Procedure, AICPA, New York, to date.

Backer, Morton (ed.): *Modern Accounting Theory*, Englewood Cliffs, N.J., Prentice-Hall, Inc., 1966.

Cashin, James A., and Garland C. Owens: *Auditing*, 2d ed., New York, The Ronald Press Company, 1963.

Lenhart, Norman J., and Philip L. Defliese: *Montgomery's Auditing*, 8th ed., New York, The Ronald Press Company, 1957.

Rappaport, Louis H.: *SEC Accounting Practice and Procedures*, New York, The Ronald Press Company, 1966.

Silvoso, Joseph A., and Royal D. M. Bauer: *Auditing*, 2d ed., Cincinnati, South-Western Publishing Company, Incorporated, 1965.

Stettler, Howard F.: *Auditing Principles*, 2d ed., Englewood Cliffs, N.J., Prentice-Hall, Inc., 1961.

Herrick, Anson: "Balance Sheet Presentation of Treasury Shares," *The Journal of Accountancy*, April, 1963, pp. 74–75.
Lauver, R. C.: "The Case for Pooling," *The Accounting Review*, 1966, pp. 65–74.
Suttle, C. William, and William G. Mecklenburg: "Pooling of Interests," *World* (Peat, Marwick, Mitchell & Co., New York), parts 1 and 2, Winter, 1967, and Spring, 1968.
Cohen, Manuel F.: "Some Problems of Disclosure," *The Journal of Accountancy*, May, 1968, pp. 61–63.
Imdieke, LeRoy F., and Jerry J. Weygandt: "Classification of Convertible Debt," *The Accounting Review* (AAA, Evanston, Ill.), October, 1969.
Fox, Kenneth L., and Phillip E. Fess: "Suggested Refinements of Procedures in Determining Earnings per Share," *The Journal of Accountancy*, January, 1970.

Chapter 30

Sales and Other Revenues

EDWARDS B. MURRAY

Manager, Corporate Audit Staff, General Electric Company

BASIC CONSIDERATIONS

Introduction. The summary of financial operations (income statement) has become increasingly significant to investors, creditors, governmental agencies, and management as a means of measuring past profitability and earning power of a business. The balance sheet, once given primary emphasis, is now generally considered of collateral rather than predominant importance as a factor in investment and credit decisions. Despite this trend, verification of balance sheet accounts has continued to be the principal concern of independent auditors with only such review of revenue and expense accounts as may be required to insure that balance sheet accounts are properly stated.

The principal reasons for the limited review of revenue accounts are:

1. Verification of balance sheet accounts at the beginning and end of the accounting period will substantiate the net income of the period, although the validity of specific revenue and expense accounts may not be established in this manner.
2. Verification of many balance sheet accounts (Cash, Accounts Receivable, Securities, Inventories, and Fixed Assets) necessarily entails some examination of related income accounts (e.g., Accounts Receivable and Bad Debt Expense; Notes Payable and Interest Expense).
3. Although fraud may be accompanied by a misstatement of revenues and expenses, major defalcations involving dissipation of assets will usually be detected by verification of the asset accounts.

Nonetheless, a comprehensive audit should include a thorough examination of revenue and expense accounts to detect irregularities, errors, inconsistencies, or indications of laxity which may not be disclosed by audit of balance sheet accounts.

Definition of Revenue. According to APB Statement No. 4, *Basic Concepts and Accounting Principles Underlying Financial Statements of Business*

Enterprises, paragraph 134, issued October, 1970, revenue is defined as follows:

Gross increases in assets or gross decreases in liabilities recognized and measured in conformity with generally accepted accounting principles that result from those types of profit-directed activities of an enterprise that can change owners' equity.

According to the Statement, revenue under present generally accepted accounting principles is derived from three general activities, described in paragraph 148 as follows:

(*a*) Selling products (*b*) rendering services and permitting others to use enterprise resources, which result in interest, rent, royalties, fees and the like, and (*c*) disposing of resources other than products—for example, plant and equipment or investments in other entities.

The above definition supersedes the definition of revenue in Accounting Terminology Bulletin No. 2, paragraph 5. Revenue is realized when an asset (usually cash or a claim to receive cash) is received, or a liability is extinguished, when a company provides goods or services to another entity. According to Davidson, *Handbook of Modern Accounting,* p. 10-7, there are two main kinds of revenue.

1. Operating revenues result from the company's providing its main products or services to its customers—those products or services that it is in business to provide.
2. Non-operating revenues are incidental gains, such as those which result from sales of noncurrent assets and from retirements of noncurrent liabilities.

Recognition of Revenue. Revenue is usually recognized at a specific point in the earning process, generally when assets are sold or services are rendered. According to APB Statement No. 4, paragraph 150, "Revenue is generally recognized when both of the following conditions are met: (1) the earning process is complete or virtually complete, and (2) an exchange has taken place." The rules and conventions of revenue accounting are concerned primarily with (1) the timing of recognition of income in the accounts and (2) determination of the amount of revenue to be recorded.

Timing. According to APB Statement No. 4, paragraph 151:

Revenue from sales of products is recognized under this principle at the date of sale, usually interpreted to mean the date of delivery to customers. Revenue from services rendered is recognized under this principle when services have been performed and are billable. Revenue from permitting others to use enterprise resources, such as interest, rent and royalties is also governed by the realization principle. Revenue of this type is recognized as time passes or as the resources are used. Revenue from sales of assets other than products is recognized at the date of sale.

Amount. The amount of revenue to be recorded is usually based upon the arrangement between buyer and seller, as indicated by Finney and Miller (in *Principles of Accounting—Intermediate,* p. 150): "Most revenues arise from bargained transactions, and the price agreed upon by the parties to the transaction is an appropriate measure of the resulting revenue."

The amount of revenue to be recorded may be exactly determined where recording occurs at the time of receipt of cash. In other circumstances (in the case of charge sales, price-redetermination contracts, payment in kind, etc.), the ultimate amount of revenue to be realized may necessarily be based upon an estimate. In such cases, the gross amount of revenue as provided by contract or other basis of the transaction is generally recorded in the income accounts and a conservative estimate of any expected losses or allowances is provided for by establishment of appropriate allowance or liability accounts. The timing and amount of revenue are discussed as follows in Davidson, *Handbook of Modern Accounting*, p. 10-7: "Revenue is recognized when these three tests are met: (1) the revenue is captured (2) the revenue is measurable and (3) the revenue is earned."

The revenue is captured. The company is "certain to retain the related inflows of assets, or the portion that might be lost is small and susceptible to estimate." Thus accounts receivable are captured: uncollectibles may be estimated. In contrast holding gains such as an increase in market value of site land is not recognized until the land is sold.

The revenue is measurable. There must be "no serious difficulty in valuing the assets received." While cash presents no valuation problem, other assets do present valuation problems. Some transactions involve exchanges of assets for plant assets, or for the capital stock of another company. If the assets are not readily marketable and the inflow cannot be reasonably measured, the accountant will value the assets received at the amount of the assets given and may not recognize a revenue.

The revenue is earned. Generally revenue is earned when no "significant activities remain to be performed for the customer being provided with the related product or service." At the end of an accounting period, revenue which has been captured but only partly earned should not be recognized, for example, where the product requires installation and testing before acceptance.

Bases of measurement. Revenue is recognized at the earliest point at which it is captured, measurable, and earned. There are three principal points at which this may occur and three bases of recognition. These are the (1) sales basis, (2) production basis, and (3) collection basis.

Sales basis. In most cases revenue recognition occurs at the time the company's products or services are sold. The time of sale is usually considered the time of delivery to the customer or the time at which title to goods and risk of loss thereon pass to the customer.

Production basis. APB Statement No. 4, paragraph 152, provides that revenue may sometimes be recognized before the earning process is complete or an exchange has taken place, for instance, in the case of (1) long-term construction projects or (2) production of products with assured sales prices.

The use of the production basis requires that the total revenue be virtually assured and measurable and that it be possible to estimate the amount of earned revenue. For long-term construction contracts the recognition of revenue based on percentage of completion results in a more equitable net income for the period. There must be reasonable expectation of the profit margin and its future realization. Revenue sometimes may be recognized at the completion of production and before a sale is made (for example, for certain precious metals and farm products with assured sales prices).

Collection basis. With the collection basis revenue is not recognized until cash is actually collected from customers. This method is generally used by professional men and for retail installment sales.

Objectives of Audit. Audit of revenues may be undertaken (1) for the sole purpose of developing a competent opinion with respect to the fairness and consistency of their presentation in the client's financial statements and permitting certification of the statements, (2) for the sole purpose of aiding management in control and operation of the business or business functions involved, or (3) for both purposes. For verification of the financial statements, the audit program should be directed toward determination that:

Revenues have been recorded and reported in proper income accounts on a consistent basis;

Revenues have been recorded and reported in correct amounts;

Revenues recorded have been earned;

Revenues have been recorded and reported in proper fiscal periods;

Revenues have been properly recorded in related balance sheet accounts;

All revenues to which the business is entitled have been received and recorded;

Control procedures are adequate to provide assurance of proper recording and reporting of revenues.

Cashin and Owens (in *Auditing*, 2d ed., p. 487) concisely summarize the normal objectives of the audit of revenues as follows:

Internal Control	To determine that procedures are established to insure that all revenues due are received and recorded
Auditing Procedures	To determine that all revenues have been recorded and that all recorded revenues have been earned
Statement Presentation	To determine that revenues have been properly and consistently shown.

In addition, in order to aid management, the program should provide for determination that:

Revenues have been maximized within the framework of objectives and policies of the business;

Controls over revenue-producing operations are adequate to prevent loss from error, fraud, or lack of attention, and that control procedures are being followed;

Revenue-producing operations are being conducted efficiently and economically;

Revenue-producing operations are being conducted lawfully and do not expose the business to major liability, loss, or hazard to reputation;

Revenues have been accurately and meaningfully analyzed, classified, and reported to management.

Most examinations include elements of both verification and management control (operational) audit.

GENERAL PRINCIPLES OF CONTROL

A broad definition of internal control is contained in AICPA's Statements on Auditing Procedure No. 33: "Internal control comprises the plan of organization and all of the co-ordinate methods and measures adopted within a business to safeguard its assets, check the accuracy and reliability of its accounting data, promote operational efficiency, and encourage adherence to prescribed managerial policies."

The statements further categorize controls as *accounting controls* and *administrative controls.* The independent auditor, concerned primarily with verification and certification of the financial statements, ordinarily reviews and tests the *accounting controls,* which are established to assure the reliability of the financial records and to safeguard the assets of the business. The internal auditor or operational auditor may properly extend his review to the adequacy and efficacy of *administrative controls,* which have to do with compliance with management policy, measurement of operational efficiency, and appraisal of progress toward business objectives.

Some of the more common organizational and procedural mechanisms utilized to provide effective control of revenues include:

Segregation of Responsibilities. Insofar as practicable, the functions of originating, processing, collecting, depositing, recording, and internal audit (internal check) of revenues should be segregated so that fraud or error on the part of any one individual will be subject to disclosure in the normal course of operations. As an example, the several functions involved in the processing of a customer's order might be segregated among different organizational units as follows:

Activity	*Performed by*
(*a*) Receipt of customer's order and preparation of a stock withdrawal or production order	Sales department (or order service department)
(*b*) Approval of customer's credit; collection activity	Credit and collection section of the finance organization
(*c*) Shipping and preparation of shipping documentation	Shipping or traffic department
(*d*) Preparation of the invoice	Billing section of the finance organization
(*e*) Maintenance of accounts receivable records	Accounts receivable section of the finance organization (may be combined with credit and collection)
(*f*) Write-off of uncollectible accounts and authorization for returns and allowances	Accounting section of finance organization after approval by a manager not responsible for any of the preceding functions
(*g*) Receipt, deposit, and initial recording of customers' remittances	Cashier or a separate section of the finance organization not involved with any of the preceding functions.

In smaller companies or branch offices, the organization may not be large enough to provide for a full segregation of principal duties. In these instances, the duties of individuals performing the functions should be segregated to the extent feasible to assure current disclosure of significant fraud or error. Internal audits or test checks by management should be made with greater frequency in such situations.

Internal Control Questionnaire. The following internal control questionnaire is taken from *Auditing*, 2d ed., by Cashin and Owens, p. 490.

INTERNAL CONTROL QUESTIONNAIRE

1. Are there written policies and procedures for sales?
2. Have sales forecasts, budgets, individual quotas, and other controls been established?
3. Is actual sales performance as compared with projected sales performance reported regularly to management?
4. Is an established price list available?
5. Do responsible officials approve any changes in established prices?
6. Does the Credit Department approve all orders?
7. Is the Credit Department independent of the Sales Department?
8. Do all shipments out of the plant, whether for regular sales, returns, or other items, clear through the designated shipping department?
9. Are all shipments authorized by duly executed serially numbered shipping orders?
10. Are all shipments accounted for through sales invoices, charges to suppliers, purchase orders for repairs, and other documents?
11. Are sales invoices serially numbered, and are all numbers accounted for?
12. Are prices, terms, extensions, and postings of invoices periodically checked?
13. Is the total sales amount checked by means of sales analyses by product, salesman, etc.?

14. Are receiving reports prepared for returned goods?
15. Is there a written returned-goods procedure?
16. Is the issuance of credit memoranda properly controlled?
17. Are sales other than regular products properly controlled?
18. Are sales quantities reconciled with inventory credits?
19. Is there adequate control of transportation allowances?
20. Is the approximate quantity of scrap accounted for in recorded scrap sales?

Internal Check. Many companies establish routines to check revenue transactions either on a test basis or, if the hazard of loss on individual transactions is significant, by a current 100 percent examination. These procedures, which may involve some duplication of work, provide a continuous safeguard against error, negligence, and fraud. Although internal auditors may be assigned to perform these postaudits or checks on a regular basis throughout the year, this work is part of the accounting system and should not be confused with periodic general audits performed under professional audit standards by public accountants or internal auditors. Where accounting work is processed largely on EDP equipment, it may be possible to incorporate in the computer programs provision for printing out or otherwise calling attention to revenue transactions or groups of transactions of abnormal amount, beyond arbitrarily specified limits, or bearing an abnormal relationship to other data (e.g., to related costs or average selling price extended by quantity). The effectiveness of internal check may be enhanced by this or other means of identifying unusual transactions for review and verification.

Budgets. Periodic budgets of revenues should be part of the business plans of the organization. Those directly responsible for realization of the budgets should be parties to their preparation, and management should be informed of the assumptions on which the budgets are based. After approval by higher management, the budgets should become the basis for measurement of actual results, appraisal of performance of those responsible, and highlighting of deviations for intensive analysis, study, and changes in organization or planning.

Accounting and Reporting Systems. The accounting and reporting systems should be designed to inform financial and general management of the results of revenue-producing activities and to alert them to any unusual deviations. The systems should include provision for recording, classification, and summarization of revenue and periodic reporting to management in meaningful form. Reports to management should include comparisons with results for prior periods and budgets.

AUDIT PROCEDURES

General Audit Procedures. Specific audit procedures and techniques have been devised or may be developed for various types of organizations and revenue-producing activities. Most of these specific approaches are adaptations, modifications, expansions, or variations of the following general audit procedures:

Examination of controls. Procedural and accounting controls designed to ensure proper recording of revenue transactions and proper disposition of resulting cash receipts should be reviewed and tested for efficacy.

Comparative analysis of revenues. Analysis and comparison of current revenues with revenues for past periods and with budgets may disclose significant fluctuations.

The relationship between revenue and direct costs, expressed as gross profit ratio, tends not to vary markedly from period to period or among companies within an industry. Ratios of certain expenses, such as commissions, to sales may also be expected to remain quite stable from period to period. Comparative analyses of these relationships and others, such as the ratio of credit sales to accounts receivable and that of sales to average inventory (i.e., turnover), are useful in highlighting areas which the auditor should examine in greater detail. Abnormal variations may be indicative of errors in classification or recording of revenues, deficiencies in procedures, and irregularity in handling of collections, as well as of changes in underlying revenue-producing activities (e.g., price changes, introduction of new products, or initiation of new methods of distribution). Comparisons are most effective if classified as finely as practicable, by type of revenue, product classification, department, source, geographical area, or other meaningful grouping. Comparisons may be made by months, weeks, or days for detection of significant deviations within the audit period as well as of fluctuations from results for prior fiscal periods.

Examination of recorded transactions. Revenues reported in the financial statements should be verified by analysis of the general ledger accounts in which revenues are recorded and examination (on a sampling basis) of underlying records of individual transactions. The following general procedures are usually applicable:

1. Abstract and analyze general ledger accounts in which revenues are recorded.
2. Obtain source documents supporting journal entries selected for review (e.g., invoices, sales tickets, or cash register tapes) and examine for (*a*) accuracy of computation, (*b*) correctness of summarization and classification, (*c*) propriety, (*d*) authorization, and (*e*) allocation to proper fiscal period.
3. Account for selected blocks of consecutively numbered source documents and trace them to journal entries and the general ledger to determine that all documented transactions have been recorded on the books.
4. Verify disposition of revenues by comparing entries in revenue accounts with corresponding offsetting entries in directly related balance sheet accounts (e.g., cash, accounts receivable, sundry receivables, or deferred income). This part of the examination may be performed at the same time as the analysis, review, and verification of the related balance sheet accounts.

These approaches may be supplemented by audit procedures directed toward the maximization or optimization of revenues. These procedures are an extension of the three approaches outlined and are designed to determine: (1) that all revenues to which the organization is entitled have been received or otherwise accounted for, (2) that all available sources of revenue have been explored, considered, and exploited to the extent practicable and consistent with the organization's charter and objectives, and (3) that revenue-producing operations have been conducted with maximum efficiency and effectiveness.

These procedures require a determination of sources of revenue available to the organization by such means as (1) inquiry of management and others, (2) physical observation of factory, warehouse, office, and remote-site operations and facilities, (3) analysis of recorded cash receipts or credits to cash accounts, (4) review of credits to other asset accounts (to identify dispositions of assets which should have resulted in revenue), and (5) general review of accounts in which revenue-producing assets might be recorded (e.g., facilities rented to others, loans, installment accounts, inventories, etc.). Individual sources of revenue may then be studied in appropriate depth by (1) examination of original documents recording revenue-producing activities, (2) physical observation of such activities, (3) comparison of the activities, in terms of profit margins, yield, and efficiency, with available industry information or data on similar activities elsewhere and with statistics for prior periods, (4) consideration and evaluation of alternative means of conducting the activities, and (5) discussions with interested management and employees.

Analytical Review of Sales. Supplementing the financial audit of the accounts, an analytical review of sales should be made to disclose significant unusual conditions or transactions which have not been otherwise detected.

This review is based on comparison of sales for current periods with those of comparable prior periods and the budget. These comparisons may be refined to the extent that sales may be segregated by product lines, departments, territories, or other classifications. Explanations for significant fluctuations should be obtained from management and reviewed for validity. Such fluctuations may arise from accounting or classification errors, price changes, introduction of new products, discontinuance of products, competitive influences, product quality problems, work stoppages or plant closings, for other reasons, economic conditions or other causes.

Ordinarily, comparative sales analyses of this nature are regularly prepared by the client organization for management information and use. However, in small businesses such standard analyses may not be available and it may be necessary to derive them from ledger and subledger accounts.

As a minimum, the following four types of sales analyses are generally prepared or obtained:

1. Annual sales in total
2. Annual sales by product or department
3. Monthly sales in total
4. Monthly sales by product or department

If such analyses are not a normal part of the client's management information system, the auditor's examination may provide useful information or perspective to management. However, the principal purpose of this review is to provide the auditor with a broader understanding of the financial statements, the business which they portray and the major changes which have taken place during the period under audit. For example, sales analyses might provide initial clues to manipulations of the accounts, misappropriations of cash sale or C.O.D. collections, unrecorded liabilities, overvaluation of obsolete stocks, misstatements of commission accruals, a breakdown in customer service or other significant situations which could affect the financial statements or should be brought to the attention of management and possibly of owners or shareowners.

Operational Audit Procedures. The normal examination of recorded sales transactions should provide reasonable assurance that sales have been accurately and properly recorded in the financial statements, but it is only incidentally concerned with the efficiency of sales and related activities and with the maximization or optimization of sales revenue. Supplementary operational audit procedures directed toward the latter ends are an extension of the normal examination of controls over and documentation of the chain of transactions set in motion by the acceptance of a customer's order.

The following supplementary procedures may be combined with the basic audit program outlined in the preceding paragraphs. These operational audit procedures are organization-oriented rather than transaction-oriented, i.e., primary emphasis is placed on the effectiveness with which essential functions are performed rather than upon the transactions themselves. Selected transactions are examined in depth but principally for the purpose of testing the operation of prescribed controls and appraising the efficiency and effectiveness of the functional activity under examination.

1. Order service
   a. Determine point at which orders are first documented (e.g., by telephone logs, serially numbered order forms, order confirmations, etc.) and select a representative number of orders for audit, including completed and open orders.
   b. Compare selected orders with quotations to determine that quantities, prices, and terms are in agreement.
   c. Trace selected completed orders to shipping and billing documents. Trace billing to summaries and entries in general ledger sales and receivable accounts.
   d. Review selected completed orders and related correspondence and contract files to determine that proper billing, in accordance with provisions of orders or contracts, has been issued for:
      (1) Price escalation
      (2) Specification changes
      (3) Direct shipments from vendors
      (4) Installation, consultation, or other services performed on customer's premises
      (5) Premium transportation, special export packing, and similar extra costs incurred at customer's request
   e. Review selected cost-plus or cost-based government contracts to determine that all costs and related profits or fees have been billed.
      (1) Review cost-accumulation and cost-allocation instructions and procedures to determine their adequacy.
      (2) Review price-redetermination proposals and settlements for reasonableness, accuracy, and completeness.
      (3) Review pricing data submitted to governmental agencies as a basis for establishment of firm prices to determine that estimates of costs and profit are adequately supported by latest valid cost data as required by government regulations.
      (4) Review coding and accumulation of sales and cost data on renegotiable business to ensure proper reporting to the government as a basis for renegotiation settlement.
   f. Review all old open orders to determine reasons for failure to ship or bill.
2. Shipping
   a. Select a number of representative closed shipping authorizations (memoranda of shipment, shipping notices, or gate passes) and perform the following:
      (1) Check approvals and ascertain that authorized signers are responsible employees independent of those physically handling shipments.
      (2) Check quantities and description against billing, and trace billing to general ledger entries.
      (3) Compare with transportation bills, bills of lading, loading tallies, or other corroborating evidence of quantities and products shipped. In this connection, obtain and verify explanations for any alterations of quantities or descriptions.
      (4) Determine that necessary information is indicated on shipping

documents to ensure proper billing and payment of transportation charges (quantities, descriptions, weights, carriers, freight bill references, prepaid transportation charges, terms, etc.).

(5) Check canceled shipping authorizations, and if not supported by adequate approval and supporting evidence of nonshipment, consider confirming cancellations with customers.

b. Observe warehousing and shipping procedures to ascertain whether division of responsibilities, limitation of access to warehouse and shipping docks, guard surveillance of building or plant exits, alarm systems, and protection of doors, windows, skylights, etc., are adequate to prevent unauthorized or unrecorded removal of products.

c. Review log or other record of open shipping authorizations to determine reasons for failure to ship or failure to record shipments. Appraise adequacy of follow-up and discuss with management any indications of laxity or delay in completing shipments.

d. For products billed by weight or for which standard shipping weights are used, select representative packages or products and weigh. This is particularly important where changes have occurred in product design or packaging. Failure to review and adjust standard weight records may result in incorrect billing of products or overpayment of outgoing transportation charges.

e. Review selected gate passes, truck passes, and similar documents authorizing removal of products or property from premises; compare with duplicate copies and determine disposition of material (return to stock, charge to consignment account, or issue of billing). Review open documents and appraise adequacy of follow-up.

f. Determine source of prenumbered shipping authorization forms and account for selected blocks of used and unused forms.

g. Review procedure for routing and determining mode and classification of shipments for greatest economy consistent with customer requirements. Current or periodic review by traffic specialists may be desirable. Review selected transportation bills and compare with shipping documents for quantities, weights, descriptions, etc.

3. Billing

a. Account for selected blocks of bills in numerical sequence and compare missing numbers with shipping log and billing summaries.

b. Trace selected blocks of bills to billing summaries and entries in general ledger sales and receivable accounts.

c. Compare costs applied to selected bills with cost records, and test the classification and summarization of sales and costs to verify the reliability of classified profit and loss reports to management. (Verification of cost records may be performed in connection with the audit of inventory valuations.)

d. Review and test stockroom or receiving department records of returned material. Determine that procedures are adequate to ensure that all returns are recorded in these records and that prompt disposition (repair and return, scrapping, issuance of credit, billing for repairs, etc.) is made. Verify disposition of selected items.

e. Review customer complaints or claims disclosed by replies to receivable confirmation letters and determine whether prompt, courteous, and proper disposition is being made.

f. Consider opportunities for using available data processing equipment to facilitate the audit of billing. (The following applications are illustrative only, as the audit procedures in each case must be adapted to the particular system, equipment, and business involved.)

(1) Tabulate bills for a selected period in order by catalog or model number, showing bill numbers, quantities, unit prices, and total prices as an aid to detecting pricing discrepancies and major extension errors.

(2) Tabulate recorded bills for a selected period in bill-number order to detect unrecorded bills (missing bill numbers).

(3) Tabulate bills for a selected period by shipping document serial number to detect unbilled shipments.

(4) Tabulate bills by bill number for a selected period, indicating shipping dates as an aid in determining promptitude of billing and billing cutoff at the end of the fiscal period.

4. Efficiency

a. Review reports of costs and number of employees engaged in order service, shipping, and billing operations. Compare with:

(1) Budgets

(2) Reports for prior periods

(3) Comparable data on other divisions of the company or other companies

b. Review routines and reports concerned with measurement of productivity of employees in these operations and investigate apparent subnormal performance. Consider appraising productivity by observation on a random sampling basis for measured time periods.

Specific Audit Procedures. A major source of revenue is sale of tangible property (materials, commodities, products, and real estate), nontangible property (securities, computer programs, etc.), or services. (Revenue may also be derived from intangibles, such as patents, licenses, etc., but such income is ordinarily classified as operating revenue or sundry income rather than as sales.) A general program for audit of sales of products is outlined below and important variations applicable to other specific types of sales are outlined in subsequent paragraphs.

SALES OF PRODUCTS

Sales of products entail the transfer of inventories to customers in the ordinary course of business and ordinarily involve physical delivery and passage of title. For our purposes we may group sales of products into (1) primary products and (2) by-products.

Primary Products. Primary products are defined as those products which are the principal sources of sales revenue of a business.

General audit program. Following is a condensed program applicable to both manufactured and purchased products as shown in Cashin and Owens, *Auditing*, 2d ed., p. 492:

1. Examine sales transactions.
2. Compare invoices with shipping records.
3. Determine that shipments are made only on authorized orders.
4. Determine that all revenue due has been received.
5. Determine that revenue total does not include improper items.
6. Examine cutoff of shipping and receiving records.
7. Test footings of sales records.

8. Determine that shipments are promptly billed.
9. Examine credit approvals.
10. Test invoice prices with price lists.
11. Verify footings and extensions of invoices.
12. Trace postings of sales to general ledger.
13. Examine credit memoranda above a given dollar amount.
14. Examine discounts and freight allowances.
15. Review handling of intercompany, interdivision, interplant, and interdepartment sales.
16. Examine the basis of recording profit on installment sales.
17. Examine treatment of consignment sales.
18. Determine that proper accounting is made for partial shipments, non-customer shipments, etc.
19. Examine the handling of prepaid transportation charges.
20. Review reasonableness of quantity and price of scrap.
21. Determine that, where practicable, quantities shipped are reconciled with inventory credits.
22. Examine miscellaneous revenues reported.

Manufactured products. Following is a detailed program applicable to manufactured products. It could be adapted for broader application where desired.

Preliminary audit work. Effectiveness of the sales audit is dependent upon the auditor's comprehensive understanding of (1) the nature of the business and (2) operating policies and procedures for solicitation and acceptance of orders, shipment of products, issuance of billing and credits to customers, and recording of sales transactions. Preliminary audit work should include the following:

1. Determine what products are sold and source of these products by:
   a. Discussion with management
   b. Review of classified statements of sales
   c. Physical observation of manufacturing, warehousing, and shipping areas
   d. Review of billing to customers
   e. Review of purchases of products purchased for resale (may be done in connection with review of accounts payable vouchers and purchasing)
2. Review organization charts, instructions, and summaries of physical and paper work procedures for:
   a. Solicitation or taking of orders from customers
   b. Recording and processing of orders
   c. Shipping of products
   d. Pricing
   e. Billing to customers
   f. Issuance of credits for returns and allowances
   g. Recording of billing and credits
   h. Internal check of order, shipping, and billing activities

Review of internal controls. Study of the information obtained through the preliminary work described above should permit the auditor to draw tentative conclusions with respect to the adequacy of *prescribed* internal controls. (Whether prescribed controls are in actual operation will be determined in connection with detailed examination of recorded transactions and relevant source activities.) Representative elements of normal internal control of sales revenue and protection against loss by fraud or error are suggested by the following questions. In each case, the auditor should be concerned not only with the procedures but with possible conflicting duties and with the organizational independence of those responsible for internal check.

1. Do routines for *acceptance and processing of customers' orders* provide for:
   a. Comparison of orders (before acceptance) with quotations, price lists, etc., to ensure that prices and terms are correct?
   b. Consecutive numbering of orders and establishment of a consecutive order log or order file?
   c. Issuance of consecutively numbered price adjustment notices or equivalent documentation of changes in orders (such as changes in specifications, quantities, or delivery method)?
   d. Closing of completed orders by attachment of copies of shipping or billing documents, or posting of shipment or billing references to a consecutive order log to permit current follow-up of open orders?
   e. Regular independent internal check of closed-order file to determine that closed orders have been fully and accurately shipped and billed?
   f. Regular independent internal check of open-order file to determine that open orders are being promptly and properly followed for shipment and billing?
2. Do *shipping* and related routines provide for:
   a. Routing of all shipments through a designated shipping department?
   b. Preparation of consecutively numbered memoranda of shipment or equivalent shipping authorizations?
   c. Establishment of a log of shipments or consecutive file of memoranda of shipment?
   d. Closing of log or file of memoranda of shipment by recording of billing references or attachment of bill copies?
   e. Regular independent internal check of closed-shipment file to verify issuance of billing or authorized cancellation?
   f. Regular independent internal check of open memoranda of shipment to determine adequacy of follow-up or reasons for delay in billing?
   g. Periodic or regular independent verification of products loaded on outgoing trucks or freight cars?
   h. Limitation of access to warehouse and factory stocks?
   i. Periodic inspection of vehicles and trucks leaving premises?
   j. Periodic test-weighing of standard packages (where applicable) and comparison with weights shown on bills to customers and transportation bills?
3. Do routines for *billing to customers* provide for:
   a. Serial numbering of bills and current accounting for all sequential numbers in billing files?
   b. Independent internal check of summarization of bills and comparison with journal entries to determine that all bills issued have been recorded in sales and receivable accounts?
   c. Independent comparison of billing with orders and memoranda of shipment to verify quantities, prices, and terms?
   d. Identification and billing of transportation charges where appropriate?
   e. Billing of sales and excise taxes where applicable and accumulation of such billing for reports to taxing jurisdictions?
   f. Assurance of accuracy, completeness, and propriety of billing where billing procedures involve the use of automatic data processing? Such assurance is dependent upon the existence of independent controls over ADP input and output, outside the data processing

function. Controls should be evaluated in the context of the specific application and business. Examples of independent checks which may be performed regularly or periodically by employees outside the data processing operation are listed below:

(1) Obtain periodic printouts of unit prices stored on tapes, disks, or other storage media and check prices against authorized price lists or handbooks.

(2) If there is a limited number of product types and models, obtain total number of units of each model billed daily, extend quantities by prices, summarize, and compare with computer-produced billing totals.

(3) Maintain a log of shipments or control totals of shipments and compare the total dollar value with the total of machine-prepared billing schedules.

(4) Maintain independent record of total number of units shipped and compare with machine-prepared total.

(5) Match outgoing freight bills (manually or by automatic equipment) with machine-prepared list of shipments.

(6) Prepare independent total of dollar amounts of all bills and credit memoranda issued and compare with machine-prepared billing schedules and entries to accounts receivable.

(7) Examine randomly selected bills; compare selling prices with costs for reasonableness of relationship; compare transportation terms, discount terms, and prices with orders or order acknowledgments.

(8) Examine selected credit memoranda; compare with related bills for prices, quantities, and terms; examine authorization.

Analysis of statements and accounts. Analysis of the sales account and examination of underlying transactions are essential to evaluation and verification of the sales amount shown in the financial statements for the period under audit. Audit procedures generally include the following:

1. Compare sales amount reported in financial statements with balance in general ledger sales account.
2. Review financial statements and classified sales and margin reports and compare with sales and margins for prior periods and with budgets.
   a. Obtain explanations for major fluctuations and confirm the validity of the explanations by examination of supporting documentation and by discussion with appropriate personnel.
   b. Determine by inquiry and review whether there have been any changes in the client's practices with respect to the timing and determination of amount of sales recorded and reported. Determine the effect of any such changes on reported revenues and net income.
3. Abstract, analyze, and verify arithmetical accuracy of general ledger sales account for one or more months.
   a. Review journal entries for propriety.
   b. Determine that the standard or regular sales entries are offset by charges to receivables, cash, or other appropriate general ledger accounts. Check posting of these entries to the general ledger accounts involved.
   c. Examine all correcting entries and nonstandard entries for propriety.
   d. Obtain details of selected standard entries and all significant non-

standard entries, test arithmetical accuracy of summarization, and select appropriate groups of transactions (e.g., billing and credit memorandum schedules) for detailed examination.

Examination of recorded transactions. Analysis and review of statements and general ledger accounts provide a key to detailed source documentation of recorded sales transactions. These records must be adequately tested to provide a basis for verification of the sales account. These tests should be directed toward providing reasonable assurance that all recorded revenues have been earned and all earned revenues have been properly recorded.

1. Account for all sequential numbers in selected blocks of copies of bills and credit memoranda. Verify and trace totals into schedules or summaries and thence into the general ledger entries.
2. Select a number of bills and credits from these blocks and perform the following procedures.
3. Verify (*a*) extensions of quantities by unit prices and (*b*) footings.
4. Verify prices and terms.
   a. Compare prices and terms (cash discount, method of transportation, f.o.b. point) with price lists, handbooks, contracts, orders, or other designated sources.
   b. Determine reasons and approvals for deviations from price lists, handbooks, or other pricing source. Determine that pricing policy and procedures and the means of obtaining competitive information have been approved by legal counsel, inasmuch as vulnerability to legal action under the antitrust laws may represent a substantial exposure to loss. Review cost studies supporting price differentials for varying quantities or customer classifications and ascertain that these have been approved by legal counsel.
   c. Review comparative classified analyses or reports of profit margins on product sales. Obtain explanations for significant fluctuations and give particular attention to the pricing basis for the products involved to determine that changes in cost or other conditions have been taken into account in price-change decisions.
   d. Determine that transportation charges have been billed in accordance with terms of sale and in correct amounts.
   e. Determine that sales taxes and excise taxes have been billed, where applicable, and properly recorded and accumulated for payment to taxing jurisdictions. Determine the criteria for tax exemptions; review the procedure for identifying tax-exempt transactions, obtaining any necessary exemption certificates and filing necessary reports or refund claims; and test the effectiveness of the procedure by reviewing the handling of selected tax-exempt transactions.
5. Verify quantities billed by comparing selected bills with related customer orders and shipping documents.
6. Determine that bills have been recorded in the proper fiscal period by examining shipping dates shown on selected bills issued before and after the end of the fiscal period under audit and verifying these dates by reference to shipping documents. In the case of contract sales, review contract terms with respect to passage of title or other factors relevant to the timing of recording of sales.
7. Test the accuracy of classification of selected sales in specified categories (product lines, distribution channels, geographical areas, classes of

customers, customer industries, etc.) to determine that classified sales reports are meaningful for intended management use.

8. Review selected credit memoranda for sales returns, allowances, and adjustments.
   a. Determine that they have been properly approved and have been issued for bona fide reasons.
   b. Verify receipt of returned products by reference to receiving records, stock records, or other records maintained independently of billing and sales organizations.
   c. Compare amounts of credits with related bills.
   d. Review reasons and approvals for price concessions. If these concessions are substantial or recurrent, they may be indicative of underlying deficiencies in product quality, service, credit extension, collection activity, etc., which should be investigated and brought to the attention of management with appropriate supporting statistics.
   e. Review promotional or advertising allowances to dealers or others; examine published plans for such allowances; review required documentation (tear sheets for space advertising, certifications and scripts for radio and television advertising, bills from advertising media, receipts for payments to product demonstrators, etc.). Determine that plans have been approved by legal counsel and review any significant deviations from plans with counsel.

Sales of By-products. By-products or secondary products produced incidentally to primary manufacturing processes may be an important source of supplementary revenue. The revenue from sales of by-products may be recorded as sales, if significant, or as a reduction of the cost of the primary product. In addition to the normal audit procedures applicable to sales of manufactured products, the auditor may perform the following:

1. Physically observe the manufacturing process to determine whether procedures are adequate to record all by-product production and to segregate, accumulate, and safeguard the by-product.
2. Determine by discussion with manufacturing and engineering personnel what measurements or standards are available with respect to quantities, types, and quality of by-product production (e.g., the standard relationship of by-product quantity to primary-product production). Investigate significant deviations of actual from standard production of the by-product.

Sales of Scrap. Scrap produced in connection with the manufacturing process is usually segregated by type (to the extent economically advantageous), accumulated, and sold to scrap dealers or scrap users. Revenue from scrap sales is generally treated as a reduction of manufacturing costs. The auditor should be concerned with determination that (*a*) all valuable scrap is used or accumulated for sale, (*b*) maximum revenue is being obtained from scrap sales, and (*c*) billing is issued or cash received for all scrap removed from the premises. Audit procedures should include the following:

1. Review instructions and routines and physically observe manufacturing operations to determine that scrap produced is properly segregated, accumulated, safeguarded, and accounted for.
2. Review possibilities of (*a*) more efficient use of materials to reduce amount of scrap produced, (*b*) utilization of remnant material in other manu-

facture, (*c*) reworking of items rejected on inspection and scrapped, and (*d*) purchasing materials in optimum dimensions to minimize waste.

3. Review operating reports and statistical data analyzing trends in scrap generation and sales in comparison with product production and with standards or norms. Investigate significant deviations in either direction, which might indicate either excessive scrap losses in the manufacturing process or failure to accumulate and sell all scrap produced.

4. Determine that high-value scrap is segregated from low-value scrap to obtain highest possible net revenue (after deduction of cost of segregation).

5. Review and test procedure for obtaining and verifying periodic competitive quotations for scrap. Compare prices received with trade journals or other sources of market prices.

6. Review reports of cost and number of people employed in the scrap and salvage operation and compare with budgets, reports for past periods, trends in quantity of scrap handled, and revenue from scrap sales. Investigate significant deviations from normal relationships or other indications of inefficiency or subnormal productivity of salvage employees.

7. Review, observe, and test procedure for weighing and shipping or scrap dealer pickup of scrap to determine that all scrap shipments are recorded accurately.

SALES OF SERVICES

Sales of services (as opposed to sales of products) are generally designated as "(gross) operating revenue" if they represent the principal business of a concern, but they may be classified as "sales" if, as in the case of installation and repair services, they are incidental to product sales. Services may include a heavy proportion of personal labor or work, or they may be performed in large part by electrical, electronic, or mechanical means. The audit approach in each instance must be tailored to the nature of the service and the manner in which it is rendered, the objectives being the same as for other forms of revenue.

Personal Services. Services with a heavy proportion of personal labor or work include professional services (e.g., medical, legal, engineering, accounting, systems analysis, etc.), computer programming, clerical services, installation and repair work, and day labor. They are often sold on the basis of time expended or of a fixed fee for a project or undertaking. The audit program should provide for:

1. Audit and review of the seller's payroll records, job records, and billing procedures to determine that:
   a. Time of all employees is accounted for, i.e., classified and allocated to individual jobs or overhead tasks.
   b. Billing is issued for all allocated time and for all completed fixed-fee projects.
   c. Billing rates are in accordance with contracts or quotations for each work classification involved.
2. Review of traveling, living, and other expenses and their accumulation and allocation to jobs, where arrangements provide for billing of time *and expense.*

Public Utilities. Revenue of public utility companies is derived from the sale of such services as transportation, electric power, gas, water, steam, telephone and telegraph, and grain storage and handling. These companies are subject to regulation by governmental agencies, which specify in detail the uniform methods of accounting and reporting to be used. Effective audit requires a comprehensive knowledge of applicable regulations and principles.

Revenues of transportation companies are derived from numerous sources, such as freight, passenger service, dining service, sleeping accommodations, mail, express, excess baggage charges, storage, demurrage, switching, and apportioned revenues of other carriers involved in interline traffic. Adaptation of normal audit techniques to the special problems of revenue accounting in this industry would include (1) review and testing of procedures for initiating and collecting charges for services through sale of tickets and issuance of such shipping documents as bills of lading and waybills, (2) testing of charges against approved tariff schedules, (3) examination of procedure for allocation of income among participants in the use of joint facilities and from transportation service involving movement of people or goods by more than one carrier, and (4) determination that classification and reporting of revenues are accurate and in conformity with the requirements of regulatory agencies.

Utilities engaged in selling electric power, gas, water, telephone, and telegraph service often employ meters or other automatic means of measuring the quantity of service rendered. Special audit procedures would include examination of the utility's procedures for (1) testing accuracy of metering devices, (2) reading of meters and reporting of readings, (3) billing of charges, (4) estimating and accounting for service rendered for which meter readings have not been taken, and (5) reporting to regulatory agencies.

Construction Contracts. Construction contracts generally provide for the furnishing of supervision, labor, and materials as well as purchased or subcontracted services (such as steel erection, electrical and plumbing work, and rental equipment such as cranes, scaffolding, etc.). The auditor should examine and test procedures for accumulating and allocating to individual construction contracts all labor (including overtime premiums), material, and other costs incurred. He should be particularly alert for erroneous inclusion in overhead of labor, materials, or other costs directly chargeable to construction contracts. Overhead is generally billed to the customer as a fixed percentage of direct costs, determined and agreed upon in advance. The AICPA Committee on Auditing Procedure's booklet *Auditing in the Construction Industry* outlines special features of contractor audits.

Other Services. The multitude of other services from which revenue may be derived includes leasing of equipment; advertising or promotional service; financing on an installment basis or otherwise; computer service bureau or time sharing service; vending machine and good service; office or plant maintenance; guard, security and alarm service; and product repair service. If the provision of a service is a significant part of a business, the revenue therefrom is generally classified as "sales" or "operating revenue." However, if the service is only an incidental part of the business, the revenue may be treated as "nonoperating revenue" or a reduction of cost or expense.

OTHER REVENUE

In most companies the following types of revenue will be incidental to the principal business of the company and will be *nonoperating revenue.* If it is a main service of the firm such as interest income in the case of a financial institution then it will be *operating revenue.*

Rental Income. Rental income may be derived from long-term leasing or short-term rental of real property, office equipment, construction equipment, manufacturing or mining machinery, automotive equipment, or other physical assets. Classification of rental income depends upon the nature of the business involved. Companies (e.g., computer manufacturers) regularly offering customers the option of outright purchase or lease of their products may classify rental revenue as sales. Companies regularly engaged in the rental of property ordinarily classify rental income as operating revenue or, more specifically, as revenue from rentals. Where rental of property to others is occasional and only incidental to the principal operations of the business, rental income is classified as "other revenue."

Audit procedures should include:

1. Review of listings, inventories, floor plans (in the case of buildings), or other records of property or equipment available for leasing. Physical inspection of selected items to determine whether they are on lease, being utilized by the owner, or idle.
2. Examination of selected leases and comparison of specified rentals with credits to rental income accounts and charges to rentals receivable. Rentals for past periods may be confirmed with selected lessees.
3. Review of lease terms to determine that obligations of lessee and lessor are clearly defined, with particular attention to casualty and liability insurance coverage, cost of maintenance and repairs, leasehold improvements, taxes, and utility costs.
4. In the case of subleases, determination that relevant provisions of principal leases are not violated.
5. Determination that rent received in advance is not reflected as income unless and until earned.

Interest Income. Interest income may be derived from loans, notes receivable from customers, past-due accounts, installment receivables, or bonds and other investment securities. Audit of revenue from these sources includes:

1. Physical inspection or confirmation of instruments evidencing interest-bearing obligations.
2. Determination that income specified in the terms of the obligation has been recorded in the accounts.
3. Confirmation with debtors (*a*) in the case of notes, installment accounts, and past-due accounts receivable, and (*b*) where interest payments are delinquent. The status of delinquent bond interest may be confirmed by reference to financial journals or correspondence with issuer.

Dividend Income. Dividends on investment securities must be audited in conjunction with the related asset account. The auditor should determine that all dividends to which his client is entitled have been received and recorded. The amounts may generally be verified by reference to financial journals or other independent reporting services and by comparison with dividend statements and copies of information returns received from issuers.

Royalty Income. Royalties may be received from patent licenses, books, mining properties, or other property used or exploited by an outside party under agreement with the owner of the property. The basic approach to audit of royalties is summarized by Cashin and Owens (in *Auditing*, 2d ed., p. 372) as follows:

> The auditor should examine and make excerpts of all royalty contracts covering patents or copyrights, and of other similar contracts entered into by his client. The principal points of interest to the auditor are the description of the subject matter, the

royalty rates and method of computation, the periodic credit dates of entry of earned royalties, and the provisions relating to interim payments on account and in advance of the periodic credit dates.

Royalty agreements generally provide audit rights for the licensor or an independent auditor engaged by the licensor. Such audits should be directed toward verification of the completeness and accuracy of the licensee's reports on which royalty payments are based. Adequate examination should be made of the licensee's records supporting the royalty reports. Such records may include production, billing, or shipment records of the licensee. The audits may involve questions of identification of products utilizing the techniques, designs, or formulae covered by the patent claims. Such questions are ordinarily referred for resolution to patent counsel of the licensor and licensee.

Fees for Technical and Management Services. Fees for these services may consist of (*a*) service charges based on purchaser's sales or production of designated lines of products, (*b*) directors' fees for participation of individual representatives on boards of directors, or (*c*) retainer or consulting fees charged on the basis of time spent or accomplishment of specified projects. Supporting agreements specifying compensation rates and arrangements should be examined and compared with revenue recorded from these sources. Independent corroboration of amounts recorded should be sought by reference to such sources as reports of purchasers of the service certified by independent accountants, or payroll records and expense accounts of employees involved in providing these services. Consideration may be given to confirmation of the amount of fees paid with the purchasers of service.

Sales of Used Equipment or Other Property. Except in the case of dealers in used equipment or other property, such transactions are infrequent and the net gain or loss is considered as other revenue or expense. In connection with the audit of fixed assets, periodic inventories or catalog records of major equipment and other property should be examined, compared with ledger control balances, and tested by physical inspection. From this examination, comparison with prior inventories or workpapers, and review of dismantlement entries in general ledger and supporting records, selected dispositions may be identified and traced to billing or cash collections. Particular attention should be given to the procedure for obtaining, opening, and recording competitive bids and for obtaining appropriate management authorization for disposition. Equipment incorporating unique or valuable proprietary design or features should not be sold without evaluating the competitive disadvantages of disclosure in comparison with the potential revenue from sale.

Consideration should be given to any available options with respect to tax treatment of used equipment and property sales (e.g., favorable taxation as capital gains). Routines should provide for separate recording or other identification of such transactions for tax purposes.

For sales of real estate, the auditor should be particularly concerned with (1) competitive bids or other basis for price, (2) approval by the board of directors or authorized management, (3) accuracy of description of property conveyed in the deed, and (4) allocation of cost to property sold if a partial disposition.

Sales of Securities. Except in the case of brokers and investment firms regularly engaged in the sale of securities (which is treated in *Audits of Brokers or Dealers in Securities*, a pamphlet prepared by the AICPA's Committee on Auditing Procedure), profit on security transactions is generally considered as other revenue. Profit is determined by deducting from the sale price the applicable commissions, brokerage fees, transfer taxes, and cost of the securities. The cost of securities sold is generally determined on the basis of (1) the actual acquisition cost of securities represented by specific certificates or (2) cost on a first-in, first-out basis. The cost basis for determination of *taxable* profit must be reduced by the amount of distributions designated by tax law or regulation as tax-free or otherwise to be considered as a reduction of the cost basis.

Audit of revenue from sales of securities should include verification of revenue on selected sales by examination of brokers' advices and comparison with market quotations in financial journals. The examination must be made in conjunction with the audit of the related asset account. Through examination of the security account, verification of securities on hand at the audit date, and testing of disbursements during the audit period, assurance may be obtained that all security sales have been recorded and the proceeds properly disposed of.

TYPES OF SALES

Cash Sales. Over-the-counter sales, whether for cash or on a charge basis, may be controlled initially through use of cash registers or serially prenumbered sales slips. Cash sales are particularly susceptible to misappropriation of proceeds. Control may be strengthened by segregation, to the extent feasible, of the duties of (*a*) preparing sales slips, (*b*) delivering merchandise, and (*c*) collecting cash. Regular accounting for sales slips, register readings, and recording of collections should be performed by an individual independent of the sales operation. The auditor should test the effectiveness of this internal control procedure by accounting for serially numbered sales slips, comparing these with cash register tapes or readings, and tracing the latter to bank deposits and ledger entries. He should also test relevant inventory transactions and stock records and ascertain that merchandise for which the operation is responsible is on hand or accounted for by sales or otherwise. Major discrepancies should be investigated by other applicable techniques.

As a safeguard against withholding of cash collections and concealment by falsification of sales slip copies, failure to issue sales slips, failure to record sales on cash registers, etc., outside "shopping services" may be employed periodically to purchase merchandise and observe the handling and recording of the sale.

Charge Sales. As in the case of cash sales, internal control over charge sales is based upon an adequate segregation of duties related to shipping or delivery of merchandise, issuance of billing, recording of charges, and collection and deposit of proceeds. Audit of charge sales is closely related to the audit of receivables and is frequently done in combination with that part of the examination.

C.O.D. Sales. Collect-on-delivery sales have certain characteristics of both cash sales and charge sales. The principal distinction is stated by Meigs (in *Principles of Auditing,* p. 657): "Companies making substantial amounts of C.O.D. sales usually handle these transactions separately from cash sales and charge sales. The problems involved in entrusting both merchandise and cash collections to deliverymen require specialized bookkeeping routines and control procedures."

Audit and control procedures for C.O.D. sales are outlined in:

Cashin and Owens, *Auditing* (2d ed., pp. 208–209)
Meigs, *Principles of Auditing* (3d ed., pp. 657–658)

The auditor should examine control procedures in effect, trace selected C.O.D. sales to cash receipt records or the receivable subsidiary record maintained for such sales, and investigate C.O.D. shipments for which collection has not been made promptly. Special attention should be given to any C.O.D. invoices which have been canceled to determine that cancellation was valid and that the merchandise was not delivered.

Conditional Sales. Sales under extended or installment payment terms frequently involve retention of title or protective lien through conditional sales contracts, chattel mortgages, or another arrangement. The auditor should determine that the requirements of law in the states or countries involved have been interpreted and set forth in operating instructions by legal counsel. He should examine documentation of selected transactions and evidence of any filing or registration of the contracts which may be required by law.

Installment Sales. While installment sales are usually recorded in the same manner as regular charge sales, the tax laws have offered the option of reporting the income from such sales ratably as collections are made. Where this optional installment method of reporting revenue is in effect, the auditor should determine that deferred income has been accurately and consistently computed and recorded. If interest and carrying charges are involved in the installment sales, the interest should be entered in the revenue accounts as earned or as collected, on a consistent basis. The portion of revenue from carrying charges representing cost of servicing an installment account (initial documentation, recording, legal work, collection work, etc.) is ordinarily allocated to the period in which the related costs are deemed to have been incurred.

Cost-plus Sales. Sales of new or nonstandard products or services for which it is not feasible to establish firm prices in advance may be made on the basis of (1) actual costs incurred plus fixed or variable (percentage) fees or (2) other cost-based formulae. Such sales are particularly prevalent in governmental procurement of research and development services and new defense products. The auditor should review and test the accumulation and allocation of costs to specific contracts. Proposed or completed settlements of negotiable contracts (e.g., price-redetermination contracts) should be examined to determine that cost data furnished are complete and accurate and that settlements are computed in accordance with contract terms.

Consignment Sales. Consigned stock represents inventory of the consignor until sold to customers by the consignee as agent, distributor, or dealer, for the consignor. Such sales are ordinarily reported on a regular basis by the consignee, who deducts commission and expenses from his remittance.

Consignments out. The audit of the consignor should include a check of procedures and accounts to determine that shipments on consignment are segregated from sales. The following may indicate that consignments are included as sales and call for additional investigation:

1. Invoices labeled as consigned, entered as sales
2. Unusually frequent or relatively large "sales returns"
3. Extremely late payment of accounts if measured by usual credit terms

The consignees' periodic reports which generally include sales, commissions, and related expenses chargeable to the consignor, are compared with the consignor's records and these are confirmed by direct correspondence.

If consignment contracts so provide, periodic physical inventories are taken at the stock locations to test the validity of consignee's reports.

Consignments in. The audit of a consignees' revenues from sales of consigned merchandise includes the following steps:

1. Review of consignment contracts and relevant correspondence with consignors and determination of compliance with terms of the agreements.
2. Review of routines for identification or physical segregation of consigned merchandise and for separate recording of consignment sales in the accounts. Procedures should provide for physical and accounting control of consignment operations, whether the consignee elects to report as revenue only commissions earned on consignment sales or to include these transactions in sales and cost of sales in the financial statements.
3. Comparison of consignment reports sent to consignors with accounting records and verification of commission computation.
4. Direct confirmation with consignors of (*a*) merchandise for which the consignee is accountable, (*b*) amounts owing consignors for consignment sales, and (*c*) any commissions or compensation due from consignors.
5. Inspection and test count of inventory of consigned merchandise on hand and reconciliation with consignment reports.

SALES ADJUSTMENTS

Sales Returns. A representative sample of transactions involving returns of merchandise for credit or refund should be reviewed as outlined under "Examination of recorded transactions" (item 8, page 30-17). As in the case of gross sales, comparative analyses of sales returns in relation to gross sales for current and past periods may provide clues to underlying deficiencies such as deteriorating product quality, misappropriations of cash or merchandise or inadequacies in control procedures. If analysis of returns indicates the prevalence of merchandise defects, the auditor should determine that this fact is recognized in valuation of merchandise inventories and, in the case of defective resale products, that procedures for filing claims against responsible vendors are adequate and are being followed.

Sales Allowances. Sales allowances are often closely related to sales returns in that customers may frequently accept a price allowance in lieu of returning the merchandise. Goods damaged in transit or with minor defects may be found to be usable by the customer and a price allowance may be less costly to the seller than the transportation and repair or replacement costs which would be incurred if the merchandise were returned. Allowances may also be granted for failure to ship merchandise of the exact quantity, size, color or other specifications ordered by the customer. It is the practice of most manufacturers to maintain records of allowances according to functional or departmental responsibility. The auditor should review and obtain explanations of large fluctuations in allowances and bring to the client's attention any indications of laxity or weakness in organization or control procedures which have contributed to the abnormality.

Cash Discounts on Sales. These are to be distinguished from trade or quantity discounts which are ordinarily deducted from the list price in calculating the gross invoice price. The preferred treatment (*Accountant's Handbook*, 5th ed.) is to regard cash discounts as sales adjustments either by deducting from sales the discounts taken or by recording the sales at net prices and treating forfeited discounts as additional income. The auditor may find it useful to obtain or prepare a comparative analysis of total sales discounts allowed and their percentage relationship to sales for current and past periods. Explanations should be obtained for major fluctuations and management's attention should be directed toward any indications of significant laxity or inconsistency in enforcement of discount terms with resultant loss of revenue.

Sales Freight. As a general rule, outbound transportation costs are considered as selling and distribution expenses. Where the seller prepays the transportation and adds this cost to the invoice to the customer, this transportation charge to the customer should be treated as an offset to the cost incurred and should not be recorded as sales. If the merchandise is sold at a fixed price, delivered but with freight collect and the purchaser is allowed to deduct from his remittance the freight paid by him, such freight allowance should be treated as a deduction from sales. (There may be exceptions to this rule in some industries.) Freight allowances of this nature should be the subject of comparison and investigation.

Warranties and Guarantees. Product warranties may be of varying terms from as little as a month or two to five years or more. Standard warranties are often supplemented by optional extended warranties or service contracts for which an extra charge is made. Appropriate provision for warranty costs may be made in the liability or reserve accounts on the basis of experience or estimates of probable product failures and service requirements. These provisions are generally charged to operating expenses. However, the net revenue from extended warranties or service contracts for which an extra charge is made is sometimes deferred and amortized as earned. The auditor should review warranty cost experience and estimates and satisfy himself that appropriate adjustments of liability and deferred income accounts have been made to reflect the situation at the balance sheet date.

Deferred Credits. Deferred credits are obligations resulting from advance collections for goods or services and are classified as liabilities until the goods are delivered or the services performed. Further classification as current or long-term will depend upon the period in which the obligation is to be discharged.

Among the types of deferred credits are:

1. Unearned rent
2. Interest charged in advance on discount-basis loans, including bonds issued at a discount
3. Gift certificates, tickets, tokens, coupons, and similar items redeemable in goods or services
4. Unearned insurance premiums
5. Subscriptions received in advance
6. C.B.D. (cash-before-delivery) merchandise sales

In each case, the auditor determines by computation and test check of the records that the amount of income received but not yet earned is reflected in deferred credit accounts. At the same time, he must determine that deferred credits are transferred to revenue as they are earned.

The auditor must be alert to distinguish between advance payments and deposits which may have to be refunded. On the other hand, in the case of rents, so-called "deposits" may represent deferred rent applicable to the final lease period.

In some cases, such as redeemable coupons, no records may be retained from which the amount of unearned revenue can be computed. In these cases the auditor must see that a reasonable amount of liability is reported.

Intracompany and Intercompany Sales. Sales among organizational components of a business (intracompany sales) or affiliated companies (intercompany sales) may be billed at cost, commercial prices, or other agreed prices to permit a proper presentation and measurement of the operating results of individual departments or affiliated companies. Such transfers do not constitute sales for the consolidated enterprise and should be eliminated in preparation of the consolidated financial statements. If the transfer prices include a profit factor, the amount of such profit applicable to merchandise inventory or other assets held by the purchasing component should also be eliminated by revaluation of the assets.

STATEMENT PRESENTATION

The income statement ordinarily shows the net sales, cost of sales, selling expenses, general and administrative expenses, income taxes, income before extraordinary items, extraordinary items, and net income.

The earnings per share of common stock should be disclosed in accordance with APB No. 15, *Earnings Per Share.* The computation should be based ordinarily on the weighted average number of shares outstanding during the year. A pro forma earnings figure should be reported on the assumption of full conversion of all outstanding convertible debentures, convertible preferred stock, warrants and stock options.

Segmented Reporting. There has been much discussion concerning the adequacy of disclosure of the operating results of conglomerate companies engaged in diverse unrelated businesses. It has been argued that unsegmented income reports of such companies and of other multi-line businesses do not provide the investing public with sufficient information to permit informed investment decisions. On the other hand, segmented (divisional or product line) reporting of revenues introduces difficult problems of cost, expense and tax allocations and the possibility of damage to company competitive interests. In September 1967 the Accounting Principles Board issued APB Statement No. 2, *Disclosure of Supplemental Financial Information by Diversified Companies,* recommending voluntary disclosure of divisional data. The Board did not lay down any specific requirements pending further study. The problem was considered by the Financial Executives Institute and a research study was undertaken by R. K. Mautz. The results were published by the FEI in 1968 as *Financial Reporting by Diversified Companies.* Among other recommendations the study suggested that diversified companies report sales or other gross revenue and the relative contribution to net income of any separate industry segment producing 15 percent or more of gross revenues. This is somewhat higher than required later by the SEC.

SEC Requirements. The SEC has announced a series of major changes that relate to the reporting and registration forms required under the Securities Act of 1933 and the Securities Exchange Act of 1934. The changes conform closely to earlier proposals by the SEC. These changes which become effective for fiscal years ending on or after December 31, 1970, are discussed in detail in Chapter 45, "Securities and Exchange Requirements." We are concerned in this chapter primarily with requirements with respect to reporting revenue. The new Form 10-K requires the reporting of information as to lines of business, and classes of products or services. Where a company has more than one line of business, it must report for each line of business the approximate amount or percentage of (1) total sales and revenues and (2) income or loss before income taxes and extraordinary items. The test for reporting the chosen line is whether during either of the last two fiscal years it accounted for (*A*) 10% or more of total revenues (*B*) 10% or more of income before income taxes and extraordinary items or (*C*) a loss which equalled or exceeded 10% of the income specified in (*B*). If total sales and revenues did not exceed $50 million in either of the most recent two years, the percentage to be used is 15%. The auditor now has additional responsibilities in determining that sales and other revenues is properly reported in SEC filings.

BIBLIOGRAPHY

Accounting Research and Terminology Bulletins, final edition, AICPA, New York, 1961.

APB Statement No. 4, *Basic Concepts and Accounting Principles Underlying Financial Statements of Business Enterprises,* AICPA, New York, October, 1970.

Aspley, John C.: *The Sales Promotion Handbook,* 3d ed., Chicago, The Dartnell Corporation, 1962.

Cadmus, Bradford: *Operational Auditing Handbook,* New York, The Institute of Internal Auditors, 1964.

Cashin, James A., and Garland C. Owens: *Auditing,* 2d ed., New York, The Ronald Press Company, 1963.

Davidson, Sidney: *Handbook of Modern Accounting,* New York, McGraw-Hill Book Company, 1970.

Lenhart, Norman J., and Philip L. Defliese: *Montgomery's Auditing,* 8th ed., New York, The Ronald Press Company, 1957.

R. K. Mautz: *Financial Reporting by Diversified Companies,* New York, Financial Executives Institute, 1968.

Meigs, Walter B. and E. John Larsen: *Auditing,* 4th ed., Homewood, Ill., Richard D. Irwin, Inc., 1969.

Schiff, Michael, and Martin Mellman: *Financial Management of the Marketing Function,* New York, Financial Executives Institute, 1962.

Challis, D. A.: "How the Internal Auditor Can Assist the Sales Department," *The Internal Auditor,* Winter, 1965.

Saul, Ralph S.: "Corporate Disclosure," *The Internal Auditor,* September/October, 1969.

Skousen, K. Fred: "Standards for Reporting by Lines of Business," *The Journal of Accountancy,* February, 1970.

Kensey, John P.: "Dividing the Incentive Pie in Divisionalized Companies," *Financial Executive,* September, 1970.

Pacter, Paul A.: "Line-of-Business Earnings Disclosures in Recent SEC Filings," *The Journal of Accountancy,* October, 1970.

Chapter **31**

Procurement

DUANE E. WILSON

Chief Auditor—Chicago, Standard Oil Company (Indiana)

THE PROCUREMENT FUNCTION

In the modern business world, the procurement function has become a key function of almost every enterprise. Goods and services with a value of many billions of dollars are purchased each year by industrial, governmental, and service organizations. Such goods and services acquired from others frequently become a large portion of the total cost of operating an organization. Although volumes vary widely depending on the size and nature of the enterprise, the degree of astuteness applied to the procurement function sometimes makes the difference between success and mediocrity or failure of the enterprise. Further, the dynamics of the procurement function are such that there is always an opportunity for continuous improvement. This chapter will discuss some of the many and complex factors involved in this vital function and how management controls over procurement can be evaluated and improved.

Purpose and Objective. "Procurement" is the function of securing from outsiders the facilities, equipment, materials, and services required by an organization. It is the function of supply, from determining and defining a need to the delivery of the item to the user.

"Procurement" has also been defined as:

> . . . the act of obtaining the right product at the right price, in the right quantity, at the right time, and at the right place. In this definition, it is evident that the word "right" is a relative one, reflecting a basic standard for evaluating the activities related to obtaining materials, supplies, and services from others. In most profit-seeking businesses, "right" is interpreted to mean that which is to the best long-term interests of the business as a whole.[1]

Implied in both of these definitions is the receipt of maximum value for procurement expenditures, assurance of supply, and efficiency of the procurement function.

The procurement function, therefore, may include all of the following:

Recognizing a need
Determining what to buy
Designating where to procure
Determining the time to buy
Determining the quantity to be procured
Determining the quality to be procured
Determining the price to pay
Arranging for transportation
Expediting and follow-up
Receiving of material and services
Processing invoices for payment
Disbursement of cash

For the purpose of this chapter, we will exclude the recognition of a need, as this is an operating function in most organizations, and the disbursement of cash, which is covered in another chapter. All of the other functions mentioned above will be included in our consideration, although some may be performed by the purchasing department, some may be the responsibility of other departments, and others may be shared by the purchasing and other departments.

[1] Bradford Cadmus, *Operational Auditing Handbook*, New York, The Institute of Internal Auditors, 1964, pp. 43 and 44.

Activities of the Purchasing Department. Top management policy, of course, governs how much of the procurement function is performed by the purchasing department and how much is vested in other operating and staff departments.

The following are responsibilities which may typically be given to the purchasing department:

Purchase goods and services
Develop sources of supply
Assist in standardization of materials
Expedite the delivery of material and equipment
Handle complaints and return of material
Assist the determination of the proper time and quantities to buy
Assist in transfer of excess inventory stocks between departments
Dispose of surplus and obsolete materials
Participate in the development of specifications for equipment, etc.

In addition, some organizations make the purchasing department responsible for the following activities:

Traffic
Operation of warehouses
Inspection and receipt of incoming materials
Review of invoices for payment
Control of finished goods and in-process inventories
Purchases for employees' personal use

Procurement by Others. In the interest of efficiency, portions of the procurement function will usually be performed by personnel other than those of the purchasing department. Examples of those activities most frequently performed by others are:

Field purchases. The activities of many organizations are such that local personnel must procure material and services for efficient operations. When operations are dispersed geographically, it is frequently not practicable for the purchasing department to make all purchases. Authority to procure routine contract services is commonly delegated to local operating personnel.

Emergency purchases. Provision is commonly made for emergency purchases of material, services, and repairs to be arranged by local personnel when efficient operations are at stake.

Specialized purchases. Specialized purchases are frequently more appropriately handled by the department involved because of the particular expertise required. These may include:

Advertising services
Auditing services
Computer services
Engineering services
Transportation
Raw materials
Consulting services
Insurance
Real estate

Small quantities. Repetitive purchases of small quantities of material are often more economically and efficiently consummated by local personnel.

Although administrative responsibility for such procurement activities may have been delegated to others, the purchasing department often retains functional responsibility for guidance, assistance, and counsel in any or all of these areas.

MANAGEMENT CONTROL AND EFFICIENCY

Management's Expectations and Policy. Because of its key role in most organizations, procurement deserves direct attention from top management on a continuous basis. Typically, there is no other functional area of an organization where the potential savings are so great or where the effect on operations is so significant. The efficiency and operating costs of all departments are involved. Further, innumerable relationships outside the company are involved in obtaining the materials, services, and special skills of others. Accordingly, top management must define its policies as to how these responsibilities will be carried out. Further, the essential elements of the policies must be in writing if there is to be continuity in the procurement activity throughout the organization and over a period of time. Also, it is fundamental to good management control that written policies be the basic tool for measurement of performance.

Such written policies are usually referred to as a "purchasing policy manual." Such manuals take a variety of forms and serve a variety of purposes.

The following are typical section headings for such a manual:

General Policy
Responsibility
Departmental Relations
Supplier Relationships
Business Ethics

Each of these topics involves important management decisions that can have profound effects on the enterprise.

General policy. This is a statement of top management's general attitude toward the procurement function. It may be a brief statement that the general policy of the organization is to procure equipment, supplies, and services when needed, at the lowest ultimate cost, consistent with appropriate standards of quality and service. The many implications involved in each phase will be subject to management decision and delineation in subsequent sections of the policy.

Responsibility. Responsibility of the purchasing function should be established in this section. The extent to which the purchasing department will participate in the total procurement function must be defined.

For instance, the purchasing department may have all, partial, or no responsibility for determining what to purchase, when to buy, vendor selection, price to pay, quantity to purchase, and the size of inventories. In a large organization, these decisions are very complex, and some flexibility is necessary for changing conditions. However, it is most important that clear responsibility be established if duplication is to be avoided and performance is to be evaluated. Figure 1 is an example of this section of the policy appropriate for a large company.

Departmental relations. Relationships between the purchasing department and other departments should be clearly spelled out. This includes defining channels for requisitions, contacting suppliers, expediting, and all of the other functions that involve both purchasing and other departments. The authority vested in other departments should be specified. This is particularly important in areas where purchasing shares responsibility, such as in negotiating construction contracts, guidance on field purchases, determining quantities, and establishing quality requirements. Figure 2 illustrates a statement of policy on construction contracts.

Supplier relationships. Since relationships with suppliers have important implications involving public relations, proprietary information, and contractual agreements, management's intent in this area should be made known to all those involved. There is a desirable balance where a working relationship is established to mutual advantage without excessive contact and familiarity.

Business ethics. Management's attitude toward gifts, entertainment, and conflict of interest should be explained in this section.

The purchasing policy manual may specify operating procedures and uniform practices for negotiations with vendors, inquiries and bids, and

Figure 1 PURCHASING POLICY BULLETIN

Responsibility for the design and the execution of operating policies and procedures to accomplish purchasing objectives rests with the chief purchasing officer. He is accountable for the functional performance and efficiency of the overall purchasing organization, for development of effective complementary centralized and decentralized purchasing programs, and for staffing, training, and evaluation of professional personnel for headquarters and decentralized purchasing offices.

Within monetary limits and responsibilities set by executive authority, it is the responsibility of the purchasing department to provide (or except as delegated to others to provide) procurement services to:

Initiate, conduct, and conclude negotiations for the purchase of facilities, equipment, goods, and services, and execute all contractual documents required;

Continually develop sufficient and reliable sources of supply for present and known future needs;

Promote and recommend use of standard materials whenever possible, and assist in standardization of materials, supplies, and equipment;

Explore the markets, in connection with its work, for new sources, products, processes, ideas, and materials which will lower costs. Disseminate to other departments information which may promote improved operations;

Evaluate (with the assistance of others when necessary) the capabilities of manufacturers, suppliers, and contractors;

Expedite the delivery of material and equipment to meet the requirements of the using department;

Obtain priority assistance from the appropriate governmental agencies during periods of governmental control of materials;

Handle complaints concerning purchased material, and negotiate for the return of the material or other settlement;

Assist in supervision of company inventories and the determination of the proper time and quantities to buy;

Assist in transfer of excess inventory stocks between departments of the company and between affiliates;

Dispose of surplus and obsolete materials, including scrap; provide guidance for disposition of materials by others under delegated authority;

Promote, in cooperation with vendors and personnel of other departments, purchasing research and value-analysis programs to effect savings;

Determine final specifications only if requested. Provide assistance and guidance in development of such specifications for equipment, facilities, materials, and supplies.

Figure 2 CONSTRUCTION, INSTALLATION, AND ERECTION CONTRACTS POLICY BULLETIN

Purpose. To set forth the general policy relating to the authorities and responsibilities for construction contracts.

Policy. The following are the policy responsibilities which are assigned to the principal divisions, departments, or management areas concerned with construction. These responsibilities will be met whenever either a specific project manager is assigned to supervise a construction job or the normal location/division management supervises a construction job. The Executive Vice-president—Operations has delegated to the Director of Purchases the authority to correlate all activities on construction, installation, and erection contracts up to the start of the work. The procedures and forms necessary to implement this policy will be prepared by the appropriate staff unit. The individual needs of each division will be considered in preparing the various procedures.

Engineering

1. Select the architects and/or consulting engineers.
2. Prepare the necessary specifications to be used in soliciting bids and, ultimately, in the actual construction.
3. In concert with other departments, evaluate and select the contractors.
4. Prepare the engineering aspects and specifications for the contract and for subcontracts, when applicable.
5. Supervise the architects and/or consulting engineers and contractors in the performance of their work under the contract.
6. Establish and administer proper contract supervision in the areas of quality of materials and equipment, subcontracts, quality and progress of work, changes in the work, and amendments to the contract.
7. Control all aspects of actual prosecution of the job to ensure acceptable completion within the funds and time allocated.

Legal

1. Review the proposal made to, or received from, the contractor, or
2. If competitive bidding, review the invitation and bid proposal to be accepted.
3. Consult with representatives of engineering, purchasing, accounting, and the contractor to finalize the agreement.

Purchasing

1. Provide a list and evaluation of qualified contractors and subcontractors.
2. Solicit the bids from qualified contractors on a uniform basis.
3. Notify bidder of the award of the contract and issue all related purchase orders and commitments.
4. Administer the purchasing aspects of the contract in accordance with the XYZ Company purchasing policy.

Treasurer-comptroller

1. Review the financial responsibility of potential contractors and determine when surety bonds are required.
2. Determine the insurance coverage required and the tax liability under the contract.
3. Approve the accounting and auditing aspects of the proposal and contract and establish cost records and cost controls.
4. Establish disbursement controls and procedures and effect payments required by the contract.

The final selection of the contractor shall be an engineering decision and shall be approved by authorized representatives of the Purchasing and the Treasurer-comptroller Departments. Authorization for the XYZ staff to proceed will be issued by designated representatives of the Operations Management Department.

other similar matters. In some cases, the manual will include specific information regarding allocation of business, quality standards, transportation matters, etc.

From the auditor's standpoint, the more explicit the purchasing policy manual, the better. If management has clearly set forth its intent in the various areas mentioned above, the auditor's job of evaluating management control will be facilitated considerably.

Organization and Responsibility. As mentioned in the previous topic, top management must establish a general policy toward procurement and specify where and by whom the procurement activity will be performed. The placement of the purchasing department in the organization structure and the level of the executive to whom the purchasing manager reports are basic decisions in this regard. Further, they are key decisions because much of the management control over the function revolves around this placement. From this base are generated the definitions of procurement responsibility, assignment of authority, etc.

Procurement is frequently a coordinated effort involving both operating and staff personnel, a fact which gives rise to some rather complex relationships. The necessity for these relationships to be clearly defined is obvious. Such definitions are made by means of formal organization charts, job descriptions, and delegations of authority. These documents, when carefully conceived and developed, can avoid duplication of work, encourage efficiency, and provide the tools for management control over performance.

The organization within a purchasing department involves decisions regarding centralized versus decentralized procurement; allocation of duties based on geographical areas or by types of commodity; providing for administrative and staff functions most efficiently; delegations to subordinates; and coordination of the entire effort. The quality of these decisions will have a profound effect on how well purchasing management is able to control and evaluate purchasing performance.

If management's organizational plans are to be effective, it is, of course, essential that they be disseminated to all those concerned. This fact underscores the need for formal organization charts, job descriptions, and authority delegations. Further, there must be some means of regularly advising all concerned so that they understand their duties, authority, and responsibility, as well as their relationships to others involved in the procurement activity.

Yardsticks of Performance. Good management does not assign responsibilities and goals and then forget about them; it expects results. As in other functions of an organization, management must have methods of evaluating performance. Standard criteria are out of the question, of course, because of the nature of the function. However, yardsticks can be formulated which will serve as a basic tool of evaluation. These yardsticks must be established in advance if meaningful comparisons are to be made.

Many of these standards of performance, particularly in the general management area, will necessarily be based on subjective judgment as to how well specific activities have been conducted. This qualitative evaluation can be made of such areas as the following:

Establishing plans and goals for implementing overall objectives of the procurement function

Developing sufficient and reliable sources of supply

Developing supplier relationships that are conducive to mutual benefit and respect

This list can be expanded, of course, to include all of the important activities related to procurement. There are also some quantitative yardsticks that can be developed. These include:

Number of requisitions handled
Average cost per requisition
Average time required per requisition
Number of purchase orders placed
Average cost per purchase order
Average time required per purchase order
Number of inquiries and bids solicited
Number of visits by vendors
Total amount spent
Cost of purchasing per dollar spent

These statistics will be meaningful only if they are accurately prepared and carefully used. Comparisons with previous periods, other locations, or other companies can be very useful in evaluating relative work loads and efficiency.

These are tools of management control and should be utilized by management on a regular basis. They are also useful considerations for the auditor in his task of appraising the management controls over the function.

Purchasing Research. In the interest of improving procurement efficiency on a continuing basis, most organizations include purchasing research in the activities of the purchasing department. The success of the activity is usually directly related to the approach taken. A systematic allocation of time and expertise is essential for effectiveness. In large organizations, it is often found desirable to segregate this research function from regular operations and to vest it in certain individuals who have no other duties. One of the more important projects that may be assigned in this area is the design and implementation of programs to evaluate the performance of procurement duties. This involves establishment of the yardsticks discussed in the previous topic, gathering data, drawing conclusions, and making recommendations for improvement. Other activities that may profitably be included in this function are:

Study and conduct research in procurement techniques to improve efficiency and reduce clerical costs.

Prepare and interpret statistical reports in the procurement area.

Design and administer savings programs.

Develop programs to optimize recoveries from scrap, salvage, and waste materials.

Evaluate supplier performance.

Develop new sources of supply.

Conduct make-or-buy studies.

Investigate new products and services and determine their significance to the organization.

Develop programs for control of quality of purchased goods.

Analyze and interpret market trends and conditions.

Participate in value-analysis studies.

Study opportunities for standardization and substitution.

Conduct research with respect to long-range prospects and business conditions as they affect procurement policy and personnel requirements.

Disseminate pertinent information throughout the organization for the guidance of all those involved in the procurement activity.

As indicated by these examples, purchasing research activities can be a vital element in management control of the procurement function.

Value Analysis. The basic concept of value analysis is a traditional one in procurement and engineering activities. However, beginning in the late 1940s, the concept began receiving increased emphasis to the extent that it has become a much more sophisticated and effective technique in reducing costs.

As a result of some rather phenomenal successes in using the technique, the United States government has given impetus to its use by strong encouragement to or requirement for value analysis on defense contracts. Reported savings on defense work alone amounts to billions of dollars.

"Value analysis is systematic study applied to any item used, the objective being to maintain adequate quality but at a lower cost."[2] It relates value to the function rather than to the cost. A value-analysis program does not replace other cost-reduction efforts; rather, it supplements them. The usual connotation of the term "cost reduction" normally involves evaluating the worth of an item, while "value analysis" evaluates the worth of a function.

Professor Edward Blake describes one company's use of value analysis in an article in *Management Services:*

> This approach to the problem of cost is well summarized in the check list of ten "Tests for Values" compiled and used in the purchasing department of the General Electric Company. This code is widely circulated and used throughout the various divisions and departments of the company. Every part, material, operation, and service must pass these tests:
>
> 1. Does its use contribute value?
> 2. Is its cost proportionate to its usefulness?
> 3. Does it need all the features it possesses?
> 4. Is there anything better for the intended use?
> 5. Can a usable part be made by a lower-cost method?
> 6. Can a standard product be found that will be usable?
> 7. Is it made on proper tooling, considering quantities used?
> 8. Do material, reasonable labor, overhead, and profit total its cost?
> 9. Will another dependable supplier provide it for less?
> 10. Is anyone buying it for less?[3]

In large organizations, with extensive potential for benefits from a value-analysis program, the responsibility may be vested in a special segment of the engineering department. In other organizations, the purchasing department may be wholly responsible for the program. In any case, the technique has application in any procurement function. The purchasing department, whether wholly or partially responsible for the program, can have significant influence on its implementation throughout the organization.

Because of its significant potential benefits, those responsible for procurement should be knowledgeable in this area. The auditor will be concerned with whether or not a program of value analysis has been established, its place in the organization, that all personnel involved in procurement are trained in its use, and that benefits are properly evaluated.

[2] Victor H. Pooler, Jr., *The Purchasing Man and His Job*, New York, American Management Association, 1964, p. 91.

[3] Edward Blake, *Management Services*, New York, AICPA, September–October, 1964, pp. 45–46.

Electronic Data Processing Applications. The procurement function tends to generate the large number of repetitive transactions which are characteristic of a successful data processing operation. Therefore, it is quite common, and should be a reasonable expectation, that the auditor will encounter a computer in a portion of the procurement activity.

A wide range of applications may be confronted. Depending on the size of the company and the desires of management, automation may encompass only a single facet of the operation, such as expense distribution, or a complete systemization from generation of the purchase document to payment of the invoice, including automatic inventory control. The latter may be described as an information system and would be concerned with all aspects of requisitioning, i.e., shipping, receiving, routing, paying, cost distribution, inventories, and the economics of each. Figure 3 is an illustration of a system encompassing these features.

The prime target of a computerized purchasing system is almost always a reduction in inventory. Precise mathematical formulas dealing with

Figure 3 CENTRAL COMPUTER APPLICATION—PROCUREMENT AND INVENTORY MANAGEMENT

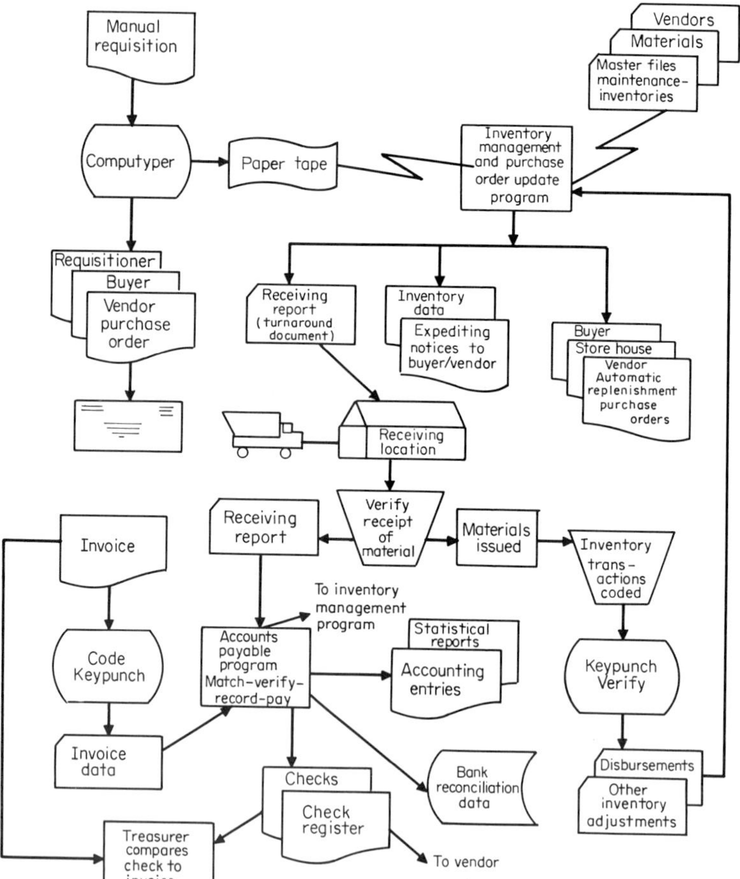

probabilities can be applied to determine optimum inventory levels. The rapid processing ability of the computer permits a repetitive analysis of each transaction. This, in connection with a projection of future activity, allows the computer to initiate reordering at the most desirable time.

Other advantages, such as clerical savings, improved buying, and utilization of available computer time, may influence a conversion to EDP, but they are usually of a secondary consideration and normally do not accrue in the short run.

If the opportunity presents itself, the auditor should make use of the computer by having audit routines built into the normal processing runs. Items may be selected for audit or exception information may be generated for further review.

Of particular significance to the auditor, in automated systems, are the effects on internal control. If the computer is used only as a high-speed calculator, control considerations will not be materially different from those in a manual system except that another department is involved in the process. However, if "online" systems with communication capabilities and/or direct-access storage are encountered, the control problem becomes unique in that the audit trail becomes obscure. The auditor must then be concerned with an entirely new set of considerations, which are covered in another chapter. It should be stated, however, that the auditor must adjust his former control criteria and be willing to accept reasonable alternatives as his contribution to progress. Management will not condone an audit policy which is incompatible with EDP, nor, on the other hand, will they accept chaos as the result of inadequate system planning. The auditor can be a key person in plotting the middle course.

Streamlined Procurement Techniques. Where small purchases are many, it is desirable, and sometimes imperative, to devise special methods for handling these small orders. Considerations of efficiency and economy make it obvious that equal attention cannot be given to all orders irrespective of the amount involved. Several streamlined techniques are being successfully used to minimize handling of small items so that time and expertise of procurement personnel may be appropriately allocated for maximum benefit to the organization. When properly conceived and implemented, these techniques or systems can result in notable savings with no significant loss in control of dollar volumes spent. Some of these techniques are discussed below.

Purchase order draft system. This system simply involves combining the purchase order with a signed blank check to pay for the material ordered. The vendor completes the check in the proper amount, ships the material, and the transaction is complete. The advantage of reduced paper work on the part of both the buyer and seller is obvious. In addition, cash discounts are assured and the potential for automation of such purchases is enhanced considerably.

However, as Henry DeVos points out in an article in *The Journal of Accountancy*, controls must be stronger in a purchase order draft system than they need to be in a more conventional system.

Mr. DeVos outlines the following control techniques to be incorporated in the system:

> Under this system, the invoice audit function is moved from the "pre-audit" to the "post-audit" stage. Under the conventional system an invoice is audited before it is paid, while under the purchase order draft system the invoice is audited after payment.

The purchase order and check are prenumbered with the same number and the two documents are perforated where they are joined together. This nullifies the danger of sending one vendor a blank check with another vendor's purchase order. A prefix on the number identifies the purchasing office from which the order was issued. The canceled check therefore gives positive identification of the vendor and the issuing office.

Another important control in the purchase order draft system is not normally found in conventional systems. The reverse side of the check is imprinted "For deposit only to the account of the payee." Therefore the check can only be redeemed by deposit to a bank account of a named payee. The check is worthless to any unauthorized person if lost or stolen.

In addition, two other limitations have been included. First, a monetary limit is established. Kaiser started by limiting its use to purchase orders of $200 or less (which accounted for 75 per cent of the purchase orders) and has subsequently raised the limit to $1,000, now accounting for 92 per cent of the purchase orders. The second limitation is that of time. The checks have been so printed as to make void any payment after ninety days. This limitation makes it impossible for a vendor to discover a check in his files many months later and attempt to cash it. Should the vendor file the check away by mistake or oversight, the vendee can safely pay the invoice after the ninety-day period and be certain that no double payment will result.

The usual type of internal control also exists. While a purchasing agent may sign the check, the bank is instructed to release canceled checks directly to the financial officer. Thus the originator of the check has no means of intercepting and destroying a check after payment by the bank.

It is important to note that while this is a simple check to the bank, it is a draft to the vendee. A special account is opened against which the bank charges these checks. The account is operated on the imprest fund basis and arrangements are made with the bank to transfer funds from the operating fund daily to reimburse the account. Thus, although to the bank it is a simple check, the vendee would not record the blank check in the cash disbursements journal until the canceled check is received. Hence, no outstanding checks—no checks in transit—therefore, no bank reconciliation. This eliminates another clerical chore.[4]

Blanket orders. Blanket orders are frequently advantageous for the purchase of material and services which are bought on a repetitive basis. They provide the advantage of quantity purchasing power by combining the requirements of various locations and/or by totaling the requirements for a given period of time. Such an arrangement may involve firm price agreements with the advantage of price protection. Increased efficiency is realized through the elimination of a large number of rush or small-value transactions without a loss of central authority over terms, prices, and conditions.

Traveling requisitions. The traveling requisition is used for reordering repetitive material and supplies. Its use is usually most practical in a warehouse or stockroom environment where minimum and maximum levels for the items have been established.

Traveling requisitions are printed on card stock for durability and are reused many times, sometimes for a number of years. Information needed to place repetitive orders, such as description of material, manufacturer, and location requiring the material, is entered permanently on the requisition. When reorder is necessary, the requisitioner simply enters the quantity required and a validating signature on lines provided. Those responsible for procurement respond by entering the purchase order number and date on the requisition and returning it to the originator. From that point, the purchase is handled in the conventional manner.

[4] Henry DeVos, "Management Control and Information," *The Journal of Accountancy*, November, 1964, pp. 85–86.

The use of traveling requisitions can reduce the paper work involved in repetitive orders a great deal; they provide valuable historical information, and sometimes are adapted to serving as an inventory control record. In addition, control and audits are facilitated in well-designed systems by the ready accessibility of information on turnover, ordering, and inventory levels.

Monthly charge accounts. Monthly charge accounts are often advantageous for miscellaneous small supplies, stationery, small repair services, and for other similar requirements. A typical system provides for orders to be placed by telephone or other informal means with selected cooperating vendors. The orders may be placed directly by operating personnel or by informal media through procurement personnel. Delivery tickets or counter tickets become receiving reports when signed by receiving personnel. Such tickets also serve as the authorization to pay when associated with invoices submitted monthly.

Charge account systems can eliminate significant amounts of paper work in requisitioning, ordering, and paying; however, some loss of control over price and quantity will result. Therefore, the use of such an arrangement is usually limited to small quantities of miscellaneous supplies or services where tight control is not practicable from the standpoint of ultimate economy or efficiency.

Inventory Management. All enterprises have inventories of some kind; consequently, decisions must be made with respect to inventory levels, order quantities, timing of orders, policy on stock shortages, warehousing methods, etc. These decisions can, and frequently are, made on the basis of intuition and other superficial methods. However, there are analytical techniques which many organizations have found to be highly successful in minimizing ultimate total costs of acquiring and maintaining inventories. These techniques range from simple mathematical formulas to linear programming and mathematical models utilizing the computer. The auditor will be interested in knowing that available technology is being explored and used to the maximum extent to improve decision making in this area.

An example is the popular formula for computing the economic order quantity:

$$EOQ = \sqrt{2AS/IC}$$

where EOQ = economic ordering quantity in units;
A = usage per year;
S = cost in dollars to procure each order or release;
I = annual cost of carrying inventory expressed in decimals (%); and
C = unit price of item in dollars.[5]

Calculations of both S and I should include only variable costs, and further details on the use of the formula are shown in the referenced text. However, the mathematics involved need not prevent the use of this technique regularly by clerical personnel. Victor H. Pooler, Jr., points out:

> For a given operation or plant the value of S and I may be constant, in which case there are only two variables, A and C, which change with each item considered. The basic formula can be simplified by determining the constant (K), which equals
>
> $$\sqrt{2S/I}$$
>
> The formula then becomes:
>
> $$EOQ = K\sqrt{A/C}$$

[5] Adapted from Victor H. Pooler, Jr., *The Purchasing Man and His Job*, New York, American Management Association, 1964, p. 159.

Figure 4 TABLE OF ECONOMIC ORDER QUANTITIES

Unit price in dollars	Usage/year in units: 500	1,000	3,000	5,000	8,000	10,000
0.50	316	447	775	1,000	1,265	1,414
1.00	224	316	548	707	894	1,000
5.00	100	141	245	316	400	447
10.00	71	100	173	224	283	316
100.00	22	32	55	71	89	100

This chart is based on K = 10

By reading across from the price column at the left, find the EOQ under the annual usage figure.

A $1 item with annual usage of 1,000 should be bought in lots of 316 (in practice, round off to 300).

After finding the *K* value for a department or plant operation, charts can be prepared which eliminate even simple arithmetic.[6]

An example of such a table is shown in Figure 4.

Materials Management. The concept of materials management has sparked a good deal of controversy, and the attitudes toward it are widely varied among management, procurement, and financial personnel.

The concept is basically one of organization where all functions of material procurement, material handling, material control, traffic, and sometimes production scheduling are made the responsibility of one manager. This is sometimes accomplished by establishing a title of "Materials Manager," with purchasing being one branch of his organization, on the same level as the functions of material handling and production scheduling. Other companies adopt the concept only to the extent of placing inventory control and warehousing in the framework of the purchasing department. There are an infinite number of other variations of organizing the materials management function.

The principal advantages of the concept are said to be: (*a*) improved coordination of the procurement activity, and (*b*) placing control and authority for material supply in the same hands. However, there can be special control problems where material control, requisitioning, ordering, and receiving are all vested in one organization. Proper control is a major consideration in the design of such a system and the establishment of the organization structure. Division of duties and other control measures can be established, but some special measures may be necessary to equal control that is inherent in more traditional systems.

INTERNAL CONTROL

Since procurement exercises immense influence over commitments, expenditures, quality, and timing in most organizations, it deserves very special con-

[6] Adapted from Victor H. Pooler, Jr., *The Purchasing Man and His Job*, New York, American Management Association, 1964, p. 161.

sideration with respect to control. Basic controls are established through its placement in the organization structure and the amount of authority and responsibility delegated to it, as discussed in previous paragraphs.

The objective of such assignment of responsibilities is to establish controls inherent in a situation where no individual or function has the ability to complete a transaction without accountability to others. The control obtained through segregation of functional responsibility is illustrated in Figure 5.

Procurement is typically centered in the purchasing department, which performs its functions in close coordination with operating departments on one side of the transaction and with the accounting and treasury departments on the other. Accordingly, very effective checks and balances are available simply by properly allocating responsibilities among the departments. The following division of duties might be considered ideal:

1. The need for procurement of material or services is determined and a requisition is prepared by properly authorized individuals in the operating departments.
2. The purchasing department selects the vendor; agrees on price, terms, and f.o.b. point; arranges routing; issues the order; and expedites delivery.
3. The requisitioning department or separate receiving department acknowledges receipt of material or service.
4. The accounting department receives the invoice directly from the vendor and verifies price, terms, and f.o.b. point; compares report of receipt with invoice; computes discounts, taxes, etc.; approves the invoice for payment; and sends the invoice to the disbursing officer for disbursement.

There are many circumstances, of course, where these principles are not practicable. When this is the case, the degree of additional risk should be evaluated and appropriate steps taken to compensate for weaknesses in control through division of duties. However, where these principles can be adapted to the organization, internal check will be enhanced and the need for exterior controls will be minimized. Organizational controls are generally considered to be superior to other methods of control because:

They are automatic and continuous.
They are usually the most economical form of control.
They are strong because collusion is required to circumvent them.

Procurement Authorization. The authorization for procurement of material and services involves the determination of a need, specification and description of the required material and services, and approval for acquisition. Control in this important area is sometimes difficult to establish and frequently deficient.

Before a procurement authorization is issued, decisions must be made relating to:

Justification for the expenditure
Long-range and short-range planning of requirements
"Make-or-buy" considerations
Timing of requirements
Quantity required
Quality required

Budgets and policies on standardization, etc., will provide general guidelines, but control over the majority of the decisions made from day to day in

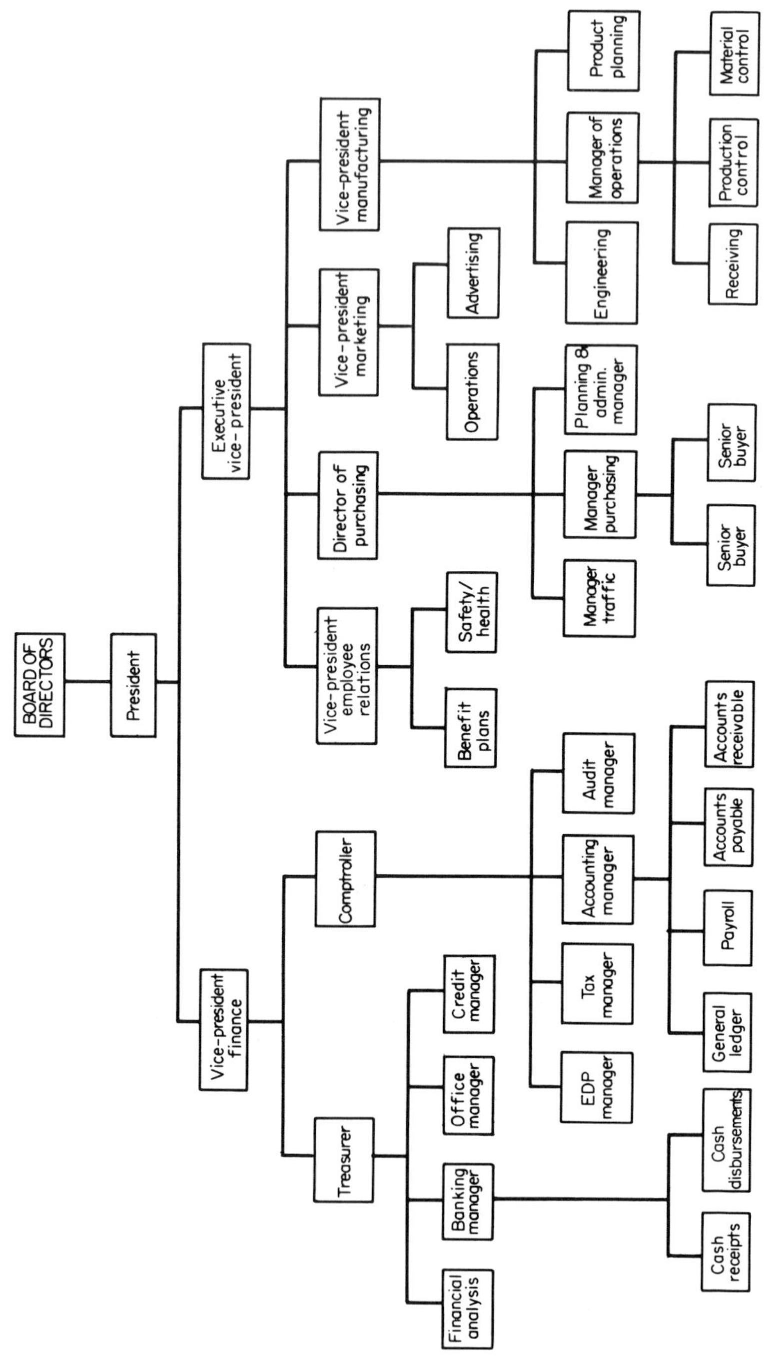
BOARD OF DIRECTORS
President
Executive vice-president
Vice-president finance
Vice-president employee relations
Director of purchasing
Vice-president marketing
Vice-president manufacturing
Comptroller
Treasurer
Benefit plans
Safety/ health
Operations
Advertising
Financial analysis
Banking manager
Office manager
Credit manager
EDP manager
Tax manager
Accounting manager
Audit manager
Manager traffic
Manager purchasing
Planning & admin. manager
Engineering
Manager of operations
Product planning
Cash receipts
Cash disbursements
General ledger
Payroll
Accounts payable
Accounts receivable
Senior buyer
Senior buyer
Receiving
Production control
Material control

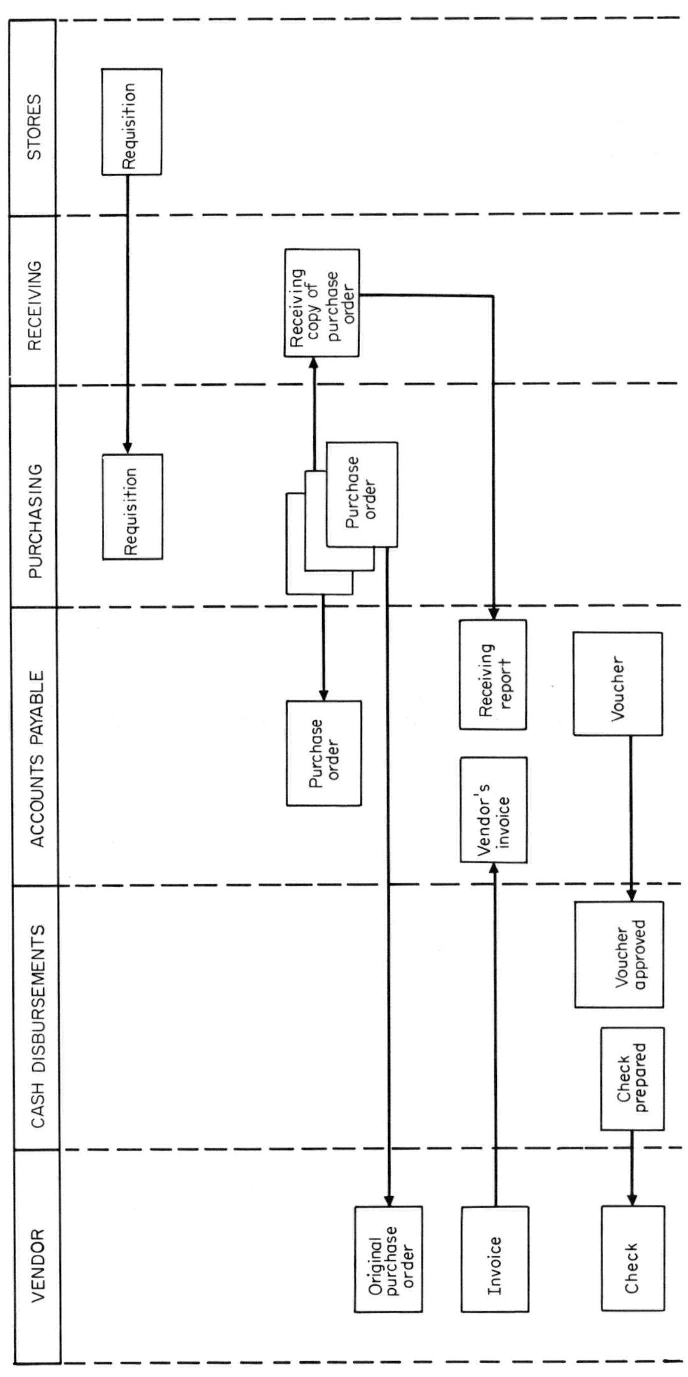

Figure 5 ORGANIZATION CHART—INTERNAL CONTROL OF PURCHASING ACTIVITIES

this area must depend on other management controls established within the organization.

The placement of the authority to make the decisions should be specific and in writing. This is accomplished through a delegation of authority approved by top management. The key to the delegation is to achieve a balance between efficiency and control. Lower management must have authority commensurate with their responsibility, but sufficient authority must be retained at successively higher levels to permit the desired control of expenditures.

The type of expenditure involved will influence the amount of authority delegated. In the interest of efficiency, more authority is usually granted for routine operating expenses than for capital expenditures.

The authorization to purchase is usually formalized by means of a purchase requisition. As discussed in a previous paragraph, it is desirable for efficiency and good control that someone other than the authorizing person, commonly the purchasing department, handle the actual procurement. This will provide:

1. An independent view of the acquisition for validity and reasonableness
2. Verification that the acquisition is properly authorized
3. Opportunity for the benefits of procurement expertise
4. Opportunity for consolidation of orders and arrangement for economic order quantities
5. Elimination of direct contact with vendors by those authorizing the acquisition

The circumvention of the purchasing department by operating personnel is one of the most frequently noted violations of policy. Symptoms of this condition may be:

1. An excessive number of confirming orders. This may indicate that the vendor selection and other arrangements for the purchase have all been made by the requisitioning department.
2. Description of the material is so restrictive that the purchase is limited to a single vendor.

There will, of course, always be circumstances where these conditions are unavoidable, and they do not necessarily indicate an intentional avoidance of established routine. However, whenever they occur, a vital link in the control system has been subverted; accordingly, exceptions should be minimal.

Placing the Order. It is in placing the order that the heaviest demands are made on the expertise of the buyer. The order is the formalization of a wide variety of decisions that involve the location of a source of supply, negotiation of price and terms, selection of the vendor, timing of delivery, and special conditions.

Good control requires that methods be established to assure that those responsible for procurement:

1. Stay abreast of sources of supply and, where volume warrants, develop multiple sources.
2. Encourage competition by effective allocation of business.
3. Be currently aware of reliability of sources of supply.
4. Utilize blanket orders, consolidation of quantity requirements, and other techniques to obtain favorable prices.

5. Consider factors other than prices and terms which may affect ultimate economics of the purchase.
6. Conform to the organization policy on obtaining bids and handle bids received so that the intended benefits and control are realized.
7. Establish prices in advance of placing the order where practicable and enter them on the order for subsequent verification.
8. Obtain maximum available discounts.

This control must be developed largely within the department placing the order and can be designed in a variety of ways. Some of these are as follows:

Organization. Buying is usually assigned by commodity so that individual buyers are involved with only a few kinds or classes of material. This permits them to become "expert" in the area by maintaining contact with market and vendors.

Approvals. Management may limit the authority of subordinates to specified quantities or amounts. Authority to negotiate blanket order prices, to place orders for certain key commodities, and to make orders above certain dollar values is retained by higher levels in the organization.

Reports of Activity. Reports to management on dollar volumes of orders placed, number of orders processed, costs per order, etc., can be invaluable tools of management control when conceived to furnish meaningful and relevant data.

Reports on Allocation of Business. Summaries of allocation of business, by commodities or groups, can give management significant information with regard to vendor selection. Actual allocations may be reviewed (*a*) for comparison with established guidelines, (*b*) to detect indications of favoritism, (*c*) as evidence that new sources of supply are being developed, and (*d*) for assurance that competition is being encouraged.

Some considerations of control over the placement and processing of orders are discussed below.

Handling Bids. Most organizations require that competitive bids be solicited for certain commodities and when certain dollar limits are exceeded. However, the control and benefits afforded by competitive bids can be subverted if they are not properly handled. Good control over the solicitation of formal bids will involve the following requirements:

1. Invitation to bid should be in writing specifying all pertinent information, such as required delivery date, transportation arrangements, delivery date requirements, and due date of bid. Omission of any of these items may result in bids that are not comparable or in unfair treatment of some of the bidders.
2. Invitations to all bidders should be identical and should be sent only to reliable vendors who are potentially acceptable winners of the bid.
3. Preferably the bids should not be opened until all are received. This is particularly pertinent to bids on engineered equipment or for construction services. Where amounts are significant, they should be opened by a bid committee or in the presence of persons independent of the transaction.
4. A bid summary should be prepared and signed by witnesses of the opening of the bids.
5. It should be ascertained that bids are comparable in all respects; otherwise, net ultimate cost should be computed before the winning bidder is selected.
6. If other than the low bidder is selected, proper explanation in writing should be made.

Control of Blank Forms. Since purchase orders constitute a firm commitment of the organization and authorized signatories are not known to vendors, the importance of control over the blank forms is obvious. The forms should be prenumbered serially, they should be stored in a safe but convenient place, access to them should be limited to a few key persons, and a control record of forms used should be maintained. It is also a good practice to account for all numbers in the completed order file as a double check on the use of order forms.

Distribution of Copies. Preparation of multiple copies of purchase orders serves to notify affected departments that the order has been issued. This practice also serves a role in the control system. For example, the requisitioning department can verify that the order was accurately prepared for the material requisitioned; the receiving department will be on notice to expect delivery; and the accounting department can trace for processing of the invoice.

Form Design. The design of the purchase order form can have considerable impact on the efficiency and control of its processing. The most important items for consideration are:

1. Arrangement of information for ease in preparation and handling
2. Provision of adequate space for all information necessary to complete the transaction by both the buyer and the seller
3. Size, shape, and colors that will contribute to efficient handling
4. Copies should be provided only as necessary for control and efficiency. One copy should be used for multiple purposes where feasible, and information copies should be kept to an absolute minimum.

Purchase orders generally must be tailor-made for each organization with respect to content and arrangement. However, certain basic information that should be called for on all forms is listed below:

1. Buyer's name and address
2. Order number
3. Requisition number
4. To be used for
5. Charge information
6. Vendor's name and address
7. Shipping and routing instructions
8. Cash discounts
9. F.o.b. point
10. Date needed and/or promised
11. Description of material
12. Quantity
13. Price
14. Conditions of purchase
15. Cancellation provisions
16. Insurance requirements
17. Conditions for work on buyer's premises

Preparation of Orders. Orders are usually written by clerical personnel using information supplied by buyers relating to the selection of the vendor, terms and conditions of the sale, and routing instructions. Internal checks must be established which will assure: (*a*) accurate and complete transcription of information to the order forms, (*b*) prompt handling of and priority attention to rush items, and (*c*) that all requisitions are processed.

Routing. Delivery costs are frequently an important factor in the total ultimate cost of material. Further, transportation arrangements can be quite complex. In most enterprises the traffic or transportation function is handled by specialists in the field.

Some considerations of control in this are discussed below.

1. Mode of transportation and routine should be specified on the order by the purchaser whenever transportation is significant. When this decision is left to the discretion of the vendor, the transportation arrangements are likely to be those most convenient for the shipper and not necessarily those most economical to the purchaser. The shipper, of course, has little incentive for economy where transportation costs are paid by the purchaser, so the purchaser is wise to exercise control over this part of the transaction.
2. Control must be established to ensure that the mode of transportation selected is appropriate for the required delivery date and the nature of the material. The unnecessary use of air transportation, special delivery, etc., can involve substantial waste which can quickly consume price advantages secured by astute buyers. Regular reviews of special transportation required by short lead time may indicate deficiencies elsewhere, such as inadequate planning by the ordering department, inefficient processing methods, etc.
3. Differences in delivery costs must be considered in awarding competitive bids to be sure that the total ultimate costs are comparable.
4. Consideration should be given to consolidating shipments, pool cars, stop-off cars, etc., where these arrangements will reduce transportation costs.
5. Transportation charges involve complex tariffs and rate schedules, and they should be verified by qualified personnel. Where large volumes of small charges are involved, however, it may not be practical to check each charge. In these circumstances, statistical sampling techniques are used very successfully for verification of all charges below a specified dollar value. This practice should be considered wherever the history of recoveries and the estimated potential loss do not justify complete verification. Some organizations find it advantageous to employ firms which specialize in auditing transportation charges with their compensation being a portion of recoveries from carriers.
6. The review of transportation charges should include verification that the vendor followed the purchaser's mode and routing instructions.

Expediting, Follow-up, and Adjustments. Expediting, follow-up, and adjustments should normally be the responsibility of the procurement function. This is usually advantageous because (*a*) it limits contacts with vendors, (*b*) procurement personnel who are familiar with the transaction handle it to its conclusion, and (*c*) the ordering department does not duplicate work of procurement personnel.

Some considerations of control in this area are discussed below.

1. The system should provide for follow-up on a routine basis through a tickler file to preclude the necessity of contact by the requisitioning department.
2. Follow-up should be limited, however, to that necessary for efficient operations. Routine tracing on the status and location of shipments can usually be limited to large or critical orders.
3. The responsibility for follow-up and the departmental relationships should be clearly defined to avoid duplication of effort.
4. The system should provide for prompt reporting of damages, incorrect

quality, over- and under-shipments, etc., so that corrective action can be initiated at the earliest possible date, preferably before payment of the invoice. This is usually handled on receiving reports and special reports of damages. Unnecessary delays can jeopardize or complicate proper adjustment.

5. Authority to approve adjustments or accept compensation for damages should be specified in the authority delegations. It is advisable to require approval of someone other than the buyer on all adjustments other than routine corrections which do not substantially affect the terms of the original order.

6. Attention should be given to ascertaining that all costs connected with the damage are included in the claim.

7. Provision should be made for recording claims for damage and adjustments in the financial records where appropriate.

8. Claims should be aged and traced on a regular basis in the interest of settling them as currently as possible.

Completing the Transaction. Accounting personnel are normally responsible for verification that the invoice reflects the terms of the transaction as indicated in the purchase order. An invoice so approved, together with proof of receipt, constitutes authority to pay for the disbursing agent.

Accounting personnel should:

1. Verify price, discount, f.o.b. point, and other terms of the purchase to make sure they are in accordance with the purchase order.
2. Associate receipt of material with the invoice and verify their agreement.
3. Ascertain the applicability and rate of sales and use taxes.
4. Check extension, compute taxes and discounts, and enter total to be paid.
5. Enter account distribution.
6. Prepare checks.
7. Prepare control totals and send to disbursing officer for validation and release of checks.

The system described above is not always practicable in small organizations, in highly computerized systems, etc. However, it affords an excellent system of internal checks, and the principles involved should be adapted to the extent possible.

Related Activities. Activities such as the handling of scrap and surplus material and the operation of warehouses are not normally considered a part of the procurement function. However, these activities are often assigned to personnel who are also engaged in procurement. When this is the case, control problems may be encountered which require special attention by management and the auditor.

Scrap and Surplus. The handling of scrap and surplus inherently is an activity which is difficult to control because of its very nature. The quality, quantity, and value of this material are frequently difficult to assess and control; attention to the matter may be inconvenient and therefore neglected; and the values involved are often minor in relation to prime products, which may encourage complacency.

Some control considerations are:

1. Authority to designate material as scrap or surplus should be clearly defined and vested in an appropriate level of management.
2. Accumulation, storage, and disposition should be handled by other personnel than those designating material as scrap or surplus.

3. Physical protection from theft or other loss and separation of material of different values should receive regular attention.
4. The system should provide for reuse within the organization where appropriate.
5. Control over sales prices, weights, and movements should be adequate to ensure disposition to the best advantage of the organization.

Warehousing. When the maintenance of warehouses is also a function of those responsible for procurement, a weakening of control may result. However, when such an arrangement is found to be advantageous, the principles of good internal check should be applied by allocating responsibilities within the department. For example, selection of the vendor and ordering should be handled by a group who have no direct supervision from the warehouse personnel who approve the requisitions. Ideally, a third group would receive the material and prepare the receiving report. Where such arrangements are not feasible, an increased level of attention from management may be necessary to assure adequate control.

CONDUCTING THE AUDIT

Approach and Objective. There are many reasons for auditing the procurement function. The particular reason will, of course, determine the approach to the project. It is vital, however, that the objective of the audit be clearly established before the audit is begun. The objective should pervade all considerations in the scope of the audit, the design of the audit program, and concomitant activities. The objective should be reduced to writing, and all those engaged in the audit should be conscious of it throughout the performance of the audit.

The objective of the audit may range from verification of compliance with written procedures to an evaluation of the effectiveness of the entire activity. If the intent is to assist management responsible for procurement, the objective will tend toward the broad scope implied by the latter. An objective of this kind might be stated:

> To evaluate the adequacy and effectiveness of the policies, procedures, and other means employed in procuring required material and services at the lowest ultimate cost consistent with appropriate standards of quality and service.

Such an objective has broad implications and, when competently carried out, can result in furnishing management with valuable information and recommendations which will assist them in improving the efficiency and effectiveness of the procurement activity. If the audit is for some other purpose, the objective should reflect the true purpose of the audit, and the audit plan should be designed accordingly.

Although the detection of fraud is not the primary purpose of the audit, the possibility should be considered throughout the review. The procurement activity, by its very nature, presents innumerable opportunities to purchasing agents for manipulations, and business history shows that many such agents have succumbed to the temptation. Although good internal control is a deterrent, controls cannot be designed which will prevent all fraud, particularly where collusion is involved. And collusion is frequently more easily arranged with outsiders than with fellow employees. As Harvey Cardwell says: "The cashier must take the initiative in his thefts, but purchasing agents are actively tempted by expert practical psychologists — salesmen from whom they buy."[7]

Some examples of methods which have been used by purchasing agents to perpetrate fraud are:

1. The purchasing agent receives a kickback in return for the award of business on a negotiated-price basis. This may be in the form of cash, gift certificates, merchandise, services, etc.
2. The purchasing agent allows a favored bidder to meet the lowest bid with a kickback arrangement.
3. Payments are authorized on fraudulent invoices with no delivery of material or services.
4. The purchasing agent owns or has an interest in a firm to which business is awarded.
5. Payments are authorized for quantities or quality in excess of that received with a collusive arrangement to split the proceeds.

There are, of course, innumerable variations on these and other arrangements, with shadings from outright theft to subtle conflicts of interest which should be watched for in the audit.

Preparation. The performance of an audit with a management viewpoint obviously requires considerable preparation. The objectives are broad and make heavy demands on the auditor to be knowledgeable about the procurement activity. Some suggested steps in this preparation are shown below.

1. Review and become familiar with the reports and other data that management in charge of procurement uses to manage the function.
2. Review organization charts of the departments involved and develop information on the responsibilities and relationships of all those involved.
3. Review written policies and procedures.
4. Review departmental objectives and plans.
5. Review authority delegations of all departments involved.
6. Review pertinent contracts and correspondence.
7. Become familiar with basic commodities involved, and study literature and current publications on market conditions, prices, etc.

This list is not represented to be complete; rather, it suggests the types of information that will be helpful to the auditor.

This phase of the audit is a critical one. The level on which the audit is conducted and, consequently, the results obtained, depend heavily on the thoroughness of preparation. It can also equip the auditor to speak knowledgeably with the procurement personnel, thereby contributing to early acceptance of his presence and program. A failure to demonstrate competence in the early stages can often jeopardize the effectiveness of the entire audit.

Audit Program. The audit program or plan should be developed only after thorough preparation as discussed above.

The audit will involve the following activities:

1. Interviews with key personnel to: (*a*) compare assigned responsibilities with actual duties, (*b*) evaluate controls that are operative in the area, and (*c*) develop an understanding of the various employees' relationships to the departmental objectives and to the other functions of the department.

[7] Harvey Cardwell, *The Principles of Audit Surveillance,* Princeton, N.J., D. Van Nostrand Co., Inc., 1960, p. 62.

2. Flow-charting work flow, with particular attention to internal control points. This technique is frequently beneficial in evaluating the efficiency of work flow and in detecting control weaknesses.

3. Sampling of requisitions, orders, invoices, and other pertinent records. Where the volume is large enough, statistical sampling will be advantageous. From this sample, important conclusions can be drawn as to the effectiveness of controls in the area.

4. Develop a summary of internal control standards as they apply to the circumstances. This summary can become the basis for comparison of actual conditions with the ideal and can form a point of reference for many of the evaluations to be made. This may be in the form of a checklist, a narrative, or a flow chart.

5. Determine how the computer may be advantageously utilized during the audit.

The computer, when used imaginatively, can save very substantial amounts of time and simultaneously achieve better results.

Advantageous applications in the procurement area may include:

1. Statistical samples of requisitions, orders, etc.
2. Stratification of order amounts for special reviews based on size.
3. Calculation of standard deviation for use in evaluating validity of samples.
4. Exception printouts, such as purchases from other than approved vendors.
5. Comparison of purchase prices with those used in inventory calculations.
6. Summaries, such as total allocation of business to particular vendors.
7. Calculation of pertinent statistical data, such as total number of orders, average size of each order, cost per order, etc.

Further, in highly automated and real-time systems, use of the computer may be essential to the conduct of an effective audit. In such systems, the computer forms a vital link in the internal control structure. The adequacy of these controls must be evaluated by appraisal of the input, output, and processing controls.

No program can be designed that will fit all organizations and circumstances. Rather, each program should be designed specifically to fit the unique characteristics of each audit. It should be dynamic and flexible. Accordingly, the following is not a program but rather some suggestions for consideration in the design of procurement audit programs.

Organization and Administration. **General policy.** Review the general policy of the organization with regard to procurement. What is the general nature of procurement needs?

Responsibility. Where has responsibility for procurement been placed? What are the responsibilities of the purchasing department? What are the responsibilities of other departments in the procurement process? Have these responsibilities and relationships been clearly defined? Are they understood by all affected personnel?

Organization. How is the purchasing department organized to carry out its responsibilities? Is the authority of individuals commensurate with their responsibility? Are duties allocated so as to develop and utilize expertise to a maximum degree?

Budgets. How are budgets used to control the procurement activity? Are budgets based on reliable data and valid assumptions? Are they regularly compared with actual, and are deviations explained?

Departmental objectives. How are objectives established for those engaged in the procurement activity? Do established objectives give proper consideration to both long-term and short-term objectives of the entire organization? How is actual performance measured against objectives? Do objectives include provision for continuously improving the efficiency, effectiveness, and economy of the procurement activity? Are the objectives adequately quantified so that the degree of achievement can be determined?

Planning. How are departmental plans regarding procurement developed? Are they specific, yet flexible? Are they based on valid data and reasonable assumptions? Do they contribute to the effectiveness of the organization with respect to efficiency and ultimate economy?

Reports. What reports and information are furnished to management concerning the procurement activities and performance? Are the data furnished valid? Are they relevant? Are they adequate for continuous evaluation of the effectiveness of the activity?

Evaluation. How is procurement effectiveness measured? Is there provision for the measurement of departmental and sectional performance as well as individual performance? Are yardsticks meaningful? Are they used effectively?

Materials management. What is the organization's policy on materials management? Who has the responsibility for inventory levels? Does the policy provide adequate and effective controls?

Purchasing research. Is there a program of purchasing research? Is it well organized and systematic? Are the techniques of linear programming, operations research, etc., being explored and used? Are scientific methods being applied to such problems as economic order quantity, inventory levels, ordering and replenishing costs, cost of stockouts, cost of warehousing, etc.? Do the results indicate that the program is effective? Are the means of dissemination to all interested personnel effective?

EDP applications. What are the opportunities for utilizing electronic data processing in the procurement function? Are they being utilized to maximum advantage? Have adequate controls been established to ensure accuracy of processing, valid data, and prompt handling?

Purchase Authorization. Authority delegations. Are authority delegations for authorizing acquisitions clearly defined? Are all those affected aware of their responsibility and authority? Are authority delegations kept current with personnel and condition changes? Are controls adequate but not excessive, considering the relative values involved for capital expenditures, operating supplies, contract services, construction, etc.?

Make-or-buy. How are "make-or-buy" decisions made? Are controls adequate to ensure that all pertinent factors are considered? Are new studies made when economic or other conditions have changed? What control is exercised over using contract services versus using employee labor?

Standardization. Is the policy on standardization of material effective in minimizing ultimate cost to the organization? Is standardization the subject of continuing study in order to maximize its benefits?

Value analysis. Does the organization have an active program of value analysis? Where is responsibility vested? Is the program effective in reducing costs? Are reported savings valid?

Requisition forms. Are purchase requisition forms designed for efficient processing? Is provision made for all required information? Are these forms designed for ease in preparation, handling, and filing? Is the number of copies prepared sufficient but not excessive?

Processing. How efficient is the system of processing requisitions? How are requisitions processed and controlled to ensure that all requisitions are received? How are approvals controlled and verified? Should specimen signatures be used for the verification? Are established approval procedures being followed?

Floating requisitions. Are "traveling" or "floating" requisitions utilized where feasible? Could the method be expanded to advantage?

Accuracy. Are incoming requisitions complete and accurate? What control measures are in effect to minimize errors and special handling? Are those responsible for preparing and approving requisitions adequately trained in this procedure?

Confirming requisitions. What is the proportion of "rush" and "confirming requisitions" previously placed by telephone? Does the ratio indicate a condition of poor planning or circumvention of established procedures?

Procurement and Order Processing. Approvals of requisitions. What controls are in effect to ensure that requisitions are properly approved before the order is placed? Are specimen signatures used? Would their use be practicable and advantageous?

Source of supply. What procedures are used to assure that all sources of supply are considered? Are new sources being developed? Do procurement practices encourage competition?

Reliability of vendors. How is the reliability of vendors evaluated? Are the procedures adequate to assure current information in this regard?

Bids. What is the policy on quotations and bids? Is documentation required, and is it adequate? What is the procedure for opening bids? Are solicitations accomplishing their intended purpose? Are they handled in a manner that is fair to all bidders?

What approval is required when the award is made to one other than the low bidder? Is an explanation required? Are the explanations reasonable and consistent with procurement policy?

Price. What methods are used to determine "best price"? What catalogs and other source and price files are maintained? Do procedures assure that these are current at all times? Are such files adequate and convenient? Are they used to best advantage? To what extent are prices shown on the order and made a part of the purchase agreement? What control is exercised over prices not agreed in advance? To what extent are premium prices paid? Are they justified? Does the extent of such prices indicate a deficiency in planning of needs, development of supply sources, etc.?

Quantity. To what extent are quantity discounts obtained? How are "economic lot quantities" determined? Do quantity decisions result in net ultimate savings, considering distribution after delivery, storage, etc.? Is there a procedure for systematically consolidating orders for like material? How are consolidations coordinated with ordering departments?

Blanket orders. To what extent are blanket orders utilized? Would increased use be advantageous with respect to quantity discounts, paper work, etc.? Is proper legal consideration given to blanket order contracts? How are deliveries against blanket orders controlled? Is their use achieving the intended advantages?

Vendors. What factors other than price and discount are considered in vendor selection? Is there evidence of favoritism toward certain vendors? Are reports summarizing allocation of business prepared for and reviewed by management? Is there evidence that the reports are used for their intended purpose? How are quality and service evaluated? Are reciprocity arrangements approved by the proper level of management? Is management kept advised of the results?

Verbal orders. What is the extent of verbal orders? Is special control exercised in those cases where control inherent in the regular procedures is circumvented? Is the volume of verbal orders reasonable and justified? Would the extension of the practice be advantageous?

Confirming orders. Does the volume of confirming orders indicate intentional circumvention of normal controls and the use of procurement personnel? Do the confirming orders serve a good purpose, or are they prepared to comply with instructions and make the paper work "look right"? Could they be eliminated in some circumstances without loss of control?

Cost-plus. What control is exercised over orders issued on a cost-plus or price-escalation basis? Is this method of pricing the best alternative in the circumstances? Do purchase contracts contain adequate audit clauses for verification of costs in the vendor's records?

Discounts. Are maximum available trade and cash discounts obtained? What control is exercised in this area? Is the information available to procurement personnel current? How are notices of change obtained?

Transportation. How is determination made as to who will absorb freight charges? Do purchase orders specify the mode of transportation and routing? Is verification made that vendors have complied with these instructions? What action is taken when they do not? Is proper consideration given to shipping in carload lots, pool cars, stopover cars, etc.?

Trade-ins. What control is exercised to ensure that maximum trade-in allowances are received? Are the benefits of sale rather than trade-in properly evaluated? Is determination made on the basis of net cost of the new material? Are there tax considerations involved in the decision?

Preparation of orders. Is the procedure for order preparation efficient? Is control over accuracy and completeness adequate? Is the flow of paper smooth and orderly? Is the purchase order form designed for efficiency and ease in handling? Does the system provide adequate handling of rush and emergency orders on a priority basis? Is the number of errors and complaints excessive? Is proper attention given to correction and prevention of errors?

Order processing. Does the system provide for an efficient method of follow-up and expediting? How are these functions coordinated with the requisitioning departments? What is the policy on direct contact with vendors by other than procurement personnel? Is the policy followed?

Substitutions. Are procurement personnel alert to "make versus buy" opportunities? To use of surplus material? To use of substitute materials? Where has responsibility been placed for these decisions? Are these considerations a regular part of the procurement activity? What results have been obtained? Is increased emphasis appropriate? Would better coordination with requisitioning departments and vendors improve the effectiveness in this area?

Receipt of material. Are positive receipts of material received? How is performance of services confirmed? Is a copy of the purchase order used for this purpose? Does the system minimize clerical work, even on partial shipments? How are differences reported? Is control adequate to ensure proper adjustment with a minimum of paper work and correspondence? Is material received by personnel who are not otherwise involved in the procurement transaction? If not, have other measures been taken to supplement control and keep the risk at a reasonable level?

Quality. What controls are operative to ensure that the quality of material received is what was ordered? How and to whom are exceptions reported and handled? Is the control adequate to detect fraud through delivering a lower quality than is charged for?

Decentralized and Field Purchasing. Decentralized purchasing. What responsibility and authority are delegated for procurement by decentralized purchasing personnel? How is control exercised by the central purchasing department? Is the control adequate to assure adherence to procurement objectives of the enterprise?

Field purchasing. What authority is delegated to field personnel? Is it adequate to efficiently procure miscellaneous small supplies, emergency repairs, etc.? Could overall procurement efficiency be improved by increasing or decreasing authority delegated to outlying locations? Is adequate information available to management to make decisions currently in this area as conditions change?

Control guidance. Is purchasing department expertise utilized in local procurement activities? Is information on sources of supply, prices, and discounts disseminated currently for the guidance of local personnel? Is information on blanket orders, national discount contracts, etc., disseminated to all those who may be able to utilize it? Are means established to ensure compliance with guidance furnished by headquarters?

Control and risk. Are the same principles of good internal control operative as are applied to purchases handled through the purchasing department? If this is not feasible, is the risk appropriately reduced by authority limitations and other means?

Related Activities. Warehousing. Where personnel engaged in procurement are also responsible for warehousing and/or materials management, have steps been taken to ensure good control? Are duties divided so that those requisitioning and receiving do not handle price negotiation and ordering? Have areas of potential conflict or risk been defined and special internal checks established?

Sale of scrap and surplus. Where is responsibility placed for handling of scrap and surplus material? What controls are in effect over the accumulation, storage, and sale of this material? Is material of different values separated for maximum realization? How is material in storage safeguarded? How are weights and quantities of sales controlled? Are controls over cash received adequate?

Purchases for employees. Many organizations do not permit purchases to be made for employees' personal use but limit assistance to referrals to reliable vendors. If such purchases are permitted, procedures should be established for billing and collection from the employees, and special controls may be necessary to prevent these purchases from being charged to expense.

Ethics. What is the organization's policy on acceptance of gifts, entertainment, and conflicts of interest? Does it clearly define what constitutes conflict of interest? Has this information been disseminated to all suppliers, contractors, and employees? Are employees required to sign an acknowledgment that they understand the organization's attitude in this area? Is the policy adequate? How is it enforced?

FINDINGS AND THE AUDIT REPORT

When all of the samples have been taken, the controls have been evaluated, and deficient conditions have been disclosed, the most important part of the audit remains to be done. This is the evaluation of the findings and the development of constructive recommendations. Whatever significant benefits are to be realized from the examination will result largely from this phase of the audit.

Evaluation of findings is particularly important. This involves putting the findings in proper perspective and interpreting their importance to management. It demands that the auditor differentiate between an acceptable level of error and a condition that needs correction through additional control. He must also be able to recognize conditions that are actually symptoms of a much larger problem. To use a medical analogy, he should avoid the pitfall of prescribing aspirin for appendicitis. Conditions of error and inefficiency may indicate deficiencies in basic policy or management control. Obviously, maximum benefit to management can be realized only by diagnosing the true deficiency rather than by correcting the errors.

The form, content, and distribution of the audit report will, of course, be governed by the purpose of the audit. This matter is discussed at length in another chapter of this volume. However, the procurement function may involve several departments, and this fact may necessitate special handling of procurement audit reports. This may be handled by wider than normal distribution in some circumstances, while in others more than one report may be in order.

The keys to a successful conclusion of a procurement audit are that:

1. Those directly involved are informed of the results of the audit;
2. Those who should take additional action are provided the information and motivation to do so.

CONCLUSION

The foregoing is an attempt to make a brief examination of the importance of the procurement function in most organizations, the implications of the function for the success of the enterprise, and the potential benefits of a perceptive audit of the activity.

Perhaps nowhere in the organization is the system of management control, internal control, and internal check more important to the effectiveness of a function. These are areas of expertise of the auditor; consequently, procurement is one of the functions in which the auditor has the opportunity to make his most meaningful contributions to management and to the enterprise.

BIBLIOGRAPHY

Aljian, George W.: *Purchasing Handbook,* 2d ed., New York, McGraw-Hill Book Company, 1966.

Arnstein, William E.: "Inventory Management," in *Management Services by Accounting Firms,* New York, The Ronald Press Company, 1967, pp. 121–151.

Cadmus, Bradford: *Operational Auditing Handbook,* New York, The Institute of Internal Auditors, 1964, pp. 39–88.

Cardwell, Harvey: *The Principles of Audit Surveillance,* Princeton, N.J., D. Van Nostrand Company, Inc., 1960.

Haas, Geo. H., Benjamin March, and E. M. Krech: *Purchasing Department Organization and Authority,* New York, American Management Association, Inc., 1960.

Hayes, Albert F., and George A. Renard: *Evaluating Purchasing Performance,* New York, American Management Association, Inc., 1964.

Moffitt, Ralph C.: "Procurement Auditing," *The Internal Auditor* (The Institute of Internal Auditors, New York), December, 1958, pp. 27–38.

Oline, Robert H.: "A Way of Determining Economical Buying Quantities," *N.A.A. Bulletin* (National Association of Accountants, New York), February, 1962, pp. 87–90.

Harman, D. R.: "Audit of Procurement," *The Internal Auditor* (The Institute of Internal Auditors, New York), Fall, 1962, p. 71.

Stephens, Harold: "Purchasing by Telephone without Confirmation or Invoice," *N.A.A. Bulletin* (National Association of Accountants, New York), June, 1963, p. 55.

Blake, Edward: "Value Analysis," *Management Services* (AICPA, New York), September–October, 1964, pp. 44–50.

Sutherland, Robert E.: "Purchase Order Numbering with Built-in Intelligence," *N.A.A. Bulletin* (National Association of Accountants, New York), June, 1965, pp. 33–37.

Gross, Harry: "Make or Buy Decisions in Growing Firms," *The Accounting Review* (American Accounting Association, Evanston, Ill.), October, 1966, pp. 745–753.

Parks, William H.: "Simplified Inventory Control for Computer," *Financial Executive* (Financial Executives Institute), May, 1968, pp. 86–93.

Smith, William F.: "An Audit of the Marketing Function—Creativity Revisited," *The Internal Auditor* (The Institute of Internal Auditors, New York), July/August, 1970, p. 14.

Chapter 32

Compensation

JOHN J. KEARNEY, JR.

Secretary and General Auditor,
Long Island Lighting Company

GENERAL

Compensation costs have tended to increase over the past few years. Besides the basic wage rate, there have been many fringe benefits which have increased the cost and the number of problems involved in payroll computation. Many additional operations and more interpretations are necessary to compute the various gross-pay elements, including call-in time, holiday pay allowances, differential pay, overtime, and various other allowances. The payroll deductions are now far more numerous than before, with social security, state unemployment, group insurance, pension plan, medical insurance, and many others. With the help of computers, the tremendous number of calculations necessary for a large company are handled readily.

Payrolls generally do not pose as many problems for the public accountant as for the internal auditor or governmental accountant. The most important problems relate to systems and internal control considerations, which are generally closely studied by management.

Audit Approach. In connection with an audit of payroll, the auditor is trying to determine that employees are paid the correct amount, properly authorized, and on time, and that payroll charges are distributed to the proper accounts. In addition, and as a vital part of his audit, he should attempt to determine whether the payroll activities are efficiently "meshed" into the overall system of the company.

The auditor, in doing a payroll audit, must not lose sight of the relationship of the payroll department to the personnel department, treasury, paymaster's department, etc., in order to perform the type of audit that management expects.

The payroll department is not isolated from other operations. It is, rather, part of a continuous operation of the business. In this connection the auditor can make a valuable contribution in terms of possible problem areas between the various departments that are involved in the preparation, distribution, authorization, and payment of payroll. In particular, he should review very closely the procedures surrounding overtime controls, out-of-class rates, wage increases, sick leave, terminations, additions, transfers, etc., even though this may require extending the audit to other departments.

Personnel Data. The personnel department is an important element in the control and audit of payroll. It provides an independent control over critical matters in connection with payroll audits. For example, it maintains independent records of hirings and firings, individual rates and rate changes, and various other records, such as employee withholding records. As a part of the overall system of internal control, the auditor has an interest in what personnel functions are carried out and how well they are performed. For the protection of the company, there should be an adequate interview and a testing program for particular jobs. Also, for proper protection, references and former employment should be verified. If the individual is employed, certain forms should be completed, such as the withholding certificate and authorization for various voluntary deductions, such as insurance, union dues, etc. Generally, an authorization from personnel is required before anyone is added to or deleted from the payroll. The independent status of the personnel department is helpful to the auditor and provides a separate source to verify payroll data. During his audit of the payroll, the auditor will review the operations of the personnel department and determine how well the department is equipped for its responsibilities and how well the responsibilities are carried out. For example, in the modern company of any size, the personnel department must subscribe to various kinds of labor services and references to help in interpreting the status and problems of various employee classifications.

Timekeeping Data. Timekeeping data provide an additional important point of control for the auditor. Most manufacturing plants require two types of time data: clock cards, showing the number of hours at work, and job cards, showing the jobs and the time on each job. For good internal control, employees who have payroll duties or supervisors who have line responsibilities should not approve time cards, to prevent the possibility of payroll padding. The auditor will usually see that there is some reconciliation between the clock cards and the job cards. The clock cards, of course, show gross time while the job cards may include only net production time. Any nonproductive, special work or idle time will have to be determined and reasonably reconciled. In some cases it may not be feasible to reconcile each payroll, but the auditor may wish to make a reconciliation periodically to assure himself that time is being properly accounted for.

Cost Data. The analysis of labor costs provides another source of control for the auditor in his review of payroll. His analysis will involve the detailed allocation of labor charges to products, departments, or activities. He will look for variances and changes in unit costs which may provide the clue to inefficiencies or irregularities in payroll procedures. The auditor may make comparisons in various classifications with previous periods, with standard allowances, or with other controls. Any unusual changes should be investigated. The total hours charged to cost operations can also be reconciled with the total hours paid according to the clock cards.

Payroll Department. The basic function of the payroll department is to prepare the payroll for salaries, wages, and commissions earned by employees. Responsibilities of the payroll department include the processing of payroll authorizations for accessions, changes, and terminations, as well as time sheets for employees with variable distribution of payroll charges to accounts and work orders. The distribution of payroll charges to accounts and work orders is processed in Payroll, along with the preparation of related journal entries. Reports are prepared for month-end and annual closings.

The payroll department maintains payroll controls, cumulative earnings records, and other necessary data relating to earnings in connection with unemployment insurance, social security, federal, state, and city withholding taxes, and other tax purposes. Reports required by management, government agencies, insurance companies, and others are also prepared by Payroll. The auditor must be aware of the relationship of the payroll department to the entire business operation. He should keep in mind various work-measurement procedures and other clerical measurement methods that may be of value in his audit. The auditor should note the extent to which payroll practices have been committed to writing in the various departments. In a large manufacturing plant with a number of separate departments, there are frequently unnecessary variations in practices among the different departments. Written operating practices are usually very helpful in standardizing the practices throughout the plant and are valuable in helping new payroll department employees to learn the job. These procedures usually cover working hours, overtime, call-in pay, special bonuses, holidays, meals, and many other matters which are essential in computing a payroll. They are also very helpful to the auditor in learning what the procedures are and whether they are actually being carried out. An audit of the payroll will naturally involve the testing of payroll data against the terms of the collective bargaining agreement and any established company rules and government regulations. During the course of his payroll audit, the auditor should be aware of other factors that may come to his attention, such as the underutilization of mechanized equipment, poor safeguarding of assets, or other actions detrimental to company interests.

Computer-oriented Payrolls. With the increased use of EDP, many companies now prepare their complete payrolls on the computer. The payroll activity is usually one of the first applications of the computer, since there are voluminous calculations to be made and much of the basic information can be stored in the computer and retrieved readily for current needs. Computerized processing requires additional controls, as well as different procedures. Certain detailed audit steps necessary when manual systems are used should be revised and reconsidered in terms of the computer.

The impact of automation on audit procedures and the expected further sophistication and effectiveness of future equipment make it extremely difficult to standardize computerized audit procedures. In terms of a specific audit approach, the auditor is still confronted with input, processing, and output. His basic objective, with or without the computer, is still the same. However, the immediate effect of the computer is to require additional knowledge on the part of the auditor in terms of computer-oriented systems before the audit actually begins. Accordingly, it is highly desirable and perhaps essential that a qualified auditor assist in the system design and implementation.

"Audit trails," which are mainly internal controls that have been built into the computer programs, should not be confused with the other requirements of a complete internal audit. These "audit trails," which in the past were sometimes called "preaudits," are effective only in controlling the checks and balances and do not presuppose the accuracy of the original source or input data.

A possible approach in connection with computer-oriented payrolls is:

1. Flow-chart all input data, outlining control functions.
2. Review work of "control group."
3. Review organizational assignments.
4. Review schedules of operations.
5. Review "hardware" controls.

The auditor must concern himself with:

1. Procedural controls over the creation and processing of input or source data outside the computer
2. Controls incorporated in the equipment
3. Controls developed within the computer programs
4. Procedural controls over data processing operations within the computer

The auditor should perform his tests to determine, in addition to those steps previously mentioned:

1. The continued existence of the audit trails within the computer program
2. That the input data are supported by original source documents
3. The accuracy of the computations
4. That the output has been developed from the input

The above may require the preparation of a "test deck." Input and output data should be completely in the control of the auditor.

The foregoing is intended as a guide. Each auditor should prepare his own detailed audit procedures, incorporating the necessary audit steps as outlined in this chapter. For further information on EDP considerations, see Chapter 16, "Computerized Systems."

EVALUATION OF INTERNAL CONTROL

Personnel Records

1. Are properly approved authorizations maintained on file for:
   a. Personnel changes?
   b. Salary and wage rates or union classifications?
   c. Payroll deductions?
2. If so, are these files maintained independently of and inaccessible to persons who:
   a. Prepare payrolls?
   b. Approve payrolls?
   c. Physically distribute payrolls?
3. Do procedures provide that all authorizations, particularly notices of separation from employment, are transmitted promptly to the payroll division?
4. Do personnel records contain signatures of employees?

Time Records

1. Are the time records and other data from which the payrolls are prepared approved independently of the employees who prepare the payrolls?
2. Are overtime hours and special benefits approved by employees who supervise the activities but who do not:
   a. Prepare payrolls?
   b. Physically distribute payrolls?

Preparation of Payroll

1. Are the persons who prepare the payroll independent of hiring and firing functions?
2. Are they excluded from the physical distribution of payrolls?
3. Is the payroll *checked* by employees who take no part in its:
   a. Authorization?
   b. Preparation?
   c. Physical distribution?
4. Is the payroll approved by a responsible employee or officer?
5. When practicable (as in the case of salary payrolls), are the totals of current payrolls reconciled with previous payrolls by showing specific changes?
6. Are well-defined procedures in effect with respect to the distribution of labor charges, particularly as between capital and maintenance?

Payment of Payroll

1. Is the payoff (in cash or check) made by employees:
   a. Who take no part in and do not control the preparation of the payroll?
   b. Who are not responsible for hiring or firing employees?
   c. Who do not approve time reports?
2. Is the payroll bank account reconciled regularly by an employee who has no connection with the:

   a. Preparation of the payroll?
   b. Physical distribution of paychecks?
3. Are endorsements compared, at least on a test basis, with the signatures on file?
4. *a.* Where payment is made in cash, are receipts required?
   b. If so, are they compared, on a test basis or otherwise, with signatures on file, by someone independent of the payroll department?
5. If the employee has left the firm, are unclaimed wages returned to a department other than the payroll division?
6. Is a report of unclaimed wages, for employees who have left the firm, made directly to the accounting department by the employees who made the payoff?
7. Are payments of unclaimed wages, for employees who have left the firm, at a later date made only upon:
   a. Presentation of appropriate evidence of employment?
   b. Approval by an officer or employee who is not responsible for the preparation of the payroll or for reporting time?
8. Are W-2 Forms accounted for and placed in the mail by persons who take no part in:
   a. Approving payrolls?
   b. Preparing payrolls?
   c. Physically distributing payrolls?
9. Are W-2 Forms which are returned by postal authorities forwarded for investigation directly to persons who took no part in:
   a. Approving payrolls?
   b. Preparing payrolls?
   c. Physically distributing payrolls?

Other Considerations

1. Is there a rotation of duties among employees?
2. Are employees required to take vacations every year?
3. Are all employees bonded?

AUDIT PROGRAM

This program is intended only as a guide. It therefore is no substitute for original and imaginative thinking.

Salaries and Wages

1. Review the last audit's working papers and the report.
2. Ascertain whether any changes were made in the payroll system, payroll accounting procedures, labor agreements, and other company policies pertaining to payroll matters since the last audit. Become thoroughly familiar with the union contract.
3. On a statistical sampling basis, select employees for detail testing. (See the chapter on statistical sampling.) All payrolls should be covered in the selection.
   Prepare worksheets for tests of individual earnings.
4. For those employees being tested, post the following to the worksheets.
   a. The total hours worked in the period and the breakdown, if any, between taxable and nontaxable hours. (Note: Sick hours are not taxable for FICA purposes.)

b. Rate paid—pick up regular and overtime hours.

c. Post from the cash book detail sheets to the worksheets the following:
(1) Gross pay
(2) Overtime hours and dollars
(3) "Sick" time (Indicate with or without pay.)
(4) FICA withheld
(5) FIT withheld
(6) State income tax withheld
(7) Amount of miscellaneous deductions
(8) Net pay
(9) Payroll receipt number or check number
(10) Petty cash paid, if any
(11) City tax

d. Post to worksheets from the time summary the following:
(1) Job title
(2) Classification
(3) Number of exemptions
(4) Regular hours
(5) Regular rate of pay
(6) Payroll code

5. For those employees being tested, perform the following steps *in the payroll division:*

a. If applicable, obtain time sheets, examine, and sight-foot hours thereon, agreeing total with total pay hours posted on worksheets.

b. Ascertain that the time sheets and/or sick-time reports have been approved by authorized persons. Compare such approval signatures with those on file in the payroll division records.

c. Post to the worksheets the monthly paid employee's overtime status from the employee's master pay card, i.e., whether on full, limited, or straight overtime, if applicable.

d. For those employees who are not required to prepare time sheets, determine that there is an authorized approval on hand.

e. Check calculation of gross pay.

f. Check calculation of FICA. (Determine applicable rates and ceilings first.)

g. Examine Form W-4 in support of exemptions now shown on worksheets and check calculation for FIT and state tax withheld.

h. Crosscast to net pay.

i. Ascertain by reference to the "cumulative earnings" record that the deduction for FICA is proper. (No deduction for FICA should be made if earnings since beginning of year exceed the authorized ceiling.)

j. For those instances encountered in payroll audits in which individuals are paid at a rate higher than their regular rates, check back with the individual's department to determine whether the temporary assignment records maintained by that department verify the use of the higher rate. (This is intended to check on possible collusion on the part of someone in the payroll department.) If the departmental records bear out payment at the higher rate, check back with the individual's supervisor to determine why the man was paid at the higher rate. Obtain specific information, including (in most cases) the name of the individual whom the test employee replaced temporarily. Check out this explanation against other records (for example, if we are told that John Doe was paid temporarily as a foreman because Sam Brown was out sick, check payroll department or departmental records to determine that Brown was actually sick on the day in question).

k. Trace overtime hours, premium time, bonus items, etc., for the individual employees from the source on hand in the payroll department to the original departmental records.

l. Determine that overtime hours, premium time, etc., have been posted in accordance with the provisions of company rules, labor agreements, and governmental regulations.

m. Check overtime, premium, and bonus rates to ascertain that they agree with the terms of the labor agreements, company rules, and governmental regulations.

n. Check the computations of the amounts of premium pay.

o. Determine that proper approvals have been obtained.

p. Agree employee's classification and rate of pay. Check against union contract (if applicable to employees being tested) or management authorization.

q. Check the date when the present rate of pay or salary went into effect against the cash book detail sheets to determine that such rate was effected on the date authorized.

r. Obtain the detail of the miscellaneous deduction amount as shown on the worksheets.

s. Examine signed authorizations for all deductions and ascertain that such deductions are correct individually and in total.

6. **Commissions**

a. Verify the accuracy of the report of compensation by checking the entry of information from the original sales order and contract to the report. These data should include the salesman's name, completion date of order, product, type of sale, net cash selling price, correct commission rate, and customer's name.

b. Check against the report all credit and return orders, thereby verifying commissions deductible.

c. Check payments for illness, vacations, holidays, training period, jury duty, etc., from records kept of such periods of absence. In this regard, an examination should be made by scrutinizing the dates of sales orders and contracts to see that a salesman did not make a sale (and receive commission therefor) on a day when he was absent (and was paid absent pay) for any of the foregoing reasons.

d. Verify the correctness of all footings on the report of compensation.

e. Check the total amount payable to each salesman to the salary roll for the corresponding period.

f. Verify that the stipulations provided by labor agreements were followed.

g. Perform steps 7, 8, and 9.

7. For those employees being tested perform the following steps *in the personnel department.*

a. Refer to Employee Service Record cards and note or agree the following on the worksheets:

(1) Note the effective date of rate or salary on worksheet.

(2) Agree the employee's classification and rate of pay or salary.

8. For the payrolls selected, perform the following (in the payroll division):
   a. Trace totals on cash book detail sheets for the payroll tested into the "Summary of Payrolls" paid during the period.
   b. Foot columns of cash book detail sheets.
   c. Foot the Summary of Payrolls.
   d. For the payrolls tested, trace the totals for the *month* shown on the Summary of Payrolls paid during each period in the month into the Monthly Summary of Payrolls.
   e. Agree the total gross payroll for the month as shown on the Monthly Summary of Payrolls to the applicable general ledger accounts.
   f. Test-check the calculation of the following accruals and determine that the percentages used in distributing such amounts appear reasonable. (This should include an examination of the amounts actually paid and tax returns filed.)
      (1) Employer's share of FICA
      (2) Employer's share of federal and state unemployment tax (Examine notice from the state in support of percentage used—copy of such notice in payroll division.)
      (3) Compensation and liability insurance
      (4) Vacation, etc., loading
      (5) Group life, hospitalization, and retirement
   g. Test-check the posting of the monthly journal entry to the general ledger.
   h. From the Monthly Summary of Payrolls select a number of work orders and accounts charged.
      (1) Obtain the time sheets for the applicable periods and take off—by time sheet—the number of hours charged to the particular work orders and accounts selected. Agree the total obtained from taping the time sheets to the total charged on the Summary.
      (2) Select a number of work orders and accounts as shown on the individual time sheets and tape the hours charged for the selected work orders on every remaining time sheet. Agree the total of this tape with the total shown on the Monthly Summary. (This step is a test to see that work orders charged on the time sheet were not "left out" of the distribution run.)
      (3) Take off the total hours and dollars charged for each selected work order and determine that the "loading" on the dollars is reasonable.
9. The possibility that a supervisor is keeping an employee's name on a payroll for a short period after the employee has actually terminated is very difficult to detect. The following steps have been devised in an attempt to make this detection:
   a. Visit the personnel department and obtain a list of all employees who have terminated during the previous month.
   b. Prepare a confirmation asking these employees to verify the termination date as shown on the personnel department's records.
10. **Distribution of Checks**
   a. Compare individual payroll checks with payroll summary for verification of amounts for those employees selected for detailed testing.
   b. Determine that payroll bank deposits agree with the total of net amounts due employees as shown by the payroll summary.

c. Observe the delivery of the pay to those employees covered by the audit. Employees must be satisfactorily identified. If personal delivery is not feasible, prepare list of employees covered by the audit, personally obtain their signatures, and compare these signatures with paycheck endorsements or other payroll records. Prepare a list of names of those employees to whom deliveries were not made or whose signatures could not be obtained, showing the reason. Compare reasons with company records, as follows:
(1) Prolonged illness—Compare with records of sick leave, correspondence, etc.
(2) Accidents while on or off duty—Compare with accident reports, time reports, correspondence, etc.
(3) Left service—Verify with termination notices and personnel records.
(4) Retired from service—Verify with pension list or personnel records.
(5) Vacations and other time off—Verify with time reports and departmental records.

d. Prepare a list showing names, dates, amounts, and approvals for any payroll advances. Review authorizations and determine whether each advance was within framework of company policy.

e. Review company treasury department procedures with respect to payrolls. Where checks are mechanically signed, ascertain that a proper record is maintained of the number of payroll check signatures and that check-signing equipment is properly protected against unauthorized usage, and examine spoiled paychecks to determine whether they are properly voided.

11. **Bank Reconciliation**

a. Bank account
(1) Reconcile bank account. Have bank send bank statements and canceled checks directly to the audit department. Utilize mechanized equipment when possible to verify payroll and list outstanding checks.
(2) Determine whether employees whose checks have not cleared the bank are still on the payrolls and determine, if possible, why their paychecks have not been presented to the bank for payment.
(3) Has the payroll department made the necessary effort to clear the unclaimed wages?

b. For wages paid in cash
(1) Determine whether pay envelopes or receipts which have not been signed are properly preserved.
(2) Ascertain whether cash is turned over to cashier for proper recording.

12. **Unclaimed Wages**

a. Check to see that all transfers from the imprest or special payroll bank account are transferred to the general ledger account within the prescribed time.

b. Inspect debits to the general ledger account to determine that the vouchers were properly authorized and approved.

c. Prepare a list to show the balance in unclaimed wages, showing period covered, employees' names, and amounts due.

d. Make a brief statement as to how long unclaimed wages are carried on the books and what happens when the statute of limitations has expired.

13. **Payroll Inspection**
   a. Review a reasonable sample of current time sheets on file and evaluate them from the standpoint of whether:
      (1) They are of such a form and prepared in such a way as to make erasures or alterations difficult, i.e., prepared in ink or by similar means;
      (2) whether all erasures, changes, and "out-of-rate" items are initialed by the approver of the time sheet;
      (3) and whether there is no possibility that additions can be made after the approval.
   b. Also ascertain whether the payroll division is checking that the approval signatures were properly authorized. (Note: In doing this step, prepare a schedule on how many time sheets were examined, how many were found to be deficient in one way or another [list these], etc.)
   c. Select a random sample of time sheets and confirm with appropriate supervision any changes or erasures thereon not supported by specific authorization.
14. **Overtime**
   a. Obtain payroll records showing the amount of overtime worked during the current year.
   b. Compare with one or two prior years and look for trends in specific departments.
   c. Compute the percent of overtime pay to regular pay and determine which departments show the largest percentages.
   d. For departments charging significant amounts of overtime, both in terms of total company overtime and in percent of overtime to regular time, determine which divisions and/or sections are contributing the most to overtime worked.
   e. Determine for the above departments the nature of, and reason for, the overtime work.
   f. Determine whether overtime was properly authorized and approved.
   g. Determine what controls are in effect governing the use of overtime, i.e., what is the extent of supervision during overtime, what records are kept of who worked and how long, etc.
15. **Vacations and Absences**
   a. Determine what controls are maintained by the various departments for vacations and absences.
   b. Review the company policies and/or collective bargaining agreements regarding vacations and absences and determine that all departments are complying with them.
   c. Review and examine the records maintained to determine how effective and accurate they are in terms of control.
      (1) Will the records point up excess vacation and absences?
      (2) Are the records checked periodically to avoid this situation?
      (3) Is there a daily sign-in sheet or time card used to control vacations and absences?
      (4) Are records uniform in all departments?
      (5) Are excessive cases of sickness reviewed periodically and discussed with the employees concerned?

PAYROLL FORMS

Various types of forms are used by the payroll department to update its records and supply information to provide the basis for payments of commissions, salaries, and wages. In connection with the authorization of payments to employees, typical forms for this purpose may be found on the following pages.

Accession to Payroll (Figure 1). This form provides the authorization for additions to the payroll for new hires. It is a four-part form which originates with the employment department, and copies are sent to Payroll, Personnel, and the department in which the employee will work. The form, when properly approved, authorizes Payroll to pay a particular person a specific rate of pay and identifies his occupation and the place where he will work.

Payroll Change (Figure 2). Another form used in connection with the authorization of payments to employees is the "Payroll Change" form. It is used by Payroll as their authorization to effect changes in the status of existing employees that may involve a change in pay or work location, occupation, etc. The form may also be used for employee terminations.

Time Sheet—Weekly—Individual (Figure 3). This form is used by employees whose payroll charges have a variable distribution, i.e., all of their time is not charged to one specific account or work order on a given day, but to several accounts. Payroll computes the employees' wages for each period by applying the pay rate to the number of hours reported. This report contains provision for hours worked on a regular, overtime, and premium-time basis, as well as vacation, legal, and holiday time, etc. There is also provision for computing additional compensation due the employee on account of work performed at a higher classification, etc.

Weekly Fixed Supplemental Pay Report (Figure 4). Employees whose pay distribution is fixed must have a form to report hours worked in addition to their regular time. A form for this purpose is shown in Figure 4. This form also provides in a second part for the reporting of expenses to be reimbursed through petty cash.

All of the above forms must be properly approved by authorized individuals. It is customary for the payroll department to have on hand a file of specimen signatures against which they may check signatures appearing on forms that authorize Payroll to make changes in pay records.

AUDIT FORM

Confirmation of Payroll Data (Figure 5). In connection with the audit of payroll records, the form shown in Figure 5 may be used to confirm information reported on the payroll time sheet. Alterations or changes made on time sheets subsequent to their approval which are not authorized may be revealed through this procedure.

Figure 1 ACCESSION TO PAYROLL

1 ORIGINAL

ACCESSION TO PAYROLL

DEPARTMENT — DIVISION — DATE RECD. IN PERSONNEL DEPT. — AUTH. NO.

SECTION — LOCATION

1 NAME OF EMPLOYEE	
2 MARITAL STATUS	
3 SOCIAL SECURITY ACCOUNT NO.	
4 EFFECTIVE DATE	
5 IS EMPLOYEE NEW, REHIRED, TRANSFERRED OR PLACED ON PAYROLL FOR SPECIAL PURPOSE.	
6 IF FORMERLY EMPLOYED BY AN AFFILIATED CO. GIVE NAME OF CO., ALSO NAME UNDER WHICH EMPLOYED	
7 RATE—HR., DAY, WEEK OR MONTH	
8 OCCUPATION	
9 SCHEDULED WORK WEEK	—DAYS —HOURS
10 STATUS	☐ REGULAR ☐ TEMPORARY ☐ PROBATIONARY
11 COMPENSATION INSURANCE CODE	☐-1 ☐-2 ☐-4 ☐-5 ☐-9
12 NON-UNION CODE	☐-0 ☐-1 ☐-2
12 UNION CODE	☐-7 ☐-8 ☐-9
13 PAPERS ATTACHED—CHECK	☐ RETIRE. ANNUITY ☐ GROUP LIFE INS. ☐ HOSPITAL PLAN ☐ FUND ☐ GOVT. BONDS ☐ WITHHOLD. EXEMPT. CERT. ☐ RESIDENCE CERT. ☐ ______

REMARKS

PAYROLL MASTER CARD

HRS.	GROSS	FICA	STATE EXEMP.	STATE TAX	FED. EXEMP.	FED. TAX	NET AMT.

DATE ______ PREPARED BY ______

DATE ______ APPROVED BY ______

STAT. CODE	PAYROLL NO.	EMPLOYEE NO.	LOC. NO.

PAYMENTS SECTION

SPECIAL PAYMENT	VISIBLE FILE	PRED. TOTALS
KEY PUNCH	CARDS COMPARED	SECTION SUPV.

EMPLOYEE OCCUPATION — CODE NO.

VARIABLE PAYROLL

ENTERED — DATE

REPORTS AND RECORDS

CARD CUT — SECTION SUPV.

Figure 2 PAYROLL CHANGE

DEPARTMENT	DIVISION	DATE RECD. IN PERSONNEL DEPT.
SECTION	LOCATION	

1 NAME OF EMPLOYEE		
2 DATE CHANGE EFFECTIVE		
3 IF REMOVED FROM PAYROLL INDICATE LAST DAY WORKED		
4 KIND OF CHANGE: RESIGNATION—GIVE REASON; LAY OFF " "; DISCHARGE " "; TRANSFER—SPECIFY NEW DEPT.; OTHER CHANGES—SPECIFY		
5 STATUS BEFORE CHANGE		
6 STATUS AFTER CHANGE		
7 IF TERMINATION AND ADDITIONAL PAYMENTS TO BE MADE FOR VACATIONS ETC. INDICATE		
8 DISPOSITION OF FINAL PAY	☐ MAIL TO HOME	☐ MAKE AVAILABLE LAST DAY OF WORK
9 COMPENSATION INSURANCE CODE CHANGE YES ☐ NO ☐	☐-1 ☐-2	☐-4 ☐-5 ☐-9
10 NON-UNION CODE CHANGE YES ☐ NO ☐	☐-0 ☐-1	☐-2
10 UNION CODE CHANGE YES ☐ NO ☐	☐-7 ☐-8	☐-9
11 PAPERS ATTACHED—CHECK	☐ RETIRE. ANNUITY ☐ GROUP LIFE INS. ☐ HOSPITAL PLAN ☐	☐ GOVT. BONDS ☐ WITHHOLD. EXEMPT. CERT. ☐ RESIDENCE CERT. ☐
12 IF TERMINATION, INDICATE CONDITION OF HEALTH	☐ GOOD	☐ POOR

REMARKS

DATE ______ PREPARED BY ______	DATE ______ APPROVED BY ______

STATE. CODE	PAYROLL NO.	EMPLOYEE NO.	LOC. NO.

TERMINATIONS	POSTED DATE - INIT.	CHECKED DATE - INIT.
RECORD CARD		
REMOVE Cross Ref. Record Card (if any)		
PREPARE 3 x 5 Cross Ref. Card (if req'd.)		
PERSONNEL FOLDER		
REVIEW CARD		
NOTIF. TO INSURANCE DIV.		
NOTIF. TO UNION		
NOTIF. TO RESTORATION		
NOTIF. TO TREASURY DEPT.		
NOTIF. TO MEDICAL DEPT.		
NOTIF. TO		
NOTIF. TO		
ENTER FROM RECORD CARD:		
CONTRACT CODE		
OCCUPATION		
EMPL. STATUS		

TRANSFERS	POSTED DATE - INIT.	CHECKED DATE - INIT.
RECORD CARD		
CROSS REF. RECORD CARD (Monthly P/R)		
REVIEW CARD		
PROMOTION CARD		
NOTIF. TO UNION (If Union Contract Code Changes)		
NOTIF. TO MEDICAL DEPT.		
NOTIF. TO		
ENTER FROM RECORD CARD:		
ADDRESS		

MISC. CHANGES	POSTED DATE - INIT.	CHECKED DATE - INIT.
RECORD CARD		
CROSS REF. RECORD CARD		
PERSONNEL FOLDER		
REVIEW CARD		
PROMOTION CARD		
NOTIF. TO UNION		
NOTIF. TO MEDICAL DEPT.		
NOTIF. TO TREASURY DEPT.		
NOTIF. TO		

Figure 3 TIME SHEET—WEEKLY—INDIVIDUAL

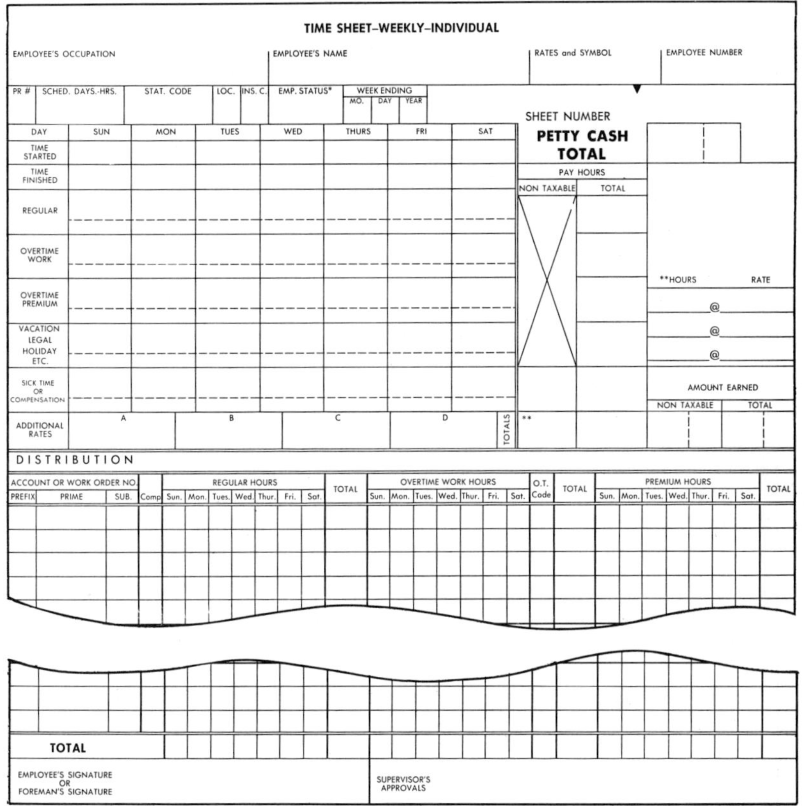

TIME SHEET–WEEKLY–INDIVIDUAL

EMPLOYEE'S OCCUPATION | EMPLOYEE'S NAME | RATES and SYMBOL | EMPLOYEE NUMBER

PR # | SCHED. DAYS.-HRS. | STAT. CODE | LOC. | INS. C. | EMP. STATUS* | WEEK ENDING: MO. DAY YEAR

SHEET NUMBER

PETTY CASH TOTAL

DAY	SUN	MON	TUES	WED	THURS	FRI	SAT
TIME STARTED							
TIME FINISHED							
REGULAR							
OVERTIME WORK							
OVERTIME PREMIUM							
VACATION LEGAL HOLIDAY ETC.							
SICK TIME OR COMPENSATION							
ADDITIONAL RATES	A	B	C	D	TOTALS		

PAY HOURS: NON TAXABLE | TOTAL

**HOURS | RATE

@

@

@

AMOUNT EARNED: NON TAXABLE | TOTAL

DISTRIBUTION

ACCOUNT OR WORK ORDER NO.				REGULAR HOURS							TOTAL	OVERTIME WORK HOURS							O.T.	TOTAL	PREMIUM HOURS							TOTAL
PREFIX	PRIME	SUB.	Comp	Sun.	Mon.	Tues.	Wed.	Thur.	Fri.	Sat.		Sun.	Mon.	Tues.	Wed.	Thur.	Fri.	Sat.	Code		Sun.	Mon.	Tues.	Wed.	Thur.	Fri.	Sat.	
TOTAL																												

EMPLOYEE'S SIGNATURE OR FOREMAN'S SIGNATURE | SUPERVISOR'S APPROVALS

Figure 4 WEEKLY FIXED SUPPLEMENTAL PAY REPORT

WEEKLY FIXED SUPPLEMENTAL PAY REPORT

ALSO TO BE USED IF EMPLOYEE WAS PAID SICK TIME AND/OR IS ENTITLED TO A PETTY CASH PAYMENT

EMPLOYEE'S NAME

DEPARTMENT	DIVISION	SECTION	LOCATION	WEEK ENDING

INSTRUCTIONS: *—To be completed by Payroll Division when required.
TO EMPLOYEES —Fill in Columns 1-2-3-7, for days you worked overtime, and Part 3, if due any Petty Cash.
TO SUPERVISORS—Fill in Column 8 for Paid Sick Time indicating number of hours for each day sick.

WEEKLY FIXED OVERTIME

7 DISTRIBUTION: REGULAR DISTRIBUTION— COMPLETE (A) AND (C) ONLY. WRITE WORD "REGULAR" IN (A) AND O.T. CODE IN (C). IRREGULAR DISTRIBUTION — COMPLETE (A), (C) AND (D) ONLY.

1	2	3	4	5	6	7 (A) ACCOUNT OR WORK ORDER			HOURS				AMOUNT			8 PAID SICK TIME		*9 DEDUCTION OF TIME	
WORK DAY AND DATE	TOTAL WORK HOURS	REG. HOURS	OVER-TIME WORK HOURS	PREM. HOURS	TOTAL O.T. PAY HOURS	PRE-FIX	PRIME	SUB	(B) REG.	(C) O.T. CODE	(D) OVER TIME	(E) PREM.	(F) REGULAR	(G) OVERTIME	(H) PREMIUM	DAY AND DATE	HOURS	DAY AND DATE	HOURS
SUN.									FILL IN WEEKLY TOTAL IN TOTAL SPACE BELOW							SUN.		SUN.	
MON.																MON.		MON.	
TUES.																TUES.		TUES.	
WED.																WED.		WED.	
THURS.																THURS.		THURS.	
FRI.																FRI.		FRI.	
SAT.																SAT.		SAT.	
TOTALS						TOTALS IRREGULAR DISTRIBUTION										TOTAL		TOTAL	
						REGULAR DISTRIBUTION													

TEMP. ASSIGN. RATE	GRADE	DATE FROM	DATE TO	* AMT. OF ADJUSTMENT	DEPT. REMARKS
$				$	

PETTY CASH $

FOR PAYROLL DIVISION'S USE ONLY ADJUSTED IN WEEK ENDING:

CURRENT WEEK		PREVIOUS WEEK		TOTAL PAY HOURS	N.Y.S. TAX	GROSS SICK TIME	GROSS PAY	TAXABLE GROSS PAY	F.I.C.A. TAX	FEDERAL TAX	NET AFTER TAXES
REGULAR PAY HOURS	DEDUCTION OF TIME CREDIT	OVERTIME PAY HOURS	SICK TIME								

WEEKLY RATE	HOURLY RATE	PAYROLL DIVISION REMARKS
$	$	

THIS IS A REPORT OF OVERTIME AND/OR AMOUNT OF PETTY CASH TO BE PAID FOR THE WEEK INDICATED. IF CORRECT, SIGN AND PRESENT THIS TO YOUR IMMEDIATE SUPERVISOR.

EMPLOYEE NO.	PAYROLL NO.	STAT. & LOC. CODE	SUPERVISOR'S APPROVAL
EMPLOYEE'S SIGNATURE			SUPERVISOR'S APPROVAL

INSTRUCTIONS: AFTER FORMS ARE COMPLETED, DETACH DEPARTMENT COPY AND FORWARD BALANCE OF SET TO PAYROLL DIVISION.

Figure 5 CONFIRMATION OF PAYROLL DATA

To:

In connection with a review of payroll procedures, we are verifying (on a test basis) certain specific information shown on the time sheet(s) of the below-named employee for the week ending ____________________:

Employee's Name	Employee's No.	PR No.	Stat. Code	Location
________	________	______	____	______

Regular Hours ____________________

Overtime Hours ____________________

Overtime Premium ____________________

Vacation, Holiday, etc. ____________________

Sick Time or Compensation ____________________

Total Hours ____________

We would appreciate your letting us know whether the above information is correct. The space below or the reverse side may be used for this purpose if you wish.

____________________ Date ____________________

Signature ____________________ Date ____________________

BIBLIOGRAPHY

Financial Manager's Job, The American Management Association, New York, 1964.
Payroll Guide, Prentice-Hall, Inc., Englewood Cliffs, N.J., to date.
Payroll Tax Guide, Commerce Clearing House, New York.
Studies in Personnel Policy, No. 81, National Industrial Conference Board, New York.
Wage and Salary Administration: A Guide to Current Policies and Practices, Dartnell Corporation, Chicago, 1969.

Brennan, Charles W.: *Wage Administration,* Homewood, Illinois, Richard D. Irwin, Inc., 1959.
Cashin, James A., and Garland C. Owens: *Auditing,* 2d ed., New York, The Ronald Press Company, 1963.
Dickey, R. I.: *Accountant's Cost Handbook,* New York, The Ronald Press Company, 1960.
Heckert, Brooks, and Harry Kerrigan: *Accounting Systems Design and Installation,* 3d ed., New York, The Ronald Press Company, 1967.
Research Report No. 4, *Internal Audit and Control of Payroll and Accounts Payable,* The Institute of Internal Auditors, New York, 1957.

Richmond, R. L.: "Labor Contracts and the Internal Auditor," Conference Papers, *The Institute of Internal Auditors,* 1963.
"Support of Payroll Deductions," Readers' Problem Clinic, *The Internal Auditor,* Fall, 1966.
Wescott, J. W.: "Motivation and Productivity," *The Internal Auditor,* January/February, 1963.
Krein, Dr. Ted J.: "People—Assets That Talk Back," *The Internal Auditor,* July/August, 1969.
King, Alfred M.: "Check-Account Payroll," *Management Accounting,* June, 1970.

Chapter 33

Production

N. T. CAMPBELL

Audit Zone Manager, IBM Corporation

ELEMENTS OF PRODUCTION COST

General. *Production cost* involves three primary elements of any company: its machinery, its material, and its manpower. Since these three elements constitute a major portion of cost in most products, it is essential that the auditor, internal or external, examine these elements from both an operational and a financial point of view. Too often, auditors have merely treated these elements as assets, usually from the intangible form of documents, that must be protected or accounted for, without considering the more important tangible operational aspects of *utilization* and *productivity*.

It is the intent of this chapter to explain the importance of operational controls concerning machinery, material, and manpower and to provide the auditor with various means of determining the existence and adequacy of such controls. If the auditor has examined the adequacy of operational controls involving product cost, then he has a firm basis for evaluating the various methods of accounting for such cost through the financial cost system. The audit considerations in this chapter are, therefore, intended to involve the auditor not only in the financial accounting for cost but, more important, in the vital workings of other areas of the organization that really make up those product costs.

The harmonious movement and integration of machinery, material, and manpower are extremely complicated and call for a great deal of control. Depending on the size of your particular organization, you may decide to make an overall audit including many of the areas specified in this chapter, or, if your organization is too large, you may elect to review the areas, one by one.

Machinery, Material, and Manpower as Elements. It is apparent, as we consider the various elements of product cost—machinery, material, and manpower—that each has a direct bearing on the others throughout the production cycle. If we control one element, we derive some degree of control over the others; and if we control all three, we have a very well-managed organization. Control of costs, whether it be a primary objective or not, leads to a definite ability to plan.

If we have established standards of measurement for machinery, material, and manpower, then we have established a means of determining, with a high degree of accuracy, the capabilities of our factory. We can then make more accurate money-making decisions on how to run the business.

It therefore behooves the auditor, whether internal or external, to consider very seriously his present involvement in the operational areas of product cost.

MACHINERY COST

Machinery as an Element of Product Cost. The capital investment in machinery is a significant element of product cost and is ever increasing as complicated, automated machinery more and more takes the place of manual effort. Because of the extraordinary cost of machinery, it is essential that management have controls to assure its maximum utilization and efficiency. Not only is the productivity of such equipment of vital concern to management, but, as it continues to grow as an important segment of the integrated production cycle, it must be well controlled to assure that delivery commitments are met.

Audit Purpose—Machinery Cost. The significant capital investment in machinery warrants an adequate basis for evaluating machine utilization and performance.

Technical limitations will, of course, prevent the auditor from making an engineering review; however, a basic and logical evaluation of measurement factors is within the scope of an audit.

Since purchase justification for such equipment is both tangible and intangible, both aspects must be considered and weighed carefully in the audit evaluation.

The audit purpose is to determine the existence of an adequate and meaningful method of comparing actual machine utilization and productivity with a measurement of standard performance, at the same time ensuring that management agrees with the evaluation measurements used and is reviewing these factors on a continuing basis.

Audit Considerations—Machinery Cost. Ideally, 100 percent machine utilization and productivity is desirable, but in practice this is unattainable.

The machine manufacturer supplies percentage factors based upon operations performed during factory tests. However, revisions of these guidelines are necessary based upon conditions and operations unique to each plant.

All companies should have some type of control report, whether it be a handwritten log for a single piece of machinery or an EDP system for a multitude of machines; the report can be in any form but should tell management, whether it be one person or 20, the following types of information:

1. Manufacturing engineering—Information on machine uptime, downtime, and idle time;
2. Industrial engineering—Information on the average time to process a part;
3. Quality engineering—The number of accepted and rejected parts;
4. Maintenance—A listing of the downtime failures and their total time;
5. Higher management—A summary of machine usage and parts processed.

Audit Procedure and Questions—Machinery Cost. Standards and labor coding. The auditor must first determine for his review:

1. What reports and analyses for machines are available to management which show utilization and efficiency figures?
2. Does management accept such figures as being realistic and conclusive?
3. Do various jobs and operations have industrial time standards assigned? Are they:
   a. Standards established by manufacturing engineering methods?
   b. Temporary standards?
   c. Educated "guesstimates"?
4. Are manufacturing and industrial manufacturing standards departments in agreement on estimated time standards being used?

   Is there an active program to review and update jobs and operations with and without time standards?
5. What was the economic justification for the original purchase of the automated machines selected for audit review? Are significant purchase justification factors being realized?

The auditor will usually find that direct labor time recording is the basic factor in determining machine utilization. However, the accuracy and reliability of these time recordings will have to be established.

If direct labor time recordings are made against various jobs and operations without established industrial time standards, then an effective and reliable comparison is *lacking.* A machine operator could be recording time against a "machine in operation" labor code when in reality he may be "setting tools," etc., and the machine is idle.

This situation raises several questions:

1. Are there enough direct labor time codes to cover any given machine situation?
2. Are established industrial time standards being prepared for machine operations?
3. What is management doing to improve time-recording accuracy and reliability?

Inaccurate labor time recording has the following adverse effects:

1. Directly affects machine utilization and performance ratings.
2. Forces production scheduling on an automated basis to be manually adjusted.
3. Unit cost of parts worked is directly affected.
4. Reduces effective report use by management.

Validity of Reports—Machinery Cost

1. Select machines for review. This is often a problem, depending on the number of machines involved. The auditor must therefore study the machining operation so that he can base his review on a sample that will be reflective of that operation. If this study is not made, there is a great danger that the results of this audit and much hard work will be meaningless. It is very prudent to discuss the method of selecting the audit sample with the operating management directly involved in the audit; management will be able to give the auditor valuable input and should, in any event, generally concur with the basis of the sample. Statistical procedures should be considered. Some elements that might be considered in performing the audit follow:
   a. Dollar expenditures by machine group.
   b. Percentage of total machines in use.
   c. Department using numerous automated machines.
   d. A combination of the above.
2. Review in detail all available reports, records, and analyses of automated machine utilization and efficiency ratings.
3. Is the measurement base used in the reports reviewed adequate and meaningful to management? Do these reports contain information on an exception basis? (Management is not normally interested in what is going as planned but what are the exceptions.)
4. Is management reviewing these reports on a continuing basis, and how timely are these reports?
5. Are future machine purchases that are contemplated based on evaluation of present machines?
6. Are significant original purchase justification factors being realized? Are proper justification records on file? Proper approvals?

7. Are the machines used on the number of shifts for which they were originally justified?

8. Is there an active industrial time standards program in effect?

9. If job and operation time estimates are found to be unrealistic, does manufacturing challenge them? What action is taken to revise and update time standards?

10. Are sufficient labor codes available to cover all machine situations?

11. If adequate or useful evaluation reports are not available, or if present measurement factors are in dispute for determining machine utilization and productivity, the following will be necessary:

a. Establish with manufacturing the total machine availability hours on those machines selected for review during a given period.

b. Compute total actual labor hours recorded against machines selected for the same period. Divide the total obtained in *a* above into the total just obtained (*b*); this will provide machine utilization percentages.

c. Prepare a schedule of direct labor time recordings which appear excessive. Discuss with the manufacturing and industrial time standards departments.

12. Are there other methods which can be implemented to better evaluate machine utilization and efficiency?

Survey—Machining Departments. Review the machining departments and the operations of these departments with the managers.

1. Discuss the number of personnel in the department as compared with the number of available machines, if idle machines are noted.

2. Review the machine utilization report with the manager if there is a sizable variance between potential and actual productive hours. Inquire as to the reason for this variance.

3. Also inquire as to the reason for orders being produced ahead of schedule and for orders being behind schedule.

4. Visually inspect the department, noting (*a*) semifinished parts orders being held on stop orders; (*b*) parts held for undue length of time; (*c*) parts without production orders; (*d*) mixed parts.

5. Review the parts being produced and locate the applicable production order. Ascertain that the initial setup expenditures and the subsequent setup caused by regrinding of tools due to order quantity are charged to production orders. Resetups occasioned by tool trouble and downtime for other reasons will be charged to factory overhead.

6. Compare the part numbers on the labor cards with the parts being worked on per production orders.

7. Compare the quantities claimed to have been produced per labor cards with the quantities shown on the posting copies of the production orders.

8. List idle machines by machine group. Determine by review of the machine load report whether any machine groups show a consistent number of available hours in the idle machine group class. Determine, if possible, if permanent subcontract work has caused this condition.

9. Note the number of "send ahead" production orders in the department. Review all production orders in the department and note send-aheads shown on each. Review previous production orders showing send-aheads above to determine if the condition is on a continuing basis. Note, by part number, number of teardowns and resetups required because of send-aheads.

10. Note special equipment, tools, etc., located in the department and inquire as to use, accountability if not tagged, and storage location when not in use.

11. Determine whether there are any items of government-owned industrial property in the department and verify the mix of government and commercial work performed on the machines. List appropriate identification information for subsequent verification that Department of Defense (DOD) approval was requested and granted for any such items used on commercial programs.

12. Note the number of small order quantities on production orders in the departments reviewed and inquire as to the prevalence of this condition.

13. Note the number of large order quantities on production orders in departments reviewed and inquire as to the prevalence of this condition, particularly when bulky material is used.

14. Note the duties performed by indirect-classified employees. Inquire as to personnel of other departments working in the department reviewed.

15. In the automatic screw machine department inquire as to the number of automatic machines which are run in batteries of two, three, and four by one operator and the number of hand-fed machines that require an individual operator for each machine. Determine whether the equipment, by machine group, is being used effectively. Inquire of the manager as to excess equipment if the machine utilization report reflects any. Note the excess equipment by machine type and serial number if possible.

16. Inquire of the manager as to work being subcontracted on a permanent basis which resulted in loss of production hours and idle equipment. List the subcontracted work by part number and quantities of parts on production orders for previous months.

17. Inquire of the manager as to work which was originally planned as a "buy" item which is now being performed in-house. List these items by part number, quantities, and job charged, for verification of appropriate budget adjustments. Prepare notes on any adverse effects that this shift in the "make-or-buy" plan has had on the department's schedule and overtime.

18. Inquire of the manager as to the existence of machinery which is subject to calibration. Determine the approximate date of such calibration for future verification against calibration records, with cross-reference to Quality Control parts rejection sheets and the machine's specification.

MATERIAL COST

Material as an Element of Product Cost. Material cost is another primary cost in any manufactured product. In order to comply with the intent of this chapter, our concern with *material cost* will be to determine that material is charged *directly* to a specific product, based on the type of raw material used, the design, and the production methods. It will not deal with inventories, as such, since that topic is covered elsewhere in the handbook.

Obviously, the type and quality of raw material used in a product, the manufacturing process, and the quantity of that material directly affect the cost of the final product. Management and the auditors should therefore assure themselves that operational controls exist to provide the required quantity and quality of material, at the least cost, when and where it is needed.

Audit Purpose—Material Cost. In order to assure that material cost is kept to a minimum, the auditor should:

1. Determine the existence of an adequate and meaningful method of comparing actual material cost with a measurement of standard cost.
2. Determine usage and compare it with that forecast.
3. Determine that the material is at the required place in the manufacturing process and at the right time.

Audit Considerations—Material Cost. The physical nature of material, as well as the manufacturing processes, will vary from company to company. It is, therefore, important to point out some differences that must be considered for an audit review.

1. In custom products or companies producing job orders with a static makeup of parts (bill of material), the method of forecasting quantity requirements lends itself to precise measurement of actual usage. If the company is involved in continuous-process production, then a comparison is more difficult. However, a measurement of "yield" can be made at various stages of the continuous process and compared with either past yield or standards of yield established by engineering studies.
2. Too often the cost of material is compared with or measured against past cost or prices. A better method of measurement is to have qualified engineers estimate the cost based upon the manufacturing process that will result in the desired quality. This method of comparison for material cost is pertinent not only when material is produced directly by the company involved, but more so when that material is purchased from another company. The use of engineering cost estimates provides an excellent management tool in deciding whether to "make or buy." It also permits the measurement of the success of manufacturing and purchasing in meeting cost targets.

   The determination of whether price or cost history will be used for comparison, as opposed to engineering cost estimates, will depend primarily on the nature of the material or product involved.

In line with a basic audit and management concept, the auditor's approach will be most effective if he selects that material which represents the high-value items, whether they are manufactured or purchased. The actual cost of manufacturing or the actual price of purchase should be compared with an engineered cost estimate; if none exists, the actual cost should be compared with past costs.

Audit Procedure and Questions—Manufactured Material. The auditor, in attempting to determine whether the areas of audit purpose are being managed well (see the section entitled "Audit Purpose—Material Cost"), will probably find it difficult to determine how he should select his audit sample. The number of parts or quantity of material, even in a small company, is often staggering. It is therefore very important that the auditor select a *sample that is reflective of the operation* being audited. To do this he must choose a sample that is not distorted by exceptional or "one-time" situations; it must include the full range of activity and not just exceptional items that are either too high or too low. He must study the nature of the business or product he is attempting to audit. It is most prudent that, when making the sample determination, he consult with the management being audited, since they will surely have valuable input and should, in any event, generally concur that the method of selecting the sample is reflective of their operation.

Too often the auditor will go blindly ahead, using only a statistical sample or something less sophisticated, only to find that he has taken either a period that is exceptional, a product that is exceptional, or material that is exceptional.

Some aspects or elements of the audit sample to consider are:

1. One or two products that are representative of the company's overall operation.
2. High dollar-value parts or material that represents the major material expenditures of the company.
3. Specific commodities that are representative of the company's operation.
4. Depending on the sophistication of the company, you might audit only those products, or materials, or commodities that reflect an overexpended condition. This will be an audit by exception.

Some audit questions pertinent to material or parts manufactured versus purchased are presented below. Depending on the size of the company or operation being audited, some of these questions may involve specific audits in themselves. In a large operation, where the auditor is more or less permanently assigned, it is often desirable to perform a specialized audit of a few elements or even a single element of concern, as represented in the following questions.

1. Does management have a means of comparing manufactured material cost with some standard? If so, is it an adequate and meaningful means of measurement? If engineering cost estimates are used for measurement, are they updated as conditions change?
2. Is there a detailed bill of material calling out material?

If so, is it accurate and up to date? (The possibility exists that product specification changes—that is, engineering changes—may not be reflected in the bill of material.)

3. Are there detailed job orders and operation routings to assure that the correct material arrives at the right place at the right time?
4. Is there a specified method of recording and accounting for scrap material during the various stages of manufacturing? (This should pinpoint problem areas.) Is every effort made by Manufacturing to assure that material classified as scrap is actually that? A determination of scrap (excluding chips, spoilage, etc.) should be made by Quality Control as a matter of good internal control. The disposition may, of course, be handled by Manufacturing.
5. Are counts or some type of measurement recorded as material moves from operation to operation in the manufacturing cycle? (This will enable management to pinpoint problem areas.)
6. Investigate the adequacy of the method used to determine material requirements, such as: (1) future requirements based on sales forecasts, (2) future requirements based on past usage, or (3) automatic requirements based on inventory balances.

Determine the effectiveness of the method of forecasting by comparing actual usage with whatever method of forecasting is used.

7. Were requested completion dates scheduled far enough in advance of need, considering balances on hand?
8. Were cancellations of open material orders or reduction of quantities ordered made promptly when requirements were deleted or decreased? When configuration changes are processed in Planning, is adequate con-

sideration given to the rework of finished parts already in the production stockroom?

9. Determine whether emergency or rush orders are increasing material cost.

10. Review Production Stockroom shortage reports to determine the extent of shortages of fabricated parts. These shortages will have an effect on the product assembly areas. List parts shortages and relate these back to the departments involved.

Audit Procedure and Questions—Purchased Material. As was the case with manufactured parts or material, the auditor will generally find it difficult to select a sample of purchased parts that is reflective of the company or operation being audited. The very large number of parts or material being purchased will usually make an audit review difficult, but, unless the sample is representative, the audit will be meaningless. In selecting his sample, the auditor should generally avoid exceptions (unless he is deliberately performing an audit by exception). Generally he should use statistical techniques wherever practicable. He therefore must study the nature of the business or operation being audited. It is very prudent to get the concurrence of the purchasing management on the proposed method of selecting the sample. Management will be able to give the auditor valuable input and to point out any exceptions (i.e., period of time, product, commodity). It is very discouraging to find out, after all the detailed audit work is finished, that the audit sample and audit results are not usable.

Some aspects of the audit sample that the auditor should consider are:

1. Select and review high dollar-value parts. Sample size should be based on Purchasing's share of responsibility.
2. Select and review parts from one or more products that are representative of the business or operation being reviewed.
3. Select parts that are representative by individual buyer.
4. Select commodities that are representative of the company or operation.

Regardless of which of the above elements are used, be sure that it will guarantee the desired result of some representative concern of the company or operation you are reviewing.

Some audit questions pertinent to material or parts being purchased as opposed to manufactured are presented below. Depending on the size of the company or operation being audited, some of these questions might involve specific audits in themselves. In a large operation, it is often very desirable to perform a specialized audit of a few elements or even a single element of concern, as represented by the following questions.

1. Does management have a means of comparing purchased material cost with some standard?

If so, is it an adequate and meaningful means of measurement?

If engineering cost estimates are used for measurement, are they updated as conditions change?

2. Are standard or engineering cost estimates available to Purchasing before the first order is placed?

3. Are there indications that the standard is merely the actual, or reworked actual price?

4. Are buyers measured on their cost performance?

5. Are problems of large cost estimates versus purchase price variances resolved through vendor negotiations?

6. Are material requisitions received with sufficient lead time to permit buyers to negotiate the best cost?

7. Investigate the adequacy of the method used to determine purchased material requirements, such as: future requirements based on sales forecast, or based on past usage, or automatic requirements based on inventory balances.

Determine the effectiveness of the method of forecasting requirements by comparing actual usage with the method of forecasting used.

8. Determine whether emergency or rush purchases are increasing material cost.

9. Review production stockroom shortage reports to determine the extent of shortages of purchased parts. These shortages will have an effect on the product assembly areas. List part shortages and relate back to the purchasing department's records of material on back order.

10. If the production stockroom is not an inventory position, review the existence of slow- or no-movement parts. List these parts for subsequent review of the total inventory position, possible reallocation to other work in-house, return of parts to seller for credit, or cancellation of open back orders.

11. Determine whether there is located in the department any discrepant purchased material to be repaired which was classified by Inspection as "seller responsibility." Consideration must be given to the proper accumulation of repair cost and subsequent billing to the responsible seller.

MANPOWER COST

Manpower as an Element of Product Cost. Although automated machinery is doing many of the jobs once done by people, the rising cost of labor continues to make it a major element of product cost.

The ratio of direct labor to indirect is also changing, with increasing automation and advanced technology. The quantity of indirect manpower as related to direct is growing and may well exceed it in some companies.

As was the case with machinery and material, as elements of cost, manpower must also be controlled through some comparison with a standard.

Audit Purpose—Manpower Cost. In order to assure that manpower cost, both direct and indirect, is kept to a minimum, the auditor should determine:

1. Does management have an adequate and meaningful method of comparing actual labor performance with specific standards?

2. Are employee wages directly related to employee performance in relation to those standards?

3. Is the number of employees justified in relation to the production plant?

Audit Considerations—Manpower Cost. While the setting of labor standards requires professional background in industrial engineering, the auditor is qualified to make some basic evaluation of the existence and validity of those standards. Some considerations that may differ from company to company are:

1. If the company is unionized, the labor rates will be controlled by collective bargaining.

2. A nonunion company has more flexibility in establishing labor rates and

labor standards but should be no less precise in using labor rate standards as a control of manpower cost.

3. Employees are paid for either time worked, or the amount of work performed, or a combination of the two.

Audit Procedure and Questions—Manpower Cost. Probably no area of a business is more *sensitive* to audit than labor. The auditor should, therefore, approach this area of cost with a great degree of prudence, tact, and management awareness.

Direct Manpower. In any audit, one of the most difficult aspects is determining the basis or sample that will result in a valid reflection of the business or operation being audited. The audit questions generally deal with business logic, as is evident from the questions that follow, and are generally easy to come by, but the task of answering those questions is complicated by the size or number of items involved, which is staggering in relation to the reality that any audit will be confined to a limited number of transactions. Wherever practicable, the auditor should use accepted statistical techniques. Therefore, before he can answer the questions below, he must find a basis or method of sampling. To do this, the auditor must study the business or operation being audited. It is most desirable that the auditor get information and concurrence from the management being audited as to the validity of the audit sample. In auditing direct labor, the auditor might consider these factors as a basis for his sample:

1. Select a department or group of departments that are representative of the direct labor of the business or operation being audited.
2. Select a statistical sample of direct employees from the payroll register.
3. Select direct employees for a specific product or manufacturing process.
4. Select by skills, for position codes that are representative of the business or operation.

Regardless of the method, be sure that it will result in a valid reflection of whatever is the prime area of concern.

Following are specific audit questions regarding direct labor:

1. Are there established standards of performance for each direct classification?
2. Are labor rates related to those standards?
3. Is the number of employees in line with the production forecast?
4. Are performance standards revised when a change in method or process occurs?
5. Is overtime in excess of standard provisions?
6. Are employees working on jobs in line with their classifications, or both under and over their classifications?
7. Is quality a factor in the performance measurement?
8. Is the flow of work and material conducive to measurement?
9. Are there clearly defined responsibilities?
10. What direct labor is not measured against a standard, and why?
11. Is total time on labor claims in balance with the time recorded on payroll records?
12. Do attendance or labor claim documents provide adequate categories for reflecting time (i.e., direct labor production, teardown and setup, waiting time, nonchargeable time, etc.)?
13. Determine what the established shift premium rates are and what controls are in effect to prevent the arbitrary change of a shift starting time

so that a premium is earned for a normally non-premium shift (i.e., normal non-premium shift, 8:00 A.M. to 4:30 P.M.; however, any shift starting between 4:00 A.M. and 6:30 A.M. is assigned a three (3) percent premium . . . ; the foreman starts his shift at 6:00 A.M. to provide for two (2) hours' overtime; therefore, the entire shift is then a premium shift).

Indirect Manpower. Some specific audit questions regarding indirect labor are:

1. Is there some method in use to evaluate the performance of indirect labor? Is there appraisal or evaluation of performance objectives?
2. Is that evaluation directly related to merit pay?
3. Are operating budgets in use to control and justify indirect labor?
4. Are there clearly defined responsibilities and authority?

Incentive Standards. An ideal method of increasing productivity and lowering cost, while at the same time rewarding the worker with increased pay, is the use of wage incentives. Some audit questions related to incentive wages are:

1. Is the incentive plan actually resulting in cost reduction?
2. Are all direct employees participating in the incentive plan?
3. Is quality directly related to productivity?
4. Are the standards changed without regard to a change in process or method?
5. Is there an actual, desirable difference (incentive) between the standard rate of pay and the rate of pay the employee can expect for performance above the standard?
6. Are employees well informed as to the responsibilities encompassed in their standards and incentives?

MANUFACTURING OVERHEAD

Manufacturing Overhead as an Element of Product Cost. The value of indirect expenses has continued to grow even though many people still associate direct labor and material as the major constituent of product cost. Manufacturing overhead, however, is as much a part of product cost as are direct labor and material. In many industries, the manufacturing overhead totals more than either direct labor or direct material costs and is, therefore, a very significant management and audit concern.

Manufacturing overhead contains a multitude of items, such as:

1. Indirect labor—salaries and wages for those not directly working on the product itself.
2. Indirect materials—materials which are not actually a part of the product but which are necessary in running the company producing the product.
3. Other plant costs—taxes, rent, utilities, insurance, depreciation, etc.

Manufacturing overhead items are generally those costs not directly associated with the product. This element of product cost has other characteristics. Some manufacturing overhead costs are *fixed* and remain generally constant regardless of changes in product volume. Other manufacturing overhead costs vary from month to month but not necessarily in the same proportion as product volume; these costs are referred to as *semi-variable costs.* Those costs which change with volume are termed *variable costs.* The type of costing in which only the variable costs are charged to inventory is called *variable costing* or *direct costing*. Under this method the fixed costs are considered a cost of the period and are charged to expense. This approach is useful in providing information for managerial decisions requiring a distinction between variable and fixed costs. It is also useful in eliminating income distortion where there are substantial differences in production and sales volumes. By excluding fixed overhead from inventory costs the income for successive periods is not affected by fluctuations in inventory and is tied in more closely with sales. Total inventory cost is thus lower under direct costing than under full or absorption costing. The exclusion of a portion of costs makes direct costing a problem for financial statement purposes. The AICPA, in Accounting Research and Terminology Bulletins, final edition, states:

> The primary basis of accounting for inventories is cost. . . . As applied to inventories, cost means in principle the sum of the applicable expenditures and charges directly or indirectly incurred in bringing an article to its existing condition and location.

For the purposes of this handbook it is desirable to discuss all production costs in this section. For further information as to the various methods of costing and the advantages and disadvantages of each method the reader is referred to the bibliography at the end of the chapter.

Overhead Distribution. It is much more difficult to accurately charge overhead than it is to charge direct labor and material. However, if inventories are to be stated correctly, if individual jobs, lots, or batches are to be correctly costed, and if sales controls and pricing policies are to be valid, then a reliable method of distributing these overhead costs must be arrived at. Overhead distribution is made through overhead rates. Overhead, added to direct labor and direct material, gives the total *factory* cost to the manufactured product. Some of the bases used to distribute overhead are:

1. Direct labor hours
2. Direct labor cost
3. Direct material cost
4. Machine hours
5. Units of product
6. Weight or volume
7. Combination of above

The auditor must seek to determine whether the best base is being used; suggested procedures are covered later under the heading "Audit Procedures and Questions."

Audit Considerations—Manufacturing Overhead. There is still a tendency for management, even financial management, to view *overhead costs* as of minor importance in relation to *direct product costs*. This attitude stems from the days when overhead was, in most instances, an insignificant element of cost. However, that is no longer the case and this attitude is no longer valid.

Another problem in dealing with the control of overhead cost is the diffusion of responsibility for it and the multitude of items making it up. Direct costs tend to be tangible in nature, whereas overhead cost becomes intangible to the extent that we become concerned with electricity versus oil heat, air mail versus regular mail, first-class travel versus tourist class, or a phone call versus a memo. In short, most direct product costs can be directly related to and measured against the product, whereas many overhead costs might be viewed as necessary versus unnecessary and reasonable versus unreasonable.

Audit Procedure and Questions—Manufacturing Overhead. The auditor's approach, like management's, is to determine whether overhead costs are under control and whether the method of accounting for such costs is the best reflection of the products involved.

Overhead cost control. It is most desirable to control overhead costs as rigidly as direct cost is controlled. To do this, these costs must be charged directly to people having the responsibility for them and means of controlling them.

The level of charge and responsibility depends on the degree of control desired. The best control of overhead cost is one in which each employee feels responsible for indirect costs. Some points to be considered by the auditor are:

1. Are there manufacturing cost elements in addition to the traditional direct labor and direct material in your plant?
2. Are different classifications of expenditures required for determining product cost and obtaining cost control?
3. How is idle labor accounted for?
4. How is idle machine time accounted for?
5. What are the primary overhead cost accounts in use?
6. To what extent might these accounts be better controlled through further subdivision?
7. How does a cost center differ from a department, and what purpose does it serve?
8. In a multiple-product industry, can there be reasonable control of overhead cost without departmentalization of costs?
9. How does the management control of overhead costs compare with that of direct costs?
10. How does a change in production processes affect the pattern of overhead costs?
11. What incentives have been developed for improved cost performance?
12. What is the method used for enforcing cost variance accountability at various levels of management?

Budgets—overhead cost control. The budget is a method of controlling overhead cost so that performance can be measured and a basis of comparison maintained. A budget for each department establishes the normal or expected cost for comparison with actual to show the department head where expenses are out of control. It is most desirable that all departments, including production departments, staff, and all service departments, be brought under budgetary control.

With the expansion of business, new products have been added and departments have been split, requiring additional audit review. Often new managers or others do not know which expenses should or should not be charged to an individual product, and cause problems in properly classifying charges. These problems, together with changes in account numbers and titles, make a systematic audit review of departmental expenses essential.

Often it is possible to detect questionable or erroneous charges or credits through a visual review of the budget statement. This is especially true where such amounts appear to be not in keeping with the operations performed in a department. For example: charges to the chemical supplies accounts in the accounts payable department statement are obviously erroneous, as would be a charge to the heat treatment department for meat, fowl, and seafood.

Visual detection of questionable items or errors is not difficult and takes very little time.

Usually, departmental budgeted expenses are based on past years' expenses and, in some cases, are in error, either as a result of over-budgeting in anticipation of an emergency or as a buffer to assure that the budgeted overall departmental expenses are not exceeded by the actual.

A properly forecasted budget is one that is based on the *future actual operations* of a department, as they can best be determined. However, in most cases the previous year's actual expenses are used as the basis for the forecasted budget for the forthcoming year.

A visual comparison of expenses to date with the budgeted amounts will show sizable variances in individual accounts if proper budgeting techniques are not used in the development of estimated operating expenses.

There are exceptions to the above statement, particularly in machining and assembly departments as operations are changed, machines are replaced, parts and assemblies are subcontracted, and other changes made, all of which will distort the anticipated expenses for a particular account or accounts.

It could be that the performance of the department, based on a regular *audit of its operations*, is acceptable. However, a more detailed insight into the *indirect cost of the operations* may disclose data which might change the entire picture. Examples are excessive overtime charges, large telephone toll expenses, subcontract charges for work previously performed in the department, and productive work time charged as indirect time.

The best approach to an audit of departmental expenses is to ask a representative number of managers of departments for their departmental operating budgets and to review the budgets with them. By so doing, it should become apparent whether the managers know what is being charged to their departments or whether they do not know.

A good approach is to select representative accounts and determine whether the charges are correct as shown. For example, if there are sizable charges for job training, a review of the individuals charging their time would be advisable. If an experienced employee has consistently charged time to job training, it would be well to review the jobs worked on during the period in question. It could be that some productive time was charged to Job Training to keep the departmental efficiency rating at an acceptable position. Other accounts could also be used to level off or not to charge one particular account in order that it would not be questioned.

A list of indirect personnel in the department should be obtained, for all shifts, and the distribution of payroll examined to verify the accuracy of charges.

When auditing machinery or assembly operations, idle equipment should be noted. Inquiry should be made as to the machines not being staffed: for example, is the operator absent because of illness, or has he been transferred to another department, temporarily or permanently, etc.? Good judgment should be used in the selection of charges and credits to be reviewed. Dollar limitations should be established, and items below the amount determined should not be audited. Experience gained from three or four audits of departmental expenses will provide a guide.

Some specific questions that should be considered in reviewing budgets are:

1. Is budgetary responsibility placed at the proper level?
2. Are budget variances analyzed and explained?
3. Do budget variances result in the intended corrective action?

Overhead distribution. If predetermined rates are used, there may be under- and over-applied absorption. The amount will depend on the cost method used. If an "actual" rate is used, the amount depends on the correctness of the estimate and the frequency of review to assure that it is representative. If a "normal" rate is used, the amount depends on the correctness of the estimate of expected expenses, budget variations, and the rate of activity. The difference between actual and absorbed variable expenses represents waste or abnormal expense and is an indication of the efficiency of the manufacturing department.

The determination of the base to be used for overhead distribution should aim to select the one which results in the most accurate distribution of overhead to the products involved. This sounds simple but it is not, and the auditor in reviewing this area will find it difficult to establish his own means of determination. What are the criteria for determining whether to distribute overhead on the basis of direct labor cost, direct labor hours, machine hours, material cost, etc.? Some aspects that the auditor might consider are:

1. Determine the relationship of the elements of cost in the total manufacturing cost.
2. In a manufacturing process which is mostly manual, the direct hour labor cost will probably be the best distribution base.
3. If wage rates vary widely, then direct labor cost might be the best distribution base.
4. If most of the manufacturing costs relate to machinery, such as depreciation, insurance, taxes, space cost, etc., then the costs may be assembled by a machine line or group and distributed on the basis of machine hours.
5. If material cost is high, then total direct cost might be used (total of both labor and material).
6. Sometimes the business or operation is very complex and no one basis is suitable. In that case a combination of the bases may be necessary.

COST SYSTEMS

Cost Systems—Financial Aspect of Product Cost. The previous sections of this chapter have emphasized the need for cost control at the operational level, on the premise that the financial cost system will be only as valid as the input to that system.

Cost systems for product cost are maintained for many reasons—to determine the cost of a product, to compare actual costs with historical, budgeted, or standard cost, and to provide management with data so that planning and operating decisions can be made.

The kind of manufacturing operation generally determines the kind of cost system used. Some of the more common cost systems are:

1. Job costing—When the manufacturing process concerns special orders produced to specifications or customer orders, job costing is employed. In this system all definable charges attributed to the job are charged to it.
2. Process costing—When the manufacturing process involves large quantities of homogeneous units in continuous production or assembly operation, process costing is used.
3. Standard costing—Predetermined costs are arrived at and later compared with actual costs. Costs are classified by both products produced and the areas involved. (Includes direct costing.)

Audit Purpose—Cost System. Regardless of the cost system used, the auditor's purpose in reviewing it should be to answer these questions:

1. Does it reflect the actual conditions, either by product or by operations?
2. Does management have confidence in it as a tool for planning and decision rendering?
3. Is it useful in controlling cost?

Audit Procedure and Questions. Operational audits of product costs will aid in determining the validity of the accounting for such costs. Some audit questions pertinent to the cost system itself are:

1. Are cost variances brought to the attention of those individuals having authority to incur costs?
2. Is there definite corrective action taken to eliminate unfavorable variances when actual costs differ from standards or budgets?
3. Are costs reflected in their proper category and during the period in which they are incurred?
4. Does cost coding positively identify each item with the group to which it belongs?
5. Does the cost system identify problem areas or unprofitable products?
6. Would the system be more effective and timely if it were automated (using EDP)?
7. Are the general and subsidiary books of account adequate and suited to the company's business?
8. Are the cost records controlled by or periodically reconciled with the general books of account?
9. If standard costs are used, can actual costs be determined through the use of variance accounts or otherwise?
10. Are work orders a part of the accounting and cost system?
11. Does the method of accruing costs and writing off deferred charges result in a reasonably correct application of cost to a designated period?
12. Do accounting procedures provide for segregation of normal expense accruals from accruals for contingencies?

BIBLIOGRAPHY

Accounting Guide for Defense Contracts, Department of Defense, 1967, chaps. 12, 13, 15, and 22.

Armed Services Procurement Regulations (ASPR), Department of Defense.

Defense Procurement Circular #60, "Authorization for Defense Contractors to Use Government-owned Industrial Plant Equipment on Industrial Work," Department of Defense, 1968.

Brink, V. Z., and J. A. Cashin: *Internal Auditing,* New York, The Ronald Press Company, 1958, chap. 18.

Buffa, Elwood S.: *Production-Inventory Systems: Planning and Control,* Homewood, Ill., Richard D. Irwin, Inc., 1968.

Cadmus, Bradford: *Operational Auditing Handbook,* New York, The Institute of Internal Auditors, 1964.

Carson, Gordon B.: *Production Handbook,* 2d ed., New York, The Ronald Press Company, 1958.

Dickey, R. I.: *Accountant's Cost Handbook,* New York, The Ronald Press Company, 1960, Sections 5, 6, 7, 8, and 9.

Heckert, J. B., and J. D. Willson: *Controllership,* New York, The Ronald Press Company, 1963, chaps. 15 and 16.

Moore, Franklin G.: *Production Control,* 2d ed., New York, McGraw-Hill Book Company, 1959.

Gross, Harry: "Make or Buy Decisions in Growing Firms," *The Accounting Review,* October, 1966.

Staab, H. A., C. W. Cissel, and B. J. Neuman: "Operational Audit of a Production Control Function," *The Internal Auditor,* Spring, 1967.

"Scope of Operational Audits," in "The Readers' Problem Clinic," *The Internal Auditor,* January/February, 1968.

King, Barry G.: "Cost-effectiveness Analysis: Implications for Accountants," *The Journal of Accountancy,* March, 1970.

McRae, T. W.: "Opportunity and Incremental Cost: An Attempt to Define in Systems Terms," *The Accounting Review,* April, 1970.

Chapter 34

Marketing

CHARLES FABRIZIO

Manager, Internal Audits, Warner-Lambert Pharmaceutical Company

GENERAL

Definition. Marketing includes those expenses incurred in planning, directing, and controlling all marketing activities. Included are marketing research, product administration, personal selling, warehousing, transportation, etc. For our purposes we are not including any share of general administration or other expenses. Audit activities related to procurement, payroll, and production costs have been discussed in earlier chapters, and the audit activities concerned with administrative and other expenses will be discussed in Chapter 36. The audit activities between these two limits are discussed in this and the following chapter. Even though advertising is a part of marketing, it is somewhat different and more impersonal than most other marketing activities. Furthermore, for companies producing consumer products and with extensive television and radio programs, the advertising costs alone will often be as much or more than all other marketing costs. In most cases advertising activities are separated from other marketing functions. There may be a full advertising department which plans, produces, and places all advertising, or there may be an advertising department, mainly executives, which has responsibility for advertising, but the production and placing of advertising and some of the planning will be performed by an advertising agency. For these reasons it is desirable for auditing purposes to have one chapter concerned with advertising and another chapter concerned with the other marketing costs.

Activities Included. The nature and number of marketing functions assigned to the marketing department vary greatly among firms. Companies producing industrial products usually have a marketing organization substantially different from that of companies producing consumer products. Again, companies producing products for general commercial use may incur substantial warehousing and storage costs which will not be required by those companies making products to special order, which usually do not require much storage. The following marketing activities will be discussed in this chapter.

Marketing administration. All expenses of those responsible for developing, directing, and coordinating all marketing activities

Marketing research. All expenses of those responsible for market forecasting, determining market position and market potential, estimating demand for new products, market surveys, analyses, etc.

Product administration. All expenses relating to the product profit responsibility such as budgeting sales volume and marketing costs, planning sales promotion and its coordination with advertising, package design, price recommendations, factory liaison, and product improvement

Personal selling. All expenses of sales supervision, salesmen, sales offices, sales service, and other expenses related to solicitation of orders

Sales promotion. All expenses incurred, especially with consumer products, to push the sales of established products through various promotion efforts such as coupon promotions and premium awards

Warehousing. All expenses of warehousing, packaging, storing, handling, etc., related to the distribution of goods to customers

Traffic and transportation. All expense of outbound goods to customers such as freight charges and the operation of outward transportation equipment

Form of Organization. As pointed out by Schiff and Mellman,[1] "In recent years there has been a significant change in the attitude of top corporate management regarding the position and responsibility of the marketing department." This changed approach has been called the new marketing concept, the total marketing concept, the integrated organization approach, and various similar terms. In essence it means a change from the traditional approach of marketing as the sales arm of the business to a customer-orientation philosophy. It means discerning what goods are needed in the market and directing all activities with the customer viewpoint in mind.

Many factors have an influence on the particular form of marketing organization selected by a company. According to Arnold Corbin,[2] these factors may be grouped into two broad categories, external factors and internal factors.

External factors. As indicated, the external factors lie outside the company but still may have a strong influence in determining the form of the marketing organization. These external factors are business environment, markets, and customer requirements.

BUSINESS ENVIRONMENT: The type of environment affects not only the marketing objectives and strategy but also the organization for implementing the objectives and strategy. For instance, the marketing organization may vary depending on whether the products are sold to household consumers or to business firms. For consumer items there is a need for preselling in mass markets. In addition there is the struggle for shelf space in retail stores. These factors tend to give emphasis to advertising and sales promotion. However, if the company produces an industrial product, there is a tendency to emphasize such factors as technical service and part replacement. Other important factors may be styling or distribution, as in the automobile industry.

MARKETS: The size, scope, nature, and location of markets have an important impact on the form of marketing organization. If there are relatively few markets, there may already be a market-oriented organization. Where there are a large number of markets, a product-oriented organization is more feasible. If there is widespread distribution, some form of geographical organization may be called for. The number of customers, frequency of purchases, size of order, and degree of service required also affect the form of organization.

CUSTOMER REQUIREMENTS: The requirements and the expectations of the customers are also important factors. With the expansion of discount stores, giant wholesalers, retail chains, and buying syndicates, new pressures are being exerted on the manufacturer. With the general trend toward centralized purchasing, there have been more requests for annual contracts, blanket

[1] Michael Schiff and Martin Mellman, *Financial Management of the Marketing Function*, New York, Financial Executives Institute, 1962, p. 12.

[2] Arnold Corbin, in H. B. Maynard, *Handbook of Business Administration*, New York, McGraw-Hill Book Company, 1967, p. 8-8.

orders, "stockless purchasing," etc. Also the special buying requirements of government agencies sometimes pose unique problems.

Internal factors. The internal factors may be grouped into the following: top management philosophy, product policy, and people.

TOP MANAGEMENT PHILOSOPHY: The philosophy of top management has a very important bearing on marketing organization. If management has maintained tight control and made most of the important decisions, it is not likely that a decentralized setup will be followed. However, in many cases the company has expanded rapidly and the point is reached where one-man control is no longer feasible. Unfortunately many top officers still hold onto too much detail. The auditor often is in a position to recommend certain steps in decentralizing operations. Sometimes this may be at the point where the company is going public. In another case it may be when bank financing is required. Often the top officer is close to retirement age or sometimes even beyond normal retirement age and the lender would like to make sure there is adequate provision for a qualified successor. The auditor may be in a position to urge a management evaluation program.

PRODUCT POLICY: As the products become more diverse, there is a tendency to move away from a functional approach to a product-group approach. This is true where there has been emphasis on new products and new markets.

PEOPLE: People problems are also a factor in marketing organization. Proper decisions cannot be made unless the people concerned are considered, such as the type of employee, number of employees, qualifications, ambitions, and many intangible factors. The organization will have to be geared to a degree to the people who will have to run it. Generally it is better to work toward the improved organization, but without disrupting the present arrangement, depending on the time element involved. Figure 1 is a representative organization chart for a marketing department.[3]

Marketing Concept. The marketing concept is often so important from the viewpoint of auditing that further discussion is warranted. Until the early 1950s very few businesses were marketing- or customer-oriented. Most were production-oriented based on a particular manufacturing skill, especially in earlier days. With the development of radio and later television, the emphasis focused on the ability to mass produce. However, this expansion at first was aimed primarily at how much could be produced, not necessarily at what the market needs were. After World War II there was increased emphasis on marketing by top management. A large number of companies began to place all marketing functions under a single executive, usually a vice-president, and to move toward a "total marketing concept." All aspects of their longer-term as well as day-to-day management decisions are based on a thorough understanding of the market and the customers. "Under the total marketing concept, the corporate objectives are established and the business managed with the sole purpose of making and selling what the customer wants, in the way he wants it, when and where he wants it, and at a price he is willing to pay."[4] The auditor will want to know what comparable changes the company has made in recent years to keep pace. What changes have competitors made in recent years? What is the form of organization used by the leading competitors? How many have converted to the total marketing

[3] As shown in Michael Schiff and Martin Mellman, *Financial Management of the Marketing Function*, New York, Financial Executives Institute, 1962, p. 16.

[4] John R. Sargent, in H. B. Maynard, *Handbook of Business Administration*, New York, McGraw-Hill Book Company, 1967, p. 8-3.

Figure 1 ORGANIZATION CHART OF A REPRESENTATIVE MARKETING DEPARTMENT

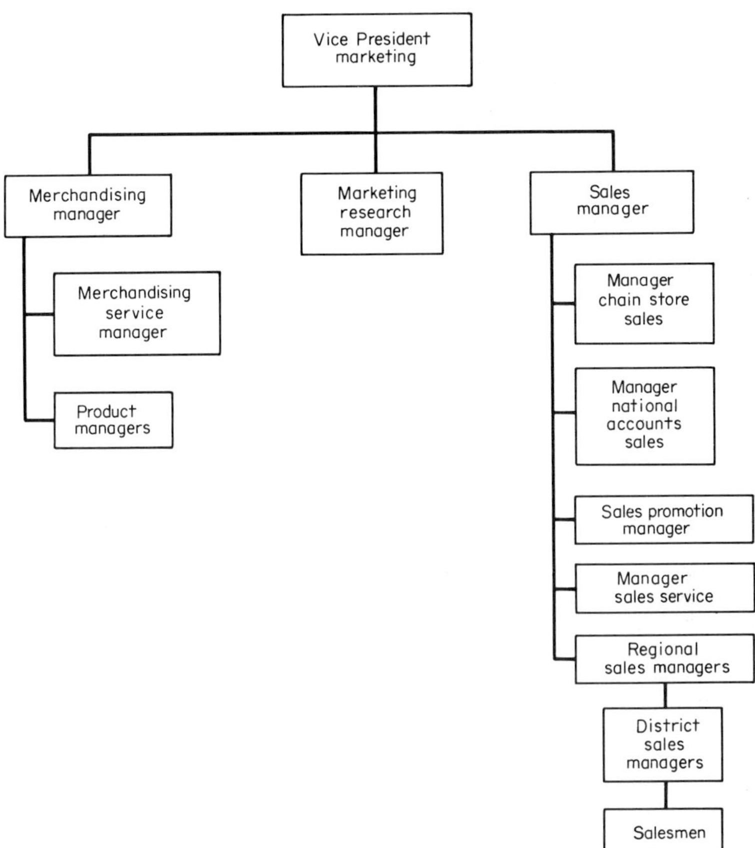

concept? Are there consultants in the field who make surveys of marketing performance and personnel evaluation? What is the cost of such a survey? These and many similar questions should be answered with respect to marketing concepts.

APPROACH TO CONTROLS AND AUDITING

Organization Structure. In the initial stage of the audit the auditor will have to become familiar with the general organization structure of the marketing department. Since much of the auditor's early efforts will be concerned with the operation of internal controls, he will have to review the lines of responsibility; that is, what are the lines of responsibility as practiced as compared with the established lines of responsibility? Recent studies have shown that most companies now tend to place all responsibility for a product under one person, the product manager. Generally he will report to the marketing vice-president and will have the additional title of assistant vice-president. Since the various products of a large company may be directed to widely different market areas—for example, one product may be for men, another for women, etc.—the product unit may operate with a substantial degree of independence. Thus the product manager may be responsible for developing the annual sales estimate, the annual advertising and marketing budget and the expense budget for his unit. Therefore, the auditor will be greatly concerned with reviewing the responsibility and performance of the product manager.

Matching Reports to Objectives. Since there may be two or more product units, the auditor will be interested in determining that the objectives are reasonably set forth and classified and that comparison with results is facilitated. He will want to relate the breakdown of the objectives to the setup of the reports. In many cases the objectives will be developed by the product manager while the operating reports will be designed and presented by the controller. Perhaps the operating reports were not designed on a profit responsibility basis and should be more closely aligned with the objectives.

In addition, the auditor will want to compare the objectives and reports of the various product units. There should be a generally uniform approach and uniform reporting. Perhaps the auditor may select the best features in each product unit report and suggest a more uniform approach embodying the best features of each unit.

From a study of the reports, the auditor may be able to show how unit marketing costs can be reduced by deriving greater volume from the marketing efforts. The auditor will often find resistance to reducing marketing costs but will find ready ears when the approach is developing more marketing effort and results for the same money.

Types of Analyses. The most important purpose of a market analysis is to provide marketing executives with necessary information in the planning, direction, and control of marketing efforts. These analyses will not provide the answers for the product manager's problems but will provide the information for sound decisions.

There are three basic methods of analyzing marketing costs, by:

1. Nature of expense
2. Functional operation
3. Manner of application

Nature of expense. Generally, marketing costs are classified by nature of expense, such as salaries, payroll taxes, supplies, and rent. This is often the first and sometimes the only analysis made. A separate coding may also provide for classifying these expenses according to product units. If individual expenses are compared month by month, it is possible to discern trends in relation to previous months and with the same month last year. In addition, the ratio of the individual expense can be determined and compared with other periods. However, comparison with past periods is often not of too much help, as the previous periods may not be representative. Inefficiencies may be included which would distort the comparison. Generally, a predetermined acceptable amount is preferable. Usually an analysis by type of expense is limited from a control standpoint, since it is difficult to identify the cause of any excess cost. Therefore, this type of analysis is not of much help in directing the marketing effort.

Functional operation. A form of analysis which is particularly useful for control is one by type of functional operation. Since it relates to the functional unit, it is possible to measure individual performance more readily, especially where the organization is large or the operation is complex.

The approach is similar to that used in various types of management studies. The principal steps are as follows:

1. *Identify functions.* Identify functions to be measured, segregating them according to individual responsibility.
2. *Segregate costs.* Classify the functions so that direct costs can be separated from indirect costs. For control, emphasis should be on direct costs.
3. *Establish units of measure.* Determine the unit, such as number of salesman's calls, pounds, or tons.
4. *Calculate unit cost.* Develop statistics by dividing the total controllable functional cost by the number of units.
5. *Promptly correct deviations.* If significant deviations from standards occur, action should be taken promptly to correct the situation.

Manner of application. While it is important that the performance of the individual functions be good in relation to the standard, that alone is not enough. For example, while the cost per salesman's call may be reasonable, it is even more important to measure income or results achieved in relation to effort or cost exerted. This type of analysis shows marketing cost by products, territories, salesmen, customers, channels of distribution, methods of sales, etc. Often these analyses will extend to various kinds of subanalyses such as the breakdown of territorial costs among different products.

To be most effective, the costs may be divided into three groups: direct costs, semidirect costs, and indirect costs. In an analysis by salesman, the salary expense is direct. However, in an analysis by product, this expense might be semidirect or indirect. Indirect expenses, such as the salaries of general marketing executives, must be allocated on a more or less arbitrary basis.

Budgetary Control. Budgeting and control of marketing costs are not satisfactory in many companies. Often the budget is established as a fixed amount based on past experience, and it does not relate the expenditures adequately to the results achieved. For example, an unbudgeted trip may have resulted in a significant amount of new, profitable sales. The basic steps in developing effective marketing budgets and control are as follows:

Obtain background data. Obtain information on the marketing program such as the organization, products, method of operation, and channels of distribution.

Segregate costs. Find out what cost data are needed for planning and control, and arrange for proper segregation of such items.

Cost responsibility. Assign definite cost responsibility, and hold the executive responsible for those which he controls.

Code subclasses. Provide for subclasses of costs for analysis by product, territory, etc.

Make cost and profit analyses. To help in selecting the most profitable channels of marketing, make pertinent cost and profit analyses.

Develop variable and fixed costs. The variable and fixed factors for each cost center should be developed to study the cost behavior.

Develop standards. Standards should be developed as applicable, for example, the cost per salesman's call, number of calls per month, automobile expense per mile.

Accumulate statistical data. The necessary statistical data should be accumulated for use with the standards.

Determine budget presentation. Consult marketing executives and ascertain whether the budget should be presented on the basis of total cost and profit, product profit, territorial profit, etc.

Report on budget performance. Set up reports on a responsibility basis to show budget performance for each cost center.

Cost Standards. While it is difficult to establish standards for some marketing activities, it should be understood that this applies to only a part of the marketing effort. A large part of marketing expenses can be measured as accurately as production costs.

Marketing cost standards may be (1) general standards or (2) individual standards.

General standards. These standards are of a general nature and apply to marketing functions as a whole, or to major divisions. Examples of this type are:

Selling cost as a percent of net sales
Cost per unit sold
Cost per customer account

Individual standards. These standards relate to individual functions or cost items which provide specific control. Examples of this type are:

Shipping cost per order
Warehousing cost per pound
Warehousing cost per shipment
Cost per mile traveled
Entertainment per customer

Audit Approach. As marketing is a specialized function which varies greatly among companies, even those in the same industry, it is essential that the auditor study the operations of the particular company. In the usual financial audit the receiving and disbursement of cash, for example, is much the same for most companies. However, for the auditor to perform a marketing audit he must have an understanding of the marketing organization structure, the marketing policies and procedures, the channels of distribution, and many other matters which are primarily operating functions.

Usually the auditor does not get this type of experience in the regular opinion audit. In some cases the public accounting firm may undertake a management services assignment pertaining to marketing, but generally the marketing audit will be performed by the internal auditor. However, it would be very advantageous for the public accountant in his opinion audit to extend his review of the marketing function, since an additional objective evaluation would be beneficial in such a subjective area.

Operational Audit of Marketing. The operational audit has been described as:

> A comprehensive and constructive examination of an organizational structure of a company, institution, or branch of government, or of any component thereof, such as a division or department, and its plans and objectives, its methods of control, its means of operations, and its use of human and physical facilities.[5]

As has been pointed out in various publications, operational auditing stresses the managerial aspects of auditing. The traditional type of financial auditing undertaken by public accountants to provide information primarily for stockholders is largely protective, to safeguard the assets of the company. The purpose of the operational audit is entirely different. Generally it is for

[5] William P. Leonard, *The Management Audit*, Englewood Cliffs, N.J., Prentice-Hall, Inc., 1963, p. 35.

the purpose of providing information to management that its objectives and goals are being carried out, that the management controls installed for the purpose of increasing efficiency are effective. This is a very important responsibility in a company with many decentralized functions. In such a case the auditor has to become familiar with actual operations and actual problems.

The auditor must be aware of the four basic steps in an operational audit. These are: (1) familiarization, (2) verification, (3) evaluation, and (4) reporting. These basic steps are discussed in some detail in the following chapter.

THE MARKETING DEPARTMENT

Marketing Objectives. The objectives established for the marketing function serve as a basis for measuring the results. Also a well-developed set of objectives aids in coordination of various segments of marketing effort. The objectives should be specific and attainable. Generally, it is preferable to state the objectives in quantifiable terms such as dollars, units, percentages, or time. Thus the objectives may be shown in condensed form as follows:

To increase performance on the following:

1. Return on assets employed to 15 percent
2. Dollar sales by 20 percent
3. Share of the market to 10 percent
4. Sales to consumers by 12 percent
5. Sales to industry by 10 percent

In his review the auditor will obtain a copy of the stated objectives and the bases on which the objectives were determined.

Marketing Department Structure. In his review of the marketing department structure the internal auditor will ask for an organization chart, or if one is not available he will prepare a chart. He will discuss with the head of the department, usually the vice-president—marketing, the general plan of organization. He will also want to know how long the basic plan has been in effect and if any changes are contemplated. If there have been no changes in some time, perhaps the present structure should be modified. The auditor may then review for the past 5 years the type of any new products launched. Into which markets did they fall? What were the changes in sales of present products? Are signs of product obsolescence shown? What new territories have been added? These and similar questions will help the auditor to get an idea whether the department structure has kept pace with the market changes.

In his review the auditor will consider the basic types of structure and how the present structure may be classified. Most company structures will fall into one of the three following groups: functional, product, geographic, or some combination.

Functional. The various functional heads under this arrangement report to the department head. For example, there may be an advertising manager, a sales manager, a marketing research manager, and a product planning manager. Below the sales manager would usually be the regional sales managers, such as those for the eastern region, western region, etc. This is a simple organization structure and is most useful when there are few products and few markets. Also there is centralized authority and responsibility. Top management may feel that specialization by function is desirable.

This type of structure will usually be found in the small or medium-sized company. Very often the general control of the company is heavily centralized. The company may be tightly controlled by a dominant personality who had a large part in building the company. As is so often the case, there may be time for a change, and the auditor should be aware of the alternative structures and the advantages and disadvantages of each type. He should be ready where the situation warrants to make a proposal for change, based on sufficient research and discussions with qualified marketing people.

Product. Where the product lines have expanded in recent years, it may be desirable to consider a structure which provides greater product responsibility. Usually the auditor will be performing an operational-type audit. The first step is familiarization with the operation. This presumably he has accomplished in discussion with the department heads and the general review of operations. Where there are a number of products, it may be desirable to have product groups. These may be related products which may be marketed in one general market such as the consumer market in which there may be joint advertising, promotion, etc. However, sometimes the manufacturing, research, and finance may remain centralized. In some cases the company may be divisionalized with separate divisions for each product or product group. This is looked upon as a separate business and has its own manufacturing, marketing, and finance components, such as for General Motors. Where the size of the operation does not warrant separate divisions, a product sales plan may be indicated. Where separate customer groups must be serviced, such as retail, industrial, and special customers, this plan is a logical approach.

Geographic. In many cases there may be a geographic organization. Often this may be influenced by the location of the manufacturing operations which may be on the West Coast, the Midwest, and the East or the South. Generally, a different product will be produced in the respective locations which may depend on the source of supply.

This particular structure should pose no additional problems for the auditor. Where the situation warrants there may be a regional internal auditor located at the regional office. If so he will usually be able to coordinate his work with that of the independent auditor, particularly with respect to cash and inventories.

Marketing Responsibilities. For purposes of discussion we may follow the general outline presented in Fig. 1. This is a simple presentation which is likely to be more helpful to the auditor in understanding the various relationships than an involved chart.

The chart is representative of the type which would be used by a company marketing consumers' goods direct to retail and through wholesale channels. As can be seen, the basic responsibilities are divided between the merchandising manager and the sales manager. The merchandising manager is responsible for impersonal selling and product administration, while the sales manager is responsible for personal selling. Much of the responsibility for impersonal selling is discussed in Chapter 35, "Advertising," and will not be covered further here. Following are the responsibilities for the principal titles.

Vice-president – marketing. Responsible for developing, managing, and coordinating all marketing activities. These responsibilities include market research, advertising, sales promotion, product administration, and personal selling. He has line authority over the sales manager, merchandising manager, product manager, and marketing research manager.

Sales manager. Responsibility for supervising the sales force through two levels of field administration: the regional manager and the district manager.

He is also responsible for the selection, training, and compensation of the field force. He may be responsible for the selection of the type, size, and location of the channels of distribution. He defines the sales job, prepares the sales program, and evaluates sales performance.

Product manager. In line with the generally greater recognition of the product manager his responsibilities are significant. His assigned duties include profit responsibility, budgeting sales volume, impersonal selling costs, planning advertising and sales promotion, package design, price recommendations, and product improvement.

Marketing research manager. Research responsibilities include forecasting the general sales trend, determining the competitive position of various products, analyzing the size of the market and the territorial sales potential, estimating demand for new products, etc. Often the research department may establish goals and also evaluate performance in relation to the goals. The research manager will often be responsible for long-range planning.

Introduction of New Products. From a marketing point of view there is almost always a need to stimulate the market by offering new products. The need may be to change the quality of the product to meet the customer's demand either by improving quality, at a possible increase in cost, or by reducing price to meet competition, which may require reducing quality so as to reduce the cost of production. There may also be need for diversification, which requires the design of more items or the establishment of new lines of products.

Description of new product. Before a new product is launched, the product manager should prepare a rationale in the form of a marketing decision for top management's approval. It should include among other things a description of the product to be introduced, estimated share of the market, list of competitors' products, 5-year profit and loss projection, selling prices and advertising copy to be tested, location of test markets, timetable for releasing the product nationwide, etc. Also, the market decision proposal should include the cost of the introductory free deals, the description of the various packaging proposals, and the break-even point.

The report should be examined as to the reasonableness and reliability of all the pertinent information included. Also, the potential loss to the company, if the project is abandoned, should be calculated. This should include the write-off of all inventory items as well as the cost of all commitments.

Progress reports. Progress reports should be prepared monthly and reviewed to determine if the new product is achieving the desired results. The actual sales should be compared with those estimated. Variances exceeding pre-established percentages should be explained fully. Office personnel as well as the field force should interrogate consumers as to their likes and dislikes, including whether they expect to become regular users. A calculation should be made to determine whether competition has been affected by the introduction of the new product.

The calculations for determining the selling price should be reviewed, taking into consideration its relationship to the cost of goods sold.

Report of results. When a final decision has been reached, a copy of the product manager's report should be examined:

1. To determine if the decision made was justified
2. To compare the actual with the estimated results
3. To decide if a new 5-year projection should be made, based on actual experience to date

To assess new product line planning properly, many points should be reviewed and evaluated. Any new product development should be oriented to the careful evaluation of market opportunities and potentials. The new products as well as product improvements should keep abreast of or at least equal the pace of competition and also should be ready before the old products become obsolete. The company should have a program for being informed of technological developments which may affect the market potential for present or new products. The profit and growth potential for each product should be evaluated as a basis for future expansion or possible discontinuance. The size, packs, and varieties of each product should be reviewed periodically for anticipated changes. Also, ordering requirements should be evaluated. Each product should be given adequate sales representation and should be moved through the most efficient distribution channel in order to reach all the profitable market centers.

Sales Forecasting. Essentially, a sales estimate provides a frame of reference for future company planning and activity. For it to be accurate, the sales forecast should be expressed in terms of dollar sales and quantities for each specific product. The methods and procedures used in forecasting sales vary greatly from company to company. Sales forecasting is generally started several months before the beginning of the year for which the sales estimate is intended. Since the final sales results of the current year are unknown, it is usually customary to project the sales for the current year. This estimate should serve as the basis for estimating next year's sales.

The current year's sales volume should be examined and evaluated for conditions and situations which tend to distort the results. For example, a strike may have depressed the results or a strike in a competitor's plant may have inflated sales. Introduction of a new product may have increased the sales disproportionately. Accordingly, the current year's sales should be adjusted to put the sales volume on a more realistic basis for estimating next year's sales.

Trend analysis of specific brands, population growth, market survey reports indicating the share of the market, contemplated promotion plans, and prior year's performance all become part of the sales estimate picture. Although some organizations still rely on rough estimates and "crystal ball" gazing as their basis of sales estimating, most companies prefer that the forecasting be based upon facts, prior performance, statistical techniques, market surveys, common sense, and good judgment.

Since the whole profit plan including the cash forecasts is based upon a reasonable accuracy of the total sales estimate, it is very important to discover as soon as possible when actual sales may differ considerably from the sales estimate. Constant monitoring is required in order to determine if the sales variances indicate that a trend is developing that will deviate significantly from the sales estimate.

Controls for Forecasting. The sales forecasting controls should be reviewed to determine:

1. Are they prepared by the product or brand managers? Who approves the final sales estimate?
2. What is their status in the marketing organization? What authority do they have as to making decisions concerning the sales forecasts?
3. What methods and techniques are utilized, for example, market survey reports, statistical techniques, population growth factors, prior year's results, analysis of economic conditions?

4. Are the forecasts used by the manufacturing department for production planning? Are the inventory levels adjusted to reflect the sales estimate? Are personnel requirements adequate to cover the sales forecast? What effect does the sales forecast have on the advertising commitments?

The basic methods and procedures used in estimating should be reviewed to determine the following:

1. Are the various available sources of information used in the preparation of the reports?
2. Are the time and expense expended in gathering the information warranted by the value of the information? Could the data have been assembled by other means?
3. Has consideration been given to having the forecasts prepared on the computer?
4. Are the sales estimates revised too often or not enough? What are the reasons requiring revisions?

Audit of Forecasting

1. Obtain the required information and make reviews as prescribed. Obtain description of sales forecasting, such as
   a. Method of preparation
   b. Sources of information used
   c. Compilation of data
2. Examine sales forecasting procedures to determine
   a. Organization
   b. Responsibility
   c. Methods and techniques
   d. Distribution
   e. Uses of the forecast
   f. Frequency of revision
3. Request organization charts for
   a. Departments preparing forecasts
   b. Departments using forecasts
4. Prepare horizontal flow charts to determine whether
   a. Sequences can be improved
   b. Steps can be eliminated
5. Obtain copies of reports and forecasts to determine
   a. Who uses the information
   b. If information is duplicated in other reports
   c. The timeliness of reports
   d. If significant variances between actual and estimated are adequately explained
   e. If recipients of reports are satisfied with contents

SALES PROMOTION

General. Under the heading of sales promotion is a wide range of activities which have the purpose of inducing customers to buy the company products.

The control and audit procedures related to sales promotion are similar in general to those pertaining to other procurement. Certain features of sales promotion require special controls and audit procedures. Generally each promotion is described in detail in a specific bulletin or proposal which is distributed to field locations and affected personnel. These bulletins or proposals generally contain the following information:

1. The promotion number
2. The geographic area in which the promotion is to be offered
3. The type of promotion
4. The dates of the promotion
5. The specifications of the promotion, i.e., how the allowance is earned, how it is calculated, etc.
6. Other details pertinent to that particular promotion such as special instructions for writing orders, procedures for making payments to dealers, and special advertising to be used in conjunction with the promotion

Types of Sales Promotions. Following are typical types of sales promotions. It is likely that not all the types listed below will be used in a particular company under audit.

Free products. A sales campaign may offer free products to distributors in a certain ratio. For instance, there may be an offer of one free item for each ten purchased.

Coupons. Frequently coupons or certificates are given having a cash value toward the retail price of a specified company product.

Price reductions. Price reductions provide credit for products distributed during the period of the campaign.

Advertising material. Various kinds of sales material are imprinted with the dealer's name and provided to him at no charge.

The Sales Promotion Program. Various methods are used to reimburse or reward the participating customers, who may be wholesalers, retailers, or the ultimate consumer. The promotions often are of the type requiring the wholesaler or retailer to undertake special selling efforts.

These promotion allowances are generally settled by one of three methods: (1) an adjustment stated on the face of the invoice (off-invoice allowances), (2) direct payment or crediting the customer's account, or (3) issuance of a premium (merchandise for the personal use of the customer).

Promotion Materials. The acquisition, inventory, and shipment problems relating to promotion materials are similar, in general, to the handling of other materials. The requirement for properly authorized documents for purchases, shipments, and billings is just as pertinent here as for other materials. Exceptions to the general procedures will be discussed below.

Purchases. The purchasing procedures for promotion materials differ from other purchases in that the selection of the vendor may be based on the total package of design, price, and production capability. Often the vendors will be provided with only general specifications, and they will be asked to suggest design, typography, and other features to make their proposal distinctive. Thus the final decision in awarding the contract will not necessarily be made on the basis of the lowest price, since a higher price may be justified for an item with greater appeal.

From an audit standpoint, when orders are placed at a higher price, based on claimed advantages, the auditor should determine that the higher price was properly authorized. Where material is purchased by an agency, the auditor should review the agency procedures to assure that company interests are protected.

Shipments. Very often promotional materials are shipped directly from the supplier to the distributor or user so that the materials will be available simultaneously in various locations at the start of a campaign. When such a shipment is made directly, the auditor should request that a receiving report be prepared and copies made available for comparison with the supplier's shipping reports. In many cases circulars or catalogs are distributed without charge by other than company employees. In most such instances there will be little incentive for economical handling. The auditor should review the storage and shipping controls with a view to minimizing wastage.

Billing. In many cases promotion materials are billed to a distributor on a basis on which he shares part of the cost. Generally the charge will cover only the imprinting of the distributor's name and the mailing cost. For example, a magazine which may have an article describing the company's products may be so distributed. The auditor in any case should determine that adequate billing and collection procedures are maintained. As with any other auditing review the auditor will compare actual results with expected results. One type of undertaking may be the printing of a book promoting sales of a company's products which may be sold to consumers at cost. The auditor may make an examination on a project basis; that is, at the completion of a particular project he may verify the cost in relation to the claims made to obtain authorization for the promotion.

Special materials. In most cases special promotion materials are produced in relatively small quantity with a resultant high unit cost. For example, a trade show exhibit or a film may cost thousands of dollars. Here again the auditor will examine the final cost in relation to the authorized cost. He must pay special attention to charges such as overtime and alterations and determine that all additions and revisions were properly authorized. In some cases the final cost may be greater than was originally expected and that would have originally been approved by management. The auditor will want to determine the cause of the overrun. Did it result from poor estimating; that is, were essential items which should have been included left out? Was any omission deliberate? Why were revisions necessary? Could such changes be anticipated through better planning? Can a recurrence be prevented? These and many similar questions could be asked by the auditor and the answers given in his report.

Distributors. Many types of plans are used to influence the distributor or other large-quantity buyers to handle more of the company's products.

Some of the allowances and credits made to the distributor under these plans were described earlier in the chapter.

Legal considerations. When price concessions or special awards are given, the general plan should be approved by the company legal department. Most large companies will issue policy bulletins as a guide to legal matters. Special attention should be given to assure that price reductions are applicable on an equal basis to all distributors. If this is not done, the company may be subject to legal action for discriminatory pricing practices. The auditor should review the various pricing concessions and determine that proper legal approval has been obtained for each. He should watch particularly for any cases where a project was not submitted for legal review because it was felt that it was covered by a legal opinion on a previous project. The auditor should not accept a layman's opinion on legal matters and should ask for written approval from the legal department.

Extra goods or free goods. Generally extra goods or free goods will be given in proportion to purchases during the period of offer. The purpose is to overload the distributor so that he will exert extra selling effort. Also it will save storage cost for the manufacturer.

The auditor should determine that the shipments made and free goods given are in accordance with the terms of the deal. He will want to make sure that any sales made for later delivery or other variations are valid. He may wish to get an interpretation of the provisions from authorized officers where the amounts are material. He should also review the company policy for items returned after expiration of the deal.

Special prices. In many cases a special price or discount may be given for sales during the promotion period. Usually the distributor would be credited at the allowance rate, e.g., 10 cents a package for all packages on hand at the beginning of the period. He would also be credited at 10 cents a package for all shipments made to him during the promotion period. He would be charged for all packages on hand at the end of the period. Since such an arrangement is based on accurate reporting by the distributor or the salesman and with a large number of distributors involved, there is a possibility of abuse but mostly on a small scale. Where the customer is to report inventories, the form should include a certification by the customer as to the correctness of the inventories. The auditor should review the terms of the promotion and visit a few distributors to review their procedures. Where a material amount of allowance is involved, the auditor may wish to review the computations.

Premiums, samples, coupons, contests (distributors). Various other types of plans are used to stimulate distributor sales, such as items given out by salesmen, free samples of company products, and various types of contests. The auditor's concern is largely to determine that the premiums or samples are properly controlled, that safeguards are provided to prevent abuses. For example, control should be exerted over free samples to determine that the amount issued is reasonable with respect to the number of customers. The items should be safeguarded from the time they are received until the time given to the salesmen. In the case of contests the auditor should review the terms to determine that reasonable safeguards are applied in the selection of the winner. He should make sure that he applies comparable auditing procedures to such contests as he does in all other cases. He should not be duped into merely opening an envelope or counting the results. He should verify the procedures in recording the points or votes, test some of the items for validity, and generally control the process as he would in similar circumstances in other phases of auditing.

Retail Customers. Various types of incentives are offered to prospective customers. Generally the purpose is to obtain new customers for the product. Often the promotion may be for the purpose of introducing a new product.

Legal considerations. Many states have restrictions against premiums, samples, or contests. The legal aspects of all such promotions should be reviewed by the legal department. The auditor should be aware of the various states and countries which restrict such promotions. During the course of his marketing audit he should determine that promotions are not allowed to move into restricted areas either inadvertently or advertently.

Premiums, samples, coupons, stamps, contests (retail customers). Various types of premiums, samples, coupons, stamps, and contests are used to stimulate sales.

Consumer promotions have reached large proportions in recent years, and we now see trading stamps being used at food stores, gasoline stations, discount stores, and many other outlets. In addition gasoline stations have used a wide variety of contests or games to increase consumer sales. Congressional hearings have disclosed abuses where the gasoline station operator was able to determine the winning tickets ahead of time.

The auditing aspects of these promotions vary with the particular type. In the case of premiums the usual plan is to have the offer pay for itself; that is, the cash sent in covers the costs of the premium and its handling. In effect the customer may get the premium at wholesale cost rather than retail price. Since a very large volume may be involved on attractive premiums, the usual practice is to have an outside agency handle premium orders. In fact many firms specialize in handling such promotions. The auditor will want to make sure that it is a reputable firm. He will also study the agreement carefully and raise questions on any matters which need clarification. He should review all complaints about nonreceipt of premiums, delays, and other problems involved in the promotion.

In the case of free samples the auditor will want to determine that unauthorized use or misappropriations by company employees are minimized. Large mailing of samples is usually handled by outside mailing agencies. Here the auditor will want to ascertain the reliability of the agency and the controls used in the mailing and handling of samples.

In the instance of coupons the employees or outside agencies should not make the coupon distribution. Coupons should be canceled immediately upon redemption. The ratio of redemption to sales of the product should be developed in total and for individual outlets.

Where contests are involved, the receipt of entries and the judging are usually handled by an outside agency because of the large volume involved. This method minimizes fraud by company employees in selecting the winners. The auditor will carefully examine the agreement with the outside agency and the services and charges to be made. Depending on the materiality of the amounts, he may wish to visit the office of the agency and review its procedures in handling the contest. He will also be concerned with the controls over the purchase and distribution of merchandise prizes.

Specific auditing procedures concerning various kinds of sales promotion plans are provided later in the chapter.

General Controls. In his review of controls the auditor will determine that there is an adequate control system and that the system is operating effectively. In addition to the specific controls and the control system there are general controls that apply to all sales promotion activities that should be considered by the auditor. He should determine that such general controls are in effect and should make adequate tests of these controls. The principal general controls are (1) responsibility, (2) coordination, (3) reporting, and (4) reviewing.

Responsibility. For each sales promotion campaign or activity responsibility should be definitely fixed. Thus a specific section or unit of the advertising department may be charged with responsibility for a particular campaign.

Coordination. A most important aspect of any sales promotion activity is coordination with related functions such as advertising, sales, and production. Unless coordination is achieved, there may be a loss of goodwill of distributors and consumers if merchandise is not available when coupons or stamps are presented for redemption.

Reporting. Progress reports are an integral part of a successful campaign. Generally there will be reports of costs to date and expected additional amounts. Increased sales should be related to costs. The results may be shown by increased sales over previous periods, new accounts opened, number of inquiries, etc.

Reviewing. Generally the auditor should review the problems involved in controlling sales activities. Usually he can become familiar with this aspect by accompanying a sales representative on visits to distributors and customers and reviewing their procedures.

Audit Objectives. In his examination the auditor will be concerned with (1) the audit objectives and (2) the audit program. Following are objectives and audit programs adapted from those used by a company with a large number of consumer products. The objectives and audit programs will differ by companies, but the following material should provide valuable help in developing a program for any company.

In connection with audit objectives the auditor's responsibilities will be to:

1. Review the system of internal control over expenditures to assure that the promotion specifications and timing are adhered to and that performance is documented and accurate. Particular attention should be given to:
   a. Promotion payments made to wholesalers who control certain retailers and who have given *written* notification that the wholesaler should receive the promotion payments.
   b. Bulletin specifications, for example, whether payment is to be based on orders received or orders shipped. This is important at the end of the promotion in determining whether the order was on hand or the shipment was made on or before the last day of the promotion period.
   c. Back orders resulting from product shortages should be controlled and the customer given an appropriate credit even though the promotion may have expired.
   d. Control records should be maintained to show payments to individual customers, particularly wholesalers and jobbers, so that duplicate payments are not made.
2. Verify the propriety of promotional expenses by establishing that expenditures are in compliance with promotional bulletins and are properly approved and adequately supported and that expenditures are classified and costed as prescribed.

Audit Program. The specific steps in an audit program will vary considerably among companies. However, the following programs are representative and should be helpful in developing comparable programs in other companies. The programs shown are for (1) headquarters and (2) company plants.

Headquarters. Following is a program for the examination of controls and promotion expenses at corporate and division headquarters.

1. Read for reference and background information:
   a. The chart of accounts
   b. The corporate accounting manual
   c. Promotion bulletins
2. At headquarters prepare a schedule of promotion costs incurred during the period being audited. Select promotions to be verified; coordinate work with any field audit in progress, particularly with respect to a specific promotion.
3. Obtain a copy of the following for each promotion to be audited:
   a. Original budget proposal
   b. Promotion bulletin
   c. Purchase orders for materials used in the promotion, such as coupons, premiums, samples, mailing lists, and packaging material
   d. Agreements with vendors supplying services such as printers, mailing houses, co-packers, and storage warehouses

e. Reports of costs and performance

4. List the names and functions of personnel who might be contacted during the audit.

5. Review selected promotion bulletins for approval by the law department for clarity of specifications, terms, and promptness of notification to the field.

6. Review the file of interpretations of promotion bulletin wording by division management.

7. Review the coordination of advertising with the timing of the promotion. The advertising should be placed in the districts just prior to or during the period of the promotion.

8. Determine the extent to which promotions are reviewed by the headquarters accounting department. Such a review should be in terms of control requirements as well as expense provision needs.

9. Ascertain the amount of promotion expense allocated for each of the promotions to be audited. In addition to reviewing the total amount, examine the basis of allocation and the amount allocated to each district.

10. Determine that expenses are correctly classified as to trade and consumer promotions and accumulated by promotion number and proper account.

11. Compare the cost of the promotions selected with similar other offers as to actual to-date and projected costs.

12. Verify the accuracy of data used to evaluate costs as they are incurred, such as a sales realization test.

13. Determine that good purchasing practices are followed in obtaining materials or services connected with the promotions selected, for example that:

a. Bids were obtained from vendors.

b. Purchases by the marketing department were adequately controlled.

c. Vendors' financial responsibility was investigated or considered before the contract was drawn.

14. Control practices of vendors supplying or mailing coupons and/or premiums were investigated prior to selection.

15. Determine the adequacy of all contracts, agreements, or purchase orders as to cost, timing, billing, reporting, insurance coverage, audit clause, and termination.

16. Determine that copies of purchase orders are received and reviewed by the accounting department.

17. Vouch disbursements to vendors noting:

a. Payments to coupon printer or premium vendor were made after comparison of signed bill of lading from printer with signed receiving report from the mailer or plant.

b. Coupon printer overrun was in accordance with the purchase order or agreement.

c. Notarized statement is on hand signed by an official of the printing company stating that the printing plates and negatives were destroyed.

18. Determine that coupons have been reviewed and cleared by the law department.

19. Determine that inventory records of coupons and premiums are in enough detail to control the movement; also, that inventory reports from outside vendors or warehouses are submitted frequently and reconciled with the inventory records.

20. Determine that adequate and timely reports are received from the outside mailer of coupons, specifically that:

a. The bulk mailing permit is taken out with the post office in the name of the company.
b. The amount of postage advances made to postmaster and monthly report of postage on hand are as submitted by the post office.
c. Subsidiary records are kept of postage advanced and used, and the balance on hand.
d. If the mailer maintains a validated permit (signature and post office stamp) "Statements of Mailing Matter with Permit Imprint" are submitted to support reported quantities mailed and postage used.

21. Review makeup of mailing lists as to:
a. Requirements of promotion.
b. Number of names required. This should be checked against the total mailings postage paid.
c. How list was compiled and kept current.
d. If company personnel are included on the lists so as to test the performance of the mailer.

22. Determine that controls over returned mail were adequate, for example:
a. That the contract or purchase order includes a provision for returned mail guarantee.
b. If returns were handled by the mailer, that a review was made by the company to ascertain that the returns were in connection with the promotion.
c. Periodic reports on returns were issued by the mailer.
d. That, at the end of the promotion, a certificate of destruction was received from the mailer for returns destroyed.

23. Test paid checks for compliance with the promotion as to dates, payee, and endorsements. The dates should coincide with the promotion period; the payee should not be an individual but a store or wholesaler, and endorsements should agree with the payee and be paid within a reasonable time of the date of preparation. When testing checks, also review reconciliation of the bank account for old outstanding checks.

Company plants. The following program is designed to test the controls over coupons or premiums at company plants. Examine controls over coupons or premiums to be inserted in or made a part of the package of finished product as follows:

1. Determine that deliveries of coupons or premiums have been counted as received, and signed receiving reports have been prepared.
2. Verify that the custodian of coupons or premiums is independent of the packing department, and that coupons are issued only on the basis of approved requisitions and signed receipts.
3. Determine that storage facilities provide adequate safeguards such as restricting unauthorized personnel access to coupons or premiums.
4. Verify that unused coupons are destroyed in the presence of another responsible employee and a signed statement to this effect prepared.
5. Determine that surplus coupons or premiums are controlled.
6. Review controls exercised in the packing department to safeguard coupons or premiums in their possession.
7. Examine the accounting for coupons or premiums, taking into consideration the:
a. Maintenance of perpetual inventory records
b. Basis for computing usage

c. Frequency of physical counts and investigation of any differences between counts and records

DIRECT SELLING

Before the consumer makes his decision to purchase, a favorable climate must be developed. This is done through direct selling. The important stage in direct selling is the retail level. Thus, the salesman concentrates much of his time at this level. It is here that a selling and merchandising job well done earns important rewards.

Salesman's Stock. There are quite a few elements that make up "detail work." The first requirement is that the salesman should carry enough of each of the company's products to transact business until the supply can be replenished. The salesman obtains stock through shipments from the company which are charged to him at the regular price. Cash payments for such stock are not acceptable—orders must be submitted crediting the salesman's account and charging a direct customer's account, thereby creating a revolving stock situation. It is desirable for each salesman to have an amount of cash and stock on hand proportionate to the size of his territory.

The salesman keeps a daily record of his activities, including other information the company may need. He is responsible for accounting for the balance in his stock account with either company products, cash, or a combination of both items.

The manager verifies the stock and funds each time he works with the salesman. In order to facilitate checking, the salesman's records must be up to date.

Review of Sales Activities. From time to time an audit is made of each salesman's account in somewhat the following manner:

1. From salesmen's statements in the office, make copies of those of the salesmen to be audited.
2. Arrange to have the district manager meet the auditor and accompany him to a meeting with the salesman to be audited.
3. The following examination should be made of the salesman's records.
   a. Count the funds belonging to the company.
   b. Make a physical count of the stock in the salesman's possession.
   c. Inspect the addresses on the cartons to determine the original consignee.
   d. Extend the value of the stock at standard company prices.
4. Compute the amount to be accounted for at the time of the audit, which should be compared with the total value of stock and cash on hand. The difference, "shortage or overage," should be indicated.
5. Determine the condition of the salesman's automobile, and submit any prescribed report.
6. Prepare a "flash" report giving the following information:
   a. Preliminary results of the verification
   b. Handling and condition of the salesman's records
   c. Attitude of the salesman
   d. Condition of stock, etc.
   e. Other pertinent comments
7. Mail confirmations to accounts listed by the salesman to verify (*a*) validity of the transactions, (*b*) whether salesman owes them stock or cash, and (*c*) validity of stock on loan.

Verify the accuracy of salesmen's reports by testing recent reports in the office.

1. Make on-the-spot visits to the stores listed in reports selected, and verify that:
   - *a.* The salesman actually visited the store.
   - *b.* The transactions took place.
   - *c.* The stock display is adequate.
2. Make sure that the salesmen are reimbursed for out-of-pocket expenses while on company business. Receipts are required for transportation, lodging, automobile expenses, and all items exceeding $25. Select a sample of expense vouchers and determine that:
   - *a.* Meal expenses are in agreement with established allowances.
   - *b.* Receipts agree with the amounts indicated on the voucher.
   - *c.* Receipts have not been altered.
   - *d.* Expenses are reasonable.

Audit Objectives. Following are the selling expense objectives as developed in one company. There may be wide differences because of varying selling organizations, selling policies, etc.

1. To determine the propriety of the costs of inducing, maintaining, or increasing customer acceptance and purchase of the product, excluding advertising costs.
2. To determine the adequacy of control over selling expense.
3. To determine the reasonableness of methods in use for allocating selling expense to products for the purpose of calculating product profitability.

Audit Program. Select one month for detailed audit (same month as that used in connection with other profit and loss accounts).

1. Prepare a schedule showing the amounts charged to this account for the month and year to date, by centers of responsibility and by natural expense.
2. By reference to invoices, expense statements, and other documents, vouch the more significant items in each category. Show the percentage vouched and explain in general terms the type of expenditures.
3. Examine the schedule prepared for item 1 above, and compare the monthly charge with the year-to-date charge. Determine any unusual fluctuations. Investigate and explain such fluctuations.
4. Obtain or prepare product profit and loss summaries. Consider the reasonableness of the basis used for distributing selling expenses to products.
5. Compare selling expense percentage with net sales by products to total selling expense percentage for the division.
6. Describe the method used to control selling expenses, such as regional expense breakdowns and monthly budget comparisons. Comment on the adequacy of this method.

OTHER MARKETING ACTIVITIES

There are a number of different kinds of expenses which may be included in the marketing group. In most cases the items other than advertising will be included under a title such as selling expense or distribution expense. It is possible that some marketing research expenses may be included in advertising or in a research and development category. In any case the auditor will review all aspects of marketing operations when he is conducting a marketing audit. It is not practical to attempt here to cover all the types of items which may be included. Following are audit procedures relating to certain specialized marketing areas. These are traffic, warehousing, and transportation.

Traffic. In a company which maintains a corporate traffic department the auditor will review the objectives and organization of the traffic function itself in addition to reviewing the operations of that department.

The corporate traffic department. The auditor will review the following operations of the corporate traffic department:

INTERNAL CONTROLS: The internal controls relating to the traffic function are as follows:

1. Is the latest organization chart available?
2. Are the duties of each employee fixed as to responsibility?
3. Are traffic manuals in use?
4. Does the department perform internal audit functions?
5. Are traffic employees' duties rotated?
6. Are all employees required to take vacations?
7. Are the traffic records adequate for the business?
8. Is adequate control exercised over field locations?
9. Are expenses and costs under budgetary control?
10. Are internal reports to management adequate to bring out abnormal transactions?
11. Is any employee associated (work or family) with an organization with which the traffic department does business?
    a. Are transactions with these enterprises routine?
    b. Are duties of the employee such that irregular transactions are improbable?

AUDIT PROGRAM: Following are the audit procedures applicable to the corporate traffic department:

1. Obtain or prepare a copy of the organization chart for the department.
2. Prepare a list of personnel together with a brief description of the duties of each.
3. Review the authorities and responsibilities of the department and determine that they are in writing and are clearly defined.
4. Prepare a listing of the major functions handled in the department.
5. Determine the method of selecting carriers.
6. Review the procedures in effect for classifying commodities.
7. Determine the extent to which traffic participates in negotiations with carriers to obtain revised classifications or reductions in rates.
8. Review contracts or lease agreements, if any.
9. Test freight rates previously approved by referring to published tariffs.
10. Determine procedures in effect to ensure compliance with published tariff regulations.
11. Review the selections and approval of public warehouses.
12. Examine procedures for utilization of transit privileges.
13. Investigate arrangements for leasing of special transportation equipment.
14. Review side-track agreements.
15. Review claims procedure.
16. Review system of verification of freight charges.
17. Review records retained by traffic for adequacy and necessity.

The plant traffic department. The auditor will review the following operations of the plant traffic department:

OBJECTIVES OF TRAFFIC AUDIT: The principal objectives of the plant traffic audit:

1. To determine that traffic procedures followed are in accordance with those prescribed by the corporate traffic department.
2. To ascertain by tests that the traffic function for the period under review has been properly executed.
3. To determine that new procedures are received promptly.

AUDIT PROGRAM: The following audit procedures relate to traffic operations at company plants:

1. *The traffic manual.* Examine the traffic manual and determine:
   a. What is its purpose?
   b. Are routings followed?
   c. Does the manual cover needs?
   d. Are changes required?
   e. Are routings used which are not included in the manual? Have they been approved by corporate traffic?
2. *Contract carrier operation.* Discuss with appropriate personnel the carrier operation and:
   a. Obtain copies of contracts for review by corporate traffic and legal departments.
   b. Determine if corporate traffic has approved or reviewed all contracts prior to their execution.
3. *Private trucking.* Review the extent of private trucking and determine:
   a. How is it used? Is special-purpose equipment required?
   b. Has a list and description of owned trucks been obtained for review of insurance coverage?
   c. Are log books or maintenance records kept?
   d. Are ICC safety and hours of service regulations being complied with?
4. *Transit.* Review transit procedure and determine:
   a. Is the application of transit being properly made?
   b. Are accurate records being maintained?
   c. Is there a possible need for additional transit? Could more raw material be received by rail to take advantage of transit on subsequent outbound shipments?
5. *Other agreements.* Has the plant entered into the following types or any other agreements with carriers: (*a*) average demurrage, (*b*) weight, (*c*) side track? Were the agreements properly approved? Are the terms of the agreements being followed?
6. *Traffic routing and procedures.* Test traffic routing and comment on the following aspects:
   a. Consolidation of shipments
   b. Leader-trailer cars
   c. Payment of freight bills within ICC regulations
   d. Ordering cars and trucks
   e. Disposition of overs, shorts, damage, and salvage
   f. Reporting and coordination with corporate traffic
   g. Cost savings in possible consolidation of area traffic functions

Warehousing. The auditor will review the following warehousing operations:

Objectives of a warehousing audit. Review the objectives and determine that:

1. Monthly charges for warehousing of finished goods are proper and relate reasonably to the goods actually stored during the month.
2. Warehousing charges are held to a minimum.

Audit program. The following audit procedures are to be applied:

1. Inquire into the method of calculating the monthly charge to this account. Describe the method.
2. Check the propriety of the calculation for one or two months, and trace the charge into the account.
3. If portions of the storage costs are deferred, prepare a schedule showing the charges to the expense account and the charges to the prepaid account each month over a 10- to 12-month period. If monthly charges to both are not significant, and expensing the charges as received would not materially distort the monthly operating results, consider suggesting the abandonment of the prepaid storage account.
4. Examine a representative number of storage invoices:
   a. By reference to inventory records determine that the goods actually were stored during the period at the named location.
   b. By reference to signed warehouse contracts make sure that charges agree.
5. If a prepaid storage account is used, reconcile the charges to the expense, with the credits to the prepaid account.
6. Where storage charges on finished goods are received from distribution-sales services, examine the charges for at least 3 months, and trace to the general ledger.
7. Inquire into the use of local warehouse facilities. If any are used, ascertain by reference to correspondence, contracts, and credit reports that the warehouse's financial worth, insurance coverage, and certified inventory reports are adequate and current.
8. Question the use of the particular warehouse. Would the rent, taxes, and other costs be less in another local warehouse? Would taxes be less in a suitable location in a nearby state?

Transportation. The auditor will review the following transportation functions:

Objectives of a transportation audit. Review the objectives to determine that:

1. The amounts charged to operations each month were proper and relate to the goods moved in that month.
2. The amounts deferred on the balance sheet relate to the accumulated transportation costs of goods not yet delivered to customers.

Audit program. The following audit procedures are to be applied:

1. Describe the system used to calculate the amount of expense chargeable each month.
2. Determine the reasonableness of the rate used. Describe the method of arriving at rates for:
   a. Goods delivered to customers
   b. Goods not yet delivered on which transportation has accrued
3. Determine the reasonableness of the charge by applying rates used for item *a* above to the quantity of goods delivered in a selected month (preferably the latest).
4. Determine the reasonableness of the balance in the "prepaid transpor-

tation" account by application of rates used for item *b* above to the quantity of goods in field storage.

5. Select a representative sample of charges to the prepaid account. By reference to supporting invoices, determine the propriety of the charges.

6. Where transportation charges on finished goods are received through distribution-sales services, check the source documents to the general ledger for at least 3 months.

7. In examining freight invoices, watch for demurrage charges on goods shipped to customers. If any are found, inquire into the reason why they were not charged to customers.

BIBLIOGRAPHY

A Survey of Marketing Research, American Marketing Association, Chicago, 1963.

Marketing Series No. 81, *Essentials of Successful Sales Management,* American Management Association, New York, 1951.

Research Report No. 13, *Internal Audit and Control of Advertising and Sales Promotion,* The Institute of Internal Auditors, New York, 1963.

Research Report No. 24, *Product Costs for Pricing Purposes,* National Association of Accountants, New York, 1954.

Research Reports Nos. 25–27, *Cost Control for Marketing Operations,* National Association of Accountants, New York, 1954.

Cadmus, Bradford: "Advertising and Sales Promotion," *Operational Auditing Handbook,* New York, The Institute of Internal Auditors, 1964.

Frey, Albert Wesley: *Marketing Handbook,* New York, The Ronald Press Company, 1965.

Hille, Robert: "Distribution Methods and Costs," *Handbook of Business Administration,* New York, McGraw-Hill Book Company, 1967.

Lazo, Hector, and Arnold Corbin: "Organizing for Marketing," *Management in Marketing,* New York, McGraw-Hill Book Company, 1961.

Mainwaring, Thomas L.: "The Distribution Function," *Operational Auditing for Management Control,* New York, American Management Association, 1969.

Schiff, Michael, and Martin Mellman: *Financial Management of the Marketing Function,* New York, Financial Executives Institute, 1962.

Scher, Irving: "An Auditor's Introduction to the Antitrust Laws," *The Internal Auditor,* Winter, 1966.

Lewis, Ronald J.: "Strengthening Control of Physical Distribution Costs," *Management Services,* January–February, 1968.

Whittaker, C. M.: "Auditing Sales Forecasting—Why Not?" *The Internal Auditor,* January/February, 1968.

Smith, William F.: "An Audit of the Marketing Function—Creativity Revisited," *The Internal Auditor,* July/August, 1970.

Chapter 35

Advertising

E. GEORGE HAKULA

General Auditor, General Foods Corporation

GENERAL

Introduction. Generally, every company incurs some advertising expense, but for some companies and especially those engaged in the sale of consumer-type products, the cost of advertising represents one of the most significant elements of expense beyond production costs. Multi-million-dollar advertising budgets are more the case than the exception for most consumer-product-orientated companies of any significance. Indeed, the annual cost of advertising may, in some cases, exceed the cost of production.

Advertising in the broad sense covers a wide range of activities. Daily we are exposed, if not deluged, with advertising on television, in the newspapers, and on the radio. But what we see and hear in the form of advertising is the end product of a series of activities ranging from program production to the preparation of commercials or hard-copy advertisements. Expenditures are made for such diverse activities as story and script writing, acting and theatrical directing, photography, and writing the commercial message, which may include catchy slogans and jingles. Not to be overlooked are time and space charges.

Advertising is a unique type of expense in that it is difficult to measure accurately what is achieved (in terms of added sales and profits). It is also very difficult to define the essentials of good advertising, and presently there is no reliable way of measuring quantitatively how good or bad advertising is. Even advertising expenditures cannot, for the most part, be evaluated in terms of ordinary procurement criteria.

This is a broad generalization, for while the results of mass advertising are exceptionally difficult to relate to changes in sales volumes, the results of other types of advertising, such as a direct-mail campaign or a newspaper advertisement for a specific product, can be determined with a considerable degree of accuracy.

With respect to advertising expenditures, those that relate to creative effort are more difficult to evaluate objectively. However, some assurance of reasonableness can be had for most other types of advertising costs. For example, a high degree of certainty is possible for such expenditures as media charges, which can be verified to established tariffs or rate cards.

Furthermore, advertising activities can also be subject to organizational controls such as objectives, procedures, and internal accounting controls. Thus, in spite of the complexity and vagaries of advertising, the auditor decidedly has a role to play, albeit one requiring him to have an understanding of the essentials of marketing strategy as well as a high degree of resourcefulness. An auditor's dispassionate probe of this activity is indispensable when consideration is given to the huge outlays of money usually involved, which are expended in an environment where change and uncertainty are more the rule than the exception.

Advertising—A Function of Marketing. Marketing may be defined broadly as including all the activities required to move the product from the point of manufacture, or purchase in a nonmanufacturing concern, into the hands of or control of the consumer, i.e., selling the product. So defined, marketing consists of advertising, sales promotions, selling, shipping, warehousing, and storage.

Advertising is the important element of the marketing effort of companies which depend on the consumer market, for advertising is the means for creating an awareness of the company's products and services. The other elements of selling or marketing effort are directed toward more specific action, the purchase of the product. These functions, which are also important to a company's success and thus deserve the attention of the auditor, are discussed in Chapter 34.

Advertising—Its Place in the Company. The position of the advertising department in a company's organizational structure depends largely on the degree of importance that the marketing effort has on a company's ability to achieve its objectives, i.e., to promote sales and profits. If the company's principal products or services are for direct consumer use, it probably can be characterized as marketing-oriented, with substantial amounts being expended on television and radio advertising. In such a case, advertising will constitute a significant portion of total marketing costs. The manager of advertising in this type of company will ordinarily report to the senior official having general marketing responsibility. In some cases, the responsibility for sales promotion activities is also assigned to the advertising manager. In other companies, only advertising is assigned to the advertising manager, with responsibility for sales promotion assigned to a marketing or sales manager.

Regardless of the division of responsibility, the auditor should ascertain that there is effective communication between advertising, sales promotion, distribution, and the selling activities.

THE ADVERTISING DEPARTMENT

Variation in Approach. Traditionally, advertising has been more closely connected to selling activities than the other aspects of marketing, and hence advertising and selling were often combined into one department. With the expansion of first radio advertising and then television advertising, it was seen that the problems related to mass communication were different from those found in direct selling and personal contact, and a separate unit to handle advertising was therefore found desirable. In some of the larger companies with very substantial consumer sales, large advertising departments came into being which assumed full and direct responsibility for the planning, preparation, and placement of advertising with the various media then available. Even with large advertising departments, companies often were required to engage outside technical experts and artistic talent, for it was not economically sound to employ such persons on a full-time basis. This led to the practice of hiring the specialists through agencies which, once formed, broadened their services to developing advertising ideas and preparing and placing advertising for not just one concern but a number of different companies. The advertising agency was born!

Whether a company develops its own programs and places its own advertising or uses an advertising agency depends on a number of variable factors. Some companies have enough advertising so that they can use their own employed talent adequately and it is thus economical to provide for their own advertising needs. In other companies, with perhaps smaller advertising budgets or diversified advertising requirements, it is not feasible to employ full time all the various types of talent needed. These needs are met by the advertising agency.

Since the auditing procedures will vary somewhat depending on whether the company uses an advertising agency or not, we shall discuss each of these arrangements separately.

Where an Agency Is Not Used. In those few companies where an advertising agency is not used, the advertising department will do all its own preparation and production work. In addition to the technical personnel: artists, copywriters, and layout experts, the department must employ specialists in various kinds of media to handle the placement of advertising. Thus, a company with this kind of department provides for itself most of the services available through an advertising agency. It must be borne in mind that even though an agency is not used for preparing and placing the advertising, an agency is often engaged to provide certain special services. For example, the company may call on an advertising agency to make a specific market survey, as the company may not be staffed with personnel qualified for such a special study.

Where an agency is not used, the department is usually staffed with supervisory level employees, each responsible for the advertising needs of a particular division or group of products. This form of delegation is normal, for products often appeal to different segments of the consuming public. Some products may be consumed by both sexes, others perhaps by men only, and still others may be for the younger generation. The advertising program for each product must recognize the market that is sought and hence must be administered by a person familiar with the advertising needed as well as with that which is available.

Additionally, such a department will usually have a financial section that is responsible for the preparation of budgets, the auditing of the advertising disbursements, the maintenance of cost and commitment records, and the preparation of reports which indicate expenditures by product line as well as by type of advertising expense.

Since most companies use advertising agencies, the illustrative audit program later in this chapter assumes that such an arrangement prevails. Should an agency not be employed, an audit program combining the operational features of the advertising department audit and the financial audit procedures of the agency audit would have to be combined.

Where an Agency Is Used. Where an agency is used, the products will generally be grouped according to the similarity of markets, and the responsibility for each group will be assigned to a particular account executive of the agency. Some of the larger companies employ more than one agency and allocate to each the products they believe that each agency can best market.

Before embarking on an audit of an agency, the auditor must familiarize himself with the manner in which advertising responsibilities have been delegated both within his own company and at the agency (or agencies). Further, with respect to his own company's organization, he must ascertain who is responsible for developing and approving the various advertising budgets, how the agency's invoices are processed, and what cost reports are issued. (Incidentally, budgets represent the key element of all advertising control systems. Because of their importance, advertising budgets are discussed in a separate section of this chapter.)

Another preliminary step for the auditor is to ascertain the arrangements existing between his company and the agency. In most cases, the auditor can refer to either a contract or the correspondence that may have been exchanged between the company and the agency outlining each party's responsibility. It is imperative that the auditor become thoroughly familiar with the services expected to be performed by the agency and the manner in which the agency is to be compensated for its efforts.

As an additional preliminary step, the auditor should determine whether his company has formally evaluated the performance of its agency. Procedures for conducting such an evaluation have been developed, and now most major advertisers annually review the performance of their advertising agency. Such evaluations generally concentrate on the agency's creative abilities, but administrative or financial problems may be identified which should be considered by the auditor when he prepares the audit program.

THE ADVERTISING AGENCY

Services Performed. An advertising agency offers a wide variety of services and strives to meet all the marketing needs of the client. Traditionally, the agency plans, prepares, and places (in various media ranging from newspaper to television) the advertising. There are many important decisions to make with respect to each of these activities, and the agency can be expected to be familiar with all the latest trends and techniques and also able to evaluate the probable effectiveness of specific approaches in particular market areas. Thus, the agency can provide expert help in developing advertising programs that have maximum appeal and suggest the media which will best meet the company's marketing objectives. A service correlated to the development of the advertising message is the planning, preparing, and purchasing of television and radio programs.

Part of these basic agency services is conducting merchandising, marketing, and research studies whenever they are considered essential to the development of an advertising program.

Finally, the agency is generally responsible for verifying and paying all charges incurred by the agency in behalf of the company.

Beyond the above basic services, the agency provides a number of related services such as the development of sales promotional plans that are coordinated with the advertising effort. So-called collateral material such as point-of-sales material, leaflets, catalogs, and even sales manuals are often prepared by the agency.

Agency Agreements. Perhaps surprisingly, many companies do not have a written agreement with their agency. Often a long-standing and mutually satisfactory relationship has developed between the company and its agency, and a contractual agreement is not considered necessary—the contention being that contracts are concerned with details whereas the basic relationship depends on the advertising that is created.

The trend among advertisers is, however, toward formalized agreements. While the content of such contracts varies considerably, the tendency is toward a contract of several sections wherein the basic part contains broad definitions of agency duties and responsibilities, termination clause, etc., supplemented by operating agreements which detail the services to be performed, compensation, and procedural matters.

Often the operating agreement sections (sometimes referred to as the billing policies) represent the formalization of the verbal and written agreements which have developed over a period of time. Such sections serve as a guide to company marketing groups in negotiating with the agency for the services to be performed, to the agency personnel for preparing the billings, and to the corporate personnel concerned with the fiscal aspects of advertising. Obviously, these sections of the agreement are of greatest concern to the auditor. Although certain understandings with the agency may have worked satisfactorily in the past, new personnel, new products, and new conditions are likely to produce problems relating to interpretation of the agreement.

If the auditor finds that there is no formal agreement with the advertising agency, he should urge that such an agreement be developed and executed. As perhaps implied, a properly prepared agreement provides a formal basis for billing and the basic structure for a cost-control system. Another important reason for reducing the terms of a relationship to writing is that it helps forestall misunderstandings and time-consuming discussions between parties. Incidentally, the agreement should contain an audit clause permitting the company auditor to review and examine the agency's records related to the billings rendered.

Agency Compensation. Traditionally, agencies have derived their income mainly from commissions received from the advertising media. Because the commission system forms the basis of most agency agreements, this discussion will center on the various aspects of this system. However, mention must be made of another form of agency compensation, which is commonly referred to as the fee system.

The fee system is of recent origin and has been adopted by a number of major advertisers (as well as dropped after a 2-year experiment, in favor of the commission system, by one of the nation's largest advertisers). The system has been the subject of much debate, and many variations have been developed in an effort to overcome some of its disadvantages and yet retain it in principle.

Basically, a fee system can be likened to the manner in which a company compensates its law firm or public accountants. Under one arrangement, the company pays its agency a fixed fee which is determined at the beginning of the year plus the cost of all out-of-pocket expenditures made by the agency (such as for media charges)—net of any commissions or discounts. Another fee system, stripped of its many special conditions, calls for the company to reimburse the agency on a cost plus basis—all payments to third parties being billed net of commissions.

An auditor faced with this kind of arrangement would be well advised to refer to the booklet entitled *Fee Methods of Agency Compensation.*[1] In addition to describing various forms of fee systems in effect, the booklet discusses the cost factors and operational matters to be considered, including that of auditing agency expenses.

Because so many variations of the fee system exist, an audit program tailored to the needs of a particular agreement must be developed. Suffice it to say, the approach to auditing a fee system agreement would be similar to that used in examining the billings of a construction firm engaged under a cost plus type of contract. As in such cases, the auditor must review the method of allocating overhead, salaries of supervisory personnel, and profit.

Returning to the more accepted, "commission system," the agency's income is derived from two types of billings—media and nonmedia billings.

[1] Association of National Advertisers, Inc., New York, 1969.

Media billings account for the major share of an agency's income, as it receives a discount—usually 15 percent and commonly referred to as commission—from the media on space or time purchased. If less than a 15 percent commission, or no commission, is allowed by a particular media, it is customary to allow an agency to bill the company on a basis which will yield it 15 percent of the gross billing. However, any rebates, volume discounts, or cash discounts received by an agency are passed to the advertiser. Similarly, credits issued by a medium because of poor reproduction, drop in published circulation, rate changes, preemption of purchased time, mechanical failure, etc., must be credited to the company's account.

The auditor must be alert to the various credits due from the media organizations. Particular attention should be given to the quantity of advertising purchased from a specific medium, for the rates drop substantially as the aggregate volume of space or time purchased by or for an advertiser increases. Importantly, the advertising done by a company's subsidiary or affiliate, as well as its various operating divisions, can be combined in determining the applicable rate.

On nonmedia billings, the agency adds a service charge (usually equivalent to 15 percent of the amount billed to the company) for certain materials and services purchased, as well as for certain services performed within the agency. Another nonmedia charge is that concerning certain television production charges for which networks allow the agency a 15 percent discount, the charges being billed to the company at the gross amount.

The auditor should recognize that the commission basis has an inherent conflict of interest. The more billings the agency renders the more it earns, and one might conclude that there is little incentive to the agency to reduce billings. In fact, proponents of the fee system of compensating agencies often cite this as one of the major shortcomings of the commission system. The auditor, cognizant of the effect of the system, can determine whether the expenditures are within the approved budget limits. He can ascertain whether the agency's procedures serve to protect the company's interests by identifying credits, volume discounts, and other amounts due, and finally, he can form some conclusions from the attitudes, professionalism, and integrity displayed by the agency personnel with whom he comes in contact.

Payments to Media. Generally the agency will assume responsibility for verifying the billings submitted by the media to the agency. This will include (1) evidence of performance and (2) determination of satisfactory performance.

Evidence of performance. In order for the agency to determine whether the advertising being billed has in fact taken place, reference must be made to some kind of tangible evidence. In the case of magazine and newspaper advertisements, the evidence would consist of "tear sheets," i.e., an actual advertisement torn from the publication. In the case of television or radio advertising, the evidence takes the form of performance affidavits issued by the station which aired or televised the commercial. As for outdoor advertisements, the locations of the various billboards are listed, thus affording the agency the opportunity of visually checking the advertisement.

Determination of satisfactory performance. In addition to obtaining evidence that the advertisement was in the newspaper or on the air, it is necessary to determine that the advertisement was in all respects satisfactory. Experienced agency personnel have the responsibility for determining this and to do so, consider such particulars as:

Space advertisements—the quality of reproduction, page position, and whether a competitor's advertisement was on the same or a facing page.

Television and radio commercials—whether the program or commercial was preempted (interrupted perhaps for a special news broadcast) or subject to a mechanical failure affecting the sound or visual transmission.

As concerns television and radio programs and commercials, several controls exist of which the auditor should be aware. First, according to FCC rules, each station must maintain a detailed program log and has an obligation to the network to report performance in accordance with that log. Second, stations have a contractual obligation to their network not to alter any of the network broadcast material, and to report all interruptions. Third, broadcasts are subject to observation by a number of interested individuals—not the least important of which are the advertisers and their agencies. Fourth, broadcasts are subject to test checks by monitoring services which issue reports such as Broadcast Advertisers Reports (BAR reports).

Rates, discounts, and credits. As part of the verification procedure, the agency must check the rates per the media's invoice to their published "card" rate or the contract rate where time or space has been so purchased. As stated before, the volume of advertising purchased by a company has an important bearing on the rate. Credits for any of the types of unsatisfactory performance described above must also be controlled by the agency.

Payment. The agency effects payment to the media, usually net of the commission earned, and bills the company for the gross amount.

Generally, agency verification procedures are well established, standardized, and usually adequate. For any particular agency this must be verified by reviewing its procedures and examining its billings and supporting documentation. Of equal importance to the auditor is whether there is a separation of the various functions such as order and billing, payment, traffic, and sales so as to afford sound internal control. Where the verification procedures and internal controls prove to be adequate, the auditor can direct his attention to determining that the charges comply with established budgets and schedules.

Companies with Multiple Agencies. Companies that employ more than one agency generally designate one of the agencies to act as a master agency and thus be responsible for all media purchases of a particular kind. To explain, a company with multiple agencies may instruct all its agencies to funnel, for example, radio time purchases through agency A and television spot commercial purchases through agency B. A variation of such an arrangement permits each agency to purchase time or space directly but requires it to report all such purchases to the designated control agency.

Arrangements of this kind provide the company with greater leverage in both purchasing and utilizing media time or space. They also facilitate the chore of determining the volume of advertising done by the company with a particular media organization, thus assuring that volume discounts are not lost.

Media billings are initially processed and paid by the master agency, which in turn bills the other agencies involved, who then bill the company.

Where a company is serviced by multiple agencies, occasions may arise where one agency performs a service for another agency in connection with the company's business. Under certain circumstances, the agency performing the service is entitled to be compensated by the other agency. For example, a program may be sponsored by products serviced by more than one of the agencies, and the "producing agency" is therefore entitled to a production fee which the "participating agency" realizes on the show talent.

Such interagency compensation agreements are often exceedingly complicated and should be subject to the prior review and approval of the company.

THE ADVERTISING BUDGET

Budgets are important to the management of most functions, but in advertising, the budget is an indispensable tool. The nature of advertising, as described earlier, is such that the effectiveness of money spent is difficult to measure and the reasonableness of many of the related costs is difficult to evaluate. The advertising budget therefore represents the most important means of planning as well as controlling such expenditures.

Defining and Classifying Advertising Expenditures. A company should have an appropriate set of accounts for advertising expenditures. Unless these charges are classified in a consistent manner and in sufficient detail, the budget will be next to useless as a control device.

A company's chart of accounts for advertising will depend on a number of factors such as (1) the level of its advertising expenditures, (2) the extent of its product line, and (3) the forms of advertising that it employs. Companies that have even a modest advertising program will find it desirable to subdivide advertising expenditures into at least the following major categories:

Magazines and newspaper space charges
Television time
Radio broadcast time
Magazine and newspaper advertising production
Television talent and commercial production
Radio talent and production

Companies that incur large outlays for advertising customarily have a very extensive chart of accounts which provide subaccounts to distinguish consumer publications from trade papers and spot radio and television commercials from network costs, and may even have subaccounts by publication, station, and other media. Additionally, the code of accounts may be so constructed as to permit charges to be categorized by product or product line.

The chart of accounts should not only provide for an appropriate classification of charges, but to be certain that it is used in a consistent manner, the accounts should be documented; i.e., a written description should be prepared for each account, indicating the charges to be included and excluded and when the expenses are to be recorded.

Developing the Advertising Plan. The effective advertising budget represents the culmination of a great amount of effort expended by both the company's advertising and marketing personnel, as well as the agency's consultants. Information must be gathered on historical and current sales, and advertising and marketing projections. Overall company goals and sales objectives must be determined as well as a marketing strategy. While the company is in the best position to accumulate the necessary data and determine goals and sales projections, the development of a marketing strategy and the related advertising plan and strategy is often done with the help of the agency.

Spending Limitations. Even the most sophisticated companies, those which approach advertising expenditures from the goals that are to be reached, generally place a ceiling on the aggregate amount that can be spent. Some companies determine the amount to be spent for advertising by employing arbitrary yardsticks such as a fixed percentage of sales or a percentage of profits or so much per unit to be sold. However the limit or amount is established, it must be considered in developing the advertising plan.

The Budget. So far we have dealt with planning steps involved in the formulation of the budget. Next (although in practice it is concurrent with strategy and media planning) is to cost out the plan. Here the agency plays an important role by providing cost estimates. In practice, the company may estimate certain of the costs, but regardless of the source of the estimates, it is important that they be accurately calculated and that an audit trail is prepared so that subsequent variances can be analyzed and explained.

Another factor to be considered in developing the budget is the timing of the expenditures. For example, certain products are seasonal and therefore should be advertised in the period or season in which the consumer can be expected to be in the mood to buy. Determining the timing of the expenditures also enables the budgeter to estimate when the funds will be needed—an important concern of the company treasurer. Incidentally, determining estimated monthly expenditures by dividing the annual budget by 12 (a technique used by some companies) does not generally produce "cash flow" data that are of any practical use.

Once the advertising plan is costed out and the timing of expenditures determined, the budget is prepared and submitted to the company's advertising executive for his review and approval. While only a summary version of the budget may be submitted to top management for their review and approval, supporting schedules provide the detail of the amounts to be spent (1) by product, (2) by type of medium, and (3) for media as distinguished from production costs. Obviously, if the budget is to serve as a control device, the details must be categorized to conform with the company's chart of accounts.

To summarize, a properly prepared advertising budget provides management with a plan of not only how much and how the advertising monies are to be spent, but when the expenditures will be made.

Budget Revisions. A budget is a management tool for planning and controlling expenditures, and while the approved budget should be strictly adhered to, it is subject to change when unforeseen developments occur. The introduction of new products or revised sales plans may justify an increase or decrease in the budget. Whether such changes affect the overall budget or merely transfer amounts between products or media, the change should not be made without the approval of top management, who should be provided with a full explanation of the reasons for requesting the change.

PURCHASING ADVERTISING

General Considerations. Although the purchase plan for the ensuing year is formulated during the budget preparation, the actual purchasing or fulfillment of the plan does not commence until the budget is approved.

The first consideration concerns the responsibility for purchasing various services and materials. While most companies delegate to their agency the responsibility for space and time purchases, the responsibility for purchasing the other items varies greatly among companies. As it is axiomatic that the control over an activity depends on responsibilities being clearly defined, the auditor's first task is that of determining how the purchasing function has been delegated. While responsibilities must be defined, the policy should recognize that close cooperation must exist between the company's advertising and marketing personnel and their counterparts at the advertising agency.

Going beyond this, the purchasing of advertising requires the exercise of the same sound judgment and the same policies and controls that surround the procurement of other types of services and supplies. The above factors notwithstanding, the all-important factor of creativity has a strong influence on advertising purchasing decisions. Peculiar also to this activity is the manner in which time and space are bought. We shall discuss the latter area first, followed by a description of the basic policies and techniques that should surround all other (nonmedia) advertising purchases.

Media Purchases. Media requirements are tentatively established at the time that the advertising plan is formulated. This information is usually prepared by the agency and takes the form of insertion schedules which detail the company's space and time requirements for the year. Usually, a separate schedule is prepared for each medium, indicating the name of the medium, date of insertion, amount of space or time, color, cost, and volume discounts, with such items based, for the most part, on published tariffs. The insertion schedule, once approved by the company, serves as the agency's authority to contract for space and time, and the schedules may be employed as blanket or annual purchase orders.

Nonmedia Purchases. This category covers a wide variety of materials and services such as art, printing, radio, and television production—which represent the costliest of the nonmedia-type purchases. (It should be noted that nonmedia purchases in the aggregate usually account for a fraction of a company's advertising budget—most of the money being spent for space and time.)

Many of the so-called nonmedia purchases involve the creative efforts of writers and artists; the talents of producers, photographers, and actors; and the craftsmanship of engravers and printers. These services, by their very nature, involve costs which are difficult to evaluate objectively, i.e., to determine their reasonableness. It is therefore important that their procurement be subject to such standard purchasing policies and techniques as the following:

Vendor selection. Only competent, adequately equipped, and reliable suppliers should be employed. However, so as to avoid overreliance on one group of suppliers as well as permit cost comparisons, alternate sources should be employed from time to time.

Competitive bidding. Bids should be sought for each project.

Requisitions. Properly prepared and approved requisitions should be on hand before commitments are made.

Planning and timing. The preparatory work should be thorough and complete. Time should be provided for the work to be done in an orderly manner.

Documentation. The project should be described in detail and each supplier provided with explicit instructions.

Consolidation of orders. To the extent practical, like projects should be grouped so as to take advantage of cost savings attributable to volume.

Know-how. Those involved with the procurement of these services should have a general understanding of how the work is performed and the problems involved. Furthermore, they should be familiar with the pricing system used by the various crafts and have readily available historical pricing data.

Whether the agency or the company's advertising department handles the purchases of these nonmedia services, the party responsible should prepare an estimate detailing the services and materials involved and their estimated cost. The estimate should be reviewed and approved by the advertising or marketing employee responsible for the product concerned, and a copy of the estimate returned to the purchasing area. Commitments should not be entered into until the estimate has been approved.

CONTROLLING AND VERIFYING ADVERTISING EXPENDITURES

General Considerations. Control and verification of advertising expenditures pose some special problems because (1) many of the costliest items represent intangible services (for example, television or radio time), (2) the purchases may have been negotiated by a third party (for example, an agency's purchase of advertising space in a magazine), and (3) the agency's compensation depends, to a great extent, on the amount of advertising placed and it thus has no special interest in minimizing its cost.

Controls. Given the environment described above and alluded to elsewhere in this chapter, advertising expenditures must be subject to adequate and effective controls. The advertising budget represents the key element of the control system. For it to be an effective form of control, periodic, but frequent, reviews must be made of the budget in relation to the amounts spent and committed to date. As this implies, it is mandatory that a system be in effect whereby not only are expenses promptly and properly classified, but commitments are also recorded and classified as they are made.

Another very important aspect of control concerns the relationships and procedures in effect between the company and its agency. The agency's responsibility must be clearly defined; a definite procedure must exist for the preparation, submission, and approval of estimates (before commitments are made); forms and documents that are exchanged between the company and agency should be standardized; the accounting classifications of each party must dovetail; and the payment procedures of both the company and its agency must assure that all bills are promptly paid and recorded.

Duties and responsibilities should be properly segregated at the agency as well as at the company. It would not do, for example, for one agency employee to be responsible for the placement of advertising orders and also the verification of the related charges.

The purchasing procedures, as previously described, provide for certain types of controls and hence should be strictly adhered to.

Mention must also be made of the insertion schedules which, once approved, authorize the agency to contract for space and time and also represent the basic documents against which invoiced rates can be checked.

Individual jobs or projects are best controlled if the related costs are first itemized on an estimate and then subject to frequent checking to the actual costs as they are incurred. Attention is thus focused at an early date on those elements of the project which may be getting out of hand, which in turn may permit corrective action or else obtaining of advance approval to incur additional expense.

Because advertising projects, such as television commercial productions, are often extremely costly, there is a tendency to ignore the cost of the various elements so long as the total cost is within the estimate. This broad brush approach is usually indicative of weak controls, for as manufacturing personnel well know, substantial savings are often accomplished by paying attention to specific items.

Federal, state, and municipal sales and use taxes represent one such minor cost item that may not be given the attention it deserves. Usually, companies purchase, consume, store, and use many different kinds of materials on which they may be subject to sales taxes in the state in which they purchase and accept delivery and may also be subject to use taxes in states where they store, consume, or distribute the materials. Some states and cities exempt some of these items from taxation; others exempt them, under certain circumstances, when a similar sales and use tax has already been paid in another taxing jurisdiction. A full discussion of the tax regulations of all the various state and municipal jurisdictions concerned is clearly beyond the scope of this chapter, but the auditor should know that many expenditures may be subject to taxes and even double taxation that can be legally avoided if proper steps are taken in arranging purchase and delivery. See bibliography reference to the booklet *Federal, State and Municipal Laws Affecting Advertising.* While the tax rates cited in this booklet are, in many cases, out of date, the principles and problems cited are, for the most part, still in effect.

Verification Procedures—Media Expenditures. Establishing that media charges represent advertising that has in fact taken place is generally not difficult. For magazines and newspaper advertisements, tear sheets can be obtained which are exact copies of the advertisement as it should have appeared in the finished publication. The agency has the responsibility for checking the layout and positioning of the advertisement. This function may also be performed by an independent bureau. Tear sheets are usually retained by the agency, although some companies insist that they be attached to the invoices.

Television and radio commercials can be verified by referring to station affidavits or reports from independent monitoring agencies. Companies sometimes request their agency to also audit the station logs.

In the case of outside billboards and signs, an independent agency can be asked to certify their existence.

Media charges can be traced to published rates, such as those published by the Standard Rate and Data Service and the rate cards issued by television and radio stations.

Checking media prices can be a complicated task, for volume discounts are generally offered and thus it is necessary to establish the total amount of advertising placed by or for a company with each medium so as to determine the applicable rate. Often, the discount is paid retroactively; that is, it is granted by the media when the level of advertising reaches a certain point, and then the discount covers all advertising placed during, say, the previous quarter. Because such discounts are significant, the auditor should make certain that procedures are in effect whereby the amount of advertising for the entire company is accumulated by media. The auditor should also keep in mind that where the volume of advertising in a particular medium has not quite reached the "break point," it may be possible to secure additional coverage for a nominal amount by purchasing merely enough more space to reach the break point. Also, it may be less expensive to advertise at chain rates on an entire network rather than on specific stations where the local station rates would prevail.

Verification Procedures—Nonmedia Expenditures. Any advertisement involves the expenditure of monies for its preparation. Hence, such charges can be related to a media commitment or expense. The documentation, some of which will be in the form of third party invoices, will establish whether or not the charges concern the company.

As for costs, where contracts have been negotiated it is a relatively simple task to verify their propriety. Third party invoices should also serve to support such costs. Not to be overlooked are the approved estimates, which ideally itemize the work and estimated costs involved in each project and which should therefore support the billing. Any unforeseen expenditures should, of course, have been reviewed and approved by a company executive prior to payment.

BILLING PROCEDURES

Submission of Bills. Advertising agencies generally bill their clients at least monthly. All such billings should cite the applicable estimate and indicate the charges by account classification and product. Often agencies submit summary billings which, so long as they can be traced to approved estimates (which in turn should provide the details), are adequate and acceptable.

Production charges are usually billed monthly and usually as they are incurred, although in some cases the agency may defer billing the company until a particular project is completed. For control purposes, progress billings are preferred, but in either case, such billings should be supported by third party invoices.

Payroll taxes applicable to talent services deserve mention, since some companies have interpreted the labor laws as requiring the advertiser to be the legal employer of such individuals except when they are employed in "package" shows. As the employer, the advertiser must withhold various payroll taxes from salary payments made to talent; file social security, unemployment tax, and federal and state information returns; and provide workmen's compensation and disability coverage on their behalf.

Where such an interpretation is in force, the agencies generally act as a withholding agent, deducting the various payroll taxes from talent salary payments. Monthly or semimonthly, the agency will prepare a statement setting forth all such payments and withholdings, including social security numbers. Statements will be accompanied by a check for the total amount withheld, and the company then incorporates the salaries and withholding data in their various payroll and tax returns.

Coordinating Payments. Charges for space and time are often of significant amounts and must be paid by the agency within relatively short periods either before or after the advertisement is run. In order not to place undue hardship on the resources of the agency, the company must closely coordinate its payments for media with the agency's cash outlays. As this implies, the company should not be placed in the position whereby in effect it is providing working capital that could be used by the agency to discharge its other obligations.

Credits issued by media organizations (for volume discounts, preemptions, poor reproductions, etc.) are usually shown as reductions on the agency's billing rendered at the end of the month in which the credit was received.

AUDIT OF ADVERTISING

General. Should reason be needed to justify an auditor's examination of the company's advertising activities, it could be found in the definition of internal auditing as promulgated by The Institute of Internal Auditors. This definition states that: [2]

[2] Statement of Responsibilities of the Internal Auditor, The Institute of Internal Auditors, New York, 1957.

Internal auditing is an independent appraisal activity within an organization for the review of accounting, financial and other operations as a basis for service to management. It is a managerial control, which functions by measuring and evaluating the effectiveness of other controls.

That advertising is an activity that falls within the above definition there can be no doubt. Support for this can be found in the preceding sections, many of which contain references to controls and describe practices the eftiveness of which can best be determined by the application of auditing procedures.

What kind of auditing should be performed, and which of the many auditing procedures would be appropriate to advertising? Suggestions and examples of audit programs are provided at the end of the chapter, but in the final analysis the most effective audit program is one that has been tailored to the company's requirements and circumstances.

Generally speaking, however, the advertising audit will include both financial and operational audit procedures. There will certainly be a need to review internal controls, verify billings, commitment and disbursement procedures, and ascertain the extent of compliance with company policies. However, the extent to which the auditor must concentrate on the verification of documents, records, and reports as opposed to evaluating managerial controls and procedures depends essentially on how adequate and effective are the established procedures and controls at both the company and the advertising agency.

Conducting the Audit. The number of transactions and the amount of record keeping associated with advertising is substantial. The fact that this characteristic is combined with disbursements that often aggregate hundreds of thousands, if not millions, of dollars suggests that financial auditing procedures would be most appropriate for advertising. And, as stated, no advertising audit program could be considered complete if it did not provide for the tests and reviews customarily associated with the financial audit. Nevertheless, since advertising is so highly specialized and involves so many technical considerations, the audit should be planned and conducted along the lines of an operational audit. The elements of such an audit, as stated in the *Operational Auditing Handbook,*[3] consist of the following four basic steps:

1. Familiarization
2. Verification
3. Evaluation and recommendations
4. Reporting

Within the context of advertising, each of these steps will be discussed. It should be noted that whether the company handles all its own advertising or engages an advertising agency, the approach would be the same.

Familiarization. For an understanding of advertising, particularly as it applies to a specific company, the auditor has available to him three major sources of information: (1) background data, (2) agency data, and (3) advertising department data. A brief explanation of each source follows.

BACKGROUND DATA: This information is generally of two types.

[3] Bradford Cadmus, *Operational Auditing Handbook,* New York, The Institute of Internal Auditors, 1964, p. 25.

1. General reference material. The company's advertising department or its advertising agency very likely has a suggested reading list of books, pamphlets, and periodicals. More particularly, the auditor should make a point of obtaining the publications of professional associations such as the Association of National Advertisers (ANA), the Broadcast Advertisers Reports (BAR), and the publications of the Standard Rate and Data Service (SRDS).

2. Company prepared material. If the company has a financial manual, this should certainly be reviewed as well as the company's chart of accounts. The company may also have a specific written procedure for the payment of advertising bills. If such exists, the auditor should become familiar with its contents. Both audit reports and audit work papers of previous audits are important sources of information for the auditor.

AGENCY DATA: Heading this list is the contract, letter of agreement, or correspondence file concerning the relationship between the company and its agency. It is imperative that the auditor become familiar with the terms of the agency contract (if such exists) and especially with the operating agreements which may serve as addenda to the agency contract. The organization chart of the agency would also be useful if for no other reason than to advise the auditor of the agency personnel that he will have to contact. If there are any procedural write-ups which describe the agency's practices, and/or flow charts depicting the flow of documents through the agency, they should be carefully reviewed.

A representative example of a flow chart is provided at the end of this chapter.

ADVERTISING DEPARTMENT DATA: An organization chart of the department would be informative, as it would indicate the names and positions of the various people comprising the advertising department as well as the department's position within the company. Job descriptions, if available, should be reviewed, especially as they pertain to the employees responsible for budgets, commitments and disbursements records, and the processing of agency billings.

Here is another area in which flow charts would be especially helpful in following the flow of work and understanding the controls in effect.

Discussions should be held with various members of the advertising department so as to (1) determine what they do, (2) ascertain the kinds of problems they may be experiencing with the agency, (3) solicit their suggestions as to what should be incorporated into the program, and (4) review with them the tentative audit program.

Verification. Having gained a general understanding of advertising and familiarized himself with the objectives, controls, and procedures, and the manner in which responsibilities have been divided, the auditor is ready to commence the verification phase. Its major objective is to determine what practices, controls, etc., are actually in effect.

The auditor might begin by requesting the agency or the company to provide him with a summary of the billings rendered during the current year. For this summary to be useful, it should distinguish media from nonmedia billings. With statistical sampling techniques, a representative number of transactions should be selected and examined, as one would audit any disbursement material, keeping in mind, however, the role of the budget in advertising and the importance of estimates as a source of authorization.

It is important that the transactions selected for examination be representative of all major types of advertising expenditures. Furthermore, it is highly desirable that a representative number of advertising projects, in their entirety, be subject to audit. In this manner, the auditor can best determine whether job records are properly set up and maintained. He may compare original estimates with final costs and obtain explanations for significant variances. He can then determine if the various phases of the project have been properly coordinated.

Not to be overlooked in the audit are the nonconsumable supplies and assets employed, for the most part, in the preparation of advertisements and commercials. For example, furniture, artwork, company products, and other props are often employed in commercials and other nonmedia-type projects. As many of these items are reusable or retain some resale value, it is imperative that the auditor determine what disposition has been made of them after they have served their initial purpose.

As explained in the previous sections, many of the transactions referred to above are initiated by the advertising agency. Hence, much of the verification work will have to be done at the agency, which in turn will afford the auditor an opportunity to view firsthand the agency's purchasing and disbursement procedures and the related controls.

Evaluation and recommendations. Throughout the verification and familiarization phases the auditor must keep in mind his basic objective, which is that of evaluating the effectiveness and the relative efficiency of the procedures and controls that surround advertising activities. Therefore, the evaluation phase of the examination is actually performed concurrently with the other two. Thus, upon completion of the verification work, the auditor should be in a position to render an opinion with respect to controls, the accuracy of the reports, and whether corporate policies and contractual terms have been adhered to. He should also be in a position to make recommendations aimed at strengthening controls and/or eliminating duplicate effort.

Reporting. The planning, writing, and presenting of the advertising audit reports are especially important to the audit of advertising. It is the most challenging as well as the most important phase of the audit.

Why are the reports so important? First of all, they are the most tangible evidence of the auditor's efforts, the core around which he plans and performs his work and the amounts of advertising involved may be in the millions.

Some essentials of a good advertising audit report are (1) planning, (2) content and arrangement, and (3) issuing the report.

PLANNING THE REPORT: The auditor must keep the report in mind throughout the audit. This cannot be overstressed, for to do otherwise will, at the very least, convert the writing task to a time-consuming chore. More importantly, failure to bear in mind the probable content of the report may make it impossible for the auditor to express a supportable opinion and offer recommendations that are both meaningful and germane. As concerns recommendations, the auditor must be prepared to describe current practices in detail and cite examples of them.

Another technique to be employed during the audit is that of drafting, at the completion of each part, both the conclusions and any recommendations that may have been developed. At this time, the findings and recommendations should be discussed with the personnel directly concerned. Often cogent reasons for not changing what might appear to be an inefficient procedure are advanced. This is the appropriate time to face up to the arguments and excuses, for not only are the facts clear in the auditor's mind, but he can explore the validity of the comments made.

CONTENT AND ARRANGEMENT OF THE REPORT: The report for an advertising audit offers greater opportunity for originality than does a report pertaining to a routine examination such as that of a warehouse inventory or a cashier's fund. While there are no hard and fast rules concerning content and arrangement—the particular needs, interests, and idiosyncrasies of a company's management must be considered—a suggested approach follows.

1. Brief introductory comments should be aimed at informing the reader of the name of the department (advertising) and/or the name of the agency together with data (such as annual billings or products advertised if more than one agency) which will provide the reader with some dimensions of the relative size and importance of the department and/or agency.
2. Scope of the audit should be briefly described together with any limitations that may have been placed on the auditor.
3. The opinion (overall) and major findings and recommendations (in outline form only) should be positioned so as to be on the first page of the report.
4. An expanded description of the audit of major activities should come next, with comments as to the relative efficiency, effective controls, etc. As an example, a comment along the following lines may be appropriate:

> Thirty percent of all nonmedia billings, which in the current year aggregate $15 million, were examined, as were the related company and agency procedures. While all billings proved to be bona fide, the agency had no effective means of independently determining the company's total use of a particular medium, relying almost exclusively on the advice of the media. We have therefore recommended an appropriate system to enable the agency to keep track of these expenditures by medium.

5. Particularly effective or perhaps unique practices which benefit the company should be cited.
6. Comments on the disposition made of prior audit recommendations, if applicable, should be included.
7. Finally, acknowledgment should be made of the assistance and cooperation rendered the auditors by the advertising department or agency personnel, should such a compliment be warranted.

It might be noted that the above outline provides for only summary-type statements of importance, the findings and recommendations to be detailed in a separate section of the report. This presumes, of course, that a number of findings and recommendations were developed during the audit. In such cases, and particularly because a report may be distributed to different levels of management, it is helpful to all concerned if the details are reported in a separate section, but preceded by an index listing the captions of each finding and recommendation.

In discussing the audit report, we have perhaps implied that this is the auditor's only means of communicating his findings and recommendations. This, of course, is not the case, especially as concerns minor deviations from established procedures or internal controls and recommendations involving minimal procedural modifications. Depending on their nature, such matters can be more effectively handled orally or in a separate memorandum directed to the personnel involved.

ISSUING THE REPORT: Even though all matters may have been discussed with the personnel involved during the course of the audit, it is a good practice to issue a draft of the completed report, and any memorandums contemplated, to the company supervisors who will be affected by their content. This gives them the opportunity to check the accuracy of the auditor's statements and, in general, determine that the circumstances are being fairly and clearly reported.

The final report should reflect any pertinent comments or suggestions offered by those who have reviewed the draft, and of course, it should not include any comments or recommendations that were not in the draft.

As to its distribution, the audit report should be directed to the chief executive responsible for advertising, with copies issued to affected company supervisory personnel. Generally, the auditor should not send the report to the advertising agency but rather should issue an extra copy to the company executive who acts as the liaison between the company and the agency. This executive should then review the report directly with his counterpart at the agency and, if he deems it appropriate, provide the agency with those sections of the report which pertain to the agency.

AUDIT OF ADVERTISING DEPARTMENT

An audit program that is developed for the company's advertising department will generally not be suitable for the company's advertising agency despite the fact that the functions of each are in many respects similar and certainly related. First, an audit of the advertising department should emphasize operational auditing techniques. The audit of the advertising agency, on the other hand, involves an examination of the procedures and records of an organization not affiliated with the company, which in itself places certain restrictions on the auditor (he cannot expect to delve into the agency's policies, objectives, etc., to the extent that he can within his own company). Second, while some procedures and practices of the agency must be reviewed and tested, the auditor can accomplish the remainder of his objectives by the application of verification techniques.

As for the audit program for the advertising department, its content depends, in the first instance, on whether an agency is employed and, if so, the extent to which the agency is responsible for the procurement of media time and space, nonmedia services, payment of bills, etc. We have assumed in the illustrative program that follows that (1) the company employs an agency and (2) the agency performs all the services outlined earlier in this chapter.

The major objective of the audit of the advertising department is to evaluate the controls surrounding advertising. The auditor wants to know (1) if the prescribed controls and procedures are both adequate and effective in implementing the company's policies and objectives and (2) that these procedures are being adhered to. To accomplish this objective, the program might be structured along the following lines:

1. Reviews of the controls and procedures concerning:
   a. General departmental activities
   b. Budgetary matters
   c. Agency relationship
2. Verification tests aimed at determining what practices and controls are actually in effect

The approach to be followed in each of the above areas is described below.

General Departmental Activities

1. Obtain the organization chart of the department and the job descriptions of the key individuals. Ascertain who is responsible for the approval of

estimates and invoices, who reviews project progress reports, and who acts as the liaison between the company and its agency.

2. Obtain or prepare flow charts depicting the flow of documents through the department. Such charts should enable the auditor to assess the general pattern of controls and procedures and then concentrate his efforts on those areas which may be weak and inefficient.

3. Obtain copies of the accounting reports that are issued, especially those pertaining to funds committed and spent as compared with budgeted amounts. Determine if the reports have been prepared as required and in a timely fashion and if they had been reviewed and approved by the appropriate supervisory employees. Determine what action, if any, has been taken with respect to variances. Determine also whether the expenditures agree, or can be reconciled to, the books of account. Finally, determine if the reports appear to be complete and whether the expenditures have been properly classified.

4. Ascertain if any advertising materials are purchased by the advertising department or by the company's purchasing department, and then review the purchasing procedures. Assess the procedures in terms of standard purchasing practices such as those concerned with the selection of suppliers (are bids obtained, are alternate sources considered, etc.). Also, are detailed requisitions required, are quantity requirements determined in a realistic manner, and are purchase orders prepared?

5. Ascertain whether the disbursement function is carried out by the advertising department or by the company's accounts payable department, and review the disbursement procedures. Ascertain whether the procedures provide for proper invoice audit, and whether invoices must be properly approved and supported before payment is made. Not to be overlooked is the period in which the outlay was expensed. Generally, the expenditures should be expensed when advertised.

6. Review inventory reports and records pertaining to advertising supplies, property, and other props used in the preparation of commercials. Determine whether physical inventories are periodically conducted and by whom. Also, are the custodians required to prepare inventory reports and are these, as well as physical inventory counts, reconciled to the books?

7. In connection with the above items, a review should be made of disposal practices.

Budgetary Controls. This area actually involves two separate budgets, (1) the advertising department budget and (2) the advertising budget.

The advertising department budget

1. Obtain a copy of the budget and compare costs and dates to determine cost areas that vary or are likely to vary significantly from the amounts authorized. Such variances should be discussed with the department manager.

2. If advertising department costs are allocated among the company's products or divisions, the basis of allocation should be reviewed and tested.

The advertising budget

1. Obtain a copy of the budget. Determine whether it has been properly approved, that the details are properly and adequately classified, and that the amounts agree with the actual and committed expenditures contained in the financial reports.

2. Review the basis for determining budget amounts. Determine whether

there is an audit trail that will permit performance to be measured against the budget objectives.

3. Determine the frequency with which budgeted amounts are compared with committed and actual expenditures, and who prepares and who reviews the comparison. Ascertain if there is evidence of appropriate reviews and if adequate action has been taken with respect to variances.

4. Determine that revisions have been properly approved. Be on the lookout for amounts that may have been diverted to other projects without proper approval.

5. Prepare an analysis of any significant variances between actual and budgeted amounts. Ascertain the reasons for material differences, the extent to which they are documented, and the steps taken to minimize added cost that may have resulted from the revisions.

6. Evaluate selected, but significant, expenditures in relation to benefits derived. Good business judgment must be exercised in the evaluation, not that of a self-proclaimed marketing expert. The auditor should look for the unusual (in terms of amounts spent vs. expectations) and then ascertain whether and how results were determined justifying the expenditures. The auditor's purpose here is twofold: (1) to determine the existence of, and then question, projects that appear unusual and (2) to ascertain whether there is a routine procedure for evaluating project results.

7. Review month-by-month expenditures in relation to the amounts budgeted. Expenditures generally should not be bunched at year end, for this suggests that budget balances were deliberately used up.

8. Determine that advertising has been properly allocated among products and divisions of the company.

9. Determine that any prepaid and deferred items are bona fide future charges.

Agency Relationships

1. Obtain a copy of the agency contract together with any addenda or correspondence relating to services to be performed, billing procedures, etc. The auditor should review these documents carefully to determine whether they provide a clear definition of (1) responsibilities, (2) services, (3) compensation (commissions and rates for billable services), and (4) the billing procedure.

The auditor should then excerpt those provisions relating to agency responsibilities, services to be performed, agency compensation, and billing and accounting requirements. These data are to be used in conjunction with the verification phase.

2. Agencies are customarily required to prepare and submit to the company a number of reports and schedules which pertain to both advertising plans (the future) and advertising that has taken place (for example, in the quarter just ended). Copies of these reports should be obtained and compared (1) with the approved budget for future advertising and (2) with the accounting records for expenditures made.

As part of this review, the auditor should determine whether the agency has complied with the company's requirements as to both content and timing of the reports.

3. Determine whether the agency has been subject to a formal evaluation. The auditor should note any critical comments concerning those activities which would be subject to his reviews and tests.

4. For the protection of their clients, agencies are normally required to

carry advertisers' liability insurance in agreed-to minimum amounts. The auditor should examine certificates issued by the carrier evidencing coverages and endorsement (requiring notification to the company prior to modification, termination, or cancellation of the policy).

5. Because of the confidential aspects of marketing, agencies must agree not to disclose any of the company's plans, and also must agree not to provide services to a competing company unless such services have been approved in advance by the company. The auditor should determine whether the agreement provides this form of protection.

Verification. Having made the reviews outlined above and examined the documents indicated, the auditor should select a representative number of invoices. Such a selection should include agency billings, direct payments to suppliers, and departmental charges. Having made the selection, the auditor should then perform an in-depth review of each transaction. That is, the auditor should follow each transaction from its inception to its payment to determine that the various functions involved have been carried out in the prescribed manner.

AUDIT OF ADVERTISING AGENCY

Objectives and Approach. The objectives of an audit of the company's advertising agency are to determine that the expenditures made by the agency in behalf of the company (1) are in accordance with and complementary to the company's advertising plan and objectives, (2) have been subject to proper controls and generally accepted business practices, and (3) are proper in all respects.

The first and second of these objectives require that agency practices be reviewed and evaluated, whereas the third objective involves the examination of agency transactions to determine the practices actually in effect and ascertain the propriety of the agency's billings. This approach is illustrated in the program that follows, which is composed of two sections, "Procedural Review" and "Verification Phase."

Procedural Review. **Preliminary steps.** The general approach is that of an operational audit wherein the auditor familiarizes himself with the overall nature of the activities involved and then sets about examining and reviewing the agency's organization and practices. Once beyond the basic familiarization steps described earlier in this chapter, the auditor should obtain (or prepare where needed) and study:

1. The agency contract together with any operational agreements and/or correspondence relating to responsibilities, billing policies, etc.
2. The agency's organization chart as well as the job descriptions for employees responsible for purchasing and procurement, estimating, production control, and accounting. The auditor should also ascertain the names and telephone extensions of those employees he expects to contact during the audit.
3. Procedural memorandums and/or flow charts describing and depicting the flow of documents through those agency departments which are of key concern to the auditor.

At this point, the auditor not only should know what is expected of the agency but should have a general impression of the adequacy of the controls and the degree of sophistication inherent in the various key functions which he is to review and evaluate.

In-depth procedural review. As stated, there are certain agency activities which the auditor will wish to examine closely and then test by examining billings and all the related records (these are discussed under "Verification Phase"). Activities for which the procedures, practices, and controls are to be determined are enumerated below. Indicated also are matters specific to each activity which the auditor should consider in the course of his review.

PURCHASING

Media purchases:

1. Are these purchases handled by a media specialist?
2. Is there an effective means of coordinating buying plans with the budget objectives of the company?
3. Are purchases made in accordance with approved insertion schedules, and are the contracts for space and time, which are negotiated at the beginning of the year, based on yearly plans (with rates at the most advantageous level)?
4. Where more than one agency is employed, and thus one acts as a "master agency," is there an effective means of communicating to the master agency the purchase of space and time planned and made by the other agency or agencies in behalf of the company?

Nonmedia purchases:

1. Is the section staffed with experienced, knowledgeable employees who can carry out this function in an efficient, informed manner?
2. Are duties properly segregated?
3. Are the lines of responsibility and authority well defined?
4. Have standards and procedures been established to govern vendor/supplier selection? In this connection, are prospective vendors/suppliers subject to credit-type checks performed by employees independent of the purchasing function?
5. Are competitive bids solicited? Are selections made for reasons other than the lowest price adequately explained?
6. Are detailed and approved requisitions needed before an order is placed?
7. Are the orders, or more ideally the requisitions, supported by or referenced to approved estimates?
8. Are purchase orders issued for all orders?
9. Have standards of acceptance been established?
10. Are contract files maintained?

ESTIMATING: Are detailed estimates prepared and submitted to the company for approval before commitments are made?

Are the estimates prepared so as to facilitate later comparison with actual expenditures? Are advertising plans costed out in a manner that would assure the accuracy of the cost estimates? (Do they work with complete plans, and do they have the needed data, rate schedules, etc., on hand?)

ACCOUNTING

General accounting section:

1. Are the payroll procedures such that they accurately record the time spent by agency personnel on billable projects?
2. Are the rates used for billing agency personnel in agreement with the billing policy?

3. Are the controls and records applicable to advertising material, property, and props (used in commercial production) adequate in the following areas:
   a. Disposal practices?
   b. Storage facilities?
   c. Adequacy and reliability of the inventory records?

Client accounting section:

1. Are duties properly segregated?
2. Has a checklist been prepared of the reports required by the company?
3. Has a billing and payment schedule been formulated indicating the dates on which billings must be rendered to the company, when payment is due to the agency, and when payment is due to the various media?
4. Are project costs periodically summarized and compared with estimates, and variances analyzed?
5. Are such reports sent to the company, and do the data contained therein agree with the approved estimates and agency accounting records?
6. Has a system been established whereby revised estimates are prepared and submitted to the company as soon as it becomes evident that expenditures and commitments will exceed the original estimate by more than the established tolerance?
7. Are the accounting records pertaining to paid but unbilled charges periodically reviewed to determine the status of items billable to the company? Likewise, is the status of all charges billed to the company but not yet paid to third parties periodically reviewed?
8. As concerns accounts payable:
   a. Are invoices subject to arithmetical check?
   b. Are media invoices checked against contracts, card rates, or SRDS data, tear sheets, station affidavits, reports of monitors, and other proof of performance data?
   c. Are nonmedia invoices routinely checked for propriety of rates (such as union rates, reuse payments, contracts, and going rates)?
   d. Are invoiced amounts compared with approved estimates to establish propriety of the charge?
   e. When progress billings are received, is the cost vs. work to date reviewed by knowledgeable agency personnel?
   f. Are invoices approved by a supervisory employee before payment?
   g. Does the agency abide by the terms of payment?
9. Is there an adequate procedure for recording the amount of advertising placed with each medium? (Because of the importance of this procedure, the auditor should prepare a written description of the procedures, accounts used, and reports prepared.)
10. Is there an adequate procedure for controlling credits arising from advertising that did not take place or which was not presented in accordance with the purchase specifications (poorly reproduced or placed, preempted time, etc.)? (The agency's procedure should be fully described in a memorandum.)
11. Are all cash discounts, rebates, and other credits recorded directly to the company's account?

Verification. Objective and scope. This phase of the audit involves examining a representative number of agency billings to (1) determine the practices actually in effect, and (2) verify the propriety of payments to the agency.

In determining the extent to which agency billings are to be examined, two factors should be considered. First, the reliability of the various systems (purchasing, accounting, etc.) must be considered, for this would have a bearing on the number of transactions selected for examination. Second, the extent of the agency's services must be considered so that the selection will include transactions representing every major agency service.

All billings selected for audit must be examined to determine that they conform to certain basic requirements. Depending on the type of charge involved, certain invoices must be subject to additional review. The detail program that follows begins with the audit steps that should be carried out for virtually all agency billings selected for audit. Additional audit steps are outlined in the succeeding sections.

Preliminary steps. The auditor should obtain from the agency a summary listing, broken down by media and nonmedia expenditures, of their billings to the company for the current fiscal year. The data on this schedule, together with the information obtained in the course of the various procedural reviews described above, should enable the auditor to decide how much verification work will be necessary.

Concurrently with his review of these data, the auditor should decide on which billings he intends to examine. It is important that this be done in the early stage of the audit, for the examination will involve such agency records as paid vouchers, job jackets for production costs, contracts, inventories of props, and films. Therefore, providing the agency with advance notification of the specific data and material needed will enable them to assemble it in a manner least disruptive to their normal work routine and also will avoid costly delays for the auditor.

Finally, the summary listing of billings may be used as a work paper lead schedule. As such, the auditor can indicate thereon the amount of each type of expenditure verified and also cross references to the work papers which pertain to the various billings examined.

Basic audit steps. To verify the propriety of payments made by the company to its agency, the auditor should determine that all the billings selected for audit represent charges that are:

1. For the account of the company
2. Legitimately billable, i.e., not expenses that should be borne by the agency
3. Levied against the proper product estimate, period, and account code
4. Supportable to detailed estimates which have been properly approved
5. Correct from the standpoint of the agency commission that may be included (reference must, of course, be made to the billing policy to determine which charges are commissionable)
6. Correct insofar as they may contain charges for agency personnel (such charges should have been calculated in accordance with the rates included in the billing policy)
7. For advertising that has actually occurred or, in the case of certain media, for space and time actually committed
8. Net of credits, rebates, and cash discounts which, per the contract or billing policy, are to be passed on to the company
9. Arithmetically correct and, where applicable, supportable by third party invoices which in turn are arithmetically sound
10. Supported by the approval signature of the agency employee responsible for reviewing the particular expenditure

All billings which involve payments by the agency to a third party should be audited to determine the appropriateness of the bill-pay sequence. That is, the auditor should note the dates on which the following documents were received, prepared, and paid.

1. Third party invoices to agency
2. Agency's billing to company
3. Company's payment to agency
4. Agency's payment to the third party

With the exception of certain media billings for which a special arrangement may have been made permitting the agency to bill the company before payment to the media, all billed charges should represent paid items. Even in the case of advertising media billings, the date of the payment by the company should be close to the date on which the agency made payment.

Additional audit steps. MAGAZINE, NEWSPAPER, AND TRADE PAPER SPACE

1. Using the estimate and the master schedule of insertions, check each selected invoice for insertion date, lineage ordered, and total lineage for the particular estimate.

2. Verify cost of insertion or line rates with space contracts and/or Standard Rate and Data Service for rate, quantity, and cycle discounts.

3. Verify a number of insertions (newspaper and magazine) against lineage and rates that appear on the invoice. This step can be accomplished when reviewing the agency's procedure for checking tear sheets and verifying that present controls in effect are adequate.

NOTE: The agencies generally retain tear sheets for 3 months unless this procedure is conducted by an outside firm such as the Advertising Checking Bureau (ACB).

4. Determine whether rebates from publishers are passed on to the company by the agency, with commission added.

5. If the company has more than one agency and one has been designated as the master control agency for magazines and Sunday supplements, that agency sets the rates to be charged by all the company's agencies. If such is the case:

   a. Secure the latest master insertion schedule for all magazines and main Sunday supplements from the media department.
   b. Review and evaluate the agency's system of control over rates and volume discounts.
   c. Determine at what volume-discount levels billings are being made and how such is determined, for example, progressively as the rate is earned, or on the basis of planned insertions during the contract year. Verify the publishers' invoices.

6. Determine if cancelable commitments are controlled.

7. There may be no master control agency for newspaper space. In this case, and if the company has more than one agency, the agency which places the initial insertion in any given contract year issues the master contract and thereby becomes the master agency for that particular publication. If such is the case, determine:

   a. Whether the agencies communicate with each other in order to coordinate planned insertions to obtain the lowest and most realistic volume rates throughout the year.
   b. Whether the agencies select trade papers and newspapers which allow volume discounts and whether they tabulate lineage insertions

and rates for the contract year, or year to date, and interchange lineage with the company's other agencies.

c. Ascertain that the company has been billed at the same rate in each agency, and if the insertion rate was revised downward, make certain that the company has, or will be, credited with the applicable rebates.

MAGAZINES, NEWSPAPER, AND TRADE PAPER PRODUCTION COSTS: The transactions selected for this category of expense should be for the same period of time as those selected for verifying magazines, newspapers, and trade paper space.

1. Verify that the charges apply to the advertisement checked.
2. Note any unusual charges, such as overtime, or any other items which may indicate inefficiency, and determine whether they were approved by the agency and the company, and whether the company or the agency may have been at fault.
3. Compare the total actual cost with the agency's estimate. Where detailed cost estimates are available, compare the variances between major categories of expense. Determine that the total billing does not exceed the approved estimates by more than a reasonable amount.
4. Check the advertisements, selected for detailed testing, to the media insertion schedule, and examine tear sheets.
5. Determine if copies of vendors' invoices are submitted to the company for review to justify billings of production costs.
6. Determine if the agency has obtained releases for the use of names, pictures, music, etc.

TELEVISION AND RADIO NETWORK PROGRAM TIME: Prior to the audit of the agency, determine the number of shows for each network, the time period covered, and the applicable discount structure in effect.

1. Determine that the discount is in accordance with each network's discount structure and that the company is securing the highest discount available based on the number of shows, etc. Verify also that the discount, as determined above, agrees with the network's billing and the estimate prepared by the agency.
2. The selection of transactions for audit should include at least one television and radio show for each major network and only those for which the agency acts as the master agency (assuming more than one agency).
   a. Verify that the approved media estimate agrees with the network station listing at the beginning of the 13-week cycle, i.e., in number of stations and in aggregate dollar amounts.
   b. Trace subsequent additions and deletions of stations or changes in rates during the 13-week cycle as shown on network invoices, to estimate revisions and network notices of rate changes. Note that any rate increases are effected subsequent to any rate protection period stipulated in the contract.
   c. Verify on a test basis station rates on the estimate to *SRDS—Network Rates and Data* booklet for the applicable period.
3. Determine that adjustments for interruptions or nonperformance are supported by credit memoranda and that the computation is in accordance with each network's billing policy.

Also, develop from the actual billings how the networks render their credits to the agency, i.e., with or without commissions; how the agency, in turn, credits the company with or without commissions.

In each case, make certain that the agency obtains the highest credit available.

4. Test check the performance of individual stations by reference to BAR reports, noting agreement of performance time with the estimate.
   a. For any cases of nonperformance or interruption, determine that the show was rescheduled per a change order, or credit was passed on to the company.
   b. Review procedure for makeup time.
   c. Ascertain the extent to which the agency uses BAR reports to check station performance.

5. Review all shows with the agency media personnel to determine if there are any unsettled matters or any outstanding commitments for which the company has not yet been billed—major interruptions, switch in product insertions, etc.

TELEVISION AND RADIO SPOT ANNOUNCEMENT TIME: The selection of transactions to audit should include several television and radio spot announcement estimates for a quarter.

1. Verify that billings to the company are in agreement with the approved estimates by checking selected stations, related rates, and number of spot announcements.

2. Determine that performance is certified by the stations by a certificate or affidavit of performance. Also, ascertain whether the agency spot checks the station log records.

3. Select a representative number of these invoices:
   a. Verify station rates listed thereon against master contracts located in the media department and to rates included in the Standard Rate and Data book.
   b. Determine that the time of performance as per the invoice agrees with the time ordered as shown on the estimate.
   c. Secure the related BAR reports, and check the time of actual performance as listed thereon with the time of performance shown on the invoice. Review the reports for possible triple spotting. Where BAR reports are not available for the stations listed, trace available BAR reports to station invoices on a test basis.

4. Test the agency's control system to determine if there is an effective reporting procedure on spot announcements to assure that the lowest possible rates are obtained. Determine if the agency refunds commissions on rebates earned on volume discounts.

5. Determine the method employed by the agency in obtaining frequency discounts; i.e., progressively from the beginning of the contract year or at a planned insertion level for the entire contract year.

6. Determine if there are any commitments outstanding for which the company has not yet been billed.

TELEVISION, RADIO, NETWORK COMMERCIAL PRODUCTION COSTS: The transactions selected should be for the same period and programs as selected for the audit of television and radio program time charges.

1. Determine that talent costs billed are in agreement with the prevailing union scales. Determine how taxes are reported and paid, and how commis-

sion has been computed (payment of reserve for union increases should be deferred until the agency is required to make payment).

2. Review the network's billing for studio rental, time, etc., to each network's published listing of charges. (Note: Networks publish a booklet with this billing data, which can be obtained from the agency's media department.)

3. Test the controls over talent payments, including reuse payments and other production charges. On package shows, examine the contract and determine:

a. That the agency is billing the company in accordance with the terms of the contract including the computation of commissions

b. If the show includes both originals and reruns, the manner in which the agency bills the company, i.e., separately for each, or at an average of the two

4. Prepare a listing of those charges which appear to be unusual or extraordinary. Review these items with appropriate agency or company personnel. Determine whether they are proper and whether they should be spelled out in detail in the billing policy.

5. Determine whether releases have been obtained (use of names, music, etc.).

TELEVISION AND RADIO SPOT COMMERCIAL PRODUCTION COSTS

1. Verify that billable time or finished work such as storyboards and jingles is at approved rates or amounts as outlined in the billing policy. List all unusual charges for review with agency and/or company personnel.

2. Determine when the producer is to be paid—after the completion and acceptance of the commercial or in partial payments, and verify that the agency's billings reflect the terms of payment.

3. Review the listing of props used in the production of film commercials, verifying the physical existence of them on a test basis.

4. Determine whether releases have been obtained (use of names, music, etc.).

ALL OTHER AGENCY BILLINGS: The expenditures covered by this section are generally minor in relation to the amounts expended for media space, time, and related production projects. Nevertheless, the aggregate amounts spent should be determined and if meaningful, or subject to weak controls, should be audited. The audit steps involved are described below.

List the annual agency expenditures for each of the following:

Outdoor
Research
Store audits
Publicity
Collateral material and other
All other billings
(specify by type)

Based on the amount of expenditures for each of the above, select a representative number of estimates or projects and complete the following audit steps.

Outdoor:

1. Determine whether the agency is a member of the national outdoor advertising bureau. If it is, ascertain if the agency uses their services.

2. If the agency purchases space directly from outdoor plants, compare the poster contract with the estimate for the accuracy of the following data: product, city, posting dates, cost per month, and total cost.

3. Ascertain whether all contracts have been accepted and any exceptions or changes are covered in revised estimates.

4. Check vendors' invoices to the approved space contract.

5. Ascertain whether lithography on outdoor posters has been ordered directly by the company.

6. In addition to reviewing affidavits of performance from outdoor plants, inquire as to what additional verification of performance and appearance is made by the agency, or perhaps the company's sales force.

Research:

1. Note whether research has been done at company's request and that the total cost of the project has been approved by the company.

2. Obtain a summary statement of expenditures and verify charges as follows:

a. Trace outside interviewing expense to time sheets submitted by interviewers.
b. Examine supporting data for field trips taken by agency personnel.
c. Examine time records for agency personnel charged to the project.
d. Examine all other charges such as telegrams and express charges.
e. Determine if there are any charges for supervision and how they are applied.

For all the above, determine that the billing is correct and that it conforms to the billing policy applicable to research.

NOTE: When a standard rate is used to compute the billing for labor and overhead, test the rate. Is any profit included in the rate? Is the rate an established and approved one? Is it current?

Store audits:

1. Obtain current charts used in determining store audit panel costs.

2. Select projects to be audited and analyze charges made to the company for store audits, e.g., number of products plus distance cost.

3. Ascertain that the applicable discounts are granted to the company based on the number of products involved.

4. Determine if the agency is compensated for this service and if it is in conformance with agency billing agreement.

Publicity:

The major part of this work handled by the agency probably relates to publicizing television and radio shows. What costs are to be billed and the amount, if any, must be agreed to by the agency and the company before work is started.

1. Determine that the amount of billings, in detail and in total, agrees with the approved estimate.

2. If billings are in excess of estimate, have they been specifically ordered and approved by the company?

Collateral material and other specified billings:

Billings under this heading should be negotiated in advance with the agency at an agreed price. The agency should render detailed estimates so that billings can be verified with the detail as well as the total cost. Perform the necessary audit steps to assure that billings are proper and agree in detail, and in total. Reasons for significant variations in cost should be investigated.

FLOW CHARTS

An excellent way for the auditor to gain an understanding and to be able to review quickly the flow of advertising activities is by means of flow charts. In addition to presenting information in concise form, the flow chart enables the auditor to review more efficiently the adequacy of internal controls. This approach is more effective in some cases than would be the internal control questionnaire, and for this reason, a number of large companies maintain comprehensive flow charts of all advertising activities. As a matter of fact, if more than one agency is used, there would ordinarily be separate sets of flow charts for each agency.

At the beginning of the advertising audit, the auditor should carefully review the flow charts and then direct his examination of the procedures and documents to determining that the flow charts represent the practices actually in effect. Should the auditor's review reveal deficiencies in the agency's system of internal control, recommendations to correct the weaknesses would have to be developed.

For a better understanding of flow charts, we have reproduced a chart set applicable to an advertising agency whose client has an extensive advertising program. The charts and exhibits are not intended to serve as a model for network time purchases and payment procedures, but rather, as an example of a flow chart and also to provide the reader with additional information on agency practices. Incidentally, these charts were prepared by a member of the company's advertising department, who might be regarded as a specialist in advertising agency accounting and control practices.

In the flow chart shown, there are three separate phases: (*a*) estimating cycle, (*b*) billing cycle, and (*c*) payment cycle. (See Figures 1*a* to 1*c*.)

Estimating cycle. This part depicts the procedure of the estimator and others involved in the development of the estimated billing for network time. The flow chart also indicates the work of the typist and the biller in connection with estimating.

Billing cycle. In the billing cycle are shown the work flow of the biller, the billing machine operator, and the accounts receivable clerk. In addition to the work flow, the distribution of copies and time schedules is shown.

Payment cycle. The third part of the chart shows the procedure of the agency in making the payment to the network. Since the billing to the company is closely related to the payment to the network for the same service, the billing clerk determines that services shown on all applicable network invoices have been billed to the company. A remittance advice and check are prepared and the necessary accounting entries effected.

Figure 1a ESTIMATING CYCLE (SEE SAMPLE FORM IN FIGURE 2)

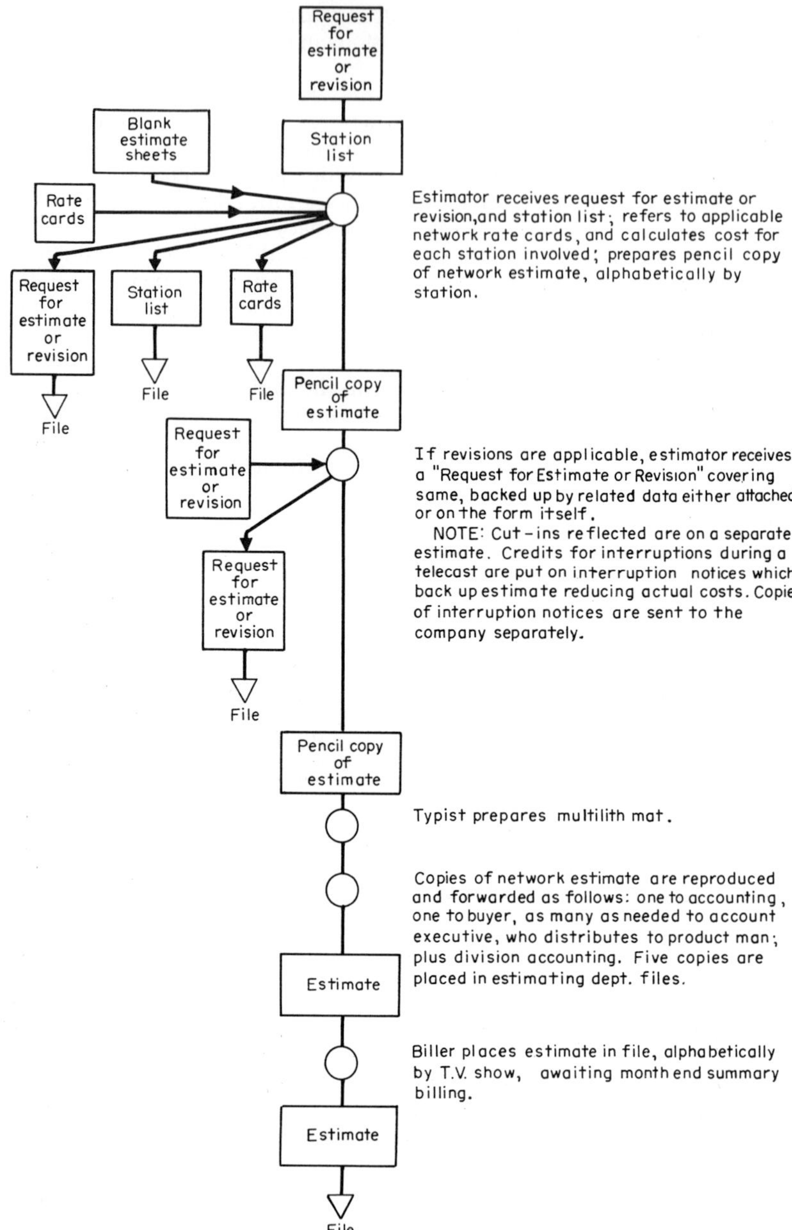

Figure 1b BILLING CYCLE

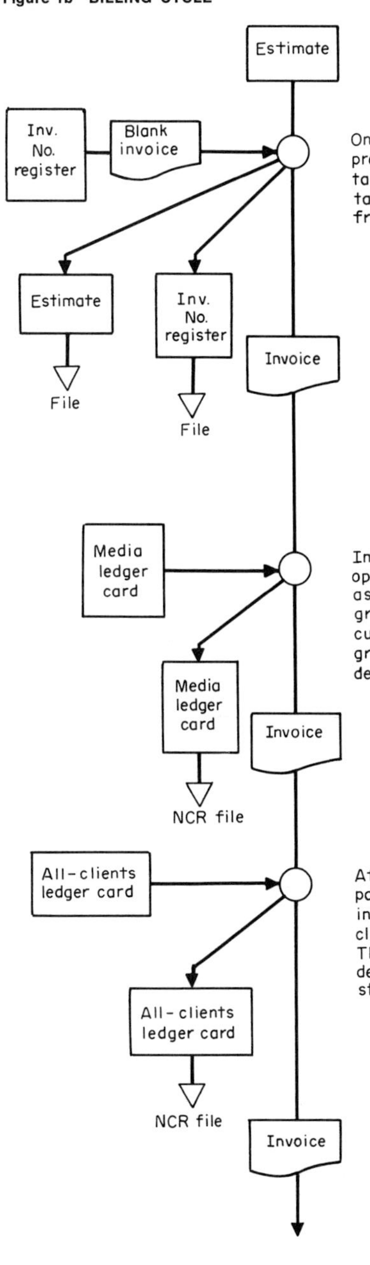

On approximately 23rd of month, biller manually prepares an invoice from the estimate. Time and talent are split apart. Biller enters net time cost, net talent cost, agency of record fee and invoice number-from invoice number register.

Immediately after preparation of 3-part invoice, NCR operator posts to media ledger card, showing by product as follows: Invoice date, invoice number, gross billed, gross cost, net cost, cumulative net payable amount, cumulative monthly sales amount, cumulative monthly gross. See end of this flow chart for detailed description of entries on media ledger cards.

After entries are completed for all clients under one particular media, the all-clients ledger card is placed in the NCR machine, and a cumulative total for all clients (for the particular media involved) is posted. This card's function in month-end proof steps is described at the end of this flow chart. Invoices are stamped as being "posted" by NCR operator.

Figure 1b BILLING CYCLE (CONTINUED)

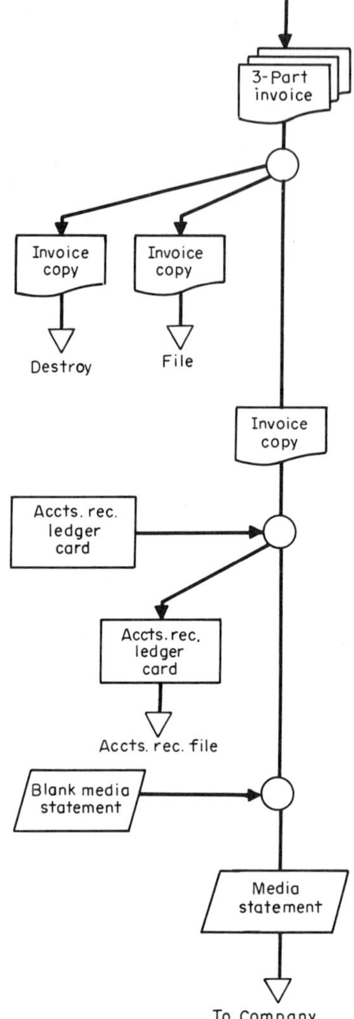

Biller receives back handwritten 3-part invoice from NCR operator; and destroys original. Places duplicate in network file and forwards triplicate to accounts receivable section.

Accounts receivable clerk receives invoice copy from biller, and posts gross invoice amount-gross of cash discount, net of agency commission -to accounts receivable ledger sheet.

On 25th of the month, accounts receivable clerk prepares a media statement -by estimate - of all items to be paid by agency in following month for each division. Statements are sent to respective divisions and a copy of each is used to support the cash requirements letter sent to corporate office.

END OF BILLING CYCLE

NOTE: Upon receipt of check from the company - per cash requirements letter - accounts receivable clerk posts credits to accounts receivable ledger card for gross invoice amount (net of agency commission) represented by the payment. Cash discounts are posted in a separate column. Individual charges and corresponding credits are then keyed off.

Figure 1c PAYMENT CYCLE (SEE SAMPLE FORM IN FIGURE 3)

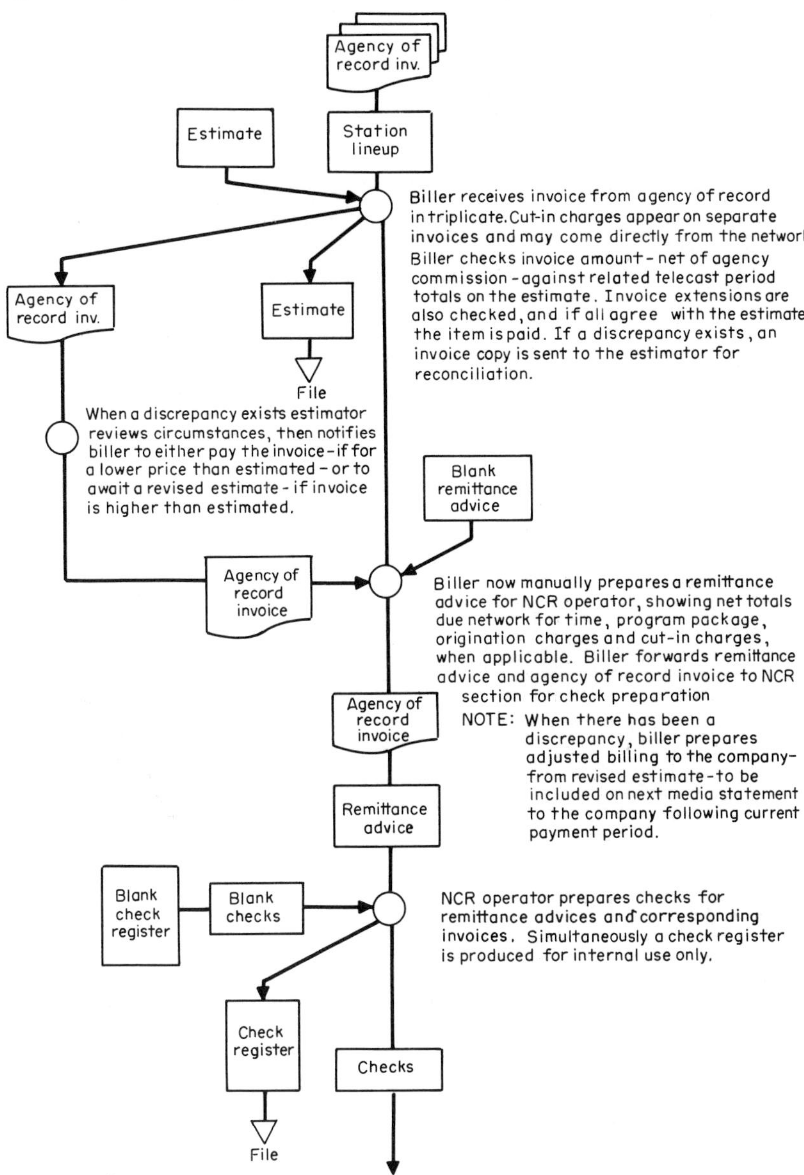
Agency of record inv.
Estimate
Station lineup
Biller receives invoice from agency of record in triplicate. Cut-in charges appear on separate invoices and may come directly from the network
Biller checks invoice amount - net of agency commission - against related telecast period totals on the estimate. Invoice extensions are also checked, and if all agree with the estimate, the item is paid. If a discrepancy exists, an invoice copy is sent to the estimator for reconciliation.
Agency of record inv.
Estimate
File
When a discrepancy exists estimator reviews circumstances, then notifies biller to either pay the invoice - if for a lower price than estimated - or to await a revised estimate - if invoice is higher than estimated.
Blank remittance advice
Agency of record invoice
Biller now manually prepares a remittance advice for NCR operator, showing net totals due network for time, program package, origination charges and cut-in charges, when applicable. Biller forwards remittance advice and agency of record invoice to NCR section for check preparation
NOTE: When there has been a discrepancy, biller prepares adjusted billing to the company - from revised estimate - to be included on next media statement to the company following current payment period.
Agency of record invoice
Remittance advice
Blank check register
Blank checks
NCR operator prepares checks for remittance advices and corresponding invoices. Simultaneously a check register is produced for internal use only.
Check register
Checks
File

Figure 1c PAYMENT CYCLE (CONTINUED)

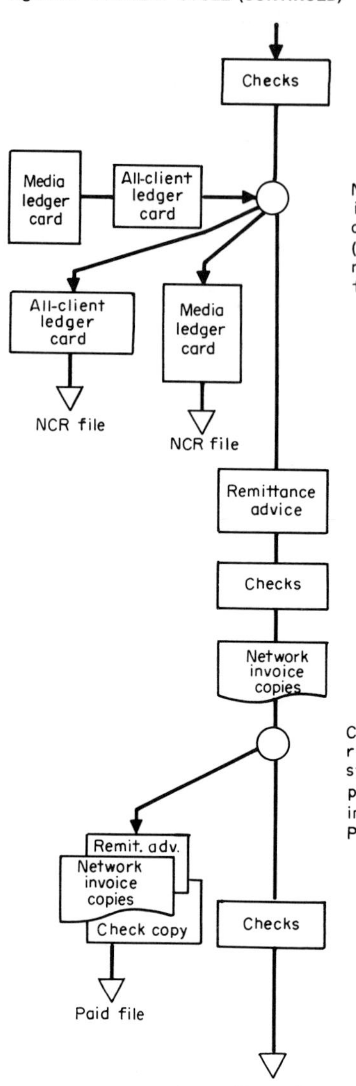

NCR operator enters amount paid to agency of record in "cost" column of media ledger card (these entries are in red). Cumulative payable amount for all clients (by media) is posted to all-clients ledger card. Checks, remittance advices and invoices are then forwarded to an accounting clerk.

Clerk verifies checks against respective invoices and remittance advices. Then, a copy of the check is stapled to its related documents, and the batch is perforated "paid". Original checks are forwarded to internal accounting for signature and mailing. Paid documents go to paid files.

END OF PAYMENT CYCLE

Figure 2 REQUEST FOR ESTIMATE OR REVISION

ESTIMATING__________

TRAFFIC__________

FORWARDING__________

ACCOUNTING__________

CONTROL__________

REQUEST FOR ESTIMATE OR REVISION

ESTIMATE NO.

DATE__________

CLIENT__________

PRODUCT__________

DUE DATE__________

PLEASE PREPARE

- ☐ ESTIMATE
- ☐ REVISED ESTIMATE
- ☐ CHANGE SHEET
- ☐ CANCELLATION
- ☐

MEDIA

- ☐ NETWORK TV/RADIO
- ☐ SPOT TV/RADIO
- ☐ MAGAZINES
- ☐ NEWSPAPER
- ☐

☐ ESTIMATE REVISION NOT REQUESTED

STATIONS—PUBLICATIONS NUMBER	STARTING	ENDING	BUDGETED TOTAL COST

SPECIAL INSTRUCTIONS

BUYER __________

Figure 3 DISCREPANCY NOTICE

(Accounting)

DISCREPANCY NOTICE

IMPORTANT: TO BE RETURNED TO ACCOUNTING DEPT. NO LATER THAN________________

TO: MEDIA DEPARTMENT Date:________________

Attention:________________

Client:________________ Product________________ Schedule or Estimate No.________________

Publication: City________________ State________________

Program:

Station:

THE INFORMATION CONTAINED ON ESTIMATE AND/OR CONTRACT FOR THE ABOVE MEDIUM IS NOT IN ACCORD WITH THEIR INVOICE OR AFFIDAVIT. WILL YOU PLEASE CHECK THE DISCREPANCIES INDICATED AND ADVISE.

SCHEDULE ORDERED				BILLING RECEIVED			
DATE	TIME	CLASS SPACE	RATE	DATE	TIME	CLASS SPACE	RATE

REMARKS:

BY________________

MEDIA REPLY:

DATE BY

ACCOUNTING DETAIL

The agency maintains three basic accounting controls. These are as follows:

1. Establishing the relationship between accounts receivable and accounts payable
2. Establishing the relationship between agency sales (total billing), and accounts receivable
3. Reconciling media ledger card balances with unbilled or unpaid items in active media billing files

The "media ledger card" referred to in this flow chart serves as a record of all media invoices to clients, and related payments to networks. There is one such ledger card for each product on each network show. One basic purpose of this ledger card is to provide the basis for comparing billing to client with payments to media.

From the over-all control standpoint, individual entries (debit or credit) to the media ledger cards are accumulated and posted to the "all clients" ledger card. This cumulative total is reconciled at month end to related accounts payable and receivable general ledger entries.

Again at month end, an "analysis of cards" worksheet is prepared from the media ledger cards—with the following entries:

1. Accumulative accounts payable (by network show)
2. Monthly sales to date (by network show)
3. Monthly cost to date (by network show)

The total of individual media ledger cards (for the above three totals) is proven to the totals on the "all clients" card.

The "analysis of cards" worksheet is then passed to the clerk assigned to the client's account, who uses same to prepare a "monthly billing analysis" worksheet. This particular worksheet shows client by client total billing figures for each media, and production account. These totals are compared to the debit column total of the accounts receivable ledger (maintained by client), and any discrepancy is resolved.

Again using the "analysis of cards" worksheet, the General Ledger Clerk applies the 85% standard to the total billing figure—to assure that cost figures are correct.

BIBLIOGRAPHY

American Association of Advertising Agencies,
Arthur Andersen & Co., *Manual of Advertising Agency Accounting*, 1952.

Association of National Advertisers, Inc., publications, New York:
- Bloede, V. G.: *How the Agencies Look at Agency Evaluation Procedures*, 1969.
- Claggett, W. M.: *Client-Agency Evaluation Procedure*, 1969.
- Eldridge, Clarence E.: *Management of Advertising and Marketing*, 1966.
- Kelly, R. J.: *The Advertising Budget: Preparation, Administration and Control*, 1967.
- Shulins, Sidney J.: *Fee Methods of Agency Compensation.*
- Tighe, E. P.: *Federal State and Municipal Laws Affecting Advertising*, 1959.

Research Report No. 13, *Internal Audit and Control of Advertising and Sales Promotion*, The Institute of Internal Auditors, New York, 1963.

Cadmus, Bradford: *Operational Auditing Handbook*, New York, The Institute of Internal Auditors, 1964.

Lamperti, Frank A., and Thurston, John B.: *Internal Auditing for Management*, Englewood Cliffs, N.J., Prentice-Hall, Inc., 1953.

Norbeck, Edward F., et al.: *Operational Auditing for Management Control*, New York, American Management Association, Inc., 1969.

Oxenfeldt, Alfred R., and Swan: *Management of the Advertising Function*, Belmont, Calif., Wadsworth Publishing Company, 1964.

Steven, Anton: "Auditing Advertising and Sales Promotion Expenses," *The Institute of Internal Auditors*, Winter, 1964.

Cleveland Chapter: "Reducing Agency Charges for Overtime," *The Internal Auditor*, Winter, 1966.

Whittaker, C. M.: "Auditing Sales Forecasting," *The Internal Auditor*, January/February, 1968.

Rayburn, Letricia, and Gale: "Cost Standards for Advertising and Sales Promotion," *The New York Certified Public Accountant*, July, 1970.

Chapter 36

Administrative and Other Expenses

WILLIAM C. LINS

Professor of Accounting, Graduate School of Business Administration, Rutgers University

GENERAL

Definition. "Administrative and other expenses" are those related to general policy determination—to the direction and control of a business enterprise as a whole, as contrasted with expenses of more definitive functions such as production and selling. The particular items included under administrative and other expenses will generally vary with the nature of the business.

Audit Objectives. The audit objectives of the examination of administrative and other expenses are to determine that expenses are:

1. Properly authorized
2. Correctly recorded
3. Properly classified, on a consistent basis
4. Properly matched against appropriate revenues
5. Properly allocated in various reports
6. Included in full and recorded as required
7. Used as a basis for constructive recommendations to management

Relation to Other Phases. Although it is the purpose of this chapter to deal exclusively with administrative and other expenses, it must be realized that the auditor cannot isolate all of these expenses from other phases of the audit. The work required to fulfill the audit objectives outlined above has in large measure already been performed for many expenses in connection with the verification of balance sheet accounts. For example, interest expense is usually verified in connection with the examination of the related liability. The examination of accounts payable and accrued liabilities requires a search for unrecorded liabilities and tests to determine that all expenses of the period under review have been recorded properly.

When the auditor considers the examination of administrative and other expenses, he must plan to concentrate on those expenses which have not been examined in connection with balance sheet or other accounts. In addition, he will want to emphasize those objectives which have not been completely fulfilled during the review of other accounts.

THE AUDIT

Extent of Examination. The extent of the examination of administrative and other expenses is highly dependent upon the:

1. Extent and effectiveness of internal control
2. Extent and effectiveness of internal auditing
3. Purpose of the audit
4. Nature of the opinion and financial statements required
5. Condition and accuracy of company financial data

For a typical business organization, the extent of examination might be somewhat uniform throughout all phases of the audit, but in some instances extra verification procedures or extensions of basic or minimum procedures may be required if certain company systems or records are substandard. The same condition would hold true if internal control or internal auditing were strong in some areas and weak in others, etc.

The auditor assures himself that the financial statements present fairly the financial position and results of operations, on a basis consistent with that of the preceding period. Although the achievement of this overall standard may require only the application of minimum auditing procedures, real contributions may be made to the success of the business enterprise if the auditor will continually search for ways of eliminating or reducing expenses, improving control systems, increasing efficiency, etc., and will report his findings and recommendations to management.

Expense Components. Administrative and other expenses may be grouped, for our purposes, into three broad expense components. These are (1) salaries, (2) supplies, and (3) other. While the various items may have varying amounts of each component, we can often isolate the largest component and verify it along with related amounts in the other items. For example, salaries may be an important component of research and development, and a less important component in most other items.

Salaries. Salaries classified as administrative or other expenses usually pertain to officers, administrative personnel, or office employees. Generally one of the most effective methods of review for salaries is by comparison with the budget or with salaries for the previous year. The auditor should also compare the number of employees with the budget or with the figure for the previous year. In addition to merely verifying what has taken place, the auditor should consider various operational auditing considerations. For example, salary increases may have been regularly given, with the result that the present salary is far in excess of what the nature and responsibility of the position call for. In some cases office salaries or the number of employees is not adequately reduced when the volume of work declines in a particular area. Most non-officer salaried jobs may be controlled through a personnel evaluation program with different grade levels and rate ranges. Top limits may be established for various jobs. The auditor will want to test the effectiveness of such a program. As in testing gross corporation figures, the auditor may select some employees from representative departments and determine whether salary changes have been made in accordance with the salary plan.

Supplies. Unless it is company policy to charge all supplies to expense as they are purchased, it is important for the auditor to satisfy himself that both the supplies inventory and the supplies expense are properly recorded. If perpetual records are maintained, the auditor should test the requisitioning of supplies and the effectiveness of the controls exercised over them. Physical control procedures are even more important when periodic inventories are used as the basis for determining expenses for the period. Employees should not have free access to office supplies.

The auditor should keep in mind various operational auditing considerations where the expense for supplies and forms is substantial. For example, where a company may have many units, each buying small quantities of bond paper, carbon paper, and hundreds of other supply items, the excess cost can be very large indeed. The auditor may want to review the volume of purchases and to suggest for those representing large expenditures that blanket orders be placed at a volume price. Very often such a volume price may be half or less what is now being paid for a comparable item. The various units of the company can then draw against the blanket order. In many instances the large suppliers have sales offices or warehouses in various parts of the country and usually are convenient to most company locations. The cost of forms may be very high, especially where different colors or many carbons are required. The auditor may wish to compile the total printing costs with a view to recommending that blanket orders be used for printed forms also. He may also wish to question the cost of certain expensive forms. Perhaps good reproductions can be used instead of typeset forms. In some instances substantial savings on forms have been made based on the auditor's review and recommendations.

Other. The third component will vary widely among the various items. This might represent a service, such as utilities, etc. These will be taken up later as we discuss the various specific items.

Types of Expense Control. The installation and operation of a specific type of expense control is a vital factor in the overall control system. In addition to the direct benefits in the form of savings, an expense control program tends to focus the attention of all personnel on the need to watch expenses. The employees should become "expense conscious."

The auditor will appraise the effectiveness of the expense control programs in the same manner that he evaluates the effectiveness of other types of control. The principal forms of expense control are (1) budgetary control, (2) established standards, and (3) a cost-reduction plan.

Budgetary control. Most modern companies will have some form of budgetary control. Such a budget may be a comprehensive budget of many parts or it may consist of only certain parts, such as a capital budget, sales budget, expense budget, etc. In any case, a well-planned budget is one of the most effective forms of control. The auditor's responsibilities with respect to the budget are described later in this chapter.

Established standards. A special type of budgetary control may involve standard costs. While standards have long proved their effectiveness in manufacturing operations, they are only beginning to be used to any great extent in clerical operations. In the last few years much research has been done in this area and various kinds of standards are available. For example, standards have been established for practically every typing operation. Where a large number of typists are employed, some kind of standards may be desirable.

Cost-reduction plan. From time to time most companies embark on some form of cost-reduction plan. In most cases it is some type of proportional cost-reduction plan. That is, a definite percentage reduction may be assigned to specific locations, particularly with respect to personnel expense. Additions or replacements of personnel may not be approved for a specific period.

Auditing Procedures. Most administrative and other expenses may be verified by either of two general methods:

1. Application of overall tests
2. Examination of individual transactions

Overall tests. Overall testing is one of the most effective devices that an auditor may apply to financial transactions, because it normally results in proving total expenses of a given type while also verifying cutoff requirements. For example, royalty expenses may be subject to overall testing. If the auditor applies the royalty rate to the applicable sales, the amount of royalty expense thus derived should equal the amount recorded. Because overall testing requires the auditor to check all such transactions for a given period, the test cannot be performed until after the period has ended and all applicable transactions have been recorded. Figure 1 is a worksheet illustrating an overall test for royalty expenses.

Individual transactions. Examination of individual transactions is the method normally used when overall procedures cannot be employed. Since testing procedures are commonly used (as opposed to complete examination of transactions, which is sometimes required because of special circumstances or for certain accounts), the reliance that can be placed on the results depends primarily upon the internal control in existence, the extent of the tests, and the results of the tests. Either traditional or statistical sampling methods may be used in testing administrative and other expenses. Methods of evaluating the results are discussed in subsequent paragraphs.

Auditing Techniques. The examination techniques may vary considerably, depending upon the nature of the expense, the method of record keeping, internal controls, etc. The following techniques are representative of those which may be employed in typical situations.

When overall testing is possible, the examination techniques are simplified. It is usually sufficient to examine copies of the documents, such as contracts, agreements, franchises, etc., under which the expenses are incurred, evidence of obligation payments during the period under review, and proper accruals at the end of the period. Examination of the latter two types of items can usually be done simultaneously when the applicable rate is applied to the base for the period under review.

When individual transactions are examined, the techniques may range from a minimum test of several items to verification of all transactions. The former is appropriate when there are numerous regular transactions, plus acceptable recording and control systems. The latter is often done for the more unique type of transaction such as professional fees and certain taxes, plus unusually large or unusual items in other accounts such as travel and entertainment, miscellaneous expenses, contributions, repairs and maintenance, etc.

For those items selected for examination, the auditor should satisfy himself that each was properly requisitioned, ordered, received, invoiced, and recorded. Depending upon the audit program, the payment may be verified at this time or in relation to the examination of cash or vouchers payable. Examination of this type may be started at an interim date but must be completed after the records have been closed for the period under review.

At some time during the audit of administrative and other expenses the auditor should scan or analyze selected expense accounts which might have re-

Figure 1 ADMINISTRATIVE AND OTHER EXPENSES

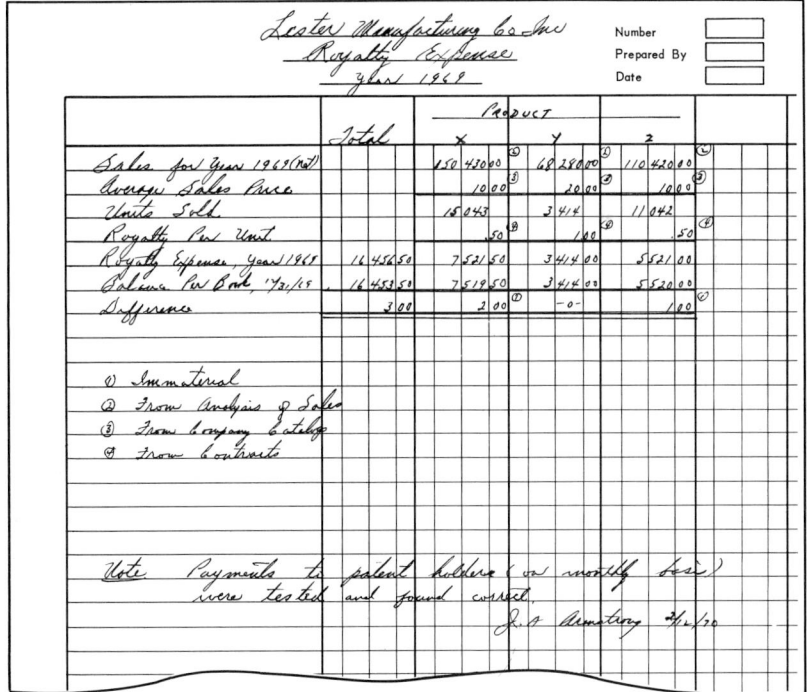

Lester Manufacturing Co. Inc
Royalty Expense
Year 1969

Number
Prepared By
Date

	Total	Product X	Product Y	Product Z
Sales for Year 1969 (Net)		150 430 00 (2)	68 280 00 (2)	110 420 00 (2)
Average Sales Price		10 00 (3)	20 00 (3)	10 00 (3)
Units Sold		15 043	3 414	11 042
Royalty Per Unit		.50 (4)	1 00 (4)	.50 (4)
Royalty Expense, Year 1969	16 456 50	7 521 50	3 414 00	5 521 00
Balance Per Book, 12/31/69	16 453 50	7 519 50	3 414 00	5 520 00
Difference	3 00	2 00 (1)	-0-	1 00 (1)

(1) Immaterial
(2) From Analysis of Sales
(3) From Company Catalog
(4) From Contracts

Note Payments to patent holders (on monthly basis) were tested and found correct.

J. A. Armstrong 2/12/70

ceived unusual or nonoperating charges. Accounts such as sundry or miscellaneous expenses, travel and entertainment, contributions, etc., may contain inappropriate charges.

Auditing Documentation. Those transactions subject to overall testing may be completely documented, as illustrated in Figure 2. It is frequently true that the amount of documentation is quite small in relation to the significance of the expenses involved.

When expense accounts are composed primarily of routine transactions and when the recording and control systems are satisfactory, the tests may be made directly on the original records. Working-paper notations may be made concerning the kinds of work performed, approximate extent, and results. When the quantity of tests is not extensive, which is often the case if statistical sampling methods are used, the auditor may prefer to list in detail in the workpapers all documents, records, etc., that have been examined, together with the results.

Those items requiring individual inspection and verification, such as fees for professional services, certain taxes, large contributions, significant repairs, etc., should be listed in detail in the workpapers. In addition to serving as proof of work performed, these listings often lead to the discovery of unrecorded liabilities (such as attorney's billings) and unrecorded assets (such as items erroneously charged to repairs). They also aid in preparing or verifying income tax returns (for contributions, etc.).

In a well-organized set of workpapers it is appropriate to include a control sheet for administrative and other expenses which would include for each expense the totals from the previous period, totals per books this period, appropriate adjustments, and final-statement balances. If budgets are used by the company, it is helpful to include the budgeted amounts also. As an aid in analyzing the changes in expenses between periods and the variations from budgets, the differences may be noted for each expense. Figure 2 illustrates such a control worksheet.

BUDGET VARIANCES

Aid to Auditing. If management uses expense budgets (and it need not be demonstrated here that budgets may prove extremely helpful as an aid to successful administration) and has used them properly, variances from budgeted amounts may be quite revealing in reviewing the propriety, accuracy, and classification of various expenses. Properly employed, expense budgets forecast not solely what expenses are expected to be, but rather what they ought to be. Often, managements do not properly evaluate the variances between budgeted and actual amounts, as they are already caught up in forecasting future periods while being concerned with present problems. Budgets usually have to be prepared for future periods before the results from present and sometimes past periods are complete or before they have been properly analyzed.

Analysis of Variances. The auditor, as well as management, should analyze in detail any significant budget variances. (Figure 2 illustrates a control workpaper for administrative and other expenses that facilitates this kind of analysis.) Through this analysis, it is easy to detect accounts requiring special attention because actual results are either substantially below or above the budgeted figure. The difference may be accounted for in various ways; some of the more common explanations are:

Figure 2 ROYALTY EXPENSE

Lester Manufacturing Co. Inc
Administrative and Other Expense
Year 1969

Number
Prepared By
Date

Expense	Year 1968	Per Books 1969	Adjustments Debit	Adjustments Credit	Final 1969	Difference 1968 and 1969	Budget 1969	Difference Actual and Budget
1-1 Salaries and Wages	101 400 00	103 562 20			103 562 20	2 162 20 (1)	103 000 00	562 20 (6)
1-2 Bonus and Profit Sharing	5 500 00	5 800 00			5 800 00	300 00 (1)	5 800 00	-0-
1-3 Supplies	867 10	1 006 32			1 006 32	139 22 (1)	1 000 00	6 32 (5)
1-4 Depreciation and Amortization	31 410 20	32 900 02			32 900 02	1 489 82 (1)	33 000 00	(99 98) (5)
1-5 Repairs and Maintenance	16 438 16	15 339 06		1 100 00	14 239 06	(2 199 10) (4)	15 000 00	(760 94) (4)
1-6 Rent	1 200 00	1 200 00			1 200 00	-0-	1 200 00	-0-
1-7 Research and Development	28 400 01	33 568 14			33 568 14	5 168 13 (2)	33 500 00	68 14 (5)
1-8 Royalties	13 462 00	16 453 50			16 453 50	2 991 50 (1)	16 500 00	(46 50) (5)
1-9 Travel and Entertainment	4 962 14	5 237 26			5 237 26	275 12 (1)	5 000 00	237 26 (5)
2-1 Professional Services	12 500 00	16 850 00			16 850 00	4 350 00 (3)	12 500 00	4 350 00 (3)
2-2 Contributions	2 500 00	2 800 00			2 800 00	300 00 (2)	2 800 00	-0-
2-3 Pension Plan	19 000 00	21 006 14			21 006 14	2 006 14 (1)	21 000 00	6 14 (5)
2-4 Insurance	15 400 00	17 009 01			17 009 01	1 609 01 (1)	16 800 00	209 01 (5)
2-5 Taxes	11 438 02	13 127 14			13 127 14	1 689 12 (1)	13 000 00	127 14 (5)
2-6 Interest	2 000 00	2 000 00			2 000 00	-0-	2 000 00	-0-
2-7 Utilities	16 438 19	18 327 22			18 327 22	1 889 03 (1)	17 500 00	827 22 (7)
2-8 Postage	11 006 10	12 003 00			12 003 00	996 90 (1)	12 000 00	3 00
2-9 Sundry	2 300 20	2 401 80			2 401 80	101 60 (1)	2 400 00	1 80 (5)
	296 222 12	320 590 81		1 100 00	319 490 81	23 268 69	314 000 00	5 490 81

1. Erroneous charges or postings
2. Change in level of business activities
3. Inefficient operations
4. Efficient operations
5. Reduced prices of goods or services
6. Increased prices of goods or services
7. Budgeting errors

Comparison with Previous Period. Simultaneously with an examination of the variances between budgeted and actual amounts, it is appropriate to examine the difference between actual for this period and actual for the previous period. (See Figure 2.) These differences are usually subject to the same explanations as budget variances.

When differences are identified as having been caused by circumstances that require managerial action, the auditor should make appropriate recommendations to management. At the same time it is appropriate for the auditor to give management any other suggestions that will result in reduced expenses or increased efficiency.

PROGRAMS

Internal Control Questionnaire. It is assumed that regular salaries and wages, materials, supplies, etc., are controlled through acceptable established procedures which are discussed in other chapters.

1. Have levels of expense approval been established?
2. Are such levels set forth in writing?
3. Are all expenses forwarded for approval to the established point for expenses or the purchasing department?
4. Are the following items verified before payment?
   - *a.* Company name
   - *b.* Receipt of material or services
   - *c.* Prices
   - *d.* Terms
   - *e.* Discounts
   - *f.* Extensions
   - *g.* Footing
   - *h.* Account distribution
5. Do non-material expense purchase orders originate in one place?
6. Are receipts of services properly approved?
7. Does the accounting department receive directly copies of:
   - *a.* Expense authorizations?
   - *b.* Purchase orders?
   - *c.* Receiving reports?
   - *d.* Expense invoices?
8. Does the accounting department match expense invoices with expense authorizations, purchase orders, and receiving reports?
9. Are the hiring and severance procedures adequate, and are they consistent with manufacturing and other areas?
10. Are the timekeeping, payroll compilation, and payment adequate and consistent with other areas?
11. Are invoices stamped or perforated to prevent reuse?
12. Are shortages and damaged goods properly reported?

13. Are all vouchers and supporting papers signed by an authorized person?

Audit Program. It is assumed that regular salaries and wages, supplies, etc., will be examined under another audit program. This program is concerned with procedures relating to administrative and other expenses.

1. Obtain a list of persons authorized to approve expenses.
2. Compare actual expenses and budgeted expenses.
3. Compare monthly expenses with prior years both in dollar amounts and as a percentage of net sales.
4. Investigate all significant variances from budget and from prior-year actual.
5. Obtain or prepare analyses of accounts selected for examination.
6. Determine that selected expenses have been properly approved.
7. Analyze selected expense accounts.
8. Scan expense accounts not analyzed, especially those in which unusual items are likely to be charged.

INDIVIDUAL EXPENSES

The following discussion concerning typical administrative and other expenses is not meant to be completely comprehensive or all-inclusive or to serve as an audit program, but has been provided merely to indicate the standard auditing procedures that may be used, or certain peculiarities common to particular expenses. For our purposes we may group the administrative and other expenses into two broad categories: (1) those common to other departments and (2) those peculiar to administrative and other activities.

Expenses Common to Other Departments. Some of the expenses included in the "administrative and other expense" category are common to those incurred in many other departments, and no special auditing procedures are required for these items. In fact, it is likely that these expenses will be verified simultaneously with those of the other departments, since the audit emphasis will relate to the type of expense rather than the particular department. Some of the usual types of such items are salaries and wages, bonuses and profit sharing, supplies, depreciation, rent, etc. Particular items may be considered here or under the following caption. Generally, if the item, such as salaries, has been treated sufficiently in other chapters, then it will be discussed only briefly here.

Salaries and wages. Salaries and wages classified as administrative and other expenses usually pertain to officers and office and administrative personnel. Other classifications of salaries and wages may be manufacturing, sales, purchasing, retail, etc. For salaries of officers, the auditor should review the minutes of meetings of the board of directors and the executive committee and determine that payments have been in accordance with authorizations. In many cases officers are permitted to maintain drawing accounts, which are actually salary advances if the account has a debit balance or current liabilities if the account has a credit balance. Generally there are agreements or understandings concerning these advances, and the auditor must be sure that such balances are not written off without proper approval. If a debit balance remains after the salary has been credited, such amounts should be approved by the directors and included in the minutes or the item should be covered in the report. Generally the auditing procedures for other salaries and wages will be described in Chapter 32.

Bonuses and profit sharing. Bonuses or profit-sharing expenses should be verified by examination of contracts and agreements and a determination made that their provisions are properly reflected in the accounts.

Amounts paid to company officers based on earnings of the period must be carefully examined to make sure that the earnings are properly calculated and that there has been no irregularity in recording revenues and no fraudulent reduction of expenses. With any bonus plan or profit sharing, the auditor has a liability to the company to determine that the correct amount has been allocated, and also a corresponding liability to the employees to determine that they have received the full amounts due. The auditor must pay close attention to all provisions of the plan to satisfy himself that all parties have been treated in accordance with the conditions.

The auditor's tests should enable him to ascertain that all bonuses and profit-sharing amounts actually earned during the period have been properly accrued.

Supplies. Supplies consumed in connection with administrative and other expenses should be reviewed by the auditor in the light of the materiality of the expenditure and the degree of internal control present. The auditor will want to make sure that proper distinction has been made between expense and inventory. If the inventory of supplies is correctly stated, then the expense is correct. Any major changes between the budgeted expense and the current actual expense should be investigated. The same is true for any substantial changes between actual for the prior year and that for the current year. Where perpetual inventory records are maintained, the auditor will determine that proper adjustments have been made to conform with any physical inventory taken. The auditor will want to review the distribution or allocation among departments to determine that the departmental charges are not overstated or understated. If the company has a practice of charging supplies to each department as they are purchased, then a supplies inventory is not usually maintained. The auditor will want to make tests to determine that material amounts are not charged to one department and used in another.

Depreciation and amortization. Depreciation and amortization charges normally are verified in connection with the examination of fixed tangible and intangible assets and their related allowance accounts. Charges to expense accounts should be reconciled with amounts credited either to the appropriate allowance account or directly to the asset. Credits to depreciation and amortization, since they are exceptional entries, should be carefully analyzed and approved. Gains or losses on dispositions of assets should not be reflected in either depreciation or amortization.

Rent. Rent expense may be verified by examination of existing lease and license agreements or contracts, by examination of rent invoices, and by inspection of paid checks. If the amount of the rental expense is based on varying factors, such as gross receipts, the auditor should ascertain that proper accruals have been recorded, and that the expense shown for the entire period is accurate.

Expenses Peculiar to Administrative and Other Activities. This category includes mainly types of items that are not generally charged to other departments. These are professional services, contributions, pension plans, insurance, taxes, interest, utilities, postage, and sundry or miscellaneous items.

Professional services. Included principally among professional services are fees for legal, accounting, and management consulting services. Because this account usually contains only several debits even though the total may be quite substantial, it is easy to analyze it completely and to prepare a workpaper which shows all entries in detail. This is particularly important in relation to legal fees because it may reveal undisclosed or contingent liabilities, or entries that should be capitalized, such as legal fees in relation to the acquisition of properties.

Contributions. All material contributions should be listed in detail in the auditor's workpapers. They should be checked back to authorizations in the minutes of meetings of the board of directors if they have been authorized by that group. The auditor must pay particular attention to the deductibility of contributions for income tax purposes.

Pension plans. When a qualified pension plan is in effect, as is common for many companies today, the auditor must satisfy himself that all conditions and provisions of the plan have been complied with. It is also important that the auditor be familiar with generally accepted accounting principles as they apply to pension plans, and that he satisfy himself that the company's accounting procedures are sound. He should make sure that APB Opinion No. 8, "Accounting for the Cost of Pension Plans," is complied with.

Insurance. Insurance expense is normally examined simultaneously with the verification of prepaid or unexpired insurance, even though certain types of insurance are not paid in advance and some require accrued liabilities.

A separate detailed workpaper for all insurance carried by a company is standard procedure. Major differences in insurance expenses between periods should be investigated. The auditor should attempt to determine whether the company is adequately insured in all areas to protect the client against loss but not so heavily insured that excessive premiums result.

Taxes. An examination of taxes may be done at the same time that tax liability is reviewed. The auditor should examine paid tax bills and city, state, and federal tax returns to determine the proper expense for the period, including appropriate accruals. The auditor must understand the nature of each different type of tax, and must verify all rates, computations, bases for assessments, etc., and be assured that the taxes have all been correctly determined. Close examination of real estate and personal property taxes may reveal unrecognized transactions for the acquisition or disposition of assets.

Interest. Interest expense is usually verified in connection with the audit of the interest-paying liability. Interest rates should be ascertained and computations checked to see that the interest expense for the period is correct. It is important to check also to see that interest payments are made when due, in order to avoid possible penalties.

Utilities. Utilities usually include gas, water, electric, telephone, and telegraph. Whenever possible, the company should verify its own usage, which can be checked by the auditor and then matched against the invoices from the supplying companies. It is then simple to multiply the usage factor by the appropriate rates to determine the expense for the applicable period. For example, an employee can read the gas meter at the same time as a representative of the gas company; the appropriate rates can be applied to the period's usage and the amount of the invoice determined before it is received. In similar manner, accruals can be prepared at year end prior to receipt of the next invoice from the supplier.

The auditor should be careful to review all utility bills to make sure they are all for services received by the company and not for personal usage of any employee. Telephone operators should maintain logs for all toll calls. These logs can be matched against charges of the telephone company. The auditor should investigate company policy concerning personal use by employees of company telephones and satisfy himself that there is adequate compliance.

Postage. The auditor should satisfy himself that postage expense is reasonable under the circumstances and in proper relationship to prior periods and the amount of mail used by the company. His testing in this area may be minimal if he finds sound control over the metered machine or loose stamps and procedures that do not permit employees to use the company mailing facilities and company postage for personal use.

Sundry or miscellaneous. All material charges to sundry or miscellaneous expense should be inspected carefully and listed in the auditor's workpapers. Contained therein may be items that should be charged to fixed asset accounts. In addition, there is a tendency to charge to such accounts items that are not proper business expenses.

BIBLIOGRAPHY

Accounting Principles Board Opinions, AICPA, New York:
No. 7. *Accounting for Leases in Financial Statements of Lessors.*
No. 8. *Accounting for the Cost of Pension Plans.*
No. 10. *Omnibus Opinion.*
No. 12. *Omnibus Opinion.*
Accounting Principles Board Statements, AICPA, New York:
No. 2. *Disclosure of Supplemental Financial Information by Diversified Companies.*
No. 3. *Financial Statements Restated for General Price-level Changes.*
No. 4. *Basic Concepts and Accounting Principles Underlying Financial Statements of Business Enterprises.*
Statements on Auditing Procedure, AICPA, New York:
No. 33. *Auditing Standards and Procedures.*
No. 39. *Working Papers.*
No. 41. *Subsequent Discovery of Facts Existing at the Date of the Auditor's Report.*

Backer, Morton: *Modern Accounting Theory,* Englewood Cliffs, N.J., Prentice-Hall, Inc., 1966.
Cashin, James A., and Garland C. Owens: *Auditing,* New York, The Ronald Press Company, 1963.
Heckert and Wilson: *Business Budgeting and Control,* New York, The Ronald Press Company, 1967.
Grinaker and Barr: *Auditing, The Examination of Financial Statements,* Homewood, Ill., Richard D. Irwin, Inc., 1965.
Holmes: *Auditing Principles and Procedures,* Homewood, Ill., Richard D. Irwin, Inc., 1970.
Meigs and Larsen: *Principles of Auditing,* Homewood, Ill., Richard D. Irwin, Inc., 1969.
Stettler, Howard F.: *Auditing Principles,* Englewood Cliffs, N.J., Prentice-Hall, Inc., 1970.

Alspach, H. E.: "Auditing the Budgetary Function," *Budgeting,* September/October, 1966.
Henry, E. J. G.: "Auditing the Adequacy of Insurance Coverage," *The Internal Auditor,* November/December, 1969.
Bernstein, Leopold A.: "Reporting the Results of Operations—A Reassessment of APB Opinion No. 9," *The Journal of Accountancy,* July, 1970.
Francia, Arthur J., and Norman J. Elliott: "Significant Differences in Accountants' Professional Liability Insurance Coverage," *The New York Certified Public Accountant,* October, 1970.
Heeschen, Paul E.: "Auditing Data Processing Administrative Activities—Operational Auditing Applied to EDP," *The Internal Auditor,* November/December, 1970.

Part Four

Reviews and Reports

Chapter 37

Concluding the Audit

BERNHARD C. LEMKE

Professor of Accounting, Graduate School of Business Administration, Michigan State University

WHAT IS "CLOSING"?

When Does Closing Begin? If the words "completion" or "winding up" are understood whenever the words "close" or "closing" are used, it is apparent that portions of the audit are being completed almost from the first day of the fieldwork. Most audits are conducted by working sequentially on a limited number of planned and well-defined segments of the audit program to the point of completion, rather than by attempting to perform a large number of audit activities concurrently. These hundreds of audit activities have a very wide range of duration periods. Some parts may only require a few minutes or an hour, such as obtaining data readily available. Other parts of the audit may require days or even weeks to complete.

Since audit review activities are described in detail in Chapter 38, the matters relating to review will not be discussed here.

When Does Closing End? Although the beginning of the closing activities can be variously signaled, the bulk of the end of the closing activities occurs toward the completion of the fieldwork, perhaps a week or two before the the fieldwork called for by the audit program is completed. Here judgment is required. Such factors as the date the audit report is promised, the purpose and length of the audit, the skill of the field staff and its size, the type and variety of problems encountered during the fieldwork, and other pressures may trigger the activities associated with "closing activities" at an earlier or later point, even within the same firm. An earlier beginning may be expected where problems have been encountered or where inexperienced staff is employed. The phrase "a week or two" is an attempt to strike an average under normal conditions. The timing and coordination of the closing activities are important factors in any audit.

The end of the closing activities should occur some time before the release of the final or formal report to the auditee. Generally, housekeeping duties such as tidying up the files and completing various tag-end routine steps can take place after the final report has been delivered.

Were Objectives Accomplished? In order to determine whether the objectives of the audit were accomplished, there are several questions which may be asked during the audit. The answers to these questions should be received before the end of the closing activities. These questions are discussed below.

1. **Time and cost.** Did we accomplish in a completely professional manner what we agreed to accomplish within the limits of time and cost as spelled out in some detail in our agreement?

2. **Completeness.** Did we overlook something of significance which another professionally competent auditor would have found? Is there any service

to management, the stockholders, and the public which we, as professionally competent auditors, can reasonably be expected to perform but failed to provide?

3. **Conclusions.** Would a professionally competent auditor arrive at the same conclusions we did on the basis of the evidence in the working paper file? If our conclusions are challenged in court or commission hearing, can we be reasonably certain of our facts in a legal sense?

4. **Cooperation.** Were we denied access to any information we considered necessary? Were we prevented from making tests or observations or performing any audit steps we considered essential? Were we, in other words, hindered from attaining our objective?

The reason for asking these questions "toward the end of the audit engagement" is that we are fast approaching the last opportunity to improve the tentative answers, if that is necessary, or to withdraw from the audit engagement completely should the answer to question 4 require such a drastic step.

Was Independence Maintained? The auditor has the right to determine the steps and procedures needed to carry out the purpose or objective of the audit. He should be "independent" in the sense that his professional competence and reliability are taken for granted.

It is important, however, not to use the word "independence" interchangeably with the word "freedom." In an auditing sense, independence does have limitations, whereas freedom may give the impression of a complete lack of restraints, restrictions, or limitations.

We must assure ourselves, as auditors, that we were permitted to investigate all areas and use all techniques and procedures we regarded as reasonably and professionally necessary to accomplish the objectives for requiring the audit in the first place.

If the auditor broadens the objective or scope of the coverage beyond the agreed-upon objective, he has gone beyond the bounds of independence into the broader realm of freedom. Within the bounds just discussed, the auditor must have the right to take such measures as are appropriate, with the cooperation and consent of the client.

Any restrictions in this area may nullify the benefits of the audit. Although independence is ordinarily associated with the public accountant, it should be recognized as an important ingredient of internal auditing as well.

Are Closing Activities Uniform? The closing activities of public accounting, internal auditing, and governmental auditing need not differ, except in degree of emphasis. It is likely that the internal auditor may be much more informal with the unit being audited in these activities, especially in such matters as conferences and the follow-up of audit recommendations, since both parties are usually members of the same company. The internal auditor may find his activities considerably broadened temporarily in certain areas as a result of audit recommendations which management may want him to implement or to supervise. Part of the similarity between the public and the internal audit may be due to the fact that the internal auditor is often recruited by management from public accounting, although the similarity of broad objectives unquestionably is the major factor.

POINT SHEETS OR STAFF NOTES

Daily Progress. In all phases of the audit there is a need to record daily progress in diary form. In addition there should be some agreement on the means of communication both among members of the field staff and between the field staff and the audit supervisor and others. In order to avoid time-consuming consultation as each point or issue arises, the audit staff may use a memorandum system of staff notes, check sheets, follow-up notes, or point sheets, sometimes called findings sheets.

Form of Point Sheet. In its simplest form a point sheet is a ruled sheet of paper divided vertically into two parts. On the left part of the page the auditor writes notes concerning points he wishes to discuss or clear with his supervisor. The space to the right of each note is reserved for the supervisor's comments or reaction.

Clean-up of Points. Depending on the urgency of the notes, to a certain extent, it is customary for the staff man and the supervisor to "clean up" the point sheets at regular intervals.

This method of point sheets can be used in all areas of the audit and is particularly useful in the review stages, in which instance the positions are reversed. Here the supervisor requests clarification from the staff man or issues further instructions to him.

Final Audit Points. One or more conferences between the audit staff and the audit supervisor or manager are usually held prior to the close of the fieldwork. The conferences are almost always held at the audit site, usually at a prearranged time. The field audit staff has meanwhile prepared a list of points pertaining to the audit which it wishes to discuss with the supervisor, or which the field audit staff must refer to him prior to taking action.

Arrangement of Audit Points. When a number of audit points are to be discussed with the supervisor, the list should be arranged in some logical order. For example, the items may be arranged according to importance, urgency, safety, or dollar value; they may be arranged according to general trial balance sequences or some other logical system. At this point, before the conference begins, the field audit staff must determine that the working papers and relevant summaries and documents are complete, adequately indexed and cross-referenced, and in substantial compliance with the audit program and general audit standards. Many of the listed points will refer to material in the audit working papers and related files in which possible cross-indexing between point sheets and working papers should be made.

Decisions on Audit Points. Since these point sheets (with the decisions of the supervisor incorporated in them) remain with and become part of the field audit working papers, the supervisor should prepare such memoranda of his decisions as he requires for follow-up purposes and for a record of his participation in this important audit step. Undoubtedly, several of his decisions will extend or possibly shorten the audit as originally programmed, which, in turn, will increase or decrease the cost of the audit from the original budget or estimate.

Review of Audit Data. A related part of the supervisor's duties at this point or at a later date, or both, is a detailed review of the audit data in order to look for loose ends, unsupported conclusions, inadequate coverage, opportunities to strengthen the audit, outright errors of procedure or fact, and deviations from auditing standards. Because the supervisor may review the audit working papers at various times and at various stages of completion, it is desirable that he avoid cumbersome and unnecessary duplication of effort. Therefore some system of indicating the nature and extent of the review of portions of the audit should be devised. This system may utilize a code mark or a distinctive signature or stamp. Care should be exercised that subsequent changes in reviewed material are not made without the supervisor's knowledge and consent.

Because these steps of the manager's review include a number of necessarily mechanical sequences, a form may well be prepared in advance which will be useful in all audits to check against the omission of one or more of the many parts of the review.

It may be suggested that perhaps the supervisor or manager is too close to the details of the audit, in spite of his essentially supervisory role, and that the review just mentioned should be made by someone selected at random from the administrative group of the audit firm who has not participated directly in the audit. While this suggestion undoubtedly has some merit, it should be noted that the person to whom the supervisor or manager reports—either a principal or partner of the audit firm or the head of the internal audit function—will have to assume responsibility for the audit report which will eventually be released. His review of the completed audit file in order to evaluate the reliability of the audit report for which he must accept responsibility will undoubtedly satisfy the need for objectivity.

COORDINATION

Avoiding Duplication. Large corporations or enterprises are likely to have comparably large internal audit staffs. Therefore both the internal audit staff and the public accounting staff will be actively engaged in auditing the same unit. In order to avoid unnecessary duplication each will accept the other's audits either in part or in total, up to a point.

Audit schedules and programs often are arranged ahead of time to avoid serious overlap and to make arrangements for the exchange of audit results. Standards for mutual acceptability are set.

However, the manager of a given audit must satisfy himself that the audit steps performed by the other auditors are pertinent, expert, conclusive, objective, and otherwise up to the standards expected in his audit.

If the other audit file is acceptable, a copy of the required segment is ordinarily made, identified, inserted in its proper sequence in the file, and treated in the same manner as if it had been prepared by the regular audit staff. At times, a report or summary is accepted in lieu of the actual working paper detail.

Comparable Audit Standards. The "other auditor's work" must be acceptable in the sense of conforming to comparable standards. The review of the working papers involved must take nothing for granted. In some instances, the two sets of auditors will have worked more or less side by side. When this is not the case, care should be taken to make such tests of the material as seem appropriate in order to verify the acceptability of the work.

Rotation of Auditors. In geographically dispersed client organizations, the various units comprising the total organization may be audited on a rotating basis by the client's internal auditors, public accountants in foreign countries, and local public accountants. Before a program of rotation is agreed upon, a study of the materiality of the units being audited by other auditors should be made.

The accounting staff of the unit being audited may prepare, under proper instruction, a number of the schedules and analyses required for the audit. The auditor must make sure that such working papers have been properly prepared and he must test the papers before they are accepted.

A description of the rotation of inventory work between the public accountant and the internal auditor may be found in Cashin and Owens, *Auditing*, 2d ed., page 257. In that example the company has a large number of widely separated locations which must be visited by either the public accountant or the internal auditor. The plan of rotation is based on the following: The inventory at each location represents a percentage of the consolidated total at the month-end prior to the date of the physical inventory. A work sheet is prepared by the internal auditor showing the dollar value of the inventory by location and percentage. In another column of the work sheet is indicated whether the inventory at the particular location had been observed the previous year by the public accountant or the internal auditor. If there is no special problem, the observation of the inventory would be rotated. If poor internal control or other problems were noticed the previous year, the public accountant may wish to observe the inventory for several years to follow up for suggested improvements. From the figures on the work sheet it is easy to determine the percentage of the total inventory observed by the public accountant and by the internal auditor. Also it is possible to readily decide which location need not be visited every year. Based on the degree of internal control and the dollar value, a number of locations may need be visited only every other year. These locations, however, should not be notified in advance that the auditor will not observe the inventory so that no lessening of care in taking the physical inventory occurs.

REVIEW OF WORKING PAPERS

The Trial Balance. Every audit has a control document to which all the audit papers are directly or indirectly referenced. Ordinarily an established coding system is adopted for this purpose from which no deviation is permitted. In a financial audit this document is in the form of a "trial balance." A multicolumn general trial balance working paper is used which has money columns headed "Preaudit Trial Balance," "Audit Adjustments," and "Postaudit Trial Balance." Corrections resulting from the audit findings in the form of journal entries bridge the gap between the Preaudit Trial Balance as submitted to the auditor by the client and the Postaudit Trial Balance. A supporting working paper should spell out each audit adjustment in detail and should be cross-indexed to relevant data. Relevant data concerning decisions reached, such as conferences with the client regarding the adjustment or disposition of items, should be tied in.

The Preaudit Trial Balance should, of course, be traced to the client's general ledger in detail. Wherever subsidiary ledgers exist for the accounts in the Preaudit Trial Balance, they should be taped or otherwise traced into the respective control accounts, and such support should be filed in the working papers. As one of the last follow-up stages of the audit, the Postaudit Trial Balance should be traced to the general ledger to verify the fact that the client has incorporated the mutually agreed-upon adjusting or correcting entries (supported by still another representation letter).

Schedules and Analyses. A review of the large number of schedules and analyses cover a variety of matters. Each schedule should be carefully inspected for obvious omissions, poor organization, inadequacy, etc. Following are a number of matters which should be included in any inspection of schedules and analyses:

1. **Heading.** Each paper should be headed with the name of the company or unit, the audit period, a title, the auditor's name and the actual date the

paper was prepared, and some indication of pagination, in addition to a logical index code.

2. **Tests, samples, or observations, etc.** Tests, samples, observations, confirmations, or representation letters and documents must be adequate, complete, consistent, competent, appropriate and meaningful. The supporting detail should be present and integrated into the account or project being audited. The conclusions should be valid and reliable.

3. **Verification.** Totals, footings, and arithmetic in general should be checked for accuracy. Tapes or other evidence of lengthy computations should be supplied, and the basis or formula should be reasonable.

4. **Description.** Any descriptive material should be specific, complete, and clear. All portions should be readily understood by an auditor unfamiliar with the particular company.

5. **Source of data.** The source of the data included in the schedule should be given and an explanation of how it may be verified, if necessary.

6. **Explanation.** Explanations should be included on the assumption that the schedule will be read by someone competent in auditing but unfamiliar with the company being audited. Whether explanatory footnotes should be used for this purpose and to what extent is a matter of choice.

7. **Tick-marks.** "Tick-marks" and other shortcuts for identifying standard processes and procedures should be used. These marks may conform to a standard pattern adopted firmwide or may apply only to the particular worksheet.

8. **Cross-references.** Cross-references to other parts of the audit file or to other sources should be complete and mutually relevant (meaningful at both ends of the cross-reference). Symbols used should be proper. Omissions of expected cross-referencing should also be checked.

9. **Completeness.** Each page or sequence of pages should be complete in the sense that it tells the complete story implied by the title. It should not be vague or confusing, nor must something be supplied to round it out, assuming, of course, that the reader is familiar with auditing standards. It is primarily for this reason that the review of working papers at some stage should be performed by a person who has not worked on the specific audit in a manner which can be typified as a routine "day-to-day" job. There should be enough lack of familiarity with the details of the audit that the confusing or the ambiguous stands out.

10. **Authenticity of evidence.** Supporting evidence in the form of schedules, exhibits, diagrams, reproductions, etc., should be carefully scrutinized as to relevancy. If supplied by the client, details of its source and the client's representation that it is accurate and pertinent should be included with some indication that it was supplied to the auditor with the full knowledge and consent of the appropriate official of the client. This assurance of the client should not preclude the auditor's independent test of the authenticity and validity of the supporting evidence. Thus a schedule supplied by the client which purports to be a summary of a subsidiary ledger should be independently tested or verified by the auditor, and such assurance should be included in the working papers.

11. **Personal references or comments.** Any references or comments included in the working papers which might reflect unfavorably on an employee or officer of the company should be specially edited. If the particular working paper might later be seen by others than the audit staff, perhaps such comments should be included in a special confidential file.

Audit Summaries. If the field auditor is expected to prepare a summary of his findings, conclusions, opinions, and recommendations for each section of the audit, these summaries should be reviewed with the following in mind.

1. **Availability.** Are such summaries, etc., included at all points where they are called for or can be expected?

2. **Competence.** Are the summaries competently prepared in a professional auditing sense? Will they be useful in writing the audit report?

3. **Support.** Are the findings, conclusions, or recommendations fully supported and cross-referenced to the supporting working papers? Does the reviewer arrive at the same conclusions from the sources to which the cross-references lead?

4. **Trivial data.** Are any of the summaries trivial, controversial, petty, or of such a nature that if inadvertently read by an employee or officer of the company will be embarrassing to the auditor? There should be some agreement about the handling of minor and major audit findings as well as about how to determine which is which. Some supervising auditors insist they be given the opportunity to make that distinction, thus requiring that the field auditor report all deviations uncovered in the audit process.

5. **Omissions.** A difficult feature of the review is the detection of omissions. The ability to detect omissions depends largely on experience and training, patience, and familiarity with the type of audit program used by the firm in similar circumstances.

6. **Cross-indexing.** A very important feature of the review is determining that the working papers are properly cross-indexed to other important papers. The following are the important papers to which the working papers should be cross-indexed. Conversely, these papers should be adequately cross-indexed to the appropriate working papers.

TRIAL BALANCE: Generally a specific audit step is the determination that each working paper is cross-indexed to the trial balance for quick reference.

AUDIT PROGRAM: The cross-indexing of the working papers to the audit program should be made with particular care to get beyond the purely mechanical to include a preliminary appraisal of the adequacy of the various audit steps in light of the findings revealed in the audit working papers and summaries.

INTERNAL CONTROL QUESTIONNAIRE: The cross-indexing of the working papers to the internal control questionnaire is an essential feature of any audit. The foundation of the audit rests on the documentation of the adequacy of internal control.

REPRESENTATION LETTERS: It is essential that representation letters from lawyers, engineers, labor negotiators, and others supporting important parts of the audit be properly cross-indexed to the working papers. Particular attention should be paid to any extension or reduction of the audit based on such material. The information in these documents should be supported by corroborating facts in the working papers and properly cross-indexed as well.

SUGGESTED ADJUSTMENTS: The audit findings generally result in a variety of adjustments and corrections to the records. Some corrections may have been made immediately upon the auditors' discovery of error. Adjustments of a minor nature may also have been made during the course of the audit. Any such correcting entries should be indicated in the working papers. While most of these corrections will be of a mechanical nature or noncontroversial character, it is desirable to note any such items which require reconciliation with previously gathered data.

SUPPORT FOR ADJUSTMENTS: The adjustments and corrections of a significant nature which are proposed by the field audit staff and the supervisors should be carefully reviewed to see that the support for them exists in the audit working papers. Often the reviewer may require further support to pass upon the materiality of the proposed adjustments and corrections because it is desirable that such proposals be made in a carefully documented manner by the manager or partner in charge.

Internal Control Review. Although mentioned at various points, it is worth repeating that as the manager reviews the audit working paper file, he should be constantly aware of the fact that he is accepted as an expert on internal control and should be on the alert for matters relating to it.

A lack of internal control would, of course, require the use of additional auditing steps to overcome the lack. A good system, on the other hand, should reduce the scope of audit effort.

It should also be kept in mind that many audit reports comment at some length on internal control matters as well as suggest ways to improve internal control. In many cases a separate letter or report detailing such internal control matters and suggested ways to improve internal controls is an important feature of the audit.

The Audit Program. Prior to the start of the audit, a formal audit program is undoubtedly prepared or made available which serves as a basic planning tool. Its subsequent importance and use varies from firm to firm. As the audit progresses, it will be modified, depending on the problems encountered, since it is impossible to forecast all audit steps in detail. The reviewer must be constantly aware of the content of the formal audit program because it often represents the minimum acceptable audit requirements. An audit program which is kept up to date as the audit progresses is a valuable tool in planning future audits.

Special Reports. Where the auditor is aided in the preparation of special reports, the basic work for this purpose is often coordinated with the various audit steps. In effect this results in a "rough" draft. Before this rough draft is released, it should be reviewed in depth and in detail by the experts, who should perform any additional specialized work required. These experts may well be either on the staff of the audit firm or brought in from outside for this purpose.

Where such additional assistance is requested by the client, it is customary to prepare a separate working paper file for that purpose rather than to make the material a part of the basic audit file. This may require the duplication of certain schedules or other data primarily intended for the basic audit file. A review of these specialized files is beyond the scope of this chapter and in practice is performed by the supervisory specialists in the relevant areas.

Interim Work. It is desirable to perform some of the audit work *during* the period under review rather than to wait until the *end* of the period or later, if the terms of the audit permit this.

Under these circumstances, the "as of" date of the audit is significantly later than the performance of the interim work. It is necessary, therefore, to be extremely careful that the interim work be as applicable as if it had been done at the end or after target date.

The review and record of the transactions carried out between the interim date and the target date must be thorough and convincing to be acceptable.

Tests should be made to assure that no events have taken place in the interim which would cast doubt on the acceptability of the interim work as representative of the conditions as of the audit reporting date. It is not unusual to find that these tests suggest a duplication or reworking of parts of the interim work.

Subsequent Events. There is a time lag between the last date of the events being audited and the actual release date of the audit reports. Hopefully, this lag or gap will be short, but in the interest of fairness and full disclosure it is likely that a review of the events which have taken place in this time gap must be made before the effective release date of the audit report. A review of some subsequent events is routine in some areas of cash, receivables, and payables, for example, but these are not primarily the groups involved in this section.

The review is intended to cover a variety of events and records. The purpose is to disclose the important and unsuspected matters which may influence the reader of the final report, or which he will regard as significant.

Such matters may include plans to shut down or retire major assets, to sell or lease major divisions, to merge or otherwise change ownership, to make major changes in the financial structure, to file lawsuits of major consequence or to be sued, or to broaden or shrink the range of products. Matters such as major damage to facilities of the company and larger commitments than are normal in the areas of purchase orders, union contracts, and other agreements may also be significant.

Events may have occurred which tell us something about the allowance for doubtful accounts, depreciation, and obsolescence. Strikes, changes in tariffs—in fact a limitless number of events may have occurred which must be considered. The question arises, Are they material enough in a financial sense to justify being "disclosed," at least as footnotes, in the final report? The list may be expanded to include the following:

Insurance coverage and claims
Lease and repurchase agreements
Trust indentures and other debt agreements
Collateral
Conditional conveyances of title
Defaults
Pension obligations
Lawsuits and damage claims
Disputed or delinquent tax matters
Unusual or excessive outstanding purchase orders and contracts
Stock options, profit-sharing and bonus agreements and arrangements
Capital stock and dividend restrictions
Conditional sales agreements
Preferred stock dividends and rights
Foreign investments
Accommodation agreements
Receivables discounted or sold
Guarantees and warranties
Compliance with wage, pollution, licensing, and other legal or regulatory requirements
Agreements to sell major units or property
Agreements to merge with other companies or vice versa
Catastrophes and their aftermath
Major managerial changes
Other

The search for significant events requires an informal extension of the audit beyond the cutoff date. This search may be supplemented by discussions with officers, company lawyers, and others; by reading reports and releases made by the company in the interim; and by reading the minutes of the meetings of the board of directors, stockholders, and major committees, if this is within the scope of the audit.

The auditor's responsibility is described in Chapter 10, Statements on Auditing Procedure No. 33, when (1) the effects of known events or transactions are not determinable at the date of his report and (2) for events which occur after the balance sheet date but before the date of his report. However, previous pronouncements did not deal with situations involving information which existed at the date of the auditor's report but of which he had no knowledge.

Since some of the recent court cases have involved this point the AICPA has issued Statement on Auditing Procedure No. 41, *Subsequent Discovery of Facts Existing at the Date of the Auditor's Report.* The purpose of the statement is to establish procedures to be followed by the auditor who subsequently becomes aware of facts which might have affected his report had he been aware of such facts at the date of his report.

The superficial resemblance between this activity and the review to determine the existence of contingent liabilities should be noted. The main difference may well be the time period to which these two factors relate: the contingent liabilities (or assets) stem from *prior* events, rather than *subsequent* ones.

Not to be overlooked are alert observations by the auditor as he goes about his duties. It should be remembered, however, that the financial reports as finally issued, including references and footnotes to subsequent events, are fundamentally the reports of the client and not of the auditor. The events reported should have a significant impact on the financial implications of management's reports to the reader thereof.

Incidentally, a subsequent event can also be a cheerful and beneficial one; the search should not be limited to the gloomy and destructive happenings.

When important matters are likely to be objectively determinable only by competent professional talent, representation letters may be required by the auditor from lawyers, engineers, geologists, and others.

Draft of the Report. Reports are drafted for various purposes from the same set of audit working papers, and may include the following.

1. **Informal report.** An informal report by the supervisor of the field audit force is a "trial run" to test the adequacy of the audit working papers in a general sense. The supervisor has a copy of the informal report as well as all other reports prepared for the previous audit. This "trial run" report may be incomplete and not intended for distribution.

2. **Working report.** A working report is one which will be used in a conference with the financial management group of the company. This group is skilled in all the matters which will be touched upon in a discussion with the auditors; and consequently the working report could be called a discussion report in the sense that its contents will form the main topic of the conference. The report lists the findings of the audit which the auditors consider important enough to obtain concurrence from the company and to receive assurance that appropriate consideration will be given to the findings. In a typical audit this means an agreement that specific adjusting or correcting entries will be incorporated in the accounts for the audit period.

3. **Final report.** The final report is distributed as the official, permanent record of the audit. It is prepared after the conference described above.

4. **Opinion.** The "opinion" of the auditor usually accompanies the financial

report. It is usually published as part of the company's annual report to its stockholders.

CONFERENCES

Preliminary Meeting. Prior to the arrival of the manager and during the course of the field audit, the field audit staff may have given informal advice and suggestions to company personnel which, if significant, were probably reported in the working papers or the staff notes. This is more likely to have happened in an internal audit than in a public audit.

When the manager arrives, conferences are arranged between the audit function and the unit being audited. At this stage the manager is in the process of assembling data for a formal audit conference report, having substantially finished his review of the audit file, and he is primarily interested in getting concurrence from management on audit findings which most likely will constitute the main body of the final report. Depending on the gravity of the findings, the manager may request his superior to be in attendance at any informal interim meetings or conferences. His superior, in turn, may ask that several appropriate line officers of the unit being audited also be in attendance or at least be represented.

In the event corrective action is promised by management, this should be noted for subsequent reports and also entered in the audit file for follow-up purposes (that is, to check later whether the promised action was taken).

These more or less informal conferences or other interim reporting formats may well be regarded as part of the audit in the sense of establishing an area of understanding which leads to confidence in and acceptance of the findings of the field auditor as reviewed or modified by the audit manager.

The manager or auditor-in-charge must assure himself that the conclusions reached as a result of the fieldwork are fair, factual, and important; that they are adequately supported by the audit working papers and documents; and that the tentatively proposed audit conference report includes a balanced consideration or evaluation of the position on both sides of each point at issue. During the conduct of the audit, the auditor may have observed instances where the internal control, information gathering, organization, and operations can be improved. Before making recommendations in these and other areas, the auditor must be certain that he has "thought through" such recommendations. It can be embarrassing and may give the client the impression of incompetence if a simple explanation will nullify what appeared to the auditor to have been a worthwhile recommendation. The auditor also must not give the impression that more work was done (and therefore charged) in the conduct of the audit than was absolutely necessary.

Conferences vary in the number held and their purpose. The conference procedure should not be regarded as similar to a legal process in which the accused is given a chance to defend himself, but rather as an educational process for improving the current and future reporting practices and operational procedures of the enterprise.

In the event that fraud or any other criminal act is suspected, the conference procedure is not appropriate. Under such conditions, whatever steps are taken must be under the direct supervision of the audit partner and the lawyer designated by the client for that purpose before any of the details are released or discussed outside the immediate audit group.

The Audit Conference. When the auditor feels ready to make a more or less formal presentation of his findings to the auditee, an audit conference is held.

The auditor-in-charge or his superior is responsible for this meeting or conference and is expected to take the initiative in making the arrangements and structuring the event.

The date and place should be selected, and other arrangements for the meeting should be made with the help of the auditee at least two weeks in advance of the event under normal circumstances.

The format of the meeting should be carefully worked out. It is especially important that the auditor and auditee be represented by persons responsible and knowledgeable in the topics to be discussed, so that full discussion can take place and agreement on points and issues can be reasonably reached without major postponement or extension of the meeting.

It is desirable that the list of persons invited to attend be made available well ahead of the scheduled time so that changes may be proposed by either party. A representative of the public accounting firm may be asked to participate in the conference called by the internal audit function, and vice versa.

Prior to the meeting a memorandum should be prepared and made available which summarizes the arrangements made and lists or spells out the purpose of the audit conference and the points to be discussed.

At the beginning of the conference, a reasonably detailed outline of the points to be discussed should be made available to the participants, and the meeting should be largely devoted to the discussion and eventual resolution of these points. This outline should not contain any major surprises (if it does, this meeting may have been called too soon), but should be devoted to audit findings already familiar to the auditee as a result of previous informal conferences or interim reporting channels. In other words, the group in attendance should be prepared to minimize the time spent in the fact-finding and familiarization steps and spend most of the time discussing plans and arriving at decisions.

A written and authenticated summary of each conference—especially when agreement is reached on specific adjustments and corrections—should be prepared, acknowledged or authenticated by the auditee, and made a matter of record as soon as feasible after the conclusion of each conference.

Use of Visual Aids. The fact that the conferences with the client are ordinarily held before the release of the final report does not mean that such conferences are to be conducted in an informal manner, if this is understood to mean casual preparation.

Depending on the time available, the type of personnel attending the conference (that is, the managerial level), and the importance of the findings, effective use should be made of visual aids and props. This is especially necessary when some of the persons at the conference are not technically trained in the type of reports traditionally prepared by auditors for the financial officers of the client.

The visual aids must be appropriate to the situation, designed to save time as well as to set forth the audit results clearly, and prepared with great care to maintain a high and rigid standard of fairness.

Follow-up. The audit report and its related conferences will produce a number of follow-up situations where the client has agreed to make corrections or changes as a consequence of the audit just concluded. One of the features of the next audit should be a review of these follow-ups to see that they were completed in a satisfactory manner and so maintained. If important enough, a follow-up may be scheduled between the audit just completed and the beginning of another, but this should not preclude making a record for use in the future audit. In most cases the auditors assigned to the next audit of the unit will determine whether the recommendations were carried out. However, when the recommendations are important enough, a follow-up may be made within a short time which may become an integral part of the present, not the future, audit.

This is particularly important where a recommendation is coupled with a possibility of an *exception* in rendering an opinion. Thus the auditor may regard a company's manner of handling a specific matter or situation as violating a principle of disclosure, consistency, materiality, or "fairness" on which he must comment in his opinion, *unless* the company agrees to remedy the defect. To avoid this form of comment or exception, the agreement to take corrective action—usually in the form of an adjusting or correcting entry—must be carried out within a very short period of time, thus requiring almost immediate "follow-up."

It is not desirable that the auditor assist directly in implementing the recommendations, if it is to be done with the intent of forcing compliance. He may at times be asked to decide whether the correction was made in a satisfactory manner, but his authority is not of such a nature that he can either design, supervise, or perform the steps involved in carrying out the recommendation. It is not desirable that he be given this authority because it would destroy part of his independence of viewpoint since he would be required in the future to pass judgment, as an auditor, on his own handiwork!

STEPS IN WINDING UP THE AUDIT

Winding Up Details

1. **Forms.** Questionnaires, checklists, and similar forms pertaining to the audit and its reports should be completed. These deal largely with ensuring that all the safeguards are taken in connection with repetitive steps in all audits.

2. **Audit problems.** A study of audit problems, complications, and unusual events should be made. A record of what to expect is often very helpful to subsequent auditors.

3. **Audit program.** The audit program should be reviewed for suggestions for modification of the scope, coverage, etc., in future audits—in effect, second-guessing the audit staff on "how it should have been done" and "how it should be done in the future."

4. **Cost analysis.** A cost analysis of the audit should be made. Prior to the audit a program and a budget were prepared in some detail. At the completion of the audit a comparison with the actual results should be made. The resulting variances should be analyzed and appropriate action should be proposed which will reduce the recurrence of unfavorable variances in future audits.

5. **Billing.** In most cases there are travel and living expenses while on a trip and other expenditures which are reimbursable. All such items have to be summarized for billing. In a few cases the field audit staff may complete the invoices to be mailed to the client. In most cases, however, the preparation of the invoice is a "top-level" undertaking because it involves policy decisions of a type not ordinarily delegated.

6. **Audit record.** A diary of events, staff participation, officers called upon, persons receiving reports, etc., should be made the responsibility of specific individuals in the audit section.

7. **Draft of report.** As part of his training the auditor should prepare a rough draft of the audit report. This is valuable training in business writing as well

as in auditing. The auditor will learn that in carrying out his audit procedures and in developing his findings he will have to keep in mind the way the findings will be presented in the report and to make sure to document adequately all findings. The final report is usually prepared in the main office using the rough draft and audit paper file as raw material. Usually a skilled auditor who is unfamiliar with the specifics of the audit will reference the final report to the audit working paper file and make sure there is complete justification for all matters included in the final report. Obviously the file must be complete and comprehensive before this is done.

8. **Audit files.** Substantial work must usually be done to prepare the audit files for review by top officials of the audit function in the event that the files are called for in a review of the final report. In addition the files may be needed as part of the continuing review of the firm's auditing standards and capability or in connection with conferences with the client.

9. **Permanent data.** The data which are of a permanent or continuing nature will have to be summarized for the permanent file. Certain data which will be needed in the next audit will also have to be summarized.

Liability Review. Before finally concluding the audit it is advisable to make an overall liability review of any areas which may involve liability claims such as stockholder suits under the 1933 or 1934 SEC Acts. Significant extensions of the auditor's liability have been set forth in recent court decisions which ought to be considered. The auditor should be familiar with the recent cases and be alert to the potential liability, if any, in the particular audit. If any indication of such liability arises the auditor should obtain the pertinent facts, study the applicable AICPA releases, and discuss the matter promptly with his superior.

Rating of Performance. An important part of every audit is the rating of the staff men who worked on the job. Such an evaluation is an essential factor in the development and guidance of the individual. In many cases evaluations are also made of the auditee staff.

The audit staff. A logical part of the closing activities is a rating of each person who worked on the audit by his immediate superior on the job. The rating should be reasonably detailed and should cover the weaknesses and strengths of each person in relationship to his duties in the audit. One basic benefit will be the improvement in the composition of future audit "teams."

Because the rating will become part of the personnel record upon which promotions and other actions are based, it should include anything else considered essential or useful.

At some regular and appropriate time, each employee should be brought up to date on the findings which result from the rating process. This should be done by a skilled member of the personnel section of the firm because a major purpose of the rating is to help the employee improve his skill and progress in the firm. The person doing the rating may suggest ways in which this might be accomplished.

The auditee staff. Unless specifically requested by the client, a rating of his staff may well be resented. Nevertheless, a rating of employees in critical or important positions from an internal control point of view cannot be avoided and to the extent that it points up weaknesses and strengths in internal control must be accepted as an essential and necessary element of the audit. In the subsequent discussion of internal control with the client, the emphasis undoubtedly will be on the distribution of duties, systems matters, organizational factors, and the like, rather than on the competence of specific employees.

Courtesy Matters. As the auditors prepare to leave the audit site there are a number of things that should be taken care of as a matter of courtesy. The following are the principal items:

1. **Courtesy visits.** It is proper to pay a courtesy call or visit on appropriate officers and department heads before leaving the job.
2. **Return of documents.** Steps must be taken to make sure that all documents, files, and other materials are returned in good order and that signed and dated receipts or releases are obtained.
3. **Copies of documents.** A check of the records and a check of the staff should be made to determine if any promises were made to supply copies of reports, publications, analyses, etc.
4. **Restoration.** A check must be made that the premises used were restored to their condition prior to the audit. Damage of any kind should be repaired before leaving.
5. **Property left.** A final check should be made before leaving to make sure that no property such as briefcases, equipment, files, or wearing apparel is left behind.
6. **Housekeeping details.** Generally a staff man is assigned to take care of housekeeping details such as shipping the files to the home office, arranging for transportation, etc.
7. **Debts.** Any miscellaneous charges for postage, meals, transportation, etc., should be settled before leaving. Receipts should be obtained for all such items.
8. **Staff conduct.** In addition to courtesy visits an attempt should be made to find out from management if the conduct of the staff was satisfactory. What can be done to improve the professional conduct of the staff?

Audit Files. The following types of files will result from practically all audits, in addition to the file relating to the terms and conditions of the audit engagement.

1. **Current file.** A current file contains the audit working papers of the current audit with its related papers, tables, reports, summaries, and other documents.
2. **Permanent file.** A permanent file contains facts uncovered or gathered in all previous audits which are of an enduring nature or which provide a background for future audits. Much of the information in this file would have had to be obtained in the course of any audit if the file had not been available. The permanent file avoids the repetition of standard and more or less unchanging facts.
3. **Next audit file.** A next audit file will include much of the material potentially useful in the next audit which is not included in the permanent file. It will also include any information which will become available as time passes up to the date of the next audit which the auditors and manager will find of use and interest. Up to the start of the new audit, this file should be fairly slim.

A fourth group of files results if the client engages the audit firm to prepare tax returns, governmental reports, etc.

Preparing for Next Audit. Ordinarily it must be assumed that the audit engagement will be repeated the next year. Based on the audit just completed and the circumstances surrounding it, it may be suggested that a future audit emphasize certain categories for stated reasons. For example, various sites or units of the audit may be rotated, especially if the enterprise has a variety of units not all of which are audited at the same time. Other advice or suggestions should be recorded in sufficient detail while the background is fresh. There is some advantage to arranging conferences between the internal auditors and the public accountants during the closing stage of the audit. It is usually beneficial for both groups of auditors to discuss their audit findings. Presumably during the year the internal auditor has supplied the public accountant with a copy of each report issued. The findings of either the internal auditor or the public accountant may influence the rotation program for the following year. If the internal control is poor in a particular unit, the public accountant may prefer to continue to visit that unit until the problem is corrected.

BIBLIOGRAPHY

Planning and Control of Audit Procedures (CPA Handbook), AICPA, New York, 1953.

Kane, Robert L.: *Duties of the Junior and Senior Accountants*, AICPA, New York, 1953.

Research Committee Report No. 15, *The Survey of Internal Auditing, 1968*, The Institute of Internal Auditors, New York, 1969.

Statements on Auditing Procedure No. 33, *Auditing Standards and Procedures*, AICPA, New York, 1963.

Statement on Auditing Procedure No. 41, *Subsequent Discovery of Facts Existing at the Date of the Auditor's Report*, AICPA, New York, 1969.

Billings, Robert E.: "The Review of Audit Working Papers," *Readings in Auditing*, 2d ed., Cincinnati, Ohio, South-Western Publishing Company, Incorporated, 1965.

Brink, Victor Z., and James A. Cashin: *Internal Auditing*, New York, The Ronald Press Company, 1958.

Directors, Accountants, Lawyers, and Others under BarChris and Related Cases, Englewood Cliffs, N.J., Prentice-Hall, Inc., 1969.

Meigs, Walter B.: *Principles of Auditing*, Homewood, Ill., Richard D. Irwin, Inc., 1969.

Palen, Jennie M., ed.: "Typical Auditing Procedures," *Encyclopedia of Auditing Techniques*, Englewood Cliffs, N.J., Prentice-Hall, Inc., 1966.

"Appraising Staff Performance," Readers' Problem Clinic, *The Institute of Internal Auditors*, August, 1968.

Bradt, John D.: "Effectively Presenting an Audit," *The Internal Auditor*, July/August, 1969.

Knortz, Herbert C.: "Economic Realism as a Reporting Essential," *The New York Certified Public Accountant*, December, 1969.

Chambers, R. J.: "Feed, Symbol and Feedback in Accounting," *The New York Certified Public Accountant*, January, 1970.

Alvarez, Abdon P.: "Positive Reporting," *The Internal Auditor*, November/December, 1970.

Chapter 38

Audit Review

MARY E. MURPHY

Professor of Accounting, California State College, Los Angeles

IMPORTANCE OF REVIEW

Business management has the responsibility for adopting sound accounting policies, for maintaining an adequate accounting system, for safeguarding company assets, and for devising an internal control system which assures the preparation of proper financial statements. The auditor's responsibility is generally limited to expressing an opinion on statements he has examined.

Pronouncements of the American Institute of Certified Public Accountants, The Institute of Internal Auditors, and other professional societies cover all phases of audit examinations. However, no codification of standards and procedures can ever replace the auditor's responsibility for deciding what is necessary in any particular set of circumstances, nor relieve him of personal responsibility in expressing his opinion concerning the reasonableness of financial data. The quality level called for by auditing standards provides guidance to the auditor as well as assurance to the public of the breadth and depth of his responsibilities.

TYPES OF REVIEW

The audit review is a very important aspect of every auditing engagement, whether it is made by a certified public accountant, an internal auditor, or a representative of a governmental agency (SEC, IRS, FPC, FCC, etc.). On this review may depend the validity of the results of an audit. In some recent court cases, the outcome has rested on the adequacy of the audit review. Unfortunately, in one or two cases very severe sentences were imposed where the court felt that the review was inadequate.

The Public Accountant. No independent audit can reach a logical conclusion without a review by the CPA who has made the examination and by a partner or supervisor of a public accounting firm which accepts final review responsibility. The reviewer is alert to errors of principle, of judgment, and of a mathematical nature.

In making his review, the CPA is aware of the possibility that fraud may exist. Financial statements may be incorrect as the result of defalcations and other irregularities, or because of deliberate misrepresentation by management, or both. The usual auditing engagement is directed to the expression of an opinion on financial statements. It is not primarily designed, and cannot be relied on, to disclose defalcations and other similar irregularities. However, their discovery may result from the examination. In addition, although the deliberate misrepresentation by management is usually more closely associated with the aim of the ordinary examination, this examination cannot be relied on to assure its discovery.

The subsequent discovery that fraud existed in a company audited by a CPA does not of itself indicate negligence on the part of the CPA. The CPA is not an insurer or a guarantor.

The review should be made by a CPA who has had close association with the audit, including preaudit planning and supervision, preparation of the audit program, review of business data and clients' representations, survey of working papers and schedules, and drafting of financial statements. Some CPA firms insist upon the use of review questionnaires and the observance of definite procedures in the appraisal of the draft of financial statements. In most cases, these statements and the independent auditor's opinion on them are submitted to clients for comment before being sent to the printer.

The CPA's review, basically, should answer the following questions concerning the audit engagement: (1) Was the audit sufficiently comprehensive? (2) Are the assets properly valued and clearly stated? (3) Has adequate provision been made for actual and contingent liabilities? (4) Are income charges and credits properly classified? (5) Have proper accounting principles been applied on a consistent basis? (6) Do working papers contain all analyses, schedules, and explanations necessary to support the financial statements and the auditor's opinions? and (7) Does the report present correctly and adequately the results of the examination?

The closeness of contact of a CPA with work pending in his office—for example, audits, tax work, management services, special investigations, and management audits—is vital to the expression of an unqualified opinion on the audit engagement.

The Internal Auditor. Internal auditing is a staff function rather than a line function, as has often been stressed by The Institute of Internal Auditors. Therefore, the internal auditor does not exercise direct supervision of other persons in a company's organization, although he does review their work. The internal auditor should be responsible to an officer of sufficient rank in an organization to ensure an appropriate scope of internal auditing activities as well as the implementation of recommendations made by the internal auditor.

The organization and administration of the internal audit and control function are essential aspects of efficient business operation. Through questionnaires, flow charts, procedures manuals, and systems surveys the internal auditor prepares the way for regular and impartial review of company procedures. On the basis of ability, experience, and special knowledge of a company's operations, the internal auditor determines that company policies and procedures are being carried out and that internal controls are adequate and are operating effectively.

Preplanning carried out by the internal auditor and his staff reduces the cost of the CPA's examination of company records and methods. However, the more important aspect is a better audit rather than a cheaper one. If the independent auditor is provided with good business records and intelligent answers to pertinent questions, his own efforts connected with audit and review can be devoted to more important matters than the routine authentication of business papers.

Coordination of the efforts of the internal auditor and those of the CPA should be a continuing objective of company policy. Through coordination of effort, improvements in internal audit and control frequently are made, discrepancies between written company procedures and actual company procedures eliminated, branch and subsidiary records enhanced, and internal accounting and auditing methods improved.

Under modern conditions, the internal auditor must know the purpose of all aspects of EDP equipment and must understand the language of this equipment and of its operators in order that he can use the equipment's capabilities to the maximum extent in his own work. He should prepare a flow chart which outlines the fundamentals of company organization and control to be incorporated in EDP procedures. This material should be evaluated by the internal auditor and modified from time to time.

The Governmental Auditor. Individuals employed as auditors by various branches and agencies of the federal, state, or municipal governments in many cases hold CPA certificates. Their audit review is concentrated on assuring the government unit employing them of the maximum revenue from business enterprise (for example, IRS); on authenticating expenditures by companies operating under government contracts (GAO); and on implementing directives covering accounting and auditing procedures to be observed by regulated industries (FCC).

In preaudit conferences with company executives, governmental auditors set the pattern for the actual review. Directives are issued from time to time by government units to aid companies in outlining accounting procedures. For instance, in February, 1964, the IRS issued EDP guidelines which specified that a general ledger and necessary subsidiary ledgers were to be written out, with source references, to coincide with financial reports for tax-reporting periods. In addition, audit trails were to provide for the identification of individual-source items included in summary data. Dependence is placed now, as in the past, on government directives, but even greater significance is directed to the governmental auditor's review of pertinent records and accounts.

If the public interest is to be adequately protected, governmental auditors must assure that private interests operate at highest efficiency, with waste reduced to the minimum. Within the government itself—national, state, or local—sufficient attention must be devoted to sound accounting principles, internal control, and audit review by governmental auditors and frequently by independent auditors to provide assurance of modern, efficient, and ethical procedures.

The audit review of government units may be conducted in the field or in the office of the government agency and of companies falling under the purview of a government agency. It has broad implications for national policy from the viewpoint of budgetary projections, contractual arrangements with suppliers, and maximum collection of revenue. Throughout, the governmental auditor supplies an overall review of data to ascertain whether these data conform with government regulations, as well as to interpret regulations to offer maximum revenue to the local, state, or national economy.

NATURE OF REVIEW

The type and extent of the review made by the internal auditor, CPA, or governmental auditor depend on the organization of the business enterprise under examination. Just how inquisitive the reviewer should be in following up details and in seeking answers to pertinent questions depends on the circumstances of each case. Based on the auditor's technical background and practical experience, a decision is reached as to the depth and breadth of the review.

The Public Accountant. Audit review practices vary according to the size and organization of a CPA firm. Some CPA firms designate review departments which concentrate on the review of the working papers and comparison of data in these papers with the report. The reviewer then sends a memorandum to the partner, outlining various matters and questions to be considered and resolved by the latter. In other CPA firms, the partner himself reviews the working papers and traces data to the report. In very large public accounting firms, the various phases of the review are carried out by different levels of personnel, with supervisors, managers, and partners accepting responsibility for specific aspects of the review.

Staff members of CPA firms come directly into contact with clients' records during the annual, interim, or continuous audit engagement. Their activities are based on preaudit planning by partners, supervisors, and seniors of the CPA firm.

From the inception to the conclusion of the audit, the staff member (who usually holds a CPA certificate) assesses accounts and methods of the client company; determines valuations of assets; ascertains whether all liabilities are on the books; evaluates written representations of the client; and examines confirmations from banks, customers, and others. In these activities the CPA is aided by the client's employees.

What is done at this stage of the engagement forms the basis for any review initiated during the examination. It is especially on this level that inquiries are noted by the CPA staff member, as well as any exceptions to generally accepted accounting principles and auditing procedures as promulgated by the AICPA, the SEC, the IRS, and other bodies. These matters are discussed by the staff member with his supervisor (a CPA), in this way transferring responsibility for accepting or rejecting the client's approach to accounting and to internal auditing.

The supervisor. Final responsibility for the adequacy of the examination and for the soundness of the opinion expressed as to the fairness of the financial statements accrues to the principal in charge of the engagement. This individual may be a sole practitioner or a partner in an accounting firm. In order to meet AICPA auditing standards, due professional care must be exercised in the performance of the examination and the preparation of the report, and the work must be adequately planned, with all staff members properly supervised.

The supervisor (in some CPA firms designated by another title) of the audit engagement prepares the audit program and is responsible for reviewing this program and working papers on completion of the audit. The audit program should be challenged each year, updated, reviewed, and approved at the time of preaudit conferences with staff members. Ideally, preaudit conferences should also be arranged with clients and constant communication maintained between the CPA firm and the client until the engagement is concluded.

Continuous supervision of the engagement by a senior member of the CPA staff is essential to the writing of an opinion on the engagement. This supervision is invaluable if any aspect of the independent auditor's work is questioned in a court case.

Comparison of the current year's program and data with those of the previous year is vital to a scientific audit. In this way, important accounting changes and trends become apparent to the CPA supervisor. Frequently, additional auditing procedures are outlined by the supervising CPA to provide depth to the engagement and to eliminate any weaknesses which appear when working papers are subjected to an independent, critical review.

Detailed discussions with the client's officers and employees occur during the audit engagement and during the review processes. The CPA's familiarity with the client company and with the industry within which it functions is important. Sometimes the supervisor suggests that the staff CPA return to the client's office to carry out additional review procedures indicated by the working papers to be essential for an unqualified independent auditor's opinion.

Tax returns, 10K forms, and other required reports should be prepared by the CPA's staff before they leave the client's office. A letter of recommendation should be prepared at the same time. In addition, exhibits and schedules to be included in the auditor's report should be written "on the spot."

The partner. Preparation of a time budget for the audit and the review is vital to the efficient completion of an auditing engagement. This step is carried out by the partner in charge of the engagement.

Each CPA firm has an established policy as to who shall carry out review procedures when an audit is completed, to ascertain whether statements and opinions are based on sufficient evidence and whether they are in accordance with generally accepted accounting principles applied on a consistent basis.

The partner compares present accounts of clients with those of the previous year. All fieldwork is completed and working papers are prepared with the written independent auditor's report in mind. In all cases, working papers must support financial statements. They must contain all relevant information necessary to complete the various schedules which are part of annual company reports and tax returns.

The CPA must be alert for notations and memoranda in working papers which may be used against him. This is part of the job of the reviewer of these papers. Where anything of importance is questioned, the reviewer should satisfy himself that the query has been answered and that the papers set forth this answer as clearly as possible. Working paper review at the completion of an audit is vitally important to minimize the legal hazards of an engagement.

The responsibility for preparing the opinion rests with the CPA partner. He must approve draft statements and release the final report. In many cases, he discusses these statements and the auditor's opinion section relative to them with the client before these documents are released to printers for annual reports or issued on CPA stationery to banks, governmental agencies, and other interested parties.

Some CPA firms observe the policy of requesting a member of their organizations who has had no immediate connection with the audit to review working papers, draft statements, letters to the client concerning weaknesses in internal control, and similar documents. In this way, a second reviewer is brought into the picture, with the CPA firm doubly protected against human error on the part of its partners and staff. This step is especially important in large corporate examinations or in audits of multinational enterprises.

A partner's review is made to ascertain whether SEC regulations are being met in a client's registration statement and prospectus and in annual reports filed with the Commission. The SEC specifically requires that CPAs' certificates filed with it state whether or not the audit was made by using generally accepted auditing standards.

No CPA should speak for his firm (through an auditor's report) unless a review has been made of his work. This review is essential to ascertain that the performance of duties by subordinates has been accurate and thorough; to ensure that the audit was completed according to the terms covering it; and to recognize developments which may have bearing on the scope, aim, and final value of the audit.

It is important for a CPA to review the work of his subordinates. If the reviewer is not a partner of the firm, the review should always be made by individuals who are independent of those actually performing or supervising the audit work as well as of those who prepared the draft of the financial statements. In addition, the review should be designed to enable the CPA firm to interpret intelligently the figures it has obtained and to which it is to certify. This part of the review should be made by a person, preferably a partner, qualified by his knowledge of modern accounting principles and acquainted with the accounting aspects of the industry and the more important problems of the company under examination.

The Internal Auditor. As the company staff member primarily concerned with internal check and control, the internal auditor is in a position to evaluate the whole accounting system, to consider matters brought to his attention by the controller, and to take remedial steps to improve accounting and review procedures. The analytical qualities of the internal auditor are brought into focus through his procedures of review. He is responsible for outlining and explaining these procedures to his staff.

The reviewing and reporting procedures of the internal auditor are integrated with those of the company executive to whom he is directly responsible. This executive, in coordination with the internal auditor, organizes his own accounting and review procedures, thus eliminating duplication of review steps and permitting concentration on overall review objectives.

The internal auditor's review of conversions of existing manual or punched-card systems to EDP is usually started by request from the data processing area or from an executive. There are five phases of the review process, namely: (1) reviewing the existing procedures; (2) reviewing the new system by means of questionnaires, flow charts, checklists, and discussions, tracing controls over data flow, and reviewing program documentation; (3) reviewing the "debugging" of new programs; (4) reviewing the conversion of existing files; and (5) reviewing the parallel run of old and new systems.

The Governmental Auditor. On-the-job reviews are an essential part of all field and office audits performed by governmental auditors. These reviews are made for every phase of government operation, from the national to the municipal level, to assure branches and agencies of the government of the correctness and authenticity of book entries.

In addition to regular review procedures, as outlined by the Federal Government Accountants Association, governmental auditors make special investigations under directives of the Atomic Energy Commission, Federal Communications Commission, Federal Housing Administration, Federal Power Commission, and other governmental bodies. There is a certain duplication between the field audits made by government agency accountants and the examinations performed by CPAs of these governmental bodies. Sometimes government agencies ask to review CPAs' working papers. Requests of this nature should be cleared with clients before working papers are released, and the CPAs themselves should be present when the working papers are reviewed to prevent extraction of data from schedules or alterations of the contents.

Although CPAs participate in the preparation of cost and other data to be submitted to various government agencies by private contractors and suppliers, these data are audited also by the permanent audit staffs of the various branches of the military services. This would appear to be a duplication of effort and cost. Field audits could be conducted economically and efficiently by CPAs, with government agency auditors focusing their attention on substantive problems and on supervision and periodic testing of the entire audit program. The FPC has substituted audits by CPAs, supplemented by test checks by the FPC's own staff, for field audits required in gas pipeline rate cases. Undoubtedly this type of coordination of the work of the governmental auditor and the CPA will be extended in the future.

The governmental audit supervisor. The governmental audit supervisor prepares the examination program followed by the staff members making field and office reviews. An overall critical review of all audits performed by government units is essential to an opinion on records and procedures expressed to the Comptroller General of the United States, to a government branch and agency, to a legislative inquiry committee, or to some other agency in authority. The apparent lag in accounting processes at the present time does not permit the achievement of rapid review for regulatory purposes. As already mentioned, the use of CPAs in regulatory surveillance programs would substantially improve the effectiveness of regulatory accountants by permitting their concentration on questions of primary interest to government commissions.

Directives issued by government branches are implemented by governmental audit supervisors. These supervisors also ascertain whether a CPA's opinion on a client company conforms with government pronouncements.

TIMING OF REVIEW

Any auditor brings to his review a background of technique and sophistication which emanates from training and experience. An important aspect of his work is the initial and continuing evaluation of the proper time for his field or office review.

Year-end Work. In many cases the review date selected coincides with the year end. Although the AICPA has stressed the advisability of companies' adopting a natural business year for their accounting periods, tax regulations have tended to concentrate the taxpayer's attention upon December 31. Therefore, most audit reviews are made as of the year-end date, with overly heavy CPA engagements concentrated on that date.

The activities of the internal auditor, to a certain extent, are also concentrated on the year-end date, since, as already emphasized, his work is correlated with the activities of the CPA. Certainly the internal auditor must prepare adequately for the independent audit. His staff has to meet certain pressures for accounting summaries as of December 31 and shortly thereafter.

Irrespective of the title of the reviewer—CPA, internal auditor, or governmental auditor—an effort is made to assure that records are maintained in conformity with generally accepted accounting principles and that they are reviewed in conformity with generally accepted auditing standards. Since the review is correlated with the closing date, there is an absence of surprise connected with the audit. This situation must be offset by preplanning by the auditor to ascertain whether records prepared by executives and staff fully authenticate any uncertainties which may emerge from the review.

Interim Work. Because of the danger of concentrating too heavily on December 31 (or some fiscal date's) financial data, CPAs usually schedule reviews in clients' offices at various other dates during the year. Thus, the element of surprise is introduced by the CPA in both his fieldwork and his office review. The uncertainty of the review date tends to stimulate greater accuracy on the part of company executives and staff and frequently forces them to maintain accounting records on a current basis.

Internal auditors plan reviews for various dates throughout the calendar or fiscal year. In some instances, the internal auditing and accounting staff members are informed of these dates, as special internal control methods are designed to ensure accuracy and integrity. However, in many companies, although the review program is projected on paper a year or more in advance, employees learn of it only when they are asked to prepare data for a review.

The governmental auditor schedules his review at a date which seems feasible to him. Usually, this date coincides with a regulated industry's fiscal closing date, but a review is also made at other dates to provide the vital element of surprise.

Adoption of an interim date for the review by the governmental auditor, internal auditor, and CPA has an added advantage, namely, that of bringing to the auditor's attention at an early date any improper accounting principles and procedures which can be corrected before the annual review. In this way, the cost and extent of the year-end review are reduced.

Continuous Audits. Through adopting the continuous auditing approach, the auditor reduces the range and cost of the annual and/or interim audit. In addition, the integrity of the accountant and of management is assured not only at a closing date but also throughout the year. Reviewing procedures at year end, under the continuous audit, can be concentrated on certain accounts or procedures, rather than on the entire accounting system. Suggestions for record improvements, critical evaluations of conformity with government regulations, and assessments of managerial and staff competence can be emphasized.

Ideally, all audits should have certain review features scheduled at year end, at interim, and at other dates throughout the year. In this way, business enterprises and government units receive the most efficient services from their auditors at a cost commensurate with duties performed and responsibilities accepted by these professionals.

The use of analytical audit methods and the increased transfer of accounting data to EDP equipment may accelerate the trend toward continuous auditing. Given adequate internal controls, supplemented by audit checks and tests (some on a surprise basis), it may be possible for CPAs to express opinions on financial statements without repetition of all audit steps now considered necessary in each accounting period. A continuous auditing process conceivably might permit CPAs to accept some responsibility for quarterly or semiannual reports.

LOCATION OF REVIEW

General. As has been noted, the audit review is performed both in the field—in a company's office or plant, nationally and/or internationally—and in the office of the governmental auditor, internal auditor, or CPA. Some aspects are best performed "on the spot," since inquiries can then be made of individuals closely connected with records and procedures.

However, the auditor's office affords uninterrupted time to review working papers and supporting schedules, clients' written representations, confirmations from customers and other individuals, and additional pertinent documents.

In both field and office review procedures, working papers have an important role. Nothing should be left to memory but all points should be incorporated in the auditor's working papers covering all aspects of the engagement. After review of these working papers, financial data are incorporated in memoranda, statements, and other documents used by internal management and stockholders and filed with governmental agencies, stock exchanges, banks, and other interested parties.

Field Review. Field review concentrates on an examination of selected business documents, on pertinent inquiries made orally or in writing of company management and personnel, and on a critical assessment of internal control procedures. It holds the objective of revealing strengths and weaknesses in the accounting system which the auditor can reevaluate in the light of other examination details. This reevaluation may lead to additional review procedures at the time of the audit or at a later date.

Proper review should occur not only after the fieldwork has been finished but also throughout the entire period of the audit engagement. Ideally, a prereview should be made before starting an audit, with supervision during the engagement, and then a review carried out at the completion of the audit. A field review should be made by someone having higher responsibility for the engagement than the in-charge accountant. Attention should be directed to a comparison of the present year's data with those of the previous year. All supporting schedules must be integrated with the working papers, with tax returns, and with SEC and other required reports written in the field. Letters of recommendation should be prepared in the field, also.

Office Review. An office review permits a more all-inclusive survey to be made by the auditor than can be carried out on a client's premises. This may be a review of specific accounts or documents which have direct bearing on the authenticity of the accounting system maintained by a company or governmental unit, or a review of the fieldwork and field review just completed by the auditor.

One reason for the review is to ascertain that information contained in working papers is correctly stated in the financial statements and that all facts disclosed in an auditing engagement are set forth in the report. The review should take place not only after the fieldwork is performed, but also throughout the entire period of control of the engagement. It should begin with acceptance of the client. Therefore, there is also prereview and supervision as well as review. This survey varies with each auditing engagement and is based on the personal judgment, responsibility, and decision of the CPA.

If there has been no field review completed, a more searching office review must be initiated. Statements and adjustments are discussed with clients, errors are corrected by clients' staffs, a clerical review is made of the final report, and auditors who have carried out the examination are apprised of the results of the office review.

AUDIT REVIEW PROBLEMS

The audit review—regardless of who performs it and where and when—is advanced by mechanization of accounting records, introduction of data processing, improvement of statistical sampling techniques, and development of depth auditing. However, reliance must always be placed on the skill and experience of the initial reviewer, as well as of all individuals who participate in subsequent stages of evaluation of the audit.

Scope of the Audit. Basically, as has been pointed out, the audit review is initiated with an examination of business documents to determine the authenticity of these documents and a determination of the accounting principles used to introduce these documents in company records.

Post-statement disclosures present a problem frequently faced by CPAs and other auditors in annual examinations. Introduction of these disclosures in the body or footnotes of financial statements has to be considered by both auditors and company managements. Sometimes a compromise is reached which is mutually satisfactory.

There is also the question of understated or undisclosed liabilities to be considered by audit reviewers. All examinations are designed to disclose actual and contingent liabilities of client companies. The internal auditor accepts primary responsibility here, with the CPA and governmental auditor basing their review upon procedures to test the adequacy of a company's system of internal control and outlining audit and review procedures to be carried out on both an internal and an external basis.

The impartial and critical viewpoint of the reviewer develops in practice, but it is founded on technical knowledge of modern trends in the fields of accounting and auditing. Public accounting experience covers a wide range of business and tax problems. This experience and the possession of a

CPA certificate afford a well-balanced approach to the audit review. In government service, it may be impossible for the reviewer to be a CPA. In corporations, however, the internal auditor and the controller usually have had the benefit of public accounting experience and frequently hold CPA certificates.

There always exists the problem of detecting collusive fraud by top management. The present size and range of national and international business operations have tended to enhance the responsibilities and hazards of the auditor. The usual auditing engagement of the CPA is directed to the expression of an opinion on financial statements. It is not primarily designed to disclose defalcations and other similar irregularities, although their discovery may result. In addition, although the deliberate misrepresentation by management is usually more closely associated with the aim of the ordinary examination, such examination cannot be relied on to assure its discovery.

Reliance for the prevention and detection of fraud must be placed primarily on a company's system of internal control. The CPA reviews this system, evaluates its adequacy by tests, and decides whether internal control and fidelity bonding provide protection against fraud on an economical and effective basis. The subsequent discovery that fraud existed in a company audited by a CPA does not of itself indicate negligence on the part of the CPA. The CPA is not an insurer or a guarantor. If he made an audit examination and review with due professional skill and care in accordance with generally accepted auditing standards, he has fulfilled the obligations inherent in his professional activities.

The law of auditors' liability needs clarification. Lawsuits brought against CPAs cannot be covered, in cost, by insurance carried by CPA firms. In the end, the cost must be met from auditors' fees, becoming indirectly a levy on the business community. Implicit in recent legal actions are two facts: (1) clients must have a greater understanding of what auditors undertake to accomplish in the usual engagement; and (2) auditors must redouble their vigilance in the performance of their work through greater supervision and more critical review of staff work to detect deficiencies.

Approach of the Reviewer. It is not sufficient for the reviewer to meet training and experience standards set by the AICPA, The Institute of Internal Auditors, the Federal Government Accountants Association, and other professional societies. The reviewer must also possess the qualities of judgment, character, and impartiality associated with independent auditing. The necessity of bringing a critical viewpoint to bear on the review, and the ability to outline, coordinate, and supervise the underlying audit are all vital to a well-organized examination. It is not too much to require that reviewers rotate their duties and responsibilities from time to time, both in the field and in the office, in order to bring a fresh approach to review techniques.

All engagements should be discussed by the firm partners with supervisors to be sure that the supervisors understand current problems and information concerning companies discovered during the course of the audit. Certain dates should be set up for cash cutoff, physical inventory, and receivables confirmation. On large audits, certain phases of the examination and the review should be cycled so that all locations and areas are examined on a systematic basis. Substantial portions of the engagement, ideally, should be completed at interim dates. Simultaneous examinations, a cash count, and confirmation of receivables might be made of certain companies. There is also a possibility of coordinating the examination at an interim date with a review to year end, with reexamination of certain areas at year end.

Examination of EDP presents additional timing problems which auditors must consider in order that their activities may be coordinated with a company's systems department. With EDP, also, attention must be directed to the experience, proficiency, and training of staff members on the engagement. The audit program must be challenged, reviewed, and updated every year in light of alterations in the client's accounting and internal auditing procedures.

Rotation of auditors on the engagement or between engagements is essential for proper staff training and audit efficiency. Constant communication must be maintained with the client, with a postaudit conference arranged between the independent auditor and the client in the latter's office. Planning and review procedures are essential to offer clients maximum auditing service at a minimum cost.

Generally Accepted Standards. The reviewer should be thoroughly familiar with pronouncements of professional societies covering accounting principles and auditing standards. These pronouncements serve as guidelines to good practice, but, to a certain extent, they are modified in practice to attain improved standards and to coincide with governmental directives. The process of modification is the responsibility of the professional—CPA, internal auditor, or governmental auditor—assigned to the audit and the review.

Generally accepted auditing standards seek to protect against errors of a theoretical, mathematical, or other nature committed by company management and/or personnel. These principles are extended and deepened by companies through manuals, training programs, and executive development courses; by government branches and agencies through indoctrination and in-training courses; and by CPA firms through training programs and establishment of policies relative to acceptance of responsibility.

Within the public accounting firm, attention is directed to policies concerning reviews of clients' branch offices and subsidiaries, on both a domestic and a foreign level. Firm policy is also developed as to who shall make the review in multinational companies, where and when the review should be made, and whether the review responsibility should cover audits performed by other public accounting firms overseas.

From the viewpoint of a company, procedures must be outlined relative to internal audit review of domestic and foreign branches and subsidiaries, and of U.S. and overseas corporations being considered as merger possibilities.

Government agency policy as to audit review is specified by legislative enactments covering the agency in question, and by directives from various government executives as to the functioning of these agencies. In some instances, the review is made of U.S. financial data only, but in others review procedures may cover foreign income of certain enterprises.

The tendency, in any case, in recent years has been to enlarge and deepen the audit review. As stated above, reliance is placed on generally accepted auditing standards promulgated by the AICPA and other professional societies and by the U.S. government. The reviewer's tasks are more complicated today than in the past, as financial data are available with greater rapidity and in greater amount because of EDP and other mechanical aids. Mathematical techniques, including statistical sampling, have made the audit review more scientific but, at the same time, have demanded greater mathematical ability and precision on the part of the reviewer.

Liability Review. The reviewer must be especially alert to matters which may cause potential liability suits. He should be thoroughly familiar with the requirements of the 1933 and 1934 SEC Acts and the facts in all the recent court decisions affecting auditor's liability. He should discuss the various points carefully with the auditor in charge who may not have been aware of certain matters that could lead to liability suits. The reviewer should also be thoroughly familiar with the recent AICPA releases relating to subsequent events such as Statement on Auditing Procedure No. 41, *Subsequent Discovery of Facts Existing at the Date of the Audit.*

Communication of Results. A continuing aim is to improve review procedures so that individuals whose work depends on the review are informed, as rapidly as possible, of the result of the review. If this tenet is observed, company and governmental accountants will have a favorable reaction to the review and the reviewer because they will receive the maximum benefit from the process. They will be able to alter procedures at an early date to coincide with improved practices outlined by the reviewer, and can aid in checking the possibility of fraud and defalcation in every phase of business operation.

The above paragraph also applies to the CPA. He and other auditors, with improvement in business procedures, can eliminate certain phases of their reviews, thus reducing review costs to corporations and the government. On-the-job training of reviewers is one method of preparing qualified individuals to be alert to discover errors in accounting principles and manipulations of accounting records.

Additional literature on the audit review is badly needed. This vital area of auditing has been "undersold" in university courses in auditing and in specialized auditing literature. An essential ingredient of the new approach to the review would be greater integration of EDP and statistical sampling techniques with the traditional audit review.

As an overall rule, there should always exist a proper relationship between the cost of making the review and the usefulness of the evidence obtained. In determining the latter, relative risk must be considered. The question of difficulty and expense involved in a satisfactory review should not in itself be a valid basis for omitting the review or certain aspects of it.

Most importantly, auditors must be trained in classes and on the job to approach the review with the objectives of reaching a logical conclusion as they examine and summarize financial facts, and of providing an opinion as to the correctness and integrity of these facts. In this way, internal auditors, management, CPAs, and the government follow efficient procedures and enhance company operations in an increasingly complex area of the national economy.

AUDIT REVIEW PROGRAM

Some CPA firms have formalized review procedures in order to provide a guide to reviewers. This usually takes the form of a checklist or questionnaire which covers an overall review of working papers and reports. Other CPAs follow the same general pattern without actually using a written questionnaire. In the main, the review checklist or questionnaire covers basic data, representations by clients, working papers and reports, and procedures leading to release of the report.

Review Checklist. An example of an audit review checklist follows:

1. Was the auditor's responsibility clearly defined with the client?
2. Was the client's organization chart examined and employees' functions noted in the working papers?
3. Was the scope of the audit examination adequate in view of the client's system of internal control?
4. Was the audit program modified or expanded as required in the circumstances?
5. Was the audit adequately planned and staff accountants, if any, properly supervised by CPAs?
6. Was due professional care exercised in performing the examination and preparing the report?
7. Was a review made of the client's accounting policies and procedures?
8. Were the client's accounting principles applied on a consistent basis?
9. Were the Opinions of the AICPA Accounting Principles Board observed by the client?
10. Was the audit made "around" or "through" computers in the examination of the financial statements of clients using EDP to process accounting data?
11. Did the supervisor of the audit satisfy himself by appropriate procedures and competent evidential matter that the audit was correctly carried out?
12. Were statistical sampling techniques used in the audit?
13. Was a variation in statistical sampling techniques made during the course of the examination, and for what reason?
14. Did the extent of observation, confirmation, and inspection of items provide a reasonable basis for an opinion relative to the financial statements under examination?
15. Were material differences that were disclosed by the procedures reconciled?
16. Did working papers adequately cover a description of the internal control in effect, an audit program, a general ledger trial balance, a list of adjusting entries, analyses of accounts, excerpts of minutes, miscellaneous recommendations, and a rough draft of the audit report?
17. Were working papers adequately reviewed and integrated with the financial statements and report?
18. Were financial statement disclosures adequate?
19. Was a test for reasonableness made by comparison and by ratio analysis?
20. Were written representations obtained from the client?
21. Were copies of contracts and legal documents reviewed to determine if they had been given effect to by the client?
22. Did the cutoff investigation of transactions for the test period indicate that transactions were recorded in the proper accounting period?
23. Did a search for post-balance sheet events reveal any financial statement adjustments or disclosures?
24. Were management services prepared for the client?
25. Were management services engagements carried out by specialists and adequately supervised?
26. Were tax returns prepared for the client?
27. Was there compliance with auditing standards promulgated by the AICPA?

28. Were the report comments and footnotes suitable?
29. Was there a sound basis for the opinion rendered?
30. Were adjusting journal entries necessary, and did the client approve these entries?

Modification of Program. The above checklist would need to be expanded in the case of a large-scale engagement, enlargement of responsibility to include domestic and foreign subsidiaries, or matters pertinent to proposed mergers, tax planning, or involved management services appointments. It will be noted that the review checklist should be prepared to elicit affirmative answers. If negative answers are obtained, they should be supplemented by satisfactory explanatory statements.

Where the above type of checklist is used, each CPA firm (or internal or governmental auditor) will add special questions arising from the engagement, the firm's or individual's own policies, and prevailing practices and procedures observed by the industry under audit. The reviewer should add any relevant questions which arise during his assessment of the various aspects of the examination. No data should be left to memory, but, instead, all points should be preserved in working papers, review memoranda, and other documents concerned with each auditing engagement.

It should be reemphasized that there is no single standard of audit review. The review is dictated by the circumstances of each examination. The reliability of the supervisor and the complexity of the client company are taken into consideration by the reviewer in judging the extent of review procedures essential to his approval of financial statements. In every case, there should be satisfactory evidence of the adequacy of audit procedures to establish the reliability of the client's accounting records, the propriety of adjusting entries made, the soundness of judgment displayed by the supervisor in decisions reached, the adequacy of disclosures in the statements and opinion, the compliance of the presentation of financial statements with professional standards, and the clarity and sufficiency of the footnotes to statements and the comments in the report.

Reviewer's Analysis. In some instances, the reviewer inspects and initials each working paper schedule, tracing the total into the working trial balance. The reviewer makes a critical analysis of financial statements and of all facts developed during the examination. He questions staff members on the audit, satisfying himself that due care has been exercised in performing the engagement and in preparing the report. By thoroughly reviewing the engagement, the reviewer (supervisor or partner) performs an internal check for the CPA firm, satisfies himself that there are no material misstatements in the report, and advances the professional training of staff members.

BIBLIOGRAPHY

Ingalls, Edmund: *Practical Accounting and Auditing Problems,* AICPA, New York, 1966.

Statements on Auditing Procedure No. 33, *Auditing Standards and Procedures,* AICPA, New York, 1963.

Statement on Auditing Procedure No. 41, *Subsequent Discovery of Facts Existing at the Date of the Auditor's Report,* AICPA, New York, 1969.

Billings, Robert E.: "The Review of Audit Working Papers," *Readings in Auditing,* 2d ed., Cincinnati, Ohio, South-Western Publishing Company, Incorporated, 1965.

MacNeill, James H.: *Accounting Practice Management Handbook,* AICPA, New York, 1962.

Mikesell, R. M. and Leon E. Hay: *Governmental Accounting,* 3d ed., Homewood, Ill., Richard D. Irwin, Inc., 1961.

Murphy, Mary E.: *Advanced Public Accounting Practice,* Homewood, Ill., Richard D. Irwin, Inc., 1966.

Powell, Weldon: *Audits—Planning and Review* (*Independent Auditing, Standards*), New York, Holt, Rinehart and Winston, 1964.

Ready, Robert D.: "The Auditor's Protection against Liability Based on Client's Fraud," *The Journal of Accountancy,* August, 1962.

Schemerhorn, Robert P.: "Supervision and Review of Accounting Engagements in a Small Firm," *The New York Certified Public Accountant,* January, 1968.

Schwersenz, Jack: "Improving Report Review Procedures," *The New York Certified Public Accountant,* April, 1968.

"Landmark Decision on Liability, *Escott et al. v. BarChris Construction Corporation,*" *The Journal of Accountancy,* June, 1968.

Coakley, Walter J.: "Accountants Legal Liability," *The Journal of Accountancy,* July, 1968.

"The Continental Vending Case Affirmed," *The Journal of Accountancy,* February, 1970.

Reiling, Henry B., and Russell A. Taussig: "Recent Liability Cases—Implications for Accountants," *The Journal of Accountancy,* September, 1970.

Chapter 39

Review of Taxes

CARL D. HARNICK

Partner, Arthur Young & Company

FEDERAL TAXES

Income Tax. Every person or entity carrying on a business or deriving income within the United States is subject to the federal income tax. The income of a partnership is generally taxed to the partners. However, a partnership whose characteristics more nearly resemble those of a corporation is taxed as a corporation.

In addition, nonresidents deriving income from U.S. sources are generally taxed at a flat rate on gross income. The tax is generally collected through withholding at the source.

In accordance with the provisions of Subchapter S (Sec. 1371 through Sec. 1378), certain corporations may elect not to be subject to federal income taxes. The election, which must be made within 30 days before and 30 days after the commencement of the corporation's taxable year, causes all the income of the corporation to be taxed to its shareholders as an ordinary dividend or a long-term capital gain, whether distributed or not. Whether the income is taxed to shareholders as ordinary income or long-term capital gains depends upon its nature in the hands of the corporation.

The election, which must be consented to by all shareholders at the time it is made, and by all future shareholders, may be made only by corporations with fewer than 11 shareholders (all of whom must be U.S. resident individuals or estates), and by corporations with only one class of stock, whose income is primarily from the active conduct of business within the United States. In addition, there are other restrictions as to the type of income which may be earned by the corporation, the subsidiaries it may own, and the composition of its shareholder group.

Affiliated Corporations. A U.S. parent corporation and its 80 percent-owned domestic (and certain Mexican and Canadian) subsidiaries may make an election, which generally is irrevocable, to file a consolidated federal income tax return and compute their tax on the basis of the consolidated income of the affiliated group. The applicable regulations impose separate calculations for certain transactions and tax attributes in certain circumstances primarily relating to changes in the membership of the affiliated group or shifts in control of the parent. (Sec. 1501 through Sec. 1504.)

The consolidated return regulations make each member corporation jointly and severally liable for the consolidated tax liability.

Until 1975 an affiliated group not filing a consolidated return (including affiliated brother-sister corporations ineligible to file a consolidated return) may make an annual election to apportion one $25,000 surtax exemption among themselves; after 1974 the surtax exemption may only be allocated in full to one member of the group. Alternatively, prior to 1975 the group may elect to claim reduced surtax exemptions, and pay an additional 6 percent tax thereon; this election will not be available after 1974. (Sec. 1561 and Sec. 1562.)

Personal Holding Companies. A corporation is required to pay the personal holding company tax of 70 percent of its undistributed personal holding company income in the event that more than 50 percent of its stock is owned by five or fewer individuals at any time during the last half of its taxable year and more than 60 percent of its income, as adjusted, is "personal holding company income." Subsidiaries of companies which meet the 50 percent ownership test are also deemed to have met the ownership test. (Sec. 542.)

"Personal holding company income" includes dividends, interest, royalties, certain rents, certain mineral, oil, and gas royalties, income from personal service contracts, and certain other types of passive income. (Sec. 543.) Undistributed personal holding company income consists of taxable income before certain special corporate deductions (including the dividends received deduction), less federal income taxes, a limited net operating loss carry-over, the excess of long-term capital gains over the applicable federal income taxes, and certain other items. (Sec. 545.)

Banks and certain other corporations are excluded from the personal holding company tax. (Sec. 542.) In certain circumstances dividends paid before or after the taxable year may be included as distributions of the current year's undistributed personal holding company income. (Sec. 561 and Sec. 547.)

International Operations. In addition to taxes imposed on operations within the United States, a federal income tax is imposed on certain earnings (generally passive income and income from related corporations) of foreign companies which are controlled by U.S. persons. (Sec. 557 and Sec. 957.) Further, transactions between U.S. companies and their foreign affiliates are subjected to scrutiny by the Internal Revenue Service in order to ensure that income and expenses are fairly allocated between related U.S. and foreign companies. (Sec. 482.)

Most foreign governments impose income taxes (collected by withholding at the source) on dividends, interest, royalties, and frequently, management fees remitted to companies incorporated outside the jurisdiction of the country imposing the tax.

The United States has income tax treaties with most of the industrialized and many of the underdeveloped nations of the world. These treaties generally limit the power of one of the contracting states to tax entities of the other contracting state to such entities which conduct business through a permanent establishment in the former state. The treaties also provide for reduced withholding taxes on dividends, interest, royalties, and other types of income derived from the state imposing the tax by entities of the other state, where such entities do not have a permanent establishment in the former state.

U.S. companies engaged in business in foreign countries through branches are generally subject to the same taxing statutes as companies incorporated in such countries. However, certain countries (Canada, for example) impose a tax on the unremitted earnings of branches of foreign corporations.

In certain countries, local interpretation and administration of the tax statutes may cause the effective rate of tax to vary from that which might be anticipated.

Western Hemisphere Trade Corporations. A domestic corporation, 90 percent of whose gross income was derived from the active conduct of a trade or business (as contrasted with the mere receipt of passive income) and 95 percent of whose gross income was derived from sources outside the United States, for the current and two preceding years, is termed a Western Hemisphere Trade Corporation provided all of the corporation's business (other than incidental purchases) is done in countries in the Western Hemisphere. (Sec. 921.)

A Western Hemisphere Trade Corporation is allowed a deduction computed by multiplying the corporation's taxable income before such deduction by a fraction, the numerator of which is 14 and the denominator of which is the normal tax and surtax rates applicable to corporations. (Sec. 922.)

Based upon current tax rates, the Western Hemisphere Trade Corporation deduction is computed as follows:

$$\begin{array}{c}\text{Taxable income before Western Hemisphere}\\ \text{Trade Corporation deduction}\end{array} \times \frac{14}{48}$$

Possessions Corporations. A domestic corporation, 50 percent of whose gross income was derived from the active conduct of a trade or business (as contrasted with the mere receipt of passive income) within a possession of the United States and 80 percent of whose gross income was derived from sources within a possession of the United States, for the current and two preceding years, is termed a Possessions Corporation. (Sec. 931.)

A Possessions Corporation is taxed only on its U.S. source income, and on its income from any source which is received in the United States. (Sec. 931.)

Accumulated Earnings Tax. The accumulated earnings tax (27½ percent of the first $100,000 of accumulated taxable income plus 38½ percent of the excess) applies to corporations (including foreign corporations) formed or availed of for the purpose of avoiding the individual income tax with respect to its shareholders or the shareholders of any other corporation, by permitting earnings to accumulate instead of being distributed. The tax does not apply to corporations subject to tax as personal holding companies or foreign personal holding companies. (Sec. 532.)

Except in the case of a mere holding or investment company, a corporation may accumulate its earnings for the purpose of meeting the reasonable (including reasonably anticipated) needs of the business, or it may accumulate $100,000, whichever is greater. (Sec. 534 and Sec. 537.)

Excise Tax—Interest Equalization Tax. The tax is imposed on the acquisition, from non-U.S. persons, of certain foreign stock or debt obligations. The rate of tax varies from 1.05 to 22.5 percent, depending upon the maturity date of the debt obligation and the rate of tax imposed by the executive order of the President. The rate of tax on acquisitions of stock varies from 15 to 22.5 percent, depending upon the executive order in effect on the date of acquisition.

The principal exemptions from the tax are:

1. Debt obligations with a maturity of less than 1 year
2. Investments in foreign entities owned more than 10 percent by the U.S. person making the investment

3. Securities of less developed countries or of corporations engaged in business in less developed countries
4. Certain new issues of Canadian securities

Other Excise Taxes. Most federal excise taxes have been repealed; however, excise taxes are still imposed on the following transactions:

1. Retail sale of special fuels
2. Manufacture of automobile and related items, firearms and shells, and fishing equipment
3. Sale of telephone and teletypewriter service and transportation of persons by air
4. Foreign insurance and reinsurance of U.S. risks
5. Highway use by certain vehicles
6. Manufacture and/or sale of alcohol and tobacco

In addition, excise taxes are imposed on certain transactions and/or occupations for regulatory purposes. These include wagering, narcotics, machine guns, etc.

Federal Unemployment Tax. The tax, 3.1 percent of covered payroll, complements the state unemployment taxes in force in each of the states and the District of Columbia by permitting a credit for all or a portion of the state taxes paid, plus taxes not required to be paid because of favorable experience ratings. For purposes of computing the tax, sick pay, retirement pay, payment for services rendered outside the United States, and annual wages in excess of $3,000 per employee are excluded.

Federal Insurance Contributions Tax. The tax is imposed on both the employer and employee. The rate for each is presently 5.2 percent of annual wages up to $7,800 and is scheduled to be increased gradually to 5.9 percent by 1987. The employees' portion of the tax is collected by the employer through withholding from wages and, together with the employer's portion of the tax, must in the case of larger corporations, be remitted on a semimonthly basis; most other corporations are required to make their remittances monthly.

Tax Preferences. Corporations are subject to a "minimum tax" computed at the rate of 10 percent on the amount by which certain designated "tax preferences" exceed the sum of (*a*) $30,000 and (*b*) the corporation's regular federal income tax (as reduced by the investment tax credit and foreign tax credit) for the year. (Sec. 56.)

The tax preferences which may give rise to liability for the minimum tax are (Sec. 57):

1. Certain interest expense and accelerated depreciation on personal property subject to a net lease. (Applicable only to Subchapter S corporations and personal holding companies.)
2. Accelerated depreciation on real property, to the extent it exceeds the amount allowable under the straight-line method.
3. Amortization of certified pollution control facilities, to the extent it exceeds the amount allowable under any accelerated method.
4. Certain amortization of railroad rolling stock. (Applicable only to railroads.)
5. Certain additions to bad debt reserves. (Applicable only to banks and other financial institutions.)
6. Percentage depletion, to the extent that cumulative depletion deductions (on a property-by-property basis) exceed adjusted basis at end of year.

7. A portion (5/12 for 1970, 3/8 thereafter) of the excess of net long-term capital gains over net short-term capital losses.

Liability for minimum tax is deferred in any taxable year in which the corporation incurs a net operating loss which is carried forward (but not back) to another taxable year. (Sec. 56.) Special rules are provided for members of controlled groups, for Subchapter S corporations, for Regulated Investment Companies, for Real Estate Investment Trusts and for tax preferences attributable to foreign sources. (Sec. 58.)

STATE AND LOCAL TAXES

Corporate Income and Franchise Taxes. A corporate income tax or franchise tax based on income is levied in almost every state and the District of Columbia. Franchise taxes are imposed for the privilege of carrying on business in a particular state whether or not any business is actually carried on in the state and whether or not the corporation qualifies itself to do business in the state. On the other hand, income taxes are imposed on income derived from the particular state in either interstate or intrastate commerce without reference to where the corporation carries on its business. In some states, a very minimal degree of activity within the state will cause the state authorities to require the filing of tax returns. However, Public Law 86-272 prohibits the states from taxing the income of corporations whose only activity within the state consists of soliciting orders.

Income is generally apportioned among the states on the basis of sales, property, and employees within the respective states. However, since each state establishes its own rules for measuring the factors, it is possible for the combined taxes of the various states to be levied on more than 100 percent of a corporation's taxable income.

Certain states require gains and losses from sales of property to be allocated directly to the state in which the property was located; other states require dividends, interest, royalties, and similar income to be allocated directly to the state in which the corporation's main office is located.

A number of cities also levy corporate income taxes. In addition, taxes based on net worth (as defined) or on officers' compensation are frequently imposed as an alternative to the franchise tax based on income, with the highest tax required to be paid.

An increasing number of states and municipalities require payments of estimated corporate income and franchise taxes.

Consolidated or combined returns for commonly controlled entities are permitted or required (this may be in conflict with Public Law 86-272 mentioned above) in a number of states, generally as a device to protect the revenue. In addition, many states permit the carry-back and carry-over of net operating losses.

License Fees. Most states and jurisdictions impose a requirement that domestic corporations pay an annual fee. The fee may be fixed at a nominal amount or may vary depending upon the number of shares authorized or outstanding and their par value. In the event of an increase in the number of shares authorized or outstanding, or a change in par value of stock, significant fees may be involved.

Corporations qualified to do business in states other than their state of incorporation are generally required to file an annual report and pay a tax on any increase in capital employed in the foreign state, or change in the par value of stock. Such an increase may occur by either a change in the number of shares outstanding or an increase in sales, employees, or property employed in the state.

Sales and Use Taxes. Sales and use taxes are levied by almost every state. In addition, a number of local jurisdictions also impose sales and use taxes. The tax is generally levied only on the sale or lease of tangible personal property; however, some states impose the tax on a limited class of services. Generally most sales for resale are exempt from tax, although exemption certificates are usually required to be submitted by the purchaser in order to relieve the seller of the responsibility for collecting the tax.

In most cases the tax is imposed upon the purchaser, but the seller is always responsible for the collection of the tax. In many states the seller is required to remit the tax on all taxable transactions regardless of whether some or all of the sales price is not collected; however, credit is usually given for sales returns and allowances.

The obligation to collect sales taxes has been imposed on taxpayers whose activities within the particular state are insufficient to require the payment of income and franchise taxes.

Real and Personal Property Taxes. Real and personal property taxes are imposed in every state and the District of Columbia, except for Delaware, Hawaii, and New York, which impose only real property taxes. These taxes are imposed at either the state or local level.

It should be noted that local interpretation and administration of the tax statutes may cause the effective rate of tax to vary from that which might be anticipated.

State Unemployment Tax. Every state and the District of Columbia provide for a tax on employers based on wages paid. The definition of wages subject to the tax varies, although most states adhere to the federal definition. The rate varies, based upon the employer's unemployment experience rating, and the particular state involved, and ranges from one-half of 1 percent to in excess of 4 percent. The maximum wages subject to tax is $3,000 in most states.

ACCOUNTING FOR INCOME TAXES[1]

Tax Allocation. The provision for federal, local, and foreign income taxes should be based on the transactions included in the determination of pretax accounting income.

Recognition of permanent differences between accounting and taxable income, i.e., dividends received deduction, municipal interest income, etc., takes place in the year the item enters into accounting income. Deferred taxes, measured by the differential between income taxes computed with and without inclusion of the transaction creating the difference between taxable income and pretax accounting income, should be provided for all *nonpermanent* differences (i.e., accelerated depreciation, installment accounting) between taxable and accounting income. In computing deferred taxes, *nonpermanent* (*timing*) differences may be considered individually, or similar *timing* differences may be grouped.

The tax effects of operating loss carry-backs (and other carry-backs) are recognized in the determination of net income (loss) of the periods in which the carry-back arose to the extent the carry-back gives rise to a refund.

[1] This section is based primarily on material from AICPA Accounting Principles Board Opinions No. 2, No. 4, and No. 11.

The tax effects of operating loss carry-forwards (and other carry-forwards) should not be recognized until they are actually received, except when realization is assured beyond a reasonable doubt. The situations in which the realization of the carry-forward is considered to be assured beyond a reasonable doubt are defined very narrowly. In the future periods in which the carry-forward is recognized, the tax benefit, if material, should be reported as an extraordinary item of net income. Deferred tax credits existing at the time the carry-forward arises must generally be adjusted in that period or in subsequent periods.

Tax allocation within a period should be applied to obtain an appropriate relationship between income tax expense and (1) income before extraordinary items, (2) extraordinary items, (3) adjustments of prior periods, and (4) direct entries to other stockholders' equity accounts.

Deferred charges and deferred credits relating to timing differences should be netted and classified as a net current amount and a net noncurrent amount in accordance with the respective assets and liabilities to which they relate.

In the income statement there should be disclosure of (1) taxes estimated to be payable, (2) tax effects of timing differences, and (3) tax effects of operating losses.

Investment tax credits (available now only under certain narrow circumstances) may be recognized in the determination of accounting income in the year of realization or amortized over the life of the asset which gave rise to the credits.

The minimum tax on tax preferences should be recognized in the determination of accounting income in the year that liability for such tax arises, which may (because of net operating loss carry forwards) be different from the year in which the tax preferences affect either accounting or taxable income.

The foregoing is not necessarily applicable to all industries.

OBJECTIVES AND PROCEDURES

General. The objectives of the review of taxes are twofold:

1. To form an opinion as to the adequacy of the tax liability shown on the balance sheet and the fairness of the classification between current and deferred taxes, and as to the adequacy of the provision for taxes appearing in the income statement
2. To comment to management on the adequacy of the procedures and practices being followed with respect to compliance with the laws and regulations of the various taxing jurisdictions to which the taxpayer is subject and on the areas for planning to reduce taxes

The tax provision is ordinarily determined by applying the tax rates in effect for the period to the income reported in the financial statements. Differences between financial and tax accounting relating to the periods in which transactions are reported affect only the balance sheet classification of taxes, not the amount of the tax provision. On the other hand, such non-timing differences between financial and tax accounting as investment credits, foreign tax credits, percentage depletion, and net operating losses affect the computation of the tax provision.

The review of taxes entails:

1. Evaluation of company tax personnel
2. Review of minutes and other documents
3. Review of accounts

Evaluation of Company Tax Personnel. It is ordinarily not possible to test the internal control of a company's tax department in the same fashion as that of other departments. Accordingly, more reliance must be placed on such factors as company representation letters to the auditor, attorneys' letters to the auditor, and the results of an evaluation of the competence of the company's tax department. While this evaluation may be subjective in many respects, there are some objective measures which may be used. Among these are the following:

1. While it may normally be expected that extensions of time in which to file annual tax returns are obtained, this would not normally occur in the case of more frequently recurring returns and often is an indication of an understaffed or poorly managed department.
2. Whether or not extensions of time in which to file returns are obtained, returns should be completed sufficiently in advance of their expected filing date to permit adequate review both by those within the company's tax department and, in the case of major returns, by the company's financial management, auditors, and counsel.
3. As with other departments dealing with the compilation and analysis of financial data, the tax department should make use of mechanical aids in the preparation of tax returns. These may range from pegboard devices for the preparation of consolidating and consolidated schedules to the utilization of computers in analyzing and consolidating accounts or in preparing segments of returns such as depreciation, foreign tax credits, and state tax allocation factors.
4. Discussion with the individuals responsible for payroll, property, and sales tax returns will usually reveal whether these taxes are in responsible hands.

The completion of this evaluation will enable the reviewer to determine the extent of the remaining procedures to be followed.

Review of Minutes. The review of minutes contemplates the review of the minutes of the board of directors' meetings and shareholders' meetings as well as those of each major executive committee, such as the finance committee and management committee.

The following are tax-significant items which may be encountered in the review of minutes:

Authorization of bonuses
Payments to widows of deceased employees
Compensation of officers and key employees
Acquisitions and dispositions of property
Acquisitions and dispositions of subsidiaries
Grants of stock options
Changes in the capitalization of the company

Review of Accounts. Most balance sheet and certain income and expense accounts must be reviewed with a view to determining the proper tax treatment of the transactions which have occurred.

BALANCE SHEET ACCOUNTS

Receivables. Interest receivable which is unlikely to be collected need not be accrued for tax purposes.

Accrued interest receivable on non-interest-bearing U.S. obligations issued at a discount and maturing within 1 year (U.S. Treasury Bills) and on similar state and local obligations does not accrue for tax purposes until payment of the obligation or its disposition. [Sec. 454(b).]

Dividends, although declared, including those whose record date is prior to the end of the year, are not includable in taxable income until actually or constructively received, or accrued.

Advances to stockholders or to businesses controlled by the stockholders of the lender may lead to the assertion that the stockholders have received constructive dividends or, even more serious from the viewpoint of the corporation's accounts, to the assertion of the accumulated earnings tax (see page 39-4 for further discussion). Either assertion is more likely where the advances are not in the form of notes and are unsecured, long-term or regularly renewed, non-interest-bearing, made in proportion to stock ownership, etc.

Advances to affiliated businesses are required (Reg. 1.482-2) to bear interest of at least 4 percent in order to avoid the imputation of interest income at 5 percent by the IRS. While the same new regulation requires the IRS to make a compensating allowance of interest expense with respect to the recipient of the advance, a net increase in tax expense may result in the case of nonconsolidated affiliates, consolidated domestic subsidiaries which operate at a loss or are taxed in lower tax brackets, or foreign subsidiaries exempt from tax and/or subject to tax in jurisdictions which will not recognize the imputed interest expense. (Reg. 1.482-1.)

Advances to foreign corporations which are less than 10 percent owned may give rise to the interest equalization tax (see page 39-4 for further discussion).

Installment accounting is available for tax purposes for sales of real property, and for casual sales of personal property where the sales price exceeds $1,000, if the proceeds in the year of sale are 30 percent of the sales price or less. For this purpose, the assumption of the seller's mortgage, and regular payments on that mortgage, are not considered proceeds; however, the satisfaction of any other lien on the property, or any other obligation of the seller, is considered a payment in the year of sale. In order to qualify for installment accounting, the taxpayer must make an election in the return for the year of the sale for each installment sale. (Sec. 453.)

Installment accounting is also available to dealers in personal property (manufacturers, wholesalers, or retailers) who sell on the installment basis regardless of the percentage of the sales price received in the year of the sale. This method may be elected in any tax return; however, generally all of the taxpayer's installment accounts receivable, including prior years' receivables, the profit on which had previously been recognized on the accrual method, is subject to tax under the installment method. There is provision for a tax credit to recognize the prior amounts included in income; however, since the taxpayer generally does not receive a sufficient credit to offset the second tax which must be paid on these prior years' receivables, dealers in personal property must generally sell to a third party all installment receivables on the last day of the year preceding the year in which the election to adopt the installment method is made. (Sec. 453.)

The gross profit from installment sales is included in taxable income in the year the installment receivable is collected (whether the taxpayer is on the accrual or cash basis for other purposes) or in the year in which the installment receivable is exchanged or otherwise disposed of. Selling an installment receivable (with or without recourse), pledging it, and exchanging it for a new note are examples of transactions which have sometimes been treated as dispositions of installment obligations.

In the case of installment obligations arising from the sale of assets subject to capital gains tax (except patents) which do not provide for an interest rate of at least 4 percent, a portion of the proceeds is treated as interest income at the rate of 5 percent. (Sec. 483.)

In the case of installment sales of depreciable, personal, or real property in which a portion of the gain is treated as ordinary income, the ordinary income must be recognized as collections are made, before any capital gain is recognized. (Reg. 1.1245-6 and Reg. 1.1250-1.)

Allowance for Doubtful Accounts. The reserve method for bad debts is available for tax purposes only if it is elected on the tax return for the year in which the taxpayer first experienced a bad debt, or if application is made to the Commissioner of Internal Revenue within 90 days after the start of the year in which it is desired to change to the reserve method. Except for the above, tax accounting for bad debts must be on the basis of actual charge-offs regardless of the method adopted for financial accounting purposes. (Reg. 1.166-1.)

In evaluating the deductibility of provisions to Reserves for Bad Debts, the Internal Revenue Service places great reliance on the relationship of prior years' charge-offs to prior years' credit sales. Difficulty is sometimes encountered in securing deductions for provisions to Reserves for specific doubtful accounts unless the account is actually charged off or prior years' bad debt experience supports the provision. Accordingly, a liberal policy in making charge-offs is indicated.

Banks, small business investment corporations, and certain other classes of lenders are permitted to compute the addition to a reserve for doubtful accounts under special rules.

Inventories. The income tax regulations recognize that inventory rules cannot be uniform for all taxpayers, and they therefore establish two tests of a proper inventory method for tax purposes:

1. The inventory method must conform as nearly as possible to the best accounting practice in the trade or business, and
2. The inventory method must clearly reflect income. (Reg. 1.471-2.)

This same regulation states that in order to reflect income clearly, the inventory practice should be consistent from year to year.

Whether inventories are valued at cost, or at cost or market, whichever is lower, goods which are damaged, obsolete, and otherwise not salable at normal prices may be valued at selling price (actual price at which offered for sale within 30 days after inventory date) less direct cost of disposition. Under either method, average cost may not be used.

The regulations indicate that in the case of manufactured goods, cost includes material, labor, and overhead (including a reasonable proportion of management expenses). (Reg. 1.471-3.) However, some courts have recognized direct costing and other consistently followed inventory methods which include less than the full absorption of overhead in inventory.

In valuing inventory at cost or market, whichever is lower, the comparison should be made for each item rather than for classes of inventory or for the inventory as a whole. "Market" means the current bid price for the particular item in the volume in which usually purchased. When no open market exists, the taxpayer must use whatever method of determining market is appropriate; however, the IRS will make reference to actual sales prices less direct cost of disposition for a reasonable period before and after the inventory date to determine the fairness of the taxpayer's estimate of market. In the *E. W. Bliss* case (6th Circuit, Sept. 29, 1965), contract price less cost to complete was held to be a reasonable method of determining the market value of work in process being manufactured to specific contract terms. (Reg. 1.471-4.)

Retailers are permitted to employ the "retail method" of pricing inventories. (Reg. 1.471-7.)

The LIFO method of valuing inventory may be used by any taxpayer provided he also uses the LIFO method in reports to shareholders, creditors, etc. (Reg. 1.472-2.) Revenue Ruling 69-17 (1969-1 CB 143) permits a subsidiary under certain circumstances to use the LIFO method, notwithstanding the fact that the difference between LIFO cost and cost or market, whichever is lower, is eliminated in consolidated financial statements, so long as separate financial statements of the subsidiary state the inventory at LIFO cost.

Any taxpayer may elect to determine LIFO cost under the "dollar value" method. (Reg. 1.472-8.)

Fixed Assets and Depreciation. Fixed asset records must be sufficiently detailed to permit the calculation of depreciation as well as a determination of allowable investment credit. While the investment credit is usually determinable from a scrutiny of machinery and equipment and furniture and fixtures, accounts such as leasehold and building improvements, and buildings must also be reviewed. Items found in these accounts, such as elevators and escalators, certain power generating equipment, fences, fixtures, and research equipment, may qualify for the credit.

Fixed asset accounting policy affects the recognition of taxable income. The regulations [1.167(a)-7 and 8] permit each fixed asset to be accounted for separately, with the result that gain or loss must be recognized upon the sale or retirement of each asset. Also authorized are methods under which similar or dissimilar assets are grouped in one account; however, under this method gain or loss is not generally recognized on normal retirements (which includes most retirements, unless the event causing retirement was not anticipated in setting the depreciable life).

There is no statutory authority for the widely followed practice of establishing a minimum dollar amount for capitalization of fixed asset acquisitions. Such a policy will normally not be disturbed by the IRS if the minimum capitalization amount is reasonable and the practice does not distort income.

In the case of a combined acquisition of land and building, the cost is allocated between the depreciable and nondepreciable property in accordance with the relative fair market values of each.

In the case of an improved leasehold of real property, no portion of the cost of acquiring the leasehold may be allocated to the improvements if the improvements were constructed by the fee owner rather than by the lessor.

Tangible personal property with a useful life in excess of 3 years, and residential real property new in use to the taxpayer, may be depreciated over its estimated useful life to the taxpayer under the straight-line, declining-balance (at no more than 200 percent of the straight-line rate), sum-of-the-years'-digits, or unit-of-production methods, or under any other reasonable method which does not, for the first two-thirds of the useful life of the property, result in depreciation in excess of the depreciation which would be allowable under the declining-balance method above. (Sec. 167.)

Used tangible personal property, new nonresidential real property, and new tangible personal property with a useful life of 3 years or less may be depreciated only on the straight-line, declining-balance (at no more than 150 percent of the straight-line rate), or unit-of-production methods. (Sec. 167.)

Used residential real property having a useful life of at least 20 years may be depreciated under the straight-line or declining balance (at no more than 125 percent of the straight-line rate) methods. All other used real property, whether residential or nonresidential, must be depreciated on the straight-line method. (Sec. 167.) If real property is depreciated under an accelerated method, the amount in excess of straight-line is treated as a "tax preference" to which the minimum tax may apply (Sec. 57.)

Property qualifying as a "Certified Pollution Control Facility" may, at the corporation's election, be amortized over a period of 60 months. This election is available for facilities placed in service prior to 1975; if made, the resultant deduction for amortization (to the extent it exceeds depreciation otherwise allowable) is treated as a "tax preference" to which the minimum tax may apply. (Secs. 169 and 57.)

Improvements to leased property may be depreciated only on the straight-line method over the life of the lease if the lease life is less than the normal useful life to the taxpayer. If the useful life of the improvement is less than the life of the lease, the improvement may be depreciated under the rules for new or used property.

Taxpayers may change from the 200 percent declining-balance method to the straight-line method by making an election in a timely filed return for the year of the change. Any other change in depreciation method may be made only upon request from the IRS within 90 days after the start of the year for which the change is requested. Such requests are normally approved.

An investment credit determined as a percentage of the basis of eligible property purchased or constructed by the taxpayer applies to reduce the tax. The property eligible for the credit is new tangible personal property, and certain other new property, plus up to $50,000 per annum (to be allocated among the members of a controlled group of corporations) of used property otherwise eligible. In general, the eligible property must be placed in service prior to 1976 and must be acquired by the corporation or constructed, reconstructed or erected under a contract which, on April 18, 1969, and at all times thereafter, was binding on the corporation. The investment credit percentage is determined as follows:

Useful life of property	Public utility property	All other property
Less than 4 years	–	–
More than 4 years but less than 6 years	1%	2⅓%
More than 6 years but less than 8 years	2%	4⅔%
More than 8 years	3%	7%

The investment credit determined above may be claimed as a credit against the income tax due; however, such credit may not exceed $25,000 (to be allocated among the members of a controlled group of corporations), plus 50 percent of the tax otherwise due (net of foreign tax credit) in excess of $25,000. (Sec. 38 and Secs. 46, 48, and 49.)

Unused investment credits may generally be carried back 3 years and carried forward 7 years. However, special limitations apply during such years. (Sec. 46.)

The premature disposition of eligible property, on which investment credit has previously been applied to reduce income tax, will cause the unearned portion of the credit to be "recaptured" as additional tax payable. If replacement of such property is made within 6 months after the date of premature disposition, by property which (but for failing the April 18, 1969, test discussed above) would itself have been eligible for the credit, such recapture shall be reduced proportionately. (Sec. 47.)

Intangible Assets. The costs of acquiring intangible assets such as goodwill, patents, licenses, trademarks, and copyrights must be capitalized. Similarly, the cost of defending or perfecting title to intangible assets must also be capitalized. [Reg. 1.263(a)-1.] However, the expense of protecting the value (as distinguished from title) of an intangible asset is deductible. (See below for further discussion of trademarks and patents.)

Intangible assets whose useful life can be estimated with reasonable accuracy may be depreciated on either a straight-line or unit-of-production basis. Typically, copyrights and patents are depreciable (over their legal life or their estimated useful life, if that is shorter). Goodwill is not subject to depreciation. [Reg. 1.167(a)-3.]

Research and experimental expenditures may be deducted as an ordinary and necessary business expense, provided this treatment is elected for the first taxable year in which such expenditures are incurred. Once elected, this treatment applies to all of the taxpayer's research and experimental expenditures and may not be changed without the consent of the IRS. (Sec. 174.)

As an alternative to the above, a taxpayer may elect to treat research and experimental expenditures as a deferred expense amortizable over a period selected by the taxpayer, but not less than 60 months commencing with the month the taxpayer first realizes benefits from the expenditures. A taxpayer may request permission to change to or from the deferred method of treating research and experimental expenditures, or to change the amortization period under the deferred method, for all such expenditures or for one or more projects, by filing an application with the IRS prior to the close of the year for which the change is to be effective. (Sec. 174.)

If neither of the foregoing methods is selected, research and experimental expenditures must be capitalized and may be amortized only if a useful life may be determined with reasonable accuracy [Reg. 1.167(a)-3]; in any event, they may be charged off when the research project is abandoned. (Reg. 1.165-2.)

As discussed above, the cost of acquiring a trademark or trade name must be capitalized and ordinarily is not amortizable. Under a special provision, however, expenditures to acquire a trademark or trade name, except for the consideration paid to acquire a seller's trademark or trade name, may be treated as a deferred expense and amortized over a period of not less than 60 months. A taxpayer may elect this treatment only in a timely filed return. (Sec. 177.)

Under another special provision, there are certain circumstances in which the consideration paid to acquire a seller's trademark, trade name or franchise may be deductible by the buyer, either when paid (in the case of contingent payments or fixed series payments) or through amortization over a 10-year (or shorter) period (in the case of lump-sum payments). (Sec. 1253.)

Prepaid Expenses and Deferred Charges. Not all expenditures which are properly treated as deferred or prepaid assets for financial accounting purposes are accorded similar treatment for tax purposes. In order for an expense to be deferrable for tax purposes, it must either relate to the acquisition of an asset whose life is substantially in excess of one year or relate to the receipt of income which is not recognizable until a subsequent year.

Some of the more common items which may be deducted for tax purposes, although deferred for purposes of financial accounting, are considered below.

Painting and other incidental repairs which neither materially add to value nor appreciably prolong life must be charged to expense. (Reg. 1.162-4.)

Advertising and similar expenditures incurred but deferred on the books to match income expected to be received in a subsequent period must be charged to expense unless the income of the future period is fixed and determinable for tax purposes at the close of the taxable year. (Reg. 1.162-1.)

Unamortized expenses of a retired mortgage must be charged to expense in the year refinanced since the asset (the mortgage) to which these expenses relate has been disposed of. The fact that the mortgage was retired in order to secure a new mortgage, although significant in determining the financial accounting, does not affect the tax accounting.

Expenses specifically deductible under a section of the Internal Revenue Code (interest and taxes, for example) must be deducted in the year incurred even though they might otherwise be capitalized. (See below for elective treatment of certain carrying charges.) For example, property taxes are generally accruable on the lien date regardless of the period benefited.

Expenses of organizing a corporation are generally deductible only in the year the corporation is dissolved; however, under a special provision, these expenditures may be amortized over a period of not less than 60 months, provided the taxpayer so elects in a timely filed return for the year in which the expenditures were incurred. (Sec. 248.) A similar election is not available for expenses of a merger or other reorganization of a corporation.

Bond discount, whether arising from the sale of bonds at less than par value or from the sale at par value of bonds with stock-purchase warrants, is amortizable over the life of the bonds. (Reg. 1.61-12.) The tax treatment of bond discount arising from the sale of convertible bonds at par is not clear. Similarly, expenses of registration and other costs of issuing bonds are amortizable over the life of the bonds; however, in the case of convertible bonds the unamortized balance attributable to bonds converted is treated as a nondeductible capital expenditure.

A taxpayer may elect, on his original return for a taxable year, to capitalize annual taxes, mortgage interest, and other expenses of unproductive real property. Similarly, with respect to real or personal property under development or construction, a taxpayer may elect to capitalize interest on a loan, employment taxes, sales and use taxes on materials, and other necessary expenditures, otherwise deductible, which are properly capitalizable. (Sec. 266.)

Investments. Investments in unrelated businesses may be indicative of an improper accumulation of earnings subject to the accumulated earnings tax. (See page 39-4 for a further discussion.) This is particularly the case where the investment is a loan or a minority interest in a corporation controlled by stockholders of the corporation under audit. The fact that the investment is sound from a financial point of view is not necessarily a defense against the accumulated earnings tax unless the investment is related to the business of the taxpayer (for example, an investment to secure a source of supply); however, this fact would probably be a defense against the assertion of a constructive dividend to shareholders.

An election is available to amortize the excess of cost over redemption value of taxable bonds; however, the premium attributable to the conversion feature of convertible bonds is not amortizable. Amortization must also be computed on the premium attributable to tax-exempt obligations; the amount thereof is required to reduce basis but may not be deducted for tax purposes. (Sec. 171.)

There is no provision for the amortization of the discount which arises when bonds are purchased below par.

Investments of certain controlled foreign corporations in U.S. securities, or loans to U.S. corporations (including a U.S. parent) are generally deemed the equivalent of dividend distributions and subject the U.S. parent to tax on the deemed dividend. (Sec. 956.)

Loans from a domestic subsidiary to its parent may also be treated as constructive dividends in certain circumstances.

Investments in stock or securities of a foreign corporation by a U.S. corporation, and under certain circumstances by a foreign subsidiary of a U.S. corporation, may subject the U.S. corporation to the interest equalization tax. (See page 39-4 for a further discussion.)

Acquisitions of 5 percent or more of the stock of a foreign corporation, while not necessarily subject to the interest equalization tax, are subject to an IRS reporting requirement.

Under the equity method of accounting, dividends from affiliates are credited to the investment account; dividends must be included in taxable income. On the other hand, charges and credits to the investment account representing profits and losses of affiliates have no tax effect.

Accounts Payable, Accrued Expenses, and Other Liabilities. In order for a liability to give rise to a deductible expense it must be payable to a specific creditor and the amount must be reasonably determinable. Hence, reserves for contingencies, reserves for guarantees and warranties, and similar reserves do not generally give rise to deductible expenses.

Reserves for vacation pay do not give rise to deductible expenses unless there exists a liability to each employee which is fixed and determinable at year end. However, under special legislation, which has been periodically renewed for more than a decade, taxpayers who have been accruing and deducting vacation pay, based on an estimate of the liability to a group of employees, although there is no fixed liability to any specific employee, may continue this practice.

Liabilities which are being contested do not give rise to deductible expenses. Upon payment of the liability, the deduction is allowable notwithstanding the fact that the contest continues. (Sec. 461.)

The retirement of a taxpayer's indebtedness at less than its face amount, either by a forgiveness of indebtedness by a creditor or by the purchase of a corporation's own bonds on the open market at less than face value, ordinarily gives rise to taxable income. (Reg. 1.61-12.) However, by filing a consent with his tax return, a taxpayer may elect not to recognize such income and to reduce the tax basis of assets by an equal amount. (Sec. 108 and Sec. 1017.)

Accrued salaries which are in the nature of deferred compensation are not deductible until paid, regardless of the corporation's accounting method. (Sec. 404.)

Deferred Credits. Unearned income, such as prepaid rent or interest, is taxable when received or accrued, whichever is earlier, regardless of the fact that it may be treated as deferred income for financial accounting purposes. (Reg. 1.61-7 and 8.)

Capital Accounts. The granting of an option to acquire the grantor's stock does not give rise to taxable income to the grantor corporation. Further, if the option is a "qualified stock option" within the meaning of the Internal Revenue Code, and the Internal Revenue Code provisions applicable to such options are observed by the grantor and optionee, no deduction is ever allowed the corporation. However, in the event that the optionee of a "qualified stock option" does not observe all of the restrictions applicable to the option, the grantor corporation becomes entitled to a deduction.

The statutory requirements applicable to "qualified stock options" are as follows:

1. The shareholders must, within 12 months before or after the plan is adopted, approve the plan, the aggregate number of shares which may be issued under options, and the class of employees (of the issuing corporation or its subsidiaries) eligible to receive options.
2. The option must be granted within the earlier of 10 years from the date the plan is adopted or approved by the shareholders, and must expire no later than 5 years from the date of grant.
3. The option price must be not less than the fair market value of the stock at the date of grant. (There is a limited relief provision for the failure of a bona fide attempt to grant the option at not less than the fair market value of the stock.) Except in corporations whose equity capital is less than $2 million, more than 5 percent shareholders (after applying attribution rules) are not eligible to receive qualified stock options.
4. The option, by its terms, may not be exercisable while there are outstanding any previously granted and exercisable qualified or restricted (under prior law) stock options, and may not be transferable during the optionee's lifetime.

Most other stock options (including options which are intended to be "qualified" but fail to meet the above requirements) are covered by provisions which result in compensation income to the employee-optionee, and a compensation deduction (subject to the rule of reasonableness) to the employer-grantor at a time determined in accordance with the following rules:

1. Upon issuance of the option, if the option is unrestricted and has a readily ascertainable fair market value
2. Upon exercise of the option, if the option is unrestricted but does not have a readily ascertainable fair market value at the date of grant
3. Upon disposition of the stock acquired pursuant to the option, by the optionee or upon lapse of restrictions if the option was granted subject to restrictions

With respect to "nonqualified" options granted prior to April 22, 1969, the deduction is measured by the difference between the option price and the fair market value of the stock on the date the deduction is recognized, except that in the case of an option subject to restrictions, the deduction may not exceed such difference on the date of exercise. A similar rule applies to "nonqualified" stock options granted after April 21, 1969; however the limitation based on the difference between the market value and option price on the date of exercise does not apply. There are transition rules which may apply to stock acquired between April 22, 1969, and April 30, 1970. (Sec. 83.)

Other transactions affecting the capital accounts may give rise to taxable events. Examples are deductions arising from the excess of purchase price over face value on the repurchase of a convertible obligation, (subject to a limitation) expenses associated with disposing of a business pursuant to an antitrust action, income arising from the redemption of outstanding stock with appreciated property, and state taxes imposed on recapitalizations and stock dividends.

INCOME AND EXPENSE ACCOUNTS

Dividend Income. An 85 percent deduction is allowable to corporations with respect to most dividends received from domestic corporations. The deduction is limited to 85 percent of taxable income, except that there is no limitation when 85 percent of dividend income results in a loss for tax purposes. In an extreme case, a $1 change in taxable income will cause almost a 15 percentage point change in the dividends received deduction. (Sec. 243.)

In certain circumstances, prior to 1975, provided the members of an affiliated group of corporations not filing a consolidated income tax return elect to allocate one surtax exemption among them, and in all cases after 1974, a 100 percent dividends received deduction is allowed. (Sec. 243.)

Property dividends received by a corporation from domestic corporations are included in taxable income at the lower of the distributing corporation's tax basis or the property's fair market value. Property dividends of foreign corporations are includable in taxable income at their fair market value. (Sec. 301.)

Distributions which are in excess of the distributor's earnings and profits (retained earnings on a tax basis) are not taxable as dividends; rather, they reduce the basis of the underlying investment. (Sec. 316.)

With respect to companies with large amounts of dividend and interest income, see page 39-3 for a discussion of personal holding companies.

Gains and Losses. Gains and losses from the sale or exchange of property other than the following are termed capital gains and losses:

1. Stock in trade
2. Depreciable personal property and real property used in the taxpayer's trade or business
3. Copyrights received in tax-free transactions from the creator
4. Accounts or notes receivable
5. Certain discount obligations of governments (Sec. 1221)

Net gains from property held more than 6 months are called long-term capital gains and, reduced by net short-term losses, are subject to favorable tax treatment. However, a portion ($^5/_{12}$ for 1970, $^3/_8$ thereafter) of the excess of such net long-term gains over such net short-term losses is treated as a "tax preference" to which the minimum tax may apply.

The gain, net of any losses, in a year, from the sale of depreciable personal property and real property used in the taxpayer's trade or business and held for more than 6 months, is added to the corporation's net long-term capital gain. (Sec. 1231.) Similar treatment is accorded banks for their net bond loss. (Sec. 582.) Net losses from such transactions in any year are treated as ordinary deductions.

Capital losses may not be claimed as deductions but may be carried back for 3 years and forward for 5 years to be offset only against capital gains.

Gains from the sale or exchange of personal property, to the extent of depreciation claimed after 1962, is taxable at ordinary income rates. (Sec. 1245.) A similar provision applies to gains from the disposition of real property, or substantial improvements to real property, depending upon the depreciation method and the length of time the property was held. (Sec. 1250.)

Gains from the sale or exchange of stock in a "collapsible corporation" formed or availed of principally for the manufacture, construction, production, or purchase of certain property (generally, property which would be included in the corporation's inventory) with a view to the sale or exchange of such stock prior to the realization by the corporation of a substantial part of the income from such property, are treated as ordinary income. (Sec. 341.) In addition, a collapsible corporation is denied the benefits of certain advantageous provisions of the Internal Revenue Code. (Sec. 333 and Sec. 337.)

Interest Income. Interest income from obligations of state and local governments and possessions of the United States is exempt from tax. (Sec. 103.)

Except for U.S. Treasury Bills and corporate obligations issued before May 28, 1969 original issue discount on corporate obligations is taxable ratably according to taxpayer's period of ownership, as the discount accrues. Accrued discount on Treasury Bills is taxable only on sale or collection of the bills. (Sec. 454.) Interest and other items of income which are doubtful of collection may be excluded from taxable income. Proceeds from the sale of capital assets under a deferred-payment plan which does not provide interest at a rate of 4 percent per annum are generally deemed to include interest income at a 5 percent rate. (Sec. 483.)

Royalty Income. Income, however denominated, from the transfer of substantially all rights to a patent is taxable at long-term capital gain rates. This provision is not applicable to transfers of patents held by individuals related to the creator of the patent or to transfers to certain related foreign corporations. (Sec. 1235 and Sec. 1249.)

However, income from the transfer of a franchise, trademark, or trade name will not be treated as long-term capital gain if the transferor retains any significant power, right, or continuing interest with respect to the subject matter of the franchise, trademark, or trade name. A right to contingent payments constitutes a significant power. (Sec. 1253.)

Interest Expense. Interest incurred to acquire or carry exempt municipal obligations is not deductible. In certain cases, the IRS has attempted to disallow interest expense to taxpayers holding municipal obligations, under the theory that the municipal obligations should have been sold to satisfy the debt. (Sec. 265.)

Interest incurred to acquire stock or assets of another corporation is subject to statutory disallowance if certain specific tests are met and if total interest expense for the year exceeds $5,000,000. (Sec. 279.)

Payments in accordance with a deferred-payment contract for the acquisition of a capital asset which does not provide for interest at a rate of 4 percent per annum results in interest expense at a 5 percent rate. (Sec. 483.) This imputed interest is treated as interest for all purposes, including the application of withholding taxes on payments to nonresidents.

Taxes. All state, local, and foreign taxes paid or accrued in carrying on a trade or business are deductible. (Sec. 164.)

Foreign taxes imposed on or measured by income may be either deducted or claimed as a credit against federal income taxes otherwise due. (Sec. 901.) The foreign tax credit is subject to the following limitation:

$$\text{Federal income tax after investment credit} \times \frac{\text{taxable foreign source income}}{\text{taxable income from all sources}}$$

The above limitation is applied on a country-by-country basis unless the taxpayer elects to compute the limitation by combining all foreign income taxes. The latter election is generally irrevocable in the absence of the consent of the IRS. (Sec. 904.)

Excess foreign tax credits may be carried back 3 years and carried forward 5 years, subject to the above limitation in each year. (Sec. 904.)

Foreign taxes imposed on or measured by the income of a foreign corporation, more than 10 percent of which is owned by a U.S. corporation, are treated, by such 10 percent owners, as creditable foreign taxes in proportion to the dividends received from such corporations. The credit is computed as follows:

From corporations in less developed countries:

$$\text{Credit} = \text{dividend} \times \frac{\text{foreign income taxes}}{\text{income before foreign income taxes}}$$

From corporations in developed countries:

$$\text{Credit} = \text{dividend} \times \frac{\text{foreign income taxes}}{\text{income after foreign income taxes}}$$

The credit (referred to as the "deemed paid credit") from developed-country corporations must be included in taxable income. (Sec. 902.)

Royalties, dividends, and interest from foreign sources are often received after deduction of foreign income taxes withheld by the payor. It is generally advantageous to ascertain the amount of withheld income taxes in order to report the income gross and claim the tax as a credit.

Contributions. A corporation may deduct charitable contributions paid or (under certain circumstances) accrued to qualifying donee organizations subject to the limitation that the contribution deduction not be greater than 5 percent of taxable income (computed without regard to such deduction and to certain other specified deductions). For contributions in the form of property, the amount of the deduction depends upon the nature of the property, the length of time held by the taxpayer and the amount by which the property's fair market value exceeds its adjusted basis to taxpayer; under certain circumstances, the full value of appreciated property may be deductible. (Sec. 170.)

Compensation. In order to be deductible, compensation must be an ordinary and necessary business expense and reasonable in amount. The IRS may assert that compensation of officers or employees who are also large shareholders (or relatives of large shareholders) is unreasonable or is a disguised dividend and hence not deductible. Bonuses based on profits of the business paid to the above persons are especially likely to attract the attention of the IRS and must be considered from that point of view.

See page 39-17 for a discussion of stock options.

The IRS has frequently attempted to disallow gratuitous payments to widows of deceased employees under the theory that the payments were gifts or (where the deceased was a shareholder) disguised dividends. The employer has been able to sustain its deduction where he was able to demonstrate that the payment was clearly related to the deceased's employment.

Depletion. The owner of an economic interest in a natural resource is allowed a deduction for the greater of cost (computed in accordance with the taxpayer's remaining basis in the property and the number of units sold) or percentage depletion (22 percent of gross income from the property in the case of oil or gas, equal or lesser percentages for other minerals). The percentage-depletion deduction is limited to 50 percent of the net income from the property, excluding depletion. The basis of the interest is reduced, but not below zero, by the depletion allowed or allowable, to the extent that the percentage depletion deduction, when added to all prior depletion deductions on a property-by-property basis, exceeds the adjusted basis of the interest at year-end, before depletion. Such excess is treated as a "tax preference" to which the minimum tax may apply.

Intangible Drilling and Development Costs. A taxpayer may make an irrevocable election to deduct all intangible costs (labor, services, etc., as contrasted with tangible costs such as equipment and supplies) necessary for the drilling and preparation of wells for the production of oil and gas.

Net Operating Loss Deduction. Generally, the excess of deductions over income in a corporation's taxable year is termed a net operating loss and may be applied to reduce taxable income of the 3 preceding years and the 5 succeeding years. A net operating loss carry-over of the corporation which incurred such a loss may generally be claimed by the successor corporation in a tax-free acquisition or liquidation (Sec. 381), subject to certain limitations (Sec. 381 and Sec. 382).

A net operating loss deduction may be disallowed if more than 50 percent control of a corporation is acquired, or if a corporation acquires the property of another corporation not previously controlled by such acquiring corporation or its shareholders in a tax-free transaction, and the principal purpose of either acquisition was to secure the benefit of a net operating loss deduction which such corporation would not otherwise enjoy. (Sec. 269.)

The number of years to which a net operating loss may be carried forward may be extended in the case of regulated transportation companies or companies which have foreign expropriation losses.

Antitrust Damages. Treble damages paid to the federal government and, in certain circumstances, the penal portion of antitrust damages paid to others, is not deductible. (Sec. 162(g).)

CERTAIN ITEMS TO BE CONSIDERED IN REVIEWING A CORPORATE TAX ACCRUAL

- Closely held corporations
  - Personal holding company and foreign personal holding company status
  - Accumulated earnings tax status
  - Constructive dividends
  - Unreasonable compensation
  - Qualification of Subchapter Selection
- Foreign operations
  - Foreign tax credits
  - Reallocation of income and expenses
  - Interest equalization tax
  - Qualification of Western Hemisphere Trade Corporation
  - Qualification of Possessions Corporation
  - Effect of foreign direct investment program on remittance of funds and resultant tax consequences
  - Investments in U.S. property by foreign subsidiaries
  - Subpart F income

- Foreign taxes
- Withholding of U.S. income taxes

Investment credit
- Qualification of property
  - Location
  - Use
- Leased property
- Life

Carry-overs
- Net operating losses
- Capital losses
- Foreign tax credits
- Investment credits
- Charitable contributions
- Pension and profit-sharing deductions

Other
- Minimum tax on tax preferences
- Dispositions of capital assets
- Natural resources
- Stock options
- Disposition of installment obligations
- "Claim of right" income
- Liabilities not fixed and determinable
- Reserve for doubtful accounts
- Depreciation
- Charitable contribution limitation
- Multiple corporations
  - Consolidated return
  - Surtax exemptions
- Sale and leaseback transactions
- Pension and profit-sharing contribution
- Accounting methods
- State and local taxes
- Payroll taxes
- Excise taxes
- Tax-exempt status of private charitable foundations, pension and profit-sharing trusts, business leagues, etc.

COMMON DIFFERENCES BETWEEN NET INCOME PER BOOKS AND TAXABLE INCOME

Item and reference	Treatment in computing net income per books	Treatment in computing federal taxable income
Bad debts	Reserve	Direct charge-off or reserve method
Installment sales	Income reported as accrued	Income reported as collections are made
Depreciation	Various	Accelerated
Goodwill amortization	Deducted	Not deductible
Research and experimental expenditures	Various	Deducted, amortized over 60 months, or charged off as abandoned
Incidental repairs	May be amortized	Deducted
Expenses related to future income (including circulation expenses)	Deferred	Deducted
Expenses of refinanced mortgage	Various	Deducted
Property taxes and certain carrying charges during development period	May be capitalized	May be deducted
Reorganization expenses	Various	Not deductible
Discount on bonds and treasury bills purchased at less than par value	Amortized into income	Not includable in income until disposition
Adjustments to reflect equity in investments	Includable in computing net income	Only dividends and dispositions recognized
Transactions affecting liabilities for expenses not fixed and determinable at year end	Includable in computing net income	Recognized when fixed and determinable
Contested payments	Includable in computing net income	Recognized upon settlement of contest or payment
Unearned income	Deferred	Taxable upon receipt
Disqualifying dispositions of stock options granted at approximately market value	Not recognized	Deductible
Dividends from domestic corporations	Recognized on record date at fair market value	Taxable upon receipt measured by lower of value or tax basis
Dividends from foreign corporations	Recognized on record date at fair market value	Taxable upon receipt at fair market value; deemed paid foreign taxes includable in income
Capital losses	Recognized in computing net income	Deductible only against capital gains
Municipal interest income	Includable in computing net income	Not taxable
Interest expense to carry municipal bonds	Recognized in computing net income	Not deductible
Foreign income taxes	Recognized in computing net income	Not deductible if claimed as a credit
Federal income taxes	Recognized in computing net income	Not deductible
Depletion	Recognized based on cost	Deduction may exceed cost, and based on gross receipts
Intangible drilling and development costs	May be capitalized	Deductible
Contributions	Recognized based on cost	Deductible based on fair market value but limited to 5% of taxable income before contributions
Insurance on life of officer where corporation is beneficiary	Recognized	Not deductible
Carry-overs of deductions	Various	Deductible subject to limitations

BIBLIOGRAPHY

Accounting Principles Board Opinions No. 2, No. 4, and No. 11, *Accounting for Income Taxes,* AICPA.

Income Tax Regulations, Internal Revenue Service, as adopted through March 16, 1970.

Internal Revenue Code of 1954, as amended through December 31, 1969.

Statements on Responsibilities in Tax Practice, AICPA Tax Committee, releases to date.

Bardes, P., W. T. Barnes, J. B. Fish, Jr., Stuetzer, Jr., and P. D. Yager: *Montgomery's Federal Taxes,* 39th ed., New York, The Ronald Press Company, 1964.

Beaman, W. H.: *Paying Taxes to Other States,* New York, The Ronald Press Company, 1963.

Bitker, Boris I., and James S. Eustice: *Federal Income Taxation of Corporations and Shareholders,* 2d ed., Federal Tax Press, Inc., 1966.

Denney, R. L., A. P. Rua, and R. J. Schoen: *Federal Income Taxation of Insurance Companies,* 2d ed., New York, The Ronald Press Company, 1966.

Miller, Kenneth G.: *Oil and Gas Federal Income Taxation,* Commerce Clearing House, Inc., 1968.

Owens, Elizabeth A.: *The Foreign Tax Credit,* Harvard Law School, 1961.

Raby, William A.: *The Income Tax and Business Decisions,* Englewood Cliffs, N.J., Prentice-Hall, Inc., 1964.

Roberts, Sidney I., and William C. Warren: *U.S. Income Taxation of Foreign Corporations and Nonresident Aliens,* Practicing Law Institute, 1967.

Taxation in the United States, Harvard Law School, Commerce Clearing House, Inc., 1963.

Wakely, Maxwell A. H., Chairman, Editorial Board: *Federal Income Taxation of Banks and Financial Institutions,* Warren Gorham and Lamone, 1968.

Wood, E. O., and J. F. Cerney: *Tax Aspects of Deferred Compensation,* Englewood Cliffs, N.J., Prentice-Hall, Inc., 1969.

Chapter **40**

Standards of Reporting

MAX BLOCK

Editor, The New York Certified Public Accountant

REPORTING RESPONSIBILITIES

Introduction. The standards of reporting discussed here are primarily those promulgated by the American Institute of Certified Public Accountants (AICPA) in its Statements on Auditing Procedure (SAP), Accounting Research Bulletins (ARB), and the releases of its Accounting Principles Board (APB). They are the guidelines for the independent auditor's report (opinion) on financial statements, departures from which must be disclosed and justified.

SAP No. 33, entitled *Auditing Standards and Procedures,*[1] sets forth initially the generally accepted standards of reporting for AICPA members (and, in a practical sense, for all other independent auditors).

Some consideration has also been given to the regulations (S-X) of the Securities and Exchange Commission (SEC) governing the form and content of financial statements filed with it, and its Accounting Series Releases.

Prevailing reporting practices and trends, with respect to both financial statements and auditors' reports, culled from the published reports of about 600 commercial and industrial corporations, are annually reviewed in the AICPA "Accounting Trends and Techniques," a valuable reference work.

A basic aim of the standards is to assure fair presentation in the financial statements and in the accompanying footnotes, in accordance with prevailing

[1] Statements on Auditing Procedure No. 33, *Auditing Standards and Procedures,* AICPA (Committee on Auditing Procedure), New York, 1963, p. 16.

generally accepted accounting principles. The major elements of fair presentation are (1) adequacy of disclosure and (2) consistency.

Standards are a bulwark of the auditor's independence, inasmuch as all professional-minded auditors are guided, largely, by the same standards. Moreover, public confidence in financial statements is based on the auditor's attestation, which rests on the profession's reporting standards.

The concern here is with the *presently* prevailing reporting standards and generally accepted accounting principles, and thus no consideration is given to concepts that are under discussion but which have not been given AICPA approval. Thus concepts such as "current value" to replace "historic cost," the "constant dollar," and others are mentioned but not discussed.

Reporting standards are in a constant state of evolution, reacting to the progressive demands of statement users for information that will better serve their needs. As economic activity increases in volume and complexity, new issues and new data needs will command attention.

Other organizations, aside from SEC, are interested in and present their views on reporting standards to the AICPA and to the public. Prominent among them are the American Accounting Association, the Financial Executives Institute, the National Association of Accountants, and Robert Morris Associates (bankers).

The AICPA Standards of Reporting (SAP No. 33). There are four basic standards of reporting, namely:

1. The report shall state whether the financial statements are presented in accordance with generally accepted principles of accounting.
2. The report shall state whether such principles have been consistently observed in the current period in relation to the preceding period.
3. Informative disclosures in the financial statements are to be regarded as reasonably adequate unless otherwise stated in the report.
4. The report shall either contain an expression of opinion regarding the financial statements, taken as a whole, or an assertion to the effect that an opinion cannot be expressed. When an overall opinion cannot be expressed, the reasons therefor should be stated. In all cases where an auditor's name appears with financial statements the report should contain a clear-cut indication of the character of the auditor's examination, if any, and the degree of responsibility he is taking.

NOTE: The term "report" as used above, refers to the "auditor's report," sometimes referred to as the "auditor's opinion" (scope and opinion). The term "auditor's report" should not be confused with "audit report," which refers to the complete financial report.

Each of these standards is discussed later.

Management's Responsibility for Financial Statements. SAP No. 33 describes the responsibility of management with respect to financial statements thus:[2]

> Management has the responsibility for adopting sound accounting policies, for maintaining an adequate and effective system of accounts, for the safeguarding of assets, and for devising a system of internal control that will, among other things, help assure the production of proper financial statements. The transactions which should be reflected in the accounts and in the financial statements are matters within the direct knowledge and control of management. The auditor's knowledge of such transactions is limited to that acquired through his examination. *Accordingly, the fairness of the representations made through financial statements is an implicit and integral part of*

[2] SAP No. 33, p. 9.

management's responsibility. [Emphasis supplied.] The independent auditor may make suggestions as to the form or content of financial statements or he may draft them in whole or in part, based on the management's accounts and records. However, his responsibility for the statements he has examined is confined to his expression of opinion on them. The financial statements remain the representations of the management.

The SEC also holds that the company has the major responsibility for the propriety and accuracy of the financial statements.

In its Accounting Series Release No. 62 (1947), the Commission stated that

Financial statements filed for the registrant and its subsidiaries have been recognized by this Commission and by public accountants generally as representations of management upon whom rests the primary responsibility for their propriety and accuracy.

This position has been confirmed by the SEC in several later decisions. In short, it takes the position that management does not discharge its obligations with respect to the accuracy and propriety of financial statements by the employment of independent auditors, however reputable.

Lastly, it is noteworthy that the New York Stock Exchange recommends that the financial statements filed with it be signed, on their face, by the company's chief financial officer. This can be construed as emphasizing the responsibility of the company for its financial statements.

The Auditor's Responsibility for Financial Statements. The auditor's responsibility is, essentially, for his opinion. Basic to it, as a minimum (and only a minimum) is his competent employment of generally accepted auditing standards and the determination that (1) the statements comply with generally accepted accounting principles (selected by the company from the available alternatives), consistently applied, (2) all material facts are disclosed lucidly and adequately, and (3) the statements constitute a fair presentation in accordance with the principles employed.

His responsibility, in the case of corporations, is to the stockholders, primarily, yet perhaps to no lesser extent to the public, those segments having a legitimate interest, as exemplified by prospective investors, advisors to prospective investors, and credit grantors. In the case of partnerships and individuals, the responsibility is to the parties at interest.

In any case, the auditor should, and no doubt largely does, try to influence clients to improve financial statement quality and extent of disclosure, and to comply with the standards laid down by AICPA except where deviation, disclosed, can be justified.

Finally, it is well to consider this important point made by Professors Mautz and Sharaf in *The Philosophy of Auditing* (p. 166):

Surely an auditor will welcome the existence of established principles because the collection and evaluation of evidence in itself is a sufficiently difficult assignment to tax his abilities. But until accounting principles are established on a more secure basis than now exists, an important part of his assignment must be to evaluate the principles applied in the accounts and statements he reviews. Whether they produce data that measure up to his concept of truth must be the question he undertakes to solve, not merely whether the reported data are in accord with what someone contends are accepted accounting principles.

To Whom the Auditor's Report Is Addressed. The addressee of the auditor's report is not uniform in practice.

In a corporation it is, variously, the company, the directors, the stockholders, and the stockholders and directors. One might say simply that the report should be addressed to the client, whoever it is. The ascendant view is that the logical addressee is the stockholders and directors.

In nonpublic companies the report may be addressed to:

Sole proprietor—to the individual.

Partners—to the partners individually or as a group.

Corporation—to the president or chairman of the board, or both. It might also be addressed to stockholders or stockholders and directors.

The Report Signature. It is logical that the responsibility for an opinion rests with the accounting firm or the sole practitioner. Accordingly, the opinion need be signed only with the firm name or, in the case of a sole practitioner, the individual's name.

Subsequent Discovery of Facts Existing at the Date of the Auditor's Report. The caption is the title of SAP No. 41 (October, 1969). It deals with the discovery, after the financial statements have been released, of material differences due to frauds or errors. This statement must be studied, because the recommendations require careful deliberation and judgment in the event of need for action.

If new information comes to the auditor's attention, he should first determine that it is "of such a nature and from such a source that he would have investigated it had it come to his attention during the course of his examination (and) he should, as soon as practicable, undertake to determine whether the information is reliable and whether the facts existed at the date of his report." Then he should discuss it with the client.

Disclosure of the discovery should be made by the company to all parties who may be concerned. This the auditor should encourage the company to do. If it doesn't, the auditor may have to act independently.

Revised statements may be necessary, and SAP No. 41 is helpful in determining the course to be followed.

Impact of the Securities and Exchange Acts on Reporting. The Securities Act of 1933 (the "disclosure" act) gives the Commission broad powers to do the following:

Define accounting, technical, and trade terms used in the law

Prescribe the form on which required information shall be presented in the financial statements

Prescribe the items or details to be included

Prescribe the methods to be followed (1) in the preparation of accounts, (2) in the valuation of assets and liabilities, (3) in the determination of depreciation and depletion, (4) in the differentiation of recurring and nonrecurring income and investment and operating income, (5) in the preparation of consolidated financial statements

The 1934 act (the "trading" act) gives the Commission essentially similar powers with respect to the preparation and content of financial statements. Under the Holding Company Act of 1935, the Commission has even broader powers. Under the Investment Company Act of 1940, the Commission has the authority to issue rules and regulations requiring some measure of uniformity in the accounting policies to be followed by subject companies in maintaining their accounting records and in preparing required financial statements.

Regulation S-X is the principal accounting regulation of the SEC. It governs the form and content of financial statements under the acts previously cited.

In addition, there are Accounting Series Releases that contain opinions of the Chief Accountant and amendments of S-X.

Legal Aspects. Accountants are increasingly involved as defendants in suits claiming damages for losses allegedly suffered in relying on financial statements, attested by them, for decisions in making investments or extending credit.

Negligence is alleged, in most cases, in the auditing process, as a result of which financial statements did not present fairly the income and financial position.

It is not practical here to describe the various cases that have received much publicity. But auditors would be well advised to read summaries or reviews, even the court record (for example, the judge's charge), not alone to learn what are alleged deficiencies but also to recognize the enlargement of the scope of the auditor's responsibility being brought about by the courts. Some fine magazine articles on this subject have been published.

Sometimes financial statements are challenged by parties involved in contract litigation, e.g., buy-sell agreements. Here, too, the auditor may be required to defend the soundness of his opinion.

AICPA STANDARDS OF REPORTING

STANDARD NO. 1

The report shall state whether the financial statements are presented in accordance with generally accepted principles of accounting.[3]

An *Inventory of Generally Accepted Accounting Principles for Business Enterprises* was prepared for AICPA by Paul Grady, CPA.[4] It was not, as the author states, "a mission to discover new or improved accounting principles." Thus, it may be expected that this area will be the subject of considerable research and discussion, and some revision and amplification. The term "principles of accounting" includes not only accounting principles but also methods of applying them.

The principles incorporated are those deemed to have reached accepted status by usage, not by design. They are not uniform, as they include "broad objectives, standards of accounting performance and measurement and standards of disclosure."

One of the highlights of the Inventory is the listing of "alternative methods of implementing generally accepted accounting principles." The alternatives are one of the major areas of the layman's difficulty with financial statements, since they may be responsible for wide variations in gain or loss, with corresponding effects on the balance sheet. Nevertheless, rigid conformity in application of the principles does not appear to be possible or desirable, as circumstances vary widely.

The independent auditor, in his examination of a company's financial statements, must ascertain that they are in accord with the prevailing standards. If there is a material departure, he may not submit an unqualified opinion but any one of the following, as appropriate; qualified, adverse, disclaimer (no opinion, for stated reasons), piecemeal (associated with a disclaimer or

[3] SAP No. 33, p. 40.

[4] P. Grady, Accounting Research Study No. 7, *Inventory of Generally Accepted Accounting Principles for Business Enterprises*, New York, AICPA, 1965.

adverse opinion), unaudited (accompanied by a disclaimer, and a footnote on each financial statement).

The adoption of an alternative principle, if its effect is material, must be disclosed in the year of change together with the economic effect. The standard of consistency, a relevant concept, is discussed later.

Application of Generally Accepted Accounting Principles to Regulated Companies. The principles applicable to regulated companies are, in the main, similar to those of nonregulated companies except with respect to the treatment of certain items specified by the regulatory agency.

Where the published statements conform to regulatory requirements but material departures from generally accepted accounting principles exist, the auditor cannot issue an unqualified opinion. He may disclose their compliance with the requirements of the regulatory agency but nevertheless must qualify his opinion.

STANDARD NO. 2

The report shall state whether such principles have been consistently observed in the current period in relation to the prior period.[5]

The above principle, while seemingly simple, can pose difficult questions, as will be observed. Consistency ranks as a major reporting standard, since it is vital to the comparability of financial statements. It is known that a change in an accounting principle can materially raise or lower earnings. Thus, a failure to disclose a material change and its effect on earnings of the current year and, where applicable, the effect on the prior reported years would be manifestly deceptive.

Comparability of Financial Statements. The comparability of financial statements is affected by three types of changes, which are: [6]

1. A change in accounting principles employed
2. An accounting change due to altered conditions, without a change in accounting principles
3. Changed conditions not affecting accounting principles

Comment on changes. A change to an alternative accounting principle (e.g., straight-line depreciation method to declining-balance method) requires disclosure because of the variation in consistency. Mention of the reason for the change is not required. This disclosure should appear in the auditor's opinion.

A changed condition also may require a disclosure, if material. Thus, a change in a depreciation rate due to a revision of the estimated useful life of an asset would require a disclosure, in a footnote.

A changed condition, unrelated to accounting, may also warrant a footnote disclosure if material. Illustrative of such situations are the acquisition or disposal of a subsidiary or plant or the initiation of a pension plan.

The inclusion of comparative financial statements covering the last 2 years in all annual reports submitted to it has been made mandatory by SEC in its amendment to the proxy rules [Rule 14(a)-3], effective Mar. 1, 1967. This requirement has tended to cause comparative financial statements to be included in annual reports to stockholders and in other external reports in which such statements are not mandatory.

[5] SAP No. 33, p. 42.
[6] SAP No. 33, pp. 43–44.

It is also of interest that the SEC requires [Rule 2-02(c) of Regulation S-X] the auditor to disclose in his report material changes in accounting principles or practices, or in their application, which affect comparability. He must state his approval or disapproval as to the general acceptance of the new principle in expressions such as "which we approve" or "which has our approval" or "in which we concur." This is not otherwise required.

Reclassifications. A reclassification of items may, in some instances, affect comparability, for example, where items are shifted from cost of sales to general administrative expense or vice versa. Where material, such revisions should be disclosed and explained in the financial statements or a footnote.

Period to Which the Consistency Standard Relates. The consistency standard covers the current and the next prior year, even if the latter year's statements are not presented.

Where 2 or more years' statements are presented, the consistency standard covers all years in the audit report. In this case, the reference to consistency in the auditor's report should be modified. Instead of "on a basis consistent with that of the prior year," it might read "consistently applied during the periods" or "applied on a consistent basis."

Reporting an Inconsistency. Where a material change is made during the year under audit, it must be disclosed in the opinion section of the auditor's report.

No reason need be advanced by the company for the change, nor is the auditor under any compulsion to disclose it. Nevertheless, there are some who feel that the reason should be disclosed as some protection against changes that may serve only special interests rather than the company and the stockholders.

Disclosure in the Auditor's Opinion of Changes in Accounting Principles

The subject of changes in methods or principles has aroused public interest to the extent that the Accounting Principles Board has on its agenda an opinion on this subject.

Change to an alternative generally accepted accounting principle. Since the change is to a generally accepted accounting principle, the auditor need not indicate whether he approves or accepts the change, though he may do so.

The auditor's expression of approval may be worded as follows: [7]

> . . . in conformity with generally accepted accounting principles applied on a basis consistent with that of the preceding year, except for the change (insert expression of approval), in pricing of inventories . . . as described in Note __ to the financial statements.

Change from a principle or practice which lacks general acceptance to a generally accepted accounting principle. In such a case the auditor should not only disclose the change but express his approval of it, in conjunction with its mention.

The same wording may be used as in the preceding paragraph.

Change to a principle or practice which lacks general acceptance. Dependent on the magnitude of its effect, the auditor should either qualify his opinion or submit an adverse opinion on the financial statements taken as a whole.

A model qualified opinion is as follows: [8]

> In our opinion, except for (brief description of the change and its effect) as explained in Note __, a practice which we believe is at variance with generally accepted accounting principles, the accompanying statements present fairly . . .

[7] SAP No. 33, p. 46.
[8] SAP No. 33, p. 47.

Changes expected to have a future effect. Where a change in accounting principles does not affect the initial year materially but, it is reasonably certain, will materially affect future years, it should be disclosed by footnote to the initial year's statements. If not disclosed by footnote, it should be disclosed in the auditor's report.

A change in the depreciation method is an example of such a change, and the following is illustrative of the footnote disclosure:

It has been the consistent practice of the company to provide for the depreciation of property on a straight-line basis over their estimated useful lives. Commencing with the current year, the company is providing for depreciation on new additions to property on the declining-balance method. This change has no material effect on the current financial statements.

Restated amounts in prior years' financial statements. Where a change has been made and the accounts have been adjusted retroactively, the financial statements for the affected years, if submitted in a report, should be restated. The financial statements or the notes thereto should disclose the change and its effect on financial position and income.

If only the year in which the change was initiated is in the report, a note such as the following is adequate: [9]

. . . in conformity with generally accepted accounting principles applied on a basis consistent with that of the preceding year after giving retroactive effect to the inclusion, which we approve, of the accounts of foreign subsidiaries as explained in Note __ to the financial statements.

If comparative reports comprising the affected years are reported on, the wording may be the following: [10]

. . . applied on a consistent basis after giving retroactive effect to the inclusion, which we approve, of the accounts of foreign subsidiaries as explained in Note __ to the financial statements.

The phrase "which we approve" is not mandatory except for certain SEC purposes.

Financial statements of prior years not restated. If a report contains comparative statements and the prior years were not adjusted for retroactive changes in accounting principles, a disclosure of their nature and effect should be made.

The disclosure varies in accordance with the circumstances here cited.

1. Where the change took place in the current year, the disclosure should appear in the auditor's report. It may be assumed that the current year's statements are fairly presented but not the affected prior years included in the comparison. This would require omission of the "consistency" reference and the addition of one on the nonfairness of the prior years' statements.

In that event the auditor's report should include a middle paragraph disclosing the deficiency of the prior years and stating that it was removed as of the beginning of the current year and that appropriate adjustments were made in the retained earnings as of the beginning of the year.

The opinion would be the standard short-form opinion, revised as indicated in the first paragraph.

2. Where the change took place in other than the current year and the auditor is reporting on all the years, he should provide a footnote describing the change and its effect, and refer to that note in the financial statements.

[9] SAP No. 33, p. 49.
[10] SAP No. 33, p. 49.

If a footnote is not used, a reference should be included in the auditor's report.

3. Where only the current year is reported, a footnote reference is sufficient.

The auditor's first report. There are two situations where the independent auditor will submit his first report, namely: (1) a newly organized company and (2) his first audit of a going concern.

In the first instance, he need only omit the "consistency" phrase from the opinion paragraph.

In the second instance, if the auditor cannot accept the prior year's statements as fairly presented, he may not include the consistency phrase in his opinion. An illustration of this disclosure, where the prior year's statements improperly were on a cash basis, is the following: [11]

Middle paragraph

The Company has kept its records and has prepared its financial statements for previous years on the cash basis with no recognition having been accorded accounts receivable, accounts payable, or accrued expenses. At the beginning of the current year the company, with our approval, adopted the accrual basis of accounting, and appropriate adjustments, where material, have been made to retained earnings as of the beginning of the year.

Opinion paragraph

In our opinion, the accompanying balance sheet and statement(s) of income and retained earnings present fairly the financial position of the X company as of ________, and the results of its operations for the year then ended, in conformity with generally accepted accounting principles.

Pooling of interests. To assure fair presentation where two corporations have joined in a pooling of interests, the following rules as to consistency must be observed:

1. Where comparative statements are presented, including statistics on earnings per share, all of the years must be on a pooled basis. Failure to do this results in an inconsistency which must be disclosed. The disclosure, in the auditor's report, should describe the nature of the pooling and its effect on net income for all of the years covered in the report.

2. When single-year statements are presented, a footnote disclosure should be made, describing the pooling transaction and reporting the net incomes of the constituent companies for the preceding year separately or in combined form. Omission of such a footnote disclosure would call for a disclosure in the auditor's report. The disclosure having been made, in either form, the reference to consistency may be included in the auditor's opinion.

In the second instance there are also the following possibilities:

If the auditor can assure himself that the accounting principles employed are consistent as between the current and the preceding year, he may retain the "consistency" reference in his opinion.

If the auditor cannot assure himself of the consistency in the 2 years' principles, he must disclose that fact and omit the "consistency" phrase.

If the auditor cannot, in addition, assure himself of the accuracy of the opening account balances, he would be unable to express an opinion on the income statement, though he might nevertheless be able to express an opinion on the balance sheet.

[11] SAP No. 33, p. 52.

In this event, the independent auditor's report might be expressed as follows:[12]

. . . and such other auditing procedures as we considered necessary in the circumstances, except as indicated in the following paragraph.

Because of major inadequacies in the company's accounting records for the previous year, it was not practicable to extend our auditing procedures sufficiently to enable us to express an opinion on the statement(s) of income and retained earnings for the year ended (current year) or on the consistency of application of accounting principles with the preceding year.

In our opinion, the accompanying balance sheet presents fairly the financial position of the X Company as of (current year end) in conformity with generally accepted accounting principles.

Multipurpose Statements. Financial statements are closely scrutinized by large stockholders, security analysts, bankers, economists, "crusading" stockholders, representatives of stockholder organizations, lawyers, and labor unions. Competitors and some customers also avidly examine published statements. Each has a different purpose in mind.

This raises the question as to whether the annual report to stockholders can serve at one and the same time all the diverse interests needing financial information.

Following are examples of some of those who may need or desire additional financial information:

1. An insurance company interested in making a 20-year debenture loan has need for much long-range financial and nonfinancial material.
2. A competitor would like to know what products and services are profitable.
3. A customer would like to know the margin of profit the seller is earning.

STANDARD NO. 3

Informative disclosures in the financial statements are to be regarded as reasonably adequate unless otherwise stated in the report.[13]

It is the objective of this standard to assure the fairness of presentation of financial statements. This means that all material disclosures necessary to achieve this quality have been made within the statements, by appended notes or in the auditor's report.

Adequate disclosure, as here contemplated, extends to every aspect of the financial statements—their form, arrangement, content, and appended notes. It also relates to the amount of detail given, the classification of items, the bases of items (e.g., inventory, fixed assets), liens on assets, dividend arrearages, restrictions on dividends, contingent liabilities, and other items of significant interest.

Fair presentation is composed of three subconcepts which, though closely related, require independent consideration. They are:

The concept of accounting propriety
The concept of adequate disclosure
The concept of audit obligation

Where Disclosures Should Be Made. The primary location of disclosure is directly in the related financial statement, adjoining the items involved. This,

[12] SAP No. 33, p. 51.
[13] SAP No. 33, p. 54.

of course, is impractical in many instances because of the size of the disclosure, and to avoid unduly complicating and enlarging the financial statements.

If the primary location is impractical, the disclosure might next be made in a note which is keyed to the related item, at the bottom of the statement. If that is impractical, the note may be placed in a section of the report immediately after the financial statements. In published reports related notes are usually off the statements, though some disclosures may nevertheless adjoin items on the statements.

However, an appended note disclosure may not be used to cure an impropriety in a financial statement. Thus, for example, if an investment has decreased in value materially and should be written down, a footnote disclosure of this fact will not justify reporting the investment at cost.

Accounting principles underlying the major items in financial statements should also be disclosed as an aid in analyzing and comparing the statements.

If a company has failed to make an adequate disclosure of a material item, the auditor should undertake to prevail on the company to make it. Failing that, he should disclose the item in his report and qualify his opinion as necessary.

Harmful Disclosures. There are instances where disclosures may be damaging to a company needlessly or may violate a "classified information" clause of a defense agency contract.

In the latter instance, the company and the auditor are legally bound to comply. Nevertheless, every effort should be made to minimize the censorship impact so as to keep the financial statements from being misleading.

In the former instance, the auditor is faced with a challenge to his judgment, experience, and tactfulness. He must satisfy himself first that a disclosure, for example, of a lawsuit for patent infringement would really harm the company significantly. He should also get an opinion from the company's counsel as to the possible outcome. Finally, if satisfied in all these respects, and the company has set up a reasonable provision for possible damages, the auditor might properly agree to the omission of a footnote disclosure.

Meeting the Needs of Sophisticated Users. Many who use financial statements frequently, such as bankers and other credit grantors, financial analysts, and attorneys in commercial practice, unless informed of the conventions on which they are based and the limitations of the auditor's attestation, have great difficulty in analyzing and comparing the statements. Many expect, for example, that the balance sheet should disclose the "fair value" of a company.

Indeed, the conventions and limitations are the public accounting profession's greatest source of criticism—the charge of unreliability and incomparability of financial statements.[14]

Their needs, particularly if diverse, will probably never be met by the conventional annual report. Such a report, even if feasible, would be uneconomic in cost and would become available too late for timely use by many persons.

Such users must seek detailed and additional data from the company directly, from SEC filings, financial services, banks, credit agencies, and other sources that may be helpful.

This does not suggest an attitude of smugness or complacency. It suggests rather a realistic limitation, one that is mindful of the fact that[15]

[14] William G. Maas, "What to Tell Security Analysts," *Public Relations Journal,* March, 1955.

[15] Committee on Accounting Concepts and Standards of the American Accounting Association, *The Accounting Review,* October, 1959.

The use by investors of published financial statements in making investment decisions and in exercising control over management should be considered of primary importance. It seems reasonable to assume that those using financial statements for these purposes will be willing and competent to read them carefully and with discrimination.

Extraordinary and Prior Period Items. APB Opinion No. 9 resolves the long-time indecision about the location of extraordinary items of income (loss) and prior period adjustments—whether in the income statement, the retained earnings statement, or both.

The Opinion upholds those advocating the "all-inclusive" income statement and the "clean" retained earnings statement.

This means that current net income should reflect all items of profit and loss recognized during the period with the *sole* exception of *rare*, and material prior period items which may, instead, adjust the retained income opening balance.

The income statement would conclude as follows:

	$	*Per share*
Income before extraordinary items (less applicable income tax)	$ x x x	$ x x
Extraordinary items (less applicable income tax)	x x x	x x
Net income	$ x x x	$ x x

Rare and material prior period adjustments are defined in paragraph 23 as material adjustments which:

(a) can be specifically identified with and directly related to the business activities of particular prior periods, and (b) are not attributable to economic events occurring subsequent to the date of the financial statements for the prior periods, and (c) depend primarily on determinations by persons other than management, and (d) were not susceptible of reasonable estimation prior to such determination.

Treatment as prior period adjustments should not be applied to the normal, recurring corrections and adjustments which are the natural result of the use of estimates inherent in the accounting process.

When prior period adjustments are recorded, the resulting effects (both gross and net of applicable income tax) on the net income of prior periods should be disclosed in the annual report for the year in which the adjustments are made.

Cited illustrations of extraordinary items are (paragraph 21):

(a) the sale or an abandonment of a plant or a significant segment of the business, (b) the sale of an investment not acquired for resale, (c) the write-off of goodwill due to unusual events or developments within the period, (d) the condemnation or expropriation of properties and (e) a major devaluation of a foreign currency.

Disclosures by Conglomerate (Diversified) Companies. The inexorable pressure for disclosure of earnings data concerning the natural "segments" of conglomerate companies is getting results. This is evidenced by the increase in the number of public company financial statements that contain, as unattested supplementary data, such facts as sales and contribution to pretax net profit, among other information of their segments.[16]

SEC now requires some such data for companies reporting on forms S-1, S-7, and 10, and with the annual 10-K report.

The AICPA has also dealt with this subject, and the Accounting Principles Board, in its Statement No. 2 (September, 1967), offers certain recommendations.

[16] Leopold Schachner, "Diversified Operations—Guidelines to Accounting Practice," *The New York Certified Public Accountant,* August, 1970.

Other organizations are seriously concerned, particularly those representing business interests. This is understandable, because the problems of disclosure are far more complex than a superficial glance discloses, e.g., what companies should report? What are the reportable segments (product, division, territory, etc.)? Is the information, because of intracompany relations or other reasons, reasonably determinable and reliable? Will the disclosure benefit competitors or otherwise embarrass the company? What kind of data should be disclosed?

Notable efforts have been made by the Financial Executives Institute in sponsoring an in-depth survey by a renowned scholar, Professor Robert K. Mautz. His findings were disclosed in a report, "Financial Reporting by Diversified Companies," published in May, 1968.

The National Association of Accountants published in September, 1969, a very useful guideline to conglomerate reporting in a work by Alfred Rappaport and Eugene M. Lerner, entitled "A Framework for Financial Reporting by Diversified Companies."

Finally, attention is drawn to AICPA's "Accounting Trends and Techniques," wherein will be found examples of conglomerate disclosures made in published annual reports.

As yet, the subject of attestation of conglomerate data is not an issue. Eventually, when such reporting becomes stabilized, a demand may arise.

Business Combinations and Intangible Assets. The accounting principles employed in merger and acquisition accounting, and in resultant subsequent accounting, created one of the greatest critical storms to harass the profession. At issue was the propriety of the optional use of the pooling-of-interests method, the part-pooling–part-purchase method, and the purchase method of accounting for mergers and acquisitions. The chief culprit was the pooling method which made possible many company takeovers with "thin" financing and which resulted in some very questionable accounting results.

The advantages of pooling accounting are considerable. Briefly, they are the following:

1. The assets of the merged company are not restated at current value, regardless of the merger appraisal, rather their book value is retained.
2. Thereby, goodwill, which usually is involved in a merger, need not be recorded and, consequently, need not be amortized by annual charges to income.
3. If appreciated depreciable assets are taken over, book value is retained. Therefore, the annual charge to income is at a smaller rate than otherwise would be required.
4. A pooling requires retroactive combination of the earnings of the constituent corporations for all periods reported.

It should be evident that supporting or increasing earnings (and therefore stock market prices and management benefits) is a major consideration.

However, as was inevitable, a bridle has been placed on poolings in APB Opinion No. 16, *Business Combinations,* effective with combinations initiated after October 31, 1970.

Poolings remain permissible under APB Opinion No. 16, in fact mandatory when the new rules apply, but specific conditions must be met. Among the significant requirements are: (1) The combination is effected in a single transaction or is completed according to a specific plan within one year, (2) a corporation issues only common stock with rights identical to those of the majority of its outstanding voting common stock in exchange for substantially all of the voting common stock interest of another company. All other transactions constitute purchases.

Partial pooling accounting is prohibited, as well as the inclusion of the profits of an acquired company in net income reported to stockholders even though the pooling took place after the end of the year reported on.

Another important consideration pertains to the amortization of goodwill emerging from the transaction. Amortization of goodwill, as well as other acquired intangibles, is required of all pertinent items arising from combinations, or otherwise acquired after October 31, 1970, per APB No. 17, *Intangible Assets.*

As to intangibles, generally, APB No. 17 holds that a company may record as assets the costs to develop *identifiable* intangible assets but should record as expenses the costs of developing intangible assets that are not specifically identifiable, such as goodwill.

Consolidated and Combined Financial Statements. Intercorporate investments require the consolidation of the statements of the affiliated companies (except where impractical or where severe restrictions exist) to assure fair presentation of the financial position and earnings of the group as a whole.

This raises questions as to:

What conditions warrant *inclusion* of a company?

What conditions warrant *exclusion* of a company?

What constitutes "control," and how much warrants inclusion in a consolidation?

The AICPA provides direction in a response to these questions, and deals with some of the accounting procedure problems, but the subject has not yet been adequately researched nor is there yet one complete, definitive guide.

The Institute's guides appear in ARB No. 51 and in an amendment thereof, APB Opinion No. 10. The SEC position appears in Regulation S-X and in its Accounting Releases.

Every annual consolidated report should contain a statement of principles of consolidation. Reference to published reports will disclose a wide variety of detail, and lack of detail. Basically, the statement should disclose what subsidiaries have been excluded, the assumption being that all others wherein there is ownership of more than 50 percent of the voting stock are included. Unusual inclusions should be disclosed, as well as the reasons for exclusion from consolidation.

Subsidiary statements that are excluded from the consolidation should be reported individually or in homogeneous groups, e.g., banks, insurance companies.

In the case of foreign subsidiaries, the conversion policies for foreign currency accounts as well as adjustments for devaluations, etc., should be disclosed.

The major amendment in APB Opinion No. 10 is the requirement that accounts of all subsidiaries (regardless of when organized or acquired) whose principal business activity is leasing property or facilities to their parents or other affiliates should be consolidated, because in such cases the " 'equity' method . . . is not adequate for fair presentation . . . ."

The other amendment deals with the "equity" method. It provides that where a domestic subsidiary is not consolidated, and unless there are valid reasons for not consolidating (e.g., control is temporary, or the company is in the hands of trustees), "the investment in the subsidiary should be adjusted for the consolidated group's share of accumulated undistributed earnings and losses since acquisition."

The SEC is vitally interested in what is included in consolidated statements, and its Regulation S-X and findings in individual cases deal with the subject both broadly and specifically. It is concerned equally with the propriety of exclusions as well as inclusions. Each must meet the test of being in the interest of fair presentation.

The SEC, because of its protective function, may be expected to be very conservative. For that reason an auditor would be well advised to "clear with SEC" borderline and unusual cases.

As an indication of the extent of SEC's concern, a decision requiring consolidation in the absence of any stock ownership has special interest. It held that because a company was in a "satellite" relationship and was effectively controlled by another, by means of dominant trade relations, their financial statements should be consolidated. (*Atlantic Research Corporation*, Securities Act Releases 4657 and 4657A.)

Combined statements. Where two or more corporations are owned by the same stockholders (common ownership), in essentially corresponding interests, but there is no intercompany investment, there may be a need for a combined statement.

Also, where subsidiaries are omitted from a consolidation, they may be grouped in a combined statement. Thus, for example, if a merchandise retailer has several credit financing subsidiaries and several insurance company subsidiaries, all of which are excluded from the consolidation, combined statements may be prepared for each subsidiary group.

The combined statement will be more meaningful than individual statements where there is common management and the intercompany transactions and executives' services are not or cannot objectively be accounted for in the intercompany allocations.

Comparative Statements. In published and nonpublished reports, comparative statements, usually 2 years, are furnished. Single-period reports are used for new companies and in special cases.

An important distinction is drawn between comparative statements as to which an opinion is expressed and those as to which an opinion is disclaimed. In addition, the requirements of the "consistency" principle must be borne in mind.

Prior period statements should be revised for material adjustments ascertained in later years. This makes the comparison more meaningful.

Where comparative statements are attested, each is subject to the same rules of disclosure. Thus, footnote references required in each instance must appear. A consolidation of similar footnotes may be made and is usually desirable as a practical matter.

Comparative statements can present problems where the prior year's statements were attested by a former auditor. The treatment of this type of situation is discussed elsewhere.

Earnings per Share (EPS) Reporting. This item of statistical data is one of the most significant financial statement guideposts. It is the basis for the price-earnings ratio constantly used by stock buyers and advisers in their evaluations of such securities.

For many years it presented no serious problem except, in instances, in the determination of the number of shares to use in the computation. This simple existence faded away as companies used claims on common stock for various purposes, such as options for executives, warrants, conversion by preferred stock and bonds, and contingent price adjustment on purchase of a business.

Moreover, the realization of extraordinary income and losses, of a nature warranting their separate location in income statements, made it evident that their impact on per share earnings should also be segregated.

Thus, in reaction to the need for more precise per share data that would reflect all the existent and prospective impacts, the Accounting Principles Board, in December, 1966, included in its Opinion No. 9 a section devoted to "Computation and Reporting of Earnings per Share."

This, however, did not settle all the issues, and the Board therefore published, in May, 1969, its Opinion No. 15 entitled "Earnings per Share," superseding No. 9.

It is now the definitive expression, but it is believed, challenges will arise as applications of the guidelines are made by accountants. In the interim, it is adequate in the large majority of cases.

It is not possible to do more, in the available space, than to deal summarily with some major aspects. Auditors should study carefully Opinion No. 15 to ascertain its full scope.

EPS reporting compulsory. Earnings per share data must appear on all income statements. Nonpublic corporations, generally, may not see a need for this information, but it may be useful to have.

Reporting EPS for extraordinary items. Earnings per share must be shown separately before and after provision for extraordinary gains and losses. Extraordinary items must be adjusted by their income tax effect.

EPS reporting for complex capital structures. Corporations with complex capital structures should make a dual presentation of earnings per share. The Opinion provides that:

> The first presentation is based on the outstanding common shares and those securities that are in substance equivalent to common shares and have a dilutive effect. [Primary earnings per share.]
>
> The second is a pro-forma presentation which reflects the dilution of earnings per share that would have occurred if *all* contingent issuances of common stock that would individually reduce earnings per share had taken place at the beginning of the period (or time of issuance of the convertible security, etc., if later). [Fully diluted earnings per share.]

EPS determination considerations. The determination of the amount per share of common stock requires allowance for:

- The inclusion of "residual securities" (common share equivalent, distinguished from senior securities) in the common stock category
- Allowance for earnings of senior securities
- Computation of the number of shares to which the residual income is to be applied.

The earnings per share is an average per share. Therefore, where changes (increases and decreases) during the year have been material, a weighted average should be used. Where the changes are insignificant, the year-end total may be used. The number of shares used in the determination should be disclosed and, where desirable, how it was determined.

Where a pooling of interests has occurred during the year, the number of shares to be used is the total of the outstanding shares applicable to both companies (weighted average, if required) for the period. Adjustments may be necessary where recapitalization of the capital stock structure of the surviving company was effected.

Where common stock has been issued as a stock dividend or stock split, or where common stock has been acquired from a "reverse" split, the computation of the number of shares would be made retroactive to the beginning of the period. Where, however, stock is acquired for the treasury, the weighting is based on the period in the treasury.

Treatment of senior securities. The term earnings per share should not be used for senior securities (preferred stock); rather the "earnings coverage" should be stated, i.e., the number of times or the extent to which the dividend requirements of senior securities have been earned.

Contingent dilution of common stock. Where convertible securities are outstanding, disclosure should be made in the Income Statement showing the prospective effect on the earnings per share if the conversion is made. Similar consideration is to be given to other contingencies, such as options and issuances under business purchase agreements. All these disclosures are conditional on materiality.

Restated prior period income. If prior period income is restated, the earnings per share should be restated correspondingly in a historical summary of earnings included in a financial report. If such prior period adjustment is included in a later year and is material, the later year's earnings per share should be adjusted and a disclosure of it made.

Price-level Change Reporting. APB Statement No. 3, entitled *Financial Statements Restated for General Price-level Changes* (June, 1969), was issued in response to increasing pressure for the disclosure in financial statements of the effect on financial position and earnings of the changes in monetary values.

When inflationary conditions are significant and prevail for extended periods, historic cost data are only historic, not realistic from the viewpoint of an evaluation of a company's current worth and real earnings.

Yet, it does not appear to be appropriate for the APB to recommend presently the integration of price-level changes directly into financial statements. If desired, adjusted statements may be included in an annual report as supplementary data.

When extreme changes occur, as happens in some countries, the effects must be recognized.

Statement No. 3, paragraph 1,

> explains the effects on business enterprises and their financial statements of changes in the general purchasing power of money, describes the basic nature of financial statements restated for general price-level changes (general price-level financial statements), and gives general guidance on how to prepare and present these financial statements.

A more detailed discussion of general price-level financial statements appears in Accounting Research Study No. 6, *Reporting the Financial Effects of Price-level Changes.*

STANDARD NO. 4

The report shall either contain an expression of opinion regarding the financial statements, taken as a whole, or an assertion to the effect that an opinion cannot be expressed. When an over-all opinion cannot be expressed, the reasons therefor should be stated. In all cases, where an auditor's name is associated with financial statements, the report should contain a clear-cut indication of the character of the auditor's examination, if any, and the degree of responsibility he is taking.[17]

[17] SAP No. 33, p. 56.

The expression of an opinion (auditor's report) is necessary to disclose the degree of responsibility assumed by the auditor.

An opinion may relate to any or all of the financial statements similarly or dissimilarly. Thus, an unqualified opinion may be expressed as to the balance sheet and retained earnings and a qualified opinion applied to the income statement.

The auditor's report contains these two basic parts: (1) the scope paragraph and (2) the opinion paragraph.

Scope—compliance with generally accepted auditing standards (and exceptions) in the examination of the financial statements

Opinion—the auditor's representation on the fairness of the financial statements

Since departures from the auditing and reporting standards occur because of varying circumstances, there are varying opinions. Applicable AICPA-prescribed opinions (SAP No. 33) are here reviewed.

The standard short-form auditor's report consists usually of scope and opinion sections, and sometimes a middle section.

In a long-form report, the auditor's representations usually open with a detailed scope section, including various remarks, and conclude with the opinion. Or the short-form opinion might be stated, followed by the scope details and other remarks.

Where a short-form report has been furnished and later a long-form report follows, the latter must include the opinion or refer to it as previously submitted.

Where financial data are included in the audit report as supplementary information (e.g., an analysis of sales by products) but as to which the auditor cannot accept responsibility, the material should be separated from the attested statements as "additional data," preceded by a disclaimer of responsibility.

Unqualified Opinion. The unqualified opinion that is commonly used is illustrated below.[18] It applies, in this example, to the three basic financial statements. It may, however, apply to less than all.

> We have examined the balance sheet of X Company as of June 30, 19__ and the related statement(s) of income and retained earnings for the year then ended. Our examination was made in accordance with generally accepted auditing standards and accordingly included such tests of the accounting records and such other auditing procedures as we considered necessary in the circumstances.
>
> In our opinion, the accompanying balance sheet and statement(s) of income and retained earnings present fairly the financial position of X company at June 30, 19__, and the results of its operations for the year then ended, in conformity with generally accepted accounting principles applied on a basis consistent with that of the preceding year.

Qualified Opinion. A qualified opinion is used to disclose an "exception" which, though worthy of mention, does not warrant a disclaimer of the financial statements.

Where the "exception" is material, an opinion must be disclaimed or an adverse opinion expressed. The test of materiality lies within the auditor's judgment and may be a crucial matter.

Adequate disclosure of the cause of the qualification should be made in the opinion paragraph of the auditor's report. If reasonably determinable, it

[18] SAP No. 33, p. 57.

should also state the effect on financial position and results of operations. If a scope limitation is involved, a disclosure should be made in the scope paragraph.

A qualification may stem from either (1) limitations in the scope of the examination, (2) the indeterminate status of accounts in the financial statements, (3) reservations with respect to the fairness of presentation in accordance with generally accepted accounting principles consistently applied, or (4) an inconsistency in the accounting principles applied.

Following is an illustrative qualified opinion based on a change to an unacceptable principle or practice:

> In our opinion, except for (brief description of the change and its effect) as explained in Note __, a practice which we believe is at variance with generally accepted accounting principles, the accompanying statements present fairly . . . .

Illustrative qualified opinion, based on the existence of undeterminable adjustments of income taxes for open years:

> In our opinion, subject to any adjustments to the balance sheet and statement of retained earnings which may result from the final determination of the company's income tax liability for prior years as indicated in Note A to the financial statements, the accompanying financial statements present fairly . . . .

In this example it is assumed that the final outcome is dependent upon the decisions of other parties than management.

Disclosures due to an inconsistency or failure to comply with generally accepted accounting principles should be such as to facilitate the comparability of the financial statements.

Disclaimer of Opinion. There are generally two grounds for the disclaimer of an opinion, namely:

1. The examination is inadequate for the expression of an opinion
2. Though the audit may have been adequate, there exist material indeterminate items that obviate fair presentation

Disclaimers are common, and properly so, where limited examinations of interim period financial statements are made. In many instances, particularly nonpublic companies, annual audits are also so limited as to preclude an unqualified or qualified opinion.

There are instances where auditors prepare financial statements without audit, frequently in connection with the preparation of tax returns. In such instances not only is a disclaimer required (whether or not the auditor's stationery is used) but each statement should carry the legend "prepared from the books without audit." The reason for a disclaimer should be stated. If it is due to the limitation of scope, the auditor should disclose the reservations or exceptions he may have regarding fairness of presentation.

One should not disclaim an opinion where an opinion has actually been formed, whether it be a qualified opinion or an adverse one.

A simple disclaimer is shown below

> We have examined the balance sheet of the XYZ Corporation as of ________ and the related statements of income and retained earnings for the year ended that date.
>
> The scope of our examination did not permit the confirmation of accounts and notes receivable nor the observation and other tests of the merchandise inventory, both material items.
>
> Because of these limitations on the scope of the examination, we cannot and do not express an opinion on the financial statements.

Adverse Opinion. Such an opinion is very drastic and is one that rarely occurs. It is required if any of these three circumstances exist:

1. A departure from generally accepted accounting principles of such materiality as to result in unfair presentation
2. A material misstatement in the statements
3. An omission of a material disclosure

In some cases the auditor may deem it appropriate to express a piecemeal opinion on those items in the financial statements which comply with generally accepted accounting principles.

The following is an example of an adverse opinion: [19]

Although the proceeds of sales are collectible on the installment basis over a five-year period, revenue from such sales is recorded in full by the Company at time of sale. However, for income tax purposes, income is reported only as collections are received and no provision has been made for income taxes on installments to be collected in the future, as required by generally accepted accounting principles. If such provisions had been made, net income for 19__ and retained earnings as of December 31, 19__ would have been reduced by approximately $______ and $______, respectively, and the balance sheet would have included a liability for deferred income taxes of approximately $______.

Because of the materiality of the amounts of omitted income taxes as described in the preceding paragraph, we are of the opinion that the financial statements do not present fairly the financial position of X Company at December 31, 19__ or the results of its operations for the year then ended in conformity with generally accepted accounting principles.

Mixed Opinion. The following example illustrates the use of different opinions in one auditor's report:

Par. 1. Scope—conventional short form
Par. 2. Disclosure of noncompliance with generally accepted accounting principles
Par. 3. Opinion

In view of the material effect of the changes noted above, which we believe are at variance with generally accepted accounting principles, we are of the opinion that the accompanying balance sheet and statement of retained earnings do not present fairly the financial position of ABC Co. at ________ in conformity with generally accepted accounting principles.

However, we are of the opinion that the accompanying income statement presents fairly . . . .

Piecemeal Opinion. A piecemeal opinion is a means of salvaging a situation where a disclaimer or an adverse opinion on the statements as a whole is submitted. Thereby the auditor can express an opinion on certain items in the financial statements but not on other material items as to which he has none or an adverse opinion.

The auditor meets the reporting requirements standard, since he has disclosed the scope of the examination and the responsibility he assumes.

A typical piecemeal opinion is the following:

Scope paragraph. Conventional form, concluding with the phrase: "except as noted in the following paragraph."

Middle paragraph

At your request we did not observe the inventory or make other tests. Because of this limitation and the materiality of the inventory to the financial position and results of operations of the company, the scope of the examination was inadequate to express an over-all opinion on the accompanying financial statements.

[19] SAP No. 33, p. 69.

Opinion paragraph

In our opinion, however, the cash, marketable securities, accounts and notes receivable, capital stock and all expense items in the income statement are fairly stated in conformity with generally accepted accounting principles applied on a basis consistent with that of last year.

In expressing a piecemeal opinion, the auditor may be assuming a greater responsibility for the covered items than in an opinion on the statements as a whole.

The wording of the piecemeal opinion should not create the impression that it contradicts the disclaimer or adverse opinion attached to it.

Unaudited Statements. An unaudited statement is one where "the certified public accountant (a) has not applied any auditing procedures to the statements or (b) has not applied procedures which are sufficient to permit him to express an opinion concerning them." (SAP No. 38.)

The AICPA committee which promulgated SAP No. 38 takes the position that a disclaimer of opinion should accompany unaudited financial statements with which the CPA is "associated." It offers the following illustrative disclaimer:

The accompanying balance sheet of X Company as of December 31, 19__ and the related statement(s) of income and retained earnings for the year then ended were not audited by us and, accordingly,we do not express an opinion on them.

The committee also holds that the disclaimer may accompany the unaudited financial statements or it may be placed directly on them. If the disclaimer is separately expressed, each page of the financial statements should be earmarked as unaudited.

An accountant may supply accounting services that do not necessarily associate him with financial statements. For example, he may merely type client-prepared statements or help in their preparation without making any examination. Or, he may make such an insignificant examination as classify the statements as unaudited.

The auditor is associated with unaudited financial statements when he does the following:

1. Consents to the use of his name in a report, document, or written communication setting forth or containing the statements.
2. Submits to client or others, with or without a covering letter, unaudited financial statements which he has prepared or assisted in preparing. It does not matter whether the stationery does or does not carry the accountant's name.

The "associated" relationship is important, for where it exists it calls for the expression of an opinion.

Where an auditor is engaged to prepare monthly or other interim period statements for only the client's internal use, it might not be necessary to include all footnotes or other disclosures that might otherwise be desirable. In that event, the disclaimer should include references to the fact that the statements are restricted to internal use by the client and therefore do not necessarily include disclosures that would be necessary for a fair presentation of the statements to other users.

If the auditor has not made an examination but is associated with the statements, he is not entirely without responsibility. If he should have knowledge that the financial statements are not a fair presentation, he should insist (except in the condition described in the preceding paragraph) upon appropriate revision and, if unsuccessful, should set forth his reservations in the disclaimer and their effect on the financial statements.

Long-form Report. The long-form report is preferred by many bankers and other credit grantors because it presents, in addition to the "auditor's report" (opinion), in considerable detail, the audit scope, comments on financial position and operations, and schedules and statistical data supporting and complementing the basic financial statements. Such data do not appear in a short-form report.

A major problem relating to the auditor's attestation limitation can arise if audited and unaudited data are not carefully segregated and earmarked.

This can be avoided by grouping all unaudited data in one section preceded by a preface entitled, for example, "Additional Information," and which contains a statement along these lines:

> The data included in the following section are presented for supplementary analysis purposes and are not necessary for a fair presentation of the financial position and results of operations. The data have been obtained from company records and other sources but have not been subjected to the audit procedures applied in the examination of the basic financial statements. Because the data have not been audited we disclaim an opinion on them.

Frequently auditors furnish a client both types of audit reports. In that event caution must be exercised to assure that:

1. The long-form report does not controvert the short-form report by including material facts that were omitted from the latter.
2. None of the comments or other data in the separate section may be construed as exceptions or reservations, as distinguished from mere explanations.

Previous Years' Statements Unaudited or Audited by Other Accountants. Where comparative statements are presented, and those for the earlier years were unaudited or did not bear an unqualified opinion, a full disclosure should be made and exceptions to comparability noted.

If the prior year's statements were examined by another auditor, that fact should be disclosed so as to absolve the current auditor of responsibility. Nevertheless, the prior year's audit report should be reviewed and inquiries made to assure that no serious misconception will develop from the comparison of the two years' statements.

Where another auditor has made a complete examination and his opinion is relied upon by the current auditor, reference should be made to the separate examination, and as further evidence of limitation of responsibility, the other auditor's report could be incorporated.

In the case of SEC registration statements, where different auditors are not uncommon for one year's statements or prior years' statements, the problem of limitation of responsibility is a very serious one.

Part of the Current Examination Made by Other Independent Auditors. It is fairly common for more than one auditor to be involved in a year's examination. This happens where a distant branch or a subsidiary is audited by other accountants than those auditing the principal company, or in business combinations where different auditors are involved.

A question arises as to the division of responsibility between the auditors. Where an auditor is willing to assume all the responsibility, having performed the major portion of the examination and properly supervised the delegated work, he need not even mention the utilization of another accountant.

Where, however, the principal auditor does not desire to assume all the responsibility, he must disclose his reliance on other auditors, as indicated in the following auditor's report:

> We have examined the consolidated balance sheet of X Company and subsidiaries as of November 30, 19__ and the consolidated statements of income and retained earnings for the year then ended. Our examination was made in accordance with generally accepted auditing standards, and accordingly included such tests of the accounting records and such other auditing procedures as we considered necessary in the circumstances. We did not examine the financial statements of B Company, a consolidated subsidiary, which statements were examined by other certified public accountants whose report thereon has been furnished to us. Our opinion expressed herein, insofar as it relates to the amounts included for B Company, is based solely upon such report.
>
> In our opinion, based upon our examination and the aforementioned report of other certified public accountants, the accompanying consolidated financial statements present fairly . . . .[20]

In the case of combined or consolidated statements, the principal auditor may rely on the reports of the other auditors, but he need not necessarily accept responsibility for the work done by them. In that event, he may nevertheless express an unqualified opinion provided the basis for his opinion is adequately described. A statement could appear either in the scope or opinion paragraph that in arriving at his opinion amounts applicable to the units examined by other auditors were included, solely upon the basis of the other auditor's report. (See preceding illustrative opinion.)

The principal auditor, in that event, should make such inquiries as will satisfy him that his confidence in the other auditor's report is not misplaced.

If the principal auditor is unwilling to utilize the other's report, he should qualify or disclaim an opinion on the fair presentation of the combined or consolidated statements. In disclosing his grounds, he should point out the percentages of the assets and revenues that are qualified.

Omission of Necessary Audit Procedure. Where it is impossible or impracticable for an auditor to confirm receivables or observe inventory and he has used other satisfactory methods, he no longer must disclose the variance (SAP No. 43). Where other satisfactory methods were not used, the omission should be noted in the auditor's opinion (scope section).

Material Uncertainties as to the Effect of Future Developments. The use of a modifying phrase such as "subject to" ordinarily is evidence of a qualified opinion, except where it refers to the use of a report of other auditors and merely discloses a division of responsibility.

There are only two circumstances when the phrase "subject to" is appropriate. One involves management's inability to estimate the probable effect on financial position and earnings of matters such as lawsuits, tax matters, and other material contingencies, the outcome of which depends on the decision of others than the client.

An illustration of an opinion embodying "subject to" is here submitted: [21]

> In our opinion, subject to any adjustments to the balance sheet and statement of retained earnings which may result from the final determination of the company's income tax liability for prior years as indicated in Note A to the financial statements, the accompanying financial statements present fairly . . .

[20] SAP No. 33, p. 68.
[21] SAP No. 33, p. 73.

Another contingency is cited in this opinion:

In our opinion, subject to the successful conclusion of X project and ultimate recovery thereby of the related deferred research and development costs in the amount of $______ described in Note __, the accompanying financial statements . . .

Where a contingency is very large in relation to a company's capital, a disclaimer such as this would be in order:

Because of the possible material effect on the financial statements of the above mentioned lawsuit, the outcome of which is uncertain, we do not express any opinion on the company's financial statements taken as a whole.[22]

The second use of "subject to" is in instances where there are uncertainties as to the valuation or realizability of assets dependent on management's judgment.

Negative Assurances. A negative assurance is a disclosure in the auditor's report such as this: "However, nothing came to our attention which would indicate that these statements (amounts) are not fairly presented (stated)."[23] It is sometimes included, unwisely, where necessary audit procedures have been omitted yet the auditor feels that the statements nevertheless are fairly presented.

Such an assurance is inappropriate, because it gives the financial statements a greater validity than the limited scope warrants.

In SEC matters a negative assurance is permissible in letters required by underwriters. There may be other special situations where it may be appropriate.

Reporting on Subsequent Events. Between the statement date and the delivery date, there is a hiatus that must not be ignored. This is so because the auditor's responsibility for disclosures of material poststatement events does not necessarily expire until the report is virtually out of his hands.

There are three broad categories of poststatement events which merit disclosure, first by the company and, failing that, by the auditor. They are:

1. Events that affect the financial statements directly and which would have been taken into account if more timely known, should be reflected in the statements directly. For example, a lawsuit settled after the balance sheet date, in an amount materially different from that anticipated, should be taken into the statements by an adjustment.
2. Some events need not be reflected directly in the financial statements; footnote reference is adequate. Some examples are a commitment for new financing or the purchase of a business; a serious fire, flood, or other casualty. The disclosure should be as informative as necessary to be meaningful.
3. Certain events will not affect financial statements, except possibly indirectly, yet if they are weighty matters they may warrant disclosure. Examples are management changes, legislation, product changes, strikes, unionization, marketing agreements, loss of important customers, and others. Such disclosures are not common and require careful deliberation in arriving at a decision.

An auditor associated with financial statements that are part of a registration statement filed with SEC has a special responsibility to maintain a surveillance over the company up to the registration date because of the liability provisions of the 1933 act.

[22] SAP No. 33, p. 73.
[23] SAP No. 33, p. 61.

How far into the future an auditor must peer is not a settled matter, nor can it be. It may be a short period or one of several months. The only guide is the accountant's experience, judgment, and intuitive powers, applied to the particular case. A case that extends an auditor's responsibility almost indefinitely is discussed in *The Journal of Accountancy,* July, 1967.[24]

Complications arise from the fact that segments of an annual audit are made during various parts of the year; other problems exist where complete interim period examinations of financial statements are made. There is no formula for dealing with these problems other than good judgment.

Date of auditor's report. The date of the auditor's report affects in some measure the extent of his responsibility for subsequent events. In general, the date of completion of all important audit procedure should be used as the date of the auditor's report. In most cases this date will coincide with the completion of his work in the client's office.

Where the report bears a substantially later date, because of a delay due to conditions beyond the auditor's control, e.g., awaiting a legal determination, it would be well for the auditor to disclose the audit completion date.

One must not assume, however, that the report date necessarily terminates the subsequent events period.

Copies of prior reports. Occasionally, a client requests copies of financial statements of prior years as to which the auditor has reported. No subsequent events inquiry need necessarily be made. Where, however, there is knowledge of important events that merit either modification of the statements or disclosure, revised statements should be submitted. In that event, the auditor should point out that the statements depart from the original in the stipulated respects.

Comparative Statements. Comparative statements covering 2 years, if attested, are both subject to the reporting standards except that the auditor's opinion need refer only to the current year. However, disclosures pertaining to the 2 years should, nonetheless, appear in the statements or in appended notes as warranted.

The prior year's statements may be revised for adjustments that make for fair presentation and improved comparability. Such revisions should be disclosed.

In the case that the prior year's statements were unaudited or were attested by another auditor, special attention (described elsewhere in this chapter) is required. Where the current auditor was "associated," a disclosure should be made.

If there is a variation in opinions between the years, e.g., one year's statements are unqualified and the other's qualified, a disclosure should be made by a note. Where the present auditor has material doubts or exceptions about the prior year, he should make appropriate disclosure in his report.

REPORT VARIATIONS

Cash Basis Statements. Only one of the four standards of reporting does not apply to statements on a cash basis, namely, the observance of generally accepted accounting principles.

Thus, where there is no question about consistency and adequacy of disclosures, the following is a satisfactory form of opinion:

[24] *The Journal of Accountancy,* July, 1967, p. 56.

We have examined the following statements of the X Company as of December 31, 19__, and for the year then ended:

Statement of Assets and Liabilities Arising from Cash Receipts and Disbursements

Statement of Cash Receipts and Disbursements on Account of Income and Expense

Our examination was made in accordance with generally accepted auditing standards, and accordingly included such tests of the accounting records and such other auditing procedures as we considered necessary in the circumstances.

In our opinion, the accompanying statements present fairly the assets and liabilities as of December 31, 19__, arising from cash receipts and disbursements and the cash receipts and disbursements on account of income and expenses for the year then ended, on a basis consistent with that of the preceding year.

If there is no accompanying note to disclose the omission of inventory, receivables, payables, income tax, and other material accruals, the auditor should disclose them, preferably in a middle paragraph of his report.

Should there still be a possibility of misleading inferences from the report, a middle paragraph, worded as below, should be included:

Because of the omission of accounts receivable and accounts payable, it is our opinion that the accompanying statements do not present fairly the financial position or results of operations of the company.[25]

Sole Proprietorship Statements. A careful distinction must be drawn between the financial statements of a business operated as a sole proprietorship and of an individual whose assets include a solely owned business. Both types of statements are common, but there is a considerable distinction in their auditing and reporting considerations.

Here we are dealing *only* with a business or professional activity conducted by a sole proprietor.

Because the sole proprietor probably has assets and liabilities independent of those of his business, the fullest disclosure of the limitation is desirable. Accordingly, the financial statements as well as the scope paragraph of the auditor's report should refer to the sole proprietorship by trade name, if any.

There probably are many situations where the auditor writes up the accounting records. This does not bar him, in the case of unlisted companies, from expressing an opinion except if he (1) controls client funds (e.g., signs checks) or (2) makes managerial decisions.

Where feasible, any staff member who performs the write-up work should not prepare the financial statements.

Among the disclosures that are desirable are the following:

1. Personal disbursements from business funds. Where material amounts are withdrawn from the business in payment of personal debts, living expenses, and income tax, a footnote disclosure is desirable. Some auditors may deem it desirable to make such a reference in their report.

2. No income tax provision. Since income tax is payable by the individual, not the business, such expense is not included in the income statement of the business. The auditor should disclose the omission of an income tax provision, but where the amount is known, it should be disclosed.

[25] SAP No. 33, p. 89.

3. Proprietor's salary. Because of his legal status a proprietor's salary is only a part of his drawings against profits, and not an operating expense. Nevertheless, some accountants recommend a reasonable annual charge for salary (regardless of drawings) to make the income statement more meaningful as a guide to accomplishment and for comparison with an incorporated company. (Of course, a corporation officer's salary is a tax-deductible expense, which affects a comparison.) The omission or inclusion of a salary provision should be disclosed unless clearly obvious from the statements.

An illustration of the reference to the sole proprietorship in the auditor's report is the following:

> We have examined the following statements relating to the accounts of the ____________ business conducted as a sole proprietorship at ____________ under the name of X Company.

An unqualified opinion is possible if all the auditing and reporting standards have been observed.

The scope section of the opinion might well include a sentence to this effect:

> Because this business entity is a proprietorship, our examination was not extended into any assets or liabilities, real or contingent, other than those reflected in the accompanying statements.

NOTE: See AICPA Industry Audit Guide, *Audits of Personal Financial Statements* for a detailed discussion of this topic.

Partnership Statements. A partnership has most of the legal-accounting conditions peculiar to a sole proprietor, namely:

1. The individual partners may have personal assets and liabilities other than their capital in the firm.
2. The partnership pays no federal income tax.
3. The partners may or may not designate some part of their drawings as salary.

Disclosure of these circumstances should be made, in footnote form or in the auditor's report, as warranted.

The financial statements and the auditor's report should append to the partnership name the legend "a partnership," unless obvious.

Disclosures, as described under "Sole Proprietorship Statements," should be made.

Statements of Nonprofit Organizations. The standards relating to consistency, disclosures, generally accepted accounting principles, and opinion are applicable in all instances. However, generally accepted accounting principles often are not employed by small institutions.

In certain cases, notably hospitals, colleges, and municipalities, pertinent accounting principles have been formalized. Thus, compliance with these standards, and with the other three general reporting standards, should warrant an unqualified opinion.

In that event, the second paragraph of the auditor's opinion might conclude with this phrase:

> . . . present fairly the financial position as of ________ of the various funds of X Hospital and the results of its operations and changes in funds for the fiscal year then ended in conformity with generally accepted accounting principles as applied to hospitals.

If there is no conformity to the generally accepted hospital accounting principles, a disclaimer or fairness exception would be necessary.

Problems of some governmental financial statements. Federal, state, and municipal governments and agencies often fix by statute or regulations the chart of accounts and format of the financial statements to be submitted and in some instances the wording of the independent auditor's opinion.

The financial statements and the wording of the opinion in some instances do not coincide with generally accepted accounting principles and reporting standards as observed by the profession.

In such cases some auditors have prevailed on the clients to make the revisions necessary to permit the expression of an unqualified opinion. Where a problem as to the wording of an opinion exists, a "straddle" may be mutually agreeable. Thereby the client's wording is combined with the auditor's expressions to achieve a satisfactory result, as illustrated below. Where no compromise is possible, a qualified opinion must be expressed.

Accounting societies have been endeavoring to get these entities to introduce AICPA generally accepted accounting principles into the framework of their regulations and statutes. Much progress has been made; much remains to be achieved.

Here is an instance where an "impossible" municipality opinion was converted into a mutually acceptable one:

Municipality's prescribed opinion:

I hereby certify that this above report is a true and correct report of the __________ of __________, county of __________, as obtained from the records submitted to me or my representatives, supplemented by personal inquiry and investigation; and I believe it to be a true report of the financial condition of the __________ as evidenced by books, records, and documents submitted for inspection.

Compromise opinion:

We have examined the financial transactions recorded in the books and accounting records of the Town of __________ for the fiscal year ended ________.

Our examination was made in accordance with generally accepted auditing standards and accordingly included such tests of the accounting records and such other auditing procedures as we considered necessary in the circumstances. Information and explanations were obtained from officials.

Accordingly, in our opinion, and to the best of our knowledge and belief based on such examination, the attached . . . accompanied by explanatory comments and recommendations, present fairly . . . in accordance with generally accepted accounting principles as applied to municipalities.

Management Service Reports (Special Services). Since management services are an integral part of accounting services, the AICPA has taken the position that the rules of ethical practice and reporting standards are applicable.

Thus, where appropriate, a report on such an engagement should disclose the scope and express an opinion. If it includes financial statements, the reporting standards would apply to them.

The scope should state the nature of the engagement, the names of the parties, and any other appropriate facts.

The opinion should disclose the responsibility the auditor is taking for the conclusions reached, or recommendations offered or whatever other data have been submitted.

An illustrative opinion for a special services report appears below:

In our opinion, the accompanying commission statement fairly sets forth the unit (dollar) sales of article(s) and the amount of commission applicable thereto in accordance with the agreement stated above.

Partial Financial Statements. Some investigations pertain to segments of financial statements, as in the case of a determination of working capital required to comply with a loan agreement. This type of investigation would ordinarily call for an auditor's opinion similar to that above covering the examination of a commission account.

The Funds Statement. SEC action in making this statement mandatory (see Accounting Series Release No. 117) requires its inclusion in published SEC annual reports. The Release summarizes the required form and content. The Accounting Principles Board Opinion No. 3 also deals with this statement. Its value as a management tool, and as a reference for security analysts, is responsible for the rapid increase in the statement's popularity and in the eventual APB and SEC actions.

Cash flow per share appears as a statistic in some reports. This is undesirable because to unsophisticated readers it may be synonymous with earnings per share. It may have financial management value, but its publication should be avoided.

Where the statement is attested by an independent auditor, the same considerations applicable to the attestation of the other basic statements prevail.

Pro Forma Statements. There is a wide variety of pro forma statements covering both balance sheets and income statements. They relate to past periods and future periods and are intended to reveal what would have been, or would be, if the impact of specified events were registered on the subject financial statements. They are also referred to as "giving-effect" and "as-if" statements.

They are common in merger and acquisition investigations and in new financing plans, to picture the effect on financial position and income of the prospective event. There are many other uses, all intended to inform or to cast more light on a proposed undertaking.

Accountants should be careful about such statements and should not give authority to speculation. The statement should not speculate about what might have been, or prophesy the future. It should disclose the determinable effect of a specific transaction. Thus, if a long-term loan is to be made to acquire the assets of a going concern, it is proper to prepare a pro forma balance sheet of the buyer, giving effect to the purchase. The prediction of future earnings is not one the accountant can sanctify.

The SEC (1933 act) formulated Rule 170 entitled "Prohibition of Use of Certain Financial Statements" dealing with security offerings. It is indicative of the care that must be given to projections to avoid misconceptions.

In addition, the SEC (1934 act) Rule X-15C1-9 reaffirms the foregoing rule and strengthens the intent of the phrase "manipulative, deceptive, or other fraudulent device or contrivance" with respect to statements giving effect to prospective financing.

Where the auditor can attest to pro forma statements, he may use these typical additions to his report:

Scope paragraph—add:

We have also examined the accompanying pro forma balance sheet which is based upon the aforementioned balance sheet and gives effect to the transactions described in footnote __.

Opinion paragraph—add:

. . . and the accompanying pro forma balance sheet presents fairly the financial position of the company as it would have appeared at ________ had the transactions described in Note __ been consummated at that date.

It is desirable that the term "pro forma" be included in the statement title, in type size equal to the rest of the caption. Here is an illustrative form:

ABC Machinery Corporation and Subsidiaries
XYZ Machinery Corporation and Subsidiaries
Pro Forma Consolidated Balance Sheet at ______ giving effect to the transactions described in the accompanying notes.

OTHER ASPECTS

Ethical Aspects of the Auditor's Opinion. Compliance with AICPA's standards of reporting, by members, is a requirement built into Article 2 of its Code of Professional Ethics. Other articles (also referred to as "rules") of the Code that contain reporting standards are these:

	Article
Independence of the auditor	1.01
Avoidance of a discreditable act	1.02
Confidential relationship with client	1.03
Observance of technical standards	2.02
Expression of opinion mandatory	2.03
Caution re opinion on forecasts	2.04
	Opinions
Prohibited self-designations	No. 5
Denial of opinion does not discharge responsibility in all cases (related to denials and disclaimers of opinions)	No. 8
Responsibility for pro forma statements and forecasts under Article 2.04	No. 10
Independence (regard for appearance to third parties)	No. 12
Ethics of tax practice	No. 13
Ethics of management advisory services	No. 14
Disclaimer of auditor lacking independence	No. 15
Retired partners and firm independence	No. 16

Reporting Standards for Nonpublic Accountants. Nonpublic accountants comprise, largely, those in government and business organizations.

Their audit programs range from limited scopes and objectives to rather broad ones, according to the needs of the individual situation. Auditors of the U.S. Defense Contract Audit Agency not only are concerned with the establishment of costs, but they inquire into managerial efficiency and offer advice in that area. Internal auditors may evaluate company policy compliance, as well as verify the accuracy of accounting. Governmental auditors examining the handling of grants will look for compliance with all the purposes and conditions of the grant. Internal Revenue agents, concerned primarily with the correctness of the reported tax, examine records and inquire into transactions in that connection.

Such reports obviously vary widely in form, reflecting the objectives of the examination and the uses to which they will be put. Though they may deal with matters of small or large size, they do not circulate externally and do not have much public utility. Because of the limited use, the format and wording are not as important as for public company financial statements.

Some agencies fix the format of their reports; others allow some latitude, particularly as to comments. Thus, a discussion of reporting standards for these widely divergent reports of necessity must be restricted to attributes common to all reports.

For the purpose of this chapter, it may suffice merely to list the desirable qualities of a report, namely,

It must serve the needs of the user.
It must be objective and reliable.
It must demonstrate the adequacy of the examination.
It should be well written, organized, and concise.
It should sum up the examiner's findings and conclusions.
Where warranted, it should report weaknesses found and, if possible, recommendations for their correction.
It should be neatly typed and, if extensive, should be indexed.

CONCLUSION

It would not be fitting, though this is a necessarily terse commentary on the standards of reporting, to omit reference to a milestone report (1966) of a committee of the American Accounting Association entitled, A Statement of Basic Accounting Theory. It has received wide acclaim as a significant forward step in the formulation of a general theory for identifying, measuring, and communicating economic information and to demonstrate its applicability in the areas of general purpose business financial statements.

These aspects are particularly significant:

1. Usefulness of information is the basic criterion by which accounting information is judged. In order to be useful, accounting information should have these four qualities:

Relevance
Verifiability
Freedom from bias
Quantifiability

2. The recommended guidelines for good communication are:

Appropriateness to expected use (relevance)
Disclosure of significant relationships
Inclusion of environmental information
Uniformity of practices within and among entities
Consistency of practices through time

The present standards of the public accounting profession, promulgated by the AICPA, are necessarily in a transitional state. First, there is a backlog of problems piled up that requires massive research and debate. Second, new problems are continually developing as companies increase in size and complexity of operation, and create new forms of doing business. Third, reporting standards continue to rise. However, a major, long awaited Accounting Principles Board Statement (No. 4), entitled *Basic Concepts and Accounting Principles Underlying Financial Statements of Business Enterprises* should provide a foundation for the necessary further development and integration of accounting principles that make for fair presentation in financial statements.

Other entities that have interest in the standards of reporting are working in this direction, simultaneously and in communication with the AICPA. Most notable is the Securities and Exchange Commission, which has made vital contributions.

Financial analysts and credit grantors, constantly in need of more and more sophisticated data, are helping by their constructive criticisms and recommendations. Stockholders and prospective stockholders would like financial statements to reveal more than historic cost, namely, current fair value. If ever this concept becomes a reality, it alone could revolutionize financial reporting and its standards, but it will create new imponderables.

Finally, the profession is confronted with an inexorable demand for an authoritative listing of generally accepted accounting principles appropriate in the best interests of the public and the economy. In this process, it is expected that the problem of alternative principles that produce widely disparate results will be resolved. Both will eventually develop and influence reporting standards of the future. However, absolute uniformity in the application of principles and in reporting still appears to be both undesirable and impractical, because there are unique differences in the operations of companies, and individual transactions may also have unique aspects. The application of broad generalities to individual situations will always require the exercise of independent judgment.

BIBLIOGRAPHY

American Accounting Association: *A Statement of Basic Accounting Theory,* Evanston, Ill., 1966.

American Institute of Certified Public Accountants, New York, releases to date:

Accounting Trends and Techniques, annually.

Opinions and Statements of the Accounting Principles Board.

Statements on Auditing Procedure.

Securities and Exchange Commission: Regulation S-X and Accounting Series Releases.

The Institute of Internal Auditors: Research Committee Report No. 10, *Internal Audit Reporting Practices,* New York, 1961.

Lenhart, Norman J., and Philip L. Defliese: *Montgomery's Auditing,* 8th ed., New York, The Ronald Press Company, 1957.

Palen, Jennie M.: *Report Writing for Accountants,* Englewood Cliffs, N.J., Prentice-Hall, Inc., 1955.

Rappaport, Louis H.: *SEC Accounting Practice and Procedure,* New York, The Ronald Press Company, 1966.

Ross, Howard: *The Elusive Art of Accounting,* New York, The Ronald Press Company, 1966.

Tuck, Clarence, and Thomas Boyd: "Interim Financial Statements," *The New York Certified Public Accountant,* September, 1969.

Davidson, Sidney: "Accounting and Financial Reporting in the Seventies," *The Journal of Accountancy,* December, 1969.

Saul, Ralph S.: "Corporate Disclosure," *The Internal Auditor,* September/October, 1969.

Norr, David: "What a Financial Analyst Wants from an Annual Report," *The Financial Executive,* August, 1970.

Gunther, Samuel P.: "Poolings—Purchases—Goodwill," *The New York Certified Public Accountant,* January, 1971.

Following are recent AICPA publications relating to Chapter 40 and some important APB Opinions and SAP in process:

I APB Opinion No. 18. *The Equity Method of Accounting for Investments in Common Stock,* March, 1971.

APB Opinion No. 19. *Reporting Changes in Financial Position,* March, 1971.

Statement on Auditing Procedure (SAP) No. 44. *Reports Following a Pooling of Interests.*

II Some important APB Opinions and Statements on Auditing Procedure in process:

Statements on Auditing Procedure

Piecemeal Opinions

Reliance on Other Auditors

APB Opinions

Imputed Interest—Receivables and Payables

Non-cash Transactions

Extraordinary Gains and Losses

Diversified Companies

Extrative Industries

Accounting Changes

and others

Chapter 41

Report Writing

JENNIE M. PALEN

Certified Public Accountant

PLANNING THE REPORT

General. To write a good audit report requires more than a thorough knowledge of accounting and auditing. It calls for considerable skill in marshaling facts and expressing conclusions in correct, current, comprehensible, and dignified yet persuasive language.

This chapter deals with commentary reports prepared by internal auditors, governmental auditors, and public accountants. All of these issue reports in great variety on substantially the same subjects. The difference is the product mix. The output of the public accountant contains a greater proportion of the so-called long-form audit reports, made up mostly of comments on financial statements, analyses of trends, recommendations, and the like. Internal and governmental auditors process a greater number of special reports dealing with miscellaneous subjects. The principles underlying good report writing apply to all. A well-planned, well-written, professionally presented report is a permanent and highly visible testimonial to the auditor's abilities. No auditor should overlook the prestige it can bring him.

Role of the Previous Report. In repeat work the prior report serves as a valuable guide, as a reminder of matters that might have been overlooked, and sometimes as a useful pattern where wording for a difficult situation has been carefully worked out. But before he adopts it as a model, the auditor should consider (1) whether it suits current conditions, (2) whether it was a good report under previous conditions, and (3) what he can do to improve it. He should not drop any material that serves a protective function or whose omission would raise a question. But he should remember that every report is a new opportunity for service.

Review of Work Papers. Before drafting the report, the auditor makes a thorough review of the papers to determine that all work has been satisfactorily done, that all loose ends have been cleared, and that he has in mind all matters disclosed by the audit that are of importance or interest.

PRINCIPLES OF GOOD WRITING

Within the confines of a chapter, only the briefest statement of the principles of good writing is possible.

Equipment. The report writer who aspires to excellence needs a good reference book on grammatical construction and an unabridged dictionary.

Tone. The purpose of a piece of writing dictates its tone (or character). The auditor's purpose is usually to inform, to assure, to alert, or to persuade. The tone should be dignified and the language simple, clear, restrained, and in current use. The road to dignity is through honest thinking sincerely expressed and supported by documented fact. Slang (which may be unintelligible at a later date) and high-flown language are equally inappropriate. By using short words, short paragraphs, good but unobtrusive transition, strong, direct, and correct sentences, strong beginnings for sentences and paragraphs, and by saying exactly what he means, no more, no less, the auditor gives his writing style and credibility.

Clarity. Accounting matters are not difficult to explain if we really understand them ourselves and if we can put ourselves in the place of a reader whose knowledge of the subject may be less than complete. These are some of the hindrances to clarity: (1) use of technical, vague, or stilted language, (2) excessive brevity, and (3) excessive detail. It is well to test each sentence carefully to see if it could possibly convey a meaning we did not intend it to have. Clarity is a matter of communication and of literary excellence. Even more, it is a matter of protection to the writer, the reader, and those written about.

Accuracy. No auditor should need to be reminded that accuracy is essential. So he will check all his figures as he takes them from the records, his draft to his work papers, and the final report to the draft, as well as assure himself that he has interpreted all figures correctly.

Conciseness. The readers of his reports are busy people. They want to get to the pith of the matter at once. By revision of written material we condense and sharpen; by cutting out unnecessary detail we give it speed, clarity, persuasiveness. (See "Wordiness" below.)

Tact. All our efforts fail if we mistake bluntness or cleverness for accuracy, or if we let personal resentments color our words. Our language should be designed to secure cooperation, not provoke resentment. (See also "Criticisms and Recommendations.")

Paragraphing. Paragraphing is designed to break up material and make it easier to read. A paragraph should develop only one central idea. The long paragraph repels the eye and often is found to violate this principle. Break it up and improve readability.

Sentence Structure. In good writing, sentences vary in length as well as in construction, with short sentences predominating. The straight declarative sentence is the most vigorous—the independent clause first, the dependent clause following it. To avoid monotony, however, sentences in the reverse order are mixed with it. Compound sentences—those in which clauses are joined by the simple conjunctions (*and, but, or, nor,* and *yet*) should be used in moderation. They are likely to ramble in a manner inimical to the tone desired in technical writing. In his search for exactness, the auditor often finds himself trapped in long, involved sentences. Granted, it is sometimes hard to speak without qualifying clauses. Careful thinking, however, will usually break these down into more digestible units.

Among common sentence faults are:

1. Failure to express parallel ideas in parallel form. Example: "The discrepancies are due to carelessness on the part of clerks and because supervision is lacking." Better: "The discrepancies are due to carelessness on the part of clerks and to lack of supervision."
2. Use of parallel form where the ideas are not parallel. Example: "The new posting procedures have proved to be faster, more accurate, and provide more information than the method previously used." Better: "The new posting procedures have proved to be faster, are more accurate, and provide more information than the method previously used."
3. Dangling modifier (often accompanies a weak switch from active to passive voice). Example: "Having decided what procedures to adopt, the drafting of a new manual is next undertaken." Better: "Having decided what procedures to adopt, we then draft the new manual." A common error is to use the participle *resulting* without a noun to which it can attach itself. Example: "Petty cash disbursements are often made without proper approval, resulting in poor control of incidental expenses." Better: "Petty cash disbursements are often made without proper approval. As a result, the control of incidental expenses is poor."
4. A series of modifiers, each tacked onto the preceding one, until all sense of direction is lost. The only remedy is complete revision.
5. Stilted phrasing. Avoid the inverted phrase. "The methods we used" is more natural than "The methods used by us." "A good goal to aim for" is more graceful than "A good goal for which to aim." It is better to end a sentence with a preposition than to use an awkward construction to avoid it.

Indefinite *It* and *There*. Excessive use of the indefinite *it* and *there* robs a piece of writing of its vigor. People who are addicted to the use of this construction unfortunately use it habitually as a paragraph opener. The effect is monotonous, trite, dull. Many of these constructions can be omitted entirely. For example, introductory phrases like "It seems appropriate to state at this point" are best just dropped. "It seems apparent" says no more than "Apparently" and says it less well. "There are many instances where" says no more than "Often" or "In many instances." Instead of saying "It is therefore recommended" or "It was noted," why not say simply "I recommend" or "I noted"? Instead of "There is generally" we need only to say "Generally."

Verb vs. Noun. Good writing derives much of its quality from the skillful use of verbs. Verbs are words of action. When honest verbs are reduced to passivity by making them into nouns, the result is appalling. Note the dullness of the following sentence: "A recommendation for the utilization of the advantages of mechanization is appropriate." This sentence has only one verb—the colorless *is*. Yet there are several verbs here, emasculated by being turned into nouns. Let us restore them: "A well-designed machine system will speed up the work as well as reduce expenses."

Active vs. Passive Voice. Active verbs are more vigorous than passive verbs. Passive verbs move backward, active verbs forward. The typical auditor's report drowns in passive verbs: "Working fund and payroll bank accounts were reconciled;" "Accounts receivable were satisfactorily confirmed by correspondence with customers;" "The more important financial and accounting functions were reviewed;" "Particular attention was given to . . . ;" "The matters which are believed to be of special interest are outlined as follows;" and so on to the end.

Some, at least, we can get rid of: "We reconciled the working fund and payroll bank accounts;" "The confirmation procedures showed satisfactory results. Sixty percent of the total number of customers, representing 79 percent of the dollar balances, confirmed their accounts;" "We reviewed the more important financial and accounting functions, giving particular attention to . . . ;" "Below is an outline of matters we believe to be of special interest."

Tense. One of the commonest of errors is the piling up of tenses. Example: "The auditor would have liked to have done this himself." Better: "The auditor would have liked to do this himself." Another is the use of the past participle with *after*. Example: "After having reconciled the bank account . . ." Better: "After reconciling the bank account . . ."

With *since* we use the present perfect tense: "We have not counted the cash since January 15." With *after* we use the past tense: "We did not count the cash after January 15." When we specify the time of action we use the past tense: "We counted the cash on January 15."

Truths that continue into the present are expressed in the present tense: "The treasurer said that the foreman distributes [*not distributed*] the payroll every Friday morning."

Agreement of Verb with Subject. Probably the most prevalent grammatical error is that of using a verb that agrees in number with an intervening noun rather than with its subject. This is an easy slip where there is a great distance between noun and verb, but there is no excuse for such errors as "The total of accounts receivable differ from the control" or "The cost of all ingredients are less than the overhead." Note, however, that a singular subject followed by a parenthetical phrase takes a singular verb. Example: "Good scheduling, as well as efficient operators, is [not *are*] needed."

Two or more singular nouns joined by *or* or *nor* take a singular verb, but if the nouns are of a different number, the verb agrees with the nearest. Example: "Neither the directors nor the president was [not *were*] informed of the action."

When *dollars* refers to a sum of money, it takes a singular verb. Example: "Five hundred dollars was paid for the option."

Wordiness. Probably the fault most disastrous to interest is wordiness. It is an insidious and progressive illness, often laboriously cultivated, and fatal to clarity as well as style. These are some of the ways to avoid it: (1) omitting words that merely repeat what has already been said, (2) weeding out pretentious words and stereotyped phrases, (3) using the right words, so that no additions or amendments are necessary, (4) constructing sentences in the way that most effectively expresses the idea, and (5) omitting irrelevant details while retaining the important ones. These are some examples:

As Used	*Suggested Revision*
Cash on hand was verified by actual count	We counted the cash
In conclusion, the implementation of the recommended system would substantially alleviate the administrative burden in the area of payroll supervision	Such a system would greatly simplify the control of payrolls
Attention is directed to delays in connection with the deposit of receipts	Receipts are not deposited promptly
Monetary amount	Amount
The true facts are	The facts are

The Right Word. To combine correctness with compactness, we need to know the exact meanings of the words we use. This is a very small sample of words often used incorrectly:

Word	*Incorrectly Used for*
Fact	Opinion, consideration, circumstance
Reiterate	Repeat
Convert	Translate, express in
Verbiage	Wording
Verbal	Oral
Enormity	Size, great size, enormousness
Forcibly	Forcefully
Convince	Induce, persuade
Realize (a loss)	Incur, sustain, experience
Confirm	Obtain confirmation of
Amount	Quantity, number

Transition. The best transitional device is an orderly progression of thought. Too leisurely transition can kill interest and is a sure sign of the unsure writer. Seldom is a whole paragraph needed, nor are such self-conscious phrases as "It is now time to consider," "Let us now proceed to the next point," "Some further consideration of this is now in order," and the like. The less evident the transition the better.

The short transitional phrases *however, also, to some extent, thus, in addition, on the contrary,* and the like should not all be used at the beginning of sentences; as many as possible should be woven into them and, to avoid a monotonous, jerky effect, preferably at different points.

One good method of transition to a new paragraph is to repeat a word or phrase from the last sentence of the preceding paragraph.

Captions. Frequent use of captions and subcaptions will solve many of the problems of transition. Of themselves, they announce a change of subject.

Developing the Audit Comments. From the moment he starts his work the auditor weighs all that he finds for its interest or value, makes a note of it, or even drafts his comment in final form for inclusion in his report while the details are still fresh in his mind. This not only saves him the trouble of looking into the matter twice but gives his material an urgency that might be lost as other problems divert his attention.

REPORTS OF THE INTERNAL AUDITOR

Reporting Responsibility. The internal auditor serves and reports to management. In the main, his work is designed to strengthen internal control, to determine that the operating procedures laid down by management are being followed, and to assure that the controls established are adequate, that they are economical, and that they are being effectively carried out. In performing these functions, he reports important deviations, recommends methods of correcting them where correction is possible, and follows up to see that his recommendations, when approved by management, are properly carried out. He concerns himself with such matters as excessive accumulations of stores, purchasing policies, shipping and billing procedures, buy or make decisions, efficient use of excess funds, protection of stores, equipment, and other assets from theft or damage, payroll procedures, insurance, even employment practices. His work may include studies of the costs of a variety of operations, analyses of trends, and the like. In some cases he makes examinations of the financial statements of a branch or plant.

Form of Internal Auditor's Report. In general, the reports fall into these classes: (1) oral, (2) questionnaire, (3) letter, (4) bound report in commentary form, (5) report containing financial statements, with or without comments on these statements.

The oral report suffers from a serious defect—it provides no record. Oral communication is best confined to minor matters or to discussion preceding or accompanying a written report. The questionnaire has its uses in that it serves as a checklist and as a record of work performed. As a report it is likely to be perfunctory and to communicate ineffectively.

The letter report is practical where the material is brief. It is often used also to augment a formal report or to convey recommendations to the persons responsible for operations. When tabulations, detailed discussion, or elaborate recommendations are needed, or wherever the report consists of more than a very few pages, a formal bound report is desirable. In this guise it creates a more favorable impression, besides being easier to identify and handle than loose stationery.

The auditor is necessarily guided by the wishes of management in choosing form and content. He need not, however, let this stop him from trying to introduce improvements in reporting procedures.

Arrangement of Content. The management executive to whom the internal auditor reports is not necessarily a trained accountant and usually will not be interested in a detailed description of audit procedures. Except, therefore, where he is reporting on the audit of the accounts of a plant or branch, the auditor may effectively begin with a summary of the problem and the recommendations he offers for its solution. He may then present a brief statement of the scope of his audit and any limiting factors. He follows with his audit findings, presenting them according to their importance—unless some other order seems especially appropriate. He gives only enough background information to substantiate the point he wishes to make. If, as a result of his discussions with the people involved, corrective action has already been taken, he will say so. If operating management has expressed other opinions, he will present these also. He will conclude with his own findings and opinions, clearly, impartially, and tactfully expressed.

If he considers it necessary to include tabular or other statistical material, he should consider the advantages of submitting it as a schedule, rather than in the comments. Then the reading of the text will not be interrupted and the reader may consult the tabulation, ignore it, or leave it for later study, as he sees fit.

Photographs, Charts, etc. Where the report relates to physical conditions, photographs are sometimes more illuminating than words. Charts, which have considerable dramatic power in showing trends and complex relationships, are discussed briefly in this chapter under the heading "Graphs."

Percentage Relationships. Percentages are one of the most potent means of driving a message home. In addition to the usual percentage breakdowns of expenses and income, the internal auditor often finds use for some of the other percentages listed in this chapter under "Percentage Relationships." When carefully selected, they are a valuable tool.

Review with Operational Management. Except where delicate situations exist, such as fraud or suspicion of fraud by the department manager, the auditor usually reviews his report with the operating personnel and local management before he issues it, not only for the psychological effect but as a precaution against errors or misconceptions on his part. In doing so, however, he should be careful not to let himself be pressured into removing a just criticism. At the same time, he may learn something about the art of criticizing without giving needless offense. It also helps to give praise where praise is due. He does not, of course, give any orders. These come from top management.

Follow-up. Obviously, the auditor's responsibility is not discharged until he has determined that the actions recommended by management have been carried out. He may wish to report on this feature only when there is noncompliance or faulty compliance, or he may report in all cases, depending on his understanding with management.

Addressing the Report. The officer to whom the internal auditor's report is addressed should be the one who is the highest-rated accounting officer in the organization and preferably a member of the board of directors. This may be the vice-president in charge of finance, the controller, or the treasurer.

Examples. The report that follows is an example of one type of report on a routine audit of the accounts of a main office.

Dear Sirs:

We report as follows on the audit of the head office accounts of XYZ Corporation for the months of February and March 19__. Our examination was conducted in accordance with the procedures prescribed in the Audit Manual for Section 1 Examinations, since it was not made in conjunction with that of the independent auditors. The audit worksheets showing the procedures followed or items covered and the signatures of those who performed each step are submitted separately. We submit herewith:

Exhibit

A – Trial Balance, March 31, 19__

Schedule 1 – Accounts Receivable, Summarized by Age

B – Major Stock Differences Shown by Test Counts

C – Suggested Forms for Record of Toll Calls and for Salesmen's Expense Reports

CASH

Because of the large number of cash sales now made at this office, a considerable amount of cash is on hand at closing each day and is left in the safe overnight. There are obvious dangers in this situation, both from fire and from burglary. As a measure of protection against these risks, we recommend that the company make arrangements for night deposits in the bank.

The cash items included an advance of $100 to Mary Adams, executive secretary, dated February 6, and bearing no official approval. This is in violation of the instructions in the Procedures Manual that all advances be approved and that they be cleared against the next payroll or else removed from cash by charging them to a loan account. At the direction of the chief accountant, the advance has since been deducted from payroll.

For the past three months the balance in the checking accounts has been more than twice what is normally needed for current use. We suggest that, rather than leaving these funds where they earn no interest, part of them be converted into bank certificates of deposit or else invested in high-grade short-term securities.

BILLING

During the months of February and March, 12 debit memos were issued to adjust incorrect prices on customer invoices, and 8 credit memos were issued on the basis of customers' complaints of overpricing. Our tests of invoices showed that extensions are carefully performed but that frequent errors occur in unit pricing that are not caught. We discussed the matter with the chief billing clerk, who has arranged to have prices as well as extensions double-checked until statistical sampling can be used.

INVENTORY SHORTAGES

In accordance with prescribed procedures, the stock clerks inventory the various stocks on hand when they reach their lowest point during the year. As part of our internal audit, we make test counts of selected items from time to time. Our counts at March 31 disclosed a few differences between the stock records and the stock on hand, some minor, others of more significance. These latter are listed in Exhibit B. They are too large to be accounted for by occasional inadvertent overissue. We checked all the issuances from these stocks to job orders and to specifications and found no differences. We were informed that the stock room is kept locked at all times. As a preliminary measure, we suggested to the plant superintendent that the lock be changed and this has been done. If shortages continue, a thorough study of the entire situation of receipts and issuances is obviously needed. We plan to extend our check in April.

INVENTORY LEVEL

We noted also that the total inventory of materials is nearly half as much again as it was a year ago this time, although sales have increased only 5 percent and the backlog of orders is normal. At present operating rates these materials represent eight months' supply and constitute two-thirds of the entire inventory. The cost of these materials has risen only 2 percent in the past year, whereas the cost of carrying excessive inventory is around 5 percent. Unless there is reason to believe that wholesale prices will rise abruptly, or that a shortage in supply is threatened, it does not appear that stockpiling in excess of needs is warranted. We recommend that no further purchases be made until the levels of these stocks reach normal.

PRODUCT AND MATERIALS INSPECTION

Returns of product for defects were twice as high in this quarter as in the previous one. Either the production process is less efficient or the product is being less carefully inspected, or both. In at least one case it developed that purchased materials were defective and that the defect should have been discovered when the materials were unpacked. In any case, steps should be taken to ensure that defective merchandise is not shipped. We recommend that stricter controls be placed on inspection procedures, both for finished product and for materials. The manufacturer should be charged for defects caused by faulty materials. We recommend that statistical sampling be instituted to supplement the present inspection procedures.

SALESMEN'S TRAVEL ADVANCES

Several salesmen's expense reports lacked supporting data for the expenses claimed, such as hotel bills, number of meals, etc. Also, in violation of instructions in the Accounting Procedures Manual, in several instances the cashier made reimbursements for expenses before the reports were approved. When handled in this manner, approval unfortunately tends to become perfunctory.

We present, as part of Exhibit C, a form that we recommend be used for reporting salesmen's expenses. It includes, among other things, provision for prior approval by the salesman's supervisor. We recommend also that a maximum per diem allowance be set, to be exceeded only upon approval.

The Accounting Procedures Manual provides that transportation be obtained, where possible, through the office. In a number of instances this was not done.

TELEPHONE TOLL CHARGES

Checking the telephone bill has been a long and unsatisfactory process, because no adequate record is kept of long-distance calls. We submit, as part of Exhibit C, a suggested form for recording toll calls as they are made. In addition to showing data necessary to check the telephone bill, it has a space for entering the name of the account to be charged.

Very truly yours

Research Committee Report No. 10 issued by the Institute of Internal Auditors, under the title *Internal Audit Reporting Practices,* contains, in addition to some excellent material on report writing, 32 pages of specimen reports taken from practice, including comments on payrolls, securities transactions, inventories, invoicing, suspected fraud, sales of scrap, shipping procedures, production controls, and the like. It contains also a useful checklist for testing the quality of a report.

Much additional material will be found in the examples of reports and of wording contained in the section on "Reports of the Independent Auditor" below.

REPORTS OF THE GOVERNMENTAL AUDITOR

Nature of Contents. In addition to reports on examinations of the financial statements of government corporations, and in addition to all types of internal audit reports (see previous section), the governmental auditor undertakes investigations of many types of business activity at the behest of the government.

Scope of Review. He may also investigate such matters as improved inventory controls, the need for more effective and economical use of electronic systems in government operation, statistical sampling techniques, systems for managing nonexpendable equipment, possible saving through use of commercial air transport in sending cargo to Asia or Europe, possibility of saving interest by advancing funds to states only as needed, improvements in controls over government-owned property in contractors' plants, and a great variety of other matters.

Importance of Good Writing. Each of these is a special writing project. Many of these reports are issued as publications of the General Accounting Office and may be consulted for procedures followed.

In preparing material for use in mergers, rate cases, and the like, the government accountant is involved with matters of great significance. His analyses and conclusions are often based on reports of outside companies and auditors, and he will be careful to state sources, using precautions such as those which independent auditors apply.

Intricate Matters Reviewed. These examinations involve numerous intricate matters that concern valuation of property, capitalizable assets, fixed charges, debt, earning capacity, financial position, capitalization, and equities. In view of their importance, the responsibility is great.

Similarity of Auditors' Reports. While the reports of internal, governmental, and independent auditors may vary in emphasis, they have more similarities than differences, and each may profit by considering what the other has written. Everything in this chapter may be read in relation to some part or other of the governmental auditor's work.

REPORTS OF THE INDEPENDENT AUDITOR

Since the clients of the public accountant include governmental bodies, corporations, partnerships, individuals, committees—anyone who wants accounting service or advice—his reports cover everything in the field. We deal here with the commentary section of the so-called long-form report and with certain of the more usual special reports, but not with financial statements or the formal opinion, both of which are very large subjects in themselves.

Adaptation to Purpose. The small and medium-sized businesses, which do not have large accounting staffs, often depend on the auditor for an annual record of their financial affairs, for details of accounts, and for information and advice about their books and controls. They may want to know what auditing procedures were performed. They need the auditor's watchful eye and welcome his comments. Big businesses, in which management receives voluminous internal reports, do not need duplication of these but do benefit from the auditor's analytical review of them from outside the arena. His long-form report and his reports on special situations can serve the large client very well indeed.

Reports for Credit Purposes. Because banks receive reports from auditing firms of all sizes and varying types of practice, they like to know what auditing procedures were followed. They welcome comments about trends, turnover, current position, cash balance, notes receivable and payable, summaries and aging of accounts receivable, inventories, accounts payable, collection policies, credit terms, insurance, source and application of funds, and the like.

Reports for Prospective Purchasers. A prospective purchaser will be interested in almost any facts the auditor can give him. They might include (1) a brief history, from the date of organization, of major capital transactions, products, plants, reorganizations, mergers, acquisitions of other businesses, etc.; (2) details of bank loans and bond issues and any restrictions, subordinations, defaults, or other significant features; (3) tabulations of plant and other physical property, as well as of patents and other intangibles; (4) aging of receivables; (5) names of large customers and type of business done with each; (6) comments on adequacy of records, internal control, and physical control of stock and plant properties; (7) summaries of earnings for a number of years; and (8) comments on the efficiency of employees, especially key employees.

Since the comments will necessarily cover a period of years, the auditor should be careful to disclose the source of any material not covered by his audit.

Reporting on Defalcations. Usually a defalcation is the subject of a separate report, because (1) it may be used in court and (2) the client may, for more than one reason, wish to keep it in a confidential file.

Great care is required here to avoid making any assertion that cannot be proved in court. No matter how convincing the evidence that someone has stolen money, the auditor does not use these words. Very often the only factual statement he can make is that there are irregularities in certain accounts or that certain amounts are unaccounted for. He should especially remember here the admonition not to let his emotions color his language.

Where practical, he should include photocopies of forged or fictitious documents—even of records, where there is danger that a record may be destroyed after it leaves his hands.

Even where these are not part of the report, it is a good idea to have photocopies of the papers to support his assertions if they are challenged.

A defalcation report might begin like this:

> We have made an examination of certain of the records of XYZ Corporation for the period from ______ to ______ for the purpose of establishing the extent of irregularities disclosed in the course of our examination for the year ended ______
>
> Total discrepancies amounting to ______ were found, as follows:
>
> | | |
> |---|---|
> | Collections on customers' accounts not accounted for | ______ |
> | Checks drawn to J. Smith and charged to repairs, not supported by bills or other evidence | ______ |
> | Petty cash slip advance, signed "J. Smith," not redeemed | ______ |
> | Total | ______ |
>
> It appears that the method used to conceal these irregularities was . . .

Criticisms and Recommendations. These sometimes appear in the long-form report under the related headings or as a separate section. Often, however, they are the subject of a separate report, in order to remove minor criticisms from a report that may be given to bankers or others, or to permit circulation of the criticisms alone to the departments affected.

Even though he may have discussed them orally with the client, the auditor does well to submit his criticisms and recommendations in writing. If the weaknesses are not corrected, he is then on record as having called attention to them.

In reporting on these rather difficult matters, the auditor faces the problem of not antagonizing his client or the client's employees to the extent that he defeats his purpose of effecting improvement. In making criticisms there are five basic rules: (1) be sure you are right; (2) as much as possible, avoid words that have unpleasant connotations, such as *mistakes, wasted time, incompetence, laziness;* (3) make your approach to the subject through the advantages that will result from the change, rather than dwelling on the evils of the present method, that is, stress the cure rather than the fault; (4) do not try to be clever; (5) imagine yourself in the place of the person criticized, and think how you would react if someone used these words to—or about you.

This sentence, for example, would arouse resentment: "Because of the poor judgment used in carrying all the accounts in one ledger, a great deal of time is wasted in looking for the bookkeeper's mistakes at the end of every month." A better and equally truthful way of saying it would be: "The ledger could be balanced more promptly and with less overtime work if it were divided into two sections with a controlling account for each section."

This sentence found in a report is incredibly bad: "Inventory turnover has dropped from 7.5 times in the previous year to 3.7. This indicates poor judgment in stockpiling materials by the vice president in charge of purchasing." Instead of the second sentence, the writer might have said, "We suggest that the company reappraise its purchasing policy to determine whether it is necessary to carry as much stock as it now has on hand. The cost of carrying excessive inventory is around 5 percent."

Note that in both these revisions the wording has been expanded rather than condensed. If there is one time when we can afford to pad our writing a little, it is when we are saying something that might not be welcome. Wrapped in a few extra words, a harsh fact may have a softer impact.

The auditor should make his recommendations only after having thought them through carefully and given consideration to all the procedures that will be affected by the change. He should be convinced that their advantages will outweigh the cost. He should not make recommendations that will save his own time but impose undue burden on others.

Illustrations of Recommendations. Below are a few illustrations of recommendations:

Employee purchases

Purchases for the account of employees are charged to inventory accounts, which are credited with cash when collection is made. These purchases should be charged to an employee account receivable, so that accounting control is established over collection.

Access to safe-deposit box

For the protection of all concerned, we recommend that the presence of any two persons be required for access to the safe-deposit box. At present any one of four people may open it.

Subsidiary investments record

No subsidiary record has ever been kept for investments, some of which have been held for many years. When an investment is sold it is necessary to go back to old ledgers and to old files, now in storage, to determine what it cost and when it was bought, as well as details of stock dividends, split-ups, and the like. This time-consuming procedure must be duplicated several times each year. An investment ledger, written up as from the time of purchase, would save much time for the bookkeeper.

Inventory shortages

At the time we observed the inventory we found that in general the stock records are well kept and that only minor adjustments were needed to bring the stock records into agreement with the counts. There were, however, sizable shortages in three items, all of which were stored in a shed, apart from the other stock. We recommend that these materials be moved to the regular stockroom where they can be controlled or that access to the shed be restricted. The shortages were in . . . .

Petty cash approvals

Petty cash disbursements are made without prior approval. As a result, the control over incidental expenses is poor. Requiring all expense vouchers to be approved before payment is not only a protective measure, it is an educational one that fosters respect for orderly procedure.

Damage to stock

The stockroom is narrow, dark, and crowded, and some of the stock has been damaged by dampness. It might be well to consider enlarging the space and providing better lighting and insulation. These, together with easier access to the materials, could not only save the stock clerk's time but prevent considerable damage to the stock.

Other examples of criticisms appear in the sample report under "Reports of the Internal Auditor."

If, instead of criticism, the auditor wishes to express approval of the system of internal control, he may choose to say something like this: "We reviewed the internal control and accounting procedures and tested their effectiveness.

In our opinion, the controls established, when carefully adhered to, afford reasonable safeguards of the accuracy of the records."

OTHER REPORT DATA

Protective Measures. Reasonable care and professional competence are of course the primary protective measures. These also help:

1. Care in disclosing the status of any unaudited figures, as, for example: "as shown by the sales journal," "as shown by unaudited reports of subsidiaries," "prepared by company employees," "at quoted market value," "as shown by a letter signed X.Y. in the Company's files."
2. Avoidance of such words as *verify* and *value*. *Verify* is a strong word. We can verify an addition, but to say "we verified the cash receipts" is to make a claim that in the usual audit is impossible. "We verified the accounts receivable by obtaining confirmations from the debtors" is too broad, even when 100% confirmation is achieved. The possibility of rigged confirmation is all too real. *Value* is a vague term, often conveying an unintended implication of worth. It needs narrowing down, as, for example, "quoted market value," "carrying amount," or "appraised value as shown by an appraisal of X Company, appraisers, dated . . . ."
3. Weighing everything said for clarity and for possibility of misinterpretation.
4. Avoiding substitution of report pages by using typewriters in the report department with specially designed type.
5. Impressing upon the client that the auditor's name may not be used in any published material unless the material has been cleared with him.
6. Quoting any quoted material verbatim, even to errors in spelling.
7. Bearing in mind at all times that what he says in his report he may have to substantiate on the witness stand someday.

In the comments, some auditors include a disclaimer of responsibility for discovery of irregularities. Others take care of the matter in a letter to the client at the time of accepting the engagement. Comment in the report might read somewhat as follows (assuming that the work has included the procedures described):

> Our examination included a review of the company's system of internal control and internal check, as a result of which we pointed out certain weaknesses in the system and suggested certain improvements. The auditing procedures we applied should assist management in discharging its responsibility for installing and maintaining an adequate internal control system. Our examination cannot, however, be relied upon to disclose defalcations and similar irregularities, although their discovery may result. No such irregularities were disclosed by our examination and we have no reason to suppose that any exist.

Supplementary Information. The auditor assumes or disclaims responsibility for the comments and schedules accompanying the financial statements by adding to the short-form report a paragraph somewhat like one of these:

> 1. Our examination was made primarily for the purpose of forming an opinion on the current year's basic financial statements, taken as a whole. The other material included herein, though not considered necessary to a fair presentation of the financial position and results of operations, is presented primarily for purposes of supplementary analysis, has been subjected to the audit procedures applied in the basic financial statements, and is, in our opinion, fairly stated in all material respects in relation to the basic financial statements, taken as a whole.

2. The supplementary information included in this report, although not considered necessary to a fair presentation of the financial position and results of operations, is presented primarily for purposes of supplementary analysis and has not been subjected to the audit procedures applied in the examination of the basic financial statements but has been taken directly from sources described therein, without verification.

Comments vs. Schedules. Long tabulations are best submitted as schedules supporting one of the statements or, if they do not tie into a statement, as an exhibit. The auditor can then refer to them in the comments and discuss them as much as he wishes. Text heavily laden with tabular material is forbidding to the eye. Unless the details are essential, they should be scaled down, relegated to a schedule, or omitted.

Tables that use more than four money columns are hard to present on a single sheet, and fold-over pages in the comments are annoying to the reader. Rounding the amounts to even dollars or to thousands may permit the use of more columns.

A trend over a period of years or a sudden change in a trend is a matter of great interest. A vertical tabulation can present such a summary in a small space, thus:

Year	Net sales	Cost of goods sold	Gross profit

Percentages, Ratios, etc. The value of percentages, or the so-called ratios, in analyzing financial data is indisputable. Of the great variety of these that have been devised, some are exceedingly valuable, others marginally so. A welter of percentages can be confusing. The good report writer chooses those most significant in the circumstances and presents them in a way that makes their import clear. If he packs them in long paragraphs in which every sentence is weighed down by percentages, he will succeed only in discouraging the eye and making them almost useless for reference purposes. If he believes that detailed percentages will be useful, he will find it effective to present them in tabular form, with a comment that emphasizes their salient points.

Ordinarily, when one ratio is out of line, others will be also. The worse the situation, the more ratios will need comment. When a bad situation improves, management will be delighted to hear about it. Even holding the line is sometimes a highly favorable achievement.

Valuable as percentages are, they reach their real potential only when compared with corresponding percentages in the preceding period or periods. By themselves they tell an incomplete story. Sometimes it is useful to compare them with *industry standard* ratios. *Standard* ratios, while they do have some flaws, show striking variations among industries and have some usefulness as a rough guide to performance.

The relationships seldom omitted are the current ratio (current assets ÷ current liabilities), inventory turnover (cost of goods sold ÷ average inventory), the rate of net income earned on proprietorship equity, and the ratio of net income to net sales. But there are many others equally useful in circumstances where they are significant. Some of these are:

1. Quick or acid-test ratio (total of cash, temporary investments, and receivables ÷ current liabilities)

2. Creditors' equity ratio (total liabilities ÷ total of liabilities and proprietorship)

3. Proprietorship equity ratio (total proprietorship ÷ total of liabilities and proprietorship)

4. Number of days' sales in inventory (inventory ÷ average daily sales—at cost, if possible)

5. Turnover of accounts receivable (net credit sales ÷ gross amount due from customers)

6. Number of days' sales in receivables (gross amount due from customers ÷ average daily sales)

7. Average collection period (average gross trade accounts receivable ÷ average daily credit sales)

8. Each asset or group of assets ÷ total assets (a balance sheet expressed entirely in these percentages is called a common-size balance sheet)

9. Each item in the income statement ÷ net sales (an income statement expressed entirely in these percentages is called a common-size income statement)

10. Earnings per share of common capital stock (net income ÷ shares outstanding, or by weighted average of number outstanding where there have been significant changes); often accompanied by earnings per share before taxes

11. Percentage of returns and allowances (returns and allowances ÷ gross sales)

12. Each element of manufacturing cost ÷ cost of goods sold (by comparison with same percentages in previous period, shows what costs are changing disproportionately)

13. Percentage of increase or decrease in any item (increase or decrease experienced in the current period ÷ dollar amount in the prior period)

The rule of 2 to 1 for the current ratio is not a reliable guide. Some businesses need more, some less. If a business is able consistently to discount its bills, a lower than 2 to 1 ratio does not of itself connote an inadequate current position. If it cannot do so on a higher than 2 to 1 ratio, it obviously needs more working capital. The acid-test ratio (No. 1 above) measures quick assets available for current debts. It can disclose a dangerously low cash position or, on the other hand, the existence of funds that could be more profitably employed.

Where there are several departments or products, inventory turnover should be computed for each, if possible. Where a cost system is in use, separate turnover rates for materials and for finished goods can show excess stockpiling of materials or overproduction of product. In commenting on these matters, the auditor should take into consideration such factors as expected scarcity of materials or a large backlog of orders.

Nos. 2 and 3 are strikingly effective in disclosing undercapitalization or any change in the stockholder-creditor relationship.

The value of the various income and expense percentages and the increase-decrease percentages is obvious. Even when percentages are shown in the financial statements, it is well to discuss the salient ones in the comments.

Graphs. Because the accountant finds figures so easy to comprehend and more exact than graphs, he is inclined to downgrade the usefulness of graphs in his own writing. For his readers, however, this is not always true. Charts often present dramatically something that might be overlooked—or underappreciated—in comment form. They also have the virtue of presenting, as an integrated whole, relationships that in a tabulation appear as unconnected detail. They can be used effectively to supplement financial statements and, with modern duplicating equipment, are easily reproduced. Charts particularly suitable for the commentary section are the line or curve chart, the bar chart, and the column chart. Line charts are good for showing trends over a period of time. The bar chart, which is readily understood and easily prepared, is excellent for comparing different components at the same time. The column chart is a bar chart with a vertical base. There are many other types of graphs. Circles, squares, spheres, and cubes are harder to interpret than line and bar charts, and some, especially pie charts and symbols, have their pitfalls. The auditor who wishes to use any but the simpler forms should be familiar with the techniques of preparing them.

Captions. In a short comment report captions may not be needed, but in voluminous reports they are necessary to facilitate reference, cut down wordage, and simplify the problem of transition. Whatever system of captioning is selected should be consistently followed, or a most untidy and unprofessional appearance will result.

DESCRIPTION OF AUDITING PROCEDURES

Various Methods Used. Auditors differ widely in the extent to which they describe auditing procedures. A great many consider that the formal opinion contains all that is necessary. Some devote one section of the comments to them, placed at either the beginning or end or treated as an exhibit. Others may describe them under the various subject headings. An auditor may employ all these methods under different circumstances, depending on the client and the purpose for which the report will be used. The purpose of this section is neither to recommend nor to discourage their use, but to furnish viable illustrations of what may be said if desired. Obviously they are subject to condensation or amplification to suit circumstances. Below is one example.

Illustrations

SUMMARY OF AUDITING PROCEDURES

In accordance with generally accepted auditing standards, our audit procedures did not comprise examination of each accounting entry or record but were based on such testing as we considered necessary in the light of the adequacy of the company's controls and accounting procedures.

We made tests, for selected periods, of recorded transactions, including cash receipts and disbursements, purchases, sales, expenses, and payrolls, by reference to records of original and supporting evidence. We inspected vouchers in support of selected charges to certain expense accounts, reviewed analyses of certain other income and expense accounts, and investigated significant variations in income and expense accounts from the preceding year.

Cash, notes receivable, and securities

We counted the cash on hand and obtained confirmation from banks for that on deposit, of bank loans and acceptances payable, and of securities pledged under the loans. Certificates representing the other investments owned and shares of the company's own stock held in the treasury were examined, together with notes receivable and the collateral held under those notes. The makers of the notes confirmed their indebtedness and the collateral pledged.

Security valuations and income from securities

We computed the market value of listed securities and were furnished with financial statements, audited by other accountants, of those companies whose securities were not listed. Income from investments was supported by published records of dividend payments or by the financial statements referred to above.

Accounts receivable

Statements of their accounts at November 30, 19__, were mailed, under our supervision, to 450 of the 600 customers with balances at that date, with requests that they confirm their balances direct to us. Total balances in these 450 accounts were 85 percent of the dollar amount of trade accounts receivable. Confirmations were received from 400 of these customers, representing 75 percent of the total dollar amount of trade receivables. To the other 150 accounts not covered by the foregoing requests we mailed requests that asked for a reply only if differences existed. All differences reported were satisfactorily explained. On the basis of our review of accounts and notes receivable we believe that the allowance for losses in collection is reasonable.

Inventory

We attended the inventory-taking as of November 30, 19__, observed the methods used, and made selected test counts. For goods in public warehouses we examined warehouse receipts, obtained confirmation from the warehouses, and observed tests made by company employees on October 28, 19__. We also tested computations and prices sufficiently to satisfy ourselves that the inventories are stated at the lower of cost (first-in, first-out basis) and market. The controller and plant superintendent have certified to us that all inventories were taken by count, measurement, or weight, that, except for liens under acceptances payable, they are the unencumbered property of the company, and that they include no unsalable items.

Prepayments

Insurance policies and tax and other bills were examined in support of prepaid expense balances.

Property

Major additions to property are in agreement with purchase invoices and are supported by the minutes. Entries for sales and retirements were reviewed. Provisions for depreciation were consistent with the policy followed in the previous year.

Accounts payable

We tested the trade accounts payable by obtaining confirmation of those showing credit balances and by circularizing others with whom the ledger showed transactions during the year. We also test-checked the computations of accrued liabilities. These procedures did not disclose any unrecorded liabilities. The president and treasurer of the company have furnished us with a written statement that, to the best of their knowledge and belief, all liabilities have been disclosed to us. The company's attorneys inform us that they know of no suits against the company or any flaws in the title to any of its assets.

Income taxes payable

The Internal Revenue Service has examined the company's tax returns through 19__, and has proposed additional assessments of $__ for 19__ and $__ for 19__. The company plans to contest these assessments and has made no provisions for them. We reviewed the return filed for 19__ and believe that the amount taken up as a liability is reasonably accurate.

Bonds payable and capital stock

Bonds outstanding were confirmed by the trustees under the indentures, and the shares of capital stock outstanding by the registrar and transfer agent.

REPORT CATEGORIES

History. The prospective purchaser or prospective lender, as well as others, find useful a brief statement of the history of the company from its inception. For this reason the auditor often includes such a section in a report on a first audit. Thereafter it is usually dropped, except sometimes for a section labeled "Major Changes."

Material for this summary comes from the certificate of incorporation, minutes, important contracts, reports of other accountants, and the accounting records. It covers, briefly, capitalization, sites of plants, types of product or activity, long-term borrowings, business expansion, formation or purchase of subsidiaries or branches, research and invention, important litigation, and other major developments, including a statement of the general area where the product is sold.

Major Changes during the Year. Some auditors use this caption to give the strategic opening position to such important matters as changes in capitalization, new bond issues, expansions, unusual increases in earnings, or even such internal but pervasive changes as mechanization, welfare plans, and the like.

Operations. Others go directly to the universally interesting topic of earnings. Whether owner, lender, executive, employee, prospective purchaser, or merely curious bystander, the first question a reader is likely to ask about a business is whether it is currently profitable. The section on operations is therefore the most likely opener, and the most-used opening sentence is that which states the net income for the year as compared with last year's income.

Even though the income statement contains comparative figures and percentages, it is well to summarize them in the comments, often in tabular form, and to point out their significance. Most of the readers of reports are less adept at analyzing statements than is the auditor and will welcome his ready-to-use interpretations. These may pinpoint trouble spots, profitable and unprofitable departments, products, or territories, or may disclose the soundness or unsoundness of purchasing and financial policies. One type of comment is illustrated:

OPERATIONS

Net income for the year amounted to $____, as compared with $____ in 19__. The figure for the current year is after an adjustment of $____ to record decline during the year in the market value of temporary investments.

After payment of dividends on the 5½ percent cumulative preferred stock, earnings on the common stock amounted to $____ a share, an increase of $____ over 19__ and of $____ over 19__. The past three years have registered a steady increase in both unit and dollar sales, accomplished in the face of a steady increase in material and labor costs. As shown in Schedule 1 of Exhibit A, sales were __ percent higher in 19__ than in the previous year, cost of goods sold was up __ percent, selling expenses rose __ percent, and general expenses increased __ percent. Although all costs were up in dollar amounts, their relationship to net sales shows a gratifying downward trend, the result of an intensive sales campaign, as well as consolidation of administrative functions.

Inventory turnover at the company's plants during 19__ and 19__ is as shown below:

Plant	Turnover	
	19__	19__

Inventories of both manufactured goods and materials and supplies at the Riverdale plant continue to be in excess of needs. At a time when the stocks at the other plants are normally at their low point for the year, the inventories at Riverdale constitute three months' supply. Since the manufacturing processes and materials used are the same at all plants, it may be well to reappraise the purchasing policies at Riverdale. The company borrows periodically to finance inventories, and overstocking can substantially increase interest costs.

Financial Position. Next most important after operations is financial position. This is a sample comment:

FINANCIAL POSITION

The stockholders' equity increased $______ during the year, including $______ added to the amount set aside for contingencies. At December 31, 19__, the asset value per share of outstanding capital stock was $______, as compared with $______ at December 31, 19__, an increase of $____ a share.

The year was marked by an expansion of facilities that resulted in a net increase in plant (less depreciation) of $______ and an increase in production that added $______ to the inventory during the year. Collections from customers against future deliveries of goods and services amounted to $______ at December 31, 19__, an increase of $______.

The increase in plant was financed largely through the sale of $______ of temporary investments.

These transactions resulted in lowering the current ratio from 3.3 to 1 at the end of the previous year to 2.3 to 1 at the end of 19__. The current position, however, is still excellent. Cash, temporary investments, and current receivables are 120 percent of all current liabilities and are 235 percent of all current liabilities exclusive of the $______ of customers' advances, much of which will be liquidated by shipment of goods now included in inventories.

Mainly because of the large increase in customers' advances, the creditors' equity in the total assets increased 9 percent and the stockholders' equity correspondingly decreased, but the stockholders' equity was nevertheless 66 percent, as against a 34 percent creditors' equity, an excellent relationship.

The comment on financial position may include a condensed balance sheet expressed in even dollars and in percentages, showing comparison with the previous year end, with comments on the individual changes.

It might also include a comment along these lines: "Trade receivables are 11.8 percent of net sales as compared with 15.8 percent last year. Apparently the increase in sales has not been accompanied by a loosening of collection standards. The allowance for losses appears to be ample."

Sometimes there is a comment on the dividend policy, for example: "The current ratio has slipped from 2.1 to 1 to a new ratio of 1.8 to 1. With a continuation of the upward trend in earnings this condition might be corrected by holding the dividend to a lower rate."

Comment on Individual Items. It is not necessary to comment on every item in the financial statements. Nor is it possible to list all the topics for comment in reports. Many of the most useful comments will arise out of problems peculiar to the business activity being audited. What the auditor communicates should not be a stereotype. However much he organizes his reporting, his reports will differ among clients, among reports for the same client in different years, and even among reports for the same year for the same client, according to the specific uses of those reports. These differences will not affect the presentation of financial position and operating results, however.

Except in those special cases where he considers it desirable, the auditor need not comment under each item on the auditing procedures used. As has been stated, his formal opinion covers use of accepted procedures or, where he chooses to use it, his summary of auditing procedures. He may, however, deal with significant exceptions, as well as breakdowns, analyses, and those recommendations which he does not decide to make the subject of a separate report.

Cash. A comment on cash might read:

CASH—GENERAL FUND
SPECIAL DEPOSITS
BUILDING FUND

A cash fund at the Denver office was not counted. We inspected the custodian's cash report and obtained his acknowledgment of the amount of the fund.

During our attendance at the Portland office we noted that, because cash sales are often made in considerable amounts after bank closing hours, large amounts of cash are often kept overnight in the office safe. We recommend that arrangements be made for a lock box, to avoid the considerable risks. We also found in the cash three post-dated checks totaling $2509.82. Postdated checks are not cash and should not be taken up as such. It appeared to us also that the petty cash fund of this office is larger than is necessary and could feasibly be reduced by as much as $500.

To achieve better use of funds, we recommend that wire reimbursements be used on payroll dates to avoid maintaining free balances to cover payroll needs.

The building fund, carried in the balance sheet among noncurrent assets, was created in December to segregate funds to be used in a plant expansion program planned for the coming year. The fund is earning interest at the rate of 5 percent.

Marketable securities. The balance sheet will show the market value of these securities. If they are few in number, the comments may list them. Any pledging, and any changes during the period, should be described. A comment might read:

These securities are listed in Schedule 2 of Exhibit B. The United States Government bonds are pledged under a note payable to __________ Bank.

During the year the company sold all its investments in common stocks and bought government and utility bonds, which were selling at advantageous prices. Profit on these sales amounted to $______.

Dividends and interest received during the year amounted to 6.3 percent on the total investment, as compared with 5.4 percent in the previous year. The increased return is due, in part, to the reinvestment of the profit realized on the portfolio sales.

Notes receivable. The auditor lists or comments on maturities, collateral held, collectibility, origin, collections since the balance sheet date, whether any are renewals of older notes, and any other pertinent matters.

Accounts receivable. The comment on accounts receivable will include (unless covered elsewhere) description of the nature, extent, and results of the confirmation procedures. These are vital matters.

An aging summary, the turnover of receivables (or the number of days' sales in receivables), comments on collectibility, comparison of terms granted with the age of the balances or the average collection period, and an evaluation of the allowance for losses are all important. The auditor should disclose large amounts due from individual customers, as well as large individual amounts not confirmed by the customers. Where feasible, he should mention the amounts collected since the balance sheet date, as shown by the ledger accounts, on each category in the aging summary. These amounts have considerable value in appraising collectibility.

He may wish to comment on collection policies and the protective devices to be used in writing off uncollectibles. He may comment on accounts written off during the year, collections on those previously written off, and the basis used in providing for losses in collections or for cash discounts.

Note that the phrase "adequate provision for all possible losses" is too comprehensive. Only a 100 percent allowance could provide for all *possible* losses. Credit insurance, if carried, should be mentioned.

Pledging of accounts will, of course, be disclosed in the balance sheet but may need further description.

A comment might read as follows:

ACCOUNTS RECEIVABLE

The trade accounts receivable represent 35 days' sales, as compared with 29 days at the previous year-end, both on the basis of sales during the last quarter.

The following summary, prepared by employees of the company and test-checked by us, shows the age of the balances and the collections on each category since the balance sheet date:

Date of charge	*Amount*	*Collections*
December, 19__	$______	$______
November..........................	______	______
October	______	______
Prior...................................	______	______
Total	$______	$______

The company makes provision for losses in collection by charges to income amounting to 2 percent of the gross credit sales. During the past five years the write-offs of uncollected balances have averaged 70 percent of the average provision. Accounts totaling $______ were written off during the year and $______ was added to the allowance account. On the basis of our review of the accounts with the credit manager and in the light of the company's excellent collection record, we believe the allowance account of $______ to be ample provision for probable losses in collection.

Inventories. The auditor may tabulate the various categories of inventory, perhaps by locations. A breakdown of inventory into finished goods, goods in process, and materials and supplies is important to any analysis. Percentages of each category to the total and the percentage of the total inventory to the total current assets will be revealing as to total inventory changes when compared with like relationships at the previous year end. Having shown turnover rates in his comment under "Operations," the auditor may now show turnovers by categories, where they are significant. He may comment on slow-moving or obsolete stock or on the basis of costing used or any changes in the basis of costing. The year in which LIFO was adopted may be of continuing interest. He may have suggestions regarding the physical or book control of stock or the inventory procedures.

He sometimes comments here on the backlog of orders as it relates to the finished stock on hand. He may comment on excessive accumulations of materials or, conversely, on inadequate supplies of scarce components. In this, of course, as in all criticisms, he should be very sure of his ground. He might say, for example, "We understand that the finished product consists of about 60 percent X ingredient, 30 percent Y, and 10 percent miscellaneous materials. Of the materials on hand, X amounted to 10 percent and Y to 80 percent of the total. Imbalance so severe as this could possibly cause serious delays, perhaps shutdowns."

Property. The auditor usually tabulates, or comments on, the changes in the various categories of property, setting out separately, of course, only major items. He may compare the carrying amount of each category with the related depreciation allowance, in dollars, and in percentages. He will describe the depreciation policy and the practices followed in accounting for maintenance and repairs, unless these are so fully covered in the footnotes as to need no amplification.

He may describe a construction program planned or in progress, any important sales, abandonments, or write-downs, property fully depreciated that is still in service, liens (other than under mortgage bonds), and installment purchases.

Intangibles. The nature of the various types of intangibles, their origin, the basis of the amount at which they are stated, the methods of amortization, the dates of expiration of patent or other rights, acquisitions, sales, or write-offs during the year, and income from any rights granted all are appropriate subjects for comment, as well as any information that throws light on the value of the intangibles.

Deferred charges. These are usually listed or summarized. The origin, basis of carrying amount, and amortization policy are important. New items created during the year such as, for example, discount on a new issue of bonds, should be described, as should the treatment of discount on bonds that were refunded.

Notes and acceptances payable. Useful for both management and credit purposes is a tabulation that shows name of lender, interest rate, due date, amount, and any assets pledged as security—unless all have been paid at the time the report is prepared. A tabulation of the range of borrowings throughout the year, showing the ledger balances at the end of each month, is often of value.

Accounts payable. An aging of accounts payable balances can be as useful as the aging of accounts receivable, both for management and for lenders. It may also justify a recommendation that the company borrow in order to discount its bills, since cash discounts yield a much higher interest rate than is paid on loans.

It may be enlightening to point out any large amounts due to one or two creditors, especially if the company's financial position is not too good. Large amounts due to officers or stockholders are also important.

Reference to the liability certificate and the letter from the company's attorneys is sometimes made here, if not covered elsewhere.

Accrued payables. Unless these are minor or routine, the auditor usually lists them and describes their nature. Accrued rents that are measured by sales, accrued royalties, accrued bonuses, and the like may require detailed comment. Accruals of liabilities under service or product guarantees will require explanation of the method of accrual and the basis for dividing the amount between current and noncurrent liabilities. Informative details not given elsewhere in the report regarding the status of income taxes are often furnished here or under Accounts Payable.

Long-term debt. If this is not detailed in the balance sheet or a schedule, the comments should show particulars regarding each issue. They may amplify information given in the footnotes respecting such matters as restrictions on dividends and maintenance of current position, or failure to comply with any of the terms of the indentures. Any new issues, retirements, or refundings during the year will be described.

Capital stock. Unless they have been covered in the opening sections of the report, the auditor will comment on such matters as authorizations for the issue of additional shares, sales of shares and compensation received for them, shares acquired for the treasury, changes in par or stated value, stock dividends, stock split-ups, and transactions in stock options. These will include also any significant changes since the balance sheet date or any contemplated changes of which the auditor has knowledge.

Paid-in surplus. Paid-in surplus should be classified by source (see Accounting Terminology Bulletin No. 1). The balance sheet description should be specific. A comment on one of the types of capital surplus might read as follows:

PAID-IN SURPLUS

The paid-in surplus was increased during the year by a credit of $50,000 arising from the issuance of 10,000 shares of no-par capital stock for the plant of X Corporation at Tucson. The directors placed a valuation of $550,000 on the property, which is $50,000 more than the stated value of the stock issued for it.

Retained earnings. Balance sheet disclosure of restrictions on earnings is sometimes amplified in the comments, especially if any restrictions (or violations) arose during the period. Other matters for inclusion here would be unusual charges or credits directly to retained earnings, dividends, dividend arrearages, the percentage of net income disbursed as dividends, and the like. Choice among these subjects would, of course, depend on prior coverage in the opening sections.

Insurance Coverage. The auditor with a clientele that includes many small and medium-sized businesses will doubtless find insurance deficiencies to comment on. Big businesses employ insurance consultants, but small businesses often buy insurance haphazardly, from friends, relatives, or to return a business favor. They may, unwittingly, be overinsured for some risks, underinsured for others, and for some completely uninsured. Where the auditor finds specific deficiencies, he may make this general type of comment:

INSURANCE COVERAGE

Although no appraisals of the company's properties are available, it is highly probable that at current price levels the fire insurance policies do not provide adequate protection. The properties are at scattered locations and are insured by several different insurers. Although there is considerable movement of property among the different locations, no floater policies are carried. There is no coverage of possible losses through business interruption after fire or other major casualty. We note that inventories are insured for an amount that equals their highest level, although that level is reached only twice during the year. Surety bonds on employees handling cash have not been increased in five years, in spite of a heavy increase in funds handled. Blanket insurance, including a feature under which the amounts in inventory are reported periodically and premiums adjusted accordingly, may offer best and less costly protection. Using a single broker may also result in economies. Aside from these deficiencies, we express no opinion respecting the adequacy of coverage and recommend that an insurance consultant be employed to make a thorough review.

Where the auditor has no specific recommendations, he will probably tabulate the coverage and add that he expresses no opinion as to its adequacy.

Source and Application of Funds. Unless included as an exhibit, a brief summary of the derivation and use of funds is a useful part of the comments, either in one of the opening sections or toward the end under the above caption. Banks especially like it, as do many clients, if it is not made too complex. There are many forms of the statement. Some show changes in cash, some in working capital; some are no more than recapitulations of the *increase-decrease* column of the balance sheet; some show the changes in all financial resources. They may be prepared to cover a period as well as a single year. Space does not permit discussion of all these types. The report writer will find it to his advantage to study them.

General Comments. Sometimes the auditor will have several brief observations, none long enough to need a section all to itself, which he groups at the end under the heading "General." They may have to do with such matters as payroll, efficiency of employees, hiring practices, commendations, and letter of representations.

Concluding Paragraphs. Does a report need a concluding paragraph, in the sense of a final summary or graceful exit line? Not unless the auditor has something more to say. Many auditors conclude by saying that the accounts have been well kept and that the auditor appreciates the courtesies extended him. There is no harm in these statements if they are true. When said, however, at the end of every comment report, such remarks become perfunctory. They are far warmer if expressed orally or in a special letter. Structurally, the auditor does not need any "concluding" paragraph. When he has said what he has to say, he needs only to stop writing.

REVIEW OF REPORT

Nature of Review. Before a report is typed, someone other than the writer should pass upon its correctness, technical soundness, and professional excellence. The review comprises:

1. Supervision during fieldwork
2. Review of papers on completion to establish (*a*) that all necessary work was done, that it was done satisfactorily, that a record was made of the procedures followed and the conclusions reached, and that those who did the work and those who reviewed it signed or initialed for having done so; (*b*) that the adjusting entries are proper and complete, have been applied to the trial balance, and have been entered by the client's employees on the books
3. Determining the mathematical accuracy of all statements and tabulations, including cross references, and checking all loose figures in the entire report to the work papers
4. Checking client name, titles of statements and of accounts, dates, and the like, to determine that they are correct and agree throughout
5. Editing the entire content of the report
6. Discussing unusual matters with a partner
7. Initialing both papers and draft, to evidence review
8. Reviewing the edited draft (or final typed copy) with the client, to ensure that it meets all the client's needs and that there is mutual understanding

Dating the Report. The short-form report normally is dated as of the completion of all important procedures, usually the date when the fieldwork ends. This marks the end of the auditor's opportunity for obtaining knowledge of significant post-balance-sheet events. To preserve this protective feature, not only the long-form report but all others issued under the engagement bear the same date, including any additional copies that may be asked for later.

Report Instruction Sheet. When the edited draft goes into typing it is accompanied by a printed form, signed or initialed by the in-charge accountant, which shows client name, engagement number, date work was completed, date draft was turned in, date delivery is required, number of copies to be rendered and to whom, whether or not the report is the final one to be rendered under the engagement , and what work, if any, is to be done or other matters cleared before rendition. The sheet should be signed by the person or persons who reviewed the papers and the report and should name any partners with whom the report was discussed. It is the authorization for typing and is the basis for other records as the report progresses.

Typing. Whether the typing is done by one typist or by a large department, a style manual for typists is necessary. It should prescribe the firm's rules regarding capitalization, indentions, margins, leaders, underscoring, dollar signs, reference marks, and the like. Only by requiring scrupulous adherence can professional-looking reports be produced. Machines should all have the same style of type, and ribbons should match in color and extent of usage on each machine used for the same report.

In addition to the rendition copies, at least one copy for the files and a proving copy (one for each writing) are required. As soon as a page is removed from the machine, the last sheet is placed over the ribbon copy, to protect it and to serve as a proving copy.

Checking. Proofreading is done by reading from the draft, which should be done by someone other than the one who typed the sheet. All additions and other computations are proved and all loose figures and names are checked to the papers, unless this had been done on the draft before typing. In this case it is necessary only to use special care in the proofreading. Corrections are made and checked on each copy separately. All who perform the typing and various checking operations sign for them on the proving copy.

Reproduction. The firm whose clients require many copies will find that one of the many reproducing machines will be of great value. It will save expensive typing and checking time, besides reducing the danger of errors. Even when only one writing is needed, many firms use the machines. Not only do they produce uniform copies; they do away with such labor as interlaying and removing carbons and making corrections on several copies. Further advantages are that corrections are easily made on the master copy and are not easily detected on the machine copies, and overtyping is easily removed from the bottom of a sheet.

Rendition. It is a courtesy to the client, as well as an opportunity for cementing relations, for the partner in charge of the engagement to deliver the report. For purposes of record, however, the report should still be accompanied by a transmittal letter. If the client has instructed that copies be delivered to others, the letter to the client should state that this has been done, and the letter to that person should say that the reports are being sent him on instructions of the client.

BIBLIOGRAPHY

Accounting Principles Board Opinion No. 3, *The Statement of Source and Application of Funds*, AICPA, New York, 1963.

Accounting Research Study No. 2, *"Cash Flow" Analysis and the Funds Statement*, AICPA, New York, 1961, pp. 51–56.

Financial Statements for Bank Credit Purposes, Robert Morris Associates, Philadelphia, 1951, 1964.

Research Committee Report No. 10, *Internal Audit Reporting Practices*, Institute of Internal Auditors, New York, 1961.

Style Manual, in *Accounting Management Handbook*, AICPA, New York, 1962.

Cashin, James A., and Garland C. Owens: *Auditing*, 2d ed., New York, The Ronald Press Company, 1963, chap. 19.

Copperud, Roy H.: *A Dictionary of Usage and Style*, Englewood Cliffs, N.J., Prentice-Hall, Inc., 1964.

Karsten, Karl G.: *Charts and Graphs*, Englewood Cliffs, N.J., Prentice-Hall, Inc.

Lutz, R. R.: *Graphic Presentation Simplified,* New York, Funk & Wagnalls Company.
Palen, Jennie M.: *Report Writing for Accountants,* Englewood Cliffs, N.J., Prentice-Hall, Inc., 1955, chaps. 20–29; pp. 298–305, 346 of chap. 15.

Davies, J. O.: "The Audit Report," *The Internal Auditor,* June, 1956.
Murray, Edwards B.: "Auditing the General Accounting Activity," *The Internal Auditor,* September, 1957.
Couperthwaite, B.: "The Fine Art of Report Writing," *The Internal Auditor,* June, 1959.
Billings, Thomas N.: "Communication Isn't Just What You Say," *The Internal Auditor,* March/April, 1969.
Bergwerk, Rudolph: "Effective Communication of Financial Data," *The Journal of Accountancy,* February, 1970.

Part Five

Education and Professional Requirements

Chapter **42**

Education and Experience

CHARLES H. ZWICKER

Professor of Accounting and Chairman, Accounting Department, C. W. Post College of Long Island University

GENERAL

Educational Trend. The great advances made in industrial processes and technical skills, together with the creation of new industries, have called for significant changes in the approach to business education. The increase in the number of conglomerate corporations and the effect of international and multinational operations have also had an impact on business education.

This past decade has seen a substantial change in the means, purposes, and results of education. Major foundations have made heavy outlays to study methods by which education for business may be made more meaningful, and the results have been reported in the influential Gordon-Howell report, Roy and MacNeill's *Common Body of Knowledge,* and Frank Pierson, et al., *The Education of American Businessmen,* among others. The impact of these studies has been significant, causing major changes in the business curricula of the universities.

Generalized versus Specialized Education. With the greater complexity of business activities there came a need for greater understanding of business operation. Colleges and universities offered additional courses to meet these needs. There came a tendency for these courses to proliferate to such a degree that some college programs became largely vocational. Much of the training was based on past experience. With the greatly accelerated rate of change, less reliance can be placed on past experience, which may already have become obsolete. In addition to the accounting subjects, the accounting student must have knowledge of broader aspects of business, such as marketing, production, industrial relations, business law, computer technology, and various applications of quantitative theory. The individual as well as the corporation must be aware of social responsibilities. The corporation and its officers must be aware that their help is just as much needed in fostering efficient social services as in the efficient production and distribution of economic goods. Business leaders find that a knowledge of industrial and economic processes is not enough. They must be able to draw on a broader understanding of the social sciences and the humanities and of the effect of change on larger groups of people.

Education Essentials. With the expanding role of the accountant in society and the resulting role of leadership that such a position entails, it is essential that the young people going into the profession be trained for such leadership. As was pointed out in *Horizons for a Profession,* many of these attributes are *qualities,* not definable as knowledge. This was a sound approach to developing a common body of knowledge that each CPA should have upon entering the profession. The ad hoc Committee on Education and Experience Requirements, in its 1969 report,[1] endorsed *Horizons for a Profession* as authoritative for the purpose of specifying the required knowledge. Since this knowledge is to be gained before entering the profession, then it must ordinarily be gained by college study.

As was pointed out in *Horizons, conceptual understanding* is to be valued over *procedural skill.* The accountant must not only know how to calculate a standard deviation but, much more important, must understand the meaning of the concept.

Another important fact pointed out in the *Horizons* study was that some of the most important and significant aspects of the auditor's services cannot be defined as knowledge or even as experience, but in more intangible terms: "wisdom, perception, imagination, circumspection, judgment, integrity."

[1] *Report of the Committee on Education and Experience Requirements for CPAs,* New York, AICPA, 1969.

These qualities are well stated in the introduction and summary of the study, as follows:

> When to speak out, when to be silent, how to say or write that which is necessary but awkward, courage to face up to the need for doing so, talent to be firm yet diplomatic, imagination to see beneath and beyond the surface, perceptivity not only for what has happened but also for what may happen, constancy in ethical behavior, sagacity to avoid errors of omission as well as those of commission: these and other attributes like them are *qualities*, not definable as knowledge but inherent in individuals. Without them a CPA can be nothing more than a technician, regardless of the scope of his knowledge; possessing these attributes plus requisite knowledge, he is a *professional.*[2]

Experience Requirements. On the basis of a thorough study of the present experience requirements, the Committee on Education and Experience Requirements for CPAs concluded that no qualifying experience should be required of those who complete the five-year program. The committee set a target date of 1975 for the adoption of the requirement of five years of study. For the transitional period the committee recommends four years of college study with one year of qualifying experience. The advantages and disadvantages of the experience requirement are discussed in detail in "The Issues Surrounding Qualifying Experience Requirements," by William C. Bruschi, which is included as Appendix C of the committee report. Presently there are wide variations in experience requirements. Eight jurisdictions require no experience for the CPA certificate, while at the other extreme nine jurisdictions have narrow requirements which recognize only public accounting experience. As mentioned, "a lifetime of accounting experience not in public practice is not considered equivalent to a year or so as a junior staff member of a public accounting firm."

The reasons for the committee's recommendation eliminating qualifying experience are summarized in the report as follows:

> 1. We have concluded that the common body of knowledge delineated by *Horizons for a Profession* can be best obtained through college study.
> 2. We recognize a clear-cut distinction between the value of experience and the value of an experience requirement. There can be no question about the value of experience but there is serious doubt about the value of present-day experience requirements.
> 3. It is unreasonable to require a period of qualifying experience for which uniform standards cannot be set and which cannot be effectively policed.
> 4. Experience requirements imply apprenticeship which is inappropriate for a learned profession.
> 5. The continuing dilution, reduction, and elimination of experience requirements is positive evidence of their ineffectiveness and of the trend toward eventual elimination of all experience requirements.
> 6. There is no evidence that CPAs obtaining their certificates in jurisdictions without experience requirements are more often guilty of infractions of the rules of professional conduct or substandard practice than those with extensive experience.
> 7. A fifth year of college study is of greater benefit to the CPA than a year or two of experience as a junior staff member of a CPA firm. While the first years of appropriate experience may enhance certain qualities such as professionalism and technical competence, a college program of at least five years permits the attainment of both breadth and depth of knowledge that is unlikely to be obtained from a four-year program and satisfying an experience requirement.
>
> While the foregoing reasons are the bases for our recommendations, there are two practical considerations which further support our position:
>
> 1. Most CPAs who plan to practice independently will take a position with an established CPA firm for a few years.

[2] Robert H. Roy and James H. MacNeill, *Horizons for a Profession,* AICPA, New York, 1967.

2. Even in the absence of an experience requirement, the time needed to pass all parts of the CPA examination will provide most candidates with a period of practical experience.

Statement of Recommendations. The *Report of the Committee on Education and Experience Requirements* was released in early 1969. The recommendations made in that report supersede those included in the resolutions adopted in 1959 and amended in 1960 and 1962. Following are the recommendations made in the 1969 report:

1. The CPA certificate is evidence of basic competence of professional quality in the discipline of accounting. This basic competence is demonstrated by acquiring the body of knowledge common to the profession and passing the CPA examination.
2. *Horizons for a Profession* [3] is authoritative for the purpose of delineating the common body of knowledge to be possessed by those about to begin their professional careers as CPAs.
3. At least five years of college study are needed to obtain the common body of knowledge for CPAs and should be the education requirement. For those who meet this standard, no qualifying experience should be required.
4. The states should adopt this five-year requirement by 1975. Until it becomes effective, a transitional alternative is four years of college study and one year of qualifying experience.
5. The college study should be in programs comparable to those described in "Academic Preparation for Professional Accounting Careers." [4] The transitional qualifying experience should be in public practice or equivalent experience in industry, government, or college teaching acceptable to state boards of accountancy.
6. Candidates should be encouraged to take the CPA examination as soon as they have fulfilled education requirements and as close to their college graduation dates as possible. For those graduating in June, this may involve taking the May examination on a provisional basis.
7. Student internships are desirable and are encouraged as part of the educational program.
8. The *Report of the Standing Committee on Accounting Education,*[5] which provides that the accreditation of academic programs is the responsibility of the academic community, is endorsed.
9. Educational programs must be flexible and adaptive and this is best achieved by entrusting their specific content to the academic community. However, the knowledge to be acquired and abilities to be developed through formal education for professional accounting are proper and continuing concerns of the AICPA.
10. The AICPA should review periodically the standards of admission requirements for CPAs.

THE MODEL PROGRAM

Introduction. In its report, the ad hoc Committee on Education and Experience Requirements for CPAs pointed out the need for the recommendations specified in *Horizons* to be adopted if accountants are to be equipped to undertake the role recommended in the study. One of the objectives of the committee was to provide more specific guidance to planners of accounting curriculums. In its report, the committee states that the recommended "program for formal education can best be determined by examining an educational program that could, in its opinion, carry out the objectives stated in

[3] Roy and MacNeill, *op. cit.*

[4] AICPA (Committee on Education and Experience Requirements for CPAs), "Academic Preparation for Professional Accounting Careers," *The Journal of Accountancy,* December, 1968. See Appendix D.

[5] AICPA (Standing Committee on Education), *Report of the Standing Committee on Accounting Education,* New York, AICPA, 1966. See Appendix E.

Horizons." These recommendations are summarized in the model program shown below. The classifications are: General Education, General Business, and Accounting. It is understood, of course, that accounting is a part of general business, but for our purposes it can be best treated under a separate caption.

Recommended Programs. The AICPA committee states that at least five years of college study are needed for optimum preparation for a career in accounting. However, for one reason or another many potential entrants to the profession must settle for a four-year undergraduate degree. The recommendation is that the five-year program should be required by 1975. Until it becomes effective, the transitional requirement should be four years of college study and one year of qualifying experience. The four-year program should match the five-year program in scope but should treat the topics at less depth. For those with the recommended five-year program, no qualifying experience would be required. The following requirements are stated in semester hours.

	Five-year	Four-year
General Education:		
Communications	6–9	6–9
Behavioral Sciences	6	6
Economics	6	6
Elementary Accounting	3–6	3–6
Introduction to the Computer	2–3	2–3
Mathematics, Statistics and Probability	12	12
Other General Education	25–18	25–18
	60	60
General Business:		
Economics	6	6
Social Environment of Business	6	3
Business Law	6	4
Production or Operational Systems	3	2
Marketing	3	2
Finance	6	4
Organization, Group and Individual Behavior	9	6
Quantitative Applications in Business	9	6
Written Communication	3	2
Business Policy	3	3
	54	38
Accounting:		
Financial Accounting	9	6
Financial Reporting Theory—Applied		
Financial Accounting Problems—Contemporary		
Financial Accounting Issues		
Cost Accounting	6	3
Cost Determination and Analysis		
Cost Control		
Cost-based Decision-making		
Taxation	3	3
Tax Theory and Considerations		
Tax Problems		
Auditing	6	3
Audit Theory and Philosophy		
Audit Problems		
Computers and Information Systems	6	4
	30	19
Electives	6	3
Total	150	120

Course Topics. The report recommends, in "Preparation for Professional Accounting Careers," that "the Institute neither specify in terms of courses or course hours how this education should be attained nor encourage such criteria to be made a matter of law or regulation."

The educational programs must be flexible to meet the needs of a changing society. As stated, business education must not only keep pace with the latest technology and developments, but must anticipate the changes that take place in business and in the accounting profession.

Accounting education is now provided in a number of ways: (1) the four-year liberal arts school, (2) the undergraduate business school, (3) the two-year junior college plus two years in a senior college, and (4) graduate school. The programs listed as either five-year or four-year programs may be completed in any one of the types of schools listed above or in any combination of these types of schools. It is the trend today for many of the survey courses to be taken in a junior or community college and the advanced courses to be taken in a senior college. The suggested program, as implied by *Horizons,* is designated as a "model program" to distinguish it from various actual programs. The captions used in various segments are *generic terms* rather than *course titles,* and the course hours are provided only to give relative weight to the various topics. The course designations and hours are provided only for *curriculum guidance.*

As in the recommended programs, the suggested course topics are grouped under (1) General Education, (2) General Business, and (3) Accounting. The numerals in parenthesis after each component are the recommended semester hours in the five-year program.

General Education. In this category are included principally the liberal arts subjects, the humanities, philosophy, history, language, and other arts and science courses. Many of the better undergraduate schools require that at least 50 percent of the total required hours be in liberal arts. The total usually is about 60 or 62 hours, depending on the total requirements for the particular school. For the five-year program, this would represent about 40 percent of the total hours. Many schools now give the students wide latitude in the selecting of the courses in this category. Certain courses in this category have a close relationship to accounting. These are the following courses.

Communications (6–9). Effective communication is an indispensable skill of the professional. The student should be able to demonstrate adequate writing ability, not alone in the communication courses, but in every one of his college courses. The emphasis should not be on literary style, but on conveying the intended message clearly, concisely, and precisely, without errors in grammar, punctuation, or spelling.

Behavioral sciences (6). The educated auditor must understand individual and group behavior, the decision process, and organization theory. Specific topics should include authority, learning, motivation, conflict, and innovation. He must know how decisions are made and the formal and informal networks of power within an organization.

Economics (6). The auditor should have a good understanding of the general field of economics, including both elementary macro- and micro-economics. Thus he should acquire an overview of the economy as a whole. This would include national income measurement, monetary and fiscal theories and policies, employment, economic growth, international economics, etc. In micro-economics, the student should gain knowledge of the economic factors that affect the firm, their effects, and their interactions. He should be aware of the relationship of price to demand, of the factor of elasticity, and of the effect of degrees of competition.

Elementary accounting (3–6). The introductory course should be in the General Education section, because an educated individual in an industrial society should know the rudiments of accounting. It is recommended that the introductory course be appropriate for both majors and non-majors. Therefore, the course should emphasize the functions of accounting in a business-oriented society and the conceptual framework of accounting. The primary emphasis of the course should not be on the mastery of procedures.

Introduction to the computer (2–3). A basic knowledge of computers, what they are and what they can do, is necessary for all students. It is desirable that this course be offered early so that the student can use it as a tool in subsequent courses. In this course the student should gain basic knowledge of at least one computer system—the functions, capabilities, and the terms associated with the system. He should acquire knowledge of at least one computer language, sufficient to permit simple programming.

Mathematics, statistics, and probability (12). The auditor should become familiar with mathematical potentials for solving business problems. He should be able to express complex relationships in quantitative terms. This group should include differential and integral calculus, modern algebra, statistics, and probability. The objective should be conceptual understanding rather than manipulative skill.

Other general education (25–18). These courses in the liberal arts area cannot be definitely tied to professional practice. These courses may be required or they may be electives. The trend today is to give the students more leeway in selecting the courses. In general, these courses should supplement the study of the humanities, the physical or social sciences, and the arts, as specified in other areas.

General Business. The general business courses are concerned with broader functions of the business society, such as production, marketing, finance, and some of the social forces which affect business. For expository purposes we are considering accounting as a separate category even though it is actually a part of general business. In the model program this category consists of 54 hours in the five-year program and 38 hours in the four-year program. The individual topics are described below.

Economics (6). The accounting major requires greater depth in economics than is provided in the elementary course (six hours). Further study is required in (1) economic theory and (2) the monetary system. Further knowledge of the operations and theory of the business society is usually included as an objective in an intermediate economics course. The auditor should be thoroughly familiar with the operations of our complex monetary system and the institutions comprising our banking system.

Social environment of business (6). This caption refers to the various social forces which affect business. Topics such as organized labor, black power, poverty programs, etc., will be covered. Courses may be titled "Government Regulation of Business," "Regulatory Agencies," "Administrative Law," etc.

Business law (6). The auditor in his work requires an extensive knowledge of business law. He should understand the meaning of constitutionality, the relationship between federal and state law, and between common law and statutory law. Certainly he should know the law of contracts, agency, commercial paper, sales, property, wills, estates, and trusts. He should be able to apply the principles of law to accounting and auditing problems, and to know when to seek legal counsel.

Production or operational systems (3). The auditor should be familiar with the nature of production and production planning and scheduling. In his work he will also need to be familiar with production terminology and production processes. He should understand how cost accounting relates to the production process.

Marketing (3). The auditor should be aware of the various channels of distribution and the advantages and disadvantages of each type. He should be familiar with the methods of pricing and should know how pricing theory relates to economics. He should be aware of ways that accounting can help in solving marketing problems.

Finance (6). Finance is closer to accounting than many of the other general business subjects. The auditor should be thoroughly familiar with the concepts and methods used in financial analysis. He should be able to evaluate capital needs and to measure the effect of depreciation and taxes on cash flow. He should be able to compute and interpret various financial ratios and the rate of return under alternative courses of action.

Organization, group, and individual behavior (9). This course should relate behavioral sciences to management problems. The topic includes various relationships: organizational, group, intergroup, and individual. As a system designer and as a consultant, the auditor must be aware of the personal factor involved in this work.

Quantitative applications in business (9). In addition to the introductory courses (12 hours), the accounting major should have courses which can help him to develop quantitative solutions to many business problems. These include courses in linear planning, queuing theory, critical-path methods, and simulation. Also, the student should be familiar with statistical sampling, statistical decision theory, and Markov processes. Generally, the courses should be problem-oriented.

Written communication (3). The material presented under General Education (6–9) should be reinforced with a course primarily concerned with written business communication. The auditor must understand how, through the presentation of the data, the selection of words and punctuation, etc., he can effect the desired reaction in the reader. He should be aware of the position and self-interest of the reader.

Business policy (3). This type of course should integrate the material covered in the separate functional fields, such as marketing, production, etc. This course is especially suited to the case method. Some schools present this course as a business game, with sales, advertising, and other decisions aided by up-to-date information supplied by the computer.

Accounting. The report points out that while breadth of understanding is desirable, it should not result in deficiencies in accounting understanding. It should not be a choice between essential and desirable education. Both can be achieved in the five-year program. Conceptual understanding is to be desired above procedural skill, but it is believed that both requirements can be met within the allotted time. The recommendation is for 30 semester hours beyond the elementary course of three to six hours, or a total of 33 to 36 semester hours. The accounting category is classified into four main areas: (1) financial accounting, (2) cost accounting, (3) taxation, and (4) auditing.

Financial accounting (9). This would be a further study of accounting principles beyond the elementary course of three to six hours included under General Education. Generally, this would include two semesters of intermediate accounting and one or two semesters of advanced accounting. While the college courses are entitled "Accounting Principles," they usually include both theory and problems. The Report recommends that the theory include the determination of periodic income, revenue recognition, cost allocation, and the flow of funds. Other areas to be studied are inventory valuation, depreciation theory, liability recognition, and equity measurement. The courses should also include a study of the content and presentation of accounting statements. Theory must be applied in solving practical problems. Corporation problems should include consolidations, conglomerates, and poolings of interest. It is important that accounting be presented as a dynamic discipline, and as directly involved with the problems of today's society.

Cost accounting (6). These courses are more related to managerial accounting. However, in order to provide management advisory services, the public accountant would have to be familiar with cost-based decision making and cost control in addition to his ordinary responsibilities for cost determination. The student should study cost accounting concepts and terminology. These concepts would include direct and indirect costs, cost allocation, allocation of overhead, and cost-volume relationships. He should also be familiar with such cost controls as flexible budgets, profit-center analysis, and standard costs. The student should also be aware of the importance of cost accounting to decision making and planning. Such decisions may be: make-or-buy decisions, product mix, capital budgeting, and inventory planning. The tools might include value analysis, models, and incremental analysis.

Taxation (3). It is neither desirable nor possible to cover the subject of taxes in detail. However, some knowledge of taxes and their impact on decision making is essential. The student should have a broad appreciation of taxes as a revenue source and as a device to control the economy. The student should be able to apply tax principles to business problems, which should be of varying complexity and should involve individuals, partnerships, corporations, trusts, estates, etc.

Auditing (6). The auditor's education should, of course, give particular attention to the audit function, including auditing theory and philosophy. Essential elements of this portion of his education include such topics as evidence, authorizations, basic techniques including sampling, review of internal control, and arithmetic controls, and reconciliations. He should also have an understanding of the role of the independent auditor, his legal responsibilities, his code of ethical conduct, and his standards of reporting, fieldwork, and competence. In addition, the role of the internal auditor as a vital control element within the management organization, whether in industry or in government, should be thoroughly understood.

One suggested outline for a course in auditing is presented by P. E. M. Standish in *The Accounting Review*. He states, "the auditor's education should provide him with an understanding of auditing principles reinforced and expanded by exposure to problems and cases." [6]

Computers and information systems (6). In addition to the introductory course of two to three hours under General Education, the student should develop skills with higher language and the potential uses of the computer. He should know how to examine complex systems and should know the techniques of flow-charting and system analysis. He should develop a basic skill in system and design and know the applicable control procedures.

[6] P. E. M. Standish, "An Appraisal of the Teaching and Study of Auditing," *The Accounting Review*, vol. 39, July, 1964.

REQUIREMENTS FOR SEPARATE FIELDS

Within the auditing profession there is considerable mobility. It is common for auditors with public accounting experience to move into industry or into governmental positions. Likewise, auditors from industry or government may go with public accounting firms. In terms of education, the differences among the three fields are not very significant. Those intending to sit for the CPA examination must complete the courses registered with the state, in some cases, or the college public accounting tract in other states. Ordinarily there are only a few courses which are different on the undergraduate level, between the public accounting tract and the industrial or private accounting tract. In some cases the industrial or private accounting program will permit more electives, since no state requirements may be involved.

Public Accounting. Certified public accountants, like physicians or lawyers, are professional people, licensed by the state and offering their services, as experts, to the general public. The area covered ranges from the individual to the giant corporation, and includes trusts, estates, municipalities, charitable organizations, unions, pension funds, and practically all units of private or public enterprises having a need for record keeping. Generally, CPA work can be separated into three broad classes: auditing, taxes, and management advisory services. However, there may be wide variations among firms, with some firms doing a high proportion of tax work and others doing a high proportion of management advisory services. In general, the CPA's principal function is the examination of the financial statements and the expression of an opinion in his report concerning the fairness of the presentation in the financial statements. Business enterprises, individuals, government, and the general public rely heavily on the integrity, independence, and competence of the public accountant. Without such reliance our business community could hardly operate as it does today. Decisions relating to the investment of funds, the issue of credit, or the operations of a business often depend on the public accountant's report. The public accountant has been held liable, under the Securities Act of 1933, for fraud and for unintentional negligence where financial statements he has examined and upon which he has expressed an unqualified opinion have contained misrepresentations.

Accounting is the youngest of the professions. While record keeping goes back to ancient times, it was not until 1896 that New York became the first state to license certified public accountants. The demand for professional accounting services has expanded to such a degree that the number of CPAs has exceeded 120,000. The number of candidates sitting for the Uniform CPA Examination is around 30,000.

Because of the greater reliance on the work of public accountants and the high degree of knowledge and integrity required, the public interest has demanded ever higher standards. The requirements for admission to the profession are continually being raised to meet the higher standards. Generally, a college degree with a major in accounting is required. In a few states a high school diploma is sufficient, but the number of states with these requirements is rapidly decreasing. Several states offer as an inducement to secure an advanced degree a reduction in the experience requirements.

The regulations for sitting for the CPA examinations and the granting of the certificate are set by the various states, but at the present time all of the states and the District of Columbia use the Uniform CPA Examination of the American Institute of Certified Public Accountants as all, or the principal part, of their written tests of candidates for the certificate. The examinations cover two and a half days and are given twice a year on the same days throughout the country in May and again in November. With a uniform examination being given throughout the country and the requirement of a high level of education to sit for the examination, it is possible to maintain high educational standards. With the expanding role of the accountant, ever-increasing knowledge, gained principally through education, is required.

The experience requirements differ among the various states. However, there is a definite trend toward requiring more education and less experience to enter the profession. The ad hoc Committee on Education and Experience Requirements for CPAs in its report included, as one of its recommendations, ". . . at least five years of college study are needed to obtain the common body of knowledge for CPAs and should be the education requirement. For those who meet this standard, no qualifying experience should be required."

Internal Auditing. Whereas the certified public accountant holds himself out to the general public and to industry for a fee, the internal auditor is allied to one entity and is part of the managerial function. His work proceeds along organizational lines. He is interested in how his organization functions—in the accounting controls which will maximize efficiency and income.

Unlike the certified public accountant, who is subject to regulation by the various states and whose admission to the profession is based on specific educational and experience requirements, no licensure is required of the internal auditor. This does not mean that the basic requirements of education, integrity, general knowledge, and ability are less. Basically, the training is the same, and in some areas it is extended.

The candidate for a career in internal auditing should give greater emphasis to the study of budgeting, controllership, and costing methods. He should give greater attention to courses in taxation. The general background of business organization is important, and the managerial point of view should be acquired.

Some large corporations prefer that the internal auditors have a major in management, with a minor in accounting principles, cost analysis, and auditing being essential. Whether a bachelor's or a master's degree is required depends on the company, although a master's undoubtedly provides the better-trained individual.

In recent years there has been a considerable change in some states in allowing credit toward the CPA degree for internal auditing experience. Formerly only experience in a CPA firm was allowed. For example, if the particular state required two years' qualifying experience, then those two years would have to be in a CPA office. The time period would have to be attested by a CPA.

While most state laws and regulations permit state boards to accept experience in industry or government, it is often not specifically stated in the law that certain experience will be accepted. Recently New York State changed its CPA regulations to permit other than public accounting experience to be allowed, if the applicant has "applied generally accepted accounting principles and generally accepted auditing standards" in his work for the required period.

Governmental Auditing. The federal government, the states, and various county and municipal governments offer a wide variety of employment opportunities for auditors. Depending on the particular agency, the work may be the usual attest function as performed by certified public accountants. For example, the General Accounting Office may audit private corporations having government contracts in somewhat the same manner as the CPA.

There are a very large number of auditors who are employed by various executive agencies such as the Department of Defense, the Internal Revenue Service, the Securities and Exchange Commission, the Federal Bureau of Investigation, etc. An "internal" audit type may involve appraising the financial management and the accounting operation of a military installation or activity, including such areas as procurement and supply, inventory controls, accounting systems and procedures, financial planning and reporting, and management controls.

There is a demand for auditors in state offices, county offices, and various other municipal units, such as school districts, water districts, and various commissions.

Education for governmental auditing does not differ substantially from that for civilian auditing. Preparation generally includes a degree in accounting with at least 24 semester hours in the major. Generally, the agencies seek graduates with high education records and a college degree.

More and more states now give credit for government experience. In some cases one year may be given for each two years of service, or one year may be allowed for each year of government service. Generally, each case is handled on its own merits, and credit will be allowed depending on the diversity of experience and the application of generally accepted accounting principles and generally accepted auditing standards in the work.

CONTINUING EDUCATION

The education of the auditor really begins rather than ends upon his receiving his college degree. As a professional man, he takes on a lifelong commitment to his profession. With the rapid developments during the past decade, this is indeed an onerous burden. He must keep up with the literature of his profession and must keep himself up to date in his field. This entails a long-term period of continuing education. He may obtain this education in a number of different ways. For our purpose, we may group this continuing education into (1) professional responsibilities, (2) employer responsibility, and (3) individual responsibility.

Professional Responsibility. In order that the standards of the profession may be raised, the profession itself, through its professional organizations, must lead the way. Thus when new technologies such as data processing develop quickly, it is necessary to provide study programs, courses, etc., to help the individual member meet the new challenge in the profession. Although the AICPA probably offers the most extensive selection of courses for the continuing education of the auditor, The Institute of Internal Auditors, the National Association of Accountants, and the various state societies of certified public accountants also offer programs which can be of benefit to the auditor. The AICPA offered the following auditing courses in a recent year:

Audits of Inventories
Audits of Savings and Loan Associations
Bank Auditing
Embezzlement—Its Prevention and Control
Fundamentals and Applications of Probability and Statistics
General Standards
Hospital Accounting and Medicare Audits
Income Tax Allocation
Statistical Concepts and Estimation of Dollar Values

Long-form Reports
Short-form Reports
Special Reports
Standards of Fieldwork
Standards of Reporting

Numerous other courses were offered in taxation, practice management, and other fields. Additional courses are continually being developed by the AICPA as well as by all other organizations of the profession.

A vital part of the auditor's continuing education is regular participation in professional development programs, whether sponsored by his employer or by professional organizations.

Employer Responsibility. The employer, whether a CPA firm, industrial company, or government agency, has a responsibility toward the auditor. It is as much to the employer's benefit as to the employee's to have the employee work to the maximum level of his capability. Therefore, various kinds of training are given to help the employee to upgrade his potential. To this end the employer may provide (1) orientation and indoctrination programs, (2) on-the-job training, and (3) staff training.

Orientation and indoctrination. Generally, this is a program offered at the beginning of employment to acquaint the auditor with significant facts about the employer. In some cases a simple guide or a first job assignment for a junior auditor may be described. In some cases the auditor may be placed in each of various departments for a short period.

Job experience. On-the-job training is vital to the development of the auditor's technical competence. Because auditing experience is the application of knowledge to practical situations, it is useful in the attainment of proficiency in the use of procedures and techniques. The auditor learns how to conduct an audit and how to apply accounting principles.

Through job experience, the auditor is able to develop a value system that can serve as the basis for professional judgment. He learns to apply the ever-elusive concept of materiality and becomes aware of professional risks. His judgment in evaluating the quantity and quality of evidence needed for adequate verification is sharpened.

On-the-job training develops the auditor's administrative ability. The auditor learns how an audit is initiated, conducted, and managed. He becomes aware of the details of scheduling staff time and talent, planning the audit work, supervising and reviewing the work, rendering the report, and closing the engagement, and of the many other functions inappropriate for the classroom.

Because through experience the auditor gains technical competence, judgment, and administrative knowledge, on-the-job training may be viewed as a vital extension of the formal educational process.

Staff training. In addition to on-the-job experience and professional development programs, an essential part of the auditor's training also encompasses staff training. Job experience cannot always be equated with staff training, nor should attendance at professional programs be construed as the whole of staff training. Staff training is this and more, and its responsibility rests with both the employer and the auditor himself.

Not all employers will be large enough or interested enough to provide staff programs for employees. Many of the large firms, both CPA and industrial firms, have excellent programs. The individual firms which have the resources to prepare and conduct their own training programs enjoy several advantages. These advantages have been listed as follows:

1. They know the past education of their professional staff personnel.
2. They can assign personnel to conduct training programs.
3. They can induce employees to participate.
4. They can evaluate the employee's increase in competence resulting from the training program.[7]

One firm states its objectives in continuing-education courses for its staff members in the following terms:

1. Improve the competence of our staff members in all technical areas so that they may provide better services to our clients.
2. Assist each person to realize his maximum potential.
3. Create new ideas for practice development.
4. Present the firm's philosophy, policies, and procedures in technical as well as administrative areas.
5. Disseminate developments not only in accounting, but in other phases of business as well.[8]

Many employers of auditors, however, do not have at their disposal the capabilities to sponsor individual firm programs. In these and other instances, programs of professional organizations can be utilized to advantage.

In addition to those firms offering their own programs, there are as many more firms, both CPA and industrial, which will pay for all or a substantial part of educational courses. For example, to encourage further education many firms will pay the tuition or reimburse the employee for college courses taken in the evening. Very often there is a requirement that the course be job-related and that the student receive a passing grade. Also, the employer may pay for tuition in courses or programs offered by professional organizations. For example, a CPA firm may pay for courses, such as staff training programs, offered by the AICPA, or for some of the programs offered by the American Management Association. An industrial company may send employees to courses offered by The Institute of Internal Auditors, the AMA, the NAA, etc.

Individual Responsibility. The individual has a major responsibility for his professional education from the very start. Beyer describes the auditor's self-development as follows:

> Self-interest suggests he learn what his university and his firm require as quickly and as thoroughly as time and circumstances allow. The man who is really determined to become a leader in his profession will learn more than mere requirements in all stages of his career.
>
> Ideally, and hopefully, the whole of one's training in the university and in the firm is accompanied by self-development. This is not something done to or for someone although the individual benefits from the process. Rather it is a stimulus, a challenge to accept personal responsibility for keeping open the door to further enlightenment.[9]

In a program of self-development, the first objective for the auditor, particularly for the independent auditor, after completion of his formal education and indoctrination into his employer's procedures, is his certification as a CPA. This certificate stands as his mark of admission to the accounting profession. Having reached this milestone, the auditor must then ready himself

[7] AICPA Planning Committee, "Education of Certified Public Accountants," *The Journal of Accountancy*, vol. 125, April, 1968, p. 51.

[8] Robert Beyer, "Professional Education for the Accountant: Whose Responsibility?" *The Quarterly*, September, 1964, p. 5.

[9] *Ibid.*, p. 7.

for the challenges thrown at him by change. He must master new techniques, overcome specific deficiencies in his previous training, and remain up to date in his area of special competence.

A program of self-development for the auditor includes a reading plan, active participation in professional and civic organizations, speeches, articles, and self-study programs such as those offered by the AICPA in statistical sampling. Self-development is a never-ending process for the professional auditor.

To paraphrase John W. Gardner in *Self-Renewal*, the exploration of the full range of his own potentialities is not something the auditor can afford to leave to the chances of life. He must pursue it systematically to the end of his professional career. He must look forward to an endless and unpredictable dialogue between his potentialities and the claims of his profession or, greater still, the claims of life—not only those claims he encounters, but the claims he invents.

COMPUTER EDUCATION

Need. Although education in computers was discussed as a part of the formal education for the auditor, rapid technological developments in electronic data processing demand that this topic be given special consideration. Davis states that:

> The auditor should understand EDP for two reasons: (1) so that he can prepare a reliable evaluation of internal control in a computer-based data processing system and (2) so that he can utilize the computer in auditing if the characteristics of the system and the relative cost of the application makes this procedure advisable. Since the computer is becoming omnipresent in all areas of information processing, there is a strong case for the position that all CPAs should have a good knowledge of EDP. A concurrent updating of audit staff computer expertise has often failed to accompany the rapid adoption of computer technology by client companies.[10]

Knowledge Recommended. The auditor who has fieldwork or immediate supervisory responsibility involving a computer should have a general understanding of EDP as provided by the following topics:

1. EDP equipment and its capabilities
2. Characteristics of computer-based systems
3. Fundamentals of computer programming
4. Computer center operations
5. Organization and management of the data processing function
6. EDP documentation
7. Controls in EDP systems
8. Auditing techniques not using the computer
9. Auditing techniques using the computer

Sources of Training. Sources of training available for the auditor of EDP-operated systems include the following:

1. Courses given by computer manufacturers. These include general orientation courses as well as courses in programming and operating particular machines.

2. Courses given by educational institutions. The nature of formal educational courses in computers is discussed in a previous section of this chapter.

[10] Gordon B. Davis, *Auditing and EDP*, New York, AICPA, 1968, p. 231.

3. Self-study and programmed learning. A major drawback of this method of EDP training, however, involves the lack of "hands-on" experience.

4. On-the-job training. On-the-job training can be gained to some degree through proper supervision.

5. Professional development programs. Recently, among the programs offered by the AICPA were the following:

Auditape System Workshop
Auditing of EDP Installations
Introduction to EDP
Principles of Computer Programming
Program Flow-charting and Decision Tables
Systems Flow-charting
Use of Service Bureaus

Many other organizations, such as the American Management Association and The Institute of Internal Auditors, offer seminars on computer topics. The auditor need not be a member to attend.

6. Internal firm programs. Many employers provide in-house training for performing an audit in an EDP environment.

The auditor's education and training should undoubtedly include a combination of some aspects of these methods for achieving continuing expertise in auditing EDP installations.

BIBLIOGRAPHY

Carey, John L.: *The CPA Plans for the Future,* New York, AICPA, 1965.

Carey, John L. (ed.): *The Accounting Profession—Where Is It Headed?* New York, AICPA, 1965.

Carey, John L., and William O. Doherty: *Ethical Standards of the Accounting Profession,* New York, AICPA, 1966.

Davis, Gordon: *Auditing and EDP,* New York, AICPA, 1968.

Report of the Committee on Education and Experience Requirements for CPAs, New York, AICPA, 1969.

Roy, Robert H., and James H. MacNeill: *Horizons for a Profession,* New York, AICPA, 1967.

Williams, Doyle Z.: *A Statistical Survey of Accounting Education 1967–68,* New York, AICPA, 1969.

Cashin, James A., and Garland C. Owens: *Auditing,* New York, The Ronald Press Company, 1963.

Littleton, A. C.: *Essays on Accountancy,* Urbana, Ill., The University of Illinois Press, 1961.

Beyer, Robert: "Professional Education for the Accountant: Whose Responsibility?" *The Quarterly,* September, 1964.

Madden, Donald L., and Lawrence C. Phillips: "An Evaluation of the Common Body of Knowledge Study and Probable Impact upon the Accounting Profession," *The Journal of Accountancy,* July, 1968.

Wheeler, John T.: "Accounting Theory and Research in Perspective," *The Accounting Review,* January, 1970.

Buckley, John W.: "A Perspective on Professional Accounting Education," *The Journal of Accountancy,* August, 1970.

Schneider, Aaron: "Selecting and Developing Internal Auditors," *The Internal Auditor,* September/October, 1970.

Campfield, William L.: "Towards Making Accounting Education Adaptive and Normative," *The Accounting Review,* October, 1970.

Chapter 43

The CPA Examination in Auditing

SAMUEL PERSON

Associate Professor of Accounting and Director of Business Administration, Dowling College

DOYLE Z. WILLIAMS

Associate Professor of Accounting, Texas Tech University

INTRODUCTION

Of the many roles the auditor fills, unquestionably the most visible is his role as an independent reviewer of management's financial reporting to the public. To meet the public's need for assurance of competence of individuals offering or who may offer their services to the public as competent appraisers of the fairness of management's financial reporting, the CPA designation has been devised. The attest function has been uniquely reserved for those who hold the CPA certificate.

As the CPA certificate is a matter of public interest, its granting to properly qualified individuals is done with great care under state rather than private control. Beginning in 1896 with New York, all 50 states, the District of Columbia, Guam, Puerto Rico, and the Virgin Islands have adopted statutes which govern the designation of those who may hold themselves out as CPAs.

Importance of the Examination. One of the most important means used by all boards of public accountancy in judging the qualifications of candidates for certification is the Uniform CPA Examination. The Board of Examiners of the American Institute of Certified Public Accountants (AICPA) has the responsibility for the preparation of the examination and the operation of the Advisory Grading Service, also used by all of the boards of public accountancy.

The Uniform CPA Examination is given in May and November each year. Specific dates and application requirements are available from the boards of accountancy of the respective jurisdictions. The subjects covered by the 2½-day examination are Accounting Practice (two parts), Business (Commercial) Law, Theory, and Auditing.

Purpose of the Examination. The underlying reason for testing the CPA candidates' competence in auditing and related matters is to safeguard the interest of the public (including clients). The purpose of the Uniform CPA Examination, therefore, is to determine that the candidates present "evidence of basic competence of professional quality in the discipline of accounting. The basic competence is demonstrated by acquiring the body of knowledge common to the profession and passing the CPA examination." The examination is designed to measure not only technical knowledge and skill but, even more importantly, disciplined judgment, perception, and objectivity.

Subject Areas. Although the content changes as conditions warrant, generally the CPA examination seeks to measure the candidate's knowledge of the following subject areas:

1. Accounting concepts, postulates, and principles
2. Generally accepted auditing standards, including auditing procedures
3. Business organization and operation, including a knowledge of the basic laws governing such organization and operation
4. Uses and reporting of accounting data for managerial purposes
5. Quantitative methods and techniques as they apply to accounting and auditing
6. Federal income taxes
7. Current professional literature and accounting issues receiving special attention at the time of the examination

In writing the examination, candidates are expected to demonstrate their ability to apply their technical knowledge with good judgment and logical reasoning to specific situations. The examination also seeks to determine the candidate's ability to:

1. Express ideas accurately, clearly, and completely, and in good English
2. Organize accounting data and present them in acceptable form
3. Discriminate among data in a complex situation, and evaluate and classify such data
4. Apply appropriate accounting concepts and auditing procedures to given situations

THE AUDITING EXAMINATION

In the auditing part of the Uniform CPA Examination, a knowledge of generally accepted accounting principles as well as generally accepted auditing standards and procedures is essential. The usual objective of an independent audit is to express an opinion on the fairness of presentation of financial statements in accordance with generally accepted accounting principles.

Although the content of the auditing examination varies, the questions usually emphasize a knowledge of the following topics:

Auditing Standards. The candidate should understand and be able to apply these standards to specific situations.

Accounting Principles. The candidate must know what the generally accepted accounting principles are, the assumptions underlying these principles, and how to determine that they have been applied on a consistent basis.

Professional Ethics. The candidate must understand that public confidence in the profession comes from high standards of performance and a high sense of responsibility to the public interest. He should know that as a CPA he will be expected to comply with the Code of Professional Ethics issued by the AICPA.

Internal Control. The candidate should know the principal elements of an effective internal control system and be able to point out deficiencies in existing controls. He should also have a clear understanding of how the results obtained from the evaluation of internal control may affect audit procedures. A knowledge of the audit effects of an electronic data processing system is essential.

Audit Programs and Procedures. Questions dealing with audit programs attempt to measure the candidate's understanding of the purposes of the programs as well as their design and application to existing situations.

Audit Evidence. Candidates should have a clear understanding of the types and relative value of evidence which may be accumulated in an audit.

Statement Presentation and Auditor's Report. Candidates should be able to evaluate financial statement presentation and disclosure and to determine and write the type of auditor's opinion appropriate to the circumstances. The candidate should also understand the standards for issuing unaudited statements.

Other Topics. Questions on the theory and application of statistical sampling in auditing appear regularly in the examination. The candidate should have a basic knowledge of a computer system and a working knowledge of at least one computer language. He should also be able to flow-chart or diagram an information system of modest complexity.

EDUCATION AND EXPERIENCE

According to "Academic Preparation for Professional Accounting Careers," published by the AICPA, the Committee on Education and Experience Requirements was charged with "reviewing the conclusions of Horizons and recommending to the executive committee a position on education and experience for CPAs as a basis for Institute policy. The report of the committee was presented in early 1969. The specific points are discussed more fully in the preceding chapter.

Education Requirements. Ideally, the candidate who is to be successful on the CPA examination will have adequate general intelligence and a college degree in accounting. His background is likely to include a course in auditing. The report of the Committee on Education and Experience Requirements for CPAs states that

> We have concluded that the common body of knowledge delineated by *Horizons for a Profession* can be best obtained through college study.
>
> A fifth year of college study is of greater benefit to the CPA than a year or two of experience as a junior staff member of a CPA firm.

The college study for those preparing for the profession should be in programs comparable with those described in "Academic Preparation for Professional Accounting Careers."

Experience Requirements. In the past, there has been some question concerning the value of experience in the passing of the auditing examination. Recent evidence, however, has clearly and conclusively established that no significant correlation exists between work experience and success on the auditing examination.[1]

When to Take the CPA Examination. Normally, it is preferable for the would-be CPA to take the CPA examination at the earliest possible moment after he completes his formal educational studies. This point is stated by the Committee on Education and Experience Requirements as follows:

[1] Doyle Z. Williams, "A Profile of CPA Candidates," *The Accounting Review*, vol. 44, January, 1969, pp. 161–162.

Candidates should be encouraged to take the CPA examination as soon as they have fulfilled education requirements and as close to their college graduation dates as possible. For those graduating in June, this may involve taking the May examination on a provisional basis.

If several months have elapsed between the completion of formal accounting study and taking the examination, the candidate will normally have the need to review extensively for the examination. To assist in the review, many candidates have participated in formal CPA review courses. These courses are usually beneficial to the candidate who needs a disciplined, defined, and guided approach to study. The candidate who is highly motivated and possesses a high degree of self-discipline can probably do well on his own.

Time and Place of the Examination. The Uniform CPA Examination is given in each of the jurisdictions in May and November each year on the dates established by the Board of Examiners of the AICPA. The candidate may find the exact date of the examination in *The Journal of Accountancy* and in professional papers and journals. For information concerning the application and the filing period see Chapter 44, "State Laws and Regulations."

Generally, the examination covers four subjects in five sessions over a $2\frac{1}{2}$-day period totaling $19\frac{1}{2}$ hours. The schedule is usually as follows:

Day	*Period*	*Hours*
Wednesday:		
Accounting Practice I	1:30 to 6:00 P.M.	$4\frac{1}{2}$
Thursday:		
Auditing	8:30 A.M. to 12:00 noon	$3\frac{1}{2}$
Accounting Practice II	1:30 to 6:00 P.M.	$4\frac{1}{2}$
Friday:		
Commercial Law	8:30 A.M. to 12:00 noon	$3\frac{1}{2}$
Theory of Accounts	1:30 to 5:00 P.M.	$3\frac{1}{2}$
Total		$19\frac{1}{2}$

In a few states a fifth subject not included in the uniform examination is required. This may be Economics, Ethics, etc.

DEVELOPING AND GRADING THE EXAMINATION

At the present time all 50 states and the jurisdictions of the District of Columbia, Puerto Rico, the Virgin Islands, and Guam use the Uniform CPA Examination and the grading services of the AICPA.

Developing the Examination. The examination is developed by the Director of Examinations of the Institute and his staff from the stockpile of questions and problems maintained. These questions and problems are contributed by accounting practitioners, state board members, and university professors. In some cases students submit questions through their professors, for which the students receive recognition. An exposure draft of the examination is prepared and sent to the Board of Examiners, who may make further revisions before deciding on the final draft.

Grading the Examination. With the exception of objective-type questions or arithmetical problems most questions and problems have no official answer. However, there must be general agreement as to reasonable answers. Thus the answers are in effect a series of points to be discussed by the candidate. These points may range from 1 or 2 to 20 or more. Not all the points have the same relative value. For each particular problem an overall weight is assigned, and then relative weights are assigned for the points within the problem. In addition credit is given for reasoning, organizing, analytical ability, etc. The individual weights are recorded with the overall weight to yield a point score for each question or problem. All graders are Certified Public Accountants. Some are accountants in practice; others are teachers. A very careful "dry-run" sample is graded and evaluated before the rest of the papers are graded. There are now about 30,000 candidates taking the examination. Each grader will grade only one question or problem. The examination papers are processed in batches of about 25. When the grading for a batch has been completed, the scores for each candidate are totaled and the related papers given to a reviewer. These reviewers usually have had several years of grading experience and look over the candidate's performance as a whole, watching for low scores in an otherwise good overall paper. Any tendencies toward erroneous grading by individual graders are noted and corrected. Generally the reviewing process is concentrated on papers in the middle ground. Those papers with scores so high that regrading could not possibly reduce them below 75 are passed fairly quickly. Those papers with scores so low that regrading to 75 is not possible are also placed aside. The Director of Examinations receives daily statistics on scoring and maintains cumulative summaries for each subject. Any unexpected change in pattern will be investigated immediately.

After the grading has been completed, the results will be posted by states, giving the candidate's number and grade on each subject. Any inconsistencies will be reviewed by the Director of Examinations, who will look for inconsistencies in grades among subjects. Further review and regrading may also be done at this point if warranted.

After all papers have been graded and all reviews made where necessary, the examination papers with grades will be returned to the state boards. The state boards will review the papers and notify the candidates of their performance. With such a painstaking grading process, it is seldom necessary to have any further regrading by the AICPA advisory grading service.

PREPARING FOR THE AUDITING EXAMINATION

There is no universal, guaranteed way to prepare for the CPA examination that will apply in every case. Each candidate must develop his own review and study programs in light of his own particular situation. Accordingly, the following suggestions are general in nature and must be appropriately considered and supplemented by each candidate.

Maintain Disciplined Program. The candidate who engages in a program of self-review for the CPA examination should follow closely a well-defined program of disciplined study. He should set aside a given period of time each day and devote that time exclusively to relentless, productive study. Assuming that the candidate has completed successfully an acceptable college program, the next most important factor is adequate preparation. With career, family, and other commitments a disciplined program requires sacrifices from the candidate, his family, and often his employer.

Allow a Sufficient Period of Time. The candidate should begin his review for the CPA examination at least 2 to 3 months, preferably longer, prior to the examination date. As with his business assignments the candidate should approach the preparation for the CPA examination in an organized and systematic manner. Generally a written schedule or time budget is desirable. Without some kind of target the time often goes by without commensurate results. Unless a sufficient time period is allowed, it may be necessary to put in long hours, evenings, holidays, and weekends in a crash program that will usually be less effective. Success on the examination requires a good study plan and an adequate commitment of time and effort.

Review All Subjects Simultaneously. If the candidate is sitting for other parts of the examination, he will find it useful to review all subjects simultaneously. Simultaneous review is possible and practical, since the subjects of the examination are interrelated. Thus, preparation for theory helps in auditing, since a vital part of the auditor's concern is the determination of consistent application of generally accepted accounting principles. Obviously, an awareness of the latter is essential for success on the Theory examination. Further, preparation for business (commercial) law aids in auditing, since much of the auditor's concern lies with such questions as the passing of title. Finally, it would seem obvious that preparation for the Accounting Practice examination aids in auditing, since it requires knowledge of accounting problems.

Review Auditing Text. As a first step for preparation for the Auditing examination, the candidate should refresh his knowledge of auditing standards and procedures. In this respect, a thorough review of a recent edition of a widely used college auditing textbook is recommended. Because of the increasing role of computers in performing the audit function, the candidate should supplement his study with a review of the text *Auditing and EDP*, published by the AICPA.

Review Official Pronouncements. The candidate should read or review all official pronouncements of the AICPA relative to accounting and auditing. For example, it is essential for the successful candidate to know and understand thoroughly the Opinions of the Accounting Principles Board and the Statements on Auditing Procedure, issued and published by the AICPA. He should study especially Statements on Auditing Procedure No. 33, *Auditing Standards and Procedures.*

Review Current Literature. The candidate should be familiar with current issues and topics in accounting and auditing. Thus, he should make *The Journal of Accountancy* (published by the AICPA) part of his regular reading diet, supplemented by *The Accounting Review* (published by the American Accounting Association), and various state society periodicals. The candidate may also find *Management Services* (published by the AICPA) helpful in keeping him abreast of developments in electronic data processing (EDP), systems and controls, and related topics.

Solve Past Problems. Solving recent CPA examination problems is widely held to be an excellent way for the candidate to prepare for the CPA examination. Official questions and unofficial answers to prior examinations are available from the AICPA.

In solving prior examination problems, the candidate should be careful to:

1. Write within the time suggested for the problem.
2. Not look at the unofficial solutions until the time allowed for a problem has been exhausted.

Review of prior examinations should be designed to pinpoint deficiencies in the candidate's knowledge and help him develop approaches to solutions.

Prepare Outlines, Notes, etc., of Important Points. During the period of study the candidate should make extensive outlines, notes, etc., of important points covered. A review of the outlines and notes helps greatly to reinforce the retention of data covering a great deal of material. If the candidate has developed a habit of taking notes in college, it will be simple to make notes for the examination. As the examination nears and the pressure increases, it reassures a candidate to be able to refer to a summary of the material studied and to refresh his memory and bolster his morale.

WRITING THE AUDITING EXAMINATION

As the candidate approaches the day he actually writes the Auditing examination, he should keep certain mechanical considerations in mind. Although some of these matters might appear trite, they have helped many candidates and thus are worthy of mention here. No importance, however, should be attached to the order of presentation of the following suggestions:

Order of Attacking Problems. A candidate should first review all questions on the examination quickly. He should then assign priority of questions as follows:

Answer first the easiest questions in terms of individual ability and knowledge.

Answer second the hardest questions. It is imperative that once a candidate has committed himself to a choice of questions, he should keep going at a steady pace. In attacking a given problem once he has selected the order of attack, he should carefully review and analyze the facts. At this second reading, the candidate should underline all pertinent data and cross out unnecessary data.

Read Questions Very Carefully. One of the essentials on the examination is a very careful reading of the question or problem. Very often a candidate, being mindful of the tight time allowances, begins the answer before he has analyzed the question. The time allowances are sufficient to permit a careful reading of the question. Before beginning the answer, the candidate should:

1. Read the requirements of the question
2. Quickly scan the facts of the question as related to the requirements
3. Read very carefully the facts of the question, using marginal notes and underlines to indicate significant facts

Interpret Requirements. Caution should be exercised in reading questions, following instructions, and determining requirements. Common sense should be used. Candidates should not "read into" questions or look for tricks. Assumptions should be made only if essential. When assumptions are made, the candidate should state in his answer what he has assumed and *why*. Questions should not be criticized. Indeed, if a fact is not stated, it should not be assumed that the fact is pertinent.

Outline Points. Before beginning the answer, an outline of the principal points should be developed either mentally or in writing. In order to secure maximum credit, all salient points pertinent to the question should be carefully considered before the answer is formulated.

Organize Answers. Answers should be thought out and organized in accordance with the outline developed. A "mental picture" of the solution should be envisioned before it is approached.

In problems requiring computations, a candidate should leave a "trail" of his work. Computations supporting formal answers should be "keyed" or cross-referenced to the answer. No more information than is absolutely essential should be copied from the material provided in the question.

Worksheets or journal entries should be utilized only when necessary. All solutions and conclusions should be supported and papers properly identified.

Budget Time. Failure to make efficient use of time is one of the most frequent causes of failure on the examination. The candidate should budget his time according to the weights of the questions and problems. The weight or estimated time for each question or problem is specifically included on the examination as a guide to the allotted time. The candidate should try to solve all the problems in the examination. A partial solution is better than none. If time grows short, it is wise to outline logically and briefly what additional steps are required or what the remainder of the approach would be. If possible notes should be given on the theory related to the problem.

Exercise Judgment. The exercise of "judgment" is a prime factor to consider in taking the auditing examination. An answer may show evidence of considerable technical knowledge but may also display a lack of professional judgment, which is vital to the auditor. For example, the candidate may memorize audit programs and procedures and list all procedures rather than only those which are relevant. A most important attribute of the CPA is his judgment in selecting the auditing procedures which are appropriate in the particular circumstance. The candidate is expected to be able to show in his answers that he possesses the required judgment at that point. The candidate must be able to distinguish important procedures from those which are relatively unimportant. He should give adequate consideration to the major points.

Use Captions, Short Sentences, etc. In answering auditing questions, the candidate should use the outline or tabular approach as much as possible. He should use captions to outline his points, then fill in additional supporting or explanatory data for each caption. Such information should be given in short sentences and short paragraphs. If these points are kept in mind, the principal points are easily identified and conflicting statements are readily apparent. The main ideas can be stated concisely and generalizations avoided. For emphasis the captions and principal points may be underlined.

Answering Procedural Questions. Questions related to auditing procedures can be answered most effectively if the candidate remains aware of some general approaches. In this connection, five items to consider are discussed below.

1. *General Internal Control Considerations.* Since evaluation of internal control is a significant objective in any audit, the candidate should be aware of the general internal control characteristics and how they relate to the pertinent auditing procedures. The basic characteristics of internal control, as stated in Statements on Auditing Procedure No. 33, are as follows:

a. A plan of organization which provides appropriate segregation of functional responsibilities

b. A system of authorization and record procedures adequate to provide reasonable accounting control over assets, liabilities, revenues, and expenses

c. Sound practices to be followed in performance of duties and functions of each of the organizational departments

d. A degree of quality of personnel commensurate with responsibilities

2. *Basic Procedural Routines.* Basic to the audit of any account is the application of procedures necessary to accomplish the outlined objectives. These may be stated broadly as follows:

a. Verification and testing of reliability of books of account and related documents

b. Physical inspection and observation
c. Confirmation
d. Securing client representations
e. Analysis, comparison, and review
f. Inquiry

This is not intended to suggest that no other procedures are applicable. These are *broad* guidelines. An alert candidate can relate these basics to every given circumstance in terms of developing audit programs. Thus, for example, the question of the applicability of statistical sampling would relate to the first basic procedural routine listed above to the extent that "testing" is involved.

3. *Audit Objectives—Assets.* As a general rule the objectives of most audits with respect to assets are to determine the reliability of internal control as it relates to the asset. Based on the reliability of internal control the audit objectives are to determine the existence, ownership, valuation, classification, and balance sheet classification.

4. *General Audit Objectives—Liabilities.* With respect to liabilities the auditor is concerned with determining existence, valuation, classification, and balance sheet presentation.

5. *Concept of the Opinion Audit.* Many CPA examination questions concern the opinion the CPA expresses in his report at the completion of his audit. The fourth reporting standard states that "The report shall either contain an expression of opinion regarding the financial statements taken as a whole, or an assertion to the effect that an opinion cannot be expressed." Often on the basis of given facts he has to determine which of the following opinions would be appropriate: (1) unqualified, (2) qualified, (3) adverse, or (4) disclaimer.

Answering Narrative Questions. A high percentage of auditing questions require narrative answers. The candidate should attempt to write clearly, logically, legibly, and to the point. He should not be too concerned with writing style. He should avoid general or vague answers to specific questions. Precise audit terms should be used, not such phrases as "check the cash receipts." The candidate should state *how* it is to be done: Are the cash receipts to be counted, vouched, footed, etc.?

BIBLIOGRAPHY

Board of Examiners, AICPA: *Information for CPA Candidates,* AICPA, New York, 1970.

Requirements for CPA Examination and Certification in 50 States and District of Columbia, Department of Defense, Washington, D.C., November, 1967.

Rules and Regulations of the particular State Board of Accountancy. (Since state requirements differ, the candidate must obtain a copy of the applicable rules and regulations from the State Board of Accountancy in his state.)

Carey, John L.: *The CPA Plans for the Future,* New York, AICPA, 1965.

Edwards, James Don, and John W. Ruswinckel: *The Professional CPA Examination,* New York, McGraw-Hill Book Company, 1963.

Newman, Benjamin: *Auditing CPA Review Text,* 2d ed., New York, John Wiley & Sons, Inc., 1964.

Public Accountancy, Law, Rules, Information, Handbook 14, The University of the State of New York, The State Education Department, Albany, 1966.

Roy, Robert H., and James H. MacNeill: *Horizons for a Profession,* New York, AICPA, 1967.

Walden, Robert E., and Ray M. Powell: *CPA Coaching, Auditing,* Boston, Houghton Mifflin Company, 1962.

Williams, Doyle Z.: *Uniform Statistical Information Questionnaire Data—A Supplementary Report,* New York, AICPA, April, 1968.

Bonderow, Simon, and Frederick E. Harzer: "Preparing for and Taking the CPA Examination," *The GAO Review,* Fall, 1969.
Bruschi, William C.: "CPA Candidates—What Are They Like?" presented at annual meeting of the Association of CPA Examiners, Sept. 18, 1965.
AICPA Committee on Education and Experience Requirements for CPAs, "Academic Preparation for Professional Accounting Careers," *The Journal of Accountancy,* December, 1968.
Williams, Doyle Z.: "A Profile of CPA Candidates," *The Accounting Review,* vol. 44, January, 1969.
Bruschi, William C.: "Issues Surrounding Qualifying Experience Requirements," *The Journal of Accountancy,* March, 1969.

Chapter **44**

State Laws and Regulations

ROBERT G. ALLYN

Executive Secretary, New York State Board of CPA Examiners

NATURE OF CPA PRACTICE

Introduction. The auditor operates within a framework of laws and regulations that govern his activities related to:

1. Licensure or certification to practice
2. The standards to be followed in the examination of financial data and statements
3. The expression of an opinion on financial statements
4. Other functions related to his professional service

It is the purpose of this chapter to outline and describe the principal features of state laws and regulations in force in the United States that specify the auditor's qualifications to enter practice and his continuing statutory responsibilities while he is engaged in practice. Although standards of professional competence and propriety embodied in regulatory codes of professional conduct or ethics have been covered elsewhere in this book, some consideration will be given in this chapter to grievance procedures that come within the rules of professional conduct. A further limitation of the scope of this chapter is that it is related mainly to the licensure or certification of independent public accountants who serve clients in the capacity of outside auditor, rather than those internal or governmental auditors who serve as employees. There are no legal requirements to render service as an internal or governmental auditor. It is the public accountant who must satisfy state statutes and regulations setting forth qualifications such as education and experience before he can hold himself out as independent and qualified to use the designation "Certified Public Accountant," "Public Accountant," or some other title permitted by statute.

Historical Background of Certification. The genesis of the auditor in western culture as an expert in accounting and as an independent observer and judge of the correctness and integrity of financial statements can be traced at least as far back as the thirteenth century. Although the origin of a professional class of auditors is mainly identified with Great Britain and the United States, records exist throughout the European continent and dating from the early days of the commercial revolution of the employment by guilds, cities, estates, and other enterprises of auditors charged with the responsibility of assuring owners of their managers' accountability and stewardship over funds and property. The early auditors were usually employees rather than independent professional accountants. With the steady and widespread growth of trade, commerce, and industry, however, auditors in Great Britain and the United States began in the eighteenth century to list their names in city directories offering their services to the public. By the middle of the nineteenth century professional societies of accountants had been formed in Scotland (1854) and in several cities in England (1870–1880). Following the organizational structure of the guilds, the professional societies of accountants and auditors were chartered by the crown. English and Scottish public accountants who comprised the membership came to be known by the designation "Chartered Accountant."

The need for the services of independent auditors was further extended in England, bringing with it legal recognition when Parliament passed laws regulating the formation of joint stock companies. These laws provided for "the appointment of auditors who would be representatives of the shareholders and report to them," and further directed that "the balance sheet and the auditors' report be sent to the registrars of joint stock companies as well as the shareholders before the general meeting."[1] Thus it was that a need for a professional class of auditors, springing from economic necessity, came to be coupled with the protection of the public welfare or interest.

The demand for accounting and auditing services and the necessity of providing a measure of protection of the public welfare were equally potent forces in shaping the evolution of the profession in the United States. Economic and political factors that shaped this country's history, however, served to bring about a somewhat different relationship among practitioners, their clients, and the public. For example, in the United States the designation comparable to the British designation of "Chartered Accountant" is "Certified Public Accountant," or "CPA." The right to use this designation is a privilege regulated by state statutes and granted to those who meet statutory or regulatory qualifications of residency, citizenship, education, and experience, and who have passed the Uniform CPA Examination that is prepared and graded by the American Institute of Certified Public Accountants (AICPA).

In Canada the Institute of Chartered Accountants of the Province of Quebec was formed in 1880. The Dominion Association of Chartered Accountants was established in 1902 and changed its name in 1950 to the Canadian Institute of Chartered Accountants.

The profession of public accountancy was given initial legal recognition in the United States by the State of New York in 1896. The first statute, which served as a pattern for other states, provided:

CERTIFIED PUBLIC ACCOUNTANTS

Laws of New York 1896 ch. 312

An Act to Regulate the Profession of Public Accountants

1. Any citizen of the United States, or person who has duly declared his intention of becoming such citizen, residing or having a place for the regular transaction of business in the State, being over the age of 21 years and of good moral character, and who shall have received from the Regents of the University a certificate of his qualifications to practice as a public accountant as hereinafter provided, shall be styled and known as a certified public accountant; and no other person shall assume such title, or use the abbreviation C.P.A. or any other words, letters or figures, to indicate that the person using the same is such certified public accountant.

In short order, the following states enacted legislation creating a professional class of auditors: Pennsylvania (1899), Maryland (1900), California (1901), Illinois (1903), Washington (1903), and New Jersey (1904). By 1968, all states, the District of Columbia, Puerto Rico, the Virgin Islands, and Guam had adopted legislation providing for the certification of public accountants.

Unlike the practice in the United Kingdom, the performance of the attest function in the United States has not been restricted solely to auditors who are members of a professional society of public accountants, nor is it restricted only to public accountants licensed by the state. Some states have not adopted regulatory legislation limiting the practice of public accountancy solely to those who meet statutory qualifications. In other words, as will be described in detail in the following paragraphs, the right to practice as a public accountant or independent auditor is not uniform in this country; it is restricted in some states and unrestricted in others. A listing of the permissive and regulatory states appears in Table 3 (page 44-20).

[1] A. C. Littleton, *Essays on Accountancy,* Urbana, Ill., The University of Illinois Press, 1961, pp. 95–96.

Certification and Licensure. Public accountancy as a certificated profession is to be distinguished from a licensed profession. Generally, most state laws have accorded public accountancy the status of a certificated profession by conferring the exclusive right to use a designation, such as "Certified Public Accountant" or "Public Accountant." Such certification does not confer the exclusive right to practice or perform certain prescribed services. The health professions exemplify those licensed professions that restrict certain defined acts to those persons who have met qualifications established by statute. One obstacle in according the profession of public accountancy the status of licensure is the lack of agreement as to what constitutes the elements of a definition of the profession. Neither the AICPA in its recommended regulatory legislation [2] nor the National Association of State Boards of Accountancy in its proposed model regulations [3] has defined public accountancy. A few states have promulgated a statutory definition of public accountancy.

A few examples appear as follows:

California

A person shall be deemed to be engaged in the practice of public accountancy within the meaning and intent of this chapter:

(*a*) Who holds himself or herself out to the public in any manner as one skilled in the knowledge, science and practice of accounting . . . ; or

(*b*) Who maintains an office for the transaction of business as a public accountant; or

(*c*) Who offers to prospective clients to perform for compensation, or who does perform on behalf of clients for compensation, professional services that involve or require an audit, examination, verification, investigation, certification, presentation, or review, of financial transactions and accounting records; or

(*d*) Who prepares or certifies for clients reports on audits or examinations of books or records of account, balance sheets, and other financial, accounting and related schedules, exhibits, statements, or reports which are to be used for publication or for the purpose of obtaining credit or for filing with a court of law or with any governmental agency, or for any other purpose; or

(*e*) Who, in general or as an incident to such work, renders professional services to clients for compensation in any or all matters relating to accounting procedure and to the recording, presentation, or certification of financial information or data. [Section 5051 amended and renumbered by chap. 310, Laws 1959.]

Indiana

A public accountant is hereby defined as a person skilled in the science of accounting, who holds himself out to the public as a professional accountant practicing for compensation, whose time during the regular business hours of the day is devoted to the practice of accounting as such professional public accountant. [Section 1 as last amended by Acts 1945, chap. 326.]

District of Columbia

For the purpose of this chapter a public accountant is hereby defined as a person skilled in the knowledge and science of accounting, who holds himself out to the public as a practicing accountant for compensation, and who maintains an office for the transaction of business as such, whose time during the regular business hours of the day is devoted to the practice of accounting as a professional public accountant. [Feb. 17, 1923, 42 Stat. 1261.]

[2] Form of Regulatory Public Accountancy Bill, approved by the AICPA Committee on State Legislation, New York, 1956, amended 1958 and 1961.

[3] Model Rules to Support Form of Regulatory Public Accountancy Bill, approved by the Committee on Legislation and Regulation, Association of Certified Public Accountant Examiners (now National Association of State Boards of Accountancy), New York, 1967.

New York

The public practice of accountancy within the meaning of this article is defined as follows: An individual engages in the public practice of accountancy who, holding himself out to the public, in consideration of compensation received or to be received by him, offers to perform or does perform for other persons, services which involve signing, delivering or issuing or causing to be signed, delivered or issued any financial, accounting or related statement or any opinion on, report on, or certificate to such statement if, by reason of the signature, or the stationery or wording employed, or otherwise, it is indicated or implied that such individual has acted or is acting, in relation to said financial, accounting or related statement, or report as an independent accountant or auditor or individual having or purporting to have expert knowledge in accounting or auditing. [Article 149, Section 7401.4 of the Education Statute.]

Registration. Registration is to be distinguished from certification and licensure. In order to continue the right to remain in practice, many states require public accountants to register and pay a fee periodically, such as annually or biennially. As of the present writing, five jurisdictions—Alabama, Delaware, the District of Columbia, North Dakota, and Vermont—do not require public accountants to register their intent to practice. Nine jurisdictions—Alaska, California, Illinois, Indiana, Massachusetts, New Jersey, New York, Pennsylvania, and Virginia—provide for biennial registration. The remaining 39 jurisdictions require annual registration.

The penalty for failure to register periodically differs among the states. Some states require registration and payment for a permit if the public accountant holds himself out to practice; if he does not practice or wish to hold himself out to practice, registration is not required (e.g., New York). Moreover, in these states certification is retained until revoked. Some other states require periodic registration to maintain the basic status of public accountant in that state (e.g., Oregon). In all states requiring registration, practice without a current authorization subjects the public accountant to penalties. The Oregon Statute states:

Failure to renew a permit before expiration thereof shall not deprive a licensee or holder of a certificate of certified public accountant of the right of renewal, but in such cases a delinquent renewal fee of $12.50 shall be paid for each year of delinquency; provided, however, that no permit shall be renewed after a period of five years from the date of expiration. [Statute Section 673.150.]

QUALIFICATIONS TO PRACTICE

The qualifications to hold oneself out to practice public accountancy differ from state to state. For a detailed and current statement of the requirements of a state, it is suggested that the reader contact the Secretary of the State Board of Accountancy of the state in which he is interested. Because state laws and regulations governing entrance into the profession are subject to constant change, a detailed outline of state laws will not be attempted here. Instead, a general discussion will be given in the following sections of the requirements found in all state laws and regulations under the headings of:

1. Citizenship
2. Residence
3. Age
4. Character
5. Education
6. Experience

In the pages that follow the basic qualification to practice as a public accountant will be related only to practice as a certified public accountant. However, in a later section of this chapter, reference will be made to those states that have enacted regulatory legislation resulting in the licensing, registration, or enrollment of noncertified public accountants.

Citizenship. With the exception of Kentucky, all states require the applicant to be a citizen of the United States or to have at least filed a Declaration of Intention. An immigrant, at least eighteen years old and lawfully admitted to the United States for permanent residence, may file a Declaration of Intention with the nearest office of the Immigration and Naturalization Service of the U.S. Department of Justice, at any time (Form N-300) after his admission for permanent residence.[4] Most state laws stipulate that the certificate will be revoked or voided if the holder does not become a citizen within a specified period of years (e.g., Pennsylvania, 6 years).

Residence. The residence requirement varies from no requirement in some states up to 2 years in others. Certain states specify 1 year (Arizona, Hawaii, Indiana, Maine, Maryland, Montana, North Carolina, North Dakota, Tennessee); California requires 3 months. Several states do not indicate a period of time but require that the applicant be a resident of the state at the time of application, or at the time of certification, or both. New York specifies that the applicant must be a resident at the time of taking the last subject of the CPA examination. Several states permit the applicant to offer the alternative of residence or having a place of business within the state. At least one state (Arkansas) requires both residence and place of employment to be within the state.

Applicants who plan to become certified public accountants occasionally find themselves in difficulty because of the failure to familiarize themselves with these requirements. For example, an applicant may be a resident at the time he is admitted to the CPA examination. During the time he is sitting, or before he formally applies for the certificate, he may change residence or transfer permanently to an employment out of the state. Under these circumstances he may be disqualified from receiving the certificate in the state where he initially qualified. Applicants transferred out of the state for military service are usually exempt from these requirements.

A further requirement to consider is that residence usually is interpreted to mean legal or voting residence, not merely a mailing address, or the place of permanent full-time employment. An applicant is well advised to correspond with his state board if he anticipates a change in residence or place of employment and request a ruling if the question of residence is one that is subject to an interpretation of the statute or regulations.

Age. With the exception of the following, most states and territories require applicants to be twenty-one or over either to qualify to sit for the CPA examination or to qualify for the certificate after passing the examination: Alaska, nineteen years; Kentucky, twenty-three years; Maine, no age specified; South Carolina, legal age; Wisconsin, over twenty-three years.

Character. All states specify that an applicant be of good moral character. Application forms invariably ask the applicant to answer a question whether he has ever been convicted of a crime or misdemeanor. An untruthful answer not only will disqualify the applicant but may subject him to a charge of perjury. It should be noted, however, that a criminal conviction does not permanently forestall the applicant from becoming a public accountant, as

[4] Naturalization Requirements and General Information, Form n-17, revised Nov. 11, 1964, U.S. Department of Justice, Immigration and Naturalization Service.

many states will accept evidence of rehabilitation to support a claim of good moral conduct. To further satisfy themselves of the good moral character of a candidate for the certificate, some state boards of examiners (New Jersey, Georgia) require the candidate to appear before the board for a personal character interrogation. The state of Georgia requires each candidate for the certificate to swear to the following oath:

I accept this certificate as a Certified Public Accountant with full realization of the responsibilities and obligations which I thereby assume.

I hereby solemnly swear to support the Constitution of the United States; and to support the Constitution of the State of Georgia so long as I remain a citizen thereof or practice therein.

I further swear that I will, to the best of my ability, perform my duties in the practice of my profession; that I will abide by the rules of professional conduct as promulgated by constituted authority; and, that I will always endeavor to uphold the honor and dignity of the accounting profession.

Education. It is difficult to describe generally the educational qualifications in effect in the 50 states, the District of Columbia, Puerto Rico, the Virgin Islands, and Guam. Table 1 outlines the requirements in effect as of January 1, 1971. It will be noted that by 1975, 30 jurisdictions will mandate the baccalaureate degree as the minimum educational qualification, or what the state

TABLE 1 States' Educational Requirements

State	College degree *	2 years college	No college
Alabama	1/72		
Alaska	......	X	
Arizona	X		
Arkansas	X		
California	X		
Colorado	X		
Connecticut	X		
Delaware	......	X	
District of Columbia	......	X	
Florida	X		
Georgia	X		
Hawaii	X		
Idaho	X		
Illinois	X		
Indiana	......	......	X
Iowa	......	......	X
Kansas	......	......	X
Kentucky	7/74		
Louisiana	9/75		
Maine	7/74		
Maryland	......	X	
Massachusetts	X		
Michigan	1/75		
Minnesota	......	......	X
Mississippi	......	......	X
Missouri	7/72		
Montana	......	......	X
Nebraska	......	......	X
Nevada	X		
New Hampshire	......	......	X
New Jersey	X		
New Mexico	X		
New York	X		
North Carolina	......	X	
North Dakota	......	......	X
Ohio	......	X	
Oklahoma	......	......	X
Oregon	......	......	X
Pennsylvania	X		
Rhode Island	X		
South Carolina	X		
South Dakota	......	X	
Tennessee	3/73		
Texas	......	X	
Utah	X		
Vermont	......	......	X
Virginia	X		
Washington	......	......	X
West Virginia	X		
Wisconsin	X		
Wyoming	......	......	X
Puerto Rico	......	......	X
Virgin Islands	......	......	X
Guam	7/73		
Totals	30	8	16

NOTE: Many states provide for substitution of college and graduate study for a portion of the experience requirement.

* Includes states accepting study at business and correspondence schools which the board considers equivalent.

X = requirement in effect. Dates indicate when requirement becomes effective.

board of examiners, or education department, or designated authority, deems is equivalent. Combinations of experience and education in business or correspondence schools are considered to be equivalent to a college degree in some jurisdictions.

Registered programs. A few states, for example, Colorado, New Jersey, and New York, in addition to requiring a college degree, require registration of the degree program with the state board or department of education. These states publish a list of colleges and universities that have registered programs in accounting leading to a baccalaureate or postbaccalaureate degree. These and other states have established standards for the registration of accounting programs in terms of quality of students admitted to the program, faculty qualifications, course of studies, grade point averages for graduation, physical facilities such as library, and other standards believed to be essential for a quality program in accountancy.

Graduate programs. With regard to future developments in the educational requirements, the computer revolution has sparked some significant changes in education for the profession. Advanced mathematical and statistical techniques are available to the accountant that were hitherto impractical without the computing capabilities of an electronic computer. This has opened up a great demand for accountants and auditors possessing a knowledge of higher mathematics and statistics in addition to a knowledge of accounting and business methods and procedures. As a consequence, the 4-year baccalaureate program may be found inadequate to cover both the arts and science courses as well as the professional courses. Several states now permit a waiver of experience if a candidate has a postbaccalaureate degree. For example, the Colorado statute provides for the waiver of three years' experience for candidates with a baccalaureate degree if the candidate

> has completed an additional thirty semester hours or the equivalent thereof and has attained a graduate degree in a college or university which is approved by the board, in the graduate study of accounting, business law, economics or finance. [Section 2-1-6, Colorado statute.]

All states that require a college degree request the applicant to have his college or university file an official transcript of studies with the appropriate board or licensing agency. Those states not requiring a college degree request proof of at least a high school diploma or secondary school educational equivalent. Candidates with foreign education are advised to have original records available with official translations for review by a board of examiners.

Experience. The profession of public accountancy is one of the few professions that has continued to demand that candidates for licensure give evidence of prescribed employment, in addition to the formal educational processes. These requirements usually cover the term and type of employment and, in a few cases, the nature of services rendered. They are to be found in the laws and regulations of the states' accountancy statutes and the rulings of the various state boards of accountancy.

The experience qualification dates back to the beginning of the twentieth century when candidates were required to have earned no more than a secondary school diploma and when accountancy and auditing practices and procedures were learned through a combination of employment and correspondence or night school study. The introduction of business and accounting courses leading to the award of baccalaureate or higher degrees by colleges and schools of business administration and the concurrent demand by the profession for more highly trained personnel have caused the profession to place less emphasis upon experience as a prerequisite for the certificate. Internship programs inaugurated by a few schools of business as part of the educational program, on-the-job training programs required by public accounting firms of its employees, and continuing professional educational programs sponsored by the AICPA and many state societies of CPAs, all have tended to reduce the ratio of experience to education in meeting the initial entrance qualifications for certification. The state regulatory bodies are slowly moving toward adoption of 1 year as the basic experience requirement, particularly if the applicant has a postbaccalaureate degree. The AICPA has proposed the following regulation, which has been adopted in principle by several states:

> At any time after the effective date of this Act the experience requirement shall be only one year . . . for any candidate holding a Master's Degree in Accounting or Business Administration from a college or university recognized by the Board, if he has satisfactorily completed such number of semester hours in accounting, business administration and economics and such related subjects as the Board shall determine to be appropriate; . . .[5]

Length of experience. The term of employment specified by the various states ranges from no experience in a few states that permit a substitution of education (usually consisting of studies beyond the baccalaureate degree) to a definite number of years either in addition to or regardless of the amount of education. The following jurisdictions allow full or complete substitution of education for experience:

Colorado
Delaware
Florida
Louisiana
Maryland
Mississippi
North Dakota
Oklahoma
Oregon
Puerto Rico
Vermont
West Virginia

Type of employment. The following tabulation was prepared by the U.S. Army Audit Agency in cooperation with the AICPA: [6]

	Number of states	
	Yes	No
Specific types of experience stated	42	11
Only public accounting experience acceptable	19	34
Accounting in private employment acceptable	10	43
Government experience acceptable	19	34
Federal only	10	
State, but not federal	5	
Federal, but not state	3	
Federal and state	7	

[5] Form of Regulatory Public Accountancy Bill, p. 10, approved by the AICPA Committee on State Legislation, 1956.

[6] 1968; cf. Provisions in CPA Laws and Regulations, U.S. Army Audit Agency, revised to July, 1968.

CPA experience. Generally when the experience requirements are expanded to include designated services, the performance of the attest function is referred to prominently.

The experience required in Section 3 (of the Form Bill) of the Act for a certificate as certified public accountant shall have been in public practice and a significant part of it shall have been directed toward the expression of an opinion on financial statements.[7]

That aspect of the CPA's work most closely identified with the public interest is the attest function, that is, adding credibility to information (usually financial statements) on which third parties may rely. It appears that the only aspect of modern public accounting practice that can be considered the exclusive prerogative of professional certified public accountants is this attest function.[8]

The following board ruling of the Minnesota State Board of Accountancy describes in detail many features of experience that boards seek in the evaluation of a candidate's experience:

It is the intent of this requirement that the applicant should have had practical public accounting experience of reasonable variety and importance, requiring independent thought and judgment on important accounting, auditing, and income tax matters, consistent with the competence generally expected of a CPA. It should include a significant amount of accounting work involving third party reliance on the financial statements.

Experience recognized by the Board will ordinarily be measured on the basis of Calendar months and days worked by the applicant as a full-time employee on the staff of a CPA or public accountant.

Part-time work in public accounting (regularly less than five working days per week, or less than a normal working day) will not be recognized unless unusual circumstances and conditions of such part-time employment or practice justify recognition as qualifying experience. Credit for recognized part-time work will be allowed in proportion to normal working time.

Governmental experience. Qualifying governmental accounting experience may have been gained through employment in one or more of the following capacities:

(*a*) As an examiner or supervising examiner in the office of the Public Examiner of the State of Minnesota, or in substantially identical offices of other governmental bodies, engaged in examining the books, records, accounts, and affairs of state or local governments or their instrumentalities;

(*b*) As an auditor or supervising auditor in the Division of Cooperative Accounting of the State of Minnesota Department of Agriculture, Dairy, and Food, engaged in examining the books, records, and accounts of cooperative organizations;

(*c*) As a field examiner or supervising examiner of federal or state tax agencies, engaged in examining the books, records, accounts, and documents of taxpayers for the purpose of verifying financial data contained in income tax returns;

(*d*) As an accountant and auditor or supervising accountant and auditor in the General Accounting Office of the United States of America, engaged in the examination of books, records, accounts, and affairs of departments, agencies, bureaus, or instrumentalities of the federal government;

(*e*) As an auditor or examiner with any other agency of government if the experience is therein at least as comprehensive and diversified as that described in sections (*a*) and (*b*) above. The burden rests with the applicant to demonstrate to the Board that other governmental experience should be recognized as qualifying. A written statement should be filed with the Board, giving a complete description of the purposes, work

[7] Model Rules to Support Form of Regulatory Public Accountancy Bill, Rule 3, approved by the Committee on Legislation and Regulation of the National Association of State Boards of Accountancy, 1967.

[8] Report to the Executive Committee of the American Accounting Association, p. 2, Committee on CPA Examinations, 1966–1967.

standards and procedures of any position believed to be qualifying. It is desirable that this statement be provided by a responsible administrative officer of the applicable governmental unit.[9]

Other experience problems. In addition to the principal features of experience related to the length of service, type of employment, and nature of required services, the state boards have been called upon to resolve questions pertaining to:

PART-TIME EMPLOYMENT: Some states have indicated in board rulings that part-time experience will be accepted under restricted conditions (Kansas); other states restrict employment to full-time (New York).

WHEN THE EXPERIENCE IS REQUIRED: Several states permit the applicant to take the four parts of the examination prior to fulfillment of the experience requirement but withhold the certificate until it is met (for example, Ohio). The 54 jurisdictions are about evenly divided in requiring the prescribed experience before the applicant is allowed to take all or any part of the Uniform CPA Examination. For example, Pennsylvania requires that the education and experience qualifications be met prior to the examination; Washington permits the applicant to take the examination before meeting the experience requirement. Illinois, Iowa, and Montana are the only jurisdictions that grant the certificate before any experience qualification. Illinois and Iowa, however, require the holder of the certificate to have at least 1 year's experience before being registered to practice.

EXPERIENCE EQUIVALENCE: Most state laws and regulations permit the state boards of examiners to accept experience in governmental, industrial, or other nonpublic employment, if deemed equivalent to the practice of public accountancy. While the determination of the nature of equivalence is discretionary, many boards are guided by answers to questions such as:

1. Has the employee followed generally accepted auditing standards based upon an audit program?
2. Has the employee's work been supervised by a certified public accountant?
3. Has the employee's experience been diversified as to the nature of the legal structure and type of industry of the organization examined?
4. Has the employee been involved in engagements in the "field" where he has made "on-the-spot" observations and confirmations and where he has examined documentary evidence supporting the books of account and financial statements?
5. Did the engagement result in an "independent" report on financial statements?

The foregoing guidelines may be explicit in the laws and regulations or may simply be implicit in the policies observed by some boards. In any case, the applicant should carefully document his application with evidence of the specific engagements that he believes will qualify as being of the nature of auditing practice as understood by the profession and as described more fully in previous chapters of this book.

OTHER REGULATORY MATTERS

In addition to meeting the initial qualifications for certification and registration to practice, the CPA or CPA candidate in the United States may en-

[9] Robert P. Behling, *C.P.A. Requirements*, Wisconsin State University, Whitewater State University Foundation, Inc., 1965, pp. 84–85.

counter the following regulations involving:

1. Conditioning credits
2. Transfer of credits
3. Reciprocity or indorsement
4. Temporary practice
5. Partnership formation
6. Grievance procedures
7. Continuing education
8. Accreditation of programs

Conditioning Credits. The states' policies dealing with conditioning requirements or retention of credits for parts of the Uniform CPA Examination passed vary considerably from state to state. It should be explained that 54 jurisdictions have adopted the Uniform CPA Examination prepared by the Board of Examiners of the AICPA. The examination is given twice a year, in May and November. All the jurisdictions subscribe to the Institute's grading service and have adopted the Institute's standard of a passing mark of 75 percent for each of the four subjects comprising the examination, namely, Commercial Law, Accounting Theory, Accounting Practice, Parts 1 and 2, and Auditing. The daily program of the examination is usually:

Wednesday, 1:30–6, Accounting Practice (Part I)
Thursday, 8:30–12, Auditing
Thursday, 1:30–6, Accounting Practice (Part II)
Friday, 8:30–12, Business (Commercial) Law
Friday, 1:30–5, Accounting Theory

Several states require an examination in ethics in addition to the Uniform CPA Examination. This part of the examination may not be transferable if based upon a state's rules of professional conduct. Broadly, the states that condition a candidate's right to retain credit for one or more subjects of the examination passed may be classified as follows:

1. States that have no conditioning requirements—North Dakota
2. States that grant credit indefinitely for two or more subjects passed at the same examination—Maryland, Minnesota, New Hampshire, New Jersey, New York, Pennsylvania, Puerto Rico, Rhode Island, South Dakota (a reasonable period of time), Vermont, Washington (one subject)
3. States that allow only a limited period of time or number of examinations during which the four subjects must be passed—Alaska, Arizona (any part), Arkansas, California, Delaware, District of Columbia, Florida, Georgia, Indiana, Kansas, Kentucky, Maine, Michigan, Mississippi (any part), Montana, Nebraska, Nevada, New Mexico, North Carolina, Ohio, Oregon, South Carolina, Tennessee, Utah, Virginia, West Virginia, Virgin Islands
4. States that limit credit for subjects passed to a period of time but subject to the attainment of an average grade—Hawaii, Idaho, Illinois, Iowa, Louisiana, Massachusetts, Texas, Wisconsin
5. States that restrict credit to two or more subjects passed at the same time to a period of time, or number of examinations, and which require evidence of further study if an average grade is not attained—Alabama, Colorado, Connecticut, Oklahoma, Wyoming

Transfer of Credits. As a generalization, it may be stated that the transfer of credit for parts of the examination passed from one jurisdiction to another under circumstances when a candidate changes residence will not occur if the candidate has lost the credits, as explained above. Nevertheless, provided the jurisdiction where the credits were earned releases the grades, the jurisdiction where the candidate is applying or reapplying can, of course, transfer grades if within its stated authority. For example, the State Education Department of New York as the qualifying agency will accept the transfer of grades, upon application of a qualified candidate, provided the applicant has passed two of the three subjects, Business Law, Accounting Theory, and Accounting Practice, at the same time. Passing grades in the subjects of Accounting Practice and Auditing will be transferred separately by New York.

In a Legislative Report,[10] the AICPA classified the policies of those states that transfer credits as follows:

1. Will grant credit to a candidate for parts of the CPA examination passed in another jurisdiction, provided that at the time the candidate took the examination he was not a resident of the state, had no place of business in the state, and was not regularly employed in the state. (Form Bill)

   Oregon Rhode Island Texas (2)

2. Will grant credit to a candidate for parts of the CPA examination passed in another jurisdiction, provided he was not a resident of the state at the time he took the examination.

   Massachusetts Missouri South Carolina

3. Will grant credit to a candidate for parts of the CPA examination passed in another jurisdiction, provided that the requirements for taking the examination in that jurisdiction are substantially the same as the state's.

   Arizona (2) Colorado (2) * Maryland (2)
   California Maine (1) * New Jersey (2)

4. Will grant credit to a candidate for parts of the CPA examination passed in another jurisdiction, provided that at the time he took the examination he could have met the state's requirements, exclusive of residence, to sit for the examination.

   * Georgia * Kentucky (1) * Tennessee (1)(2)
   * Iowa (2) * Minnesota (2) * Wisconsin

5. Will grant credit to a candidate for parts of the CPA examination passed in another jurisdiction.

   * Connecticut (2) * Kansas New York
   Idaho (1)(2) * New Mexico * Vermont (2)
   * Virginia

* Not a statutory provision. Regulations.

(1) State will grant credit for only some parts of the examination.

(2) State requires that the candidate have passed at least two parts of the examination to qualify for credit. The Accounting Practice section of the CPA examination is accepted by some states as the equivalent of two parts of the examination.

NB: The recognition of parts of the CPA examination passed in another jurisdiction is usually subject to the state's provisions governing conditional credit.

Reciprocity or Indorsement. The rapidly increasing mobility of accountants serving worldwide financial interests has made the matter of reciprocity in this country a serious one to resolve. The solution is especially difficult, largely because of the lack of uniformity in the requirements for certification among the 54 jurisdictions, as explained in the foregoing paragraphs. The problem is further compounded by the immigration of foreign public accountants whose educational and other credentials are difficult to evaluate and to equate with American standards in an attempt to find a fair basis for

[10] February, 1968.

equivalence. In approaching the problem, one is faced with the sword and buckler protecting the profession through legislation, namely, the paramount authority of the state to license the professions and the interest of the public that the state must preserve.

Again, because of the considerable diversity in state laws, regulations, and board rulings, the classification of the states' policies governing reciprocity can be attempted only in broad outline. A classification may be attempted in terms of the restrictions that are to be found in the regulations of most states:

1. Almost all states have a provision that the candidate seeking a reciprocal certificate:
   a. Possess the same or equivalent education and experience.
   b. Possess a certificate that is currently valid and unrevoked.
   c. Be a resident of the state to which he is applying (except New York, Louisiana, and North Dakota).
   d. Has passed the Uniform CPA Examination or equivalent.
   e. Furnish credentials of moral fitness and character.
   f. Meet the general requirements of age and citizenship.
2. The states are about evenly divided in having or not having a provision that the state of original certification extend the same privileges as the state granting reciprocity.
3. Most states require the candidate for reciprocity to meet the qualifications in effect at the time of application.
4. A few states permit the candidate for reciprocity to qualify on the basis of the requirements in effect at the time of his original certification.
5. A few states require the candidate to have entered into the practice of public accountancy or to have expressed an intention to do so.
6. A few states require the candidate to take the state's examination in ethics.
7. At least one state requires the candidate to have been a resident of the state of original certification.
8. A few states will not grant reciprocity on the basis of foreign credentials.

Temporary Practice. The majority of the states permit temporary practice by qualified out-of-state public accountants. Some situations in which such temporary practice is allowed by different jurisdictions are as follows:

1. When a specific accounting engagement is contracted outside the state—Alabama
2. When services which are incidental to the practice are conducted without the state, and in some cases provided the accountant registers with the board—California, Colorado, Connecticut, District of Columbia, Hawaii, Idaho, Illinois, Kansas, Kentucky, Maine, Maryland, Michigan, Mississippi, Missouri, Nebraska, New Mexico, New York, Ohio, Oklahoma, Oregon, Pennsylvania, Puerto Rico, Rhode Island, South Dakota, Tennessee, Texas, Utah, Virgin Islands, Virginia, Washington, West Virginia, Wisconsin
3. If the public accountant registers with the board of examiners—North Carolina
4. When the practice is to be limited to a period of time, such as 90 days or 6 months—Alaska, Florida (to a single specific engagement), Nevada, South Carolina (10 days)
5. If the public accountant registers on or before Jan. 1 of each year and other states extend the same privilege—Georgia

6. If the practice is incidental to regular home practice and if the name of a reliable agent is on file with the board—Iowa
7. If the practice is limited to subjects covered in the registration application on file with the board—Arizona
8. Limited to a period of 18 months to qualified persons—Massachusetts
9. No reference—Wyoming

The following states have made no provision for temporary practice or permits, so that in effect, one must hold a certificate in these states in order to practice.

Arkansas	Montana
Delaware	New Hampshire
Indiana	New Jersey
Louisiana	North Dakota
Minnesota	Vermont

The following states charge a fee for a temporary permit:

Alabama	Hawaii
Arizona	South Carolina
Florida	West Virginia
Georgia	

Organization of Public Accounting Firms. All states provide for the registration of partnerships of accounting firms. Recently some state laws have been amended to permit the incorporation of firms. Many of the following provisions usually included in partnership statutes or regulations have also been embodied in the incorporation statutes.[11]

1. All partnerships of CPAs operating in the state must register with the state board, or other appropriate state agency.
2. The partnership must comprise at least one general partner who is a CPA in good standing in the state and currently licensed to practice.
3. Each partner practicing in the state must be a certified public accountant in the state.
4. Each partner must be a certified public accountant in good standing in some state.
5. Each resident manager in charge of an office within the state must be a CPA of the state and in good standing.
6. The partnership may upon registration designate the firm as a firm of "Certified Public Accountants" or use the abbreviation "CPA."
7. The board must be notified within a specified time of the admission or withdrawal of a partner.

Other provisions found in some state laws require:

1. That the partnership must maintain an office in the state in charge of a partner registered to practice in the state.
2. That a filing fee must be paid and in some cases, an annual registration fee.
3. That the partnership name must consist only of one or more names of present or former partners; that the number of present partners be at least as large as the number of names in the firm name; that in using the designations "Company" or "Co." the number of present partners must be at least one more than the number of names in the firm name.

[11] AICPA Committee on Legislation Form of Regulatory Public Accountancy Bill.

4. That a partnership composed of noncertified public accountants must be termed a firm of "Public Accountants."

Grievance Procedures. As of this writing, all but the following jurisdictions have adopted a code of professional ethics and incorporated it in the state statutes or regulations:

District of Columbia	Maryland
Illinois	Virginia
Indiana	Virgin Islands
Louisiana	

Violations of these rules of professional conduct subject the violator to the following classes of penalties:

Administrative warning
Censure or reprimand
Suspension from practice for a period of time
Revocation of the certificate

In some states, conviction for a crime or felony mandates the board or jurisdictional authority to revoke the certificate. In other jurisdictions, it is discretionary.

A study of complaints processed by state boards from Jan. 1, 1962, to July 1, 1967, based on replies received from 49 state boards by the AICPA, appears in Table 2 (page 44-18).

In general, most boards follow a procedure in processing disciplinary cases as outlined below:

1. Investigation of the complaint, usually based on a written charge.
2. Informal hearing to determine if probable cause exists.
3. Presentment of the complaint and evidence to an indicting body, usually the board.
4. Indictment.
5. Formal hearing, usually before a trial committee appointed by the board from among its members. The respondent may be represented by counsel. The complaint is prosecuted before the committee by the state's attorney general. Both complainant and respondent may produce witnesses. A stenographic record of the testimony is taken. In some cases, the trial committee is not bound by technical rules of evidence. Following the hearing, the trial committee prepares a report to the full board with a recommendation for disposition or penalty.
6. Board decision and sentence.
7. In a few states, for example, New York, a superior state jurisdictional body reviews the board's decision and serves as an appellate body, thus providing the accused with another opportunity to be heard.

Continuing Education. Up to the present, no state has mandated further education beyond that required for initial certification in order that an accountant may maintain the right to continue in practice. Although the AICPA and several state societies offer extensive professional development courses to their memberships, attendance or subscription to these courses is voluntary. A few state societies award a certificate of merit to members who complete a given number of hours of study. Currently, the profession is considering the feasibility of amending the statutes and regulations to require all public accountants to give evidence of a certain number of hours of study in prescribed professional courses as a basis for continuing registration.[12] When one considers that most of the complaints that come before state boards involve technical violations, especially substandard work (see Table 2, page 44-18), there is a strong basis to justify a change in the licensing provisions governing the profession. On the other hand, mandated continuing education cannot be achieved until all states adopt legislation regulating the practice of the profession. Up to the present, 39 jurisdictions have passed laws restricting the practice of public accountancy. However, in 15 jurisdictions, the practice of public accountancy is unrestricted, which would make the prerequisite of continuing education for licensure or re-registration difficult to enforce.

Accreditation of Programs. Unlike most professions, the profession of public accountancy has not established a separate agency for the purpose of accrediting accounting programs designed for the profession. One reason is that neither the profession nor the institutions of higher learning have found it necessary or desirable, at this stage in the development of the profession, to establish professional schools of accountancy. Two notable exceptions are the Schools of Public Accountancy at Rutgers University and at Northeastern University. Currently, accounting programs are accredited indirectly if they are offered by a department of a school of business accredited by the American Association of Collegiate Schools of Business. The American Association is the accrediting agency recognized in the area of collegiate business education by the National Commission on Accrediting.[13]

APPLICATION TO TAKE THE CPA EXAMINATION

General. Although all 54 jurisdictions use the Uniform CPA Examination, the requirements as to education, experience, and application procedures vary considerably. While all states and jurisdictions use the same examination, each state has its own CPA laws and regulations which govern the requirements for taking the examination, the conduct of the examination, and the issuance of the certificate. Therefore, the CPA certificate is a state license to practice as pointed out earlier. The education requirements and the experience requirements are described in this chapter and can be readily ascertained. The application procedures are closely related to the education and experience requirements, since a candidate's application to take the examination will not be accepted unless those requirements have been met in the particular state. While the physical layout of the forms may vary among the different jurisdictions, the nature of the information to be filed is usually similar. Generally the first step in any state or other jurisdiction is to write to the board of accountancy and request the official application forms. Instructions for completing the forms may be included on the forms or on separate instruction sheets. On the following pages are described the requirements for New York State (Handbook 14).[14] The forms in other states may differ somewhat, but the required information probably will be comparable. A study of these forms and requirements will usually help in understanding what is to be filed and how to obtain the required data.

[12] Cf. Marvin L. Stone, Editorial, *The CPA*, November, 1967.

[13] Cf. Report on Accreditation of Accounting Programs, AICPA Standing Committee on Accounting Education, Nov. 28, 1966.

[14] Handbook 14, *Public Accountancy*, The University of the State of New York, The State Education Department, Albany, 1966.

TABLE 2 Complaints Processed by State Boards Jan. 1, 1962 to July 1, 1967 [a]

Based on replies from 49 state boards,[b] total complaints resolved, 790

Subject of complaint	Action taken: Referred to board	PD courses [i]	Revoked [j]	Suspended	Censured	Warning	Informally resolved	Referred to state society	Probation	Dismissed	Surrender of certificate [j]
Criminal convictions (80): [c]											
Income tax (23)	1		9	10					1	2	
Crime of moral turpitude (57)											
Fraud (12)			5	5						2	
Embezzlement (14)			7	4							3
Bribery (7)			5	1							1
Larceny (7)			4	1	1						1
Murder (1)			1								
Sodomy (1)				1							
Perjury (1)				1							
Contempt (1)				1							
Unspecified (13)			9	3					1		
	1		40	27	1				2	4	5
Technical violations (382): [d]											
Preparing false statements (7)			2	4	1						
Lack of independence (7)			1	2	1					3	
Substandard work (368)											
Improper opinion (317)		47		2	4	2	66			196	
Gross negligence (18)			2	11	2	1				2	
Simple negligence (12)			1	1		4				5	1
Inadequate work papers (1)						1					
Improper supervision (2)						1	1				
Irregularity in record keeping (1)											1
Improper forecast (1)										1	
Unspecified (16)			1	1	2	3	5	1		2	1
		47	7	21	10	12	72	1		209	3
Advertising and solicitation (220) [e]				10	62	93	24	2	1	25	3
Violation of partnership rules (14) [f]					5	7	2				
Confidential relationship (1) [g]									1		
Acts discreditable (46): [g]											
Commingling funds (4)	1			1	1		1				
Negligent with client's records (1)								1			
Failure to file client's tax return (2)			1	1							
Fraudulent practices and dishonesty (26)			2				1			23	
Nonpayment of personal bills (2)							2				
Miscellaneous (3)										3	
Unspecified (8)			1	1	3					3	
	1		4	3	4		4	1		29	
Holding out without a license (19) [h]	1			1	9	4	3			1	
Incompatible occupation (3) [g]						1	1				1
Corporate practice (8) [h]					2	1	5				
Competitive bidding (6) [g]					1	2	1			2	
Fictitious name (1) [h]										1	
Other (9) [g]											
Encroachment (1)										1	
Improper letterhead (2)						1	1				
Fee dispute (2)						1				1	
Retention of records (3)							1			2	
Fee splitting (1)										1	
						2	2			5	

TABLE 2 (Continued)

[a] Prepared by the Committee on Professional Ethics of the AICPA.
[b] List of reporting boards:

Alabama	Georgia	Maryland	New Jersey	South Dakota
Alaska	Hawaii	Massachusetts	New Mexico	Tennessee
Arizona	Idaho	Michigan	New York	Texas
Arkansas	Illinois	Minnesota	North Carolina	Utah
California	Indiana	Mississippi	North Dakota	Vermont
Colorado	Iowa	Missouri	Ohio	Virginia
Connecticut	Kansas	Montana	Oklahoma	Washington
Delaware	Kentucky	Nebraska	Oregon	West Virginia
District of Columbia	Louisiana	Nevada	Rhode Island	Wisconsin
Florida	Maine	New Hampshire	South Carolina	

[c] Cases classified under this heading involve a violation of a state or a federal law classified as a crime, felony, or misdemeanor, and may or may not involve a violation related to the practice of the profession. Of the 790 complaints classified in the foregoing chart, 80, or about 10 percent, arose from criminal convictions.

[d] Violations classified as technical involve situations where the practitioner did not adhere to the states' rules of professional conduct related to the practice of the profession. Most of the complaints arose in this area, namely, 382, or 48 percent.

[e] These cases do not relate to the practice of the profession, per se, but represent complaints against the practice of advertising professional services or the improper solicitation of professional services, as defined in the rules of professional conduct of the state boards. These cases also represent a large portion of the complaints processed, 220, or 28 percent. Most of these cases, being of a less serious nature, were settled by a public censure or an administrative warning.

[f] Some states, as previously mentioned in this chapter, require registration of copartnerships of public accountants. They specify, for example, the appropriate name designation. Fourteen complaints arose from failure to register as a partnership or the use of an improper name, a little more than 1 percent of the cases processed.

[g] These cases also involve violations of the state boards' rules of professional conduct and are self-explanatory. Sixty-six cases, or 8 percent of the cases processed, were of this nature. It should be noted, however, that of the 46 cases of discreditable acts, 29 were dismissed.

[h] These cases involve violations usually covered not in the rules of professional conduct but in the accounting laws or regulations of the states. Twenty-eight cases, or about 3 percent of the violations, occurred in this area.

[i] This caption refers to professional development courses prescribed by the state boards as a "penalty" for the violation of expressing an improper opinion on financial statements, a type of technical violation that accounted for the largest number of complaints, 317, or about 40 percent of all the complaints received by the state boards. Forty-seven cases, or 6 percent of the cases processed, were resolved by requiring the practitioner to take a state society or AICPA professional development course.

[j] Sixty-three certificates or licenses to practice were either revoked by the state boards or the practitioners surrendered certificates following the processing of a complaint. Most of these cases (45) were the result of the commission of a crime. Relatively few certificates or licenses were revoked (10) for violations of the standards of professional practice, however.

TABLE 3 State Public Accounting Laws

State	First accounting law	Law became regulatory	State	First accounting law	Law became regulatory
Alabama	1919	*	Nebraska	1909	1957
Alaska	1937	1949 †	Nevada	1913	1960
Arizona	1919	1933, 1955 †	New Hampshire	1921	*
Arkansas	1915	*	New Jersey	1904	*
California	1901	1945	New Mexico	1921	1947 †
Colorado	1907	1937	New York	1896	1959
Connecticut	1907	1955	North Carolina	1913	1925
Delaware	1913	*	North Dakota	1913	*
District of Columbia	1923	*	Ohio	1908	1959 †
Florida	1905	1927	Oklahoma	1917	1968 †
Georgia	1908	1943 †	Oregon	1913	1951 †
Hawaii	1923	1955	Pennsylvania	1899	*
Idaho	1919	*	Rhode Island	1906	1962
Illinois	1903	1927, 1943	South Carolina	1915	*
Indiana	1921	*	South Dakota	1917	1961†
Iowa	1915	1929	Tennessee	1913	1955 †
Kansas	1915	*	Texas	1915	1945
Kentucky	1916	1946	Utah	1907	1959
Louisiana	1908	1924	Vermont	1912	1953 †
Maine	1913	1967	Virginia	1910	1928
Maryland	1900	1924	Washington	1903	1949
Massachusetts	1909	1963	West Virginia	1911	1959
Michigan	1905	1925	Wisconsin	1913	1935
Minnesota	1909	*	Wyoming	1911	*
Mississippi	1920	1930	Puerto Rico	1927	1945
Missouri	1909	1943	Virgin Islands	1942	1957
Montana	1909	*	Guam	1967	1967
			Totals	54	39

* Law remains permissive.
† Law provides for continuing registration of public accountants.

TABLE 4 Final Analysis of Replies to Ethics Examination Questionnaire *

Item	Number
What code of ethics:	
Board	17
Board and AICPA	4
AICPA	3
NASBA	1
Total	25
When conducted:	
Subsequent	13
Prior	7
During	5
Total	25
Open book:	
Yes	20
No	3
Verbal	2
Total	25
Type of questions:	
Hypothetical	17
Hypothetical and abstract	2
Type of questions (*cont.*)	
NASBA	2
Various	2
Hypothetical and true or false	1
All types	1
Total	25
Source of questions:	
Board	7
NASBA	7
Various	5
AICPA	3
Board and AICPA	1
Florida Institute of CPA's	1
University of Wyoming	1
Total	25
Papers graded:	
Yes	23
No	1
Reviewed	1
Total	25

* Prepared by Committee on Professional Ethics of the National Association of State Boards of Accountancy and presented at the annual meeting of the Association in Washington, D.C., Oct. 12, 1968. Twenty-six out of the fifty-three states and jurisdictions now conduct an ethics examination.

Place and Time of the Examination. Examinations will ordinarily be held in the state capital and in additional locations depending on the number of applicants and distances to be traveled. In New York the examinations are held in Albany, Troy, Buffalo, New York City, Rochester, and Syracuse. The examinations are held twice a year, in May and November. There are five different examination periods in the 2½-day span, ordinarily Wednesday afternoon through Friday afternoon. There are four different subjects (Accounting Problems, Part I and Part II, are given separately). The daily program is as follows:

Day and Time	*Subject*	*Hours*
Wednesday (P.M.) 1:30–6......	Accounting Practice (Part I)	4½
Thursday (A.M.) 8:30–12.......	Auditing	3½
(P.M.) 1:30–6....................	Accounting Practice (Part II)	4½
Friday (A.M.) 8:30–12..........	Business (Commercial) Law	3½
(P.M.) 1:30–5....................	Accounting Theory	3½
		19½

In addition to the uniform examinations prepared by the AICPA listed above, some states require examinations in other subjects at the same examination. These subjects, such as Municipal Accounting and the Ethics Examination, are prepared and graded by the particular state.

General Rules Governing Examination and Suggestions to the Candidate. This sheet of helpful points in writing the examination is usually forwarded by the board when the candidate is informed that his application to take the examina-

FORM B (FRONT)

UNIFORM CERTIFIED PUBLIC ACCOUNTANT EXAMINATION

General Rules Governing Examination

1. Read carefully the identification card assigned to you; sign it; make a note of your number for future reference; and return the card to the examiner when he so indicates. Only the examination number of your card shall be used on your papers for the purpose of identification. The importance of remembering this number and recording it on your examination paper correctly cannot be overemphasized. If a question calls for an answer involving a signature, do not sign your own name or initials.

2. Answers must be submitted on paper furnished by the Board and must be completed in the total time allotted for each subject stated on the printed examinations. Identify your answers by using the proper question number. Begin your answer to each question on a separate page and number pages in accordance with the instructions on the printed examinations. Arrange your answers in the order of the questions.

3. Answers may be written in pencil or in ink. If pencil is used it should be soft enough to leave an easily visible impression. Use only one side of the paper. Use the plain sheets, Form F, for calculations, working notes, etc. Neatness and orderly presentation of work are important. Credit cannot be given for answers that are illegible.

4. Use a soft pencil, preferably #2 lead, to blacken the spaces on the separate I.B.M. answer sheets for the objective-type questions.

5. Attach all computations to the papers containing your solutions. Identify them as to the problem to which they relate. The rough calculations and notes may assist the examiners in understanding your solutions.

6. Stationery and supplies furnished by the Board shall remain its property and must be returned whether used or not. You may retain the printed examinations.

7. Any reference during the examination to books or other matters or the exchange of information with other persons shall be considered misconduct sufficient to bar you from further participation in the examination.

tion has been approved. The general rules provide information concerning the candidate's identification number, the paper to be used, the use of pencil or ink, etc. The suggestions to the candidate concern recommendations as to time allowances and the candidate's approach to the questions.

FORM B (BACK)

UNIFORM CERTIFIED PUBLIC ACCOUNTANT EXAMINATION

Suggestions to the Candidate

1. The estimated minimum time and the estimated maximum time that the candidate may need for giving adequate answers to each question or group of questions is given in the printed examinations. These estimates should be used as a guide to allotment of time. It is recommended that the candidate not spend more than the estimated maximum time on any one question until the others have been completed except to the extent that the maximum time has not been used on prior questions. No point values are shown for the individual questions. Points will be approximately proportionate to the time required. The following is an example of time estimates as they appear on the printed examination booklets:

	Estimated Minutes	
	Minimum	*Maximum*
Group I (All required):		
No. 1	25	30
No. 2	25	30
No. 3	20	25
No. 4	25	30
No. 5	25	30
No. 6	25	30
Total for Group I	145	175
Group II(One required)	30	35
Total for examination	175	210

2. If the candidate is unable to complete all the answers called for in the examination, a partial answer is better than none and will receive appropriate credit. When more questions are answered out of a group of optional questions than are required, the excess answers will not be graded.

3. The candidate should avoid explaining how to solve the problem instead of actually solving it in the best way he can. If time grows short, a brief statement to the point is permissible, but full credit cannot be obtained by this expedient.

4. Formal journal entries should not be prepared unless specifically required by the problem. Time may be saved by entering adjustments, reclassifications, etc., directly on the working papers. Elaborate working papers should not be prepared unless they are of assistance in solving the problem. If both working papers and formal statements are required and time is not adequate to complete both, the working papers should be completed.

5. In problems or questions which permit alternative treatment the credit given for the solution will depend on the knowledge and intelligence indicated by the candidate's presentation.

6. Due weight will be given to the arguments presented to support the candidate's answer even though the examiners may not agree with his conclusions.

7. All amounts given in a question or problem are to be considered material unless otherwise stated.

8. The CPA is continually confronted with the necessity of expressing his opinions and conclusions in written reports in clear, unequivocal language. Although the primary purpose of the examination is to test the candidate's knowledge and application of the subject matter, the ability to organize and present such knowledge in acceptable written language will be considered by the examiners.

Request for Application Forms. Copies of the required application forms can ordinarily be obtained from the particular state board of accountancy or the board in the special jurisdiction. The exact name and address of the board may be obtained from a practicing CPA. The address is ordinarily at the state capitol. For example, Georgia State Board of Accountancy, State Capitol, Atlanta, Ga. 30334. To minimize correspondence, state the number of years of experience the applicant has had. A large number of states require specified experience before certain parts of the examination can be taken. For example, in New York State, Group I subjects can be taken without experience; the Group II subject, Auditing, requires experience.

Forms to Be Completed. In many states the completed form is to be filed with the secretary of the board. In some of the populous states, such as New York which has a large number of registered professions, the examining board, designated as the Board of CPA Examiners, is part of the Division of Professional Education, a unit of the State Education Department. In the latter case the initial processing and follow-up of applications and preliminary documents may be made by a unit of the Division of Professional Education, which is responsible for the processing of initial applications for all professions. In this way the accountancy board is relieved of a large volume of clerical processing and follow-up and general correspondence. Where experience or education is to be evaluated or other professional matters are involved, the Board of CPA Examiners would be responsible.

As discussed earlier, there are wide variations in the subjects which may be taken at a particular time. Some jurisdictions permit the candidate to take all subjects of the examination before fulfilling the experience requirement. In other jurisdictions, New York, for example, certain parts of the examination cannot be taken before experience is gained. In that state the Auditing examination cannot be taken until experience is earned. In other states Accounting Practice cannot be taken until the experience requirement is met.

In those jurisdictions that permit all subjects to be taken before experience is earned, there are variations in awarding the certificate. For example, in a few states the certificate may be granted upon passing all parts of the examination. In others the certificate may be given but the candidate must have one or more years of experience before being allowed to practice.

Where experience is required for part of the examination, the candidate must decide whether to wait until he has received the required experience and then take all the subjects or to take as soon as possible those subjects not requiring experience. Generally it is better to take subjects such as Business Law and Theory as soon as possible after school, since the examination will relate more closely to text material. Some experience in the field often is helpful on the Accounting Problems and Auditing examinations. However, something is lost if there is a substantial span between college and the examination. With greater job responsibilities and less time and inclination to study, there may be negative effects. College study habits tend to be forgotten, and self-discipline becomes more difficult. Also, with marriage and children, family responsibilities often lessen the time available for study.

Summary of Required Forms

Group I Subjects. Accounting Theory, Business Law, Accounting Practice. In New York, the following forms must be filed *60 days before the examination* *date.* If the full examination is taken initially, these forms must be filed *90 days before the examination date.* Group I forms are to be mailed to the Division of Professional Licensing Services with the fee of $40.

Form 1—Application for Admission to Professional Examination (Figures 1a and 1b)

Form 10—Education, Undergraduate and Graduate (Figures 2a and 2b)

Group II Subjects. Auditing. The following forms must be filed *90 days before date of the examination.* Group II forms are to be filed with the Board of Certified Public Accountant Examiners, State Education Department.

Form 2— Application for Admission to the Certified Public Accountant Examination in Auditing (Figures 3a and 3b)

Form 2b—Certification of Employer (Figures 4a, 4b, 4c and 4d)

After the candidate's application has been accepted he will receive an Examination Admission Card (Identification No. 1-12) (Figure 5) that admits him to the examination room. This form is applicable for any subject, and for any re-examination. The specific identification number shown on the card is to be used on all of the candidates' examination papers. At this time the candidate is also provided with the General Rules Governing Examination and Suggestions to the Candidate.

Readmission to the Examination. If the candidate has failed any subject in Group I or Group II he will receive a form for readmission to a future examination. The form is to be filed no later than *30 days before the examination* with the Division of Professional Licensing Services, accompanied by a fee of $15.

Readmission to the Examination (Figure 6)

Application for CPA Certificate. If and when the candidate successfully completes all parts of the examination he must file an application for the certificate. The form requires data on all employment or other activities since the last experience information filed. The form is to be forwarded to the Board of Certified Public Accountant Examiners, State Education Department.

Form 4—Application for Certificate as Certified Public Accountant (Figures 7a and 7b)

Group I Subjects. If the candidate elects to take part of the examination before experience is gained, the forms to be filed and the time for filing will not be the same as if all subjects are taken the first time. For our purposes we will assume that the candidate will take any subjects as soon as permitted after leaving college. In New York the Group I subjects are Accounting Theory, Business Law, and Accounting Practice.

Form I—Application for Admission to Professional Examination (Figures 1a and 1b). This form calls for various kinds of information about the candidate, including a recent photograph. The form requires no fewer than three personal signatures of persons recommending the applicant. The references must be given by CPAs or faculty members of the school awarding the baccalaureate degree. The completed Form I and the filing fee of $40 are to be filed within the specified time. The fee entitles the candidate to "admission to one examination in the subjects of Group I and to admission to one examination in Group II." A fee of $15 is required for each re-examination in any subject or subjects.

While the candidate is admitted to a Group I examination he does not necessarily have to take all three parts. For example, he may take Accounting Theory and Business Law and leave Accounting Practice for a later examination. However, when he takes the Accounting Practice he will have to pay the re-examination fee of $15.

Form 10—Education, Undergraduate and Graduate (Figures 2a and 2b). One side of the form applies to undergraduate education; the reverse side is for graduate education data. The form is to be submitted at least 60 days prior to the examination by each institution the applicant attended. It is to be certified by the appropriate college official and must bear the college seal. The degree granted and the date granted are to be stated, and an official transscript of the applicant's work is to be attached. The forms ask for "yes" or "no" answers to three specific questions. Following are the undergraduate questions. The graduate questions are similar.

1. He has satisfactorily completed for admission a high school course or the equivalent.
2. He has completed at least 120 hours of college study as follows:

Business subjects:		
Accounting	24	
Business Law	6	
Finance	6	
Business Statistics	3	
Business and Accounting electives	21	60
Liberal arts and science courses		60
Total		120

3. He has completed a curriculum registered by the New York State Education Department for CPA purposes.

Group II Subjects. The Group II subjects differ somewhat among the jurisdictions. In some jurisdictions it may be Accounting Practice or another subject. In New York the Auditing examination cannot be taken prior to experience. The following forms are to be filed *90 days before the date of the examination.* The said experience must have been completed not less than 90 days before the examination. These forms are to be filed with the Board of Certified Public Accountant Examiners, State Education Department.

Form 2—Application for Admission to the Certified Public Accountant Examination in Auditing (Figures 3a and 3b). This form details the applicant's experience. He is to account for all time between graduation from high school and the date of the application. Accounting experience for which credit is claimed must be attested by the employer as specified.

Form 2b—Certification of Employer (Figures 4a–4d). This form is to be prepared and submitted directly to the Board of Certified Public Accountant Examiners by the employer. A Form 2b is to be submitted by each employer for which experience credit is claimed. The percentage of time is to be shown for the following categories:

Public accounting experience:
- Auditing services
- Financial statement preparation
- Bookkeeping services
- Tax services
- Management services
- Other

Experience in Other than Public Accounting:
- Equivalent auditing experience

An aggregate of 2 years of experience is required of a candidate who has completed a registered undergraduate accounting curriculum. One year of such experience is required of a candidate who has completed a registered graduate accounting curriculum.

Identification No. 1-12—Examination Admission Card (Figure 5). In New York the applicant receives a three-part prenumbered Examination Admission Card. The number stamped on the front of this card is to be used on all examination papers. His name is not to appear on any papers submitted. In some other states the applicant will be assigned a number just before the examination begins. He is to seal it inside an envelope with his name, and deliver the sealed envelope with the corresponding number on the outside to the examiner in charge. The candidate should make note of the number in either case.

Readmission to the Examination (Figure 6). All of the jurisdictions require a passing mark for each of the four subjects. Some states, including New York, require that two or more Group I subjects be passed at the same examinations. Credit will be allowed for Accounting Practice passed at any examination. If Accounting Theory and Business Law are the only subjects taken, then both subjects must be passed. No credit will be given when only one of the two is passed. If the candidate fails a subject he will be given his grade and a readmission form.

For readmission to any part of the examination the applicant must file Readmission Form (Figure 6), together with a fee of $15, with the Division of Professional Licensing Services, State Education Department. The readmission form is to be filed no more than 90 or less than 30 days before the examination.

Form 4—Application for Certificate as Certified Public Accountant (Figures 7a and 7b). After the examinations have been successfully completed, Form 4 must be filed with the State Board of Certified Public Accountant Examiners. The form requires a listing of all employment or other activities since the date of the last experience letter. Employment listed must be evidenced by employers' certificates.

BIBLIOGRAPHY

Board of Examiners, AICPA: *Information for CPA Candidates,* AICPA, New York, 1966.

Handbook 14, *Public Accountancy,* The University of the State of New York, The State Education Department, Albany, 1966.

Provisions in CPA Laws and Regulations, U.S. Army Audit Agency, revised to date.

Report to the Executive Committee, American Accounting Association, Committee on CPA Examinations, 1966–1967.

Student Education and Examinations in Chartered Accountancy as revised to November, 1967, The Canadian Institute of Chartered Accountants, Toronto, Canada.

Behling, Robert P.: *CPA Requirements,* Wisconsin State University, Whitewater State University Foundation, Inc., 1965.

Carey, John L.: *The Accounting Profession—Where Is It Headed?* New York, AICPA, 1962.

Glothen, William J.: *Patterns of Professional Education,* New York, G. P. Putnam's Sons, 1960.

Roy, Robert H., and James H. MacNeill: *Horizons for a Profession,* New York, AICPA, 1967.

Accounting Law Reporter, 2 volumes published by the Commerce Clearing House, Inc., New York, to date.

Allyn, Robert G.: "Planning for the CPA Examination in the United States," *The Accounting Review,* vol. 39, no. 1, January, 1964.

Allyn, Robert G.: "The CPA Program in New York State—Present and Future," *The New York Certified Public Accountant,* vol. 34, no. 6, June, 1964.

Allyn, Robert G.: "Accreditation of Accounting Curriculums," *The Accounting Review,* vol. 41, no. 2, April, 1966.

Ankers, Raymond G.: "Should New York Require a Master's Degree for the CPA Certificate?" *The U.S. Army Audit Agency Bulletin,* Summer, 1969.

Lembke, V. C., J. H. Smith, and V. H. Tidwell: "Compulsory Continuing Education for CPAs," *The Journal of Accountancy,* April, 1970.

ILLUSTRATIONS OF FORMS TO BE COMPLETED

Figure 1a APPLICATION FOR ADMISSION TO PROFESSIONAL EXAMINATION (FRONT)

THE UNIVERSITY OF THE STATE OF NEW YORK
THE STATE EDUCATION DEPARTMENT
DIVISION OF PROFESSIONAL LICENSING SERVICES
800 NORTH PEARL STREET
ALBANY, NEW YORK 12204

CERTIFIED
PUBLIC ACCOUNTANCY

FORM 1—APPLICATION FOR ADMISSION TO PROFESSIONAL EXAMINATION
FILING DEADLINES—90 DAYS FOR FULL EXAMINATION (FORM 2 ALSO REQUIRED)
60 DAYS FOR FORM 1 AND EDUCATIONAL RECORDS FOR GROUP I ONLY

Print name

Street address ....

City.......... State.......... Zip code..........

Birth date .... Birthplace..........

Citizen of U.S.A. (Yes or No)..........(If you were not born in the United States, your own *original certificate* of Citizenship *or* of Declaration of Intention *or* of Derivative Citizenship *must* be submitted at least 60 days before examination. Document will be returned by certified mail.)

College or University.......... Location..........

Graduate school .... Location..........

Dates graduated.......... Degrees received ....

Are you applying on the basis of 15 years experience? Yes.......... No..........

Are you presently employed?.......... If yes, give name and address of employer ....

....

If you have ever taken a New York State licensing examination, name profession ....

Has any State rejected your application?*..........

Have you ever been convicted of any crime?*..........

Have you ever been found guilty of unprofessional conduct?*..........

Applying for: Group I (Theory of Accounts, Coml Law and Accounting Problems)..........

Full examination..........

Time of examination requested: Fall..........; Spring ....

Check place of examination: New York City..........; Albany ....; Syracuse ....; Buffalo ....; Rochester ....

* If yes, explain in an accompanying letter.

Do Not Write Below
Fee Stamp

App. of Qualifications
Pre. by ....
Date ....
Prof. by ....
Date ....
Exp. by ....
Date ....
App. for cert..........

Approval of License
By ....
Date ....
By ....
Date ....
Lic. No. ....
To cand. ....

DO NOT WRITE IN THIS SECTION

FEE NO.	EX. DATE	EX. PLACE	IDENT. NO.	SUBJECTS	CARD SENT	BY

New Addresses ....

....

....

Xa442-Ja67-10,000(52436)*

Figure 1b APPLICATION FOR ADMISSION TO PROFESSIONAL EXAMINATION (BACK)

AFFIDAVIT

Under penalties of perjury, I declare and affirm that the statements made in the foregoing application, including accompanying statements and transcripts are true, complete and correct.

________________________ ________
Signature of applicant *Date*

PASTE
RECENT
PHOTOGRAPH
SECURELY
IN THIS SPACE

Write signature on light portion of photograph, not across features.

Date of photograph ________________

PERSONAL SIGNATURES OF PERSONS RECOMMENDING APPLICANT

This certifies that I have been personally acquainted with the applicant since the year indicated opposite my name; that I believe him to be of good moral character and worthy of licensure in New York State; and that any reservations I may have about the applicant I agree to send by certified mail in a confidential letter to the Division of Professional Licensing Services.

Please print name	*Personal signature*	*P. O. address (Including street and city)*	*Known since*

(Signatures are required by not fewer than three citizens unrelated to applicant who must be licensed in the profession for which applicant wishes to be examined or who are members of the staff of the school from which the candidate received his baccalaureate degree.)

Important: Please make check or money order in the amount of $40 payable to the State Education Department at Albany; *mail Form 1 and fee* to Fee Section, State Education Department, 800 North Pearl Street, Albany, New York 12204.

Figure 2a EDUCATION—UNDERGRADUATE

Form 10-CPA EDUCATION - UNDERGRADUATE

This form must be filed at least 60 days prior to examination.

Mail to: New York State Education Department
Division of Professional Licensing Services
800 North Pearl Street
Albany, New York 12204

Telephone: GR4-3824

TO BE COMPLETED BY APPLICANT:
Full Name__________
Birth Date__________
Address__________

Form 10 submitted for:
Examination___ Indorsement___

This is to certify that____________________
(Name of Applicant)

Check items below

1. Has satisfactorily completed for admission an approved four-year secondary school course of study, or the equivalent. ☐ Yes ☐ No

2. Has completed at least 120 semester hours of college study as follows:
   - Business subjects: 60
     - Accounting 24
       Including course coverage in each of the following subject areas - accounting principles, cost accounting, tax accounting and auditing.
     - Commercial Law 6
     - Finance 6
     - Business statistics 3
     - Business and accounting electives 21
   - Liberal arts and science courses . . . . 60 ☐ Yes ☐ No

   (The total should include at least 6 semester hours of economic principles which may be used to satisfy either the business electives or liberal arts requirements.)

3. Has completed a curriculum specifically registered by the New York State Education Department for C.P.A. purposes. ☐ Yes ☐ No

4. Has been granted the degree of____________________ Date: __________

5. Remarks (If the applicant has not completed a registered curriculum, please indicate the extent and nature of the deficiencies. If substitution has been allowed for any of the above requirements, please explain.): ____________________

I hereby certify that to the best of my knowledge and belief the foregoing is a true statement of the record of the applicant named above and I am attaching hereto an OFFICIAL TRANSCRIPT of his study as recorded at this institution.

Signature____________________
Official Position____________________
(College Seal) Institution____________________
Date____________________

INSTRUCTIONS TO APPLICANT: If the applicant has attended more than one college, it becomes his obligation to request each institution to submit an official transcript to the New York State Education Department (address above). This form, however, should be completed and appropriately certified by the institution in which registered accounting courses were completed and from which applicant graduated with appropriate degree.

DEPARTMENT ACTION: ( ) Approved By____________________ Date:__________

SEE REVERSE SIDE FOR CERTIFICATION OF A GRADUATE PROGRAM

January 1967 - 10,000

Figure 2b EDUCATION—GRADUATE

Form 10-CPA

EDUCATION - GRADUATE

TO BE COMPLETED BY APPLICANT:
Full Name__________
Birth Date__________
Address__________

Form 10 submitted for:
Examination___ Indorsement___

This is to certify that____________________
(Name of Applicant)

Check items below

1a. Has satisfactorily completed the requirements for a bachelor's degree or the equivalent in the field of accounting or business administration, including at least 21 semester hours of accounting and meeting the minimum semester hour requirements in the other subjects set forth in the Regulations for an undergraduate program (see over); and has completed all requirements leading to a post-baccalaureate degree, including a minimum of the following semester hours or equivalent in courses taken at the graduate level:

Accounting 9
Economic analysis 3
Finance 3
Other business and accounting electives 15
Total 30

☐ Yes ☐ No

OR

1b. Has satisfactorily completed the requirements for a bachelor's degree in other than the field of accounting or business administration, including (1) at least 60 semester hours in liberal arts and science courses, of which at least 6 semester hours shall be in economic principles, and (2) at least 6 semester hours in finance and 3 semester hours in statistics; and has completed all the requirements leading to a post-baccalaureate degree, including a minimum of the following semester hours or equivalent in courses taken at the graduate level:

Accounting 24
Economic analysis 3
Finance 3
Commercial Law 4
Other business and accounting electives 26
Total 60

☐ Yes ☐ No

2. Has completed a post-baccalaureate degree program registered by the New York State Education Department for C.P.A. purposes. ☐ Yes ☐ No

3. Has been granted the degree of____________________Date:__________

4. Remarks (If the applicant has not completed a registered curriculum, please indicate the extent and nature of the deficiencies. If substitution has been allowed for any of the above requirements, please explain.): ____________________

I hereby certify that to the best of my knowledge and belief the foregoing is a true statement of the record of the applicant named above and I am attaching hereto an OFFICIAL TRANSCRIPT of his study as recorded at this institution.

(College Seal)

Signature____________________
Official Position____________________
Institution____________________
Date____________________

DEPARTMENT ACTION: ( ) Approved By____________________ Date:__________

( ) Approved for two years experience requirement By____________________ Date:__________

Figure 3a APPLICATION FOR ADMISSION TO THE CERTIFIED PUBLIC ACCOUNTANT EXAMINATION IN AUDITING (FRONT)

Form 2 (Revised, June 1968)
C.P.A.

THE UNIVERSITY OF THE STATE OF NEW YORK
THE STATE EDUCATION DEPARTMENT
DIVISION OF PROFESSIONAL EDUCATION
ALBANY, NEW YORK 12204

APPLICATION FOR ADMISSION TO THE CERTIFIED PUBLIC ACCOUNTANT EXAMINATION IN AUDITING

(This application must be on file in the Department not less than 90 days before the date of the examination. Applications are valid for period of one year only.)

Print name in full *First name* *Middle name* *Last name*

Street address____ City____ State____ Zip code____

Date of birth____ Place of birth____ Are you a citizen of U. S.?____

By whom employed____

Business address: Street____ City____ State____ Zip code____

Date of examination requested____

Check place of examination: New York City____; Albany____; Syracuse____; Rochester____, Buffalo____

Examinations Taken:	Theory of Accounts	Commercial Law	Accounting Problems
A. Date first taken			
B. Number of times taken			
C. Date passed			

INSTRUCTIONS TO APPLICANT

THE CANDIDATE MUST READ THESE INSTRUCTIONS CAREFULLY AND COMPLY WITH ALL DETAILS.

Requirements: The following are excerpts from section 91 of the Regulations of the Commissioner, established by the Board of Regents: The examination in certified public accountancy shall consist of:

Group 1. The subjects of theory of accounts, commercial law, and accounting problems

Group 2. The subject of auditing

"A candidate shall be entitled to admission to the group II subject of the examination upon presentation of evidence satisfactory to the State Board of Certified Public Accountant Examiners, subject to review by the Commissioner, that he has had diversified experience involving the application of generally accepted accounting principles and the application of generally accepted auditing standards in the practice of public accountancy either on his own account, as a member of a copartnership or as an employee on a full-time basis on the professional staff of one engaged in the practice of public accountancy or, except with respect to applicants under section 7403, subdivision 3, of the statute, the satisfactory equivalent thereof as determined by the Board in the exercise of its discretion. An aggregate of 2 years of such experience shall be required of a candidate who has satisfactorily completed a registered undergraduate curriculum in accountancy and an aggregate of 1 year of such experience shall be required of a candidate who has satisfactorily completed a registered graduate curriculum in accountancy." (as amended February 23, 1968)

The said experience shall have been completed not less than 90 days prior to the date of the examination.

An application for admission to the examination in auditing shall be filed with the Department not less than 90 days prior to the date of the examination. Any false or misleading information in connection with any application may be cause for exclusion from the examination on the ground of lack of good moral character. If the Department finds that the application is complete and that all the requirements of the statute and of the regulations have been met, it shall issue to the applicant an admission card which shall advise him of the time, date, and place of the examination.

Supporting certification of employer forms should be mailed directly by the employer to the Board of Certified Public Accountant Examiners, State Education Department, 800 North Pearl Street, Albany, New York 12204.

(over)

Figure 3b APPLICATION FOR ADMISSION TO THE CERTIFIED PUBLIC ACCOUNTANT EXAMINATION IN AUDITING (BACK)

Date graduated from high school ____________

College ____________
Degree and date graduated ____________

Experience tabulation: Candidates must account for all time between graduation from high school and the date of this application. Employments or other activities must be listed in chronological order on this form. All accounting experience **for which credit is claimed** must be attested by a certified public accountant or a practicing public accountant on the required certification of employer form. Part-time employment not related to accounting during college vacation periods need not be included.

Extend time claimed for satisfaction of experience requirement to proper column.

NAME AND ADDRESS OF EMPLOYER (or other activities)	KIND OF BUSINESS	DATE (Month and year)		ACCOUNTING EXPERIENCE CLAIMED	OTHER BUSINESS EXPERIENCE
		From	To	Yrs. Mos. Days	Yrs. Mos. Days

Under penalties of perjury, I declare and affirm that the statements made in the foregoing application, including accompanying statements are true, complete, and correct.

Signature of applicant ____________

Date ____________

6869/1/02803/0222/Ap 10,000 Xa

Figure 4a CERTIFICATION OF EMPLOYER (PAGE 1)

Form 2b

THE UNIVERSITY OF THE STATE OF NEW YORK
THE STATE EDUCATION DEPARTMENT

CERTIFICATION OF EMPLOYER

(This Form should be mailed directly to the Board of C.P.A. Examiners)

Board of Certified Public Accountant Examiners
The State Education Department
Albany, New York 12204

Re ....
Print Name of Applicant

Gentlemen:

In order that the Board of Certified Public Accountant Examiners may have some basis on which to judge whether the candidate satisfies the experience requirement. I am pleased to furnish the following information:

1. I am a certified public accountant — public accountant (strike out the term that does not apply).

....

Name *Firm or Organization* *Status or Title*

....

Certificate or registration number *State in which certified or registered* *Date*

2. Address of applicant as shown on employer's records

....

Address *City* *State* *Zip code*

3. Places of employment:

(*City*) (*State*) Dates of employment: (*From*) (*To*)

....

....

....

4. This employment was on a full-time basis — part-time basis. (Strike out the term that does not apply.)

5. If the employment was on a part-time basis, show complete details below or attach a separate statement:

....

....

....

6. Applicant's job classification while in your employment:

(*Job classification*) (*Dates*) (*From*) (*To*)

....

....

....

[OVER]

Figure 4b CERTIFICATION OF EMPLOYER (PAGE 2)

7. **I HAVE READ THE INSTRUCTIONS** concerning the completion of the following analysis. In accordance with the categories therein setforth, the applicant's duties, while he was in our employ, are described as follows:

PUBLIC ACCOUNTING EXPERIENCE:	Percentage of time	Do not write in space below
A. Auditing services		
1. Examination of financial statements of clients for the purpose of expressing an opinion	....	....
2. Examination of financial statements of clients when certain auditing procedures have been applied but a disclaimer is expressed	....	....
B. Financial statement preparation	....	....
C. Bookkeeping services	....	....
D. Tax services	....	....
E. Management services	....	....
F. Other (describe below in detail)		
....		
....		
....	....	....
EXPERIENCE IN OTHER THAN PUBLIC ACCOUNTING:		
G. Equivalent auditing experience. (Attach a separate statement as outlined in the instructions.)	....	....

8. Is the applicant related to you? Yes No
(if yes, explain relationship)

9. Does the applicant, in your opinion, possess good moral character and have other attributes required of a C.P.A.? Yes No
(if not, attach a separate statement explaining the reason for withholding an affirmative approval)

....

Under penalties of perjury, I declare and affirm that the statements made in the foregoing certification, including the accompanying statements are true, complete, and correct.

....
Signature *Date*

6869/1/02803/0254
5/20,000/54002*

Figure 4c CERTIFICATION OF EMPLOYER (PAGE 3)

INSTRUCTIONS FOR COMPLETING ITEM 7 OF CERTIFICATION OF EMPLOYER

§ 91. (of the regulations of the Commissioner) A candidate shall be entitled to admission to the Group II subject of the examination upon presentation of evidence satisfactory to the State Board of Certified Public Accountant Examiners, subject to review by the Commissioner, that he has had diversified experience involving the application of generally accepted accounting principles and the application of generally accepted auditing standards in the practice of public accountancy either on his own account, as a member of a copartnership or as an employee on a full-time basis on the professional staff of one engaged in the practice of public accountancy or, except with respect to applicants under section 7403, subdivision 3, of the statute, the satisfactory equivalent thereof as determined by the Board in the exercise of its discretion. An aggregate of 2 years of such experience shall be required of a candidate who has satisfactorily completed a registered undergraduate curriculum in accountancy and an aggregate of 1 year of such experience shall be required of a candidate who has satisfactorily completed a registered graduate curriculum in accountancy.

It is the responsibility of the Board of Certified Public Accountant Examiners to determine whether this requirement has been met. For this reason, it is essential that the employer clearly describe the nature of the candidate's experience under the categories listed below. *The approximate portion of the applicant's time devoted to each category must be furnished to the Board.* If these portions cannot be reasonably estimated, a range of percentage may be given.

INSTRUCTIONS TO PUBLIC ACCOUNTING FIRMS

Question 7:

A. Auditing Services:

1. Examination of financial statements of clients where the application of generally accepted auditing standards have been employed for the purpose of expressing an opinion that the financial statements are presented in accordance with generally accepted accounting principles. The extension of the examination to the preparation of *related* income tax returns by the applicant who participated in the examination and to other *related* services, such as the design and installation of accounting and cost systems, may also be included in this category.

2. Examination of financial statements of clients when certain auditing procedures have been applied but an opinion is disclaimed because certain required auditing procedures have been omitted. The extension of the examination to the preparation of *related* income tax returns by the applicant who participated in the examination and to other *related* services, such as the design and installation of accounting and cost systems, may also be included in this category.

B. Financial Statement Preparation: The preparation of financial statements from the books of account without audit, including the preparation of *related* income tax returns and the performance of other *related* services, such as the design and installation of accounting and cost systems, in which the applicant has demonstrated a knowledge of generally accepted accounting principles.

C. Bookkeeping Services (i.e. write-ups): This service consists of work on the books of original entry, the preparation of payrolls, checks, payroll tax reports, sales and other similar tax returns, and posting to subsidiary ledgers. Posting to the client's general ledger in connection with the preparation of financial statements should be classified under A or B above, depending upon the extent of auditing procedures applied.

(OVER)

Figure 4d CERTIFICATION OF EMPLOYER (PAGE 4)

D. Tax Services:

1. Preparation of corporation, fiduciary, partnership and individual tax returns from information compiled in an audit engagement *by others*, or from unaudited data furnished by clients.
2. Research in tax law; tax planning for clients; preparation of protests, Tax Court petitions, and briefs; and representation of clients before taxing authorities.
3. Examining tax returns.

E. Management Services:

1. Design and installation of accounting or cost or other systems, when *not related to* or *an extension of* auditing assignments, as A1 and A2 above.
2. Other management advisory services.

F. Other (including but not limited to the following):

1. Checking or comparing reports and tax returns
2. Other services for clients not included in bookkeeping services
3. Other work not in connection with services to clients, e.g., filing tax law services, keeping employer's records, filing, etc.

INSTRUCTIONS TO OTHER EMPLOYERS

G. Equivalent Auditing Experience:

1. In order for the Board to equate the experience of other than those in public accounting, please attach a statement describing the individual fieldwork engagements performed for which experience credit is claimed, setting forth as much of the following as is practical, and indicating the extent to which the applicant has applied generally accepted accounting principles and generally accepted auditing standards:
   a. The nature, purpose and location of the engagements.
   b. The approximate time the applicant was involved on each engagement.
   c. The relationship between the organizations examined and the applicant's organization.
   d. The type of reports issued.
   e. The addressees of the reports.
   f. The engagements which were under the direct supervision of the certifying person (who should be a CPA), and the periods covered thereby.

6869/1/02803/0255
Ap/20,000/Xa/53912*

Figure 5 EXAMINATION ADMISSION CARD

CERTIFIED
PUBLIC
ACCOUNTANCY

1970

May 6, 1:30 p.m.
Accounting problems—part I
(4½ hours)

May 7, 1:30 p.m.
Accounting problems—part II
(4½ hours)

6970/02802/1/9568

EXAMINATION ADMISSION CARD

Identification No. I - 12- 1148

Name ....

.... New York City — State Armory, 216 Fort Washington Ave.

.... Albany — State Armory, 195 Washington Ave.

.... Buffalo — South Entrance, Memorial Auditorium, 140 Main St.

.... Syracuse — Onondaga County War Memorial, Montgomery St. entrance

.... Rochester — Armory, 900 E. Main St.

SPECIFIC INSTRUCTIONS (See reverse side)

1. Bring pen, ruler, No. 2 pencils, and eraser.
2. Admission card with photograph attached must be submitted for admission to each session of examination scheduled.

CARDS MUST NOT BE DETACHED AND THEY MUST BE FILLED OUT BEFORE GOING TO EXAMINATION CENTER.

DO NOT DETACH

PRINT LAST NAME FIRST NAME MIDDLE NAME C.P.A.

Examination Identification No. I - 12- 1148

SIGNATURE

Street address ....

City .... State .... Zip code .... County ....

Date of birth ....

Place of birth .... Citizen of ....

College or university certifying accounting program or where accounting study completed ....

Degree, if granted, and date ....

For Division Use Only ➧ Certificate Number .... Dated ....

DO NOT DETACH

C.P.A. IDENT. No. I - 12- 1148

BIRTH DATE MONTH DAY YEAR

PLEASE PRINT

Name (Last) (First) (Middle)

Street address

City State ZIP code

To be filled out by all applicants: College or university (certifying accounting program or where accounting study completed)

N.Y.S. County Code
To be filled out by N.Y.S. residents only
(See reverse side)

For Division Use Only

FRONT

FOR ADMISSION
TO EXAMINATION
CANDIDATE IS REQUIRED
TO PASTE
2 x 3 PHOTOGRAPH
IN THIS SPACE
(FULL FACE)

Conducted by
State Education Department
Albany, New York 12204

GENERAL INSTRUCTIONS

NO CREDIT will be given for this examination if educational requirements have not been fully completed.

Conduct of the examinations. Licensing examinations shall be conducted in accordance with the following rules and any candidate violating such rules may be dismissed from the examination room by the Department representative or otherwise disciplined.

(1) No candidate shall enter the examination more than 45 minutes after the question papers have been distributed nor shall any candidate leave the examination until 45 minutes have elapsed.

(2) During the examination no candidate shall communicate with any other candidate in any way except upon the express permission of the Department representative.

(3) A candidate shall not bring books or help of any kind into the examination room unless directed to do so by the Department because of the character of the examination.

(4) After handing in his last paper in any examination each candidate shall make and subscribe to an affidavit to the effect that he has violated none of the rules.

(5) The STARTING TIME for each examination is printed on the front of this card. Candidates who arrive after the starting time will not be given extra time.

Not to be completed by applicant

Exam. date	Exam. No.	Aud.	Com. law	Theory of accts.	Acct. problems	Result

Certificate mailed ....

CODE NUMBERS OF COUNTIES OF NEW YORK STATE

01 — Albany	16 — Franklin	41 — Oneida	55 — Schuyler
02 — Allegany	17 — Fulton	42 — Onondaga	56 — Seneca
31 — Bronx	18 — Genesee	43 — Ontario	57 — Steuben
03 — Broome	19 — Greene	44 — Orange	58 — Suffolk
04 — Cattaraugus	20 — Hamilton	45 — Orleans	59 — Sullivan
05 — Cayuga	21 — Herkimer	46 — Oswego	60 — Tioga
06 — Chautauqua	22 — Jefferson	47 — Otsego	61 — Tompkins
07 — Chemung	32 — Kings	48 — Putnam	62 — Ulster
08 — Chenango	23 — Lewis	34 — Queens	63 — Warren
09 — Clinton	24 — Livingston	49 — Rensselaer	64 — Washington
10 — Columbia	25 — Madison	35 — Richmond	65 — Wayne
11 — Cortland	26 — Monroe	50 — Rockland	66 — Westchester
12 — Delaware	27 — Montgomery	51 — St. Lawrence	67 — Wyoming
13 — Dutchess	28 — Nassau	52 — Saratoga	68 — Yates
14 — Erie	33 — New York	53 — Schenectady	
15 — Essex	40 — Niagara	54 — Schoharie	

BACK

Figure 6 READMISSION TO THE EXAMINATION

NEW YORK STATE EDUCATION DEPARTMENT— Application for Readmission to Examination in Certified Public Accountancy

Print name in full ______________________________

Birth date __________ Birthplace __________ Citizen of __________

Home address __________ City __________ State __________ Zip code __________

Employment address __________ City __________ State __________ Zip code __________

Name of employer ______________________________

Circle place of examination requested: Albany; Buffalo; New York; Rochester; Syracuse.

Circle subjects: Theory of Accounts; Law; Accounting Problems; Auditing.
(Do not circle Auditing unless you have filed Form 2.)

Under penalties of perjury, I declare and affirm that the statements made in the foregoing application are true, complete and correct.

__________ *Date* __________ *Signature of applicant*

Important: This request must be filed with the Division of Professional Licensing Services, State Education Department, Albany, New York 12204 *not more than 90, nor less than 30 days* prior to the date of the examination or admission card cannot be sent. Reexamination fee is $15.

Xa452-J1 67-10,000 (7A2-256)

Figure 7a APPLICATION FOR CERTIFICATE AS CERTIFIED PUBLIC ACCOUNTANT (FRONT)

Form 4
C.P.A.

THE UNIVERSITY OF THE STATE OF NEW YORK
The State Education Department
Division of Professional Education

APPLICATION FOR CERTIFICATE AS CERTIFIED PUBLIC ACCOUNTANT

You have successfully completed all parts of the examination required as preliminary to the issuance of a certificate as Certified Public Accountant. Before your certificate may be prepared, this application must be completed in full and returned to the State Board of Certified Public Accountant Examiners, State Education Department, 800 North Pearl Street, Albany, New York 12204.

____
Print name in full First name Middle name Last name

____

Street address____________ City____________ State__________ Zip Code__________

Date of birth____________________ Place of birth____________________

By whom employed____

Business address: Street____________ City____________ State__________ Zip Code__________

____

Instructions for Completion

READ these instructions and comply with all details

Account for ALL time between the date of your last experience letter filed as of ____________________ and the date of this application.

This application must be supported by a letter from your employer or employers certifying to the dates of your employment from the date of the last experience letter to the present.

Employer letters are to be mailed directly by the employer to the State Board of Certified Public Accountant Examiners, State Education Department, 800 North Pearl Street, Albany, New York 12204.

(over)

Figure 7b APPLICATION FOR CERTIFICATE AS CERTIFIED PUBLIC ACCOUNTANT (BACK)

EXPERIENCE

List ALL employment or other activities since the date of your last experience letter in chronological order.

NAME AND ADDRESS OF EMPLOYER (or other activities)	KIND OF BUSINESS	DATE	
		From	To

Under penalties of perjury, I declare and affirm that the statements made in the foregoing application, including accompanying statements and transcripts are true, complete and correct. Under the penalties of perjury, I further declare and affirm that I have read Section 94 of the Regulations (Unprofessional Conduct and Unprofessional Advertising) pertaining to public accountancy, and that I will adhere thereto.

______________________ Signature of applicant

______________________ Date

Do not write below this line

Board Action

Approved - Date______________________

Disapproved - Date______________________

Reason______________________

Chapter 45

Securities and Exchange Commission Requirements

B. BERNARD GREIDINGER

Professor of Accounting, New York University Graduate School of Business Administration

FINANCIAL STATEMENTS TO BE FILED

The heavy losses incurred by investors following the 1929 stock market crash resulted in federal regulation of security issues and trading. One of the major objectives was to make available to investors a full and fair disclosure of the financial position and earnings of all corporations whose securities were publicly held. Under the Securities Act of 1933 and the Securities Exchange Act of 1934, as amended,[1] companies offering new issues of securities for sale in interstate commerce and companies whose securities are listed or traded on a national securities exchange or on over-the-counter markets are required to register with the Securities and Exchange Commission. At registration and annually thereafter, these companies are required to file a set of financial statements certified by independent public accountants.

To aid issuers and independent public accountants in the preparation and certification of the required financial reports, the SEC prescribes certain rules governing the form and content of the balance sheet, profit and loss statement, surplus statement (retained earnings and capital surplus), supporting schedules, footnotes, and the accountants' certificate. In addition, the Commission and key members of its staff from time to time express their opinion in official decisions, reports, accounting releases, informal conferences, and "letters of comment" on the proper treatment in the financial statements of major accounting problems of a controversial nature. The Commission examines all statements filed to determine whether they comply with these reporting requirements and whether they have been prepared in accordance with recognized and generally accepted accounting principles established by the profession, as reflected in the official pronouncements of the AICPA and authoritative writings in the field. Those which fail to meet these standards are rejected with the request that appropriate corrections be made. Unless this request is complied with, new issues may not be offered to the public, and trading in securities already issued may be suspended.

This has had a most profound effect on both corporate management and the accounting profession. As a result, financial statements filed with the SEC and the national securities exchanges today contain the most comprehensive, dependable, and informative data on the financial and operating conditions of American corporations anywhere publicly available.

Responsibility for Financial Statements—Examination Procedure. It is impor-

[1] On Aug. 20, 1964, the Securities acts were amended to afford investors in publicly held companies whose securities are traded over the counter the same fundamental disclosure protections as have been provided to investors in companies whose securities are listed on an exchange.

tant to note, however, that the Commission does not warrant or assume responsibility for the fairness of the statements filed with it. Such responsibility rests with the issuer and independent accountants certifying the financial statements. This view was made emphatically clear in a recent SEC release outlining the Commission's policy to expedite registration statements and financial statements contained therein, filed under the Securities Act of 1933.[2] The release reads in part as follows:

> A Division officer will make a cursory review of every registration statement and will make one of the following three decisions:
>
> 1. That the registration statement is so poorly prepared or otherwise presents problems so serious that no further review will be made. Oral or written comments will not be issued for to do so would delay the review of other registration statements which do not appear to contain comparable disclosure problems. Counsel will be notified;
> 2. That counsel shall be advised that the staff has made only a cursory review of the registration statement; no written or oral comments will be provided; and review by the staff whether extensive as is customary or cursory as in this case, may not be relied upon in any degree to indicate that the registration is true, complete or accurate. Particularly, with respect to companies which have never before been subject to the registration process, *counsel will be requested to furnish as supplemental information letters from the chief executive officer of the issuer, the auditors, and the managing underwriter on behalf of all underwriters. These letters shall include representations that the respective persons are aware that the staff has made only a cursory and not a customary review of the registration statement, which may not be relied upon in any degree to indicate that the registration statement is true, complete or accurate, and are also aware of their statutory responsibilities under the Securities Act.* Counsel will be advised that upon receipt of such supplemental information in satisfactory form, the staff will recommend clearance of the registration statement upon request, not earlier than 20 days after the date of the original filing; or
> 3. That the filing will be subject to the regular review process.
>
> With respect to (1), the company's counsel will be advised that acceleration of the effective date of the registration statement will not be recommended and should it become effective in such form, the Division would then decide what action, if any, to recommend to the Commission. Such action could include recommendations for examination or private investigation under Section 8(e) or 20(a) of the Securities Act of 1933, stop-order public hearing under Section 8(d) of the Act, and an injunctive proceeding or criminal reference under Section 20(b) of the Act.
>
> With respect to both (1) and (2), counsel for the companies will be advised that the *statutory burden of full disclosure is on the issuer, its affiliates, the underwriter and experts, that as a matter of law this burden cannot be shifted to the staff,* and that the current work load is such that the staff cannot undertake additional review and comment. Attention is directed to the case of *Escott v. BarChris Construction Corporation, et al.,* 283 F. Suppl. 643 (DC, S.D.N.Y., 1968).

A brief discussion is presented below of the financial statements required to be filed with the SEC for industrial and commercial companies and the basic references employed in the preparation and certification of these statements.

Registration of New Issues. Financial statements of registrant. BASIC REQUIREMENTS: Most corporations making a public offering of securities register these securities on SEC Form S-1. In that form, the issuer, ordinarily, is required to file the following certified statements: a balance sheet as of a date within 90 days prior to the date of filing; profit and loss and source and application of funds statements for each of the three fiscal years immediately preceding the balance sheet date and for the period, if any, between the close

[2] Securities Act of 1933, Release No. 4934, dated Nov. 21, 1968.

of the latest fiscal year and the date of the latest balance sheet filed. The purpose is to reveal the current financial position of the company and to make available operating data of a comparative nature which will permit the investor to judge for himself the growth and progress of the particular corporation whose securities are being offered for sale. If the 90-day balance sheet is not certified, there must be submitted in addition a certified balance sheet as of a date within one year of the date of filing, unless the fiscal year has ended within 90 days of such date. In the latter event, the certified balance sheet may be as of the end of the preceding fiscal year.

Where, however, a company meets *all* of the following conditions, it may omit its 90-day balance sheet and submit in lieu thereof a balance sheet as of a date within 6 months prior to the date of filing:

1. The registrant has at least one class of its securities listed and registered on a national securities exchange, and files annual and such other financial reports as are required under the Securities Act of 1933 and the Securities Exchange Act of 1934.
2. The total assets of the registrant and its subsidiaries, as shown by the latest consolidated balance sheet filed, less any valuation or qualifying reserves, amount to $5 million or more, exclusive of intangibles.
3. No long-term debt of the registrant is in default as to principal, interest, or sinking-fund provisions.

Similarly, if this "6-month balance sheet" is not certified, there must be submitted in addition thereto a certified balance sheet as of a date within 1 year of the date of filing.

Actually, the thrust of this requirement has resulted in the submission of certified financial statements as of a date within 1 year (in practice, the end of the last fiscal year) *and* uncertified statements as of a date within 90 days or 6 months of filing, as the circumstances required.

SUMMARY OF EARNINGS: Part 1 of the registration statement (Form S-1) prescribes the information to be included in the prospectus. Item 6, entitled "Summary of Earnings," is generally regarded as the most important single part of the prospectus. The instructions read in part as follows:

> Furnish in comparative columnar form a summary of earnings for the registrant and its subsidiaries consolidated, or both, as appropriate, for each of the last five fiscal years of the registrant (or for the life of the registrant and immediate predecessors, if less) and for any period between the latest of such fiscal years and the date of the latest balance sheet furnished, and for the corresponding period of the preceding fiscal year. In connection with such summary, whenever necessary, reflect information or explanation of material significance to investors in appraising the results shown, or refer to such information or explanation set forth elsewhere in the prospectus.
>
> Instructions—1. Include comparable data for any additional fiscal years necessary to keep the summary from being misleading. Subject to appropriate variation to conform to the nature of the business or the purpose of the offering, the following items should be included: net sales or operating revenues; cost of goods sold or operating expenses (or gross profit); interest charges; income taxes; net income; special items; and net income and special items. The summary shall reflect the retroactive adjustment of any material items affecting the comparability of the results. See Item 21(b).

While the instruction quoted above calls for a series of condensed earnings statements, setting forth in comparative form the major income and expense items applicable to the enterprise, a review of hundreds of filings each year discloses that, in fact, over 90 percent of the prospectuses include profit and loss and retained earnings statements in their entirety, as prescribed by Rule 5-04 of Regulation S-X. Since fully completed income statements are included in the Summary of Earnings for the period covered by the registration, there is no need to file separately, as part of the financials called for by the form, the income statements for the latest three years and stub period, if any, because they are already included in the prospectus. This optional filing, which is widely followed, is provided for in Form S-1 under "Item 21—Financial Statements," which reads as follows: "(b) If either the profit and loss or earned surplus statements required are included in their entirety in the summary of earnings required by Item 6, the statements so included need not be otherwise included in the prospectus or elsewhere in the registration statement."

In order to avoid any misleading inferences and to assure that the historical operating data are fairly presented, appropriate care must be taken to recast the operating figures originally reported for prior years, so as to give effect to transactions and adjustments made in subsequent years which are properly applicable to the operations of respective years included in the summary earnings statement. Where necessary, attention should be directed, by means of explanatory footnotes or otherwise, to the effect on the yearly net earnings resulting from significant nonrecurring or extraordinary items.

Where the summary of earnings, or any part thereof, is presented on an audited basis, it must be covered in the accountants' certificate. Accordingly the introduction to the "Summary," quite often captioned "Consolidated Statement of Income and Retained Earnings," generally states that the income statements for the periods covered have been examined by the named independent public accountants and reference to their opinion is made elsewhere in the prospectus. The following are illustrative:

SUMMARY OF EARNINGS

The following statements of income of J. L. Clark Manufacturing Co. for the seven years ended November 30, 1967, have been examined by Lybrand, Ross Bros. & Montgomery, independent certified public accountants, whose report thereon appears elsewhere in this prospectus. The statements of income for the six months ended May 31, 1968 and 1967 have not been audited, but in the opinion of the Company, include all adjustments (consisting only of normal recurring accruals) considered necessary for a fair presentation of earnings for those periods. This summary of earnings should be read in conjunction with the other financial statements and Notes to Financial Statements included elsewhere in this prospectus.

(Dollars in thousands except per share data)

	Six months ended May 31 (unaudited)	
	1968	*1967*
Net sales	$16,322.5	$15,136.5
Cost of sales	12,937.7	12,114.2
Gross profit from sales	3,384.8	3,022.3
Selling and administrative expenses	1,678.9	1,578.6
Operating profit	1,705.9	1,443.7
Other income:		
Interest from marketable investments	.8	3.4
Net gain on sale of plant assets	.7	2.7
Miscellaneous	2.0	14.8
	3.5	20.9
	1,709.4	1,464.6
Other deductions:		
Interest	155.0	25.2
Miscellaneous	–	–
	155.0	25.2

	Six months ended May 31 (unaudited)	
	1968	*1967*
Earnings before provision for state and federal income taxes	1,554.4	1,439.4
Provision for income taxes (Note A):		
State	22.0	22.1
Federal:		
Current	788.9	689.9
Deferred	(10.0)	(30.6)
	800.9	681.4
Earnings before extraordinary item	753.5	758.0
Extraordinary item – life insurance proceeds received in excess of cash surrender value of policies (Note B)	–	–
Net earnings (Notes A, B, and E)	$ 753.5	$ 758.0
Per common share (Note C):		
Earnings before extraordinary item	$1.18	$.94
Extraordinary item	–	–
Net earnings	$1.18	$.94
Pro Forma Net Earnings (Note D)	$1.07	–
Cash dividends declared	$ .40	$.37½
Average number of shares outstanding during the period (Note C)	640,355	803,157

	(Dollars in thousands except per share data) Year ended November 30 (unaudited)						
	1967	*1966*	*1965*	*1964*	*1963*	*1962*	*1961*
Net sales	$29,958.6	$30,418.9	$26,480.0	$23,208.4	$23,481.0	$23,424.8	$21,572.3
Cost of sales	24,115.0	24,364.0	21,439.9	18,834.4	18,932.7	19,182.5	17,650.8
Gross profit from sales	5,843.6	6,054.9	5,040.1	4,374.0	4,548.3	4,242.3	3,921.5
Selling and administrative expenses	3,059.8	3,019.2	2,767.0	2,425.2	2,397.7	2,335.5	2,417.3
Operating profit	2,783.8	3,035.7	2,273.1	1,948.8	2,150.6	1,906.8	1,504.2
Other income:							
Interest from marketable investments	2.8	4.0	2.2	20.3	16.2	17.3	18.1
Net gain on sale of plant assets	4.0	9.4	13.7	8.4	23.8	25.0	2.1
Miscellaneous	23.7	60.2	10.2	15.8	29.0	10.9	26.3
	30.5	73.6	26.1	44.5	69.0	53.2	46.5
	2,814.3	3,109.3	2,299.2	1,993.3	2,219.6	1,960.0	1,550.7
Other deductions:							
Interest	58.0	6.3	12.7	3.9	6.8	18.7	59.5
Miscellaneous	–	.1	1.7	.1	4.6	4.3	4.9
	58.0	6.4	14.4	4.0	11.4	23.0	64.4
Earnings before provision for state and federal income taxes	2,756.3	3,102.9	2,284.8	1,989.3	2,208.2	1,937.0	1,486.3
Provision for income taxes (Note A):							
State	40.3	48.1	34.2	22.8	22.7	24.8	17.0
Federal:							
Current	1,319.0	1,503.9	1,007.9	877.6	974.6	926.7	723.6
Deferred	(60.2)	(69.9)	43.8	63.7	76.0	47.4	–
	1,299.1	1,482.1	1,085.9	964.1	1,073.3	998.9	740.6
Earnings before extraordinary item	1,457.2	1,620.8	1,198.9	1,025.2	1,134.9	938.1	745.7

	(Dollars in thousands except per share data) Year ended November 30 (unaudited)						
	1967	*1966*	*1965*	*1964*	*1963*	*1962*	*1961*
Extraordinary item—life insurance proceeds received in excess of cash surrender value of policies (Note B).........	–	–	–	–	–	–	78.8
Net earnings (Notes A, B, and E)...............	$ 1,457.2	$ 1,620.8	$ 1,198.9	$ 1,025.2	$ 1,134.9	$ 938.1	$ 824.5
Per common share (Note C):							
Earnings before extraordinary item.......	$1.81	$2.02	$1.50	$1.28	$1.42	$1.17	$ .93
Extraordinary item.....	–	–	–	–	–	–	.10
Net earnings	$1.81	$2.02	$1.50	$1.28	$1.42	$1.17	$1.03
Pro Forma Net Earnings (Note D)...........	–	–	–	–	–	–	–
Cash dividends declared..................	$.77½	$.70	$.65	$.60	$.37½	$.43¾	$.30
Average number of shares outstanding during the period (Note C).....................	805,762	800,385	800,000	800,000	800,000	800,000	800,000

NOTES TO SUMMARY OF EARNINGS:

(A) The federal income tax provision for the six months ended May 31, 1968, includes the 10 percent surcharge which was enacted retroactively, effective January 1, 1968.

The Company has purchased equipment which entitles it to investment tax credits against its federal income taxes, otherwise payable.

During the year ended November 30, 1964, the Company adopted the practice (and has since followed such practice) of accounting for the investment tax credit as a reduction of federal income taxes in the year in which such equipment was placed in use.

In accordance with the above change in practice of accounting for the investment tax credit, the summary of earnings for the years ended November 30, 1962 and 1963, was restated to reflect the reduction of the provision for federal income taxes (with corresponding increases in net earnings) from those amounts originally reported by the following amounts:

Year ended November 30, 1962 $ 33,343. Year ended November 30, 1963 $104,663.

(B) In compliance with the opinion of the Accounting Principles Board, the life insurance proceeds originally reported as a special item in 1961 have been restated as an extraordinary item.

(C) Based upon the weighted average number of shares outstanding throughout the period after giving retroactive effect to the recapitalization in October, 1963, in which each previously outstanding $100 par value share was exchanged for 800 new shares of $1.00 par value.

(D) After giving effect to the sale of 115,000 treasury shares offered hereby, the proceeds of which will be used to reduce the Company's 7% bank loans outstanding under a revolving line of credit (see "Use of Proceeds" elsewhere in this Prospectus), the net earnings per share for the six month period ended May 31, 1968, would have been reduced 11 cents to $1.07. Net earnings used in this per share calculation has been adjusted for the interest expense, and the tax effect thereof, related to the debt to be retired.

(E) Reference is made to the text below for information concerning operations in the 1967 fiscal year.

The decline in sales in the fiscal year ended November 30, 1967, as compared with 1966 was caused, in the Company's opinion, primarily by inventory reductions by several major customers. The sales decline and a five weeks strike at the Company's Lancaster plant in May and June 1967 were, in the Company's opinion, the principal causes of the decline in earnings in fiscal 1967 as compared with 1966.

REPORT OF INDEPENDENT CERTIFIED PUBLIC ACCOUNTANTS

To the Board of Directors
J. L. Clark Manufacturing Co.
Rockford, Illinois

We have examined the balance sheet of J. L. Clark Manufacturing Co. as of November 30, 1967, the statements of income (included under "Summary of Earnings") for the seven years then ended, and the related statements of retained earnings and capital surplus for the three years ended November 30, 1967. Our examinations were made in accordance with generally accepted auditing standards, and accordingly included such tests of the accounting records and such other auditing procedures as we considered necessary in the circumstances.

In our opinion, the aforementioned financial statements present fairly the financial position of J. L. Clark Manufacturing Co. at November 30, 1967, and the results of its operations for the seven years then ended in conformity with generally accepted accounting principles applied on a consistent basis, as restated (See Notes A and B to "Summary of Earnings").

Lybrand, Ross Bros. & Montgomery
Rockford, Illinois
January 10, 1968

CONSOLIDATED STATEMENT OF INCOME AND RETAINED EARNINGS

The following statement has been examined by Price Waterhouse & Co., independent accountants, whose opinion thereon appears elsewhere in this Prospectus. The statement should be read in conjunction with the Consolidated Balance Sheet and Notes to the Consolidated Financial Statements included elsewhere in this Prospectus.

	Year Ended December 31				
	1967	*1966*	*1965*	*1964*	*1963*
	(In thousands of dollars)				
Net sales	$390,919	$353,402	$341,752	$291,216	$304,711
Rentals	60,003	47,815	33,984	25,079	16,412
Machine service and other operating revenue	99,691	88,436	80,931	73,951	66,282
Gain on sale of land	–	1,378	–	–	1,672
Other income	3,273	2,747	2,747	2,216	1,697
	$553,886	$493,778	$459,414	$392,462	$390,774
Cost of products and services sold and rentals, exclusive of research and development expenses shown separately below (Notes 2 and 9)	$309,224	$272,389	$279,371	$234,779	$242,265
Research and development expenses (Note 9)	22,228	18,776	15,768	15,185	16,189
Administrative, selling and general expense (Note 9)	146,473	134,020	120,829	114,833	109,893
Interest expense					
Long-term debt	7,224	4,516	4,069	4,223	3,874
Short-term borrowings	3,346	3,212	2,679	1,980	2,369
	$488,495	$432,913	$422,716	$371,000	$374,590
Income before income taxes and provision for foreign operations	$ 65,381	$ 60,865	$ 36,698	$ 21,462	$ 16,184
Estimated taxes on income:					
United States (b)	$ 18,705	$ 15,700	$ 8,116	$ (1,542)	$ (2,570)
Foreign	11,633	14,200	9,286	10,300	8,732
Deferred U.S. and foreign income taxes (Note 3)	(1,670)	(2,144)	(896)	1,796	631
State	642	624	414	196	167
	$ 29,310	$ 28,380	$ 16,920	$ 10,750	$ 6,960
Provision for foreign operations	1,250	1,500	2,250	500	715
	$ 30,560	$ 29,880	$ 19,170	$ 11,250	$ 7,675

	Year Ended December 31				
	1967	*1966*	*1965*	*1964*	*1963*
	(In thousands of dollars)				
Net income for the year (Note 1)	$ 34,831	$ 30,985	$ 17,528	$ 10,212	$ 8,509
Retained earnings at beginning of year	114,074	91,255	81,120	78,315	76,857
Dividends declared	(8,178)	(8,166)	(7,393)	(7,407)	(7,051)
Retained earnings at end of year (Note 4)	$140,727	$114,074	$ 91,255	$ 81,120	$ 78,315
Net income per share (c)	$4.26	$3.85	$2.37	$1.38	$1.22
Cash dividends per share	$1.00	$1.00	$1.00	$1.00	$1.00
Ratio of earnings to fixed charges (d)	5.7	6.7	4.7	3.4	2.8

NOTES:

(a) Numerical note references are to Notes to Consolidated Financial Statements.

(b) Deferred rental income from assigned leases is carried on a net of tax basis. As a result, the provisions for U.S. income taxes exclude taxes payable of $5,400,000, $1,500,000 and $6,000,000 in 1963, 1964 and 1967, respectively, and includes $5,100,000 and $5,400,000 in 1965 and 1966, respectively, which were paid in prior years.

(c) Net income per share is based on the average number of shares, exclusive of treasury shares, outstanding during each year.

(d) For the purpose of computing the ratio of earnings to fixed charges, earnings represent net income plus estimated income taxes and fixed charges. Fixed charges represent interest, amortization of debt discount, premium and expenses, and one-third of all rentals.

The pro forma ratio of earnings to fixed charges in the year ended December 31, 1967, would have been 5.9, if adjusted to give effect to the issue of the Debentures and the borrowing of $13,800,000 from the consortium of Swiss banks on April 1, 1968, and to the application of the proceeds of the sale of the Debentures to the retirement of short-term debt.

The initial annual interest requirement on the Debentures offered hereby will be $2,812,500. If the Company is required in the future to recognize and amortize as discount an amount assigned to the convertibility feature of the Debentures, then based on an estimate that such discount would amount to about $26,000,000, initial annual financial charges in respect of the Debentures would be increased by approximately $650,000 as a result of amortization thereof on the "interest" method. The Company does not intend to impute any discount to the Debentures by reason of the value of their convertibility feature unless it is required to do so and, if so required, the amount ultimately imputed may be different from that stated above.

Consolidated net income for the quarter ended March 31, 1968, was $6,231,000 or $.76 per share compared with $5,152,000 or $.63 per share in the same period of 1967. Consolidated net revenue for the quarter ended March 31, 1968, was $140,396,000 compared with $111,227,000 for the same period in 1967. In the opinion of the Company, all adjustments, consisting only of normal recurring adjustments, necessary for a fair statement of consolidated net revenues and consolidated net income for the unaudited three month periods have been made.

OPINION OF INDEPENDENT ACCOUNTANTS

To the Shareholders of Burroughs Corporation:

In our opinion, the consolidated balance sheet and consolidated statement of income and retained earnings appearing elsewhere in this Prospectus present fairly the consolidated financial position of Burroughs Corporation and its consolidated subsidiary companies at December 31, 1967, and the results of their operations for the five years then ended, in conformity with generally accepted accounting principles consistently applied. Our examination of these statements was made in accordance with generally accepted auditing standards and accordingly included such tests of the accounting records and such other auditing procedures as we considered necessary in the circumstances.

Price Waterhouse & Co.
Detroit, Michigan
January 17, 1968

For the protection of persons relying on such representations, and in answer to inquiries by representatives of the accounting profession, the chief accountant of the SEC issued an opinion,[3] the pertinent part of which is presented below, indicating the circumstances under which independent public accountants may properly express an opinion, and the form of such opinion, with respect to summary earnings statements included in the registration statements and prospectuses:

It is generally improper and misleading for an accountant to permit his name to be used in connection with any period covered by a summary earnings table or to undertake to express his professional opinion as to the fairness of the representations made for such period in a summary earnings table unless he has made an examination for such period in accordance with generally accepted auditing standards applicable in the circumstances. When the independent accountant has been the auditor for the company throughout the entire period covered by the summary, and his several examinations conformed to generally accepted auditing standards, he would ordinarily need to make only such additional review as would be necessary to satisfy himself as to whether any recasting of the statements originally prepared would be necessary to reflect transactions and adjustments recorded in later years but clearly applicable to prior operations. If the instant work represents the first engagement of the accountant by the registrant and he is to express his expert opinion with respect to the earlier periods contained in the summary, it would, in my opinion, be necessary for him to apply to the operations and transactions of each of the earlier periods with respect to which he is to express an opinion substantially the same auditing procedures as those employed with respect to the first 2 years of the 3-year certified profit and loss or income statement included in the registration statement.

In cases where the accountant has performed sufficient work to make it appropriate for him to permit the use of his name in connection with a summary earnings table there remains to be considered the form in which he should indicate his opinion. Under the rules promulgated by this Commission, the customary method used by accountants in expressing their expert opinion takes the form of a certificate conforming to the requirements of Rule 2-02 of Regulation S-X. Such certificates make appropriate representations as to the work done, state the opinion of the accountants as to the fairness of the statements presented, and describe clearly any exceptions which the accountants may wish to take. Since, as pointed out earlier, summary earnings tables are a species of income statement it would appear that the accountant's certificate thereon should assume a comparable form, and should be included with the summary or made a part of his report as to the 3-year certified statement. If exceptions have been taken by the accountant with respect to any of the information contained in the summary earnings table, special care should be exercised in selecting the language used to introduce the summary to indicate clearly that such exceptions exist and to direct attention to the opinion of the accountant.

DESCRIPTION OF BUSINESS: As supplemental information, Item 9 of Form S-1 requires an analysis of (*a*) total sales and revenues and (*b*) income (or loss) before income taxes and extraordinary items, by major lines of business and/or classes of products or services, disclosing the approximate amount or percentage of each which contributed at least 10% to (*a*) or (*b*) above during either of the last two fiscal years. Where total sales and revenues do not exceed $50 million, then 15% is to be used.

OMISSION OF STATEMENTS: A registrant, filing on Forms 10 or 10-K, which meets either of the following conditions may omit its individual statements and file in lieu thereof the required consolidated statements described below: (1) The registrant is primarily an operating company and all subsidiaries included in the consolidated financial statements filed are wholly owned subsidiaries and are not indebted to any person other than the parent or the consolidated subsidiaries in an amount which is material in relation to the total

[3] Accounting Series Release No. 62.

consolidated assets at the date of the latest balance sheet filed, excepting indebtedness incurred in the ordinary course of business which is not overdue and which matures within one year from the date of its creation, whether evidenced by securities or not. Indebtedness of a subsidiary which is guaranteed by or secured by leases of its parent or the parent's consolidated subsidiaries is to be excluded for the purpose of this determination. (2) The registrant's total assets, exclusive of investments in and advances to the consolidated subsidiaries, constitute 75% or more of the total assets shown by the latest consolidated balance sheet filed *and* the registrant's total gross revenues for the latest period for which its profit and loss statements would be filed, exclusive of interest and dividends received, or equity in income, from the consolidated subsidiaries, constitute 75% or more of the total gross revenue shown by the consolidated profit and loss statement filed.*

The primary purpose is to obtain an earnings picture of the combined enterprise and to avoid individual statements which are meaningless in and of themselves. In condition 1 above the wholly owned subsidiaries would, in effect, be operating divisions of the parent. And in condition 2 where the parent's assets and revenues exceed 85 percent of the consolidated group and the consolidated statements are submitted, it is the considered view of the SEC that the additional statements of the parent are not essential for a fair appraisal of the financial and operating position of the combined enterprise.

Consolidated statements. An issuer which holds a majority interest in the outstanding voting stock of one or more subsidiaries ordinarily is required to file consolidated statements. These statements are subject to the same requirements as the parent, cover the same periods, and must be certified to the same extent. Under certain conditions financial statements of majority-held subsidiaries may be excluded from consolidation and filed separately. Such might be the case because of long-standing practice, because a dissimilar type of operation is involved, or because the subsidiary is located in a foreign country which restricts the free transfer of funds to one parent company, or where the political or economic situations prevalent create uncertainty as to the status of the enterprise.

Statements of unconsolidated subsidiaries and 50 percent owned affiliates. Separate or combined financial statements of unconsolidated majority-owned subsidiaries and 50 percent owned affiliates are required to be filed unless they are, in the aggregate, not significant. Rule 1-02 of Regulation S-X defines a "significant subsidiary" as one which meets any of the following conditions:

1. The assets of the subsidiary, or the investments in and advances to the subsidiary by its parent and the parent's other subsidiaries, if any, exceed 15 percent of the assets of the parent and its subsidiaries on a consolidated basis.
2. The sales and operating revenues of the subsidiary exceed 15 percent of the sales and operating revenues of its parent's subsidiaries on a consolidated basis.
3. The subsidiary is the parent of one or more subsidiaries and together with such subsidiaries would, if considered in the aggregate, constitute a significant subsidiary.

Unconsolidated subsidiaries. Where significant, statements of majority-owned unconsolidated subsidiaries are to be filed on an individual basis or consolidated or combined in one or more groups pursuant to principles of inclusion

* Conditions 1 and 2 above are effective for financial statements filed on Forms 10 and 10-K, on and after Dec. 30, 1970. Form S-1 still shows the percentage requirement as 85%. The revised Form S-1 will probably reduce this to 75%, conforming to Forms 10 and 10-K.

or exclusion which will clearly reflect the financial position and results of operations of the group or groups. The filing of consolidated or combined statements is mandatory, however, where such presentation is essential to an informative and dependable presentation of the facts.[4] Thus, for example, where subsidiaries in related fields are considered, the submission of a combined or consolidated statement would be preferable, since such presentation ordinarily would reflect most clearly the financial and operating condition of the group. These statements are subject to the same provisions as to dating, periods covered, and certification, as would be required if each unconsolidated subsidiary were itself a registrant.

Fifty percent owned affiliates. Where a parent company owns, directly or indirectly, approximately 50 percent of the outstanding voting stock of an affiliate and the remaining approximate 50 percent is owned by another single interest, a complete set of financial statements of such affiliates must be filed, subject to the same reporting requirements as those of the parent.

Additional or other financial statements. The financial statements specifically prescribed for inclusion represent the minimum reporting requirements. The primary intent of registration with the SEC is a full and fair disclosure of all material facts affecting the value of the security registered. If, however, it is determined that the statements prescribed are either inadequate or inappropriate in that they fail to reveal the financial data considered essential for a proper appraisal of the value of the security being registered, the Commission may (1) approve the registrant's request to substitute appropriate comparable statements for those prescribed or (2) direct the registrant to file other appropriate and comparable statements in addition to or in substitution for those prescribed in its standard instruction.

Thus, in addition to the basic financial statements called for, other special statements and disclosures are required to be submitted in the following specific situations: (1) reorganization of registrant; (2) registrant's succession to one or more businesses through merger, consolidation, or otherwise; (3) business acquired or to be acquired by registrant subsequent to the filing of its latest balance sheet.

Historical financial information. At registration, each company whose balance sheet is filed is required to submit, in addition, certain historical financial information, where material, relative to the following: (1) revaluation of property, (2) capital shares, (3) debt discount and expense written off, (4) premium and discount and expense on securities retired, (5) other changes in surplus, and (6) predecessors. The information called for is to be given for all the accounts specified whether they are presently carried on the books or not, and need not be certified. Since an audit is not required, these data ordinarily could be gathered from a survey or review of the accounts specified and need not be detailed beyond a point material to the investor. Companies which have one or more issues already registered with the SEC and have on a previous occasion filed equivalent information for the required period, need not file again, but instead incorporate this information by reference to preceding reports.

Annual Reports. All companies with securities registered under the Securities Exchange Act of 1934 and most companies which have registered securities for sale under the Securities Act of 1933 are required to file an annual report containing, in comparative columnar form, certified balance sheets as of the close of the last two fiscal years and certified profit and loss and source and application of funds statements for such fiscal years. In addition, to keep

[4] Regulation S-X, Rule 4-03.

current the financial information first filed, Item 1 of the form requires that there be included a "summary of earnings" for the last five fiscal years, or longer if necessary to keep the information from being misleading, supplemented in Item 2 by an analysis of (*a*) sales and revenues and (*b*) *net* income (or loss) by lines of business, substantially similar to that required to be furnished in the regulation statement as discussed above.

The annual report on Form 10-K is to be filed within 90 days following the fiscal close. However, all schedules required by Regulation S-X may, at the option of the registrant, be filed as an amendment to the report not later than 120 days after the close of the fiscal year.[5]

Where a company finds it impracticable to file its report within the time specified, an extension may be granted to a later date not exceeding 60 days after the date it would otherwise have to be filed, if it is demonstrated to the satisfaction of the Commission that such request is reasonable and will not adversely affect the interests of the investor.[6] Except for the fact that these statements are to be for the latest fiscal year only, all other requirements as to their submission are substantially the same as at registration.

In addition, there is to be furnished to the SEC copies of any annual report issued to stockholders covering the registrant's last fiscal year. The required number of copies are to be mailed to the Commission not later than the date on which the report is first sent or given to stockholders. This stockholder's report is for informational purposes and is not deemed to be "filed" with the Commission, or otherwise subject to the liabilities of Section 18 of the act (see below), unless the registrant specifically requests that this stockholder's report be incorporated as part of its annual 10-K report. If no annual report is submitted to stockholders, the Commission should be so informed.

Periodic Reports. Quarterly reports are required to be filed on Form 10-Q within 45 days of the close of the period and consists of four parts, of which II and III and the instructions thereto relate to the financials. Part III is to be filed only in the event of a reportable acquisition during the quarter and requires the submission of specified financial statements of the acquired business. Part II calls for the submission of the following summarized financial information for the quarter under review, which need not be certified and is not subject to the liability provisions of Section 18 of the Securities Exchange Act.

A. Summarized Financial Information

Company or group of companies for which report is filed:
Profit and loss information for the ____ months ended:

	______ (Current year)	______ (Preceding year)
1. Gross sales, less discounts, returns and allowances	$______	$______
2. Operating revenues	$______	$______
3. Total of captions 1 and 2	$______	$______
4. Costs and expenses:		
(*a*) Cost of goods sold	$______	$______
(*b*) Operating expenses	$______	$______
(*c*) Selling, general and administrative expenses	$______	$______
(*d*) Interest expense	$______	$______
(*e*) Other deductions, net	$______	$______
Total costs and expenses	$______	$______

[5] General Instructions to Form 10-K.

[6] Rule 12b-25, General Rules and Regulations under the Securities Exchange Act of 1934.

5. Income (or loss) before taxes on income and extraordinary items	$______	$______
6. Provision for taxes on income	$______	$______
7. Income (loss) before extraordinary items	$______	$______
8. (*a*) Extraordinary items, less applicable income tax	$______	$______
(*b*) Minority interest	$______	$______
9. Net income (or loss)	$______	$______
10. Earnings per share data:		
(*a*) Per share of common stock and common stock equivalent:		
(1) Income before extraordinary items	$______	$______
(2) Extraordinary items, net of tax	$______	$______
(3) Net income	$______	$______
(*b*) Per share of common stock, assuming dilution:		
(1) Income before extraordinary items	$______	$______
(2) Extraordinary items, net of tax	$______	$______
(3) Net income	$______	$______
11. Dividend declared, per share	$______	$______

The instructions further prescribe for the disclosure of "any material information necessary to make the information called for not misleading, such as a statement that the results for interim periods are not necessarily indicative of results to be expected for the year, due to seasonal or other specified factors, or an explanation of an unusual increase or decrease in *net* sales or income."

Furnish, insofar as practicable, in the manner described on the following page, a summary of capitalization and stockholders' equity as at the end of the latest fiscal quarter.

B. Capitalization and Stockholders' Equity

Debt	______ (Date)	Amount
Short-term loans, notes, etc.		$______
Long-term debt, including parenthetically portion due within one year (list separately convertible debt)		$______
Total debt		$______
Deferred credits		$______
Stockholders' equity	Shares Outstanding	Amount
Preferred stock (list separately convertible and non-convertible preferred stock)	______	$______
Common stock	______	$______
Capital in excess of par value		$______
Earned surplus		
Balance at beginning of current fiscal year		$______
Prior period adjustments, if any (show credits and charges) separately		$______
Net income (Item 9, above)		$______
Dividends		$(______)
Other credits (charges) (explain nature and amounts)		$______
Balance at end of interim period		$______
Treasury stock (identify class of security, number of shares and basis at which stated)	______	$(______)
Total stockholders' equity		$______

Instructions:

1. The form and content shall conform generally with that in the balance sheet and notes thereto appearing in the annual report filed with the Commission.
2. Minority interests shall be stated separately.
3. The number of shares of each class of security reserved for conversion, warrants, options and other rights shall be separately disclosed.

Proxy Statements. Where action is to be taken with respect to mergers, consolidations, acquisition, authorization or issuance of securities, modification or exchange of securities, or other similar matters, certified financial statements are required to be included in proxy material furnished stockholders. The financials are such as would be required to be filed in an original application for the registration of securities of the issuer under the Securities Act, except that all schedules other than the schedules of supplementary profit and loss information may be omitted.[7]

Where the solicitation is made on behalf of management of the issuer and relates to an annual meeting of security holders at which directors are to be elected, the proxy statement is required to be accompanied or preceded by the annual report to stockholders which contains comparative financial statements for the last two years. Any differences in the financials between those submitted to stockholders and those filed with the Commission must be disclosed. Specifically Rule 14a-3 provides that "any differences, reflected in the financial statements in the report to security holders, from the principles of consolidation or other accounting principles or practices, or methods of applying accounting principles or practices, applicable to the financial statements of the issuer filed or proposed to be filed with the Commission, which have a material effect on the financial position or results of operation of the issuer shall be noted and the effect thereof reconciled or explained in such report."

SEC Guides. Special forms. Special forms are provided for the different classes of issuers registering with the SEC as well as for different types of issues registered by the same issuer. For example, a major utility company might use Form S-1 for sale of common stocks, Form S-8 for an employee savings plan, and Form S-9 for sale of debt. Each of these forms contains detailed instructions applicable to the financial statements required to be included therein. By far the greater number of such registrations and annual reports are filed on Forms S-1 and 10-K, respectively.

Regulation S-X. Regulation S-X sets down the basic rules to be followed in the preparation and certification of the financial statements required to be filed with the SEC. These rules, together with the pronouncements contained in the Accounting Series Releases issued at intervals by the office of the Chief Accountant of the SEC, as well as specific instructions, relate to (1) the qualifications of independent public accountants, as well as the form and content of their certificate; (2) the form and content of balance sheets, profit and loss statements, and surplus statements, together with their supporting schedules and footnotes; and (3) the principles to be followed in the preparation of consolidated or combined statements.

While setting down certain minimum requirements as to the type of information to be included in the financial statements as well as certain basic rules for their preparation, Regulation S-X does not attempt to prescribe accounting methods or even reporting methods in detail. This policy is dictated by the realization that sufficient leeway must be permitted varying types of business, from small merchandising establishments to the far-flung empires of United States Steel Corporation or American Telephone and Telegraph Com-

[7] Rule 14a-3, Regulation 14A, under the Securities Exchange Act of 1934.

pany, to express adequately their financial position and operating results. The ultimate responsibility, therefore, for the preparation of fully informative and dependable financial statements in accordance with recognized and generally accepted accounting principles rests with the company and its independent public accountants.[8] A clear statement of the Commission's policy in this area is contained in its Accounting Series Releases Nos. 4 and 96, published 25 years apart. The former, dated Apr. 25, 1938, reads as follows:

> In cases where financial statements filed with this Commission pursuant to its rules and regulations under the Securities Act of 1933 or the Securities Exchange Act of 1934 are prepared in accordance with accounting principles for which there is no substantial authoritative support, such financial statements will be presumed to be misleading or inaccurate despite disclosures contained in the certificate of the accountant or in footnotes to the statements provided the matters involved are material. In cases where there is a difference of opinion between the Commission and the registrant as to the proper principles of accounting to be followed, disclosure will be accepted in lieu of correction of the financial statements themselves only if the points involved are such that there is substantial authoritative support for the practices followed by the registrant and the position of the Commission has not previously been expressed in rules, regulations, or other official releases of the Commission, including the published opinions of its chief accountant.

The latter, dated Jan. 10, 1963, reads in part as follows:

> In Accounting Series Release No. 1, published April 1, 1937, the Commission announced a program for the purpose of contributing to the development of uniform standards and practice in major accounting questions. Accounting Series Release No. 4 recognizes that there may be sincere differences of opinion between the Commission and the registrant as to the proper principles of accounting to be followed in a given situation and indicates that, as a matter of policy, disclosure in the accountant's certificate and footnotes will be accepted in lieu of conformance to the Commission's views only if such disclosure is adequate and the points involved are such that there is substantial authoritative support for the practice followed by the registrant, and then only if the position of the Commission has not been expressed previously in rules, regulations, or other official releases of the Commission, including the published opinions of its Chief Accountant. This policy is intended to support the development of accounting principles and methods of presentation by the profession but to leave the Commission free to obtain the information and disclosure contemplated by the securities laws and conformance with accounting principles which have gained general acceptance.

Accounting series releases. In the early days of its administration, the Commission held deficient and returned for correction numerous financial statements certified by leading firms of independent public accountants. The primary reasons for rejection included failure to meet the Commission's standards as to full and fair disclosure of financial and operating data, and failure to follow what the Commission's examiners considered to be "recognized and accepted principles of accounting" in the presentation of various controversial items in the balance sheet, profit and loss, and surplus statements.

With a view toward clarifying for the profession its concepts of major accounting problems, the SEC on Apr. 1, 1937, announced a program for the publication, from time to time, of opinions of accounting principles "for the purpose of contributing to the development of uniform standards and practice in major accounting questions."

Many accounting and auditing problems have arisen during the course of

[8] Regulation S-X, Rule 3-01.

the Commission's administration of the Securities Acts which have general application. In such instances the Commission has published its opinions as they arose in specific cases, and has made them available to the general public in the form of special releases entitled Accounting Series Releases. These opinions are prepared by the Commission's chief accountant and in the greater number of cases have been, prior to publication and general release, reviewed by and commented on by the AICPA, the American Accounting Association, the various state societies of certified public accountants, as well as other interested persons and agencies. As a result, these pronouncements have come to be generally recognized as sound and accepted practice for the preparation of informative and dependable financial statements. In December, 1950, the Commission directed that these Accounting Series Releases be considered an integral part of Regulation S-X requirements for the preparation and certification of financial statements.[9]

It should be pointed out, however, that for every matter covered in an Accounting Series Release, a dozen or more equally important accounting matters could be cited where the SEC has a policy well known to regular practitioners in the field which is not expressed in any official publication. The Commission's position on accounting and auditing problems generally is not prescribed to any great extent in its rules and regulations because of its reliance on the profession itself to develop sound and generally accepted principles and practices governing the audit, preparation, and certification of financial statements.

Official decisions and reports of the SEC. The Commission examines all financial statements included in registration statements and annual reports filed to determine whether they have been prepared in accordance with recognized and accepted principles of accounting, and whether they meet the basic requirements of full and fair disclosure. Financial statements have been rejected and formal public hearings held, where examination of the financial statements disclosed willful intent to deceive through (1) the inclusion of untrue, inaccurate, or misleading information of a material nature; (2) the omission of essential material information, or the application of improper accounting principles and methods which materially distort the financial and earnings position of the registrant and its related affiliates. At these hearings before a trial examiner, counsel for the Commission presents the alleged accounting deficiencies, and the registrant and its experts are given an opportunity to testify. In its official decision, the Commission reviews the deficiencies found in the financial statements or the accountants' certificate and expresses its opinion as to what accounting or auditing principles and methods would have been proper under the circumstances. These findings have been compiled in a series of bound volumes entitled "Decisions and Reports of Securities and Exchange Commission," and reflect the official opinions of the SEC on accounting and auditing problems. This is a most valuable source of information, not only for persons charged with the responsibility of preparing, reviewing, or certifying financial statements required to be filed with the SEC, but also for others concerned with the preparation and analysis of informative and dependable statements.

Letters of comment—prefiling and postfiling conferences. Where the examination reveals deficiencies in the form and content of the financial statements, or in the

[9] Accounting Series Release No. 70 and Article 1, Rule 1-01(a), entitled "Application of Regulation S-X" reads as follows: "This regulation (together with the Accounting Series Releases) states the requirements applicable to the form and content of financial statements required to be filed. . . ."

methods followed in their preparation, obviously not intended willfully to deceive or to distort the financial and earnings position of the company, the examining division of the Commission will advise the registrant of its findings by means of a "letter of comment" and request the filing of appropriate amendments to correct these deficiencies. This correspondence is confidential between the Commission and the registrant and is not ordinarily available for public inspection.

The majority of the accounting and auditing problems which arise are resolved through these "letters" and the correspondence which follows. In many instances, the alleged deficiencies become the subject of informal conferences between the Commission's staff and the registrant's independent public accountants. It is a common occurrence, also, for persons intending to file financial statements to arrange for prefiling conferences in an effort to agree upon a solution to the more difficult accounting problems involved in proposed statements. These "letters" and the correspondence or conferences which follow have proved to be a most satisfactory and expeditious means of effecting corrections and improvements in financial statements, as well as resolving difficult or unusual questions where the accounting problem presented is not covered by a specific rule or where the application of existing rules is uncertain.

Enforcement of Reporting Requirements. Unless the financial statements filed are prepared in accordance with what the Commission considers to be recognized and accepted accounting practice, the registration statement will not be permitted to become effective, and a registration statement already effective may be revoked. Since both the Securities Act of 1933 and the Securities Exchange Act of 1934 make it unlawful for any security to be sold in interstate commerce or through the mails, or traded on any national securities exchange unless a registration statement is in effect, the Commission in the final analysis has the authority to determine whether the principles followed in the preparation of financial statements filed with it are in accord with "recognized and accepted accounting practice."

Relationship between SEC and AICPA. The closest cooperation exists between the Securities and Exchange Commission and the AICPA. The Commission, through the office of its chief accountant, and the AICPA, through its committees on cooperation with the SEC, the Accounting Principles Board, and the Committee on Auditing Procedure, meet at intervals to review, discuss, and resolve major current accounting and auditing problems. With few notable exceptions, the official pronouncements of each have the approval of the other. The differences have usually concerned matters of form rather than substance. This exchange of views between the Securities and Exchange Commission and the AICPA has contributed materially to the gradual development of a body of universally recognized and accepted accounting doctrine.

INDEPENDENCE OF ACCOUNTANTS

Qualifications of Accountants. Many local accounting firms, because of their lack of familiarity with SEC requirements for the audit, preparation, and certification of financial reports, frequently find themselves replaced by national accounting firms when a client decides to obtain additional financing through a public offering of securities. Another reason for the change is that clients and underwriters may decide to switch from a small to a large firm when they "go public" because of the belief that it makes the offering more merchandisable. The SEC expresses no preference between the smaller and larger accounting firm, other than to require that the certifying accountant be duly registered and in good standing as such under the laws of the place of his residence or principal office and that he be in fact independent. Specifically, Rule 2-01 of Regulation S-X prescribes in part as follows:

(*a*) The Commission will not recognize any person as a certified public accountant who is not duly registered and in good standing as such under the laws of the place of his residence or principal office. The Commission will not recognize any person as a public accountant who is not in good standing and entitled to practice as such under the laws of the place of his residence or principal office.

(*b*) The Commission will not recognize any certified public accountant or public accountant as independent who is not in fact independent. . . .

Independence—Meaning and Significance. Unless the certifying accountants are completely independent, they cannot be expected to approach their assignment and report thereon with that degree of impartial objectivity which stockholders, creditors, and the general public have been led to believe they have a right to expect of the public accounting profession. The SEC rejects financial statements certified by accountants who are not independent in relation to the particular company whose statements they certify. The chief accountant, in one of his opinions, declared:

Independence tends to assure the objective and impartial consideration which is needed for the fair solution of the complex and often controversial matters that arise in the ordinary course of audit work. On the other hand, bias due to the presence of an entangling affiliation or interest, inconsistent with proper professional relations of accountant and client, may cause loss of objectivity and impartiality and tends to cast doubt upon the reliability and fairness of the accountant's opinion and of the financial statements themselves.[10]

Disclosure of the frauds in McKesson & Robbins, Inc.,[11] resulted in an unprecedented public interest in the adequacy of the protection afforded investors by the certification of financial statements. Here was a situation where during a period of nearly 15 years fraudulent transactions totaling some $20 million were being carried on by management, without detection by a nationally prominent firm of independent accountants who audited the accounts and certified to the fairness of the financial statements year after year throughout this entire period.

Recommendations for Independence. Based on its findings in the McKesson & Robbins affair and other investigations, the SEC offered the following recommendations to help ensure the complete independence of accountants from management control:

1. Election of the auditors for the current year by a vote of the stockholders at the annual meeting followed immediately by notice to the auditors of their appointment.
2. Establishment of a committee to be selected from non-officer members of the board of directors which shall make all company or management nominations of auditors and shall be charged with the duty of arranging the details of the engagement.
3. The certificate (sometimes called short-form report or opinion) should be addressed to the stockholders. All other reports should be addressed to the board of directors, and copies delivered by the auditors to each member of the board.
4. The auditors should be required to attend meetings of the stockholders at which their report is presented to answer questions thereon, to state whether or not they have been given all the information and access to all the books and records which they

[10] Accounting Series Release No. 22.

[11] Securities and Exchange Commission, Report on Investigation in the Matter of McKesson & Robbins, Inc., Washington, D.C., Government Printing Office, 1940.

have required, and to have the right to make any statement or explanation they desire with respect to the accounts.

5. If for any reason the auditors do not complete the engagement and render a report thereon, they shall, nevertheless, render a report on the amount of work they have done and the reasons for noncompletion, which report should be sent by the company to all stockholders.[12]

Many corporations have adopted all or part of these recommendations since they were first made public. It cannot be too strongly emphasized that accountants certifying the financial statements of publicly owned corporations need to recognize that they have a definite responsibility to the large number of investors to report not alone on the financial condition and operating results of the corporate enterprise, but also on the activities of management itself.

Regulation 14 under the Securities Exchange Act of 1934, which relates to proxy statements furnished stockholders, provides that where action is to be taken with respect to the selection or approval of auditors, or where it is proposed that particular auditors should be recommended by any committee to select auditors for whom votes are to be cast, the auditors should be named in the proxy statement together with a brief description of any direct financial interest or any material indirect financial interest in the issuer or any of its parents or subsidiaries, or any connection during the past 3 years with the issuer or any of its parents or subsidiaries in the capacity of promoter, underwriter, voting trustee, director, officer, or employee.

Relationships Preventing Independence. In determining whether public accountants are in fact independent as regards the particular company whose statements are covered by the certificate, appropriate consideration should be given to all relevant circumstances, including evidence bearing on the relationships between the accountant and his client. As to accountants certifying financial statements filed with the SEC, the Commission has instructed its staff to give appropriate consideration to the propriety of the relationships and practices involved in all services performed for that particular company by such accountants, including the certification of any financial statements which have been published or otherwise made generally available to security holders, creditors, or the public. In this connection Rule 2-01 of Regulation S-X specifically provides:

(*b*) . . . An accountant will be considered not independent with respect to any person or any of its parents or subsidiaries in whom he has, or had during the period of report, any direct financial interest or any material indirect financial interest; or with whom he is, or was during such period, connected as a promoter, underwriter, voting trustee, director, officer, or employee.

(*c*) In determining whether an accountant may in fact be not independent with respect to a particular person, the Commission will give appropriate consideration to all relevant circumstances, including evidence bearing on all relationships between the accountant and that person or any affiliate thereof, and will not confine itself to the relationship existing in connection with the filing of reports with the Commission.

Quite concerned about the manner in which the Commission's staff might interpret this directive, representatives of the accounting profession requested further clarification and specific illustrations which might be used as a guide. In discussions and conferences arising out of such inquiries, the SEC made it clear that it is interested in relationships between a certifying accountant and the company only insofar as the existence of particular rela-

[12] Accounting Series Release No. 19.

tionships might be relevant to its determination whether the accountant was in fact independent. Certain relationships between an accountant and his client, such as referred to in Rule 2-01(b) and (c) of Regulation S-X, may tend to prevent the accountant from reviewing the financial statements and accounting procedures of a client with complete objectivity, and the Commission has taken the position that the existence of these relationships will preclude its finding that the accountant is in fact independent. Accounting Series Releases Nos. 2, 47, and with appendix thereto, briefly summarize a significant number of representative cases, involving director, officer, and employee relationships, financial interests, and other so-called "entangling alliances" which resulted in the disqualification of certifying accountants from being considered independent in the circumstances.[13] It should be emphasized, however, that a finding in a particular case that an accountant is not independent does not necessarily reflect on his professional standing or qualification to serve other clients registered with the SEC.

Relationships Not Preventing Independence. In the ascertainment of whether accountants or members of their families have entered into one of these relationships with remote affiliates of the persons whose statements are being certified and whether, in some instances, they hold indirectly any financial interest in the registrant or any of its parents or subsidiaries, there is an area in which some latitude of judgment is necessary in order to avoid undue hardship and expense to registrants and to accounting firms having a widespread accounting practice, or whose clients have numerous affiliates. As to these borderline cases, the Commission has applied the test of materiality. In the final analysis, therefore, the question of independence is one of fact that can be determined only in the light of all pertinent facts in a particular case.

Another Accounting Series Release summarizes a number of representative situations involving director, officer, and employee relationships, financial interests, and certain other relationships which the SEC held to be *not* of material significance to disqualify certifying accountants from being considered independent in the circumstances.[14] The following interpretations of the independence rule were given to an accounting firm which submitted two hypothetical situations:

1. Company A proposed to file a registration statement and merge with or acquire company X, which has been entirely independent of company A. Financial statements of each company certified by different accounting firms were to be included in the registration statement.

In this situation if partners of the firm of accountants for company X had a financial interest in company A, that accounting firm could be considered independent for the purpose of certifying the statements of company X to be included in a registration statement filed by company A. This conclusion assumes that company A's shares are widely held and the partners' interest is similar to any public investor's. A different conclusion would be indicated if the partners of the accounting firm were in a position to influence the action of company A.

If company X were to continue as a subsidiary of company A, the accounting firm would not be considered independent for subsequent audits unless

[13] See also Accounting Series Releases Nos. 82, 87, 91, 92, 97, 99, 101, 105, 110 and in *The Matter of Cornucopia Gold Mines* 1 SEC 364; *The Matters of American Terminals and Transit Company* 1 SEC 1 701; *Rickard Ramore Gold Mines Ltd.*, 2 SEC 377; *Metropolitan Personal Loan Company*, 2 SEC 803, and Accounting Series Release No. 28; *A. Hollander & Sons Inc.*, 8 SEC 586.

[14] Accounting Series Release No. 81.

the partners of the firm promptly disposed of their financial interest in company A.

2. In a situation similar to that described above, the accounting firm which had certified the statements of company A generally would have no knowledge of the investments of its partners in nonclient corporations such as company X. In some large national accounting firms the determination of such holdings can be a time-consuming and burdensome task. Under these circumstances, Item 24 of the requirements of a registration statement under the Securities Act of 1933 (disclosure of relationships between registrant and experts whose opinions are included in the registration statement) may be answered in the negative with a disclaimer of knowledge as to whether or not the certifying accountants of company A had any interest in company X.

SCOPE OF THE AUDIT

Responsibility of the CPA. Determination of the scope of the audit necessary in a particular case is the absolute responsibility of the independent accountant, and one which he cannot avoid, whether or not an SEC filing is involved. Subordination of his judgment in this matter to that of management or other persons in control disqualifies him completely from being considered independent for purposes of certifying the financial statements of such company.

In coming to a final conclusion as to the area to be covered, the independent accountant should give proper consideration and due weight to the adequacy of the systems of internal control and audit maintained by the company. He should review transactions between the company and its officers, directors, and affiliates to determine the nature and extent of the examination which may be required under the circumstances. He should also review the accounting procedures followed by the company and satisfy himself that such procedures are in accord with recognized practice, have been consistently maintained during the period under review, and are not inconsistent with those of prior periods. The scope must be sufficiently comprehensive to enable the independent accountant to express an informed, objective, and impartial judgment as to whether the statements covered by his certificate present fairly the financial position of the company and the results of its operations, after giving due consideration to the effect of any significant events or transactions between the fiscal close and the date of the certificate, in conformity with generally accepted accounting principles applied on a basis consistent with that of the preceding year. Unless the scope is sufficiently adequate for this purpose, the independent accountant should refrain from expressing an opinion. Instead he should clearly state in his certificate that he is in no position to express an opinion and should indicate his reasons therefor.[15]

Illustrative Cases. The following three cases are illustrative:

1. In the case of the *Associated Gas & Electric Company*,[16] the SEC held that the certifying accountants failed to make audits sufficiently comprehensive in scope to justify their expression of an opinion as to the financial statements in question. In justification of the scope and nature of their audit, independent accountants argued that to have made a more comprehensive ex-

[15] Statements on Auditing Procedure No. 33, *Auditing Standards and Procedures*, AICPA (Committee on Auditing Procedure), New York, 1963, p. 19.

[16] 11 SEC 975.

amination would have involved a disproportionate amount of time and expense to make reasonably accurate determinations of the dollar amounts involved. In view of the distorted, confusing, and misleading financial statements which were finally presented, the reasons advanced by the accountants were considered to be without merit.

2. In the case of *Resources Corporation International*,[17] it was held that the certifying accountants failed in the performance of their duty by not broadening the scope of their examination to resolve serious doubts, expressed by the senior accountant to the partner in charge of the engagement, as to the legitimacy of the bookkeeping methods employed by the company and the nature of the relationship which existed between it and Hoover, its principal promoter and stockholder. Had they expanded their examination, the independent accountants would have discovered that the representations made in the financial statements with respect to the cost and acquisition of properties acquired by the corporation from Hoover, the source of corporate income, and the direction of its activities were materially misleading. Further, they would have discovered the huge personal profits made by Hoover in transferring to the corporation the timber properties which constituted substantially all of its assets. Observed the Commission:

> In view then of those grave doubts (expressed by their senior accountant) and of the information which came to the attention and which was at the disposal of the accountants, they were, in our opinion, under an affirmative duty to examine, most carefully, into the relationship between Hoover and the Syndicate subscribers and between Hoover and R.C.I. and to disclose the true facts. . . .

3. In the case of the *Red Bank Oil Company*,[18] the scope of audit was held to be inadequate for the purpose of certifying the financial statements for two reasons: First, the accountants failed to examine the accounts and activities of a subsidiary which accounted for about 70 percent of the consolidated sales and almost 50 percent of the consolidated assets, or to make a proper review and study of the audit report of such company prepared by other accountants, prior to the inclusion of these figures in the consolidated statements. Observed the SEC in its formal opinion:

> We think it wholly clear that where an accountant undertakes to express his opinion in part in reliance on reports of other accountants, it is essential that he have far more knowledge of the underlying facts and of the accounting principles followed than was exhibited here. Lacking such knowledge, it is impossible for him to express an informed judgment as to whether the figures reported to him by other accountants have been properly included in the consolidated statements.

Second, the accountants failed to examine the transactions and indebtedness between the parent company, its affiliates, promoters, directors, principal stockholders, and key management personnel. In one instance, the wife of the president of the corporation and one of the officers who was also a director sold to such company their stock interest in another company which cost them $3,000 and received in exchange $150,000 par value stock of the parent company. The acquired stock was set up in the accounts at the latter figure. Although the circumstances indicated a lack of arm's-length bargaining, the independent accountants made no attempt to review or disclose the details of the transaction and further failed to express any opinion

[17] 7 SEC 689.
[18] Securities Act of 1933, SEC Release No. 3110; see also 21 SEC 695 and 25 SEC 334.

as to the value at which the acquired stock was shown in the Red Bank statements. Said the Commission:

> We think it clear in any event that it is materially misleading to reflect this stock at the par value of the Red Bank shares issued therefor without full disclosure of the circumstances under which it was acquired.

AUDITING STANDARDS AND PROCEDURES

Auditing standards and procedures applicable in SEC filings are not substantially different from those in other audit engagements by independent accountants. In addition, however, and as a guide to proper SEC practice, the auditor should become familiar with the Commission's findings in representative cases wherein, after examination and opportunity for hearing, it was held that generally accepted auditing standards and procedures were, in fact, not complied with, as explained below.

Auditing Standards. No matter how adequate the scope, unless the audit is planned and executed in a thoroughly competent and expert manner, by a well-trained and fully qualified staff under the direction and supervision of persons of broad training and experience who are wholly conversant with the activities of the particular enterprise and the auditing procedures applicable in the circumstances, the judgments based thereon can be neither sound nor reliable. Since the reputation and status of the profession and its members rest in large measure on the confidence with which creditors, stockholders, the financial community, and the public in general accept the representations and opinions contained in the certificate, independent accountants must exercise the highest degree of vigilance, objectivity, and impartiality in the performance of their engagement and in the expression of their informed judgments.

Cognizant of its responsibilities in this matter to the public and profession alike, the AICPA has adopted the following definition and description of the term "generally accepted auditing standards" as they apply to (1) general standards, (2) standards of fieldwork, and (3) standards of reporting: [19]

> Auditing standards may be said to be differentiated from auditing procedures in that the latter relate to acts to be performed, whereas the former deal with measures of the quality of the performance of those acts, and the objectives to be attained in the employment of the procedures undertaken. Auditing standards as thus distinct from auditing procedures concern themselves not only with the auditor's professional qualities but also with his judgment exercised in the conduct of his examination and in his reporting thereon.

The following situations briefly illustrate wherein the examination, investigation, or review failed to measure up to accepted standards:

1. In a recent case,[20] the SEC instituted proceedings under its Rules of Practice to determine whether an accounting firm and two of its partners had violated the professional rules of conduct in the audit, preparation, and certification of the financial statements of Oleon Company, Inc., and its successor, the Oleon Division of H. L. Green Company, Inc., in 1958 and 1959. Based upon its investigation, the Commission's staff issued a report which concluded that the conduct of the accounting firm in its audit of the Oleon accounts, books, and records represented a complete abdication of the re-

[19] SAP No. 33, pp. 15–17.

[20] Accounting Series Release No. 105.

sponsibilities of an independent public accountant. Subsequent to the institution of such proceedings, the partnership was dissolved, the senior partner died, and the remaining partner, without admitting the allegation against him, agreed that he would not appear or practice before the Commission in the future, with the understanding that the proceedings would be dismissed against him and that the Commission might issue a statement with respect to its actions.

1*a*. In another case involving a nonpublic investigative proceeding, the SEC held that there may have been a lack of adherence to auditing standards by a certified public accountant in connection with the preparation and submission of certain material to the Commission. In the circumstances the accountant submitted his resignation, in which he agreed that he would not appear or practice before the Commission in the future.[21]

2. In the case of the *Red Bank Oil Company,* referred to on the preceding pages, the SEC pointed to the failure of accountants to investigate and disclose fully the items in the financial statements relating to transactions and indebtedness existing between the parent company and its officers, directors, and their affiliates; the readiness of the accountants to accept without question the statements of management in these matters; the lax procedures followed in reviewing the results of the audit and the working papers of other accountants prior to the preparation of the final consolidated report; and the complete lack of independence in the performance of the investigation. The Commission concluded its report with the following observation:

> We find that the audits for the years under consideration were inadequate and not performed in a manner consistent with generally accepted auditing standards. The issues of independence and scope of audit tend to merge since it is highly doubtful whether an accountant lacking in independence can ever exercise the objectivity, vigilance and inquisitiveness essential to his task required by generally accepted auditing standards.

3. In the case of *McKesson & Robbins, Inc.,*[22] the SEC, after a thorough investigation of all the facts in the case, including the testimony not alone of the certifying accountants but of other experts as well, concluded that the frauds involving some $20 million would have been discovered by the auditors if their examination had been efficiently performed by competent and qualified personnel in accordance with acceptable standards. The Commission said:

> Their failure to discover the gross overstatement of assets and of earnings is attributable to the manner in which the audit work was done. In carrying out the work they failed to employ that degree of vigilance, inquisitiveness, and analysis of the evidence available that is necessary in a professional undertaking and is recommended in all well-known and authoritative works on auditing.

The accountants maintained that a balance sheet examination is not intended and cannot be expected to detect a falsification of the records concealing an inflation of assets and earnings if accomplished by a widespread conspiracy carried on by the president of a corporation, aided by others within and without the recognized ranks of a corporation's operating personnel, and that no practical system of internal check can be devised, the effectiveness of which cannot be nullified by criminal collusion on the part of a chief executive and key employees. Such cases, the accountants argued, are so rare that, in their opinion, there is no economic justification for the

[21] Accounting Series Release No. 104.
[22] Accounting Series Release No. 19.

amount of auditing work which would be required to increase materially the protection against it. Rejecting these views, the Commission said:

The inference to be drawn from this position and from statements made by others in connection with this case is that a detailed audit of all transactions as distinguished from an examination based on tests and samples would have been necessary to reveal the falsification. However, as we view the situation in this case, a detailed audit of all transactions carried out by the same staff would merely have covered a larger volume of the same kinds of fictitious documents and transactions. While this might have brought under review more instances of what we have listed as circumstances suggesting further investigation, there is little ground for believing that this alone would have raised any greater question as to the authenticity of the transactions.

Moreover, we believe that, even in balance sheet examinations for corporations whose securities are held by the public, accountants can be expected to detect gross overstatements of assets and profits whether resulting from collusive fraud or otherwise. We believe that alertness on the part of the entire staff, coupled with intelligent analysis by experienced accountants of the manner of doing business, should detect overstatements in the accounts, regardless of their cause, long before they assume the magnitude reached in this case. Furthermore, an examination of this kind should not, in our opinion, exclude the highest officers of the corporation from its appraisal of the manner in which the business under review is conducted.

4. A most interesting case in this respect is that of *Associated Gas & Electric Company*,[23] because of material deficiencies both in the financial statements and in the certificate of the independent public accountants. The SEC severely criticized the work of the certifying accountants. The scope of the audit and the nature of the examination were held to be wholly inadequate for the purpose of certifying the financial statements. The opinions expressed in the accountants' certificate were characterized as not clear and so qualified by exceptions and explanations as to render those opinions nugatory. As to the financial statements themselves, it was the Commission's judgment that they were principally intended to mystify, baffle, and mislead, and that the audits and certificates of the accountants did nothing to prevent the accomplishment of that purpose.[24]

In his testimony before the SEC, one of the senior partners of the accounting firm declared: "We certainly thought that our certificates to the financial statements at all times were informative and were in compliance with the regulations of the SEC." The Commission replied:

We emphatically disagree . . . that the certificates of (accounting firm) comply with our requirements. Nor do we believe that the company and its professional accountants may properly plead that these certificates conformed to standards followed by the profession at the time.

Auditing Procedures. In the course of his review and examination of the financial statements and the underlying books, records, accounting procedures, and corporate transactions with officers, directors, affiliates, etc., the independent accountant should apply all accepted auditing procedures generally recognized as normal and applicable in the circumstances. Failure to do so should be clearly disclosed, with reasons therefor, including a description of the alternate procedures employed to satisfy himself as to the propriety of the items involved. Where facts disclosed during the course of the examination raise serious doubts as to the validity of any of the items, transactions, or other activities which may have a significant bearing on the final report, the independent accountant should extend the normal procedures or employ

[23] SEC 975.

[24] Tenth Annual Report of Securities and Exchange Commission, p. 204.

additional procedures deemed essential in the circumstances, in order to satisfy himself completely and resolve all doubts. Failure to do so should be clearly spelled out in the certificate, including a disclosure of all pertinent facts. The independent accountant must be prepared to assume full responsibility for the omission of any procedures ordinarily deemed necessary in a particular case for the purpose of expressing an informed and impartial judgment as to the fairness of the financial statements covered by his certificate.

Inventories and receivables. Following the disclosures of the frauds by the management of McKesson & Robbins, Inc.,[25] which conceivably would have been discovered had independent auditors at that time followed the practice of observing inventory taking and confirming receivables in the normal course of their examination, the membership of the Institute in 1939 approved the extension of auditing procedures to require the observation of inventories and confirmation of receivables where either of these assets represents a significant proportion of the current assets or of the total assets of a concern.[26] Failure to apply them, where they are practicable and reasonable, would ordinarily preclude the expression of an opinion on the fairness of the financial statements taken as a whole.

Appropriate disclosure should be made in the general scope paragraph of the accountants' certificate where such extended procedures are omitted, whether or not they are reasonable and practicable in the circumstances, even though the independent accountant may have satisfied himself by other auditing procedures. In the latter case an affirmative statement to that effect should be included in the second sentence of the scope paragraph, somewhat as follows:

> Our examination was made in accordance with generally accepted auditing standards, and accordingly included such tests of the accounting records and such other auditing procedures as we considered necessary in the circumstances; however, it was not practicable to confirm receivables (to observe the physical inventory taking), as to which we have satisfied ourselves by means of other auditing procedures.

In the above circumstances, no exception would be required in the opinion section of the report. Since in particular instances the omission of such procedures may be entirely proper, the explanations resulting therefrom are not to be considered exceptions or qualifications unless specifically so designated by independent accountants in their certificate. In this connection the following cases are of major interest:

1. As a result of its failure to apply accepted auditing procedures recognized as normal in the circumstances, a nationally prominent firm of independent public accountants certified financial statements in which both inventories and earnings were overstated. Under the circumstances the SEC held hearings to determine whether the accounting firm, its branch manager, and the senior in charge of the engagement were "lacking either in requisite qualifications to represent others, or in character or in integrity, or have engaged in unethical or improper professional conduct; and whether they, or any of them, should be disqualified and denied temporarily or permanently the privilege of appearing and practicing before the Commission."[27]

[25] Accounting Series Release No. 19.
[26] SAP No. 33, pp. 38, 39; see also SAP No. 36.
[27] Accounting Series Releases Nos. 64 and 67.

The discovery of the overstatements came to light some months after the statements had been certified and filed with the SEC. The Commission's hearings resulted in a finding "that each of the respondents acted in an improper professional manner in ignoring and disregarding generally accepted auditing standards and procedures applicable in this case and applicable rules and regulations and long settled decisions of the Commission with respect to the matters referred to above."

While deciding to take no further action against the accounting firm, the resident manager, or the senior accountant in charge, beyond the release to the general public of the findings in the case, the SEC concluded its opinion on this ominous note:

> It seems highly desirable that the public, and particularly the accounting profession be informed that where a firm of public accountants permits a report or certificate to be executed in its name, the Commission will hold such firm fully accountable.

2. In another case involving inventory valuations, it was discovered that subsequent to the certification of the financial statements, management had padded the inventories, with the result that both inventory and earnings were overstated and the statements were false to that extent. From the testimony of employees of the company and the independent accountants, the Commission concluded that the inventory shortage and the methods used to conceal it would have been discovered if the auditors had employed in their examination accepted procedures recognized as normal in the circumstances:

> The record establishes, beyond peradventure, that at least one of the company's principal officers, the president, deliberately manipulated and falsified the accounts in order to create the picture of a good operating record. The malfeasance was so carefully veiled that even the auditors were misled.
>
> There is nothing to indicate that the accountants were aware of the practices in question at the time they certified the financial statements. So far as appears, they were the innocent dupes of designing corporate officials. This fact, however, cannot exonerate them of all blame in connection with the false and misleading financial statements filed with the registration statement. Had they been completely alive to their functions as independent auditors, they would have discovered many of the improper practices and accounting improprieties. Too much reliance was placed on statements of the principal officers regarding many important matters. They apparently made no comprehensive effort to substantiate those statements by contact with employees having first-hand knowledge of the facts or by observation of the physical aspects of the business. And even their analysis of the records was lacking in thoroughness. In short, the audit, as conducted, did not measure up to the type of audit to which stockholders are entitled.[28]

Inventory observations in initial or "first" audits. To be applicable, the extended audit procedures described by the Institute's Committee on Audit Procedure must be *both* practicable and reasonable. From an auditing viewpoint, practicable means "capable of being done with the available means" or ". . . with reason and prudence"; *reasonable* means "sensible in the light of the surrounding circumstances." By this definition, it is clear that the observation of physical inventories at the beginning of the period, or for the year under review, in an initial or first audit where independent accountants are retained following the close of the fiscal period, would be neither practicable nor reasonable in the circumstances. However, for the purpose of expressing an opinion, independent accountants must satisfy themselves as

[28] *Illinois Zinc Company,* 6 SEC 850.

to such inventories by appropriate methods. Having done so, an exception as to failure to observe beginning inventories is not warranted and should be omitted. In such cases, a middle paragraph explaining that the certificate covers a first audit is informative and, in some cases, essential to describe the alternative procedures applied. These procedures, however, must be adequate to support an unqualified opinion as to the fairness of the financial statements. The following is illustrative:

The Villager, Inc.
Philadelphia, Pa.

We have examined the balance sheet of The Villager, Inc., a Delaware Corporation, as of August 31, 1965, and the related statements of income and retained earnings combining the results of operations for the five years and seven months then ended. . . .

We were not engaged as auditors until June 1965, and therefore we were not present to observe procedures used in determining inventory quantities as of dates prior to August 31, 1965. However, based on tests of prices and computations and other auditing procedures, the amounts stated for such inventories appear to be reasonable.

In our opinion, the accompanying balance sheets present fairly . . . and the statements of income and retained earnings . . . present fairly . . . in conformity with generally accepted accounting principles applied on a consistent basis.

Ernst & Ernst

Omission of or failure to extend accepted normal auditing procedures. A certificate is of doubtful value, and can at times be outright misleading, if it is based upon an examination and review which fail to follow accepted normal audit procedures or, where the circumstances require, fail to extend such normal procedure or employ additional procedures, in order to establish a sound basis for arriving at an informed judgment of the position of the company and the fairness of the financial statements. The following selected cases are illustrative:

1. A defalcation of approximately $500,000 was discovered some time after the financial statements of a small loan company were certified and filed with the SEC.[29] Investigation disclosed that the independent accountants had never visited any of the branch offices for audit purposes, did not examine any of notes or applications pertaining thereto held at the branch offices, and did not verify any branch-office loans by direct confirmation with borrowers. A partner of the accounting firm testified that the original records at branch offices were not examined because the engagement called for an audit of the home-office accounts alone. Although he considered the examination of the branch accounts desirable and necessary, and had so informed the management on many occasions, he did not insist upon such examination because he was "reasonably satisfied" that the company's system of internal control was adequate. In rejecting the accountants' certificate, the Commission said:

In our opinion, the accountants did in fact omit, in all of their audits of the registrant's accounts, procedures recognized as the essentials of an audit of a financial company such as the registrant; procedures which, had they been employed, as admitted by the accountant in charge of the audit of the registrant, would have resulted in an early discovery of the defalcations at the Philadelphia branch office of the registrant. We feel that the accountant's certificate in stating that their "examination in respect to the branch office records was sufficient in scope to satisfy ourselves as to the correctness of these accounts" fell short of the requirements of [our rule]. Moreover, *the omission of an adequate examination constituted so complete a disregard of recog-*

[29] *Monroe Loan Society*, 3 SEC 407.

nized accounting practice as to invalidate the accountant's original audit certificate and to impugn the integrity of the financial statements contained in registration statement as it became effective. [Italics supplied].[30]

2. Normal audit procedures should include an examination of the corporate minute books. This was brought out quite forcefully in connection with hearings held in the matter of a mining company whose certified balance sheet contained misstatements of facts. Investigation disclosed that the certifying accountant had failed to make an adequate examination of either the books or the supporting vouchers; that, with the exception of the option agreements which he had seen, the accountant obtained his information primarily from affidavits submitted to him by officers of the corporation; and that he had made no examination of the corporate minutes. The Commission said:

> The apparent omission of any examination of the minute books of the corporation raises some doubt as to whether the accountant has in fact made a reasonable examination. . . . If an accountant submits a balance sheet without having access to the minute books and to proper disbursement vouchers, he should most certainly qualify his certificate by stating the basis upon which he made his audit, and the reasons why such investigation is deemed by him to be reasonable.[31]

Review of Audit Working Papers. A well-planned audit program provides for thorough supervision and review by qualified top personnel of the accounting firm of the working papers of the field auditors prior to the certification of financial statements. In one case an independent accounting firm certified the financial statements of its client, whose assets had been deliberately overstated some $2 million by the senior accountant assigned to perform the audit. The SEC in its formal opinion expressed the view that these irregularities would have been discovered had the working papers been reviewed by a qualified partner in accordance with the following procedure:

> As a matter of principle, a review should be designed with two objectives in mind: First, to insure the integration of the original work papers with the financial statements; second, a searching analysis of the ultimate facts developed in the course of the actual audit. An adequate review with the first purpose in mind should serve not only to disclose intentional or accidental misstatements but should also serve as a method of internal check and control on the work of the firm's subordinates. This branch of the review need not necessarily be carried out by a partner but should at least be done by one well versed in the procedures adopted by the firm and in the general principles and terminology of auditing and accounting. If not a partner of the firm, such review should be made by persons who are independent of those actually performing or supervising the audit work as well as of those who prepared the draft of the financial statements. The second branch of the review is designed to enable the accounting firm to interpret intelligently the figures it has obtained and to which it is to certify. This part of the review should be made by a person, preferably a partner, qualified by his knowledge of sound accounting principles and his familiarity with the accounting phases of the industry and the more important problems of the particular company. In this manner the facts ascertained by competent employees can be subjected to the independent and broader judgment of a more experienced person who can by searching inquiry of the supervisor or senior and by examination of significant items in the work papers and schedules reach an informed judgment both as to the adequacy of the audit work done and as to the integrity and clarity of the financial statements themselves.[32]

[30] See also in *The Matter of Personal Loan Company,* 2 SEC 803.

[31] *Franco Mining Corporation,* 1 SEC 285. See also in *The Matter of Big Wedge Gold Mining Co.,* 1 SEC 98.

[32] *Interstate Hosiery Mills, Inc.,* 4 SEC 706.

In the *BarChris* case discussed in detail below the court severely criticized the auditors' work papers as lacking in clarity, completeness, accuracy, and consistency. In evaluating the qualifications of the senior accountant on the audit, the judge commented: "He was not yet a CPA. He had no previous experience with the bowling industry. This was his first job as a senior accountant. He could hardly have been given a more difficult assignment."

ACCOUNTANT'S CERTIFICATE

Form and Content. The degree of reliability which may be attached to the representations and opinions contained in the accountant's certificate depends in large measure on the answers to the following four questions: (1) Were the accountants completely independent of management and others in control in determining the scope and nature of the examination? (2) Were the review of the financial statements and the examination of the underlying books, records, and procedures, including the activities of management itself, made in a thoroughly expert manner by qualified personnel, in accordance with recognized and generally accepted auditing standards? (3) Were all accepted auditing procedures recognized as normal or deemed necessary in the circumstances fully performed? (4) Are the accountants' opinions impartial, objective, and based upon informed judgments?

Aware of the great reliance placed on the accountant's certificate by in-investors and creditors alike, the SEC, as a result of its findings in the *McKesson & Robbins* affair[33] and after obtaining the views representative of the accounting profession and other interested parties, formulated a set of instructions governing the form and content of the accountant's certificate. Specifically, Rule 2-02 of Regulation S-X provides as follows:

(*a*) Technical requirements.—The accountant's certificate shall be dated, shall be signed manually, and shall identify without detailed enumeration the financial statements covered by the certificate.

(*b*) Representations as to the audit.—The accountant's certificate (i) shall state whether the audit was made in accordance with generally accepted auditing standards; and (ii) shall designate any auditing procedures generally recognized as normal, or deemed necessary by the accountant under the circumstances of the particular case, which have been omitted, and the reasons for their omission.

Nothing in this rule shall be construed to imply authority for the omission of any procedure which independent accountants would ordinarily employ in the course of an audit made for the purpose of expressing the opinions required by paragraph (*c*) of this rule.

(*c*) Opinions to be expressed.—The accountant's certificate shall state clearly: (i) the opinion of the accountant in respect of the financial statements covered by the certificate and the accounting principles and practices reflected therein; (ii) the opinion of the accountant as to any material changes in accounting principles or practices or method of applying the accounting principles or practices, or adjustments of the accounts, required to be set forth by rule 3-07; and (iii) the nature of, and the opinion of the accountant as to, any material differences between the accounting principles and practices reflected in the financial statements and those reflected in the accounts after the entry of adjustments for the period under review.

(*d*) Exceptions.—Any matters to which the accountant takes exception shall be clearly identified, the exception thereto specifically and clearly stated, and, to the extent practicable, the effect of each such exception on the related financial statements given.

[33] SEC Report on Investigation in *The Matter of McKesson & Robbins, Inc.*, and Accounting Series Release No. 19.

These rules cover financial statements included in registration statements and annual reports filed with the Commission. While not at first generally observed by independent public accountants in certificates prepared for other purposes, the AICPA some two years later voted in favor of eliminating this double standard in accountants' certificates and adopted the substance of the Commission's requirements, after observing "that many, if not the majority, of practitioners follow the Commission's rule in all cases regardless of whether the listed or unlisted companies are involved."[34] The current form of the certificate in use by the profession as set forth in SAP No. 33 is generally acceptable to the SEC except as specifically noted therein.

Date of Certificate. Where the date of the completion of all significant phases of the audit and the date of the submission of the financial statements are within a reasonable time of each other—time ordinarily required for final review and preparation of report—it is customary for the certificate to bear the completion date. However, where the submission of the report is unduly delayed beyond the date of completion, and a subsequent development requires a major change in the financial statements prior to submission, it would then be necessary to change the date of the certificate to the later date.

Representations as to the Audit. The scope and nature of the work done may be described as the auditor deems proper, provided the description is reasonably comprehensive. No specific wording is prescribed other than that the certificate state clearly and unequivocally: (1) whether the examination was made in accordance with generally accepted auditing standards; and (2) whether all accepted auditing procedures recognized as normal or deemed necessary in the circumstances were included. The omission of any such procedures, particularly as they relate to inventories and receivables,[35] should be specifically designated, together with reasons therefor. Where alternate procedures were employed by independent accountants to satisfy themselves as to the fairness of various items in the statements, that fact should be stated.

The extent to which principal independent accountants relied upon the financial statements audited by other independent accountants for inclusion in the consolidated statements may have to be indicated. Rule 2-05 of Regulation S-X applies:

> If, with respect to the certification of the financial statements of any person, the principal accountant relies upon an examination made by another independent public accountant of certain of the accounts of such person or its subsidiaries, the certificate of such other accountant shall be filed . . . , however, the certificate of such other accountant need not be filed (a) if no reference is made directly or indirectly to such other accountant's examination in the principal accountant's certificate, or (b) if, having referred to such other accountant's examination, the principal accountant states in his certificate that he assumes responsibility for such other accountant's examination in the same manner as if it had been made by him.

Full disclosure also should be made in the certificate of the existence of those areas of information included in the financial statements about which independent accountants entertain serious doubts. And where independent accountants, or members of their staff, actually performed any of the bookkeeping functions necessary to bring the accounts into readiness for the preparation of the financial statements, the nature and extent of such work should

[34] SAP No. 12.

[35] SAP No. 33, pp. 59–60.

be clearly described. Depending upon the circumstances in the case, accountants performing such functions may be considered not independent for the purpose of certifying the financial statements resulting therefrom.[36]

Where the scope and nature of the examination have been in accordance with accepted auditing standards, and where all recognized and generally accepted auditing procedures deemed necessary in the circumstances have been applied, no useful purpose is served by a lengthy description of all detailed procedures employed by the independent public accountants in their examination, confirmation, investigation, testing, and review of the various items included in the financial statements. The technical phraseology ordinarily used in such exposition may well tend to confuse rather than assure the reader that the scope and nature of the audit were adequate for the purpose of expressing an informed opinion. Under the circumstances the Institute recommends the following simple, clear, forthright, and unqualified representation of work done:

> We have examined the balance sheet of the X Company as of December 31, 19__, and the related statement(s) of income and surplus for the year then ended. Our examination was made in accordance with generally accepted auditing standards, and accordingly included such tests of the accounting records and such other auditing procedures as we considered necessary in the circumstances.[37]

A more detailed explanation and a much more comprehensive description are called for where either the scope or nature of the examination deviated from generally accepted auditing standards, where the independent accountants failed to resolve their doubts as to certain areas of information, or where they included in the consolidated statements the unaudited accounts of certain subsidiaries and the accounts of other subsidiaries audited by different independent accountants. In such cases the specific deviations or omissions should be clearly stated; the procedures followed should be indicated; doubtful items or areas of information included in the statements should be pointed out; accounts included in the consolidated report not audited by principal independent accountants should be clearly identified; the specific nature of work performed on basic records ordinarily outside the scope of independent audit should be fully explained; and any other information which the independent accountants obtained during the course of their examination which they feel is of material importance to investors should also be included.[38] A few selected illustrations are presented below:

1. In this case principal accountants assumed responsibility for the examination of the financial statements of certain foreign subsidiaries audited by other independent accountants included in the consolidated statement but as to the audit of another foreign subsidiary indicated that the latter statements were included in reliance on the report of the accountants who certified these statements. This certificate reads in part:

> We have reviewed the reports of other independent public accountants who have examined the accounts of the foreign subsidiaries and foreign branches and assume responsibility for such examination. As to Amerline Corporation, we have reviewed the report of other independent public accountants who have examined the accounts of such company.

[36] SAP No. 33, pp. 59–60.
[37] SAP No. 33, p. 57.
[38] SAP No. 33, pp. 62–74.

In our opinion, based on such examination and the report of other independent public accountants relating to Amerline Corporation, such financial statements present fairly the consolidated financial position. . . .

2. In the following instance the principal independent public accountants specifically disclaimed responsibility for financial statements examined by other independent public accountants and submitted for inclusion in the financial report:

The financial statements and applicable notes presenting the position of The Chesapeake and Ohio Railway Company as of August 31, 19__, and the results of its operations for the eight months then ended, as well as the comparative figures presented for the eight months ended August 31, 19__, have been prepared from the books of the company; financial statements covering operations prior to January 1, 19__, have been prepared from the annual statements published by the company and Pere Marquette Railway Company which were examined by other public accountants. These financial statements have not been examined by us and are not covered by this report.

3. An accountant who performs both the bookkeeping and auditing functions for a client cannot be considered independent for the purpose of certifying the financial statements resulting therefrom. The whole purpose of an independent audit is lost if a certifying accountant is permitted to do the original work. An audit should be a check by an outside independent expert of original work done by a client's employees. It is of the utmost importance, therefore, that a reasonably detailed explanation be included in the certificate, where applicable, of the nature and extent of any original work done on the basic records. Failure to disclose such information renders the certificate false and misleading.

Accounting Series Release No. 13 deals with a critical analysis of a certificate submitted in a particular case in which the client had not maintained cash books, journals, other books of original entry, or ledgers during the period covered by the financial statements. The client's files, however, contained original underlying data such as canceled checks, check stubs, bank statements, purchase orders, vendors' invoices, sales orders, and duplicate sales invoices. In order to prepare financial statements, it was deemed necessary by the independent public accountants who certified the statements that the cash transactions and sales be recorded in books of original entry and in turn posted to a general ledger and that the books then be adjusted to an accrual basis. The entry and analysis of the transactions in formal books of account were carried out by one of the accounting firm's junior accountants, loaned on a per diem basis, and by an officer of the company.

The accountants maintained that this preliminary work consisted merely of classifying and summarizing records of transactions prepared by employees of the company at the time of the transactions. However, in many cases notations as to the purpose of disbursements had not been made on the check stubs simultaneously with the transactions, and accordingly it was necessary to rely in such cases upon the memory of an officer of the company in classifying the recorded disbursements. Upon the completion of this preliminary work, the certifying accountants found that satisfactory determination had not been made of the balances in certain of the asset, liability, and income and expense accounts. In the second, or audit, phase of the engagement, the accountants therefore considered it necessary to undertake work of a special nature and in some instances to make original determination as to the amounts of such accounts.

Notwithstanding these unusual circumstances, the certificate furnished by the accountants followed the standard form and represented that the accountants' opinion was based upon a test-check audit. In discussing this certificate, the chief accountant of the SEC stated:

> . . . when a (company) during the period under review has not maintained records adequate for the purpose of preparing comprehensive and dependable financial statements, that fact should be disclosed. If, because of the absence or gross inadequacy of accounting records maintained by a (company), it is necessary to have essential books of account prepared retroactively and for the accountant to enlarge the scope of the audit to the extent indicated in order to be able to express his opinion, these facts also should be disclosed and . . . it is misleading, notwithstanding partial disclosure by footnotes as in the instant case, to furnish a certificate which implies that the accountant was satisfied to express an opinion based on a test-check audit.

4. In the case of *Interstate Hosiery Mills Inc.*,[39] independent accountants had certified to the accuracy of the financial statements which, unbeknown to them, had been falsified by their senior accountant to the extent of some $2 million. The SEC held that the procedures upon which the accountants' certified report was based could not be described as an independent audit.

5. In another case the accountants' certificate was rejected because it failed to disclose that very little of the financial data had been verified from corporate records and that much of the data had been reconstructed on a basis which was largely arbitrary:

> . . . an accountant certifying financial data in a registration statement is under a duty to disclose the existence of areas of information about which there is considerable doubt.[40]

Opinions to Be Expressed.[41] **Unqualified opinion.** The most vital part of the certificate is the accountants' opinion of the financial statements and the accounting principles and practices on which they are based. Where, on the basis of their examination and review, independent accountants are completely satisfied that the financial statements, schedules, and summary of earnings included in the registration statement and prospectus are fairly presented in accordance with generally accepted principles of accounting consistently applied, the short-form unqualified report recommended in SAP No. 33 (Chapter 10, par. 6) ordinarily will apply, appropriately modified to cover the period of the report, as illustrated in the J. L. Clark Manufacturing Company and Burroughs Corp. presentations in the preceding pages.

Qualified opinion. The Commission ordinarily will not allow a registration statement to become effective where the accountants' opinion is qualified because of limitations on the scope of the examination, exceptions based on acceptability of accounting principles reflected in the financial statements, schedules, or summary of earnings, or where there is a disclaimer of opinion. On the other hand, a "subject to" type of qualification in the accountants' opinion ordinarily will be acceptable where there is uncertainty as to the outcome of negotiations or litigation concerning income taxes, renegotiation, or other controversies, recovery of research and development costs or other deferred charges, or similar matters which are not susceptible to reasonable accounting determination but might have a material effect on financial position or results of operations.

[39] 4 SEC 706.

[40] *Platoro Gold Mines, Inc.*, 3 SEC 872. See also in *The Matter of Livingston Mining Company*, 2 SEC 141; and *Resources Corporation International*, 7 SEC 689.

[41] Regulation S-X, Rule 2-02(c).

It is also recognized that within the framework of accepted accounting principles different bases or methods may be employed for pricing inventories, determining periodic depreciation charges, taking up profits on installment sales or long-term contracts, determining the inclusion or exclusion of subsidiaries in consolidation, eliminating intercompany profits in inventories, etc. Failure to maintain consistent policies in such matters distorts comparisons and impairs the integrity of the accounts. From the viewpoint of investors and credit grantors it is of the utmost importance to know the customary accounting policies of the company and whether such policies are in fact being consistently observed.

Where, however, for good and valid reasons changes or retroactive adjustments are made which materially affect comparisons with the preceding period, the nature and effect of such changes should be disclosed, either in the certificate or in a note to the appropriate statement referred to in the certificate. Independent accountants should express their opinion as to the propriety of such changes.[42]

Exceptions.[43] Any reservations which independent accountants may have as to the manner in which the financial statements have been prepared, the accounting principles upon which they have been based, the integrity of any of the items contained therein, or any other area of information covered by the certificate should be clearly and explicitly stated. Thus the omission of any accepted auditing procedures recognized as normal or deemed essential in the circumstances should be briefly explained. No exception need be taken, however, if by means of alternate procedures the independent accountants have satisfied themselves as to the fairness of the statements presented. Exceptions must be taken, and their effect clearly indicated, in cases where significant items in the statements are presented in accordance with accepted accounting principles which have not been consistently applied. If the nature and extent of the improper accounting practices or other exceptions are of such proportions as seriously to impair the fairness of the statements as a whole, or if the examination has not been sufficiently comprehensive as a basis for an informed judgment, the independent accountants must refrain from offering any opinion. Instead the report should be limited to a statement of findings and an explanation as to why no opinion is offered. To do otherwise would tend to confuse and misinform, since any expression of opinion as to the fairness of the financial statements would be completely negated by the numerous exceptions taken (Accounting Series Release No. 115).

A selected number of cases are briefly summarized below wherein the certificates of independent accountants were held to be defective and in some instances false and outright misleading. Such action resulted in part from the following circumstances: failure on the part of independent accountants to take exception to various items in the financial statements based upon improper accounting principles or on accepted principles not consistently applied; expressing an opinion as to the fairness of the financial statements, represented as being based upon an examination made in accordance with accepted auditing standards, when in fact such standards were not fully complied with; and expressing an opinion based upon an examination which was not sufficiently adequate for the purpose, or which revealed the nature and extent of the improper accounting practices followed by the company to be so serious as materially to impair the integrity of the statements as a whole.

[42] Regulation S-X, Rule 3-07.
[43] Regulation S-X, Rule 2-02(d).

1. The Metropolitan Personal Loan Corporation[44] failed to follow a consistent policy in its periodic amortization of deferred charges and provision for doubtful accounts. In prior years unamortized cost of establishing branches was systematically reduced by periodic charges to income. In the latest fiscal period covered by the accountants' certificate the balance of the unamortized cost was written off in its entirety to earned surplus, and similar treatment was accorded provision for bad debts. Notwithstanding this inconsistent and improper treatment, the certificate contained the following opinion:

> In our opinion based upon the examination described above and subject to the foregoing, the accompanying balance sheet and related statements of capital and earned surplus and of income and expense fairly present, in accordance with accepted principles of accounting consistently maintained by Metropolitan Personal Loan Corporation during the period under review, its position at December 31, 19__, and the results of its operations for the three years ended that date.

The SEC rejected the certificate on the ground that under the circumstances it was materially misleading to certify that the financial statements were fairly presented "in accordance with accepted principles of accounting consistently maintained."

2. Testimony and other evidence disclosed that the accounting and bookkeeping records of the Automatic Telephone Dialer, Inc.,[45] were grossly inadequate. No journals were kept, the general ledger was not kept up to date, the expenses were not properly classified, and the records were kept with a minimum of detail. In addition, the balance sheet contained an asset described as "Patent $500,000" which had been acquired from the promoter, who was also the principal stockholder, in exchange for the corporation's total authorized stock of 50,000 shares, par value $10. It was agreed that 30,000 of these shares would be donated back to the corporation as treasury stock. At the balance sheet date, 20,000 shares had been issued and 5,000 donated back.

The property was set up at the par value of the total stock issued therefor, instead of at the net amount after deducting the par value of the stock returned to the corporation in the form of a donation. At the time of the transaction, this stock was being sold to the public at $2 per share. It was further revealed that approximately half the shares were issued not for the patent but actually for promotional services and fees. The accounts showed no such distinction.

In view of the above, the certification of the accountant that the financial data "fairly represents the position of the Automatic Telephone Dialer, Inc., . . . in conformity with generally accepted principles applied on a consistent basis throughout the period under review" was rejected by the SEC as "wholly unwarranted and materially misleading."[46]

3. In the case of *Illinois Zinc Company*,[47] it was established by testimony of expert witnesses that the charges for depreciation, depletion, and amortization of development costs were arbitrary, lacking in scientific basis, and completely inadequate. On the basis of provisions made for the 5-year period under review, it would have taken from 80 to 94 years to write off the cost of the mine, even though witnesses were in agreement that the life expectancy of the mine was 15 to 20 years.

[44] 7 SEC 234.

[45] 10 SEC 698.

[46] See also *Thomas Bond, Inc.*, 5 SEC 60; and *Finger Canadian Lumber Company Ltd.*, 5 SEC 543.

[47] 6 SEC 850.

The certificate contained an explanation of the basis and methods employed by the company in determining its charges but included neither qualification nor exception. The accountants sought to justify their position on the ground that they relied upon the judgment of the management in matters of depletion and amortization of development. This view was held to be without merit under the circumstances. The Commission said:

> We agree that managerial judgment is one factor to be considered. But that factor is not to be considered to the exclusion of other factors. In the instant case, a proper investigation of (company's) policy of depreciation, depletion, and amortization of development costs would have revealed the glaring inadequacy of charges for these purposes. *Absent an adjustment of (company's) policy in line with the realities of the situation, the accountants should have expressed in their certificate, in a definite and forthright manner, their disagreement* with that policy. [Italics supplied.]

4. In the case of the *Red Bank Oil Company*,[48] the independent accountants failed to audit the accounts of one of the largest subsidiaries which accounted for approximately 70 percent of consolidated sales and 45 percent of consolidated assets. Instead they accepted for inclusion in the consolidated report the statements of this subsidiary certified by another firm of independent accountants, without review or test check of either their working papers or audit procedures. In expressing their opinion as to the fairness of the consolidated statements, the certifying accountants failed to disclose their reliance on the reports of other independent accountants. Holding that under the circumstances the nature and scope of the audit were not sufficiently comprehensive for the purpose of expressing an opinion, the Commission said:

> We doubt the propriety of the principal accountant undertaking to express his opinion with respect to financial statements when, as to so large a percentage of the revenues and assets, his opinion is founded merely on the reports of other accountants not subject to his supervision, control or direction. . . . We think it wholly clear that where an accountant undertakes to express his opinion in part in reliance on reports of other accountants it is essential that he have far more knowledge of the underlying facts and of the accounting principles followed than was exhibited here. Lacking such knowledge, it is impossible for him to express an informed judgment as to whether the figures reported to him by other accountants have been properly included in the consolidated statements. We have no hesitancy in finding (principal accountant's) examination deficient in this respect. We also believe that the principal accountant is not in a position to express an informed opinion as to the financial statements where he excluded from his review so large a part of the revenues and assets.

5. In the case of the *Associated Gas & Electric Company*,[49] the work of the independent accountants was severely criticized as failing to conform with accepted standards. Testimony and other evidence presented at the hearings disclosed that the company had completely disregarded accepted principles of accounting in the preparation of the accounts and failed to maintain any consistent policy in the application of principles once adopted. This was particularly true in regard to the revaluation of fixed and intangible assets; the treatment of intercompany profits; the recording of losses on investments; the allocation of charges between income, earned surplus, and capital surplus, the treatment of interest, debt discount, and expense; the creation of various revaluation reserves out of capital surplus to absorb current operating charges; the reflection of adjustments in value of assets

[48] Securities Act of 1933, Release No. 3110.
[49] 11 SEC 975.

and net worth arising out of the quasi-reorganization; and other transactions too numerous to mention. Improper accounting practices permeated the accounts to such an extent that independent accountants testified that they considered it impracticable to determine what the company's financial and operating position would have been if accepted principles of accounting had been followed.

Failure to obtain this vital information resulted in a finding by the Commission that the examination made was not sufficiently comprehensive to justify the accountants in certifying the financial statements. Further, the accountants were charged with failing to state their exceptions clearly and unequivocally. Rather than take a clear exception, independent accountants would state a "preference" for another method of treatment. In the circumstances, the opinion of the independent accountants as to the fairness of the financial statements was completely negated by the many exceptions enumerated in the earlier part of the certificate. The Commission said in its formal opinion:

> Under the circumstances such as those presented in this case, we hold that (independent public accountants) have not put themselves in a position to certify; for the statements neither present the financial condition in accordance with accepted principles of accounting nor adequately indicate the effects of the practices followed, nor provide the reader with the means by which he may work out the financial condition for himself. We are left with the feeling that the principal purpose of the company was not to disclose frankly, but to mystify, baffle, mislead and conceal and that the audits and certificates of the accountants did nothing to prevent the accomplishment of that purpose.

SUBSEQUENT EVENTS

Review of Subsequent Events. Since a considerable portion of the auditor's examination necessarily must take place subsequent to the balance sheet date, a sound audit program should give due consideration to a review of any significant events or transactions occurring between the date of the fiscal close and the date of the certificate, which may have a material effect on the financial statements requiring adjustment or annotation thereto so as not to make them misleading. Under ordinary circumstances, such procedures would include cash cutoffs, confirmation follow-ups, review of subsequent collections and disbursements, reading of available minutes and interim reports, discussions with management, etc. Where as a result of such examination, or from any other source, the accountant comes into knowledge of material facts adversely affecting the position of the company, either (1) retroactively, so as to make the financial statements already prepared either untrue or misleading, or (2) in the intervening period between the fiscal close and the date of the certificate, he is duty bound to disclose such information in his certificate or in some appropriate section of the report referred to in the certificate. Under such circumstances the date of the certificate assumes major importance.

Date of Certificate. For statements filed with the SEC, independent accountants' responsibility for the disclosure of "subsequent events" extends even beyond the date of the certificate—to the effective date of the registration statement. The SEC requirement in this connection is clear and unequivocal:

> If anything comes to the attention of such accountant, or he obtains knowledge of any facts before the effective date of the registration statement which would make any of the material items therein untrue, or indicate there was an omission to state a material

fact required to be stated, or necessary to make the statements therein not misleading, he shall bring such immediately to the attention of the Commission.[50]

Experience has demonstrated that delays of weeks and frequently months may occur between the date of filing and the date that the registration statement becomes effective. These delays may result from the processing procedures of the SEC or from causes brought about by issuers or underwriters necessitating continued deferral of the effective date. To avoid any possible liability in the circumstances, the independent accountant must be able to sustain the burden of proof that

he had, after *reasonable investigation*, reasonable ground to believe and did believe, at the time such part of the registration statement became effective, that the statements therein were true and that there was no omission to state a material fact required to be stated therein or necessary to make the statements therein not misleading[51]

Supplemental Auditing Procedures. To sustain the burden of proof that he has made a "reasonable investigation," the auditor should supplement his audit procedures by performing certain additional procedures with respect to subsequent events up to, or reasonably close to the effective date, to the extent reasonable and practicable in the circumstances. Ordinarily these supplemental procedures should include the following:

1. Read the entire prospectus and review other pertinent portions of the registration statements.
2. Read the latest available interim financial statements in conjunction with similar statements of an appropriate prior period or periods.
3. Read the available minutes of meetings of stockholders, directors, and committees of officers or directors, as appropriate; as to meetings for which minutes are not available inquire as to matters dealt with at such meetings.
4. Obtain a letter of representation from an officer (or officers) as to whether or not there have occurred any events subsequent to the date of the financial statements included in the registration statements and reported upon by the independent auditor which, in the officer's opinion, would have a material effect upon those financial statements or would require mention in the notes thereto; if such a letter has previously been obtained as part of the examination, obtain written confirmation that there have been no material changes to the date of inquiry.
5. Inquire of officers and other executives having responsibility for financial and accounting matters (limited where appropriate to major locations) as to:
    a. Whether the principal items in the latest interim financial statements mentioned in (2) above were treated in conformity with generally accepted accounting principles and practices applied on a basis consistent with that of the latest period reported on by the author.
    b. Whether all adjustments necessary for a fair presentation of the financial position at the interim date and the results of operations for the interim period have been made and reflected in such interim financial statements.
    c. Whether any adjustments other than for normal recurring items had been made during the interim period or to the date of inquiry.
    d. Whether any substantial contingent liabilities or commitments existed at the date of the interim financial statements or at the date

[50] Securities Act of 1933, Release No. 324.
[51] *Ibid.*, Sec. 11(b)(i).

of inquiry; where appropriate, this inquiry should also be directed to legal counsel.

e. Whether there was any material adverse change in the financial position or results of operations subsequent to the date of the financial statements covered by the report of the auditor, or any change in the capital stock or long-term debt, to the date of inquiry.

f. The current status of items which were accounted for on the basis of tentative, preliminary, or inconclusive data.

In the *BarChris* matter discussed below,[52] the court, after a careful review of all the evidence, concluded that while the written audit program conformed closely with the procedures outlined above, the auditors, by their failure to apply these procedures as required in the circumstances, failed to sustain the burden of proof that they had *in fact* made a "reasonable examination" of events occurring between the date of the certificate and the effective date of the registration statement as required under the statute.

COMFORT LETTERS FOR UNDERWRITERS

Purpose. Events occurring in the period subsequent to the balance sheet date and prior to the effective date of the registration statement which may adversely affect the financial position or operating results reflected in the financial statements appearing in such registration statement should be disclosed promptly to the SEC and the investing public and reflected by appropriate amendments to the prospectus and registration statement. What the underwriters want is assurance that there have been no developments through the effective date which would make the registration statement misleading and not complete. Failure to disclose such information may subject all persons who signed the registration statement, or consented to the inclusion of their name therein, to civil and/or criminal liabilities. In the BarChris case previously referred to, the court held that underwriters, lawyers, auditors, and directors were all to blame for false information contained in the prospectus. Particularly as it related to independent auditors, the court ruled that they were liable for the portion of the prospectus they had worked on because of their failure to ascertain, and thereby fail to report, that significant changes had occurred in the registrant's financial situation between the date of the audited statements and the effective date of the registration. This, in the opinion of the court, was due to the independent auditors' failure to apply "due diligence" in their review and examination of subsequent events as required in the circumstances. It is believed to be the first time that a judge had strictly defined standards for persons involved in procedures routine to the preparation of a prospectus.[53]

Scope. The underwriting agreement usually contains the provision that independent accountants shall perform certain additional procedures with respect to subsequent events up to the effective date, to the extent deemed reasonable in the circumstance and to furnish a "comfort letter" for the underwriters. Such a letter is regarded by the underwriters as one means of learning promptly of any event subsequent to the date of the latest financial statements appearing in the registration statement which may require disclosure. Typical of the matters covered in "comfort letters" are the following: [54]

[52] See the section on "Liabilities of Accountants."
[53] *Forbes*, Sept. 1, 1968, p. 23.
[54] SAP No. 35.

1. The independence of the accountants
2. Compliance of the audited financial statements and schedules with the applicable accounting requirements of the Securities Act of 1933 and of the published rules and regulations of the Securities and Exchange Commission
3. Unaudited financial statements and schedules in the registration statement
4. Changes in capital stock and long-term debt
5. Material adverse changes in the financial position or results of operations during a period subsequent to the date and period of the latest financial statements, summary of earnings, or related financial data in the registration statement
6. Tables and other compilations of financial information in the registration statement

The "comfort letter" may be addressed to the registrant, underwriter, or both and ordinarily is dated on or shortly before the "closing date" on which the related securities are delivered to the underwriters in exchange for the net proceeds from their sale.

Form and Content. Independence; Compliance. In its simplest form the underwriting agreement may require from independent auditors nothing more than a "letter" containing a representation as to their independence and their opinion that audited statements filed as part of the registration statement and prospectus comply with SEC requirements. Addressed to the registrant and/or underwriters, the letter may read somewhat as follows: [55]

Date__________

Dear Sirs:

This letter, written at your request, is to enable the ABC Corporation to comply with Section 5 of its agreement of March 23, 1969 with Bacon & Smith, underwriters.

We have examined the consolidated financial statements of The ABC Corporation (the "Company") and its subsidiaries as of December 31, 1968, and for the three years then ended, and of the related Summary of Consolidated Earnings for the five years ended December 31, 1968, and our opinion with respect to the foregoing is included in the registration statement (No. 2 . . .) filed by the Company under the Securities Act of 1933 (the "Act"). Such registration statement and the related prospectus, as amended at the time such registration statement became effective, are herein referred to respectively as the "Registration Statement" and the "Prospectus."

We are independent accountants as required by the Act and the applicable published rules and regulations thereunder.

In our opinion, the financial statements and summary of earnings examined by us and included in the Prospectus comply as to form in all material respects with the applicable accounting requirements of the Act and of the published rules and regulations thereunder with respect to Registration Statements on Form S-1.

Negative assurance. Comments in the comfort letter concerning unaudited financial statements appearing in the registration statement and comments as to subsequent changes should always be made in the form of negative assurance.[56] Subsequent changes usually relate to any change in capital stock or long-term debt, or any material adverse change in financial position or results of operations subsequent to the period covered by the financial statements examined by the accountants, or in some cases subsequent to the

[55] *Ibid.*

[56] This is a unique exception to the prohibition against negative assurance in reports of independent auditors. See SAP No. 33, chap. 10, pars. 19 and 20, also SAP No. 35.

date of the latest available unaudited financial statements. Since the limited procedures followed in the review and examination of events covering this comfort period preclude the expression of a positive opinion, only a negative assurance is possible in the circumstances. This may be expressed in a number of ways. The following is illustrative and should be read as a continuation of the letter immediately above.

We have not made an examination in accordance with generally accepted auditing standards of the financial statements of the Company or any of its subsidiary companies that relate to any period subsequent to December 31, 1968 nor have we attempted to audit any of the transactions or records for any such period and, therefore, we do not express an opinion thereon. In this connection it should be noted that interim financial statements for any period subsequent to February 28, 1969 were not available.

You have requested that we make a limited review for the period from December 31, 1968 to April 2, 1969 and, accordingly, we have: (a) read the unaudited interim financial statements for the period from December 31, 1968 to February 28, 1969; (b) read the minutes of the meetings of the stockholders, Board of Directors and Executive Committee held during the period from December 31, 1968 to April 2, 1969; and (c) had discussions with officials of the Company responsible for financial and accounting matters as to transactions and events subsequent to December 31, 1968. It should be understood that this limited review does not constitute an examination made in accordance with generally accepted auditing standards and would not necessarily reveal adverse changes in the financial position or results of operations of the companies or inconsistencies in the application of generally accepted accounting principles. *Subject to this explanation and based upon the limited review described above, nothing has come to our attention which in our judgment would indicate that during the period from December 31, 1968 to April 2, 1969 there has been any change in the capital stock or funded debt of the Company and its consolidated subsidiary companies or any material adverse change in the consolidated financial position or results of operations of the Company and its consolidated subsidiary companies except as set forth or contemplated in the above-mentioned Registration Statement, including the related Prospectus.* [Italics supplied.] The terms "financial position" and "results of operations" are used above in their conventional accounting sense; accordingly, they relate to the financial statements of the business as a whole and have the same meaning when used in this letter as they have when used in our opinion contained in the Prospectus.

Distribution. Comfort letters are not required under the acts administered by the SEC, and copies of such letters are not filed with the Commission. Comfort letters are prepared solely to enable the registrant to comply with the terms of an agreement with the underwriters, and their distribution is restricted to the parties to the underwriting agreement. Accordingly, the letter concludes with a closing sentence or paragraph somewhat as follows:

This letter is solely for the information of the Board of Directors of the Company and the Underwriters and is not to be quoted, or referred to, in whole or in part, in the Registration Statement or Prospectus or otherwise in connection with the registration under the Securities Act of 1933 or the sale of securities.

LIABILITIES OF ACCOUNTANTS

Civil Actions. Under the Securities Act of 1933. Independent public accountants preparing or certifying financial statements filed with the SEC which contain untrue statements of a material fact, or which fail to include information of a material nature required so as not to make the financial statements false or misleading, may be held liable for losses incurred by any person who, in reliance on such statements, purchased or sold the security of such issuer. Specifically, the Securities Act of 1933 provides as follows:

Sec. 11(a) In case any part of the registration statement, when such part became effective, contained an untrue statement of a material fact or omitted to state a material fact required to be stated therein or necessary to make the statements therein not misleading, any person acquiring such security (unless it is proved that at the time of such acquisition he knew of such untruth or omission) may, either at law or in equity, in any court of competent jurisdiction, sue . . . every accountant, who has with his consent been named as having prepared or certified any part of the registration statement, or as having prepared or certified any report or valuation which is used in connection with the registration statement, report or valuation, which purports to have been prepared or certified by him;

To escape such liability, independent accountants must prove that:

as regards any part of the registration statement purporting to be made upon his authority as an expert or purporting to be a copy of or extract from a report or valuation of himself as an expert, (i) he had, after reasonable investigation, reasonable ground to believe and did believe, *at the time such part of the registration statement became effective*, that the statements therein were true and that there was no omission to state a material fact required to be stated therein or necessary to make the statements therein not misleading, or (ii) such part of the registration statement did not fairly represent his statement as an expert or was not a fair copy of or extract from his report or valuation as an expert; [Sec. 11(b)(3)(B).]

The Securities Act extends independent accountants' responsibility for financial statements filed with the SEC to include a disclosure of material events adversely affecting these financials occurring between the date of the certification and the effective date of the registration statement. (See section above entitled "Subsequent Events.")

BarChris case. In this connection the recent U.S. District Court's decision in the BarChris[57] case further extending independent auditors' liabilities to third parties under the federal Securities Act is being viewed with grave concern by the accounting profession. Among other things, this landmark decision deals with issues involving failure to disclose matters of a material nature which developed between the date of the certification and the effective date of the registration, and clarifies the criteria for judging the falsity or misleading omissions of material items as of the balance sheet date, as well as the criteria for judging the auditor's defense of freedom from ordinary negligence, often referred to as due diligence. Briefly the facts in the case are as follows:

The registration statement of an offering of 5½ percent convertible subordinate 15-year debentures of the issuer became effective Mar. 16, 1961. On Oct. 29, 1962, the corporation filed a petition in bankruptcy and on Nov. 1, 1962, defaulted in the payment of interest. The action was instituted by purchasers of these securities against the corporation, its auditors, officers, directors, legal counsel who was also a director, and the underwriters. The court held that all defendants were responsible to some extent and that none had proved the defense of due diligence. Discussion as to the extent of liability attaching to each was reserved pending the outcome of cross claims filed among the defendants. As it relates to independent accountants, no question of fraud was involved. Their liability rested solely on their failure to apply due diligence in the examination and presentation of the financial statements filed. The court dealt at length with the scope, nature, and *quality* of the audit; the accounting principles and practices governing the

[57] *Escott v. BarChris Construction Corporation et al.;* U.S. District Court, Southern District of New York, Mar. 28, 1968.

valuation, classification, disclosure, and materiality of items to be included in the financial statements; and the auditor's responsibility therefor.

Particularly with respect to events subsequent to the date of the balance sheet, the court found that while the written audit program in this case conformed very closely to the procedures for such review outlined in SAP No. 33, the manner of its performance was wholly deficient in that in certain major respects the auditors actually failed (1) to read the prospectus, (2) to read any contract documents, (3) to have knowledge of or read the minutes of executive committee meetings, and (4) to examine "important financial records" other than the trial balance. Other areas of the audit which came under the court's critical review included the quality of the evidence obtained by inquiry, the adequacy of the sample selected for audit, the review of the work papers, and the qualifications of the senior personnel assigned to the job. The conclusion which may be drawn from this case is that while the courts will give due weight to the auditing standards established by the profession in judging the auditors' freedom from negligence, *the court will not hesitate to supply its own standards where those of the profession are not specific enough or fail to meet the criteria essential for the protection of the public interest.*

Under the Securities Exchange Act of 1934. Independent accountants' exposure of liability for "misleading statements" is contained in Section 18 of the 1934 act, which provides in part as follows:

> . . . any person who shall make or cause to be made any statement in any application, report, or document filed pursuant to this title or any rule or regulation thereunder or any undertaking contained in a registration as provided in subsection (d) of section 15 of this title, which statement was at the time and in the light of the circumstances under which it was made false or misleading with respect to any material fact, shall be liable to any person (not knowing that such statement was false or misleading) who, in reliance on such statement, shall have purchased or sold a security at a price which was affected by such statement, for damage caused by such reliance, unless the person sued shall prove that he acted in good faith and had no knowledge that such statement was false or misleading. . . .

Criminal Actions. Under both acts the Commission may institute proceedings in the federal courts to enjoin and may request the Attorney General to prosecute persons who violate any of the provisions of the Securities acts or of any of the rules or regulations thereunder. Section 21(e) of the Securities and Exchange Act reads as follows:

> Whenever it shall appear to the Commission that any person is engaged or about to engage in any acts or practices which constitute or will constitute a violation of the provisions of this title, or of any rule or regulation thereunder, it may in its discretion bring an action in the proper district of the United States . . . to enjoin such acts or practices, and upon a proper showing a permanent or temporary injunction or restraining order shall be granted without bond. The Commission may transmit such evidence as may be available concerning such acts or practices to the Attorney General, who may, in his discretion, institute the necessary criminal proceedings under this title.[58]

Continental Vending case. [59] A case in point involves the certification by a national firm of independent public accountants of the financial statements for the fiscal year ended Sept. 30, 1962, of Continental Vending Machine Cor-

[58] Section 20(b) of the Securities Act of 1933 has substantially the same wording.

[59] *United States v. Simon*, F 2d. CCH Fed. Sec. L. Rep. 91 (2d Circuit, 1969), and decision of Court of Appeals, 397 U.S. 1006 (1970); see also *The Journal of Accountancy*, February, 1970, and May, 1970, pp. 69 and 71.

poration which subsequently went into reorganization under Chapter 10 of the Bankruptcy Act. Three members of the accounting firm, two partners and the audit manager, as well as the former chairman and president of the company, were indicted by a federal grand jury in October, 1966, on five counts of mail fraud and one of conspiracy for violating a section of the Securities Exchange Act barring the filing of false and misleading documents with the SEC. The accounting firm, which agreed in October to pay $2.1 million settlement in a civil suit arising out of the same statements, was named as co-conspirator in this criminal action but not as a defendant. The case against the three members of the accounting firm went on trial in the U.S. District Court in December, 1967, and resulted in a hung jury. On retrial in May, 1968, before another federal judge, the jury returned a verdict of guilty on all counts. A federal Appeals Court affirmed the decision and the U.S. Supreme Court declined to review the conviction.

At issue in the appeal was the accountant's assertion that conformity to generally accepted accounting *was* a complete defense. The trial judge, on the other hand, held that if the jury found Continental's financial statements false and misleading, (which the jury did) then conformity to generally accepted accounting standards *was not* a complete defense.

The charges concerned loans made by Continental Vending to Valley Commercial Corporation, an affiliated company, which Valley in turn made to Harold Roth, president of Continental. The accountants were charged with concealing in Continental's 1962 financial report the fact that Roth, as of September 30, 1962, owed more than $3 million. It was further charged that the collateral Roth posted was inadequate to secure his borrowings from Valley, but that Continental's financial statement made it appear that the amount due Continental from Valley was adequately secured. The central point of the government's case rested on a footnote to the balance sheet appearing in the 1962 annual report of the corporation which indicated that an asset item of $3.5 million in the form of receivables due from Valley Commercial was more than adequately secured. According to the footnote, the money due from Valley was "secured by the assignment to the company of Valley's equity in certain marketable securities. As of February 15, 1963 (the date of the accountant's certification), the amount of such equity at current market quotations exceeded the amount receivable." The government contended that it was the intention of the defendants to tell the readers that this was a fully collectible receivable when they knew that Valley could not pay the debt; that in fact approximately 90 percent of the "marketable securities" backing the asset consisted of common stock and convertible debentures of Continental, owned by Mr. Roth and his family which could not be sold without a registration statement filed with the SEC; that independent accountants were aware of these facts in February, 1963, when they wrote this footnote and certified the 1962 annual report. The federal attorney further charged that another "false" statement in the annual report was the listing of $285,966 in cash in the balance sheet. Instead, he said, "there was a cash deficit of over $1,000," by creating cash through a "float of outstanding checks."

Counsel for the defense conceded that independent accountants had made "a perfectly honest mistake" in a footnote to the 1962 balance sheet and that the certification of the company's report "may not have been an exemplary audit." The basic question in the case, it was argued, was whether the three accountants on the engagement knew that the financial report was incorrect but still certified it as fairly representing the company's financial status in an effort to commit a fraud. In denying the criminal charge, the defense contended (1) there was no motive on the part of the auditors to commit fraud since theirs was a fixed fee and thus they had nothing to gain or lose in the preparation and certification of the financial report; (2) the financial statements of Continental, viewed as a whole, presented a fair picture of the corporation; and (3) under generally accepted accounting principles, the auditors were under no obligation to find out what Valley was doing with the money which Continental advanced to it—to do otherwise would require an audit of Valley's books.

At the trial, the defense called eight expert witnesses who testified that generally accepted accounting principles *did not require* the disclosure in Continental's financial report of the transactions between Valley and Roth. The government's attorney introduced testimony of two SEC accountants who asserted that sound accounting principles and practices *did require* the disclosure; the jury apparently accepted the SEC viewpoint. In urging the U.S. Supreme Court to review their conviction, which was denied, the accountants asserted that the real question in the case "is whether professional men may be convicted of crime for professional services performed in conformity with generally accepted professional standards." The American Institute of Certified Public Accountants also urged review in a friend-of-the-court brief. The Institute, which is responsible for writing accounting principles, said the case "for the first time squarely presents a far reaching issue of criminal liability for professional conduct."

It is clearly evident that there is an urgent need for a thoughtful and continuing review and appraisal of (1) the standards governing independent accountants' responsibilities to third parties, and (2) the "generally accepted" auditing standards and accounting principles, practices, and procedures governing the preparation and certification of financial reports.

BIBLIOGRAPHY

Accounting Series Releases of the SEC, to date.
Official Decisions and Reports of the SEC, to date.
Regulation S-X.
The Securities Act of 1933.
The Securities Exchange Act of 1934.
(All of the above are available from the Superintendent of Documents, Government Printing Office, Washington, D.C. 20402.)

Filings with the SEC—With Special Emphasis on First Filing, AICPA, New York, to date.
Greidinger, B. Bernard: *Accounting Requirements of the SEC,* New York, The Ronald Press Company, 1950.
SEC Service, New York, Pandick Press, to date.
Prentice Hall Tax Service and *CCH Tax Service,* New York, to date.
Rappaport, Louis H.: *SEC Accounting Practice and Procedure,* 2d ed., New York, The Ronald Press Company, 1966.

Barr, Andrew: "Accounting and Auditing Problems with Particular Reference to New Registrants with the SEC," *The New York Certified Public Accountant,* January, 1961.
Cary, William: "The SEC and Accounting," *The Journal of Accountancy,* December, 1963.
Greidinger, B. Bernard: "Holding Accounting Firm Accountable to Investors," *Commercial and Financial Chronicle,* May 2, 1968.
Reiling, Henry B., and Russell A. Taussig: "Recent Liability Cases—Implications for Accountants," *The Journal of Accountancy,* September, 1970.
Pacter, Paul A.: "Line-of-Business Earnings Disclosures in Recent SEC Filings," *The Journal of Accountancy,* October, 1970.

Part Six

Horizons for Auditing: A Look Ahead

Chapter **46**

The Common Body of Auditing Knowledge

JEROME K. PESCOW

Assistant Professor, Hofstra University

GENERAL

Introduction. A recent cartoon depicted a football coach lecturing to the board of trustees of a large university. With his massive weight being supported by his left hand resting on the long conference table and his right hand waving authoritatively in the air, forefinger extended toward the high ceiling of the austere room, he proclaimed, "If you want a winning football team there's only one way to do it . . . de-emphasize education." [1]

It would be comfortable to paraphrase the old coach and say, "If you want a winning audit team there's only one way to do it . . . emphasize education." However, just as organizing a winning football team is not really only a question of emphasizing football—as many owners and coaches of professional football teams will sadly attest—neither can the problem of training auditors be reduced to a simple formula of emphasizing education. Education is the result of the complex interaction of curriculum, faculty, and student body, further complicated by the educational and noneducational milieus—past, present, and future.

Nature of the Study. The first step toward determining the optimum educational background for the future accountant and auditor was taken by Robert H. Roy and James H. MacNeill in their study of the common body of knowledge for CPAs sponsored jointly by the Carnegie Corporation of New York and the American Institute of Certified Public Accountants (AICPA).[2]

Objectives. The prospectus for the study of the common body of knowledge set forth three objectives. These were:

1. To determine the knowledge which the CPA must have at the outset in order to provide the public with service of the minimum scope and quality which the public needs and has a right to expect from him at the start of his career.
2. To define the knowledge and intellectual habits which the beginning CPA must have to be able to keep pace with the growth of general knowledge of the profession in the next generation and to work into one of the present or future specialties of the profession.
3. To investigate the capabilities of the several types of educational institutions and processes—colleges and universities, in-training education and experience, and continuing adult education—for imparting the various kinds of required knowledge.

The study has gained wide acceptance as a basis for the education of accountants and auditors. The study did not specify how and where the common body of knowledge was to be obtained, but it is accepted that

[1] *Wall Street Journal,* December, 1968.

[2] *Horizons for a Profession, The Common Body of Knowledge for Certified Public Accountants,* New York, AICPA, 1967.

ordinarily this knowledge will be acquired as a part of the formal college program. The study has been supplemented by more specific recommended course topics. The specifics are referred to later in this chapter and discussed in detail in Chapter 42, "Education and Experience," and Chapter 43, "The CPA Examination in Auditing." A model program for accounting and auditing education is presented in Chapter 42.

Collecting the Data. The study is based on a questionnaire on public accounting practice, a review of college catalogs, interviews with practicing CPAs, educators, executives, government officials, and others, and a unique card-deck experiment. In the card-deck experiment, selected knowledgeable respondents ranked 53 subjects in order of importance by physically arranging a deck of cards, each bearing an individual subject. It is interesting to note that Written and Oral English received a composite first-place ranking, Advanced Natural Science ranking last. It is also telling that Auditing Principles, Standards, and Ethics ranked fourth, while Auditing Practice and Procedures ranked seventh. Educators, however, felt somewhat less strongly about the worth of these two subjects than had the other respondents, ranking them ninth and fourteenth, respectively.

One must fight against the impulse to be overly intrigued by the novelty of the mechanical aspects of the card-deck experiment and to be lulled by the comfortable numerical rankings resulting from this aspect of the study, remembering that this was merely one part of the comprehensive study. For a better understanding of this study, the author recommends that the book *Horizons for a Profession* be read carefully, particularly the summary of recommendations.

UNDERLYING CONCEPTS

Professional Attributes. The professional man must acquire a number of professional attributes in addition to a body of specialized professional knowledge.

Conceptual Understanding. The professional must achieve conceptual understanding of the body of knowledge as opposed to procedural skill.

Flexibility of Mind. The professional man should develop a flexibility of mind which permits him to adapt to change. Of course, the previously mentioned conceptual training will better equip an individual to cope with change than a training in set procedures.

Interdisciplinary Aspect. A narrow education in accounting is not adequate. The development of perception and judgment requires a much broader base of education.

MAN, HIS HISTORY AND PHILOSOPHY

The Humanities. General. The humanities concerns itself with man himself, his *history*, the *philosophies* by which he lives, the *languages* by which he communicates, and the *arts* which give expression to creativity. The humanities are the hallmark of cultivated men and women, and it is expected that the CPA will voluntarily develop an appreciation of these cultural areas.

Logic and ethics. Accounting itself is a logical construct, and everything done in accounting must be bound by the rules of logic. Ethical precepts are the foundation on which the profession rests.

Written and oral English. The responses to the questionnaire used showed that written and oral English was overwhelmingly indicated as the most important of all attributes of the accountant and auditor. Whatever a CPA may do in behalf of his clients must be communicated, usually in writing, sometimes orally. Those who cannot perform above a minimum threshold should be denied admission to the profession. English should be graded for every subject, not only the specific subject matter such as accounting, economics, history, or psychology.

Economics. General. There are two areas of social science knowledge which are necessary for the auditor. These are (1) economics and (2) the aspects of social science which are concerned with the behavior of formal organizations.

Microeconomics. Accountants are more concerned with microeconomics than with macroeconomics. The knowledge of microeconomics should encompass the nature of economic forces which affect the firm: relationship of price to demand, the behavior of costs, cost concepts, productivity, and the role of government and government regulation.

Macroeconomics. This includes an understanding of monetary and fiscal theories and policies, national income measurement, employment, economic growth, international economics, business cycles, forecasting, institutions which comprise the economy, and the interaction of government, industry, unions, financial institutions, and the like.

Behavioral Science. General. The beginning accountant should be required to have knowledge of the fundamentals of behavior and motivation.

Fundamentals of behavior. In addition to instruction in business and industrial management the auditor must have knowledge of the fundamentals of individual and group behavior.

Motivation. Behavioral research is providing important information concerning communication, decision making, innovation, conflict, leadership, authority, learning, perception, and creativity.

Law. General. The beginning CPA should have a good knowledge of business law. He should be familiar with the relationships between parties, the concepts involved, and the terminology employed.

Law in society. He should have a general knowledge of the role of law in society. He should be familiar with the law of contracts, negotiable instruments, the title to property, the legal distinctions between the various forms of organization, etc.

Mathematics, Statistics, and Probability. General. As in other parts of the report the authors place much higher value upon conceptual understanding than upon procedural skills.

Symbols of language. An auditor should have the same facility with the symbols of mathematics that he has always had with numbers, the symbols of arithmetic. He should be able to think in the language of mathematics, just as a Frenchman thinks in French.

Recommended topics. The authors have drawn upon the recommendation of a committee charged with making recommendations for the improvement of college and university mathematics curricula. That committee, formally called "A Panel on Mathematics for the Biological, Management, and Social Sciences," recommended that the following topics be included in the college program. The authors of *Horizons* believe the recommendations would be just as appropriate for the CPA. The eight recommendations are:

1. Probability (finite sample spaces)
2. Differential and integral calculus

3. Probability (infinite sample spaces, discrete and continuous)
4. Linear algebra
5. Analysis
6. Difference and differential equations
7. Computation
8. A probability and statistics sequence

THE FUNCTIONAL FIELDS OF BUSINESS

Finance. General. Since finance is so closely related to accounting, one cannot understand accounting without understanding finance. The body of financial knowledge may be separated into two broad classes.

Concepts and analytical approach. The beginning auditor should be thoroughly familiar with the concepts and analytical approaches necessary to evaluate capital needs and alternative sources of capital. He should be able to understand the effect of depreciation and the impact of taxes on cash flow.

Tools. He should be able to use the tools of financial analysis. For example, he should be able to make projections of cash and working capital. He should be able to compute financial ratios, rates of turnover, comparison of discounted cash flows under alternative capital investment decisions, and the cost of capital related to the capital sources.

Terminology. The auditor should have a good knowledge of the terminology of finance, the exact meaning of the terms used in finance. He should be able to communicate his recommendations both in technical terms for the professional and in understandable terms for the layman.

Institutions. He should have a fair knowledge of the institutions that comprise the marketplace. He should understand their relative position in the financial community and the various services they offer. He should also have a fair knowledge of governmental activities that influence the operation of the financial market.

Production. General. A significant part of the work of many auditors is related to production. He may be a public accountant with a number of manufacturing companies as clients, he may be an internal auditor employed by a manufacturing company, or he may be a governmental auditor determining production costs for a government contractor.

Production process. The authors recommend that the auditor understand the processes by which work flows through the production process. He should comprehend the fundamental difference between the continuity of successive operations in process industries and the interrupted sequences in jobbing manufacturers.

Cost system. He must understand the nature of the process and the cost system as a kind of model of the factory in numeric terms. He should know if the cost system used is adequate for the particular company and whether it is operating as expected.

Terminology. The auditor must understand the terminology of production and be able to communicate with production employees in connection with his work. He must be able to appreciate the problems and complexities of production, and he should be understanding and constructive in reporting any findings in the production area.

Marketing. General. The beginning auditor's work in connection with marketing is orientation. The key rules of sales management, physical distribution, and the like should be understood so that the information system and reports adequately meet their needs.

Solving marketing problems. The new auditor should understand marketing well enough to know the kinds of problems encountered. He should also understand the ways in which accounting can contribute to their solution.

Marketing system. He should have broad understanding of the retailing-wholesaling systems. He should understand the marketing institutions and the marketing environment.

Relationship with other disciplines. The auditor should understand the relationship of marketing to engineering, production, finance, and law.

Personnel Relations. Principles of management. The auditor must have an understanding of the principles involved in the management of the many individuals who comprise today's formal organizations. This knowledge is important in connection with his own firm as well as with the clients served.

Relation to behavioral sciences. This knowledge for beginning auditors is best given a sound foundation through the behavioral sciences.

Business Management. Where knowledge is acquired. It is stated that the knowledge necessary for this functional field can best be acquired through study in the behavioral sciences. Often the auditor himself becomes a business manager as an officer or executive in his firm.

Foundation for growth. These points are not considered essential for the beginning CPA, but they are important. He will build on them as he progresses in his profession.

ACCOUNTING

Functions of Accounting. General. Accounting operates in a broad social and economic environment and cannot be compartmentalized. The auditor must understand the relationship of his discipline to various other related disciplines.

Nature of function. The auditor must know who uses the product, the nature of the decisions to be made, and in what way accounting can aid the process. He must understand that accounting is an integral part of the decision-making process.

Nature of tax knowledge required. The beginning auditor is not expected to be a tax expert but should understand the nature of various taxes. For example, upon whom they are imposed, the tax base, range of rates, and their characteristics. He should have a detailed knowledge of the federal income tax.

Concepts of Accounting. General. The beginning auditor should have a good knowledge of accounting theory.

Accounting principles. He should know what is meant by "generally accepted accounting principles," the principles themselves, their applicability, their limitations, and the conflicts involving them. He should know the various approaches to asset measurement, the recognition of liabilities, and the concepts that comprise periodic income measurement.

Other concepts. The auditor must know the ways in which information is made reliable. The principle of objectivity must be known and its application and limitations. He must know sampling techniques and their limitations. He must know the concept of internal control and how it can be achieved.

Application of Concepts. General. Before the auditor can apply accounting concepts, he must thoroughly understand those concepts. For example, before dealing with asset measurement, one must understand what constitutes an asset.

Unique characteristics. The auditor must not alone be familiar with the kinds of assets he may encounter but must be familiar with their characteristics and their problem areas. For example, collectibility is an essential factor in the valuation of receivables, whereas cost flow is an essential factor in inventory presentation. They are both assets, but each has its unique characteristics.

Methods and Techniques. General. Accounting employs numerous methodologies to carry out its functions as described below.

Range of methods. The auditor has a wide range of methods and techniques that are available to him. While there is no need to be a machine operator or mathematician, the beginning CPA must understand the nature, uses, and limitations of the various methods and techniques. These range from the debit-credit structure to complex data processing systems.

Computer Science. General. In view of the pervasive impact of the computer on the field of accounting, the following recommendations are made.

Should know one system. The beginning CPA should have basic knowledge of at least one computer system. This implies a knowledge of the component parts, the general capabilities of the system, and the related terms.

Should know one language. He should also have knowledge of at least one computer language, for example, COBOL.

Should be able to chart a system. He should be able to chart or diagram a system of modest complexity. This includes the ability to understand the steps in a system and to use proper symbols to describe the system.

Should be able to design a program. With his knowledge of the language and the equipment, he should be able to design a simple system, program it, and proceed to debugging and testing of the program.

RECOMMENDED ACCOUNTING KNOWLEDGE

In outlining the knowledge which the beginning auditor should have, Roy and MacNeill use three categories as a guide in understanding the degree of knowledge required. These three categories are (1) thorough knowledge, (2) good knowledge, and (3) fair knowledge. The topics under each category are listed below.

Thorough Knowledge

The functions of accounting: who uses accounting information and for what purposes

The communication of accounting information: statement presentation for maximum utility and clarity

Double-entry structure: theoretical basis and application as an analytical tool

Auditing standards: general standards, standards of fieldwork, standards of reporting

Internal control: principles and applications

Professional ethics

Good Knowledge

Accounting theory and terminology, including income and asset measurement

Cost classification and cost behavior

Major categories of resources

Major sources of capital

Auditing methodology
Sampling, statistical inference
Income taxes
Business law

Fair Knowledge

Computer: systems, functions of components, programming, internal control features
Other accounting equipment and bookkeeping tools
Quantitative techniques
Types of formal organizations
Organization design: authority, responsibility, information handling, retrieval, and communication
Taxes, other than income taxes
Governmental agencies: kinds, basic objectives, jurisdiction requirements

IMPACT ON THE INFORMAL TRAINING OF AUDITORS

General. The common body of knowledge study primarily considers the formal educational training of accountants. Figure 1 illustrates the complementary function of formal and informal education. In this section, we will consider the implications of the study to the informal training of auditors.

On-the-job Training. Since the recommendations of the common body of knowledge study are now being increasingly implemented in university curricula, it is almost certain that beginning auditors will generally have a more rigorous conceptual education than previously, most likely at the expense of having only a peripheral familiarity with procedural techniques. This development will place more responsibility on the employer for en-

Figure 1 THE TOTAL EDUCATION PROCESS[3]

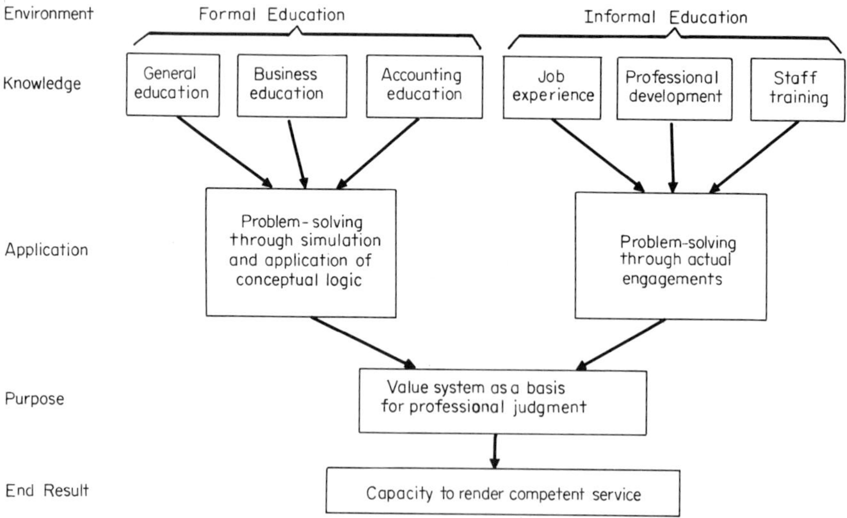

[3] Donald L. Madden and Lawrence C. Phillips, "An Evaluation of the Common Body of Knowledge Study and Its Probable Impact upon the Accounting Profession," *The Journal of Accountancy*, February, 1968, p. 88.

suring that the term "on-the-job training" will not be just a euphemism for "Who knows, if you work hard enough and long enough, you just may learn something of value."

A well-administered and organized on-the-job training program usually involves:[4]

1. Assessing strengths and weaknesses of each auditor trainee and assigning the work accordingly.
2. Ensuring that the trainee's immediate supervisor will properly instruct him as to the nature, purpose, and methods of his assignment, and offer constructive criticism.
3. Arranging for timely review and appraisal of work performed.
4. Rotating assignments both within a given audit and from audit to audit to give each trainee maximum exposure to all phases of a job and to different kinds of jobs.
5. Assigning increased responsibility to auditors as they are ready for it.
6. Providing time after the completion of an audit to review the completed job and to research material related to the next assignment.
7. Holding regular staff meetings.

Educational Obsolescence. At least of equal importance to the training of beginning auditors is the need to ensure that the entire staff is kept abreast of changing techniques and advancing technologies. The battle against educational obsolescence is a continuing one. As an experienced military man will tell you, it is easier to fight one or two larger battles than continue a series of smaller ones.

Large concerns can cope with the problem by offering their own educational courses. Smaller concerns can utilize professional-development courses offered by accounting societies. Both types of concerns can encourage their staffs to continue formal education by tuition-remission programs.

SUMMARY

After perusing the summary of recommended subjects which the study advises a beginning auditor to master, one feels that the aspiring accountant should proclaim loudly and confidently as Francis Bacon did, "I have taken all knowledge to be my province." Or to murmur with humility like Socrates, "One thing only I know, and that is I know nothing." Roy and MacNeill might well reply in the words that were originally directed to their recommendations in the areas of mathematics, statistics, and probability: "While the proposals of this report may seem excessively severe to some, it is more likely that they are too modest for CPA's who may begin their careers ten years hence."[5]

There is little doubt that the recommendations of the common body of knowledge study have a great deal of merit. The knowledge explosion is profoundly affecting the field of auditing. Many professional journals now carry a number of articles relating to the use of mathematics in auditing. The audit of online computer systems with ever-decreasing quantities of hard copy challenges the auditors' understanding of computer controls,

[4] Kimble Henbree, "On-the-job Training," *The U.S. Army Audit Agency Bulletin,* Winter, 1967, pp. 44–48.

[5] *Horizons for a Profession, The Common Body of Knowledge for Certified Public Accountants,* New York, AICPA, 1967, p. 257.

hardware, programs, and flow charts. Total information systems will bring the auditor into direct contact with mathematical models that will be integral parts of the systems under audit. The growing use of objective means of sampling and evaluation of results demands knowledge of statistical theory. The increasing popularity of management auditing brings into play the full spectrum of the common body of knowledge. If the auditor confines himself to the narrowly procedural portions of the audit, allowing data processing specialists to evaluate computer programs, mathematicians to evaluate models, statisticians to evaluate test results, and so on, he will find himself playing Trilby to someone else's Svengali.

The pressures and demands of the daily workload, complicated by the usual travel exigencies, make it easier to give lip service to the need for continuing education than actually to find time for it. Matthew Arnold might have had the modern-day auditor in mind in his poem *The Scholar-Gipsy:*

> That thou wert wander'd from the studious walls
> To learn strange arts, and join a Gipsy tribe:

The need to return to the studious walls, to be nourished by the study of burgeoning technology, is not merely important; it is vital for the continual regeneration of the auditing profession. To sacrifice this to everyday expediency is to exchange the future for mere dross.

BIBLIOGRAPHY

Report of the Committee on Education and Experience Requirements for CPAs, American Institute of Certified Public Accountants, New York, March, 1969.

Report of the CPA Examination Appraisal Commission, Association of Certified Public Accountant Examiners, New York, 1961.

Storey, Reed K.: *The Search for Accounting Principles,* The American Institute of Certified Public Accountants, New York, 1964.

Statements on Auditing Procedure No. 33, *Auditing Standards and Procedures,* AICPA (Committee on Auditing Procedure), New York, 1963.

Tentative Recommendations for the Undergraduate Mathematics Program of Students in the Biological, Management, and Social Sciences, Mathematics Association of America, 1964.

Leavitt, Harold J.: *Managerial Psychology,* Chicago, University of Chicago Press, 1964.

Likert, Rensis: *New Patterns of Management,* New York, McGraw-Hill Book Company, 1961.

McGregor, Douglas: *The Human Side of Enterprise,* New York, McGraw-Hill Book Company, 1960.

Springer, Clifford H., Robert E. Herlihy, and Robert I. Beggs: *Basic Mathematics,* vol. 1, Homewood, Ill., Richard D. Irwin, Inc., 1965.

Rush, Harold M. F.: "What Is Behavioral Science," *The Conference Board Record,* September, 1965.

"Academic Preparation for Professional Accounting Careers," *The Journal of Accountancy,* December, 1968.

Bruschi, William C.: "Issues Surrounding Qualifying Experience Requirements," *The Journal of Accountancy,* March, 1969.

Hofstedt, Thomas R., and James C. Kinard: "A Strategy for Behavioral Accounting Research," *The Accounting Review,* January, 1970.

"A Readback on 'Horizons for a Profession,'" *The Journal of Accountancy,* April, 1970.

Buckley, John W.: "A Perspective on Professional Accounting Education," *The Journal of Accountancy,* August, 1970.

Chapter 47

Quantitative Analysis

JOHN E. ULLMANN

Chairman, Department of Management, Marketing and Business Statistics, Hofstra University

GENERAL BACKGROUND

Quantitative analysis has entered the accounting and auditing fields in two major ways. First, it allows the use of accounting information in a variety of business analysis and planning tasks. It permits a more viable appraisal of such information, especially insofar as it has to be estimated rather than measured precisely. Secondly, quantitative analysis permits an understanding of the flow of resources through the business itself, permitting us to view it as an entity subject to certain outside influences and providing an interaction by which inputs become outputs. In the former group of applications, the principal tools are those found in operations research, management science, and statistics. In the latter, these are also found, in addition to which we have an increasing overlap with managerial economics, microeconomics, and econometrics.

Optimal Solutions. These techniques have two immediate objectives. The first is the specification of choices in the organization of production, marketing, or other activity, with their respective costs and a mathematical model which defines their response to varying business conditions, physical variables in the production process, etc. By successfully accomplishing this task, decisions may, in the long run, be made on a basis which *optimizes* some specifiable indicator of performance; e.g., costs or time may be minimized, or profits maximized. Now, this is *not* the search for the "one best way" of an earlier generation of efficiency experts. Rather it is the recognition that knowledge of certain business characteristics and their interaction can assist us in responding appropriately to changing environments by systematically improving the quality of our decisions.

Dealing with Risk and Uncertainty. The second objective is the ability to deal with risk and uncertainty in business. The decisions mentioned above cannot usually be made under certainty. The new techniques explicitly take risk and uncertainty into account. Indeed, they distinguish between them. Risk is the possibility that outcomes may take on a number of specified forms or values, but the probability of each of them happening is known. In uncertainty, we cannot usually enumerate the possible results of our actions, and even if we can, we cannot assign probabilities to them. Still, there are ways of dealing with such situations as well.

Because of its importance and versatility, quantitative analysis has developed intensively in the period after 1940 and, during the 1950s and 1960s, has become an almost universal subject for study by business executives and students. The 1970s are likely to bring broader applications of quantitative analysis techniques. In a single chapter, it is not possible to do justice to all of the major ones that have been developed. However, there are certain topics which have particular interest to auditors, especially if they are empowered to ask questions about operations as well as financial data and are alert to the potentials of quantitative analysis.

Techniques Discussed. The principal techniques that are of interest to auditors are:

1. *Regression.* The derivation of relationships between business variables and the assessment of their significance.
2. *Control charts.* The use of statistical methods for purposes of establishing limits of acceptability to product quality and to variance accounts.
3. *Acceptance sampling.* The procedures followed in sampling to determine the acceptability of delivered products.
4. *Waiting lines.* The evaluation of service quality and economic analysis for determining the number of facilities to be provided.

5. *Allocation.* The transportation method of minimizing transportation costs between several plants and several warehouses.

6. *Production control and inventory theory.* The analytical tools provided by mathematical models and the computer.

Quantitative Analysis and the Auditor. In Part VI, "Horizons for Auditing—The Look Ahead," are included seven chapters relating to those phases of auditing that are likely to feel the greatest impact of change in the immediate years ahead. These discuss new or improved techniques such as quantitative analysis, ratio change and trend analysis, flow charting, new directions in auditing such as performance auditing and operational auditing, and new controls such as planning, programming, and budgeting systems and other new developments described in the chapter on the common body of knowledge. These phases of coming change are discussed throughout *Horizons for a Profession* but are summarized on page 98 as follows: [1]

1. Increasingly accounting information will be stored in forms retrievable only by machines.
2. The means of presenting accounting information will become increasingly probabilistic.
3. Utilization of mathematics, statistics, and probability by accountants will increase.

In this chapter we are concerned indirectly with item 1 but very directly with items 2 and 3. As indicated in item 2 and discussed at the beginning of this chapter, accounting information will become increasingly probabilistic as opposed to the present deterministic stance. Also as indicated in item 3 the use of mathematics, statistics, and probability by accountants will increase. We are already witnessing a trend in that direction. We hope that this chapter will help that trend.

Basically, the auditor of the future must be able to think in the symbols of mathematics as he does now in numbers, the symbols of arithmetic. The *Horizon* study, page 247, recommends that the beginning CPA "be required to have the same kind of facility with the symbols of mathematics that he has always had with numbers, the symbols of arithmetic" and very persuasively on the same page, "that he be required to understand mathematics as a language to that degree which will lead him to use it, not bending reluctantly to compulsion but rising willingly to opportunity."

Most accountants out of college for some years and not being able to brush up or retread their earlier exposure to quantitative analysis will probably be "bending reluctantly" to greater use of quantitative analysis. As pointed out on page 251 of *Horizons,* "mathematics, statistics and probability are essentially deductive; they are therefore of that class of knowledge best imparted by instruction. Expressed differently, these are disciplines which are best taught; this portion of the common body of knowledge for CPAs should be acquired in school."

Most of the other subjects in Part VI of the Handbook can be learned in practice or by independent study or instruction. However, the fundamental preparation for quantitative analysis is most efficiently acquired in school. It is recognized then that the beginning CPA, one with no experience and just out of school, should have knowledge of differential and integral calculus, probability, linear algebra, differential equations, and related topics. Therefore these quantitative topics and various other matters covered in a four year accounting program, or in the recommended five year program can hardly be taught in one chapter of a handbook. A handbook is a convenient place to

[1] Robert H. Roy and James H. MacNeill, *Horizons for a Profession,* AICPA, 1967.

find essential knowledge on any particular subject; it is not an elementary treatise. If the auditor has had college subjects in recent years relating to the topics discussed in this chapter he will have little difficulty. All accredited college programs in accounting will probably cover the topics in this chapter. Therefore only a review of the basic concepts and principles will be required to make full use of the material in this chapter. For those with less exposure to quantitative analysis we recommend some of the basic books referred to in the bibliography at the end of the chapter.

REGRESSION AND CORRELATION

Definition. Regression is the determination of a statistical relationship between two or more variables. In this respect, regression can only interpret what exists physically. Since underlying its theory is that one variable, defined as *independent*, is the cause of the behavior of another one, defined as *dependent*, there must be a physical way in which independent variable X can affect dependent variable Y. Unless such a connection exists, what follows is merely a useless exercise in arithmetic.

The following analysis will deal first with simple regression and correlation involving one independent and one dependent variable, designated X and Y, respectively. Their relationship may be depicted in a scatter diagram (Figure 1). Also, the following relationships are useful:

The mean

$$\bar{X} = \frac{\Sigma X}{N}$$

where ΣX is read as "the sum of all N values of X." A relationship like ΣX^2 means "square each of the N X's and add the N squares." ΣXY means "multiply each X by its corresponding Y and add the products." Today it is usually unnecessary to perform such operations line by line, since modern desk calculators can accumulate products so that ΣX^2, ΣY^2, ΣXY, etc., can be obtained directly.

The basic relationship between X and Y is given by

$$Y_c = a + bX$$

where the suffix c denotes "calculated value." It means that each unit change in X produces a change of b in Y, which is positive for direct and negative for inverse relationships.

Figure 1 SCATTER DIAGRAM AND TREND LINE FOR SIMPLE CORRELATION

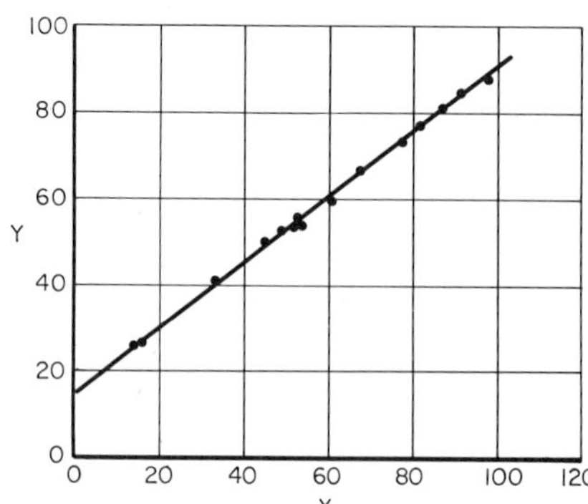

Least-squares Method. The generally used method to find the "best" fit that a straight line of this kind can give is the *least-squares* method. To use it efficiently, one first determines

$$\Sigma x^2 = \Sigma X^2 - N\bar{X}^2 \qquad \Sigma xy = \Sigma XY - N\bar{X}\bar{Y}$$

$$\Sigma y^2 = \Sigma Y^2 - N\bar{Y}^2$$

Then

$$b = \frac{\Sigma xy}{\Sigma x^2} \qquad a = \bar{Y} - b\bar{X}$$

These measures define a and b which will give the best possible fit through the original X and Y points. The problem now is how to determine whether this line accounts for a significant amount of variability of Y.

This is done by defining

$$r^2 = \frac{b^2 \Sigma x^2}{\Sigma y^2}$$

and then determining

$$t_c = r\sqrt{\frac{N-2}{1-r^2}}$$

This calculated value of t is then compared with the value in Table 1 which is entered with $n = N - 2$. If the calculated value of t, t_c, is less than the value in the table, we can assert with no more than 5 percent probability of error that there is *no* relationship of statistical significance. The coefficient

TABLE 1 Extract from Table of Student's t Distribution *

n	Significance Level 0.05	n	Significance Level 0.05
1	12.71	20	2.09
2	4.30	21	2.08
3	3.18	22	2.07
4	2.78	23	2.07
		24	2.06
5	2.57		
6	2.45	25	2.06
7	2.36	26	2.06
8	2.31	27	2.05
9	2.26	28	2.05
		29	2.04
10	2.23		
11	2.20	30	2.04
12	2.18	40	2.02
13	2.16	50	2.01
14	2.14	60	2.00
		80	1.99
15	2.13		
16	2.12	100	1.98
17	2.11	200	1.97
18	2.10	500	1.96
19	2.09		
		∞	1.96

* From B. J. Winer, *Statistical Principles in Experimental Design*, New York, McGraw-Hill Book Company, 1962, used by permission.

r is termed the *coefficient of correlation,* and r^2 is the *coefficient of determination.*

Simple Correlation. When it is desired to obtain r directly without first finding b, it is given by

$$r^2 = \frac{(\Sigma xy)^2}{\Sigma x^2 \Sigma y^2}$$

r can vary between -1 and $+1$. The nearer to these extremes, the better the correlation. A value of r of -1 indicates perfect inverse correlation, a value of $+1$, perfect direct correlation. When r is zero, there is no correlation and the t test actually measures the likelihood that r is insignificantly different from zero.

The data in Table 2 give the cost Y of a certain activity in terms of a certain input X to it. A relationship of the form $Y = a + bX$ is believed to exist, on the basis of the physical relationship and the preliminary plot of the scatter diagram in Figure 1. The following calculations are made ($N = 15$, obtained by line count):

From the table:

$$\Sigma Y = 883.84 \qquad \Sigma X = 880$$

$$\bar{Y} = \frac{883.84}{15} = 58.923 \qquad \bar{X} = \frac{880}{15} = 58.667$$

$$\Sigma Y^2 = 57{,}280.69 \qquad \Sigma X^2 = 60{,}896$$

$$\Sigma XY = 58{,}787.88$$

From the formulas:

$$\Sigma x^2 = 60{,}896 - 15 \times 58.667^2 = 9{,}269.3310$$

$$\Sigma y^2 = 57{,}280.69 - 15 \times 58.923^2 = 5{,}201.3805$$

$$\Sigma xy = 58{,}787.88 - 15 \times 58.667 \times 58.923 = 6{,}935.313$$

$$b = \frac{6{,}935.313}{9{,}269.3310} = 0.7482$$

$$a = 58.923 - 0.7482 \times 58.667 = 15.028$$

$$r^2 = \frac{0.7482^2 \times 9{,}269.3310}{5{,}201.3805} = 0.99763$$

$$r = \sqrt{0.99763} = 0.99881$$

$$t = 0.99881 \sqrt{\frac{13}{1 - 0.99763}} = 74.128$$

Since this is greatly in excess of the tabular value for t with $n = 13$ (2.16, from Table 1), the correlation can be considered highly significant.

Time series. A simple modification of the foregoing method is used to determine linear trends in time series. In the relationship $Y = a + bX$, X then means time, which is in turn expressed by a simple coding procedure. An odd number of years (or other periods) is chosen as a base, forming an uninterrupted series of integers, with zero in the middle. The X's are then coded as shown for a typical series of years

	1964	1965	1966	1967	1968	1969	1970
$X =$	-3	-2	-1	0	1	2	3

TABLE 2 Data for Simple Correlation

Y Cost (Dollars)	X Input
53.42	53
84.53	91
80.87	87
52.45	49
25.60	14
87.12	98
72.93	78
76.50	82
55.14	53
41.00	33
49.51	45
53.16	52
26.22	16
66.04	68
59.26	61

What we have done is to take the origin of X in the middle of the series. This makes the average of X, $\bar{X} = 0$, and the formulas for a and b are simplified:

$$a = \bar{Y} \qquad b = \frac{\Sigma XY}{\Sigma X^2}$$

Because the X's are a regular series of integers, we can also write

$$\Sigma X^2 = \frac{N(N^2 - 1)}{12}$$

which is convenient to use when N is large.

Important extensions of this principle are found in the general study of time series in which seasonal, cyclical, and irregular factors may be decomposed and studied separately. The procedures are shown extensively in the literature.

By putting the Y data (e.g., sales or usage) in the form of logarithms and proceeding exactly as above, we can obtain growth rates which would be given by

$$b = \log(1 + i)$$

where i is the growth rate as a decimal fraction.

Multiple Correlation. When there are two or more independent variables, the analysis is known as *multiple correlation.* In the present chapter, only the case of two independent variables is presented. Convenient computer programs exist for dealing with a greater number of variables, and in any event, the results are interpreted in the same way as those below.

The regression equation is

$$Y_c = a + b_1X_1 + b_2X_2$$

The constants are determined by solving simultaneously

$$\Sigma yx_1 = b_1\Sigma x_1^2 + b_2\Sigma x_1x_2$$

$$\Sigma yx_2 = b_1\Sigma x_1x_2 + b_2\Sigma x_2^2$$

where

$$\Sigma x_1^2 = \Sigma X_1^2 - N\bar{X}_1^2 \qquad \Sigma yx_1 = \Sigma YX_1 - N\bar{Y}\bar{X}_1$$

$$\Sigma x_2^2 = \Sigma X_2^2 - N\bar{X}_2^2 \qquad \Sigma yx_2 = \Sigma YX_2 - N\bar{Y}\bar{X}_2$$

$$\Sigma y^2 = \Sigma Y^2 - N\bar{Y}^2 \qquad \Sigma x_1x_2 = \Sigma X_1X_2 - N\bar{X}_1\bar{X}_2$$

With more than one independent variable, one can distinguish between the collective effect of the two independent variables and the individual effect of each of them taken separately. The collective effect is given by the *multiple coefficient of correlation* $R_{Y.X_1X_2}$ defined by

$$R^2_{Y.X_1X_2} = \frac{b_1\Sigma yx_1 + b_2\Sigma yx_2}{\Sigma y^2}$$

To test $R_{Y.X_1X_2}$ for significance, one computes

$$F_c = \frac{R^2_{Y.X_1X_2}/(k-1)}{(1 - R^2_{Y.X_1X_2})/(N-k)}$$

where k is the number of variables involved; in this case $k = 3$. The test is performed by entering tables of the F distribution (Table 3) with

$$n_1 = k - 1 = 3 - 1 = 2$$

$$n_2 = N - 3$$

Again, if F_c is less than the tabular value, there is *no* significant statistical correlation.

Each *partial coefficient of correlation* measures the effect of its independent variable on the dependent variable. To obtain it, it is first necessary to have the *simple* coefficients of correlation between each independent variable computed as shown before. These are denoted r_{YX_1} and r_{YX_2}, and the corresponding partial coefficients are

$$r_{YX_1.X_2} = \frac{R^2_{Y.X_1X_2} - r^2_{YX_2}}{1 - r^2_{YX_2}}$$

This measures the effect of X_1 on Y, or more precisely, that proportion of the variation of Y *not* explained by X_2 which is explained by X_1. Also

$$r_{YX_2.X_1} = \frac{R^2_{Y.X_1X_2} - r^2_{YX_1}}{1 - r^2_{YX_1}}$$

in which X_1 and X_2 are simply interchanged, gives the added effect of X_2 on Y. The statistical significance of such a coefficient is measured by

$$t_c = r_p\sqrt{\frac{N-k}{1-r_p^2}}$$

where r_p is any partial coefficient of correlation and the t table (Table 1) is entered with

$$n = N - k \qquad \text{(here } N - 3\text{)}$$

Again, if t in the table is greater than t_c, there is no correlatión.

Example. A set of data appears in Table 4 which repeats the first two columns from the simple correlation in Table 2 but adds X_2, another independent variable. The steps are as follows:

From the table ($N = 15$):

$$\Sigma Y = 883.84 \qquad \bar{Y} = \frac{883.84}{15} = 58.923$$

$$\Sigma X_1 = 880 \qquad \bar{X}_1 = \frac{880}{15} = 58.667$$

$$\Sigma X_2 = 7{,}662 \qquad \bar{X}_2 = \frac{7{,}662}{15} = 510.8$$

$$\Sigma Y^2 = 57{,}280.69 \qquad \Sigma YX_1 = 58{,}787.88$$

$$\Sigma X_1^2 = 60{,}896 \qquad \Sigma YX_2 = 470{,}793.3$$

$$\Sigma X_2^2 = 5{,}211{,}451 \qquad \Sigma X_1X_2 = 474{,}227$$

From the formulas:

$$\Sigma y^2 = 57{,}280.69 - 15 \times 58.923^2 = 5{,}201.3805$$

$$\Sigma x_1^2 = 60{,}896 - 15 \times 58.667^2 = 9{,}269.3310$$

$$\Sigma x_2^2 = 5{,}211{,}451 - 15 \times 510.8^2 = 1{,}297{,}700.6$$

$$\Sigma yx_1 = 58{,}787.88 - 15 \times 58.667 \times 58.923 = 6{,}935.313$$

$$\Sigma yx_2 = 470{,}793.3 - 15 \times 58.923 \times 510.8 = 19{,}322.76$$

$$\Sigma x_1x_2 = 474{,}227 - 15 \times 58.667 \times 510.8 = 24{,}721.20$$

Equation:

$$6{,}935.313 = 9{,}269.3310b_1 + 24{,}721.20b_2$$

$$19{,}322.76 = 24{,}721.20b_1 + 1{,}297{,}700.6b_2$$

Solving:

$$b_1 = 0.74642$$

$$b_2 = 0.00066$$

$$a = 58.923 - 0.74642 \times 58.667 - 0.00066 \times 510.8 = 14.791$$

$$R^2_{Y.X_1X_2} = \frac{0.74642 \times 6{,}935.313 + 0.00066 \times 19{,}322.76}{5{,}201.3805} = 0.99774$$

$$F_c = \frac{0.99774/2}{(1 - 0.99774)/(15 - 3)} = 2{,}655.22$$

This is greatly more than the corresponding F value in Table 3 with $n_1 = 2$, $n_2 = 12$, which equals 3.88. Hence the coefficient of multiple correlation is significant.

It is known from the example in simple correlation that $r^2_{YX_1} = 0.99763$ and, using the same method on Y and X_2, $r^2_{YX_2} = 0.05531$. The two partial coefficients of correlation are then obtained from

$$r^2_{YX_1.X_2} = \frac{0.99774 - 0.99763}{1 - 0.99763} = 0.9976$$

$$r_{YX_1.X_2} = 0.9988$$

$$t_c = 0.9988\sqrt{\frac{12}{1 - 0.9976}} = 70.821$$

TABLE 3 *F* **Values at 0.05 Probability Level**

n_2	n_1 = degrees of freedom 1	2	3	4	5	6	7	8	9	10	11
1	161	200	216	225	230	234	237	239	241	242	243
2	18.51	19.00	19.16	19.25	19.30	19.33	19.36	19.37	19.38	19.39	19.40
3	10.13	9.55	9.28	9.12	9.01	8.94	8.88	8.84	8.81	8.78	8.76
4	7.71	6.94	6.59	6.39	6.26	6.16	6.09	6.04	6.00	5.96	5.93
5	6.61	5.79	5.41	5.19	5.05	4.95	4.88	4.82	4.78	4.74	4.70
6	5.99	5.14	4.76	4.53	4.39	4.28	4.21	4.15	4.10	4.06	4.03
7	5.59	4.74	4.35	4.12	3.97	3.87	3.79	3.73	3.68	3.63	3.60
8	5.32	4.46	4.07	3.84	3.69	3.58	3.50	3.44	3.39	3.34	3.31
9	5.12	4.26	3.86	3.63	3.48	3.37	3.29	3.23	3.18	3.13	3.10
10	4.96	4.10	3.71	3.48	3.33	3.22	3.14	3.07	3.02	2.97	2.94
11	4.84	3.98	3.59	3.36	3.20	3.09	3.01	2.95	2.90	2.86	2.82
12	4.75	3.88	3.49	3.26	3.11	3.00	2.92	2.85	2.80	2.76	2.72
13	4.67	3.80	3.41	3.18	3.02	2.92	2.84	2.77	2.72	2.67	2.63
14	4.60	3.74	3.34	3.11	2.96	2.85	2.77	2.70	2.65	2.60	2.56
15	4.54	3.68	3.29	3.06	2.90	2.79	2.70	2.64	2.59	2.55	2.51
16	4.49	3.63	3.24	3.01	2.85	2.74	2.66	2.59	2.54	2.49	2.45
17	4.45	3.59	3.20	2.96	2.81	2.70	2.62	2.55	2.50	2.45	2.41
18	4.41	3.55	3.16	2.93	2.77	2.66	2.58	2.51	2.46	2.41	2.37
19	4.38	3.52	3.13	2.90	2.74	2.63	2.55	2.48	2.43	2.38	2.34
20	4.35	3.49	3.10	2.87	2.71	2.60	2.52	2.45	2.40	2.35	2.31
21	4.32	3.47	3.07	2.84	2.68	2.57	2.49	2.42	2.37	2.32	2.28
22	4.30	3.44	3.05	2.82	2.66	2.55	2.47	2.40	2.35	2.30	2.26
23	4.28	3.42	3.03	2.80	2.64	2.53	2.45	2.38	2.32	2.28	2.24
24	4.26	3.40	3.01	2.78	2.62	2.51	2.43	2.36	2.30	2.26	2.22
25	4.24	3.38	2.99	2.76	2.60	2.49	2.41	2.34	2.28	2.24	2.20
26	4.22	3.37	2.98	2.74	2.59	2.47	2.39	2.32	2.27	2.22	2.18
27	4.21	3.35	2.96	2.73	2.57	2.46	2.37	2.30	2.25	2.20	2.16
28	4.20	3.34	2.95	2.71	2.56	2.44	2.36	2.29	2.24	2.19	2.15
29	4.18	3.33	2.93	2.70	2.54	2.43	2.35	2.28	2.22	2.18	2.14
30	4.17	3.32	2.92	2.69	2.53	2.42	2.34	2.27	2.21	2.16	2.12
32	4.15	3.30	2.90	2.67	2.51	2.40	2.32	2.25	2.19	2.14	2.10
34	4.13	3.28	2.88	2.65	2.49	2.38	2.30	2.23	2.17	2.12	2.08
36	4.11	3.26	2.86	2.63	2.48	2.36	2.28	2.21	2.15	2.10	2.06
38	4.10	3.25	2.85	2.62	2.46	2.35	2.26	2.19	2.14	2.09	2.05
40	4.08	3.23	2.84	2.61	2.45	2.34	2.25	2.18	2.12	2.07	2.04
42	4.07	3.22	2.83	2.59	2.44	2.32	2.24	2.17	2.11	2.06	2.02
44	4.06	3.21	2.82	2.58	2.43	2.31	2.23	2.16	2.10	2.05	2.01
46	4.05	3.20	2.81	2.57	2.42	2.30	2.22	2.14	2.09	2.04	2.00
48	4.04	3.19	2.80	2.56	2.41	2.30	2.21	2.14	2.08	2.03	1.99
50	4.03	3.18	2.79	2.56	2.40	2.29	2.20	2.13	2.07	2.02	1.98
55	4.02	3.17	2.78	2.54	2.38	2.27	2.18	2.11	2.05	2.00	1.97
60	4.00	3.15	2.76	2.52	2.37	2.25	2.17	2.10	2.04	1.99	1.95
65	3.99	3.14	2.75	2.51	2.36	2.24	2.15	2.08	2.02	1.98	1.94
70	3.98	3.13	2.74	2.50	2.35	2.23	2.14	2.07	2.01	1.97	1.93
80	3.96	3.11	2.72	2.48	2.33	2.21	2.12	2.05	1.99	1.95	1.91
100	3.94	3.09	2.70	2.46	2.30	2.19	2.10	2.03	1.97	1.92	1.88
125	3.92	3.07	2.68	2.44	2.29	2.17	2.08	2.01	1.95	1.90	1.86
150	3.91	3.06	2.67	2.43	2.27	2.16	2.07	2.00	1.94	1.89	1.85
200	3.89	3.04	2.65	2.41	2.26	2.14	2.05	1.98	1.92	1.87	1.93
400	3.86	3.02	2.62	2.39	2.23	2.12	2.03	1.96	1.90	1.85	1.81
1,000	3.85	3.00	2.61	2.38	2.22	2.10	2.02	1.95	1.89	1.84	1.80
∞	3.84	2.99	2.60	2.37	2.21	2.09	2.01	1.94	1.88	1.83	1.79

SOURCE: *Chemical Engineering*, vol. 63, no. 3, March, 1956, p. 186.

for variance in numerator

12	14	16	20	24	30	40	50	75	100	200	500	∞
244	245	246	248	249	250	251	252	253	253	254	254	254
19.41	19.42	19.42	19.44	19.45	19.46	19.47	19.47	19.48	19.49	19.49	19.50	19.50
8.74	8.71	8.69	8.66	8.64	8.62	8.60	8.58	8.57	8.56	8.54	8.54	8.53
5.91	5.87	5.84	5.80	5.77	5.74	5.71	5.70	5.68	5.66	5.65	5.64	5.63
4.68	4.64	4.60	4.56	4.53	4.50	4.46	4.44	4.42	4.40	4.38	4.37	4.36
4.00	3.96	3.92	3.87	3.84	3.81	3.77	3.75	3.72	3.71	3.69	3.68	3.67
3.57	3.52	3.49	3.44	3.41	3.38	3.34	3.32	3.29	3.28	3.25	3.24	3.23
3.28	3.23	3.20	3.15	3.12	3.08	3.05	3.03	3.00	2.98	2.96	2.94	2.93
3.07	3.02	2.98	2.93	2.90	2.86	2.82	2.80	2.77	2.76	2.73	2.72	2.71
2.91	2.86	2.82	2.77	2.74	2.70	2.67	2.64	2.61	2.59	2.56	2.55	2.54
2.79	2.74	2.70	2.65	2.61	2.57	2.53	2.50	2.47	2.45	2.42	2.41	2.40
2.69	2.64	2.60	2.54	2.50	2.46	2.42	2.40	2.36	2.35	2.32	2.31	2.30
2.60	2.55	2.51	2.46	2.42	2.38	2.34	2.32	2.28	2.26	2.24	2.22	2.21
2.53	2.48	2.44	2.39	2.35	2.31	2.27	2.24	2.21	2.19	2.16	2.14	2.13
2.48	2.43	2.39	2.33	2.29	2.25	2.21	2.18	2.15	2.12	2.10	2.08	2.07
2.42	2.37	2.33	2.28	2.24	2.20	2.16	2.13	2.09	2.07	2.04	2.02	2.01
2.38	2.33	2.29	2.23	2.19	2.15	2.11	2.08	2.04	2.02	1.99	1.97	1.96
2.34	2.29	2.25	2.19	2.15	2.11	2.07	2.04	2.00	1.98	1.95	1.93	1.92
2.31	2.26	2.21	2.15	2.11	2.07	2.02	2.00	1.96	1.94	1.91	1.90	1.88
2.28	2.23	2.18	2.12	2.08	2.04	1.99	1.96	1.92	1.90	1.87	1.85	1.84
2.25	2.20	2.15	2.09	2.05	2.00	1.96	1.93	1.89	1.87	1.84	1.82	1.81
2.23	2.18	2.13	2.07	2.03	1.98	1.93	1.91	1.87	1.84	1.81	1.80	1.78
2.20	2.14	2.10	2.04	2.00	1.96	1.91	1.88	1.84	1.82	1.79	1.77	1.76
2.18	2.13	2.09	2.02	1.98	1.94	1.89	1.86	1.82	1.80	1.76	1.74	1.73
2.16	2.11	2.06	2.00	1.96	1.92	1.87	1.84	1.80	1.77	1.74	1.72	1.71
2.15	2.10	2.05	1.99	1.95	1.90	1.85	1.82	1.78	1.76	1.72	1.70	1.69
2.13	2.08	2.03	1.97	1.93	1.88	1.84	1.80	1.76	1.74	1.71	1.68	1.67
2.12	2.06	2.02	1.96	1.91	1.87	1.81	1.78	1.75	1.72	1.69	1.67	1.65
2.10	2.05	2.00	1.94	1.90	1.85	1.80	1.77	1.73	1.71	1.68	1.65	1.64
2.09	2.04	1.99	1.93	1.89	1.84	1.79	1.76	1.72	1.69	1.66	1.64	1.62
2.07	2.02	1.97	1.91	1.86	1.82	1.76	1.74	1.69	1.67	1.64	1.61	1.59
2.05	2.00	1.95	1.89	1.84	1.80	1.74	1.71	1.67	1.64	1.61	1.59	1.57
2.03	1.98	1.93	1.87	1.82	1.78	1.72	1.69	1.65	1.62	1.59	1.56	1.55
2.02	1.96	1.92	1.85	1.80	1.76	1.71	1.67	1.63	1.60	1.57	1.54	1.53
2.00	1.95	1.90	1.84	1.79	1.74	1.69	1.66	1.61	1.59	1.55	1.53	1.51
1.99	1.94	1.89	1.82	1.78	1.73	1.68	1.64	1.60	1.57	1.54	1.51	1.49
1.98	1.92	1.88	1.81	1.76	1.72	1.66	1.63	1.58	1.56	1.52	1.50	1.48
1.97	1.91	1.87	1.80	1.75	1.71	1.65	1.62	1.57	1.54	1.51	1.48	1.46
1.96	1.90	1.86	1.79	1.74	1.70	1.64	1.61	1.56	1.53	1.50	1.47	1.45
1.95	1.90	1.85	1.78	1.74	1.69	1.63	1.60	1.55	1.52	1.48	1.46	1.44
1.93	1.88	1.83	1.76	1.72	1.67	1.61	1.58	1.52	1.50	1.46	1.43	1.41
1.92	1.86	1.81	1.75	1.70	1.65	1.59	1.56	1.50	1.48	1.44	1.41	1.39
1.90	1.85	1.80	1.73	1.68	1.63	1.57	1.54	1.49	1.46	1.42	1.39	1.37
1.89	1.84	1.79	1.72	1.67	1.62	1.56	1.53	1.47	1.45	1.40	1.37	1.35
1.88	1.82	1.77	1.70	1.65	1.60	1.54	1.51	1.45	1.42	1.38	1.35	1.32
1.85	1.79	1.75	1.68	1.63	1.57	1.51	1.48	1.42	1.39	1.34	1.30	1.28
1.83	1.77	1.72	1.65	1.60	1.55	1.49	1.45	1.39	1.36	1.31	1.27	1.25
1.82	1.76	1.71	1.64	1.59	1.54	1.47	1.44	1.37	1.34	1.29	1.25	1.22
1.80	1.74	1.69	1.62	1.57	1.52	1.45	1.42	1.35	1.32	1.26	1.22	1.19
1.78	1.72	1.67	1.60	1.54	1.49	1.42	1.38	1.32	1.28	1.22	1.16	1.13
1.76	1.70	1.65	1.58	1.53	1.47	1.41	1.36	1.30	1.26	1.19	1.13	1.08
1.75	1.69	1.64	1.57	1.52	1.46	1.40	1.35	1.28	1.24	1.17	1.11	1.00

TABLE 4 Data for Multiple Correlation

Y, cost (dollars)	X_1, input I	X_2, input II
53.42	53	147
84.53	91	815
80.87	87	613
52.45	49	639
25.60	14	222
87.12	98	995
72.93	78	360
76.50	82	86
55.14	53	822
41.00	33	357
49.51	45	997
53.16	52	205
26.22	16	587
66.04	68	254
59.26	61	563

This is greatly more than the tabular value of t with $n = 12$ (2.18, from Table 1) and thus is significant.

$$r^2_{YX_2 \cdot X_1} = \frac{0.99774 - 0.05531}{1 - 0.05531} = 0.04489$$

$$r_{YX_2 \cdot X_1} = 0.21188$$

$$t_c = 0.21188\sqrt{\frac{12}{1 - 0.04489}}$$

$$= 0.75103$$

This is less than the tabular value of 2.18, and thus the hypothesis that the input X_2 significantly affects cost Y must be rejected.

CONTROL CHARTS

The State of Control. Control charts serve the function of alerting those responsible to the possibility that a process is not performing as expected. In doing so, they make use of measurements of a particular dimension, performance characteristic, or other continuously scaled variable, such as diameter of a bolt or current output of an electronic component. Alternatively, control charts may be based on attributes, i.e., the fraction defective within a sample, or simply a count of the number of defectives in a sample. All of these are based on the same statistical principles.

A control chart is a device for recording these characteristics on a continuous chart in which the horizontal scale is either time, if samples are taken at regular intervals, or simply batch serial numbers. It consists of a horizontal central line which represents a mean value of the variable and of an upper control limit (UCL) and a lower control limit (LCL) (Figure 2). Once the mean, UCL, and LCL have been determined and the chart prepared, it is possible to enter on it the values for succeeding samples, whether these are sample means, sample ranges (i.e., the differences between the highest and lowest values in the sample), a fraction defective in the sample, or num-

Figure 2 A TYPICAL CONTROL CHART

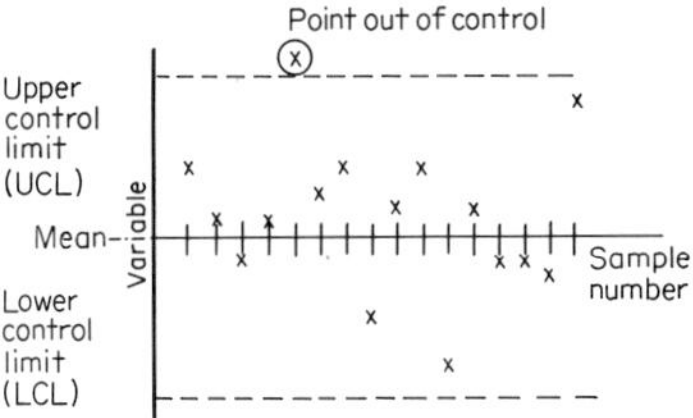

ber of defectives. In the illustration, all points except one fall within the limits set.

If a point falls outside the limits, then, according to statistical theory, and as a consequence of the wide limits that are generally used, there is a very strong chance that something is wrong with the process or operation which is being monitored. Such a physical occurrence may be a flow controller or thermostat improperly set in a chemical process, or tool wear in parts manufacture. In any event, a point falling outside the charts calls for direct investigation of the process, until the cause of the deviation has been determined and remedial action taken.

Statistical quality-control charts are generally developed in the same way. A large number of samples are taken and the mean is derived. The limits are then set in accordance with the simple formulas noted in the next sections.

Fraction-defective Charts. If samples of size n are taken at intervals and in each of them is computed $p = c/n$, where c is the number of defective items, the fraction defective p can be used in a control chart in which

$$\mathrm{UCL}(p) = \bar{p} + 3\sigma_p$$

$$\mathrm{LCL}(p) = \bar{p} - 3\sigma_p$$

where $\bar{p}$ is the mean value of p and must be obtained from a large number k of initial samples. For each of these, p is determined, which leads to

$$\bar{p} = \sum^{k} \frac{p}{k}$$

and

$$\sigma_p = \sqrt{\frac{\bar{p}(1-\bar{p})}{n}},$$

from which the chart can be prepared. Before using it, it is important to plot on it all the k points that have gone into its preparation and to eliminate all that fall outside the limits, finally recomputing $\bar{p}$ using only samples whose value of p has fallen within the limits. Note that in order to be able to use the statistical theory underlying these particular charts, it is essential that $n > 60$.

Example. The series of k preliminary tests on samples of 121 each has produced a mean fraction defective $\bar{p} = 0.04$. This is also the centerline of the control chart. From above,

$$\sigma_p = \sqrt{\frac{0.04 \times 0.96}{121}} = 0.0178$$

$$\mathrm{UCL}(p) = 0.04 + 3 \times 0.0178 = 0.0934$$

$$\mathrm{LCL}(p) = 0.04 - 3 \times 0.0178 < 0 \text{ and is therefore set at } 0$$

Number-defective Charts. It is also possible to use the number of defectives c in control charts rather than the fraction of defectives. To make the chart initially, k samples of n each are taken and the number of defectives for each is determined. The following relationships obtain:

$$\bar{c} = \sum^{k} \frac{c}{k}$$

The mean value $\bar{c}$ is the centerline.

$$\text{UCL}(c) = \bar{c} + 3\sqrt{\bar{c}}$$
$$\text{LCL}(c) = \bar{c} - 3\sqrt{\bar{c}}$$

Example. The series of k preliminary tests on the samples shows a mean number of defectives per sample of 40.96. The control chart is then

$$\text{Centerline } \bar{c} = 40.96$$
$$\text{UCL}(c) = 40.96 + 3 \times 6.4 = 60.16$$
$$\text{LCL}(c) = 40.96 - 3 \times 6.4 = 21.76$$

Variables Charts. Control charts for variables make use of actual measurements X in samples of size n, treating a single variable. For each sample the mean $\bar{X}$ is determined, from

$$\bar{X} = \frac{\Sigma X}{n}$$

and the range R, which is given by

$$R = X_{\max} - X_{\min}$$

To establish the control chart, k samples of size n are first taken, and the mean of the means, which serves as the centerline, is given by

$$\bar{\bar{X}} = \frac{\Sigma \bar{X}}{k}$$

It is also necessary to compute the mean range $\bar{R}$ of the k samples, from

$$\bar{R} = \frac{\Sigma R}{k}$$

The control limits are then given by

$$\text{UCL}(\bar{X}) = \bar{\bar{X}} + A_2\bar{R}$$
$$\text{LCL}(\bar{X}) = \bar{\bar{X}} - A_2\bar{R}$$

where A_2 is obtained from Table 5 and depends on the sample size n. In addition to the control chart for the mean, it also usually is necessary to prepare a control chart for the range itself. This is designed to assure that the variability within samples does not exceed prescribed limits. For the range control chart, $\bar{R}$ serves as centerline. The limits are

$$\text{UCL}(R) = D_4\bar{R}$$
$$\text{LCL}(R) = D_3\bar{R}$$

The coefficients D_3 and D_4 appear in Table 5.

TABLE 5 Factors for Determining from $\bar{R}$ the 3-sigma Control Limits for $\bar{X}$ and R Charts

No. of observations in subgroup n	Factor for $\bar{X}$ chart A_2	Factors for R chart	
		Lower control limit D_3	Upper control limit D_4
2	1.88	0	3.27
3	1.02	0	2.57
4	0.73	0	2.28
5	0.58	0	2.11
6	0.48	0	2.00
7	0.42	0.08	1.92
8	0.37	0.14	1.86
9	0.34	0.18	1.82
10	0.31	0.22	1.78
11	0.29	0.26	1.74
12	0.27	0.28	1.72
13	0.25	0.31	1.69
14	0.24	0.33	1.67
15	0.22	0.35	1.65
16	0.21	0.36	1.64
17	0.20	0.38	1.62
18	0.19	0.39	1.61
19	0.19	0.40	1.60
20	0.18	0.41	1.59

Reprinted from E. L. Grant, *Statistical Quality Control,* New York, McGraw-Hill Book Company, 1965, p. 562.

Some practitioners advocate dispensing with the range chart because in many practical forms of deterioration of quality, such as tool wear, the mean $\bar{X}$ of later samples drifts toward and then over the control limits; it is less likely that the means of the samples remain satisfactory while the range, which is by its statistical nature a rather coarse measure, is out of control. The decision depends on the practical form which a process breakdown would typically take.

Cost Charts. Control charts for costs are similar to control charts for variables. They make use of the deviation d of the actual cost C_a from the expected cost C_e, so that

$$d = C_a - C_e$$

The values of d may be derived from a long series of variance accounts for a particular cost center, but it is even better if they are the result of the sort of correlation study which was presented under "Regression and Correlation." In that case, the initial values of d would be given by

$$d = Y - Y_c$$

However derived, the objective is to have a control chart for the d's. Such a chart is superior to rules of thumb like requiring justification of any variance account more than 5 percent over, or the like, because the chart takes into account the inherent variability of the cost involved. Actually, a 5 percent overrun may be excessive for some tightly predictable costs and may set an impossible standard for others.

The preparation of control charts for costs is complicated by the fact that in each period there is only one "sample point" in the form of the accounting entry; i.e., $n = 1$. Accordingly, the following procedure is necessary:

1. Obtain k values of d, preferably taken over k successive time periods, with k an odd number. This simplifies step 2.

2. Order the k values in a time series, with time taken as t and centered, such that, for example, when $k = 19$, t is taken as $-9,-8,-7, \ldots ,-1,0,1, \ldots ,7,8,9$. Hence $\bar{t} = 0$. The series is then given as

$$d = a + bt$$

and the coefficient of correlation is obtained from (see "Time Series" above)

$$r = \sqrt{\frac{12\,\Sigma dt}{(\Sigma d^2 - k\bar{d}^2)(k^2 - 1)k}}$$

and tested for significance as shown under "Regression and Correlation." When d has been obtained from the residual of a least-squares regression, i.e., $d = Y - Y_c$, $\bar{d} = 0$. If r is not significant, then the d's do not vary with time, and one can go to step 3. If the d's form a time series, it is necessary to determine why this is so; normally, variance accounts are expected to show more or less random variations and not increase or decrease systematically with time.

3. The d's are next tested to see whether or not they follow the normal distribution. This is most conveniently done by plotting them on normal probability paper (Figure 3). Since it is advisable to make k, the number of cost determinations that serve as the basis for the control charts, rather large, it is most convenient to arrange them in class intervals as shown in Table 6. The last entry in the F column is k, in this case 150. It will be noted that the class intervals are *cumulative*. The upper limit in the first column and the ratio F/k in the third are used as plotting positions on the probability paper (Figure 3). The fit is seen to be most satisfactory.

4. Find the standard deviation of d, s_d. This may be done by using the

TABLE 6 Data for Normality Test

Amount of variance d less than (dollars)	F	$\frac{F}{k}$
−45	1	0.007
−35	3	0.020
−25	9	0.060
−15	22	0.147
−5	52	0.347
5	90	0.600
15	119	0.793
25	137	0.913
35	146	0.973
45	149	0.993
55	150	1.000

Figure 3 NORMALITY TEST ON DEVIATIONS d

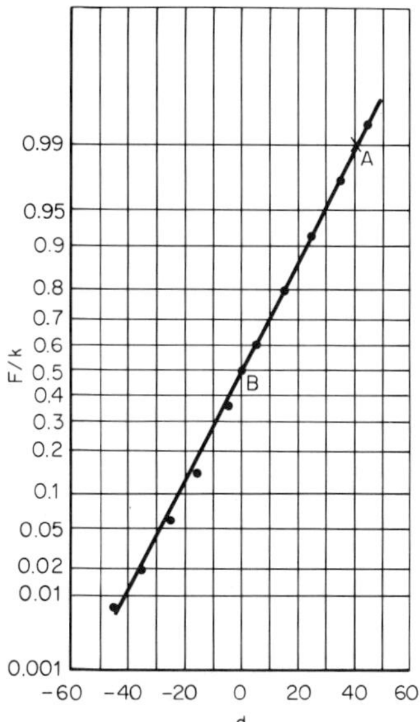

original $k = 150$ readings of d by means of

$$s_d^2 = \frac{\Sigma d^2 - k\bar{d}^2}{k}$$

noting that when d is derived from a least-squares relationship, $\bar{d} = 0$. Alternatively, s_d can be found graphically by means of Figure 3. First the point A is determined which has coordinates $0.99, d_A$ and then B with $0.50, d_B$. In this case d_B (which in a normal distribution equals $\bar{d}$) is zero. One then sets

$$s_d = \frac{d_A - d_B}{2.326} = \frac{41.3}{2.326} = 17.75$$

5. Prepare control charts, using the control limits

$$\text{UCL}_d = 2s_d$$

$$\text{LCL}_d = -\, 2s_d$$

In addition, warning limits are advisable. These are set at

$$\text{UWL}_d = s_d$$

$$\text{LWL}_d = -\, s_d$$

The warning limits serve the function of alerting the auditor to possible future troubles. Whenever two points in succession fall between the upper warning and control limits, or the lower warning and control limits, the event is considered the same as if a value of d had fallen outside the control limits (see Figure 4).

For the data of Table 6, $s_d = 17.75$.

$$\text{UWL}_d = 17.75 \qquad \text{UCL}_d = 35.50$$

$$\text{LWL}_d = -\, 17.75 \qquad \text{LCL}_d = -\, 35.50$$

Figure 4 CONTROL CHART FOR COSTS

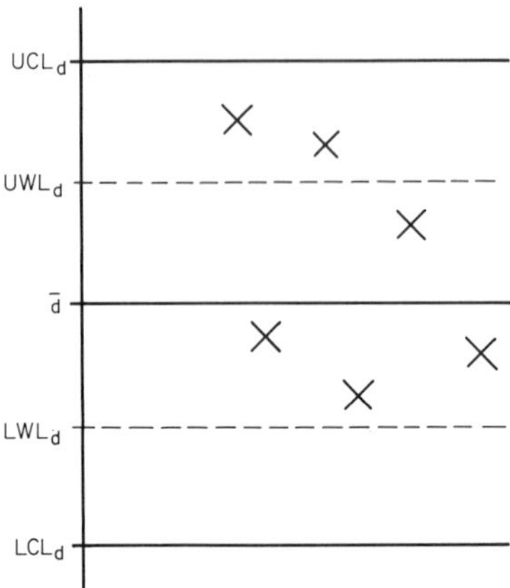

The control limits for costs are thus set at 2 sigma rather than at 3 sigma as in quality control. The reason is that whenever a point falls outside the control limit in a quality-control situation, production lines must be stopped and possibly material in process may be wasted. The costs, in any event, may be considerable. In cost control, on the other hand, the danger comes from *not* taking action against a possible deviation from expected costs, in the belief that costs are in line. The risk of starting an audit or industrial engineering study of the operation and then finding everything in order is considered acceptable. The chance of being *wrong* when stating that a process or cost is out of control is 0.270 percent with the 3-sigma limits in process control and 4.55 percent with the 2-sigma limits in cost control.

6. The applicability of the chart must be periodically tested to assure that it continues to be valid. Let this be done after m additional points have been plotted. One then determines

$$s^2_{d,k} \quad \text{and} \quad s^2_{d,k+m}$$

i.e., the first one is the variance which went into the original control chart while the second is the variance of all the $k + m$ deviations that have been tested. Their ratio is then computed by putting the bigger one into the numerator; i.e., the ratio is made larger than 1. This is then tested against the F ratio in Table 3, entering it with

$$n_1 = k - 1$$

$$n_2 = k + m - 1$$

if $s^2_{d,k}$ is in the numerator, and the other way around if it is in the denominator. As long as the calculated value is less than the tabular value, the chart continues to be suitable.

ACCEPTANCE SAMPLING

Definition. In acceptance sampling random samples of a population are examined in a systematic manner and, on the basis of acceptance and rejection criteria established for the sample, the lot is either accepted or rejected. In recent times, these procedures have been strongly influenced by a convenient document, MIL-STD 105D, originally prepared by the U.S. Department of Defense but now so widely used in all kinds of manufacturing in the United States and abroad that it is also known as the ABC Standard (for America, Britain, Canada). This discussion will focus on its use, more particularly on its single-sampling plans.

The extent of nonconformance of product is expressed either in percent defective, i.e., 100*p* as previously defined, or in defects per hundred units:

$$\text{Defects per hundred units} = \frac{\text{number of defects}}{\text{number of items inspected}} \times 100$$

Sampling Plans. The sampling plans are used as follows:

1. A code letter for sample size is first determined from Table 7. Unless otherwise specified, Inspection Level II is used. Level I may be specified when less discrimination is needed and Level III for greater discrimination. The special levels S-1, S-2, S-3, and S-4 may be used where permitted by the client and where relatively small samples with great sampling risks can or must be tolerated. The sample size is seen to depend on the lot or batch size.

2. Pick a suitable sampling plan from Table 8, entering it with the sample size code letter and the acceptable quality level, measured in percent defective or defects per 100 units inspected. The AQL is defined as the maximum percent defective or defects per 100 units that can be considered satisfactory as a process average. However, the plans provide that material no better than AQL will be rejected with a probability of 20 percent in the smallest samples to 0.2 percent in the largest. Especially when small samples are used, therefore, the maintenance of a standard no better than AQL would lead to unacceptably high rejection rates. In practical cases, the AQL is usually determined by agreement between supplier and customer.

TABLE 7 Sample Size Code Letters

	Special inspection levels				General inspection levels		
Lot or batch size	S-1	S-2	S-3	S-4	I	II	III
2–8	A	A	A	A	A	A	B
9–15	A	A	A	A	A	B	C
16–25	A	A	B	B	B	C	D
26–50	A	B	B	C	C	D	E
51–90	B	B	C	C	C	E	F
91–150	B	B	C	D	D	F	G
151–280	B	C	D	E	E	G	H
281–500	B	C	D	E	F	H	J
501–1,200	C	C	E	F	G	J	K
1,201–3,200	C	D	E	G	H	K	L
3,201–10,000	C	D	F	G	J	L	M
10,001–35,000	C	D	F	H	K	M	N
35,001–150,000	D	E	G	J	L	N	P
150,001–500,000	D	E	G	J	M	P	Q
500,001 and over	D	E	H	K	N	Q	R

SOURCE: U.S. Department of Defense, MIL-STD 105D, Apr. 29, 1963, Table I.

TABLE 8 Single-sampling Plans for Normal Inspection (Master Table)

Sample size code letter	Sample size	Acceptable quality levels 0.010	0.015	0.025	0.040	0.065	0.10	0.15	0.25	0.40	0.65	1.0	1.5
		Ac Re	Ac Re	Ac Re	Ac Re	Ac Re	Ac Re	Ac Re	Ac Re	Ac Re	Ac Re	Ac Re	Ac Re
A	2	↓	↓	↓	↓	↓	↓	↓	↓	↓	↓	↓	↓
B	3	↓	↓	↓	↓	↓	↓	↓	↓	↓	↓	↓	↓
C	5	↓	↓	↓	↓	↓	↓	↓	↓	↓	↓	↓	↓
D	8	↓	↓	↓	↓	↓	↓	↓	↓	↓	↓	↓	0 1
E	13	↓	↓	↓	↓	↓	↓	↓	↓	↓	↓	0 1	↑
F	20	↓	↓	↓	↓	↓	↓	↓	↓	↓	0 1	↑	↓
G	32	↓	↓	↓	↓	↓	↓	↓	↓	0 1	↑	↓	1 2
H	50	↓	↓	↓	↓	↓	↓	↓	0 1	↑	↓	1 2	2 3
J	80	↓	↓	↓	↓	↓	↓	0 1	↑	↓	1 2	2 3	3 4
K	125	↓	↓	↓	↓	↓	0 1	↑	↓	1 2	2 3	3 4	5 6
L	200	↓	↓	↓	↓	0 1	↑	↓	1 2	2 3	3 4	5 6	7 8
M	315	↓	↓	↓	0 1	↑	↓	1 2	2 3	3 4	5 6	7 8	10 11
N	500	↓	↓	0 1	↑	↓	1 2	2 3	3 4	5 6	7 8	10 11	14 15
P	800	↓	0 1	↑	↓	1 2	2 3	3 4	5 6	7 8	10 11	14 15	21 22
Q	1,250	0 1	↑	↓	1 2	2 3	3 4	5 6	7 8	10 11	14 15	21 22	↑
R	2,000	↑	↑	1 2	2 3	3 4	5 6	7 8	10 11	14 15	21 22	↑	↑

SOURCE: U.S. Department of Defense, MIL-STD 105D, Apr. 29, 1963, Table II-A.
↓ = use first sampling plan below arrow. If sample size equals, or exceeds, lot or batch size, do 100 percent inspection.

Changes in Inspection Standards

3. The ABC Standard also provides for tightened (Table 9) and reduced (Table 10) inspection, under the following rules:

a. Normal inspection is used at the outset.

b. Normal inspection continues unless switching procedures below require change.

c. When normal inspection is in effect, tightened inspection shall be instituted when two out of five consecutive lots or batches have been rejected on original inspection.

d. When tightened inspection is in effect, and five consecutive batches are accepted, normal inspection is reinstituted.

e. Normal inspection is changed to reduced when (1) 10 consecutive lots on normal inspection are accepted, (2) the total number of defectives in the 10 batches is less than given in Table 11, (3) production is at a steady rate, or (4) reduced inspection is approved by the client's representative.

All these conditions must obtain before reduced sampling is permitted.

f. Reduced inspection is changed to normal whenever *one* of the following occurs: (1) a lot or batch is rejected, (2) the number of defectives in a batch or lot is less than the rejection number but more than the acceptance number of the reduced plan (the lot is accepted under these conditions but normal inspection is reinstated), (3) production becomes irregular or delayed, (4) other specified and agreed-upon conditions.

(normal inspection)

2.5	4.0	6.5	10	15	25	40	65	100	150	250	400	650	1,000
Ac Re	Ac Re	Ac Re	Ac Re	Ac Re	Ac Re	Ac Re	Ac Re	Ac Re	Ac Re	Ac Re	Ac Re	Ac Re	Ac Re
↓	↓	0 1	↓	↓	1 2	2 3	3 4	5 6	7 8	10 11	14 15	21 22	30 31
↓	0 1	↑	↓	1 2	2 3	3 4	5 6	7 8	10 11	14 15	21 22	30 31	44 45
0 1	↑	↓	1 2	2 3	3 4	5 6	7 8	10 11	14 15	21 22	30 31	44 45	↑
↑	↓	1 2	2 3	3 4	5 6	7 8	10 11	14 15	21 22	30 31	44 45	↑	↑
↓	1 2	2 3	3 4	5 6	7 8	10 11	14 15	21 22	30 31	44 45	↑	↑	↑
1 2	2 3	3 4	5 6	7 8	10 11	14 15	21 22	↑	↑	↑	↑	↑	↑
2 3	3 4	5 6	7 8	10 11	14 15	21 22	↑	↑	↑	↑	↑	↑	↑
3 4	5 6	7 8	10 11	14 15	21 22	↑	↑	↑	↑	↑	↑	↑	↑
5 6	7 8	10 11	14 15	21 22	↑	↑	↑	↑	↑	↑	↑	↑	↑
7 8	10 11	14 15	21 22	↑	↑	↑	↑	↑	↑	↑	↑	↑	↑
10 11	14 15	21 22	↑	↑	↑	↑	↑	↑	↑	↑	↑	↑	↑
14 15	21 22	↑	↑	↑	↑	↑	↑	↑	↑	↑	↑	↑	↑
21 22	↑	↑	↑	↑	↑	↑	↑	↑	↑	↑	↑	↑	↑
↑	↑	↑	↑	↑	↑	↑	↑	↑	↑	↑	↑	↑	↑

↑ = use first sampling plan above arrow.
Ac = acceptance number.
Re = rejection number.

g. If 10 batches have to remain on tightened inspection, the inspection process is discontinued pending remedial action on the production process itself.

Reduced inspection means substantially smaller sample sizes and hence reduced inspection costs and thus is a strong incentive for attempting to meet its criteria. MIL-STD 105D also provides double and multiple sampling plans, each with tightened and reduced procedures, which also serve the purpose of reducing the sample size in the long run. They are somewhat more complex to administer, however. Readers are referred to the full standard for details.

Acceptance sampling is further discussed in Chapter 15, "Statistical Sampling." This method and other methods useful to the auditor are discussed in detail in that chapter.

WAITING LINES

Definition. Waiting lines occur whenever a group of arriving customers must seek service in one or more stations ("serving channels") that perform some task for them. For example, machinists must draw tools from a tool crib; orders for merchandise must wait their turn; salespeople must be adequate in number to serve customers effectively; supermarket checkout counters must be adequately manned.

The study of waiting lines is quite complex, since in practice they may take many forms, depending on the mode of arrival (e.g., single customers or groups), the number of channels (single or multiple), queue discipline (e.g., first come first served, random choice, or several schemes of priorities) and the rate of servicing.

In the present section a simple and quite general model will be presented, based on single arrivals, multiple channels, and service in arrival or random order. Service and arrival intervals follow statistical distributions which hold for a wide variety of circumstances.

The following notation is used:

A = intervals between arrivals
$\lambda = 1/A$ = number of arrivals per-unit time
S = service time (holding time)
$\mu = 1/S$ = number of customers serviced per unit of time
k = number of service stations in system
L = expected length of waiting line *including* those being served
L_q = expected length of queue (i.e., L minus the expected number receiving service)
W = expected waiting time including service
W_q = expected waiting time excluding service
ρ = channel utilization = $S/kA = \lambda/k\mu$

TABLE 9 Single-sampling Plans for Tightened Inspection (Master Table)

Sample size code letter	Sample size	Acceptable quality levels																							
		0.010		0.015		0.025		0.040		0.065		0.10		0.15		0.25		0.40		0.65		1.0		1.5	
		Ac	Re	Ac	Re	Ac	Re	Ac	Re	Ac	Re	Ac	Re	Ac	Re	Ac	Re	Ac	Re	Ac	Re	Ac	Re	Ac	Re
A	2	↓		↓		↓		↓		↓		↓		↓		↓		↓		↓		↓		↓	
B	3	↓		↓		↓		↓		↓		↓		↓		↓		↓		↓		↓		↓	
C	5	↓		↓		↓		↓		↓		↓		↓		↓		↓		↓		↓		↓	
D	8	↓		↓		↓		↓		↓		↓		↓		↓		↓		↓		↓		↓	
E	13	↓		↓		↓		↓		↓		↓		↓		↓		↓		↓		↓		0	1
F	20	↓		↓		↓		↓		↓		↓		↓		↓		↓		↓		0	1	↓	
G	32	↓		↓		↓		↓		↓		↓		↓		↓		↓		0	1	↓		↓	
H	50	↓		↓		↓		↓		↓		↓		↓		↓		0	1	↓		↓		1	2
J	80	↓		↓		↓		↓		↓		↓		↓		0	1	↓		↓		1	2	2	3
K	125	↓		↓		↓		↓		↓		↓		0	1	↓		↓		1	2	2	3	3	4
L	200	↓		↓		↓		↓		↓		0	1	↓		↓		1	2	2	3	3	4	5	6
M	315	↓		↓		↓		↓		0	1	↓		↓		1	2	2	3	3	4	5	6	8	9
N	500	↓		↓		↓		0	1	↓		↓		1	2	2	3	3	4	5	6	8	9	12	13
P	800	↓		↓		0	1	↓		↓		1	2	2	3	3	4	5	6	8	9	12	13	18	19
Q	1,250	↓		0	1	↓		↓		1	2	2	3	3	4	5	6	8	9	12	13	18	19	↑	
R	2,000	0	1	↑		↓		1	2	2	3	3	4	5	6	8	9	12	13	18	19	↑		↑	
S	3,150			↑		1	2															↑		↑	

SOURCE: U.S. Department of Defense, MIL-STD 105D, Apr. 29, 1963.
↓ = use first sampling plan below arrow. If sample size equals or exceeds lot or batch size, do 100 percent inspection.

Analysis. The basis for the analysis is Figure 5, which gives the average delay W_q as a multiple of mean service time S for given channel utilization and number of channels. It will be noted that ρ must be less than 1, because otherwise the waiting line will only go on growing; it is a characteristic of the usual queuing problem that at times the system is idle.

For example:

$\lambda = 16$ arrivals per hour
$\mu = 4$ customers served per hour, i.e., $S = 15$ minutes
$k = 5$ service stations

Entering Figure 5 with $k = 5$ and reading across from $\rho = 16/(5 \times 4) = 0.8, W_q/S = 0.57$ and $W_q = 0.57 \times 15 = 8.55$ minutes.

The other pertinent characteristics of the system are obtained from

$$L_q = \frac{W_q}{A} = \lambda W_q = 8.55 \times \frac{16}{60} = 2.28 \text{ customers}$$

$$W = W_q + S = 8.55 + 15 = 23.55 \text{ minutes}$$

$$L = \frac{W}{A} = 23.55 \times \frac{16}{60} = 6.28 \text{ customers}$$

(tightened inspection)

2.5		4.0		6.5		10		15		25		40		65		100		150		250		400		650		1,000	
Ac	Re	Ac	Re	Ac	Re	Ac	Re	Ac	Re	Ac	Re	Ac	Re	Ac	Re	Ac	Re	Ac	Re	Ac	Re	Ac	Re	Ac	Re	Ac	Re
↓		↓		↓		↓		↓		↓		1	2	2	3	3	4	5	6	8	9	12	13	18	19	27	28
↓		↓		0	1	↓		↓		1	2	2	3	3	4	5	6	8	9	12	13	18	19	27	28	41	42
↓		0	1	↓		↓		1	2	2	3	3	4	5	6	8	9	12	13	18	19	27	28	41	42	↑	
0	1	↓		↓		1	2	2	3	3	4	5	6	8	9	12	13	18	19	27	28	41	42	↑		↑	
↓		↓		1	2	2	3	3	4	5	6	8	9	12	13	18	19	27	28	41	42	↑		↑		↑	
↓		1	2	2	3	3	4	5	6	8	9	12	13	18	19	↑		↑		↑		↑		↑		↑	
1	2	2	3	3	4	5	6	8	9	12	13	18	19	↑		↑		↑		↑		↑		↑		↑	
2	3	3	4	5	6	8	9	12	13	18	19	↑		↑		↑		↑		↑		↑		↑		↑	
3	4	5	6	8	9	12	13	18	19	↑		↑		↑		↑		↑		↑		↑		↑		↑	
5	6	8	9	12	13	18	19	↑		↑		↑		↑		↑		↑		↑		↑		↑		↑	
8	9	12	13	18	19	↑		↑		↑		↑		↑		↑		↑		↑		↑		↑		↑	
12	13	18	19	↑		↑		↑		↑		↑		↑		↑		↑		↑		↑		↑		↑	
18	19	↑		↑		↑		↑		↑		↑		↑		↑		↑		↑		↑		↑		↑	
↑		↑		↑		↑		↑		↑		↑		↑		↑		↑		↑		↑		↑		↑	

↑ = use first sampling plan above arrow.
Ac = acceptance number.
Re = rejection number.

TABLE 10 Single-sampling Plans for Reduced Inspection (Master Table)

Sample size code letter	Sample size	Acceptable quality levels 0.010		0.015		0.025		0.040		0.065		0.10		0.15		0.25		0.40		0.65		1.0		1.5	
		Ac	Re	Ac	Re	Ac	Re	Ac	Re	Ac	Re	Ac	Re	Ac	Re	Ac	Re	Ac	Re	Ac	Re	Ac	Re	Ac	Re
A	2	↓		↓		↓		↓		↓		↓		↓		↓		↓		↓		↓		↓	
B	2	↓		↓		↓		↓		↓		↓		↓		↓		↓		↓		↓		↓	
C	2	↓		↓		↓		↓		↓		↓		↓		↓		↓		↓		↓		↓	
D	3	↓		↓		↓		↓		↓		↓		↓		↓		↓		↓		↓		0	1
E	5	↓		↓		↓		↓		↓		↓		↓		↓		↓		↓		0	1	↑	
F	8	↓		↓		↓		↓		↓		↓		↓		↓		↓		0	1	↑		↓	
G	13	↓		↓		↓		↓		↓		↓		↓		↓		0	1	↑		↓		0	2
H	20	↓		↓		↓		↓		↓		↓		↓		0	1	↑		↓		0	2	1	3
J	32	↓		↓		↓		↓		↓		↓		0	1	↑		↓		0	2	1	3	1	4
K	50	↓		↓		↓		↓		↓		0	1	↑		↓		0	2	1	3	1	4	2	5
L	80	↓		↓		↓		↓		0	1	↑		↓		0	2	1	3	1	4	2	5	3	6
M	125	↓		↓		↓		0	1	↑		↓		0	2	1	3	1	4	2	5	3	6	5	8
N	200	↓		↓		0	1	↑		↓		0	2	1	3	1	4	2	5	3	6	5	8	7	10
P	315	↓		0	1	↑		↓		0	2	1	3	1	4	2	5	3	6	5	8	7	10	10	13
Q	500	0	1	↑		↓		0	2	1	3	1	4	2	5	3	6	5	8	7	10	10	13	↑	
R	800	↑		↑		0	2	1	3	1	4	2	5	3	6	5	8	7	10	10	13	↑		↑	

SOURCE: U.S. Department of Defense, MIL-STD 105D, Apr. 29, 1963, Table II-C.

↓ = use first sampling plan below arrow. If sample size equals or exceeds lot or batch size, do 100 percent inspection.

↑ = use first sampling plan above arrow.

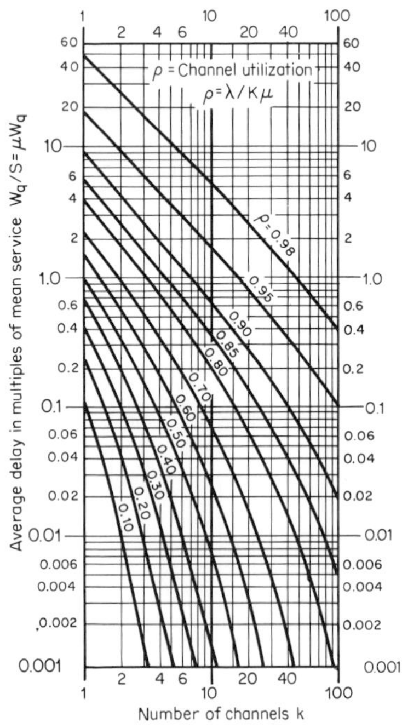

Figure 5 AVERAGE DELAY OF ALL ARRIVALS, POISSON ARRIVALS, EXPONENTIAL SERVICE TIMES, SERVICE IN RANDOM OR ARRIVAL ORDER. (Reprinted by permission from John R. Shelton, "Solution Methods for Waiting Line Problems," ***Journal of Industrial Engineering,*** **vol. 9, no. 4, 1960, pp. 293ff.**

(reduced inspection)

2.5	4.0	6.5	10	15	25	40	65	100	150	250	400	650	1,000
Ac Re	Ac Re	Ac Re	Ac Re	Ac Re	Ac Re	Ac Re	Ac Re	Ac Re	Ac Re	Ac Re	Ac Re	Ac Re	Ac Re
↓	↓	0 1	↓	↓	1 2	2 3	3 4	5 6	7 8	10 11	14 15	21 22	30 31
↓	0 1	↑	↓	0 2	1 3	2 4	3 5	5 6	7 8	10 11	14 15	21 22	30 31
0 1	↑	↓	0 2	1 3	1 4	2 5	3 6	5 8	7 10	10 13	14 17	21 24	↑
↑	↓	0 2	1 3	1 4	2 5	3 6	5 8	7 10	10 13	14 17	21 24	↑	↑
↓	0 2	1 3	1 4	2 5	3 6	5 8	7 10	10 13	14 17	21 24	↑	↑	↑
0 2	1 3	1 4	2 5	3 6	5 8	7 10	10 13	↑	↑	↑	↑	↑	↑
1 3	1 4	2 5	3 6	5 8	7 10	10 13	↑	↑	↑	↑	↑	↑	↑
1 4	2 5	3 6	5 8	7 10	10 13	↑	↑	↑	↑	↑	↑	↑	↑
2 5	3 6	5 8	7 10	10 13	↑	↑	↑	↑	↑	↑	↑	↑	↑
3 6	5 8	7 10	10 13	↑	↑	↑	↑	↑	↑	↑	↑	↑	↑
5 8	7 10	10 13	↑	↑	↑	↑	↑	↑	↑	↑	↑	↑	↑
7 10	10 13	↑	↑	↑	↑	↑	↑	↑	↑	↑	↑	↑	↑
10 13	↑	↑	↑	↑	↑	↑	↑	↑	↑	↑	↑	↑	↑
↑	↑	↑	↑	↑	↑	↑	↑	↑	↑	↑	↑	↑	↑

Ac = acceptance number.
Re = rejection number.
* If the acceptance number has been exceeded, but the rejection number has not been reached, accept the lot, but reinstate normal inspection.

A frequent problem is the one in which a number of channels must be provided at a fixed cost C_1 per channel per unit time so that the total cost of operation per unit time is kC_1. The cost of waiting per customer before service is C_2W_q, where C_2 is cost of idle time. Since it is inevitable that anyone being served must wait and since only incremental costs are relevant in a problem of this kind, W_q only can be reduced and thus W_q rather than W enters into the computation of cost of waiting. For a total of λ customers per unit time, therefore, the cost of waiting is $C_2\lambda W_q$ and the total cost is

$$C = C_1k + C_2\lambda W_q$$

This cost must be minimized, a task which is most readily accomplished by a trial method. In the following example,

$\lambda = 16$ arrivals per hour $C_1 = \$3$ per hour

$S = 15$ minutes $C_2 = \$10$ per hour

For ρ less than 1, the minimum number of channels is 5. The calculations appear in Table 12. Clearly, 7 channels give minimum total costs. The cost components and the total are also shown in Figure 6.

ALLOCATION—THE TRANSPORTATION METHOD

Definition. A frequent set of business problems involves the allocation of finite resources among different claimants. These have led to the development of such techniques as linear, dynamic, and integer programming.

TABLE 11 Limit Numbers for Reduced Inspection

Number of sample units from last 10 lots or batches	Acceptable											
	0.010	0.015	0.025	0.040	0.065	0.10	0.15	0.25	0.40	0.65	1.0	1.5
20–29	*	*	*	*	*	*	*	*	*	*	*	*
30–49	*	*	*	*	*	*	*	*	*	*	*	*
50–79	*	*	*	*	*	*	*	*	*	*	*	*
80–129	*	*	*	*	*	*	*	*	*	*	*	*
130–199	*	*	*	*	*	*	*	*	*	*	*	0
200–319	*	*	*	*	*	*	*	*	*	*	0	0
320–499	*	*	*	*	*	*	*	*	*	0	0	1
500–799	*	*	*	*	*	*	*	*	0	0	2	3
800–1,249	*	*	*	*	*	*	*	0	0	2	4	7
1,250–1,999	*	*	*	*	*	*	0	0	2	4	7	13
2,000–3,149	*	*	*	*	*	0	0	2	4	8	14	22
3,150–1,999	*	*	*	*	0	0	1	4	8	14	24	38
5,000–7,999	*	*	*	0	0	2	3	7	14	25	40	63
8,000–12,499	*	*	0	0	2	4	7	14	24	42	68	105
12,500–19,999	*	0	0	2	4	7	13	24	40	69	110	169
20,000–31,499	0	0	2	4	8	14	22	40	68	115	181	
31,500–49,999	0	1	4	8	14	24	38	67	111	186		
50,000 and over	2	3	7	14	25	40	63	110	181	301		

SOURCE: U.S. Department of Defense, MIL-STD 105D, Apr. 29, 1963, Table VIII.

* Denotes that the number of sample units from the last 10 lots or batches is not sufficient for reduced inspection for this AQL. In this instance more than 10 lots or batches may be used for the

These methods are highly useful but quite complex and do not readily lend themselves to a capsule presentation. However, there is one simple yet widely useful method that can be simply presented and which affords a useful way of solving a virtually universal business problem.

Minimizing Transportation Costs. The transportation method is an allocation model useful for solving problems related to the transportation of product from several plants to several warehouses. The objective is the minimization of transportation costs, but the method can also be applied to many other business problems. The solution of problems of this kind follows an iteration procedure, whereby a start is made with a feasible solution which is then improved by means of a set of simple rules known as an *algorithm,* until the analysis shows that no further improvement is possible. The best way of

TABLE 12 Calculations for Waiting-line Analysis

	$k = 5$	6	7	8	9
$\rho = \lambda/k\mu$	0.8	0.67	0.57	0.5	0.44
μW (from Fig. 5)	0.57	0.16	0.047	0.016	0.0058
W	0.1425	0.0400	0.0118	0.0040	0.0015
λW	2.38	0.64	0.1888	0.064	0.024
$C_2\lambda W$	\$23.80	\$ 6.40	\$ 1.89	\$ 0.64	\$ 0.24
Ck	\$15.00	\$18.00	\$21.00	\$24.00	\$27.00
C	\$38.80	\$24.40	\$22.89	\$24.64	\$27.24

quality level

2.5	4.0	6.5	10	15	25	40	65	100	150	250	400	650	1,000
*	*	*	0	0	2	4	8	14	22	40	68	115	181
*	*	0	0	1	3	7	13	22	36	63	105	178	277
*	0	0	2	3	7	14	25	40	63	110	181	301	
0	0	2	4	7	14	24	42	68	105	181	297		
0	2	4	7	13	25	42	72	115	177	301	490		
2	4	8	14	22	40	68	115	181	277	471			
4	8	14	24	39	68	113	189						
7	14	25	40	63	110	181							
14	24	42	68	105	181								
24	40	69	110	169									
40	68	115	181										
67	111	186											
110	181												
181													

calculation, provided that the lots or batches used are the most recent ones in sequence, that they have all been on normal inspection, and that none has been rejected while on original inspection.

Figure 6 COST FUNCTIONS FOR ANALYSIS OF MULTIPLE-CHANNEL SYSTEM

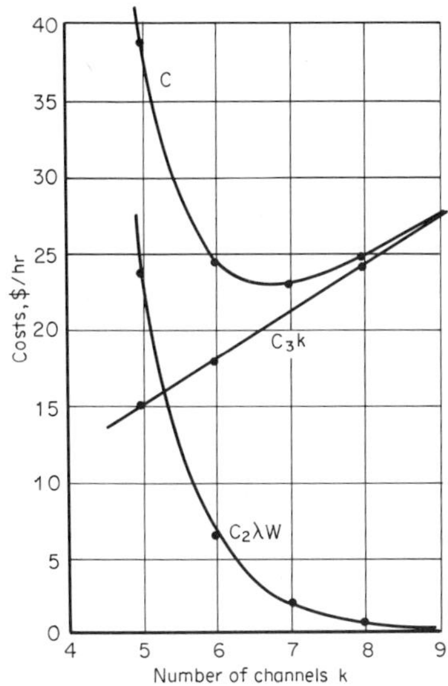

TABLE 13 Given Information

	WAREHOUSE				
PLANT	A	B	C	D	PLANT OUTPUT
	UNIT TRANSPORTATION COSTS				
I	12	13	10	11	10
II	10	12	14	10	9
III	14	11	15	12	7
WAREHOUSE REQUIREMENTS	6	5	7	8	26

explaining the method is by a worked example. Except for the fact that it uses simple numbers, it is perfectly general and can be used as a model for other work.

The body of Table 13 contains the transportation costs; e.g., it costs $10 to ship one unit from plant I to warehouse C. Because the analysis is based on incremental reasoning, we may conveniently deduct 10 (the minimum cost) from all the transportation costs and obtain Table 14.

TABLE 14 Revised Cost Matrix

	WAREHOUSE			
PLANT	A	B	C	D
I	2	3	0	1
II	1	2	4	0
III	4	1	5	2

Assignment Methods. The next task is to make *any* feasible assignment. One method is by the northwest-corner scheme, whereby maximum assignments are made, beginning in the northwest corner and continuing in this manner. In Table 15 the numbers in parentheses indicate the order in which the cells are filled. This procedure has the advantage of always following the same pattern, and some computer programs use it as a result. However, for hand computation, it is an advantage to try to come closer to the true answer. Accordingly, it is better to start with the maximum assignment in a lowest-cost cell and to continue in this manner until the requisite number of assignments has been made. In general such an assignment means filling a total of $n = r + c - 1$ cells, where r and c are the numbers of rows and columns, respectively. As will be seen later, there *can* be fewer assignments but there *cannot* be more. Table 16 uses the estimated lowest-cost method outlined above. It does not necessarily lead to an optimum assignment, but it cuts

TABLE 15 Northwest-corner Assignment

	WAREHOUSE				
PLANT	A	B	C	D	PLANT OUTPUT
I	6(1)	4(2)			10
II		1(3)	7(4)	1(5)	9
III				7(6)	7
WAREHOUSE REQUIREMENTS	6	5	7	8	26

TABLE 16 First Assignment

	WAREHOUSE				
PLANT	A	B	C	D	PLANT OUTPUT
I	5(3)		5(4)		10
II	1(2)			8(1)	9
III		5(6)	2(5)		7
WAREHOUSE REQUIREMENTS	6	5	7	8	26

the work greatly. Again, the assignments show the order in which they were made.

Next, values are given to the above assignments. First, the costs are entered from the cost table in each cell in which there is an assignment. These are underlined in the next table. Then, the marginal entries are completed in accordance with the relationship

$$p(i,j) = r(i) + c(j)$$

where $p(i,j)$ is the cell entry and $r(i)$ and $c(j)$ are row and column marginal entries, respectively. The entry in each cell is the sum of its two marginal entries. To start the process, any one marginal entry, in the present example the one for row I, is arbitrarily set at zero. The other marginal entries are then completed in sequence as outlined, and then the above relationship is used to complete the diagram, thus obtaining values also in those cells in which no assignments were made. All computations are shown following Table 17, with each number followed by its cell or marginal position.

TABLE 17 First-value Table

	WAREHOUSE				
PLANT	A	B	C	D	ROW ENTRY
I	2	−4	0	1	0
II	1	−5	−1	0	−1
III	7	1	5	6	5
	−4			−2	
	2			4	
COLUMN ENTRY	2	−4	0	1	

1. Set 0(I)
2. 0(C,I) − 0(I) = 0(C)
3. 5(C,III) − 0(C) = 5(III)
4. 1(B,III) − 5(III) = −4(B)
5. 2(A,I) − 0(I) = 2(A)
6. 1(A,II) − 2(A) = −1(II)
7. 0(D,II) − (−1)(II) = 1(D)

This completes the marginals. Now the remaining cell entries are computed.

8. 0(I) + (−4)(B) = −4(B,I)
9. 0(I) + 1(D) = 1(I,D)
10. −1(II) + (−4)(B) = −5(II,B)
11. −1(II) + 0(C) = −1(II,C)
12. 5(III) + 2(A) = 7(III,A)
13. 5(III) + 1(D) = 6(III,D)

TABLE 18 First Stepping-stone Reassignment

PLANT	WAREHOUSE A	B	C	D	PLANT OUTPUT
I	5(−)		5(+)		10
II	1(+)			8(−)	9
III		5	2(−)	(+)	7
WAREHOUSE REQUIREMENTS	6	5	7	8	26

The next step is to subtract each corresponding cost entry from the value entry and to see if any of the differences are positive. If any of them are not zero or negative, then an assignment in that cell would reduce total costs. It is not necessary to perform this subtraction in those cells in which there was an original assignment, i.e., in the six underlined entries in Table 17, because these are simply the corresponding costs so that the subtraction yields zero in each cell. It is also unnecessary to subtract any costs from table entries that are themselves zero or negative, again because the result would be zero or negative. This leaves the two cells in the table for which the computations are shown; they yield results of 2 and 4, respectively. Hence an assignment to (D,III) would serve to reduce costs.

Such an additional assignment can only be made by removing another one so that the total number of assignments remains the same. The *stepping-stone* method for doing this calls for first laying out a change path with the desired entry marked (+) and then proceeding to the next assignment, which is marked (−), at each step changing direction (Table 18). The amount reassigned is that which will make the smallest (−) cell equal zero, i.e., 2 in this case, in (C,III). The assignment then looks as in Table 19.

The value table for this assignment is prepared just like the first one, and the result is as in Table 20. Since all subtractions required give negative results, the second assignment is *optimal.*

The discussion concludes with two modifications which may occasionally be necessary. The first is the *degenerate* case in which a stepping-stone assignment removes *two* other assignments instead of one. To illustrate, let the requirements and output be slightly changed to be as in Table 21. The same stepping-stone procedure is also shown. Here both 2(I,A) and 2(III,C) are eliminated. If the assignment is left that way, it will be found that the marginals of the value table cannot be completed. It is then necessary to assign some small amount ϵ to the empty cell 2(I,A) so that the value

TABLE 19 Second Assignment

PLANT	WAREHOUSE A	B	C	D	PLANT OUTPUT
I	3		7		10
II	3			6	9
III		5		2	7
WAREHOUSE REQUIREMENTS	6	5	7	8	26

TABLE 20 Second-value Table

PLANT	WAREHOUSE			D	ROW ENTRY
I	2	0	0	0	0
II	1	−1	−1	0	−1
III	3	1	1	2	1
	−4		−5		
	−1		−4		
COLUMN ENTRY	2	0	0	1	

table can be completed. The assignment then becomes as shown in Table 22. Since all other conditions of the problem have remained the same, this solution is optimal.

A second extension of this problem occurs when plant output and warehouse requirements do not match because it is desired either to build up or to draw from inventory. The problem then is not only which warehouse shall be supplied from which plant but also which warehouse shall use inventory or, alternatively, which warehouse shall receive more than it needs immediately. Table 23 deals with the former situation. There are now only two plants, with output 10 and 9, respectively, supplying four warehouses needing 6, 5, 7, and 8 units as before. The difference is made up by establishing a dummy plant, with zero costs. Any assignment made to the dummy plant is simply not produced. Here one must work with the unit costs as shown; clearly, one cannot deduct 10 from the costs, as in Table 14.

TABLE 21 Modified Assignment to Show Degeneracy

PLANT	WAREHOUSE A	B	C	D	PLANT OUTPUT
I	2(−)		5(+)		7
II	1(+)			8(−)	9
III		5	2(−)	(+)	7
WAREHOUSE REQUIREMENTS	3	5	7	8	23

TABLE 22 Second Assignment, with Degeneracy

PLANT	WAREHOUSE A	B	C	D	PLANT OUTPUT
I	ϵ		7		7
II	3			6	9
III		5		2	7
WAREHOUSE REQUIREMENTS	3	5	7	8	23

TABLE 23 Given Information, with Dummy Plant

	WAREHOUSE				
PLANT	A	B	C	D	PLANT OUTPUT
	UNIT SHIPPING COSTS				
I	12	13	10	11	10
II	11	12	14	10	9
Dummy	0	0	0	0	7
WAREHOUSE REQUIREMENTS	6	5	7	8	26

The first assignment (Table 24) is chosen as identical to the optimal assignment of the first (general) problem; this choice is arbitrary and any other feasible solution would be just as good as a starting point, though it might involve more work to get to the optimal answer. It is therefore necessary to make an assignment to (Dummy,A). This is done by (+)2 in (Dummy,A), (−)2 in (Dummy,D), which is thereby eliminated, (+)2 added to 6(D,II), (−)2 subtracted from 3(A,II). The final assignment is then as in Table 26. In the

TABLE 24 First Assignment, with Dummy Warehouse

	WAREHOUSE				
PLANT	A	B	C	D	PLANT OUTPUT
I	3		7		10
II	3			6	9
Dummy		5		2	7
WAREHOUSE REQUIREMENTS	6	5	7	8	26

last value (Table 27), the first zero has been set in the dummy row. The table indicates that the solution is optimal.

If it is desired to allow for overtime at one plant or more, a new "plant" is established with the premium for overtime for each unit added to the transportation cost. The problem is then solved as shown in the general case (Table 13). For example, there would be a plant I and a plant I(OT), with

TABLE 25 First-value Table, with Dummy Warehouse

	WAREHOUSE				
PLANT	A	B	C	D	ROW ENTRY
I	12	0	10	11 −11 0	0
II	11	10 −12 −2	9 −14 −5	10	−1
Dummy	1 −0 1	0	−1	0	−11
	12	11	10	11	

TABLE 26 Second Assignment, with Dummy Warehouse

PLANT	WAREHOUSE A	B	C	D	PLANT OUTPUT
I	3		7		10
II	1			8	9
Dummy	2	5			7
WAREHOUSE REQUIREMENTS	6	5	7	8	26

TABLE 27 Second-value Table, with Dummy Warehouse

PLANT	WAREHOUSE A	B	C	D	ROW ENTRY
I	12	12 −13 −1	10	11 −11 0	12
II	11	11 −12 −1	9 −14 −5	10	11
Dummy	0	0	−2	−1	0
COLUMN ENTRY	0	0	−2	−1	

the former having its present output and plant I(OT) an output corresponding to the overtime capacity of plant I.

PRODUCTION CONTROL AND INVENTORY THEORY[2]

New Tools. Mathematical models and the computer have combined to give many powerful tools for the control of operations. Though some problems remain either unsolved or too difficult or uneconomic to compute, a wide variety of managerial decisions can now be routinely made with the aid of new methods that go much beyond the elementary formulations of the past. While detailed applications are matters for special study (see the references at the end of the chapter), it is possible to describe the structure of these new approaches and to explain a few which have been found useful. Essentially, production control may be classified for our purposes according to (1) its *sequence*, (2) its *scope*, (3) its *model inputs*, and (4) *the extent to which risk and uncertainty are considered.*

Sequence. The classification by sequence is in many respects the traditional one. The first step is that of planning and routing, essentially an industrial engineering operation in which the production operations are defined and related to the machines on which they are to be carried out. These procedures are laid out in some detail; they involve every operation to be done and also list the tooling required.

[2] Most of this section is reprinted by permission from J. E. Ullmann and S. E. Gluck, *Manufacturing Management: An Overview*, New York, Holt, Rinehart and Winston, 1969, pp. 126–129.

The next step is that of *loading*. The total machine needs are aggregated and adjusted for overloads. At this stage, such techniques as linear programming or the theory of waiting lines may be used so that all machines are used to maximum advantage and economy, or that total elapsed time for a given lot of output is minimized. Linear programming involves the solution of a set of linear equations and inequations, the latter representing capacity or output constraints in the system. The theory of waiting lines (queuing theory) deals with the distribution of waiting periods and the capacity of systems to serve customers when waiting is involved.

The next step is that of *scheduling*, which is the specification of the time sequence in which each job is to be done in each machine. The task of scheduling has always been facilitated by the use of graphic aids such as the time-honored Gantt Chart. More recently, network methods such as PERT and its many descendants have greatly extended the usefulness of such approaches by establishing planning methodologies for large and complex single projects, including in some versions a careful consideration of the extent to which extra cost (for example, in the form of overtime) may be traded off against a time saving. Given a viable schedule, the task of *despatching*, the actual ordering of a specific operation at a specific time, becomes a routine function for the foreman or lower manager.

Scope. The second way of classifying production control systems is by their scope, that is, by what is being controlled. The simplest systems only control a single aspect of operations, such as inventory. More elaborate mathematical models have been formulated for simultaneous considerations of inventory, production and work force requirements which can ultimately provide such additional information as an optimal overtime schedule. Other computer based models, involving in part the simulation on a computer of business operations, have been devised for interpreting the behavior of virtually all major costs of the enterprise. The adaptation of such methods to a specific firm often requires extensive studies at high cost and thus a preliminary evaluation of what the firm stands to gain from such a system.

Model Inputs. This method distinguishes between model inputs, identifying those which the model can handle, without concern over how many of these are treated simultaneously. The inputs are as follows:

1. Costs
   a. Costs and quantities independent
   b. Discounts for purchased parts
   c. Other discontinuities (overtime, excess storage costs, for example)
2. Demand
   a. Single transactions ("newsboy" models)
   b. Single time periods
   c. Special demand structures (slow-moving items, etc.)
   d. Several time periods
3. Labor
   a. Single categories
   b. Full allocation of different categories
   c. Discontinuities (overtime, learning effects)
4. Facilities
   a. Single machines or machine categories
   b. Full systems allocation

This list is by no means exhaustive. One could propose yet another subdivision by classifying the analysis of each of the above inputs into *deter-*

ministic and *probabilistic* models. In the former the inputs are assumed fixed so that the problem is generally one of simple cost minimization. Consider, for example, the economic order quantity. The problem is to find the best quantity (batch size) Q, in which to make the given product, given its total annual demand in units s, the cost of setting up the machine for one batch A, and the carrying cost c per unit per year, which is the cost of storage, interest and insurance on the inventory carried. If the quantity made at one time is larger, the number of batches in a year decreases and so does the setting-up cost; on the other hand, if the batches are larger, the average inventory increases too and so does the cost of carrying it. The result of minimizing these two costs in a given year is the well known formula $Q = \sqrt{As/c}$.

Among the probabilistic models, one of the best known is the "newsboy" model: Knowing the probabilities of selling a given number of papers on a given day, that is, the probability distribution of demand, how many papers should be stocked so as to minimize the combined effects of lost profit on items that could have been sold, if available, and salvage losses on useless inventory? Here we determine a level of inventory which, in the long run, will handle all the demand K percent of the time, where $K = d/(s + d)$, d being the lost profit per unit and s the salvage loss per unit. In effect, we establish a *service level* of K, ignoring the $(1 - K)$ percent of unsatisfied customers; the expected profit to be made from them is too small to warrant stocking the extra inventory. In the example below, a numerical application is presented.

Example. Let $d = 60$ cents/unit, $s = 40$ cents/unit. Then $K = 0.6$. Assume that according to past records demand is such that on the days listed in the "probability" column below, the number of papers sold is that given in the first column. We first make up the third column which is simply the middle one cumulated.

Demand (Dozens)	*Probability (0 Except as Listed)*	*Cumulative Probability*
30	0.05	0.05
31	0.08	0.13
32	0.19	0.32
33	0.28	0.60 ←
34	0.15	0.75
35	0.10	0.85
36	0.10	0.95
37	0.05	1.00
	1.00	

The correct answer is 33 dozen, read off directly from the cumulative data; its cumulative probability is the closest (identical, in fact) to $K = 0.6$.

This is only a simple example; the cases encountered may be much more complex. Still, the principle is quite similar. A policy is chosen which will assure the maximum satisfaction of customers consistent with optimizing the firm's operating characteristics.

A CAUTIONARY CONCLUSION

Quantitative analysis has considerable accomplishments to its credit but it is not a panacea, and hence is in occasional danger of being oversold. Its principal limitations are:

1. *Competence.* Competent quantitative analysis calls for the careful specification of alternatives, a full comprehension of the underlying mathe-

matical relationships, and a wealth of data. These are expensive, and the improvements obtainable by the analysis may not always justify this expense.

2. *Bias.* The analysts must be unbiased. An attempt to "shoehorn" results into a confirmation of management's prior preferences can greatly increase the likelihood of failure.

3. *Nonquantitative Variables.* Many business variables are not quantifiable at all, or only by some arbitrary value system which may itself determine the result. Quantitative analysis thus cannot "computerize" decisions in which these elements are controlling.

4. *Inadequate Objective Functions.* The use of a single objective function (e.g., minimizing costs) is often an insufficient basis for decisions. Laws, regulatory commissions, public relations, market strategies, may all serve to overrule a choice arrived at in this way.

5. *Internal Resistance.* The implementation of an "optimal" decision may also confront internal obstacles, such as labor organizations or individual managers with strong preferences for other ways of doing the job. (Cf. item 2 above.) Objections and predictions of failure of the proposed method often seem to turn into self-fulfilling prophecies under such conditions.

BIBLIOGRAPHY

U.S. Department of Defense, MIL-STD 105D, Apr. 29, 1963.

Buchan, J., and E. Koenigsberg: *Scientific Inventory Management,* Englewood Cliffs, N.J., Prentice-Hall, Inc., 1963.

Croxton, F. E., D. J. Cowden, and S. Klein: *Applied General Statistics,* 3d ed., Englewood Cliffs, N.J., Prentice-Hall, Inc., 1967.

Fabrycky, W. J., and P. E. Torgersen: *Operations Economy,* Englewood Cliffs, N.J., Prentice-Hall, Inc., 1966.

Goetz, B. E.: *Quantitative Methods: A Survey and Guide for Managers,* New York, McGraw-Hill Book Company, 1966.

Grant, E. L.: *Statistical Quality Control,* 3d ed., New York, McGraw-Hill Book Company, 1964.

Horowitz, I.: *An Introduction to Quantitative Business Analysis,* New York, McGraw-Hill Book Company, 1965.

Jelen, F. C. (ed.): *Cost and Optimization Engineering,* New York, McGraw-Hill Book Company, 1970.

Loomba, N. P.: *Linear Programming: An Introductory Analysis,* New York, McGraw-Hill Book Company, 1964.

Sasaki, K.: *Statistics for Modern Business Decision Making,* Belmont, Calif., Wadsworth, 1969.

Schlaifer, R.: *Introduction to Statistics for Business Decisions,* New York, McGraw-Hill Book Company, 1961.

Tuttle, A. M.: *Elementary Business and Economic Statistics,* New York, McGraw-Hill Book Company, 1957.

Ullmann, J. E. and S. E. Gluck: *Manufacturing Management: An Overview,* New York, Holt, Rinehart and Winston, 1969.

Mansfield, E., and H. W. Wein: "A Regression Control Chart for Costs," *Applied Statistics,* vol. 7, no. 1, 1958, p. 48.

Tracy, John A., "Bayesian Statistical Methods in Auditing," *The Accounting Review* (American Accounting Association, Chicago), January, 1969.

King, Barry G.: "Cost-effectiveness Analysis: Implications for Accountants," *The Journal of Accountancy,* March, 1970.

Chapter **48**

Ratio, Change, and Trend Analysis

LEOPOLD A. BERNSTEIN

Professor of Accounting, Baruch College,
The City University of New York, and Research Consultant,
Lybrand, Ross Bros. & Montgomery

THE OVERALL VIEW

Introduction. Over the years we have witnessed continuous advances in the basic conceptual framework as well as in the tools and techniques of auditing.

The development of audit tools and techniques has generally been geared to the growing complexity and quantity of business transactions and the development of data processing. Recently, innovations and refinements of modern tools of data analysis and the increased ability to apply them effectively with the aid of electronic data processing have opened new avenues of improvement in the audit process.

Present-day auditing theory envisages three major steps in the conduct of an audit:

1. Internal control review. Determination of the existence of a reliable system of *internal control.*
2. Procedural tests. The application of *procedural tests* which provide primary evidence of, and insights into, the nature of a company's system of internal control and the degree of adherence thereto.
3. Validation tests. Based on the findings in (1) and (2), the application of *validation tests* whose purpose it is to obtain direct assurance that specific account balances or components are properly stated. The extent of these tests depends on the results of the performance of procedural tests, and they provide assurance in addition to that provided by the procedural tests.

There are, however, basic limitations to a complete reliance on the system of internal control. These are:

Complexity of data. The examination of the system of internal control is an examination of the means by which data are handled and processed. A focus on the processing mechanism must be strictly distinguished from a focus on the complex facts and data which it processes.

Limitations of internal control. Although the system of internal control has a governing influence on the recording and summarization of routine transactions, reliance on the system to produce the "right statements" must be seriously qualified because:

1. Nonroutine transactions, which are the most important and critical variety, do not necessarily fit the mold of the system.
2. Omitted items do not necessarily affect the system, nor are they necessarily affected by it.

Changed conditions. The internal control system does not encompass the effect of external factors, nor does it tell us about the particular pressures under which management operates and the resultant tendencies and propensities. Thus the changing conditions to which an entity is subject are not necessarily reflected by the system of internal control. Yet the degree of testing necessary and especially its emphasis could be greatly influenced by such changing conditions.

Limitations of tests. Assurance with regard to the working of the system during selected test periods does not constitute assurance about the workings of the system throughout the entire period covered by the examination. Thus audit tests which provide assurance regarding the entire time span under audit are needed as supplements.

Effect of external factors. The system of internal control is just that—it is *internal.* Yet the ramifications of today's problems and challenges in auditing extend beyond that. In fact, the new challenges to the attest function, such as those related to problems of conflict of interest, intercompany pricing, etc., begin precisely where the *internal* system of control ends. As demonstrated by recent cases, the repercussions of external factors can be considerable.

The limitations of reliance on the system of internal control suggest that there is need for new approaches oriented toward an overall assessment of the data and their relationship to the environment, economic and otherwise, under which the enterprise operates.

Ratio, change, and trend analysis is such an audit approach designed to strengthen and supplement the tools available to the auditor. It is based on analysis and evaluation and stresses these over mechanical or procedural approaches. This is also in line with the thinking expressed in *Horizons for a Profession, the Common Body of Knowledge for Certified Public Accountants* (New York, AICPA, 1967, p. 20), which states that "the beginning CPA should be capable of making financial projections; he should understand and know how to develop the various ratios, turnovers, and use other analytical tools."

Increasingly, then, the auditor will be called upon to utilize modern tools of data analysis in the conduct of his examination.

Nature of Ratio, Change, and Trend Analysis. The use of ratios, indexes, percentage relationships, and comparisons is an important analytical tool designed to highlight the abnormal, the changing, and the unexpected variations in data. It involves the critical examination, interpretation, and explanation of the relationships that exist between sets of business and financial data at a certain point in time or their comparison over a number of periods.

A ratio measures the relative magnitude of two related factors within or without an enterprise. Ratios have no intrinsic significance. They are useful in highlighting significant changes and relationships. They do not in and of themselves form a basis for reaching informed conclusions.

Ratio, change, and trend analysis is useful for different reasons. Investors are concerned with financial strength and operating performance, creditors with solvency and financial structure, management with performance and deviation from what was planned or what is considered normal. Here we are concerned with the use the auditor can make of this method of analysis. Unlike outsiders, he has at his disposal a wealth of internally developed detailed facts and figures. He can utilize them from two distinct points of view:

1. That of the auditor trying to obtain in the most efficient manner evidential matter about the data
2. That of highlighting managerial problems and trouble areas, thus being of assistance to the company

The two objectives have many similarities, and much can be achieved through common tests.

Obtaining a broad view. The auditor uses the overall checks resulting from ratio, change, and trend analysis to obtain a broad view of the data under audit. In addition to testing the *precision* or *accuracy* of any one item by use of test checks, the auditor uses overall checks to establish the *reasonableness* of the data and their validity and consistency in the light of all attendant circumstances. By means of overall checks, then, the auditor views the audit as an examination of a business entity as a whole and uses to advantage the many necessary and inevitable interrelationships that occur in it. One significant aspect of many of these interrelationships is that any manipulation of them cannot remain disguised and is very likely to be detected.

Detecting the problem. The problem-detection point of view aims at using ratio, change, and trend analysis as a tool for finding areas requiring attention and thus offering an additional opportunity to be of service to the business. The diagnosis of a problem, indeed the recognition that a problem exists, goes a long way toward its solution. Thus the auditor does not, if possible, wait until a problem manifests itself, is detected by management, or is evident through the damage it has already inflicted. Instead he takes a reading of the business data available and assesses the possibility of the existence of problems. Ratio, change, and trend analysis helps greatly in such reading and detection.

Planning the program. The audit program, no matter how well planned, is, of necessity, rooted in the experience of the past. Yet, to be most effective, it has to be highly attuned to the characteristics and problem areas of the data to be audited. Only in retrospect do we know whether things are vital facts or trivial data. The submission of the data at the audit planning stage to ratio, change, and trend analysis will greatly help the auditor to:

1. Devote the greatest percentage of time and effort to areas where the most significant changes have occurred
2. Determine the greatest areas of vulnerability in the accounts and thus devote time in proportion to exposure and vulnerability

Many tests used by the auditor have, strictly speaking, validity only for the specific time span encompassed by the test. Ratio, change, and trend analysis, by subjecting the entire period under audit to a test, ensures that no significant time span or data are completely omitted from scrutiny.

Most recent endeavors to improve audit tools and techniques have been in the direction of finding the most effective ways of coming to grips with the great amount and diversity of data that we must assimilate, understand, and evaluate. Ratio, change, and trend analysis is one of a number of tools to help with the job.

Approaches to the Use of Ratio, Change, and Trend Analysis. The analysis of ratios and relationships involves two distinct steps:

1. The determination and measurement of changes and interrelationships in data
2. The critical examination, explanation, and evaluation of the changes and relationships revealed and their significance in the light of attending circumstances

For any type of business of a given size in a particular industry, there are expectations of what relationships would be considered normal and which would be abnormal. For example, it is normal to expect a higher inventory turnover in a high-volume low-margin discount store than in a regular department store. Similarly, one would expect the ratio of delivery expenses to sales to be lower in the former than in the latter.

Expectations such as the above can be derived from knowledge of the industry and the nature of the operations. However, in order to measure and assess the meaning of deviation from normal, more definitive yardsticks are needed. These can be obtained from two major sources:

1. Comparison with internal data—the company's experience
2. Comparison with external data—industry statistics, etc.

Comparison with internal data. Comparison is a very important analytical process. It focuses on the exceptions and on variations, thus saving us from evaluating the normal and expected. However, lack of change by no means indicates normalcy. The data compared must be adjusted to reflect changing conditions. (Example: An unchanged amount of scrap is suspect if the volume of activity has turned up or down.) Adjustments must also be made for longer-term trends.

Comparison can be made against actual company experience adjusted as above or, recognizing that the past is not in and of itself a right yardstick for the present, against a standard, a budget, or a forecast. Much useful data can be obtained from the accounting department, the cost department, or other functional departments of the company (such as sales, production, purchasing) and can be used as a basis for comparison and evaluation. Whether the data are assembled by the client or whether the auditor has to assemble them in a manner useful for comparative purposes, he has the advantage of the fresh point of view of the competent outsider familiar with the overall operations of the company. The auditor's ability to detect departures from the expected or normal is also enhanced by his exposure to a number of diverse companies in many industries.

Comparison with external data. Useful comparisons can also be made with external data. The advantages of external data may be (1) that they have an objective and independent character; (2) that they have been derived from similar operations, thus performing the function of a standard of comparison; and (3) if current, that they reflect experience during an identical period, having as a consequence similar business and economic conditions in common.

External information must, however, be used with great care and discrimination. The basis and method of compilation, the period covered, and the source and author of the data must be known in order to arrive at the decision of whether the information is comparable. At times sufficient detail may be available to adjust the data to make them comparable. In any event, a choice of a proper standard of comparison must be made from among the ones available. Differences between situations compared must be noted. Such differences may be in accounting practices or specific company policies. It must also be borne in mind that the past is seldom an unqualified guide to the future.

In addition to the various industry and trade associations, the Small Business Administration, Dun & Bradstreet, Inc., and Robert Morris Associates and others publish comparative ratios and other data of selected industries.

There are, of course, a great many ways in which ratio, change, and trend analysis can be applied. They will vary with different industries and companies and with specific circumstances.

There are many ratios in use, and care must be taken to determine that they are appropriate to a given situation, as misleading inferences may be drawn. Later in this chapter a number of common ratios and some of their uses will be presented. The ratios shown do not by any means represent a complete list and are only illustrative. Additional ratios can be developed at different levels of operations, for different subdivisions of costs, and to suit the particular conditions and requirements of various industries. The test is always the significance and usefulness of ratios utilized and the conclusions that can be derived from their comparison over a period of time.

Ratios are but one tool in the analysis of data. Comparison can also be aided by indexes, percentage relationships, correlation analysis, etc. Variable budgets and standard cost systems in use by the company are an important category. Statements of source and application of funds and break-even charts are others. Comparison can be made in many different ways. We can, for example, compare elements on a per unit basis (such as in the case of labor or raw-material costs) or period by period, depending on the circumstances and objectives of the analysis.

Determining significant variations. It is the significant variations that we are after in most cases. For instance, significant variations may arise from:

1. Period changes. Changes over a number of periods, e.g., changes in bad-debt write-off experience, changes in gross profit ratio

2. Variations from standards. Variations from present standards, e.g., variations under a standard cost system, budgetary variances

3. Inconsistency. Inconsistency with other data, e.g., overtime payments during a period of low-capacity operations, higher scrap attending lower production

4. Basic differences. Different assumptions, e.g., a method of production bonus payments that is inconsistent with management's assumption of the basis of payments

5. Relationships. The comparison of one function with another, e.g., the relationship of inventories to sales, sales to fixed assets

The plotting of ratios on graph paper can be a highly useful aid in analyzing trends. The analysis of trend is often just as valuable and instructive as the analysis of change. Generally the visual presentation of data covering a longer span aids in its understanding. Company ratios can be plotted together with comparable industry ratios so that the relative trends are clearly evident. When worthwhile, the comparison can be made with upper, median, and lower quartiles of industry ratios such as those published by Dun & Bradstreet, Inc.

The correlation of two independent variables can best be followed on scatter diagrams. For example, we can put on one axis the scrap generated by production and on the other the raw-material input. If a correlation does exist, the scatter diagram will clearly point up departures from past relationships. Other examples of items that can be so correlated are debt and interest expense, plant and depreciation, sales and bad debt expense, sales and sales expense, miles traveled and fuel consumption.

The use of ratio, change, and trend analysis presupposes the possession of a good background of industry and company operations information. Gaining the necessary background and gathering the information that must precede the intelligent application of ratio, change, and trend analysis will of necessity represent an investment of substantial time and effort on the part of the auditor. Such knowledge is indispensable to the proper performance of such an audit.

Developing comparisons and using ratios, indexes, and relationships are, of course, not ends in themselves. They are tools of major value only when they are evaluated, integrated, and properly interpreted. *Evaluation* means weighing the significance that these manifestations portray. *Integration* involves the arrangement of all these phenomena in such a way that they are put in proper and useful perspective. And in the final analysis, it is the satisfactory explanation and *interpretation* of all these that will lead to insights and informed conclusions. The following summary, "Industry and Company Information and Related Sources," describes various kinds of information useful in this type of audit and the sources where such information may be obtained.

Industry and Company Information and Related Sources

Type of Information	*Source*
BACKGROUND INFORMATION:	
A. The business, the economics governing it, and the industry group to which it belongs	1. Basic books on the industry 2. Trade journals 3. Technical articles 4. House organs 5. Price lists and manuals 6. Trade statistics 7. Internally generated data on trends, profitability, and break-even charts 8. Information on current developments (strikes, cost increases, shortages, new techniques, etc.) as reported in various sources
B. Management—its philosophy and objectives	1. Management manuals stating objectives and philosophies 2. Annual reports 3. Minutes of board meetings 4. Articles written by members of the management team 5. Information on directorships in common with other companies
C. Accounting practices peculiar to the industry and the business	1. Trade manuals and recommendations on uniform systems of account 2. Rules imposed by regulatory bodies 3. Articles in accounting publications 4. Internal accounting procedure manuals 5. The chart of accounts
D. Organization of the major departments, including the accounting department	Written descriptions, procedure manuals, etc.
E. Systems of internal control and internal check, and the existence of an internal audit staff	1. Company manuals on auditing procedures 2. Internal audit programs 3. Internal audit reports
SPECIFIC INFORMATION:	
A. The company organization chart	The client, or it may be prepared by the auditor and confirmed by the client
B. Flow charts depicting company operations	Same as for the organization chart

APPLICATION OF RATIO, CHANGE, AND TREND ANALYSIS

The application of ratio, change, and trend analysis focuses on departures from normal, expected, or established relationships in order to reach significant audit conclusions and reinforce the auditor's confidence in such conclusions.

The following types of applications illustrate this approach in practice.

Comparison by Elements. The main purpose of comparison by elements is to determine whether the components bear a normal relationship to each other and to their total. If such a relationship can be found, the pattern becomes a valuable standard against which the future behavior of such components can be compared. While there may be good reasons for deviations from these accepted patterns, it is the satisfactory explanation of these reasons that the auditor can employ as a useful tool. The least that an explanation of such reasons will do is add to the auditor's understanding of the business unit being audited and add to his knowledge of factors that can cause such changes. In many cases, however, such changes in patterns will alert the auditor to a wide variety of irregularities.

Example 1: Sales Data. Sales figures can be broken down in many meaningful ways. In many instances the auditor will find that such sales analyses are available outside of the accounting department proper. It is a reasonable expectation that the components of sales will bear a certain relationship to their total and that the rate of change in certain sales categories will show a meaningful and orderly trend over the years. Thus, the analysis of sales over a longer period of time will reveal these patterns and relationships, and any deviations from them will alert the auditor to further investigation. Examples of categories by which sales could be broken down are territory or geographical area, physical volume, major consumers or customers, major product categories, groups, and departments.

Example 2: Gross Profit. The elements going into the making up of the gross profit will in many instances exhibit expected relationships to each other and to the total sales figure. A tabulation of those elements and a determination of the relationship among them and their total will enable the auditor to establish standards on the basis of which to evaluate future gross profit ratios and components.

Example 3: Expense Components. The components of expense groups is another area where definite relationships usually exist. Thus, each component of administrative expenses may bear a constant relationship to the total. Here the auditor can again measure against established patterns of the past in looking for deviations that ought to be explained.

Comparison by Units. Unit costs are a valuable measure in establishing standards and for future comparisons. The auditor can expect to find many such figures available in the client's cost department. Variations in unit cost may be expected, but the explanation of the reason for these variations will be of real value to the auditor.

Example 1: Material. Material unit cost changes may be explained in terms of new methods of production, material mix or material quality, changed rates of rejection, changed prices, changed quantity usage or manufacturing efficiency.

Example 2: Labor. Labor unit cost variations may be explained in terms of changes in efficiency, pay rates, overtime work, downtime or setup time, and learning curves.

Example 3: Other Unit Costs. In service industries one could find such unit costs as passenger revenue mile or income per guest. Changes here can be explained in terms of the variables that affect these units. Examples of such variables are fares, rental rates, and occupancy rates.

Comparison by Periods. Most comparisons discussed here will be made over a number of periods, although in some cases the time element is not of major importance. Where the time element is of importance, recognition should be given to the fact that longer time series are more reliable, as they eliminate and smooth out the unrepresentative ups and downs that are bound to occur. In addition, recognition must be given to trend. Trend may reveal a fixed rate of change or a compounding growth factor. In either case, it has to be considered when comparisons with past periods are made. One example of a meaningful and valuable comparison with the past would be the trend of the current ratio over a number of years. The auditor would want to ascertain reasons for any sharp changes in that ratio. They may be explained by such factors as changes in credit extension policies or better investment opportunity. However, the auditor must also be alert to any inconsistency in the classification of current assets and liabilities over the years. Use may also be made of a statement of source and application of funds which would explain changes in working capital. Other examples of ratios to be compared over the years would be the ratio of cost to sales, the ratio of numbers of day's purchases to accounts payable, and the ratio of receivables to sales.

Analysis of Variances. The analysis of variances is an important function. In many cases, the auditor will find that management has already established effective variance accounts for internal control purposes. Whether the auditor establishes variances on his own or whether he adopts and verifies the variances developed by the company is not important. The usefulness of variances is in their interpretation and help in understanding the client's operational problems and in the detection of serious errors.

Examples of variances the auditor will find of great value are spending variances (i.e., variances in the rate of expenditures adjusted for rate of activity where such expenditures are of a variable nature), variances under a standard cost system, or budgeting variances.

Relationships between Accounts. In a business of any size, the auditor will find certain relationships existing between one account and another which, compared over periods of time, will allow him to gain insight into the reasons for change. For instance, the relationship of the inventory on hand and merchandise cost of sales and the comparison of such inventory turnover figures over the years may help in finding reasons for changes in profitability or may alert the auditor to the possibility of obsolete items in the inventory. As with any ratio, great care must be taken to evaluate the reasonableness of its computation and the validity of its comparison. Thus, the adoption of LIFO inventory valuation will greatly distort inventory turnover. Other relationships that are valuable to analyze are inventory levels vs. sales, consumption of materials vs. production, scrap generations vs. production, gasoline consumption vs. mileage traveled, brokerage house mail expense vs. trading activity. Examples of related accounts are sales and accounts receivable, payroll taxes and payroll total, bad debts and accounts receivable, depreciation and fixed assets, sales and sales expenses.

FINANCIAL RATIOS

Following are examples of commonly used ratios and brief descriptions of how they are used. These ratios relate to (1) financial position, (2) capital utilization, (3) profitability, (4) income, (5) cost, and (6) expense.

Ratio	*Comments*
Financial-position ratios:	
Current ratio	Widely used as a criterion of solvency, this ratio of current assets to current liabilities is a guide to the magnitude of financial margin of safety. The acid test of this ratio is accomplished by leaving out inventories.
Current debt to net worth	Indicates what proportion of financing is obtained from suppliers. Overtrading on suppliers' capital may be dangerous and may also involve loss of valuable discounts.
Total debt to net worth	This supplements the preceding ratio and compares the indebtedness with the capital base on which it was incurred.
Inventory to working capital	Shows how the least liquid portion of current assets relates to the total. When inventories exceed net working capital, the current liabilities (debts that must be paid generally within the year) exceed cash, marketable securities, and accounts receivable which represent claims on funds

Ratio	*Comments*
	due within 1 year. Thus liquidation of inventory may become necessary in periods of stress.
Fixed assets to net worth	These are criteria by which to judge the proportion of fixed assets to be financed out of equity capital in various industries. The higher the fixed asset investment, the higher the fixed costs and consequently the company's break-even point, and the greater the company's vulnerability if sales drop off.
Working capital to sales	An indication of the proper relationship of working capital to business transacted can be obtained from judicious use of industry statistics. As with most ratios, there is no rule of thumb. However, overtrading can lead to serious solvency problems.
Capital utilization ratios:	
Cash to sales	Measures the ratio of cash to volume transacted. Increases over a period may indicate, for example, that too much cash is kept on hand to support a level of sales, given no change in basic conditions.
Cost of sales to inventory	Shows the number of times the inventory is turned over. It is, of course, an aggregate ratio with components of inventory varying widely as to their individual turnover rates.
Day's sales in inventory	This is also an inventory turnover measure.
Sales to net worth	This is a measure of the adequacy of the investment in relation to volume of business and also a measure of the efficiency of capital utilization.
Sales to inventory	Measures relationship of inventory to volume of sales. Could indicate too much or too little inventory to support a given level of sales.
Fixed assets to sales	Measures the size of fixed assets investment in relation to sales volume. It may disclose excess capacity or too small a plant for a given volume. Before comparisons with external data are attempted, the age of the assets and the price levels obtaining when they were acquired must be determined.
Average collection period	Average collection period is a good measure of a company's success in enforcing its credit policy. This ratio can be compared with industry ratios. The computation is as follows: Divide annual net credit sales by 365 to obtain average daily credit sales; then divide trade notes and accounts receivable (including those discounted) by the average daily credit sales.

Ratio	*Comments*
Profitability ratios:	
Net profit to net worth (return on invested capital)	This is a prime measurement of management's ability to earn a return on the invested capital. It can be compared with other companies in the industry and evaluated in relation to risks taken. In the case of closely held corporations, adjustments may have to be made for such factors as owner salaries.
Net profit to total assets	A measure of the return earned on all assets used in the business. Since net profit reflects deductions for interest on indebtedness which also finances these assets, this is a meaningful measure. Price level changes may make it necessary to adjust fixed asset values to a common basis for comparative purposes.
Net income per unit of service	This measures profit per unit of capacity available or service rendered—as per ton-mile in freight haulers, per room in hotels, per bed in a hospital, or per alley in a bowling-alley operation. This ratio gives significant clues to the profitability or lack of it with which available resources have been used.
Income ratios:	
Sales per unit of capacity	Measures gross revenue per unit of capacity or service given by the company. It is a measure of capacity, of potential utilization and gives important clues to profitability or the lack of it.
Net profit to net sales	Measures net profit margins. Where available, meaningful comparisons can be made with external data.
Gross profit ratio	Basic measure of the margin left for general and selling expenses, research and development, and net profits. The thinner the margin, the more vulnerable the profit position usually is.

Cost ratios:

GENERAL NOTE: There are many ratios portraying cost relationships, of which these are only illustrative examples. Generally cost as a percentage of sales is a useful measure of the proportion of sales devoted to the coverage of an element of cost. Similarly the percentage that a cost bears to its cost group (such as labor to cost of manufacturing) is also of significance, and the trend in it bears watching. Finally, the comparison of unit cost figures over the years can be very instructive. Thus, variations in unit costs of material may be explained in terms of new methods of production, material mix, material quality, changed rates of rejection, etc.

Direct labor:
- Percent of sales
- Percent of cost of manufacturing
- Per finished unit

Material:
- Percent of sales
- Percent of cost of manufacturing
- Per finished unit

Ratio	Comments
Manufacturing overhead:	
Percent of sales	
Percent of cost of manufacturing	
Per finished unit	
Expense ratios:	
Commissions to sales	Measures one important cost of distribution.
Bad debts to sales or to accounts receivable	Measures the quality of the credit job. Must be related to sales success.
Sales expenses to sales	Measures the cost of the selling effort.
Ratio of various expenses to the related group total	Measures the changes in costs. Many times there is a significant relationship between expenses and the total of the group of which they are a part. (Example: machine oiling as a percentage of total maintenance.)

BIBLIOGRAPHY

Management Services Technical Studies, AICPA Committee on Management Services, to date.

Management Services (magazine), AICPA, to date.

Roy, Robert H., and James H. MacNeill: *Horizons for a Profession*, New York, AICPA, 1967.

Brink, Victor Z., and James A. Cashin: *Internal Auditing*, New York, The Ronald Press Company, 1958.

Cadmus, Bradford: *Operational Auditing Handbook,* New York, The Institute of Internal Auditors, 1964.

Foulke, Roy A.: *Practical Financial Statement Analysis,* New York, McGraw-Hill Book Company, 1968.

Skinner, R. M., and R. J. Anderson: *Analytical Auditing,* Toronto, Sir Isaac Pitman (Canada) Ltd., 1966.

Bernstein, Leopold A.: "Overall Checks in Auditing," *The Journal of Accountancy,* June, 1960.

Colegrove, Reed L.: "A New Look at the Approach to Auditing," *The New York Certified Public Accountant,* October, 1960.

Hogan, Thomas B.: "Constructive Auditing Services," *Haskins and Sells Selected Papers,* Haskins & Sells, 1961.

Bernstein, Leopold A.: "Ratio, Change and Trend Analysis as an Audit Tool," *The Journal of Accountancy,* September, 1964.

LeBlanc, N. P.: "The Preliminary Audit—Key to Audit Planning," *The Canadian Chartered Accountant,* November, 1966.

Bergwerk, Rudolph: "Effective Communication of Financial Data," *The Journal of Accountancy,* February, 1970.

King, Barry S.: "Cost-Effectiveness Analysis: Implications for Accountants," *The Journal of Accountancy,* March, 1970.

Chapter **49**

Analytical Auditing—The Flow-chart Approach

R. J. ANDERSON

Partner, Clarkson, Gordon & Co.

INTRODUCTION

General. The material in this chapter was adapted from the book *Analytical Auditing—An Outline of the Flow Chart Approach to Audits* by R. M. Skinner, F.C.A., and R. J. Anderson, F.C.A.[1] For a more comprehensive treatment of the flow-charting approach, a study of the book is recommended.

Auditing theory has for a long time stressed the need for a proper study and evaluation of internal control and the desirability of selecting the required audit procedures on the basis of this evaluation. This is clearly stated in the second standard of fieldwork of the American Institute of Certified Public Accountants (AICPA) in *Auditing Standards and Procedures*, as follows:

> There is to be a proper study and evaluation of the existing internal control as a basis for reliance thereon and for the determination of the resultant extent of the tests to which auditing procedures are to be restricted.

But what have been the means of achieving the desired goal? If the auditor verifies all the transactions for a given test period, such as 1 month, when internal control is average, what specifically should he add to his program when control is poor, what specifically should he omit when control is excellent? Apart from the general advice to do more when control is poor and less when control is good, auditing textbooks have given little guidance. It is desirable that the audit work be designed so that the linkage between control evaluation and the detailed audit procedures is explicit. Each individual audit step must either confirm the systems information on which the auditor's evaluation of control was based or explore the possibility of material errors permitted by specific weaknesses discovered in the course of his evaluation.

The Analytical Approach. The analytical auditing approach has been used in a large variety of audit engagements over the past ten years, and appropriate modifications or refinements have been made in the light of this experience.

[1] New York, Pitman Publishing Corporation, 1966.

The book referred to above is the result. In recent years there has also been much discussion of flow-charting techniques. If this indicates an increasing use of flow charting as a regular audit tool throughout the accounting profession, the trend is indeed welcomed. The only caution which might be urged is that *significant problems arise if charting techniques designed for systems specialists are applied to the quite different purposes of auditors.* There is a real need for a flow-charting approach *designed specifically for auditors.* The author hopes that both students and practitioners in the auditing field will find this chapter of use in helping to fill that need.

Confirming the System Data. The purpose of this chapter is to present a practical systems-oriented auditing technique based on flow-chart analysis and limited procedural tests. Since the emphasis is on systems analysis, the technique is referred to as "analytical auditing." The analytical audit so described represents a means of carrying out that portion of the auditor's work which is directed at an assessment of the reliability of the accounting system and which provides a basis for planning the usual verification of assets and liabilities. As such it constitutes not the whole program, but a very important part of the program, for the normal audit. Analytical auditing will be shown to be a useful tool for the *external auditor* on all but the smallest engagement. In addition, the techniques outlined will be found, with certain modifications, to prove equally effective in *internal* audit and *governmental* audit applications. The modifications required in the particular case will be indicated.

It is only in the last ten years that the systems and flow-charting approach has been used on a large number of audits of varying types. With the greater complexity of business and the automation of accounting functions, it is essential that the auditor utilize modern techniques in his work. It would certainly be surprising if the audit techniques of 30 years ago were still the most efficient ones today. Auditors must continually update their methods to suit the changed environment or else risk serious obsolescence. Greater orientation toward systems is one of the steps demanded by this new environment. Any orientation toward systems leads logically to flow charting. One of the objectives here, therefore, will be to demonstrate that the flow-charting technique is perfectly consistent with generally accepted auditing standards and, in fact, derives naturally from the acknowledged need for a proper study and evaluation of internal control.

Finally, those who have investigated this field will be aware that many pitfalls await the first exploratory attempts. It is one thing merely to design a set of charting symbols; quite another to develop a complete audit approach fully exploiting the flow-chart technique yet avoiding the many preliminary problems. It is with the thought of saving the interested practitioner these difficulties and delays that this chapter has been written. It is also the hope that, by setting forth the various procedures and their justification, it may hasten the day of full acceptance of analytical auditing and flow charting as routine audit techniques.

OBJECTIVES OF THE ANALYTICAL AUDIT

It is not the purpose of this chapter to discuss at length the responsibilities and functions of the independent auditor, the general definition of auditing standards, or the nature and uses of audit reports. This has been treated thoroughly in many publications. It will be assumed here that the reader is familiar with such material. Nevertheless, in order to explain analytical auditing and flow-charting techniques, audit objectives must be given at least a brief consideration. Any new audit procedure, after all, must first be examined from the viewpoint of what it is intended to accomplish and why.

This may sound too axiomatic to warrant serious attention, but consider the following question. Is a given audit procedure designed to:

1. Measure the extent of a known error?
2. Detect the existence of a suspected error?
3. Provide confirmation that no errors have occurred?
4. Discover what the accounting procedures are?
5. Establish that prescribed controls are operating?
6. Justify a recommendation for a systems change?

Each of these six distinguishable purposes could arise at some point in any audit, but each one calls for either a different audit procedure or a different way of applying a given audit procedure. Measuring known errors with tests designed for discovering unknown ones or investigating weaknesses with tests designed for assessing controls is about as efficient as using a shovel to cut wood. The audit tools should not be selected before the job to be done has been defined. The *purpose* of the audit step must be the first consideration. To dispense with this is to invite unnecessary audit steps and wasted hours. Why draw flow charts? The answer must be sought within the auditor's objectives.

General Audit Objectives. The main objective of the ordinary audit engagement of an independent auditor is:

To determine whether or not he may report that the financial statements present fairly the financial position and results of operations of his client, following generally accepted accounting principles applied on a consistent basis.

In the majority of cases this is the most important service rendered by him. Whenever there are people who have an interest in an enterprise but who are not familiar with its day-to-day operations, it is essential that some assurance be provided that the financial statements are not misleading. The auditor's work is therefore important to the shareholders of public companies who do not participate in management; to banks, bondholders, and other creditors; to prospective investors; and to income tax and other governmental authorities. The importance of this "attest function" of the auditor is, of course, one of the basic tenets of the profession.

It is to this "attest function" that the analytical audit is primarily directed. This does not mean, however, that its use is limited to engagements conducted by external auditors. The objectives of both internal auditors and governmental auditors usually contain many "attest" elements.

Thus, the audit objectives of the internal auditor may be:

Reviewing and appraising the soundness, adequacy, and application of accounting, financial, and operating controls

Ascertaining the extent of compliance with established policies, plans, and procedures

Ascertaining the extent to which company assets are accounted for and safeguarded from losses of all kinds

Similarly, the primary objectives of audits by the United States General Accounting Office are:

To make for Congress independent examinations into the manner in which Government agencies discharge their financial responsibilities. Financial responsibilities of Government agencies include the administration of funds and the utilization of property and personnel only for authorized programs, activities, or purposes, and the conduct of programs or activities in an effective, efficient, and economical manner.

Clearly, while the latter two sets of objectives may go beyond those of the external auditor, they contain many of the same elements of analyzing internal controls and attesting to the reliability of financial reporting. To the extent that they contain these elements the analytical audit approach will be equally valid. Thus, although some of the following description is phrased in the context of an external audit, the flow-charting technique described will be just as practical and useful whether applied by the public accountant, the internal auditor, or the governmental auditor.

Audit Components. The analytical audit consists of two basic components, (1) checking that business transactions are correctly recorded and (2) that the balances shown in the records and presented in the financial statements are fairly shown and that the assets and liabilities actually exist. The first phase is sometimes termed "interim work," "audit of transactions," or "procedural audit," the second phase the "year-end procedures" or "balance sheet program."

The timing of the two procedures can vary depending on the circumstances. In most cases the principal part of the interim work will be completed before the year end. Analytical auditing is a method of performing the procedural review on all but the smallest audit. It is in this phase of the work that flow-charting techniques can best be applied. The second phase is referred to only in passing. The latter is outlined at length elsewhere in this Handbook.

Need for the Analytical Audit. Why is the second phase or balance sheet audit not sufficient in itself? In the usual audit there are at least four reasons why the balance sheet audit by itself is not and cannot be sufficient without the analytical audit.

They are:

1. No matter how carefully the auditor counts the net assets on hand at any one time there can be no certainty as to what *should* have been there unless reliance is placed on the accuracy of the accounting records. For instance, if the accounting records are known to be generally reliable, then the close concurrence of a book figure and a physical inventory figure would help to confirm the accuracy of the latter, whereas a wide discrepancy might call for additional audit investigation. Neither conclusion would be as tenable, of course, without the previous knowledge of the accounting reliability. Again, most tests for possible undisclosed liabilities must be drawn in part from evidence in the accounting records and depend, therefore, on the latter's reliability.

2. As long as the net assets are to be valued on a going-concern basis, it is impossible to determine the appropriate valuation without relying very substantially on the accounting records. The most common example of this is the valuation of the historical costs accumulated in year-end inventories. There is little point in the auditor's checking the quantities, extensions, and additions of inventory listings if he cannot also ensure that the unit costs employed were obtained from a reliable cost system which has given accurate measurements and allocations of inventoriable costs throughout the year.

3. When, as is often desirable to spread the workload, some assets are

verified at a date other than the statement date, the reliance on the accounting accuracy becomes greater still. If the auditor verifies accounts receivable at the end of October in order to express an opinion on statements at the end of December, his opinion on the December accounts receivable figure must rest not only on his October work together with a special scrutiny of the intervening period, but also on his evaluation of the reliability of the sales-receivables-receipts system in general.

4. Finally, the accuracy of the individual components of the profit and loss statement cannot be determined merely from the verification of net assets at the beginning and end of the year. Even if the auditor's balance sheet procedures include (as they must) a number of scrutiny, review, analysis, and verification steps directed at the profit and loss components, much of his opinion on the income accounts must still be derived from an assessment of the reliability of the accounting records.

Thus, however thorough the balance sheet audit, it must, for most engagements, be based upon this first step of establishing the reliability of the accounting system. Moreover, the conclusions reached during the interim or analytical audit period directly affect the program selected for the audit. If the accounting reliability is found to be high, minimum balance sheet steps will suffice to support an opinion, and these can probably be scheduled at convenient dates over the course of the year. If, on the other hand, the accounting reliability is less satisfactory, then more extended balance sheet audit steps may be necessary to support an opinion, and many of these may have to be performed at the year end rather than at other dates. If, in the extreme, the accounting system is found to be quite unreliable, then the entire burden of proof is thrown upon special, extended or detailed audit steps. Should it happen that these still cannot adequately compensate for the weaknesses in control, the auditor would have to deny any opinion on the financial statements.

Analytical Audit Objectives. The primary objective of the analytical audit, then, is support for the expression of opinion on the financial statements. This is the reason for there being an audit in the first place. The complete fulfillment of this objective is mandatory. At the same time, it is unlikely that in the performance of the necessary work to satisfy this first requirement the auditor will not encounter areas where improvements could be made in his client's systems or controls. Service to his client in this area should be a very important by-product of the analytical audit. This subsidiary purpose is, however, quite separate from the auditor's basic aim of supporting an opinion. There is no fixed requirement as to how much of this collateral service is appropriate. Certainly, there will be some situations sufficiently serious that the auditor has an absolute duty to bring them to his client's attention. Beyond this point, however, the amount of additional assistance and advice will vary from engagement to engagement depending upon the needs and desires of the individual client. In general, these collateral services are increasing in importance, and in many cases, it is the presence of these services which makes the audit an economical package from management's point of view.

The two objectives of an analytical audit conducted by an independent auditor can thus be summarized as follows:

Primary objective (mandatory). To determine, through an analysis of the accounting system and the internal controls, the accuracy and reliability of his client's accounting records and thus to provide a basis for planning the audit steps necessary to support an opinion on the financial statements.

Secondary objective (discretionary). To give him sufficient knowledge of his client's affairs that he can offer timely suggestions for strengthening the system of internal control, for increasing the efficiency of the accounting system, and for improving the client's financial and tax planning.

Obviously, it is important that the two objectives not be confused. No amount of concentration on useful recommendations can make up for an inadequacy in the audit. Conversely, unnecessary extension of the audit will not compensate for lost opportunities to provide useful service. This chapter will examine the fulfillment of these two objectives through the use of the flow-charting approach.

The foregoing objectives have been defined in terms of the independent, external auditor. Analytical auditing can also be (and has been) used to advantage by *internal auditors*. When it is, however, certain modifications of some of the techniques are appropriate. These arise out of the slightly different audit objectives of the respective auditors. With respect to the primary objective of the analytical audit stated above, any auditor will be concerned with assessing the reliability of the organization's financial reporting in general. But his concern may not be directed as exclusively to the year-end financial statements as is that of the external auditor. With respect to the secondary objective stated above, the internal auditor and governmental auditor will have at least as much responsibility as the external auditor. His different terms of reference, and his closer continuing association with his own organization, will require him to pursue possible systems suggestions to a degree of detail beyond the scope of the external audit. Finally, the internal auditor is likely to have a third objective. His terms of reference usually require him to fulfill some *policing* function to ensure that prescribed management policies and laid-down procedures are being duly followed (even in areas where these do not have a bearing on financial reporting or internal control). In this objective, again, he is likely to reach beyond the scope of the external audit. Frequently, observed deviations from prescribed procedures will prompt him to investigate situations which, while justifying some corrective action, would be immaterial with respect to the overall statement presentation on which the external auditor reports.

The differences just mentioned are more of degree than of kind. The fields of the internal, governmental, and external auditors necessarily overlap, but the relative emphasis they place on the component parts of their program usually differs. In addition, the terms of reference themselves vary from one organization to another.

THEORY OF ANALYTICAL AUDITING

The primary objective of the analytical audit is to assess the reliability of the accounting system. In theory, this evaluation could be approached in two different ways. One could judge an accounting system by an examination of the documents and records it has produced or by an analysis of the structure and design of the system itself. These two approaches might be described as the *end-result theory* and the *method theory*.

End-result Theory. The *end-result theory* would look not at the means but at the ends. For instance, one could, in the extreme, check documentary evidence for every recorded transaction for the year. Even this, however, might not be infallible since some procedural errors might not be evident from the individual documents. In any case, on all but the extremely small engagement it would be prohibitively expensive. It would mean duplicating every step performed by the entire accounting staff over 12 months—and the cost would come close to duplicating the total accounting expense for the year too. The end-result theory can be modified, however, by arguing that it is unnecessary to check *every* transaction for the year if the auditor is able to rely on the system of internal control. Under this modified end-result theory a large sample of accounting results could be examined and if they were all correct, this could be taken as an indication that the rest of the results produced by the same system were accurate. For example, if one were to examine all the 1,000 canceled checks for one month and find them to be legitimate and properly supported, it might be inferred from this that the other 11,000 checks for the other 11 months were proper as well.

Method Theory. The *method theory,* on the other hand, would look not at the ends but at the means. Here one could attempt to explore inside the system and discover exactly how it produces its results. If the mechanics of the system were analyzed intensively and the detailed survey showed it to be designed with appropriate controls, checks, and balances to forestall errors, then this too would be a good indication that the results produced by this system (such as a year's checks) were accurate. This latter method, in other words, would go *through* the system while the former went *around* it.

Each approach, in practice, contains some elements of the other. The modified end-result approach, while concentrating on extensive tests, must include some preliminary review of internal control to justify the examination of less than 100 percent of the books and documents for the year. Similarly, the method approach, while concentrating on intensive analysis, must include some examination of documents to determine what the system to be evaluated is. The difference is one of emphasis. All current audits must consist of an *analysis* of internal control and a *testing* of documentary and other evidence. This much is implied in the standard wording of every audit report. The question is only one of the relative proportions between analysis and testing.

What is called the end-result approach has been the one most commonly described in auditing texts and, apparently, most commonly employed throughout the auditing profession in the past. As far as the primary objective of supporting an opinion is concerned, it is true that either approach, the end-result theory or the method theory, has a certain validity. The former makes an inference about the whole of the accounting results from a knowledge of a substantial part of them. The latter makes an inference about the whole of the accounting results from a knowledge of the detailed system which produced them. Neither inference is infallible, but both can be reasonable ones, if carefully made. The method approach, however, is likely to be more assured and generally much more efficient. What the auditor is trying to do in his interim audit examination is to diagnose the strengths or weaknesses of the accounting system. Thorough analysis together with a concise, well-chosen program of testing should provide a better diagnosis of the accounting reliability than restricted analysis together with indiscriminate amounts of testing. As far as the secondary objective of making useful suggestions is concerned, the method approach has a very great advantage. Armed with a more intimate knowledge of the flow of paperwork and the relationship between different procedures, the auditor is in a much better position to make realistic recommendations not only on internal control but also on systems efficiency. For these reasons the emphasis on systems analysis is bound to increase as modern auditing techniques develop. For these reasons, too, the analytical auditing technique to be described in this chapter is based on the *method* or *analysis* approach to auditing.

Standardizing Flow Charting. A systems-oriented audit plan must include some method of recording systems information accurately and comprehensively. A narrative form, which might be the first thought, proves unduly cumbersome in practice. Narrative may be suitable for some purposes—company procedure manuals or clerical job descriptions—but for the auditor's needs it is too unwieldy. As soon as any degree of detail is attempted, narrative swells to too large a size. The large quantities are difficult to absorb, related points are hard to integrate mentally, and annual changes are awkward to record. In addition, some unique problems are usually posed by the handwriting.

To these problems a standardized method of flow charting is the logical solution. First, this is the most concise way of recording the auditor's review of the system. The flow chart minimizes the amount of narrative explanation and thereby achieves a condensation of presentation not possible in any other form. It gives both a bird's-eye view of the system and an efficient documentation of the auditor's testing of it. Secondly, the flow chart is the most efficient tool for doing the actual *analyzing.* The charts clearly show what is taking place and provide an easy method of spotting weaknesses in the system or areas where improvements could be introduced. Of the different styles of charting that have been in existence for various purposes for some time, the one described here for use in analytical auditing is a horizontal charting approach. This approach has the advantage of making it easy to visualize the relationship between different parts of the integrated system. Those internal control strengths or weaknesses which arise from the way in which duties are divided can thus be readily seen on the flow charts themselves, whereas they would be hard to extract from many pages of narrative. A standardized charting technique is essential if the flow charts are to be clear and orderly and if the audit staff working together on the same engagement are to understand each other's charts. Also with a standardized approach the internal auditor and governmental auditor can more easily understand the charts and possibly exchange flow charts. In any case, their work can be more effectively conducted with standardized charts.

Investigating Weaknesses. Having analyzed the system on the flow charts and evaluated the control, the auditor can then direct additional audit investigation *specifically at those areas where the internal control is found to be weak.* This ensures a direct relationship between the evaluation of internal control and the allocation of more extended audit procedures. An audit opinion is not and could not be equivalent to 100 percent certainty with respect to every item in the financial statements. Absolute certainty on all points is not economically feasible in the audit opinion any more than absolute precision is feasible in the accounting measurement of all items. In effect, the auditor has a fund of justified audit effort, and it is his job to use that fund most efficiently. By directing audit time toward an investigation of weaknesses in the system—and in proportion to the seriousness of those different weaknesses—this end is achieved. It makes sense, obviously, to spend more time looking for errors in areas where there is a significant danger of their occurrence than in casting about for those whose occurrence appears unlikely and remote.

Limited Tests Suffice. Before the system can be evaluated and the weaknesses investigated, however, the auditor must have some assurance that the system to be evaluated is really in force. To do this he can trace a very limited number (four or five) *of each type of transaction* throughout the system from "cradle" to "grave"—or, alternatively, from grave to cradle. This should be done at the time he completes his flow charts so that he will know he has not wasted time charting a "blueprint" system which is not in operation. This "cradle-to-grave" audit, or "walk-through" audit, or "auditing in depth," which includes both the tracing of books and documents and the discussion with all employees involved, is designed to assure the auditor that every path of the system he has drawn on his flow charts is really being followed in practice.

Why is this limited procedural test of four or five transactions enough? The reasons are as follows:

1. The auditor is not just testing four or five transactions in total but four or five examples *of each type* that is processed in a different manner. This assures him that *every path* on his flow charts (both for normal transactions and for special, less frequent ones) is an accurate description of the system.
2. The auditor is not attempting, at this point, to prove that errors never occur but merely to establish what the system in operation is. Had he wanted to prove by his examination of sales invoices, for instance, that pricing errors were less than 1 percent, he would have had to examine several hundred. Fifty or one hundred would not be enough to establish a reasonable confidence concerning a 1 percent frequency. Therefore, there would be little point in his testing thirty, fifty, or even one hundred invoices; such samples would be generally too little to establish the frequency of occasional errors, yet too much merely to establish the nature of the system in force. Since, *at this point*, he is only attempting to establish the latter, a minimum test is all that is required. A test of one transaction might, of course, happen to be an unusual case. Even the results of a pair of transactions might, by chance, be misconstrued. But if four or five, selected randomly, are examined and all correspond to the system as described to him, then this constitutes reasonable *prima facie* evidence of the system in operation.
3. Because the auditor is examining every path of the system in detail, the cradle-to-grave audit tests over related parts of the system have a reinforcing effect. This reinforcing effect of related parts compensates for the fact that the extent of the test over any individual part is quite limited. If the auditor were examining only a few of the paths in the system, this conclusion would not be justified and he might have to do more extensive tests. The comprehensiveness of the systems audit, in other words, can provide assurance, even with a limited test, that the system is operating as described.
4. The auditor's investigation for occasional errors is conducted *after* the system has been evaluated. This allows him to concentrate his audit time on the riskier areas and minimize his time on the relatively strong areas. To perform extended procedural tests for occasional errors *before* the system is evaluated is to audit blindly. A *directed investigation* based on systems evaluation should be more effective and more efficient.
5. Finally, in addition to his audit investigation of apparent weaknesses, the auditor also performs a few extensive supplementary tests on a cyclical basis (which will be discussed later) in areas where he has concluded that control is satisfactory. These supplementary tests provide additional confirmation that the system initially tested by his cradle-to-grave audit is reliable.

The internal auditor may wish to go beyond the restricted extent of systems audit tests suggested inasmuch as he is concerned with detecting errors of a smaller size. Often, however, it will be useful for him to follow the restricted basis initially to assess the accuracy of the financial reporting in all material respects. Then, as a later stage, he can plan extended systems tests to guard against smaller errors to whatever degree is considered desirable. This is just another way of saying that the internal auditor may want to extend the "supplementary tests" beyond the scope suggested for external audit purposes.

Two Audit Stages. Analytical audits can logically be divided into two stages. The first stage is aimed at systems evaluation; the second, at weakness investigation. The two stages can (although this is not essential) be performed at different times during the year—thus permitting a greater flexibility of scheduling. The first stage (or "systems audit") can be performed early in the year. The auditor's flow charts are completed, or updated, the limited systems audit performed, and the system evaluated. The second stage (or "follow-up audit") can then be performed later when most of the year's results are available for review. The weakness investigation is carried out and conclusions drawn, preliminary ideas for suggested improvements are rechecked, and a memorandum of recommendations is issued to the client. This structure of the analytical audit is illustrated in Figure 1 in simple form.

The division of the audit conveniently allows for file review between the two stages, when more senior judgment can be brought to bear on the proposed weakness investigation before it is carried out. The timing of the two stages also avoids the problem of having a detailed audit directed at the same one or two months of the records year after year. The relationship of the different components in an analytical audit is illustrated in more detail in Figure 2. The next few paragraphs review the philosophy underlying

Figure 1 PROFILE OF THE ANALYTICAL AUDIT

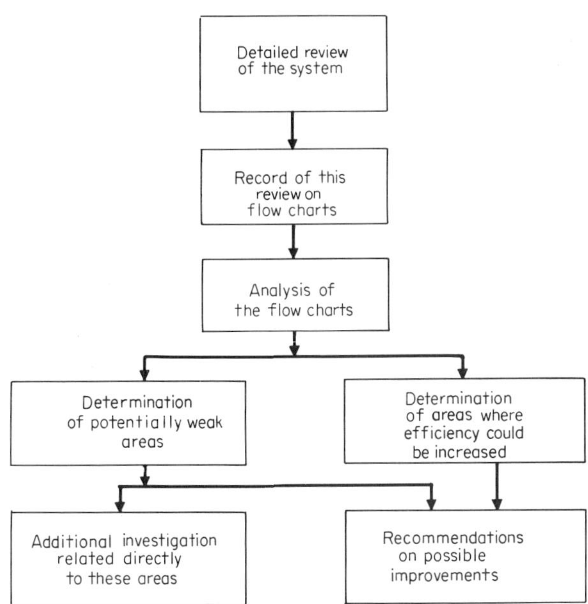

Figure 2 DETAILED PROFILE OF THE ANALYTICAL AUDIT

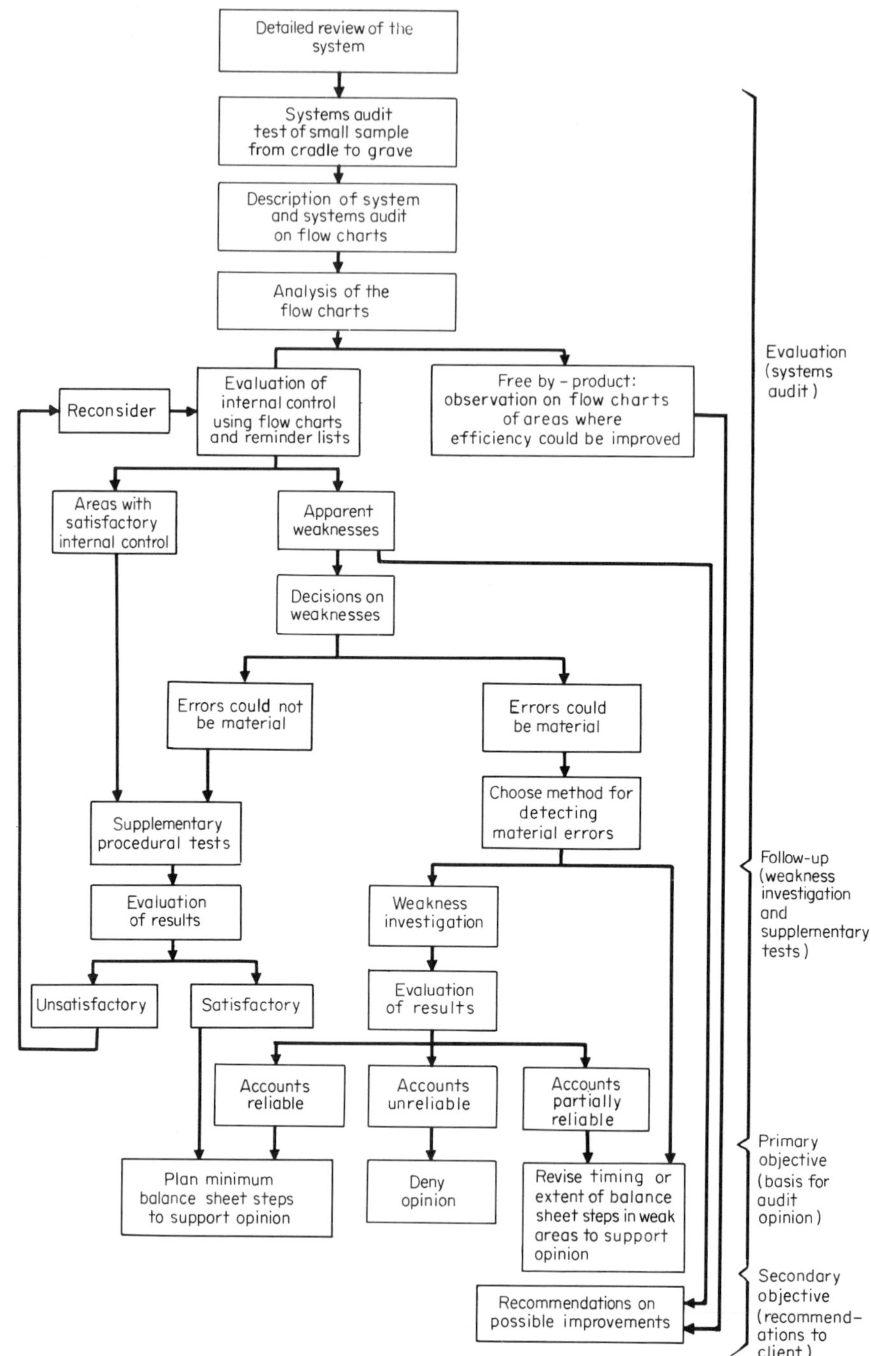

these various components. More detailed explanations of all the procedures are given later in the chapter.

Systems Audit Visit. As Figure 2 indicates, the systems audit visit begins with a review of the system, testing of it with a small sample from cradle to grave, description of the system and the test on flow charts, and an analysis of the flow charts to determine apparent weaknesses or inefficiencies.

During the evaluation of control some areas are likely to be observed where efficiency could be improved. These observations are a free by-product of the charting already required for assessing the system of internal control (primary objective). They can lead to useful suggestions on efficiency, which should be an integral part of the regular audit service. They cannot, of course, be expected to yield the results of a major systems survey—although they provide an excellent base for such a survey should it be requested by the client as an extra assignment outside the basic audit.

The evaluation of internal control, however, is where the main emphasis must be placed. This is because the auditor's primary objective is to support his opinion on the financial statements, and this depends on the internal control. While the evaluation can largely be done by an analysis of the flow charts themselves, a set of reminder questions is useful to ensure that no point is overlooked. These same questions can serve as a guide in preparing the flow charts, since they raise the points which the charts must resolve. An example of such reminder questions is illustrated in the sectional lead sheet in Figure 6.

The control evaluation will distinguish areas with satisfactory internal control from those with apparent weaknesses. These latter areas can be further subdivided. Most apparent weaknesses will give rise to suggestions for improvement to the client (secondary objective). From an audit point of view (primary objective) the auditor must, however, distinguish between weaknesses which could not permit material errors and those which could. For the latter, some additional audit work is necessary. Additional audit work required for a significant weakness may consist of either (or both) a revision in the timing and extent of certain balance sheet audit steps or a special weakness investigation to be performed during the analytical audit. Such a weakness investigation would be designed, of course, with a view to determining not whether any errors are occurring at all but whether any *material* amount of error has occurred because of the weakness.

The planning of the weakness investigation and the drafting of the memorandum of recommendations to the client completes the systems audit visit. These plans and drafts can then be approved (or amended) when the analytical audit file is reviewed between stages. The systems audit procedures are described in detail later.

Follow-up Audit Visit. The approved weakness investigation is carried out during the second stage of the analytical audit. The results of this investigation, in turn, affect the next step. If they reveal that the accounts are reliable, minimum balance sheet audit steps can be planned. This point will usually be less relevant for internal auditors since some internal audit programs may include no, or only a few, balance sheet audit steps in any case.

If the audit steps reveal that the accounts are unreliable (to the extent that no revised balance sheet audit steps can help), then an opinion will have to be denied. If, finally, they reveal that the accounts are partially reliable, then some revised balance sheet audit steps must be planned to compensate for the remaining weakness.

While the main emphasis is on investigation of the apparent weaknesses, the follow-up audit should also include a *few* supplementary tests in those areas where control is believed satisfactory. These can be selected on a cyclical basis so that over a period of 3 or 4 years all key areas of the system are covered. The purpose of these "supplementary" tests is to confirm, by reference to objective data, the auditor's evaluation of internal control. It is unnecessary for him to confirm each point each year or to spend extensive time on this supplementary program, for his evaluation (using the flow charts and reminder lists) should be reasonably reliable. Nevertheless, all evaluations are subjective, and human judgment is fallible. It would be imprudent for the auditor to continue year after year theorizing that some particular element in the system of internal control was adequate to prevent errors if he never tested this conclusion by checking to see whether, in fact, any errors did occur. The value of these supplementary tests is that they provide an automatic "feedback" of objective results to confirm or correct the auditor's subjective evaluation of the system. Naturally, if a number of errors were discovered in an area he had concluded would prevent errors, he would have to go back and reconsider his initial evaluation of internal control. If significant, this could, in turn, necessitate some weakness investigation.

Finally, the follow-up audit visit should end with the making of plans for the audit program (primary objective—for external auditors) and the issuing of a memorandum of recommendations (secondary objective).

PREPARING FLOW CHARTS

It was seen earlier that the preparation of flow charts was one of the first steps in the analytical audit. In this section these flow-charting techniques are described. Drawing flow charts is not difficult. Any standardized technique, of course, is bound to involve a number of charting symbols and conventions—but these do not take long to learn. Producing the optimum chart for the greatest readability is the main problem for the beginner, but this ability too can be quickly acquired with experience.

Basic Design. The flow-charting technique employed in analytical auditing is a form of "horizontal charting." The movement of documents and accounting information between different employees and departments is charted as a horizontal flow between different vertical columns. The advantage of this method for the auditor's purposes is that it shows the division of duties clearly and therefore helps him to evaluate internal control.

It is helpful to have special charting paper for preparing the final flow charts. This paper should be divided into about six vertical columns; a light squared background is convenient. (Typical overall dimensions would be about 14 by 17 inches.) The vertical columns are used to represent departments, sections within a department, or individual employees, as appropriate. Judgment must be employed in choosing the level of subdivision which one column should represent. For instance, in a small company the billing clerk might be represented by a separate column. In a larger company the whole billing department might be represented by one column. In a still larger company there might be distinct sections within the billing department which should each be allotted separate columns. The criterion is the significance of the division of duties from a control point of view. If the separation of two given sets of procedures is important, they should be assigned two different columns.

If the flow charts are to be prepared in an orderly manner, the total system of any organization must first be divided into logical sections. A convenient division is as follows:

Systems Section	*Section Reference Used in This Chapter*
Sales-receivables-receipts	B
Purchases-payables-payments	C
Payrolls	D
Cost records	E
Books of account and monthly statements	F

Most organizations sell some sort of goods or services (section B), purchase other goods, materials, supplies, or services (section C), pay their own employees (section D), keep some sort of record of their costs (section E), and summarize the results of all these activities in their books of account and monthly statements (section F). Obviously, there will be some organizations where a slightly different division is appropriate, but for the vast majority the above scheme is serviceable. For convenience, the same reference letters as noted above will be used throughout this chapter (section A being reserved for a description of the business).

Selection of Symbols. Horizontal charting has been used by systems men for many years. A certain number of the symbols are virtually universal among them—e.g., a rectangle representing a document or a solid arrow indicating physical movement of the document. As might be expected, however, other symbols are subject to considerable variation. Some charters use a triangle standing on its base to represent a file of documents; others stand the triangle on its apex. Some indicate document destruction by an "X" (as in the royal family trees of countless history books); others show it by a solid square. The symbols selected for analytical audit charting attempt to follow the most common conventions where practicable.

Certain of the symbols, however, were modified, or new ones developed, where this seemed expedient for auditing purposes. For instance, the symbols for a book or ledger (which are distinguished from those for documents), the symbols for a general ledger posting source (which are distinguished from those for other books), the symbols for signing and initialing (which have been singled out for special emphasis), and the symbols for the check or absence of check on numerical continuity were all created because they represent different types of audit evidence or have a particular bearing on internal control. These symbols, therefore, have a relevance for the auditor preparing a flow chart which they might not have for a systems specialist.

Conversely, there are some symbols common among systems men which are less appropriate for auditors. For instance, charting systems employed by analysts show a circle as a symbol for every "operation" performed—whether it be adding, approving, reconciling, agreeing, checking, or posting (all of which in the analytical auditing system are indicated by a word or two under the relevant document). The "operation" analysis produces a more expanded type of chart with circles appearing every few inches and revealing considerably greater detail. Such a chart is useful for formulating detailed procedures or for measuring the volume of clerical work—but this detail is rather more than the auditor needs. The auditor's charts must be designed primarily to assess internal control. Charting the mechanics of how a clerk searches a file, locates a desired card, compares it to a document being processed, and reinserts the card in the file complicates a chart whose main purpose is to analyze control. It is enough for the auditor if the chart shows merely that the clerk checks the document in question against a master card file. In other words, the nature of the charting symbols and conventions employed is bound to vary with the purpose for which the chart was prepared. Auditors' flow charts serve a different purpose from systems analysts' charts, and so their charting techniques can be expected to be slightly different too.

The Complete Chart. Because of the limited space permitted in a handbook, the various symbols recommended will not be detailed. However, an example of a complete systems chart, or walk-through audit chart, is illustrated in Figure 3, and most of the symbols can be seen to be reasonably self-explanatory. This particular flow chart does not cover the whole sales-receivables-receipts system (for instance, it omits credit note initiation, cash sales, and cash receipts). Usually, it is desirable, as here, to divide a complete systems section (such as sales-receivables-receipts) into logical components to avoid overcrowding any one chart. A complete description of the flow charting symbols and conventions employed on this chart is included in *Analytical Auditing*, pages 24–31.

The Outline Chart. Flow charts are not intended for skim reading. They are designed for intensive analysis. But with the concentration of information on the average flow chart it is desirable to have some guide to its general content before beginning to read it in detail. Such a purpose can be fulfilled by an outline chart of the type illustrated in Figure 4. The outline chart should have exactly the same column headings as the flow chart (Figure 3), the same starting arrows and concluding circles (posting sources), a line indicating the main path the reader should follow in reading the flow chart, and a bare minimum of words to indicate the major events on the chart ("orders received," "goods shipped," "invoices prepared," etc.). The outline chart should orient the reader by telling him what the flow chart covers before he starts to read it in detail and by keeping him on the right track while he is reading it. It should also assist the charter in detecting any awkwardness or confusion in his flow charts before they are completed. The outline chart is a convenient place to record any apparent weaknesses in control or inefficiencies observed in the charted system.

Recording the Systems Audit. In conducting the systems audit the various procedures will have been discussed, of course, with the employees involved. It is useful for the auditor to indicate that this has been done by initialing beside the appropriate employees' names at the head of each column on the flow charts (as in Figure 3). In this way he can ensure that he has not overlooked any key employee and has in fact obtained the information directly—and not secondhand from employees not involved in a given procedure. As for the record of the actual transactions tested during the systems audit (on the audit strip at the bottom of the flow chart), a system audit *number* is assigned for identification purposes to each book, ledger, or permanent file of documents shown on the chart. A systems audit *letter* is assigned to each temporary file of documents.

These systems audit numbers and letters are placed (as in Figure 3) below or at the lower corner of the symbol to which they relate. To make it easier to locate particular steps in the audit, the top two lines of the audit strip at the bottom of the flow chart serve as a "record index" showing the horizontal positioning of all the systems audit numbers and letters. Thus, in Figure 3, file number 6 (invoice second copies) is directly above the number 6 in the record index.

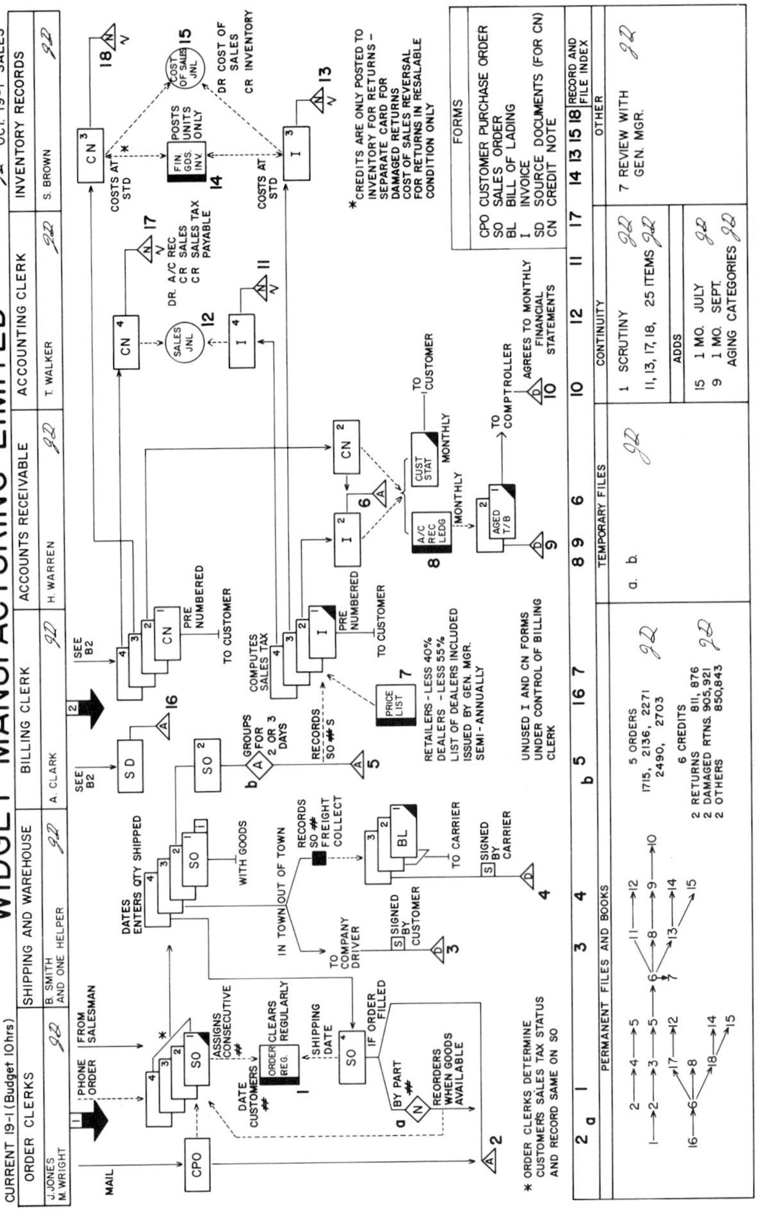

Figure 3 COMPLETE FLOW CHART

WIDGET MANUFACTURING LIMITED

CURRENT 19-1 (Budget 10hrs)

B1

JD OCT. 19-1 SALES

ORDER CLERKS	SHIPPING AND WAREHOUSE	BILLING CLERK	ACCOUNTS RECEIVABLE	ACCOUNTING CLERK	INVENTORY RECORDS
J. JONES M. WRIGHT JD	B. SMITH AND ONE HELPER JD	A. CLARK JD	H. WARREN JD	T. WALKER JD	S. BROWN JD

MAIL
PHONE ORDER
FROM SALESMAN
CPO
SO
ASSIGNS CONSECUTIVE #
DATE CUSTOMERS #
ORDER REG.
CLEARS REGULARLY
1
SHIPPING DATE
SO
IF ORDER FILLED
a BY PART #
N
REORDERS WHEN GOODS AVAILABLE
A 2

DATES ENTERS QTY SHIPPED
SO
WITH GOODS
IN TOWN OUT OF TOWN
TO COMPANY DRIVER
S SIGNED BY CUSTOMER
D 3
RECORDS SO # FREIGHT COLLECT
BL
TO CARRIER
S SIGNED BY CARRIER
D 4

SEE B2
SD
A 16
SO
b GROUPS FOR 2 OR 3 DAYS
RECORDS SO #S
A 5
SEE B2
CN
PRE NUMBERED
TO CUSTOMER
COMPUTES SALES TAX
I
PRE NUMBERED
TO CUSTOMER
PRICE LIST 7

RETAILERS - LESS 40%
DEALERS - LESS 55%
LIST OF DEALERS INCLUDED
ISSUED BY GEN. MGR.
SEMI - ANNUALLY

UNUSED I AND CN FORMS UNDER CONTROL OF BILLING CLERK

I
CN
6 A
8 A/C REC LEDG
CUST STAT
MONTHLY
TO CUSTOMER
MONTHLY
AGED T/B
TO COMPTROLLER
D 9

CN
N 17
SALES JNL 12
DR. A/C REC
CR SALES
CR SALES TAX PAYABLE
I
N 11
D 10 AGREES TO MONTHLY FINANCIAL STATEMENTS

CN
18 N
COSTS AT STD
FIN. GDS. INV. 14
POSTS UNITS ONLY
COST OF SALES JNL 15
DR COST OF SALES
CR INVENTORY
COSTS AT STD
I
N 13

* ORDER CLERKS DETERMINE CUSTOMER'S SALES TAX STATUS AND RECORD SAME ON SO

*CREDITS ARE ONLY POSTED TO INVENTORY FOR RETURNS - SEPARATE CARD FOR DAMAGED RETURNS
COST OF SALES REVERSAL FOR RETURNS IN RESALABLE CONDITION ONLY

FORMS

- CPO CUSTOMER PURCHASE ORDER
- SO SALES ORDER
- BL BILL OF LADING
- I INVOICE
- SD SOURCE DOCUMENTS (FOR CN)
- CN CREDIT NOTE

RECORD AND FILE INDEX: 2 a 1 3 4 b 5 16 7 8 9 6 10 12 11 17 14 13 15 18

PERMANENT FILES AND BOOKS		TEMPORARY FILES	CONTINUITY	OTHER
2→4→5; 1→2→3→5→6→8→9→10; 6→11→12; 6→7; 6→13→14; 13→15; 16→6→17→12; 6→8; 6→18→14; 18→15	5 ORDERS 1715, 2136, 2271, 2490, 2703 JD 6 CREDITS: 2 RETURNS 811, 876; 2 DAMAGED RTNS. 905, 921; 2 OTHERS 850, 843 JD	a. b. JD	1 SCRUTINY JD 11, 13, 17, 18, 25 ITEMS JD ADDS 15 1 MO. JULY JD 9 1 MO. SEPT. AGING CATEGORIES JD	7 REVIEW WITH GEN. MGR. JD

Figure 4 OUTLINE FLOW CHART

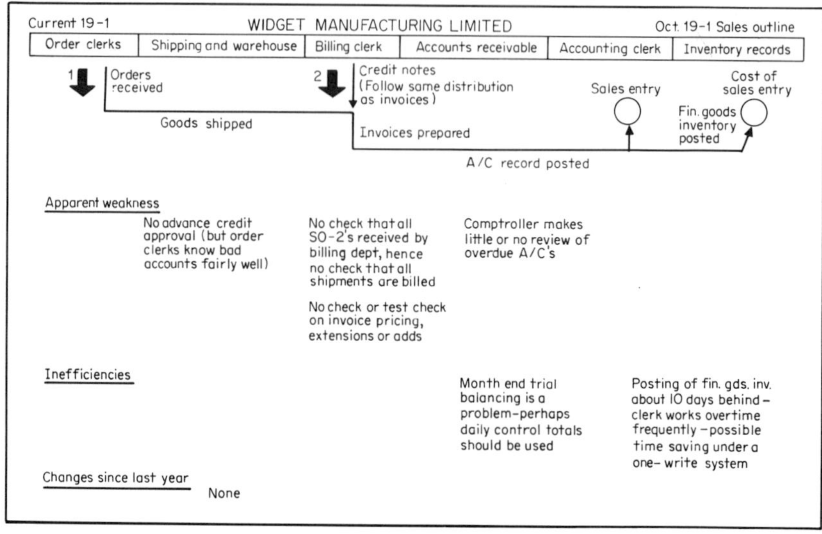

The main portion of the systems audit consists of examining and comparing the various permanent files and books while *tracing four transactions along each path of the charted system.* This audit examination and comparison can be described symbolically:

$$1 \rightarrow 2 \rightarrow 3 \rightarrow 4 \rightarrow \ldots \qquad \text{4 orders}$$

The notations in this figure mean that for a sample of four orders, items selected in record 1 were checked to related documents or information in record 2, which in turn were checked to record 3 and thence to record 4, etc.

The interpretation of the basic step

$$1 \rightarrow 2 \qquad \text{4 orders}$$

where 1 and 2 are both files of documents, is that:

1. Four documents were selected out of file 1.
2. Each such document was carefully examined, and any information or arithmetic which was verifiable without reference to any other source was checked (e.g., extensions, additions, name and address, reasonableness of amount, nature of item).
3. If sets of matched documents were contained in file 1 (such as purchase invoices and receiving slips matched and filed together), then four such sets were selected and, in addition to the examination of each document, all common or related information was agreed between the documents of a given set (e.g., receiving date, quantities, descriptions, amounts).
4. File 1 was then *scrutinized* briefly to see that it did not contain significant types of transactions not covered on the flow charts and to see that other documents in the file appear to have been processed in the same way as the sample examined.
5. Then the related documents or sets of documents were located in file

2 and all common or related information agreed between the file 1 documents and the file 2 documents selected.

6. Then steps 2, 3, and 4 above were carried out for the file 2 documents by themselves.

The systems audit numbers should be assigned in a logical "audit flow order" so that the consecutive numbers represent the consecutive audit steps. In this way the systems audit can really be read without constant cross reference to the audit strip at the bottom of the chart, since it is known that the steps flow consecutively. Conventionally, a sales audit is conducted in a cradle-to-grave direction (as in Figure 3) while a disbursements audit is conducted in a grave-to-cradle direction. The audit numbers should therefore be assigned accordingly. Occasionally, of course, the systems audit will not lead in a completely straight line but will appear as follows, say:

$$\begin{array}{ccccccccccc} 1 & \to & 2 & \to & 3 & \to & 5 & \to & 6 & \to & \ldots \\ & & & & \downarrow & & & & & & \\ & & & & 4 & & & & & & \end{array}$$

Here, record 3 is checked both to record 4 and to record 5, while 4 cannot be checked to 5 itself. This could occur, for instance, if 3 was a sales invoice, 4 the accounts receivable ledger, and 5 a sales summary. In general, the tracing of transactions from cradle to grave should be done in one continuous chain, as Figure 4 shows. It should not be broken up into segments such as

$$\begin{array}{ccccc} 1 \to 2 & \quad 2 \to 3 \quad & 3 & \quad 3 \to 5 \quad & 5 \to 6 \\ & & \downarrow & & \\ & & 4 & & \end{array}$$

since this is both slower and less effective than tracing the same transactions throughout the whole path.

When the extent of a particular systems audit is indicated as four items, it must be understood that four items will be checked along each segment of the system trail from cradle to grave or from grave to cradle. With a sales audit this is fairly unambiguous: four shipping reports are checked to four invoices that are traced to the sales summary, etc. With a disbursements audit, however, the auditor might select 4 checks, where each supporting voucher contains 20 suppliers' invoices and each invoice covers 5 purchase orders. The intention is not to check 4 vouchers, 80 invoices, and 400 purchase orders but rather to check 4 checks to the supporting vouchers, 4 invoices from among these vouchers to purchase orders, 4 purchase orders from among these invoices to requisitions, etc.

Whenever there is a fork in the system there must be a corresponding set of alternatives in the audit. For example, in:

$$\begin{array}{ll} 1 \to 2 \to 3 \to 5 \to 6 \to 7 & \quad \text{4 domestic orders} \\ \phantom{1 \to {}} 2 \to 4 \to 5 & \quad \text{4 foreign orders} \end{array}$$

domestic orders affect record 3 and foreign orders record 4. In this case an additional four transactions should be traced over the alternate path of the variable section (2 to 5) so that every charted path on the flow chart will be covered by the systems audit. It does not matter whether domestic or foreign orders are traced over the rest of the chain (1 to 2 and 5 to 7) as long as four transactions are traced in total. Preferably, the four transactions for the overall path should be selected randomly and then further transactions selected to bring those tested over each branch (2-3-5 and 2-4-5) up to four in number.

The foregoing has dealt with the systems audit relating to permanent files and books—which generally should be the largest part of the systems audit. However, the complete systems audit consists of:

1. Test and scrutiny of permanent files and books
2. Test and scrutiny of temporary files
3. Test of continuity
4. Test of additions
5. Other tests (if any)

Sometimes it is possible to trace a chain of related documents in temporary files:

$$a \rightarrow b \rightarrow c \rightarrow d \rightarrow e$$

but more often the checking of related temporary files is likely to be disjointed:

$$a \rightarrow b \qquad e \rightarrow b \qquad h \rightarrow 4$$

However, in any case, all the temporary files should be scrutinized to (1) see that the temporary files are being processed in the way outlined on the flow charts, (2) see if all the items are as current as they should be, and (3) see if any irregular items or problems are accumulating in them.

A check of serial continuity of appropriate files should be made, but for a very limited extent, say 25 items. The purpose is merely to see if, at first glance, the client is accounting for continuity and not, at this point, to conduct an extensive audit to detect the occasional missing number. Test adds should be done where appropriate but only to a very limited extent. The purpose is to ascertain the system and not, at this point, to detect the rare manipulation. Often some alternative test may be more appropriate and faster, such as agreeing two independent totals made by different employees in different departments.

Finally, a space is provided in the audit strip for any other audit steps not covered in the above categories. These will occur, say, where an alternative procedure has been described in a footnote and the systems audit of this procedure has not, therefore, been covered in the symbolic description of the main systems audit related to the charts. For each section of the recorded systems audit the auditor's initials can be entered to indicate that he has carried out the program described.

The method outlined for recording the systems audit provides a complete yet concise description of the audit steps performed. In contrast, were all the audit steps to be spelled out in detailed narrative style the systems audit program would become, in effect, a lengthy description of the client's systems. Such a result would be inefficient and would defeat the whole purpose of avoiding lengthy systems narrative by adopting flow charting.

THE SYSTEMS AUDIT

The division of an analytical audit into two stages (systems audit and follow-up audit) has been explained and each of these stages discussed in general terms. Earlier flow-charting techniques and the method of recording the systems audit on the flow charts themselves have been described. The various audit procedures constituting the systems audit can now be considered in more detail.

In conducting an analytical audit there are certain obvious differences between a systems audit being made in the initial year (when the flow charts are being prepared for the first time) and one being continued in repeat years (when the flow charts are merely being revised and updated). The following pages will describe the procedures primarily in the context of a first-year audit, but reference will be made where necessary to changes appropriate for an audit in repeat years.

Description of the Business. Systems analysis must begin with a knowledge of the physical operations of the business being audited. It is too easy to float about in a sea of statements, figures, and journal entries without a grounding in what is really going on in the business. If management sometimes shows signs of exasperation at the sight of new faces among the audit staff, it is because new faces so often mean new minds full of ignorance of what the business is all about. Some might argue that the desired knowledge can be inferred from a careful review of the accounts. This is putting the cart before the horse. It is the propriety of the accounting entries that should be derived from a reasonable knowledge of the business, not vice versa. The intention in preparing or updating a description of the client's business (section A) should therefore be to give a bird's-eye view of the physical processes and transactions that underlie the accounting entries and financial statements. The description should tell briefly what the business is and what various factors have an important bearing on its operating results. This section need not be concerned with accounting procedures (which should be covered on the flow charts). Some suggestions of what this description might include are set out below. Not all the specific points mentioned can be determined quickly for every client. Only those points should be covered, of course, where useful information is obtainable and can be summarized in a reasonable amount of time. Finally, this section will be of use to the auditor as he conducts his systems analysis only if he has it in advance. It must therefore be completed before the flow charting begins. This point is less critical for the internal auditor and the governmental auditor, who may have a closer familiarity with the operations than the external auditor can hope for without some aid.

Nature of business. A one-sentence introduction stating what business the client is in.

Ownership. One sentence again, stating briefly whether the business is owned privately or publicly, by individuals or by a corporation.

Industry. Such points as the nature of the industry; the economic factors affecting the industry (consumer disposable income, etc., competing products, cyclical or seasonal demand); the position of the company in the industry (proportion of total unit sales, number of domestic and foreign competitors, names of major competitors, comparisons with specific competitors, growth potential or outlook).

Plant facilities. Such points as the locations and approximate extent of plant, warehouse, and office space, branch locations; whether owned or leased; the age and condition of buildings, room for expansion, present plans for improvement; the nature and extent of equipment (extent of automation, age and condition of machinery); appraisals; capital expenditure budgets; comparisons with competitors.

Products. Such points as description of main product lines, relative volumes, product mix, number of products; the extent of manufacturing in relation to the finished product (and extent of purchases for resale); in which plants the various products are manufactured; service operations; warranty; extent of custom manufacturing vs. production for stock; general demand for company's products; plans for new lines, etc.

Production. Such points as the nature of the manufacturing or processing operations; plant capacity; normal operating schedule (peak and slack periods); production planning; storage facilities; engineering program (design, product development, experimental, etc.); research and development budget.

Purchasing. Such points as annual volume; main materials purchased; main suppliers and alternate sources; proportion of purchases from affiliated companies; unloading facilities; receiving operations.

Personnel. Such points as the number of employees (office, warehouse, and plant—average and range from slack to peak periods); union agreements; daywork and piecework proportions; average wage rates (comparison with industry if possible); employee benefits, pension plans, etc.; strike history and employee relations; employment contracts, bonus plans, etc., for senior personnel; organization chart of key personnel.

Sales. Such points as the method of distribution; the type and number of the company's customers; geographical location of company sales including exports; comparison with industry and specific competitors; sales force, method of remuneration, commissions, bonuses, retainers; seasonal trends; sales promotion and advertising; sales policies; selling and administrative budget; price trends and method of setting prices, proportion of sales to affiliated companies.

Operating results. Such points as current trends in gross profit and net profit rates; break-even point analysis if available (fixed costs in relation to total costs); comparison of profitability with industry and with specific competitors.

Budgeting. Such points as who is in charge of budget preparation; method of sales forecasting; production scheduling, etc.; cash requirements; reports to management (and follow-up of deviations).

Flow Charting and the Systems Audit. In beginning the systems review of a particular section (such as sales-receivables-receipts), the auditor must first obtain a general idea of what is included in that section. This can be done by (1) reading the description of the business (section A) to see what types of transactions should be expected; (2) discussing the overall system briefly with the comptroller or chief accountant; and (3) reviewing any accounting manual, procedure books, comptroller's circulars, and systems department memoranda outlining the system. Detail in these preliminary steps must be avoided. Information from (2) and (3) may be out of date. In any case it represents what senior officials think is happening or should be happening; the actual system in operation may be considerably different. The internal auditor, however, may wish to flow-chart all standard procedures laid down in company manuals and then measure all deviations from these prescribed procedures encountered during his systems audit.

In repeat years, the auditor should review the previous year's flow charts for the given section and discuss any subsequent changes briefly with the comptroller or chief accountant. This preliminary information is to be used for orientation. It should show where the careful systems review can logically begin. The preliminary information is usually best recorded in the form of a rough flow chart, which can be added to and amended during the course of the systems audit. It should not be charted in elaborate detail, since extensive corrections are almost certain to be required.

The next step is to read the internal control questions on the related lead sheet. These are the questions for which the charts will have to furnish the answers. The answers cannot, of course, be given as yet but the questions should serve as a *guide* in the actual charting. Procedures having a bearing on basic control points will have to be charted in sufficient detail to ensure that the control is accurately described. Procedures having little or no bearing on control should be charted with a lesser degree of detail or omitted entirely—at least, as far as external auditors are concerned. It must be remembered, however, that not all control procedures are located within the accounting department. Many procedures performed by other departments—perhaps "administrative controls" aimed primarily at promoting efficiency—may provide some important check on the accuracy or reliability of the accounting system.

It is common to divide internal control into *accounting controls,* which safeguard assets and accounting reliability (some would subdivide this further into *internal check* and *accounting controls*), and *administrative controls,* which promote operational efficiency. Some administrative controls may have little effect on the accounting reliability; others may compensate for deficient accounting controls and thus have a very important effect. In this chapter all the controls are referred to under the generic term, "internal control." Any procedure which provides a significant check on the accounting reliability or on the safeguarding of assets (whether direct or indirect, whether an accounting or an administrative control) should be covered in the auditor's review and recorded on his flow charts.

In repeat years the auditor must review the answers given on the previous year's lead sheets, since these will indicate where particular attention should be focused during the current year's review. He should also review the disposition of recommendations made to the client in the previous year. Adopted suggestions will necessitate flow-chart revisions. Unadopted ones may require further investigation to locate any apparent obstacles to their implementation.

Bearing in mind these internal control points, the auditor should then begin at the "cradle" and trace through to the "grave" (or vice versa) for each type of transaction. In tracing each transaction, he should discuss the procedures with the employee who performs them. That is, he should ask A rather than accept B's assertion as to what A does. As he questions each employee with respect to the transaction being traced, he should ask what that employee's procedures are, what books he keeps, what documents he processes, from whom he receives them, and to whom he sends them. In repeat years the employees need not be questioned as fully as in the first-year analytical audit. All employees, however, must still be questioned *briefly* to confirm that the previous year's system is still in force or to discover the extent of any changes. If this inquiry is combined with questions concerning the particular sample of transactions being traced, the necessary review can be completed without giving the impression of repeating the "first-year" survey all over again.

Another important step is to establish that the rough charts have in fact covered *all the possible types* of transactions occurring in the system. It is essential that all parts of the system be covered so that they will be (1) checked during the systems audit and (2) evaluated from a control point of view. Therefore, the auditor should look to see if any relevant transactions described or implied in the description of the business (section A) do not appear in the accounting system charted. Secondly, while the systems audit is being done, he must *scrutinize the books, ledgers, and document files* carefully for types of transactions not covered as yet on the charts or in the audit. Thirdly, he should refer to the flow-charting guide on the sectional lead sheets (see Figure 6) for possible variations in transaction type, and ensure by scrutiny of records and questioning of employees that all variations occurring have been covered. In repeat years there will not be the same risk that the chart has omitted any type of transaction. Nonetheless, the auditor should review section A and the charting guide on the lead sheet and consider whether any change in the current year has resulted in new types of transactions which must be added to the charts.

Volume Summary. The flow charts indicate the *design* of the system, but they do not show the physical *volume* of accounting work. Yet in assessing internal control and efficiency the auditor must be able to see the different procedures in perspective. It is therefore useful to summarize such data as the number of customers, products, and inventory accounts, and the monthly volumes of checks, vouchers, purchase invoices, sales invoices, shipping orders, credit notes, and journal entries. A more detailed list of the volume statistics which might be considered for incorporation in this summary is as follows (although only a selection of these would probably be appropriate in any individual case):

Section	*Monthly volumes of*	*Total number of*
B	Sales orders	Customers—active accounts
	Sales invoices	Customers—inactive accounts
	Shipments	Customers—by category
	Units shipped	Salesmen
	Back orders	Order clerks
	Credit notes	Billing clerks
	Checks received	Accounts receivable clerks
	Accounts receivable postings	
	Cash sales slips	
C	Purchase requisitions	Purchasing department employees
	Purchase orders	
	Purchase invoices	
	Receiving slips	
	Suppliers' debits	
	Vouchers	
	Checks issued	
D	Daily work tickets	Office employees (monthly, semi-monthly)
	Payroll checks	Plant employees (weekly) (range and peaks during year)
	Piece work tickets	Employees by category or by location
		Payroll department employees
E	Production orders	Products
	Units produced	Manufactured parts, sub-assemblies
	Production change notices	Inventory accounts (by category)
	Scrap reports	Cost ledger accounts
	Perpetual inventory postings	Cost department employees
	Cost ledger postings	
F	Journal entries	General ledger accounts
	General ledger postings	Accounting department employees

Comparative figures can be added in subsequent years so that any marked trends in the volume of accounting work will be evident.

The Internal Audit Department. Where an internal audit department exists, a new element of control is added, which the external auditor is entitled to take into account in designing his audit. The scope of the internal audit function can vary from one employee occasionally checking some petty cash funds to a fully organized department covering all phases of the client's operations. The internal audit function may be directed solely to branch locations, or it may cover the client's head office procedures as well. The external auditor should first, therefore, determine the scope of the internal audit. Then he can consider the department's independence, to whom they report, their competence, the amount of training given, the amount of laid-down audit instructions or programs, the frequency of reporting, and the quality of their reports. His findings and conclusions should be summarized and included in his working papers.

After this general assessment, the internal audit procedures should be reviewed in more detail to see to what extent the external auditor may rely on this work and reduce his tests accordingly. He should review the internal audit reports for confirmation of his conclusions on apparent weaknesses or for indications of any additional weak areas. Based on this, he may have to revise his notes of apparent weaknesses to allow for the extent to which previously noted weaknesses are offset by internal audit procedures or, conversely, to incorporate additional weaknesses uncovered by the internal auditors. Finally, it is axiomatic that great gains in efficiency can be achieved if there is close cooperation between internal and external auditors. The external auditor should consider the extent to which his work can be coordinated with that of the internal auditors. He might examine the possibility of joint use of his flow charts or the possibility of *the internal auditors updating the flow charts throughout the year.* It is particularly convenient, of course, if both internal and external auditors are using the same analytical auditing approach.

Weakness Follow-up Sheet. Once the apparent weaknesses have been determined and are noted on the outline charts throughout the file, the auditor must decide what he is going to do about them. It is useful to summarize these decisions in one place. A convenient way is on a weakness follow-up sheet of the type shown in Figure 5. This schedule represents a complete record of all apparent weaknesses in control discovered during the systems audit visit. (A new weakness follow-up sheet should be prepared each year, but it may be useful to retain the schedules for a few immediately preceding years in the file for reference.) For each weakness recorded, the schedule should state the kind of error which might occur (and remain undetected) because of the apparent deficiency in control. This is an essential intermediate step. A suitable audit program cannot be devised to compensate for a weakness unless it is first decided what one is looking for. Moreover, it would be foolish to waste a major audit investigation looking for minor errors or, conversely, rely on a minor audit step to detect major errors. Therefore, the auditor must decide not only the kind but also the seriousness of the error for which he is looking. In some cases the auditor can decide that although errors could occur owing to a given weakness, none of them could be material. In other cases the errors could, perhaps, become material, but only if there were a very high frequency of them. In still other cases even a low frequency of errors might represent a material total.

Weakness Investigation. In drafting a proposed weakness investigation for approval, the auditor should remember the following points. The purpose is not to see whether any errors are occurring at all but whether any *material amount* of error has occurred over the year. The weakness investigation may, but it *need not always,* be an extended procedural test—that is, the checking of a larger sample of sales invoices, canceled checks, purchase invoices, or other documents. Many times such checking would detect only a few minor errors and still leave unanswered the question of whether any

Figure 5 WEAKNESS FOLLOW-UP SHEET

X COMPANY LIMITED

Current 19 — 1 | DH Dec. 19 — 1 Weakness follow-up

Chart reference	Weakness	Could material errors occur?	Weakness investigation: Description	Weakness investigation: Initial	Weakness investigation: Results	Revision to balance sheet program
B_1	No advance credit approval	Could run up large accounts with doubtful risks.	No detailed audit but reviewed to see if any apparent accumulation of bad accounts.	DH	Slight increase in overdue accounts but no specific problems apparent as yet.	Emphasize verification of allowance for doubtful accounts.
B_1	Keypunching of special, non-standard prices not checked	Non-standard prices account for 10% of total sales value. A high frequency of errors could be material but a limited frequency would not be significant.	Examined 120 non-standard invoices (10 per month) and checked to price list.	DH	1 small error found (invoice No. 23691). Due to carelessness. Decided frequency of such errors must be well under, say, 5% of non-standard sales (e.g. ½% of total sales) and hence could not be material in total.	None.
B_1	Lost sales order (after shipping) would not be detected	Material amount of unbilled shipments might occur.	None. (More efficient to add year-end test).	—	—	Check client's annual yearend tab listing of outstanding order cards and trace to sales control orders and to order register.
B_1	Shipping area not guarded and is accessible to outsiders	Inventory is high bulk low value. Material amount of theft would be noticed.	None.	—	—	None.
C_2	Suppliers' statements not reconciled on a regular basis	Significant errors in accounts payable could go uncorrected.	Examined 10 larger and 30 smaller suppliers' statements and reconciled to accounts payable.	DH	15 branch purchase invoices not set up although 2 months old. Many discrepancies on reconciliation of debit and credit notes. See details on 5b. 10 of missing invoices subsequently found in inventory records (misfiled); copies of other 5 obtained from supplier.	Unless (a) statement reconcilation is instituted (as recommended) and (b) inventory record processing revised prior to year-end, extend accounts payable confirmation and statement reconciliation work at year-end to cover larger proportion of accounts.
D_1	Check of work tickets for piece work to production records not adequate	Significant overbooking of direct labor could occur.	Analyzed labor variance for 7 months to date.	DH	All but $4,000 of the total variance can be accounted for (see 5c) in terms of wage rate increase. Decided any overbooking could not therefore be material in amount.	None.

material amount of error had occurred over the year. Instead, the weakness investigation may often consist of:

1. Analysis of certain variance accounts
2. Analysis of budget performance of certain items
3. More intensive scrutiny of certain records
4. Reconciliation of certain operating statistics
5. Further questioning of certain employees
6. Examination of larger documents only, for the entire year
7. Any other appropriate steps that can be devised

It is, in other words, up to the ingenuity of the auditor to devise the investigation which has the best chance of detecting any errors *material enough to distort the financial statements* should they occur. No set verification steps can be specified in advance, and extended procedural tests will not always be the best answer.

Supplementary Tests. Even when the weaknesses have been covered by planned weakness investigations or by revised audit steps, it is desirable to do some further work to support (on a test basis) the conclusion that control in other areas is satisfactory. A convenient plan is to select one or two supplementary tests from each section of the system: sales-receivables-receipts (B), purchases-payables-payments (C), payrolls (D), cost records (E), etc. Each of these steps should consist of a procedural test in a key area where the internal control has been judged satisfactory. A key area is one that has a significant effect on internal control. Tests of weak areas are not called for here, however, since these should already be covered in the weakness investigation. Since the tests are only supplementary confirmation of the auditor's initial evaluation, only a small portion of the total audit time should be devoted to this section. Except where internal control is almost ideal the auditor should expect to spend more time on the weakness investigation than on the supplementary tests. For external auditors, the extent of the supplementary tests may be reduced where reliance can be placed upon the testing procedures of the internal audit department. In repeat years the supplementary tests selected from each section should be different from those of the preceding one or two years. The aim should be over a period of three or four years to have these cyclical tests cover all key areas in those parts of the system judged to have satisfactory internal control.

Memorandum of Recommendations. At the conclusion of the systems audit visit (the first stage of the analytical audit) the auditor can draft a memorandum of recommendations to the client covering all apparent weaknesses and inefficiencies noted on the outline charts.

Each recommendation should be drafted by the audit staff who reviewed the part of the system affected, and it should be done *during*, not after, the systems audit visit. This makes maximum use of the systems knowledge acquired during the flow-charting stage while it is still fresh. It is suggested, however, that the memorandum not be issued at this time but be held for more senior audit review between the visits and for further consideration during the follow-up audit.

Oral Review. Because of the concentration of information in analytical audit working papers a review of such a file encounters certain difficulties not present in the review of other types of working papers. A few comments on review methods for analytical auditing may therefore be of use. The best reviewing technique seems to be that of an *oral review* between audit senior and reviewer. The reviewer should *not* examine the analytical audit file

Figure 6 LEAD SHEET FOR SALES, RECEIVABLES, RECEIPTS

CURRENT 19

LEAD SHEET FOR SALES, RECEIVABLES, RECEIPTS

SYSTEMS SUMMARY

INDEX OF SECTION

B1 –
B2 –
B3 –
B4 –

INTERNAL CONTROL EVALUATION

("Yes" answers represent apparent weaknesses)	Answer (Yes or No)	Flow chart reference
1. Can goods be shipped but not invoiced?	____	____
Consider – (a) independent follow-up of serial continuity of *shipping or sales order* numbers?		
(b) shipping, billing segregated from cash receipts?		
(c) control of access to shipping area?		
(d) non-routine sales: scrap, fixed assets, consignment, employee sales, "direct" shipments from supplier to customer?		
2. Can goods be shipped to a bad credit risk?	____	____
Consider – (a) credit approval prior to shipment?		
3. Can sales be invoiced but not recorded in the accounts?	____	____
Consider – (a) independent follow-up of serial continuity of sales invoices?		
(b) shipping or sales order numbers tied up to documents processed *through* posting to receivables *or through* entry in sales summary?		
(c) billing segregated from receivables?		
(d) daily billing total *direct* to general ledger posting source?		
(e) daily billing total reconciled with total receivable postings?		
4. Can receivables be credited improperly?	____	____
Consider – (a) prenumbered credit note approval independent of receivables clerks?		
(b) proper support for credit notes?		
(c) independent approval of bad debt write-offs?		

FLOW CHARTING GUIDE

Ensure that the flow charts cover all types of transactions involving significant differences in procedures. Consider:

1. Type of order
   - telephone, written, salesman; credit, C.O.D., cash;
2. Type of customer
   - domestic, foreign; consumer, distributor; consignment; affiliated company;
3. Type of shipment
   - shipping location, warehousing;
   - type of carrier, customer pick up, direct from supplier to customer;
   - complete, partial, backorder;
4. Type of product
   - stock, custom; product class;
5. Miscellaneous
   - fixed asset sales, scrap sales, employee sales;

Ensure that the flow charts cover all significant phases of each transaction, e.g.;

- quoting, price determination, pricing, sales tax, outward freight, costing, returns, types of credit notes, write-offs, accounts receivable procedures, credit control, collections, discounts, etc.

Consider—(a) receivable trial balancing, aging, review, follow-up of delinquent accounts independent of posting clerks? ____ ____
(b) checking and mailing of statements independently of posting clerks, control where no statements?
(c) customer queries followed up independently?

6. Can payments be received and not deposited? ____ ____
Consider—(a) cashier and receivable ledger functions separated?
(b) checks stamped "for deposit only" when mail opened, bank accepts only for deposit?
(c) mail receipts direct to cashier, listed, or control totals taken immediately?
(d) deposits checked, deposited promptly?
(e) control over branch deposit accounts?

7. Can overdue accounts escape attention? ____ ____
Consider—(a) aged trial balances?
(b) independent follow-up?

8. Can sales be invoiced but not costed? ____ ____

9. Can invoicing errors occur? ____ ____
Consider—(a) pricing, quantities, extensions checked?
(b) standard price list, exceptions approved?

10. Can cash sales proceeds be misappropriated? ____ ____
Consider—(a) locked-in register invoice copy *or* prenumbered receipts?
(b) independent check of prenumbered invoices to cash book?
(c) control over drivers' collections, C.O.D. sales, etc.?

11. Can miscellaneous receipts be missed? ____ ____
Consider—(a) set up as receivable or independent check of collections?

EVALUATED BY: ....

prior to the oral review with the senior. Such an advance examination is likely to be time-consuming and less effective. It is more efficient for the reviewer, and a useful discipline for the senior, if the latter leads the reviewer through the file, explaining the system, and justifying his evaluation of the system by reference to the flow charts as he goes. The time spent on this review should not be excessive once some experience has been gained.

The oral review should be done as soon after the completion of the systems audit as possible and, best of all, at the client's office where additional information is available if needed. A suggested form for the oral review is as follows:

1. The reviewer takes the first 5 minutes to read the description of the client's business (section A).
2. For each section, starting with B and ending with F, the senior leads the reviewer briefly through:
   a. The systems summary on the lead sheet
   b. Each flow chart and related outline chart describing what the system is (a few details can be omitted)
   c. The apparent weaknesses and inefficiencies noted on the outline charts
   d. Then, the primary internal control questions and his answers to them on the lead sheet
3. In reviewing the primary internal control questions on the lead sheet the senior should
   a. For each answer that the control was unsatisfactory, refer the reviewer to the indicated flow chart and to the weakness described on the related outline chart
   b. For each answer that the control was satisfactory, refer the reviewer to the indicated flow chart and demonstrate to him, on the flow chart, how the particular control is achieved
4. The senior should then refer the reviewer to the weakness follow-up sheet and explain how each proposed weakness investigation or audit program revision will be sufficient to detect any material errors that the apparent weakness might allow.
5. Finally, the memorandum of recommendations, the supplementary tests, and the remaining sections in the file can be reviewed, ending with the analytical audit report itself.

The reviewer cannot expect to have the detailed knowledge of the system that the senior has, but he should, by a process of skeptical cross examination throughout the above review, be able to establish whether or not the system has been properly evaluated and whether the proposed program for the follow-up visit is reasonable. During the review he should consider the following questions:

1. Is the flow chart reasonably clear? Will next year's senior be able to read it?
2. Is it too detailed or, conversely, not detailed enough?
3. Does the flow chart support the senior's conclusions on the system evaluation?
4. If a flow chart neither indicates an apparent weakness nor documents an internal control strength, was it really necessary?
5. Is the apparent weakness more serious or less serious than the senior has concluded?

6. Are the senior's answers indicating satisfactory control justified? Does the senior's justification make sense?

7. Will the proposed weakness investigation or proposed audit program revision really detect material errors if they have occurred? Are the proposed steps too extensive or not extensive enough?

8. Are the proposed supplementary tests reasonable (but not excessive) as an additional test confirmation of the senior's evaluation?

9. Are the proposed recommendations to the client realistic? Do they really solve the problem? Has the proper priority been given according to relative importance? Have the recommendations been phrased intelligibly and persuasively?

10. Have the other sections of the file been completed properly?

This review may well result in a number of changes to the internal control evaluation, the proposed follow-up audit, or the drafted recommendations. Or it may result in the senior's being requested to obtain additional information on some point, rephrase certain recommendations, etc. Alternative recommendations raised during the review can, however, be investigated during the follow-up audit. After the oral review has been completed the reviewer may, if he feels it necessary, reexamine any sections of the file about which he is unsatisfied. Many times this will be unnecessary, but where it is, the rereading of certain working papers should take place *after*, and not before, the oral review with his senior.

THE FOLLOW-UP AUDIT

In the previous section the components of the first stage were discussed at length. This section reviews the steps to be performed in completing the second stage (the follow-up audit). Less need be said about this second stage, since the drafting of the weakness investigation itself has already been discussed in describing the systems audit.

Statistics Analysis. Before completing the programs of weakness investigation and supplementary tests which were drafted during the systems audit, it is useful for the auditor to do some checking of the self-consistency of financial figures, ratios, trends, and other statistics pertaining to the client's operations. It is true that analyses and comparisons of various profit and loss components are traditionally included in the auditor's work following the year end. These are still needed. But the analytical audit is a convenient time to conduct a more fundamental analysis of the statistics available before the annual rush to meet audit deadlines. The nature of and amount of emphasis to be placed on this statistics analysis will vary from audit to audit, and no precise rules can be given. The purpose is (1) to gain assurance as to the accuracy of the accounting system through the reasonableness and consistency of the various statistics, reports, comparisons, budgets, analyses, etc., which most businesses produce and (2) to locate in these reports and statistics any unusual or unexpected relationships which would warrant additional audit investigation. This might be called a "businessman's approach to auditing." Frequently, statistics analysis will provide the auditor with important information faster than an examination of large samples of documents.

Weakness Investigation. The weakness investigation as drafted during the systems audit and as reviewed can now be performed. It should include any additional work necessary to cover unresolved statistical discrepancies (as discussed above). The results should then be summarized on the weakness follow-up sheet (Figure 5). Where errors are encountered in doing the weakness investigation, it may be necessary to extend the scope of the work to resolve the matter one way or the other. It should be remembered, however, that the purpose is to establish whether or not a material amount of error has occurred over the year. Immaterial errors may not matter in themselves unless their frequency in the investigational work raises the possibility of a material total of such errors over the year. The results found in the weakness investigation may also necessitate changing the proposed revisions in the balance sheet audit program. After completing the weakness investigation, the supplementary tests as drafted during the systems audit and as reviewed can then be performed.

Informal Discussion of Recommendations. When the follow-up audit has been completed, the auditor can discuss the comments and suggestions made in the draft memorandum with the employees who might be affected thereby (using reasonable discretion). The purpose is to ensure that the suggestions are realistic and workable before they are formally presented.

Oral Review. An oral review can be done upon the completion of the follow-up audit. This oral review will normally be quite short (much more so than that following the systems audit visit). It is limited to (1) reviewing the design and results of the statistics analysis; (2) reviewing the results of the weakness investigation and supplementary tests and considering whether any additional action taken by the senior, as a result of errors found, has been adequate; (3) discussing any modifications made since the original, approved draft of the memorandum of recommendations. Following this, the memorandum of recommendations can be issued to the client. As the issuing of audited financial statements marks the end of the normal opinion type audit, so the issuing of a letter of recommendations marks the end of the normal analytical audit.

Practical Advice. **Planning.** In scheduling the follow-up visit, it should be remembered that the follow-up audit can usually be done late in the year so that as many as possible of the year's results are available to audit. Normally this visit involves far less time than the systems audit. The late scheduling does not therefore create serious peak problems. On the other hand, the longer the follow-up visit occurs after the systems audit, the less detailed familiarity with the system can the auditor retain. On some analytical audits the statistics analysis may assume major proportions and so should not be left too late in the year. Hence, some compromise between these different factors is necessary. For clients at locations some distance from the auditor it may be impractical to make two analytical audit visits; the systems audit and follow-up audit may have to be done on the same visit. In these cases, it is desirable that the working papers from the systems audit be reviewed on location, before the follow-up audit is commenced.

Work assignment. The weakness investigation and the supplementary tests can be assigned to junior audit staff provided they are adequately supervised. The statistics analysis is best left, however, for more senior audit staff to perform. Senior audit staff should also be used to bring up to date the scrutiny of appropriate books and records begun in the systems audit.

APPLICATION TO COMPUTER SYSTEMS

The larger the organization and the greater the volume of transactions the greater the savings which should accrue from the use of a systems-oriented auditing approach. Checking all transactions for a specified test period becomes excessively time-consuming while, on the other hand, the system of internal control is likely to be stronger and therefore to repay more generously a thorough analysis of control. But large organizations are the very ones most apt to have computer applications. Can analytical auditing be adapted to these data processing systems? The answer is that it can. In fact, such systems are model subjects for this type of audit. In data processing installations the procedures are more formalized, the systems more reproducible. If auditing "through the system" makes sense for a manual system, it makes even more sense for a punched card or computer system.

Computer Systems. While punched-card systems do not present the auditor with any fundamental problems not common to manual systems, with computer systems the situation is different. Computers have a much greater influence on the nature of the accounting and management reporting system surrounding them. In addition, they involve a considerable number of logical decisions and important controls within the actual internal processing of the computer. It is not the purpose of this chapter to give an extensive description of all the audit techniques which may be appropriate for particular computer systems. This would necessitate a discussion of each control feature in an EDP system and a consideration of when and how special techniques such as the use of test decks or tape dumps should be applied. The intention here is merely to demonstrate how the analytical auditing approach can be generally adapted to the audit of computer systems.

Three general premises should be stated at the outset. First, the computer is an integral part of the total accounting system and must therefore be considered in the context of the system of which it is a part. The computer hardware and personnel provide processing services for many departments and for many different kinds of information. However, as each type of data is processed, the computer uses programs and is operated under instructions specifically designed for that transaction type, and so the computer becomes inextricably part of the total system of processing for that particular type of information. For each type of transaction the computer must therefore be looked at in conjunction with all the other operations performed on the data. A so-called "computer audit" designed to treat the computer as a separate and independent entity cannot lead to an intelligent evaluation of the total control system. Secondly, if the computer is part of the system, then a systems-oriented approach (such as analytical auditing) can, with certain modifications, be used to audit it. Thirdly, the auditor does not have to be able to read program logic or "block diagrams" in order to perform the audit—although a limited background knowledge of how computers work and what they can do is an advantage. This last premise, perhaps the most contentious one, will be further examined on the following pages.

Flow Charting for Computer Systems. In computer systems, unlike manual or even punched-card systems, a considerable amount of processing, analyzing, comparing, decision making, and checking takes place *within the computer.* Much of this internal processing, and the controls built into it, must be of concern to the auditor. In other words, the auditor must consider two systems: the *internal system* (which goes on inside the computer) and the *external system* (which goes on outside the computer). This necessarily leads to some modifications in flow-charting techniques when applied to EDP systems. The external system in part lends itself to the same type of flow charting described above. The internal system requires different treatment. EDP personnel customarily document the internal logic of a computer program by means of "block diagrams." Block diagrams, however, are too detailed for what the auditor needs to know, and so a different alternative for the auditor is required. An example of such a chart of the computer processing phase can be seen in Figure 7.

Because of the division of a computer system into internal systems (or EDP phases) and external systems (or manual phases), the whole system is often more difficult to visualize, and yet it is important that the system be seen as a whole. The auditor, as has been said, cannot split the computer out from the rest of the system for a special "computer audit." Rather he must follow the normal analytical audit plan and consider each section (such as sales-receivables-receipts) as a unit—even though it involves both manual and computer phases. For this reason a summary chart is usually helpful.

Conducting the Systems Audit. The normal analytical systems audit can be performed by tracing a few transactions (1) from their source through the input phase, (2) from last visible input to first visible output, and finally, (3) through the output phase. The complete trail must be checked, including additions and calculations. (Sometimes, provided there is adequate control against the possibility of fraud, the accuracy of addition can be checked faster by a test deck designed specifically for that purpose.) Again, the systems audit can be recorded in the usual way, using file numbers and arrows. It is usually best to record the entire audit on one systems audit working paper instead of on each flow chart. Because, unlike a manual system, a complete transaction does not appear on one flow chart, a piecemeal systems audit recorded on each flow chart individually is difficult to follow. Recording the

Figure 7 COMPUTER PROCESSING CHART

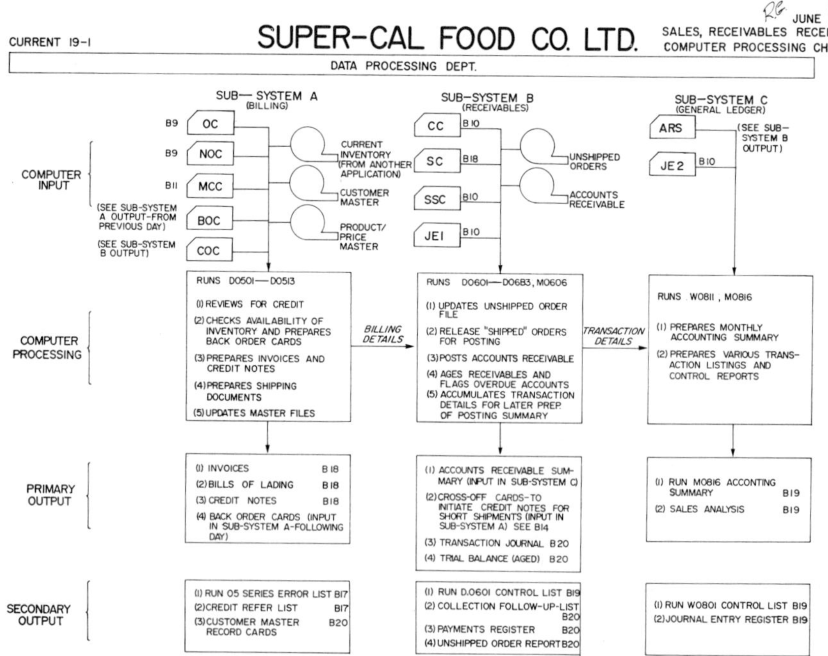

whole systems audit on one schedule enables the auditor to determine more easily whether or not the complete system has been tested.

In performing the systems audit, the computer processing phase normally presents no difficulty because the computer is only calculating, posting, or accumulating, and these operations can easily be performed manually on the data selected for the flow audit. However, when the computer is performing calculations such as invoice pricing, the systems audit must be extended to encompass all factors affecting the calculation. For instance, if the pricing varies with color, size, quantity, customer category, and sales district, all these factors must be tested and proved to be influencing the pricing as purported.

Occasionally audit-trail problems may develop, although this does not occur as frequently as has sometimes been suggested. When these difficulties do occur, special printouts or tape dumps can usually be arranged to bridge the gap. The details of such procedures, however, are beyond the scope of this chapter.

Other Effects of the Computer. The presence of a computer may have other effects on the auditor's work as well. It may affect the direction of audit steps he performs at the year end. It may well offer scope for audit use of the computer itself—such as in making random selection of accounts receivable for confirmation. The auditor must naturally be alert to these possibilities. The purpose of this section, however, has been to point out that the same analytical auditing approach can, with certain modifications, be employed just as efficiently for computer systems as for manual systems. Because of the limited space permitted in a handbook a complete description of the application of analytical auditing techniques to a computer environment is not possible; such a description can be found in *Analytical Auditing*, pages 121 to 147.

CONCLUSION

The basic design of the analytical audit was illustrated in Figure 2, and the general theory of analytical auditing was explained. The discussion has reviewed in considerable detail the techniques of flow charting and the various steps comprising the systems audit and follow-up audit for both manual and automatic data processing systems. A summary of the whole approach can be seen in the suggested analytical audit report forms (Figures 8*a* and 8*b*). Does this description of the analytical audit approach conform to generally accepted auditing standards?

Conformity to Generally Accepted Auditing Standards. There can be little dispute about the necessity of the auditor's assessment of internal control as an integral part of the audit work. The importance of such assessment has been well accepted throughout the auditing profession for a great many years. Among the generally accepted auditing standards is the AICPA second standard of fieldwork quoted on page 49-2.

Auditing Standards and Procedures (AICPA Committee on Auditing Procedure) also states, page 33:

> Where feasible, the independent auditor's review of internal control may be conducted as a separate phase of the examination, preferably at an interim date, by applying appropriate auditing procedures directed particularly to appraising the effectiveness of the client's system. Where this is not feasible, the review will usually be made in conjunction with other phases of the audit program. A record of the independent auditor's review should be prepared in some suitable form.

Figure 8a ANALYTICAL AUDIT REPORT (SYSTEMS AUDIT)

ANALYTICAL AUDIT REPORT
DESCRIPTION

SECTION I (to be completed at conclusion of systems audit) INITIAL

I have prepared or up-dated a description of the client's business as a preliminary step to my systems review.

I have prepared or up-dated a brief organization chart of the client's personnel.

I have reviewed the systems with the employees involved, traced a few transactions over all paths of each system, and prepared or revised our flow charts to document the systems and my systems audit.

I have considered the system of internal control in the light of the flow charts, my systems audit, the lead sheet reminder questions and our previous recommendations to the client. I have described all apparent weaknesses, errors discovered and inefficiencies on our outline charts and have completed the evaluation sections on the lead sheets.

I have entered the volume statistics for the current year on the volume summary.

I have scrutinized such books of account as practical for the year to ________

I have reviewed the fidelity insurance, fire insurance, and other insurance carried by the client and have completed the fidelity bond and insurance coverage questionnaires. Other possible coverage for consideration might be:

I have reviewed the reports and procedures of the internal audit department (where one exists) and have taken these into account in my assessment of the internal control.

I have taken all apparent weaknesses described on the outline charts, summarized them on the weakness follow-up sheet, and drafted a proposed weakness investigation and/or revised audit program needed to compensate for these weaknesses (taking into account any reports and procedures of the internal audit department).

I have also proposed four supplementary tests (different from last year's selection) in those areas where the control appeared adequate, to serve as a test confirmation of my assessment of the controls.

I have prepared a draft memorandum of recommendations covering the apparent weaknesses and inefficiencies summarized on the outline charts. During the audit I reported to the manager any major recommendations which should be attended to immediately. Copies of relevant memoranda from previous years are also included in the file and I have indicated thereon the disposition of each of these previous recommendations.

I have reported orally to the client any important errors I discovered and also any minor inefficiencies or system weaknesses which I thought the client might wish to attend to immediately. All significant oral suggestions have also been incorporated in my draft memorandum of recommendations.

I have completed the pertinent sections of the income and sales tax questionnaire and filed it behind my draft memorandum. Any tax recommendations arising out of this review have also been incorporated in my draft memorandum.

I have completed a time summary for the audit to date, including a suggested budget (by individual flow chart) for next year.

I have listed any uncleared notes on ________

The following significant changes have occurred in:

(i) the client's operations

(ii) the client's systems

In my review I noted the following inconsistencies in application of accounting principles:

In my review I noted the following items you would be interested in:

Date.............................. ....
Senior in charge

File reviewed
Draft memorandum of recommendations reviewed
Proposed weakness investigation approved
Proposed supplementary tests approved

Date.............................. ....
Manager

Figure 8b ANALYTICAL AUDIT REPORT (FOLLOW-UP AUDIT)

DESCRIPTION

SECTION II (to be completed at conclusion of follow-up audit) INITIAL

I have further scrutinized such books of account as practical from ______ to ______

I have considered the consistency of statistical and financial data and followed up any apparent discrepancies to my own satisfaction as indicated, except:

I have carried out the weakness investigation (including additional work necessary to cover any unresolved statistical discrepancies). The results and my conclusions are outlined on ______________ I have made a note at the front of last year's balance sheet file of any revised audit program steps indicated on the weakness follow-up sheet.

I have also enquired from officials of the company whether changes in personnel or systems have occurred that would affect the internal control, and where any new weaknesses were apparent have considered these in the weakness investigation.

I have carried out the four supplementary tests in those areas where the control appeared adequate. The results and my conclusions (including reconsideration of my previous control evaluation if any errors were encountered) are outlined on ______

I have discussed the comments and suggestions made in our draft memorandum with company employees who might be affected thereby, (using reasonable discretion), and their reaction and my resulting suggestions for modification are noted on the draft.

I have completed the time summary and the suggested budget for next year.

I have listed any uncleared notes on ______

I have reviewed all audit files on branch operations and have taken these into account where necessary in the weakness investigation and in the memorandum of recommendations.

During my follow-up audit I noted the following additional items you would be interested in:

Date.............................. ....
Senior in charge

Weakness investigation reviewed
Supplementary tests reviewed
Memorandum of recommendations issued and copy filed herein.

Date.............................. ....
Manager

The approach to analytical auditing which has been outlined in this chapter can be seen to conform with the above statements for the following reasons:

1. A review of the system is carried out at the very beginning of the analytical audit. This review is recorded on the flow charts. Thus there is a proper study of control, and it is documented.

2. A check or walkthrough audit is made immediately following to prove that the charted system is really in operation—i.e., to appraise the effectiveness of the client's system. This systems audit is recorded on the flow charts as well.

3. The flow charts assist in the actual evaluation of the existing internal control by making weaknesses easy to spot.

4. Subsequent investigation is directed specifically at the weaknesses in control discovered during the systems audit. Thus there can be no question but that the review of control is defining the scope of the audit, as it should. Provision is also made for the results of weakness investigation to cause modifications in the audit steps where appropriate.

5. The initial extents of tests in the systems audit are very restricted, but this is consistent with intelligent allocation of audit effort. Strong areas are subjected to the limited systems audit tests every year together with more

extended "supplementary procedural tests" on a cyclical basis every few years to confirm the auditor's judgment on control. Weak areas are subjected to a careful weakness investigation every year to establish that no material errors have occurred because of the weakness. In other words, the study and evaluation of internal control has been used to maximum advantage in determining "the resultant extent of tests to which auditing procedures are to be restricted."

Analytical auditing and the flow-charting approach involve, then, no change in principles but merely a new mechanism for serving these accepted principles in the most efficient manner.

When Analytical Auditing Can Be Used. The analytical audit approach can apply to all but the very small audit engagement. Where there is a formal system of office procedures and internal control, an efficient audit must place reliance on the controls in force, and this, in turn, implies some interim or analytical audit to evaluate their reliability. The larger and more complex the system the more such reliance becomes essential. The very size of the system usually produces a more impregnable system of control, while the complexity of the system leads to a greater waste of audit time if the accounting reliability is ignored.

In analytical auditing the auditor is placing reliance on *structural* control: that is, the design of the system, the division of duties, the accounting controls, etc. There may, of course, be a number of weaknesses in the system, but if so, these would be investigated as a regular part of the analytical audit —as was discussed. Provided the basic framework of a control system is there, in other words, the auditor should be able to place sufficient reliance on it that he need not examine all transactions for the year. Where this is so, the analytical audit approach can provide a more thorough and, in the long run, a more efficient way of assessing the control than vouching one or two month's transactions in detail. This situation is likely to be found in all large and medium-sized audits and in some small audits.

Advantages of Analytical Auditing. Throughout this chapter analytical auditing has been described as a systems-oriented approach to auditing, and most of the advantages of such an approach have been stated or implied in the course of explaining how the technique is used. It may be useful, however, to conclude with a brief summary. The advantages inherent in a systems-oriented approach are:

1. A better understanding of the client's business and accounting system
2. A more comprehensive appreciation of the system of internal control
3. Avoidance of the risk of perfunctory and unimaginative treatment that long procedural questionnaires and audit lists may invite
4. Many more valuable and more realistic recommendations to clients both on internal control and on systems efficiency
5. Greater use of initiative on the part of audit staff in the field
6. A more rational allocation of audit time over those areas of the accounts requiring attention
7. Less chance of going through the formal motions of checking without understanding
8. Increased client goodwill both because of the greater productivity of audit time and because of the better briefing of new audit staff

Of course, these advantages are not achieved without some time and effort. Clearly, a greater amount of staff training is required when this technique is employed. Moreover, there is a greater need to ensure that *all* steps in the audit program have been properly carried out. It can be seen in Figure 2 that the drawing of the flow charts themselves, while the key to the audit, is just the beginning of it. The charting can be thought of as the one-eighth of an iceberg that is visible above the surface. It is the other seven-eighths that really matters: the analysis of control once the system has been charted, the investigation of weaknesses once they have been analyzed. Without these latter steps the flow charting itself is completely useless. The charts are only a means to an end and not the end itself. Like any sophisticated technique, analytical auditing is dangerous if misused. Properly applied, however, in the hands of intelligent audit staff adequately trained, such dangers can be avoided and the many advantages realized. The technique then serves as an extremely efficient approach to the audit and a much more stimulating one for the audit staff employing it. The latter point can be of some considerable significance as the profession continues to seek increasing numbers and higher qualifications among students entering its ranks.

The flow-charting approach, in short, offers both greater challenges and greater potential benefits. It is hoped that the practitioner will find, as many have already, that analytical auditing can be applied successfully in practice and that the advantages to be obtained more than repay the effort required to master the technique.

BIBLIOGRAPHY

AICPA: "A Graphic Illustration of Internal Control, in *Internal Control—Elements of Coordinated System and Its Importance to Management and the Independent Public Accountant,* AICPA, New York, 1949.

Statements on Auditing Procedure No. 33, *Auditing Standards and Procedures,* AICPA, New York, 1963.

Anderson, R. J.: "An Approach to Auditing Income Accounts," in *Annual Conference Papers,* The Canadian Institute of Chartered Accountants, Toronto, 1964.

Brink, Victor Z., and James A. Cashin: *Internal Auditing,* New York, The Ronald Press Company, 1958.

Cadmus, Bradford: *Operational Auditing Handbook,* New York, The Institute of Internal Auditors, 1964.

Chippendale, Warren, and Norman P. LeBlanc: "Progressive Audit Philosophy—The Practical Application," in *Annual Conference Papers,* The Canadian Institute of Chartered Accountants, Toronto 1963.

Skinner, R. H., and R. J. Anderson: *Analytical Auditing, An Outline of the Flow Chart Approach to Audits,* New York, Pitman Publishing Corporation, 1966.

Stettler, Howard F.: *Systems Based Independent Audits,* Englewood Cliffs, N.J., Prentice-Hall, Inc., 1967.

Anderson, R. J.: "Analytical Auditing," *The Canadian Chartered Accountant,* November, 1963.

Turley, Vernon: "Flow Charting—A Modern Technique in Auditing," *The Canadian Chartered Accountant,* May, 1964.

Twede, F. L.: "Decision Tables: A Useful Technique for Documenting Internal Audit Control Systems," *Arthur Young Journal,* January, 1965.

Mitchell, George: "Flow Charting—What It Is and How You Can Use It Effectively," *Office Equipment and Methods,* March and April, 1965.

Blaney, A. L. J., and J. C. Lemminn: "Flow Charting—An Audit Tool," *The Internal Auditor,* Winter, 1965.

Schneider, A. J.: "Flow-Graph Notation in Accounting," *Accounting Review,* April, 1967.

Kirchheimer, H. N.: "Flow Charting: The Modern Method of Evaluating Internal Control and Procedures," *The Internal Auditor,* Fall, 1967.

Chapter 50

Management Performance Auditing

ELLSWORTH H. MORSE, JR.

Director, Office of Policy and Special Studies, U.S. General Accounting Office

GENERAL CONCEPT

Nature of Management Auditing. Auditing of management performance or management auditing is usually regarded as an extension of the more traditional financial auditing which encompasses audits of financial accounts, transactions, and reports including related internal control procedures. The boundaries between these two broad categories of auditing are not sharply definable, since comprehensive financial auditing requires the auditor to concern himself with many aspects of management performance and control. In fact, it is often contended that inasmuch as all activities and operations of an organization have financial aspects, the term financial auditing itself can properly embrace all that is contemplated by those who adopt the term "management auditing." The term "operational auditing" is also often used to characterize auditing that extends beyond the conventional financial and accounting areas of auditing.

Expansion of Concept. This chapter describes some of the concepts and practices that have evolved in auditing procedures which have extended beyond the customary scope of audits of financial transactions, accounts, and related reports.

Experience in such extended procedures has been gained by internal audit organizations, both in private enterprises and in government agencies; in some aspects of public accounting practice; and in the U.S. General Accounting Office in its audits of the affairs of federal agencies.

INTERNAL AUDITING

The Institute of Internal Auditors defines the responsibilities of the internal auditor broadly and in a manner which embraces the auditing of management performance.

> Internal auditing is an independent appraisal activity within an organization for the review of accounting, financial and other operations as a basis for service to management. It is a managerial control, which functions by measuring and evaluating the effectiveness of other controls.[1]

The statement describes the overall objective of internal auditing as assistance to all members of management, thus requiring the internal auditor to concern himself with any phase of business activity wherein he can be of service to management. Appraisal of the quality of performance in carrying out assigned responsibilities is suggested as one of the specific areas with which the internal auditor's scope of auditing should be concerned.

Private Industry Practices. Actual practices of internal auditors in private enterprise in extending the scope of their work vary widely. A survey[2] of 177 companies in connection with a National Industrial Conference Board study in 1963 summarized the following as the principal objectives of the auditing programs of the companies studied:

Determine the adequacy of the system of internal control.

Investigate compliance with company policies and procedures.

Verify the existence of assets, see that proper safeguards for assets are maintained, and prevent or discover fraud.

Check on the reliability of the accounting and reporting system.

Report findings to management and recommend corrective action where necessary.

[1] Statement of Responsibilities of the Internal Auditor, p. 1.

[2] Francis J. Walsh, Jr., *Internal Auditing*, Business Policy Study No. 111, New York, National Industrial Conference Board, Inc., 1963.

The same study notes that, where internal auditing is not confined to financial and accounting matters, the procurement function is regarded as an especially important area for the application of operational auditing techniques. Review of staffing of operations that are examined and observations on competence and general level of performance of personnel are also often included in the scope of the internal auditor's work.[3]

Internal Auditing in Federal Agencies. The statement of basic principles and concepts of internal auditing for federal agencies, issued by the Comptroller General of the United States, also sets forth a broad scope of auditing which takes the internal auditor into the realm of management performance.[4]

> Internal auditing should extend to all agency activities and related management controls. Although it should include the audit of accounts and financial transactions, its scope of operation should not be restricted to accounting and financial matters. The internal auditor should also review operations and activities in order that he may provide management with information on the effectiveness, efficiency, and economy with which they are being carried out. . . .
>
> The scope of internal auditing should include the following general types of work and areas of inquiry.
>
> *Appraising Performance*
>
> A necessary function of management is to establish and prescribe policies, plans, and procedures for carrying out programs and activities in pursuit of the objectives of the organization and to establish organizational or management systems for review of operations.
>
> The internal audit function can provide a highly valuable service to management by reviewing, appraising, and reporting on the extent and nature of internal compliance with management's policies, plans, and procedures as well as with applicable legal and external regulatory requirements.
>
> The internal auditor's work should include the review of the operation of the whole system of management controls over operations and resources to ascertain whether they are functioning in accordance with their design and are functioning effectively. . . .
>
> In making such examinations, the internal auditor should be alert to possibilities for improving operations and identifying opportunities for bringing about greater efficiency and economy.
>
> As a result of his familiarity with management plans and policies, intra-agency relationships, and procedures and with the manner in which they are working out, the internal auditor should also report observations as to their adequacy and effectiveness in relation to top management objectives together with such recommendations for improvement he considers appropriate.
>
> *Evaluating Efficiency and Economy*
>
> The internal auditor should be concerned at all times with minimizing unnecessary or wasteful practices in the use of the agency's resources. He should be watchful for and report on such possibilities as:
>
> Procedures, whether officially prescribed or merely followed, which are ineffective or found to be more costly than justified.
>
> Duplication of effort by employees or between organizational units, which, if eliminated, could increase overall efficiency.
>
> Performance of work which serves little or no useful purpose.
>
> Inefficient or uneconomic use of automatic data processing equipment.
>
> Overstaffing in relation to work to be done.
>
> Faulty buying practices.

[3] *Ibid.*, pp. 49–50.

[4] *Internal Auditing in Federal Agencies,* a statement of basic concepts and principles, published in pamphlet form by the U.S. General Accounting Office in 1968. Also included in Title 3 of the GAO Policy and Procedures Manual for Guidance of Federal Agencies.

Procurement and accumulation of unneeded or excess quantities of property, materials, or supplies.

Wasteful use of property.

SCOPE

The scope of management auditing can be as broad as the management process itself. At the present state of the art, there is no particular agreement in either concept or practice on how far the auditor may or should go.

Internal auditors are bound by the management concepts and attitudes within the organization they serve. Even though their charter may be unlimited, there are practical constraints on their competence to examine into everything. These constraints are particularly applicable in the scientific and technical phases of management and operations. They may also be applicable to the level of management performance within an organization, since the internal auditor's scope of operation is one to be set by the top management itself and not one of functional right. Top management may prefer to have the internal auditor concern himself with other phases of operation than top management performance.

One writer[5] has proposed a concept of management auditing as "an informed and constructive analysis, evaluation, and series of recommendations regarding the broad spectrum of plans, processes, people and problems of an economic entity." He then suggests the following approach, which sets the scope of inquiry to be pursued in a management audit.

Approach

1. *Studying the Prescribed Organization*—reviewing formal organization structure, personal interrelationships, policies, procedures, information systems and flows, and decision centers in order to determine what management has established as optimum arrangements for running an entity.
2. *Evaluating the "Live Entity"*—determining such problems as what operating people are really trying to accomplish, the schedules and routines they have established to attain objectives, and a measure of the results achieved in the light of predetermined goals and standards of performance.
3. *Searching for Profit Inhibitors*—uncovering poor organizational structuring and responsibility assignment; breakdowns in operations, programing and work flow; inadequate or ineffective communications, evaluations and measurements; and disclosing results that fall significantly below established standards.

Functions. The writer then suggests how the management auditor might be helpful to management in a number of broad functional areas of primary concern to top management.

Policies—The auditor might be useful in synthesizing accounting, economic, and other data needed by management in constructing its basic policy framework.

Plans—The auditor can assist in establishing and reviewing the planning system. He can help establish an orderly planning system, assist in allocating responsibility for planning, review progress of the planning, and evaluate its effectiveness.

Decision-making—The auditor can help management in goal-setting and strategy, including reviewing the decision-making machinery and ascertaining whether top management is given adequate information for correct decisions.

Authority Structure—The auditor can aid in the design and maintenance of an adequate position and authority structure, including rendering assistance in strengthening and expediting the flow of information between responsibility centers.

[5] William L. Campfield, "Trends in Auditing Management Plans and Operations," *The Journal of Accountancy*, July, 1967, pp. 41–46.

Communications—The auditor can help improve the entire communications system.

Results Measurement—The auditor can help management pinpoint key functions or operations in the profit-making process and establish better criteria for measuring results.

With respect to the last-named function, the writer outlines the following broad areas in which the auditor might work:

1. Furnish guidance in the development of format and related instructions pertaining to revenue and expense budgets for each responsibility center.
2. Review or give guidance in the preparation of complete statements of the performance standards and yardsticks for measurement applicable to each major decision or performance area. The auditor should carefully reexamine each set of statements to make sure that they are consistent with policies, plans, procedures and standards established at higher levels of responsibility; e.g., assure that they are compatible with and properly support the company-wide profit budget.
3. Critically examine and refine the units of measurement commonly applied in each major performance or decision area. In this regard, the auditor should help management in pinning down and interrelating the performance standards and measurements with the operating responsibilities of each person affected.[6]

It should be noted that where an auditor is involved in these broad functional areas, his objective is to help the management improve its system and to do a better managing job. His approach is initially one of evaluation of what is being done and the quality of performance. On the basis of such evaluation, he is in position to make constructive recommendations in these broad areas which, if adopted, should contribute to a more effective system and better performance in the organization.

The audit function is primarily one of evaluation. An auditor's involvement in providing assistance in any area should not result in his diversion from his primary role of the independent analyst, appraiser, or evaluator. His constructive assistance comes from his evaluative work and the translation of his observations and findings into recommendations for constructive improvement.

Another observer[7] defines the management control review as a management audit with emphasis on identification of problem areas. The purpose of such auditing is described as identifying "the management practices or policies requiring improvement and further organized detailed study." Solving problems identified is not considered a part of the process. This comes later, to be performed by the management, the company's audit staff, the management services department of the public accounting firm, outside consultants, or some combination of these.

The writer suggests that the basis of the auditor's extended investigation should be a questionnaire which is used as an interview tool in obtaining information on management controls. Major management areas to be reviewed are general information about the organization, its objectives and policies; organization and personnel; financial management; marketing; and systems and procedures.

Another writer, commenting on the probable evolution of auditing of corporate management performance, suggests the need to construct a framework for the management audit.

In developing such a framework, four areas must be examined. First, the criteria for a management audit must be considered. Second, standards of managerial perform-

[6] *Ibid.*, p. 45.

[7] Arthur E. Witte, "Management Auditing: The Present State of the Art," *The Journal of Accountancy,* August, 1967, pp. 54–58.

ance must be developed if the evaluation of management stewardship is to have meaning. Third, a method of reporting must be established so that the auditor can have a structured means of disclosing the results of his examination. Finally, it will be necessary to develop management auditing procedures and standards of documentation to support the report given.[8]

In analyzing the need to develop management auditing procedures, this writer notes that the review of management controls becomes considerably more important than in an audit of financial statements. In a financial audit, the auditor is more concerned with satisfying himself about the reliability of the financial information system than about whether the system produces appropriate information for management use. In a management audit, however, the auditor

will look to see whether management is getting information relevant to the decisions and actions which it must take. This will require a much more intensive analysis of information needs and the efficiency of the existing system in meeting them. In the marketing and production areas particularly it is likely that the auditor will have to develop increased familiarity with the information needed to make decisions, including that which is not part of the conventional books of account. The auditor will not have to decide whether management is making the *right* strategic and operative decisions but rather whether management has available to it and is using the relevant information and techniques necessary to evaluate rationally the various alternatives that exist.[9]

The author's suggestion that the auditor's concern should be with the availability of relevant information to the management for decision-making purposes but need not be with the correctness of management decisions themselves is one of the highly debatable points in the field of management auditing.

The writer in this case also notes that in a management audit the auditor will be required to make a financial analysis of the company for comparison with appropriate financial standards of performance.

In this connection, the auditor must consider the operating results of the various parts of the firm. He must select that data which are most significant in the evaluation of corporate performance and array them in an understandable fashion so that the investor and the outside analyst can use such data for their purposes. In this connection, data will have to be accumulated about the company and its environment from the accounting and other records of the firm and from outside industry and government sources.[10]

PERFORMANCE STANDARDS

One of the most difficult aspects of auditing management performance is the identification of criteria or standards against which performance may be judged by an outside reviewer. A very useful discussion of this subject will be found in Knighton's book, *The Performance Post Audit in State Government.*

Categories of Standards. This writer cites two categories of standards.

Two kinds of standards are particularly relevant: standards of effectiveness and standards of efficiency. Standards of effectiveness are those which permit judgment concerning the achievement of objectives, whereas standards of efficiency relate to the manner in which men and resources are used to pursue objectives. In the first case,

[8] John C. Burton, "Management Auditing," *The Journal of Accountancy*, May, 1968, p. 41.
[9] *Ibid.*, p. 44.
[10] *Ibid.*, p. 44.

the relevant statistics concern program output; in the latter the relevant statistics concern program composition. In both cases, the specification of standards is an integral part of the planning process and should be specified at the time objectives are chosen and programs are designed.[11]

In discussing performance auditing specifically, Knighton emphasizes the auditor's responsibility with respect to inquiring into performance standards established by management and evaluating them. He states:

First, the auditor must determine if standards have been set in the agency. If so, he must evaluate them to determine if they are relevant, sufficient, and reliable. That is, the auditor must do more than identify the standards; he must evaluate them. He must next determine the extent to which they are used by internal management. Unless they are used, the most carefully prepared standards in the world are ineffective as control devices. Finally, the auditor must determine how effective the standards have been when used. Again he is testing the effectiveness of administrative performance in an important area.

Performance standards, while designed primarily as control devices for internal management, can also be used in many cases to evaluate performance after the fact. Indeed, without some type of standard or performance indicator, it is impossible to render qualitative opinions on performance. Thus the auditor must not only determine whether performance standards are effective for internal management, but also whether they are useful for his post-performance review.[12]

Specific Criteria. Another analyst, in a case study on audit recommendations and management auditing made for the Department of the Navy, states that specific criteria for use by the auditor are necessary if the auditor is to avoid, "20-20 hindsight auditing."

In order to avoid the practice of second guessing management . . . the auditor must rely on criteria that are sufficiently well specified so that he can evaluate the procedures management has taken rather than the results produced. . . . Consider the possible effects that might result from preoccupation with results. Continued harping on errors committed, on decisions which events proved wrong, will not only make management cautious but lead to non-innovative behavior which can be ineffective if not downright dangerous in the long run.[13]

Decision Process. The author in this case then suggests that a management audit should be more concerned with the practices followed in making decisions than with the decisions themselves.

What seems to be a more appropriate concern of a management audit is how the decisions were made rather than how a particular decision turned out. It is perhaps more important to find out if good managerial practices were followed, if scientific decision-making techniques were utilized to the extent possible, if the relevant information was available and utilized, if proper controls were established to implement the decision, and if feedback was provided than to determine whether or not the particular decision was correct. (Except as this would provide information for improving the decision-making process.) The focus would be on the process, not the result.

Even if the results were right, if all the decisions turned out correctly, but the methodology flew in the face of all known managerial principles, the audit report would be of great value. . . .[14]

[11] Lennis M. Knighton, *The Performance Post Audit in State Government,* MSU Business Studies, Bureau of Business and Economic Research, Division of Research, Graduate School of Business Administration, Michigan State University, 1967, p. 84. Reprinted by permission of the publisher.

[12] *Ibid.,* pp. 112–113.

[13] Neil C. Churchill, *Audit Recommendations and Management Auditing: A Case Study and Remarks,* Management Sciences Research Report No. 85, Graduate School of Industrial Administration, Carnegie Institute of Technology, October, 1966, p. 33. This study was made with reference to the Naval Audit Service, Department of the Navy.

[14] *Ibid.,* pp. 33–34.

Not all practitioners or students of the audit function will agree that the primary concern of the management auditor should be with processes and not with the substance or results of those processes. The term "performance" itself contemplates concern not only with "input" (what is done) but with "output" (what resulted).

The differing viewpoints that can be cited as to the proper scope of management auditing illustrate that this function is still evolving, and much actual exploratory and development work remains to be done before its true role in management control systems can be adequately defined. The extent of internal management auditing as contrasted with audits of management performance by external auditors represent two aspects of the problem which can be expected to receive increased attention in the future.

MANAGEMENT AUDITING BY EXTERNAL AUDITORS

Enlarging Scope of Audit. Officials of the American Institute of Certified Public Accountants (AICPA) have raised the question from time to time as to whether the scope of auditing by independent public accountants should not be enlarged to embrace evaluations of management performance. John L. Carey, Executive Director of the Institute, wrote in 1965 that "No one is in a better position than CPAs to advise and assist management in developing objective, quantitative standards for measurement of management performance in accordance with whatever goals and policies may be established." [15] He concluded that CPAs may eventually be called upon to audit management performance.

Evaluation of Total Process. A former president of the AICPA [16] has suggested that the traditional attest function of the public accountant may be dissociated from the financial processes as such and "may well be applied to the total management process."

AUDITING PROCEDURES

Audit procedures should be tailored to the specific needs of each situation examined. The general approach in a management audit may be outlined as follows:

1. A preliminary survey of the activity being examined should be made to obtain necessary background and other working information for use in making the audit.
2. The basic charter or assignment of responsibility for the activity being examined (applicable laws and related legislative history in the case of a government activity) should be studied to ascertain the authorized purposes and related authorities of the acitivity and any applicable restrictions or limitations.
3. Pertinent parts of the system of management control should be reviewed by studying the policies established to govern the activities under examination, testing the effectiveness of specific operating and administrative procedures and practices followed, and fully exploring all significant weaknesses encountered.
4. Reports on results of the audit work performed should then be prepared

[15] John L. Carey, *The CPA Plans for the Future,* New York, AICPA, 1965, pp. 211–213.
[16] Robert M. Trueblood, "Communication and Cooperation," *The CPA,* October, 1966, p. 3.

and submitted to those responsible for receiving or acting on the auditor's findings and recommendations.

Identification of Problem Areas. Some of the techniques by which the auditor can identify problem areas warranting more penetrating examination are as follows:

Identification of possible control weakness by survey. During the preliminary survey work through which practical working information is obtained on how the activity is supposed to function and on how control procedures are supposed to work, key features or aspects can usually be identified which appear to be difficult to control effectively or to be susceptible to abuse.

In a purchasing organization, for example, the key points in the purchasing process may well be (1) the determinations made of the quantities and the quality of materials to be purchased, (2) the procedures followed in obtaining the best prices, and (3) the methods for determining whether the correct quantities and quality are actually received.

If, in relation to the total purchasing operation, the auditor concludes that these processes are the most critical from the standpoint of the need for good performance, he would be justified in concentrating his testing work on them.

Review of management reports. The auditor's review of internal reports which the management itself regularly uses to obtain information on progress, status, or accomplishment of work can be valuable sources of information on possible problem areas suggesting audit attention.

Review of internal audit or inspection reports. These reports can also be a valuable source of information on problem areas. Of particular interest to the management auditor are those reports which bring to light significant findings on which the management has taken no action. Inquiry into the reasons and justification for inaction in such cases and an evaluation by the management auditor should be made, since these circumstances could throw light on weaknesses in the management system that have not previously been referred to the top management for resolution.

Physical inspections. Physical inspections of the organization's activities and resources can be a useful way of identifying possible inefficiencies that should be given audit attention. Examples are apparently excess accumulations of equipment or material, idle or little used equipment, employee idleness, rejections of product by inspectors (or customers), extensive rework operations, or disposal of apparently useful materials or equipment.

Test examination of transactions. A very useful way to obtain a practical working insight into the efficacy of procedures is to pursue a number of transactions pertaining to the organization's operations completely from initiation to final disposition. This kind of testing will provide the auditor with valuable information on the way the organization's business is actually transacted, on the usefulness (or pertinence) of prescribed procedures, on the capabilities of personnel involved in the various operating phases, and on possible weaknesses in procedures or practices which could represent an unnecessary drain on the organization's resources (i.e., ineffective or inefficient performance).

Discussions with officials and employees. The management auditor can obtain valuable information on problem areas warranting audit attention through discussions with responsible officials in the organization and other employees concerned with the operations being examined. The degree of success in obtaining useful information in this way is in large part dependent on the auditor's reputation for independent and constructive inquiry. If he is regarded with fear because of overly critical reporting in the past, this source of information may not be productive.

Testing Procedures and Practices. Testing procedures and practices first requires some preliminary review work to obtain information on how they actually work and an insight into their effectiveness and usefulness. On the basis of such review, specific matters may be identified as problem areas or weaknesses needing further probing.

The general factors to be considered by the auditor in his preliminary review work on management controls are:

Whether the policies of the organization comply with its basic charter or grant of authority

Whether the system of procedures and management controls is designed to carry out those policies and result in activities being conducted as desired by the top management, and in an efficient and economical manner

Whether the system of management controls provides adequate control over the organization's resources, revenues, costs, and expenditures

Specific factors which may well be considered by the auditor in assessing the management control system and identifying problem areas warranting more detailed audit include:

The use by management of standards or goals in judging accomplishment, productivity, efficiency, or use of goods or services

Lack of clarity in written procedures, resulting in misunderstandings or inconsistent interpretations in the organization

Capabilities of personnel

Failures to accept responsibility

Duplication of effort

Improper or imprudent use of funds

Cumbersome or extravagant organizational patterns

Ineffective or wasteful use of employees and physical resources

Work backlogs

This listing is indicative of the kinds of factors that an alert management auditor must keep in mind in all his work. The knowledge gained in preliminary review that is conducted in recognition of these kinds of factors provides a solid basis for more detailed examination work that can lead to constructive improvements in the management system.

Development of Audit Findings. If, during the auditor's preliminary review, apparently adverse conditions or results of practices or procedures are observed, further examination will usually be warranted. Specific cases, transactions, or other units of operation should then be examined in depth to the extent deemed necessary to reach valid conclusions, to report fairly on results, and to support satisfactorily any recommendations made.

Developing specific findings is the core of this type of audit. Essentially, this process involves obtaining as much pertinent, significant information about each finding as is practicable and evaluating it in terms of cause, effect, and possible courses of corrective action.

After a specific problem area is identified for more detailed examination, a program should be developed by the auditor, for use in making a thorough, systematic examination into the matter. In the development of his specific findings and conclusions, the auditor will need to:

Identify specifically what the problem is, i.e., what is deficient, defective, in error, etc.

Determine whether the condition is isolated or widespread

Determine the significance of the deficiency in terms of cost, adverse performance, or other pertinent effects

Ascertain the cause or causes for the condition

Identifying persons in the organization responsible for the deficiency

Determine possible lines of corrective or preventive action as a basis for constructive recommendations

Wherever practicable, the auditor should review his work and his findings with management officials responsible for the area being examined so that he can obtain as much information as possible bearing on the problem and consider their views of the findings. He can then formulate his conclusions and recommendations for the audit report.

Standards for Judging Performance. The general standards which may be used in judging most kinds of management performance are effectiveness, efficiency, and economy. Particularly in government organizations, these are applicable because, except as tempered by special requirements imposed by law or pursuant to law that contribute to a contrary effect, the conduct of the public's business effectively, efficiently, and economically is an implicit responsibility of those charged with its management.

In reviewing pertinent parts of the management control system, the auditor should first ascertain how management officials themselves determine whether prescribed policies are being followed, whether authorized and prescribed procedures are effective, and whether they are being applied in an efficient and economical manner.

In addition, if the management has developed, as part of its control system, techniques for measuring or evaluating performance against internally predetermined objectives or criteria, the auditor should use such standards as a starting point in reviewing performance. However, the auditor must be satisfied as to the basis on which such standards are established and their validity as a basis for judgment.

If specific measures of internal performance are not available, the auditor has a much more difficult job of appraisal. He must then develop his own methods of examination and evaluation, utilizing all available pertinent facts and factors, in arriving at supportable opinions, conclusions, and recommendations.

Over and above the broad standards of effectiveness, efficiency, and economy, in reviewing management performance the requirements of applicable laws have to be considered. For some types of procedures or practices, specific standards exist in the form of provisions of law or regulation by an authorized superior control agency, such as the Bureau of the Budget or the Civil Service Commission in the federal government. In other cases, only general provisions of law or general policies established pursuant to law, either by the operating agency or by a control agency, are available for management guidance. In either case, a basis for independent appraisal of performance in relation to such requirements is provided. However, where only general guidance is provided by law or related policy declaration, the independent review has to be more comprehensive and penetrating because of the greater degree of latitude granted to the management in its efforts to accomplish its objectives.

Often, under these circumstances, instead of trying to measure performance against precise standards, the auditor's job resolves itself into ascertaining whether any wasteful or uneconomical operations are performed. He will want to determine if a less costly or more effective alternative is practicable in such cases. Management auditing which is carried out with this objective can be a highly useful and constructive part of any management system.

Where the possibility of wasteful, unnecessary, or extravagant use of resources exists, several factors may have to be considered in arriving at independent judgments on the quality and effectiveness of performance. Some of these are very closely interrelated. For example:

Prudence in the use of resources
Cost consciousness in using the organization's funds
Effective coordination of work or procedures
Good planning
Efficient procedures
Competent and diligent employees
Effective supervision of performance
Arrangements for detecting incompetence or irregularity

Any one or a combination of factors such as these may be found in a problem area being probed. The auditor may find, for example, that funds are not being prudently managed because spending decisions are being made that result in acquiring goods and services that may not really be needed by the organization. Or, the procedures followed in determining whether materials and supplies are needed may be faulty and may produce inaccurate or otherwise unreliable information. This may lead to decisions to buy unnecessarily large quantities that cannot be effectively used except over a long period. In this case, storage and handling costs, as well as risks of obsolescence and deterioration, are unnecessarily incurred.

The auditor must consider all pertinent factors in appraising performance where there may be several criteria or other measures of adequacy of performance to be considered. Objective judgments under these circumstances are particularly difficult to make where some of the factors to be considered may have contradictory values. Fairness, objectivity, and realism also require that the auditor avoid making judgments and conclusions on performance based solely on hindsight.

If all significant factors are appropriately considered, reasonable recommendations can be offered by the auditor concerning the discharge of specific kinds of management responsibilities, which can be of value in promoting improvements in management performance. They can also be useful to third parties in connection with their evaluations of such performance.

GAO AUDITS OF MANAGEMENT PERFORMANCE

In recent years, the U.S. General Accounting Office, an independent agency in the legislative branch of the federal government, has obtained considerable experience in expanding the scope of its audits of federal agencies beyond the boundaries of conventional financial auditing. In the federal government the General Accounting Office is the independent external auditor of the individual departments and agencies, most of whom also have internal audit units as a part of their management control systems.

The Comptroller General of the United States, who heads the General Accounting Office, is appointed by the President for a term of 15 years and is subject to confirmation by the Senate. Once confirmed, he is accountable to Congress for the operations of the General Accounting Office, of which the making of audits and investigations is a large part.

Since its creation in 1921, the scope of audit and investigative responsibility has been quite broad. The law creating the Office, the Budget and Accounting Act, 1921, directed the Comptroller General, among other things, to investigate all matters relating to the receipt, disbursement, and application of public funds. Later legislation extended and clarified his audit authority, particularly with respect to government corporations, but the 1921 law laid the primary foundation for a broad scope of auditing that went beyond accounting, financial matters, and legal compliance.

Basic Audit Policies. The Comptroller General has established broad audit policies to achieve the objectives sought by the Congress. The primary purpose of these audits is to examine independently the manner in which federal agencies discharge their financial responsibilities. These responsibilities are broadly defined to include administration of funds and utilization of property and personnel only for authorized programs, activities, or purposes, and the conduct of such programs or activities in an effective, efficient, and economical manner. In examining federal agency affairs, particular emphasis is placed on any matters suspected or found to require correction or improvement and on the means of accomplishing it. This general policy emphasizes the point that these audits are performed for the Congress as a third party, that the auditors are completely independent of the agencies audited, and that the audit work embraces not only financial matters but also operating and other management areas. This policy recognizes the desirability of focusing primary attention on weaknesses in internal control or possibilities for improvement in agency management procedures or practices.

While efficient and economical operations of government agencies are to be commended, it is even more desirable to devote management attention (including congressional attention) to promoting better performance.

Reporting. A large number of audit reports are submitted by the Comptroller General to the Congress each year. These reports become public documents.[17]

An annual report of the Comptroller General on the work of the General Accounting Office is also required by law to be submitted to the Congress.[18]

Another type of summary report sent to the Congress by the Comptroller General each year is a compilation of audit findings and recommendations for improving federal government operations. These reports summarize a great variety of findings pertaining to the discharge of federal agency management responsibilities such as contract negotiation and administration; storage, inventory, and warehouse operations; determining requirements for supplies and services; property disposals; buildings management; leasing; motor vehicle and motor pool operations; equipment utilization; management of automatic data processing equipment; utilization of employees; internal auditing; and administration of loan and grant programs.

These annual reports also provide a convenient reference source of information on management improvement possibilities, not only in other government organizations but anywhere that management improvement is an important objective.

[17] Information on the availability of copies of these reports may be obtained from Publications Branch, Office of Administrative Services, U.S. General Accounting Office, 441 G Street, N.W., Washington, D.C. 20548.

[18] Printed by and available from the Superintendent of Documents, Government Printing Office, Washington, D.C. 20401.

Examples of Findings. Examples of findings relating to federal agency management performance that have been reported to the Congress follow. These illustrate some of the subject areas in which GAO auditors have conducted examinations, evaluated the quality or effectiveness of management performance, and produced constructive recommendations.

Building construction. During an examination into inspection controls over concrete placements at three federal building projects (costing about $76 million) in Washington, D.C., it was found that the inspection procedures followed did not ensure compliance with contract specifications as to water content of concrete delivered to one of the project sites. Discrepancies were also found at this site in the use of a concrete curing compound and in performance of concrete testing. These failings were considered significant, since weaknesses in inspection and deviation from specifications in a large public building project could result in adverse effects which might not appear until many years after completion of construction.

The auditors concluded not only that the quality of inspection varied between project sites but that the deficiencies found could have been avoided if headquarters officials had exercised greater supervision over their site inspectors. The agency concerned, the General Services Administration, agreed with the auditors' proposals that frequent, systematic reviews of onsite construction inspection should be made and that site inspectors' recording procedures should be improved.

In making this examination, the auditors observed actual concrete placement operations at building sites and related inspection practices; interviewed contractor and agency officials and employees; examined records pertaining to construction supervision and contract administration; and consulted standards promulgated by technical societies for design and control of concrete mixtures.

Management of inventories. A review of Department of Defense inventory management policies and practices revealed that the department was unnecessarily managing hundreds of thousands of low-volume minor items that were readily available from commercial sources. The auditors suggested that elimination from the inventory systems of all items which could be efficiently and economically procured directly from commercial sources by the using activities would eliminate an unwarranted investment of millions of dollars in inventories and related unnecessary and continuing costs of managing such inventories.

This examination included visits to or correspondence with manufacturers and distributors to determine the availability of inventory items from established commercial sources. Costs of inventory management and of procurement from local commercial sources were also analyzed.

Heating costs. Based on an examination into heating costs incurred at a number of military installations, the auditors concluded that such costs could be reduced by several million dollars a year if manually operated coal furnaces were converted to automatic gas or oil heating units. The estimated saving was attributable to releasing for other duties military personnel assigned to tend the manually operated furnaces.

The auditors also observed that the use of coal increased the cost of property maintenance and interfered with the training of troops.

In making this examination, the auditors made detailed cost studies at a number of military installations to see whether manpower savings and other benefits were realizable by converting from coal heating. These studies were reviewed and discussed with installation and other agency officials.

Effectiveness of a housing program. To meet the needs of middle-income families desiring cooperative-type home ownership, the Federal Housing Administration insures long-term mortgage loans obtained by sponsors of such projects.

The GAO review of this program led to the conclusion that it was not fully effective in serving the middle-income segment of the population for which it was intended. Prospective purchasers of the cooperatives generally had to be from the higher income segments of the population. The program was also found to be of limited financial success since about one-half of the housing projects were either in financial difficulty or were not operating as cooperatives.

Factors identified as contributing to the program's limited success included (1) inadequate evaluation of prevailing surplus housing conditions, (2) inadequate consideration by FHA of its debt service criteria, (3) inadequate analysis of the financial ability of project sponsors to deal with financial deficits, and (4) lack of adequate management of cooperative projects.

In making this examination, the auditors analyzed the basic laws and related legislative history; reviewed the agency's policies and procedures relating to insuring mortgages; examined local, regional, and headquarters records of the agency pertaining to insuring projects at the different levels; and interviewed agency officials and employees engaged in the program.

Research and development project planning. In reviewing the management of a spacecraft project, the auditors found that shortly after a contract was awarded for the design, integration, and test of the spacecraft, available information showed that the estimated weight of the spacecraft exceeded the design weight. The design weight, in turn, exceeded the reported capability of the launch vehicle to be used to orbit the spacecraft.

The contractor was allowed to continue working toward the original design weight goal for several months, even though it was clear that attainment of that goal would be futile because of the limited capability of the launch vehicle. The auditors concluded that had prompt management action been taken on the basis of available information, substantial costs could have been saved on tasks performed by the contractor that had to be redone to develop a lighter-weight spacecraft.

In making this review, the auditors examined federal agency records on project management and contract administration, examined contractor records, and interviewed agency and contractor officials and employees.

Utilization of personnel. A review of the utilization of personnel at a military depot led to the conclusion that the depot was overstaffed with employees. The overstaffing resulted from failure (1) to identify and discontinue the practice of assigning employees to perform nonessential work; (2) to identify and eliminate inefficient work procedures; and (3) to reduce the number of assigned employees as workloads decreased.

In making this examination, the auditors reviewed the manpower used on selected work assignments. Accomplishment reports, manpower availability, work standards, work and production schedules, and work analysis reports were reviewed. Time spent on selected work assignments in relation to reported work accomplished was analyzed.

Management of equipment. The Army operates a substantial number of aircraft in maintaining readiness proficiency for combat flying and in carrying out administration, executive, and inspection functions.

In an examination of the management of 500 of such aircraft, the auditors found weaknesses which led to authorizing 25 percent more aircraft than were actually needed at the locations visited. Inadequate criteria and procedures for determining aircraft requirements, plus insufficient evaluation of aircraft justifications submitted by user organizations, were found to be basic causes for the overauthorizations.

The auditors also found that aircraft were being used for purposes contrary to the transportation and traffic management policies of the Department of Defense. Lack of effective procedures at Army installations resulted in use of aircraft for administrative purposes where commercial airline service would have been satisfactory and more economical.

In making this examination, the auditors examined records of utilization and authorization requests and interviewed officials and employees at numerous field locations where the aircraft were managed.

Motor-vehicle maintenance. In reviewing maintenance policies in selected motor-vehicle pools, the auditors found that significant savings could be achieved by adopting the specific programs of preventive maintenance developed by automobile manufacturers for their vehicles as a means of achieving the best performance, long life, and trouble-free operations in place of the requirements of the federal agency operating the motor pools. These requirements provided generally for more frequent preventive-maintenance work.

In making this examination, the auditors made comparisons of maintenance performed on government vehicles and the frequency thereof with the standards suggested by the vehicle manufacturers.

THE FUTURE

Experience Gained. A great deal of experience has been gained in extending the scope of the auditor's operations beyond financial matters into other aspects of management performance, both in government organizations and in private enterprises. Much more development will be needed before a recognized body of underlying principles and standards for such expanded auditing can be agreed upon.

Interested Parties. There are many parties of interest in obtaining reliable information on management performance—internal management officials; external regulatory organizations; policy-making and supervisory organizations, including legislative bodies; owners or investors; and labor and consumer organizations. The needs of groups such as these with their varying concerns and interests in the overall management processes for better information will largely determine the scope of management auditing of the future.

BIBLIOGRAPHY

GAO Manual for Guidance of Federal Agencies, Title 3, U.S. General Accounting Office, Washington, 1966.

Internal Auditing in Federal Agencies, U.S. General Accounting Office, Washington, 1968.

American Institute of Management: *Manual of Excellent Managements,* New York, 1966.

Statement of Responsibilities of the Internal Auditor, The Institute of Internal Auditors, New York, 1957.

Walsh, Francis J. Jr.: *Internal Auditing,* Business Policy Study No. 111, National Industrial Conference Board, New York, 1963.

Churchill, N. C.: *Audit Recommendations and Management Auditing: A Case Study and Some Remarks,* Empirical Research in Accounting: Selected Studies, Supplement to vol. 4, *The Journal of Accounting Research,* 1966.

Greenwood, William T.: *Business Policy: A Management Audit Approach,* New York, The Macmillan Company, 1967.

Knighton, Lennis M.: *The Performance Post Audit in State Government,* Bureau of Business and Economic Research, Graduate School of Business Administration, Michigan State University, 1967.

Martindell, Jackson: *Appraisal of Management for Executives and Investors,* New York, Harper and Row, 1965.

Neilsen, Oswald: "Internal Auditing in Modern Management," *Federal Accountant,* Spring, 1966.

Pinkelman, F. C.: "Development of Performance Auditing in Michigan," *The Florida CPA,* May, 1967.

Witte, Arthur E.: "Management Auditing: The Present State of the Art," *The Journal of Accountancy,* August, 1967.

Staats, Elmer B.: "The Growing Importance of Internal Audit in the Federal Government," *The U.S. Army Audit Agency Bulletin,* Winter, 1968.

Gillis, Jerry F.: "The Management Audit: Developing Specific Causes and Recommendations," *The U.S. Army Audit Agency Bulletin,* Fall, 1969.

Mead, George C.: "A Managerial Approach to Governmental Accounting," *The Journal of Accountancy,* March, 1970.

Chapter 51

Operational Auditing

LAWRENCE B. SAWYER

Supervising Auditor, Lockheed-California Company

GENESIS OF OPERATIONAL AUDITING

Definition. One of the earliest uses of the term "operational auditing" is found in an interesting article by F. E. Mints in *The Internal Auditor.*[1] The term sprang from the then Statement of Responsibilities for Internal Auditors, which stated that the internal auditor is concerned with accounting and financial matters but may also deal with matters of an operating nature. At that time operational auditing was equated with nonfinancial auditing.

New Aspects. With the passage of time, however, operational auditing assumed new breadth and scope. It began to mean more than a mere exploration into areas previously off limits to the traditional auditor. The fundamental nature of auditing began to take on new aspects.

THE NATURE OF OPERATIONAL AUDITING

Frame of Mind. Operational auditing is essentially a frame of mind, a method of approach. Under this concept, there is no such thing as a strictly financial audit or a strictly operational audit. One can approach any audit in any area either from a financial or accounting point of view or from an operating or management point of view.[2]

In sum, it can be said that the same subject can be viewed through the eyes of a public accountant and result in a traditional financial examination, or it can be viewed through the eyes of a manager (or a management-oriented auditor) and result in an operational audit.

Relationship to Internal Auditing. Operational auditing is not different from internal auditing; it is merely an extension of internal auditing into operational areas. And it is characterized—in both financial and operational areas—by the auditor's approach and state of mind.[3]

Operational auditing logically evolved from the initial delegation of responsibility to the auditor for the protection of the interests of his company. It came about when the internal auditor applied his techniques of analysis and appraisal to nonfinancial activities. As the internal auditor began to realize that he could appraise controls in any segment of his company, he developed an expertise both in arraying nonfinancial data in a manner to which he had been long accustomed and in examining the results from a management point of view. This expertise could then be carried back to the traditional financial areas, and the financial controls could be studied through the eyes of general management, instead of through the eyes of an accountant.

[1] F. E. Mints, "Operational Auditing," *The Internal Auditor,* June, 1954.

[2] E. R. Evans, "Approach—The Key to Operational Auditing," *The Internal Auditor,* Spring, 1966, p. 29.

[3] Bradford Cadmus, *Operational Auditing Handbook,* New York, IIA, 1964, p. 5.

Operational auditing is exemplified in the rules laid down to the internal auditor by two executives. The first said, "I want you auditors to regard your job as that of doing the things for management that the managers would be doing for themselves if they had the time to do them." The second said, "I want you to assume that you are the owner of this business, that the business and all its profits belong to you. Before you recommend a change, before you criticize an operation, ask yourself whether you would do this if the business was yours."[4]

Operational auditing is not, therefore, a distinct and separate type of auditing which is characterized by special programs and techniques. It is rather a manner by which the internal auditor approaches his assignment, analyzes the subject of his review, and regards the results.

Some auditors look for special manuals which will tell them how to make operational audits—when all that is really necessary is a change in their own manner of approach and analysis.

Contrast with Financial Auditing. Financial auditing, in the classic pattern, is concerned primarily with the verification of financial statements. It deals with establishing the reasonableness of certain accounts. It restricts itself to accounting controls. It is practiced chiefly in the financial areas of a company. It is concerned essentially with historical, financial data.

Operational auditing, on the other hand, is concerned with operating (administrative) controls. It may be applied to all parts of an enterprise and is equally at home in financial and nonfinancial areas. It interprets and uses operating as well as financial data. It analyzes historical data as a means of finding ways of improving future business operations.

Contrast with Methods and Procedures. The internal auditor's work in operating departments requires him to become familiar with their problems and operations. There may therefore be some confusion as to his responsibility and that of the people who are engaged in work on organizational structures, methods, and procedures. The two functions are quite separate and distinct.

Methods and procedures people study the work of an operating department with the objective of developing procedures, devising records and reports, and establishing other routines and controls to govern the day-to-day work of the department. The internal auditor, on the other hand, appraises the operation of the control system that has been established. He points out the strengths and weaknesses, but he does not install the controls. That is not his job.

This separation of responsibilities is expressed in the Statement of the Responsibilities of the Internal Auditor: "Internal auditors should not develop procedures, prepare records, or engage in any other activity which they normally would be expected to review and appraise."

This separation of responsibilities should not, however, inhibit management from calling upon the auditor, in certain instances, to review complex installations in order to determine that appropriate controls are being provided. Such a concurrent review is often found in the installations of electronic data processing (EDP) applications. The auditor, acting in an advisory capacity, may point to the kind of controls which would be needed for the successful functioning of the system. The systems people, nevertheless, have the final responsibility of deciding whether or not the suggested controls will be incorporated into the system.

[4] *Ibid.*, pp. 8, 9.

Financial Activities and Operational Auditing. Operational auditing is often regarded as dealing solely with nonfinancial areas. This is not true. It is as much at home in a financial activity as it is in a nonfinancial activity. Since it is more a method of approach than a separate body of rules and programs, it may have as much applicability to the audit of cash as it does to the audit of production control. Some examples follow.[5]

Audit of cash accounts. The operational audit does not stop with account verification and cash counts. It is concerned with cash management policies and considers how effectively they are being carried out. The operational auditor may ask, for example: "Is unemployed cash properly invested?" "Are unnecessary bank charges being experienced in certain accounts?" "Are the operating controls adequate to ensure maximum protection of company funds?"

Confirmation of receivables. The operational audit goes beyond determining the accuracy of amounts. It is interested in the comments and criticisms which may be written on the confirmations returned by customers. It includes an investigation of complaints to determine whether some action is needed to improve the entire operation. It is also interested in collection practices and in the means provided to ensure the follow-up of old and slow-moving accounts.

Observation of inventories. Besides making the necessary audit review and reconciliations, the operational auditor is interested in the character of the inventories. He questions such matters as reorder policies and procedures, the relative size of the investment in inventories, the treatment of obsolescent items, and the general management of the inventories.

In the field of operations, no area within the company need be outside the scope of the operational audit. In financial areas, the operational audit brings a new outlook and a whole new set of questions. In technical operating areas, the operational audit brings an ability to evaluate administrative control.

Through the examination of the nature, extent, and functioning of control, the auditor may perform a service to management in assessing the way in which the control has been established and is being exercised through all elements of the enterprise.

OBJECTIVES OF OPERATIONAL AUDITING

The objectives of operational auditing vary among auditing organizations. The objectives may be dictated by the degree of acceptance by management. They may be dictated by the background, training, and education of the auditors themselves. And they may be dictated by the fundamental philosophy of the auditing organization itself.

Indeed, in the same organization, the objectives may change as the auditors develop an understanding of and a familiarity with operations and as they broaden their technical competence to deal with operational matters as readily as they have dealt with financial matters.

The different objectives—some of which may be overlapping and others mutually exclusive—are as follows.

Appraisal of Control. One widely accepted view of operational auditing holds that it is directed toward control rather than performance and hence avoids technical involvement. It deals with the administrative controls exercised

[5] O'Ferrell, Estes, "The Audit of Operations," *The Internal Auditor,* December, 1956, p. 7.

over all phases of the business, and its purpose is to determine whether the controls provided are adequate and are proving effective in accomplishing management's objectives or plans of operation.

The auditor examines and reports directly on the controls involved. For example, consider a production report in which the data accumulated are found to be inaccurate. The auditor's primary concern is the control deficiency that permitted the improper accumulation of the data. By improving the control, he would be instrumental in improving future reports. He is not so much concerned with the one-time effect of financial implications of excessive production costs (such costs resulting from a bad management decision that was based on the faulty schedule information in the report he examined) as he is with the long-range effect of permitting the poor controls to stand and affect future decisions.[6]

Adherents of this operational audit philosophy believe that the auditor does not have the responsibility for evaluating how well the operation of a particular activity is performed. The auditor is interested in making sure that the established controls bring out to departmental and general management whether the department is operating in conformity with prescribed standards, with the standards and controls that it has set for itself, or with those that are generally agreed upon as applicable to such operations.[7]

By concentrating on the control aspects of an operation, the auditor seeks to provide information and assurance to management on the adequacy and effectiveness of controls not only for the time of the audit, but also for the future, assuming no significant change in the control system.

For example, in an audit of a procurement activity, the auditor would not be concerned with whether a buyer purchased a particular item at the lowest possible cost consistent with requirements for quality and delivery. His prime concern would be whether management, through the installation of a satisfactory control system, has provided assurance that the buyer will take those steps which are calculated to result in a satisfactory purchase. That is, whether there is provision for competitive bids, a system of supervisory approvals, cost and price analyses, and the like. If the auditor sees that such controls have been established and are working, he considers the controls adequate. If he learns, through appropriate tests of transactions, that the buyers are following the prescribed procedures, he considers the controls effective.

Evaluation of Performance. The evaluation of performance is properly within the province of the auditor of operations. When the subject of the audit is outside his technical competence, he may retain the services of a technician to supplement his own auditing knowledge. He may often develop a competence of his own in nonfinancial areas through exposure or study. Besides, when it is sufficiently important to him, the auditor may become reasonably conversant with such technical matters—not usually associated with auditing—as scientific management, production methods and scheduling, blueprints, industrial engineering, EDP programming, and the like.

And even when the auditor does not have technical knowledge, he still may make some appraisals of performance that are within his normal competence. To achieve this objective of evaluation, the auditor seeks to devise programs that will provide department management with the kind of information which

[6] C. N. Inman, "Managerial Auditing of Operations," *The Internal Auditor,* June, 1958, p. 44.

[7] D. E. Dooley, "Planning for Operations Auditing," *Operations Auditing,* Seventeenth Annual Conference Proceedings of the IIA, p. 46.

will show how well or how poorly the department has performed. In addition, the information will supply general management with the bases for decisions on whether to revise its planning and improve its control.

In evaluating performance, the auditor generally addresses himself to accumulating quantitative information to measure the effectiveness, efficiency, and economy with which the work is being done. He will be concerned with performance in such areas as personnel, work load, productivity, quality of work, and cost. Some of the matters to which he will direct his attention are as follows: [8]

Personnel. The auditor can apply quantitative measurements to many significant aspects of the work force. Quantitative data readily available to him include the number of employees, personnel turnover, total regular hours worked, total overtime hours expended, and ratios of regular to overtime hours and of direct to indirect employees.

In considering the number of employees he may ask: "Are we overstaffed—if so, why?" "Are we anticipating losses in the near future?" "Are we training employees for expanded operations or advancement?" "Are we understaffed—if so, why?" "Are we unable to obtain qualified employees?" "If so, what is the effect on operations?" "If the situation is critical, what steps are being taken to remedy it?"

In analyzing the turnover rate he may ask: "Is it high or is it low?" "What are the reasons for a high turnover rate?" "Are wages too low?" "Are working conditions unfavorable?" "Are we losing experienced workers?" "What is the quality of new employees?"

When looking at man-hours he may ask: "What is our ratio of overtime to regular man-hours?" "What should the norm be?" "Why are overtime hours necessary?" "Is it due to shortage of personnel, inexperienced personnel, increased work volume, backlog of work, or absenteeism?" "What plans are being made to combat excessive overtime?"

Work load. The auditor can apply quantitative measurements of performance to such matters as the volume of work handled, the volume of new work, the amount of work completed, and the backlog at the beginning and end of a reporting period.

Some of the kinds of quantitative data available, to name very few, are orders received, stores requisitions processed, payroll checks prepared, complaints handled, maintenance jobs deferred, invoices processed for payment, and purchase orders issued.

In evaluating the work load as a whole or in any particular activity, the auditor may ask: "What is the volume of new work?" "Is it increasing or decreasing?" "How do we meet an increase in the work load?" "Do we accomplish this by working overtime, by adding new employees, or by rescheduling work?" "Are we completing current work on schedule?" "What is our backlog?" "Is it increasing or decreasing?" "Are we deferring critical maintenance work in trying to meet schedules?"

Productivity. The auditor can apply quantitative measurements to productivity by determining units of work expended for the units produced. Some of the measures are man-hours per customer and man-hours per job applications processed. Sometimes it may be more meaningful to consider the reciprocal of this measurement: the units produced for each unit of work expended.

The kinds of data available include such information as customers' bills or

[8] W. T. Hamilton, "Appraising Operating Performance," *The Internal Auditor*, June, 1954, pp. 8–11.

payroll checks prepared per man-hour, purchase orders issued per man-day, invoices processed per man-day, and even man-hours devoted to inventory audits per dollars invested in inventory.

Some of the questions that arise in examining productivity are: "At what level should our productivity be?" "How does it compare with past performance?" "Is it good or bad?" "How does our productivity affect our backlog?" "What are the factors affecting productivity?" "Is unsatisfactory productivity due to shortage of materials, shortage of personnel, inexperienced personnel, poor quality of personnel, or lack of proper equipment maintenance?" "Can we improve our work methods?" "Can we further mechanize our operations?" "What has been the performance of our equipment?" "Do we have a good load factor on all equipment?" "How do we stand on man-hours per customer—is the trend up or down?"

Quality. The auditor applies quantitative measurements to quality to determine how well the job is being done. Some of the quantitative data available are the number of complaints received from customers (as a gauge of overall company performance); the number of union grievances (as a gauge of supervisory capabilities in the employee relations field); the number of errors per customer bill produced; the number of typing errors per 100 words typed; the amount of scrap generated; and the number of rejections by inspectors.

Some of the questions the auditor may ask are: "Is the quality of our work improving or deteriorating?" "How is the quality of the work affected by the caliber of employees, employee training or morale, condition of equipment, working conditions, work load?" "Can it be improved by introducing new equipment?" "Would it be helped by changing work methods?"

Cost. Cost offers the most readily available units of measurement. It is up to the auditor to appraise the available data intelligently through the eyes of management. The kinds of costs are legion, included under such broad classifications as labor costs, material costs, administrative costs, equipment costs, and the like.

In examining labor dollars, the auditor may ask: "Is the trend up or down?" "What are the reasons for significant changes?" "Are all the activities necessary?" "Can the cost of each department or division be justified?" "Should the company make or buy particular items?"

In examining costs relating to classifications other than labor, he may ask: "What is the relation of cost to forecast?" "Is it over or under forecast, and what are the reasons for wide variances?" "What are the units making up the costs?" "Are they necessary?" "Are people as cost-conscious as they should be?" "Is there a better method of obtaining results?"

Appraisal of Objectives and Plans. The objective of the operational audit may go beyond an appraisal of control or an evaluation of performance. It might concern itself with the very foundation stones of the company's operations—the objectives and plans devised by management.

Before controls can be established, there must be objectives and plans toward and through which the company's activities will be guided by its systems of control. The appraisal of objectives and plans requires a high degree of business ability and acumen on the part of the auditor. But there are standards which he can use as yardsticks.

The auditor may consider the following matters in analyzing his company's objectives and plans.[9]

[9] R. E. Seiler, "The Internal Auditor's Appraisal of Company Objectives and Plans," *The Internal Auditor*, Winter, 1960, pp. 15, 16.

Evaluating objectives. The auditor might be concerned with determining whether:

1. The objectives are clear and understandable.
2. The objectives are sufficiently inclusive or whether major areas have been overlooked.
3. The objectives are reasonable and properly reflect the company's responsibilities to stockholders, employees, community, and government.
4. The objectives have been sufficiently communicated to the proper operating personnel.
5. The objectives are compatible with each other and are in proper balance with each other.
6. The objectives have been sufficiently divided and subdivided to make them more clearly understood and more easily followed.
7. The objectives are not being changed so frequently that confusion and frustration result.

Evaluating plans. In evaluating plans, which are in essence the projected actions needed to meet objectives, the auditor might be concerned with whether:

1. The subject matter is of sufficient importance to warrant formal plans.
2. The plans are compatible with the related objectives of the company.
3. The plans improve the coordination of various objectives.
4. The plans anticipate trouble spots.
5. The plans are flexible, leaving room for developing more efficient methods.
6. The plans permit the proper delegation of responsibility.
7. The plans capitalize on the abilities and ideas of individuals in a way that will build morale and ensure successful attainment of objectives.
8. The plans assist in achieving uniformity of action in the various divisions.
9. The benefits of the plans more than offset the cost of drawing them up.
10. The plans are properly communicated.
11. The plans are made subject to measurement to determine their success or failure.

Under this audit objective, the auditor raises his sights to the evaluation not of operating controls but of the highest executive controls in the organization.

Appraisal of Organizational Structure. The company's organizational structure is part of the means by which management controls the enterprise's operations. The very structure itself, therefore, including assignment of duties and responsibilities and delegation of authority, may be a proper subject for the auditor's review. Among other things, he would want to know whether: [10]

1. The organizational structure is in harmony with the objectives of the company, division, department, or unit.
2. Clear lines of responsibility have been established which extend from the top of the organization to the lowest level of supervision.
3. The structure enables authority to be commensurate with responsibility.
4. The structure provides reasonable spans of management—neither too much nor too little.

[10] R. R. Zimmerman, "Auditing the Organization Structure," *The Internal Auditor,* Fall, 1965, pp. 59–62.

5. The structure provides for unity of command—each person reporting to no more than one supervisor.
6. The structure clearly defines responsibility for every management person in the organization.
7. Compatible functions are grouped together.
8. The structure assigns operating responsibilities to individual managers rather than to groups or committees.
9. The structure has proper balance—no function being excessively weak or excessively dominant.
10. The organization permits flexibility in daily working relationships.
11. The structure is as simple and economical as possible.
12. The structure provides for perpetuation of management through replacement by persons in training for each higher position.

THE AUDITOR OF OPERATIONS

The qualities, attributes, responsibilities, and status of the internal auditor of operations are somewhat similar to those of the traditional financial auditor. But they are more oriented toward the management point of view. They are essentially as follows:

Qualifications. In the audit of operations, an accounting background may be desirable, but it is not indispensable. Many auditing organizations include on their rosters people whose backgrounds lean toward industrial engineering and systems analysis. The accountant's ability to accumulate, array, and analyze data of an operational nature, however, is just as significant in operational audits as it is in financial audits.

More important is the auditor's expertness in the appraisal of control. Through his knowledge and familiarity with internal control, the auditor may find himself at home in any area of the company's operations. To this familiarity should be tied a good knowledge of the company, of the interface of the various activities within the company, of the flow of work, and of the people who do the work.

Probably the most important qualification is the auditor's ability to think like a manager. After he has accumulated his information and analyzed it, he must then weigh the results as a manager would and suggest improvements. It is only by thinking like a manager that he can truly serve management.

Attributes. The auditor of operations must have curiosity and persistence. He must be adaptable, and he must have both a constructive approach and business sense. Finally, he must be cooperative. These attributes are examined further in the following paragraphs.[11]

Curiosity. The auditor of operations must be interested in and curious about all operations. As he looks at an operation he should ask himself: "What is being done?" "Do we need to do this at all?" "How does it fit into the rest of the business?" "Is someone duplicating the work?" "Is there a better, easier, less expensive way?"

Persistence. He keeps on until he is sure that he understands a situation. He tests, checks, or otherwise satisfies himself that things are actually done in the way they were described to him or in the way that they should be done.

Adaptability. Since his work takes him into every area of the company's operations, he must feel comfortable in widely diverse environments. For

[11] Cadmus, *op. cit.*, p. 20.

example, he must be able to adapt rapidly and easily to the ways and jargon of the production department, the engineering department, and the advertising department. For his strength lies in his ability to deal with all manner of people on their own ground.

Constructiveness. He does not view errors or deficiencies as the end of his search. He is interested in seeing how their repetition may be avoided, rather than in emphasizing their existence. He considers the deficiency as a guide to improvement for the future.

Business sense. He looks at everything from the broad viewpoint of the effect on the efficient and profitable operation of the business. When evaluating any particular area, he keeps in mind the interface of that operation with others and its relationship to the business as a whole.

Cooperativeness. He sees himself as a business consultant, not a rival or critic of those with whom he deals. He works with them, consults with them, and reviews his recommendations with them. His concern is to improve the operation of the business rather than to receive credit for finding mistakes.

General Responsibilities. The auditor of operations has a responsibility to serve both operating and general management. He serves operating managers by offering constructive recommendations that look toward the improvement of operations. He serves general managers by providing them with a picture of what he has seen and by expressing an opinion on the matters he has reviewed.

In performing his function, the auditor has the responsibility for observing professional auditing standards in his reviews and appraisals. These auditing standards concern the thoroughness and comprehensiveness of the fieldwork and the adequacy of reporting practices.

Responsibilities for Policies and Procedures. The auditor has certain basic responsibilities to management with respect to the management policies, procedures, and other means of control that have been established. In reviewing these policies and procedures, here are some of the things he considers:

Consistency. The chain of procedures, starting with general policy statements and ending with detailed departmental policies, should be consistent within itself. The auditor is responsible for seeing that all procedures are coordinated.

Adequacy. The procedures should be so constituted as to provide a means of accomplishing management's objectives. The auditor is responsible for determining that the procedures are adequate for that purpose.

Compliance. The actual work performed should be in accordance with the prescribed procedures. The auditor is responsible for measuring this compliance.

Effectiveness. The results desired should be obtained. The auditor is responsible for devising tests which will indicate whether the procedures are truly effective.

Organizational Status. It is essential that the auditor of operations be able to deal as an equal with operating managers—not as a subordinate who is trying to persuade them that he may be able to help. As a general rule, the auditing function is assigned organizationally to the financial division under the direct supervision of a senior executive—such as a financial vice-president, controller, or treasurer. This position in the company is satisfactory, provided that the executive to whom the auditor reports has entrée to all operating departments and is not the immediate supervisor of the accounting operations.

Inadequate status usually creates major problems in obtaining corrective action for the deficiencies disclosed by the usual audit report. When the auditor's findings are ignored, the auditor cannot function effectively.

Relationship with Independent Accountants. It is difficult for operating personnel without financial background to distinguish between the work of the internal auditor of operations and the work of the independent public accountant. They observe that both the auditor and the public accountant use similar techniques in testing the reliability of records and the adequacy of protective controls. They often see that both the auditor and the public accountant seek to satisfy themselves that the assets are properly protected and accounted for.

The responsibilities of the two are different, however. The public accountant, engaged by the board of directors, is responsible for reporting to stockholders, management, and the public on the fairness of management's presentation of the financial condition of the business and the financial results of the operations over a specified period. He examines and tests records and internal controls—including internal auditing—until he is satisfied that the financial statements he is examining are fairly presented.

The internal auditor of operations, on the other hand, is responsible to general management for the adequacy and effectiveness of the system of control throughout the entire organization. His concern with financial records is generally directed toward how well they serve management in the profitable operation of the business.

While these basic responsibilities differ, there is nevertheless a community of interest and concern between the auditor of operations and the public accountant. The public accountant has long made use of the work of the financially oriented internal auditor. Both operate under comparable programs, and these programs can be readily coordinated so as to achieve a mutually acceptable division of the work of analyzing accounts and verifying financial transactions.

The public accountant's involvement with the auditor of operations is more recent. But here too there can be close cooperation. The auditor's reviews of internal control over financial and accounting matters can be used by the public accountant to supplement his own. In that area, coordination can be improved if both use the same methods of analyzing control systems. For example, both could employ similar flow-charting techniques and flow-charting symbols in their working papers. Also, the internal auditor of operations may schedule his reviews so that there is no duplication of effort and so that the public accountant may make use of those reviews at the time that he needs them.

The auditor's reviews of nonfinancial operations are also of interest and concern to the public accountant. The latter has long realized that almost anything occurring within an enterprise has some effect on the books of account and the financial statements. Through the work of the auditor of operations, the accountant may receive assurances of the adequacy and effectiveness of the operational aspects of the control system. Such assurances may well affect the public accountant's approach to his own audit.

Where the efforts of the two are properly coordinated, they may be mutually helpful and can eliminate possible confusion or duplication of effort.

ADMINISTRATIVE CONTROL

The auditor of operations must be an expert in the review of administrative—as distinguished from technical—controls. Since this is his stock-in-trade, he must be familiar with the nature and the various aspects of control. In all the diverse activities in a company, control remains a common denominator. The auditor's knowledge of control is therefore his most useful and versatile tool.

Definition of Control. Control comprises all of the means devised in a company to direct, restrain, govern, and check its various activities for the purpose of determining that company objectives are met. These means of control include, but are not limited to, form of organization, policies, systems, procedures, instructions, standards, committees, charts of account, forecasts, budgets, schedules, reports, records, checklists, methods, devices, and internal auditing.

Control may be subdivided into executive control, management control, internal control, financial control, and administrative control. Any differences that may exist arise more from the breadth and nature of the objectives management is seeking to achieve through control than from any inherent ambiguity in the term "control" itself. What is more significant is for the auditor of operations to understand that for control to have meaning it must have as its purpose the attainment of an objective.[12]

Definition of Objectives. An objective may be any value or values that are sought by an individual or group who are willing to exert some effort to attain those values. A company's objectives are a mixture of many things. Survival and maximizing profits may seem to be the most obvious. But standing alone they do not constitute clear statements of the overall objectives of the company, for they leave unsaid what the objectives are toward the employees, the community, and the economy as a whole. Company objectives must be set for market standing, innovation, productivity, physical and financial resources, profitability, managerial performance and development, worker performance and attitude, and public responsibility. Management objectives state the specific accomplishment expected of the managers of each unit in a particular period of time so that the work of the whole management group is directed towards a single goal.

Viewed by the auditor, whose concern is the adequacy and effectiveness of control, objectives are the goals toward which any function or organization is guided and directed by means of the associated systems of control.

Objectives should not be confused with the various means designed to achieve them. They should not be confused with *policies,* which are general statements or understandings that guide or channel the thinking or action of subordinates in an enterprise. They should not be confused with *plans,* which are the measures devised, within the guidelines laid down by policies, to attain an objective. They should not be confused with *procedures,* which set forth the routines to be followed in the execution of the plans and which regulate the methods employed in working toward a particular objective. They should not be confused with *methods,* which describe or constitute the mechanics of a system. Finally, they should not be confused with a *system,* which comprehends all the methods, procedures, and routines devised to reach a given objective, within the framework of existing policies and in accordance with established plans.

Objectives may relate to functions or to organizations. Some illustrations follow:

In terms of a function, the objective of scheduling, for example, is determining when or at what rate the principal phases of a plan must be completed. Similarly, the objective of corrective action is assuring the prompt removal of any interference with the planned execution of an activity.

[12] L. B. Sawyer, "The Anatomy of Control," *The Internal Auditor,* Spring, 1964, p. 15.

In terms of an organization, the principal objective of an Accounts Payable department, for example, may be thought of as paying for materials and services actually ordered and received, at prices properly agreed upon, in a timely manner.

Before the control needed to guide operations toward goals or objectives may be intelligently appraised, it seems clear that the particular objectives involved must be understood.

Nature of Administrative Controls. Once objectives have been set and the organization has been established, the administrative controls are provided to make sure the objectives will be reached in accordance with the plans set by management. There are an infinite number and variety of means and methods to accomplish overall control and detailed control, and the auditor should have a ready familiarity with them. Some of these means and methods are as follows:

Creative planning. Setting the objectives by defining what should be done, how and where it should be done, and who should do it; and deciding what is needed to accomplish the objectives in terms of human and physical resources. The means of control include long-range plans and forecasts exemplified by broad policy statements, charts, correspondence, and reports.

Organizing. Providing the capital, plant, staff, and materials necessary to gain the objectives and providing the basic guidelines within which the objectives will be pursued. The means of control include organization charts, statements of functions and responsibilities, policy and procedure manuals, charts and texts of accounts, master schedules, personnel policy statements, appropriate division of duties, and financial approval authorizations together with associated monetary limitations.

Control functions. Constraining and regulating action in accordance with the requirements of established plans for the accomplishment of objectives through the use of the following eight control functions:

1. *Routine planning.* Providing the data and information needed to carry out a particular plan. This is accomplished through directives and procedures, job assignment sheets, methods outlines, systems specifications, documents and reports, budgets, and statements of activities.
2. *Scheduling.* Establishing when or at what rate the principal phases of a plan must be completed. This is accomplished through sales, production, procurement, and performance schedules; logs and registers; and charts, documents, and reports.
3. *Preparing.* Assuring the availability, when needed, of all matters required for the execution of the plan. This is accomplished through correspondence, follow-up reports, logs and registers, documents and reports, and committees and conferences.
4. *Coordinating.* Providing for the timely release of authority to act so as to integrate the operation of related activities. This is accomplished through order control systems, logs and registers, and documents and reports.
5. *Directing.* Providing instructions needed by the performing organizations to execute the plan properly. This is accomplished through job instructions, memorandums, forms, and records.
6. *Supervising.* Making sure that all necessary action is undertaken to carry out the plan. This is accomplished through supervisory review, written reports, checklists, forms and records, and logs and registers.
7. *Obtaining feedback.* Determining the degree of agreement between actual and planned results. This is accomplished through budgets, standards, records and reports, charts, and inspection documents.

8. *Achieving improvement.* Promptly removing any interference with the execution of the plan and making appropriate changes to the plan when necessary. This is accomplished through correspondence, committees and conferences, commendations, and disciplinary actions.

PLAN FOR THE OPERATIONAL AUDIT

Approach. There are two basic operational auditing approaches: (1) organizational and (2) functional.

Under the *organizational approach,* the auditor is concerned with the administration of a department or other organizational unit. He examines not only the functions or activities within an organization but the administration of the organization itself. He will be interested in the framework of the organization, its staffing, its method of reporting, its method of evaluating personnel, its budgets, and its place in the company's scheme of things. He is able to take a picture of a microcosm within the company structure and study it from many angles.

The auditor's concern will tend to gravitate toward the problems of administration, and he will be able to provide assistance to the department manager on the administration of the department as a whole. While he should be interested in how the organization's product is used by other units within the company, his primary concern is directed toward the administration of this one unit in the company structure.

In contrast, under the *functional approach* the auditor is concerned with following a major activity or activities from inception to conclusion. He traces the functions through all the units involved with them and is less concerned with the general administrative activities within the units than with their effect upon the functions under review. Where the function is significant enough, his overview of it can be of great assistance to general management, for seldom can general management follow an activity through the organizational maze as thoroughly as the auditor can.

Each approach has much to offer. An organizational audit can be of great help to departmental management, where the auditor has a firm grasp of the management and administrative controls and where departmental management can benefit from this knowledge. In well-established, well-run departments, obviously, the degree of assistance needed or offered might be slight.

Functional audits are often more difficult. While the organizational audit offers the auditor a microcosm to examine, the functional audit challenges him with an often long and devious trail. In a large company, the function's impact on many units, and the units' impact on the function, can be tremendously frustrating in simply trying to visualize the many aspects of the work flow. And that does not begin to encompass the evaluation of the operation of the function. For that very reason, the competent auditor who manages to achieve familiarity with the function in all its complexities and to evaluate its effectiveness is performing a signal service to management, since there are probably few in his company who will ever see the problem in the same depth and breadth.

Method. The audit of any operation, be it organizational or functional, involves four distinct steps. They are: [13]

1. Familiarization
2. Verification

[13] Cadmus, *op. cit.,* pp. 25–32.

3. Evaluation and recommendation
4. Reporting the results to management

Familiarization. First the auditor must learn from operating management what the objectives of the operation are, how they are to be accomplished, and how the results are determined.

This learning is accomplished in many ways. The auditor will discuss the operation with knowledgeable people. He will seek to find out how management determines whether the activity is functioning correctly; how it reports results; how it evaluates its employees; and what effect the activity has on other activities. He will "walk through" the department or follow the function until he has a reasonably good idea of what is being done, how it is being done, and why it is being done, so as to meet the company's objectives. The auditor cannot fulfill his assignment to appraise the controls unless he knows what is being controlled.

When he has an adequate understanding of the specific objectives, he then tries to familiarize himself with the controls that management has established to see that its objectives are being attained.

First the auditor examines the organizational structure, the place of the units in the company, their relationship with other units, and the assignment of functions and responsibilities. Then he traces significant activities by flow-charting them or by following selected documents through the key control points.

Next the auditor will review the policies and procedures that govern the unit or function being examined. Written procedures, understood by employees and reasonably calculated to carry out company plans and achieve company objectives, are an indication of a well-controlled activity. Where the procedures are not in writing, the auditor will have to determine from discussions with management what it expects of its people and how the assigned activities are to be carried out.

The auditor then reviews the records generated or affected by the activity in which he is interested. He wants to know what the records are supposed to do, why they are needed, and whether they are duplicated by other records.

Finally, the auditor asks what management itself does to appraise the work performed—what kinds of reports it receives from its people and what kinds of reports it submits to higher management.

The process of familiarization is, of course, carried on throughout the entire audit. Sufficient familiarity is necessary at the outset, however, to prepare a workable audit program. Audit programs will be discussed later in this section.

Verification. By verification of transactions, just as in a financial audit, the auditor is able to determine the degree to which controls and actual operations conform to the written and oral descriptions and understandings which management has given to the auditor.

Verification requires the auditor to examine in detail a selected sample of transactions, preferably by statistical methods. The sample size will depend on the judgment of the auditor as to the degree of reliance he needs that the sample reasonably represents the population from which it was selected.

In making his verification, the auditor is usually concerned with three things: quality, timeliness, and cost. When he has established the degree to which transactions have been handled correctly, promptly, and economically, he will be determining whether or not in actual practice:

1. The organization structure and the assignment of responsibility follow the control plans of departmental management.
2. Procedures prescribed by management are being followed.
3. Prescribed internal checks are being enforced.
4. Prescribed procedures and other controls prove effective in coordinating the work with that of other departments.
5. Operating records and reports are complete, timely, factual, and meaningful.
6. Standards of performance provide an effective basis for the appraisal of operating results.

Evaluation and recommendation. Evaluation begins as the knowledgeable auditor starts his review and even takes place during the familiarization phase. Often a mere glance at an operation causes the auditor to sense that the activity is well controlled or, on the other hand, that something is wrong. Through verification these feelings may be confirmed; or his tests may disclose conditions that were not apparent from the initial survey. Final evaluation, or confirmation of the initial evaluation, usually awaits the results of such tests.

Recommendations should be made only when the auditor is completely satisfied that he understands the operation, that his appraisal has taken the true measure of the operation, and that his recommendations take into account all the factors that affect the operation.

As a result of his examination and evaluation, the auditor should be in a position to answer the following questions:

1. Do the established controls operate effectively? If not, what constructive steps can be recommended?
2. If there are numerous deviations from established policies and procedures, does the reason lie with the policies and procedures or with other factors?
3. Do departmental controls and practices conform to company policy? If not, what should be recommended?
4. Do the established controls help management in attaining operating objectives?
5. Does operating management understand and utilize its controls to best advantage?
6. Does the structure of accounts, records, and reports follow the pattern of operating responsibility, and does it conform to the way management looks at its operations?
7. Is there adequate coordination and cooperation with related departments? Are there duplications or gaps in control?

In making his recommendations to management, the auditor must see the problems as management would see them. *He must weigh the benefits of the safeguards afforded by increased control against the costs that will be incurred.* He must weigh the extent of risk against the amount of potential loss.

Of course, there will be occasions when the auditor meets a situation which is beyond his experience or training—when he is not in a position to make a practical suggestion to cure an apparent deficiency. Here the auditor must present his findings to management, making certain that all facts have been fairly presented, and leave the determination of the action to be taken to management itself.

Reporting. Reporting should not be reserved for the conclusion of the examination. The auditor provides the best service to general management and maintains the best rapport with operating management when he discusses currently and candidly the things that he has found.

Minor matters usually can be cleared up as the audit progresses and need not be included in the formal report. Referring to them in the working papers and showing there how they were corrected should suffice. Generally, matters of greater import should be discussed currently with the lowest level of management capable of taking corrective action. Any formal report that tells general management that all deficiencies were corrected before the report was issued finds a friendly acceptance by both operating and general management.

Also, while the auditor is not bound to offer solutions for the problems he has encountered—the responsibility for correcting defects must ultimately rest with operating management—his findings will receive a more sympathetic hearing if they are accompanied by reasonable, economical suggestions for curing deficient conditions.

The preparation of the formal report will be discussed later in this section.

PROGRAM FOR THE OPERATIONAL AUDIT

The program for the operational audit is best prepared after a preliminary survey. The experienced auditor usually rejects standardized programs because operations, unlike most accounting systems, often change from audit to audit.

The operational audit generally includes the evaluation of the adequacy and effectiveness of the controls designed to carry out management's objectives for the organization or function under review. To permit such an evaluation, the program must encompass both those key concepts: the objectives and the controls.

The auditor normally prepares the program after the preliminary survey has given him reasonable familiarity with the objectives of the activity and with the controls designed—or needed—to carry them out.

The reason for the program is to establish guidelines by which the auditor may carry out the purposes of his audit assignment and adduce the evidence needed to provide the basis for an audit opinion.

For some activities, the auditor has sufficient familiarity with the operation to be able to express an opinion on the effectiveness with which the activity is being performed. On other activities, which are beyond his technical competence, he will be able to express an opinion solely on the adequacy and the effectiveness of the administrative controls. For example, on one side of the spectrum may be a clerical activity, like the filing of blueprints. Here the auditor would be qualified to express an opinion on the effectiveness of the activity itself. On the other side may be the preparation of the engineering drawings from which the prints were prepared. Here the auditor most likely would restrict his opinion to the adequacy and effectiveness of the controls over the activity.

In either event, the audit program best suits the auditor's purpose if it sets forth the key objectives of the operation, determines the controls that are or should be installed, and enumerates the tests of transactions that should be made.

A program for a purchasing function, which shows in telescoped form how the objectives of the operation, the related key controls, and the tests of transactions are tied together, is described below.[14]

Objectives of the Operation. The principal objective of the purchasing function is to obtain the right product, at the right price, in the right quantity, at the right time.

Key Controls over the Operation. The system of controls devised by management to meet this objective includes procedures, instructions, reports, records, methods, and devices. These means of control usually operate as follows:

1. To make sure that the right product is obtained, control in the form of written procedures provides that the buying organization may act only upon the receipt of a properly approved request to purchase, supported when necessary by engineering specifications for the product to be obtained.
2. To make sure that the right price is obtained, the following means of control have been established:
   a. Written procedures that require competitive bids for purchases in excess of stipulated dollar amounts
   b. A form of organization providing for supervisory approval of the bidders to be solicited and methods providing strict surveillance over bid requests and bids received
   c. Records in the form of price cards showing all previous purchases for the same product and a requirement that the price cards accompany the buying package to supervisors for review
   d. Written instructions that the purchase orders be signed at appropriate supervisory levels, depending on the amounts involved
3. To make sure that the right quantity is ordered, written procedures provide that quantities stipulated by the requesting unit may not be changed (except within certain narrow limits) without written authorization from that unit.
4. To make sure that the products purchased are obtained in time, control in the form of procedures, devices, and reports has been provided. Each buyer is required to place colored identifying tabs on the copies of his own purchase orders in such a fashion as to show immediately when scheduled due dates are approaching and when orders are behind schedule. In addition, control in the form of a periodic report to management has been provided to show the steps being taken to correct schedule slippage.

Tests of the Operation. After his examination and appraisal of the system of control in the light of the principal objectives, the auditor would then perform appropriate tests to determine if the present controls are operating as intended. He would then want to see if any present controls can safely be eliminated or whether additional controls are needed. The tests may include:

1. A verification that purchase orders are supported by proper authorizing documents and specifications
2. A review of the operation of the bidding practices by a test of approval of bidders selected, by a determination that adequate justification has been supplied for the failure to request bids or the failure to award orders to low bidders, and by an examination of supervisory approvals
3. A verification that significant changes in quantities ordered are supported by approvals from the requesting units

[14] Sawyer, *op. cit.*, pp. 19, 20.

4. An examination of the tabs on open purchase orders, a verification of the accuracy and timeliness of the periodic behind-schedule report, and an appraisal of the effectiveness of the steps taken to correct schedule slippage

Summary. The program segment just discussed shows how key controls must be evaluated in terms of the objectives of the operation, and how tests of transactions must be designed to establish the effectiveness of the control system. The auditor will rarely be wide of the mark if he organizes his program along these lines, particularly in areas where he has no particular technical competence.

REPORTING THE OPERATIONAL AUDIT

Writing reports on the operational audit is not too much different from writing reports on other kinds of audits. The same rules apply. The report should be factual, clear, concise, tactful, and persuasive. These matters have been covered in other sections of this handbook.

In some respects, however, the report on an operational audit differs from reports on strictly financial activities. The reasons are twofold: first, the subject matter of the audit; second, the degree of acceptance that the auditor of operations enjoys within his company.

Subject Matter. The difficulties encountered in writing the operational audit report stem from the infinite variety of the subject matter. Each activity requires a different kind of explanation, because for each activity there are different readers with different backgrounds and different needs. Yet, if the audit report is to be read by general management as well, it must be understandable to any reasonably intelligent reader, no matter what his background may be. The auditor of operations must therefore be an expert "translator" who renders technical jargon and complex concepts into plain English.

Audit Acceptance. In financial and accounting areas the auditor is usually accepted as an expert. His opinion on financial and accounting matters is therefore seldom subject to question, and the basis for the opinion may be couched in general terms and still be found entirely acceptable. The same does not apply to reports on operational activities. It is rare that an audit opinion on, say, production control, engineering, or traffic would have the same degree of acceptance as an audit opinion on the handling of cash. This reluctance on the part of the readers to accept such opinions without question is particularly strong in companies which have not yet completely accepted operational auditing.

The auditor of operations can usually overcome such reluctance in several ways: (1) by delineating clearly the *scope* of his examination, (2) by explaining the *standards* he used in measuring performance, (3) by setting forth explicitly the *evidence* on which his opinion is based, and (4) by reviewing all *drafts* of reports with the supervisors and managers of the activities audited. These matters are discussed more fully in the following paragraphs.

Scope. The statement of scope requires careful drafting to tell the reader what the auditor did and, of special significance in an operational audit, what he did not do. Here the auditor can set forth the limitations of his audit opinion when he wishes to disclaim responsibility for opinions on technical areas beyond his competence. For example, in a review of engineering drawings, the auditor may well express an opinion on the control devised by management to ensure the accuracy of drawings, but he may wish to point out specifically that he is not expressing an opinion on the quality of the drawings themselves.

Standards. The auditor of a report on a technical area gains better acceptance if he sets forth the standards that he used in measuring the function or activity he has reviewed. He may determine these standards from statements of policies and procedures, from discussions with management personnel having responsibility for the activities, or from authoritative writings on the subject. Again using the accuracy of engineering drawings as an example, he might establish that he considered the following means of control to be basic to a good control system:

1. An engineering standards manual, available to all draftsmen, setting forth the company's drafting requirements
2. A system of review by supervisors and by design specialists for every drawing before it is released to production
3. A system of review of drawings by independent drawing reviewers to provide assurance that the company's drafting instructions have been followed and that the work is accurate.
4. A system of reporting to management on the number of drawing corrections required by the production organization to correct drawing defects

These are well-established standards. Their application by the auditor will be difficult to quarrel with. Their use as yardsticks to measure performance will form the basis for an audit opinion that should gain attention and acceptance.

Evidence. Opinions on operational activities, particularly adverse opinions, will gain better acceptance if they are supported in the report by adequate evidence of reviews and tests. Still using the engineering drawings as an example, the report could set forth the following reviews made:

1. The number of draftsmen interviewed to determine whether they had handbooks readily available to them, and the number of handbooks in use that were compared with a master volume to make sure that they were up to date
2. The number of drawings examined for initials of prescribed reviewers
3. The number of drawings examined for evidence of engineering check and of compliance with corrections requested by the checkers
4. The verification of the statistical data given to management on the number of drawing corrections required by production departments

Draft review. This review is of special importance in operational audits. It is essential that the auditor make sure that he has stated his facts correctly and, of equal significance, that he has properly interpreted them. Also, since the auditor's training is seldom in operational areas, he must be certain that he has considered all the factors that touch upon a particular operation. Finally, he must be sure he has translated the technical jargon accurately; operating management may attach meanings to certain words which the auditor has perhaps not clearly apprehended.

CONCLUSION

New Problems. Operational auditing is just beginning to be recognized by the layman. Even those auditors who have been practicing it for years can sense and foresee a broadening in their scope and a refinement in their methods. We cannot foretell all the services to management that the auditors will be called upon to provide. This is because we do not know now all the new kinds of problems that management will be required to cope with. The auditor's destiny is tied to that of management. And as management enters into new fields, the auditor will have to keep pace with it so as to continue to provide needed services.

Management's problems in the future are bound to be increased and accentuated by the impact of such matters as total information systems, new industries, new products and services, new laws, new management techniques, and increased foreign operations. The extent of the auditor's services in helping solve these problems will be challenged by management's needs and circumscribed only by the auditor's own capacity to act and his own judgment as to how he should act.

New Techniques. Today the auditor has many sophisticated management techniques to help him. Operations research techniques, electronic data processing, statistical inference, and indirect work measurement are just a few. In future years, many new techniques are sure to come over the horizon. To the extent that management sees a demonstration of the ability of the auditor to perform a service in any sector of his company, so will the auditor of operations find greater acceptance by management and improved stature in his company and his profession.

BIBLIOGRAPHY

Cadmus, Bradford: *Operational Auditing Handbook*, New York, The Institute of Internal Auditors, 1964.

Dooley, D. E.: "Planning for Operations Auditing," *Operations Auditing*, Seventeenth Annual Conference Proceedings of The Institute of Internal Auditors.

Hayes, Albert F., and George A. Renard: *Evaluating Purchasing Performance*, New York, AMA Research Study No. 66, 1964.

Norbeck, Edward F., et al.: *Operational Auditing for Management Control*, New York, American Management Association, Inc., 1969.

Sollenberger, Harold M.: *Major Changes Caused by the Implementation of a Management Information System*, Research Monograph No. 4, New York, National Association of Accountants, 1968.

Jerome, William Travers, III: *Executive Control—The Catalyst*, New York, John Wiley & Sons, Inc., 1961.

Lamperti, F., and J. B. Thurston: *Internal Auditing for Management*, Englewood Cliffs, N.J., Prentice-Hall, Inc., 1953.

Leonard, William P.: *The Management Audit*, Englewood Cliffs, N.J., Prentice-Hall, Inc., 1963.

Inman, C. N.: "Managerial Auditing of Operations," *The Internal Auditor*, June, 1958.

Seiler, R. E.: "Operational Auditing and Motivating Executive Action," *The Internal Auditor*, Fall, 1962.

Sawyer, L. B.: "The Anatomy of Control," *The Internal Auditor*, Spring, 1964.

Zimmerman, R. R.: "Auditing the Organization Structure," *The Internal Auditor*, Fall, 1965.

Evans, E. R.: "Approach—The Key to Operational Auditing," *The Internal Auditor*, Spring, 1966.

Carolus, Roger N.: "Some Challenges of Operational Auditing," *The Internal Auditor*, November/December, 1969.

Otto, James W.: "Operational Auditing Applied to Data Processing Facilities," *The Internal Auditor*, May/June, 1970.

Chapter 52

Planning, Programming, and Budgeting Systems

KENNETH S. CALDWELL

Principal, Ernst & Ernst

A NEW DIMENSION IN PLANNING AND MANAGEMENT

Allocation of Resources. How do you allocate and manage resources so as to best accomplish your goals and objectives? This is a critical question which faces the governmental official and businessman alike. In a primitive society, it is a relatively simple task, but in a society as complex as the one we live in, it is an art and science in itself.

In government, as programs multiply and federal, state, and local spending mushrooms—it now totals nearly $250 billion a year—there are increasing pressures from all sides for better planning, allocation, and management of scarce resources. Similar pressures in industry call for an increasingly higher level of skill in planning and management.

Many of the management practices pioneered in industry have been applied to or adapted for government in recent years. Planning-programming-budgeting systems, or PPBS, as it is known in governmental circles—the budgetary and financial management process largely pioneered by the Department of Defense—represents a shift in the other direction.

PPBS not only holds the promise of radically altering traditional governmental budgeting and accounting concepts and practices but has great potential for some segments of business and industry as well.

Responsibility for assisting his clients to improve operational and management systems falls on the independent accountant in his professional role as both auditor and financial and management adviser. And PPBS can be the vehicle through which the independent accountant can better discharge this important responsibility.

What Is PPBS? PPBS has been defined in a report of a Senate subcommittee [1] in these words:

> PPBS focuses on the output of programs whereas traditional budgetary approaches tend more or less to emphasize expenditure inputs. It assesses as fully as possible the total costs and benefits—both current and future—of various alternatives. It endeavors to determine rate of return per program as well as the rate of return that may have to be foregone when one program is chosen over another.
>
> PPBS is a refinement of existing procedures rather than a completely new budgetary approach. In PPBS attention is focused on programs—rather than on type of expenditure or organizational entities.

PPBS is an evolutionary, not a revolutionary, step in improving financial planning and management. It provides a framework within which a government or a commercial enterprise can more effectively allocate scarce resources among competing programs, and do a better job of planning and management.

In a PPB system, the key elements—planning, programming, and budgeting—are linked together in a systematic approach.

Planning involves establishing objectives and evaluating alternative ways of achieving them. It is done on a multiyear, agency-wide basis.

Programming defines the programs required to attain desired goals and objectives. Emphasis is shifted from inputs (how much an agency is spending) to outputs (the specific services to be provided through the programs).

Budgeting establishes the cost of carrying out each program in terms of both capital and operating budgets including personnel, facilities, and other costs on a multiyear basis or over the life of the program.

[1] *Subcommittee on Economy in Government of the Joint Economic Committee, Congress of the United States, 90th Congress, The Planning-Programming-Budgeting System; Progress and Potentials,* Washington, Government Printing Office, 1967.

A common misconception about PPBS is that its application is limited solely to governmental units. Although PPBS, as such, has evolved within government, the approach and concepts involved have important implications for virtually any form of economic activity.

The fact is that many of the concepts and techniques basic to PPBS had their origin in business and industry. However, it has been primarily within the framework of government that they have been integrated into a systematic approach to planning and management.

While some nongovernmental organizations have planning and management systems fully comparable with a comprehensive PPB system, many others do not. It is to this sector of private business and industry that PPBS holds appeal.

Recent years have seen an increased use by business, industry, and government alike of more sophisticated techniques involving the management sciences in planning and decision making. PPBS can help accelerate this process.

As Smalter and Ruggles[2] point out:

> Executives in both government and business environment have as their primary responsibility the allocation of resources to maximize long-run effectiveness.
>
> To the entrepreneur, effectiveness may mean return on investment or increased market penetration, while to the military it may imply nuclear retaliatory capability. But, in each case the process of creating objectives, the technique for analyzing alternative courses of action, and the system for establishing strategic plans have many elements in common.

PPBS concepts, with their focus on outputs or programs, can:

Contribute to the development of more effective information systems

Provide the framework needed to link and coordinate information systems properly

Help management resolve organizational, geographic, and other problems which affect the efficient use or allocation of resources

Provide the means for developing and better utilizing improved measures of effectiveness

While primary emphasis in this chapter is placed on PPBS in government, the reader should recognize its potentials for nongovernmental activities.

Traditional Government Budgets. The typical government budget is a "line-item, object-of-expenditure" budget with emphasis placed on year-to-year changes in revenues and appropriations—not on accomplishments. Revenues are summarized by source. Expenditures are classified by object—e.g., salaries and wages, contractual services, repairs and maintenance, debt service, capital improvements—for each department or agency.

Line-item, object budgetary concepts represented a substantial step forward over the formerly widespread practice of budgeting on a "lump-sum" basis. However, in too many instances, all the line-item, object budget provides is a uniform framework for maintaining a set of orderly records. These satisfy legal requirements and safeguard the public trust, but they provide, in themselves, little useful planning or financial management information.

[2] "Six Business Lessons from the Pentagon," *Harvard Business Review*, March–April, 1966, vol. 44, p. 64.

KEY ELEMENTS IN A PPB SYSTEM

The budgetary philosophy of PPBS is in sharp contrast to these traditional practices. A PPB system builds on and expands the line-item, object budgetary process to achieve improvement in two areas of management: resources and operations.

A comprehensive PPB system involves several key elements:

Development of program budgeting
Introduction of effective management information systems
Use of the management sciences (systems analysis)
Management itself

Program Budgeting. The program budget is the cornerstone of PPBS. It focuses attention on outputs or programs and on the development of related cost and performance information.

In a typical governmental program structure, activities are classified or grouped on a multilevel basis as follows:

I. Objectives
  A. Major program areas
    1. Programs
      a. Program elements

Figure 1 shows the relationship in a typical program structure.

OBJECTIVES

At the *objectives* level, broad classifications are established corresponding to overall agency goals. In a typical state government, or even a larger municipality, these might include:

I. Human resources development
II. Land and water resource development
III. Transportation development

Figure 1 TYPICAL LONG-RANGE PROGRAMMING STRUCTURE.

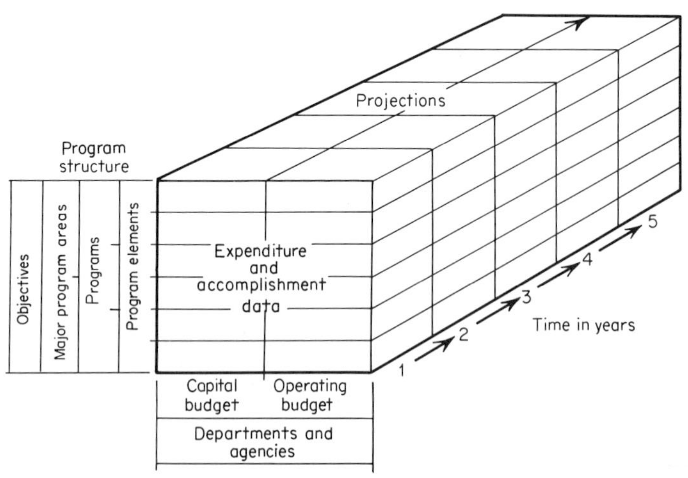

IV. Environmental service and development
V. Commercial and industrial development
VI. General government

MAJOR PROGRAM AREAS

Major program areas are established within each of these classifications. For example, in "Human resources development," major program areas would include:

A. Education
   1. Elementary and secondary
   2. Higher
   3. Special and other
B. Health
   1. General services
   2. General facilities
   3. Mental health
C. Welfare
   1. Public assistance
   2. Other
D. Employment

PROGRAMS

Within the major program area B1, Health—general services, specific *program elements* are established for:

a. Tuberculosis control
b. Venereal disease control
c. Communicable disease control
d. Cancer control
e. Chronic disease control
f. Health education

PROGRAM ELEMENTS

Within each program, the *program elements* in turn define the services to be provided in planning and implementing it, considering both immediate and long-term capital needs and operating expenditures.

Many public jurisdictions are introducing a program structure into their budgetary and accounting framework and developing the coding system necessary to link line-item appropriations, organizational structure, and programs. The state of Wisconsin, for example, has converted to a program format and no longer uses a line-item budget.[3]

Some PPB systems have been developed independently from the agency's basic budgeting and accounting systems. Such systems can only be considered as "stopgap" measures. To be effective, the program structure should be integrated or made compatible with the agency's basic budgetary and accounting structures.

This may require substantial modification or expansion of the agency's present coding systems. The proposed financial management system for the state of Kentucky requires a 16-digit coding structure as shown below:[4]

[3] Chapter 20, Wisconsin Statutes, 1967, Appropriations and Salaries.
[4] Ernst & Ernst, *Financial Management System for the State of Kentucky,* Louisville, 1968.

	No. of Digits
Fund	1
Agency	2
Responsibility unit	4
Program	6
Object of expenditure	3
	16

The concept of program budgeting is not a new one in government. It dates back as far as the year 1912, when President Taft's Commission on Economy and Efficiency in Government recommended the adoption of a program budget for the federal government. The emphasis placed on program or "performance" budgeting by the Hoover Commission in 1949 led to its introduction in several federal agencies as well as in a number of state and local governments.

However, until the advent of PPBS—with its emphasis on program budgeting—many governments paid little attention to this useful management tool.

In a sense, program budgeting is an adaptation of industrial cost-accounting concepts to the governmental budgetary and financial management process. For example, a manufacturer needs product cost information before he can set prices and devise the marketing, distribution, and manufacturing programs needed to achieve marketing goals and objectives. In the case of government, however, the "product" is a program of public service.

Management Information Systems. Like any other organization, a government agency must have information if it is to be effective—prompt and timely information which answers two primary questions: What are the citizens' needs? How well are they being met?

A government agency can develop effective management information systems without PPBS. PPBS, however, helps shape the nature of these systems and requires that information needs be defined and supporting systems developed which will:

Collect data about needs and resources

Provide information needed for planning and programming

Furnish cost and other information required to improve the resource allocation and decision process

Provide information needed for program management and for evaluating accomplishments

These information needs and supporting systems pose more problems to the governmental administrator than to his counterpart in business or industry. While some systems are common support systems, involving the planning and management of finances, workload, and personnel of all departments or agencies, others are unique to the needs of a particular agency, program, or function.

PPBS provides a common framework within which information needs can be met on a planned and coordinated basis. Figure 2 shows the interaction of the key information system elements in a PPB system—data collection, data processing, information reporting, and management action.

The Management Sciences. PPBS requires that an agency systematically identify and analyze alternative ways of reaching desired goals and objectives. Together with this goes the development of multiyear plans, with resources allocated to programs according to priority.

Figure 2 TYPICAL PPBS MANAGEMENT INFORMATION SYSTEMS RELATIONSHIPS.

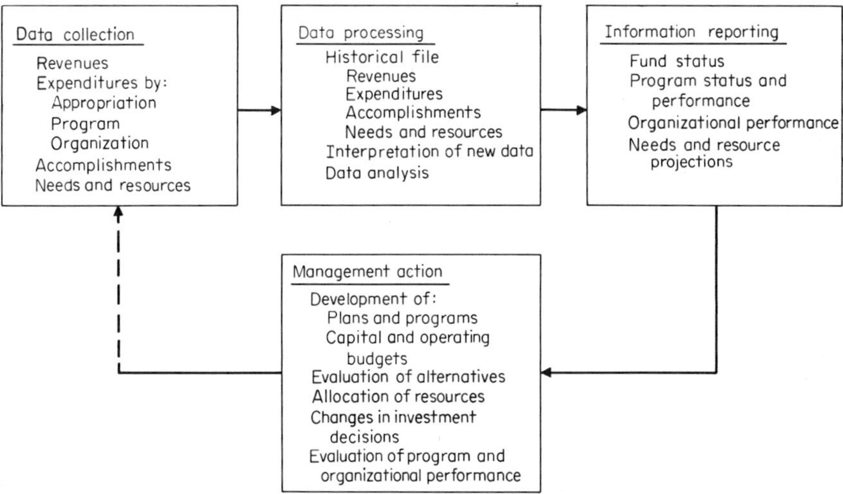

The process through which this is accomplished, often referred to in PPBS literature as "systems analysis," involves the use of the management sciences.

Government and industry alike can make effective use of the management sciences wholly apart from PPBS. PPBS has, however, served as a catalyst in helping place the management sciences in an understandable and useful perspective to governmental decision makers.

In a presentation before a Senate Committee in 1966,[5] Alan Enthoven of the Department of Defense stated:

> Systems analysis is nothing more than quantitative or enlightened common sense aided by modern analytic methods. What we seek to do in the systems analysis approach to problems is to examine a problem in its broadest sense, including its reasonableness or appropriateness from a national policy point of view, and then develop for the responsible decision maker information which will best help him select the preferred way of achieving it.
>
> This process of selection requires that we first identify alternative ways of achieving the objective and then estimate in quantitative terms the benefits (effectiveness) to be derived from and the cost of each alternative.

The use of the management sciences in PPBS is based on the fact that economic systems have a substantial amount of orderliness and regularity. Relationships between significant factors or variables can be established and used to answer questions about the operation of a system under a wide range of conditions. In this way, alternatives can be evaluated, cost-benefit and cost-effectiveness relationships established, and decision making improved.

Although most governmental as well as nongovernmental programs are complex and involve many departments or agencies, the judicious use of management sciences makes it possible to place in a useful perspective such considerations as competing objectives, many variables, limited resources, and risks.

[5] Alan C. Enthoven, Assistant Secretary of Defense, "Systems Analysis, The Systems Analysis Approach," a presentation before Special Senate Subcommittee, May 17, 1966.

The management sciences are not the answer to every situation encountered; systems analysis produces reliable results only when sufficient data are available. For this reason, the management sciences can be best applied to those critical problems about which sufficient information can be gathered at reasonable cost.

Management of PPBS. To program budgeting, management information systems, and the management sciences must be added one vital additional ingredient—management itself.

There is a widespread assumption that if an administrator is provided with better information, he will automatically put it to good use to improve his decision making. But systems are no substitute for management. Information provided by a PPB system is of little value unless the system also takes into account the way that information is used.

Thus, orientation and training of management personnel in PPBS concepts must be a part of the PPB system. The system should also be designed to provide decision-oriented information on an "exception" basis. This is common practice in industry, and it has even greater potential for government.

EXPANSION OF PPB SYSTEM

Evolution in the Federal Government. PPBS was formally introduced into the federal government by the Department of Defense in 1961, and has been applied to defense budgets for fiscal years 1963 and later. In August of 1965, President Johnson directed [6] that PPBS be installed throughout the executive branch of government under the supervision of the Bureau of the Budget, to enable the government to:

> Identify our national goals with precision and on a continuing basis;
> Choose among those goals the ones that are most urgent;
> Search for alternative means of reaching those goals most effectively at the least cost;
> Inform ourselves not merely on next year's costs, but on the second, and third, and subsequent years' costs of our programs;
> Insure a dollar's worth of service for each dollar spent.

In 1967, President Johnson further stated: [7]

> Under PPBS each department must now: develop its objectives and goals, precisely and carefully; evaluate each of its programs to meet these objectives, weighing the benefits against the costs; examine, in every case, the alternative means of achieving these objectives; shape its budget request on the basis of this analysis; and justify that request in the context of a long-range program and financial plan.
>
> This new system cannot make decisions. But it improves the process of decision-making by revealing the alternatives—for decisions are only as good as the information on which they are based.
>
> PPBS is not costly to operate, but the dividends it will yield for the people of America are large.
>
> The system has taken root throughout the government, but it will not be able to function fully until more trained men and women, more data, better cost accounting and new methods of evaluation are available.

Federal-State-Local Governmental Relationships. Far more than the federal government, state and local governments have clung to the traditional line-item, object budgetary and accounting practices. This has occurred in

[6] Lyndon B. Johnson, *Public Papers of the Presidents of the United States*, 1965, Book II.

[7] Excerpt from the President's Message to the Congress, *The Quality of American Government*, Mar. 17, 1967.

the face of ever-mounting problems of population explosion, revenue limitations, demands for more and better governmental services, lack of cooperation between local governments in planning to meet area-wide needs, and the socioeconomic ills of our urban areas.

As a result, the federal government has taken an increasingly stronger role in its relationship with state and local governments and is introducing basic PPBS concepts into many federal assistance programs.

"Creative federalism," as this changing relationship is sometimes called, is bringing about significant changes in the administration of federal assistance programs. Many of these programs, formerly based on line-item appropriations, now take the form of "bloc grants," and require a state or local government, as a condition of eligibility, to develop a "master plan." In a typical plan, objectives must be defined, specific programs developed for achieving them, alternatives evaluated, and program costs computed on a multiyear basis. This is PPBS!

These planning requirements inevitably have a profound impact on the information needs and the supporting budgetary, financial management, and data processing systems of state and local governments. The federal government, in most instances, has not prescribed uniform accounting systems for assistance programs. But it can, and does, as a condition of assistance, make informational demands on a lower-level government which virtually force that government to a drastic modification of its accounting and budgetary procedures to conform with federal requirements.

As a result, significant changes can be expected in accounting and budgetary practices of state and local governments, including:

1. The widespread introduction of program budgeting to supplement (or replace) the line-item, object budget
2. The development of more effective management information systems to meet both resources management and operating management needs, and their conversion for processing on high-speed electronic data processing equipment
3. The modification of present accounting and financial management systems to conform with federal information requirements and to meet program planning and managing needs
4. Increased emphasis on the use of sophisticated techniques for resources allocation and management, program formulation, priority determination, and program management

PPBS and State and Local Government. Despite strong pressures from the federal government on state and local governments to modernize their budgetary and financial management processes, and despite the sound rationale underlying PPBS, introduction of PPB systems into these governments can be a slow and difficult process. This is largely due to the fact that state and local governments have limited informational resources. Thus, it is to these governments that PPBS offers the greatest benefits but poses the most problems.

Problems are involved in properly defining governmental objectives and stating them in quantitative terms. The development and evaluation of alternative programs for accomplishing objectives appears to be a simple process; but unless enough relevant cost and other information is available, the question is largely academic.

Introducing program-type budgets, making the necessary changes or improvements in supporting information systems, and converting these systems for processing on computers may be an almost overwhelming task in itself.

The human element, too, enters strongly into the picture. Much PPBS literature is highly sophisticated and "systems-oriented." This has misled some legislators and administrators into a belief that PPBS is an attempt to substitute an impersonal, computerized octopus for human judgment, experience, and intuition.

Many state and local governments do not have personnel who are technically qualified to develop a good PPB system. Many administrators, even when improved systems have been developed, do not know how to make the best use of the increased information output.

Further, an administrator may not control all or even a large proportion of the financial resources of his agency or of the funds expended.

These and a multitude of other considerations must be kept in perspective in evaluating the problems, as well as the benefits, inherent in PPBS.

That there are problems is undeniable. Equally true is that they are solvable. Growing needs, mounting pressures, and the increasing complexity of society combine to make inevitable the change to PPBS or its equivalent in state and local governments.

AUDIT IMPLICATIONS OF PPBS

What are the implications of PPBS in relation to the typical governmental audit and the role of the auditor?

Few changes can be expected in the very limited role of the independent accountant in examining the records of departments of the federal government. The potentials lie with state and local government auditors, both in the examination of historical financial statements—the "financial audit"—and in the evaluation of administrative controls and procedures—the "operational audit."

Financial Audits. A wide diversity exists among state and local governmental units with respect to reporting practices, sophistication in accounting procedures, and scope of the financial audit. Various groups, such as the Municipal Finance Officers Association (MFOA), in their publications have done much to upgrade governmental financial reporting and accounting practices by stressing accrual accounting, program budgeting, etc.[8] But there still remain a vast number of governmental units which account for and report on a cash receipt and disbursement basis, without adequate attention to the establishment of appropriate funds. Furthermore, the scope of financial audits for governmental units in many instances is limited to determining that receipts and expenditures have been accounted for in conformance with legislative intent.[9]

In this context, because PPBS is primarily concerned with financial and management controls, it has, at best, only limited application to those financial audits done in conformance with generally accepted auditing standards.

The audit implications stemming from PPBS are significant, however, when viewed in relation to changes imposed in accounting structure, internal

[8] Municipal Finance Officers Association, *Governmental Accounting, Auditing, and Financial Reporting,* Chicago, Ill., 1968.

[9] For an excellent account of the variations in the scope of governmental financial audits, see Sister Maureen Dougherty, CSJ, "State Supervision of Local Governmental Audits," *Municipal Finance,* February, 1968.

controls, report context and format, federal assistance reporting requirements, etc.

Internal Controls. A key factor in any financial audit done in accordance with generally accepted auditing standards is the study and evaluation of the existing internal accounting controls as a basis for reliance thereon and for the determination of the resultant extent of the tests to which auditing procedures are to be restricted.

Under a PPB system, as in the management control systems found in business, cost and operating data are developed to measure the effectiveness of programs as well as to plan and control operations. To the extent that a PPB system reinforces the financial and accounting controls in a government unit, the auditor will have greater confidence in the unit's financial records and, consequently, can reduce the amount of test checks in the audit that would be required in the absence of such controls. For example, performance standards developed in connection with a city's snow- and ice-removal program might be the basis for limiting the number of test checks of road-department expenditures for payroll, materials, and supplies.

If, as is the case with commercial enterprises, the auditor can establish that PPBS procedures and controls have an important bearing on the reliability of the financial records, he should consider the need for evaluating such controls. For example, performance or program cost records may require evaluation to determine that funds were appropriately expended.

Audits of Program Accomplishments. Need for better reporting. Users of government financial statements (taxpayers, legislators, the federal government, etc.) are becoming increasingly frustrated by the lack of meaningful information provided by these statements. Most of them are limited to line-item summaries, by departments, of the amount of wages paid, materials and supplies purchased, etc. Users want government financial reporting to move closer to commercial financial reporting practices with emphasis on the relationship of *input* and *output*.[10]

Under the combined stimulus of increased user interest and the emphasis on PPBS by the federal government, it is likely that more and more governmental units will expand their external financial statements to include results of operations expressed in terms of program costs and accomplishments. As a result, there could be a corresponding demand upon the independent accountant to express an opinion on a governmental unit's program costs (and measures of performance) as well as on its financial transactions.

Although this possibility is conjectural, the following statement[11] taken from the MFOA publication, *Operating Budget Manual*, may be prophetic:

> It is recalled that in a number of cities, annual reports either for the whole city, for departments, or both are issued. Understandably, these reports seek to put a best foot forward. It would be unrealistic to expect otherwise. However, just as we have taken steps through the independent financial post-audit to verify the accuracy of the representations in the annual financial report, it would appear in order to have a system for verification of the claims made in the annual activity reports.
>
> The design of a system of post-audit for performance will require a great deal of time, experimentation, and trial and error before it reaches an acceptable level. However, perhaps the time is overdue when we should begin to get this step underway in some of our progressive cities.

[10] See "New Approaches in Public Education," *The Journal of Accountancy*, July, 1968, for one example of the dissatisfaction with traditional government reporting methods.

[11] Lennox L. Moak and Kathryn W. Killian, *Operating Budget Manual*, Municipal Finance Officers Association of the United States and Canada, 1963, p. 340.

It is important that the independent auditor give careful consideration to the implications of such a requirement. The following discussion does not attempt to resolve, but only to highlight, the problems that may confront him in rendering an opinion on program costs, operations, or effectiveness.

Allocation of costs. How, on a uniform basis, do you account for and allocate those costs that cut across programs, organizational lines, and even lines of managerial responsibility? This is a major question. Assignment of these costs to programs requires appropriate bases for allocation. Many governmental units now make such allocations for budgeting, control, and planning purposes. But there appears to be little uniformity of approach. The auditor need only review the debate between the proponents of absorption and direct costing in industry, or the current discussion on the problem of reporting on conglomerates on a segmented basis, to get a taste of the allocation problems that program costing presents to the governmental unit.

The allocation problem raises the specter of comparability. Ideally, the operations and costs of programs of one governmental unit should be directly comparable with those of other governmental units. However, until agreement can be reached, if this is at all possible, on goals and objectives, program structure, and bases of cost allocation, such comparisons can be worse than misleading. Yet, auditors may have to accept more, not less, diversity because of the great variety of circumstances, operating policies, and managerial judgments which influence financial planning and management.

Criteria for the audit. Another problem involves the criteria an independent accountant needs in order to express an opinion on program information. No such criteria presently exist. The MFOA has taken an initial step, however, toward establishing some standards. Their publication, *Governmental Accounting, Auditing, and Financial Reporting,*[12] sets forth a series of functional program classifications to be used to collect and report information. The program information and guidelines developed by the "5-5-5" project may also have applicability.[13]

Disclosure of assets. Still another problem involves the balance sheet of a governmental unit. Disclosure of program costs alone, without disclosure of program assets, could be misleading. Development of balance sheet information by programs may also require a multitude of cost allocations, many of them arbitrary.

Measures of performance. Aside from the problems of reporting and allocating program costs, a question remains concerning measures of performance. The accounting profession may be able to resolve the problems inherent in allocating costs among programs. But to achieve general agreement and comparability in measures of program performance is much more difficult. In this regard, Moak and Killian [14] point out:

> Studies and experience . . . show that although a considerable part of municipal activities are subject to statistical measure through workload and other measures, a significant part of the municipal work program is not easily handled on the basis of quantitative measures.

Clearly, the reporting of governmental programs on a uniform basis poses many interesting problems which will not easily be resolved but which must

[12] *Ibid.*

[13] The George Washington University, *State-Local Finances Project,* has been developing guidelines for introducing PPBS into state and local government in collaboration with five states, five counties, and five municipalities.

[14] *Loc. cit.*

be solved before the auditor has a reasonable basis for rendering an opinion on program costs and performance.

Audits of Assistance Programs. Audits of federal and state assistance programs are giving many independent accountants direct exposure to the problems of auditing program costs and accomplishments. In many such audits, specific consideration is given to:

1. Whether the expenditures are made only for established projects and programs
2. Whether administrative reviews have been made to evaluate the operations and effectiveness of the programs

As an example, the cost audits required under Title XVIII of the Social Security Act (Medicare) are used to fix reimbursements to medical facilities of incurred program costs. These audits help medical institutions develop effective financial and cost procedures and controls. They are also used to support requests for cost reimbursements.

Audits of this type can be expected to become more widespread and to a degree—dependent on federal and state policies—to focus more on programs and financial and management controls and less on objects of expenditure.

Operational Audit of a PPB System. On the premise that the independent accountant, as well as the internal auditor, has a responsibility to review and evaluate major financial and management controls, what are the major considerations involved in relation to a PPB system?

First, it is important to recognize the wide variations among PPB systems; a system designed for one agency may not be well suited to another. Second, because PPBS involves the entire governmental process, it is difficult to develop (or audit) a PPB system without considering all related aspects of a government's operations. Moreover, most PPB systems are still in a state of evolution, and consequently, some of the important considerations involved in a comprehensive operational audit of a PPB system may not apply.

Operational Audit Questionnaire. Set forth below are some of the important points that should be considered in developing an operational audit program for a PPB system in a typical governmental organization. The same criteria can be also readily adapted for a nongovernmental organization.

Organization and planning

1. Does an overall plan exist for the application of PPBS in the organization?
2. Does the PPB system have the support of the legislative body and top management?
3. Are the legislative body and top management informed and knowledgeable concerning the PPB system?
4. Has appropriate responsibility been assigned within the organization for overall development and operation of the PPB system?
5. Are qualified personnel available in the organization to develop basic PPBS concepts, and to develop and introduce necessary systems, procedures, and controls?
6. Does the PPB system involve the participation of key personnel from finance, data processing, planning, and major departments?
7. Have orientation seminars with key personnel been conducted?

Goals and objectives

1. Have goals and related objectives been established in quantitative terms?

2. Do goals and objectives provide the policy guidelines necessary to establish specific program objectives?

3. Have the major departments concerned participated in defining goals and objectives and in establishing the basic assumptions underlying them?

4. Have goals and objectives been reviewed and approved by the department heads involved?

5. Do formal procedures exist for assuring that goals and objectives are periodically reviewed and reevaluated?

Program and accounting structure

1. Has an adequate program structure been developed?

2. Has a uniform account coding structure been developed to compile needed program information?

3. Is this program structure realistic? Does it properly link and interrelate programs, line items, and organizational units?

4. If a separate account coding structure exists for programs only, have plans been developed for integration with the basic accounting and organizational coding structure?

5. Is adequate consideration given to compiling both direct and indirect program costs?

6. Do major organizational or responsibility reporting problems exist which conflict with the coding structure?

7. Are well-defined criteria and procedures available for:
   a. Collecting program costs?
   b. Allocating costs to programs?
   c. Preparing management reports?
   d. Analyzing and interpreting management reports?

Revenue available

1. Have comparable procedures been developed with respect to revenues?

2. Have studies been made of revenues available or revenue sources and potentials?

Program development

1. Are programs defined and developed in conformance with established procedures?

2. Are programs responsive to stated goals and objectives?

3. Are programs developed or expressed in quantitative terms?

4. Do quantitative measures of program performance exist?

5. Have accurate program costs or resource data been compiled?

6. Have alternative programs been developed or explored?

7. Have techniques of cost-benefit or cost-effectiveness analysis been used in evaluating alternatives?

Resource allocation

1. Has a system of establishing program priorities been established? Is it in quantitative terms? Is cost-benefit or cost-effectiveness analysis used?

2. Are there legislative or other limitations or restrictions which materially affect revenue allocations to programs?

3. Do procedures exist for identifying misoriented or ineffective programs?

Budgeting

1. Are written procedures available for budget preparation? Do these procedures cover both the capital and operating budgets?

2. Do these procedures properly integrate program budgeting with existing procedures?
3. Are these procedures being followed by departments?
4. Is centralized control exercised in budget formulation, review, and approval?
5. Do adequate program and performance data and criteria exist to support budget requests? Are the data applied in quantitative terms?
6. Do program budgets include all direct and indirect costs and capital and operating costs?
7. Are realistic forecasts of program output used to project program costs?
8. Is budget planning on a multiyear basis?
9. Are sufficient qualified personnel assigned to the budgetary process to make it effective?

Information systems

1. Have effective systems been developed for workload, budgetary and operational planning and management?
2. Are these systems properly integrated?
3. Is data processing equipment available?
4. Are systems and procedures adaptable to EDP processing?
5. Are reports decision-oriented and on an exception basis?
6. Are reports furnished on a timely basis?

Management and performance evaluation

1. Are program accomplishments reported against plans as well as against expenditures?
2. Are these measures of performance realistic?
3. Does the system utilize existing methods of workload or performance measurement?
4. Have actual accomplishments been in accordance with the plan?
5. Are major changes indicated in the nature or scheduling of programs?
6. Have managers operated within budgetary restrictions? If not, why not?
7. Does a program exist to train managers in use of the systems output?
8. Do organizational-program conflicts exist which make management of programs difficult, if not impossible?

IMPORTANCE OF PPBS TO THE INDEPENDENT ACCOUNTANT

It is not within the purview of this chapter to more than briefly touch on internal controls, operational or management audits, or the audit of computerized systems—all of which are of importance in relation to PPBS.

Improvement Potential. PPBS can act as a catalyst in helping to bring deficiencies in internal control, management control, organization, and planning to the attention of management. It can also help in defining the needed changes. While PPBS is not a tool for reorganization per se, a PPB system may require the realignment of organizational and managerial responsibilities to permit effective program planning and management.

The independent accountant must therefore understand the organizational and reporting relationships and responsibilities within the governmental unit, as well as the political and operational framework within which the unit operates.

Effects of the PPB System. The independent accountant must also understand the changes in internal and operating systems, procedures, and controls, together with their audit implications, involved in a PPB system. Further, he has the responsibility to help place planning and financial information needs in an understandable perspective to management in relation to PPBS.

For governmental units, this may result, in some instances, in the adoption of the uniform accounting procedures recommended by the MFOA. In others, the unit may be persuaded to take the first step to PPBS and introduce program budgeting concepts. Some units may be able and willing to plan for the full-scale introduction of PPBS.

For nongovernmental organizations, PPBS can result in improved planning and programming techniques, and in the expanded use of systems analysis as an aid in decision making.

Better Service to Clients. The public accountant who takes the time to understand the use and potentials of PPBS can better serve his clients—both governmental and industrial—and better equip himself to discharge his total responsibilities both as auditor and as financial and management adviser.

BIBLIOGRAPHY

"Planning-Programming-Budgeting," U.S. Bureau of the Budget, Bulletin No. 68-2, Washington, D.C., July 18, 1968.

Subcommittee on Economy in Government of the Joint Economic Committee, Congress of the United States: *The Planning-Programming-Budgeting System: Progress and Potentials,* Washington, Government Printing Office, 1967.

Subcommittee on National Security and International Operations of the Committee on Governmental Operations, United States Senate: *Internal Memorandum, Planning-Programming-Budgeting; Hearings, Parts 1 and 2;* Government Printing Office, Washington, 1967.

Alfandry-Alexander, Mark: *Analysis for Planning, Programming, Budgeting, the Second Cost-effectiveness Symposium,* Washington Operations Research Council, Potomac, Md., 1968.

Brown, Paul L.: *An Operational Model for a Planning-Programming-Budgeting System,* Bureau of Budget and Management, State of Wisconsin, Madison, Wis., 1968.

Shick, Allen: *The Road to PPB—The States of Budget Reform,* Program Evaluation Staff Publication, U.S. Bureau of the Budget, August, 1966.

U.S. Bureau of the Budget: *Program Analysis Techniques, a Selected Bibliography,* Washington, D.C., 1965.

Hitch, Charles: *Decision-making for Defense,* Berkeley, University of California Press, 1965.

Hovey, H. A.: *Planning-Programming-Budgeting Approach to Government Decision-making,* New York, Frederick A. Praeger, Inc., 1968.

Novic, David (ed.): *Program Budgeting,* Cambridge, Mass., Harvard University Press, 1965.

State of Washington and Ernst & Ernst: *Planning-Programming-Budgeting Systems for State and Local Governments,* Olympia, Wash., 1968.

Smalter, D. J., and R. L. Ruggles: "Six Business Lessons from the Pentagon," *Harvard Business Review,* March–April, 1966.

"Planning-Programming-Budgeting System: A Symposium," *Public Administration Review,* December, 1966.

De Vos, Henry, John Dyment, and Bruce Mahon: "Planning-Programming-Budgeting System—What Value to Business?" *The Journal of Accountancy,* December, 1967.

Millward, Robert E.: "PPBS: Problems of Implementation," *Journal of the American Institute of Planners,* March, 1968.

Index